# TECHNIQUES OF THE GREAT MASTERS OF ART

# TECHNIQUES OF THE GREAT MASTERS OF ART

Quantum Books

A QUANTUM BOOK

This book is produced by
Quantum Books Ltd
6 Blundell Street
London N7 9BH



This edition printed 2003



ISBN 1-86160-561-7

QUMGMA

Printed in Singapore by
Star Standard Industries (Pte) Ltd.

# CONTENTS

# EDITOR'S NOTE

This book is divided into three sections, each of which contains chapters analyzing a specific work of a major figure in Western painting. Sections II and III are divided into subsections covering, respectively, decades and twenty-year periods. Thus some artists are represented, with pictures from different points in their career, in more than one chapter.

Preceding section I is an introduction that provides a general background to the whole book. Sections II and III are each introduced by extensive summaries of the eras under consideration, and in addition each periodic subsection is given special attention with an introduction of its own.

Each chapter contains:—

**1.**

Textual introduction to the artist, his work and techniques.

**2.**

A reproduction of the whole picture under discussion.

**3.**

An actual size detail from the work under discussion, giving a clear indication of the scale of the work.

**4.**

Other details, drawing attention to relevant aspects of the artist's technique, together with a key to indicate the exact part of the picture being shown.

**5.**

An outline of the painting process (known or presumed), with specific reference to materials, tools, palette and methods of application.

**6.**

Exact dimensions and other technical details of the painting.

# INTRODUCTION

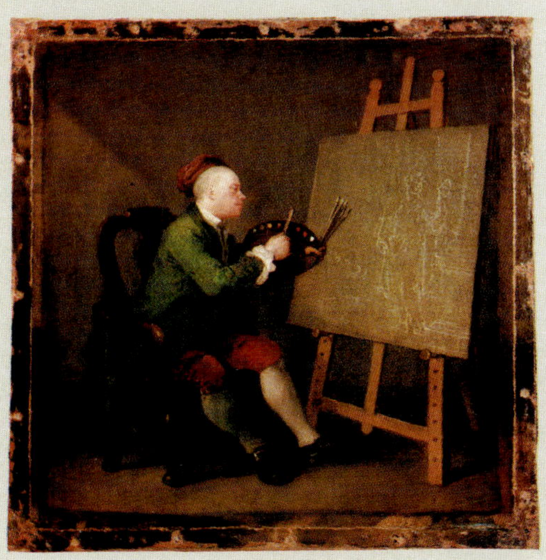

The history of painting techniques is as realistic and accurate a guide to the development of Western art as any aesthetic assessment or biographical essay. Indeed, technical considerations perhaps provide more crucial insights into the history of art than a bookcase crammed with artistic biographies. For instance, the reason artists had been painting landscapes for 500 years without becoming Impressionists lies not so much in subject matter, or even in aspiration, but in technique.

Major developments in technique have tended to go hand in hand with innovations in the materials available to the artist. Jan van Eyck may not have been the inventor of oil paints, as has traditionally been supposed, but he was the first great master of the medium — a medium without which it would have been impossible to produce the smooth, glassy surfaces and the brilliant illusionism of his Arnolfini marriage portrait. Before van Eyck, artists working in fresco or in tempera did not have the means at their disposal to achieve the dazzling *trompe l'oeil* effects which he attempted.

Van Eyck's Arnolfini portrait is the first great demonstration of the reasons why oil paints were to become the Western artist's favourite medium, unchallenged in popularity until the arrival of synthetic polymers in the last 30 years or so. Although the very slow drying time might have appeared the medium's major disadvantage, this in fact proved a crucial aid to the painter. X-rays reveal that van Eyck was able to make changes in his composition during the painting process while the fresco painter could never allow himself this essential freedom, and those who worked in tempera found that their colors did not have the necessary covering power.

The new medium gave rise to a quest for increased naturalness which preoccupied artists in the fifteenth and sixteenth centuries and which found a perfect champion in Leonardo da Vinci. This quest could best be conducted with paint which dried to a shell-like hardness, but which, as the Venetians discovered, could also soak up and reflect real light, as did the sea ringing the city in which they worked.

The high humidity of Venice made fresco painting difficult, but the flexibility of oils and the replacement of wooden panels by canvas meant that the work could be done in the studio, rolled up and finally installed in its proper location. Working in the studio ensured not only that the lighting could be controlled, but also that models could be used to increase a previously limited catalog of poses and to provide the gods and heroes painted in Venice with accurate human anatomies.

However, it was not until Titian in his old age began to deal in more reflective moods that oil paints gained a measure of independence from the task of imitating the visible world. The freedom of the brushwork in Titian's late paintings revealed the medium's hitherto unleashed powers of expression. For the first time, individual brushstrokes

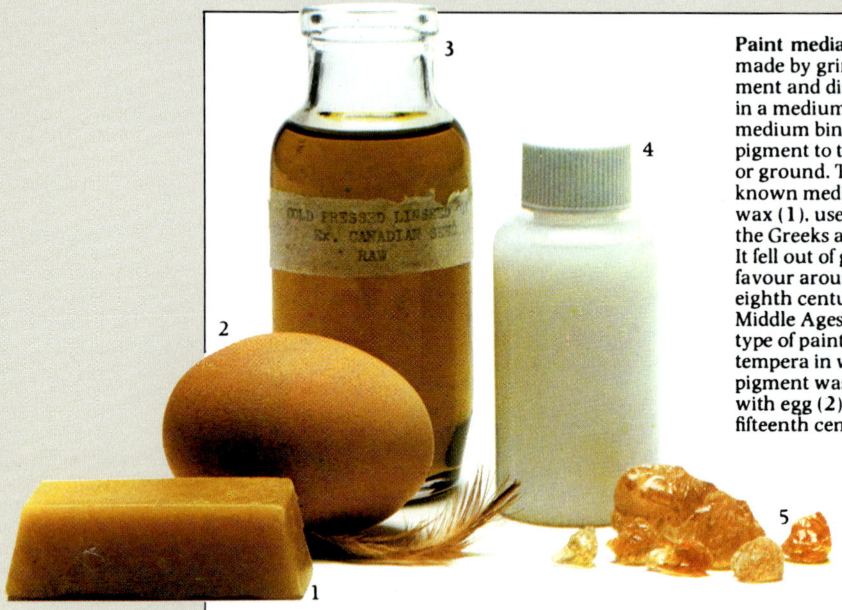


**Paint media** Paint is made by grinding pigment and dispersing it in a medium. The medium binds the pigment to the support or ground. The earliest known medium was wax (1), used mainly by the Greeks and Romans. It fell out of general favour around the eighth century. In the Middle Ages the main type of paint was tempera in which the pigment was bound with egg (2). From the fifteenth century, oil (3) became increasingly popular as a medium. The slow drying time, despite the addition of drying agents, was both an advantage and a disadvantage. Corrections were easier to make than with the faster drying tempera, but the painting could not proceed so quickly. As a medium, oil has dominated painting ever since. During this century acrylic medium (4) made from polymerized resin has become popular thanks to its quick drying time, resilience and flexibility. Watercolor is bound with gum arabic (5). When mixed with water, the paint can be applied smoothly and it adheres to the surface when dry.

were allowed to show through and disturb the illusions.

Rubens and Rembrandt took the next steps. While Caravaggio's dramatic studio light effects had already put light and shadow through their expressive paces, Rembrandt was the first painter who took a highly sensuous pleasure in oil paints. The biographer Houbraken wrote that one could take a late Rembrandt portrait by the nose, so thickly were the colors applied. Looking at a detail of Rembrandt's treatment of drapery, it becomes possible to trace a line of descent from these swiftly modelled brushmarks through van Gogh to Jackson Pollock.

Rembrandt's revolutionary late style was the result of practical as well as aesthetic considerations. While some of their contemporaries accused Rembrandt and Titian of leaving their pictures unfinished, these artists persisted in trying to find ways of speeding up the painting process. Other painters also found ways of avoiding the laborious processes involved in producing a picture. Rubens and the English portraitists, for example, relied on increasingly specialized contributions from studio hands. Gainsborough's feathery touch dwelt on faces and hands, but seems to have hardly ever settled on the rest of the canvas while Constable skimmed over the surface and hunted for elusive atmospheric conditions. But it was the Impressionists who set themselves the sternest task of all when they attempted to find a technique with which to capture a mere instant in time.

The apparently loose system of dabs and dashes employed by Monet and Renoir to preserve the spontaneity of an autumn moment at Argenteuil, or to capture the dazzle of sunlight on a woman's torso, involved the spectator more directly than ever before. Colors laid down separately, side by side, mixed not on the canvas but in the spectator's eye. Rather than a solid carefully built-up surface, the eye perceives a mosaic of fragmented brushstrokes which only form a vibrant whole from a distance. Other artists had intuitively achieved similar effects in details, but the whole of Impressionist painting chases after an elusive moment, aided only by a scholarly color theory and the sudden rush of scientific activity which left the nineteenth century artists rich in new pigments. No matter how energetically the spectators squinted, they could no longer pretend to be looking through an open window. The colors, squeezed liberally from a tube, seem to have settled on the surface of the canvas as impermanently as snow flakes.

The Post-Impressionists subsequently felt the need to challenge this impermanence, but, nevertheless, the methodical working up of a picture in layers had been irrevocably challenged and replaced by a system of work that focused evenly across the canvas. As Cézanne said, the painter could now treat the entire work all at once and as a whole. The gates were open for an idea to reach the surface of the canvas without undue delay.

Seurat turned a spontaneous Impressionist technique into a system by purifying the colors still further and reducing the dabs to dots. Van Gogh was more concerned with the expressive brushstrokes with which the Impressionists had begun to apply their colors: Gauguin noticed that, just as these brushstrokes no longer modelled themselves on visible forms, so colors were endowed with their own expressive values and need not mirror those outside the canvas.

However, these technical innovations were concurrent with, and, to a great extent, dependent on developments in artists' materials. The general availability of ready-made canvases and mass-produced brushes, and the dramatic expansion of the artist's palette in the nineteenth century had a far more profound effect on the course of Western art than the career of any one artist. It is easy to go painting out of doors when all you have to do is pack a bag with canvas and tubes of paint; it is quite a different matter if the canvas first has to be measured, stretched and primed, the colors mixed and then stored in unreliable containers.

In this century, it is debatable whether, had synthetic household paints not been developed, Jackson Pollock could have found a paint which flowed so freely from the can that it responded to his every instinctive movement, and dried quickly and effectively into puddles and dripped lines. Similarly it is unlikely that if David Hockney had not had acrylics at his disposal, Mr and Mrs Ossie Clark could have been treated to such a cool, modern interior, so unlike the cluttered home shared by the Arnolfinis.

The greater part of *Techniques of the Great Masters of Art* (sections 2 and 3) deals in detail with the frantic activity on the surface of the canvas which characterises the art of the nineteenth and twentieth centuries. In the artistic deluge that followed the Impressionist breakthrough in the 1860s and 1870s, when the canvas came to be recognized as a self-sufficient object, then abstraction became possible. Picasso introduced foreign elements such as pieces of newspaper and chair caning onto the surface; Max Ernst invented new techniques such as *frottage,* which allowed chance to play a major part in the appearance of the image. Technique increasingly became not only a painter's language but also his subject matter, a process that found its ultimate expression in the drip paintings of Jackson Pollock. The actual production of pictures — the subject of this book — had become as important as the final product.

Our contemporaries, then, can hardly be accused of feeling intimidated by the materials that they select to serve their cause. They deploy them without inhibition to achieve the efects they want. How this freedom contrasts with the practice's of their pre-Renaissance forebears! Painters of frescoes such as Giotto (1267-1337) had to proceed according to a strict scheme by which the tasks of each creative day were preordained, while the devotional triptychs of painters such as Duccio (active 1278-1319) are the products of a highly organized artisanal system in which skills were passed on from master to apprentices and the tasks necessary to prepare and complete the commission were carefully allotted to assistants.

This is where our story begins, and the first, shorter, section concerns itself with the greater possibilities of working on a canvas rather than on a prepared wooden panel or wet plaster, and with the techniques that successive masters such as van Eyck, Titian, Velazquez, Rubens, Rembrandt, Constable and Turner developed in achieving their distinctive effects in the endlessly versatile medium of oils.

SECTION 1

# OLD MASTERS

1300-1860

# GIOTTO

*The Nativity* (1302-5)
Fresco Arena Chapel, Padua

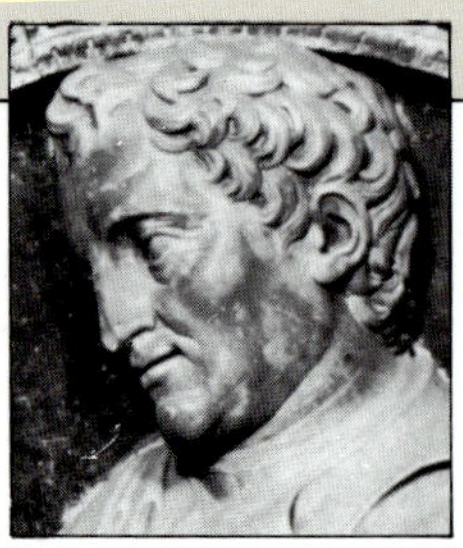

Giotto, regarded by many as the founder of modern painting, was a major exponent of fresco, a technique of wall painting known in classical antiquity and revived in the thirteenth century in Rome, where Giotto worked as a young artist. In scale and scope, wall painting was the most important art form in fourteenth century Italy. Giotto's paintings in the Arena Chapel in Padua are among the most perfectly preserved examples of fresco. *Buon fresco* or true fresco, is brush painting on freshly applied, wet lime plaster, using water as the vehicle so that the substance of the paint penetrates the plaster, and, as the plaster dries, the pigment is bound into the crystalline structure. A second main type of fresco is *secco fresco* in which pigment is applied to dry plaster using an organic medium such as egg or size which acts as both vehicle and binder. The *secco* technique had to be used with certain pigments, such as azurite and malachite. *Secco fresco* may be less permanent than *buon fresco* because the paint only forms a crust on the smooth plaster and tends to flake off. Giotto used both techniques for the Arena Chapel.

Fresco was an orderly, methodical process involving the application of several layers of plaster and one of paint. The first preparatory layer, the *arriccio*, made of coarse lime and sand plaster, is applied to the bare masonry. The drawing/called the *sinopia*, is made on this. Next, a smooth layer, the *intonaco*, is applied. The paint is laid on this plaster while it is still wet. This meant that only that area of plaster which could be painted over in one day was laid down. For this reason, this stage was termed the *giornata*, from *giorno* meaning day. To avoid splattering and damaging subsequent sections, work proceeded from the top left-hand corner, across and downwards.

It is likely that, for a design as complicated yet unified as the Arena Chapel, some preparatory drawings were done. The technique makes design changes and extensive alterations difficult – for an extensive change, whole sections of plaster had to be lifted out. Minor alterations would have been executed in *secco fresco*. Because the painting had to be completed while the plaster was still wet, the fresco painter needed a well-trained, rapid and resolute hand. These complexities gave fresco its prestige.

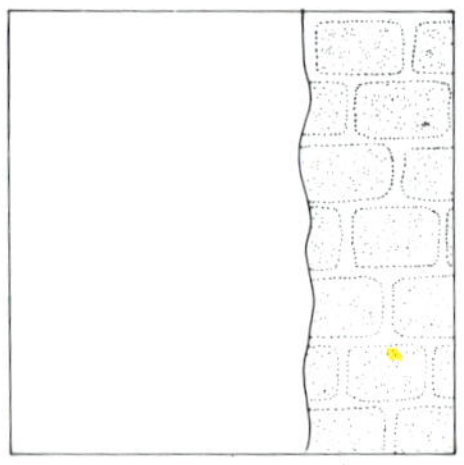

**1.** The bare masonry was first covered in a coarse, thick layer of lime and sand plaster, called the *arriccio*.

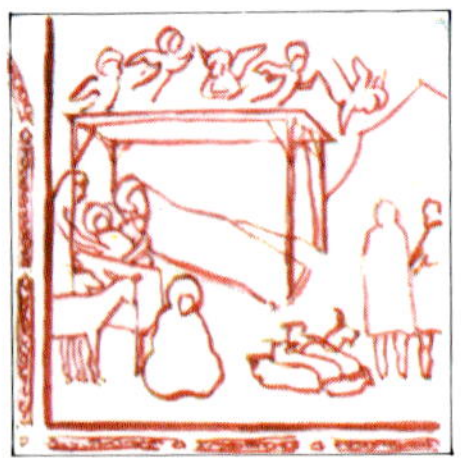

**2.** The composition may then have been drawn in on the plaster. This stage is called the *sinopia* because of the red earth pigment, sinoper, which was used generally mixed with ochre.

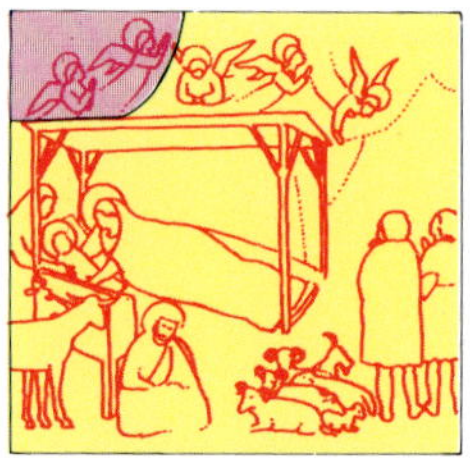

**3.** The painter then applied as much smooth plaster, the *intonaco*, as he could paint in one day and rapidly redrew the outlines. The normal painting process began at the top left-hand corner.

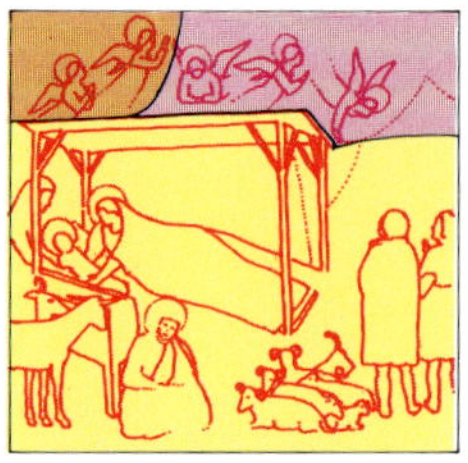

**4.** On day two, angels and the top of the mountain were painted. The artist worked systematically across the wall and downwards. The sky was added later in *secco fresco* after the *intonaco* had dried.

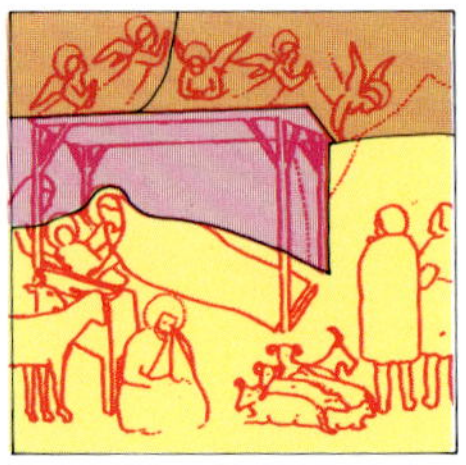

**5.** On the third day, the large, but relatively uncomplicated area of the stable and background was executed.

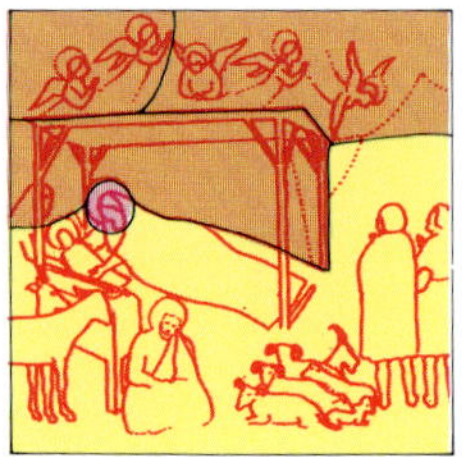

**6.** Day four was devoted to painting the Virgin's head.

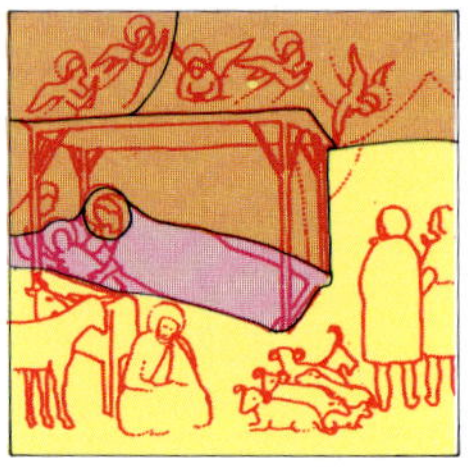

**7.** On day five the figure of the Virgin was worked on. The figure was underdrawn in *buon fresco*, and the blue robe then painted in *secco fresco* which did not follow the contours of the underpainting.

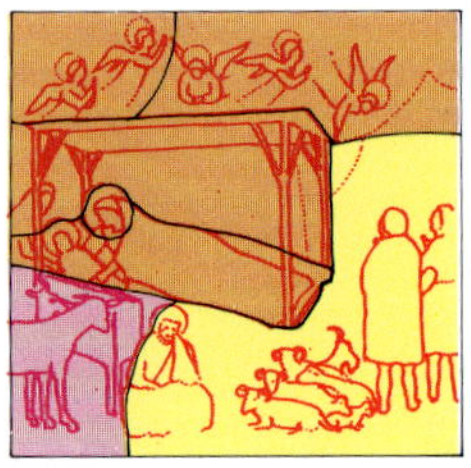

**8.** On day six the ox and ass were painted.

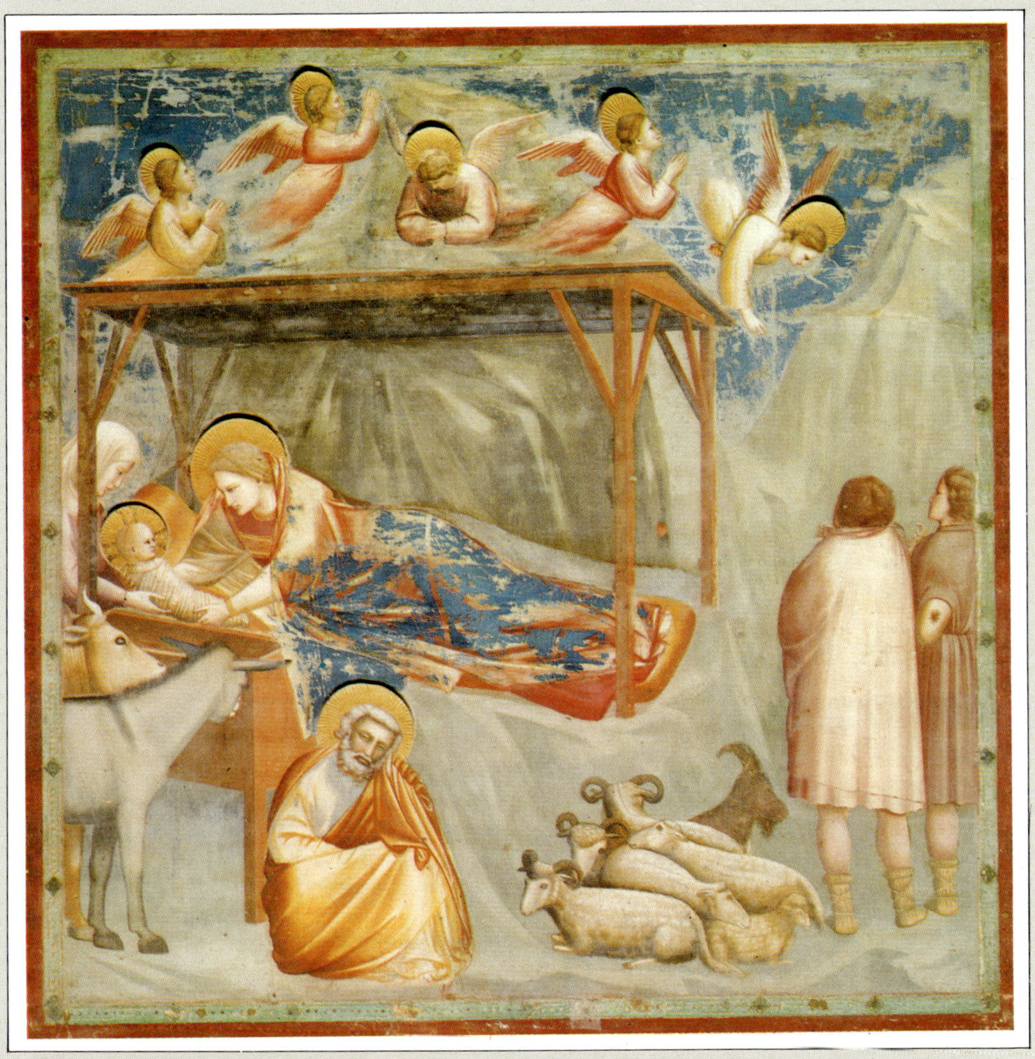

*The adjustment made to the upper contour of the reclining Virgin's body is clearly visible. The final form, painted using* secco fresco, *is visibly lower than was intended when the layer of plaster was applied and the underdrawing painted in. The red undermodelling is also visible on the figure of the Virgin where the blue paint has flaked off. Around 1390, Cennino Cennini wrote the earliestknown Italian treatise on painting techniques. It is a valuable source of information on both fresco and tempera techniques.*

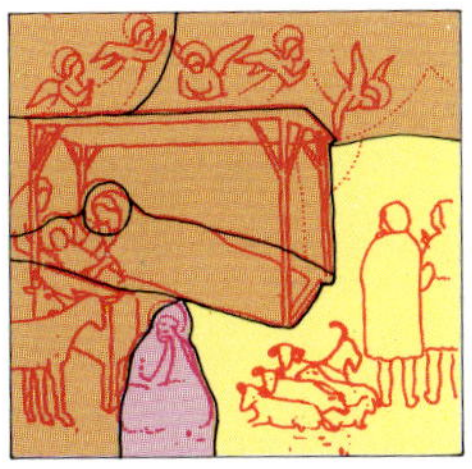

**9.** On day seven the figure of Saint Joseph was painted. His blue tunic was executed in *secco fresco*.

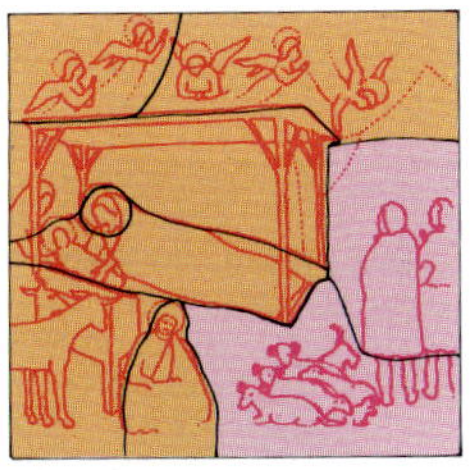

**10.** On day eight the sheep were painted, followed by the shepherds on day nine.

In fresco painting, the work was divided into daily sections, the *giornate*. This was because the paint had to be applied to the *intonaco* layer while it was still wet. The edges of each day's section were undercut to help dovetail the joins. The daily stages in *The Nativity* are shown (right).

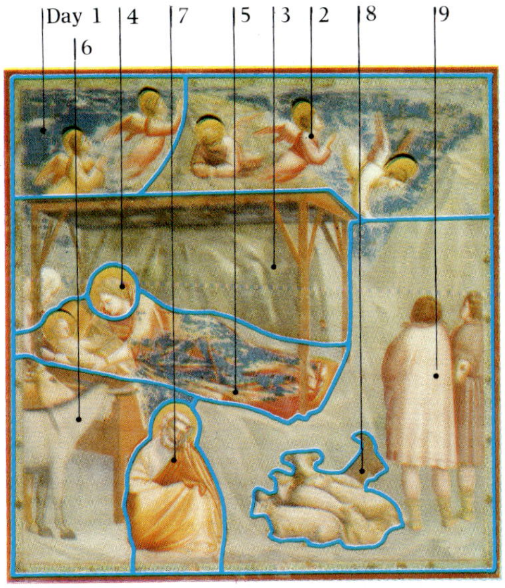

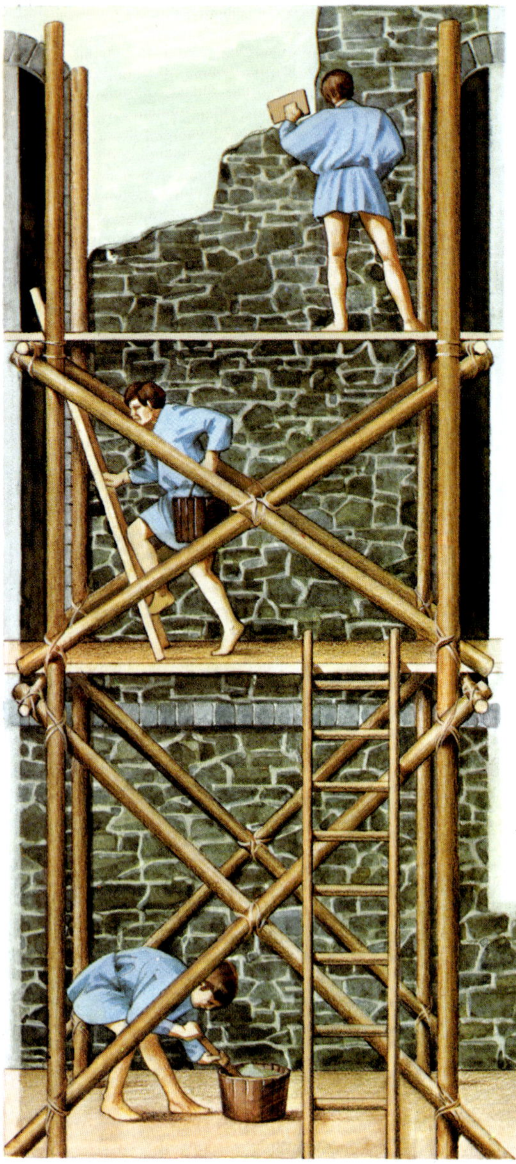

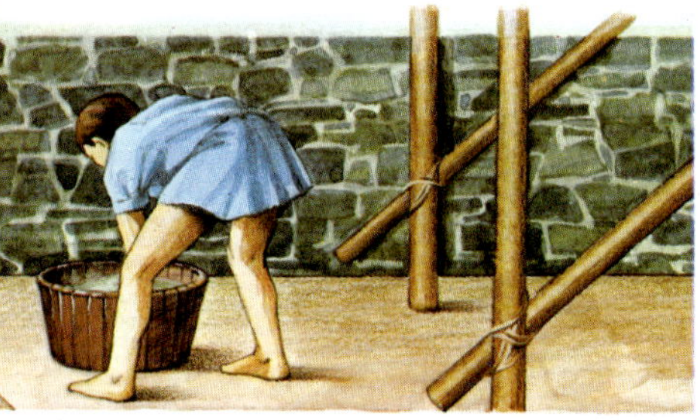

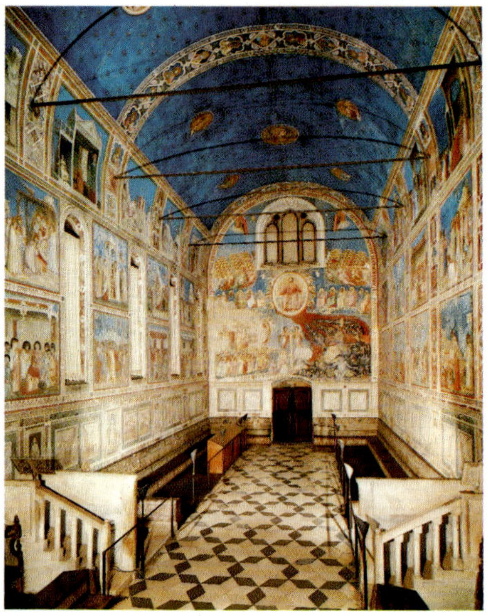

*The* Nativity *is the first scene in the second tier on the South wall of the Chapel. The entire fresco cycle is one unit, like one enormous painting. It is likely that the very bare architecture was designed specially to receive a fresco cycle. The remarkable good state of preservation of the frescoes is testimony to the durability of the technique. No lead white pigment was used because it tends to blacken in fresco. Lime white was used instead and this has contributed to the lasting purity and brilliance of the colors.*

*The paint in these details* (right, far right*) from the* Flight into Egypt *section of the Arena Chapel fresco sequence was applied using* secco fresco. *Cennini's instructions stipulate: 'If the blue is good and deep in color, put into it a little size . . . likewise put an egg yolk into the blue; and if the blue is pale, the yolk should come from one of these country eggs for they are quite red. Mix it up well. Apply three or four coats to the drapery with a soft bristle brush.' Paint applied in this way forms a thin crust over the dry plaster and is prone to flaking off. Where this has occured here the red*

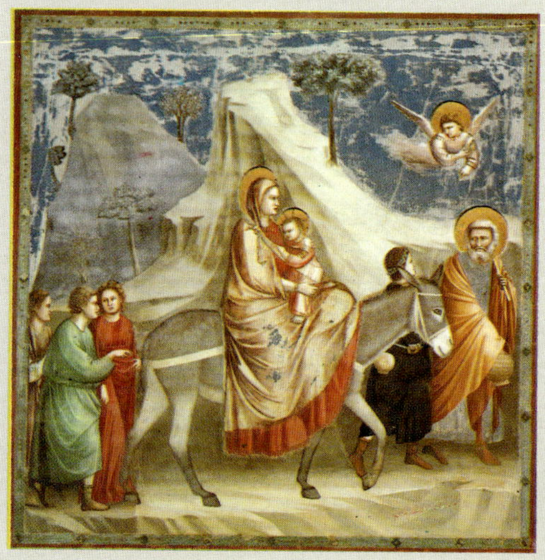

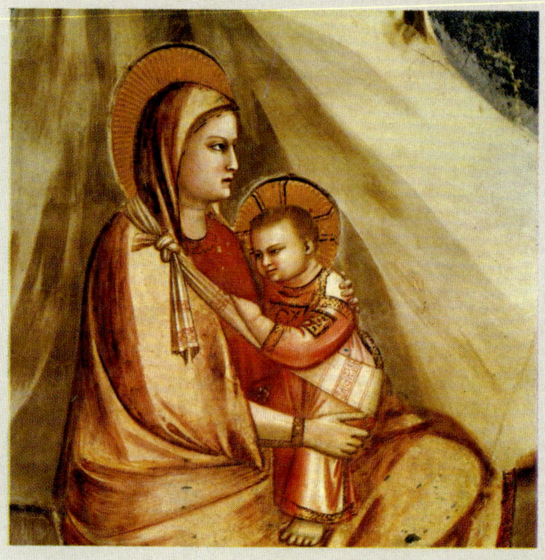

*undermodelling is clearly visible.*
*The white pigment which Giotto would have used was lime white. However, some problems have occurred, for example in the* Flight into Egypt *some of the blue pigment azurite has flaked off. It had been applied using* secco fresco.

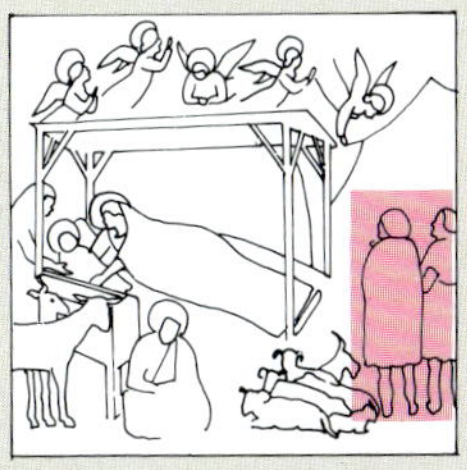

*In fresco, colors are premixed and applied in a direct manner; strokes cannot be altered by overpainting, and effects of color gradation are achieved by hatching or placing separate strokes side by side. A methodical system using a sequence of five measured tones for each individual pigment was evolved to describe form and volume. Cennini described it and frequently warned the artist never to abandon 'the sequence of colors by yielding or invading the location of one color for another.' Cennini also advised the artist to use glazed goblets with 'a good heavy base . . . so as not to spill the colours,' and to use a combination of pointed minever and bristle brushes, either broad flat brushes or fine bristles, which would have been fitted into a quill.*

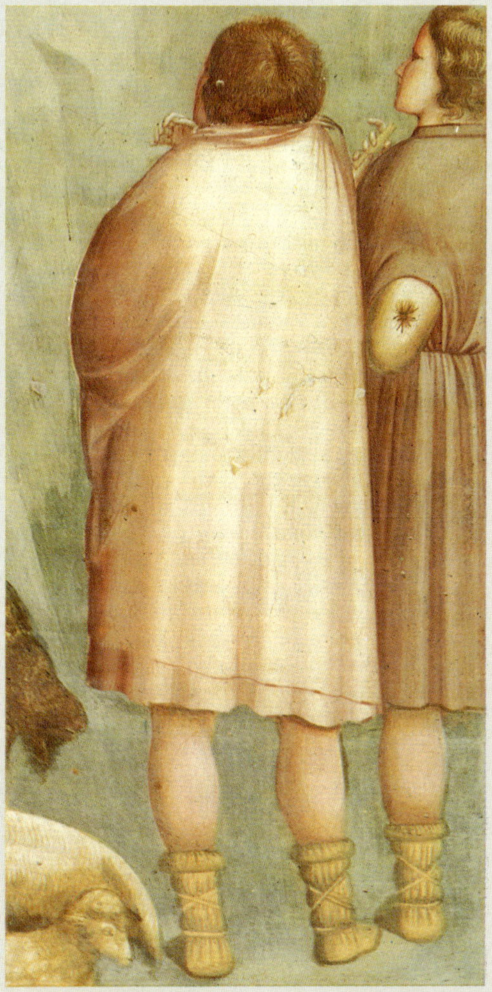

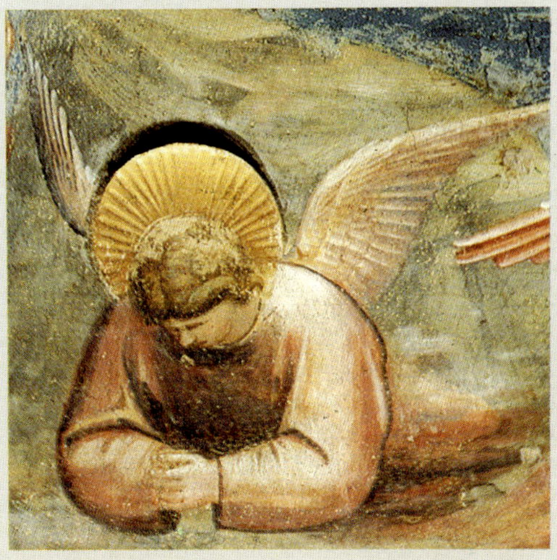

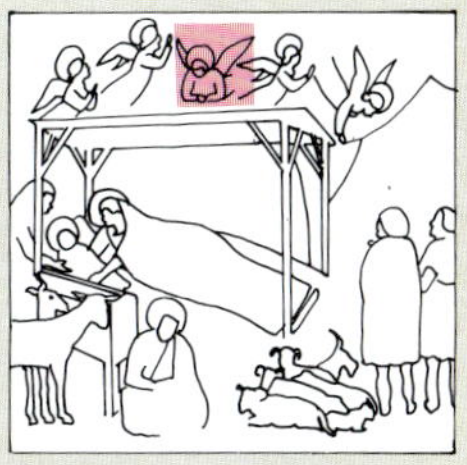

*The haloes of the Angels were modelled in thick plaster, like 'ointment or dough', as Cennini put it. The radiating beams were indented with a wooden slice. They attempt to convey an effect of perspective.*

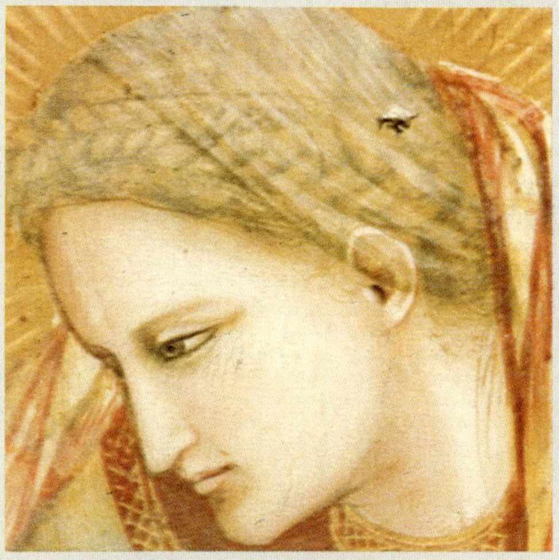

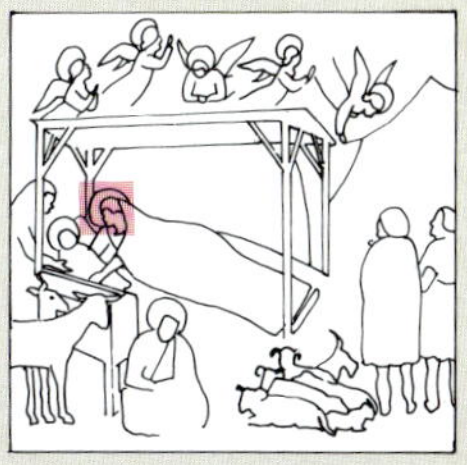

*The flesh areas on the figures were under-drawn in brown — a mixture of yellow ochre, red earth, lime white and black. They were then painted over in green earth to emphasize the shadows. The modelling was painted in tones of red and white. To differentiate between old and young, less white was used in the flesh and more in the hair of the older figures.*

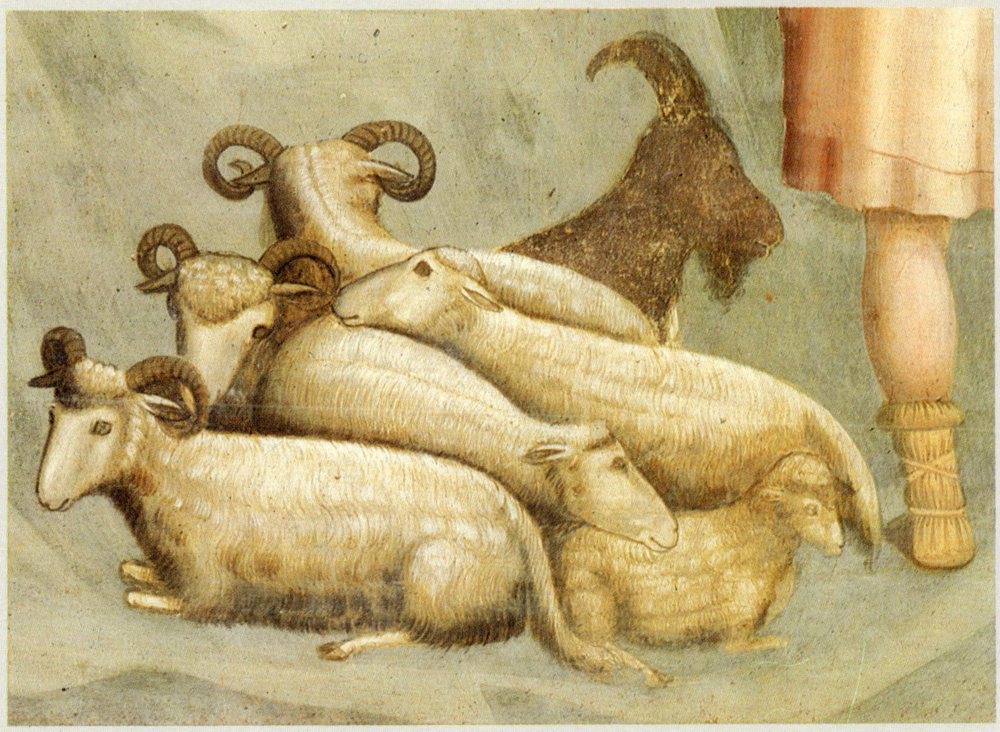

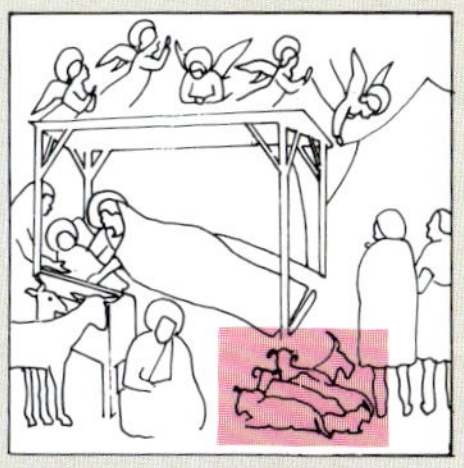

*When the paint for the sheep had been applied to the wet plaster, the artist had, as always, no opportunity to work it. Brushstrokes were applied side by side. They were blended by hatching with the point of a brush.*

# DUCCIO de BUONINSEGNA

*The Virgin and Child with Saints Dominic and Aurea* (c. 1300)
Egg tempera on wood, central panel, 62cm × 38cm/24⅛in × 15⅜in

This tabernacle by Duccio was painted in egg tempera. After walls and parchment, wood was the most important support for medieval painting. It was readily available, easy to cut and carve, and the final object was as substantial as the metalwork, sculpture, or even architecture which it was sometimes intended to imitate.

The uneven surface of the wood was first covered by preparatory layers of gesso, which is made of gypsum mixed to a thick paste with animal glue. The gesso was applied with a slice and then with a brush all over the wooden structure, beginning with the rougher *gesso grosso*, and finishing with the smooth *gesso sottile*. To ensure that the gesso adhered well, the wood was sized and sometimes strips of linen applied to cover any knots or joints. When it was finished, the ground was brilliantly white, rather thick and polished to an ivory-like smoothness. These qualities were important for the final effect of the painting.

A careful drawing was executed on this ground, first in charcoal and then in black paint. The main outlines were incised into the gesso. Design changes were difficult after this.

The gilded areas were prepared with several coats of red bole. It provided a slightly elastic underlayer for the subsequent burnishing and decoration of the gold and its color gave the gold a rich, warm tone. The gold leaf was made to adhere with egg white and burnished until it was 'dark from its own brilliance .

Painting, beginning with drapery and then flesh, was the final stage in this orderly sequence. The pigments were ground with water on a porphyry slab and the egg yolk was added as they were used. Each color was treated individually, and mixtures, except for white, were generally avoided. In modelling the form, a series of pre-mixed tones, ranging from dark to light for each pigment, was used in strict sequence.

The painter kept methodically to the tonal sequence and worked with small, hatching brushstrokes which followed the form being described. The rapid drying of tempera paint was an advantage because one stroke could be painted over the next almost immediately. However, this meant that the artist had to rely on the network of brushstrokes to achieve blended tonal transitions and it was difficult for the artist or his assistants to make adjustments at any stage in the procedure. Thus tempera painting needed discipline and method.

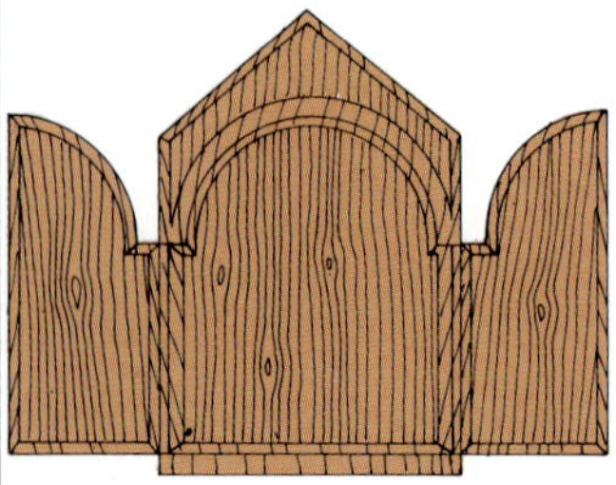

1. Painters and carpenters were organized in different guilds. A carpenter would have completed the bare wooden structure to order and delivered it to Duccio's shop.

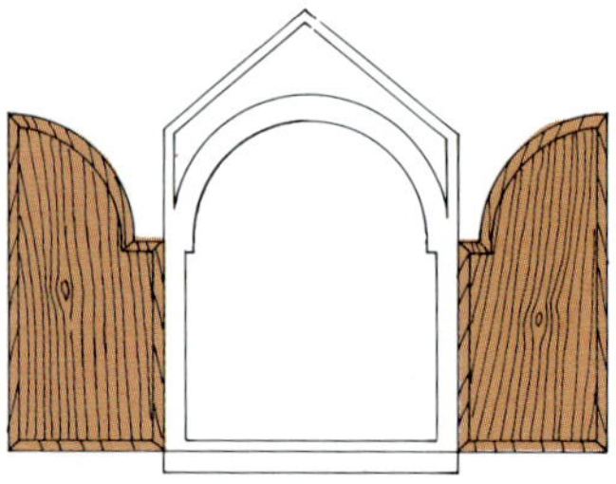

2. Faults in the wood were corrected and often a layer of linen was put over the entire structure. This was then covered with up to eight coats of gesso.

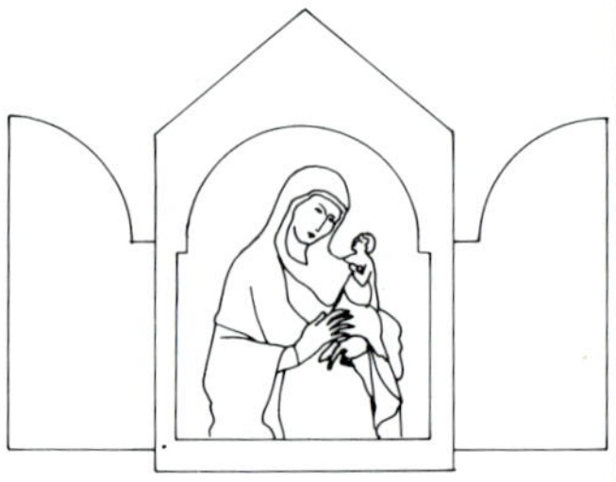

3. The gesso layer was scraped and polished smooth, and the design then defined in paint. Contours and major drapery folds were incised with a metal point.

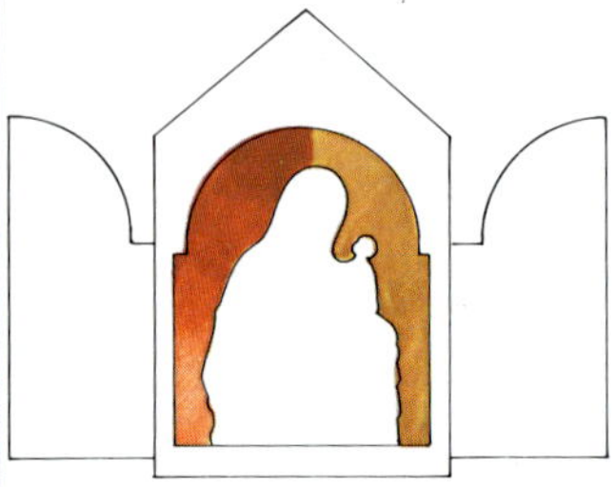

4. Up to six coats of red bole bound with egg white were brushed on and gold applied leaf by leaf. The gold was burnished and designs inscribed or punched onto it.

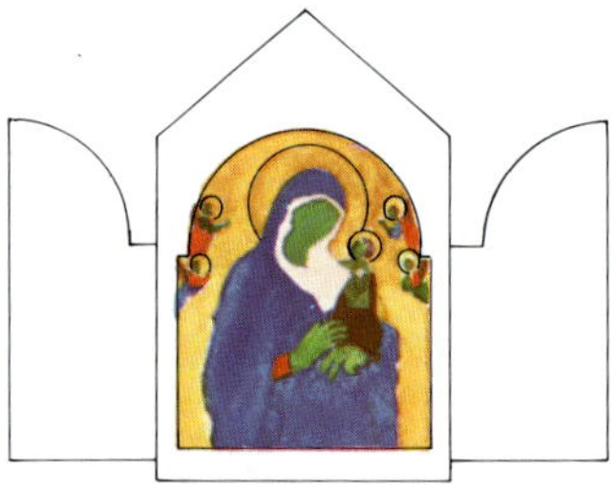

5. Drapery painting was completed before flesh painting began. All flesh areas were underpainted in one or two coats of green earth and lead white. The green earth was intended to be left uncovered in the shadows.

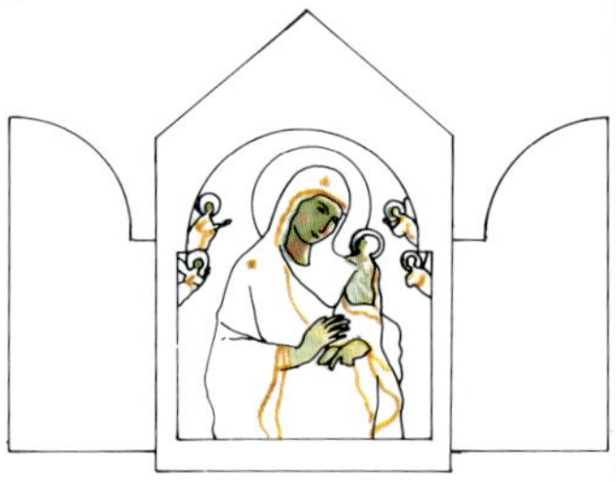

6. The flesh colors were finally painted in and details reinforced in black and sinoper. Gold lines were applied on top of the drapery by adhering scraps of gold to a sticky oil mordant.

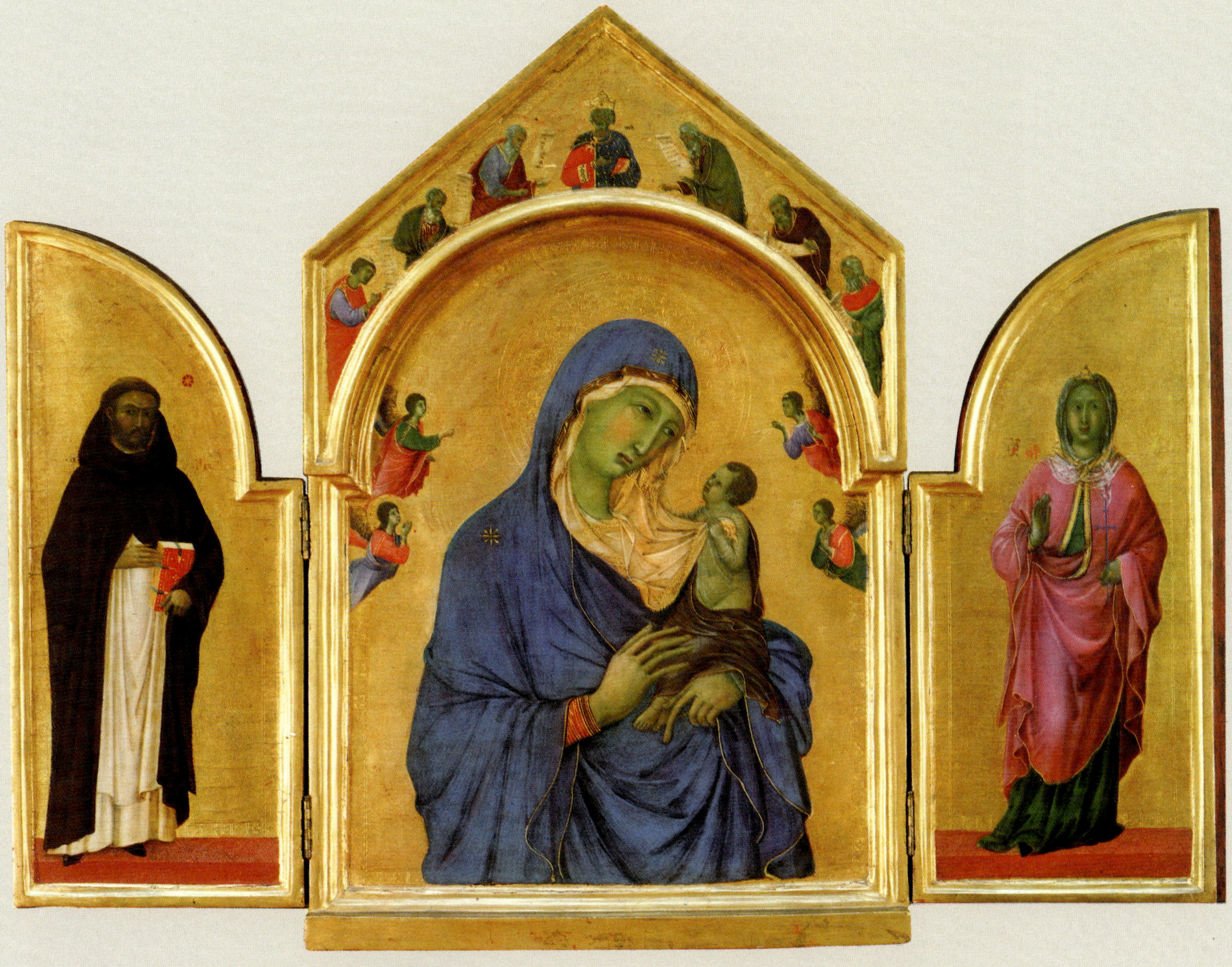

*Tabernacles were painted and decorated inside and out. The shutters protected the image when it was not being venerated. The close similarity between this tabernacle and another by Duccio indicates a degree of mass production by carpenters for painters. Not all paintings were commissioned, and it is likely that a workshop would have kept some panels in stock.*

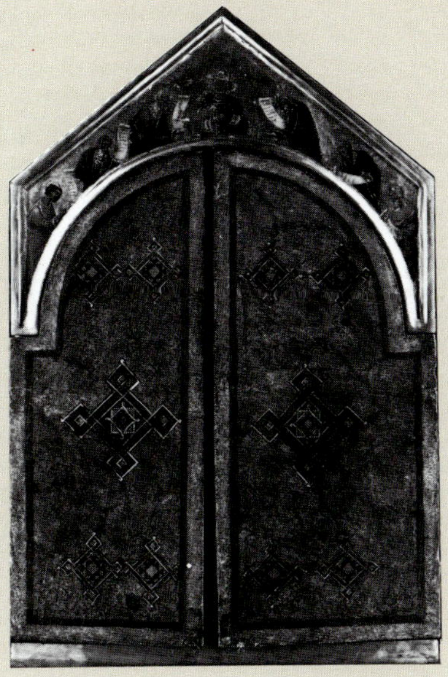

*Painting of this period can only be understood if it is realized that 'Duccio' was also a trademark. A master coordinated a workshop with apprentices and assistants, and a painting was a collaboration involving the distribution of work during all stages of production, even on small paintings. In tempera painting, the complex combination of different materials — wood, gesso, gold, and pigments bound by egg yolk — required a particularly orderly and methodical technique. This remained little changed by several generations of artists. Writing around 1437, Cennini described with pride the technique as it had been handed down from master to pupil since Giotto. The technique of painting in tempera was founded on an intimate understanding of the individual properties of the materials used.*

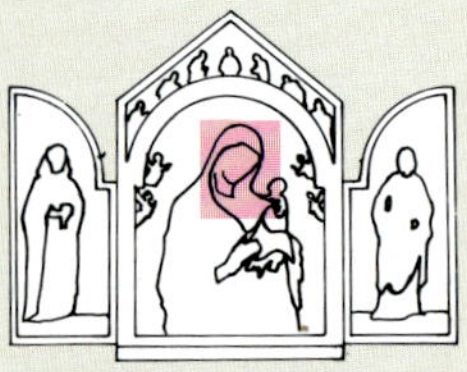

*The outer circles of the Virgin's halo were drawn using a compass. The decorative areas within the circles were executed using a single horseshoe-shaped punch, freehand drawing, and using a point for the hatched areas. Ultramarine, obtainable from the semi-precious stone lapis lazuli, was used for the Virgin's robe. This was the most expensive pigment available and, in order to show off its quality, the amount of white used in the under-modelling was limited.*

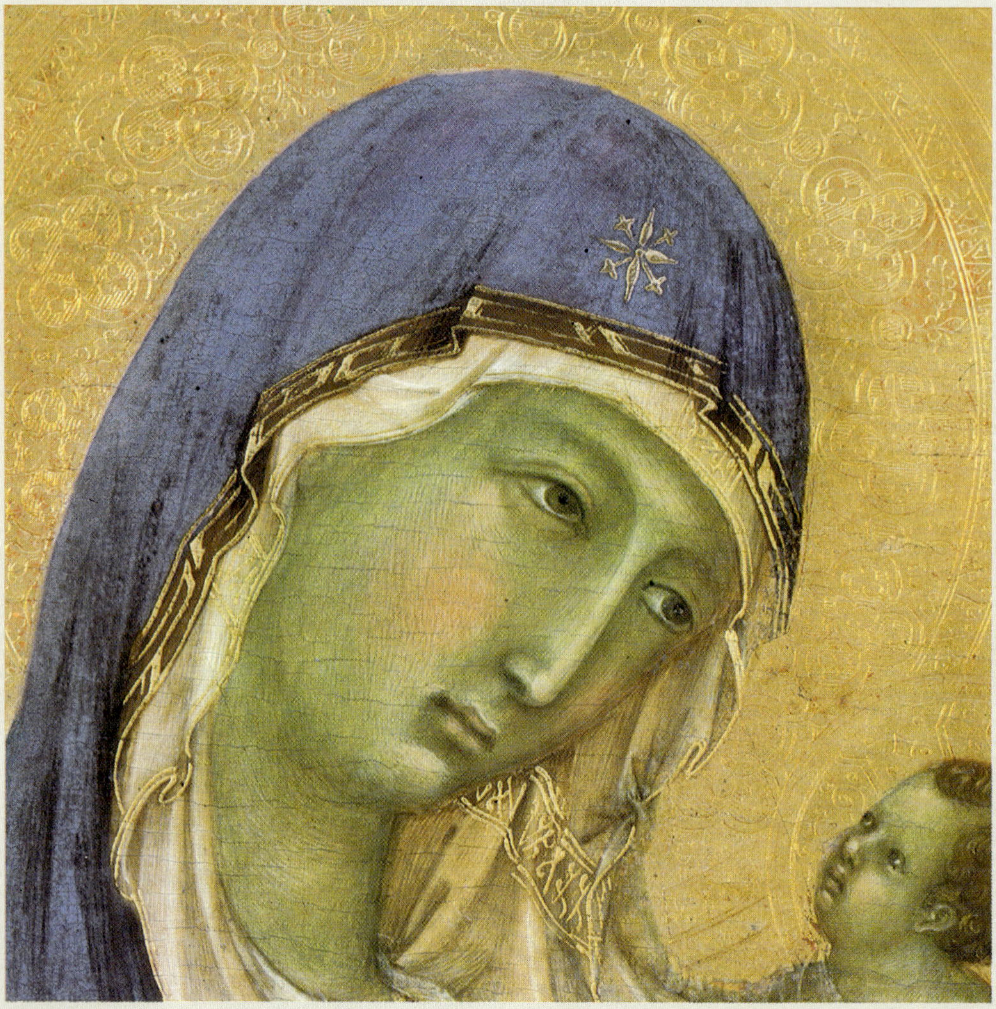

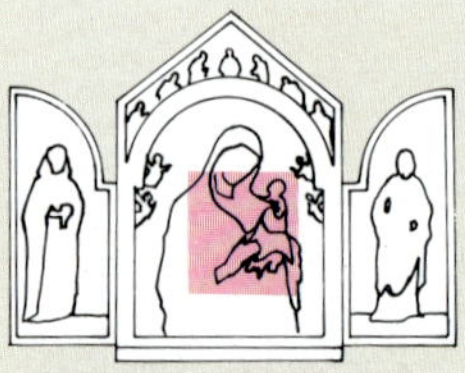

Actual size detail
*Egg tempera paint was applied in thin, flat layers and dried to a smooth enamel-like surface texture. Brushwork is not a feature of the technique but the small hatching strokes are typical and inevitable. They are anonymous rather than expressive of an individual personality. Three tones of flesh color were often used but did not obscure the green earth under-painting. A lighter flesh tone followed by pure white was used for the highlights. Sinoper and black were used for the accents of the eyes, nose, and other details.*

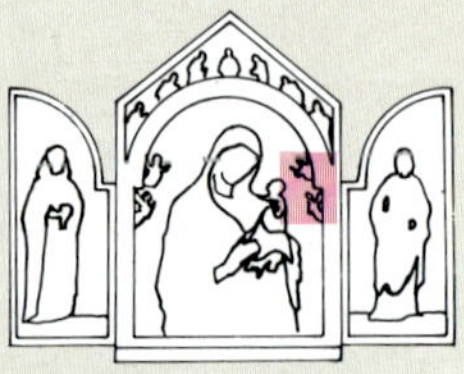

*The glittering effect of the angels' wings was achieved by painting solidly over the gold background and then carefully scratching the dry paint away to expose the gold again. The fine web of lines over the drapery was achieved in the opposite way. When the painting was finished, a thick, sticky oil mordant was painted on top, and scraps of gold leaf were stuck on to it. When the mordant was completely dry, the excess gold leaf was brushed away.*

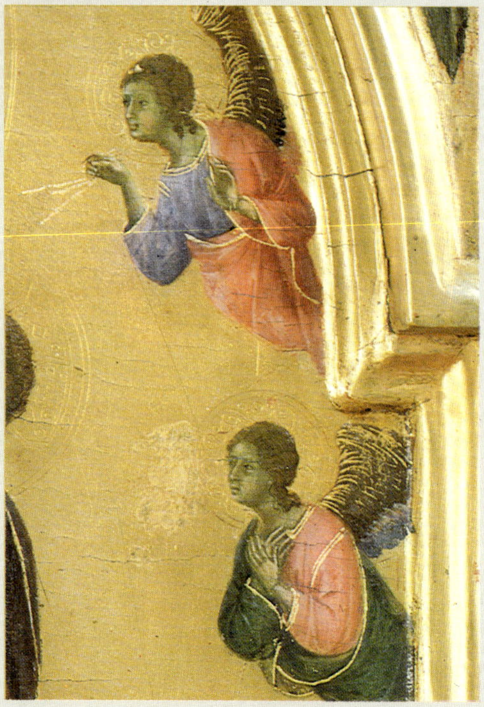

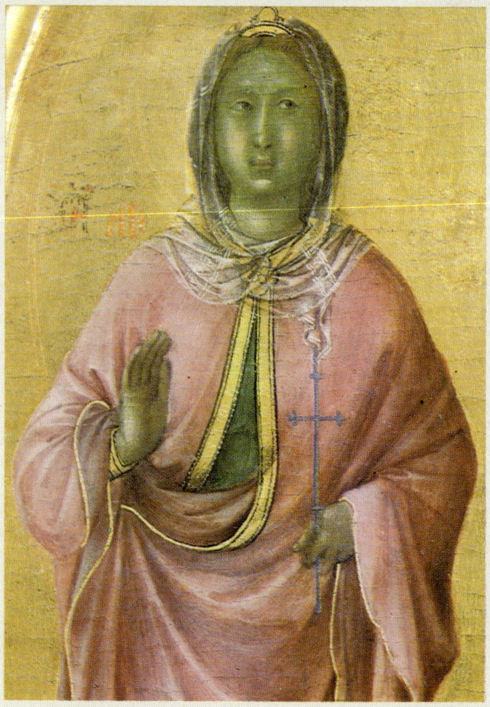

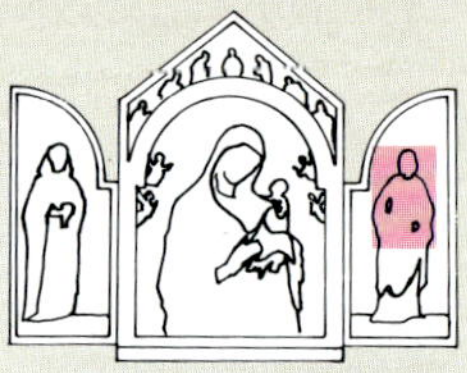

*Drapery painting followed a methodical sequence, using five pre-mixed tones which ranged from pure color in the shadows to white in the highlights. The variations in tone and brushwork were calculated to create the effect of blended modelling. However, because egg tempera dries fast, the small pointed brushstrokes which always follow the form are clearly visible.*

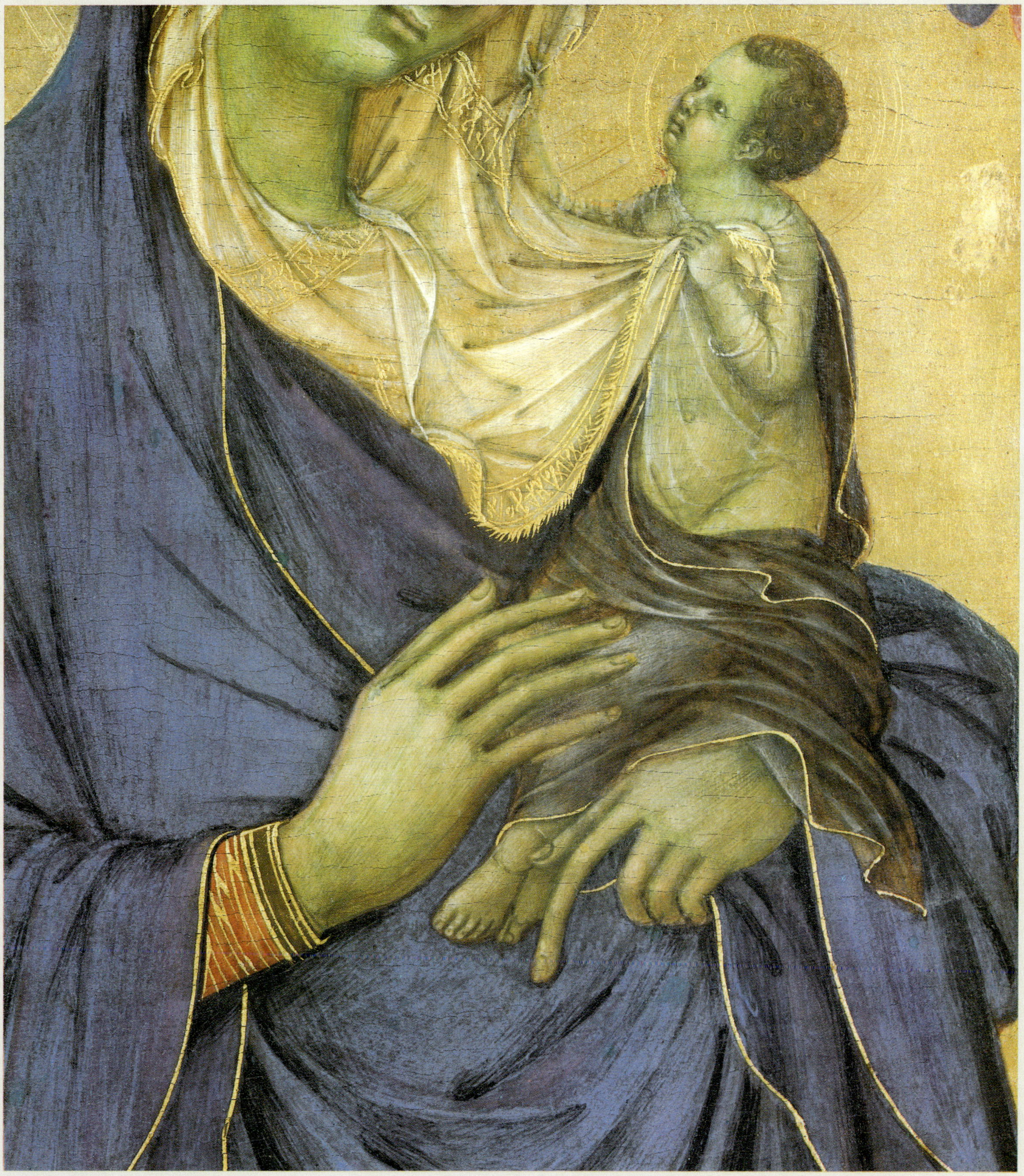

# JAN VAN EYCK

*The Arnolfini Marriage* (1434)
Oil on oak, 84.5cm × 62.5cm/33⅕in × 24¼in

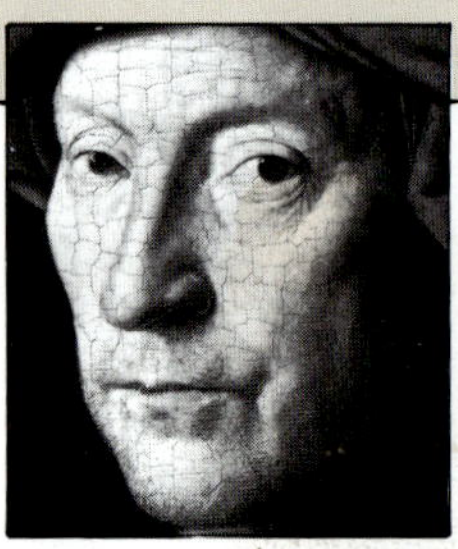

Jan van Eyck did not 'invent' oil painting, although he is frequently credited with so doing, as a new type of painting did emerge around 1420. Oil painting on panel was first described by a German monk, Theophilus, in a treatise on medieval arts around 1100. The main limitation of oil was its slow drying time which, in Theophilus' view, was 'excessively long and tedious in the case of figures'. There followed three hundred years of experiment and improvement. A particular advance was the introduction of metallic drying catalysts in the late fourteenth century.

There is considerable technical consistency among early Netherlandish painters. They painted on oak panels, on white chalk grounds; the drawing was generally done on a preparatory layer which was then rendered impermeable by a preliminary coating of oil. As in Italian panel painting, the ground was bound with animal skin glue, which completely obscured the wood grain and was polished smooth. The smoothness and whiteness of the ground, which provided a source of reflected light, plays a vital part in the final effect. Netherlandish artists used the same range of pigments as Italian artists painting with egg, but the oil gave the colors greater saturation, and increased the range of both transparency and opacity. Paint was prepared in individual workshops; pigments were ground in oil, usually linseed, on a stone slab and, when required, more oil was added to make a workable paint. It is not known whether a volatile diluent such as turpentine was used. A crucial factor in understanding the appearance of van Eyck's paintings is the optical effect of oil on the pigments and how the layered application of the paint exploited this. The painting proceeded from light to dark, from opaque to transparent. The paint is thinnest in the light areas and thickest in the shadows. It is still 'medieval in that each color area is treated individually and its boundaries respected; pigments are rarely mixed together and paint is applied in flat thin coats. This picture, the first full length double portrait in a naturalistic interior, is a fine example of van Eyck's technique. Van Eyck's superlative mastery of oil painting rapidly gave rise to the legend that he invented the process.

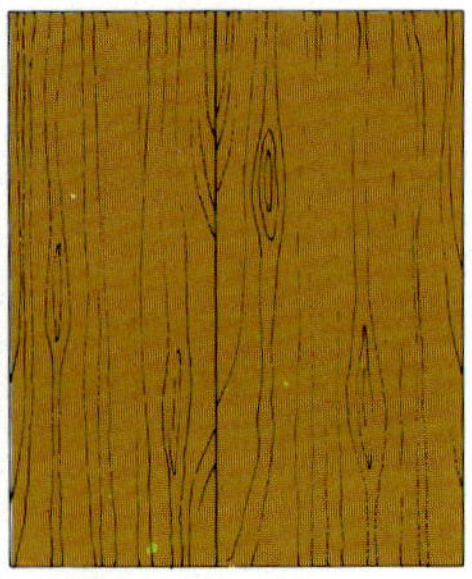

**1.** The painting was executed on a panel made of two pieces of oak with the grain running vertically. Oak has a close grain.

**2.** The animal skin glue and chalk ground was applied in a uniform layer, and polished smooth. It totally obscures the wood grain.

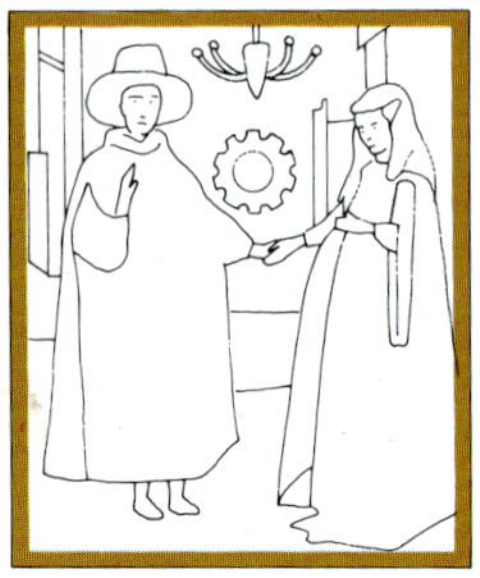

**3.** Van Eyck next began the underdrawing which was very detailed. It was painted on in an aqueous medium with a fine brush.

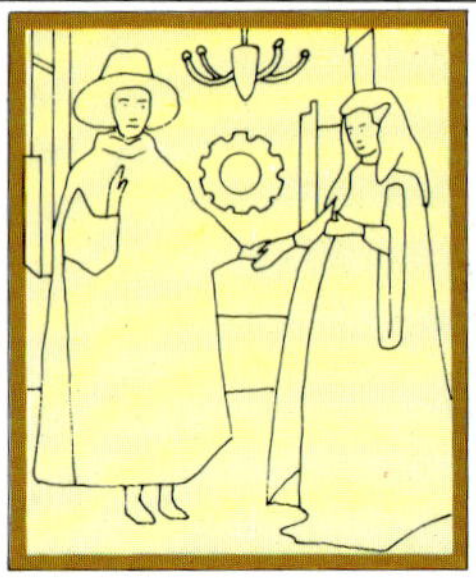

**4.** Van Eyck next made the ground non-absorbent by applying a film of drying oil.

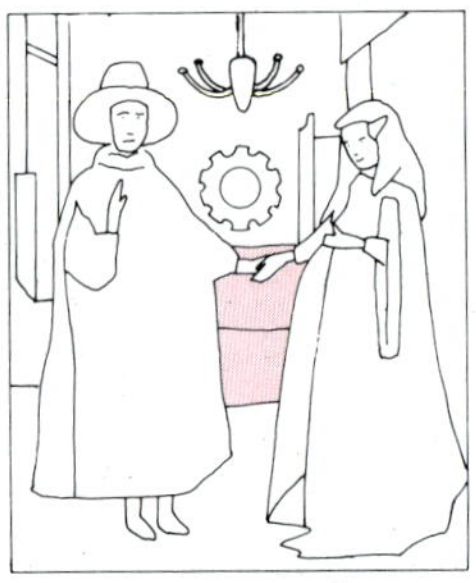

**5.** Van Eyck's technique can be described in general terms. In the lower layers of the painting the color areas were blocked in. The pigment was mixed with a limited amount of opaque white.

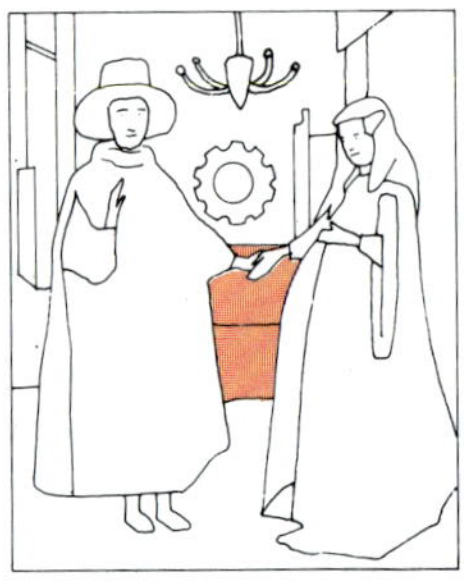

**6.** A middle tone was achieved in a second layer, which used less white and proportionately colored pigment.

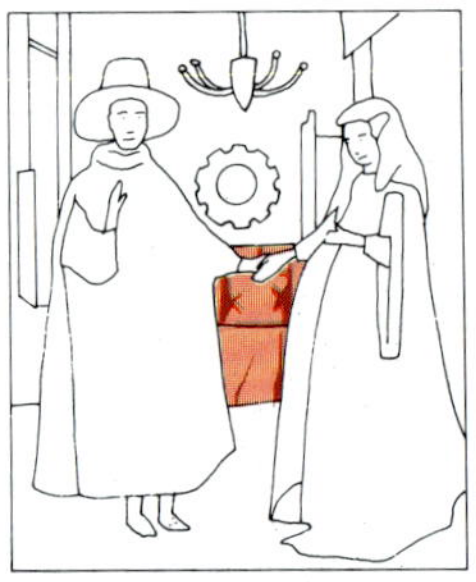

**7.** The final description of form and volume was created in the upper layers using transparent pigments which, by their varying thicknesses, enhanced the modelling.

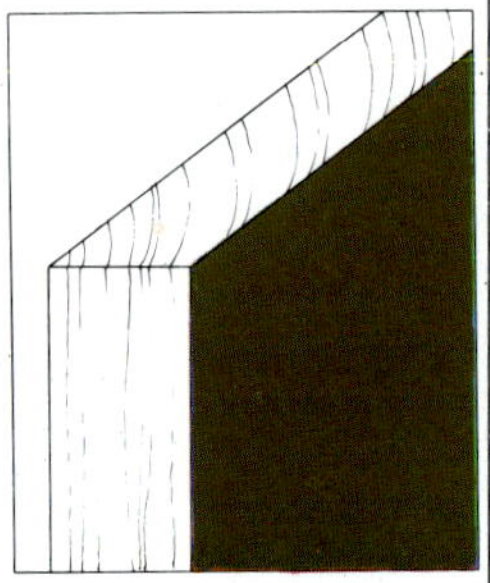

**8.** The back of the panel was covered by a thick white layer containing vegetable fibers which was covered by a thin, black painted layer. This helps prevent the panel from warping. It is not known if this layer is original.

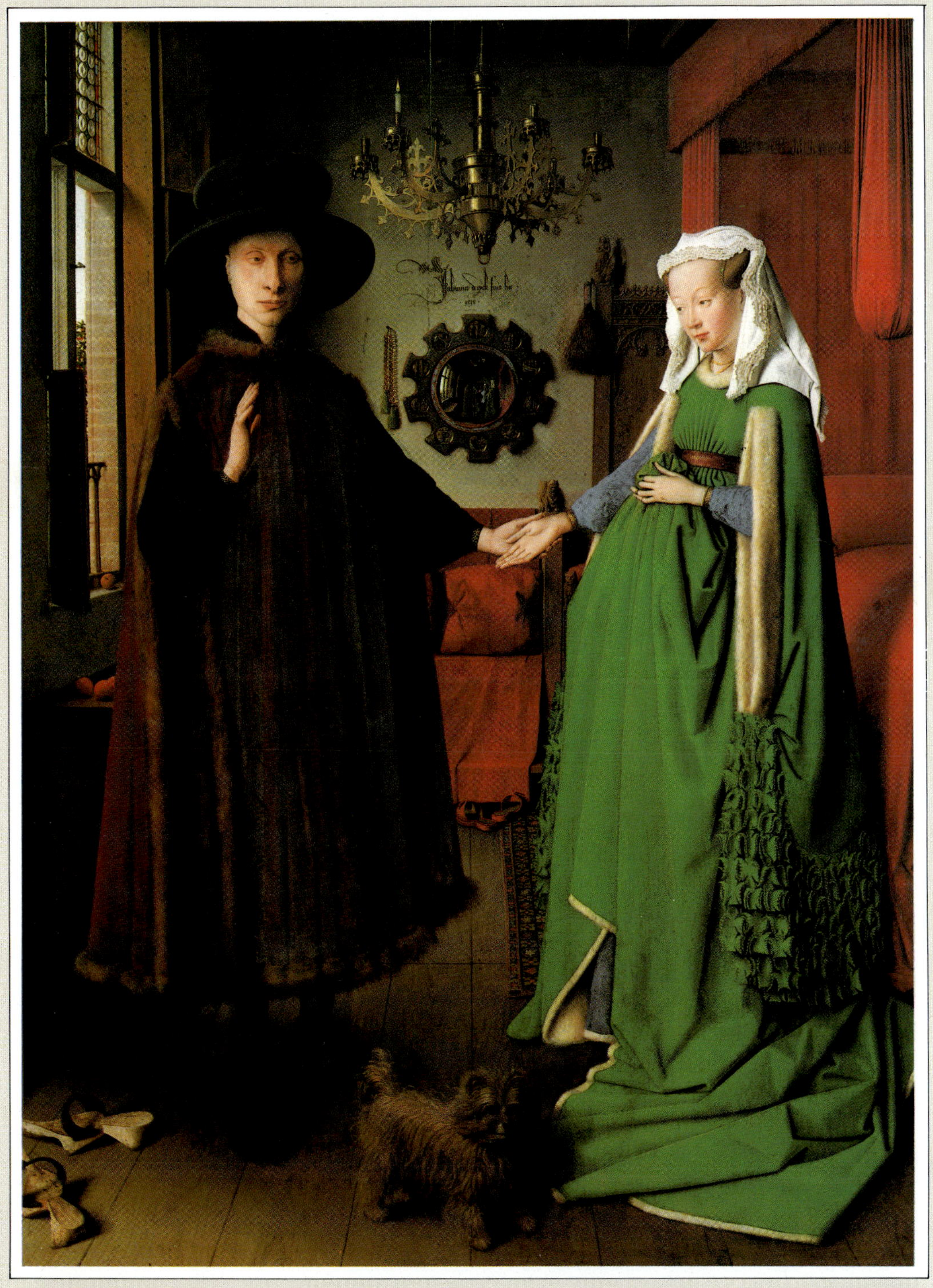

*The principle of construction in this picture is to use the effects of light reflected back from a pale opaque base, through layers of paint, which increase in transparency and saturation and act as filters. The amount of opaque white pigment in the lower layers was lessened in successive applications, so that the upper layers might rely on transparent pigments to enhance the modelling and modulate the optical effects. The brilliance and transparency of these layers may have been increased by the addition of a little varnish to the paint. In the red cushion the painting sequence was probably from an opaque vermilion and white through to a transparent red lake in the shadow area.*

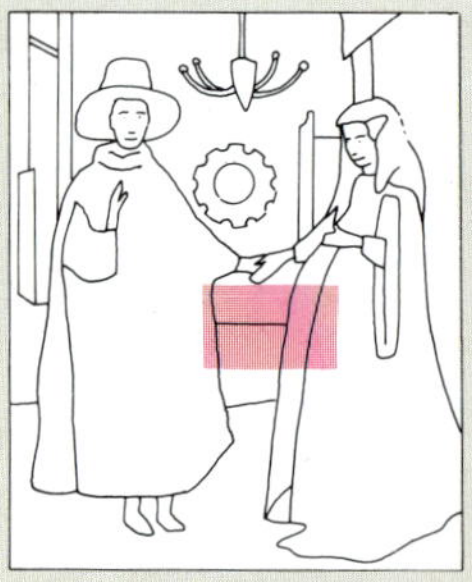

*The modelling may have been achieved by applying first a pale opaque layer of malachite, a traditional green pigment, mixed with lead white, then malachite with less white followed by more saturated, transparent layers of malachite, perhaps mixed with some yellow. Final glazes of verdigris (copper resinate) may have been painted on. All the layers are superimposed.*

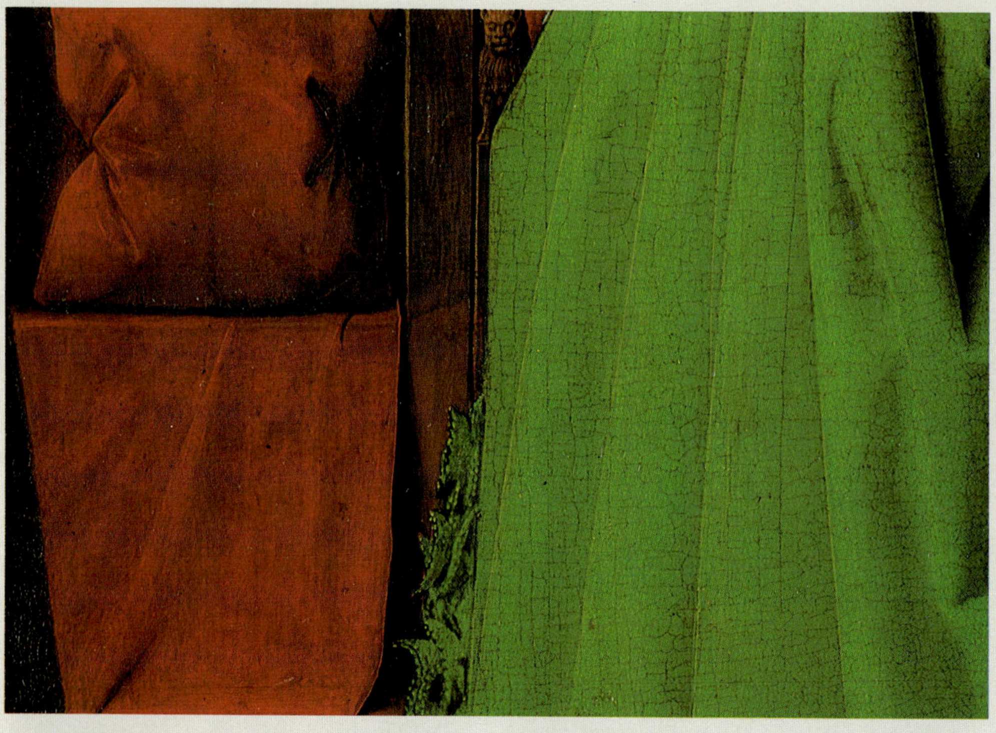

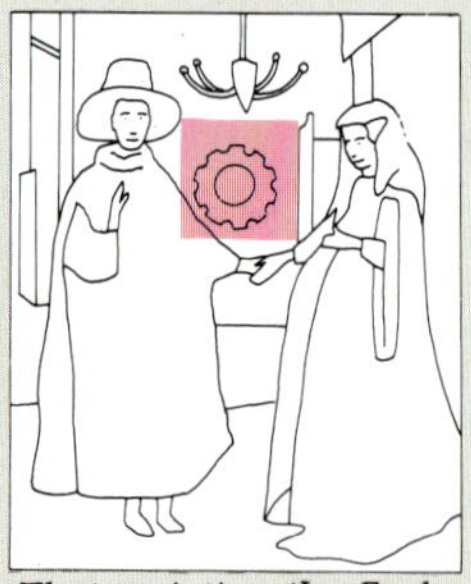

*The inscription, 'Jan Eyck fuit hic 1434' ('Jan Eyck was here 1434'), is juxtaposed with his picture in the mirror. However, the artist's presence is not emphasized. The paint surface is smooth and there are no traces of brush-strokes. Tonal transitions are blended imperceptibly. Every object is described in equally focused detail, as it is revealed by the light. Paintings in oil look more realistic than works in egg tempera. The drying process gave the artist time to study and invisibly adjust final effects. The optical properties of oil encouraged a more accurate reproduction of light, texture and color.*

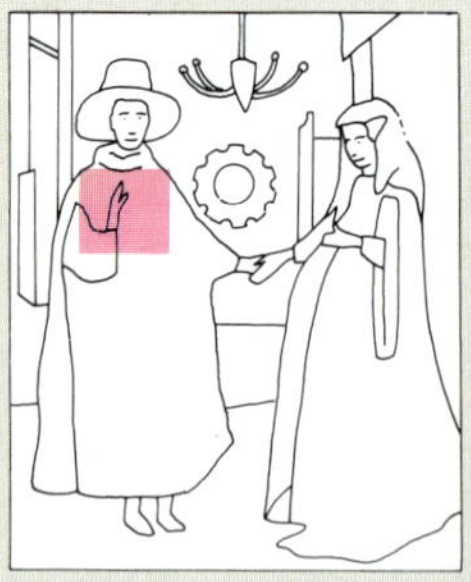

*Infra-red photography can be used to reveal some of the under-drawing or alterations in a painting. Here, adjustments to the position of the hand are clearly visible.*

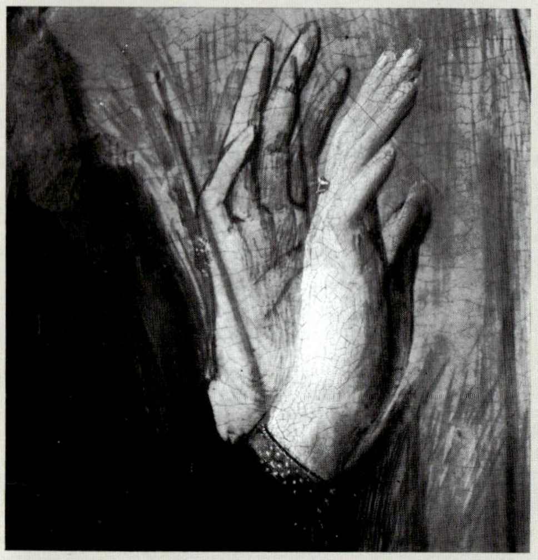

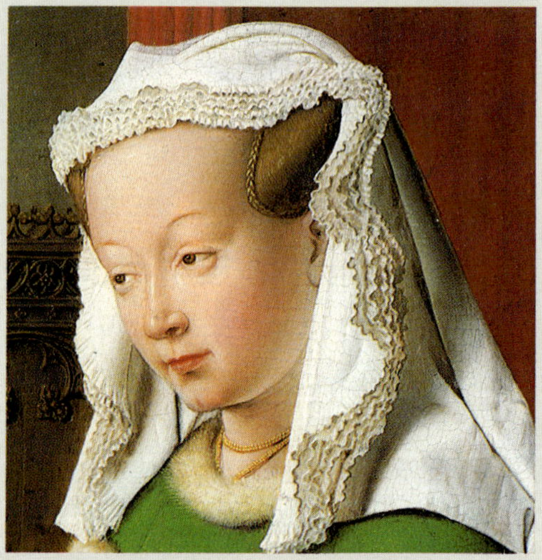

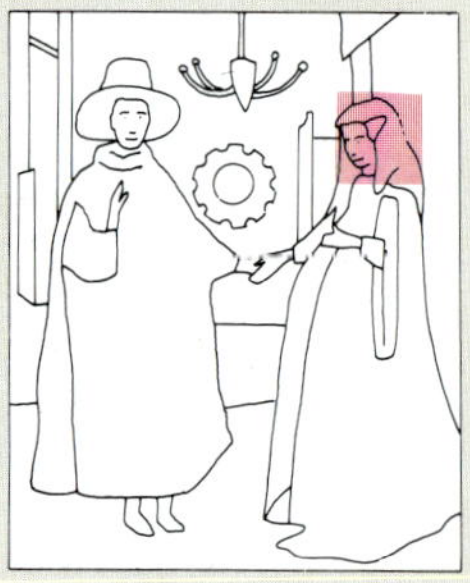

*The flesh painting relies on the effect of the white ground shining through thin layers of pinks and browns. White pigment is used very sparingly and is mostly confined to the accented highlights.*

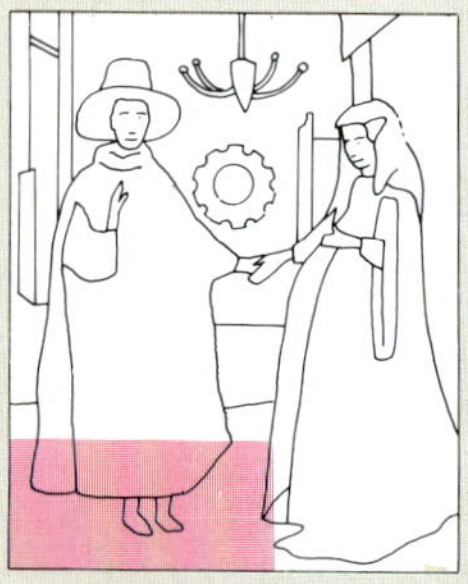

*Alterations in the position of the foot have become visible because oil increases in transparency as it ages.*

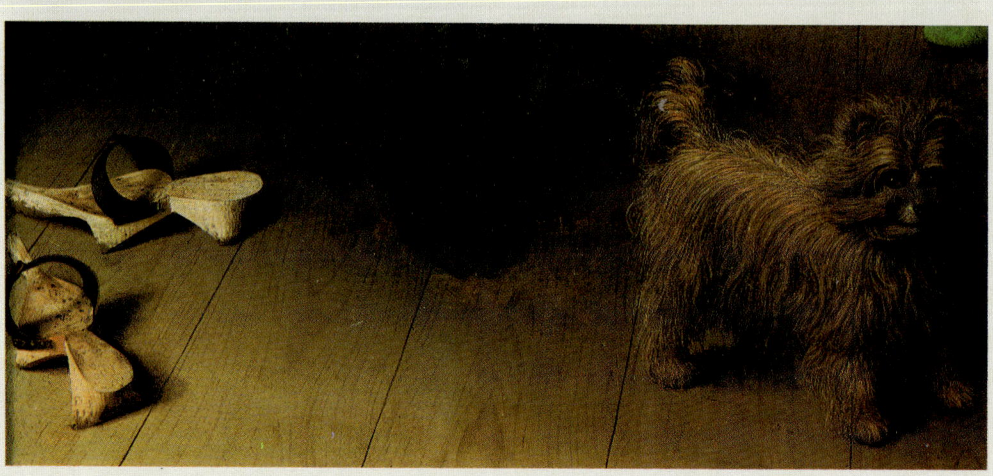

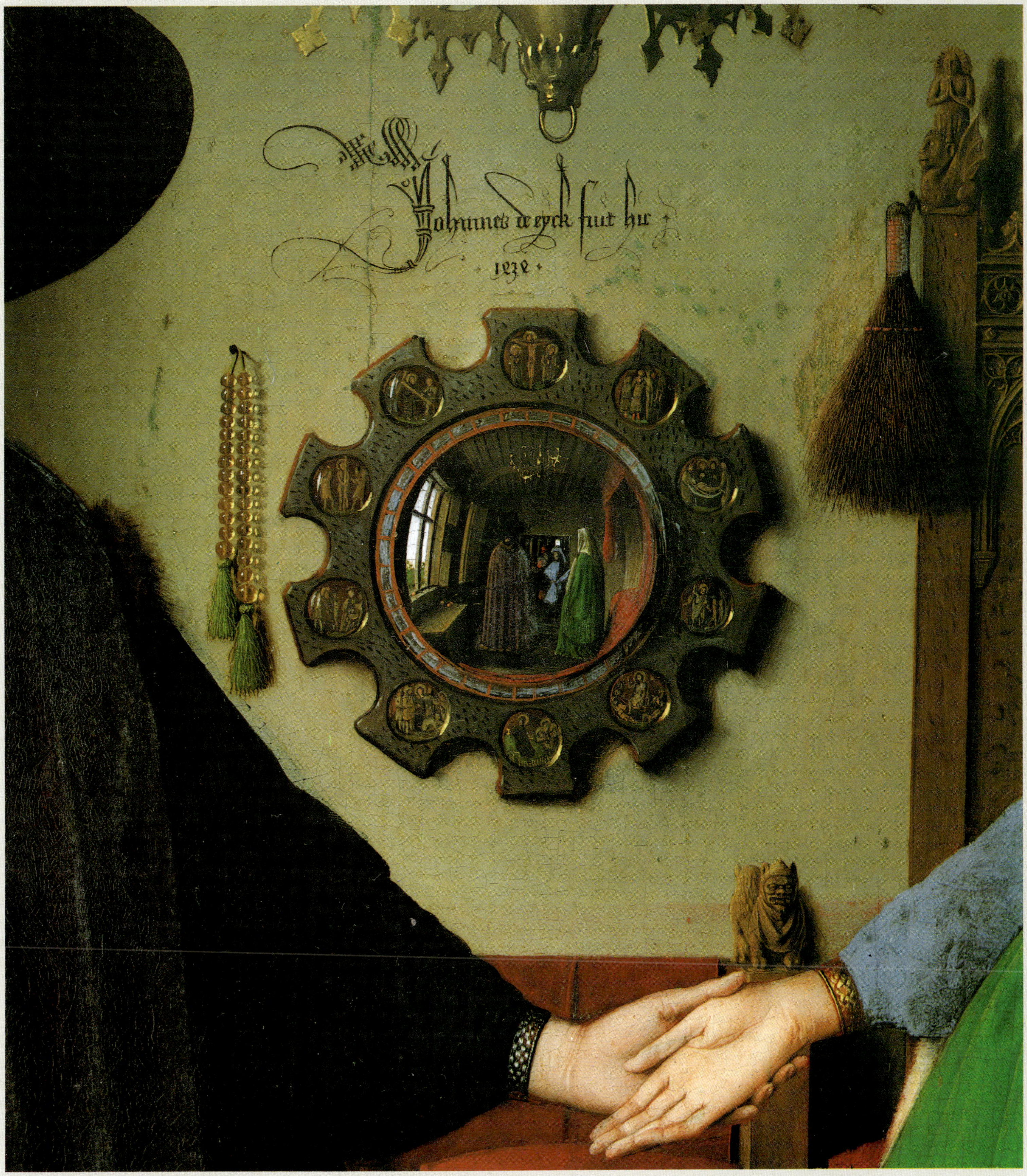
Johannes de eyck fuit hic

# PIERO DELLA FRANCESCA

*The Baptism of Christ* (c. 1442)
Egg tempera on oil on wood, 167cm × 116cm/66in × 45¾in

Piero della Francesca is now considered one of the most important painters of the fifteenth century Italian Renaissance, although his work was overlooked for a long time. Piero came from Borgo San Sepolcro – a small town in Umbria. *The Baptism* was thought to have been painted for a church in this town. Piero worked in Florence under the Venetian master Domenico Veneziano and Piero's early work shows in particular how he assimilated for example Florentine ideas on perspective and the organization of space.

Some of Piero's later paintings reflect a strong Flemish influence, most likely due to the presence of Flemish paintings and artists in Italy at the time. Although he lived until 1492, Piero appears to have stopped painting in the 1470s which was probably due to an overriding interest in perspective and mathematics on which he wrote two treatises.

The fifteenth century artists, Perugino and Signorelli, were probably both pupils of Piero's; and his influence was to be felt not only by them, but also by many other artists particularly in the areas in which he worked, for example Ferrara and Umbria. This reflects the important communication of ideas and techniques which obviously promoted the growth and development of Renaissance art.

Piero worked both in egg tempera, as in *The Baptism*, and in oil. He was working at the time when the emphasis in painting was shifting from tempera to oil. However, there is a growing body of evidence which indicates that this transition took place gradually rather than suddenly as was traditionally thought. Many artists at the time of Piero used both tempera and oil, even combining the two in one painting.

For this reason, it is generally dangerous to assume that all works in tempera by a particular artist must be from an early period and those executed in oil from a later one. Nevertheless, with further research and improving methods of scientific analysis, it may one day be possible to prove that Piero was as important and innovative an artist in fifteenth century Italian painting techniques as he was in other fields.

Piero's reputation languished for many years, and his work was only 'rediscovered' towards the end of the nineteenth century. *The Baptism* was bought by the National Gallery, London in 1860, at a time when Piero's works were beginning to attract more widespread attention in the art world.

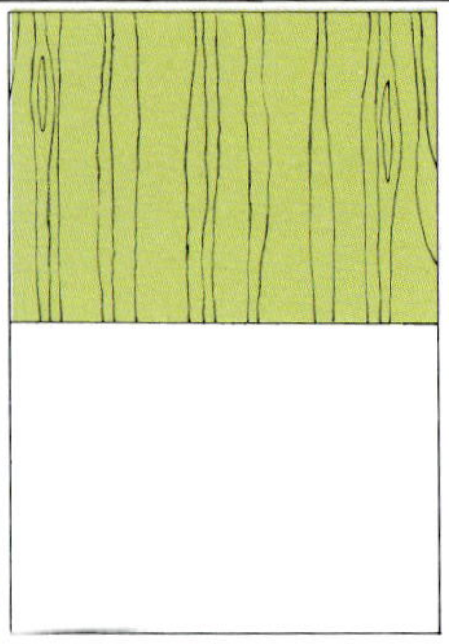

**1.** Two poplar wood planks with vertical grain were covered with white gesso. A final coat of glue was perhaps added.

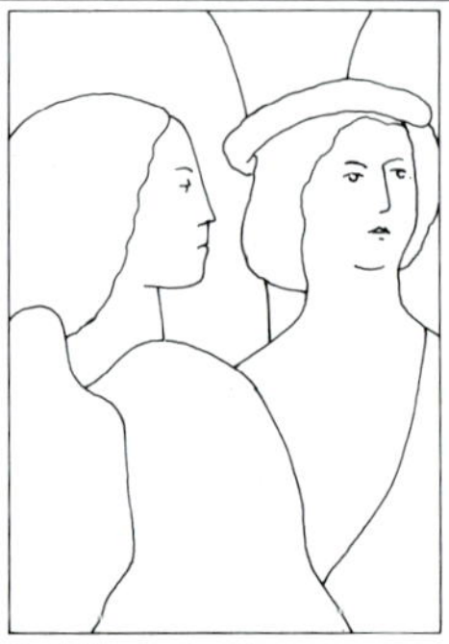

**2.** The underdrawing was done in black, simply defining the main outlines and features, which were drawn in with fine lines without hatching or shading.

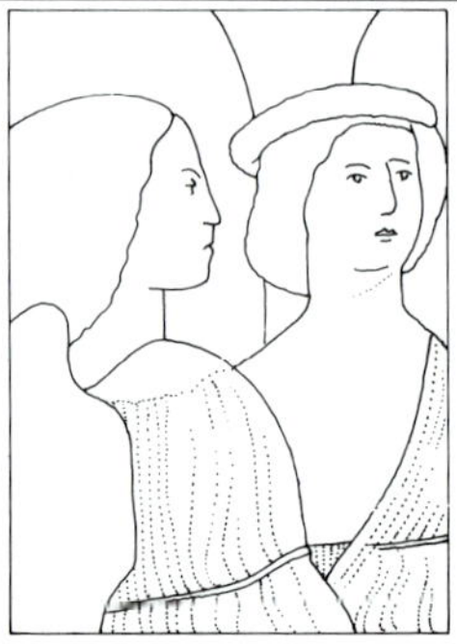

**3.** The more complicated details were most likely transferred on to the gesso by 'pouncing', a technique popular at the time.

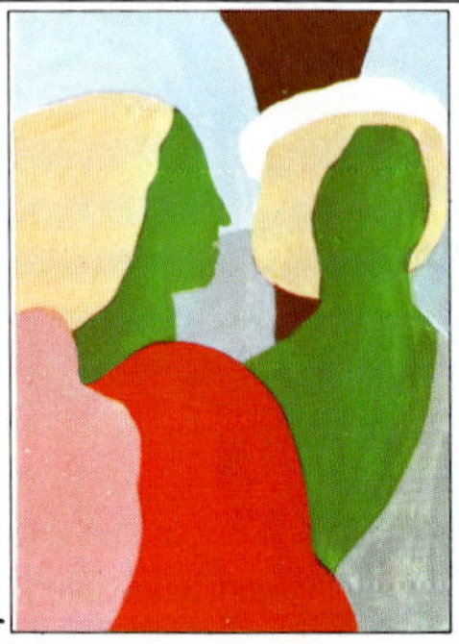

**4.** The pale blue sky was probably then added and the wreath blocked in without details. Drapery was completed but not decorated. The wings were blocked in without gold highlighting and the hair without details.

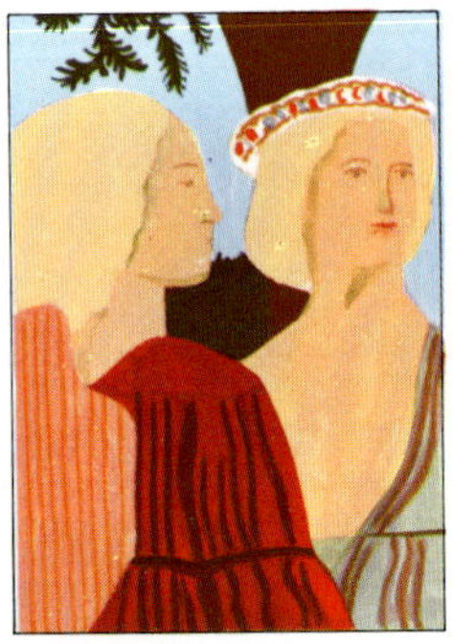

**5.** The flesh was completed allowing some of the green underpainting to show through. Leaves were put in the background and gold was added.

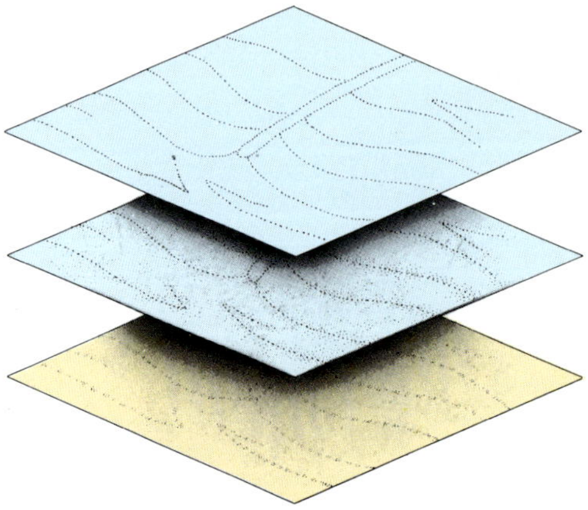

Pouncing
*Pouncing was a technique used for transferring complicated details on to the painting surface. The lines of a drawing were punctured to create a series of small perforations. The paper was then laid over the gesso ground or, in fresco, over the plaster, and dusted with charcoal powder. This penetrated the holes leaving small dots on the ground from which the artist outlined the picture.*

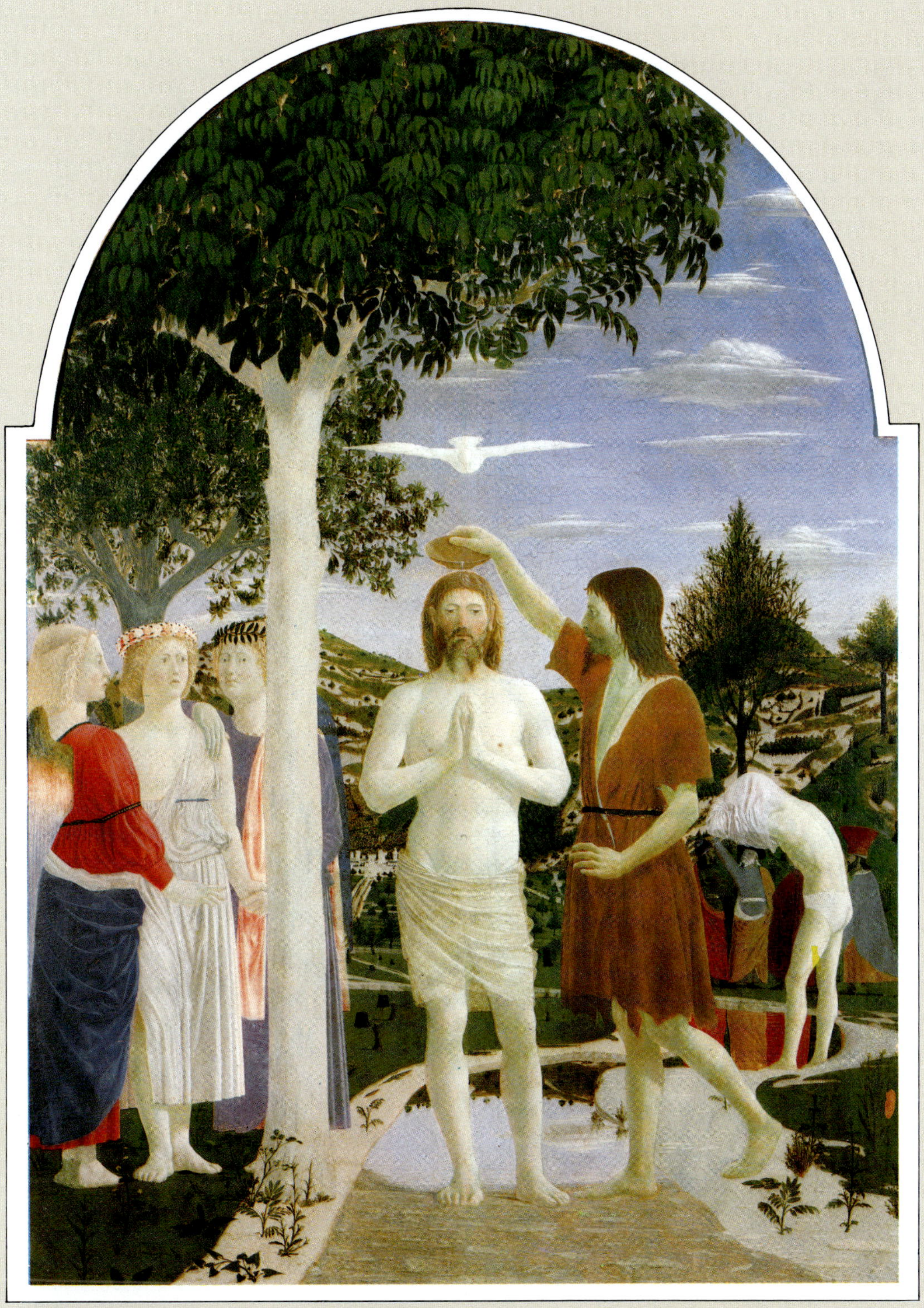

The Baptism *is painted on a panel constructed of two wide poplar planks with a vertical grain. The panel has been prepared with a thick and unusually hard ground which suggests a high proportion of glue in the gesso. The preliminary drawing is simple; however, Piero probably made full-sized cartoons for some of the more complicated details, although none of these have survived. The pigments used are standard for the period. For example, the robe of the angel on the left was painted with ultramarine, the foliage is verdigris and the flesh areas have been underpainted in the traditional green earth. That a number of forms have been painted on top of one another indicates Piero's unusual tendency to complete forms even when they were to be later covered over.*

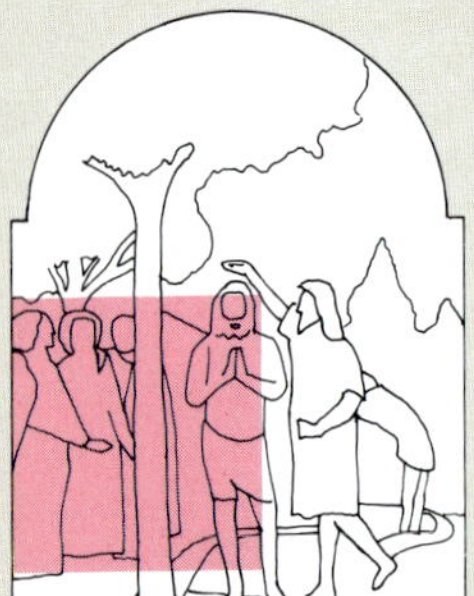

*The details of the landscape are painted over in a flat under-color. The angel's robe and wing have been extended over the landscape which is now visible due to the increase in transparency of the paint with age. Small black dots from the pounced transfer can be seen along the folds of the red fabric. The drapery has been modelled with long, hatched, unblended strokes using a system whereby the pigment is at its purest and most saturated in the fabric folds. There is some gold decoration in the angel's wings but this has been rubbed and unfortunately damaged. The green underpainting of the flesh is also now visible.*

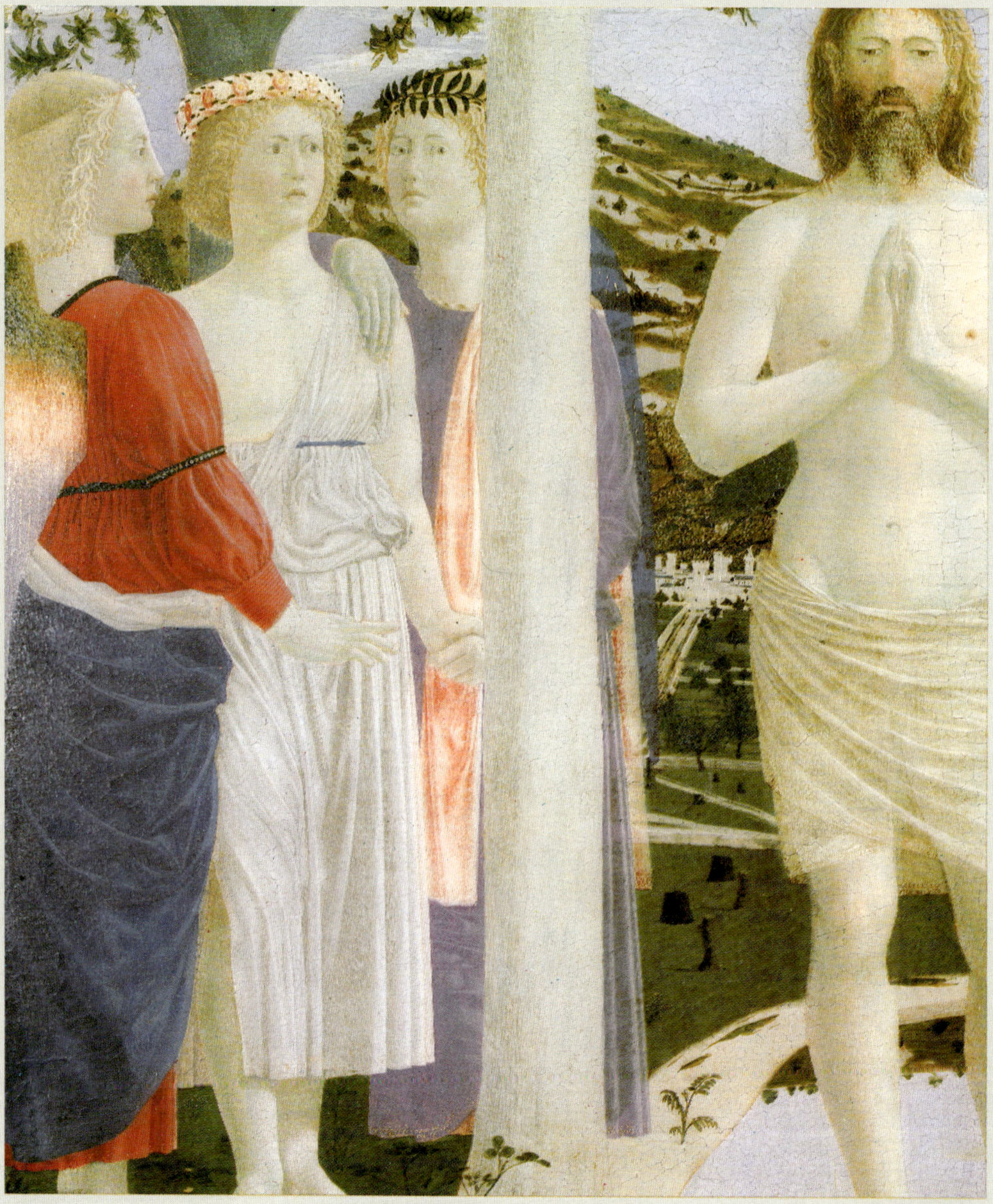

*In the head of John the Baptist, the flesh is underpainted with the green earth of traditional Italian tempera painting and then completed with a natural flesh color. The beard has been stippled over the completed flesh paint and sleeve.*

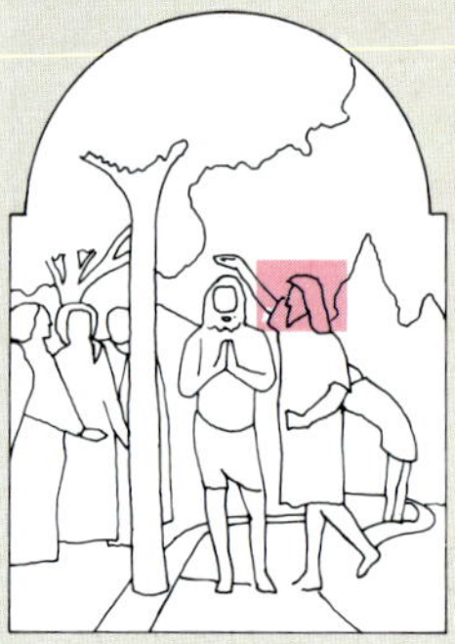

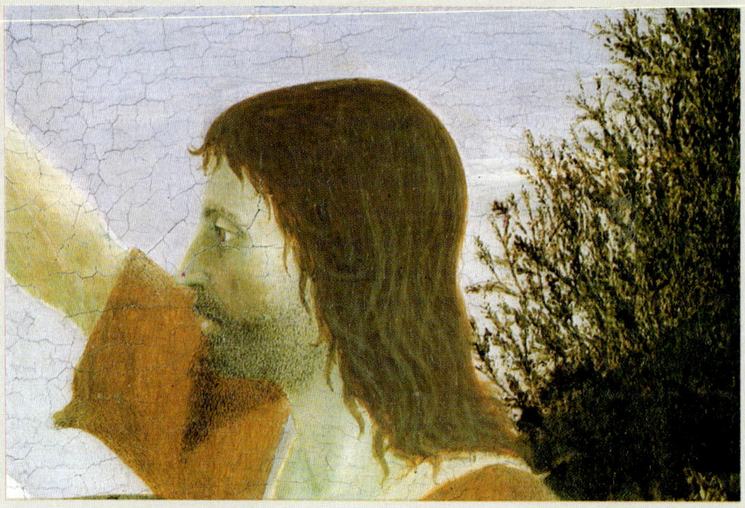

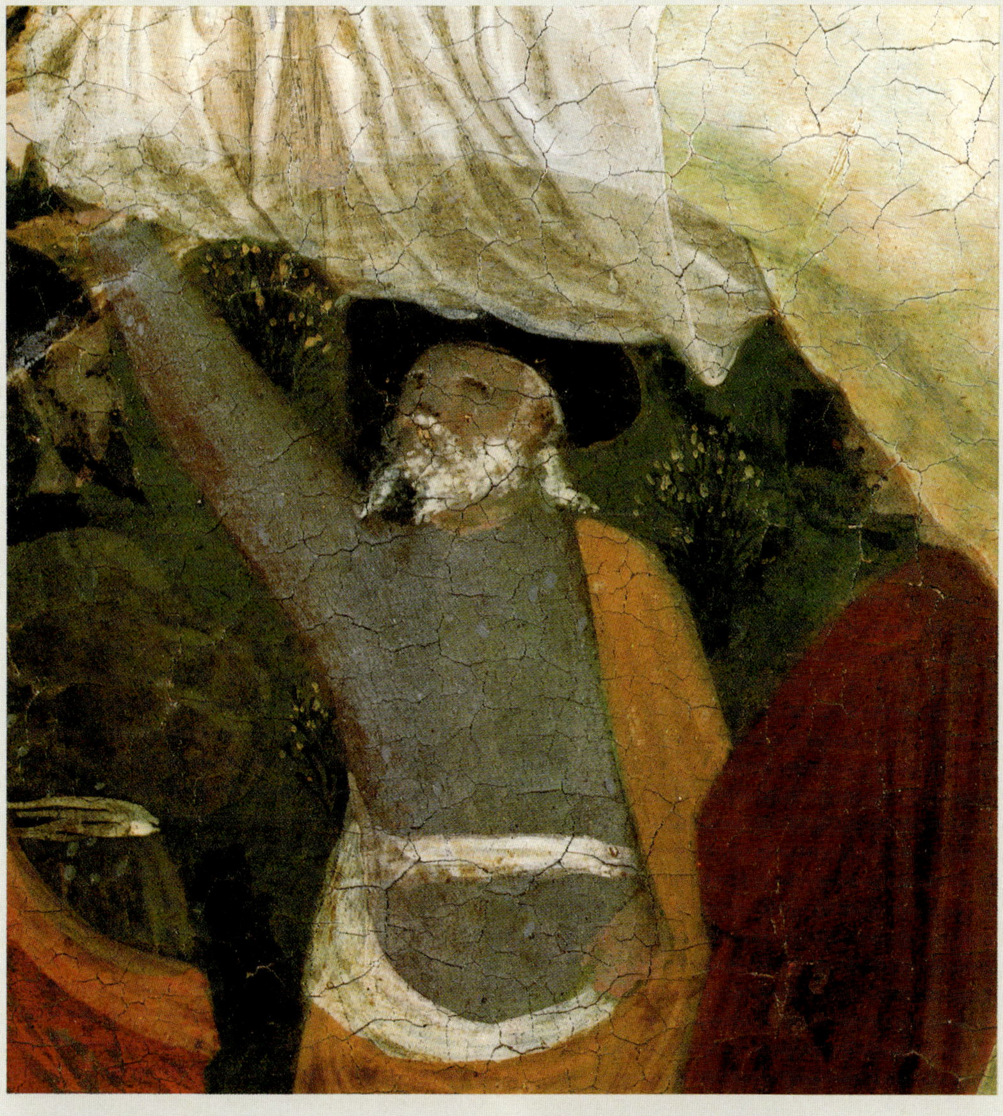

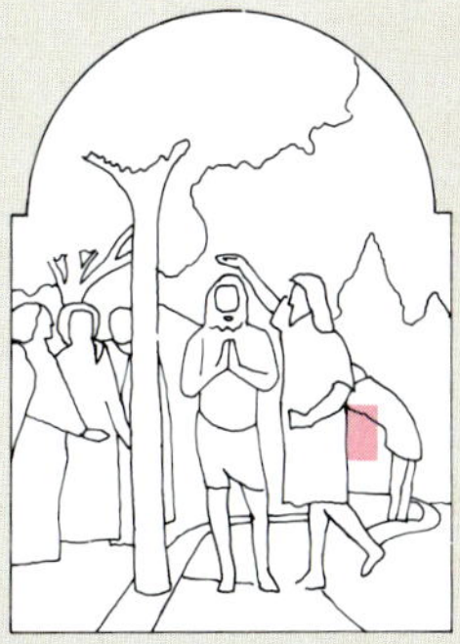

*In the heads and shoulders of the two figures in the righthand background, the upper half of the figure on the left has been painted over the landscape. In these figures the paint was applied as a fairly flat wash with a little hatched modelling.*

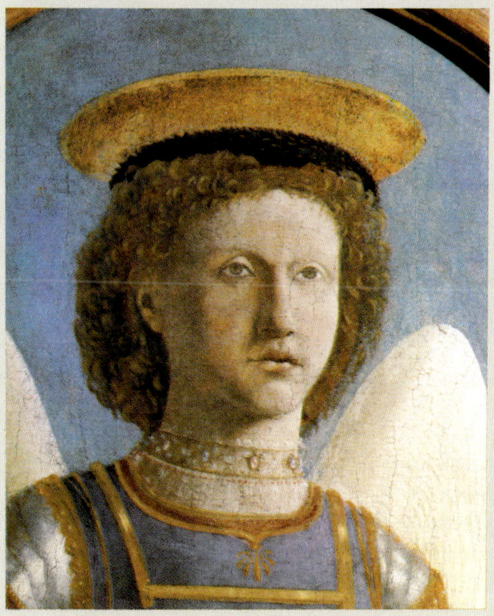

*The paint medium for* St Michael *has been identified as walnut oil. The flesh has been underpainted with a brownish under-modelling, as opposed to the green earth of* The Baptism, *although a little green has been added to the upper layers of the flesh paint to give a slightly green tinge.*

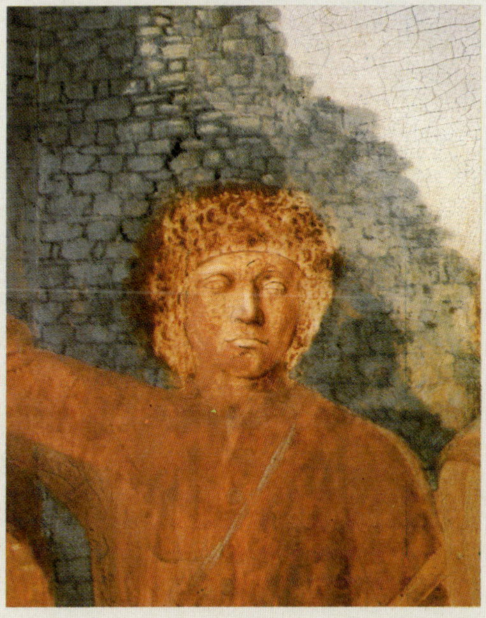

*In* St Michael *the head of the shepherd has been badly damaged in the past probably by over-cleaning, so that now little more than the brown undermodelling is left. The firm, confident underdrawing outlining the main features is typical of Piero's technique.*

# LEONARDO DA VINCI

*The Virgin of the Rocks* (c. 1508)
Oil on wood, 189.5cm × 120cm/$75\frac{5}{8}$in × $47\frac{1}{4}$in

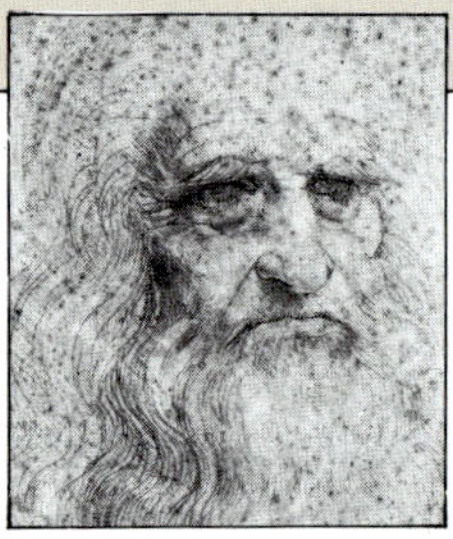

Leonardo da Vinci, one of the major figures of the Italian Renaissance, was born in 1452 and trained under the Florentine artist Verrocchio. Due to the understandable reluctance of art gallery curators to allow samples to be taken from their paintings by Leonardo, and the fact that his notebooks tend to be obscure and difficult to interpret, there is little information on the artist's techniques.

There are two versions of *The Virgin of the Rocks* – one in the National Gallery in London and the other in the Louvre in Paris. The National Gallery version is better documented and definitely came from the church of St Francesco Grande in Milan, for which it was commissioned in 1483. However, the picture has not always received the same critical acceptance as the Louvre version and it has been suggested there was a degree of studio participation. It is possible that, for some reason, the National Gallery picture was begun as a replacement for the earlier version towards the end of the century, but was never completed. Although the London version may have lost some of the immediate appeal and Florentine 'prettiness' of the Paris picture, it has gained a monumentality, depth of mood, and unity of light and color not fully attained in the first version which the artist painted.

The basic medium for *The Virgin of the Rocks* was almost certainly a drying oil as stipulated in the original contract for the work. Walnut and linseed oils are listed among the expenses for another of Leonardo's paintings and, judging from his notebooks, Leonardo was particularly concerned that his painting oils should be as clear and colorless as possible/to which end he may have prepared them himself. Unfortunately, faults in the preparation of the colors may be partly responsible for the drying defects in the paint film now visible on some works, including *The Virgin of the Rocks*.

While Leonardo would have had access to most pigments of his day, he often seems to have used a muted palette with color playing a secondary role to the modelling of forms and the organization of light and shade.

Although *The Virgin of the Rocks* has been fairly recently cleaned, many of Leonardo's other works are distorted by accumulated layers of dirt, varnish, and overpainting; and so the artist's techniques remain a mystery.

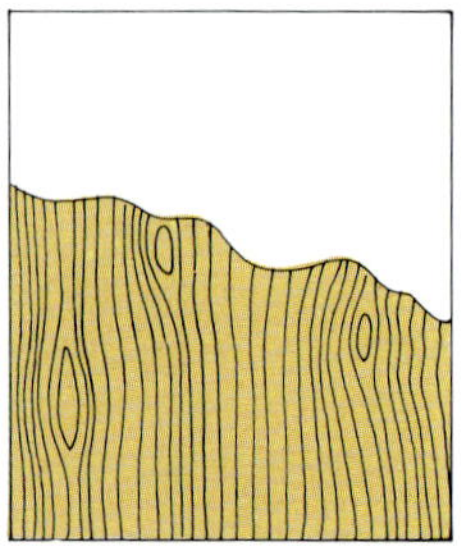

**1.** It is not possible to say exactly how Leonardo painted his works, however, a possible sequence can be worked out. First a panel would have been covered with a layer of gesso.

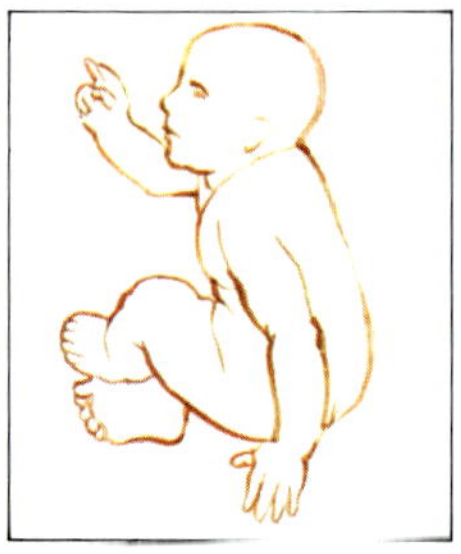

**2.** It seems that Leonardo may have first roughed in the figures on the panel.

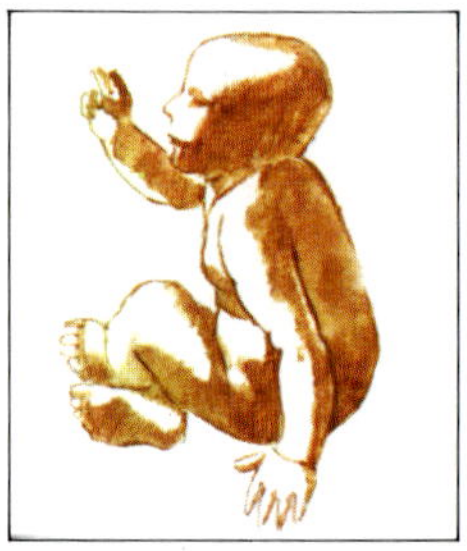

**3.** The major forms may have been modelled in a brownish tone, defining shadows and highlights.

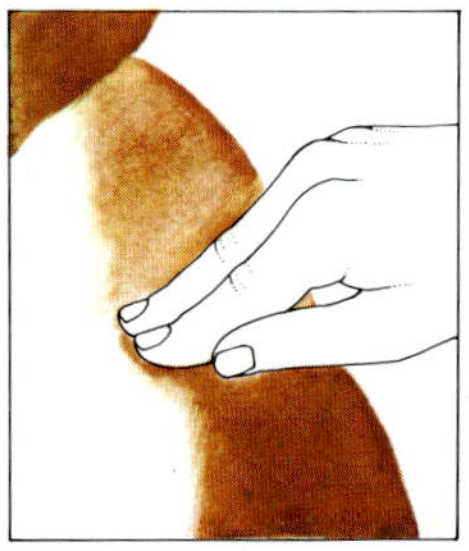

**4.** Leonardo used his fingers and palms as well as a brush, particularly for the undermodelling. This was not an unusual practice at the time.

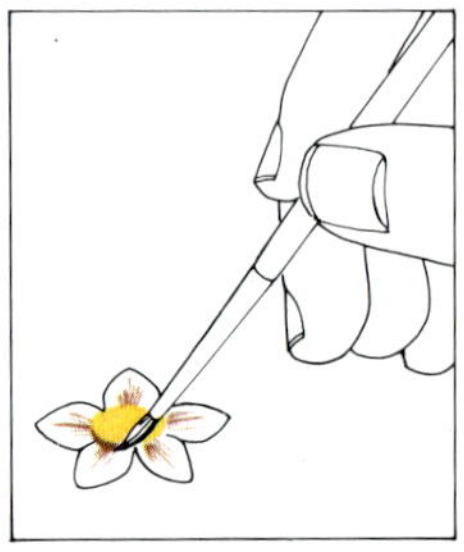

**5.** Intricate details were then put in with great precision and delicacy using fine minever brushes, similar to modern day sable brushes.

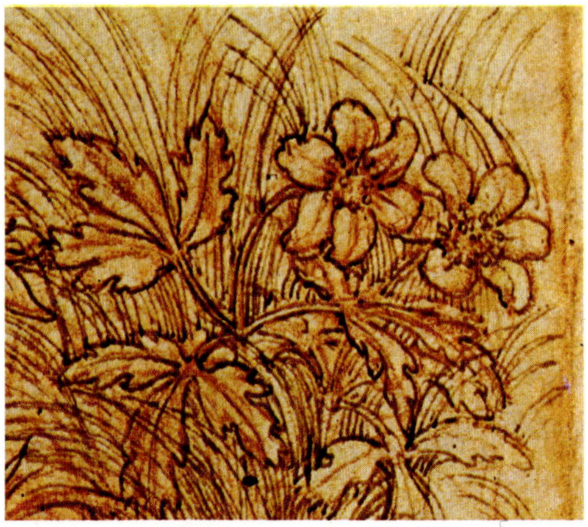

Leonardo's interest in botany was given expression in several media. There is a marked similarity between the flowers in this drawing and those in *The Virgin of the Rocks*. The detail was drawn in pen and ink over a background sketch in red chalk.

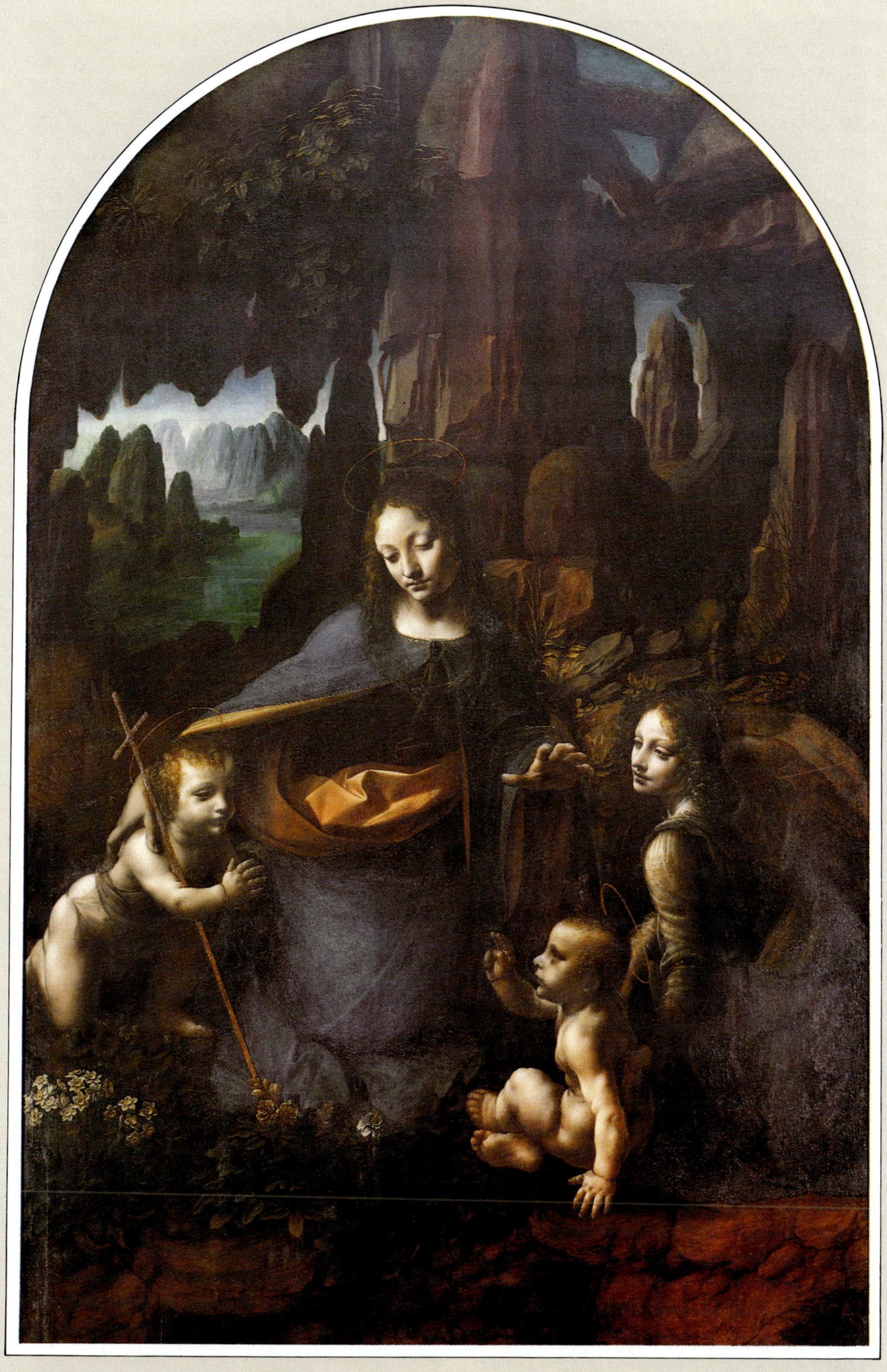

*Leonardo's preoccupation with light and shade is illustrated by his use of a brownish monochrome under-modelling visible in some of the incomplete areas of the painting. While each painting involved a number of preliminary drawings and studies, it is unlikely that Leonardo did any detailed underdrawing on the panel itself. It is possible that some of the colors in the painting have altered with time: the green foliage may have darkened and become brown, the blue robes stained and dulled by dirt and varnishes. Changes may have occurred in the flesh colors accounting for its cold and marble-like appearance. It has been suggested that Leonardo finished or intended to finish the flesh areas with very thin glazes of lake pigments, the dyes of which may have since faded.*

*This unfinished work,* The Adoration of the Magi, *illustrates that Leonardo did his undermodelling mainly in brown, using several different tones.*

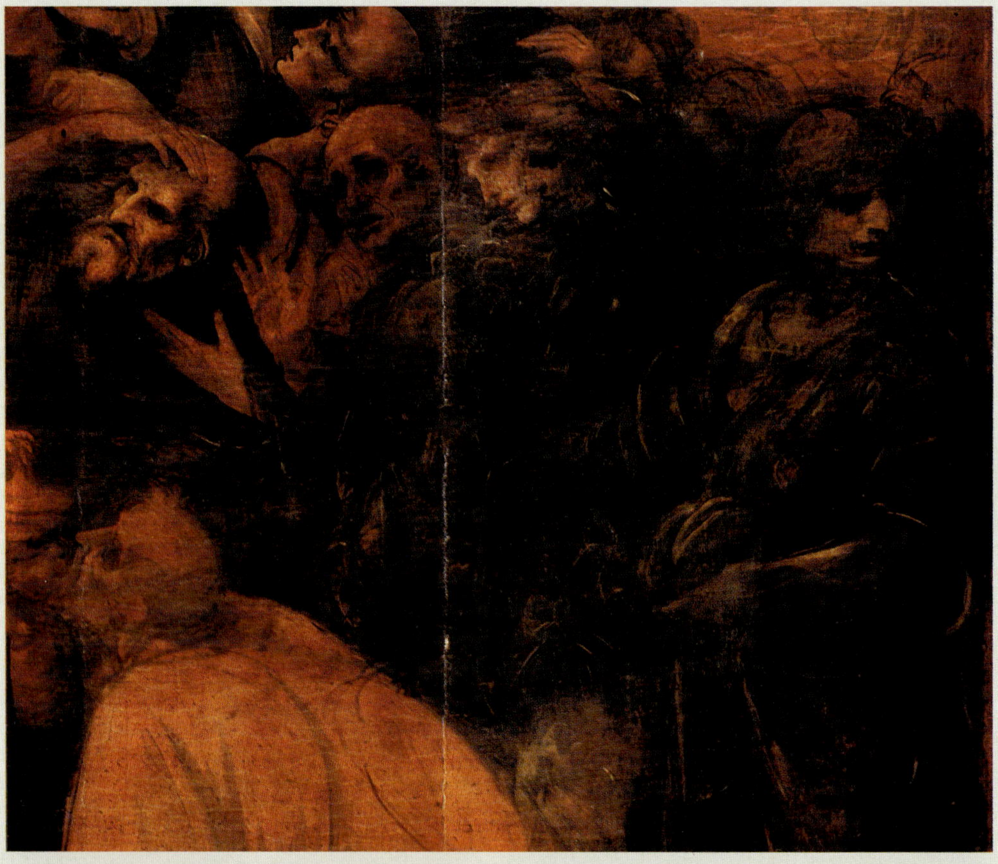

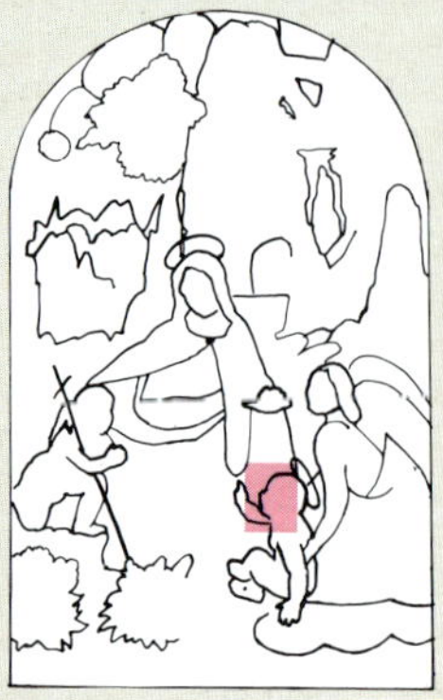

*This X-radiograph* (right) *shows that Christ's head was originally inclined more towards the spectator in a position similar to that of his counterpart in the Louvre. Both images can be seen because the white lead used in the flesh paint is opaque to X-rays, absorbing them and preventing them from reaching and blackening the film.*

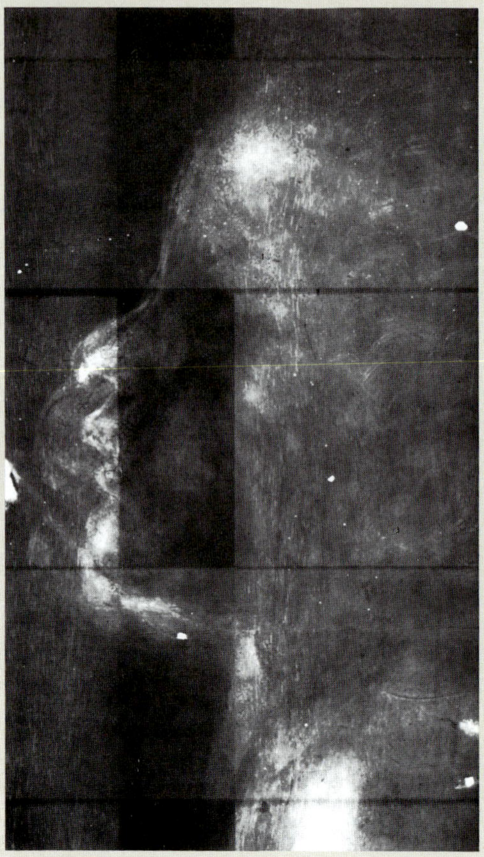

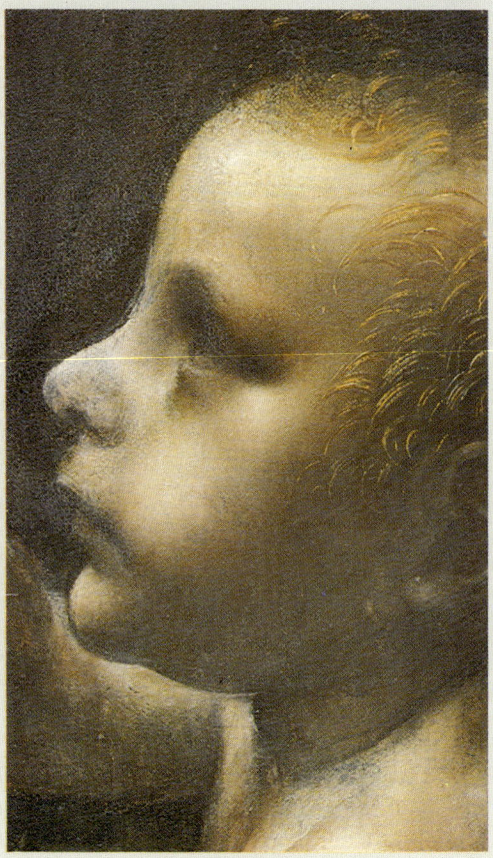

*This detail from Leonardo's painting* Virgin and Child with Carnation *shows marked wrinkling of the paint surface on the Virgin's flesh. This is caused by poor technique — Leonardo seems to have added too much oil to the paint mixture.*

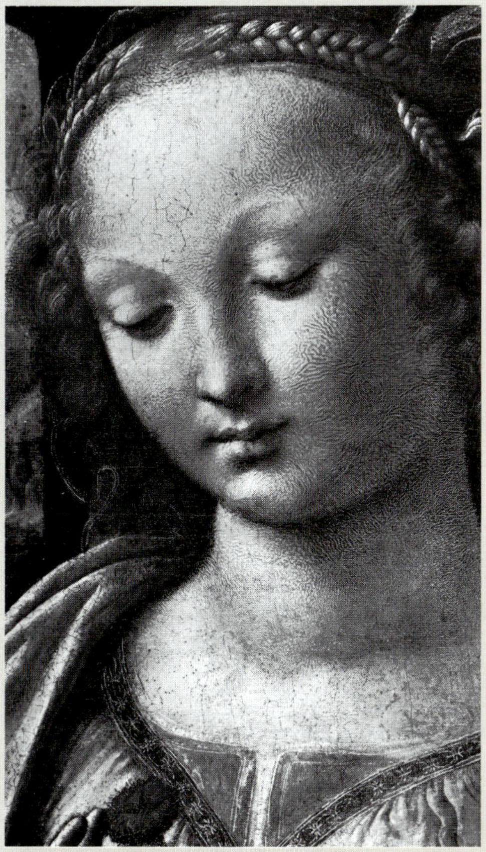

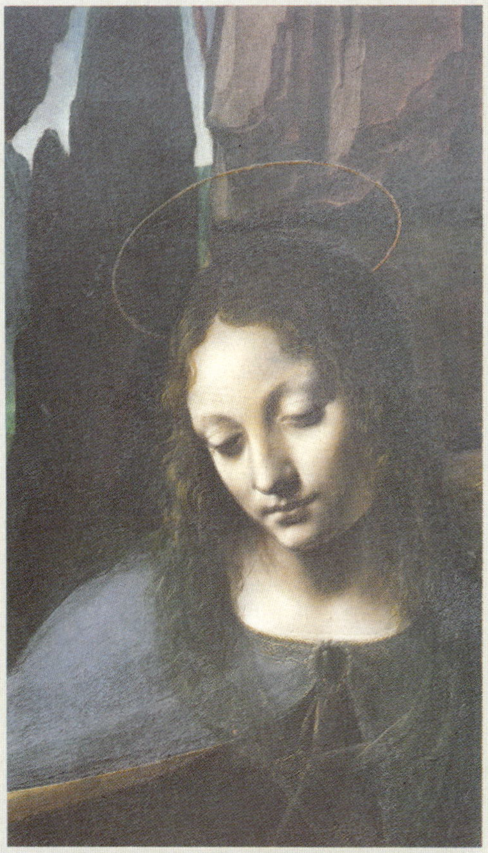

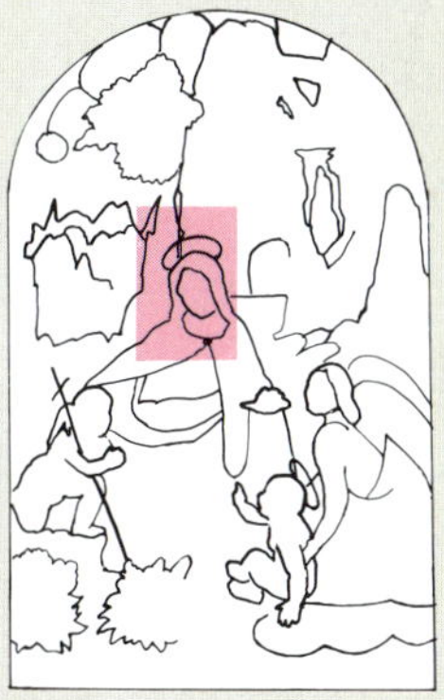

*The Virgin's head was painted using the same technique for the flesh areas as in Christ's head. In the darker shadow areas, fingerprints are clearly visible. A cross section of the robe shows that it has a complicated layer structure. An initial layer of gray was painted over with azurite before the final layer of ultramarine was applied. The use of ultramarine was stipulated in Leonardo's contract for this work; this was common practice because of the expensiveness of the pigment. The yellow in the lining of the Virgin's robe is lead tin yellow. Cracks in the robe were probably caused by drying defects. It is not known whether the gold halo is original.*

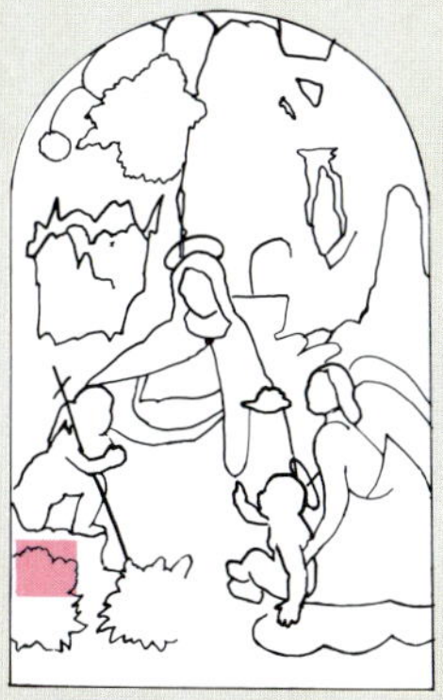

Actual size detail
*This detail shows that the plants have probably been painted over the rocks. The delicate brushwork and detail in the depiction of the flowers reflect Leonardo's keen interest in the study of botany.*

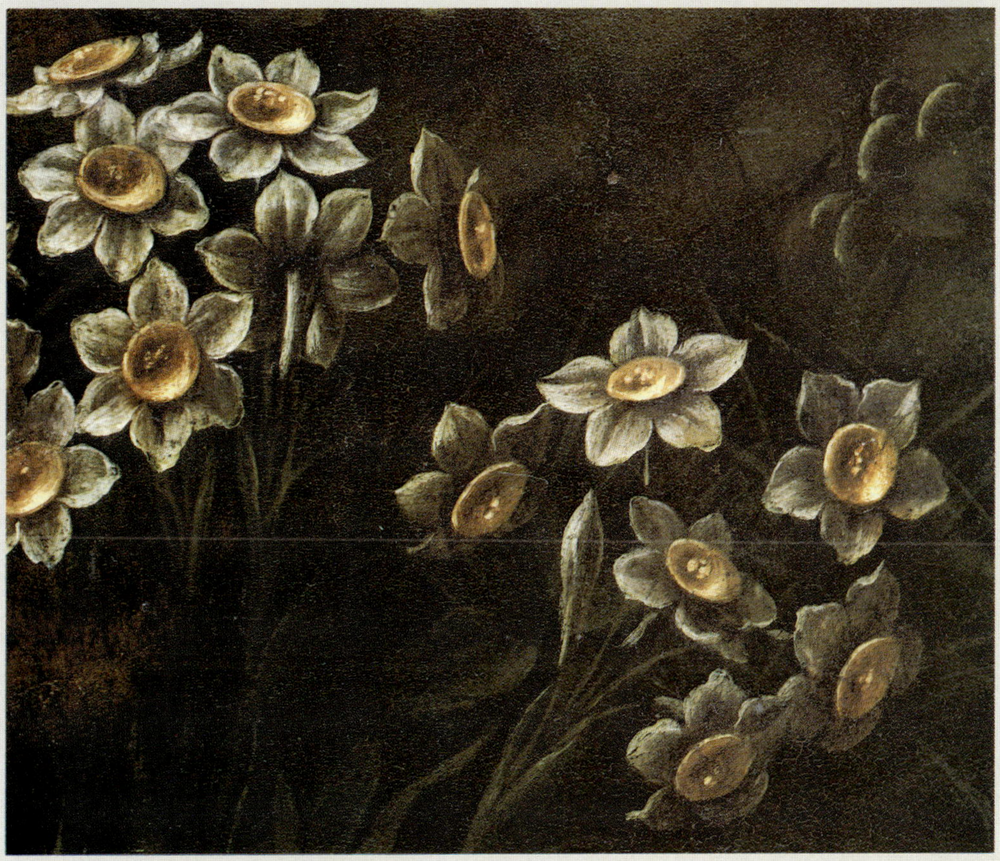

# HIERONYMOUS BOSCH

*The Carrying of the Cross* (c. 1510-1516)
Oil on oak, 76.7cm × 83.5cm/30in × 33in

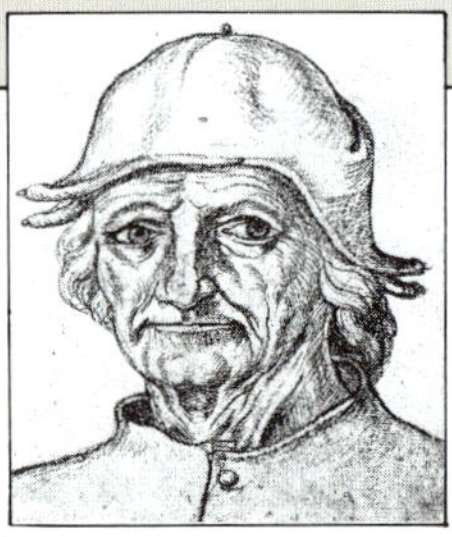

While contemporaries were fascinated by Bosch as an inventor of monsters and chimeras', they were also impressed by the originality of his technique. Karel van Mander, the first historian of Northern painting, wrote in 1604 that Bosch 'had established a very rapid, characteristic way of working, setting many of his things down at first, which nevertheless remained very beautiful without alteration. He also had, like other masters, the method of drawing and tracing out on the white of the panels and laying over this a flesh-colored priming, and he often let the ground play a part too.

The techniques which Bosch employed in his paintings were both traditional and original. Most of his works were executed on panels covered with a thin chalk ground and an oil film laid over to reduce absorbency. However, an innovatory second chalk ground was applied which added brilliance to the paint. The underdrawing was done with a brush and thin black paint. Bosch was not concerned with an objective description of detail, light, or perspective, but an expression of form. His style was rapid, sketchy, linear and often limited to single broken lines that search out the main contours of shapes in the painting. Bosch's expressive, simplified style of drawing is matched by his painting technique. He generally applied only one thin coat of paint, and it is only in the cases of red and green glazes over opaque substrates that more layers have been found in this painting. This differs dramatically from the complicated, stratified construction of earlier Netherlandish paintings.

Bosch's use of white also illustrates his original technique. Firstly, white is used much more abundantly and to achieve color effects in a single application rather than relying on the traditional method of repeated, transparent modulations of underpainting. This is linked to a diminished interest in surface textures and detail and an unusual choice of unsaturated colors. In addition, white is often used graphically and expressively in a mass of accented, loaded brushstrokes. The texture of these strokes marks the surface of the painting in a highly individualized way that contrasts with the smooth finishes of van Eyck and marks a departure in Northern painting. This is one of the major technical characteristics of Bosch's work.

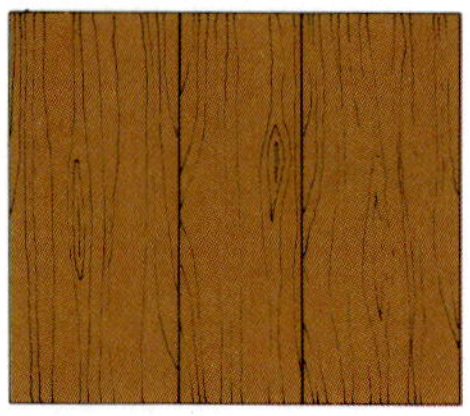

**1.** The panel is composed of three planks of oak, the grain running vertically. The center plank is narrower than the outer two.

**2.** The panel was sized and a thin chalk and animal glue ground applied which just covered the grain of the wood.

**3.** The ground was then covered by an insulating coat of drying oil.

**4.** A second, exceedingly thin layer of chalk and animal skin glue was then brushed on smoothly.

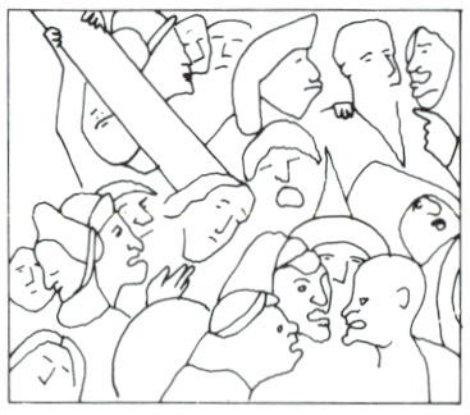

**5.** The underdrawing was sketched on the white ground using a fine brush and black pigment in an aqueous medium.

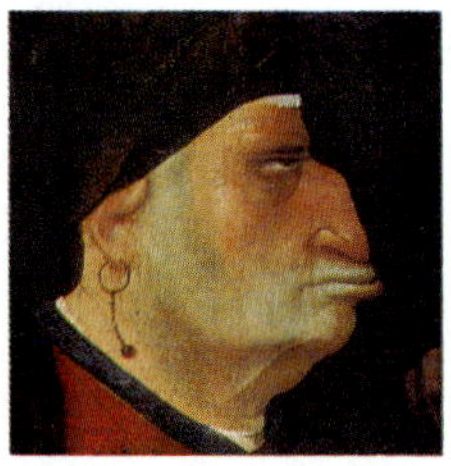

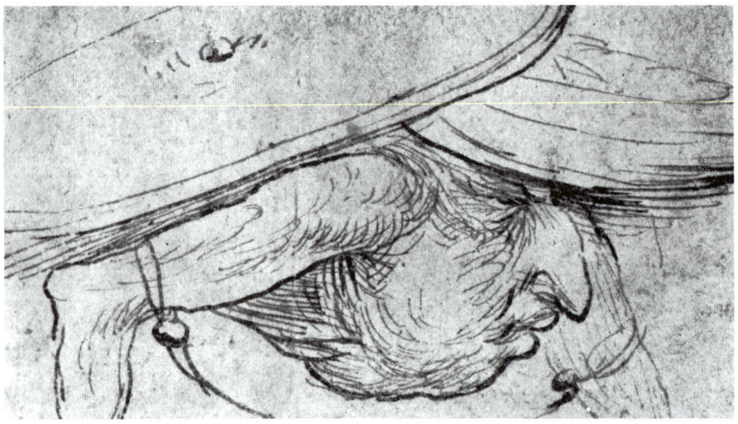

*In contrast to those of his predecessors, many rapid pen sketches by Bosch have survived. It is not clear what role these played in the creation of the painting, and preliminary studies are difficult to find. The drawings are probably an independent form of expression, but in this case there are comparisons between the underdrawing of the judge and the sketch of the fantastic toad man* (above).

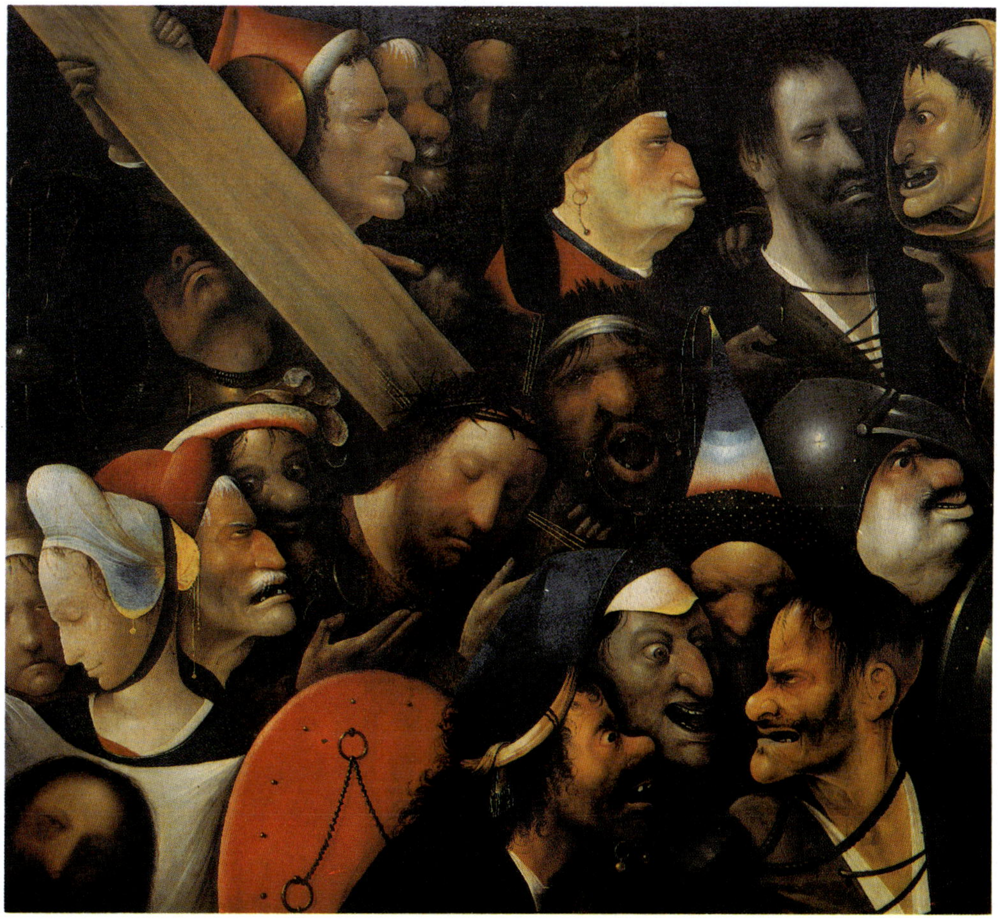

*In this picture, the paint was still applied in thin flat layers in the traditional manner, but the visibility and expressive purpose of the brushwork, the detached white highlights and the simplification of the modelling were all innovatory. There was every extensive underdrawing — usually single curving strokes without crosshatching which describe the main forms. In places, the underdrawing has become visible to the naked eye. Despite the dexterity with which the underdrawing was done, it is unlikely to have been transferred from a cartoon.*
*There is a general tendency for the paint to exceed the lines of the drawing, but there are no major alterations.*

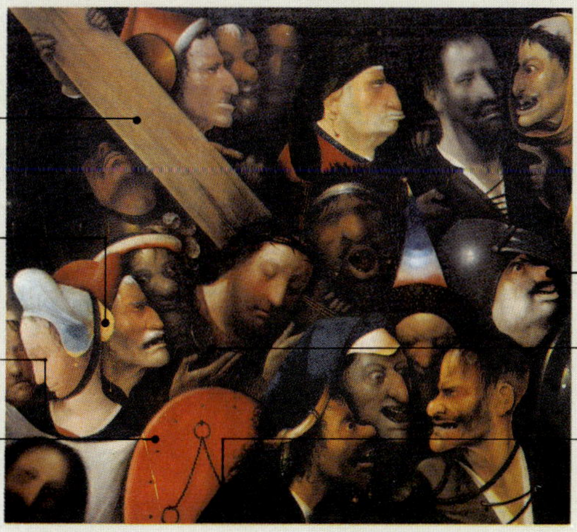

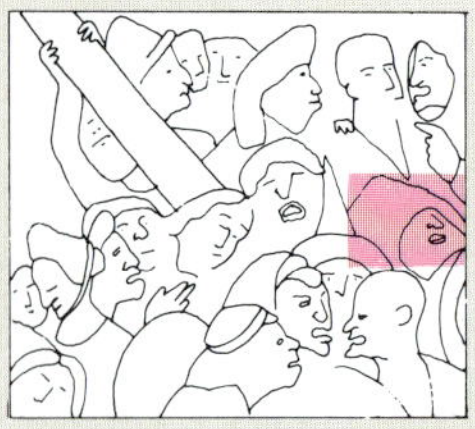

*Bosch was not generally interested in textures with the exception of metals. Instead of using abbreviated strokes of white, the highlight is surrounded by a luminous halo. This is created by opaque white paint applied over the basic gray-brown and does not rely on the effect of the ground.*

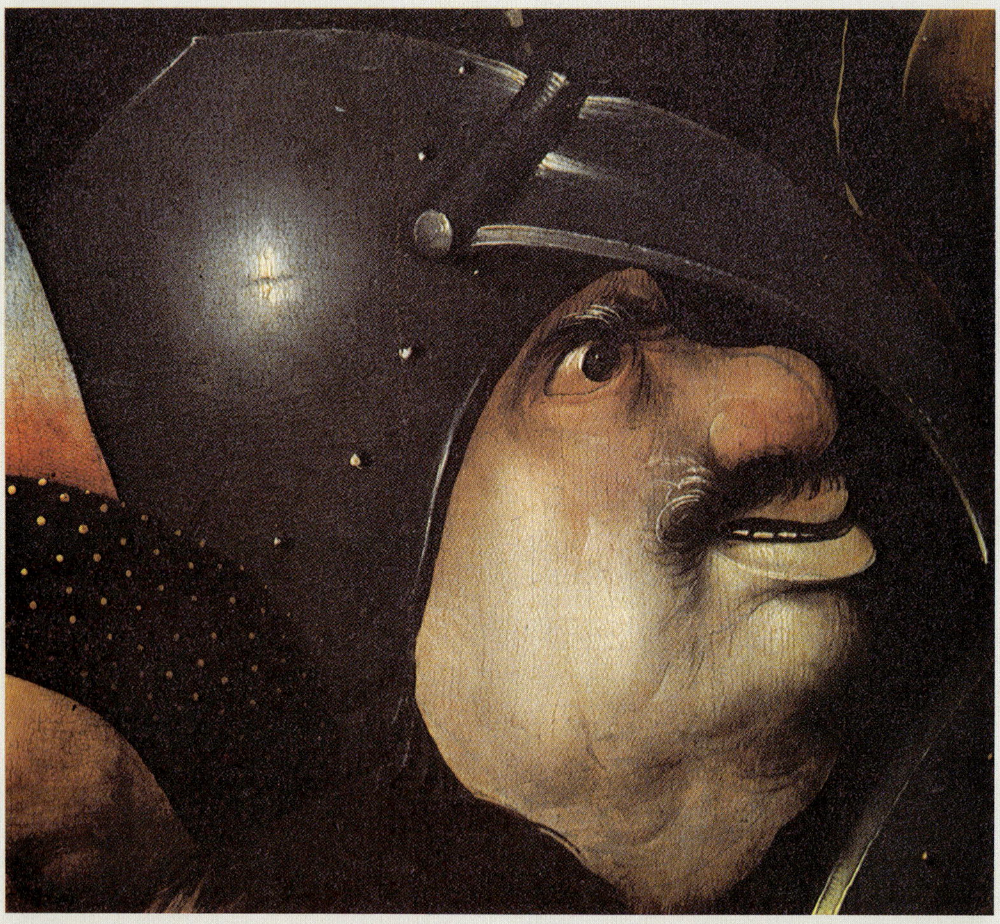

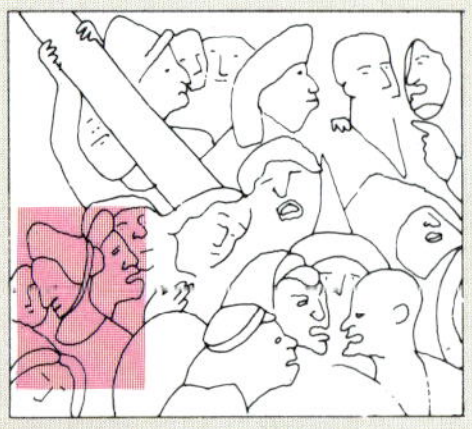

*The technique of the flesh painting is traditional. Very little white pigment was used except in the accented highlights. The lights were obtained by relying on the effect of the whiteness of the ground to shine through the thinly applied transparent flesh tones. By contrast, the lead white was freely mixed with blue and yellow pigments for the headdress.*

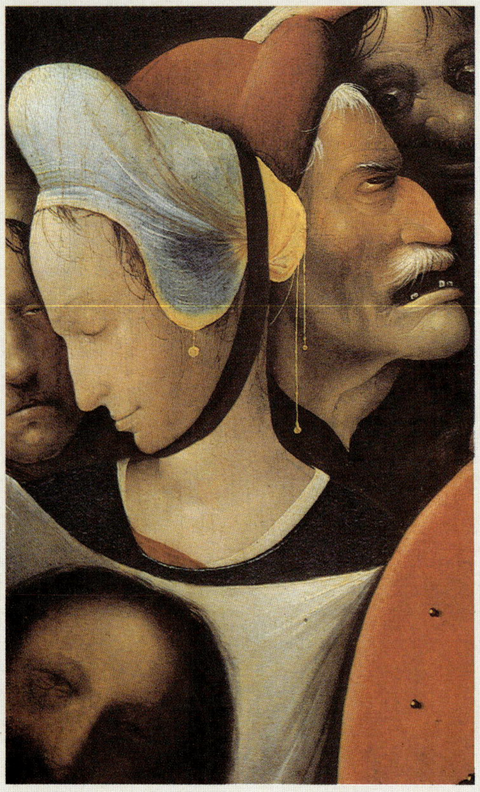

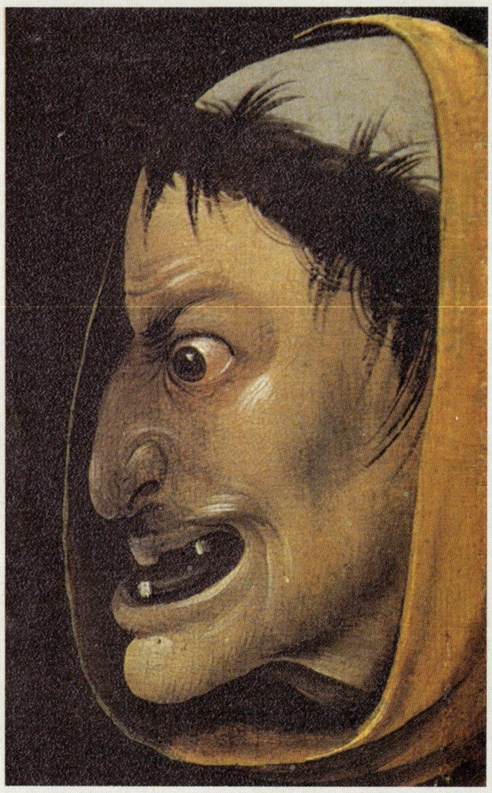

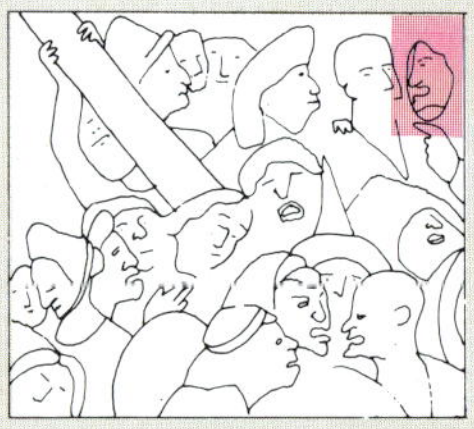

*The painting of the face is a dramatic example of the use of expressionistic brushwork and highlights.*

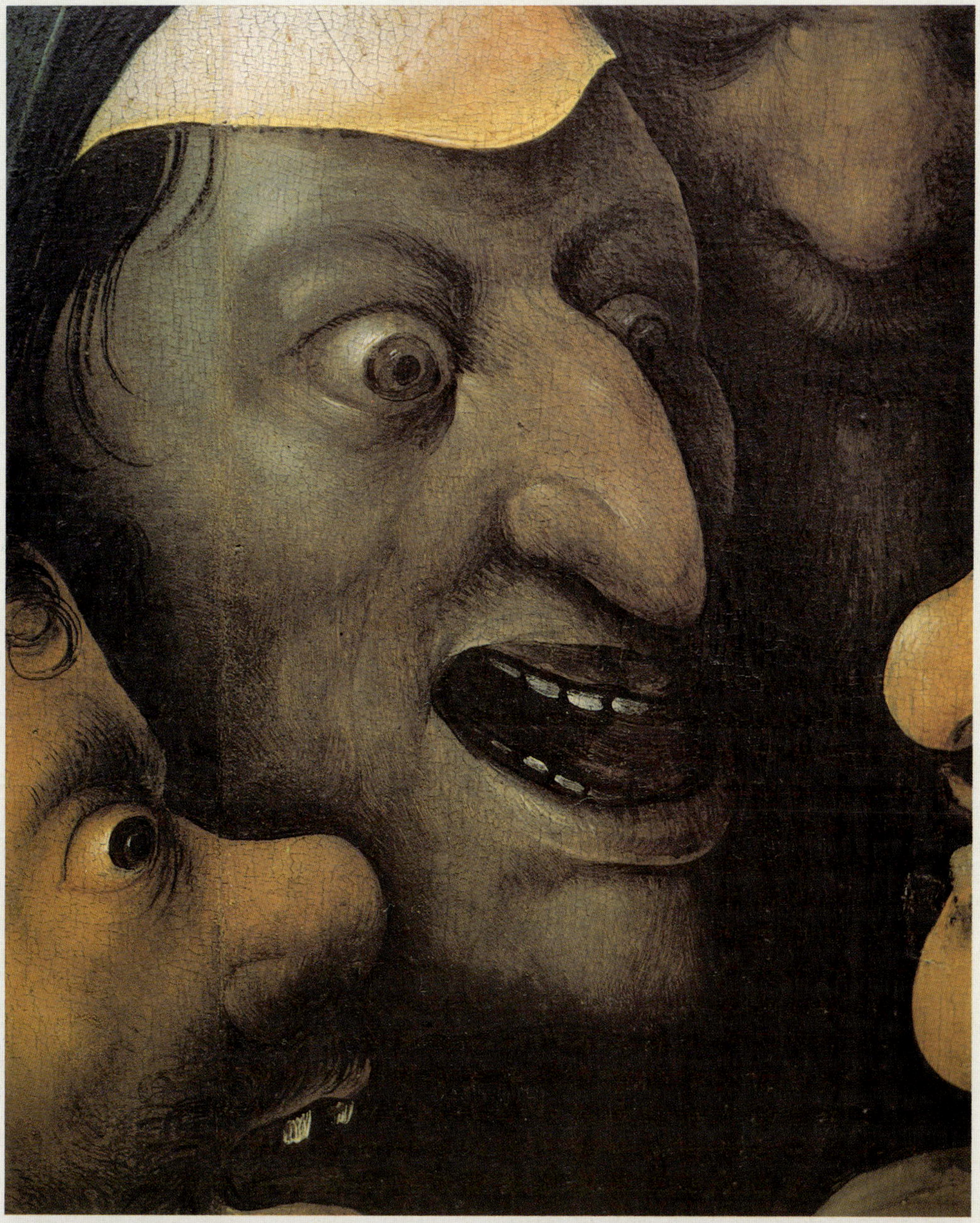

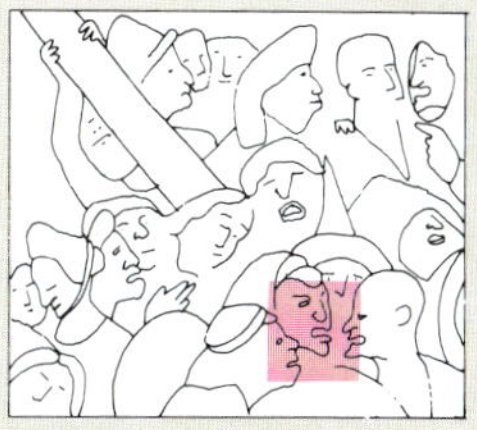

**Actual size detail**
*Four paintings of related religious themes are known to have been painted by Bosch but in this final version, the maelstrom of evil that surges around the impassive Christ and Veronica reaches a climax. Bosch's direct and simplified painting technique is shown in this actual size detail. It was perfectly suited to his intention of impressing the spectator with the immediacy of the emotional impact of the scene rather than describing in detail a tangible experience of the objective world. With great economy of means and a free, rapid handling of paint he achieves a richness of expression and a variety of pictorial handwriting that is entirely new in Northern art.*

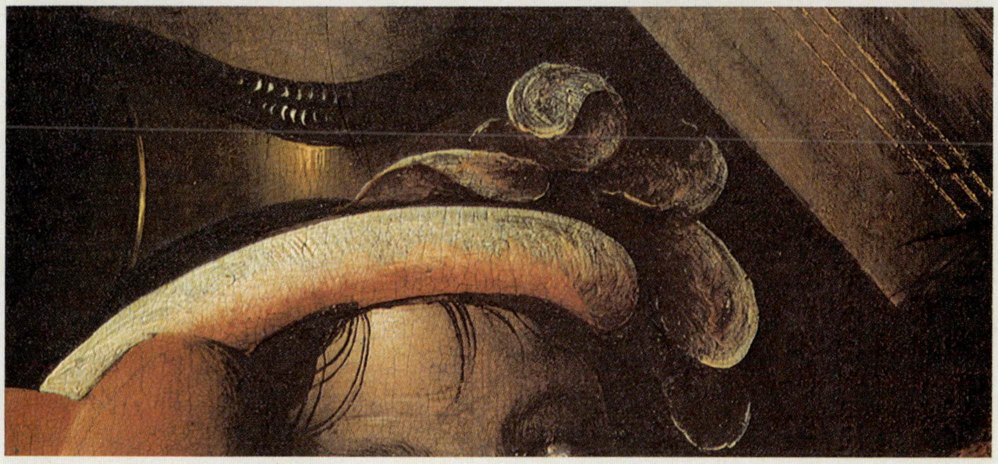

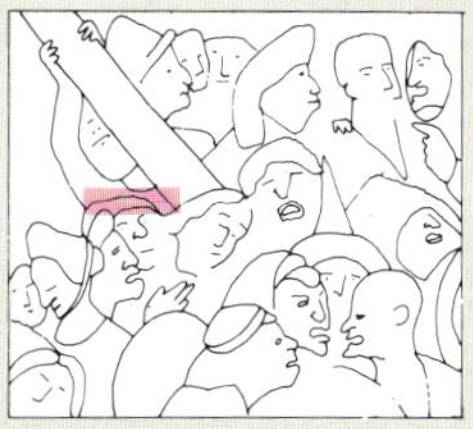

*The headdress and its ribbons are entirely described in terms of drawing. There is no illusionistic, blended, tonal modelling.*

# TITIAN

*The Death of Acteon* (1560s)
Oil on canvas, 178cm × 198cm/70⅜in × 78in

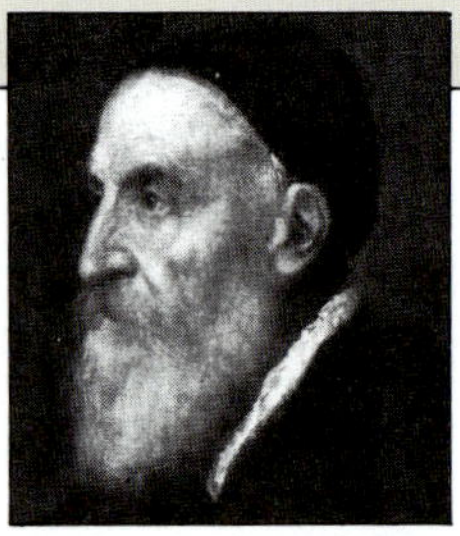

*The Death of Acteon* is probably one of the last of a series that Titian painted for Philip II of Spain. They were referred to as 'poesie' by the artist and exemplify the freedom of subject matter and treatment which characterized Venetian art from the time of Giorgione, and formed the context in which Titian's own highly individual technique evolved. Vasari visited Venice in 1566 and, like other contemporaries, was struck by the phenomenal contrast between the delicate technique of Titian's early works, which invited close scrutiny, and the vigorous brushwork of the later ones, which had to be seen from a distance for maximum effect.

In Titian's work, the separation between the drawing and painting processes has entirely disappeared. X-radiographs show how the composition was worked directly in paint. The description of Titian's working method by one of his pupils, Palma Giovene, corroborates this: 'He laid in his pictures with a mass of color, which served as the groundwork for what he wanted to express. I myself have seen such vigorous underpainting in plain red earth for the halftones or in white lead. With the same brush dipped in red, black or yellow, he worked up the light parts and in four strokes, he could create a remarkably fine figure. . . . Then he turned the picture to the wall and left it for months without looking at it, until he returned to it and stared critically at it, as if it were a mortal enemy. If he found something that displeased him he went to work like a surgeon. in the last stages, he used his fingers more than his brush. Venice, a commercial center and port, gave artists access to a wider range of high-grade pigments than elsewhere in Italy, and they were used lavishly. Titian's early works display the whole range of the palette in large juxtaposed, color blocks. In this later work, Titian broke up local color and focused on the flickering effect of light on surfaces. Complex pigment mixtures, however, were still not used, color modulations being achieved by brushwork and glazing only. The paint varied from thin washes to thick impasto, and it was applied by brushing, dabbing, scraping, smoothing and working very freely. Contemporaries commented on Titian's dramatically individual and expressive handling of the oil painting medium. Titian had a profound influence on later oil painters.

*This painting was executed on a moderately rough canvas. Large scale works of religious as well as secular subjects painted on canvas appeared early in Venice partly because the wet and salty atmosphere was so unsuitable for wooden altarpieces and frescoes. Contemporaries also commented that canvases could be rolled up and transported more easily. Titian used a wide variety of canvas weights and weaves during his long painting career and there was a general shift in his preference from a fine to a coarser weave.*

**1.** Two pieces of fairly coarse twill weave canvas were stitched together. The average loom width was about 1 meter, the distance the shuttle could be thrown easily by hand.

**2.** The canvas was stretched and sized. The size reduces the absorbency of the fibers and prevents the oil making them brittle. Size, made from kid, pigskin or glove cuttings, was especially popular because it remained soft and flexible.

**3.** Next a gesso ground made from gypsum and animal skin glue, was applied thinly and smoothly. It just filled the gaps between the weave.

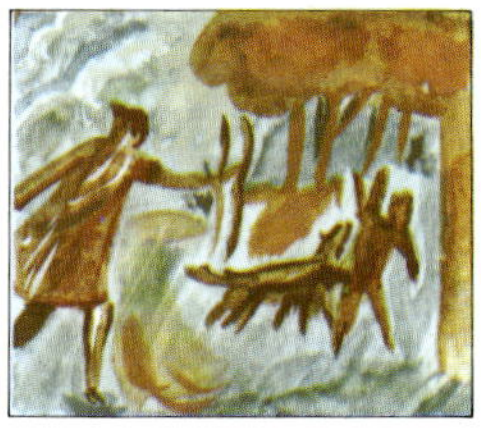

**4.** The composition was laid in using paint — mainly earth pigments and white.

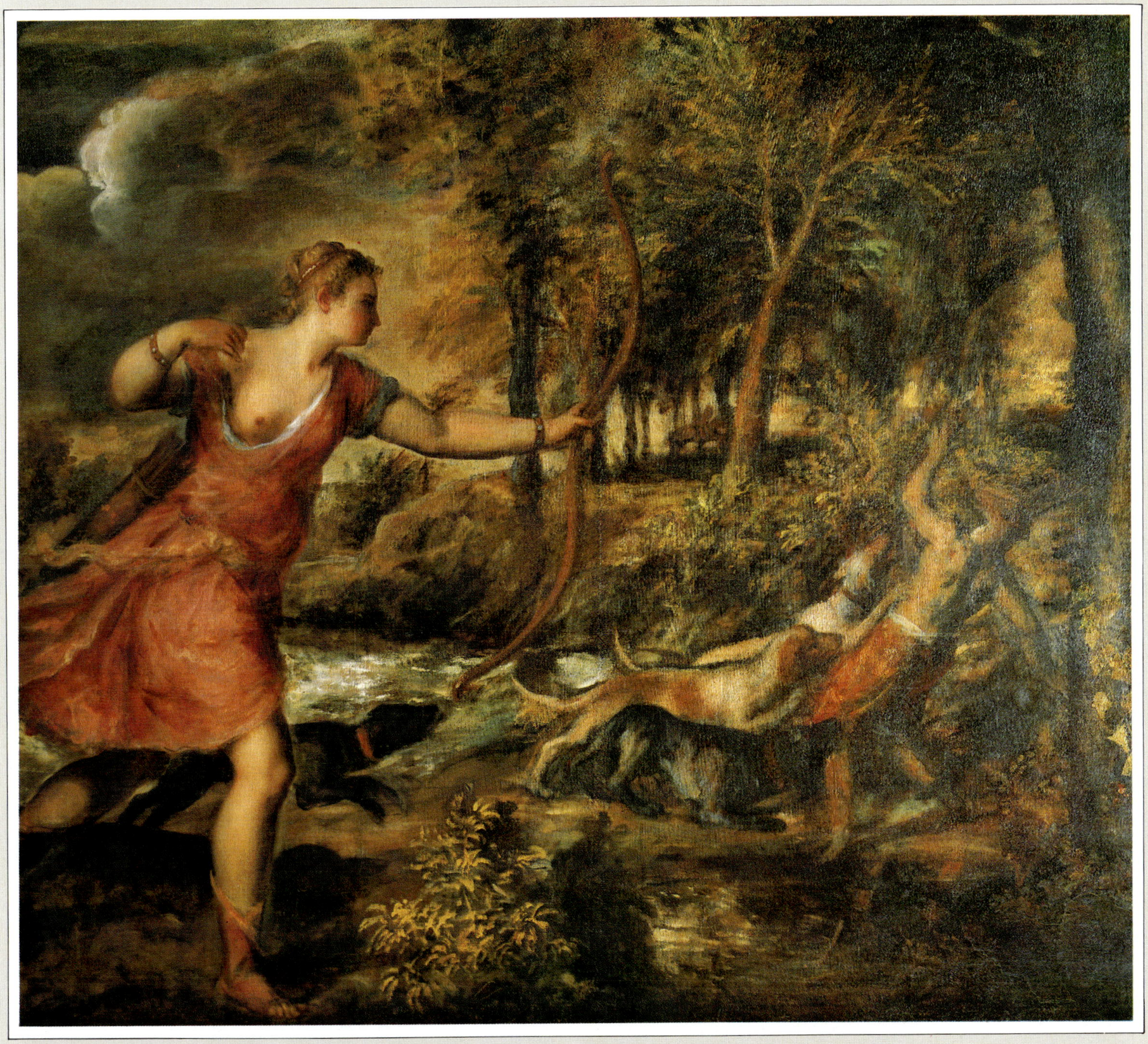

*The impression of a change towards a more restricted palette in Titian's later work is misleading. Titian used ultramarine in the sky, orpiment (yellow) and realgar (orange-red) in Acteon's tunic, crimson lakes on Diana's robe, malachite and bright green copper resinate in the foliage, as well as vermilion and lead tin yellow. The picture's present dark overall tone is the result of deterioration and discolored varnish. Until recently it was thought that Titian used a dark oil ground, which became popular during the sixteenth century; but examination has shown that it is white gesso which the heavy impregnation of lining paste has rendered translucent and caused the tone of the exposed canvas fibers to predominate.*

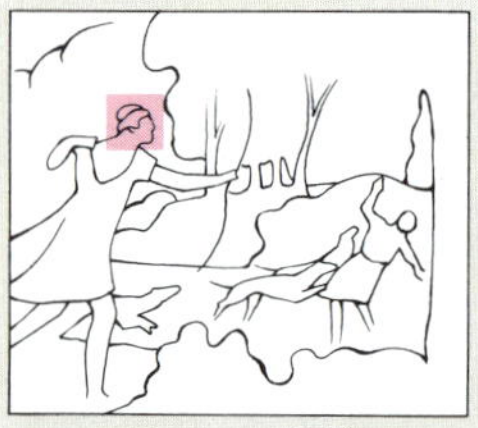

*The careful flesh modelling contrasts with the impressionistic treatment of the foliage. The lights are painted in thick opaque paint which contains a large proportion of lead white pigment, while the darks rely on a series of thin transparent glazes.*

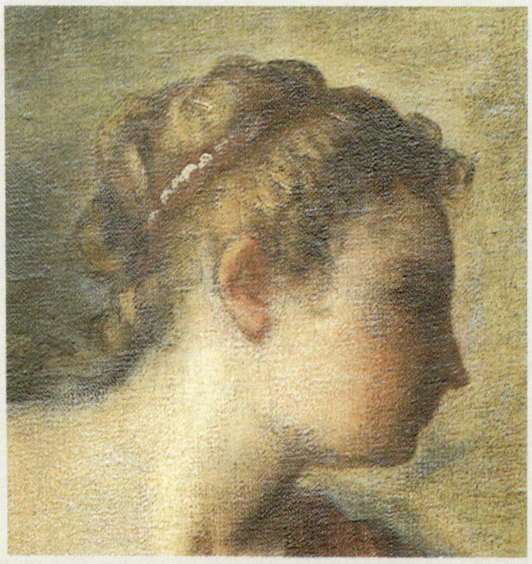

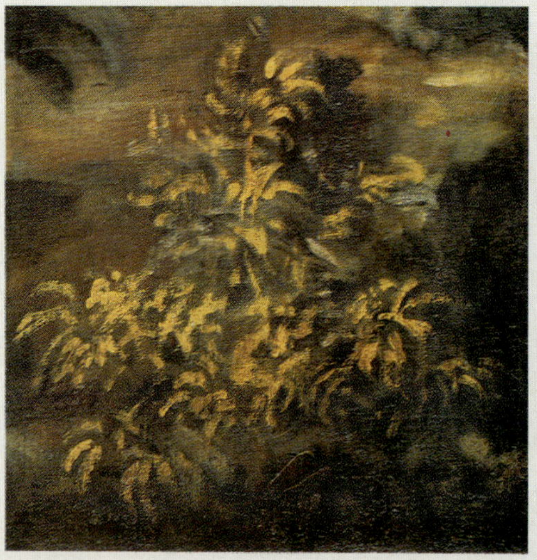

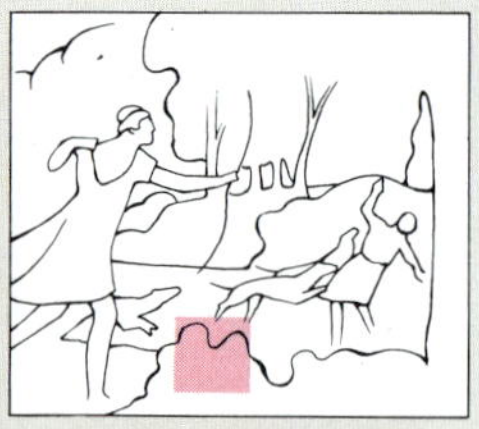

*In the foliage, form is suggested rather than naturalistically described. Contemporary critics attributed Titian's late style to poor eyesight or a shaky hand. It has also been argued that the painting was unfinished.*

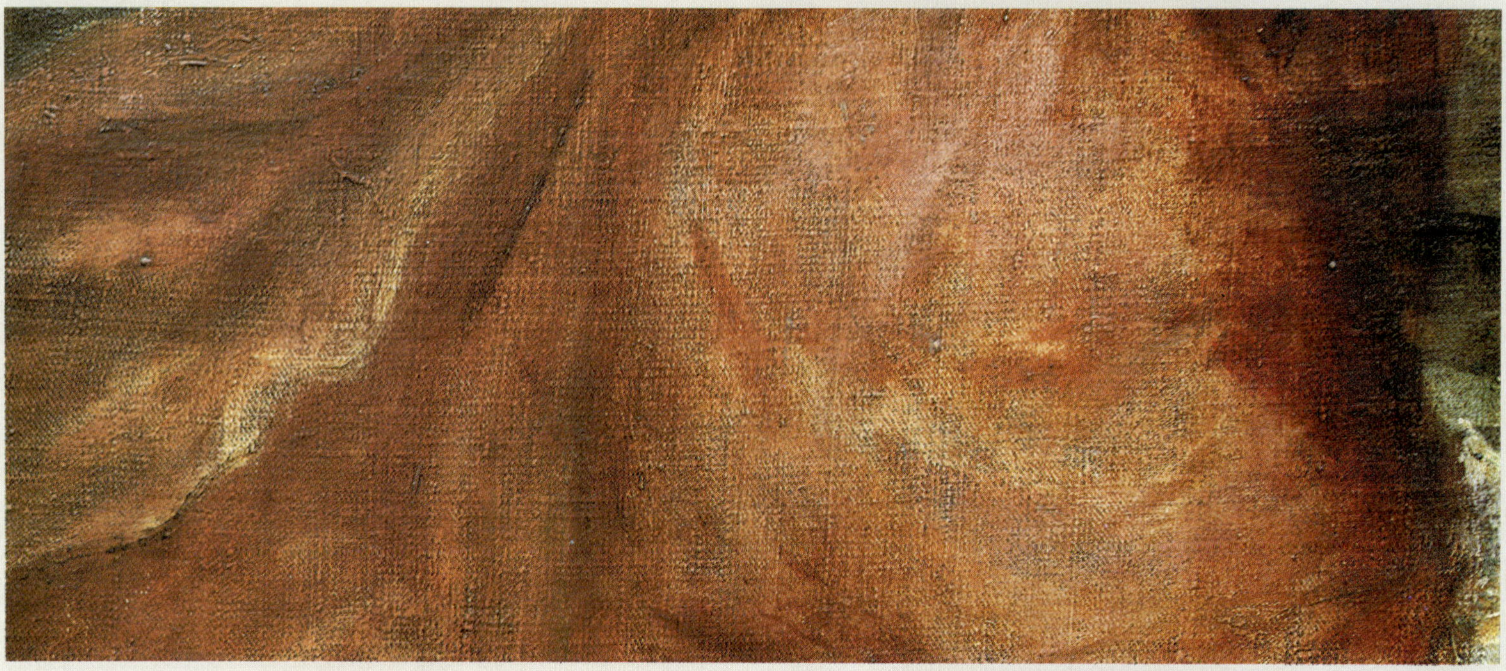

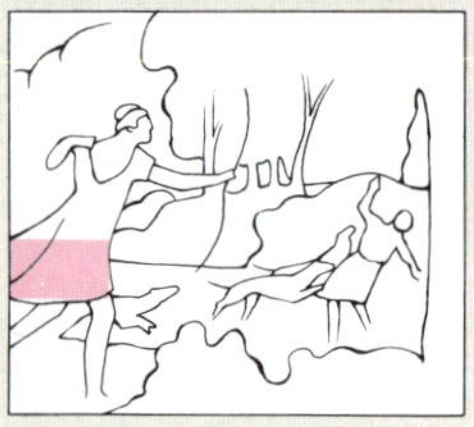

*The innumerable glazes which have been brushed, smeared or dabbed on the robe are typical of Titian's technique. They are broken up rather than applied as a smooth continuous layer. The treatment contrasts with the flesh modelling.*

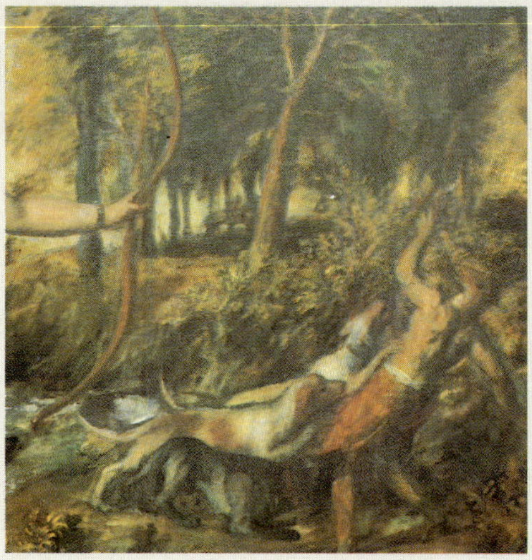

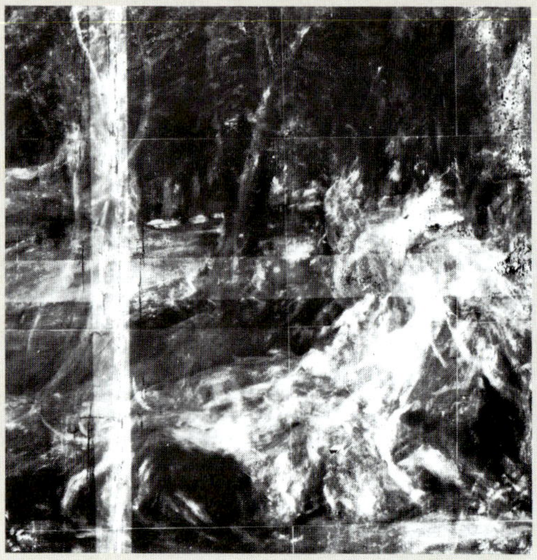

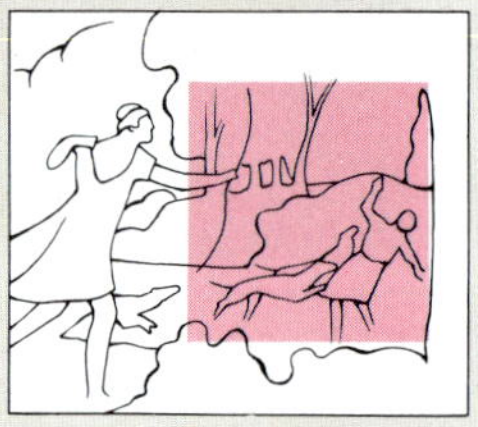

*This X-radiograph (left) juxtaposed with the detail from the final picture (far left) shows alterations made during the painting. The position of Diana's arms and the bow, finally shown without an arrow or string, changed several times. The swirling mass on the right was finally resolved into three dogs attacking Acteon.*

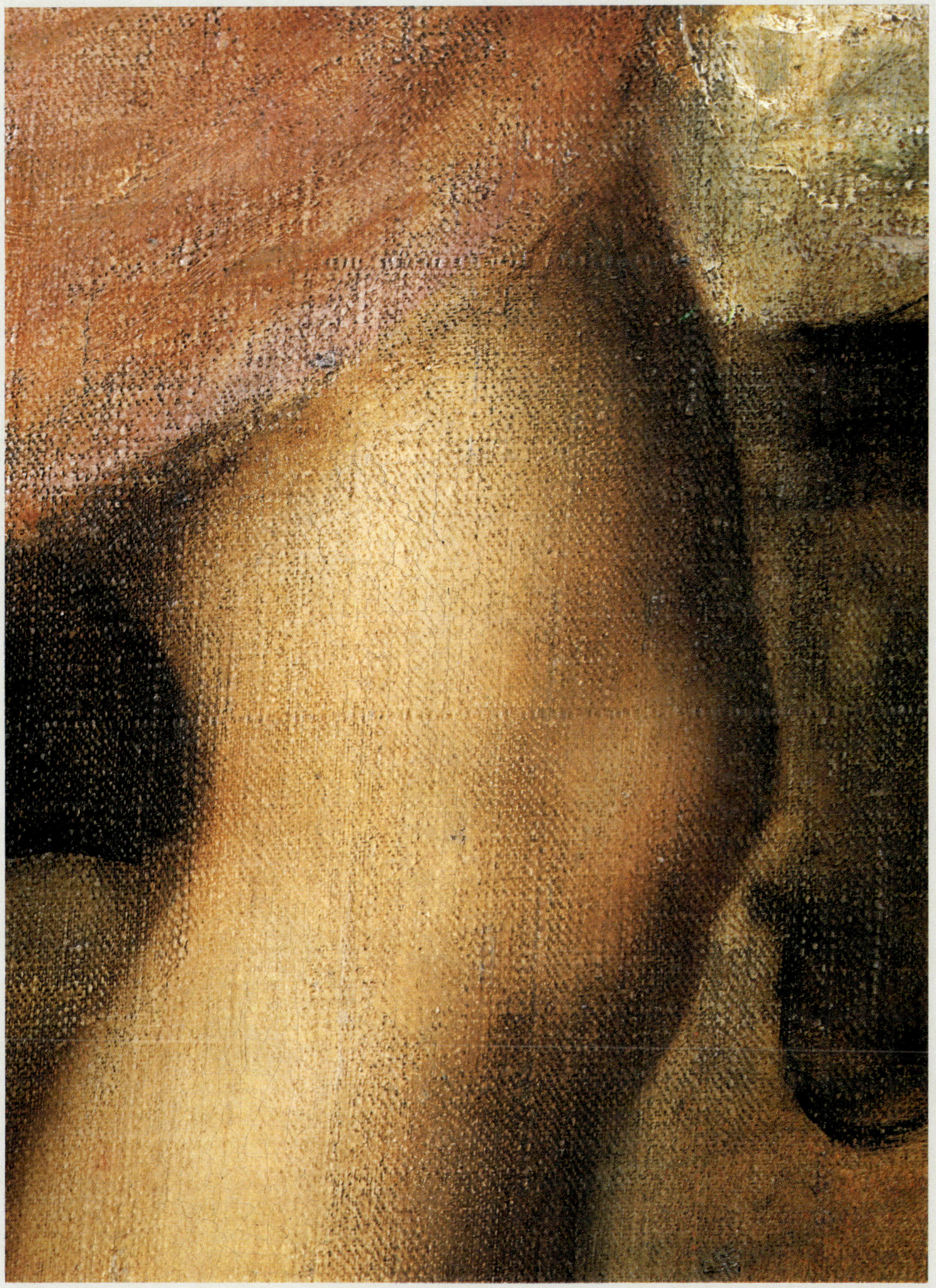

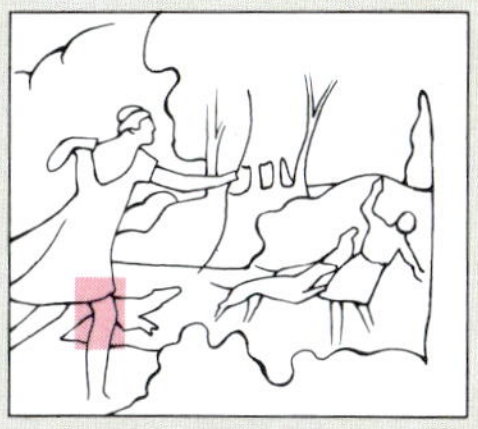

Actual size detail
*The final surface is neither even nor smooth; both the paint and surface texture are striking. Subjectively, thin paint in shadows and thick paint in light areas appears more realistic because it corresponds with an apprehension of reality, and the eye is less aware of the picture plane. There are no hard outlines, but the contours are precise and often defined by light background paint. In spite of the freedom of his technique, Titian's flesh modelling always remained careful, as Palma Giovene wrote: 'He never painted a figure* alla prima *and used to say that he who improvises can never make a perfect line of poetry.' The notion that the special quality of Titian's painting lay in a secret medium has been disproved by analysis, which has shown that he used linseed and walnut oil. Documents indicate that varnish was added to paint to increase the transparency and drying qualities of dark pigments, such as lakes and verdigris. This was traditional practice. Varnishes were made from resins either melted in hot oil or dissolved in a volatile liquid such as spirits of wine, naphtha or turpentine. The drying process of oil ensures that the surface is preserved with every expressive touch the artist makes. Contemporaries commented on the way Titian fully exploited this variable as a means of expression.*

# NICHOLAS HILLIARD

*A Youth Leaning Against a Tree Among Roses* (c. 1588)
Water-based medium on wood, 12.8cm × 7cm/5⅜in × 2¾in

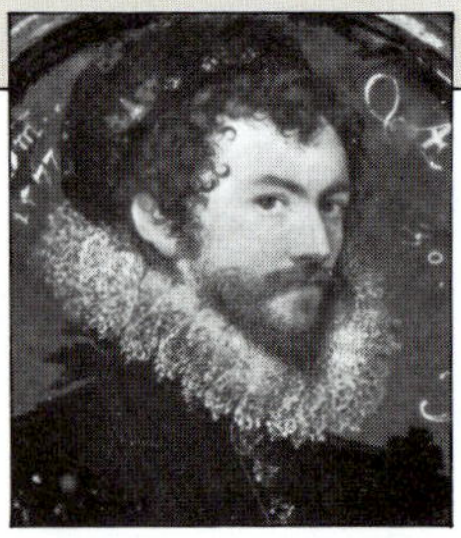

Nicholas Hilliard was originally trained as a goldsmith and this is evident in his exquisite miniatures. After spending time in France in the service of the Duke of Anjou, he emerged as a mature painter in the late 1570s in London as the Royal miniaturist to Elizabeth I and later James I. Hilliard was a declared follower of Holbein and French court portraiture, and his known *oeuvre* consists entirely of portrait miniatures which he developed with an intimacy and subtlety peculiar to the art. His linear style, incorporating naturalistic observation and modeling, found particular favor with Elizabeth I who was painted by Hilliard in 1572.

Hilliard's *Treatise on the Art of Limning* was a textbook on miniature painting based on his own methods and experience. 'Limning' was a contemporary term for this art and involved painting on vellum (calfskin). The technique was closely related to the tradition of illuminated manuscript artists.

Hilliard painted on prepared vellum, stretched over a playing card and fixed with thin paste. His brushes were made of squirrel hair fitted into a quill or handle. He cautioned against the use of too small a brush as an uneven surface would result with visible brush strokes, while too fine a tip would not take enough color. He never used a magnifying glass as this caused distortion and over-emphasis and would always work from life rather than doing preparatory drawings of his subject. Hilliard's colors were made from natural ingredients ground on a crystal block which were then mixed with distilled water and gum arabic. To give plasticity to the lakes and umbers, he would add a little sugar candy. He advised against using muddy tones and lists as his preference black, white, red, blue, green, yellow and murrey (reddish-purple). He used three types of white – 'whitlead' for body color, one for painting linen and satin, and another for faces. He also used three types of black, his preference being burnt ivory, especially for painting the eyes.

To create tones, Hilliard built up successive coats of fluid color applied in short strokes and light dabs. He did not use underdrawing as the delicate surface of the vellum made correcting difficult and advised the use of pencil dipped in a flesh tint to emphasize lines.

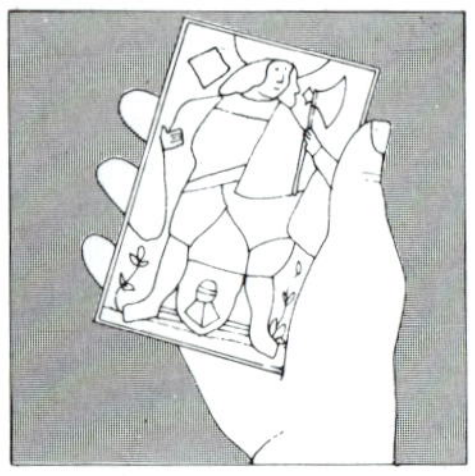

**1.** Hilliard would use a playing card cut into an oval shape, covered with sized vellum and primed with a pale flesh tint. He would work from life rather than preparatory sketches.

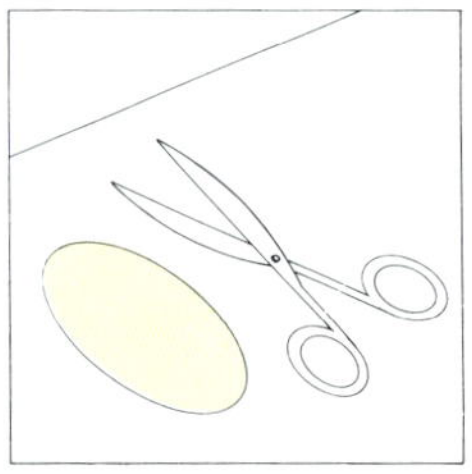

**2.** With no preparatory drawing, Hilliard would then lay in a light ground.

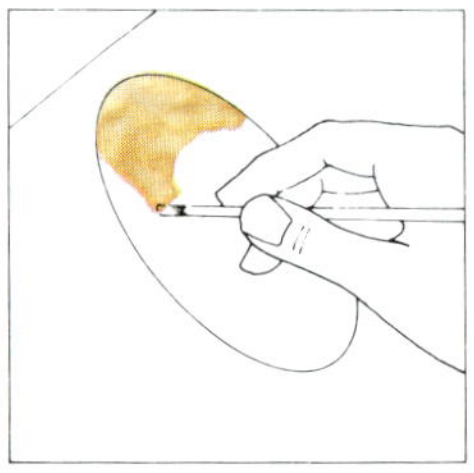

**3.** Using a series of coats of fluid color to build up tone, the colors would be illuminated by the pale vellum beneath.

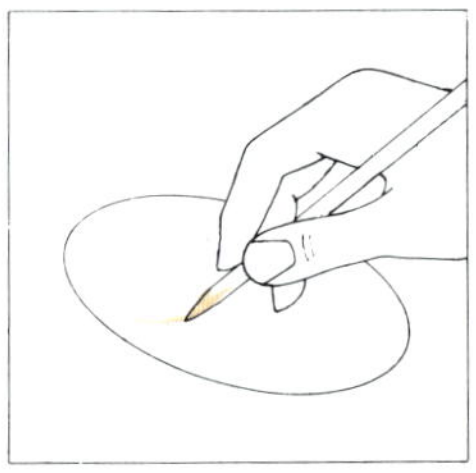

**4.** As the delicate surface of the vellum made correction difficult, Hilliard would use a pencil dipped in a flesh tint to indicate lines for further development.

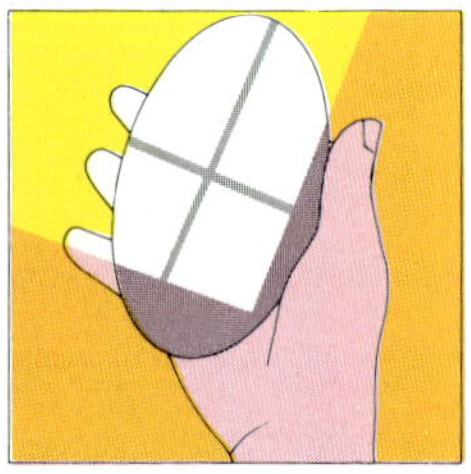

**5.** To test whether there was enough gum arabic in the medium, Hilliard would expose it to sunlight to check for crumbling and peeling.

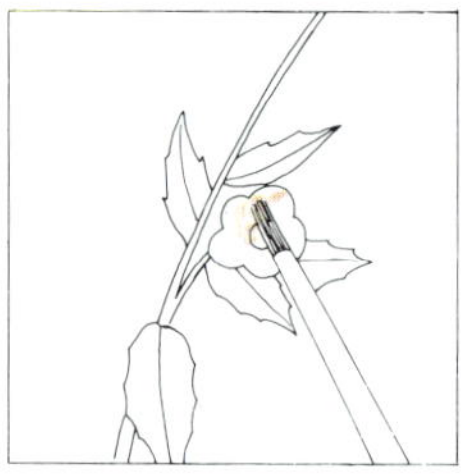

**6.** Hilliard would add the final details with minute dabs and strokes, freely applied.

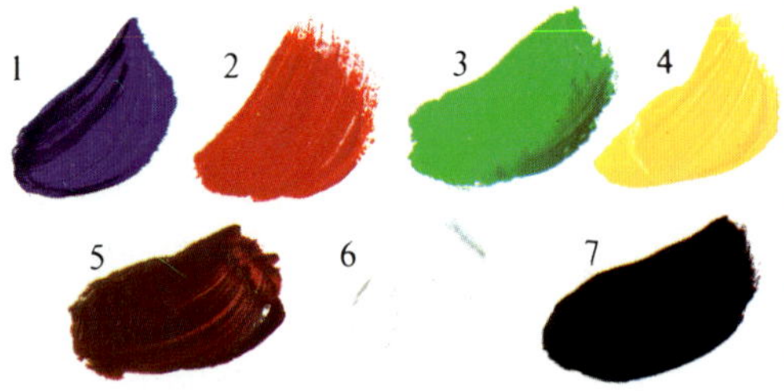


Hilliard used a limited palette and tried to avoid muddy colors. He preferred to use ultramarine from Venice (**1**), red (**2**), green (**3**), yellow (**4**) and murrey, a reddish purple color (**5**). He used three types of white (**6**) – one for faces, another for linen and satin and a third, which was called 'whitlead' for body color. He also used three types of black (**7**), preferring burned ivory for the eyes. Hilliard would have ground his pigments on a crystal block and mixed them with distilled water and gum arabic.

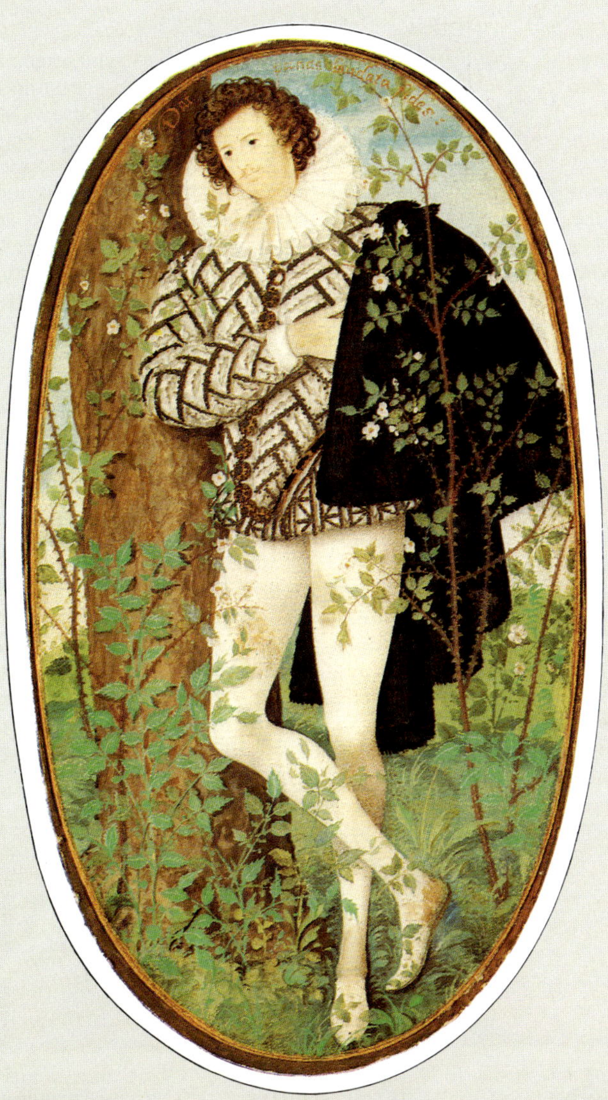

Actual size

*The majority of Hilliard's portraits show only the sitter's head and shoulders and this is one of his few full-length portraits. The sitter is thought to be Robert Devereux, the ill-fated Earl of Essex, favorite of Queen Elizabeth I who was executed for treason in 1601. Hilliard primed the vellum with a pale flesh tint. As the colors dried, light penetrated the translucent paint and was reflected back from the vellum giving a glowing purity of color. The support not only affected the color of the pigments used, but was used as a color in itself. The scale of Hilliard's work — always a primary consideration — meant that clarity of detail rather than full* chiaroscuro *modelling was essential and Hilliard used a minimum of shading and modelling, as if his subjects were illuminated in full sunlight. Hilliard's use of line and pattern enlivens and counteracts the flatness created by this lack of modelling, emphasizing the ornamental function of his work.*

*Hilliard used wild roses to create a rich, lacelike design to break up the flatness of the sitter's dark cloak. For the face and ruff, the priming coat has been modelled with flesh tints to create the features. Hilliard attached great importance to capturing the complexion of his sitters.*

*The hair is created by using a wash over which a series of minute strokes define the curls.*

*To create an elaborate ruff, Hilliard squeezed thick paint on to trace its line. When dry, this gave a raised line which cast a shadow.*

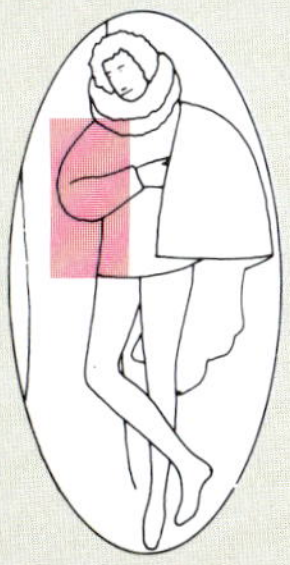

*For the buttons of the cloak, Hilliard would create a* trompe l'oeil *effect by applying silver leaf overlaid with blobs of wax and paint.*

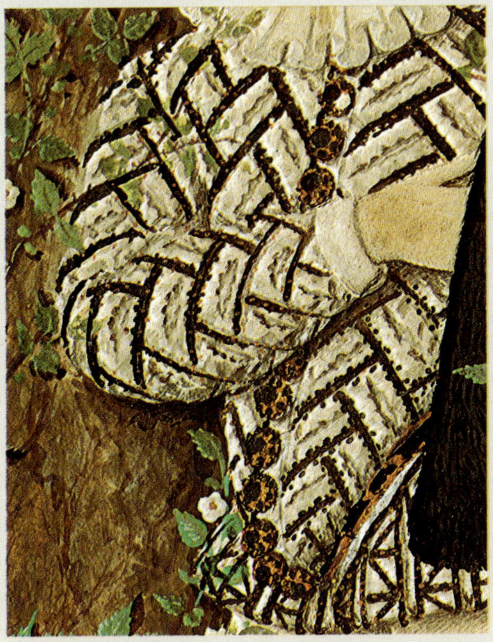

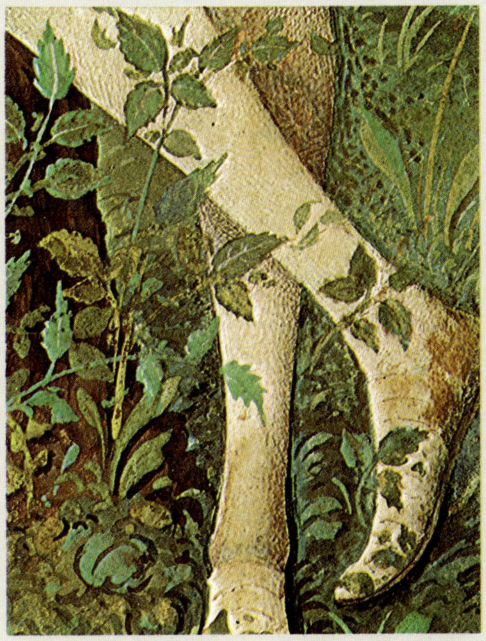

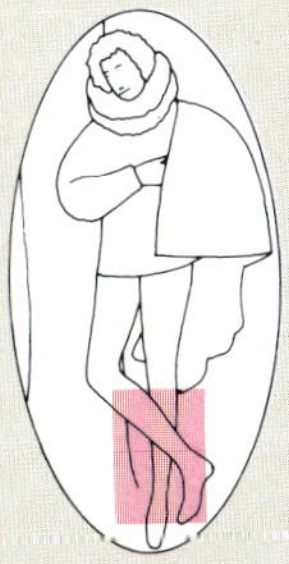

*Hilliard used tiny hatching strokes to create the shading which can be seen in the legs.*

*Light green has been used to give detail in the leaves and grasses.*

*Green was a notoriously impermanent color as seen in the patch of blue which has faded behind the sitter's raised foot.*

# CARAVAGGIO

*The Supper at Emmaus* (1596-1603)
Oil on canvas, 139cm × 185cm/55in × 77½in

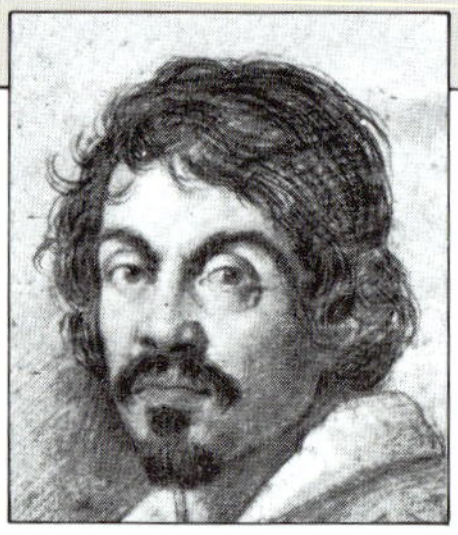

Michelangelo Merisi, called Caravaggio after his birthplace near Milan, worked chiefly in Rome. Having murdered a man, he fled in 1506, and in the last four years of his life painted in Naples, Malta, and Sicily. His violent and stormy life attracted as much attention as his controversial pictures. His vividly realistic pictures were bitterly attacked for their total rejection of idealization, which had been the chief aim of Renaissance art, and for their dramatic use of light and shadow. His style was followed by many artists, in particular those from the Netherlands, and Caravaggio had a profound influence on Rembrandt. For many conservative critics in the seventeenth century French and Italian Academies, however, his art marked 'the downfall of painting'.

Caravaggio's *The Supper at Emmaus* is generally thought to have been painted between 1596 and 1603, and is in very good condition, having been cleaned and relined in 1960. The artist's unidealized portrait of his sitters and the dark aspect of his later paintings were criticized by many of his seventeenth century biographers.

Little is known about the way Caravaggio thought out the early stages of his compositions. He sometimes re-thought his approach drastically on the canvas, although this does not appear to have been the case with this work. While the enormous care with which the positions, angles and relationships of the figures have been worked out indicates that Caravaggio made painstaking preliminary studies on paper for his composition, there is no evidence that this was his practice and no drawings have ever been attributed to him. Nevertheless, it is hard to give credence to one seventeenth century critic who described Caravaggio's technique as 'impetuous and without preparation'. X-rays have revealed that the only alteration Caravaggio made in this particular painting was a slight change in the inn-keeper's cap and profile, so he must have visualized the final composition clearly, before starting work on the canvas. The smooth, unbroken paint surface of the picture suggests Caravaggio used soft hair brushes and a fluid oil medium – probably linseed oil. Linseed tends to yellow, but this would not have adversely affected the warm earth colors of Caravaggio's works.

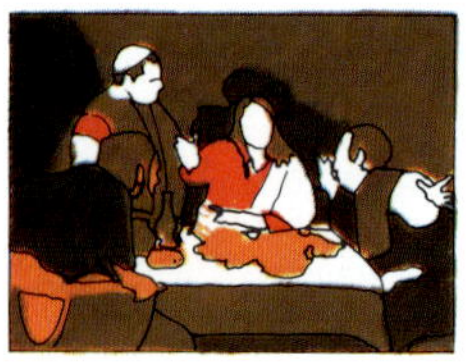

**1.** Having sketched in the outlines of the composition, Caravaggio would have blocked in the main areas of color with a large bristle brush.

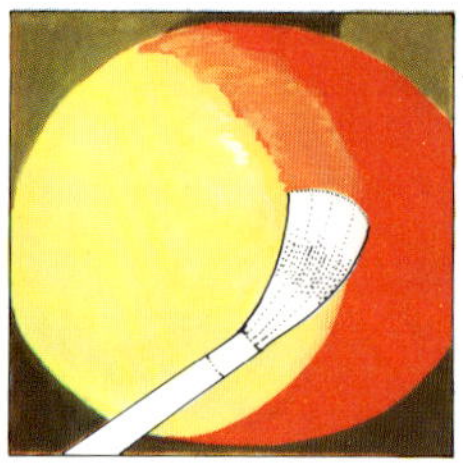

**2.** Subsequent layers of paint would have been applied with softer brushes. The contrasts of light and shadow would have been blended with a soft, broad brush.

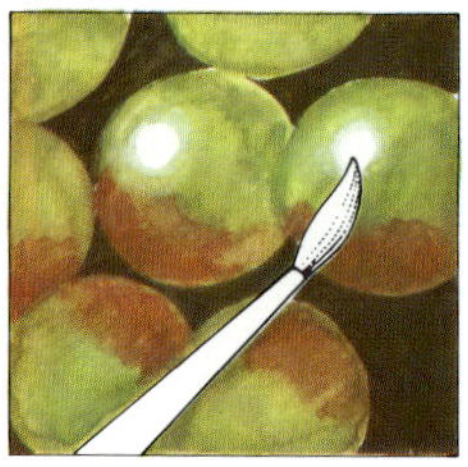

**3.** Detailed work would have been added last using fine, soft brushes with a delicate point.

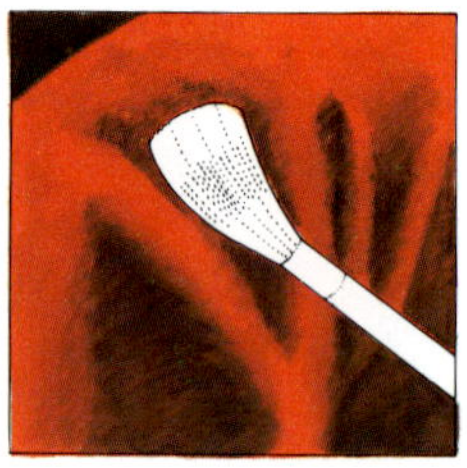

**4.** Oil glazes would have been used to modify the colors of the drapery. Christ's robe would probably have been covered with a red lake oil glaze.

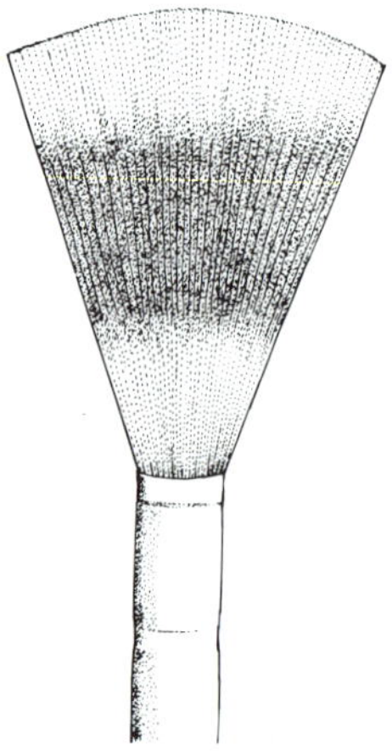

*Caravaggio could have used this type of brush for softly blending the top layer of paint and for modifying harsh contrasts.*

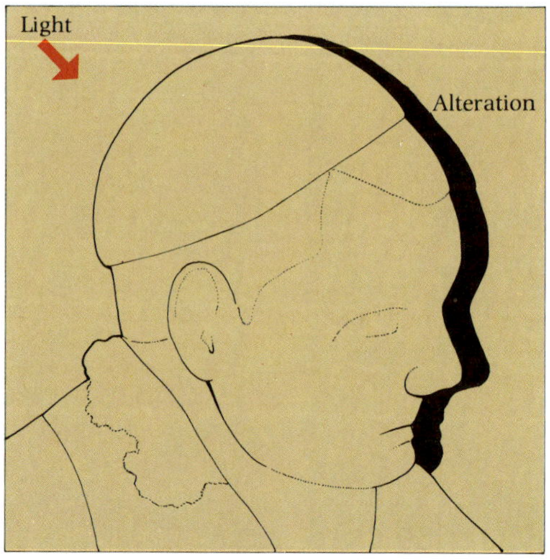


*Light falls on the figures from a steep angle. The source of light in the studio might have been an oil lamp or a small high north-facing window. The window would have been fitted not with glass but with a sheet of paper, made transparent by soaking it either in oil or animal fat. This would provide a warm, constant light ideal for artists' studios. Carvaggio's only alteration in the composition was a small change in the outline of the inn-keeper's cap and profile.*

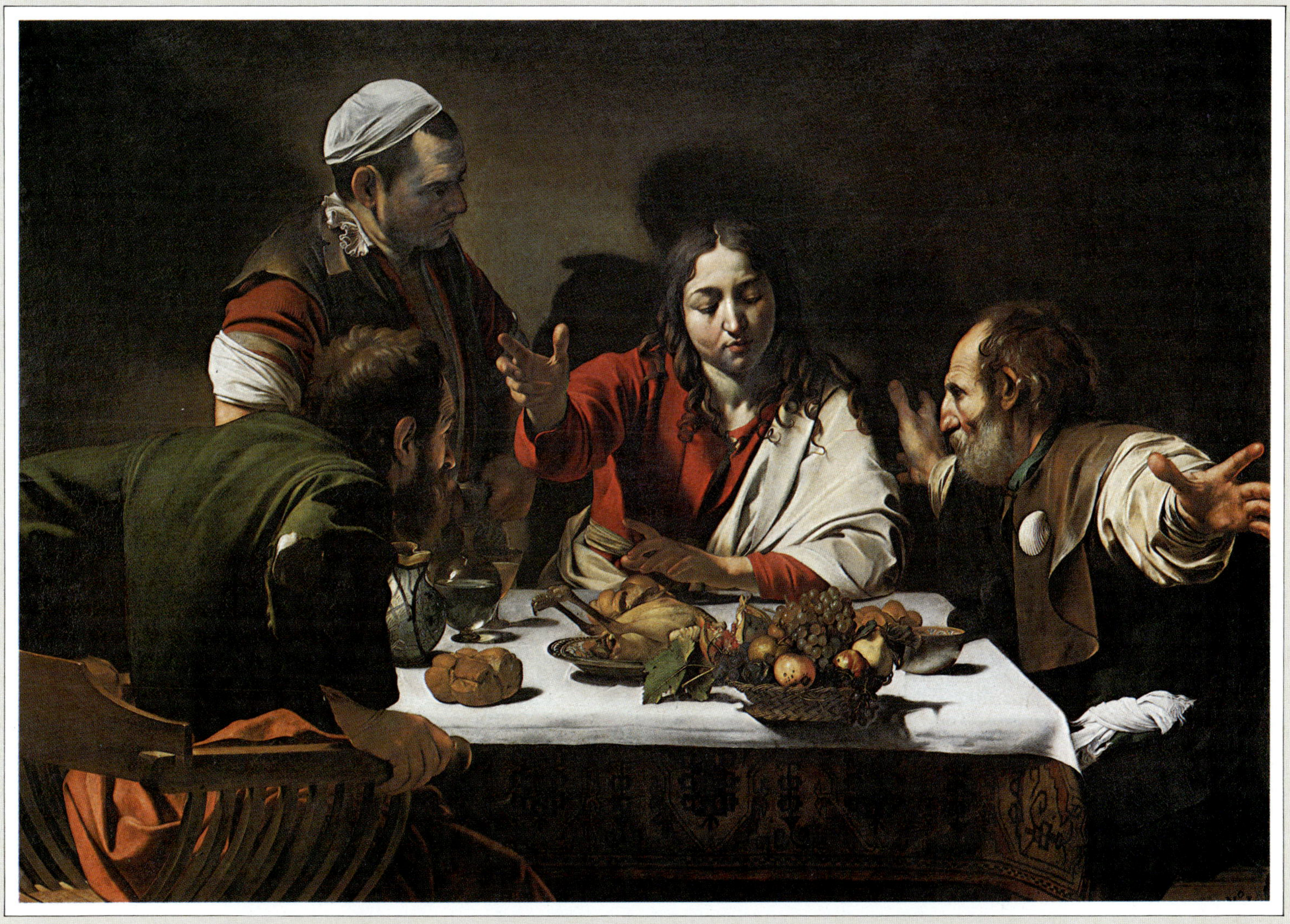

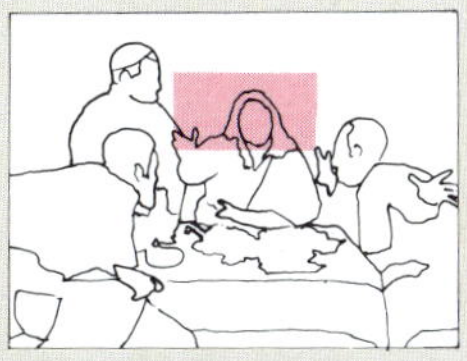

This detail of the head of Christ shows the modelling of the face and the dramatic use of light and shade to emphasize the features. The shadow cast by the servant can be seen on the wall.

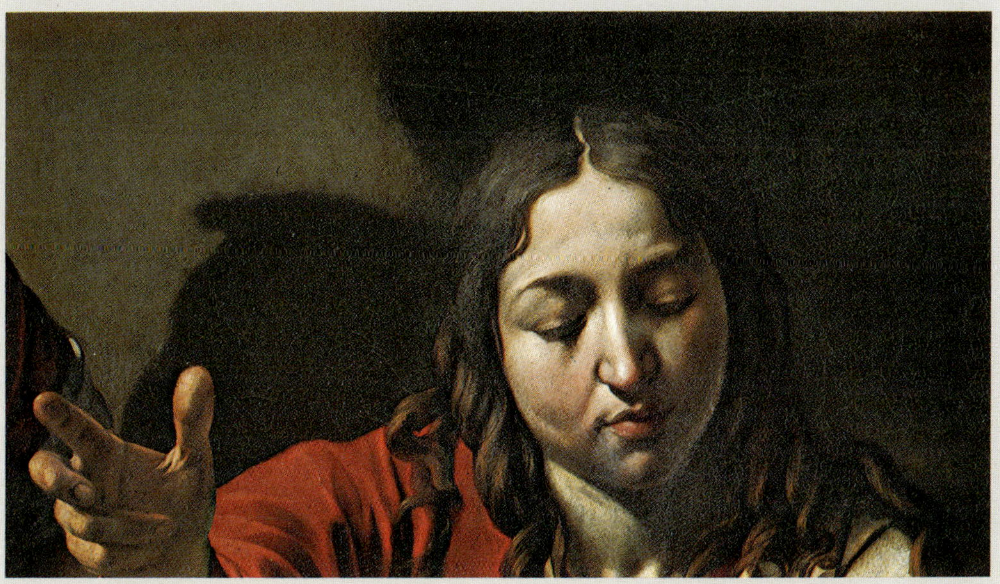

The Supper at Emmaus *was painted on smooth finely-woven canvas, probably made from flax, which Caravaggio used for many of his pictures. The ground is dark, probably a deep brown.*
*This is one of Caravaggio's most important works and shows his complete mastery and use of extreme light and shadow, arrangement of figures, and dramatic gestures to focus attention on the figure of Christ. The rich, glowing tones, which indicate a preference for warm ochres, vermilion and lead tin yellow, are characteristic of Caravaggio's color scheme.*

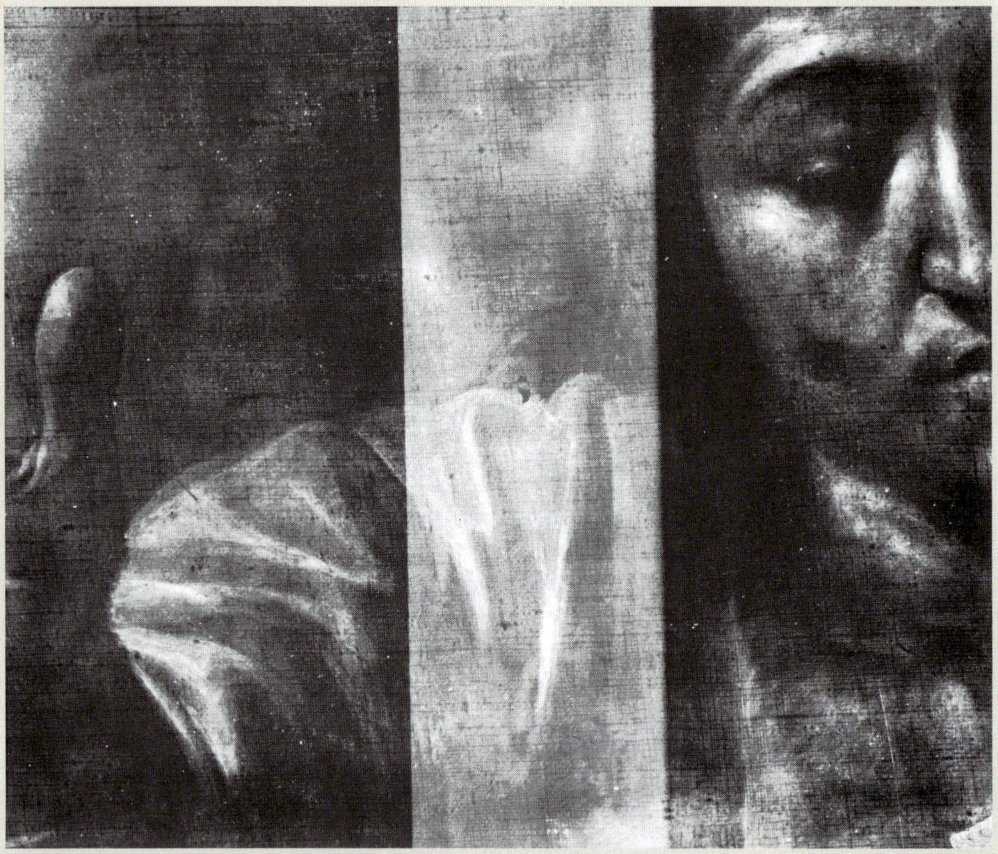

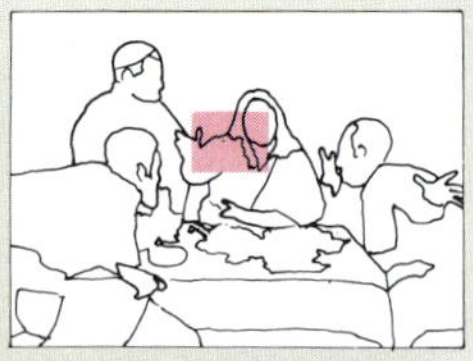

*The X-ray (left) shows that Caravaggio blocked in the highlights of the face on the dark ground using an oil paint containing predominantly lead white. Comparison with the color detail (below) shows how the oval form of the face was accentuated later. It also reveals that the harsh contrasts between light and shadow and the traces of brushmarks evident in the X-ray were modified later by softer brushes, and perhaps also by a badger-hair softener.*

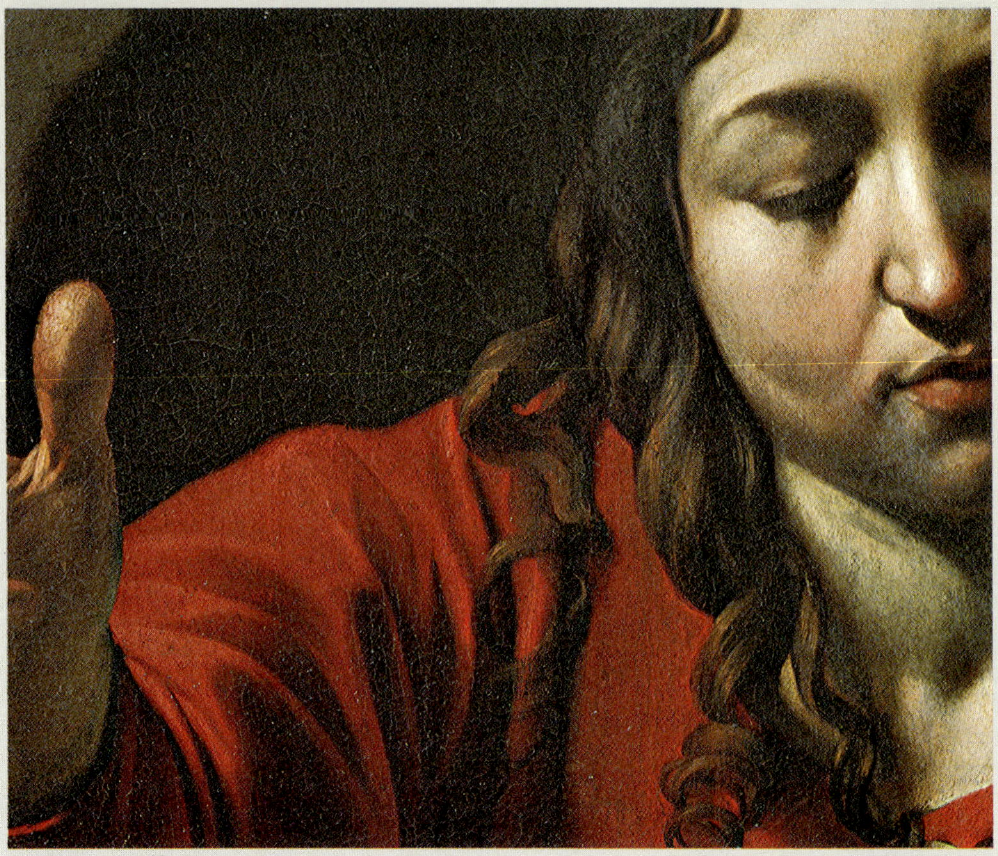

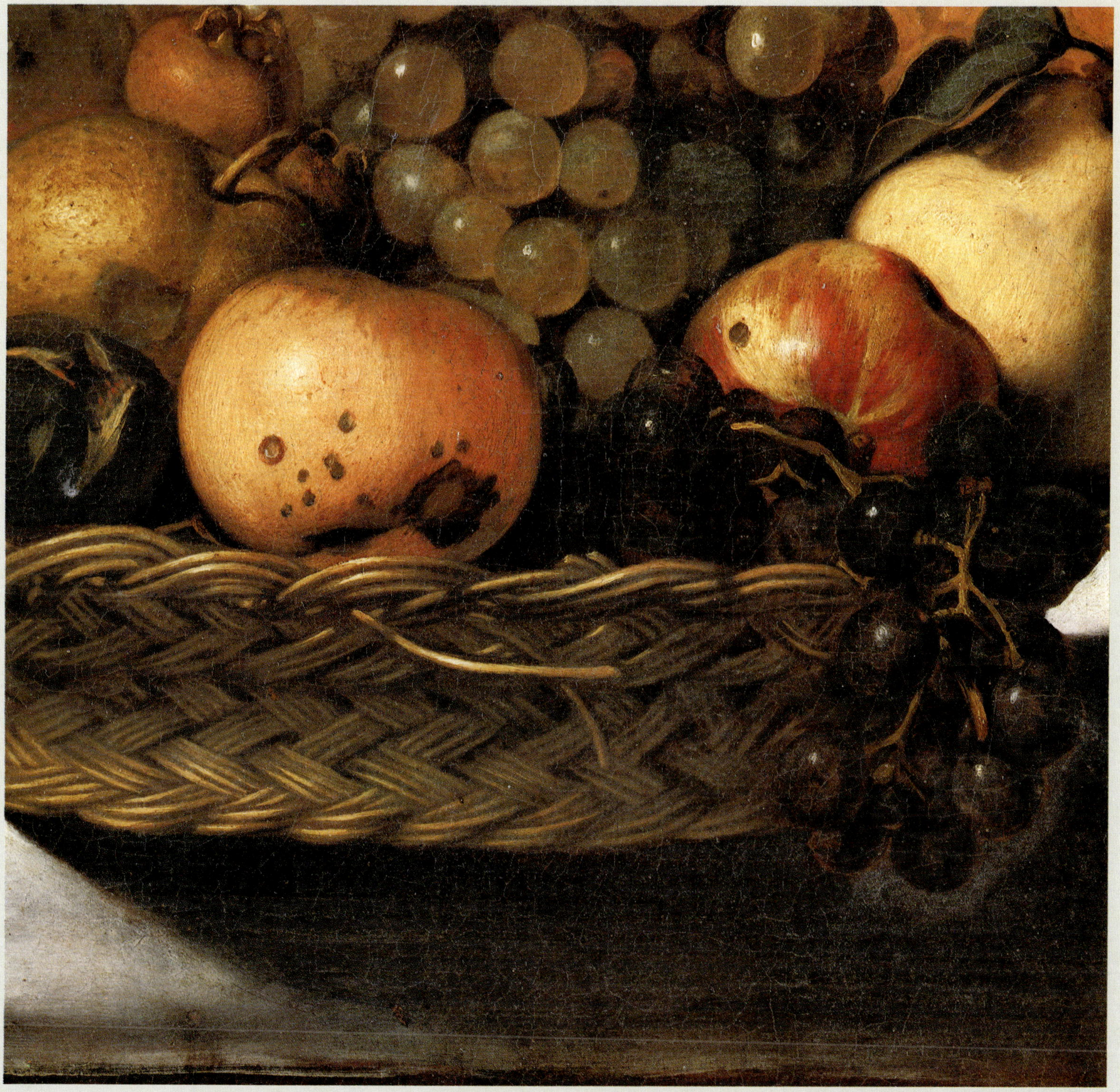

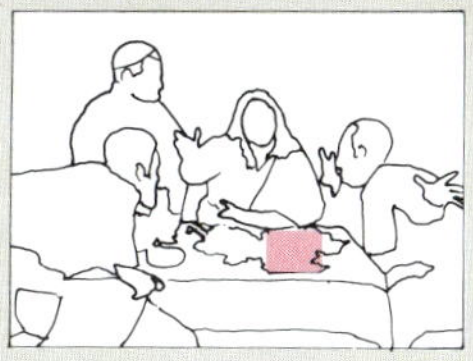

**Actual size detail**
*The enormous care which Caravaggio took over every part of the painting is well illustrated in this detail. A basket of fruit appears in many of his paintings and this detail shows Caravaggio's fascination with bruised, slightly rotten fruit.*
*It is interesting to note that Caravaggio purposely drew attention to the fruit by placing it in a very precarious position on the edge of the table.*
*Soft, fine brushes and a fluid oil medium would have been necessary to achieve this smooth, unbroken surface and detail such as the wicker basket and highlights on the grapes.*
*Caravaggio never seems to have used coarse bristle brushes or a thick oil medium to produce impasto effects, and, in this way, his technique differed considerably from that of El Greco. The smooth, unbroken paint surface suggests that he used soft hair brushes and tempered his pigments with an easily workable, quite fluid oil medium, possibly thinned with turpentine spirit. It is likely that Carvaggio used linseed oil which dried more quickly than the alternative, walnut variety.*

# El Greco

*Christ Driving the Traders from the Temple* (1600)
Oil on canvas, 106cm × 130cm/41in × 51in

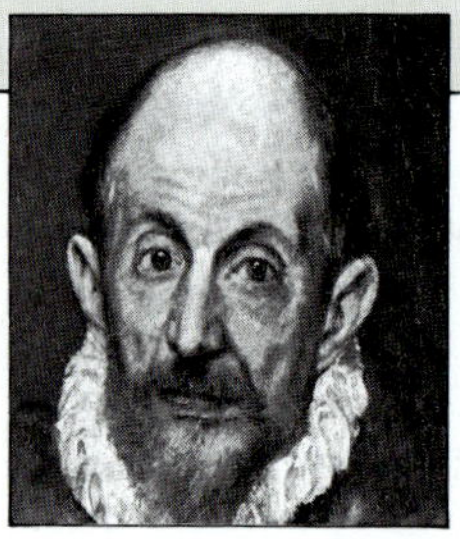

Domenikos Theotokopoulos, commonly known as El Greco, was born in Crete where he probably began to paint in the style of Byzantine icon art. He received some artistic training in Venice, but his early work shows a debt to a wide range of artists including Michelangelo. By 1577 he had settled in Toledo, Spain, where he remained until his death. El Greco failed to find lasting favor with his patron, Philip II of Spain. His distorted, elongated figures and acid, brilliant, unconventional colors made his paintings unacceptable to many, and he consequently had few followers. However, a wider appreciation of El Greco's art grew with the development of modern art during this century.

While in Venice, El Greco most certainly came under the influence of Mannerist painters, the Italian Francesco Mazola Parmigianino in particular. The elongated and elegant figures, the stress on the flowing form and pale colors all indicate that El Greco, along with most Italian artists of that time, was making the transition from the Mannerist to the Baroque period of art.

It is possible that El Greco made preparatory drawings for all of his works, but not many are known. He certainly used small clay models to work out the arrangement of figures in his compositions. This may have been a practice which El Greco learned in Venice, since Tintoretto, who had a great influence on El Greco's early style, is known to have used small wax models as well. El Greco had a cupboard full of clay models in his studio.

El Greco may also have made oil studies for his paintings, as some small-scale versions of his compositions painted on panels exist. However, it is generally assumed that these were small replicas made by the artist himself or by an assistant to provide a visual record of the finished painting after it had left the studio. Pacheco, El Greco's biographer, saw several such small versions of El Greco's works on his visits to the artist's studio.

In spite of his relatively straight-forward technique, Pacheco reports that El Greco was a slow worker, 'who took his paintings in hand many times and retouched them over and over again' to improve on his first brush strokes – a practice which Pacheco called 'working hard for a poor result'.

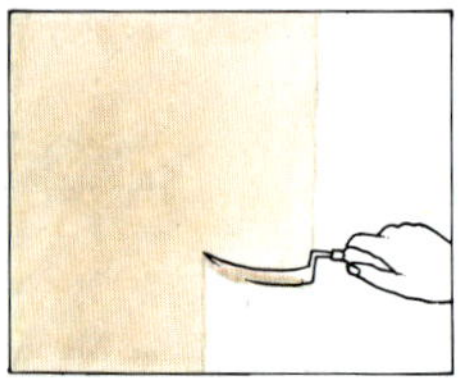

**1.** The stretched canvas was given a layer of animal-skin size applied thinly with a large, flexible palette knife.

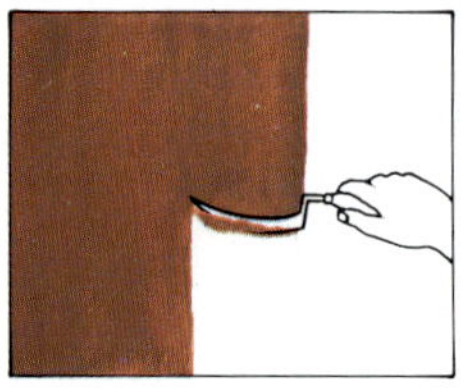

**2.** El Greco used a ground consisting of red ochre and gesso tempered with linseed oil. This was also applied with a palette knife.

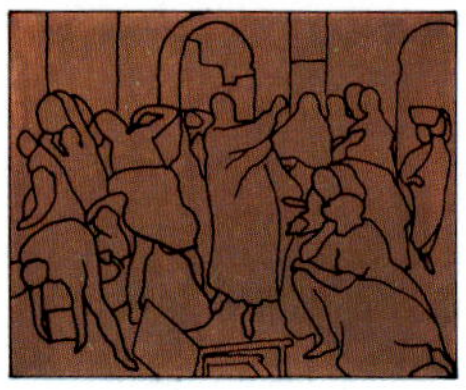

**3.** The outlines of the composition were sketched on the ground probably with black oil paint,possibly charcoal black tempered with linseed oil.

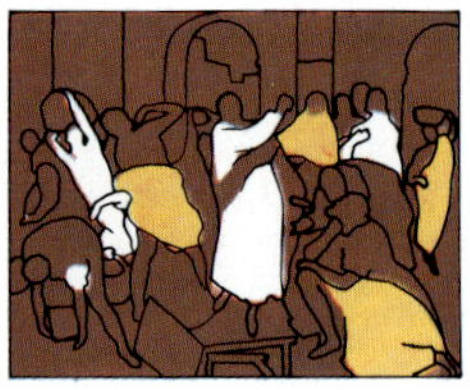

**4.** Light areas were blocked in in white or pale gray oil paint. Large areas of opaque color, such as lead tin yellow for the yellow drapery, were applied next.

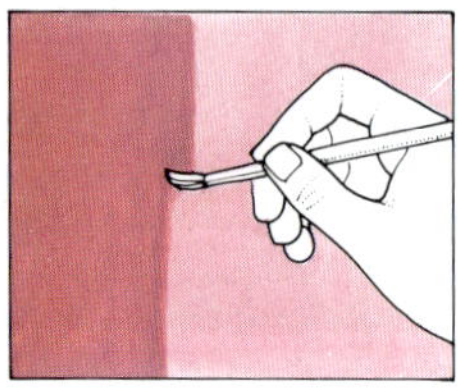

**5.** Areas of pale opaque underpainting were then modified with an oil glaze applied with a fairly stiff bristle brush.

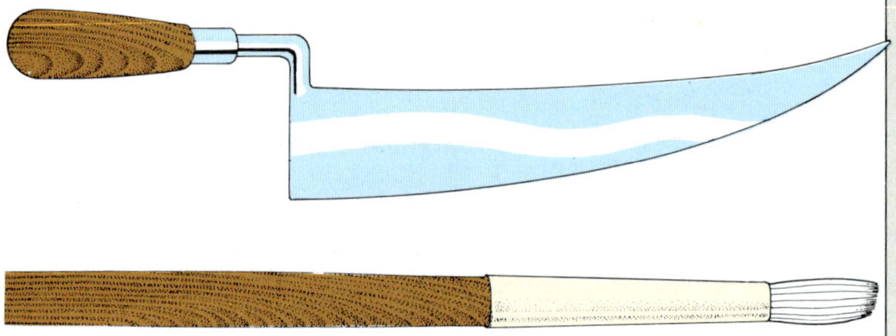

*El Greco is known to have used both a coarse hog's hair brush and an early kind of palette knife. Hog's hair brushes were first popularized in Venice because it was unsatisfactory to use softer brushes on the coarse canvas which was a common painting support in that area. The knife would have had a flexible wooden blade and a wooden handle.*

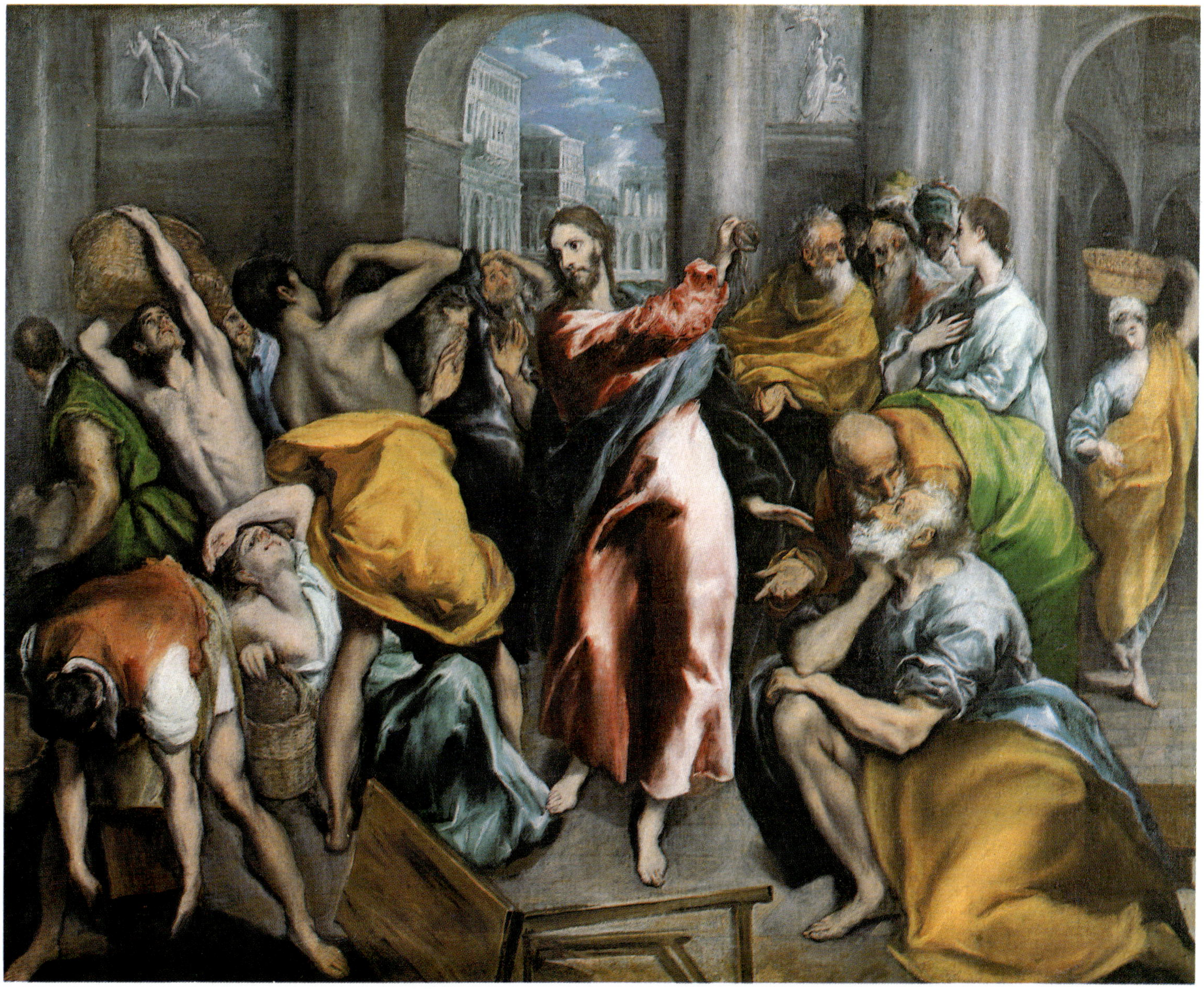

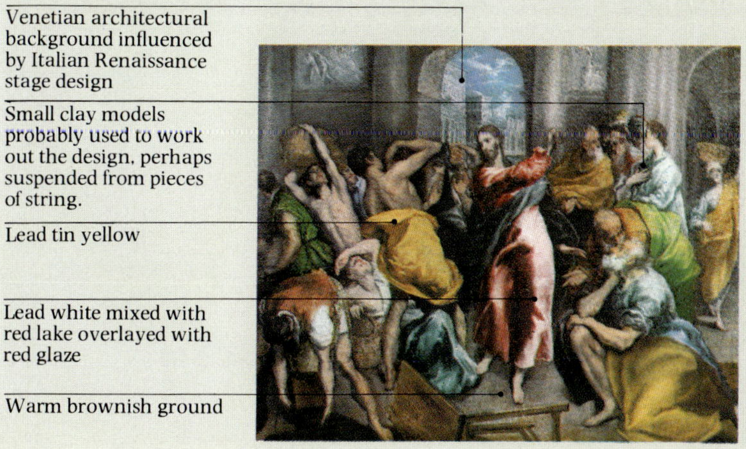


*Many of El Greco's works are painted on relatively fine canvas, covered with a warm, reddish-brown ground. This preference may have been a result of his training in Venice, where the use of such grounds became common in the second half of the sixteenth century. When tempering his pigments, El Greco used a thick oil medium of the consistency of honey, which he applied in broken strokes with a coarse hog's hair brush. His brushwork, which was considered crude by some contemporary critics, may have been developed from Titian's relatively free later style of painting.*
*The characteristic brilliance of El Greco's drapery was achieved by applying a rich, translucent oil glaze directly onto the light opaque underpainting. This was a radical simplification of the Venetian method of building up a complex series of paint layers and glazes.*

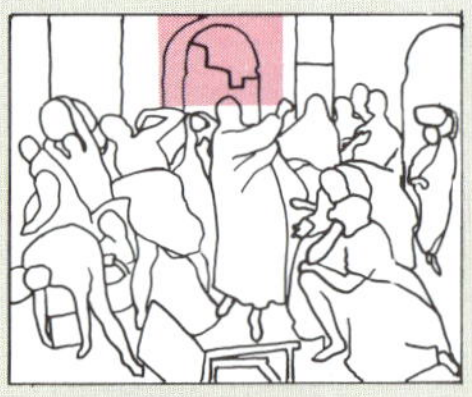

*The architecture in the background was probably based on contemporary Italian stage design which made use of perspective. The blue pigment is unlikely to have been ultramarine because of its high price; it may have been azurite.*

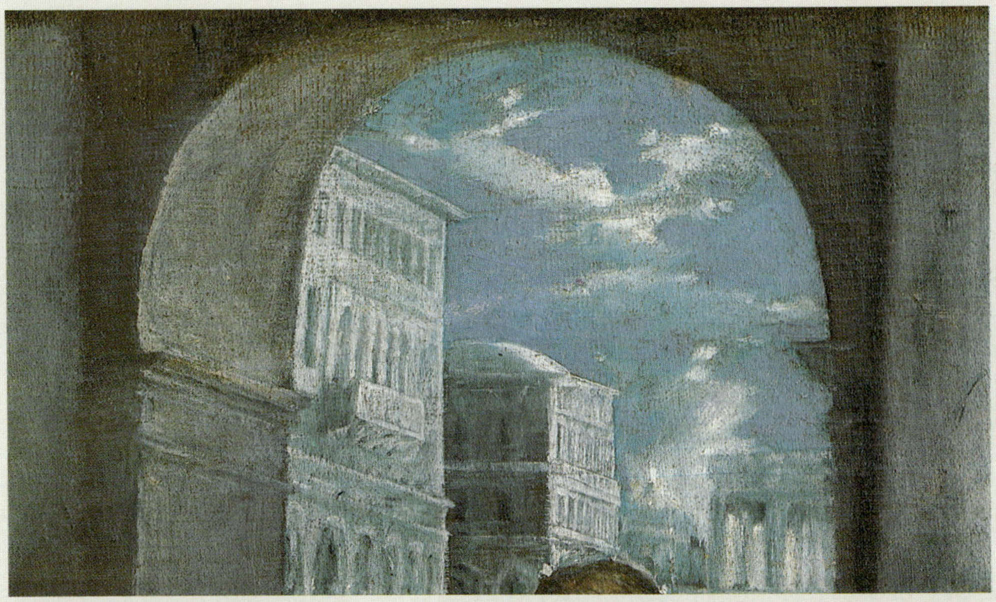

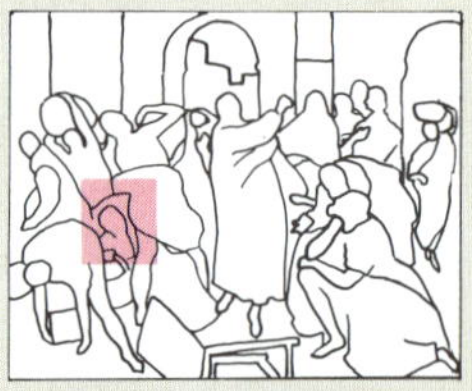

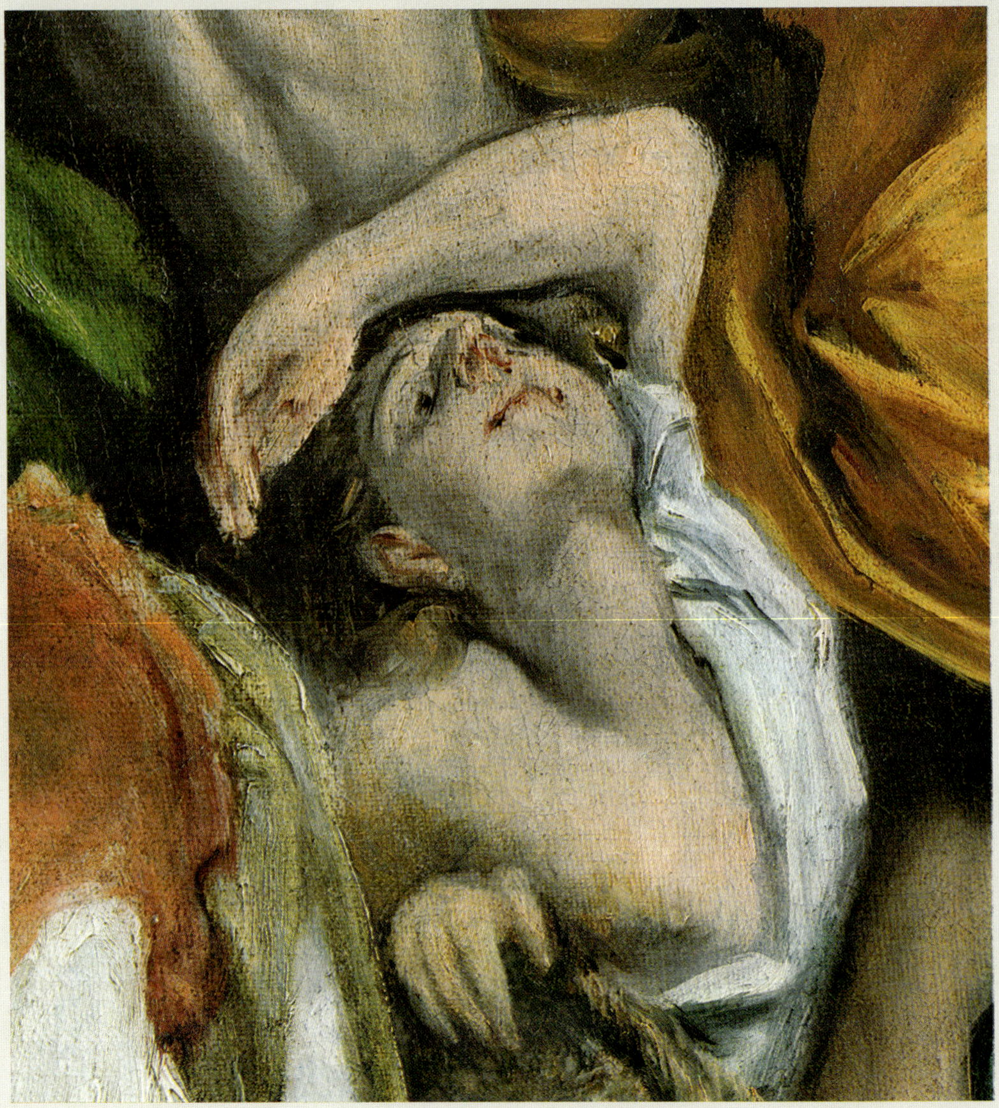

*El Greco's characteristic method of building up flesh tones with lead white and bluish charcoal black is well illustrated in the head of the boy with the basket, where the grayish tone of the shadow is well marked. The face was painted quite sketchily with the type of stiff hog's hair brush which El Greco frequently used.*

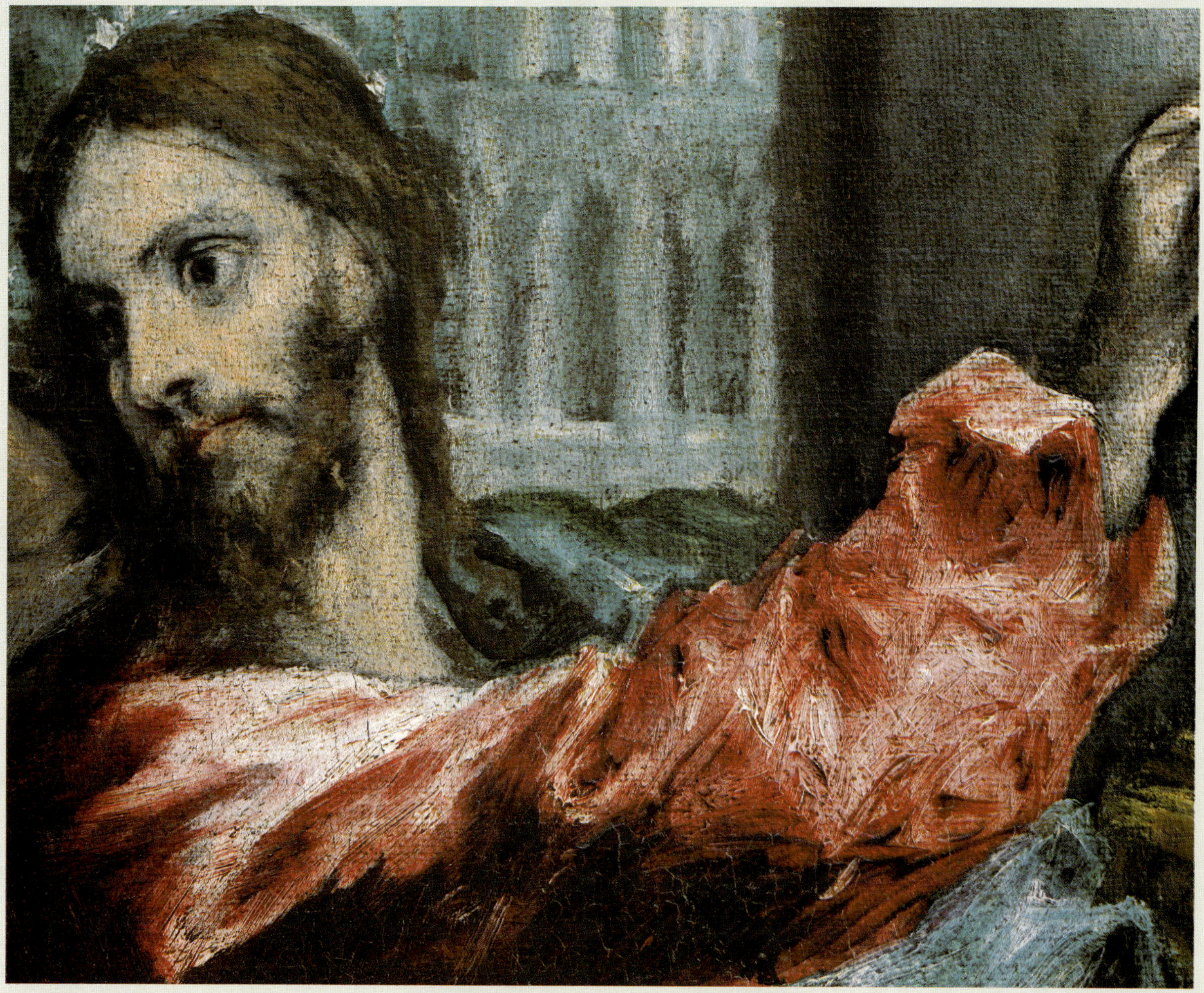

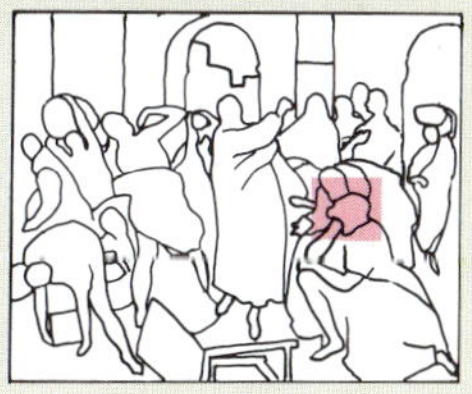

*This detail shows the way in which El Greco built up forms using broken, short strokes and dabs of thick oil paint, applied in an almost impressionistic manner with a coarse, bristle brush. No attempt was made to achieve a smooth surface by gently blending one stroke into another; indeed the marks of the individual bristles which made up the brush are clearly evident.*

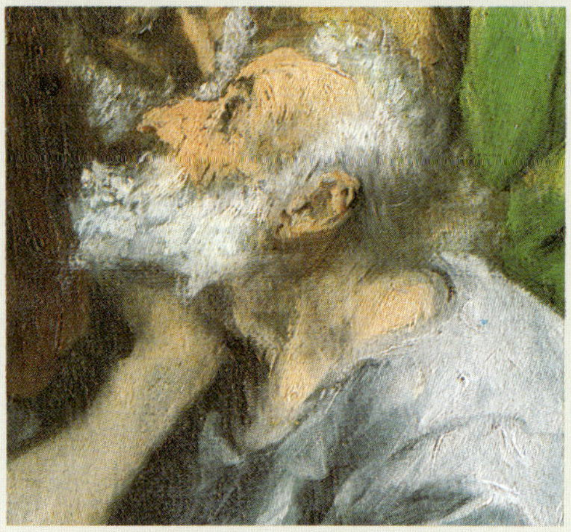

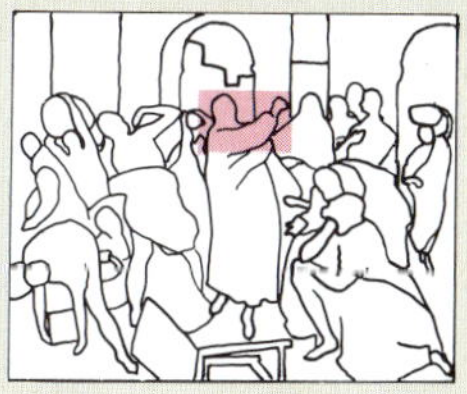

Actual size detail
*El Greco's method of building up flesh tones with lead white and bluish charcoal black is well illustrated in the head of Christ. The sleeve of the robe is an excellent example of El Greco's technique for painting drapery. The thick, opaque light layer was painted with a stiff bristle brush worked in different directions, on top of which a transparent lake was applied. The red lake was also tempered with a thick medium and applied using hatching strokes. El Greco's method differed from the common technique of the period. Most painters tempered a lake pigment with a more fluid oil medium which was applied in smooth strokes with a soft brush to achieve an unbroken glaze.*

# DIEGO VELAZQUEZ

*The Water Seller of Seville* (c. 1620)
Oil on canvas, 107cm × 81cm/42in × 31⅘in

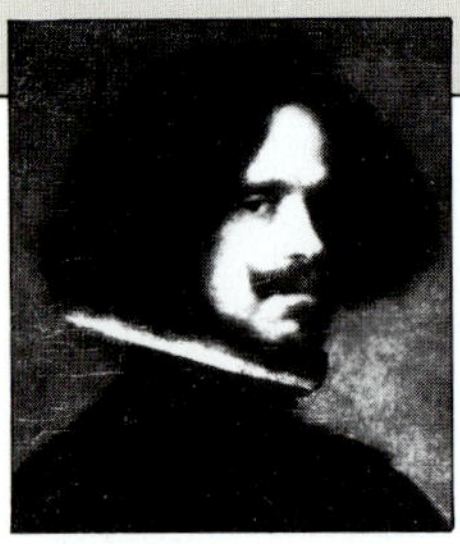

Diego Rodriquez de Silva Velazquez was born in 1599 in Seville where he lived and worked until 1623 when he was offered a post at the court of Philip IV in Madrid. Velazquez remained attached to the court until his death, but made several trips to Italy where he paid particular attention to the works of Venetian painters.

Velazquez has been a source of influence and inspiration to many artists, including his fellow countryman, Goya, more than one hundred years later, and, later still, the French Impressionist Edouard Manet in the nineteenth century. The earlier paintings of Velazquez are reminiscent of Caravaggio in their treatment of light and shade, handling of paint and attention to realistic detail. Velazquez always leaned towards a dark and dramatic style of painting. Even in his early genre paintings however, Velazquez also showed the dispassionate and objective vision which was characteristic of him.

Although few preparatory drawings of Velazquez's paintings exist, it is probable that some were made. Preliminary studies in oil were often done. This is seen in the care and detail with which many of Velazquez's paintings are executed. Many of Velazquez's canvases show that he frequently made minor alterations during painting. As he painted, he frequently wiped his brush clean on the canvas, which he later covered over as can be seen in some of his early pictures.

Velazquez probably tempered his pigments with linseed oil of a reasonably fluid consistency, only using a thicker medium for dabs of highlight. The smooth, blended brushwork in many of Velazquez's paintings indicate that, like Caravaggio, Velazquez preferred to use soft hair brushes rather than coarse bristle ones.

Velazquez's technique changed considerably during his career. By the time he was painting portraits of Philip IV of Spain in Madrid in the 1630s, his palette had become somewhat cooler in tone and his handling of paint freer, as he developed a technique of using light, feathery strokes of paint.

*The Water Seller of Seville* was painted in Seville around 1620. It was one of a series of works featuring ordinary people, eating and drinking in dark interiors. Such scenes, known as 'bodegones', were popular in seventeenth century Spain.

**1.** Velazquez often chose fine, regular weave canvas which he covered with a dark brown ground using a palette knife.

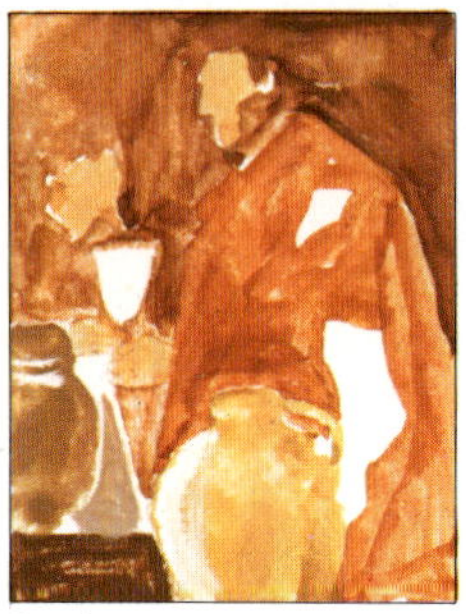

**2.** The main composition and areas of light and dark would be blocked in using a fairly large bristle brush.

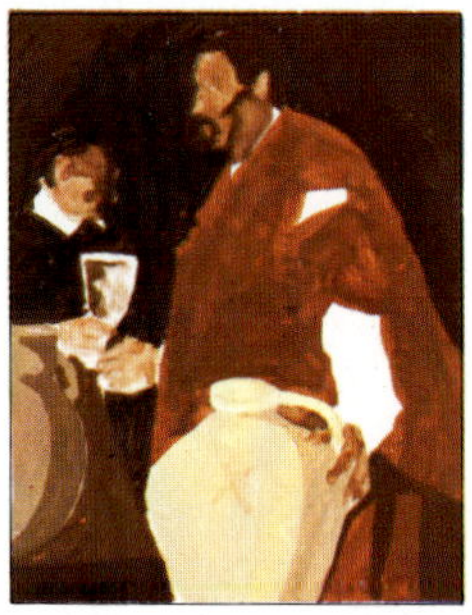

**3.** Using softer brushes, Velazquez would develop the somewhat roughly applied large areas of color.

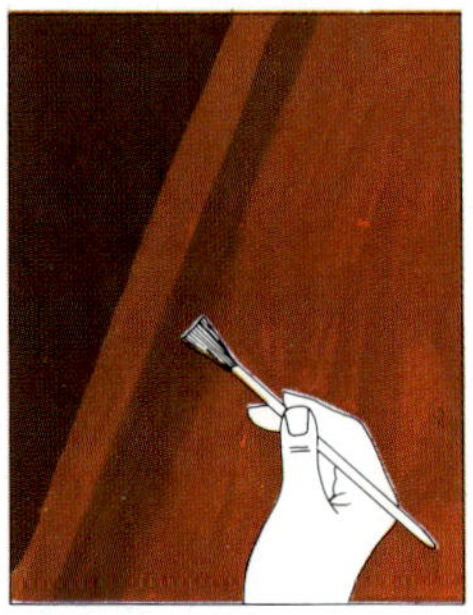

**4.** The softness of the water seller's tunic suggests that Velazquez went over the area with a blending brush.

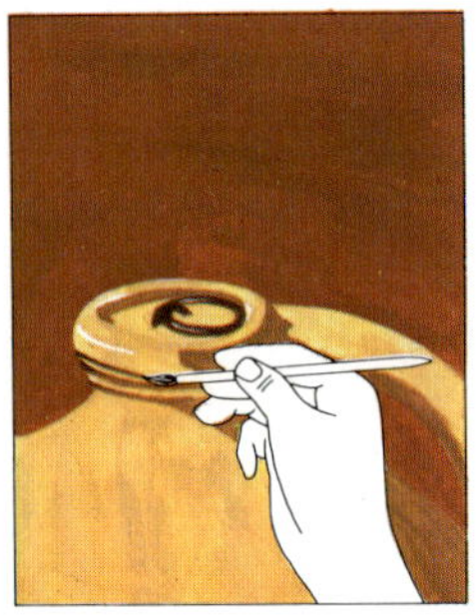

**5.** Small details, like the ridges on the pitchers, would be added with a fine pointed brush probably made of ermine or stoat.

Velazquez made only a few alterations in the painting of this picture, mainly to the figure of the water seller.

Alteration to collar

Alteration to sleeve

Alteration to left hand

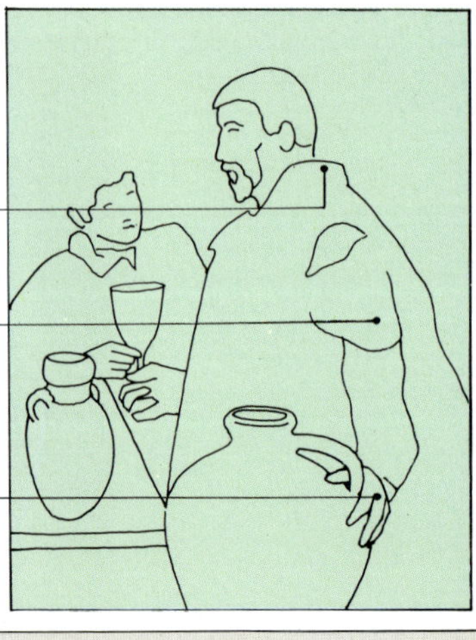

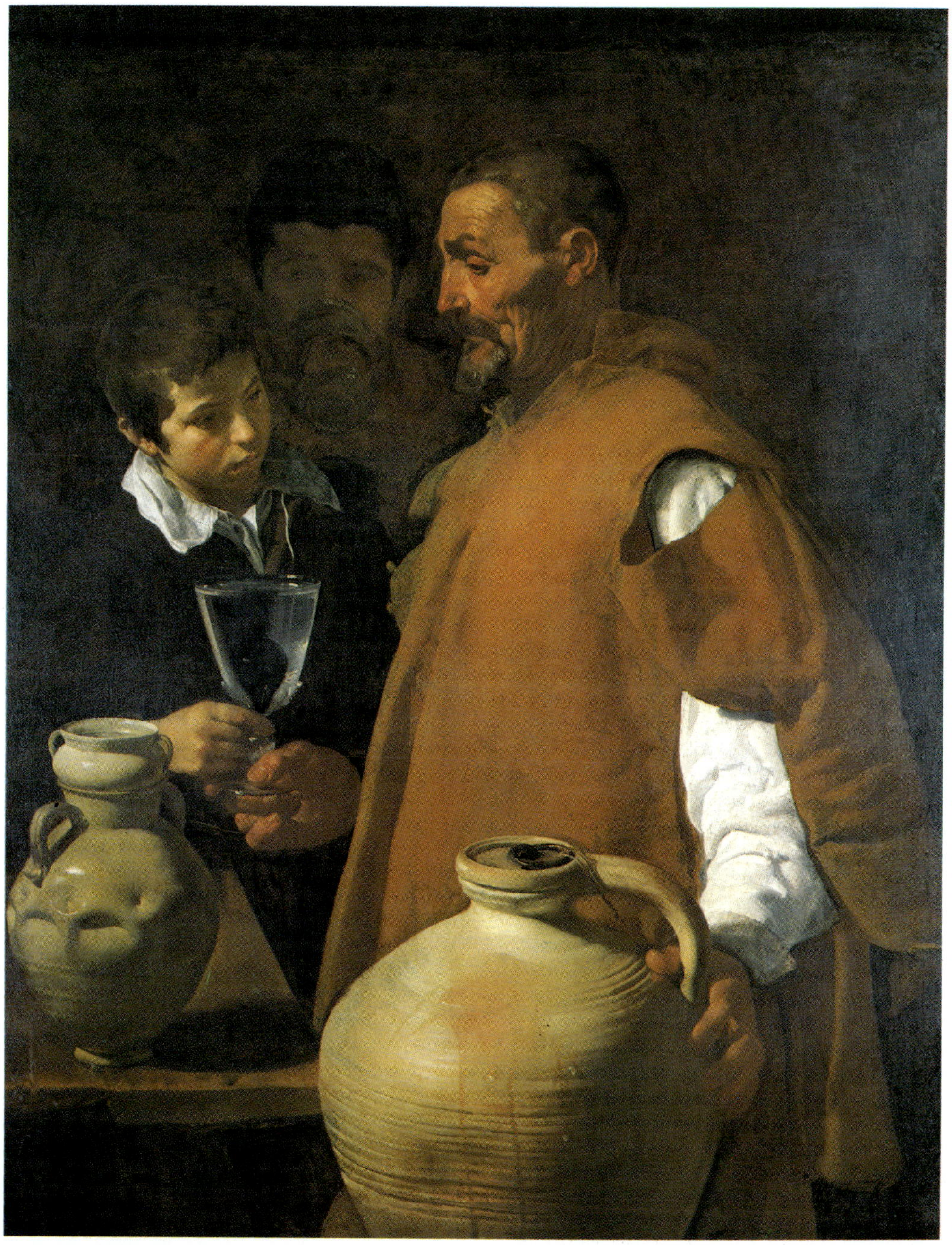

*The depiction of ordinary people eating and drinking was popular in seventeenth century Spain and Velazquez did many genre paintings of this type. The composition, with its rich ochres, earth tones, and careful attention to detail are all reminiscent of Caravaggio and show his influence on Velazquez. While no preparatory drawings for this painting survive, it is probable that they did exist. Valazquez's biographer wrote that he did many chalk sketches, probably of both the water seller and the boy. The pitchers, which occur frequently in Velazquez's works at this time, were almost certainly studio props, and the careful rendering suggests that oil studies may have been made first in the studio. In* The Water Seller of Seville *a striking, yet serene composition is achieved by the choice of warm, harmonious earth colors and the careful arrangement of large, simple shapes to form a triangle, of which the water seller's head is the apex. Velazquez may have applied a spirit varnish to protect the painting some months after it had been completed. A slightly yellowing varnish would not seriously spoil the warm colors used in this painting.*

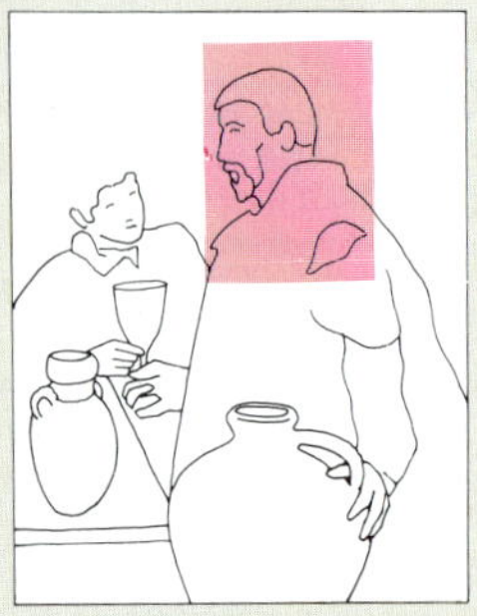

*This detail is a good example of Velazquez's study of the play of light on the weathered skin of the water seller. The whole face was painted quite thickly, but the highlights on the nose and forehead were picked out with thicker oil paint than the rest of the face. The upper paint layer of the collar of the tunic has become transparent with time, to reveal the smaller, first collar underneath.*

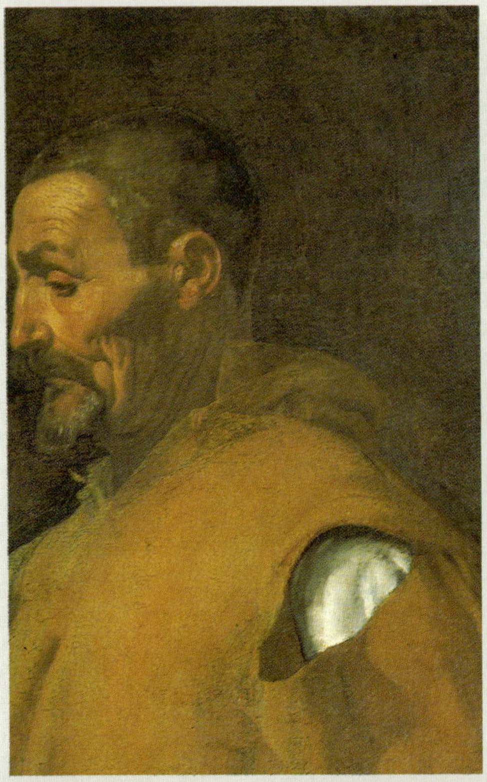

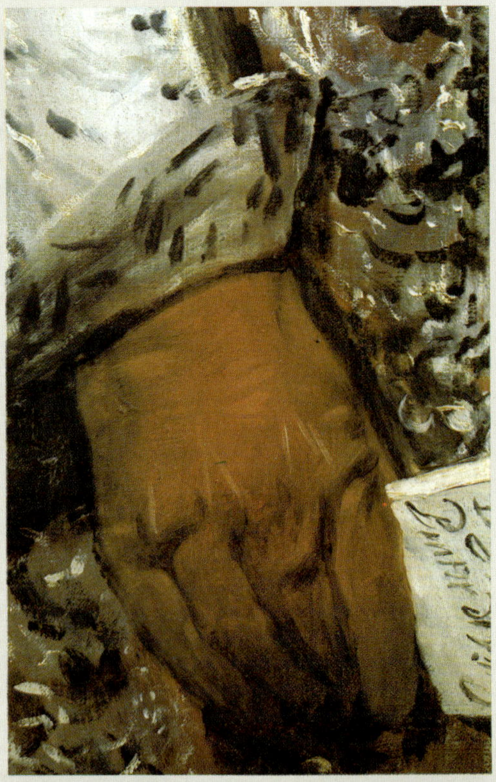

*The comparison between the hand of the water seller and the gloved hand of Philip IV in the portrait by Velazquez, painted in the 1630's shows how far Velazquez's technique developed in over 10 years. Although the paint was still quite thickly applied, the handling had become freer, lighter and more sketchy. It was such brushwork which had a marked effect on the French Impressionist Manet.*

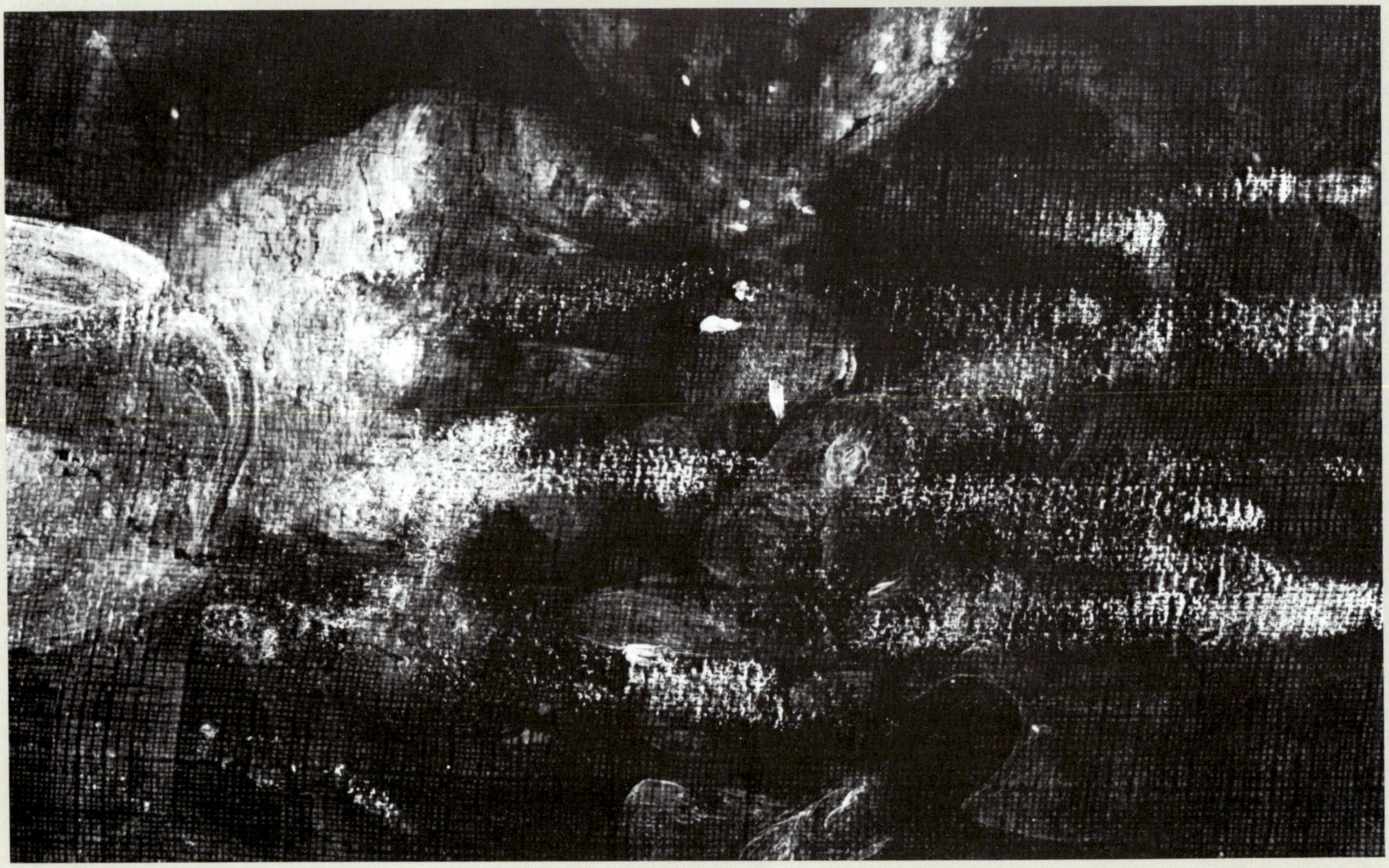

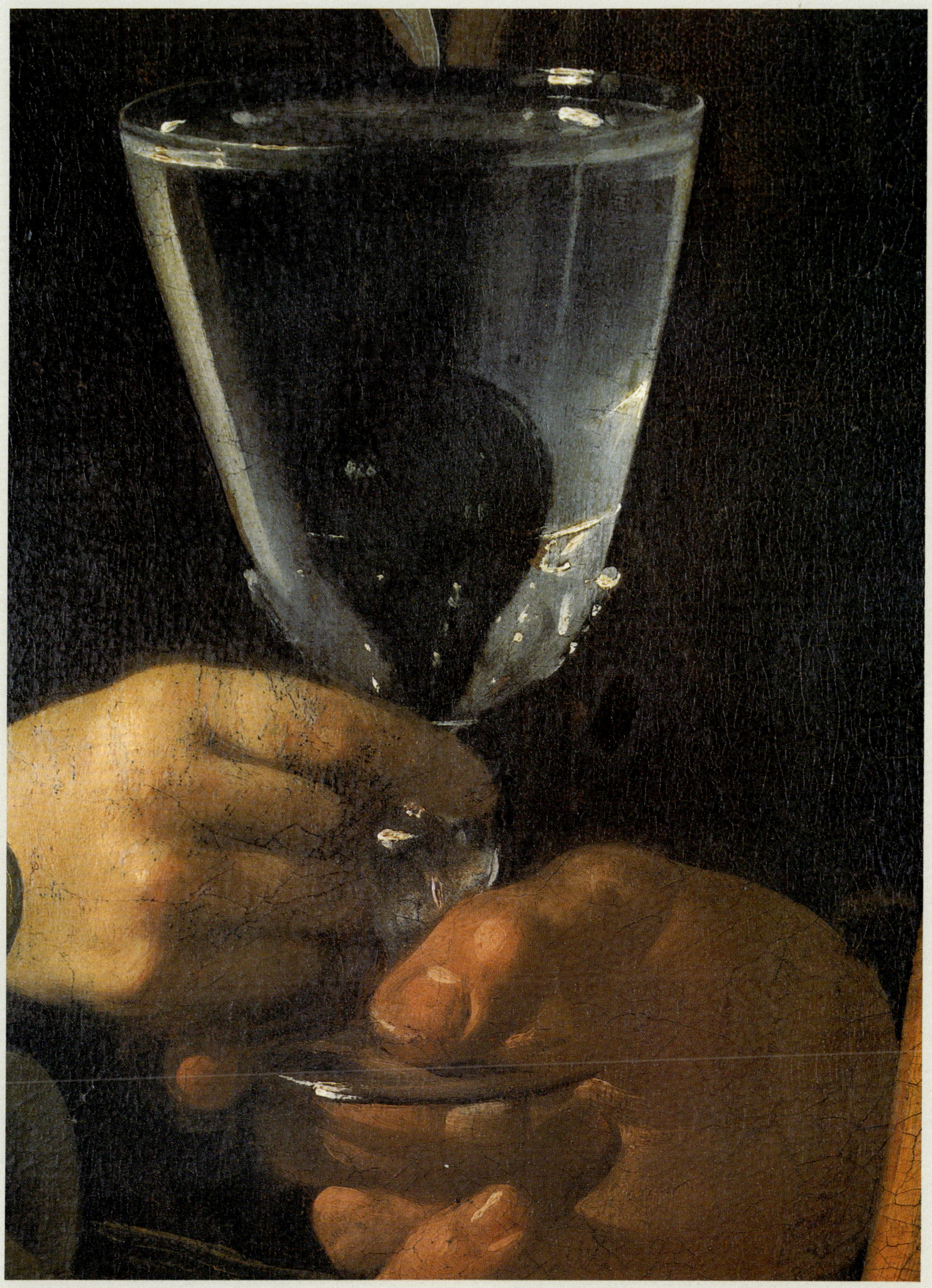

**Actual size detail**
*Unlike the water seller's head, his hands are painted quite thinly, with little lead white. The X-ray* (**left**) *reveals horizontal marks left by the artist's brush, when he wiped it clean on the canvas, which was later painted over. The interest in the effect of light on the glass is reminiscent of Caravaggio, and the delicate way it is painted points towards the finer, lighter technique developed by Velazquez later in his career.*

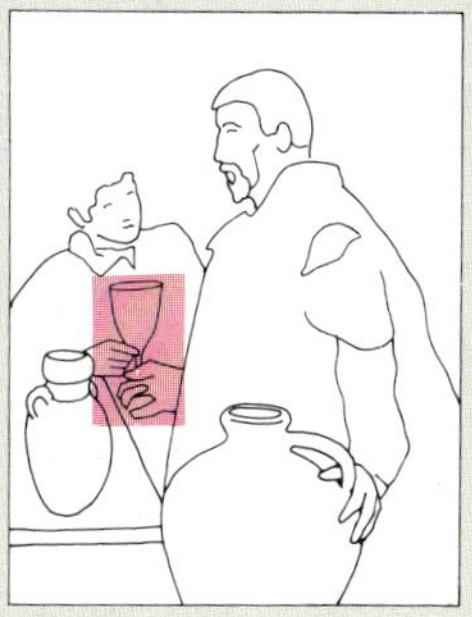

# Peter Paul Rubens

*Portrait of Susanna Lunden née Fourment* (c. 1620-25)
Oil on canvas, 79cm × 55cm/31¹⁄₁₆in × 21½in

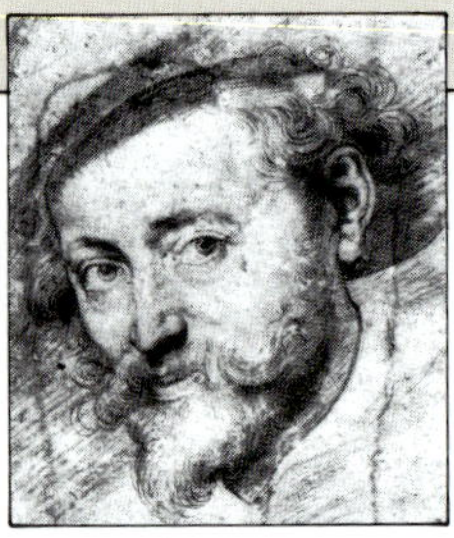

Rubens set up his studio workshop in Antwerp in 1609 and by 1611 was turning down pupils on the grounds that he already had over a hundred applicants. Even during his absences abroad, production continued uninterrupted. However, this intimate portrait of his second wife's sister has never been questioned as an entirely autograph work. Rubens worked on both wood panels and canvas, using a variety of different grounds; his general preference for panels with smooth chalk grounds may be related to the fluency of his technique. The ground on this panel is traditional – chalk bound with animal glue and impregnated with oil – but the priming is an innovation. It is brownish, and applied with long, streaked, irregular brushstrokes. Rubens probably used a lean oil medium. The effect was less monotonous than the uniform dark grounds, popularized under Italian influences, and it had the advantage, by its translucency and striped application, of allowing the white chalk ground to shine through as well.

There are no detailed preparatory underdrawings as in earlier Netherlandish painting because the composition is sketched directly in thin, fluid paint. The priming plays a crucial part in the color effects especially the flesh, where traditional procedure was reversed. The lights are painted thickly and opaquely to cover the ground priming whereas the shadows are scumbled thinly and translucently over it. The optical effect is cool and pearlized in the shadow, warm in the lights. This warm-cool modulation, the modeling, is achieved entirely by controlling the thickness of the flesh paint.

These effects required great virtuosity of brushwork. Rubens is described as painting with a pot of turpentine beside him, frequently dipping his brush into it in order to thin or work the paint. This is the first documented reference to turpentine as a diluent for oil paint and helps explain the variety of Rubens' brushwork. Rubens and his contemporaries were obsessively concerned with the color and purity of their oil media. Linseed oil was most commonly used, but walnut oil, which yellowed less, was employed for delicate tints. Resin-oil varnishes were considered to be more suitable for harsher Northern climates than those made from spirits.

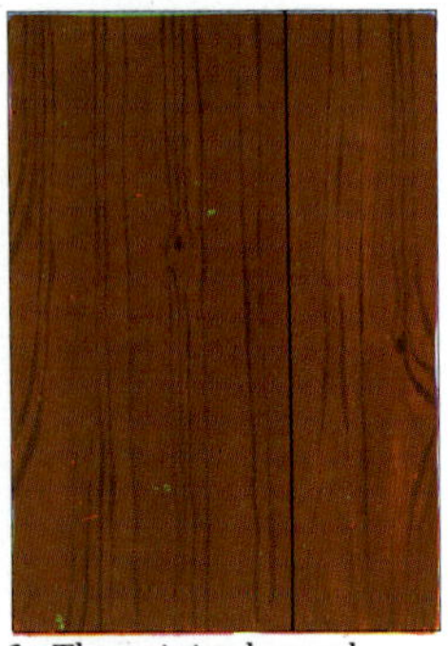

**1.** The original panel was made of two oak planks with vertical grain.

**2.** The wood was sized, and a chalk and animal skin glue ground applied and scraped smooth.

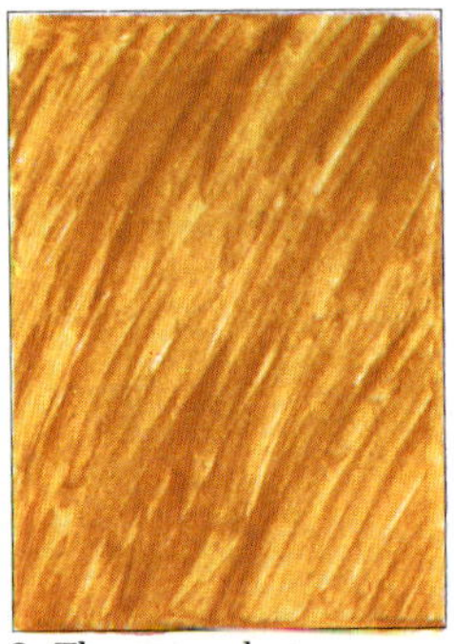

**3.** The ground was then impregnated with oil and a brown priming brushed on with long, irregular strokes.

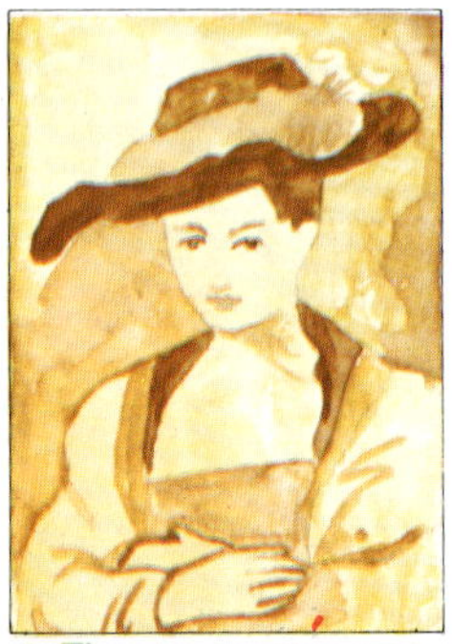

**4.** The composition was sketched in using very thin fluid paint and tones of yellow ochre and umber.

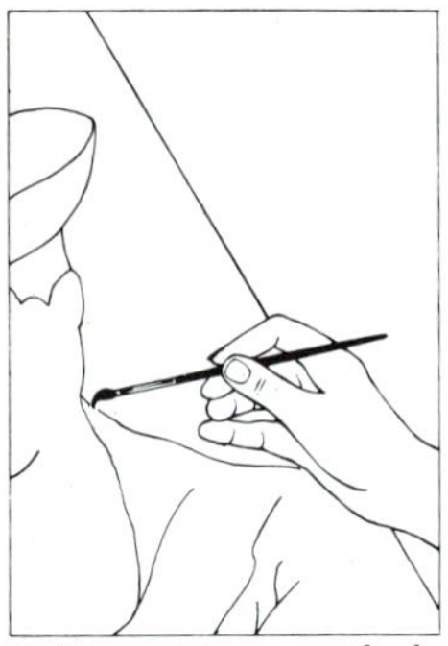

**5.** The paint was applied in a continuous process. Shadows were achieved by exposing the priming or scumbling lighter shades over dark.

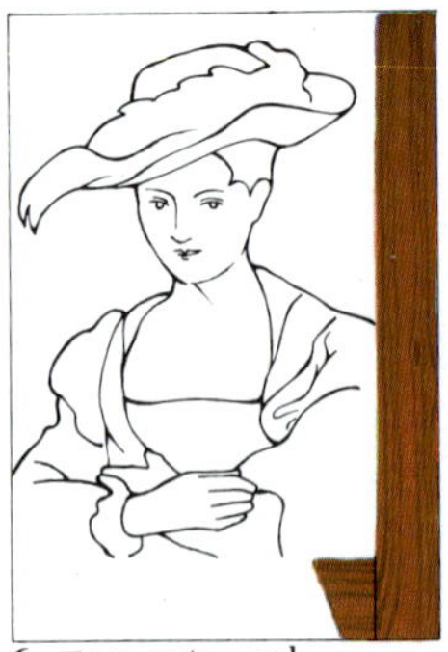

**6.** Two extra oak planks were attached. The additional strips do not have a dark priming.

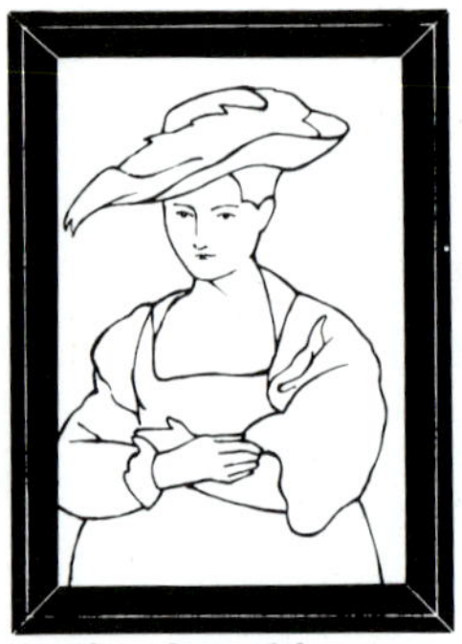

**7.** The edges of the additional planks only were unpainted. This indicates that the portrait was framed before the painting was finished.

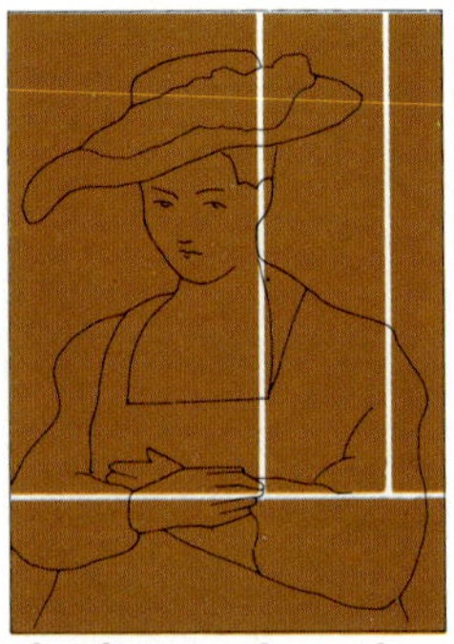

This diagram shows the construction of the finished work.

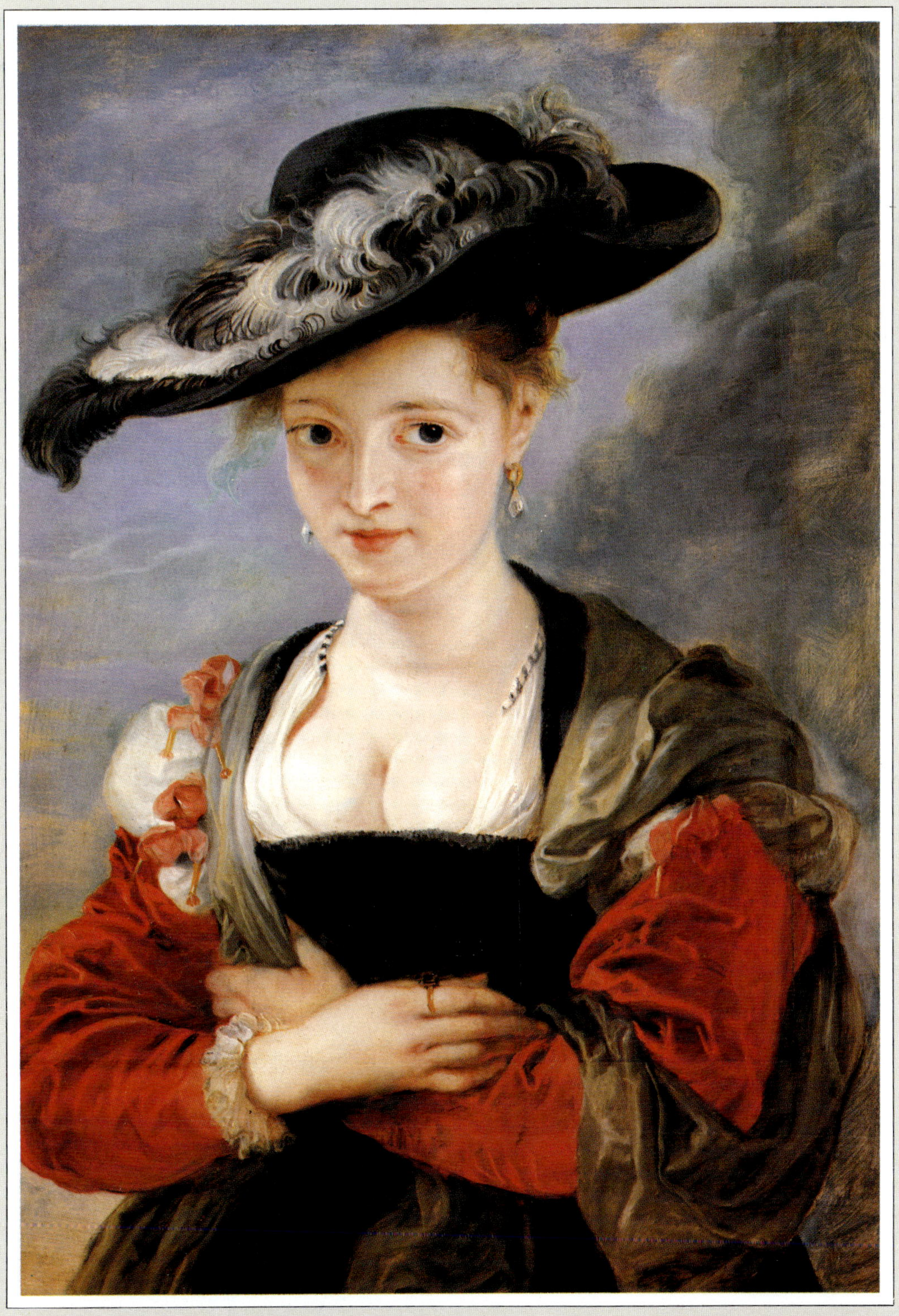

*This picture was painted on four planks of oak prepared outside the studio by a well-known panel-maker whose monogram is branded on the back. It is particularly characteristic of Rubens that the composition has apparently expanded spontaneously from a relatively unchanged central core. A strip of wood was added on the right expanding the sky and reducing the formality of the composition, while another at the bottom gives the figures more substance. Rubens' technique contrasts with earlier Netherlandish methods in the use of a dark ground, the abandonment of detailed underdrawing, and the reversal of painting procedure, working from thin darks to thickly applied lights. His preference for a thin, fluid oil medium, prepared so as to remain as colorless as possible, is typical and he fully exploits its potential variety of handling.*

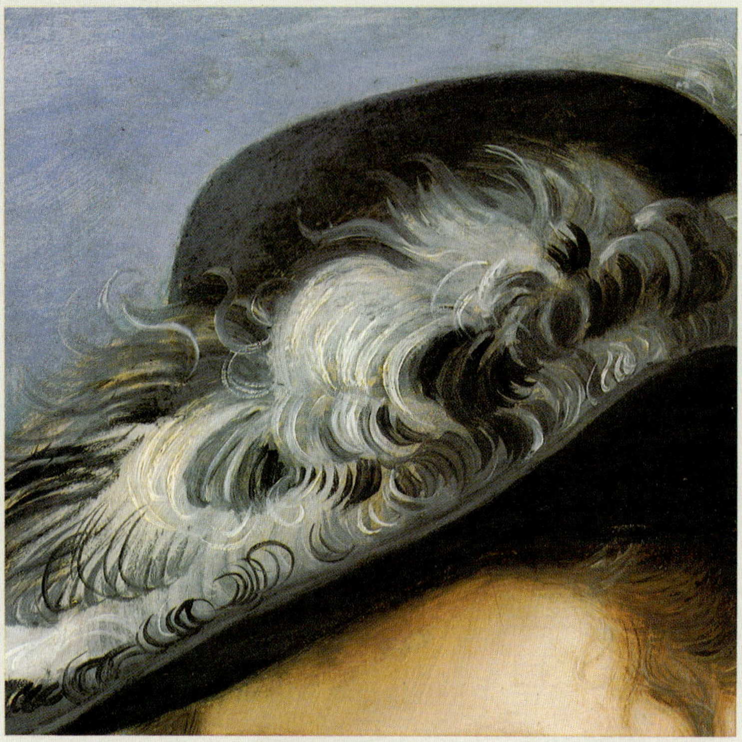

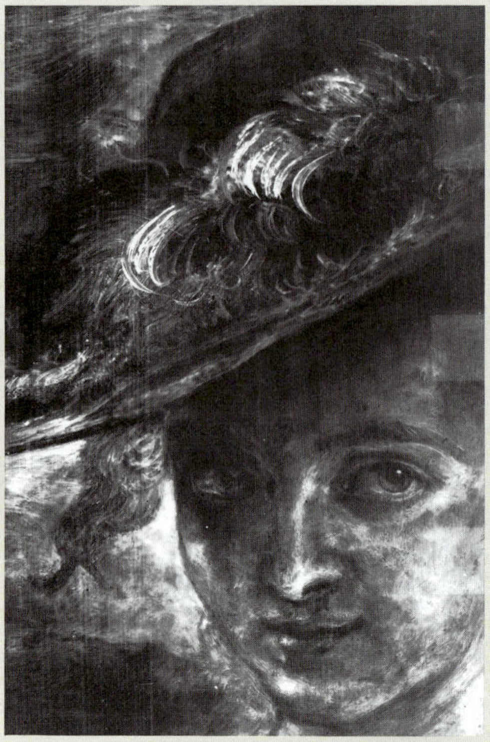

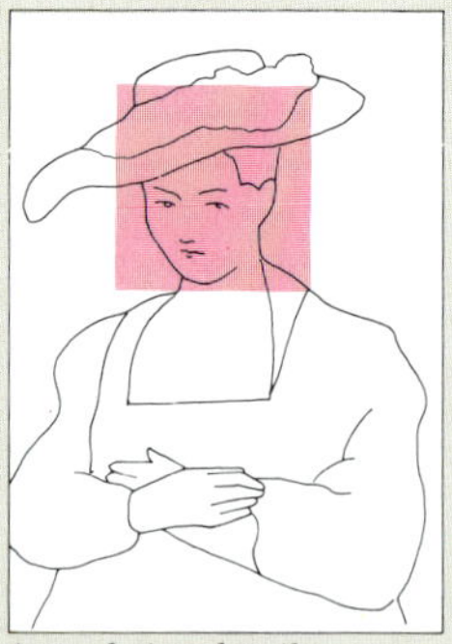

Actual size detail
*Rubens' contemporary biographer, Descamps, includes among the artist's maxims that in flesh painting the strokes of color should be placed side by side, and only lightly blended, Rubens painted the lights yellow-white, the complexion pink-red and the shadows optical blue-gray. In this actual size detail there are separate red accents around the eye, while blue pigment is mixed into the whites and the blue background paint dragged into the shadows on the right.*

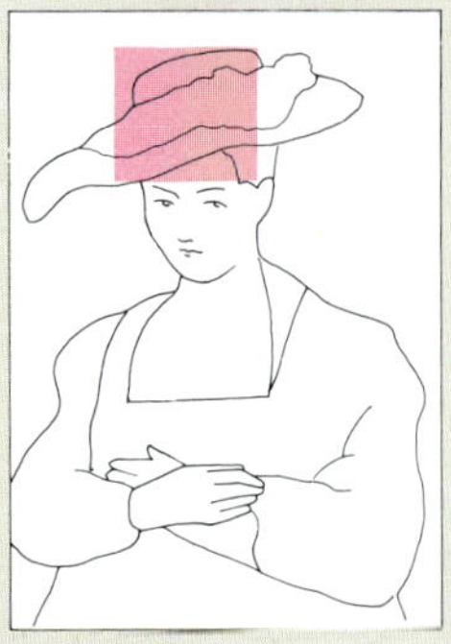

Top left
*The hat is of a type frequently worn by both men and women in the 1620s. In painting the feathers, each plume was described with a single, confident stoke.*

Top right
*The X-radiograph reveals clear variations in the handling of the paint. The combinations of long, fluid strokes and shorter, blunt strokes are highly characteristic of Rubens' working methods. The flesh highlights appear light because of Rubens' reliance on lead white pigment to cover over the dark ground.*

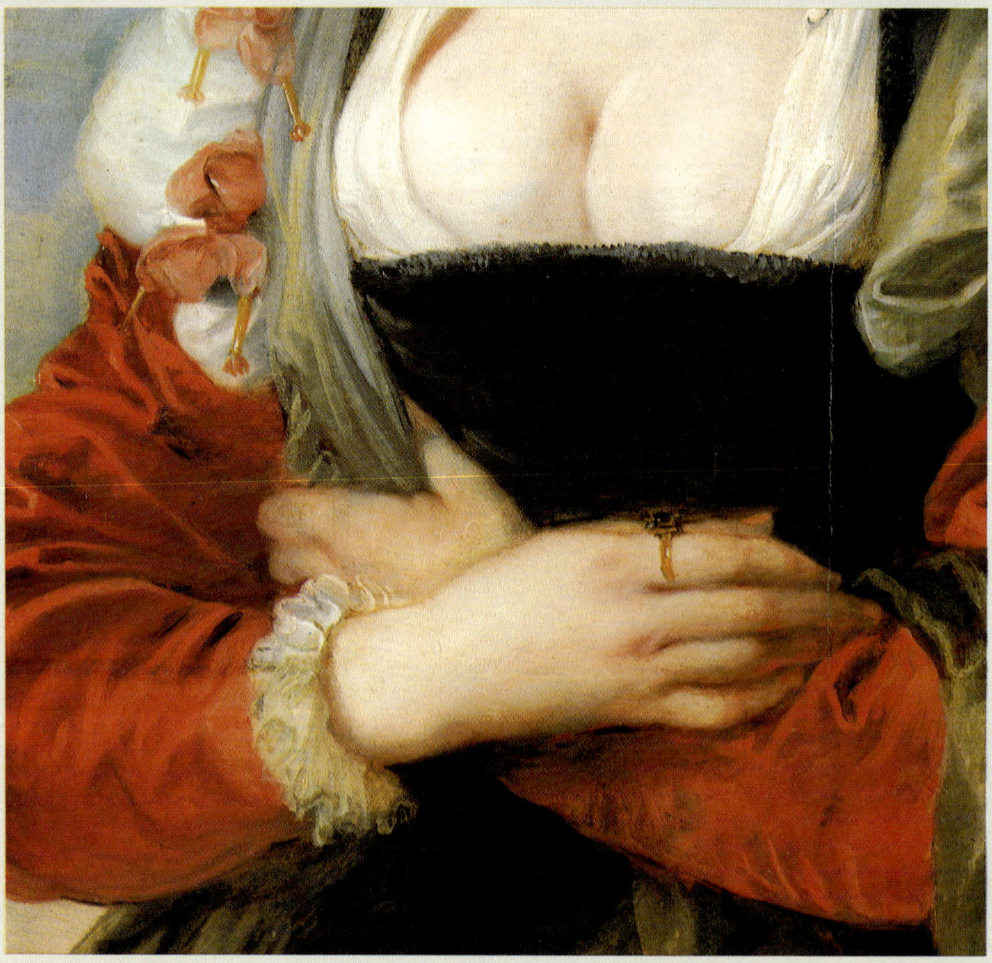

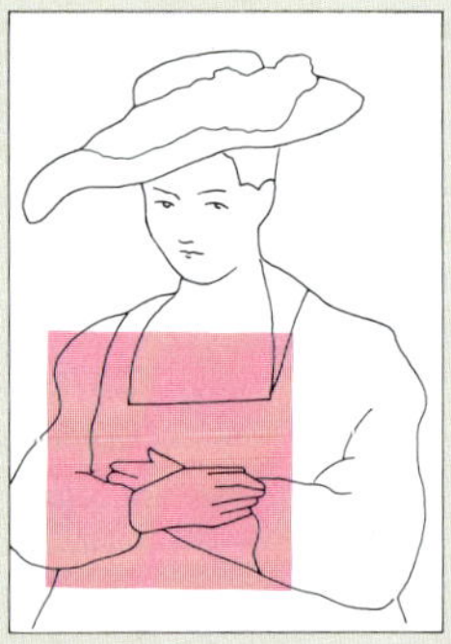

Left
*The join between the planks is clearly visible in the area of the hands. There were several alterations — only the thumb and forefinger of the left hand were originally shown: the right thumb was higher at first and the sleeves have been altered. The use of red to light up the shadows and separate colors is characteristic of Rubens. In the seventeenth century, Holland was the centre for the manufacture of high-quality, dry process vermilion. In the sleeve, vermilion and crimson lakes are mixed together, juxtaposed and superimposed.*

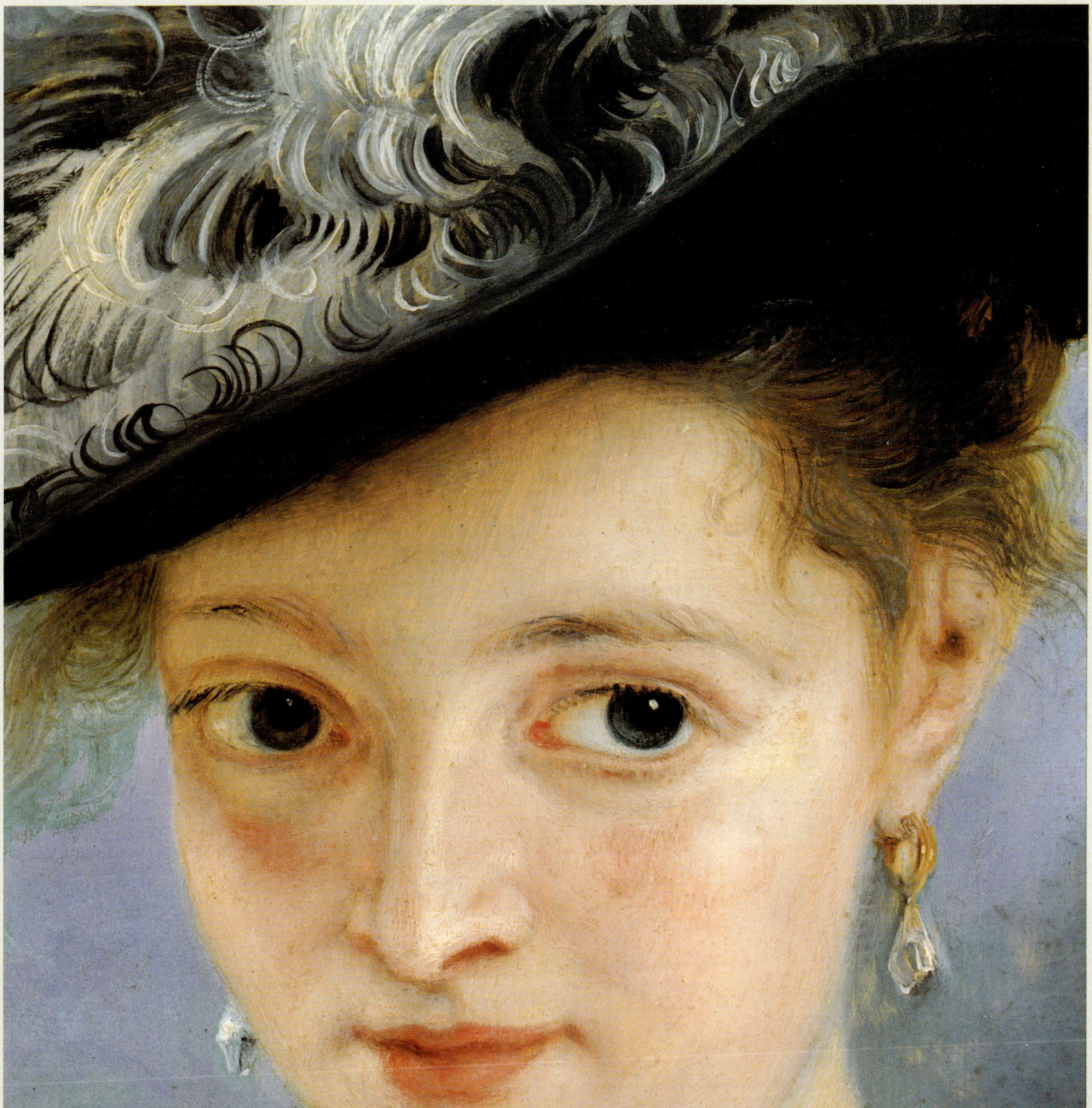

# Rembrandt van Rijn

*The Feast of Belshazzar: The Writing on the Wall* (c. 1635)
Oil on canvas, 167cm × 209cm/66in × 82⅓in

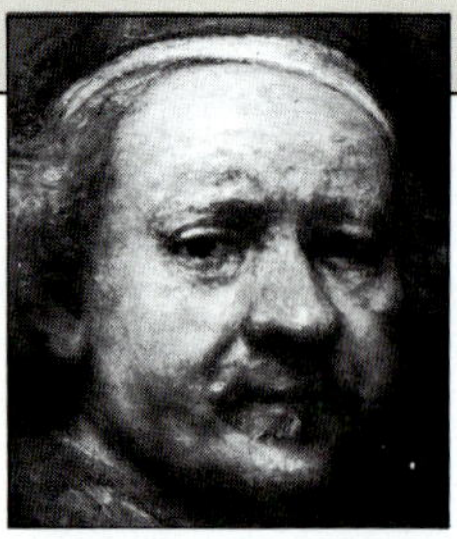

Rembrandt never visited Italy but by the time he left his native Leyden to settle in Amsterdam in 1631, he had already been exposed to the latest developments in Baroque painting. The Dutch followers of Caravaggio had ensured that the thunderous use of light and shade and dramatic figures filling the picture surface had become familiar, as had the fluid, vigorous brushwork of Rubens and the thirst for grand, painterly illusions. Like Rubens, Rembrandt would have noted that Titian in his late work had gone in search of more reflective moods and discovered a new and glorious freedom in his brushstrokes.

Of all the Baroque masters, it was Rembrandt who evolved the most revolutionary technique and who seemed to grow into Titian's spiritual heir. By the middle of the 1630s he had long since abandoned conventional Dutch smoothness and his surfaces were already caked with more paint than was strictly necessary to present an illusion. He was weighing his sitters with jewelry solid enough to steal, vigorously modelled with a heavily loaded brush. Where others needed five touches he was using one, and so the brushstrokes had begun to separate and could sometimes only be properly read from a distance. The exact imitation of form was being replaced by the suggestion of it; to some of his contemporaries, therefore, his paintings began to look unfinished. It was from the Venetians that he had learned to use a brown ground so that his paintings emerged from dark to light, physically as well as spiritually. Yet, despite a palette that was limited even by seventeenth century standards, he was renowned as a colorist for he managed to maintain a precarious balance between painting tonally, with light and shade, and painting in color. Just as form was suggested rather than delineated, so the impression of rich color was deceptive.

He worked in complex layers, building up a picture from the back to the front with delicate glazes that allowed light actually to permeate his backgrounds and reflect off the white underpainting, and generously applied body-colors which mimicked the effect of solid bodies in space. Never before had a painter taken such a purely sensuous interest and delight in the physical qualities of his medium, nor granted it a greater measure of independence from the image.

**1.** The canvas was sized with animal glue to seal it against the binding medium of the ground, which would otherwise have been absorbed and could have damaged the canvas.

**2.** A medium-brown ground was laid on consisting of ochre bound with resin and animal glue. Introduced by Titian, the use of a brown rather than white ground ensured that the artist had to work from dark to light.

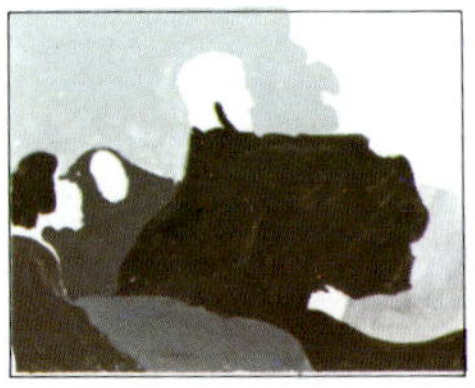

**3.** Rembrandt left no sketches or preliminary studies. Composition and distribution of light and shade are mapped out in a monochrome underpainting. The completed image is not so much a sketch as a dead-color painting ready to be worked up.

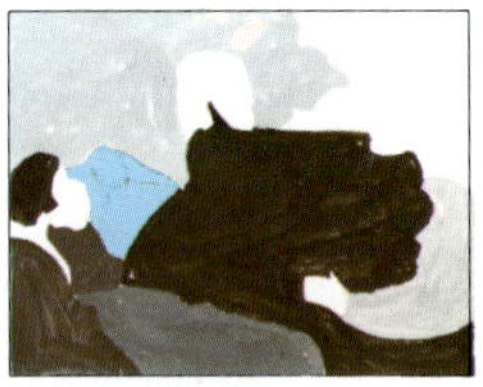

**4.** With the dead-color painting as his guide, Rembrandt then applied the body colors working from background to foreground, leaving the figures at the front monochrome silhouettes until their turn came.

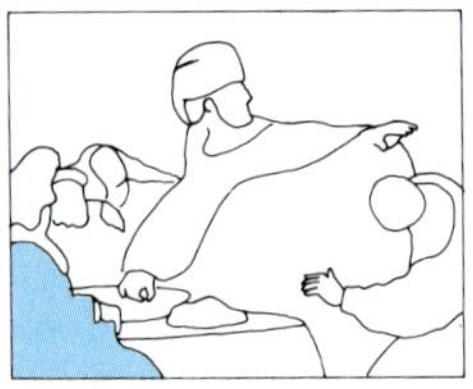

**5.** Rembrandt relied on body color. Where glazes are applied, they build up the rich blackness of the velvet worn by the figure on the extreme left and soften the contour of Belshazzar's body so that it recedes into the darkness under his outstretched left arm.

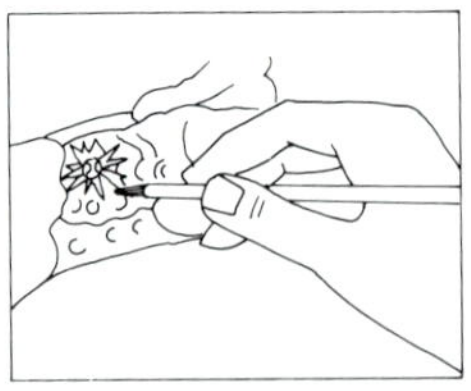

**6.** With the ground work completed, Rembrandt would set about applying the finishing touches to the painting as a whole. Working in stiff impasto, he dabbed in highlights so the twinkle of jewelry and shiny metal drew the composition together.

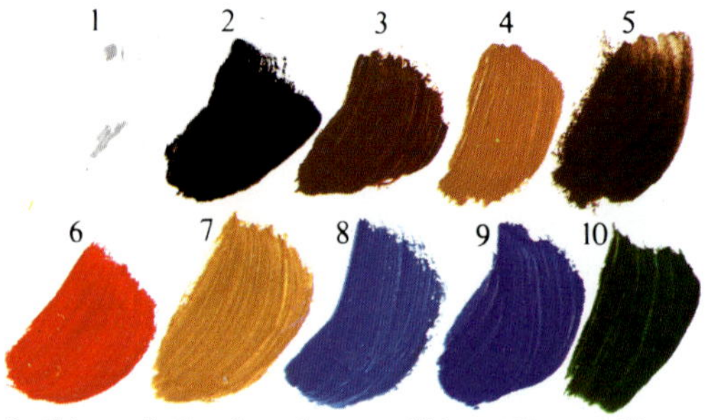


In this work, Rembrandt used the following colors: lead white (sometimes mixed with 25% chalk) (**1**), black (**2**), brown (**3**), red ochre (**4**), unidentifiable transparent browns, probably Cologne earth and bistre (**5**), vermilion and organic red lakes (**6**), lead tin yellow (**7**) usually mixed with lead white azurite (**8**) and smalt (**9**). Greens (**10**) were made by mixing lead-tin yellow with azurite or smalt.

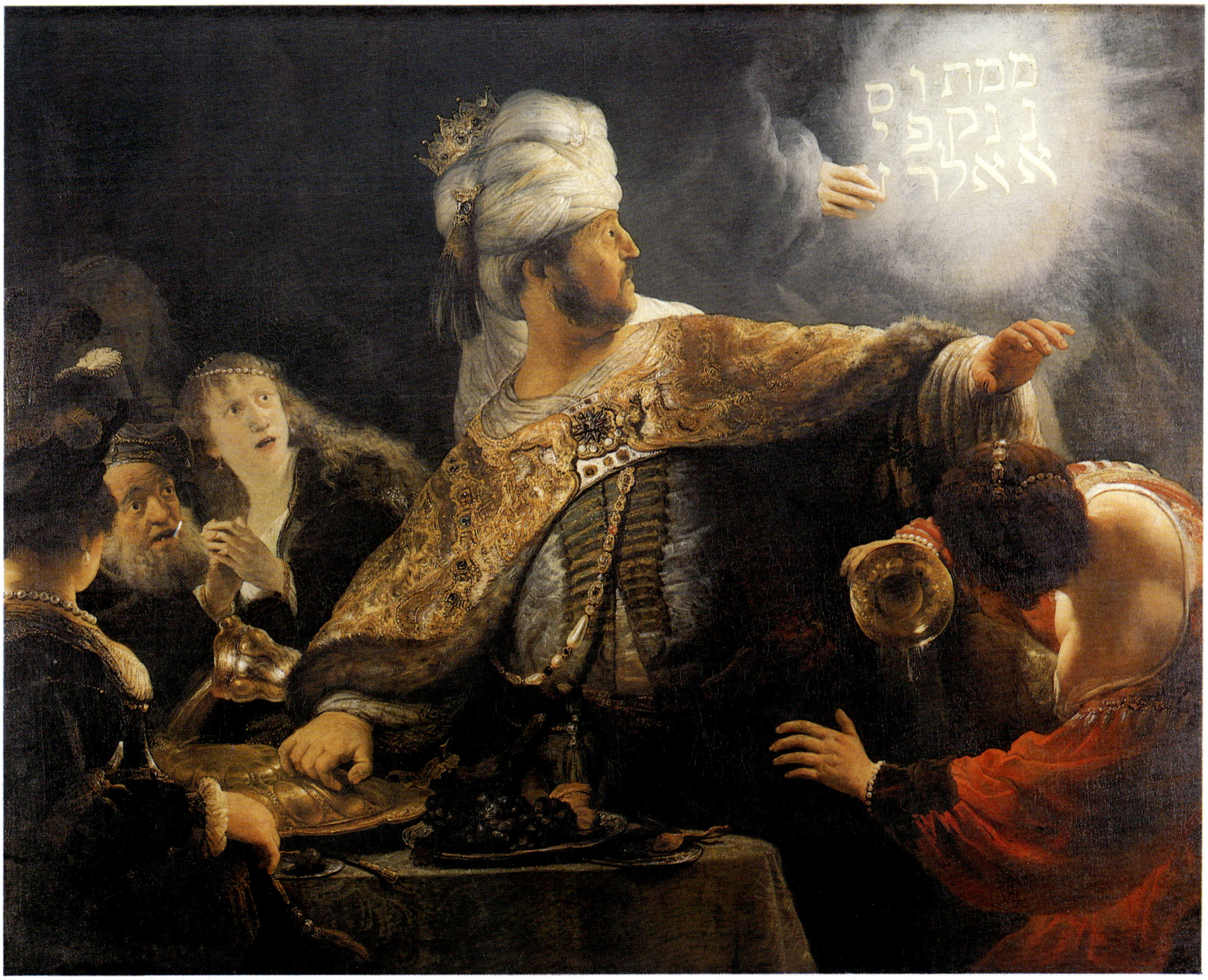

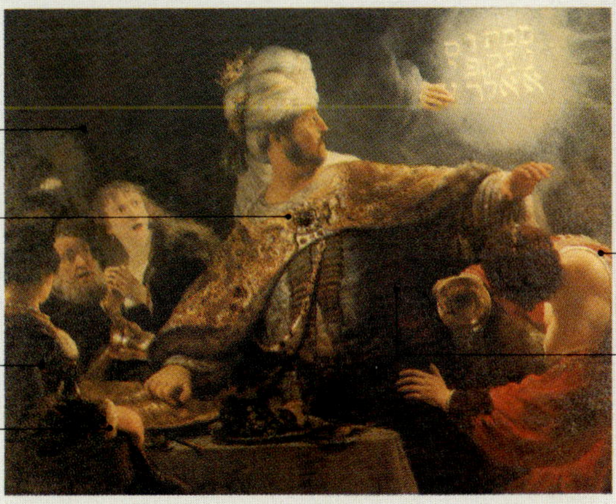


*This is the most overtly theatrical of Rembrandt's biblical scenes. Not one, but two goblets of wine are spilling their contents and the great jewelled clasp on Belshazzar's cloak is the artist's most extravagant attempt at recreating jewelry in thick, wet impasto. The picture's predominantly green-gray coloration is dictated by the underpainting, the most crucial component of a Rembrandt painting. It takes the place of a preliminary sketch and also plays an important role in the appearance of the finished painting, providing the bulk of his intermediate tones. Underpainting provides the basic color for Belshazzar's tunic, the tablecloth, the clouds of smoke in the background and the shadowy figure of the musician.*

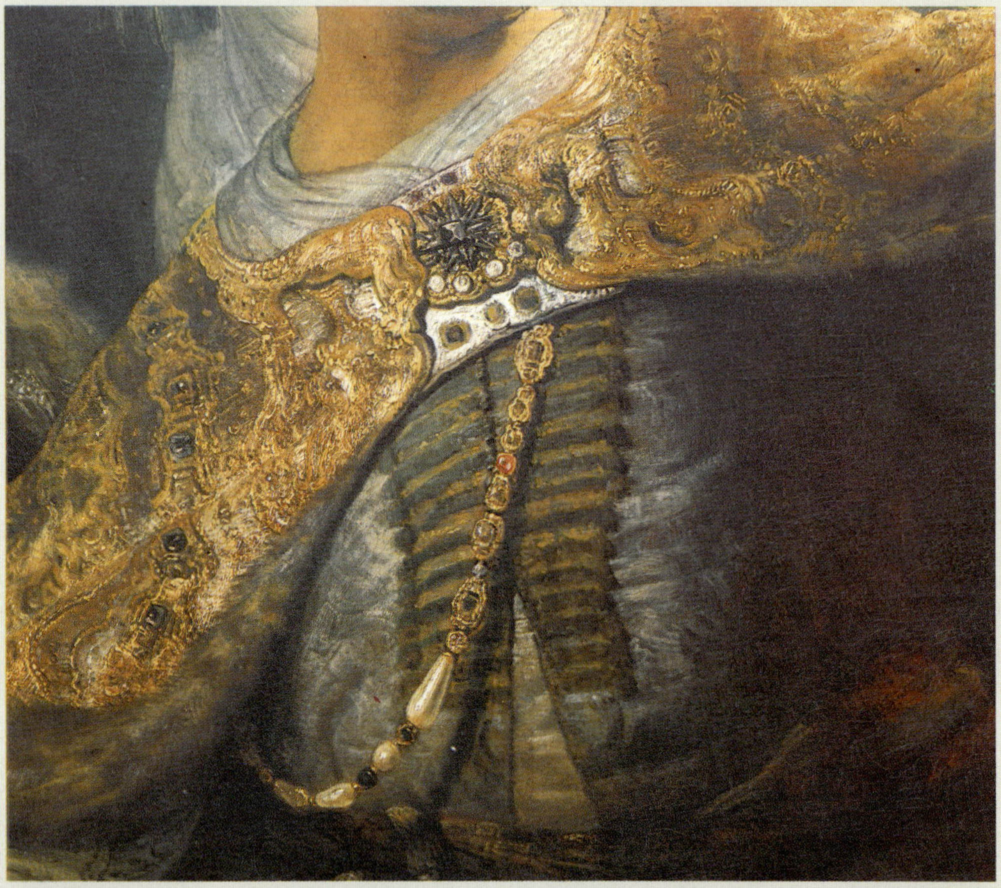

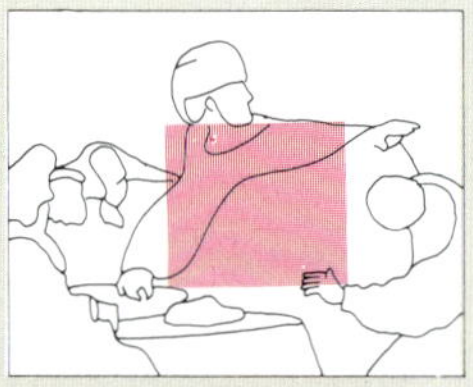

*The richly decorated cloak and the jewelled clasp show Rembrandt at his most vigorous in his painting of accessories. Working with two basic brushes — one thick, blunt and rounded, and the other fine, and pointed — he first molds the jewelry with the blunt brush into ridges, which reflect actual light, and shadowy troughs, sometimes using the handle of the brush to scrape textures into the paint surface. With the thin brush he then deposited wet yellow and white paint along the ridges so that real and painted light combine in the highlight. From very close up the clasp is a mass of illegible marks which only begin to take shape from a distance. Rembrandt worked in layers, overlapping his paint surfaces, so that Belshazzar's clothes would actually have been painted in the order in which he put them on. The gray tunic consists mostly of underpainting on which the artist has scumbled a design in very dry white paint, which has caught in the ridges of the underpainting. The brocade at the front of the tunic is loosely painted in much wetter impasto and mostly single brushstrokes; the alternating light and dark stripes are allowed to blur together. The thickest impasto of all is saved for the sumptuous cloak and the exquisite gold chain which shows Rembrandt again dealing almost exclusively in yellow and white highlights. The left side of Belshazzar's body would originally have been a deep red but the artist has applied brown glazes to push it gently back into the shadows without completely smothering its color.*

*Recent restorations have shown that Rembrandt was not as compulsive a glazer as has been suggested in the past. These flesh tones have been achieved with accurately mixed body paint (usually lead white, ochre, a small amount of black, a transparent brown pigment and vermilion) rather than thin glazes. The translucence is heightened by the yellow-white highlights under the woman's neck and along her bosom. The shadow at the back of her neck does blend into an area of glazed flesh color but the modelling underneath is inexact and results in an unusually formless back. The white edging of her dress consists of single brushstrokes allowed to break up at their ends: and the drapery on her arm prefigures Rembrandt's late work in the breadth of its execution. The single red brushstroke which joins the top of her elbow to her left shoulder has been enlivened — a slash of yellow has been worked into its edge so that a glowing orange is achieved not by mixing the pigments on the canvas but by allowing them to mix in the spectator's eye.*

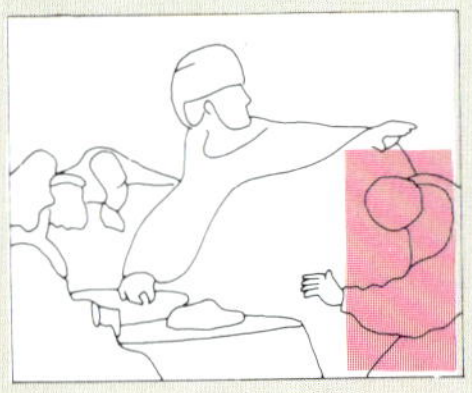

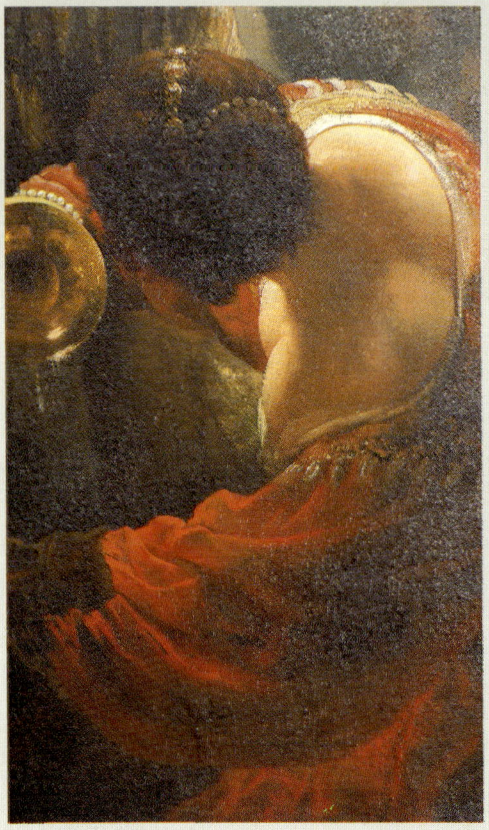

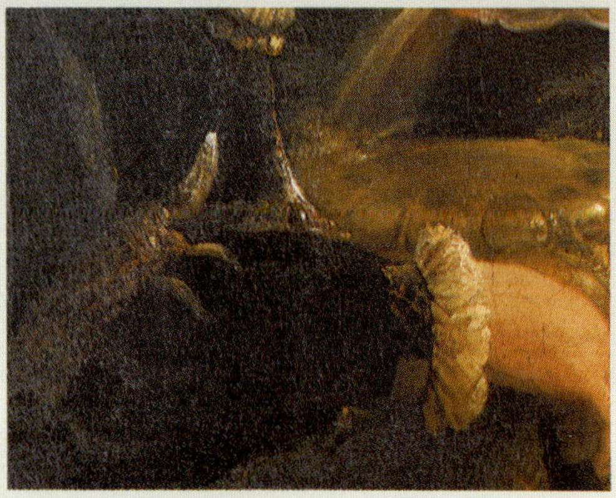

*Rembrandt and Frans Hals were the first great masters of directional brushstrokes. The strokes which make up the cuff consist of alternating dark and light strokes, turned up abruptly at the ends to suggest the pleats and rounded off along the ruffled edge of the cuff with white highlights. A similar technique is less successfully used in the rather shapeless white bodice. The dress is made up of smooth, glazed black recreating the rich textures of velvet and receding deeply into the shadow under the woman's arm.*

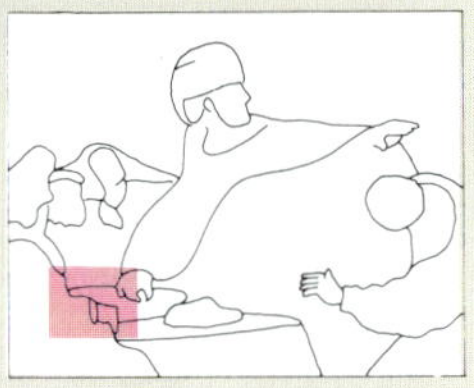

*The lace trimmings again consist almost entirely of highlights which stay firmly on the surface of the dress to suggest the texture of filigree decoration.*

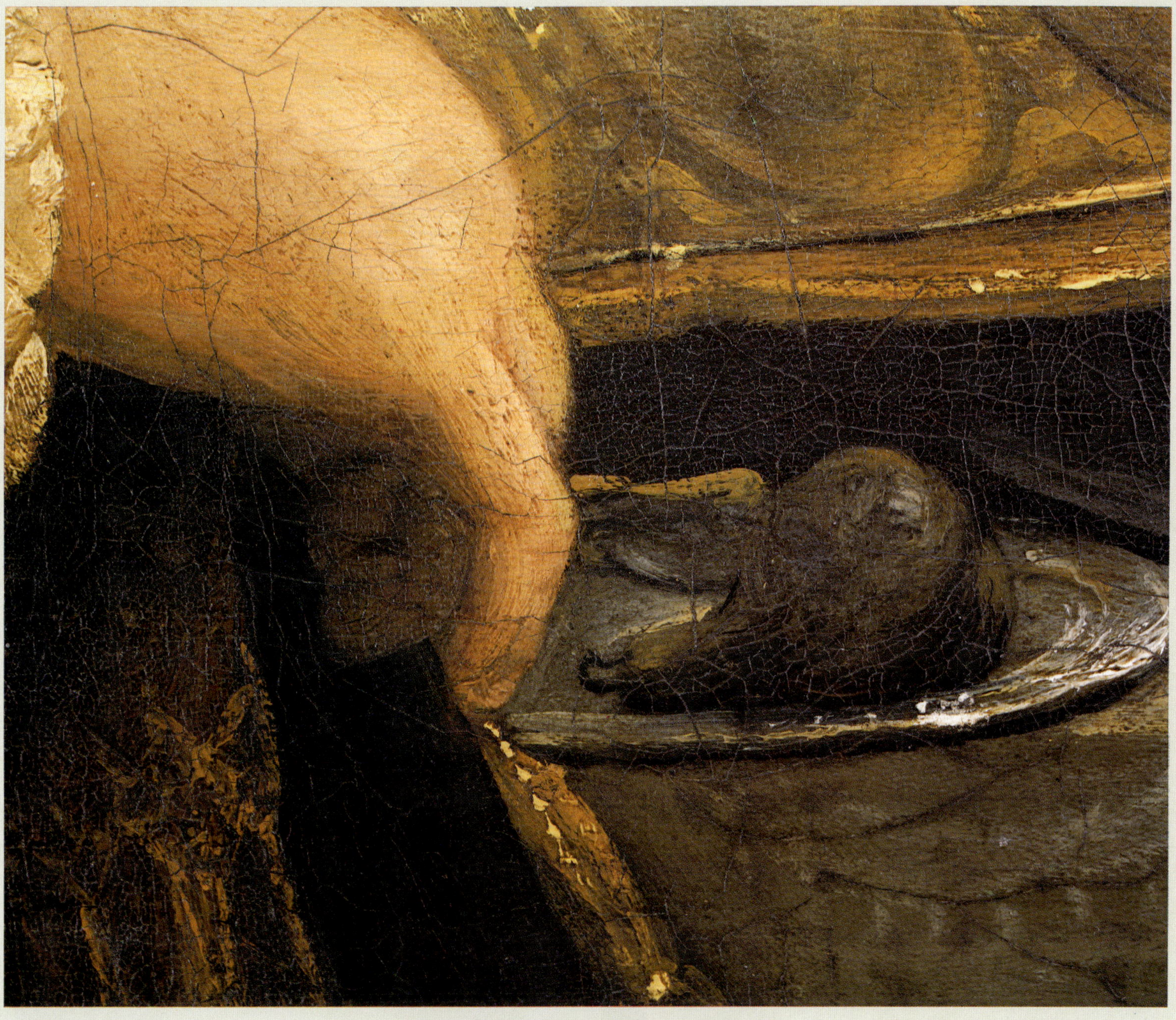

*All the figures in the painting would at one time have looked like the shadowy silhouette of the musician in the background. Rembrandt's underpainting was remarkably exact and he needed only to highlight a string of pearls in the hair to bring this figure to life. Its coloring ensures that it remains firmly in the background in complete contrast to the feathers belonging to the figure on the left, which emerge from the foreground. Rembrandt often used ceruse (white lead mixed with chalk) in both his underpainting and in some highlights.*

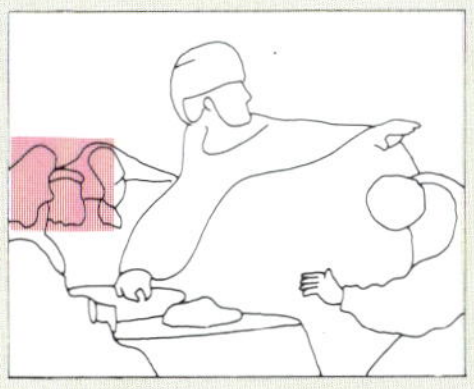

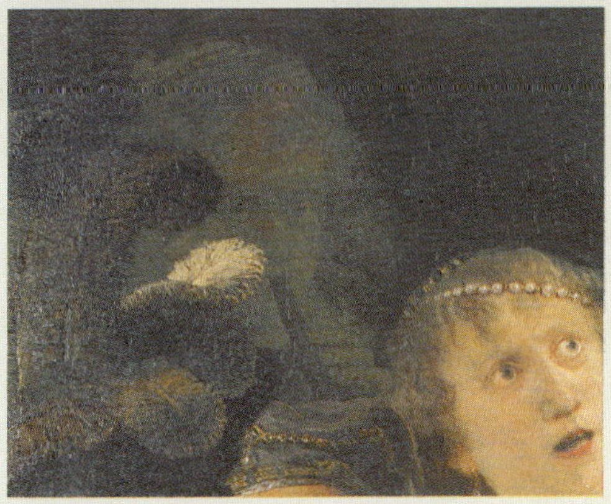

Actual size detail

*Rembrandt was the most economic of painters. The plate is no more than a white highlight, the wet paint swept along its edge catches in the grooves of the underpainting to give the plate its shape. A single, fluid black brushstroke under the rim lifts it up off the top of the tablecloth. The pear is basically a silhouette which interrupts the sparse outline of the plate. The shadow at the front edge of the tablecloth has been effortlessly achieved by going over the underpainting, on which a pattern has already been suggested in white with a darker glaze.*

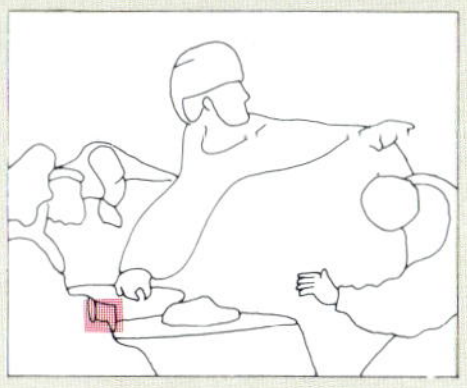

# JAN VERMEER

*The Guitar Player* (1660s)
Oil on canvas, 53cm × 46.3cm/20⅞in × 18¼in

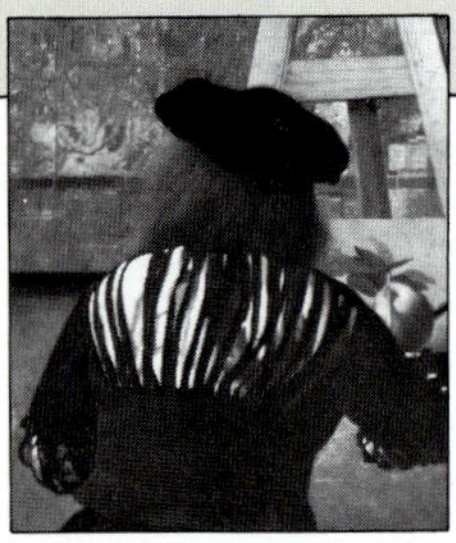

The celebrated scenes of everyday life by Vermeer mark the high point of seventeenth century Dutch genre painting. Vermeer was an art dealer and occasional committee member of the Delft painters' guild and, despite the enigmatic reputation he and his paintings have acquired, may be seen as part of a flourishing artistic generation. Together with such contemporary genre painters as Gerard Ter Borch, Gabriel Metsu and Pieter de Hoogh, Vermeer was working in a tradition influenced by Caravaggio through the Utrecht school and the painters of Rembrandt's circle.

Although early documentary sources have no recorded details of Vermeer's working methods, modern scientific investigation has revealed much about the 30 or so paintings reliably attributed to him. Before painting *The Guitar Player*, Vermeer sized the canvas and then applied several coats of a gray-brown ground consisting of chalk mixed with lead white, umber, and charcoal black pigments suspended in an oil and glue emulsion. There are no known preliminary drawings by Vermeer and infra-red photography does not reveal any black underdrawing on the ground layer beneath the paint surface. There is, however, convincing stylistic and circumstantial evidence that Vermeer frequently made use of a *camera obscura* – an instrument made up of lenses and mirrors in a box or chamber. A reduced image of the subject is reflected or traced from the mirrors onto the painting surface which the artist used as a 'drawing' to work from. Vermeer may have either laid preliminary colors directly on the projected image or traced the outline in white lead paint.

Vermeer painted light as it fell on the subject using a variety of techniques ranging from thin layers of glazes or flat underpainting to thick opaque *alla prima* paint. Visible brushwork and texture are minimal except for the impasto and some areas of drapery, and the stippled dots of light-colored paint were a characteristic light-reflecting device.

Smalt, a deep blue pigment made from powdered cobalt glass, or azurite were commonly used by painters of this period, but Vermeer made extensive use of the costly pigment ultramarine which is extracted from the semi-precious stone lapis lazuli. Vermeer's signature can be seen below the curtain.

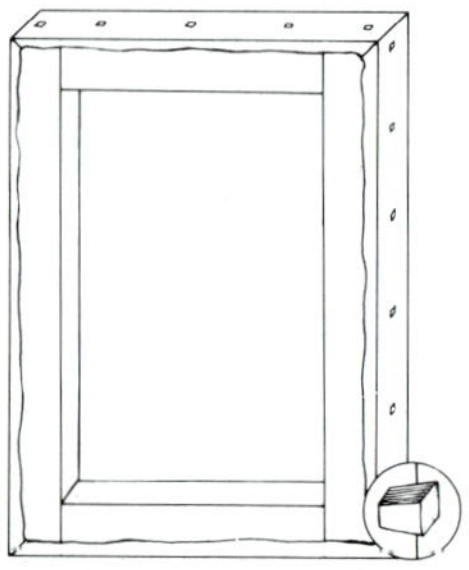

**1.** The canvas was first fixed onto the stretcher with small, square-headed wooden pegs at about 3–4 in intervals.

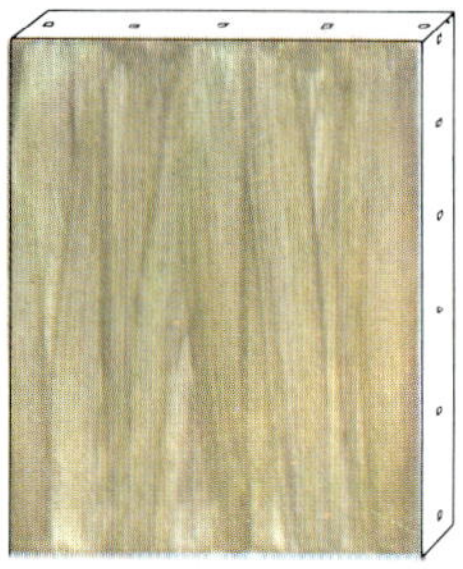

**2.** The canvas was then sized. Several coats of gray-brown ground consisting of chalk mixed with lead white, umber and charcoal in an oil and glue emulsion were then applied.

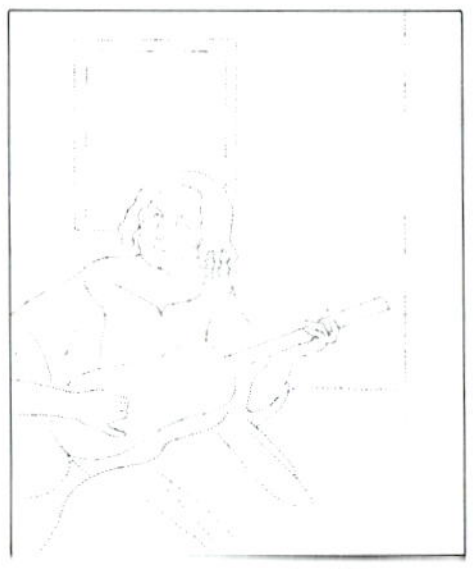

**3.** Vermeer probably used the *camera obscura* at this stage and worked from the image reflected onto the surface.

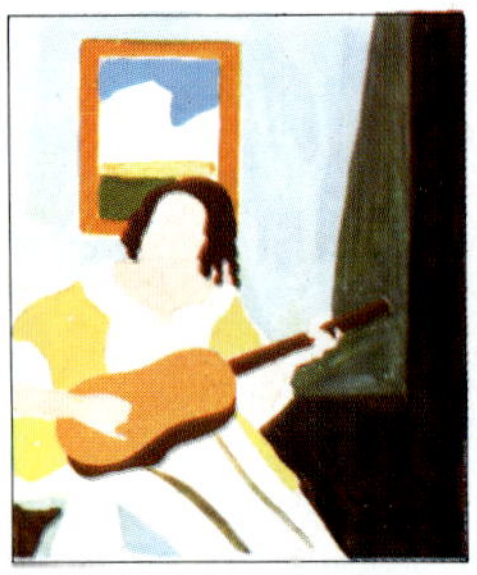

**4.** Rather than doing a detailed underdrawing, Vermeer may have laid down broad areas of flat color.

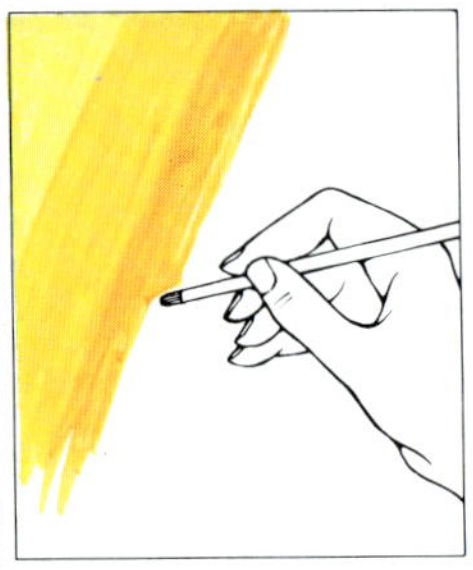

**5.** Modelling was achieved with the *alla prima* method or by building up layers of thin glazes; usually both were used together.

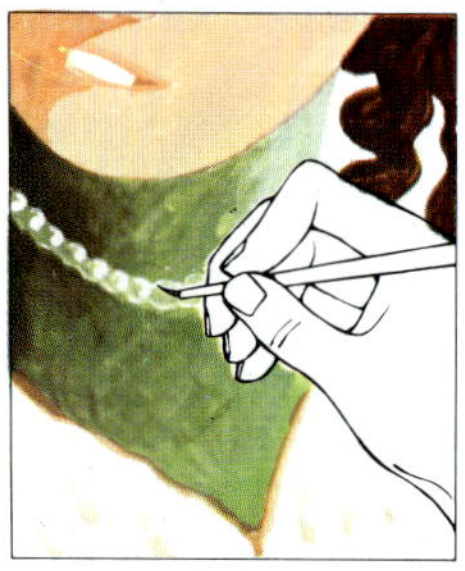

**6.** Small points of highlight were then put in with lead white or lead tin yellow.

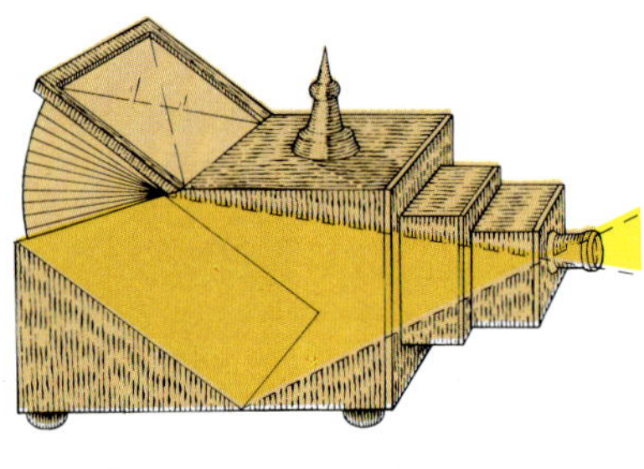

*The* camera obscura *was a sixteenth century invention which consisted of a darkened box or chamber containing an arrangement of lenses and mirrors. These would project a reduced image, similar to that of a modern reflex camera, onto a flat surface from which an artist could trace a precise and detailed drawing. Depending on the type of instrument used, this drawing in turn may have been transferred onto the surface which was to be painted.*

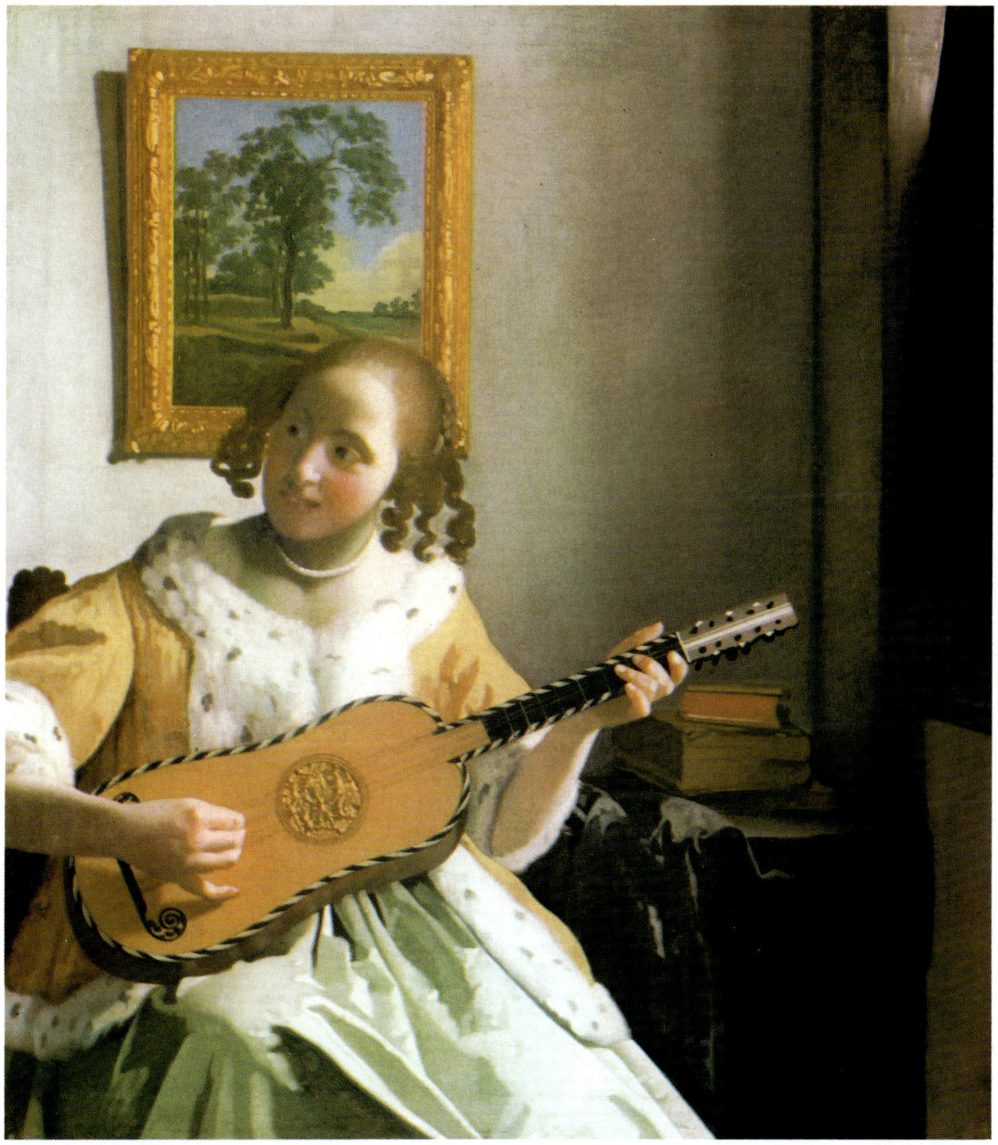

*The Guitar Player is a late work by Vermeer and this relaxed everyday scene in a domestic setting is typical of his subject matter. The subdued colors increase the optical realism which results from Vermeer's technique of painting form and detail as they appear rather than as they are known to be — the arms and hands, for instance, are not painted with anatomical precision but in terms of light and shadow. The painting is in excellent condition with minimal restoration and is one of the few seventeenth century paintings which has not been lined. The hand-spun and hand-woven canvas has never been removed from its stretcher, to which it still remains attached by the original small, square-headed wooden pegs.*

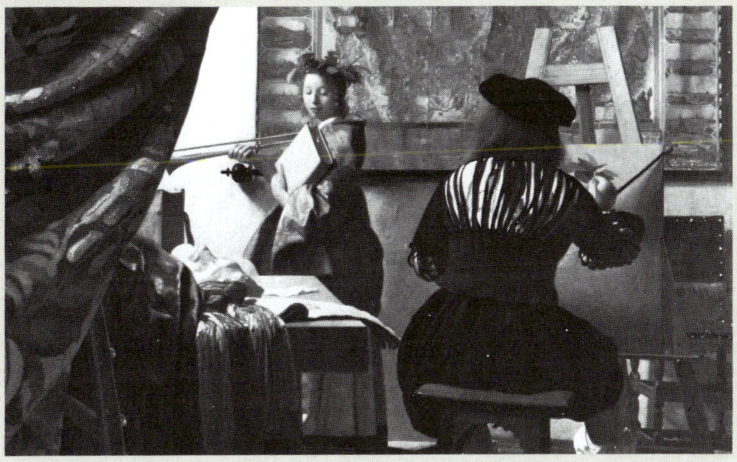

*This detail from The Artist's Studio by Vermeer shows an artist sitting at his easel painting the portrait of a girl. His hand rests on a mahl stick. On the easel is a stretched canvas with a light gray ground showing an outline sketch in white. Only the wreath on the model's head has actually been painted, and there is no sign of any preliminary drawing.*

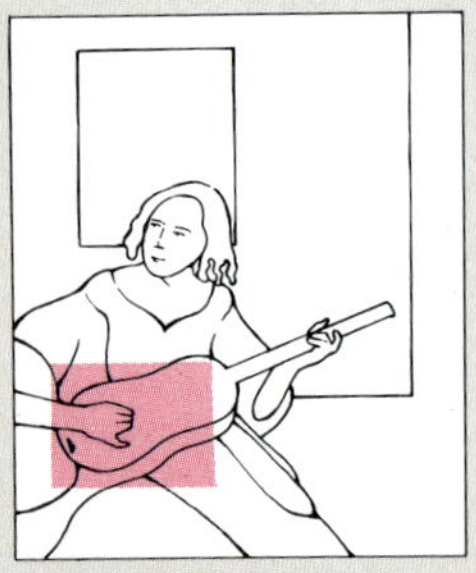

*Gray underpainting forms the basis of the skirt, over which broad, flat areas of white paint and dark gray-green glazes create the modeled effect of folds in the fabric. There is minimal texture or brushwork and interest lies in Vermeer's handling of tone to describe areas of light and shadow. The position of the guitar along the lower contour was altered, and the changed line can be seen.*

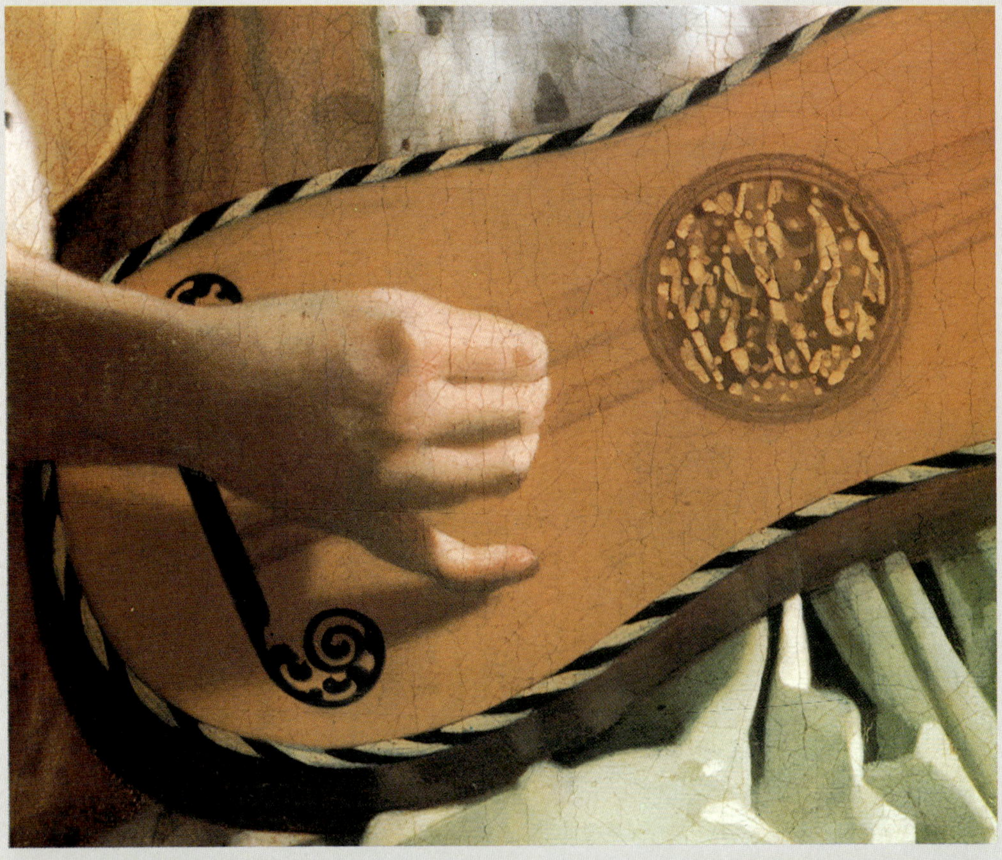

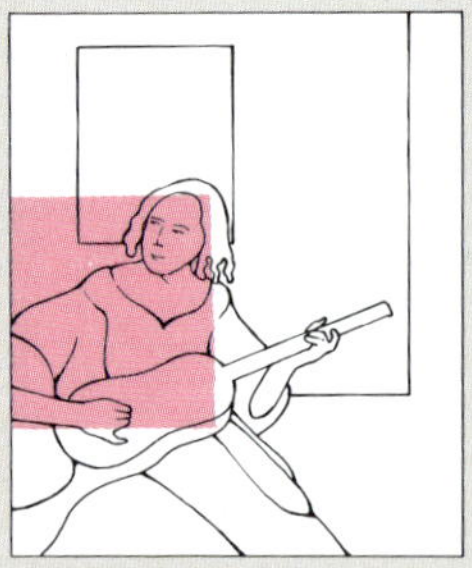

Actual size detail
*This detail is a fine example of the striking variations in Vermeer's paint texture and brushwork.*
*Thin dark glazes barely cover the gray-green underpainting of the shadowed right side of the face and throat. This contrasts vividly with the white lead dots of paint on the pearls and the impasto of the gilded frame and guitar 'rose'. The textured paint of the impasto creates an abstract light-reflecting pattern rather than a meticulous record of the objects. X-ray photographs show an emphasis of white lead on the knuckles of the right hand, which is held above the blurred lines of the vibrating guitar strings.*

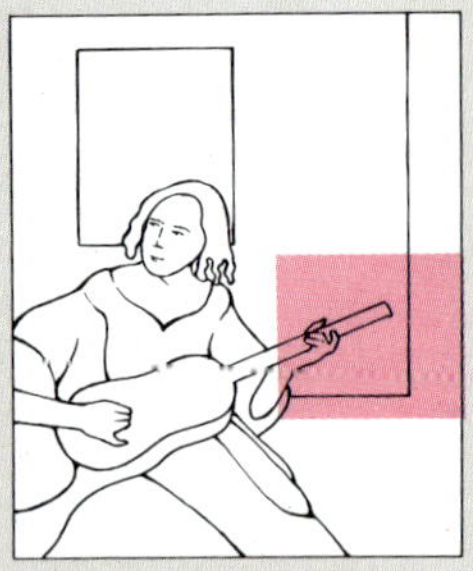

*The fingers of the left hand are painted with three or four flat, broken dabs of flesh-colored paint emphasizing the intensity of light falling on the model. The pegs on the guitar head are an abstract pattern of brilliant white, gray and black which stand out vividly against the featureless architecture of the wall and window. Ultramarine was used for painting both the curtain and the draped cloth.*

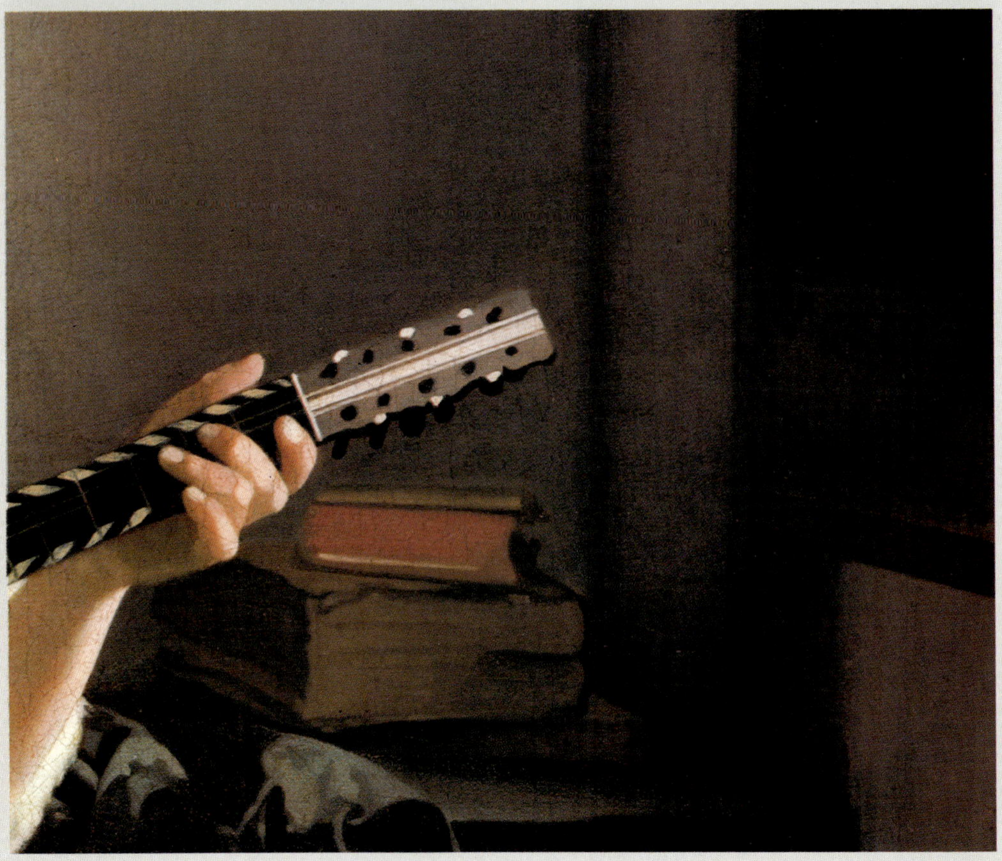

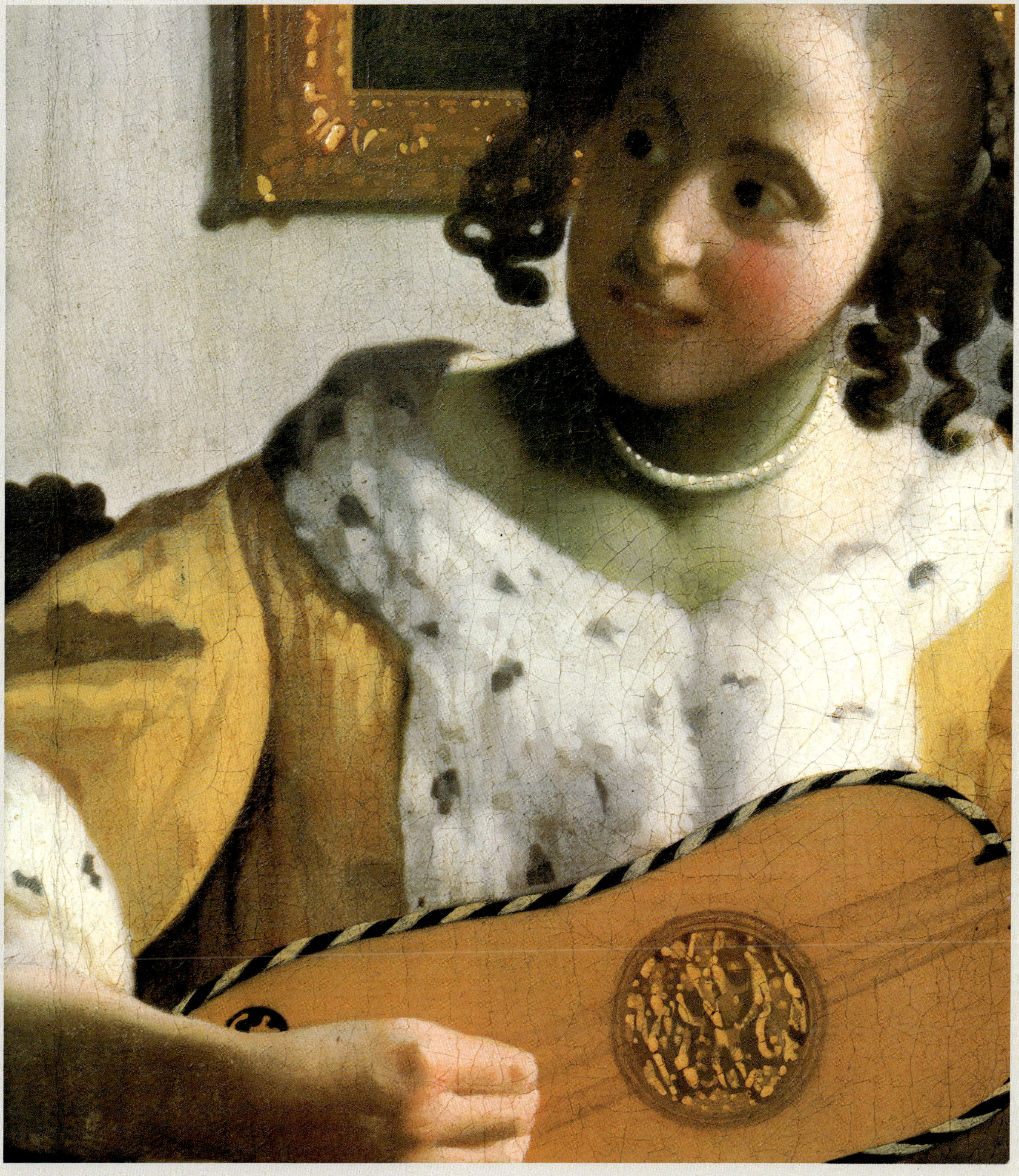

# ANTOINE WATTEAU

*Fêtes Vénitiennes* (c. 1718-19)
Oil on canvas, 55.9cm × 45.7cm/22in × 18in

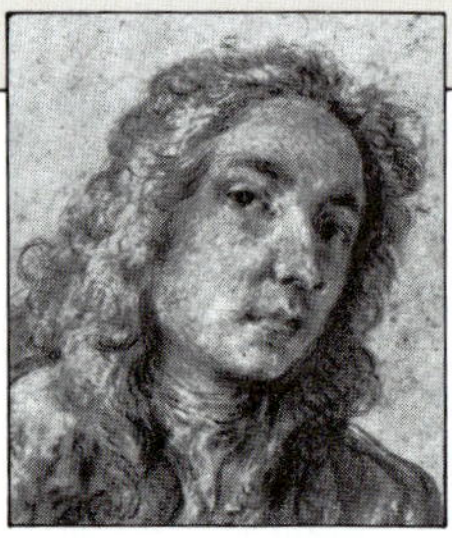

In Watteau's work there is a reconciliation of the opposing Flemish and Venetian influences which divided the artistic world of eighteenth century France. Watteau's paintings also capture the elegant, capricious and superficially charming qualities of Rococo, a fashion which suited the early skills Watteau acquired as a painter of decorative interiors. Themes from the *commedia dell'arte* were a frequent source of inspiration to him.

Watteau was remembered by his contemporaries as a fast, messy and impulsive painter. His palette was rarely cleaned, his brushes were dirty and, as he painted, they dripped with oil from a pot full of debris, dust and paint particles. Speed was of the essence and much comment was made on Watteau's excessive use of oil which has left some of his paintings in poor condition. Watteau's contemporaries claimed to notice tonal discoloration and deterioration in the paint only a short time after Watteau had completed it.

Watteau frequently made corrections and adjustments to his paintings which he often only thinly disguised. In the case of *Fêtes Vénitiennes*, most of these changes can be seen as easily with the naked eye as with infra-red photography or X-ray. Although Watteau was a prolific draftsman, there is almost a total absence of preliminary drawings or outline plans for his works. However, Watteau kept hundreds of figure studies and landscape sketches in bound volumes. The models were often dressed in fancy or theatrical costumes and these supplied Watteau with motifs from which he developed many of his paintings. He arranged the figures in groups which were usually dictated by a landscape background. Sometimes such figure studies were used for more than one painting, and it is known that a few were portraits of friends. In *Fêtes Vénitiennes* the male dancer is known to be a portrait of a painter and friend, Nicholas Vleugels, and it is thought that the melancholy figure of the bag-piper may be a self-portrait.

Despite the relatively poor condition of many of Watteau's paintings, *Fêtes Vénitiennes* is in exceptionally good condition and has only been minimally restored. In this instance, the artist's use of the excessively oily medium can be seen as a characteristic of Watteau's technique rather than a problem.

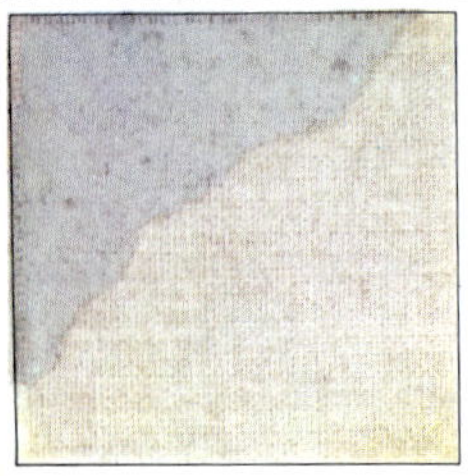

**1.** After the canvas was sized, a warm gray ground was applied.

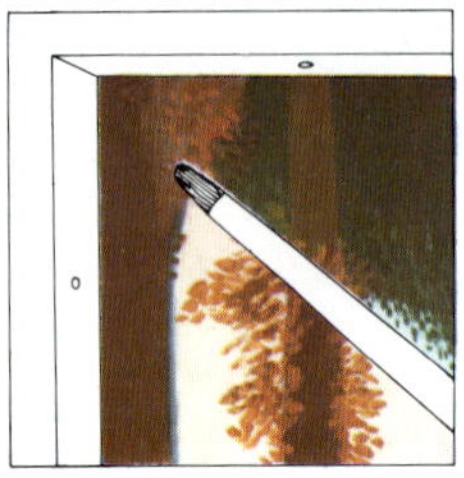

**2.** If there was no preliminary drawing, Watteau would apply paint directly to the canvas. Watteau worked quickly

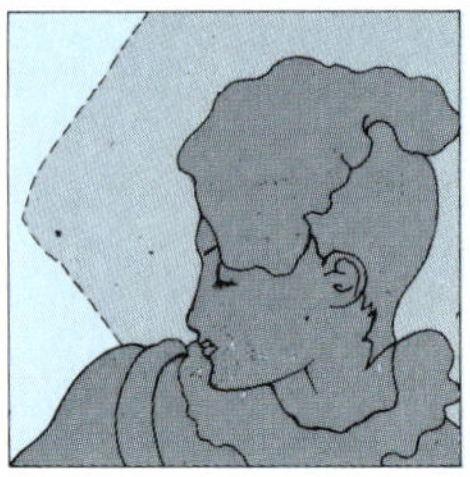

**3.** Alterations and changes were made and painted over during the painting process.

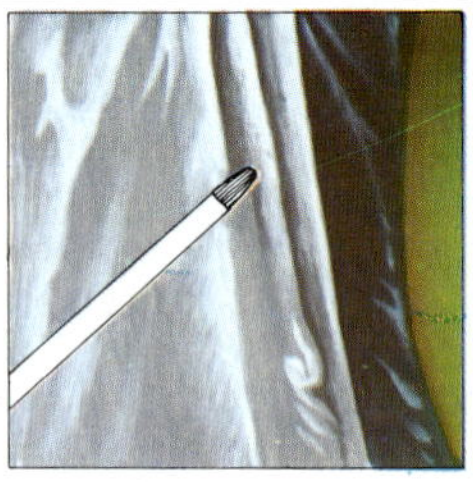

**4.** Final glazes and shadows were painted with the same speed as the rest of the painting.

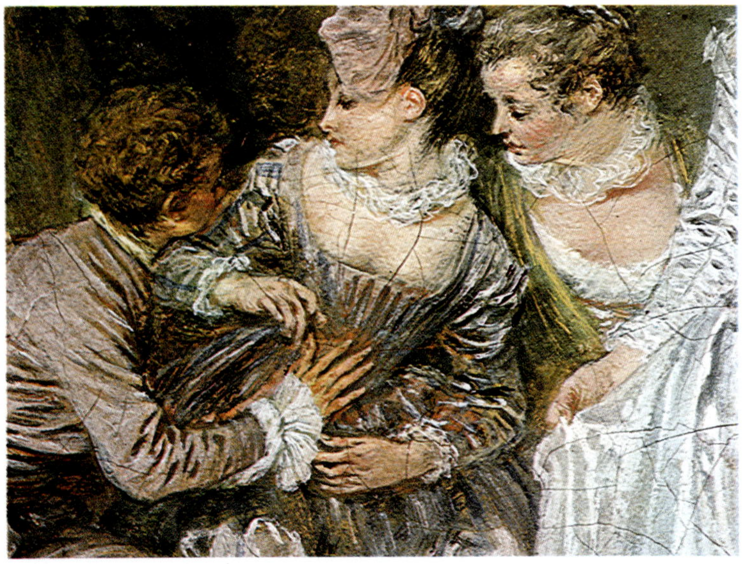

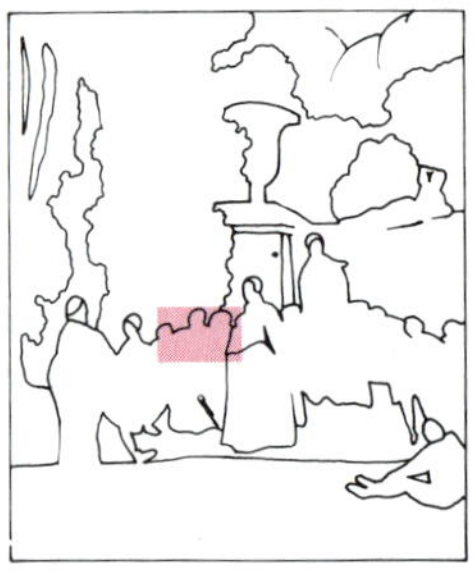

Actual size detail
*The brushwork is quick and free, the paint perceptibly modelled and Watteau has interspersed the pigments to produce streaky effects. The glazed blue stripes are a quick finishing touch. The outlines are emphasized by dark, shadow-like glazes.*

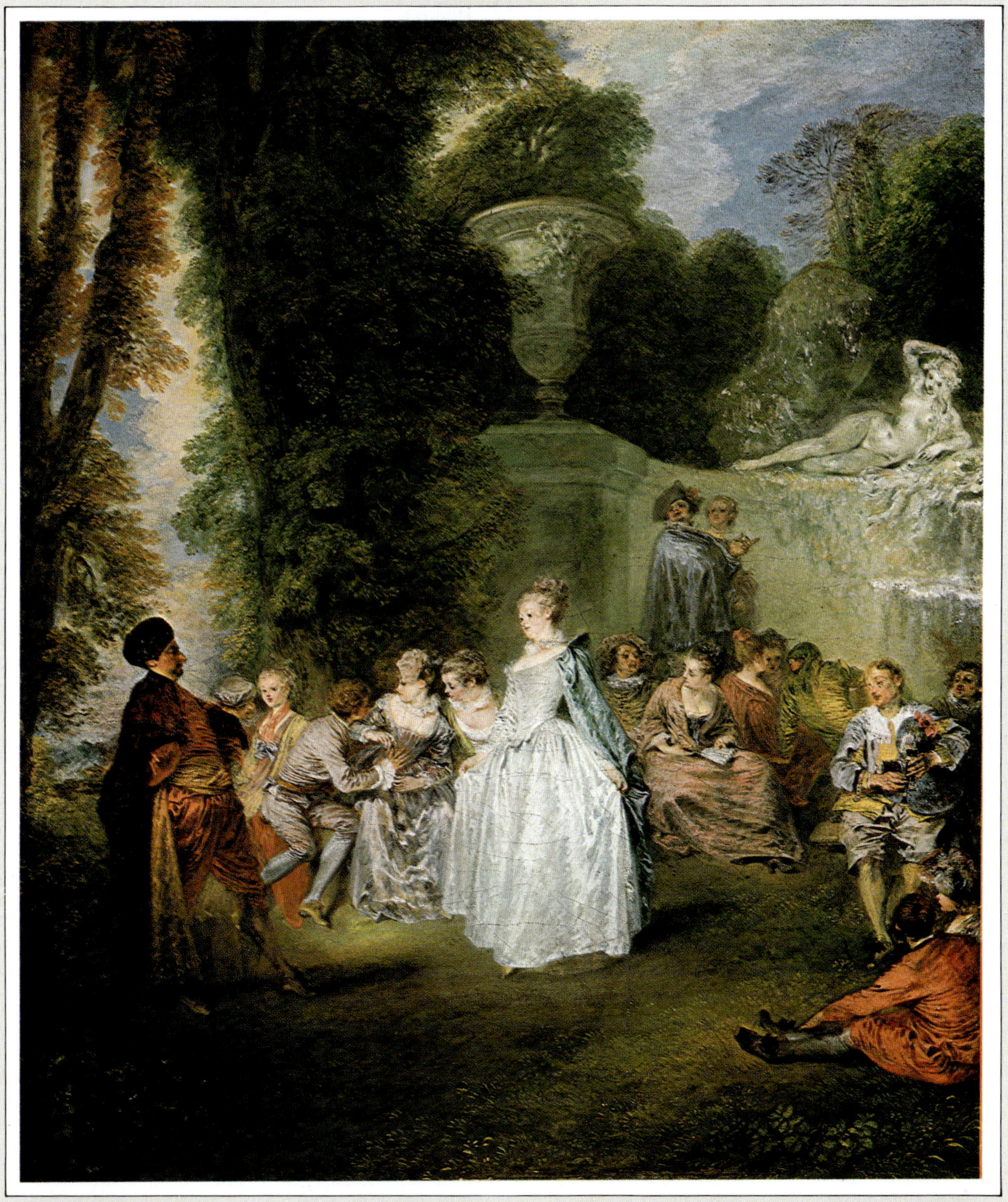

Fêtes Vénitiennes *is a typical later work. The idealized garden shows beautifully costumed people dancing and making music. The painting is on a plain-weave linen canvas which, when sized, was prepared with a gray ground containing white lead. Watteau made little use of the ground color or the canvas texture but applied his paint* alla prima. *Its texture is most pronounced in the clouds, drapery and flesh-painting, and the brushwork is free and varied. The figures were painted more precisely and the portrait of Vleughels, the dancer, contrasts with the sketchy execution of the sculpted naiad. The tall trees were thickly painted, and the dark colors built up in semi-transparent layers with more restrained brushwork. Watteau's excessive use of oil as the paint medium has caused the fine wrinkling in the paint layer and the pronounced pattern of cracks in the dark green foliage.*

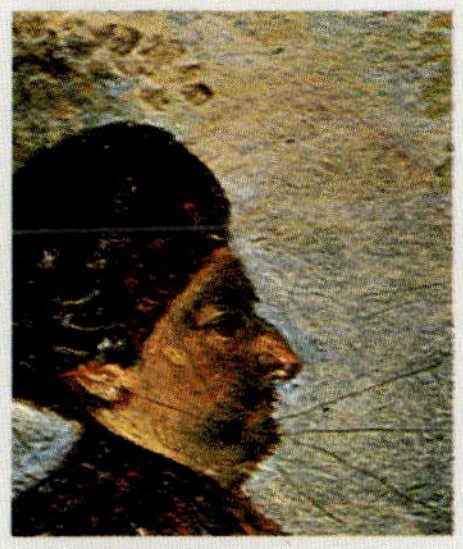

*The profile of this figure, the artist's friend Vleughels, was altered.*

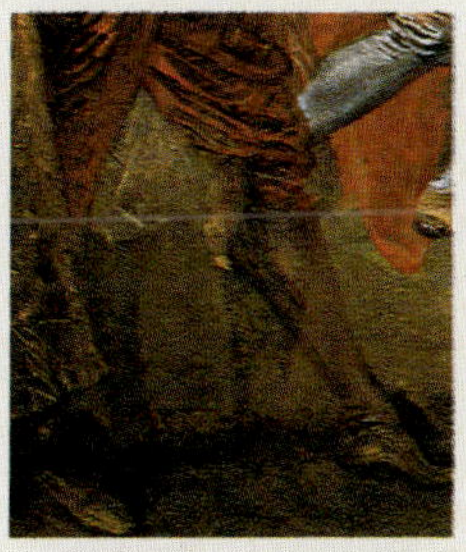

*The legs of the figure were repositioned.*

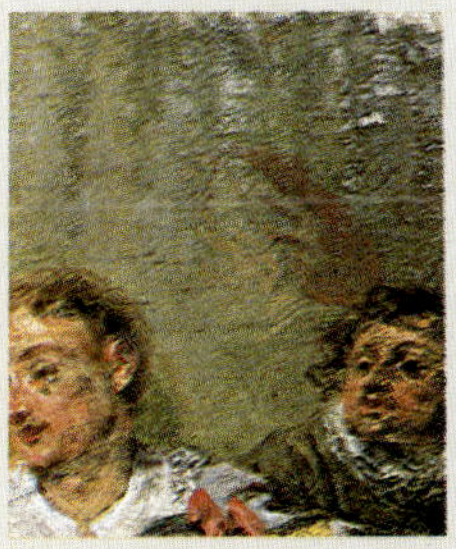

*The profile on the wall was thinly covered.*

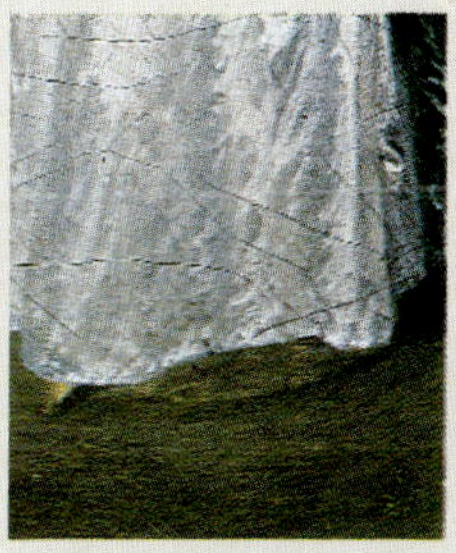

*The position of the woman's dress was altered at the hem.*

*Watteau often made changes to his paintings and in* Fêtes Vénetiennes *many of these can be seen with the naked eye.*

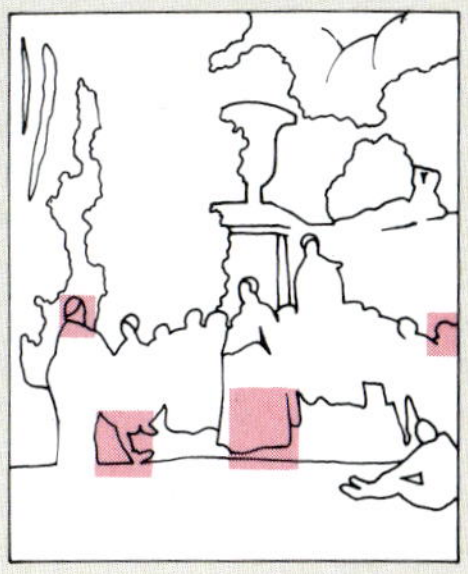

# JOSHUA REYNOLDS

*Mrs Hartley as a Nymph with Young Bacchus* (1772)
Oil on canvas, 89cm × 68.5cm/35in × 27in

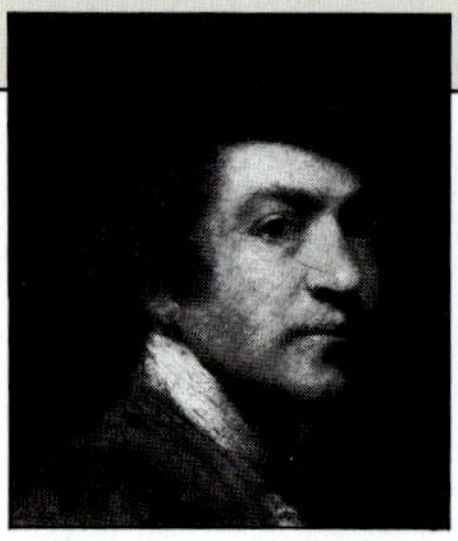

The two main periods of Reynolds's life which influenced his painting technique were his apprenticeship with the portrait painter Thomas Hudson from 1740 to 1743 and his trip to Italy from 1749 to 1752. The latter profoundly affected the artist and, for most of his career, Reynolds used poses borrowed from Classical sculpture, Michelangelo, Correggio and Van Dyck, amongst others.

Unfortunately, Reynolds was neither a careful nor systematic painter and because of his consuming passion for experimentation with various pigments and media, few of his later works have survived in anything like their original condition. Within his lifetime, several pictures were returned to his studio for repair and many have clearly suffered from later unsuccessful attempts at restoration.

Reynolds's broad aim was to duplicate the effects of the Old Masters in the shortest possible time and, as conventional media were thought to dry too slowly in the damp British climate, he would add quantities of driers. From the notes he made in muddled Italian, we find that Reynolds, like Turner, was interested in the effects of wax as a medium. He would probably melt the wax and add spirits of turpentine to produce a paste which could be mixed with colors ground in oil. This relatively quick-setting paste would enable him to produce effects ranging from the boldest impasto to the thinnest glazes, depending on the quantity of diluent added. As well, he experimented with various media and varnishes, often recklessly superimposing several media, each with a different drying rate within the same picture.

Reynolds was no less rash in his choice of pigments and would mix incompatible colors like orpiment and white lead or make use of recently invented but untested colors and 'fugitive' lakes and carmines.

His brushes were nineteen inches long, and his palette an outmoded type with a handle. Information regarding his choice of colors is contradictory and he himself wrote that 'four [colors] are sufficient to make every combination required'. One source says he preferred carmine, ultramarine, Naples yellow and black. Another says that he chose white, Naples yellow, yellow ochre, vermilion, light red, lake, black and Prussian blue. In his notes, Reynolds called Prussian blue 'Turchino'.

**1.** For one of his standard portraits Reynolds would choose a light colored canvas with an off-white or pale gray priming. Without a preliminary drawing, he would apply a rough patch of white paint where the head was to be.

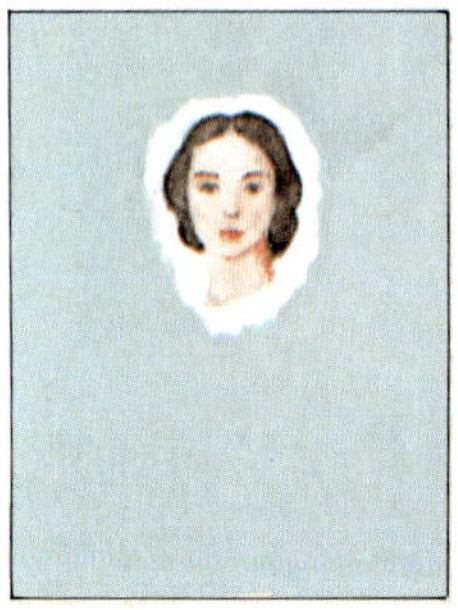

**2.** Using lake, black, and white, he would block in the main features, working wet-in-wet to produce a pallid likeness. An assistant said the face would resemble 'a beautiful cloud; everything was in its right place, but as soft as possible'.

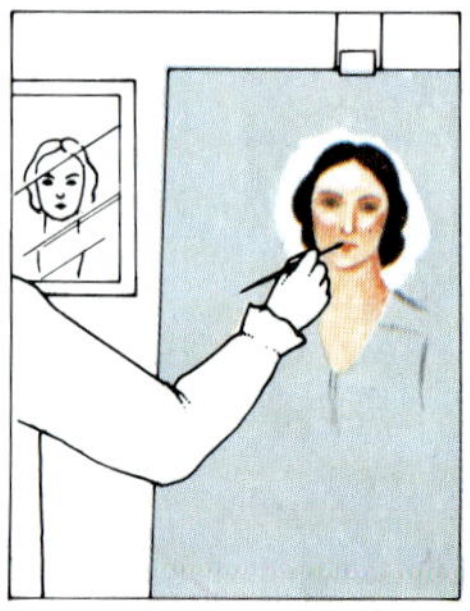

**3.** In subsequent sittings, Reynolds would create warm flesh tones sometimes using opaque colors, like Naples yellow, but more often using thin, fugitive glazes which would not obscure the underpainting. He would sometimes paint from his sitter's image reflected in a mirror.

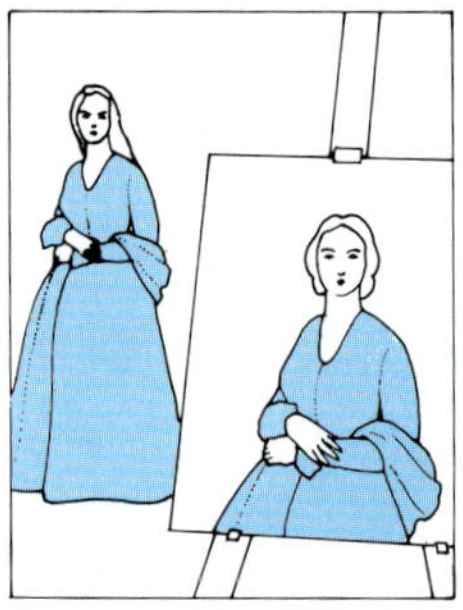

**4.** Once the head was finished, Reynolds would then pass the picture on to an assistant who would fill in the drapery from a life-size figure dressed in the sitter's clothes. Another assistant would often fill in the landscape, and Reynolds would probably add the final touches.

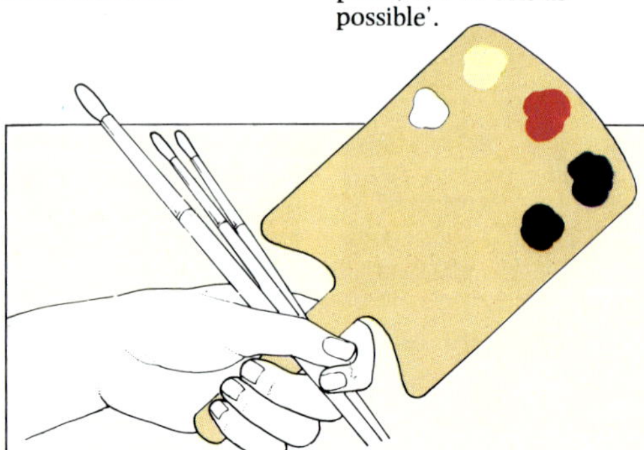

*Reynold's brushes were up to 19in (47cm) long so that he could work standing well away from the canvas. He used an outmoded type of palette with a handle. Although Reynolds himself wrote that 'four colors are sufficient to make every combination required', one of his biographers states that he used the following colors which he would place on his palette in this order: white, Naples yellow, yellow ochre, vermilion, light red, black and Prussian blue (which he called 'Turchino').*

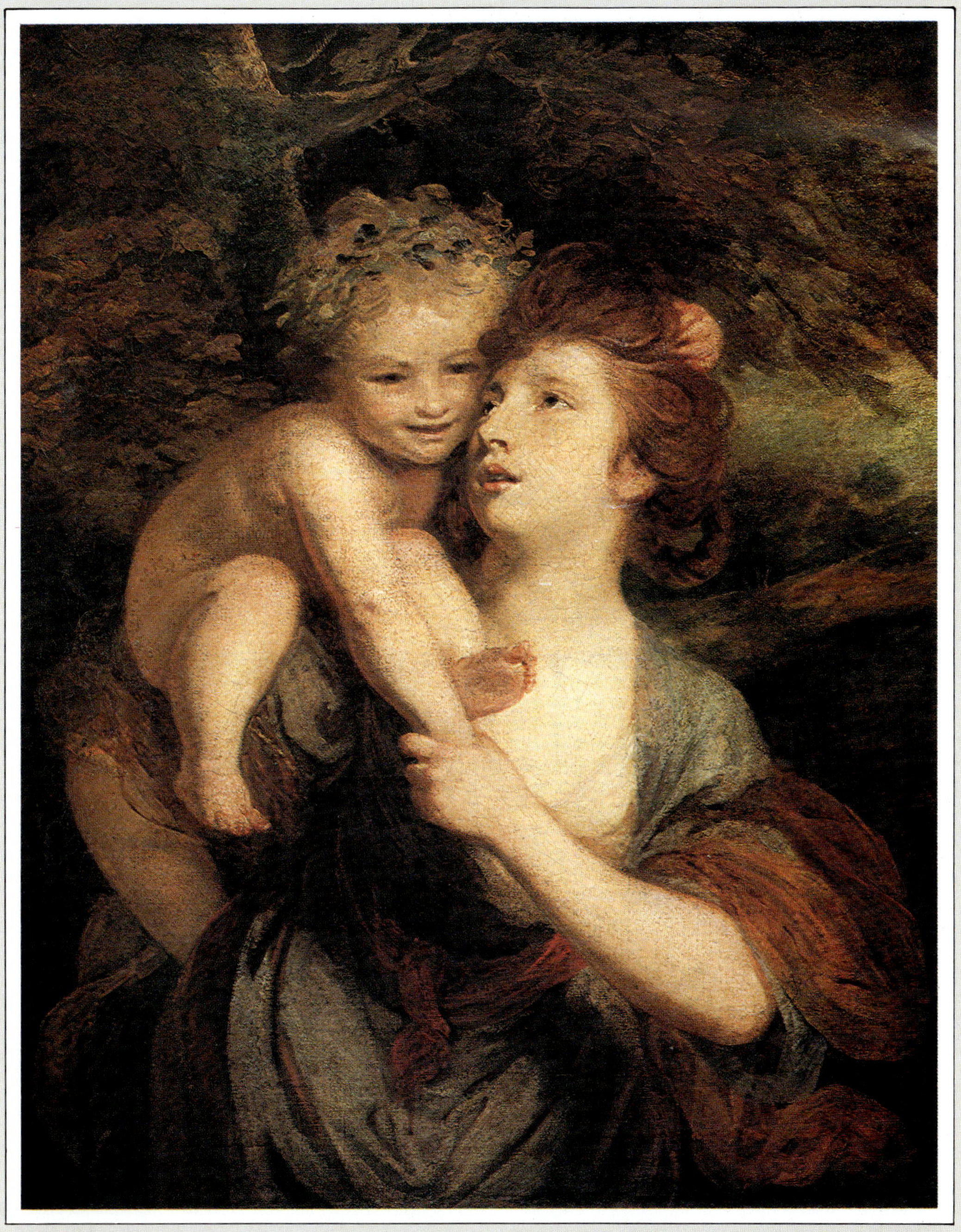

*The head in this picture suffers from serious craquelure perhaps due to Reynolds's use of 'white virgin wax' (bleached beeswax) which 'caused his colors to scale off from the canvas in flakes'. It seems that he melted the wax and then added colors ground in oil. He reportedly told one connoisseur 'Mix a little wax with your colors, and don't tell anybody.' A cross-section of the various layers of this picture indicate that Mrs Hartley's drapery was originally violet achieved by superimposing a lake glaze on top of blue, but apparently Reynolds changed his mind and applied a very thick layer of white to obliterate it. A thin layer of blue served as the shadow of a fold line, followed by a layer of orange-brown.*

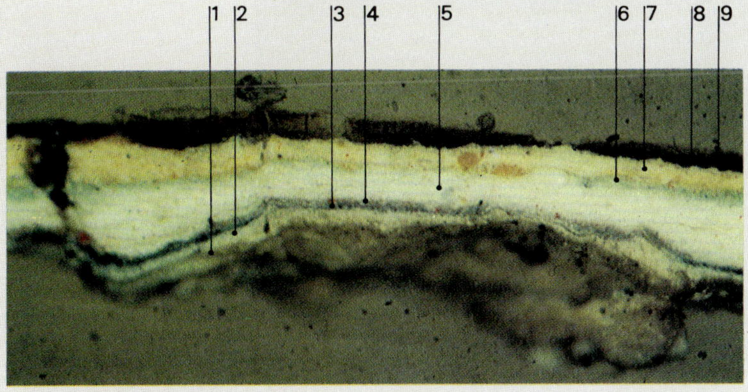


*Cross-sections of most of Reynolds's paintings reveal a complex layering of pigment and media. Shown here, working from the bottom-most layers up, are: traces of a layer of size (1); thin whitish ground, perhaps in two layers (2); Prussian blue with black particles (3); lake pigment (4); thick opaque white (5); pale blue painted wet-in-wet to the previous layer (6); yellow with some vermilion and large white lumps (7); discolored yellow-brown varnish (8); surface dirt and dust (9).*

*This complex layer structure indicates that Mrs Hartley's drapery was originally violet in hue, made by superimposing a lake glaze (4) on top of blue (3). However, Reynolds changed his mind and applied a thick layer of white to obliterate it. He then painted on a very thin layer of pale blue (6), perhaps to serve as the shadow of a fold line, followed by a layer of brown-orange paint.*

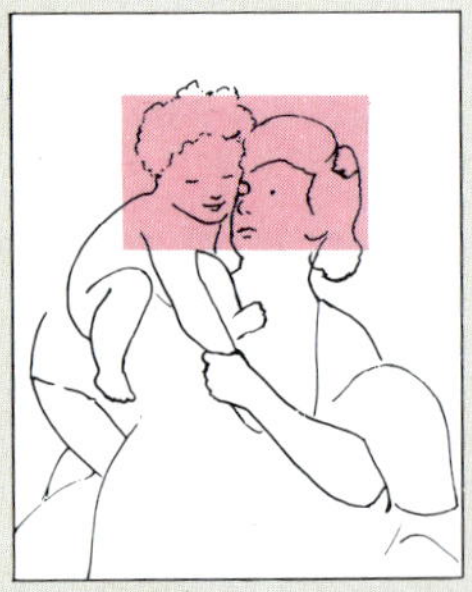

*Reynolds used assistants to complete the backgrounds of many of his pictures. However,* Mrs Hartley *is an experimental work and it is almost certain that Reynolds painted it completely himself.*

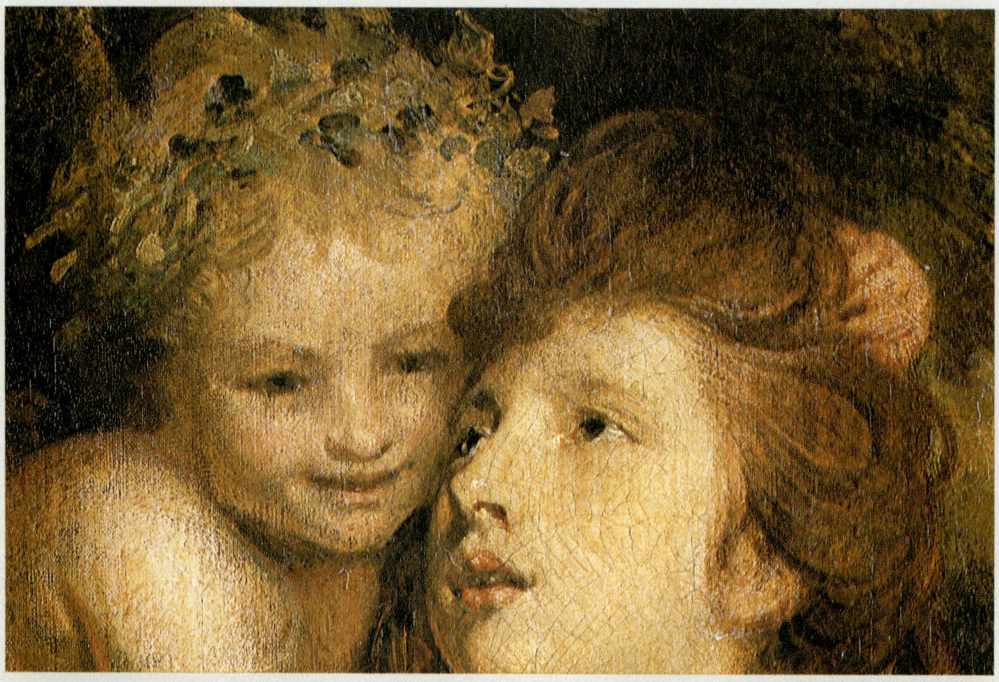

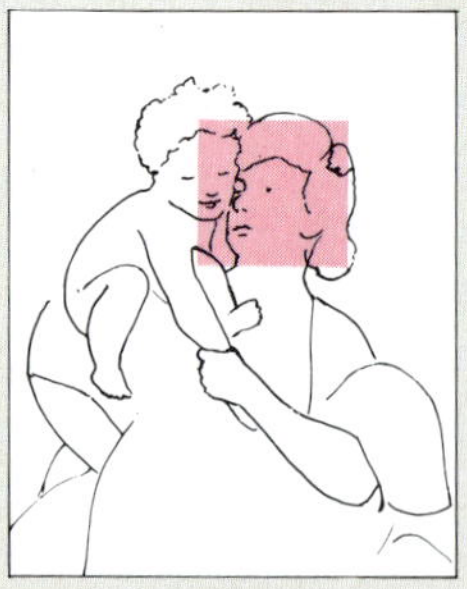

Actual size detail
*Despite a heavy layer of varnish and extensive retouching, this detail shows how the head of Bacchus has been painted in a radically different way from that of Mrs Hartley. With the latter, the traces of blue-black undermodelling near the temple creates shadows, and the added blue pigment in the white of the eye lends brilliance and liveliness to the entire face. Note that the white highlights and brushwork have been flattened during the lining process which is likely to happen if the paint contains a large amount of wax.*
*In Bacchus, the warm flesh colors have been applied thinly and the plain weave of the canvas and white ground are visible throughout. This, however, may be due to attempts to clean the picture, as many of Reynolds's experimental media are soluble in the mildest of solvents.*

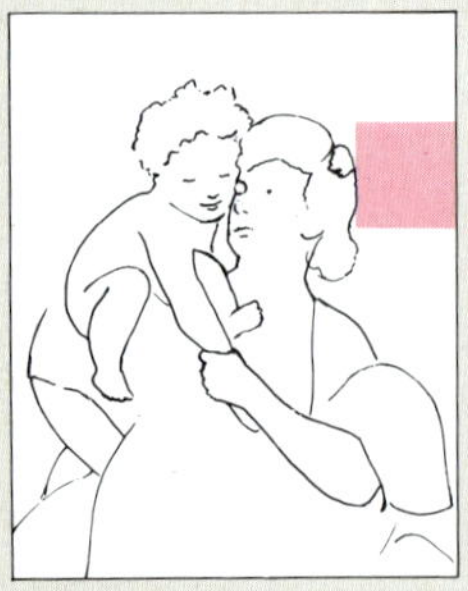

*Beneath the layers of discoloured varnish, it is likely that Reynolds built up the foliage in this area with a series of thin glazes which may have discolored. Marchi, one of Reynolds's biographers, noted that he would sometimes apply just a layer of megilp (a solution of mastic resin in a mixture of turpentine and linseed oil). Marchi commented that Reynolds used this to 'serve as a tint. This did not answer, for in a few months it was sure to become yellow and was obliged to be taken off.'*

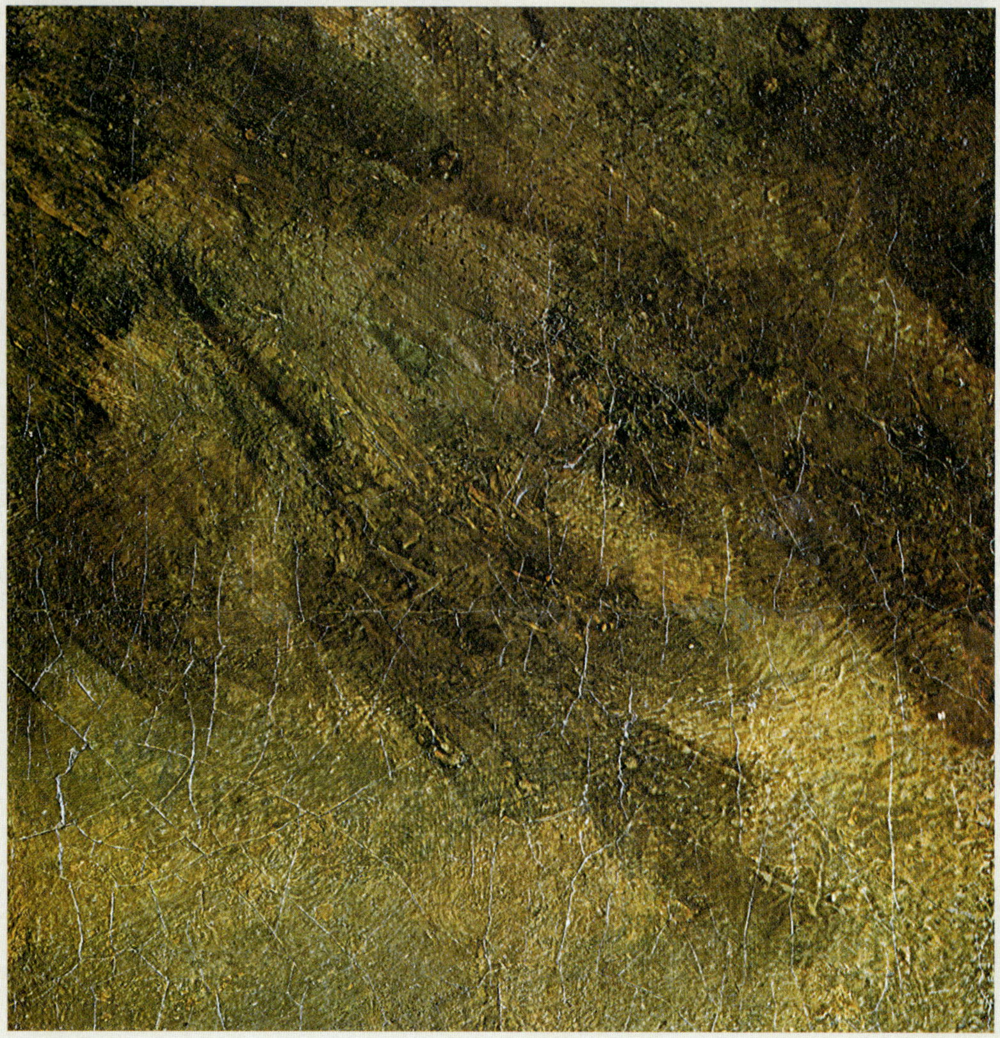

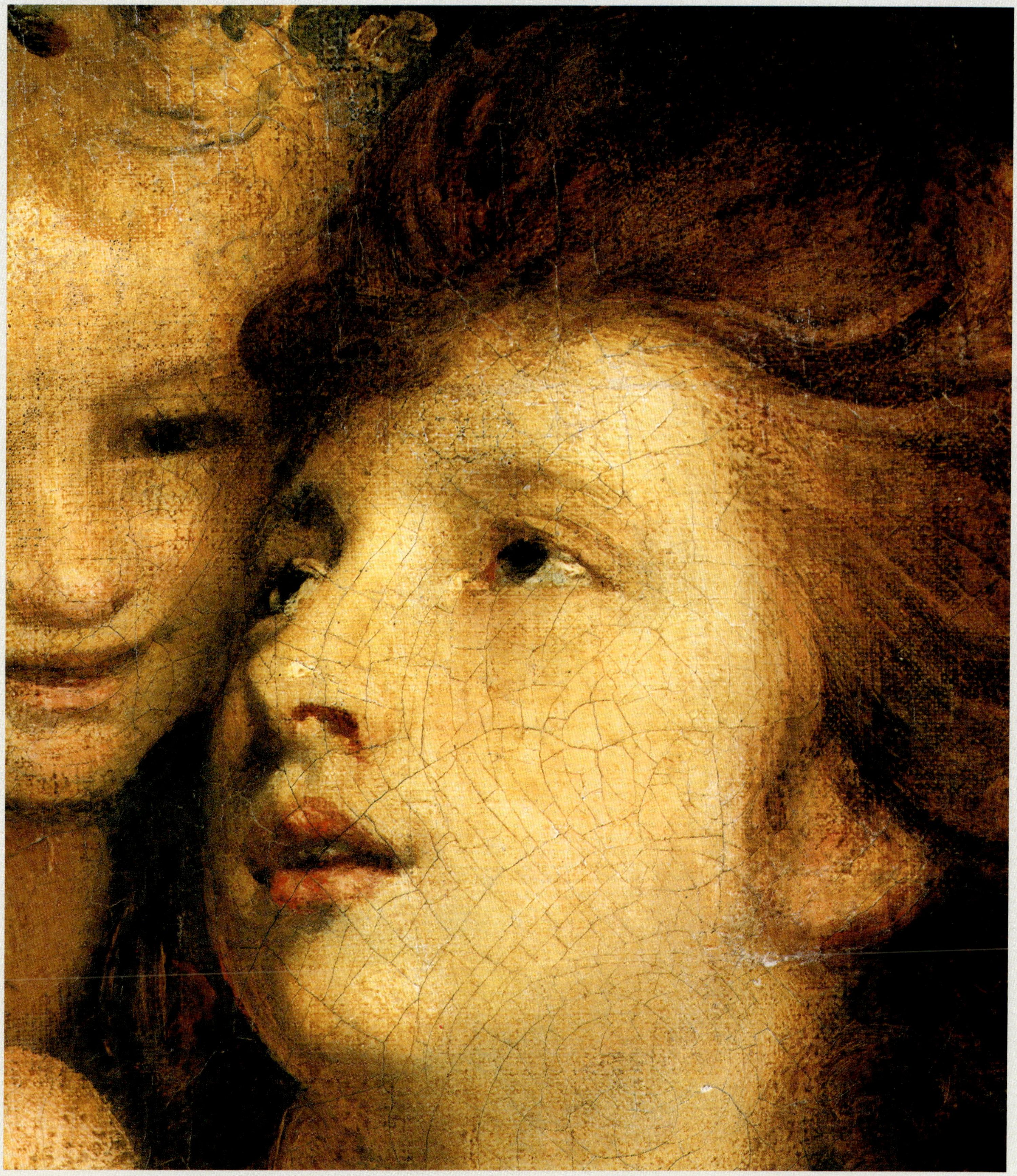

# THOMAS GAINSBOROUGH

*Portrait of the Artist's Wife* (c. 1778)
Oil on lined canvas, 77cm × 64.5cm/30¼in × 25¼in

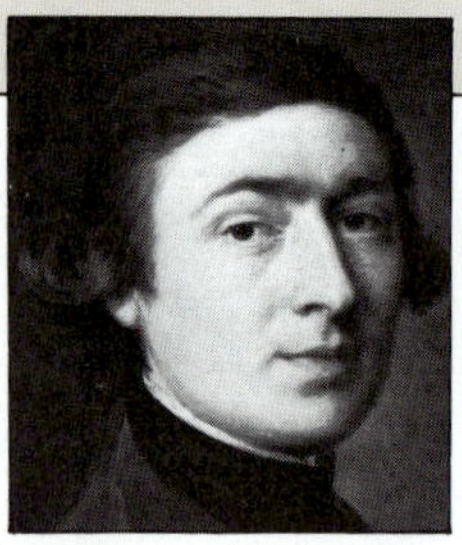

Gainsborough was apprenticed around 1740 to a French engraver, and this training is reflected in his style. His main introduction to painting came through the copying and restoration of seventeenth century Dutch paintings. Besides being a prolific artist, he became a founder member of the Royal Academy in London in 1768.

Unlike Reynolds, Gainsborough confined his experiments with technique largely to paper. The majority of his easel paintings, however, testify to the wisdom of painting 'fat over lean' and to this day, many of the portraits done in his later years remain in sound condition and are almost free of craquelure and surface deterioration.

Our knowledge of the artist's materials is scant and unreliable, but his letters indicate a fastidiousness in the choice of pigments and varnishes. Gainsborough normally favored varieties of a warm, red-brown color for a ground described in contemporary texts as resembling 'tanned leather' and particularly recommended for landscapes.

Contemporaries of Gainsborough describe how he would begin work in a very subdued light, 'a kind of darkened twilight', which enabled him to assess his subject in terms of basic shapes and broad tonal areas, free from distracting detail. Probably over a preliminary cursory chalk drawing, he would set to work on the canvas with rapid strokes of black, umber, lake or white paint, followed by washes of thinned color to 'block out' the form. These transparent washes, often so thin that they resembled watercolor, were to serve as a tonal underlay for further development.

The thin underlayers and half tones would begin to dry quickly, enabling Gainsborough to apply translucent, opaque, and glazing colors very rapidly in a largely wet-in-wet technique, either working into the washes or over them with translucent layers.

The drapery and background would be completed last by the artist applying color in a welter of glazes and loose, dazzling, scumbled strokes – 'odd scratches and marks' – which, as Reynolds observed, only assumed form when viewed from a distance. Very often alterations can be seen with the naked eye, and X-rays reveal that changes were often undertaken when the painting was close to completion.

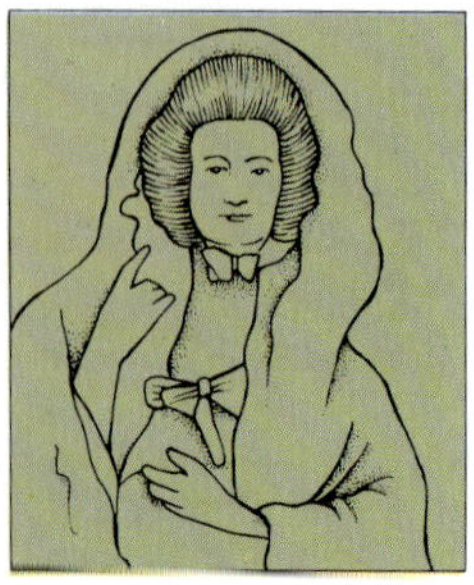

**1.** Gainsborough would place his model in a subdued light so as better to assess the overall composition.

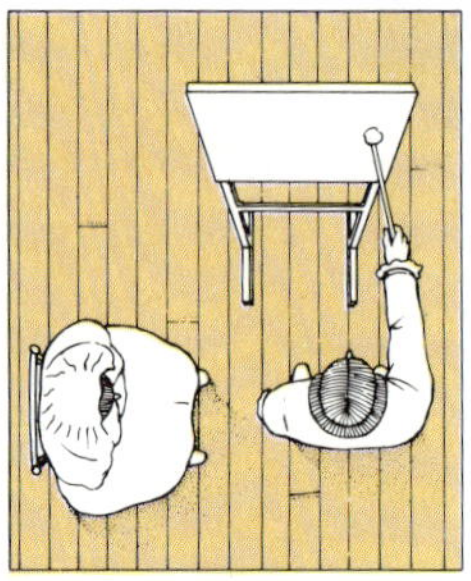

**2.** According to a contemporary, the artist would place himself and his canvas at a right angle to the sitter so that he stood still and touched the features of the picture at exactly the same distance at which he viewed the sitter.

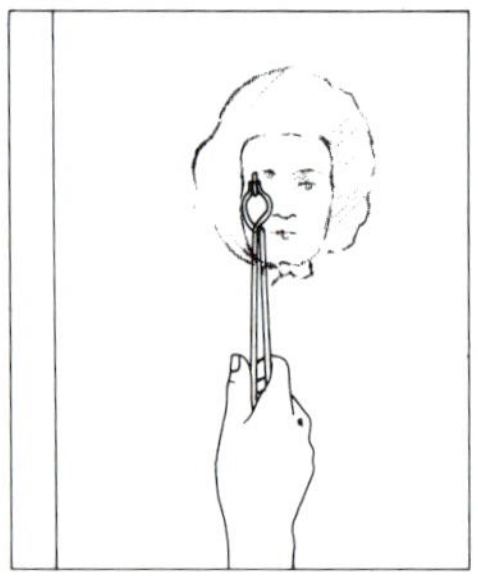

**3.** Gainsborough would initially mark the position of the sitter's head in chalk often held in a pair of tongs to allow him to stand back from the canvas. When the painting was near completion, he would again use the chalk to mark alterations.

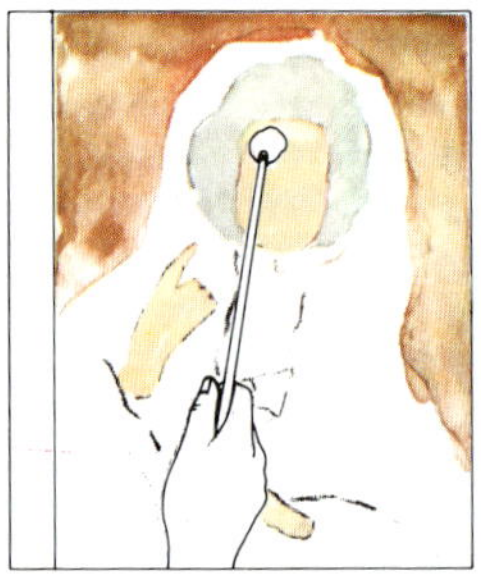

**4.** He would then block in the painting in thin paint. His daughter claimed that his 'colors were very liquid, and if he did not hold the palette right, would run over.'

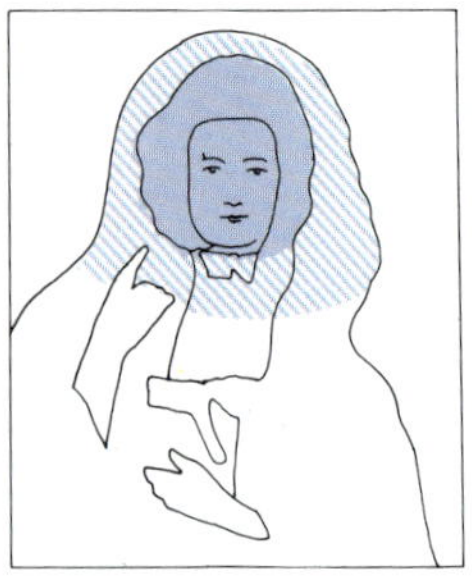

**5.** Having blocked in most of the composition in thin paint, Gainsborough would concentrate on the head and the area around it, before returning to complete the drapery and background.

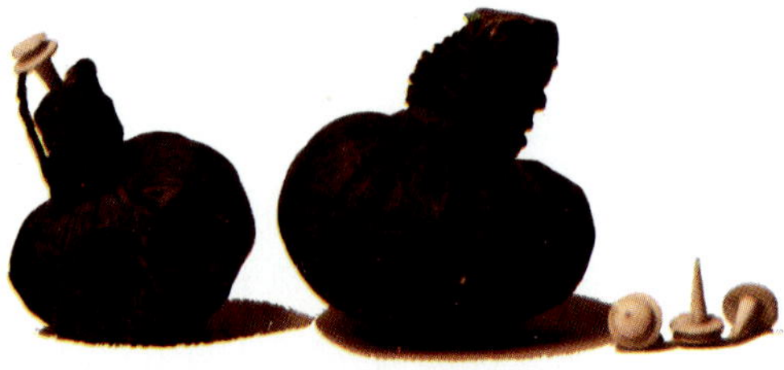

*During the seventeenth and eighteenth centuries, artists kept their paints tied in small bladders. To extract some paint, the artist would prick the side with a sharp tack which had to be replaced to seal the hole.*

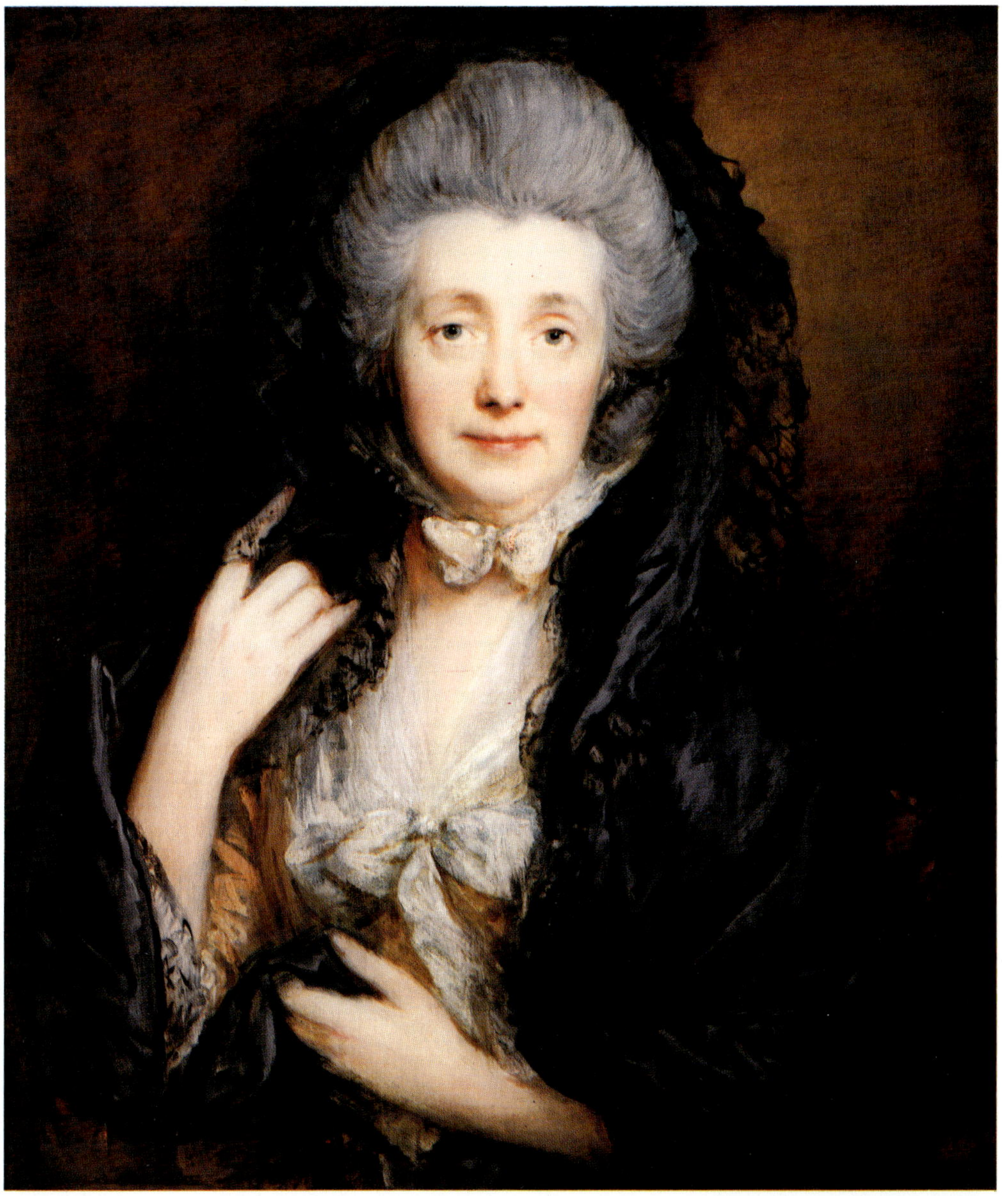

*Gainsborough would first work from the model in a dim light allowing him to lay in the general tones of the larger areas, working quickly in rough washes of very thin oil which served as an under-painting for the subsequent development of flesh and drapery. Allowing more light on the subject, he would complete the head of the model. In this case, the eyes, nose and mouth appear to have been put in using a wet-in-wet technique, while the overall smoothness of the surface suggests the artist may have used a blender before applying the last touches as seen in the highlights in the eye, the strokes of red-brown in the curve of the eyelid, the line of the mouth and the dabs of color for the nostrils.*

Right
*Gainsborough's use of a pale ground in this picture perhaps relates to his interest in transparencies lit from behind. As well as constructing an illuminated box, he and other artists painted some larger-than-life figures for a theater in 1775 and one contemporary noted that 'these pictures are all transparent and are lighted behind'.*

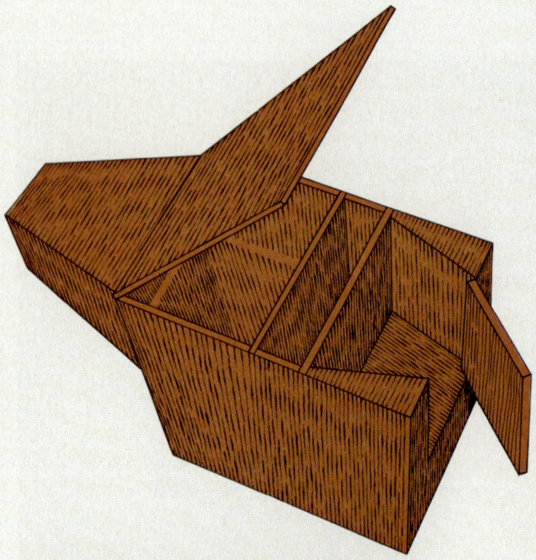

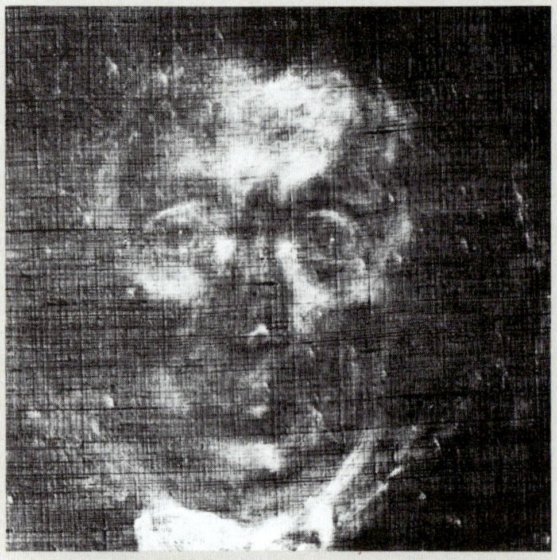

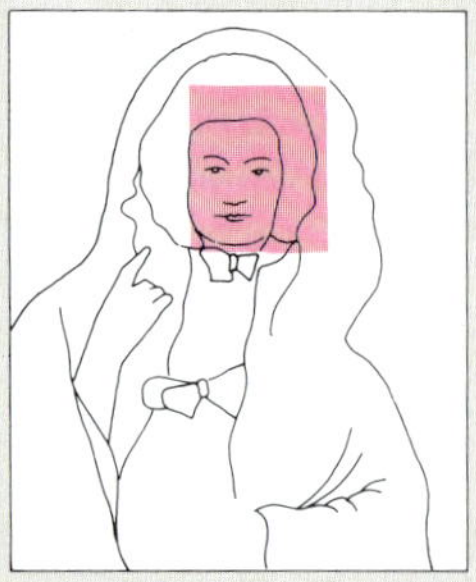

Actual size detail
*In a technique resembling that of the watercolorist, Gainsborough has achieved enhanced luminosity in his flesh tones by painting thinly and allowing the pale color of the ground to shine through. He is believed to have used a particularly pure white pigment, Cremona white, which he may have bound in poppy oil, as this was noted for its transparency and non-yellowing qualities. In view of Gainsborough's interest in creating a luminous effect, it is significant that, only a year or so after painting this picture, he constructed an ingenious illuminated box to show transparencies which were painted in oil and varnish on glass and lit from behind by candles. In this detail, a single, fine line in gray paint is perceptible down the shadowed side of the nose, whilst the nostrils have been completed with two dabs of the dark pigment which is also to be found in one mantle on the left. On the right, below Mrs Gainsborough's ear, a stroke of thin flesh color has been applied over black to soften the illuminated edge of her cheek.*

*This detail encapsulates much of the astonishing variety of Gainsborough's impulsive brushwork. It ranges from the brown washes of the bodice to the bravura scumbles and thick impasto of the bow to the bold zig-zag of the orange sleeve, which was applied with a hog's hair brush. In addition, the limpid flesh tones of the hand were painted* alla prima *with a bold stroke of red paint, outlining the thumb; and touches of black paint, rich in medium were applied over the scumbled strokes of the white ribbon. Traces of blue paint can be seen in the bow. The pigment is probably Prussian blue, although earlier in his career Gainsborough is known to have used indigo, which often behaves unsatisfactorily in oil.*

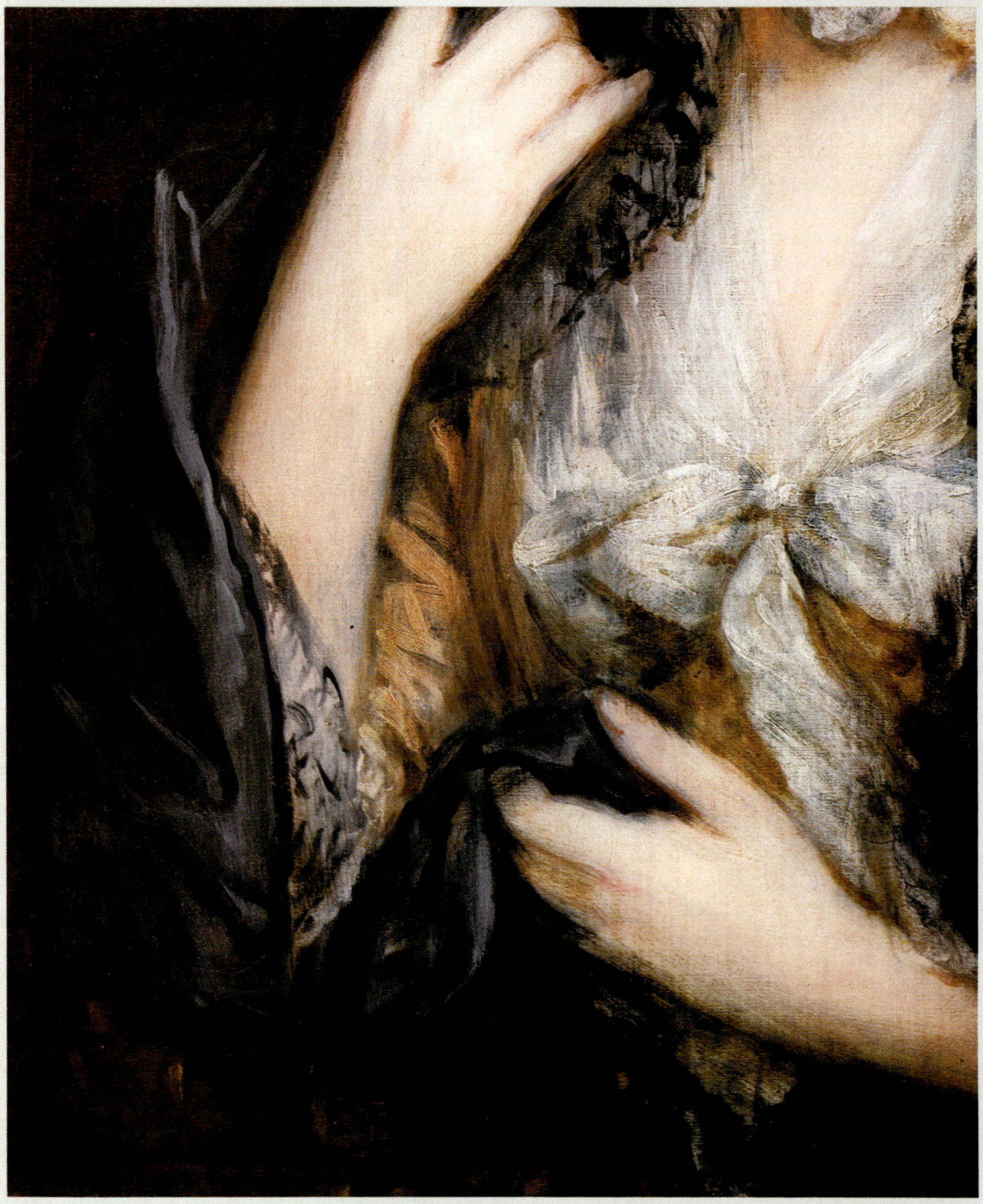

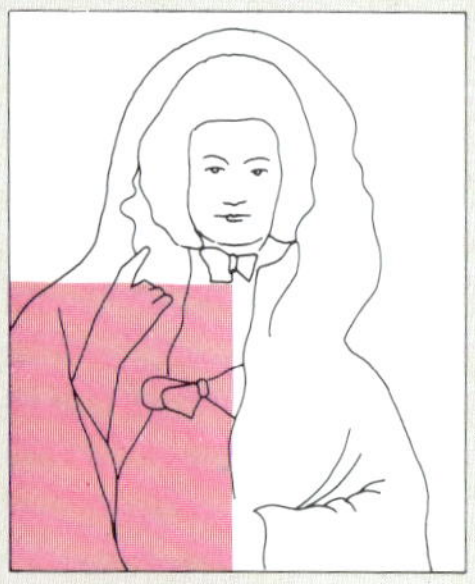

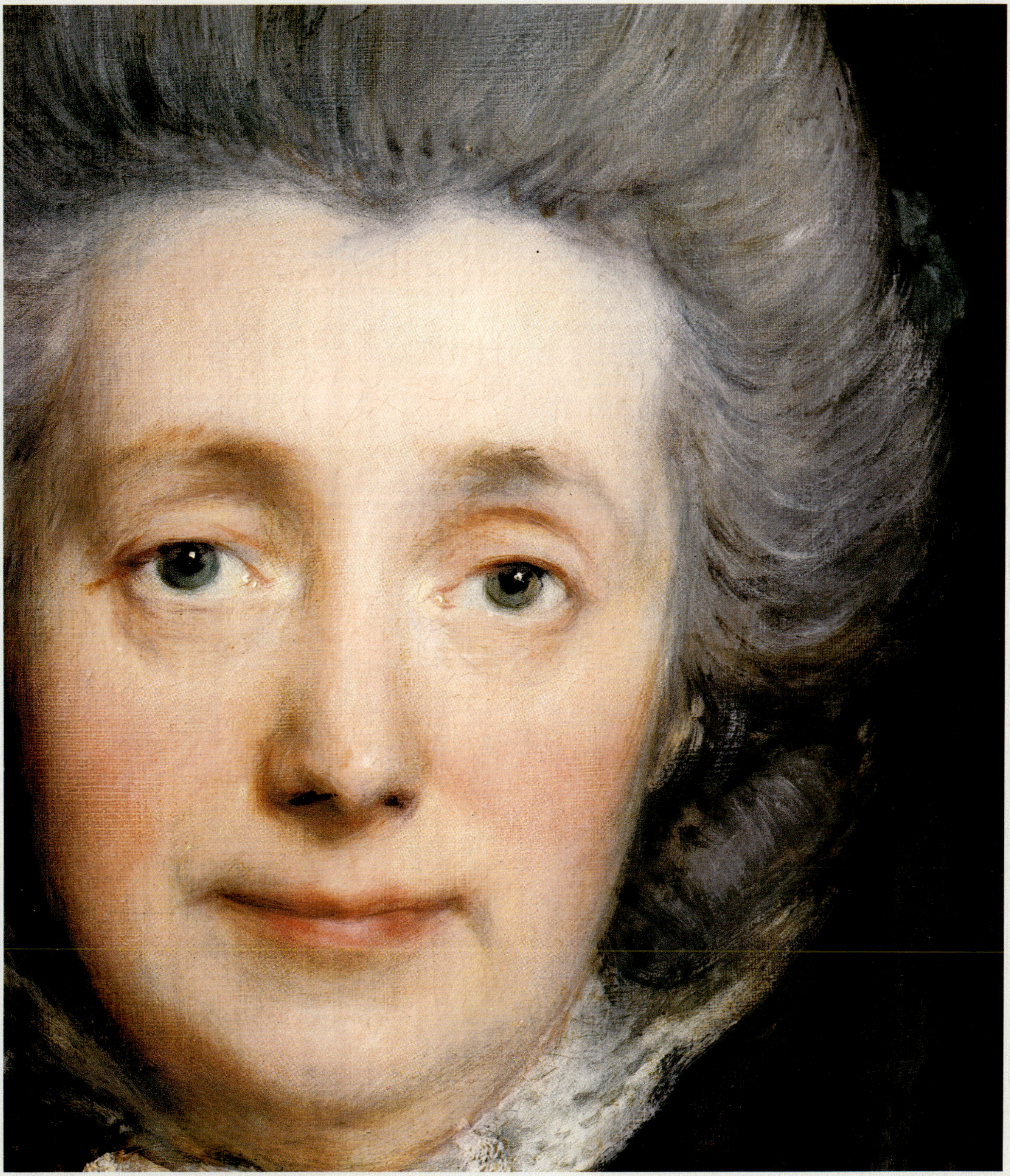

# WILLIAM BLAKE

*The Body of Abel Found by Adam and Eve* (c. 1825)
Watercolor on wood, 32cm × 43cm/12¾in × 17in

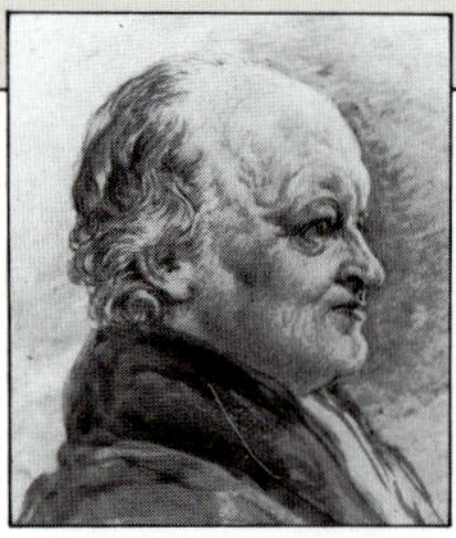

William Blake was one of the most intensely individualistic of British artists. His works combine poetic visions and dramatic religious allegory in a sinuous drawing style. Blake, who trained as an engraver, is well known for his book engravings, watercolors, and for his poems. It is significant that he chose not to paint in oils at a time when this was the most acceptable medium, rejecting it in favor of a technique which he, inaccurately, described as 'fresco'. The words 'fresco W. Blake' are incised in the priming at the bottom right of this picture but this is not what is generally accepted as fresco. It is painted in a water-based medium more properly called tempera or distemper. Unlike egg tempera where egg is the medium, or gouache and watercolor where gum is used as the medium, Blake's medium was probably rabbit-skin or carpenter's glue. The glue would have to be applied very diluted or warmed.

Blake tried to produce the maximum brilliance and purity of color in his works. It is important to remember that in Blake's formative years the artist's palette was still limited. Only later, with the development of new colors, could the artists experiment more.

Blake's tempera style, which was closely related to that of his engravings, watercolors and illustrations, relied heavily on line drawing. So Blake used a method which allowed the underdrawing to show through. He also avoided the heavy, opaque forms which characterized the work of most contemporary oil painters. Because of the brittleness of the glue medium when it dried, the final paint film was thin and Blake was unable to use impasto or to leave any thick, flowing brushmarks. The lightness of the ground which formed the highlights and emphasized the ground was crucial to Blake's technique.

Although Blake had read Cennini's work on tempera techniques, his understanding of the Old Masters' techniques was suspect. This caused him to make many mistakes before he found a satisfactory method, and, for this reason, most of his works have deteriorated. Movement of the support, ageing of the varnish and drying out of the glue have led to fine surface cracks and many small losses of paint. Nevertheless, Blake, over the years, evolved a method which allowed him to preserve the subtlety of his drawing and to use his skills as a colorist to achieve the effects he desired.

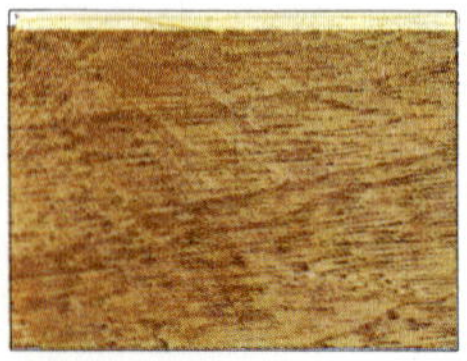

**1.** For this 'fresco', Blake used a mahogany panel. Good cuts of mahogany were readily available, and the wood usually made an excellent and stable support. However, this piece has since developed a marked convex warp.

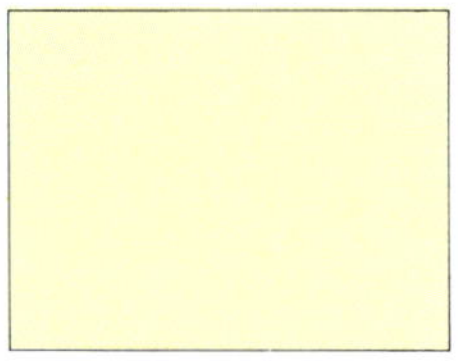

**2.** Blake applied several layers of glue and whiting to the panel to cover the wood grain with an even, warm white, gesso ground. He probably rubbed the surface down and sealed it with more glue, as the surface is smooth and non-absorbent.

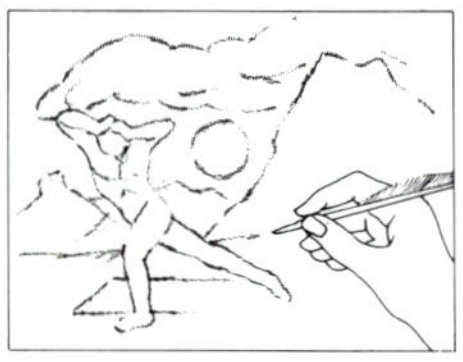

**3.** Next Blake drew a rough sketch probably with graphite pencil, working it up to a more precise drawing in heavier pencil, and black color applied with a fine brush. A fine reed pen or quill may also have been used. There are no major alterations, and the drawing is clearly visible in the finished picture.

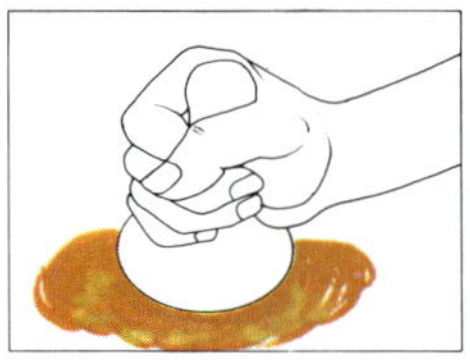

**4.** Blake then ground his pigments by hand in a dilute solution of the glue. The range of pigments was quite small and relied on traditional watercolor materials. The pigments seem to have been ultramarine, ochres, madder, black, Prussian blue, gamboge, vermilion and gold.

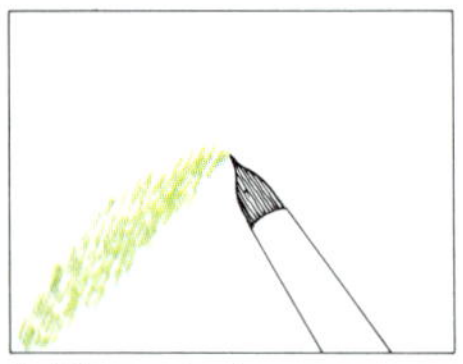

**5.** The painting was built up by applying paint in small strokes, each little more than a stain on the white ground. The white highlights of exposed ground have been left, like the unpainted paper in a watercolor.

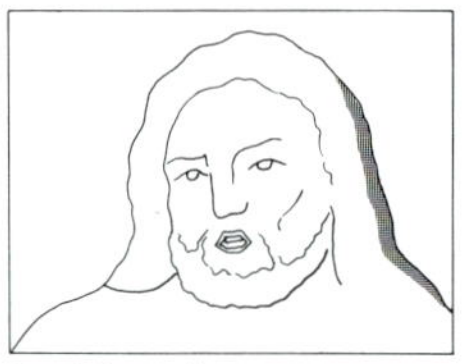

**6.** When the painting had almost been completed, a few details were re-worked and strengthened.

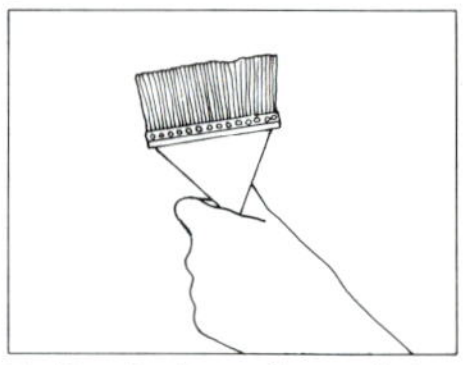

**7.** On drying, the paint would lose much of its shine, so Blake applied further layers of glue and then a spirit varnish. The varnish was probably mastic in turpentine which would give the painting a glossy surface and saturate all the colors.

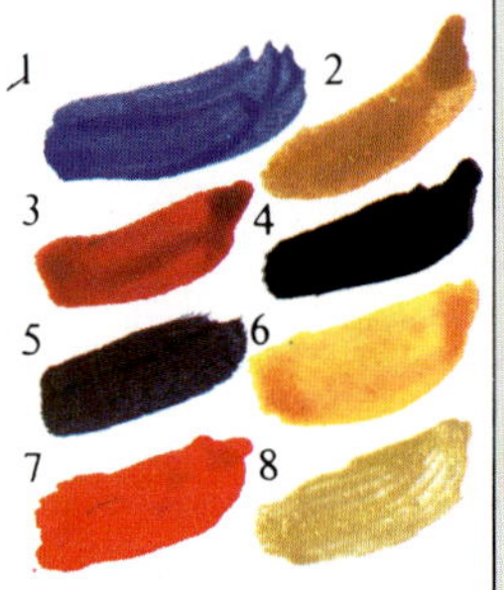


In this work, Blake used the following pigments: ultramarine (**1**), ochres (**2**), madder (**3**), black (**4**), Prussian blue (**5**), gamboge (**6**), vermilion (**7**), and gold (**8**).

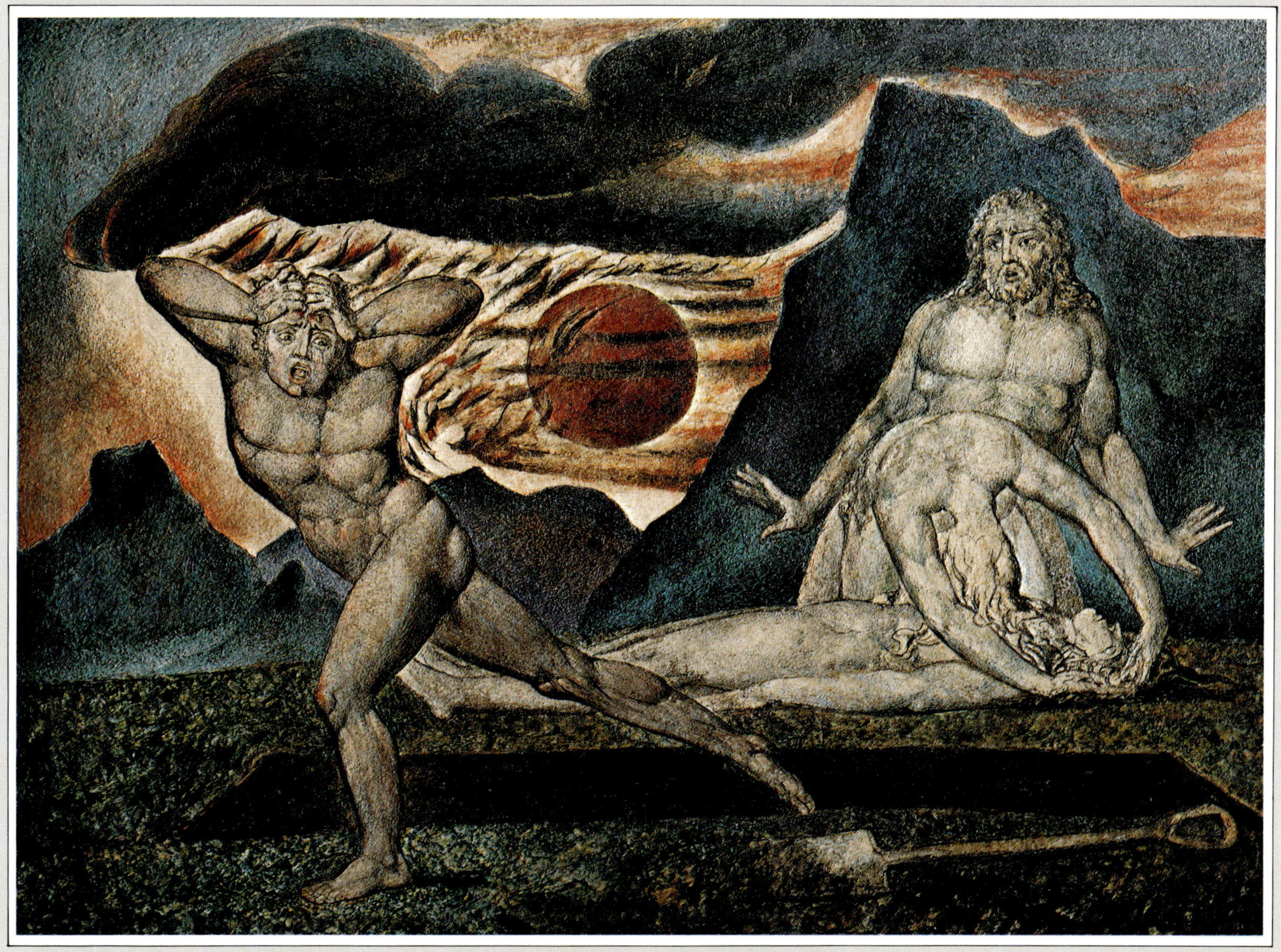

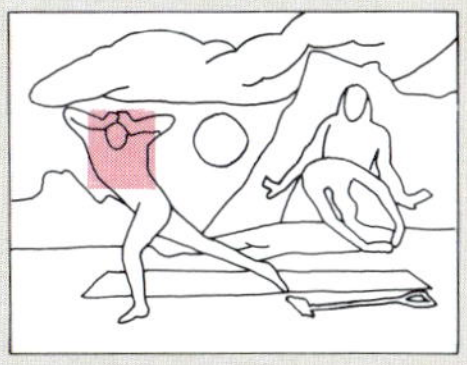

Actual size detail
*The detail shows the finished ink drawing of the figure of Cain. The rough underdrawing can be seen. Most noticeably, minor changes have been made to the hands; the original positions show through quite clearly. The light area to the left of Cain shows the exposed gesso ground. The mountain has been painted slightly thicker, but the colors are still transparent. The blue-green shadows and thinly scumbled flesh tints on the figure were applied with a small brush. The flames around Cain's head, originally painted in vermilion and blacks, have, in many places, flaked away. The dark cloud is virtually opaque with shell gold highlights applied on top.*

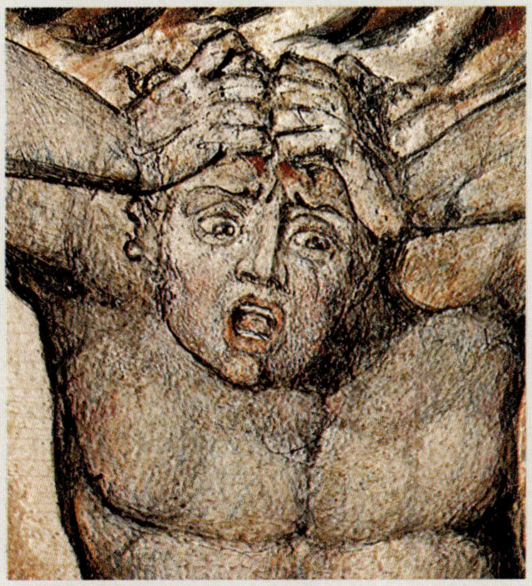

*On the finished painting the paint film is thin and even, and there is virtually no impasto. The brittleness of the dried glue limited the thickness of the paint and Blake could not rework without first rubbing down to the ground. The light ground is basic to Blake's technique, acting both to form the highlights and also to bring out the colors. The blue-green shadows on the flesh may be derived from the Italian true fresco paintings which Cennini had described. Blake has also used a fine powdered gold, called shell gold, which would have been applied in the same glue medium. The foreground green is made by applying a yellowish green glaze over the blue modelling. The color probably includes a yellow lake or gamboge. Blake was not totally consistent in using the transparency of color which his method created. For example, the gold painted over the black and the vermilion in the sky are both opaque pigments whose color is not dependent on the white ground.*

# John Constable

*Chain Pier, Brighton* (1827)
Oil on canvas, 127cm × 183cm/50in × 72in

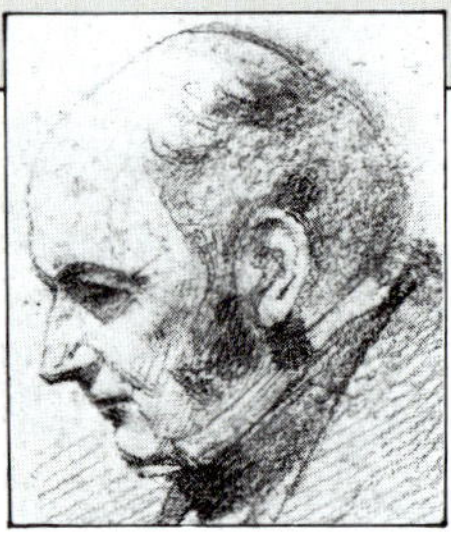

The child of a prosperous Suffolk miller, Constable's youth had a profound influence upon his art and, long after he had moved, the landscape of his childhood continued to inspire his paintings. Many of his mature works were created from memory and also from many drawings and sketches of his early environment.

Constable was greatly influenced by the landscapes of Rubens and Claude and, although he had a formal art education, he found the copying of Old Masters the surest means to gain technical expertise in a period when traditional, practical knowledge was all but extinct. A contemporary recalled Constable's dual preoccupation with nature and the Old Masters: 'No one perhaps has given a greater look of studying Nature alone . . . than John Constable, but he told me he seldom painted a picture without considering how Rembrandt or Claude would have treated it.'

The degree to which Constable worked out of doors is debatable, as the practical problems of working on large, finished canvases outside would have been great. Constable painted only in daylight and a contemporary recorded his working methods, which involved working on the whole together . . . beginning with a faint dead colour in which the masses only are laid in, and proceeding with the details gradually, and without suffering one part to advance much beyond the rest, until the whole is finished . . . Indeed, in landscape, it seems impossible that those almost imperceptible gradations of colour and light should be obtained by any other process.'

For Constable, *chiaroscuro* was an effect to be obtained at all costs; and, in the pursuit of this, he evolved an expressive and unfinished execution, including the impasted flecks of white which offended many of his contemporaries.

This was particularly true of Constable's work after the 1820s when his subjects moved away from the logic of external reality. Delacroix commented that 'Constable says that the superiority of the greens in his meadows is due to the fact that they are made up of a large number of different greens. What gives a lack of intensity and life to the verdure of the ordinary run of landscape painters is that they do it with a uniform tint.' This is one of Constable's major technical achievements.

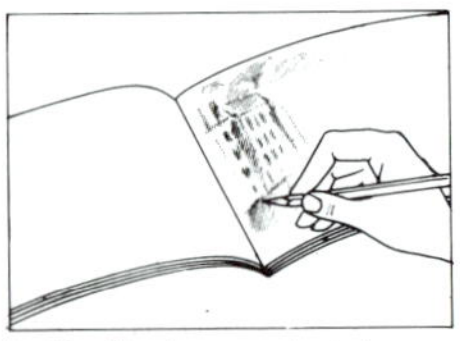

**1.** Preliminary sketches and oil studies were first done.

**2.** The stretcher with linen support and pink oil ground were probably made to order for the artist.

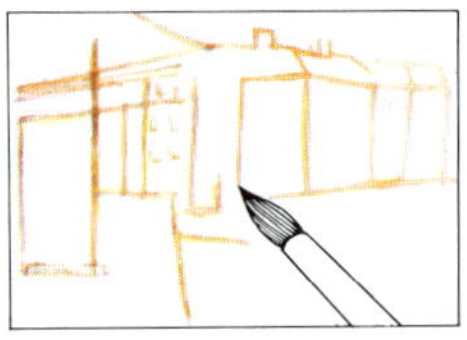

**3.** A pencil underdrawing was first made and then the masses established with washes of subdued color.

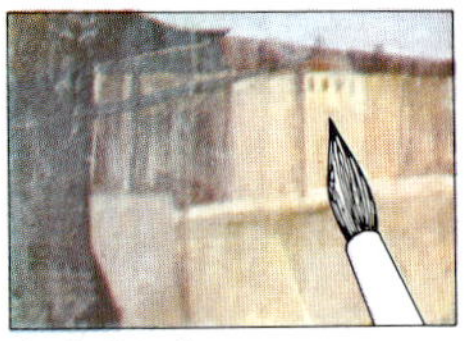

**4.** A thin but opaque building-up of the surface commenced with details added.

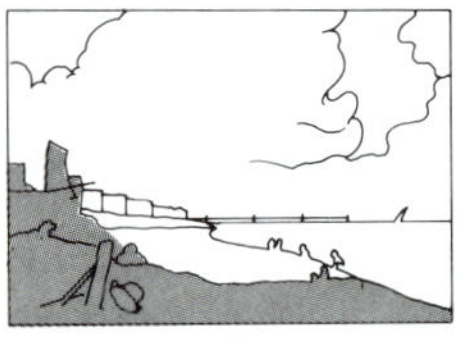

**5.** Glazings of burnt red lakes and transparent earths were used to add depth and richness to shadows and foreground.

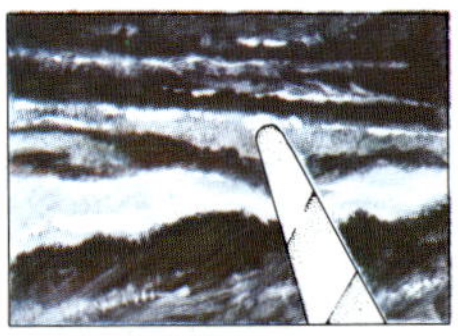

**6.** Freely knifed and brushed touches of off-white were used to give the quality of reflective light and sparkling of waves.

*This drawing, executed in pencil and strengthened with lines in pen and ink on two sheets of paper watermarked 1824, was made by Constable when he visited Brighton in 1825 or 1826, in preparation for his painting. The elongated format captures the panorama of the Pier and the Parade, which recedes in a wedge shape into the distance.*

*Concentrating upon the complex central motif, the drawing serves to record accurately the salient features and perspective, which could then be transferred to the larger canvas. In the finished painting, the areas of both sky and foreground were greatly extended. While additional buildings, boats and figures gave compositional strength and unity.*

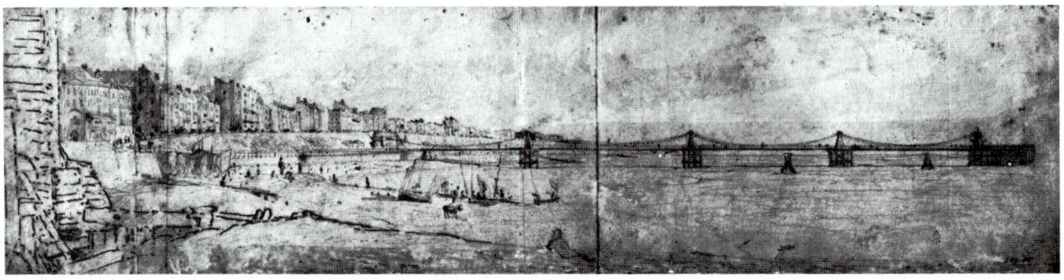

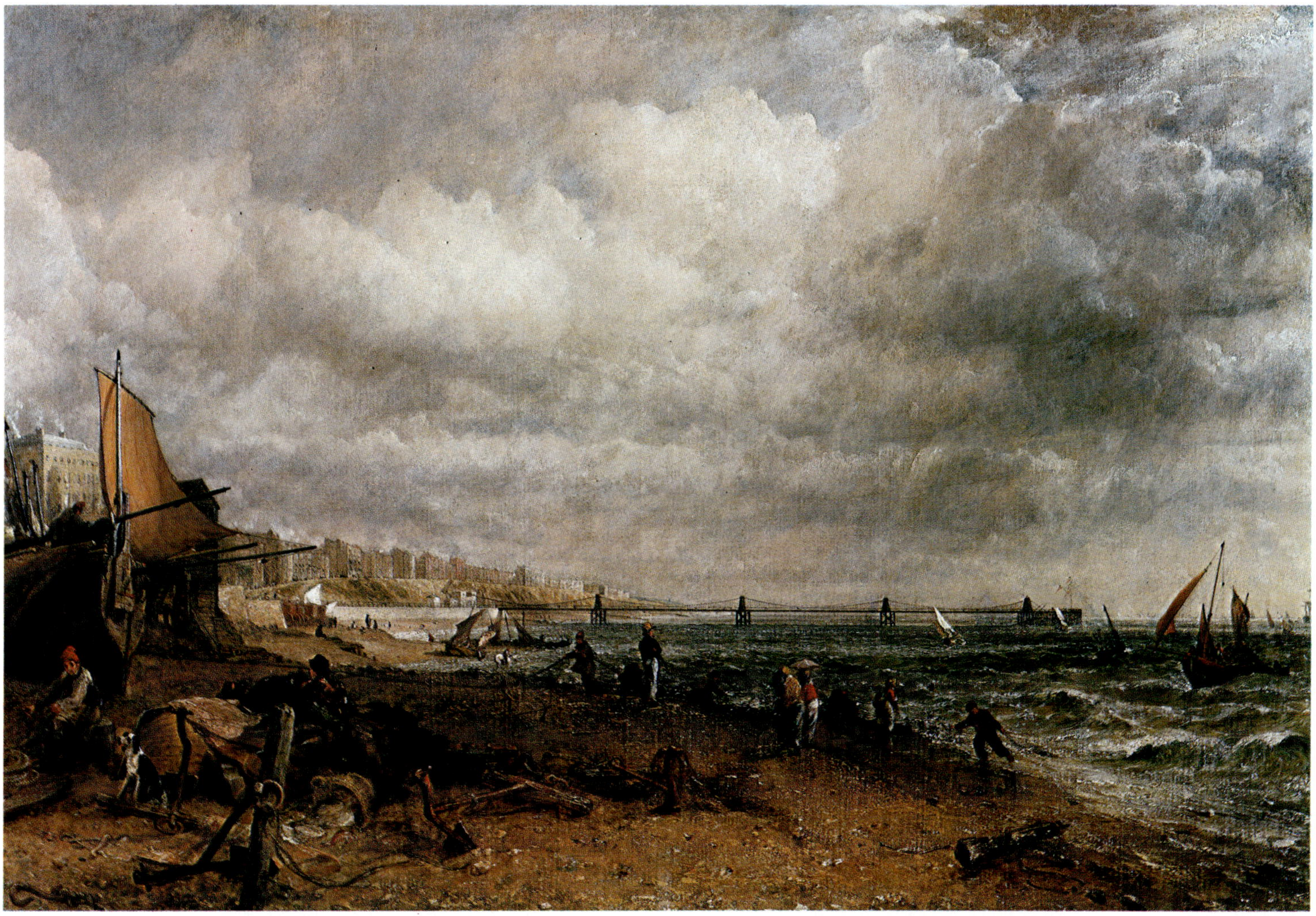

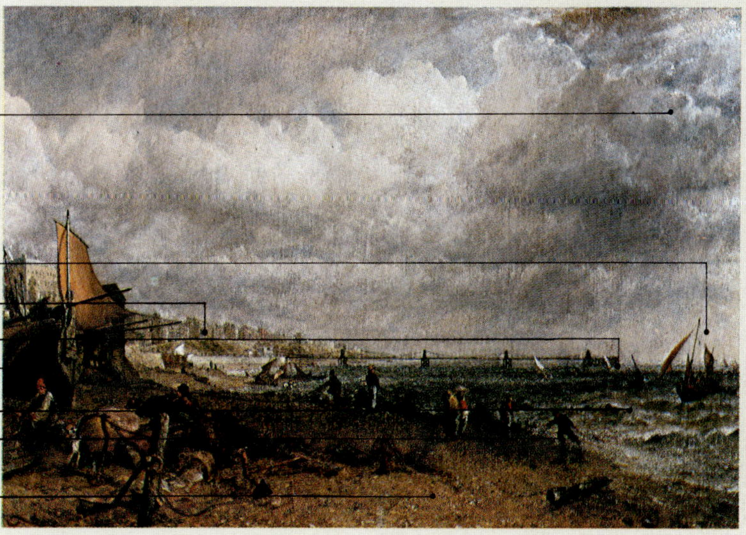


*Many changes were made in this painting during the course of its execution, with the overall format being reduced by about one-eighth of its original length. The length of the pier was extended by the artist, which necessitated painting out a sail boat which cut across the new position. Other adjustments included the addition of highlights along the horizon which have obliterated part of a small boat; the shape of the upturned hull in the left foreground has been softened and rounded, and some of the incidental figures superimposed on the completed picture. A plain canvas with pink oil ground has been used and irregularities in the weave appear where paint has been dragged across the surface. Very fine sable brushwork is contrasted with delicate and free, but controlled, flicks and dashes of color laid on with a knife to enliven the foreground and water. The flecks of off-white were used to create atmosphere, and Constable was heavily criticized for this. The dry paint consistency, used for distant, hazy buildings, contrasts with the richness of the foreground and varied scumbles and thin impasto of the sky. The palette is dominated by earth colors with touches of bright red.*

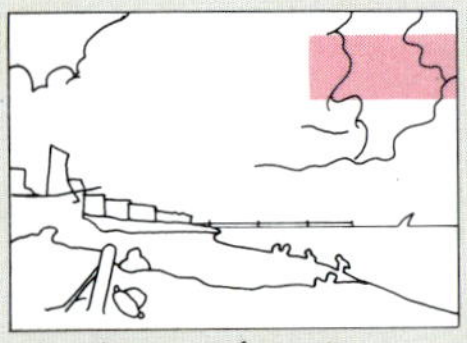

*The sky was of great importance to Constable who stated that 'It will be difficult to name a class of landscape in which the sky is not the key note, standard of scale, and chief organ of sentiment.' Constable devoted the larger proportion of his composition to sky which, through delicately scumbled veils of whites and blue-grays, captures the sullen moody light which pervades the scene.*

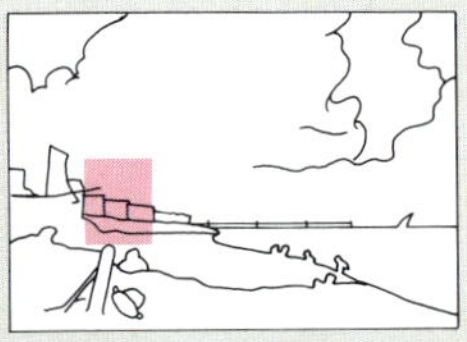

Actual size detail

*This detail illustrates Constable's varied and expressive handling which evokes a natural atmosphere. Delicate brushwork can be seen in the pier and outlines of the buildings and bathing machines which contrasts with the rich, dark paint in the foreground and thin impasto of the sky. Umber glazes were added to give the darkest shadows depth, and thin knifed layers of opaque earth colors were punctuated with flecks and dragged strokes of creamy off-white, giving atmospheric accents of light. Delicate, free touches of greens enliven the bank and add awnings to the hotel windows. They appear loose when viewed close-up but come into focus when seen from a distance. Superimposed tiny figures animate the scene.*

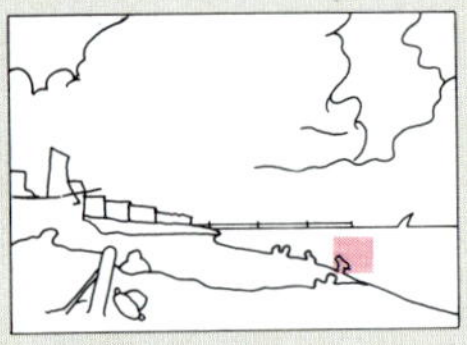

*Unlike the smaller incidental figures, most of the active foreground figures were anticipated in Constable's compositional layout. This dark figure was integrated amongst the sparkling lights reflected off the turbulent waves by the superimposition of flecks of off-white. Dark transparent greens give the deep sea effects, while scattered touches of knifework and blended strokes of stiff white depict the waves.*

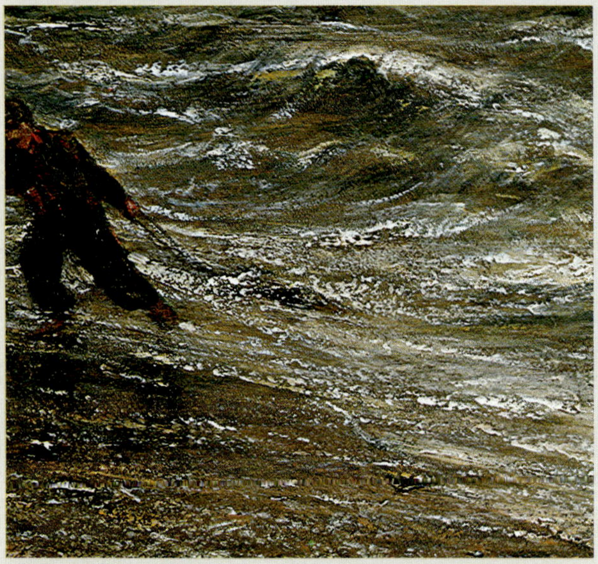

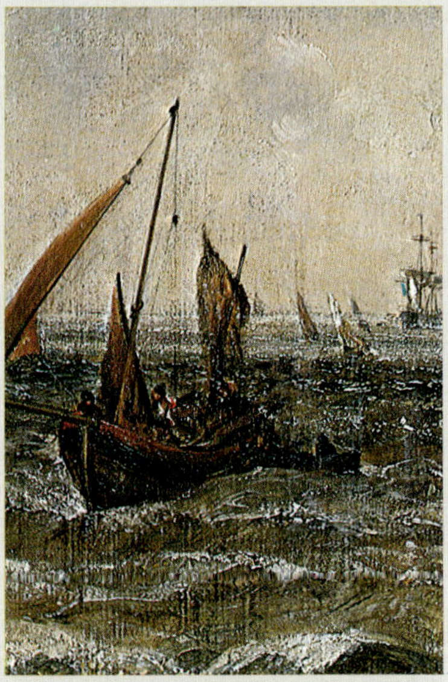

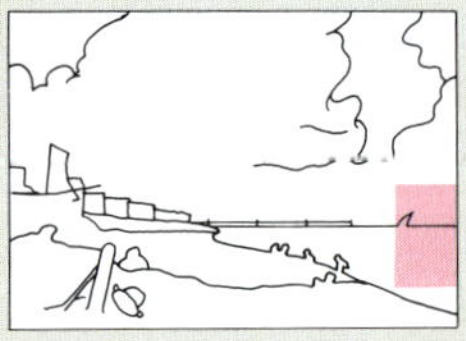

*Layers of reworking characterize the skyline, where tiny sailing boats added for interest have themselves been partially over-painted when the highlights on the horizon were strengthened.*

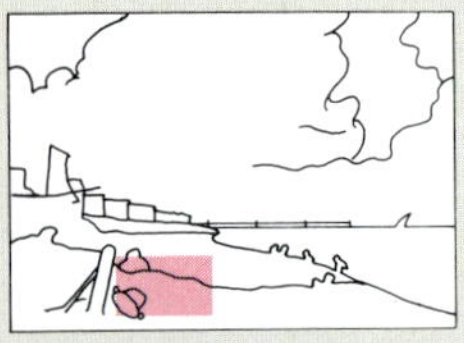

*Finely controlled over-laid films of knife-applied earth colors create the broken color and texture of the beach. The handling is boldest in the foreground to suggest its proximity to the viewer and to contrast with the subtler work which is intended to evoke distance. The accessories were freely executed with brush and knife.*

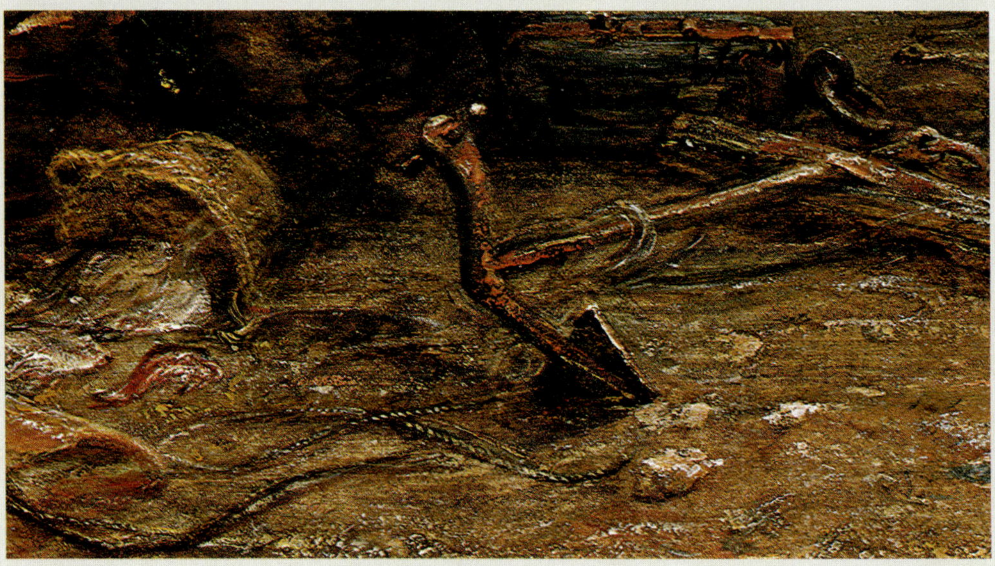

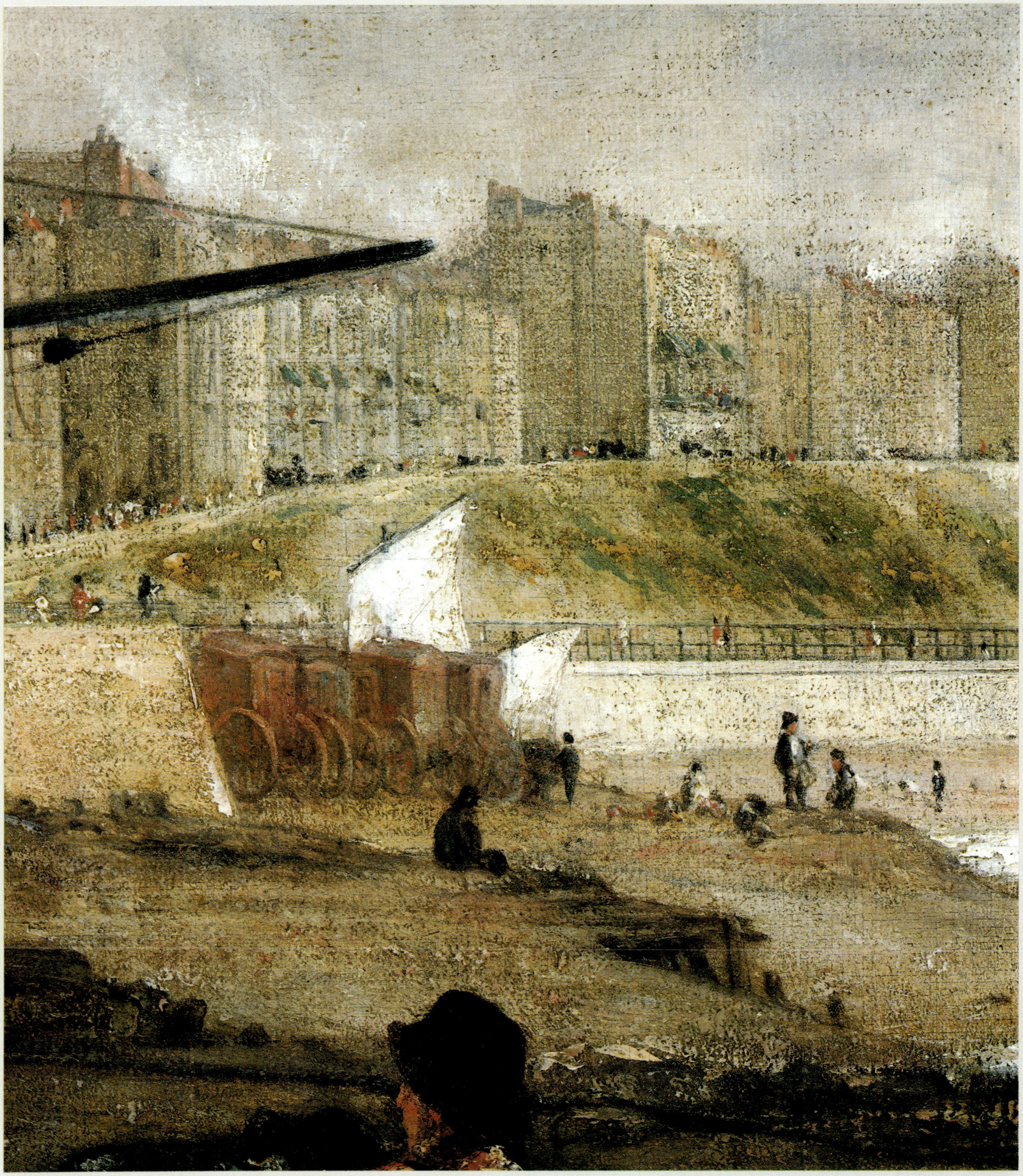

# JEAN AUGUSTE DOMINIQUE INGRES

*Oedipus and the Sphinx* (1828)
Oil on canvas, 17.8cm × 13.7cm/6⅞in × 5⅜in

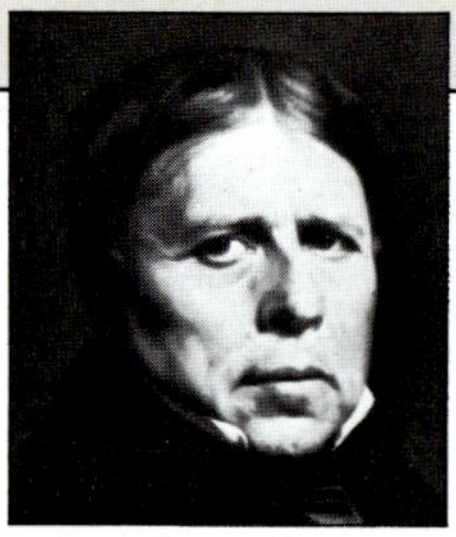

Ingres, the first great radical of the nineteenth century, created a personal, sensual style that moved away from the grand manner of the late eighteenth century Neoclassicists and evolved a new, individual idealization of form through an expressive use of line. Thus, despite a formal and academic training, Ingres' technique was unconventional and brought an intuitive and intimate grace to the stoic Neoclassical ideal.

Reacting against the sombre brown and red earth grounds of Rococo art, the Neoclassicists used pale preparations which ensured luminosity and durability. As oil paint tends to become transparent with age, pictures done on dark grounds appear to 'sink' as the ground becomes increasingly visible. Thus, on dark grounds, much of the subtlety of transparent shadows and delicate half-tones disappears with time. Artists had long been aware of this problem and felt that paler grounds had obvious advantages. However, they were more difficult to work on as they made the calculation of tones difficult unless the entire surface was covered. Dark grounds also expedited the artists' work by acting as a middle tone when left exposed between opaque highlights and any dark, transparent shadows. Ingres had a preference for strong, fairly coarse canvas, a rarity among Neoclassical painters who had followed the common rule that figure painting should be executed only on finely woven canvas the weave of which was invisible at the viewing distance.

In addition to his use of pale grounds and rough canvas, Ingres also broke with tradition by using white in his shadows. *Chiarascuro* painters had felt that transparency was essential for producing depth, and Ingres' innovative use of white created a new low-relief flatness. As well, Ingres' opaque shadows reflect his preference for soft, full-faced lighting which differed from the dramatic cross-light found in the work of earlier Neoclassicists.

Ingres' paint was thin and fluid, his touch, lively and descriptive, only blended in the figures. Although he was often considered a 'monochrome' painter who used color as an afterthought, Ingres' flat areas of bright color have a powerfully emotive and visually seductive effect not yet seen in painting of that century which influenced many later artists.

1. A medium weight, irregular weave canvas was primed with a thin darkish red ground.

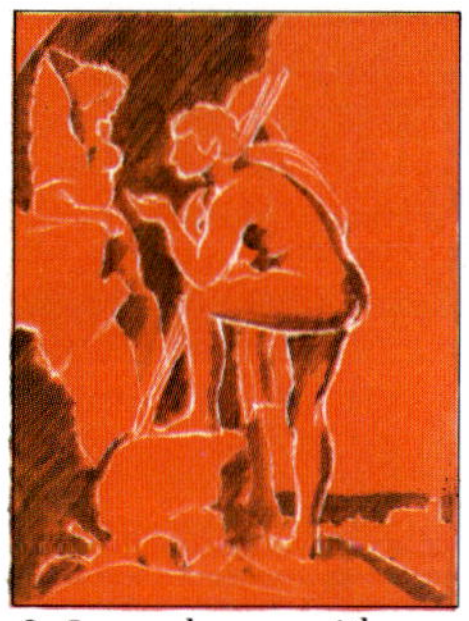

2. Ingres began with a graphite or chalk drawing to establish contours.

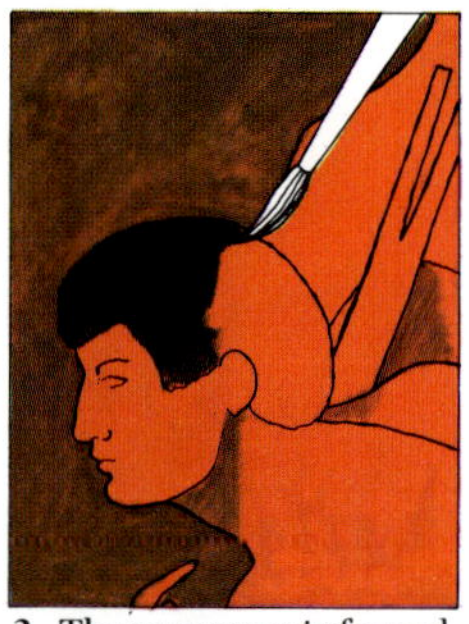

3. These were reinforced and thin shadows executed in a dark brown, probably raw umber. Also with this fluid wash the main features, such as the hair, were drawn in with a fine soft brush and fluid wash.

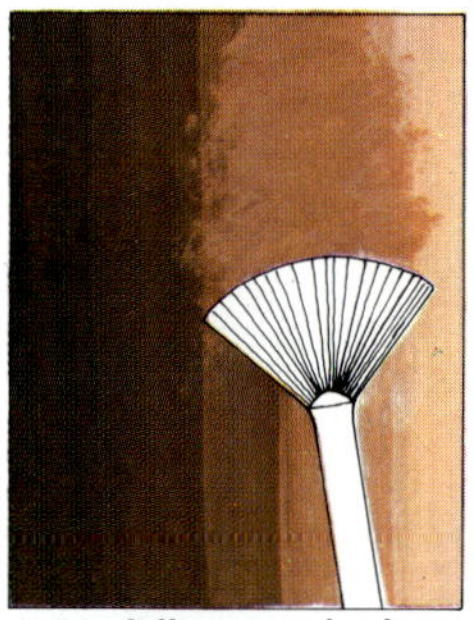

4. Modelling was built up in carefully gradated tones of light and shade. Flesh areas were smoothed and tones blended with a fan brush while the paint was still wet.

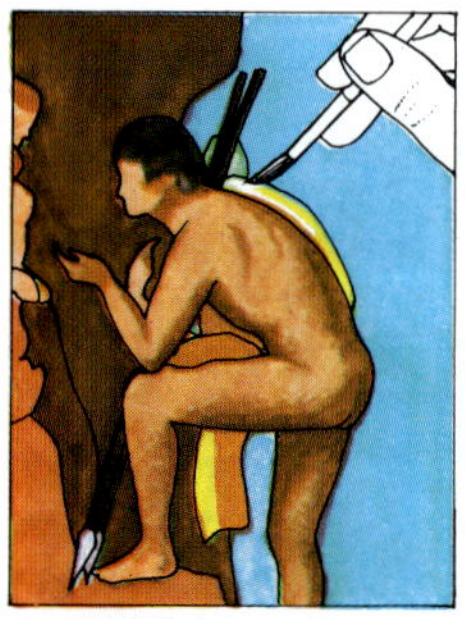

5. Highlights and individual accents of thick paint were added last.

Actual size detail
*Backgrounds, such as the sky and rocks, were created with thin unevenly brushed opaques which allowed the red ground to show through.*

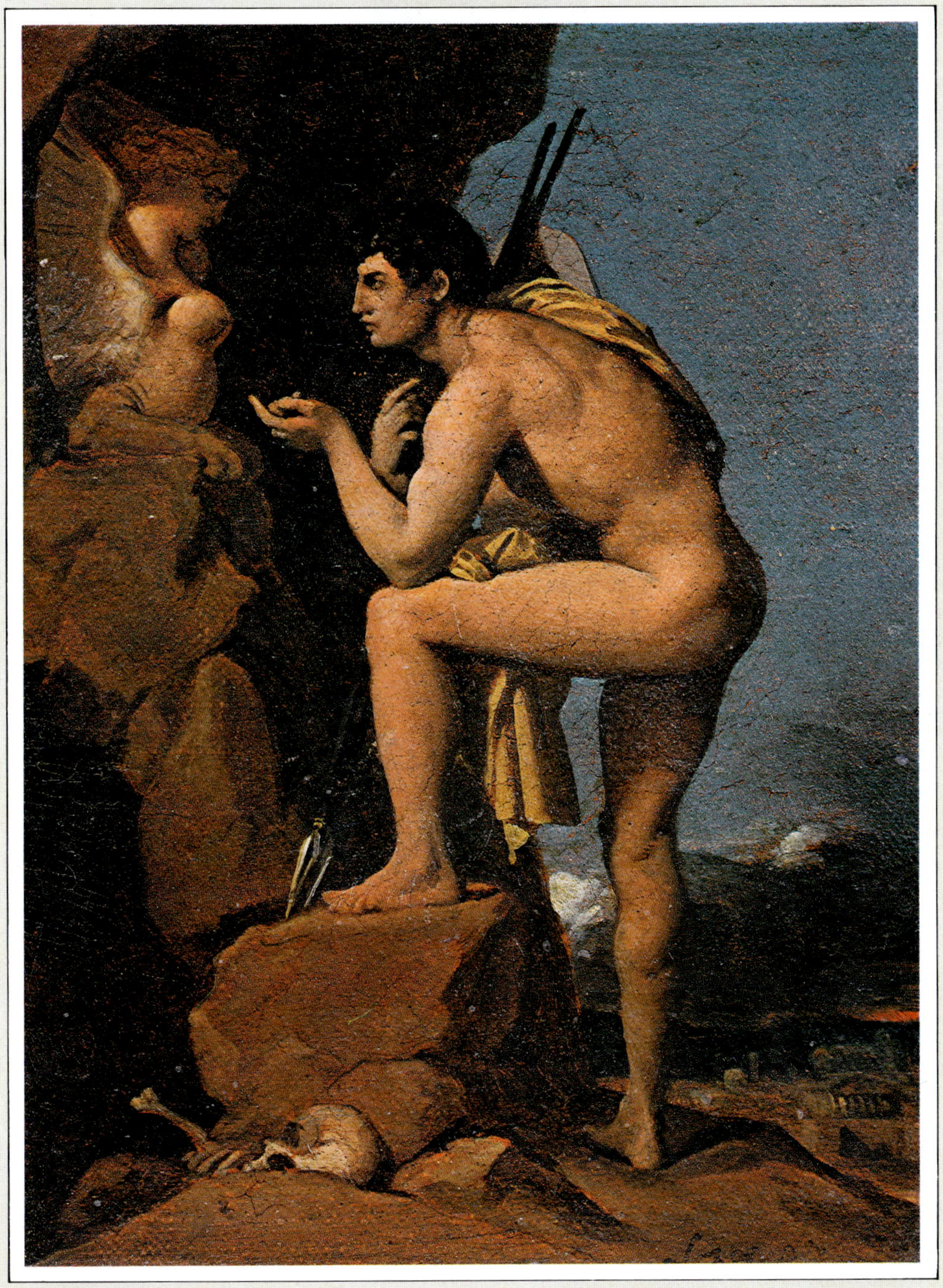

*The exposed canvas texture in this painting was unconventional for Neoclassical painting in which smoothness of finish was advocated. The weave is consistently visible in the painting and must have made the delicate handling of the paint difficult. Unusual for Ingres is the use of a dark red ground. The paint layer is thin and opaque. The ground is actively used to create an atmosphere of dark foreboding and warms the flesh tones. It is not, however, used as a middle tone as was common in* chiarascuro *painting. The paint quality is generally fluid and rich, and the background thinner and leaner. Ingres has used a sombre palette dominated by browns and earth colors, occasionally punctuated with brighter colors. Ingres rejected the then commonplace use of bitumen as a brown, because he recognized the dangers of using this transparent dark brown which never dried thoroughly and caused serious cracking and bubbling on numerous paintings of the period.*

# EUGÈNE DELACROIX

*Taking of Constantinople by the Crusaders* (1840)
Oil on canvas, 410cm × 498cm/161½in × 196in

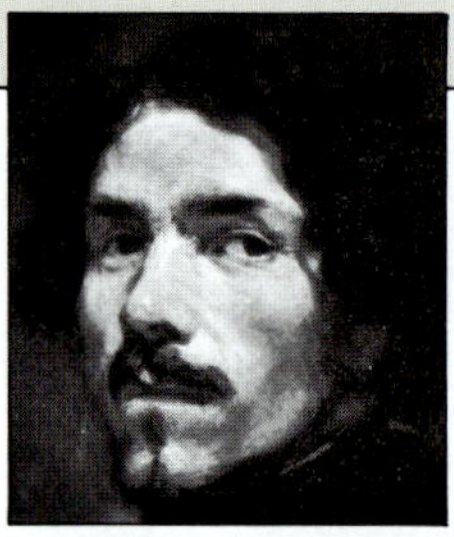

Delacroix, the great Romantic artist of nineteenth century France, received a Neoclassical training and, while his first major work reflected this in its frieze-like composition and sculpted modelling, the passionate, melancholic themes and coloristic genius that were to characterize the artist's mature work were already visible. Delacroix's handling of color in this early work was influenced both by Rubens and observations of nature, and was the starting point for his experiments in the juxtaposition of complementary colors, so influential to later painters like the Pointillists.

Delacroix's use of color combines the results of observing nature with a personal abstract quality. Thus, while the overall harmony created may owe little to recorded nature, the touches of complementary colors in the shadows and the rendering of reflected color show the artist's careful observation of natural effects. Despite his awareness of natural light, however, Delacroix never entirely abandoned the cool, studio light with its warm shadows.

Delacroix understood the importance of color in bringing a natural appearance to a picture and this, linked with the luminosity of shadows, which he observed in the work of Veronese, led him to replace the darks of traditional *chiaroscuro* with a more natural representation of outdoor shadows and reflected color. Delacroix made numerous watercolor studies and annotated drawings out of doors, was familiar with color theory, and experimented with absorbent grounds in the Venetian tradition. As well, he experimented with various media, and some of his recipes for working in oils over washes of water-based paint came from friends who were known to have painted theatrical scenery.

Delacroix's brushwork, like his color, has an existence almost independent of the forms represented, yet it is vigorously descriptive in evoking texture and building solidity. The paint is often thinnest where it depicts the turning of form in space, and thickest where it appears nearest the spectator. The handling of foreground and background are similarly contrasted, with immediate subjects painted thickly and boldly and distance created with a diminishing touch, thinner paint, and hazier definition.

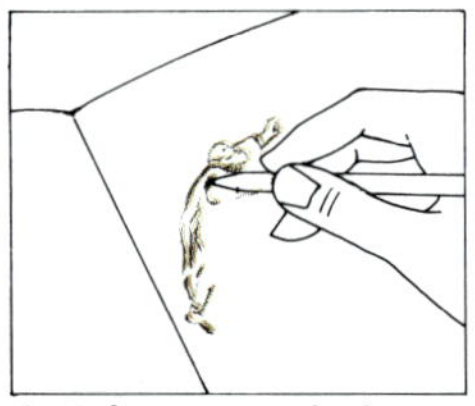

**1.** Delacroix worked from many preparatory compositional sketches, oils, and studies of individual figures.

**2.** The canvas was made to order and may have been one of Delacroix's experiments with absorbent glue-chalk grounds in which he wished to emulate the techniques of the Venetians or Rubens.

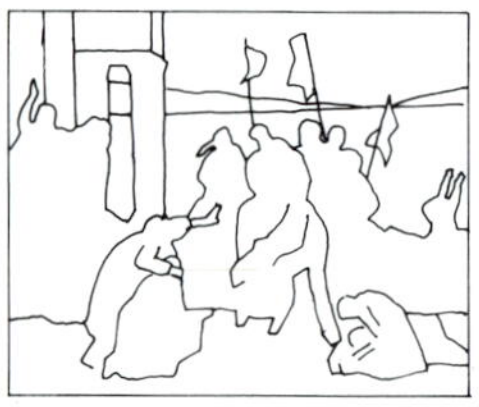

**3.** Preparatory drawing is no longer visible; dark brown contours and the main lines of the composition were put in followed by thin washes to establish masses of light and shade.

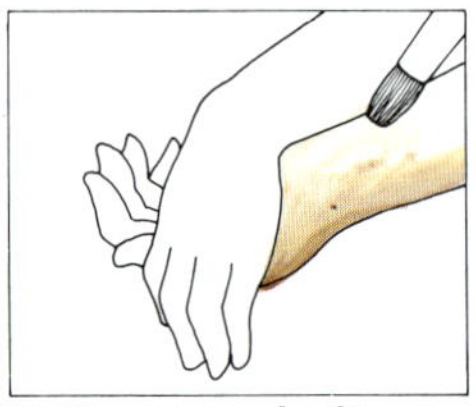

**4.** Forms were built up working from dark to light and both fairly loaded with color.

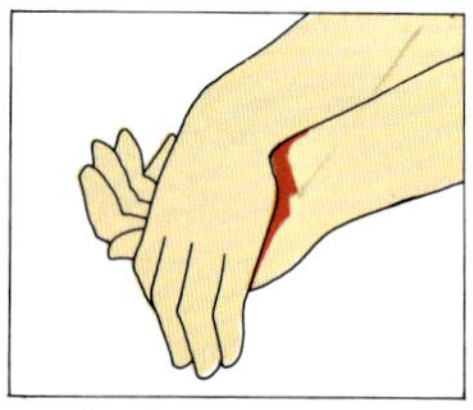

**5.** Shadows were reworked later in the painting process with additions of reflected color.

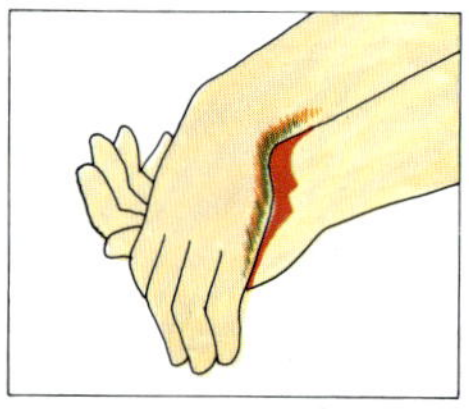

**6.** Contrasting individual strokes of orange and green were then added over dry paint to enliven shadows in the flesh.

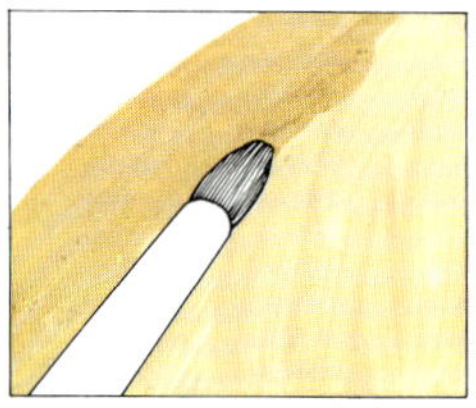

**7.** Contours were left thinnest with paint built up, for example on the flesh areas, to imitate the roundness of form.

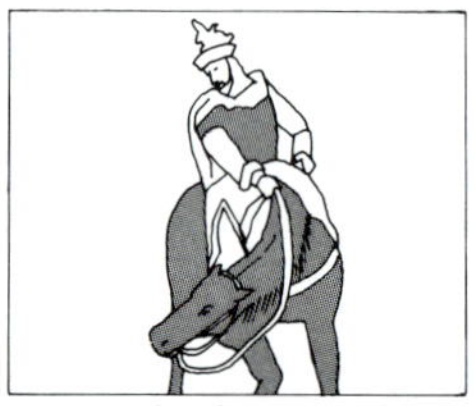

**8.** Details of texture, like the armor and horse's hair, were added loosely and thickly. Glazes were added, and, when these were dry, the painting was varnished.

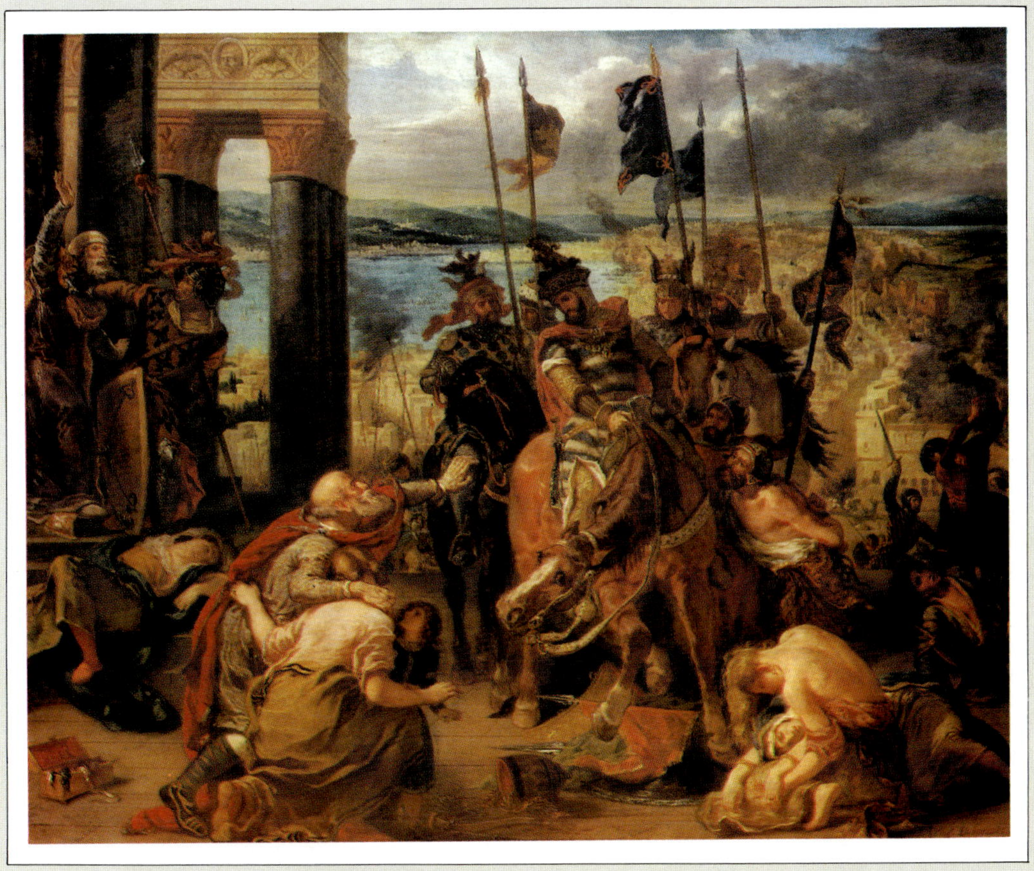

*The painting was executed on a pale ground which shows through where the paint is thinnest and most transparent. Colors are built up thickly and opaquely even in the shadows. The paint is thinnest where the contours depict the turning away of form, and most thickly applied where rounded forms project towards the viewer. The composition is split into foreground and background, with little middle ground. Generally, brushwork follows form and, on flesh areas, highlights are applied in a dry, pastel-like paint. Color contrasts are widely exploited with an extensive palette and color mixing.*

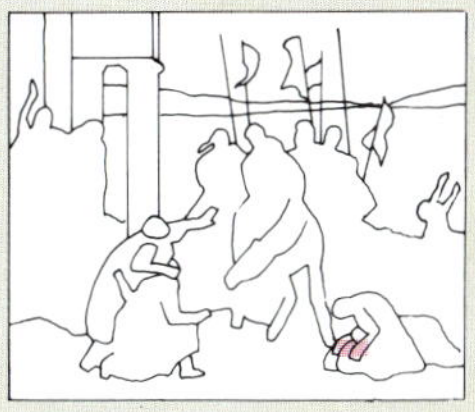

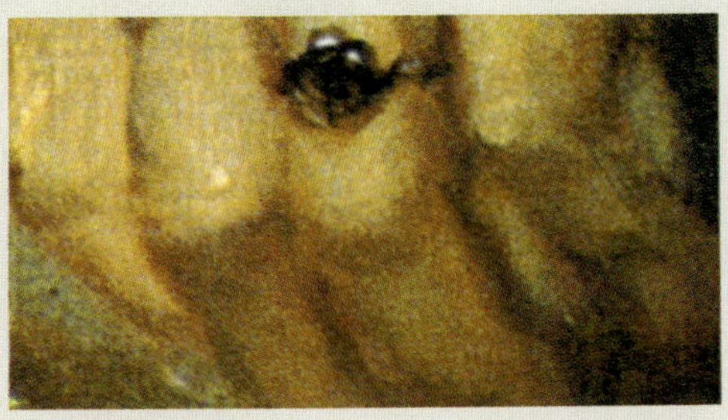

Actual size detail
*Delacroix's brushwork is lively and crisp in the foreground becoming softer, and more blurred to render distance in the background. The thick, juicy texture of the foreground paint changes to a thin, dry and scumbled passage in the background.*

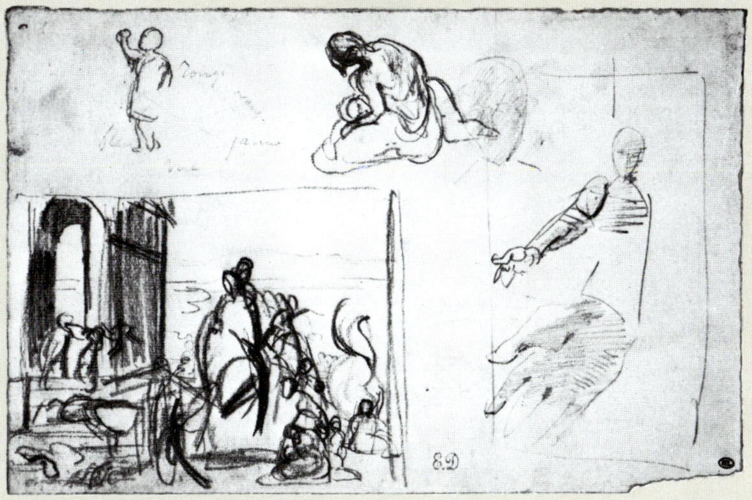

*This study for the* Taking of Constantinople by the Crusaders *was drawn in pencil by Delacroix in 1839 or 1840. The annotated color circle shown here as two overlapping triangles is the earliest definite proof of the artist's knowledge of the theories of complementary color contrasts published by Chevreul in 1839. Chevreul's theory reinforced Delacroix's own intuitive handling of color.*

# WILLIAM TURNER

*Snowstorm* (1842)
Oil on canvas, 91.5cm × 122cm/36in × 48in

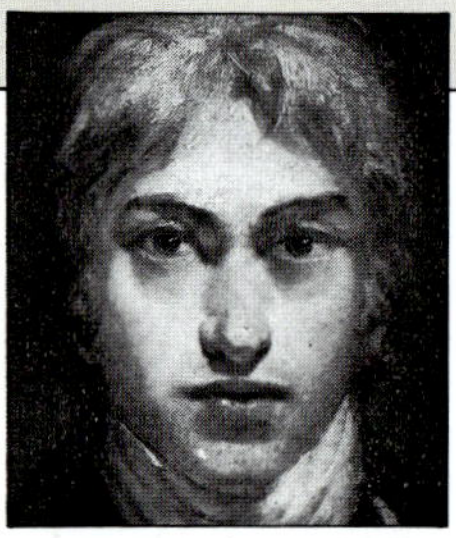

Born and bred a Londoner, Turner's precocious talent took him at the age of fifteen to the Royal Academy Schools and the Royal Academy Summer Exhibition of 1790. Nine years later, at the youngest permissible age, he was elected an Associate of the Academy which supported him through the criticism and misinterpretation which was to plague his career.

Turner was influenced by the architectural watercolorists with whom he worked as a boy, and his mature style combined a respect for the Old Masters, the ideals of eighteenth century artists, and the originality born of the individualism of the Romantic movement. He was also fascinated by the scientific ideas of his age and studied color and light theory, particularly the importance of yellow which was felt to be the closest color to 'the production of a white light'.

Turner's atmospheric light effects have been described as being 'invented', despite his commitment to work from nature. He preferred using pencil outdoors, as he found even watercolor time-consuming and inhibiting. In his early work, Turner exploited the dark warm grounds typical of eighteenth century landscapists; later, his grounds became paler and his mature works were generally executed on a white ground which enhanced and extended the brilliant colors which characterized Turner's palette. From the start, Turner adopted broad underpainting, using a variety of washed colors, rather than the more usual monochrome. Pinks, blues and yellows predominated in his underpainting which both established the composition and gave an emotive atmosphere to the coloring which was added subsequently.

Turner's use of colors, overlaid on the canvas rather than mixed on the palette, was described by a friend as approximating to 'the excellencies of Venetian coloring'. Turner depended as much on the use of scumbling as on glazing, but always the softness of these effects was counteracted by the tough and abrupt application of a thick, dense paint surface. This process of superimposing thick layers, toning them down and then returning to them was a source of fascination in Turner's technique which produced, in the in the words of a contemporary: 'solid and crisp lights surrounded with ethereal nothingness'.

**1.** A white, fairly thick oil ground was first applied on a plain linen canvas.

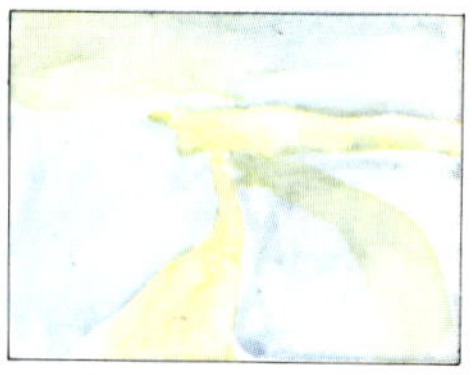

**2.** Underpainting followed using bright colors diluted with turpentine.

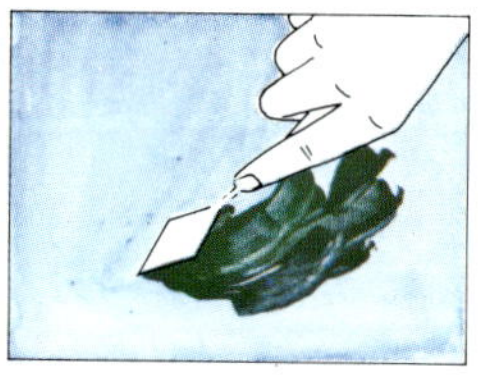

**3.** Stiff, thick layers were brushed on or applied with a knife, sometimes wet over dry to create jagged, swirling effects.

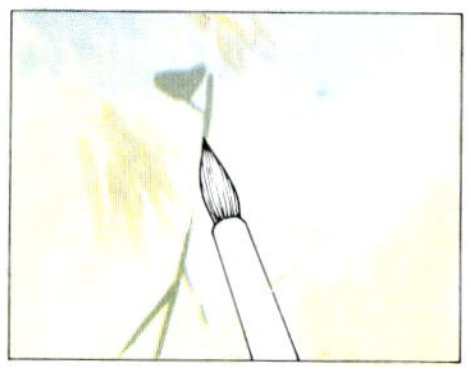

**4.** Thinner paint was applied with a brush to delineate outlines and details, and compositional changes made.

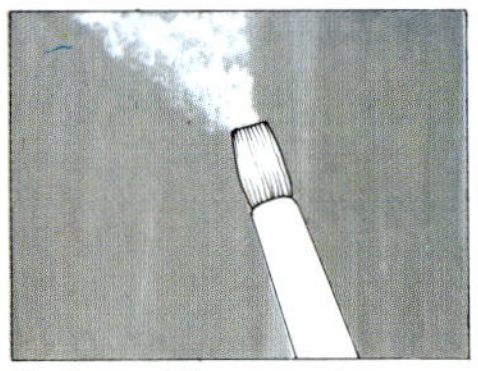

**5.** Scumblings and glazings were then worked over dry paint to enhance the richness of the color and evoke an ethereal quality.

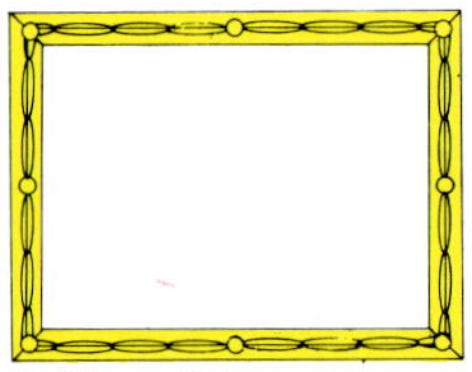

**6.** The painting was varnished and framed, gold being Turner's preference.

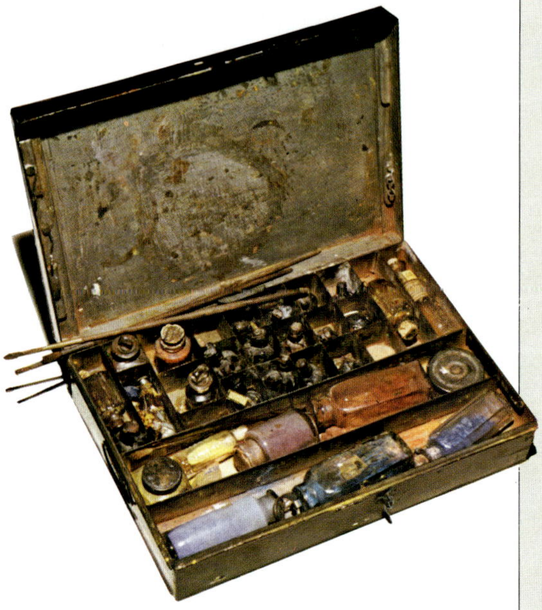

Above
*Turner's paintbox shows some of the main equipment and materials he used. Powdered pigments were kept in glass bottles with cork stoppers. Prepared paint was stored in small bladders which can be seen at the back of the box. These containers were not very reliable, and metal tubes introduced from around the 1840s proved much more satisfactory.*

*Turner seems to have used fairly large round and flat bristle brushes.*

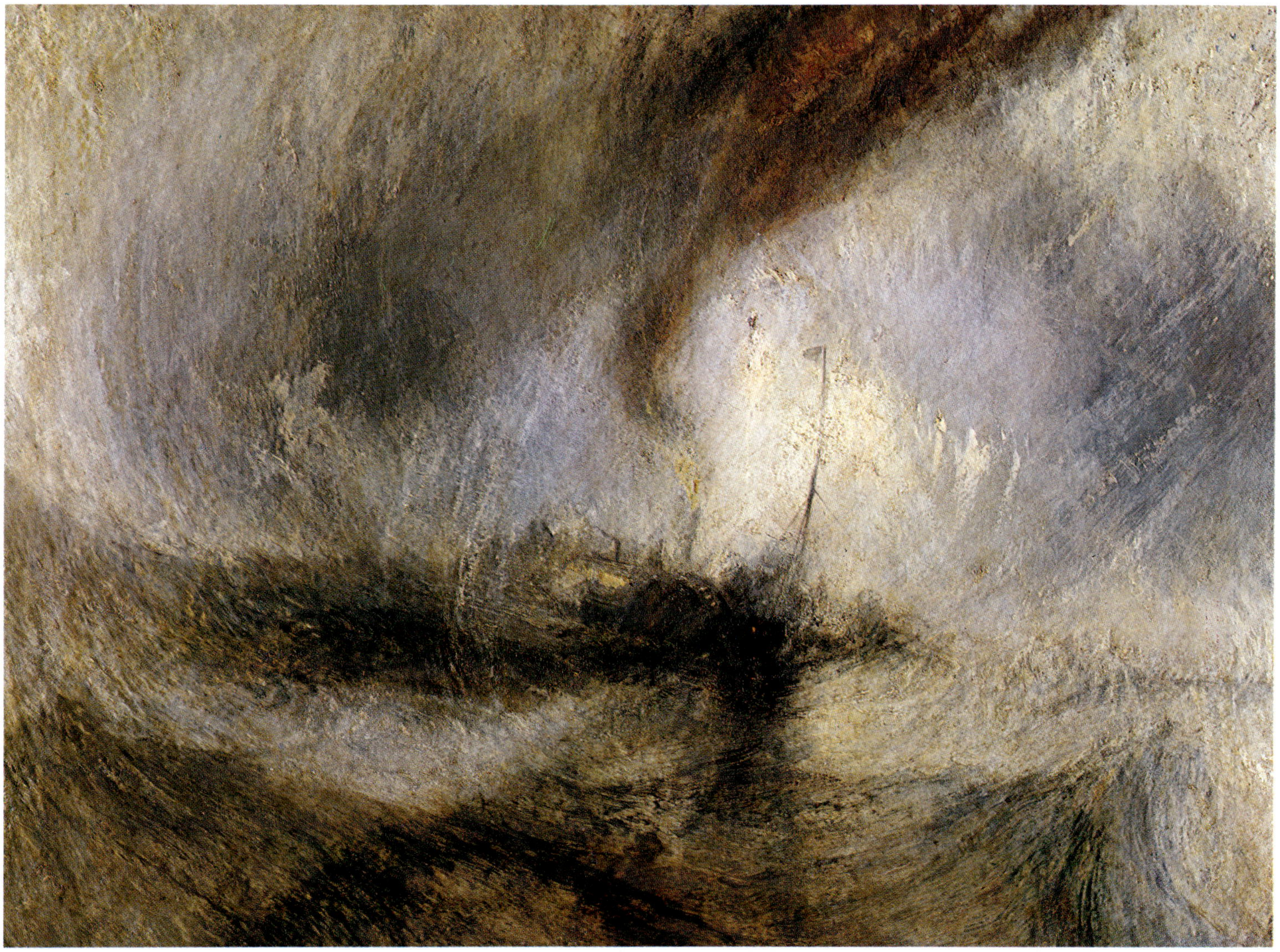

*Turner often used double canvases with two layers of linen left loose. These were often primed on both sides for protection. The canvas texture was not used in the painting process due to the thick ground. Thin washes were probably used to create the chief compositional structure, although they are no longer visible. The paint surface has been built up by the over-laying of stiff, impasted colors dragged over one another to create a broken effect. The paint quality is dryish with blacks and dark glazes added in a thin consistency. The paint is concentrated mainly on the development of lights using dirty white and yellows in scumblings and impasto worked wet over dry.*

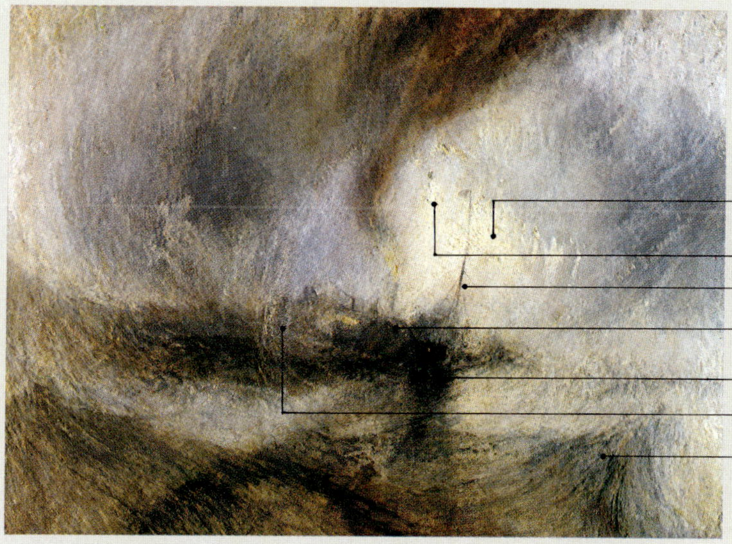

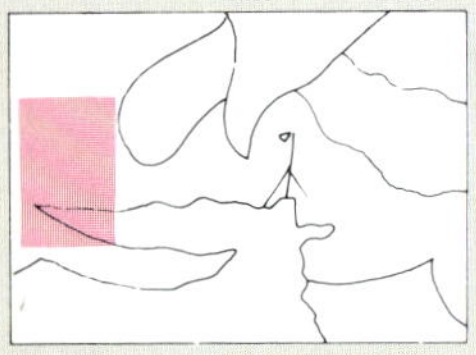

**Right**
*Thick layers of stiff impasted color were reworked with scrapings of dryish off-whites and creams, which were dragged across the irregular surface to give a jagged, crusty effect. Thin darks and scumbled whites were built up over dry color in alternate partial layers. Both a painting knife and stiff hog's hair brushes were used.*

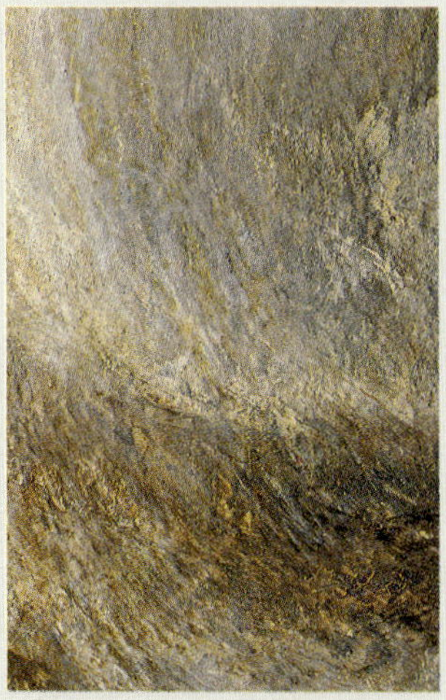

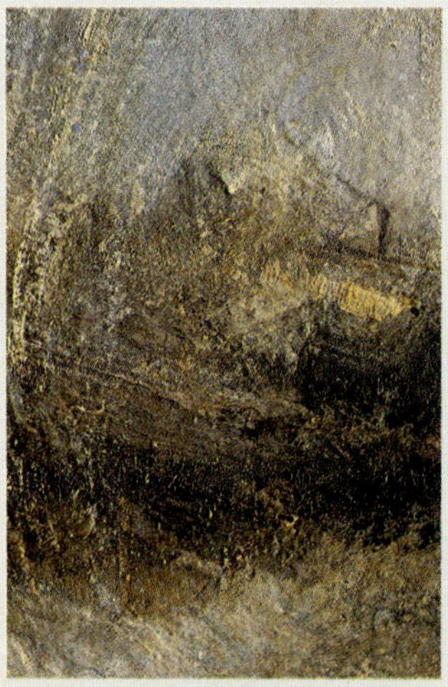

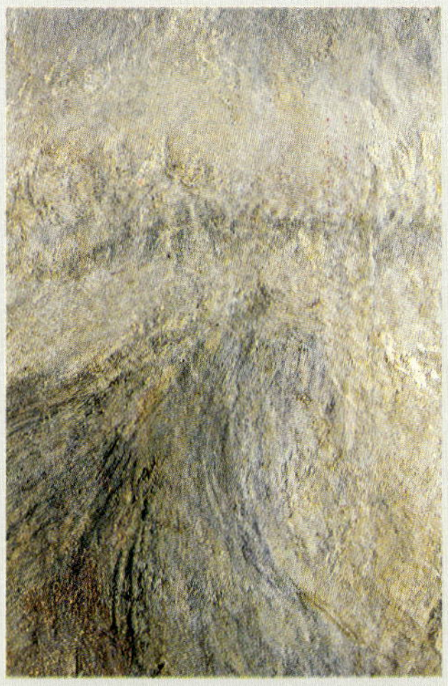

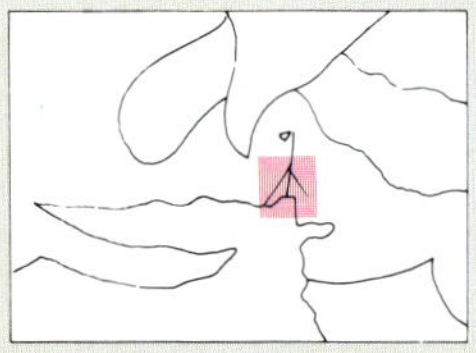

**Actual size detail**
*Turner's thick application of paint can be readily seen in this detail. While the lighter yellow areas have been applied almost certainly with a knife and stiff brush, the fine details of the mast and rigging were done with a soft, sable brush. Turner built up broken whites and yellows first with scumbles and thinner glazes of darks applied after. Turner would rework these with thick scrapings of dryish white paint, dragging further layers of thick, dryish paint across the textured layer to create his atmospheric, hazy effect. The fine cracks in the paint surface indicate its thickness, and perhaps Turner's tendency to add extenders and stiffeners to the paint.*

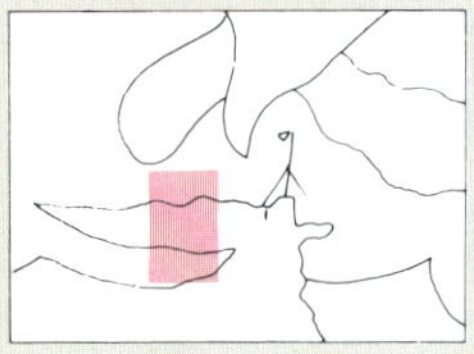

**Top middle**
*Although Turner is considered to have referred less frequently to nature in his mature and late works, he did stress the importance of observation in this picture, recounting that he had himself been lashed to the mast of the packet-boat Ariel to record the scene. However, the impracticability of such a method would suggest the record was imprinted in his excellent memory rather than on canvas on the spot.*

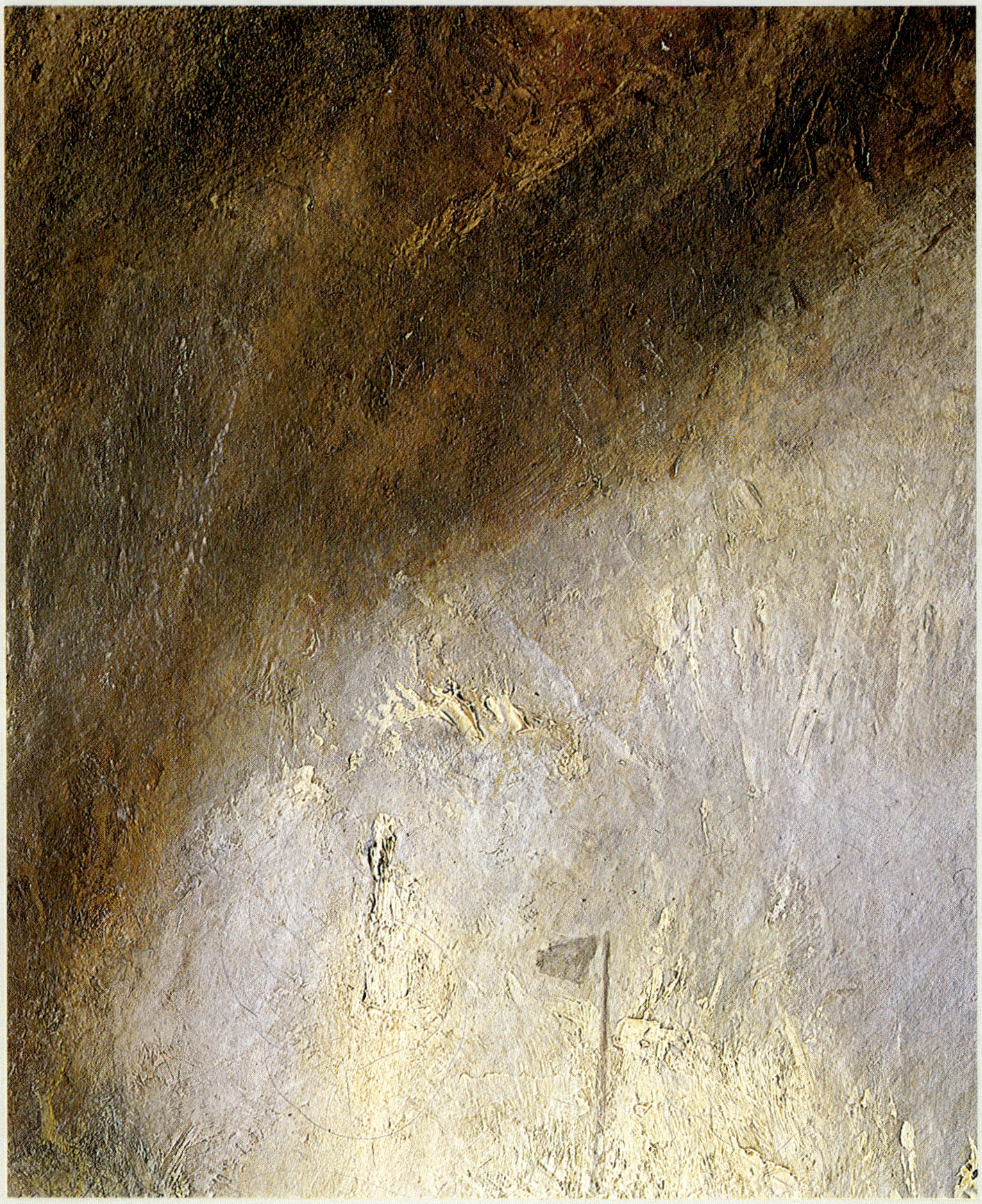

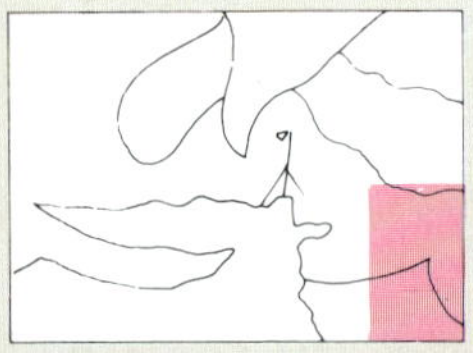

**Top right**
*Turner's almost feverish striations of irregularly applied thin and thick, dark and light paint evoke the swell and movement of the stormy sea. This builds up over the whole canvas, where the marks suggest a clockwise movement around the central pivot of the boat. This creates a swirling vortex which depicts wind-whipped sea and snow.*

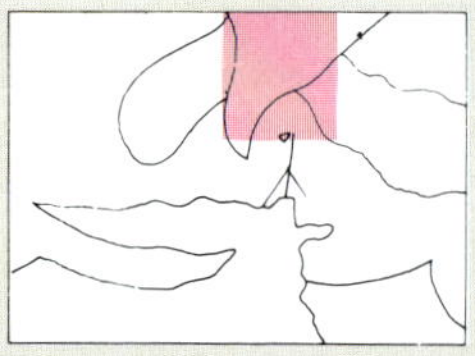

**Left**
*The stiff, buttery yellowish paint knifed on here as part of the central focus of the composition is a reminder of Turner's notion, culled from contemporary scientific theory, that yellow was the color which most closely approximated the phenomenon of white light. Using a variant of classical landscape compositions, he concentrated the lightest parts in the cente rof the picture.*

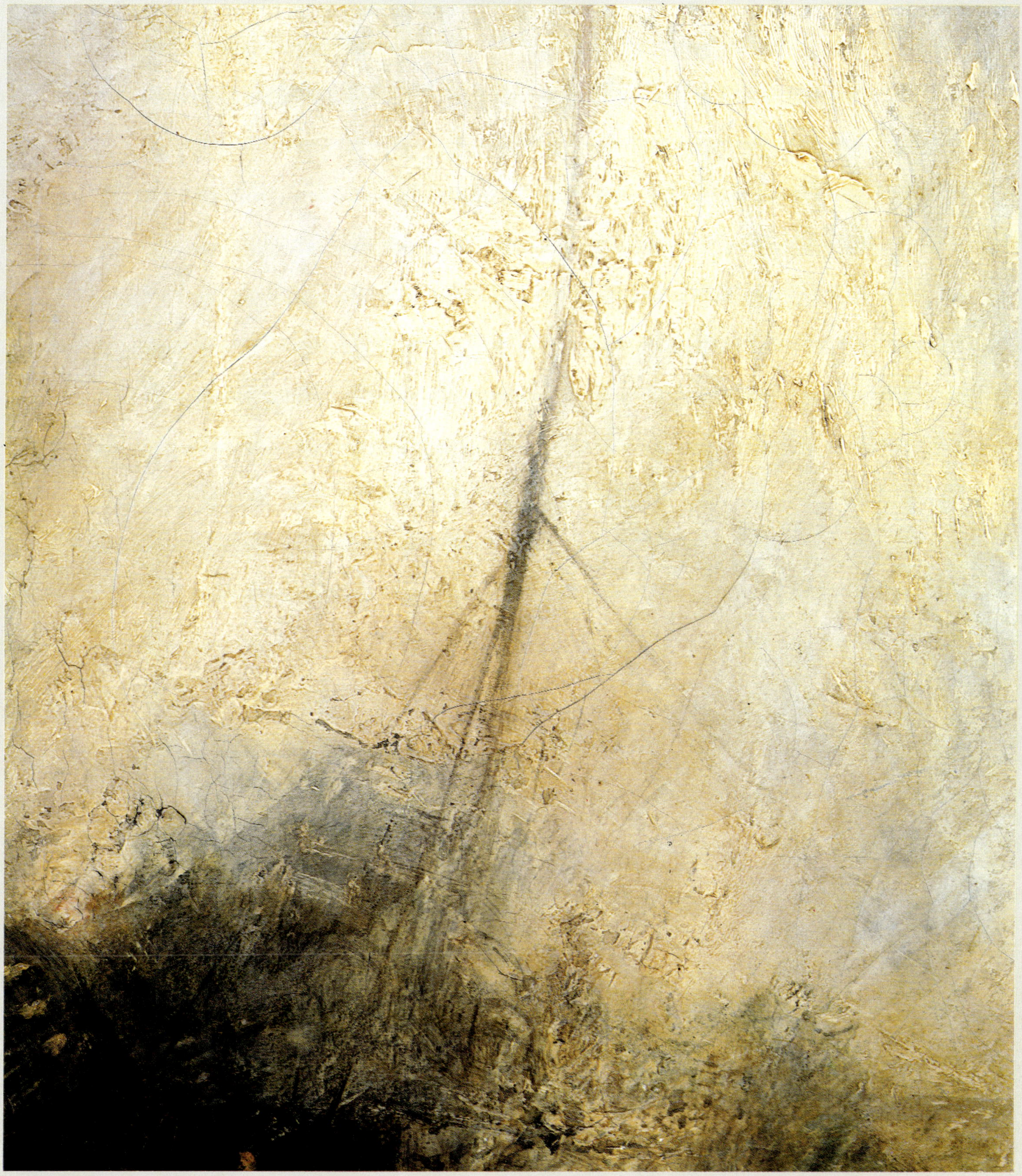

# JEAN MILLET

*The Walk to Work/Le Départ pour le Travail* (1851)
oil on canvas, 55.5cm × 46cm/21⅞in × 18⅛in

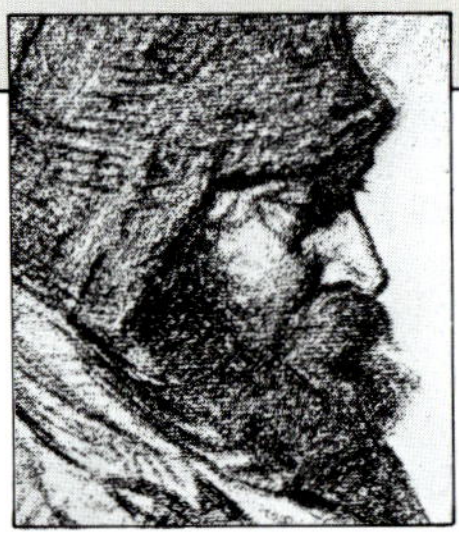

Influenced by Poussin, Michelangelo, Dutch seventeenth century painters, and French eighteenth century art, Millet immortalized the agricultural worker brought to the fore by the Revolution in 1848. Although a well-read and educated man, Millet's Realist subject matter reflects his peasant origins. His subjects included the labors of the field, times of day and seasons and, generally, the unending toil of the laborer on the land.

Millet worked from memory, studies from life, and models posed in the studio. He was not an out-of-doors painter, and his is the cool light of the studio with its warm, contrasting shadows. Often employing the earth colors, Millet's paint surfaces echo the soil which he painted. His heavily worked shadows and lights are in the tradition typified by the eighteenth century French still-life and genre painter Chardin. Late works exploit brightly tinted grounds giving an effect of colored light.

The paint quality is stiff and impasted in the highlights, thin and fluid in the middle tones and shadows – a traditional method, although elsewhere, Millet's shadows are unconventional in the heavy use of impasto. There is an active dialogue between the paint layer and ground in the darks and middle tones; impasted areas obliterate the ground but maintain the brilliance of pale areas which, over a dark ground, would sink with time. Modelling of flesh is handled with simple contrasts of light and shade with most of the middle tones suppressed. Millet's crusty paint surfaces were enlivened by dragging stiff, dryish color across dry paint on textured canvas, creating a characteristic stippled, broken effect.

Millet's graphic techniques were comparable to his oil techniques in their power to evoke texture and light. His large pastels in particular were built up with a web of pale powdery color strengthened by firm, fluent outlines of skilled draftsmanship, which are alsoseen in his paintings.

His handling of water in oil paint exploits the transparency and opacity of the pigments to imitate natural effects. Thus, the transparency of water in the shade of dark reflections is rendered with fluid, thin, transparent browns over a pale ground, while the surface reflections of sky and light are represented by opaque, broken whites and blues.

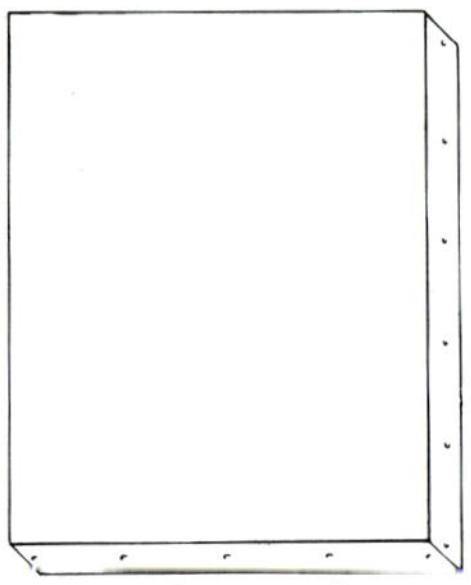

**1.** A ready-primed canvas was used on which a thin ground of white or off-white had been applied.

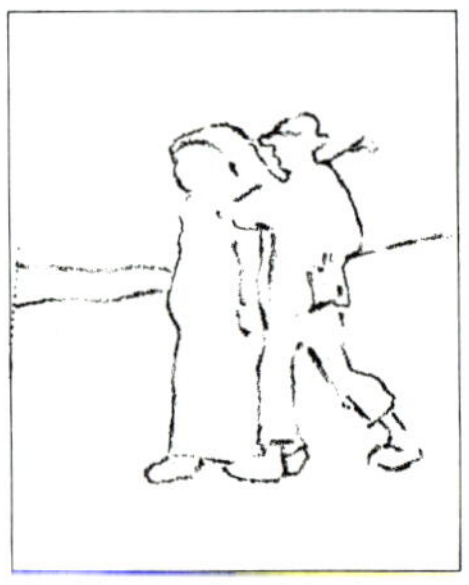

**2.** Charcoal or black chalk was used to establish the main compositional lines.

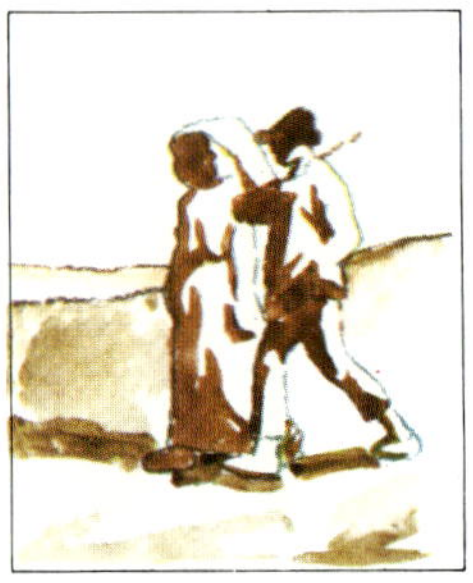

**3.** A thin wash was used to strengthen outlines and lay in main shadows: raw umber for landscape and burnt umber for figures.

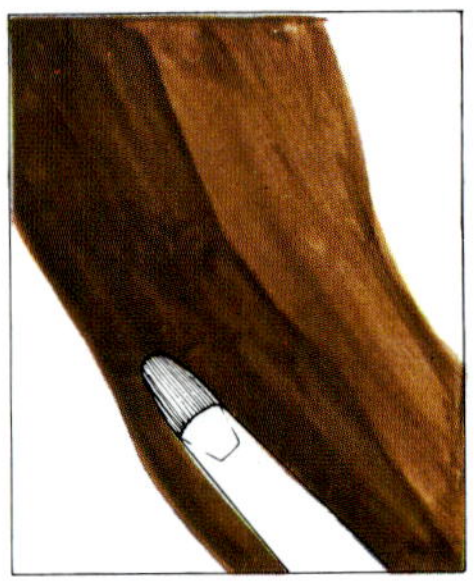

**4.** Highlights and deeper shadows were then added, with the initial wash showing through to create the middle tones.

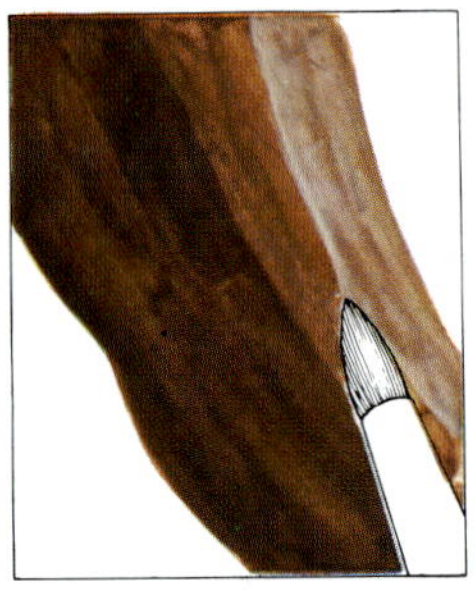

**5.** Thick, opaque lights were applied in a dryish crusty paint consistency.

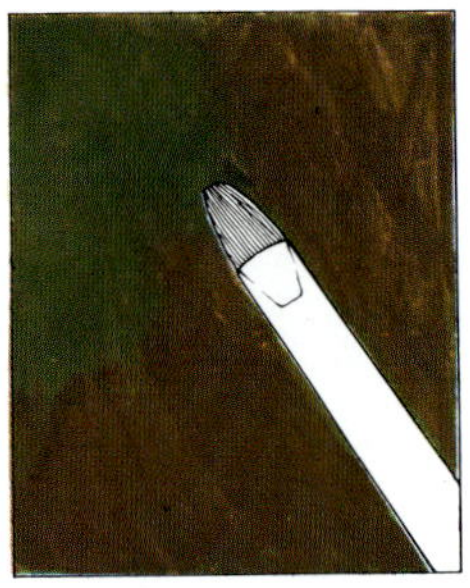

**6.** The landscape was worked very lightly with an opaque greenish scumble whose translucency allowed the initial wash to show through.

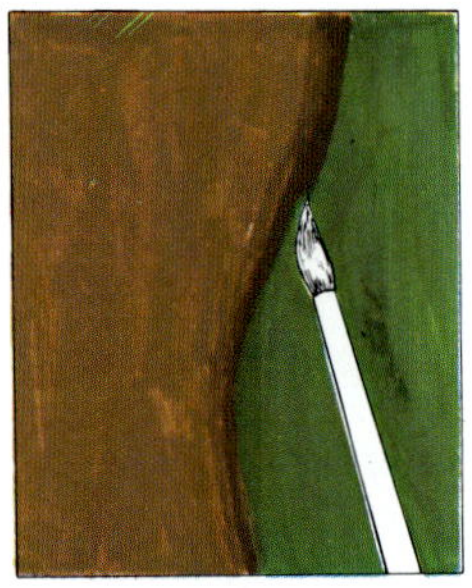

**7.** Contours were worked and strengthened with a soft-haired brush and diluted umber.

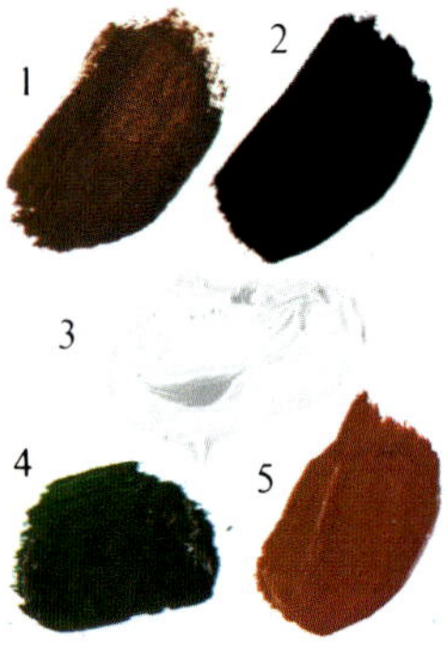


In this work, Millet used the following colors: earth colors (**1**), black (**2**), white (**3**), a mixed blue-green (**4**), iron oxide red or vermilion (**5**).

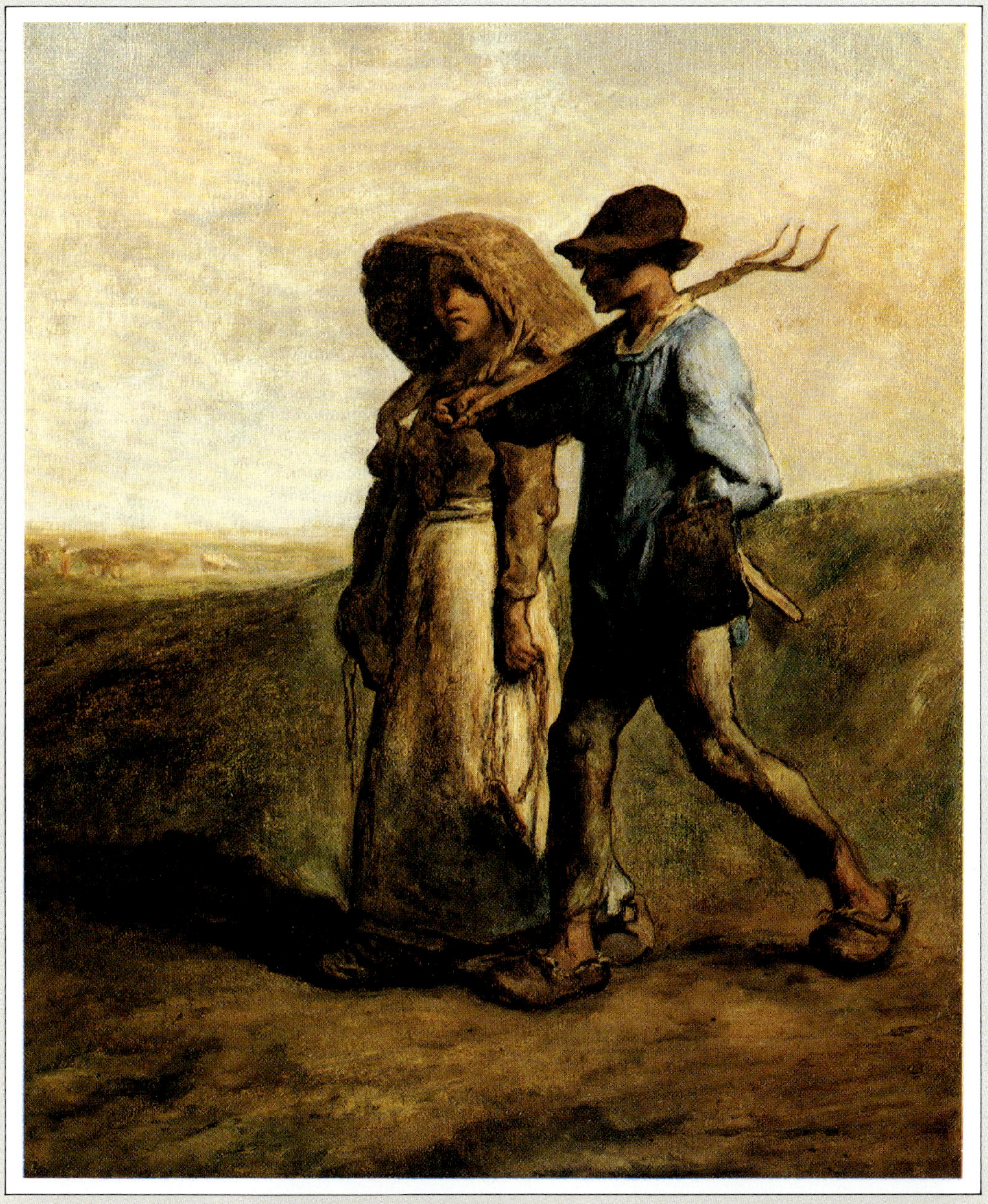

The Walk to Work *is typical of Millet's treatment of light in the stiff impasto and contrasting use of thin, transparent passages which reveal the pale ground beneath. The light comes from two conflicting sources, the back and side. Millet used a* chiaroscuro *technique in the manner of Dutch and Flemish painters to create this dramatic lighting. The brushwork is graphic and descriptive, evoking forms and textures. Millet used a limited, subdued palette dominated by earth colors, black and white. A mixed blue-green recurs throughout Millet's work, and an iron oxide red is used to add warmth.*

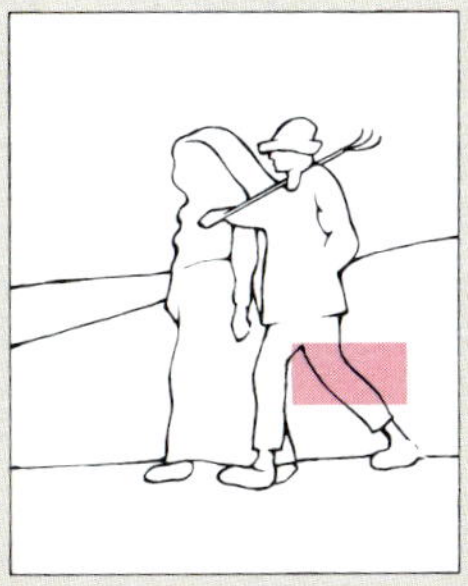

*This detail shows how Millet used the initial blocking-in of forms with a thin umber wash as a middle tone. The dark paint has gathered in the interstices of the canvas weave, giving a speckled appearance where the white ground glows through the thin transparent umber to create depth in the shadows. A thin scumble of opaque green has been laid over the browns to indicate the grassy background.*

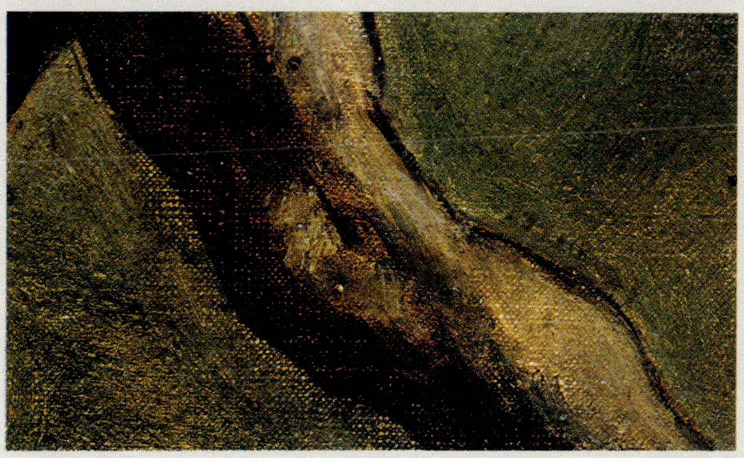

The Gooseherdess *is another painting in which Millet exploited contrasts between loaded impasto in the lights and thin transparent films in the shadows. The contrast is here used effectively to imitate the natural appearance of water with its transparent depths and reflected opaque lights; it makes an interesting comparison with Monet's entirely opaque handling which also creates a remarkable illusion of water.*

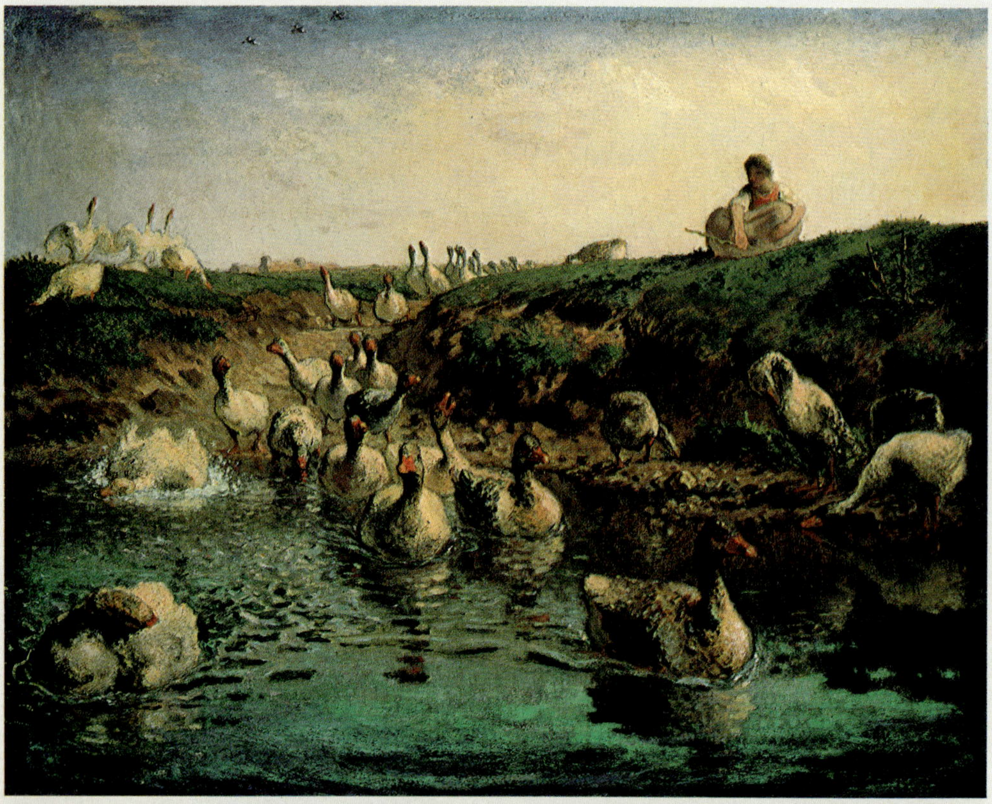

*In Millet's confident, draftsmanly execution, the brushstrokes follow the form of the clogs, while the man's legs are sculpted in strong contrasts of light and shade concentrating upon the muscular form beneath the barely indicated trousers. Further working might have built up the texture of fabric on the underlying form. Thin transparent darks reveal the white of the ground and the texture of canvas, and thin opaque scumbles separate the background from the figures.*

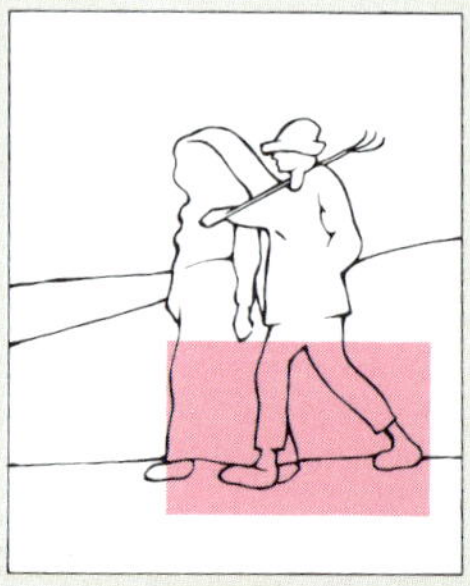

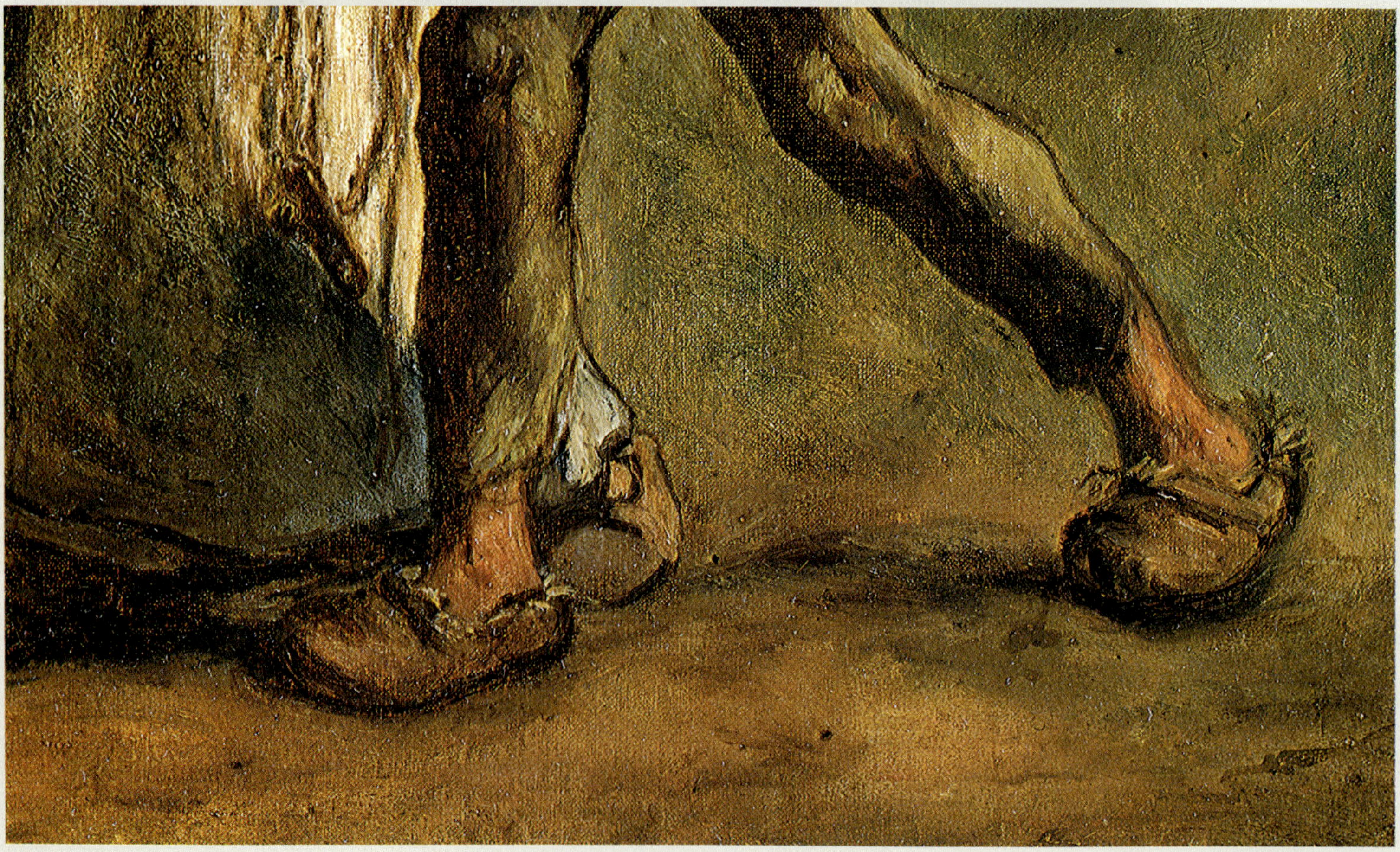

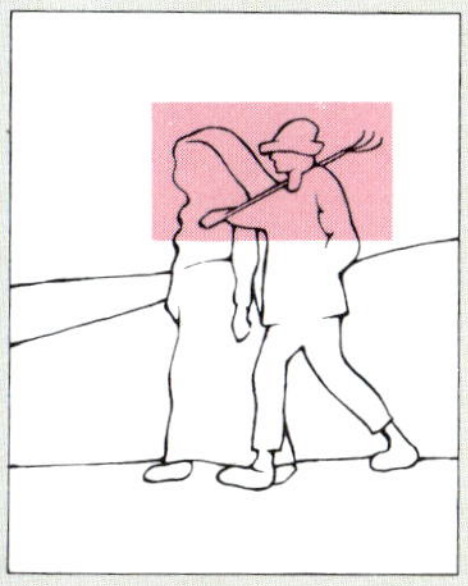

*The side light catches the heads, sculpting them in simplified blocks of opposed light and shade; both are equally loaded. Stiff brushwork is clearly visible in the creamy paint of the sky, which was worked up around the outlines of the heads. A strong dark contour has been left visible following the line of the man's neck. The shape of the pronged fork has been accentuated, the original curve of which has become visible with time as the stain of raw umber has appeared through the pale paint of the sky. The power of the image is enhanced by the shadows which add weight to the figures.*

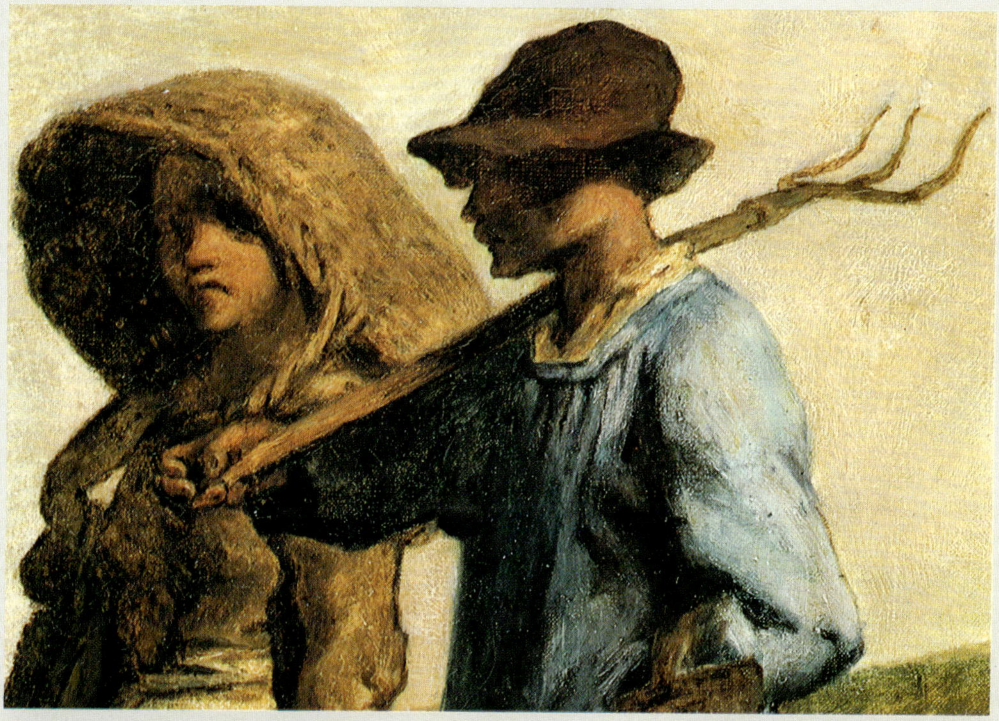

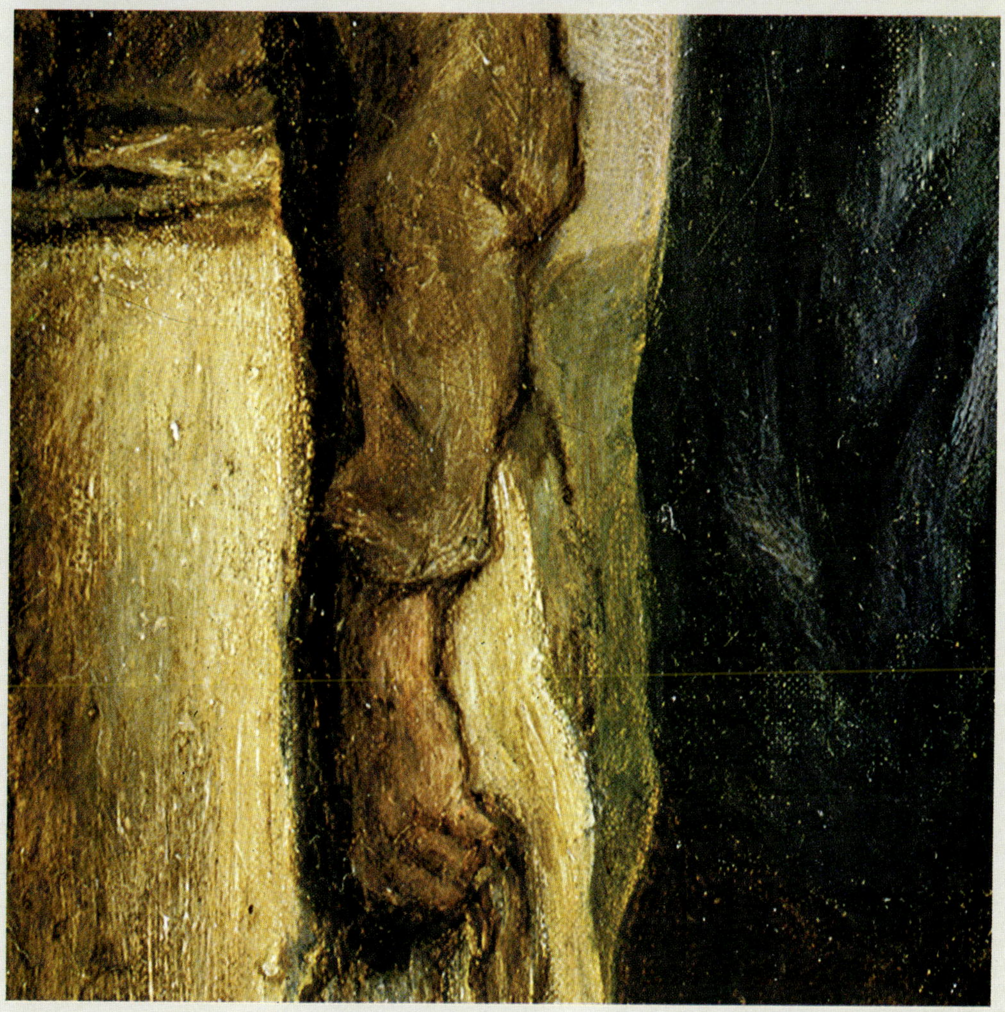

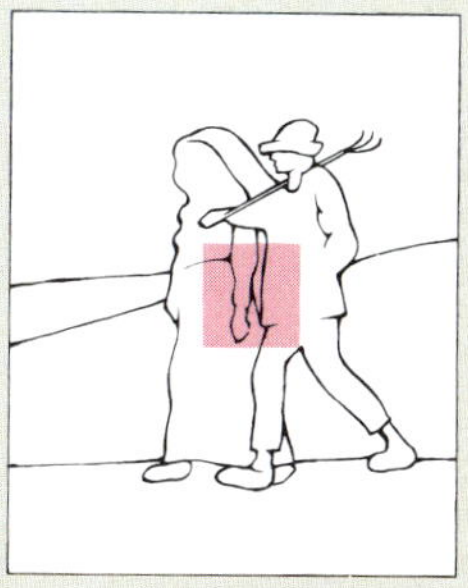

*Millet's vigorous handling and simplified, statuesque forms give a timeless grandeur to the harsh reality depicted. The stiff, buttery paint consistency retains each mark of the brush, which is exploited to convey the rough texture of home-produced fabric and the coarseness of work-hardened skin. Millet's surfaces were described by a critic as of 'a paste thick like mortar, on a harsh rough-grained canvas, with a brush broader than a thumb . . . this dish-cloth canvas daubed with och e r and black.' However, this summary underestimates the subtlety and delicacy of Millet's techniques.*

# WILLIAM HOLMAN HUNT

*The Awakening Conscience* (1853)
Oil on canvas, 76.2cm × 55.8cm/30in × 22in

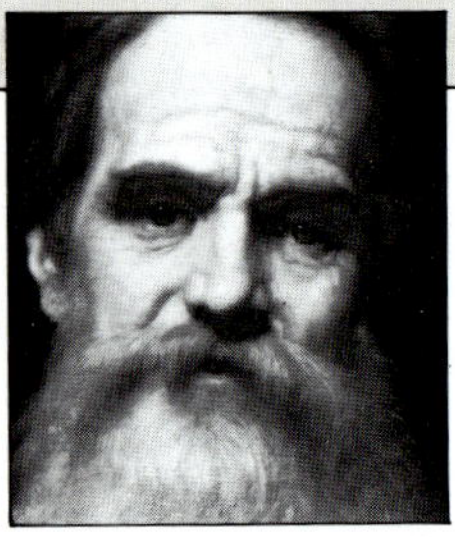

This painting had been chosen as a relatively early example of the work of the Pre-Raphaelite Brotherhood which was founded in 1848 and of which Holman Hunt was a founder member. Other members included John Everett Millais and Dante Gabriel Rossetti. The Pre-Raphaelites, as their name suggests, tried to emulate works of the *Quattrocento*, but, to achieve their results, they used the newest possible materials. For example, Hunt used recently introduced pigments such as emerald green, which had first been prepared in 1814. The group discussed the kind of painting which they felt would revolutionize their art and also shared their experiences with materials and techniques. The members of the group later diverged, but Hunt stayed closest to their original aim of rejecting the idealization of nature associated with Raphael and his successors and returning to a more immediate and realistic representation of the world, combined with a rather romantic view of medievalism.

Technically, Hunt was both well-informed and cautious, comparing his use of materials with those of the Old Masters. Hunt placed great importance on the permanence of his support, medium and pigments, and rejected those which he knew to be faulty. For example, he avoided the mistake of using bitumen as a brown, which has caused many nineteenth century paintings to deteriorate. He followed closely the experiments of the chemist George Field, who was concerned with the permanence of colors. Hunt used a rich and relatively thick medium made of poppy oil and copal resin. Hunt found that this medium was easy to work and did not contract excessively on drying; it remained tough and flexible even when applied thickly. This indicates the quality Hunt desired in an oil painting, which is illustrated by his criticism of the thinness of Gainsborough's paint, which gave an effect 'too like that produced by a watercolor to be satisfactory in a large painting'. *The Awakening Conscience* is typical of Pre-Raphaelite work in its moral emphasis and realistically depicted detail. The lavishness of the room and of the woman's dress and jewelry reflect the material rewards of her sin in becoming the man's mistress. The gilt frame is an integral part of the effect of tonal and textural richness which Hunt wished to create.

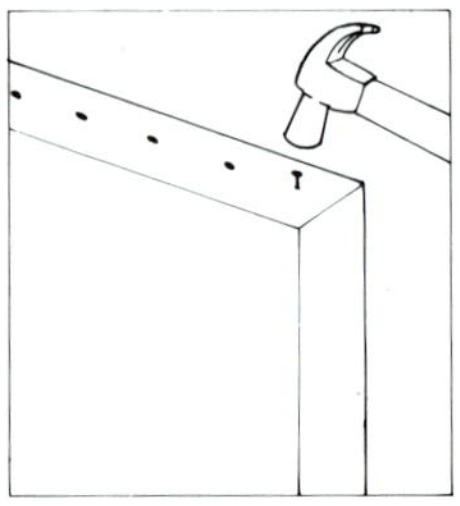

**1.** The original canvas was made of fine plain linen, ready primed with a thin white oil ground. It was probably ready stretched with a 'blind' stretcher, which protected the back of the canvas.

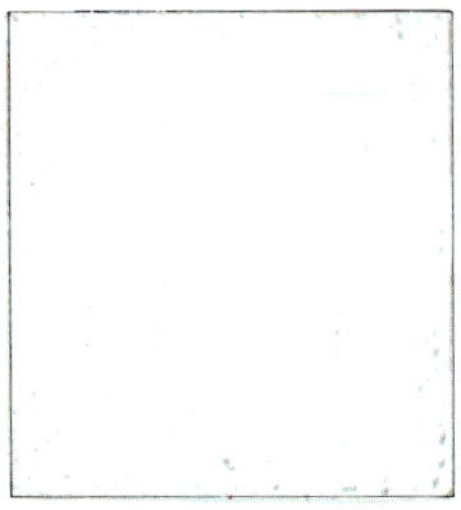

**2.** Although the canvas and stretcher came from a good and expensive colorman, Hunt was not satisfied with the ground. He applied at least one further layer of white pigmented oil ground. This produced a thick, smooth layer.

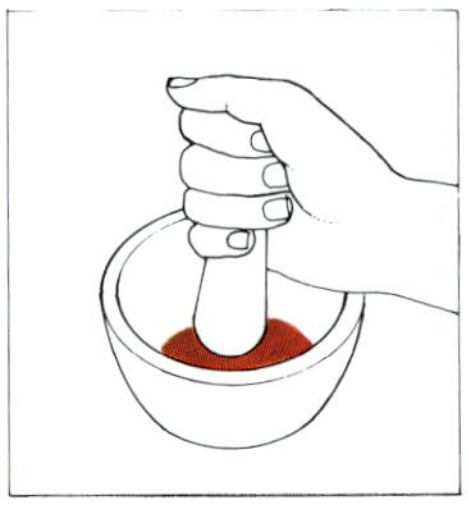

**3.** To make his medium, Hunt melted copal resin, dripping it into warmed turpentine and then added equal amounts of oil. He probably used either poppy or stand oil. He then ground the pigments into this medium.

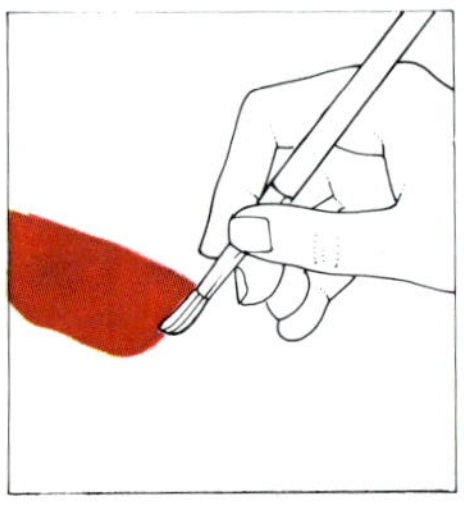

**4.** He chose the medium as it is easy to work, does not contract too much on drying and stays tough and flexible even when applied thickly.

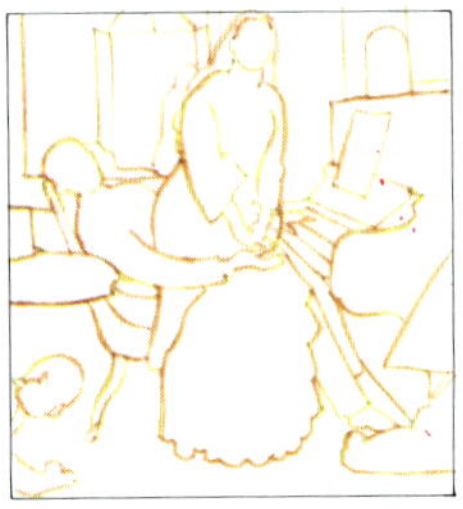

**5.** Hunt now drew the composition using paint thinned with rectified spirits of turpentine.

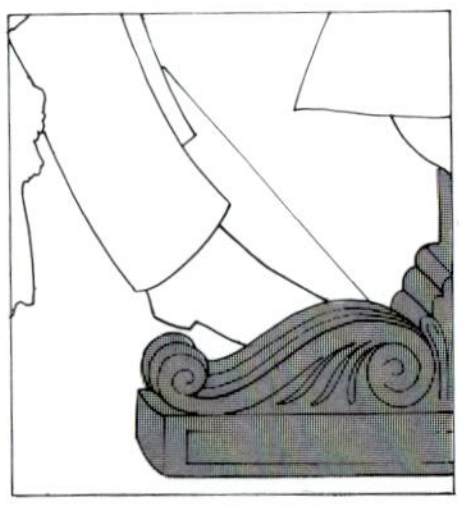

**6.** Hunt applied the paint to an area and worked until the finished effect was achieved before moving on to the next area. The shadows were created by applying scumbles and glazes over the priming.

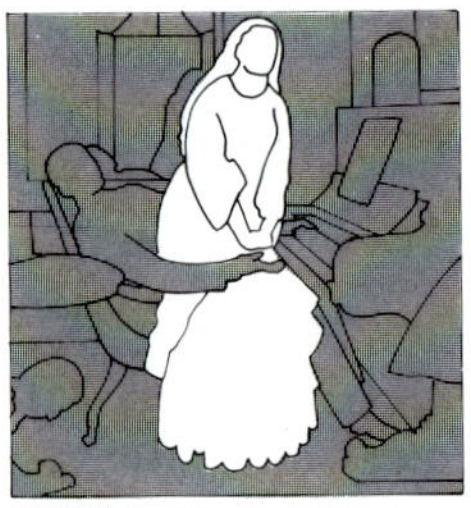

**7.** When the painting was complete, Hunt applied mastic varnish to all the painting except the main figure. Varnishing was standard practice; it was intended to be glossy and saturate the colors.

**8.** The picture was placed in a carved and molded wooden frame which had been applied with gilt. Hunt designed, and possibly made, the frame himself.

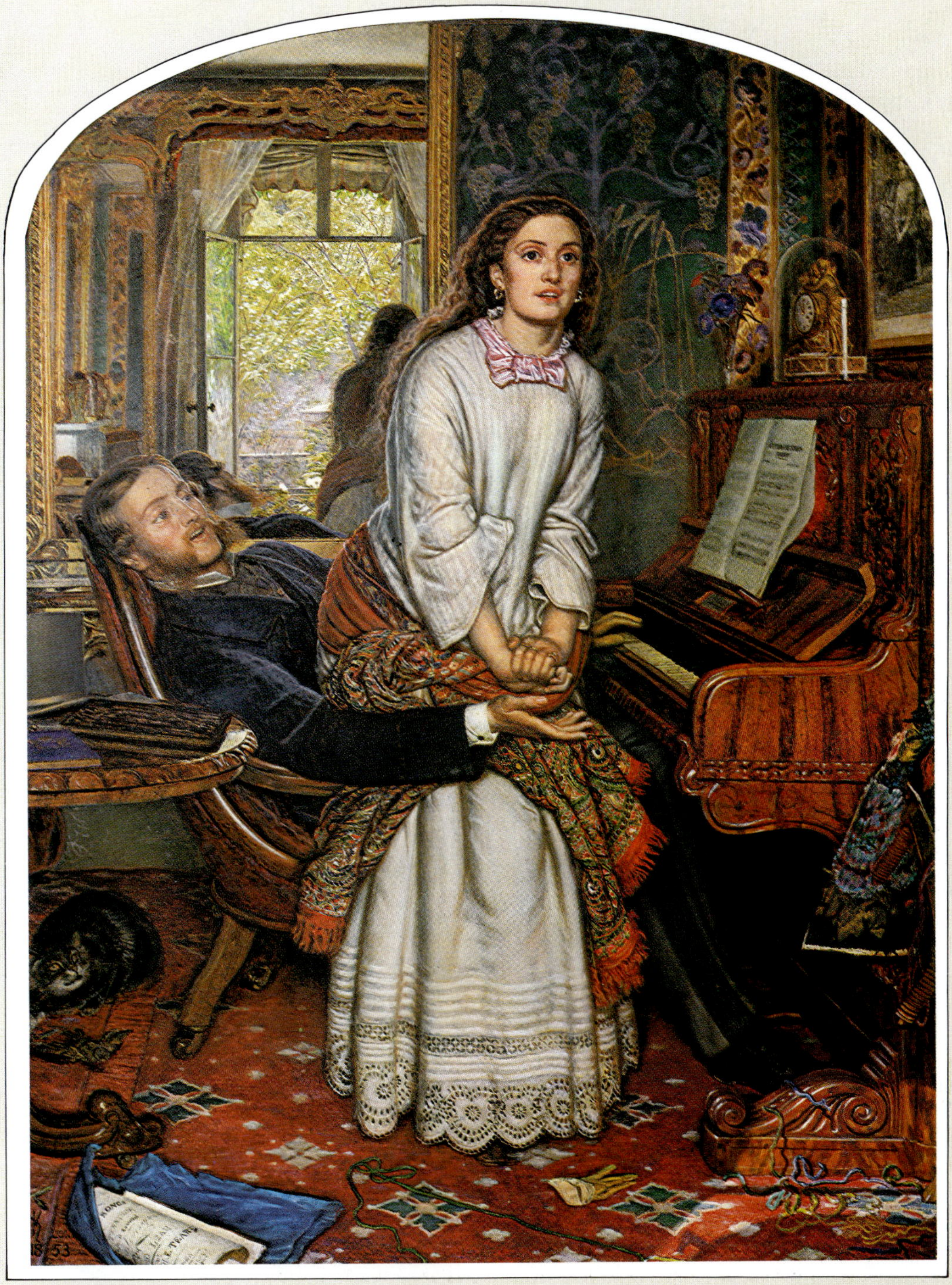

*The picture illustrates a moral in a heavily emphasized way. The woman, who wears no wedding ring, is the man's mistress. She is shown at the moment of realizing her sin. Her face was originally more contorted, but Hunt was persuaded to change it as the owner of the work found it too distressing. Hunt later regretted making the change. The alteration, however, cannot be detected in the picture. The painting is realistic in detail but not in terms of proportion or perspective. All the important objects are in focus and given equal priority. The draftsmanship appears uncomfortable when viewed from a distance. Hunt had problems in placing the man's arm, the reflections in the mirror are confusing and the folds on the woman's dress are a little contrived. At the end, a layer of mastic varnish was applied to the whole area, except the face; this led to the paint cracking. This area was later retouched. Nowhere is the ground exposed. It lends intensity to the strongly colored areas, but the light highlights are completely opaque. This technique combines well with the versatile medium and bright pigments which Hunt used.*

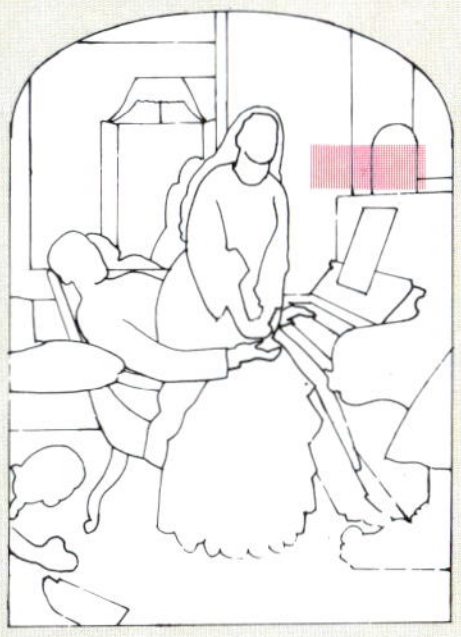

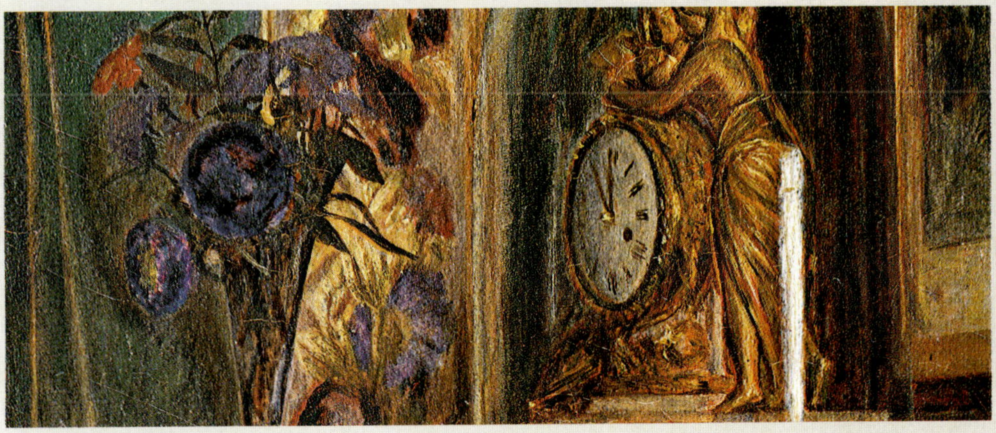

Actual size detail
*This detail shows different styles of painting. The imprecise treatment of the picture and the wall contrasts with the precision of the clock and flowers. A thick, treacly medium was applied evenly and worked patiently until the correct effect was produced. The highlight on the clock case is a thick, white brushmark, applied on top of the rest of the paint, while the flowers were painted relatively thinly with no impasto.*

# GUSTAVE COURBET

*The Meeting or Good-day Monsieur Courbet* (1854)
Oil on canvas, 129cm × 149cm/57in × 58¾in

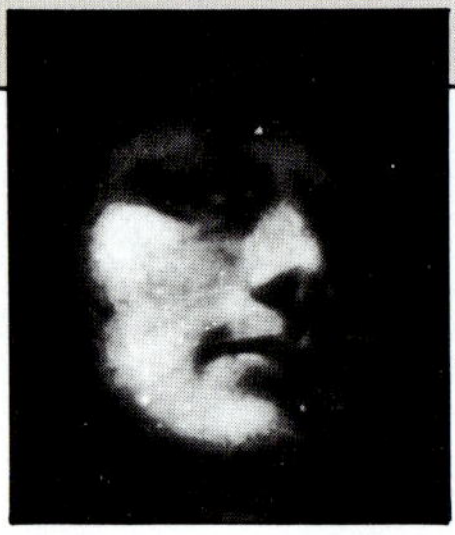

Leader of the Realist movement in painting, Courbet brought new meaning to a style which, during the 1830s and 1840s, had given a rustic and charming view of rural life to the Parisian public. Not only was his class-conscious subject matter alien to both public and critics, but his uncompromising and vigorous painting technique, evolved specially to treat rural themes, was highly innovative. Courbet's subject matter was largely autobiographical, immortalizing the common people, the middle and labouring classes of his provincial home town.

Monet recalled that Courbet 'always painted upon a sombre base, on a canvas prepared with brown'. This statement, however, is deceptive. While Courbet used earth-colored grounds for his largest works, for smaller pictures he bought commercially available, ready-primed canvases with pale grounds and, when the ground did not suit his requirements, he simply added his own. In some of Courbet's works, especially the seascapes, where a dark ground was used under a thin paint layer, increasing transparency of the latter has allowed the ground to dominate and darken the original effect.

Courbet's robust paint surfaces echo the subject matter of his pictures and his frequent choice of shallow pictorial space was complemented by the rich plasticity of paint handling. He was renowned for his dexterity with a palette knife with which he applied thin skins of opaque color that snagged previous layers, producing a delicately, color-modulated surface. The application of paint with a knife draws the oil binder to the surface and, while susceptible to yellowing with age, the technique gives a smooth buttery look unobtainable by other means. Courbet contrasted knifework with textured brushwork, which he often reserved for flesh, fabric and hair. Other methods, like dabbing color with a rag to create the texture of foliage, were also used.

Courbet's sombre, predominantly tonal handling gave his landscapes the browns of studio shadows, imposing the *chiaroscuro* of interiors even on his outdoor studies. His late seascapes, however, show a move towards the cool blue shadows and diffuse light which are associated with natural atmospheric contrasts and effects.

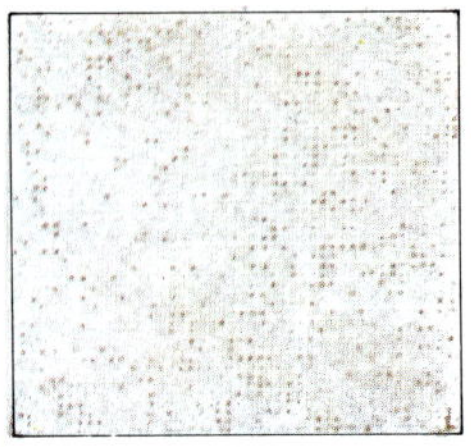

**1.** A ready-primed, non-standard format canvas was used with a thin white ground, leaving the canvas texture strongly in evidence.

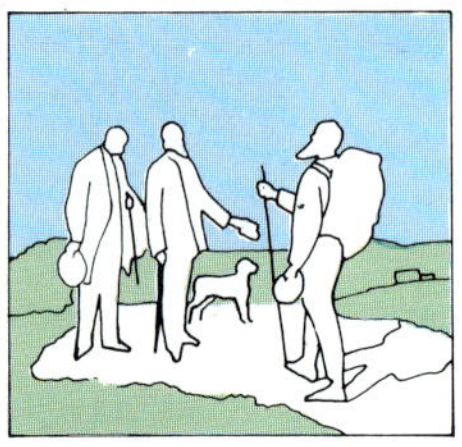

**2.** Figures and details were sketched in with thin brown paint and the background indicated with finer brushwork.

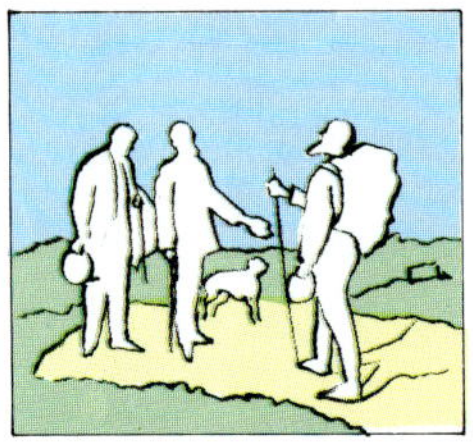

**3.** A thin, knife-applied skin of raw umber provided the base color under the road; elsewhere scumbles of local color were laid in broadly.

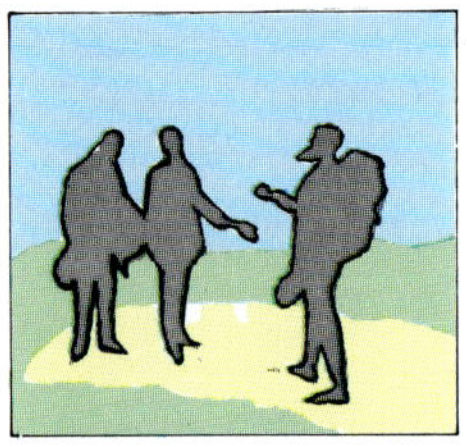

**4.** Figures are carefully and fully worked up with bold but delicate brushwork.

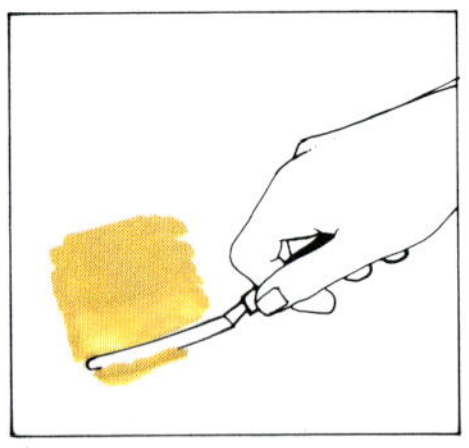

**5.** Courbet used a knife for the layered ochres of the road and fine dragged brushstrokes to evoke the distant landscape.

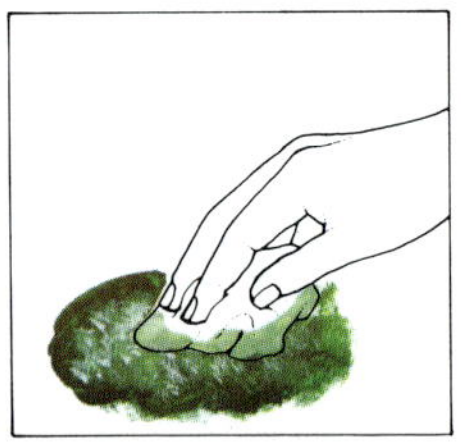

**6.** Texture of foliage was created by dabbing the picture with a crumpled rag dipped in paint. The painting was varnished upon completion.

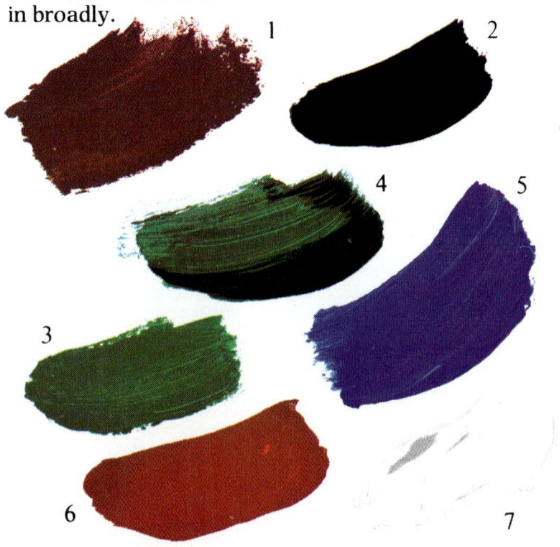


In this work, Courbet used a fairly sombre palette of: earths (**1**), black (**2**), viridian (**3**), mixed greens (**4**), cobalt blue (**5**), iron oxide red (**6**), lead white (**7**).

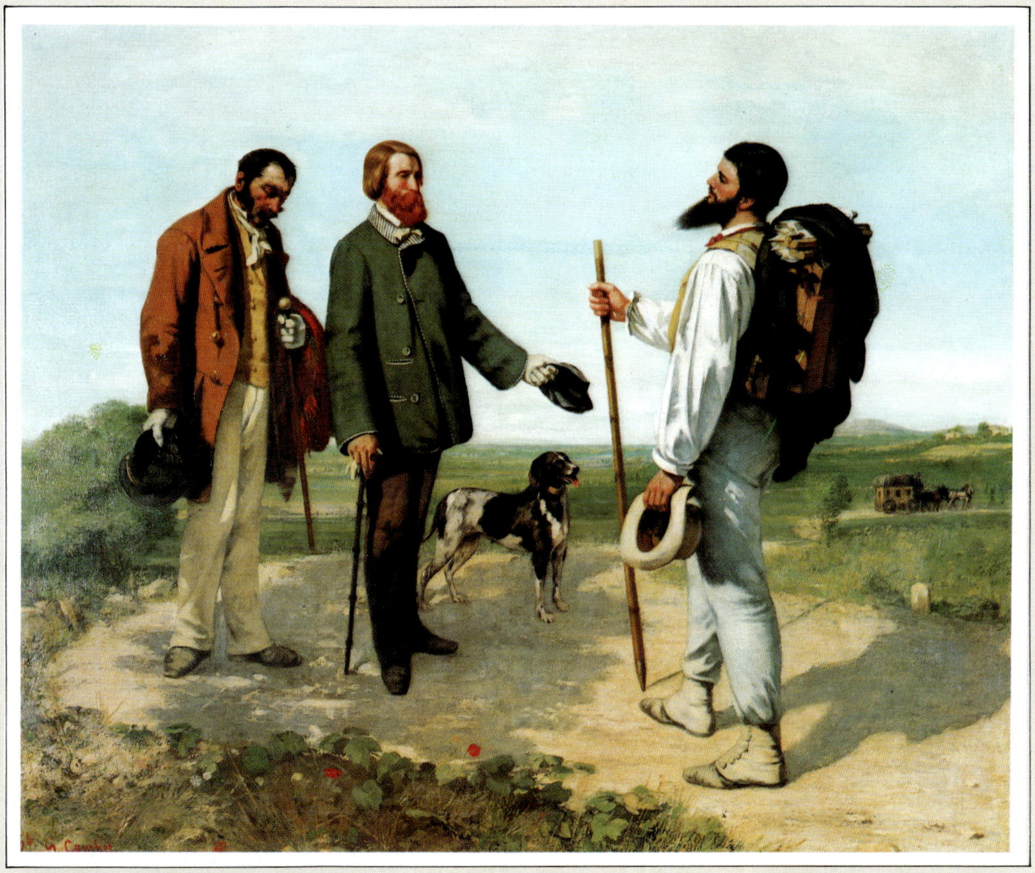

*In this painting, Courbet's practice of laying in a dark ground over the pale commercial priming has been abandoned to convey the luminosity of the bright, Southern light. A variety of techniques evoke form and texture; dragged layers of knife-work, wet-in-wet, and color dabbed on with a rag. The paint layer is varied in thickness, but uniformly opaque, with white lightening a subdued palette dominated by earths, black, viridian, mixed greens, and blue, probably cobalt. Concentrating on the figures, Courbet worked from dark to light and shadow to highlights, with constant adjustments to both.*

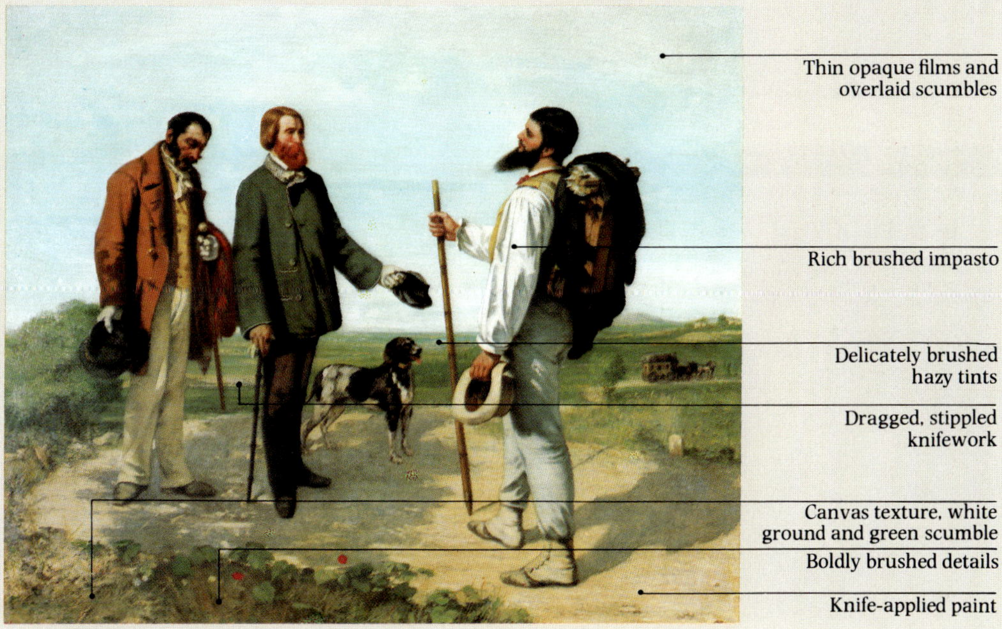

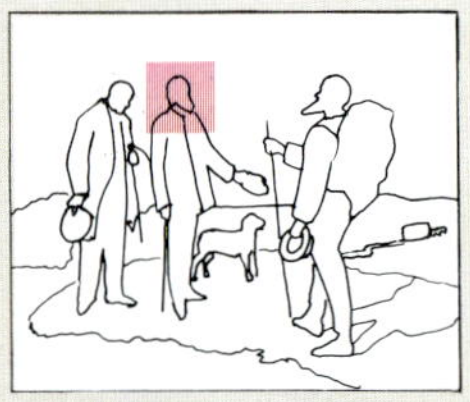

*The light comes from front left, accentuating the central figure's strong nose and profile. Colors are opaque and broadly but deftly handled in general masses of light and shade, stark against the pale blue of the sky.*

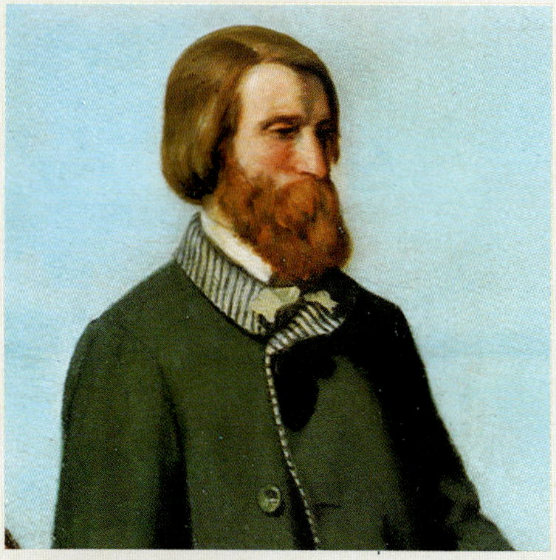

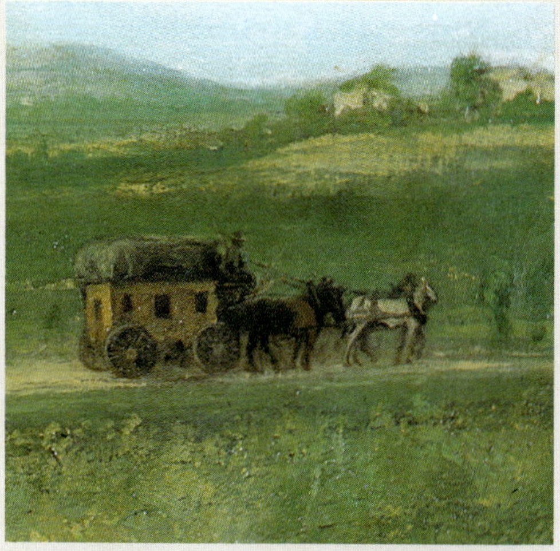

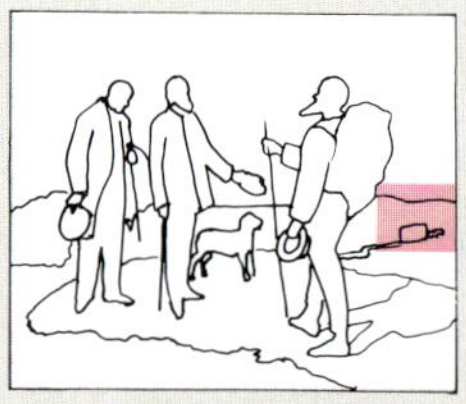

*The receding carriage gives the only articulation of middle-ground in the abrupt landscape. The grass at the bottom was depicted by dabbing color over the initial blocked-in green with a rag dipped in paint. This produces an effective, rugged texture.*

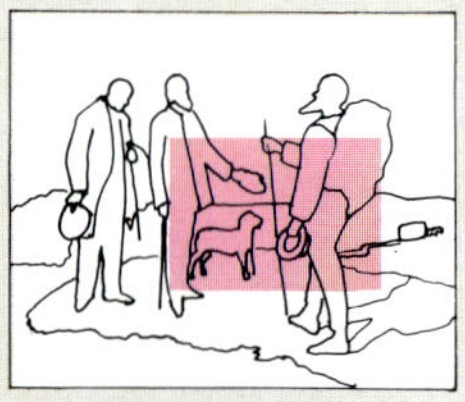

*The dog, executed in lively, hair-evoking brushwork, seems to have been completed after the landscape and the shadows were added around the dog. The broad colorful handling of the foreground contrasts with the pale delicate skyline.*

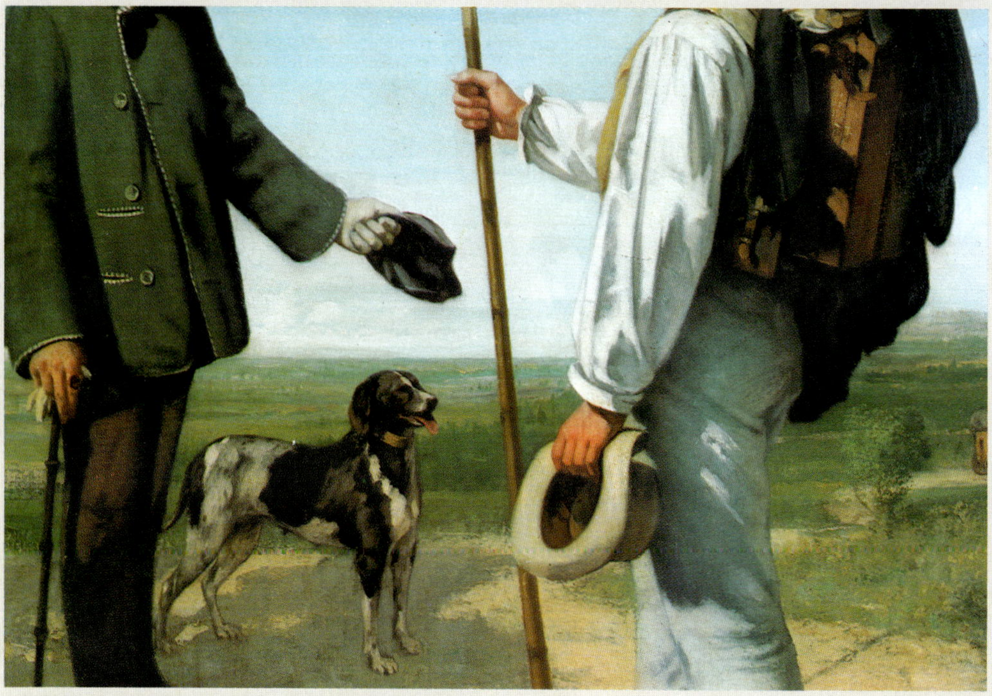

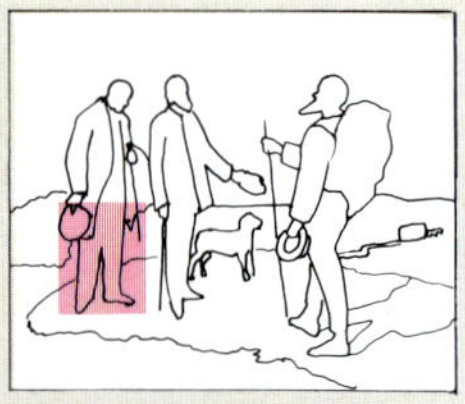

*Light and shade on this figure were rendered in stark flat areas. The shadows around the feet were also a late reworking, and the shrub was rendered by dabbing paint on with a rag.*

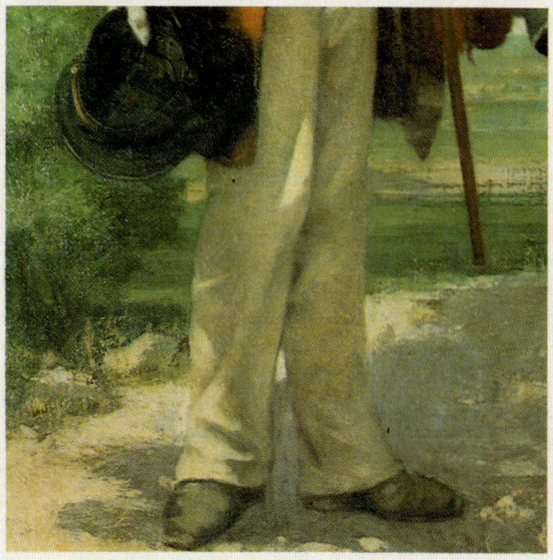

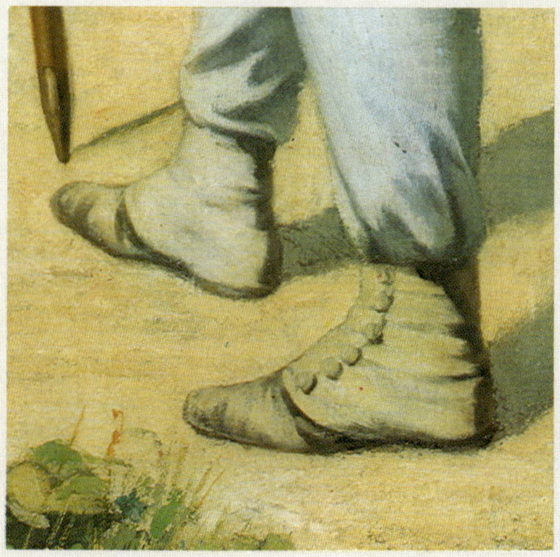

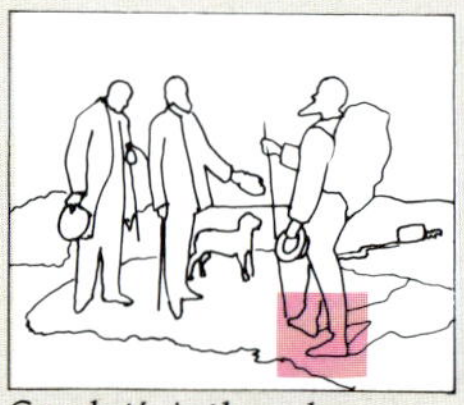

*Courbet's is the only uninterrupted shadow in the painting. His spatted shoes were freely brushed on, while the creamy ochres of the road were applied in superimposed irregular films with a flexible painting knife. This area had a knife-applied underlay of brown umber.*

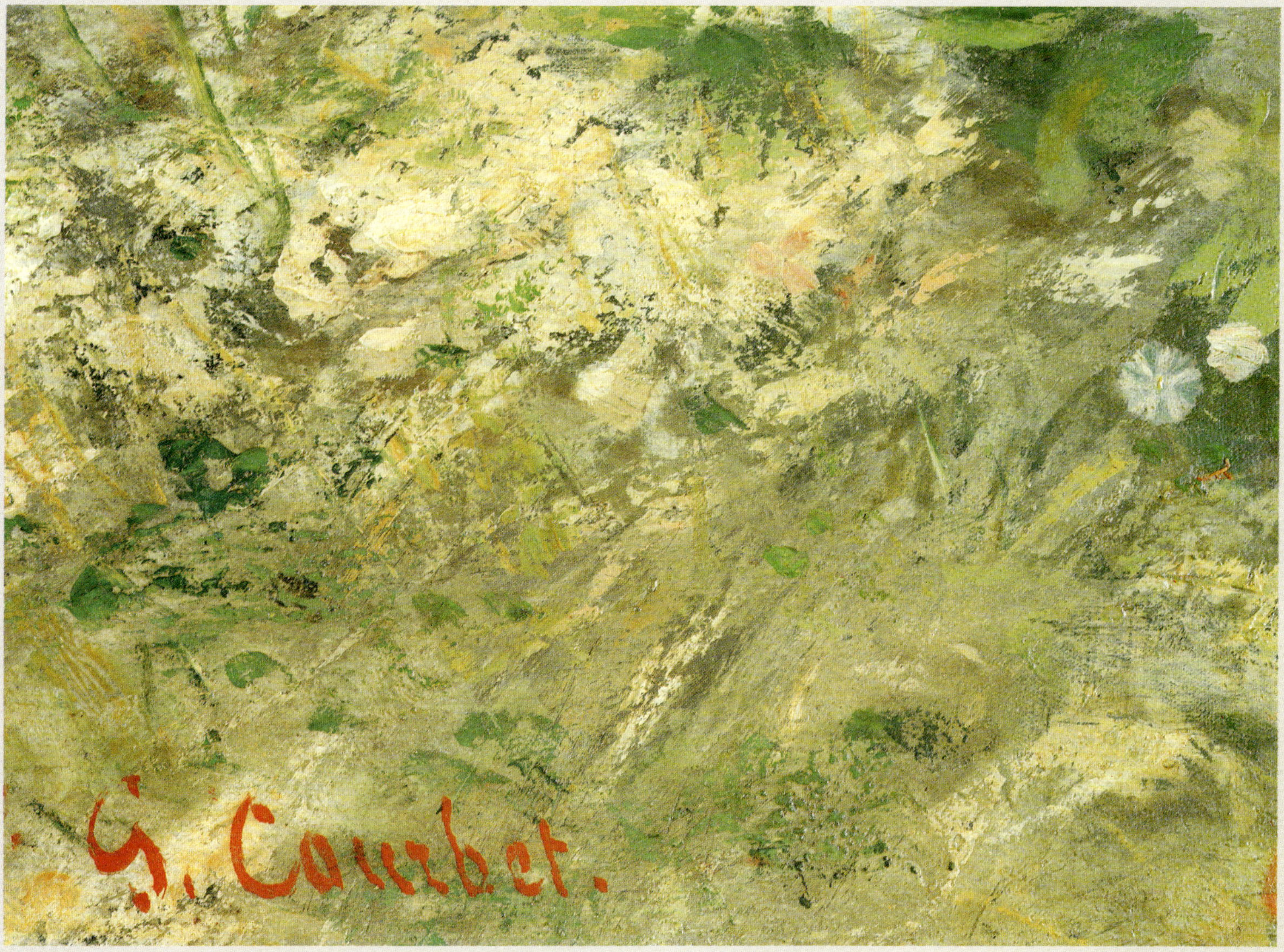


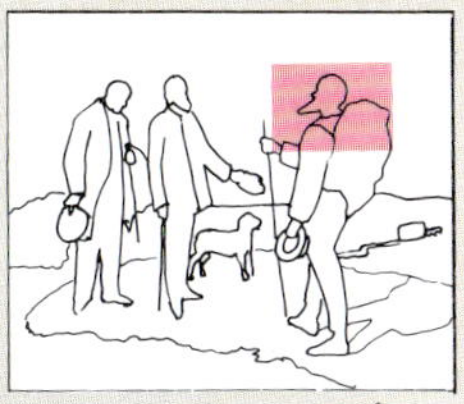

*In this detail, a stain of umber or of black mixed with umber is beginning to appear through the sky paint. This had been applied at a late stage in the painting because Courbet adjusted the length of the beard on his self-portrait. Originally it was longer and jutted out even further than it does in the final version.*

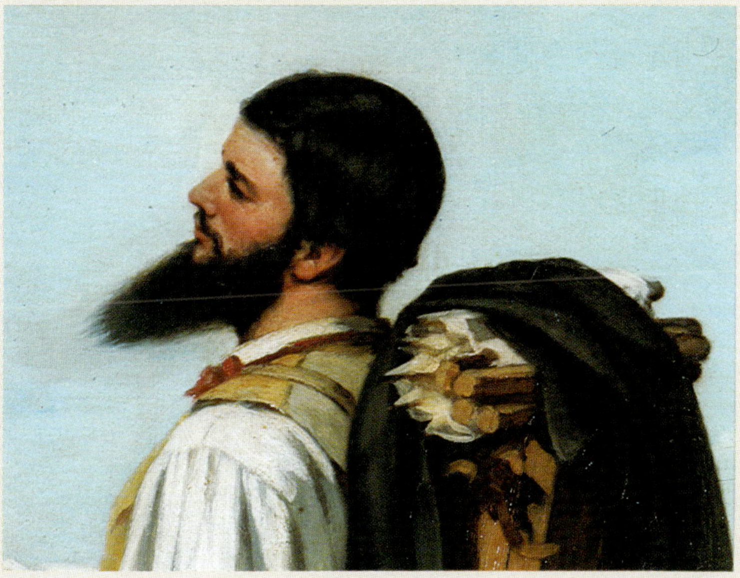

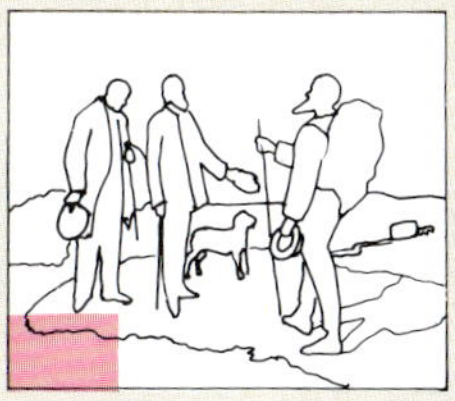

**Actual size detail**
*The loose ochres were rapidly and stiffly applied, exploiting the canvas texture and revealing patches of the luminous ground. The detailed grasses were worked on top with thicker brushed paint, and the carefully observed flowers were added. The broad but detailed handling of the foreground contrasts with the smudged soft skyline which creates the rapidly receding flat landscape.*

# SECTION 2
# THE IMPRESSIONISTS
# 1860-1905

'In a new age, new techniques. It's a simple matter of good sense', commented the young French writer and critic J. K. Huysmans (1848–1907) extremely perceptively on the innovatory Impressionist group in 1879. However, it had taken almost a century of social, political and artistic upheaval, and of struggle against the extreme stranglehold of the French Academy, for all but a few to recognize this fact. Traditional conventions in French art were deeply ingrained, and the whole established structure of the art world dug in its conservative heels against change, novelty and the needs of the new age. From the French Revolution of 1789 onwards, three generations of young, independent artists were forced to seek their own alternatives in style, training, patronage and painting methods, against the power monopoly invested in the Academy. The rise of Impressionism, with its radical new aims and painting techniques, can only be understood against the background which dictated artistic taste, and against which these young artists reacted.

**The rise of the Academies**

During the Italian Renaissance, artists like Leonardo (1452–1519) and Michelangelo (1475–1564) had struggled to raise the status of the artist from the medieval position of humble artisan. Because painting was felt to soil the hands and involve manual labor, it had not been accorded the status given to such scholarly pursuits as music, mathematics and literature. In order to rectify this, when the first art academies were founded in the sixteenth century, they taught only the most intellectual aspects of art – the scientific study of anatomy, the geometry of perspective for constructing an illusion of space and, most importantly, drawing. Although color is a real presence in nature, line as such does not exist. The outlines, contours and shading used in drawing are technical devices intended as a way of enabling artists to translate the appearance of three-dimensional objects onto a flat surface. Therefore by stressing the superiority of drawing artists were emphasizing the most intellectual and abstract aspect of their work, that element in which the humanizing, rationalizing influence of the human mind could best be seen. Painting, or coloring, was relegated to a secondary role because of its association with the senses and with the vulgar imitation of raw nature, as well as with the dirty, practical side of art. At all costs painting had to be seen to appeal to the higher, moral side of the human mind, not merely to satisfy sensual appetites.

This split between the intellectual and the senses, between line and color, artist and artisan, was perpetuated in seventeenth century France, when the Royal Academy was founded there in the 1640s. The most famous artists of this period, like Nicolas Poussin (*c* 1594–1665) and Claude (1600–1682), spent

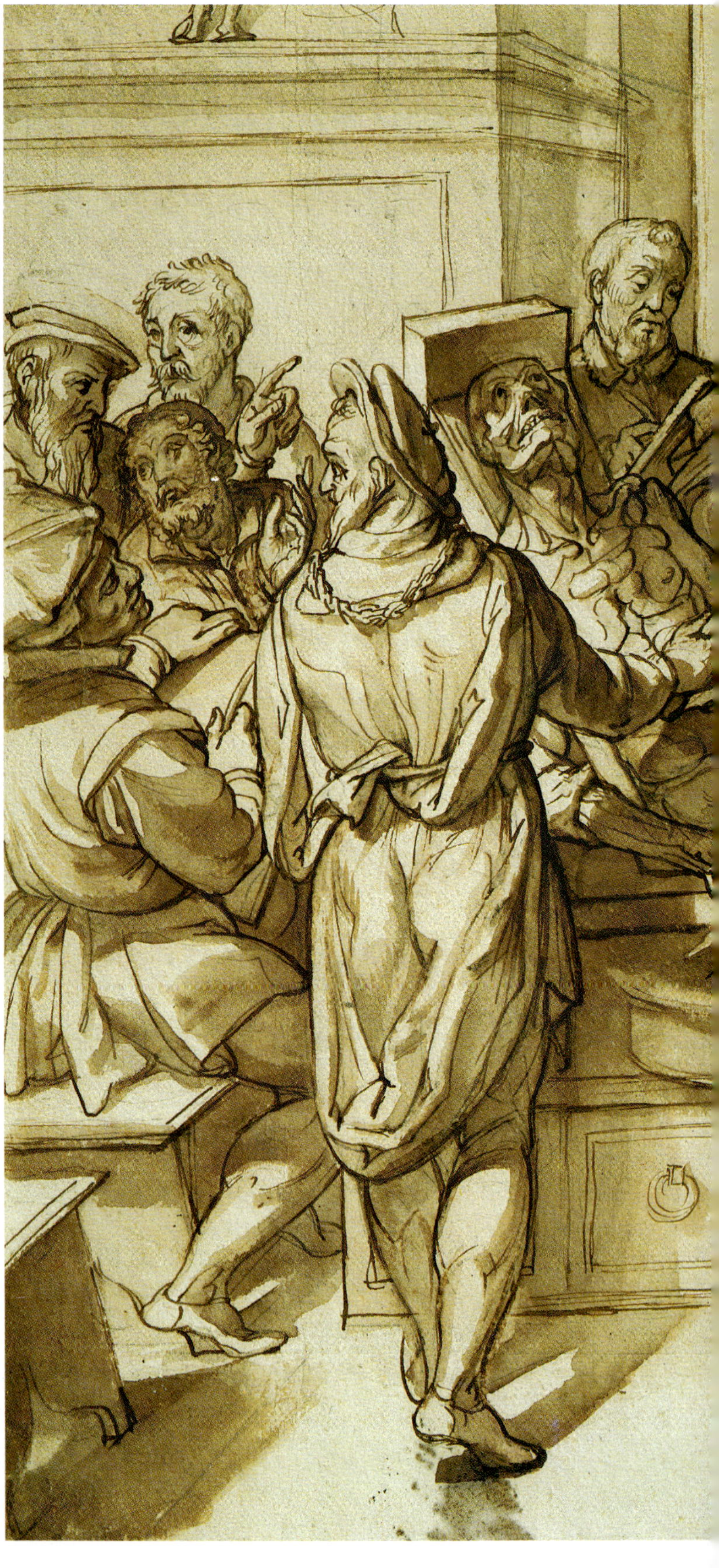

Right *This sixteenth century drawing,* The Anatomy Lesson *by Bartolomeo Passarotti (1529-1592), was executed in pen, ink and wash on paper. It shows the concern of Renaissance artists with the scientific and intellectual aspects of their trade. A hand written inventory of the Cabinet de Dessins in the Louvre notes that this shows an anatomy lesson jointly held by all the famous Italian masters of the period. Portraits of Michelangelo, Raphael, Sebastiano del Piombo, Jules Romain, Titian and Andrea del Sarto can be recognized among them.*

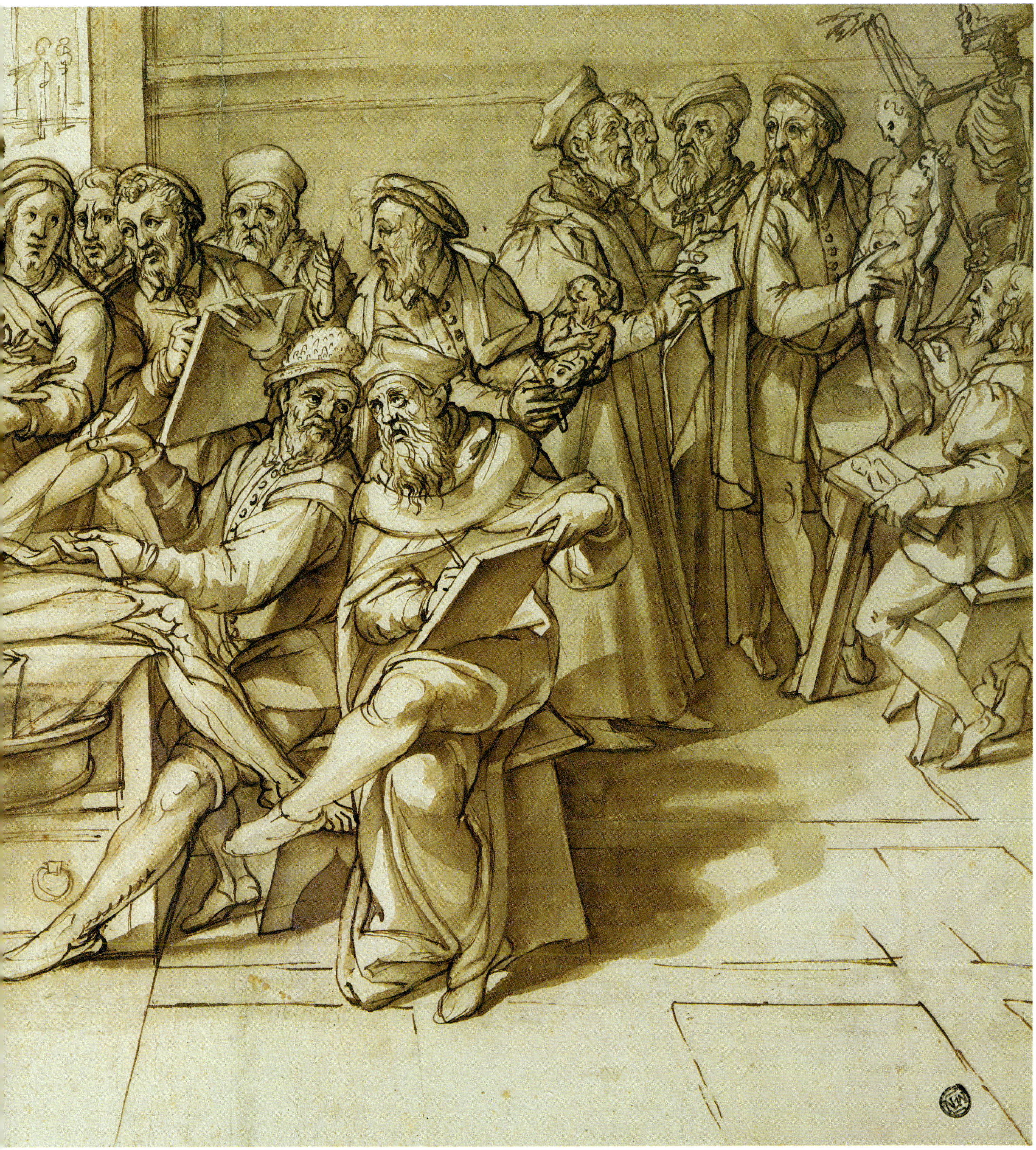

most of their lives in Italy, enjoying the privileged status by then accepted as due to the greatest talents. The renowned theorists of the period took up the debate between the mind and the senses, transforming it into the contemporary division between those in favor of the classicizing Poussin, and those behind the flamboyant colorist from Flanders, Peter Paul Rubens (1577–1640). The Academy had been founded to improve the status of French artists, to bring art within the control of the absolute monarch Louis XIV, and to free artists from what they considered the retrogressive stranglehold of the traditional guilds. While the guilds, established during the Middle Ages, stressed thorough practical training and craftsmanship, the Academy concentrated upon drawing, in particular from the human figure which was considered the principal vehicle for embodying and expressing the highest human ideals.

The human form was not simply to be 'imitated' in drawing, but to be idealized – in conformity with ancient Greek, Roman and Renaissance art – to represent the purest forms of an ideal of truth and beauty upon which the mind could reflect and thus be elevated.

These attitudes influenced the choice of subject matter which, as a result, fell into a distinct hierarchy according to the degree of spiritual elevation it was felt to display. Lowest on the scale were still life, animal painting, rural landscape and genre or domestic scenes. Historical landscape painting, by which was meant a heroic landscape with a moral or classical theme, together with portrait and religious subjects, were more highly regarded. However, the most highly respected type of painting was history painting, which represented heroic deeds from the history of the Greeks and Romans. Through this type of work, the artist could best show skill in depicting both the nude and draperies. To this end, the Academy encouraged students to familiarize themselves with details of classical history and mythology and to study and copy the works of suitable Old Masters.

Paralleling this high ideal, academic artists – unlike their guild counterparts – were from the first forbidden to advertise or hawk their products. Such lowly, mercantile activity was considered beneath the dignity of fine artists. Instead, a regular venue, the Salon, so named after the *Salon Carré* in the Louvre where the first exhibitions were held, was established as the sole acceptable market place for the work of Academy-trained artists. The power of the Salon grew, and it retained its monopoly as the main outlet for artists' work until the latter part of the nineteenth century.

**Teaching under the Academy**

By the nineteenth century, the academic training of the artist had become ritualized into a rigid formula, which was self-perpetuating and changed only with great reluctance to meet the new needs of the age. The Academy was renamed the Ecole des Beaux-Arts in the reign of Napoleon I, and it only accepted students who already showed proven ability in drawing. Drawing instruction at the Ecole was given by members of the Academy, by then an honorary elite body of artists who were elected to life membership by other academicians and who advised the government on all artistic matters. Academicians controlled not only the curriculum at the Ecole, but also the competitions students had to enter and win to achieve success and consolidate their careers. Academicians were also jurors dictating entry to and medals awarded at the annual Salon exhibitions. The Academy thus effectively dominated art production and was able to perpetuate its conservative style and taste.

Academic control of teaching was not limited to drawing instruction at the Ecole; academicians prepared students for entry into the Ecole with drawing lessons in their private teaching studios or *ateliers*, where they also instructed advanced students in painting practice. The great encyclopedia, compiled by the French writer Denis Diderot (1713–1784) and published in the latter half of the eighteenth century, shows the typical progress of students through the various stages in the hierarchical drawing curriculum, which would give them access to the Ecole. The first stage involved copying either drawings or engravings, first in terms only of outline, then with hatched shading. This was known as work 'from the flat' because students had merely to imitate the

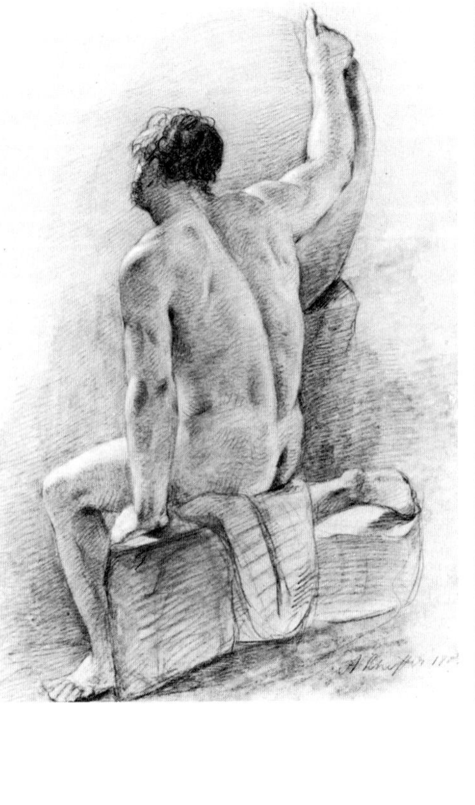

Left *Born in Holland, the artist Ary Scheffer (1795-1858) was – with Delacroix and Géricault – one of the three prize pupils at the studio of Guérin (1774-1833), where he enrolled in 1812. This life study of 1807, drawn in black crayon and white chalk on paper, is obviously a very youthful work, presumably done in Holland. If the date is correct this shows the artist began his training at a very tender age. The academic technique of parallel hatched strokes contained by contours is seen here, built up to create subtle tonal gradations which are finally heightened with white chalk. Because life drawings became so closely associated with academic training, they became known as* Academies. *The full title of this work is* Academy drawn after Life.

simple lines to which the form had already been reduced.

Once this was successfully mastered, the student moved on to drawing low-relief sculpture. Here the fall of light and shade on the simple raised forms had to be translated into shading. This shading followed strict conventions and formed an important part of the approach to painting approved by the Academy. It was called *chiaroscuro*, which means light-dark in Italian. To achieve the subtleties of *chiaroscuro* shading, series of distinct, hatched parallel marks indicated shaded areas, while the white of the paper was left blank to represent highlights. For this, pencil or graphite, a crisp precise medium, was preferred during the first half of the century. Chalk or charcoal, which were softer and more suited to the rubbed

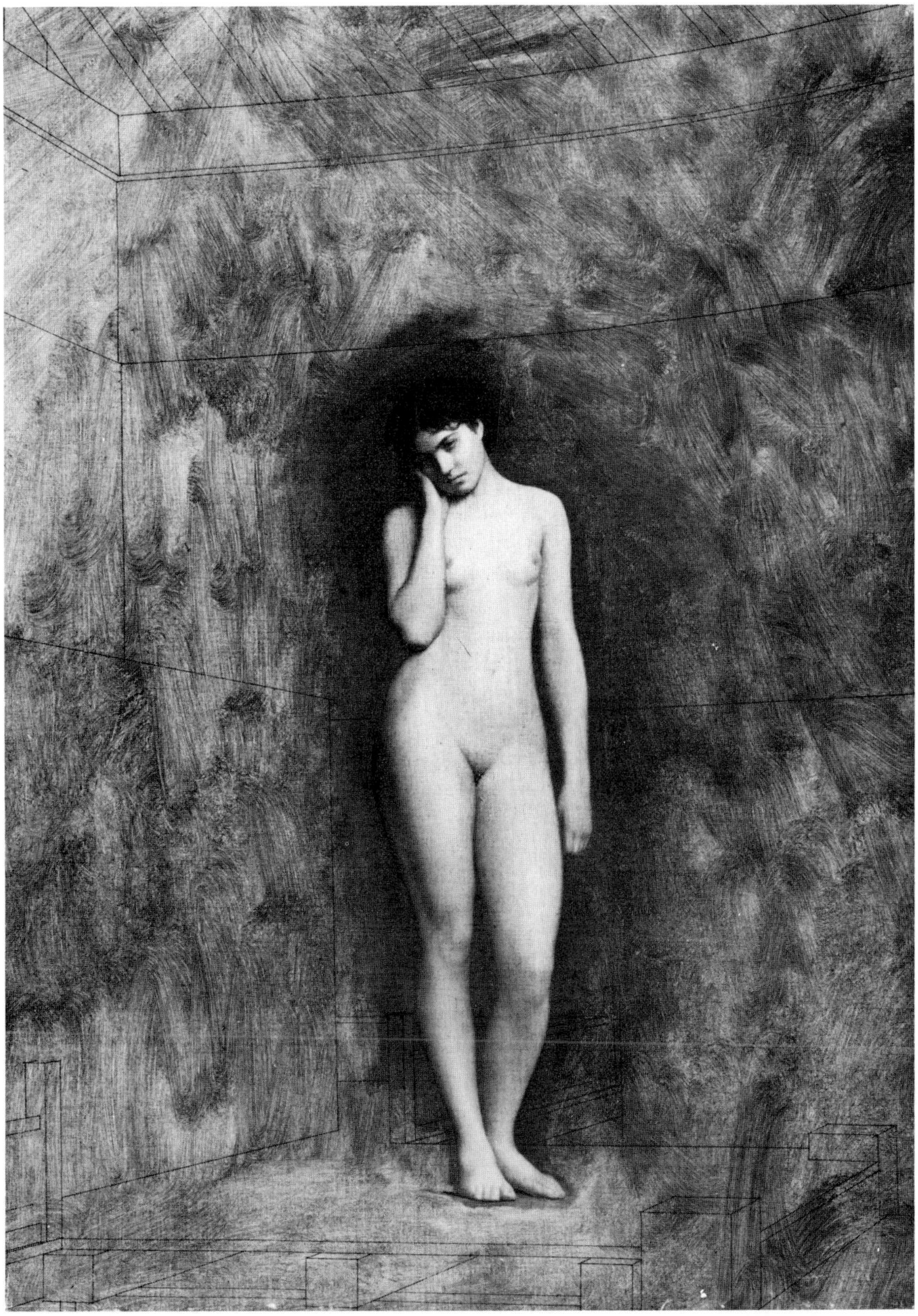

Right Greek Slave *(c1869) by Jean-Léon Gérôme (1824-1904) is an example of* ébauche *in oil on canvas. The title added to this academic nude study immediately suggests that it was intended to be seen in the classical tradition, although the contemporary appearance of the woman's face makes no concession to classicism. The ennobling title and slight idealization of the form simply vindicate the subject. The figure has been most tightly and completely worked, and the* ébauche *stage is shown complete there. The carefully laid, gradated tints for the flesh are fully blended until individual brushmarks are imperceptible. This creates a stark contrast with the background, which remains only roughly laid in. A thin wash of translucent color was rubbed on loosely in the early stages of execution. This shows the marks of the broad bristle brush and the pale ground glowing through. It also reveals the lines, drawn with a ruler, which indicate the interior in which it was intended to situate the completed figure.*

blending which was used to create tonal gradations, became the popular media as the system liberalized.

The next step was for students to draw from sculpture in the round. First only parts of, and then complete statues, usually cast after antique examples, had to be translated into delicate patterns of line, built up to recreate on flat paper the illusion of form in space. Because the reliefs and sculptures were cast in white plaster, no color was present to distract the eye; the form presented itself simply in monochrome gradations of tone from light to dark. As the models from which the students worked were already idealized works of art, they helped to inculcate in the students a mannered vision of nature, which encouraged them to draw the live model in a conventional, idealized and unindividual way. Thus, by the time students graduated to work from the live figure, their drawing style had already been formed.

Although the real color and anatomical idiosyncracies of the human figure were a shock to the students' unaccustomed eyes, the tendency to see the form only in abstract line and tonal gradations was already well ingrained. Models were commonly posed in noble stances derived from antique statues, which both aided the transition from cast to live model, and maintained the emphasis on the classical tradition. Such exercises were designed to give students the competence to tackle complex figure compositions based on classical themes, which would prepare them for the grand Rome Prize, the final competition toward which all their studies were directed.

Only when students were thoroughly proficient in drawing from the live model were they permitted to use color. The master generally gave a brief introduction to the materials and tools of painting and their care, and then the students began copying a painted head. This was either an example specially executed by the master, or, occasionally, students were sent to the Louvre to copy an Old Master head. Venetian or Flemish artists were usually chosen because their lively handling and color were simpler to imitate. Students were then put to work from a live head, before going on to attempt to paint the nude model. The first stage in the painting process was the thinly painted laying in of the lines, broad masses and halftones of the subject, which provided the base for the finished painting. This stage was called the *ébauche*. This first layer had to be 'leaner', in other words contain less oil, than the final reworking, to adhere to the rule 'fat over lean', essential to competent oil painting. This rule is important because, if an oily layer is laid over an even oilier base, the latter will continue drying after the final coat is dry, thus causing the top layer to shrink and crack, exposing the underpainting.

Students were taught to prepare their palette in advance, using mainly earth colors plus Prussian blue, black and lead white. As the nineteenth century progressed, the use of the earth colors, which were relatively stable chemically, gave way to a preference for the impermanent beauties of tarry colors, like bitumen, which destroyed many paintings. Carefully prepared tints, which were thoroughly mixed with a pliant knife on a palette, were arranged in separate rows aligned with the outer edge of a clean palette – lights, darks and intermediary halftones. Once the palette was ready, light charcoal lines were drawn onto the primed canvas to indicate the contours of the form. The canvas was then gently tapped or blown on to remove excess dusty particles of the charcoal, to prevent their muddying the wet oil colors.

Next a dilute red-brown mixture was prepared by adding turpentine to an earth-color mixture, and with this transparent tint the charcoal contours were reworked and strengthened using a fine sable-hair brush. Again with the dilute mixture, called the 'sauce', the main areas of shadow were broadly laid in, normally with a larger, stiffer hog's hair brush, following the guidelines provided by the contours. Backgrounds were generally roughed in as early as possible, to block out the pale priming color which, because of its glaring brilliance, made it difficult for the student to judge the correct tonal values in the picture. Detail was avoided in this early stage, only the general effects of light and shade were sought.

Then, with thicker paint and usually a stiff brush, the lights – or parts of the painting directly illuminated by the fall of light – were added, but not at full strength. Next came the careful work of building up the delicately graded halftones between the lights and the

Below *These scale pictures show typical nineteenth century artists' brushes, taken from French color merchants' catalogs of the period. The fan-shaped sable hair blending brush* (1) *was designed to be used dry to blend the mosaic-like touches of wet color on the* ébauche *of the figure. Most writers on technique scorned the use of the blending brush, finding its effects too soft and facile. Instead artists were supposed to use deft strokes of each appropriate tint to link the gradated tones of the flesh. The fine hog's hair bristle brushes* (2-9), *have round or flat ferrules. They are long-haired, to permit deft, flexible handling. They come with round, pointed or squared ends These shapes all exploit the natural taper and curve of the hair, so that*

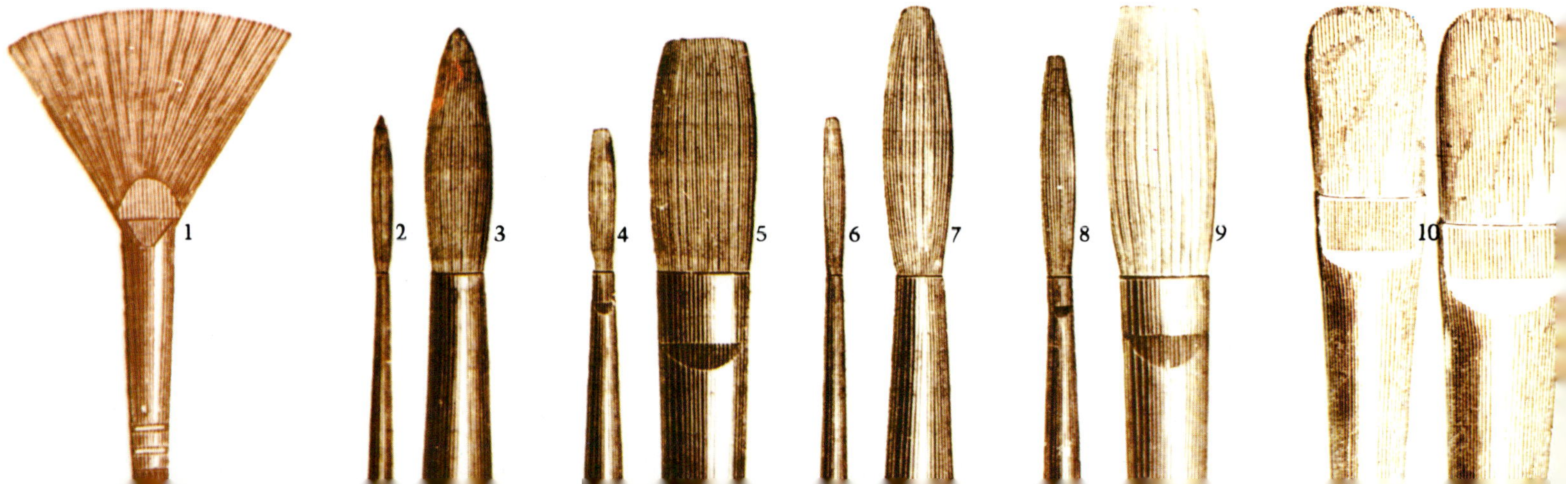

darks, to give relief to the form. These were placed side by side in separate, mosaic-like touches of color, which were finally blended until the changes in tone were imperceptible and the brushstrokes no longer visible. After blending the halftones, a few lively, expressive brushstrokes of color were applied to both lights and darks, to help the work retain a feeling of spontaneity.

Once this stage was complete, the work was left to dry thoroughly. The most thinly painted, dilute areas of color – the shadows and general background – would dry fairly rapidly due to evaporation of the turpentine spirit. The more thickly applied halftones and highlights could take a week, more usually two, to dry. The *ébauche* stage was then finished by first scraping down the dry surface, to remove any irregularities which might interfere with the smooth movement of the brush during reworking. Then the mosaic application of halftones was repeated, the highlights brought to full strength, and the color of the shadows deepened and enriched.

When painting from the live nude, students had to work rapidly to complete the *ébauche*. They had also to work in relatively thin paint, or it would not dry in time to be finished in the week allotted to each pose. Many unfinished life paintings survive, indicating how difficult it was to complete a figure study in so short a time. Backgrounds were generally left loose and vague, the greatest care being devoted to working up the precise tonal and color values on the figure itself.

The technical formula most widely recommended for executing the *ébauche* in the *ateliers* was to paint the lights thickly, in opaque impasto and, in contrast, to wash in the shadows thinly and transparently. This technique, normally retained for the finishing as well as the *ébauche* stage, aided the rendering of form in two important ways. First, the subtle transition from balanced light to shadowed areas created a convincing illusion of form in space – a sculpture-like solidity. Secondly, the physical character of the finished surface, with projecting impasted lights and flat shadows, gave a relief-like authenticity to the actual paint surface. The raised, light parts of a picture were intended to pick up and reflect back to the spectator the actual light in the room where the work was hung, thus reinforcing the illusion of light in the picture itself. For this reason, artists preferred to hang their work under a light source comparable to that under which it had been executed, preferably with the actual light source falling at the same angle as the painted fall of light so they would not contradict each other.

**The art student's life**

Students usually started to study at the Ecole between the ages of 15 and 18. Training would last for at least five years. The art student's day began early. In summer the long daylight hours permitted drawing classes in the *ateliers* to begin as early as 7am. The *rapin* – the newest student – arrived even earlier to tidy and organize the studio, and in winter to light the stove. Classes in the *ateliers* lasted only for the morning, finishing usually around noon or 1pm. The *atelier* masters normally visited their students only once or at most twice each week, to advise and to criticize their work and to set 'homework', such as compositional exercises or copying, to prepare students for Ecole competitions.

The afternoons were spent in the painting and drawing collections of the Louvre, making copies from the Old Masters. This was a crucial element in the Ecole program. Copying was intended to familiarize students with the techniques of the past, and to inspire them to emulate the compositional ideas and devices of the great masters. Students also collected and copied engravings and lithographs after Old Master paintings.

Drawing classes at the Ecole, for those advanced enough to register there, began in the late afternoon, usually at 4pm. Students normally worked from casts or the live model at the Ecole. During the summer months, most students were encouraged to draw and paint from nature, doing outdoor landscape work. A knowledge of landscape was considered essential even for students primarily interested in figure painting, as they needed to be able to paint authentic landscape backdrops to their figure compositions. It was also thought important in training the students' powers of observation.

Constrained by the tightly organized teaching program, students learned to work at

*the brush retains its shape when full of color and springs back into shape even after vigorous use. A cheap, poor brush rapidly becomes splayed, losing its shape and its ability to hold the paint. With such a brush, it is difficult to control the marks made. Each of the brush forms creates a distinctive mark. The six shorter haired bristle brushes* (10-15), *are stubby and square ended. They were ideal for use with the stiff paint consistency preferred by most of the Impressionists. They are graduated in size, for varying size of mark and suited to different scales of canvas size. The broad, flat brush* (16) *is for varnishing. The full, soft badger-hair brush* (17) *is another blending brush with a round ferrule. It serves the same function as the fan shaped blender.*

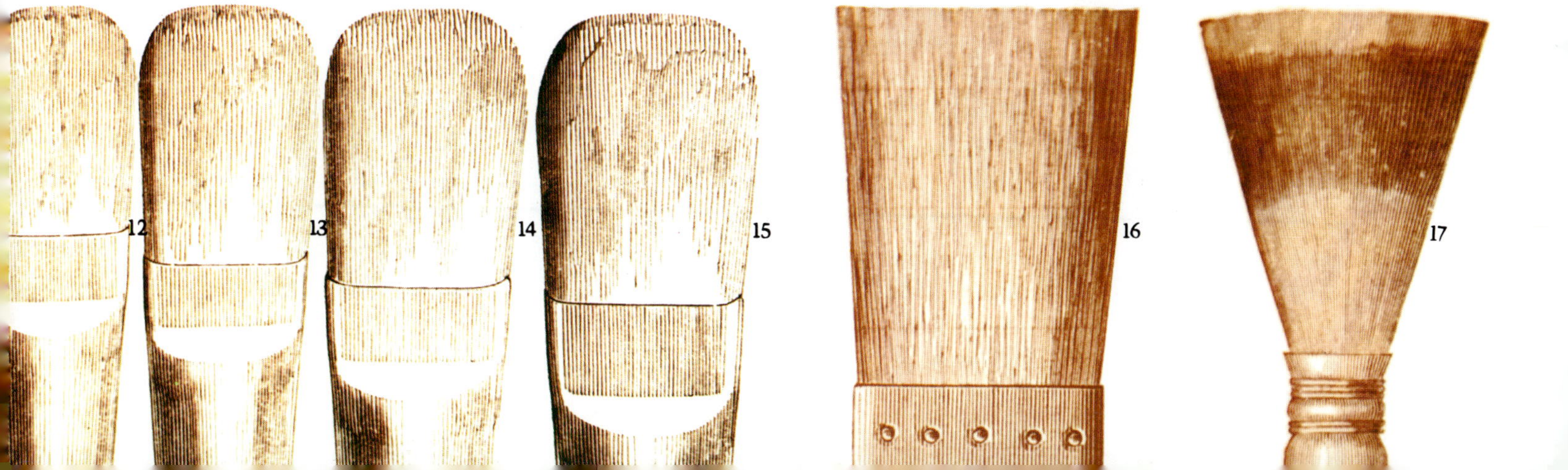

speed in order to succeed in the numerous timed drawing and painting competitions around which their studies were structured. Each competition marked a progressively more demanding step on the ladder toward the most coveted award, the Prix de Rome, which assured the winner fame after four or five years' study at the French Academy in the Italian capital. Until the early nineteenth century, only one Rome Prize – in history painting – was awarded every year and thus, because of the large numbers of students involved, few students had any real chance of success in this outdated system. Neither consistent application, nor even talent guaranteed advancement. Each master backed a protégé, and this often encouraged servile imitation in preference to independent originality on the part of the young artists.

**The Academy's authority questioned**

Although the overall program of teaching at the Ecole remained little changed from the seventeenth century until the reforms of 1863, new emphases were apparent in the nineteenth century system. The powerful impact of Jacques Louis David (1748–1825), who headed the classical revival and whose influence dominated art training and practice from the 1790s, led to a greater stress on life drawing and on the use of halftones to create 'sculptural' forms. His famous pupil Ingres (1780–1867) followed him, albeit with somewhat different concerns, as the major influence on French art through his teaching. Since many of the older independent artists, such as Delacroix (1798–1863) and Corot (1796–1875), did not run teaching *ateliers*, they produced no 'schools' of followers as such.

Another new factor was the marked increase in competitiveness resulting from the rapid growth in numbers of would-be artists from the late eighteenth century onwards. The collaborative studio-workshop training and practice still common in the seventeenth century had disappeared. The new individualism, inspired by the French Revolution of 1789 and the rise of the bourgeoisie, found its parallels in the career structure of artists. Professionalism, reinforced by a rigorous, quantifiable training, gradually gave artists a new middle class respectability and social acceptability.

By the early nineteenth century, certain more liberal changes were essential to the survival of the academic system, confronted as it was with growing dissention and dissatisfaction among independently minded artists. Some recognition of new trends had to be given by the Academy, for social and economic upheaval had created new official state and bourgeois patrons, whose needs and taste were often at variance with academic ideals. In 1816 the Academy introduced an official four yearly Rome Prize in historic landscape painting, to placate the taste of public and artists for this increasingly popular genre, and at the same time to bring it within the Academy's control. How-

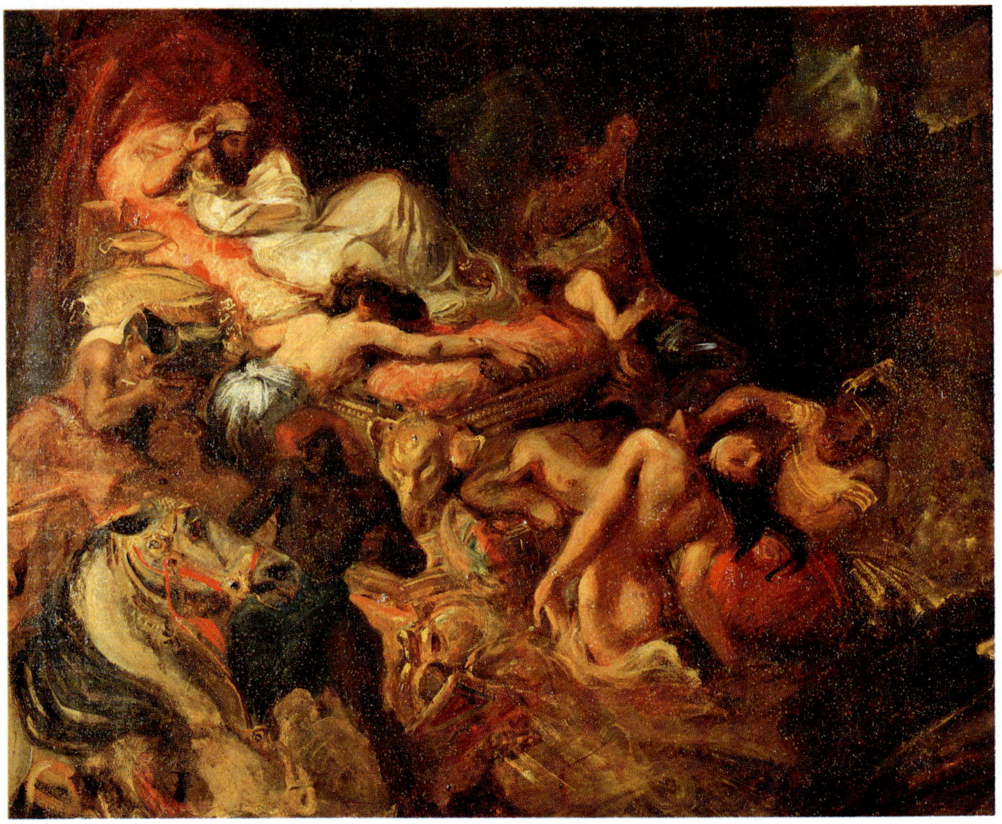

Right *This version of* The Death of Sardanapalus *by Delacroix is the oil sketch painted on canvas (c1827). Delacroix's painting is an example of the compositional* esquisse, *the smallish broadly handled preparatory oil in which color and composition for a large painting were worked out. This was usually preceded by drawn compositional sketches, also worked from the imagination, and ideas for individual figures or groups, such as the small ink drawing, or thumbnail sketch* opposite. *Precise details for figures were then worked out in drawn and painted studies from posed life figures, and changes were often made.*

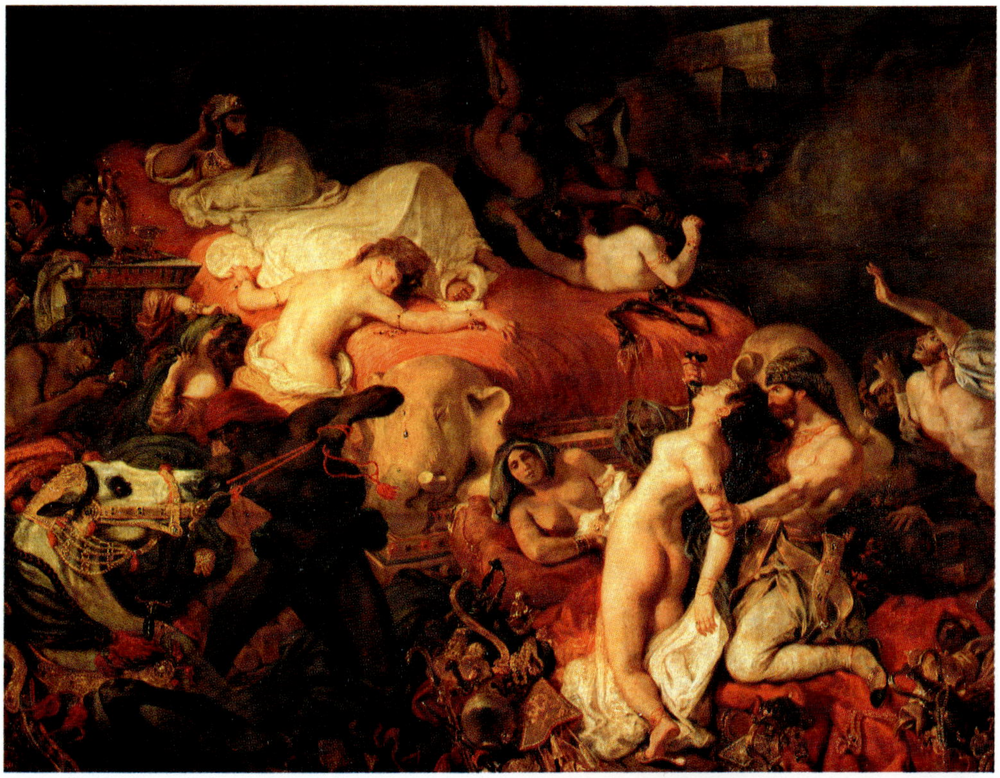

Right *The final painting of Delacroix's* The Death of Sardanapalus *(1828) was executed in oil on canvas. The subject of this huge work was inspired by the English poet Byron, whose tragedy* Sardanapalus *– based on a classic theme – was published in London in 1821, and in a French translation in 1825. However, Byron does not describe any scene like that depicted by Delacroix. This picture was painted for the Salon exhibition of 1828, and is an excellent example of the artist's romantic style. Subtle details of naturalistic color worked out in preparatory pastel drawings, were finally subsumed to the dominant warm harmonies which give the painting its emotive power.*

ever, this fostered only the classical landscape tradition, and was thus later to force the budding schools of Romantic and Realist landscape painting into open opposition to the Academy. However, in 1863, when most of the Impressionists were students, the Rome Prize for landscape was abolished.

Ironically, some aspects of the academic curriculum itself laid the foundations for the independent stylistic innovations which led to Impressionism and which eventually eroded the Academy's supremacy. The concentrated nature of the academic training ensured that students spent the majority of their time on the freely worked stages of painting – the *ébauche* of the life model, and the *esquisse*. This was the compositional sketch in oils intended to prepare students for the Rome Prize competitions. This sketch was adopted as a preliminary competition for the Rome Prize in 1816, indicating a new officially approved emphasis on the looser, preparatory stages of the painting process, as against previous concentration on the tightly methodical finishing procedures.

The compositional *esquisse* was broadly and expressively handled. Masses of light, shade and color were laid down to create the design which embodied the artist's first inspired idea for the final painting. Careful finish was not expected for this sketch, in which – on the contrary – spontaneity and originality were the prime qualities sought. The painted sketch was normally preceded by drawn sketches and, if and when the final work was to be executed,

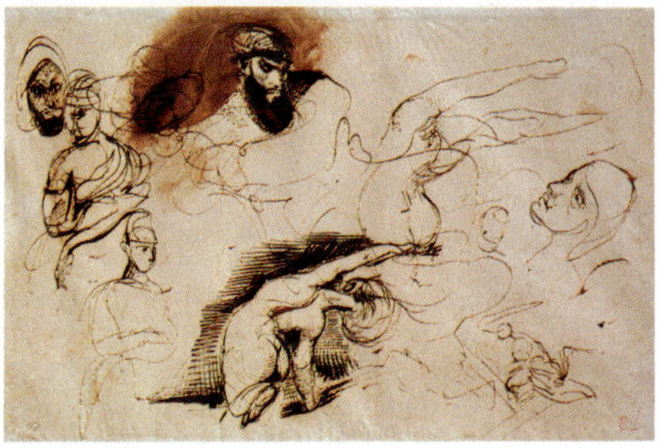

Left *This small thumbnail sketch or* croquis *for Delacroix's* Death of Sardanapalus *shows the artist toying with ideas for the poses of his figures, later to be planned in greater detail. The expressive energy of Delacroix's handling is just as apparent in this drawing medium as in his oil sketch and the final canvas.*

the artist followed up the painted *esquisse* with a series of carefully drawn and painted *études*. These were studies from life of individual elements in the composition, which refined and tightened the original idea. The compositional scheme was then transferred by drawing onto the final canvas, and the slow, meticulous process of executing the finished picture began. Critics of the academic system argued that this laborious process resulted in a sterile and mannered final product. They felt that this meant the artist's original inspiration was inevitably lost because touches of individuality were eliminated on the smooth surface where individual brushstrokes should not be discernible.

The concept of originality was a major issue much debated in nineteenth century artistic circles. Conservative traditionalists, on the one hand, associated originality with the elitist idea of genius, the inventive spark which set one individual apart from the common herd. On the other hand, a new definition of originality, with its roots in Revolutionary and post-Revolutionary democratic thinking, saw it as an innate characteristic of every human being – the uniqueness of each separate personality. These opposing definitions reflect the continuation of the deep division between the intellectual and the manual which had its roots in Renaissance ideals and aspirations.

In terms of artistic practice, the academic notion of genius was embodied in the later stages of finishing a painting, when the artist's mind refined and perfected the first, inspired idea. The newer and more 'democratic' idea of originality held that the artist's uniqueness was most apparent during the preparatory stages, when personal expression and inspiration, rather than intellect, guided the artist's hand. Thus, by unwittingly creating a program which stressed (at least in terms of time) the preparatory stages of painting – the *ébauche* and the *esquisse* in particular – the Academy fortuitously promoted the modern definition of the idea of originality.

**The Independents and new ways of training**

It was among the independent artists and movements that the new concept of originality was consciously adopted and striven after, which placed them in opposition to the ideals laid down by the Academy. There were some *atelier* masters who fostered new methods and original talent, remaining unconvinced that the Academy's program of directing students exclusively towards the Rome Prize was the best way to produce good artists. Among those who offered alternatives were Charles Gleyre (1806–1874) and Thomas Couture (1815–1879), neither of whom belonged to the Academy. They are therefore referred to as 'independent' artists. Gleyre, whose pupils in the early 1860s included Monet, Renoir, Sisley and Bazille, encouraged his students to make outdoor studies, communicating an admiration for landscape painting, and an appreciation of craftsmanship, which proved especially relevant to Renoir. Couture's most famous pupil was Edouard Manet (1832–1883), who remained with his master from 1850 to 1856, absorbing his unconventional attitudes to light and shade, handling, and immediacy.

Couture encouraged his students to work rapidly and simply to 'keep the first vivid impression'. He often suppressed detail and halftones in the interests of direct spontaneity. His brushwork was lively, his colors often dragged in thick confident strokes, and his forms, reduced to broad masses, outlined in strong contours. Couture passed on his love of the Old Masters to Manet, and their friendly association ended only in 1859, when Couture saw that Manet had abandoned the master's commitment to historic guises for his subject matter. Under the influence of writers like the poet Charles Baudelaire (1821–1867), Manet turned to fusing Old Master themes with modern life subjects. That year he exhibited in his studio his rejected Salon entry, *The Absinthe Drinker*, a modern dress subject which Couture considered lacking in the refining moral overtones of the classical tradition.

Other alternatives for art students sprang up as the century progressed. Around the time of the restoration of the monarchy in 1815, Suisse, an ex-model in David's studio, established an open life studio on the corner of the Quai des Orfèvres. There, unfettered by teaching or competitions, artists as diverse as Ingres, Courbet, Manet and Cézanne were to find access to life models, both male and female, to further their own training and interests. The *atelier* of Rodolphe Julian, which came to be known as the Academy Julian, founded in 1868, became internationally renowned among independent artists. While it did prepare students who wished for the Ecole, Julian's liberal program became for many an alternative to that formal training. Horace Lecoq de Boisbaudran's classes from 1841 to 1869 provided another option for drawing instruction. He invented a method of training by drawing from memory, which encouraged originality in a way unknown in servile copying from the model. His most famous students were the sculptor Auguste Rodin (1840–1917) and painter and lithographer Henri Fantin-Latour (1836–1904).

Another extremely influential figure in the challenge to the Academy was Eugène Delacroix who was regarded as an independent artist. Delacroix considered himself as a painter who was simply bringing new energy and vitality to a tired classical tradition. However, conservatives criticized him as an innovator, while his works were revered by younger artists for their expressive color and bold brushwork. The visible sign of the brush, which was suppressed by academic 'finish' came to represent for the Impressionist generation the outward mark of the artist's individuality – a personal calligraphy which identified originality and uniqueness. Delacroix founded no school of followers as did Ingres and the academic masters, but his example was important to many younger independent artists, particularly the Impressionists.

Corot was another extremely important independent artist who, although he kept no formal teaching studio, frequently taught and encouraged young artists, including the leading Impressionists Camille Pissarro (1830–1903) and Berthe Morisot (1841–1895). Corot had trained in the classical landscape tradition, but he abandoned the traditional *chiaroscuro* way of rendering light and shade in landscape. He was also innovatory and influential in advocating immediacy and the importance of the first impression as evidence of the artist's most genuine personal response to the subject. His maxim was 'Always the masses, the whole, . . .

Right Horace and Lydia *was painted in 1843 by the French artist Thomas Couture. Not a member of the Academy, he was extremely influential as a teacher. His most famous pupil was Manet and Couture's influence can be seen in some of Manet's work. This work is broadly handled with strong contrasts between light and dark and few halftones. As in Manet's* Luncheon on the Grass *and* Olympia, *the shadows form contours round the figures. However, unlike Manet, Couture used brown in his shadows, following the traditional practice, whereas Manet used black which was considered revolutionary.*

that which strikes you. Never lose the first impression which has moved you.' Significantly, such advice had become common currency by the 1870s, when the Impressionist style was at its height.

**New approaches to landscape painting**

In nineteenth century France, landscape painting, especially rural landscape, was the type of painting least fettered by the rules of academic tradition. This was the key reason why it became the leading area for the stylistic and technical innovations which reached their peak with Impressionism.

Many older independent artists – like both Delacroix and Corot – did not break completely with the academic tradition because they continued to maintain the importance of the highly finished work of art. However, they made technical innovations by emphasizing the sketch element in their work. Thus Corot adapted the opaque shadows taught by his neoclassical masters to represent more truthfully the delicate nuances of tonal value he perceived in nature. In his experimental outdoor studies, Corot concentrated on the overall effect of natural light and shade, choosing distant subjects in order that excessive detail should not detract from this general effect. He added white to all his colors to heighten the overall luminosity in his paintings, thus bringing them closer to a faithful rendering of outdoor light effects. By contrast, the conventional academic *chiaroscuro* technique dictated that, in landscape

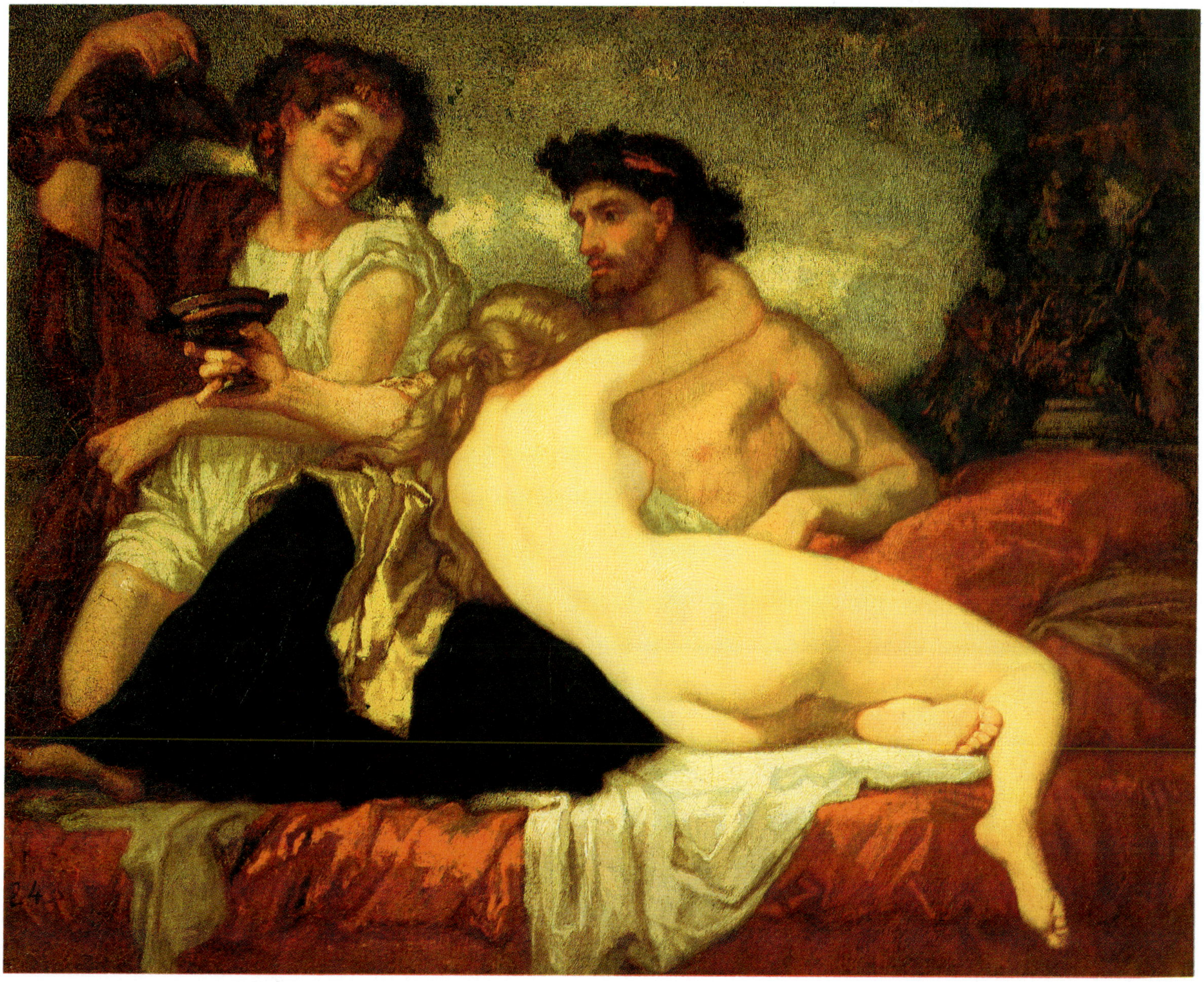

Below Two Poplars at the Villa Farnese *(c1783) by Pierre-Henri de Valenciennes (1750-1819) was executed in oil on paper. Valenciennes rounded off his academic art training in Paris with a period in Italy from 1777 to 1786, during which he studied the Italian Masters, and also made open-air studies in oil. The oil study recorded the artist's impression before the natural scene outdoors. It was intended to sharpen the powers of observation and the facility of swift execution, and to serve as a memory aid for studio landscapes. During the nineteenth century, outdoor studies gradually replaced studio-finished landscapes as the final work.*

painting, artists should artificially darken the pale range of tones found in nature and, correspondingly, lighten the pitch of the naturally somber tonal values found indoors, when painting interior scenes.

Academic landscape painting made little direct reference to real light effects in nature. Instead, a classical formula was advocated, which arbitrarily placed darks in the foreground, with somber theatrical 'wings' of trees or buildings to right and left, the scene growing systematically paler toward a luminous horizon. The lights and darks were a schematized studio invention intended mainly to direct the viewer's eye into the pictorial space. The whole was planned to represent an idea, a human ideal, not real raw nature – indeed the unidealized imitation of nature was condemned as being base and purely mechanical. Whereas in academic figure painting the *esquisse* was the most freely and spontaneously executed stage, and *études* of individual compositional elements were relatively slowly and carefully worked under static studio lighting conditions, in landscape painting the *étude* formed the loose stage, in which the artist's response to the natural effect was captured. Speed in the outdoor *étude* was essential, because of the fast changing, ephemeral lighting effects which had to be translated into paint.

In the academic landscape program, these small *études* from nature provided the raw material and visual vocabulary which aided the artist's memory when the final work was undertaken in the studio. This large-scale piece subjected the initial ideas embodied in the *études* to the classicizing process, in which the classical compositional formula dictated the pictorial structure. This, in turn, dictated the balance and tonal range of light and shade, and most of the original effects were lost in the search for an internal pictorial coherence. An elevating heroic theme, either historical or biblical, was another requirement of academic landscape painting. As accurate observation of particular rural sites in natural outdoor light gained in importance, so artists gradually abandoned studio reworking, preferring more truthful studies executed entirely before nature.

**The loss of traditional technical knowledge**

Delacroix was one among many nineteenth

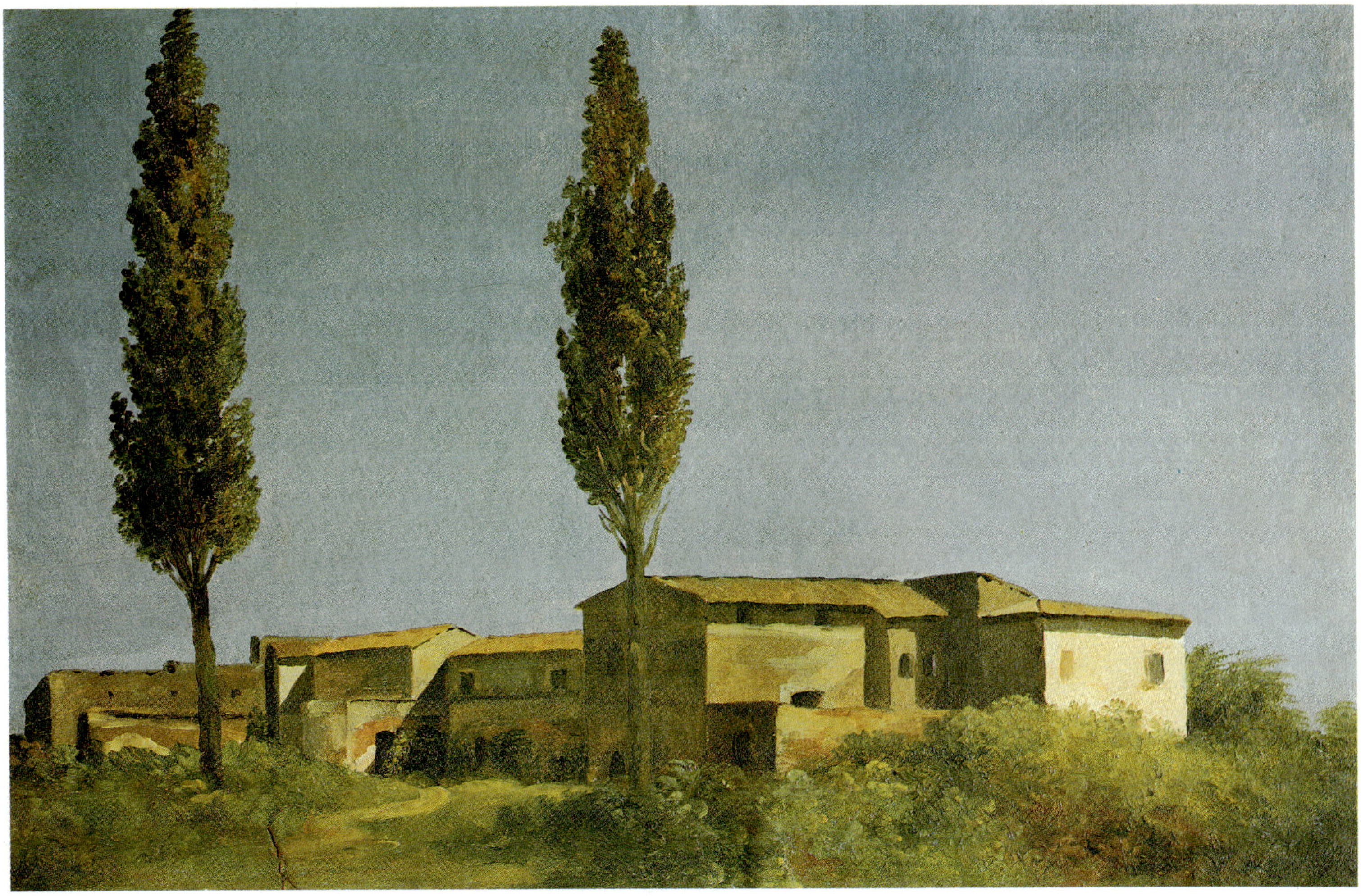

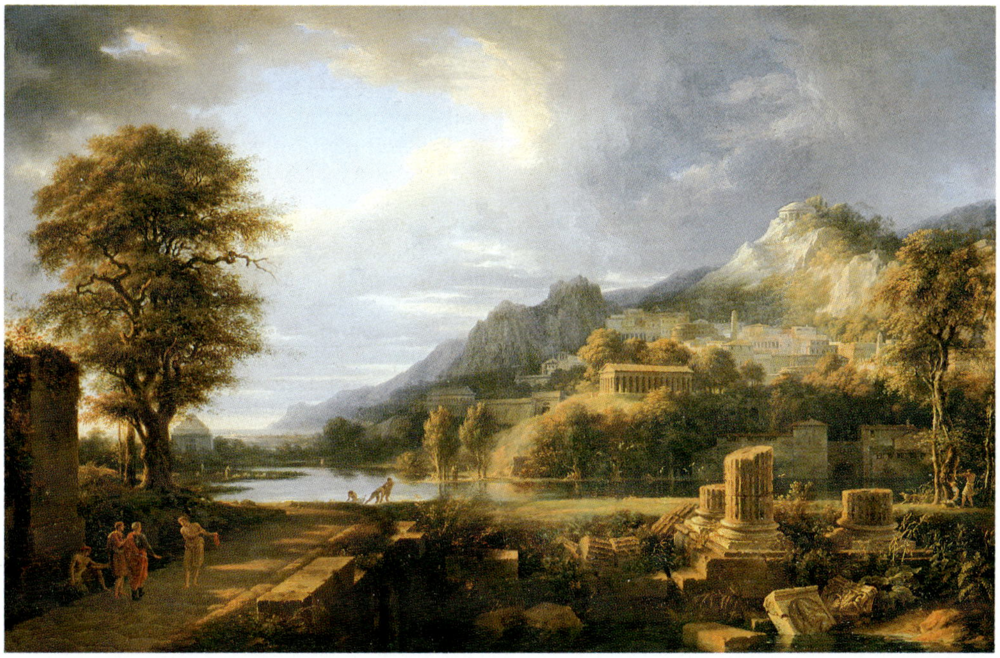

Left *Valenciennes was responsible for the revival in the 1780s of the ideal 'historical landscape' in the seventeenth century manner.* The Ancient City of Agrigentum: Ideal Landscape *(1787) was painted in oil on canvas. In 1800 he published an important treatise on landscape painting, and his ideas dominated French landscape painting for decades afterwards. His work led to the founding of the Rome Prize in landscape painting in 1816. The studio executed, historical landscape was lit by a contrived* chiaroscuro, *and usually contained small figures and classical ruins.*

century artists who held David responsible not simply for the classical revival but, more importantly, for the complete rupture with the tradition of technical expertise. It is true that David discouraged his students from studying and learning from their eighteenth century Rococo predecessors, but the breakdown in traditional painting methods was by then in any case virtually total.

David's affected disdain for technical tradition simply echoed the age-old split between the intellectual and manual aspects of art. The dissolution of traditional practical know-how had gone hand in hand with the rise of academic training in the seventeenth century. The craft-based guilds had fostered practical expertise, which was handed down by the apprenticeship system from master to pupil. Apprentices had originally to learn all the skills of the trade before they began studying drawing and painting, and thus they were well versed in the chemistry of their materials.

In the early days of the Academies, painting techniques were similarly picked up from the master in whose *atelier* students worked. However, as the preparation of materials was taken out of the hands of trainees and taken over by professional merchants and specialists, there was no longer a need for this side of the trade to be learned, leaving artists with no practical knowledge of their materials. Nothing was introduced into the students' training to replace this lost knowledge, and awareness of the basic constituents and properties of their tools-in-trade was soon lost to artists.

This development is not surprising in view of the attitude of artists to the sordid practicalities which had long linked their profession to that of the common artisan. But not only was the knowledge of materials lost, techniques for handling them survived only to become sterile rules, meaningless and misunderstood by those who used them. Artists' problems were further complicated in the nineteenth century by the introduction of mass-production into the artists' materials trade, which transformed their equipment almost beyond recognition.

Contemporary writers disagreed as to the cause of this technical malaise. Some traditionalists felt inadequate training of the artist was to blame. Color merchants, like the famous English paint chemist George Field, were quick to take this side to defend their profession. He wrote in 1835 that the 'odium of employing bad articles attaches to the artist if he resorts to vicious sources or employ his means improperly'. However, as the French specialist on artist's techniques J. F. L. Mérimée had pointed out in 1830, artists 'no longer learning the nature of their colors were incompetent to detect fraud or to distinguish the good from the inferior sort.' Many therefore used whatever came to hand and some even preferred the cheapest materials available.

Couture also believed that artists themselves rather than poor materials were to blame for the loss of sound painting. He wrote that it was a great prejudice to think that modern colors were less good than those used by the Old Masters. He naively considered that the best paints were the simplest, like those used by housepainters, and, for this reason, he felt that the excessive care and complicated preparation employed by artists' colormen were detrimental to the resulting colors. For Couture, the solidity of Old Master paintings came not

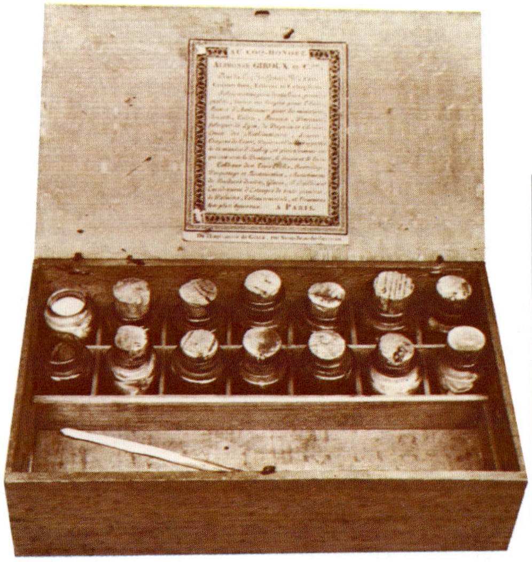

Right *This box of powder pigments in bottles was packaged and sold by the French color merchant Alphonse Giroux around 1800. The label on the lid lists materials supplied by this dealer.*

from superior materials, but simply from better painting methods. Renoir (1841–1919) had similar views, which he expressed forcibly on several occasions.

**The rise of the color merchant**

From about the mid eighteenth century onwards, artists thought that Old Master methods had been lost as a result of jealously guarded professional secrecy among practitioners. This notion derived from the existence of published volumes of *Secreti*. These were books of assorted chemical and medicinal recipes originating from medieval and later writers. Despite their title, however, these were expressly intended to make knowledge widely available. Thus the traditional recipes and handling techniques had been lost not as a result of any mean tight-fistedness among earlier practitioners, but through the changes in structure of artists' training which left them ignorant of such things, and deprived the printed knowledge of its practical meaning. By the time the guilds had been superseded by professional colormen, the concern was for profit rather than for durability. Preparation of materials became exclusively the business of traders, who, in the words of Mérimée 'had a stronger feeling toward their own immediate profit, than any regard to the preservation of pictures'. This resulted in the deterioration and rapid changes that took place in many eighteenth century pictures.

From about the early to mid seventeenth century up until the mid eighteenth century, the trade in artists' materials was associated with the more general trades of pharmacy and grocery. Although the influential late seventeenth century art theorist Roger de Piles mentioned 'color vendors', it was apparently only after the mid eighteenth century that artists' colormen began appearing as an independent class of trader. Most early color merchants concentrated on the manufacture of a particular commodity – watercolors, varnishes, particular oil colors or pastels, for example, and often bought their raw materials from different manufacturers. However, they all retailed a complete range of items essential to the artist, including supports, frames, brushes, drawing materials, paper, palettes and easels which were ready made by other specialist manufacturers. Thus a particular colorman could be engaged in the specialized production and improvement of one product – like the 'artificial crayons' perfected in the late eighteenth century by Conté – which would then appear amongst the merchandise retailed by other color merchants. Many merchants who began by selling artists' materials soon diversified, moving into picture dealing and restoration by way of renting out engravings and pictures for amateurs to copy. A famous example was the Durand-Ruel family, who began as paper retailers and became the first, most loyal and most important dealers in Impressionist paintings. Other firms began as small manufacturers or retailers and expanded into large-scale mass-producers and entrepreneurs, supplying their goods to the retail side of the trade.

**New techniques**

A further disincentive to French artists to pursue more scientifically the bases of their materials and methods, was the ever present association of craft skills with demeaning manual work. This was an especially pertinent stigma at a time when most academic and independent artists were struggling to be accepted into the bourgeois social class. Added to this, craftsmanship in the nineteenth century seems to have become inextricably, though mistakenly, linked in the minds of independent artists, with the laborious finishing procedures of Academic painting. Thus craftsmanship, in the latter third of the nineteenth century, came to be seen by many artists as a restraint upon personal expression and creativity. These were precisely the features held to be so important among independent painters. In his discussion of the need for careful craftsmanship in the build-up of the paint layer, the artist and paint scientist Vibert all but apologized for his concern, keenly emphasizing that it would not inhibit inspiration. Rather it would aid originality by providing a sound technical basis for the enduring expression of the artist's personality.

Vibert recommended *alla prima* or 'at-a-single-sitting' painting as the most durable and safe method, but, as he considered it an extremely difficult technique that few could master, he insisted upon careful underpainting. The methods promoted by academic training were in fact contradictory. On the one hand, hasty execution was encouraged because students were pressured by time. However, on the other hand, speed was incompatible with the reworked, multilayered finishing techniques fostered by the Academy, because slow and thorough drying of each successive layer in an oil painting is essential to the work's durability. These successive reworkings resulted in a complex paint layer which was extremely vulnerable because of the increased number of unpredictable chemical reactions involved. The independent rural landscapists, and later the Impressionists, discouraged repeated reworkings by advocating *alla prima* painting and landscape *études* executed rapidly before nature. This meant that they were simultaneously insisting upon the importance of permanency in their works.

Thus, from the 1850s on, the growing popularity of the rapid, sketch-like *alla prima* painting technique – which facilitated the recording of natural effects – had clear practical advantages. In addition to its aesthetic attraction in reflecting the artist's originality, it was also more suited to the new, mass-produced materials available. Many independents, like Manet in the 1860s, were to attempt a compromise between old and new methods, trying to fuse traditional elements with the search for immediacy, for the effect of spontaneity in their work. It was as a result of the lively experimentation which dominated artistic activity during this decade, that the obsolete *chiaroscuro* techniques were finally superseded by the novel techniques of Impressionism.

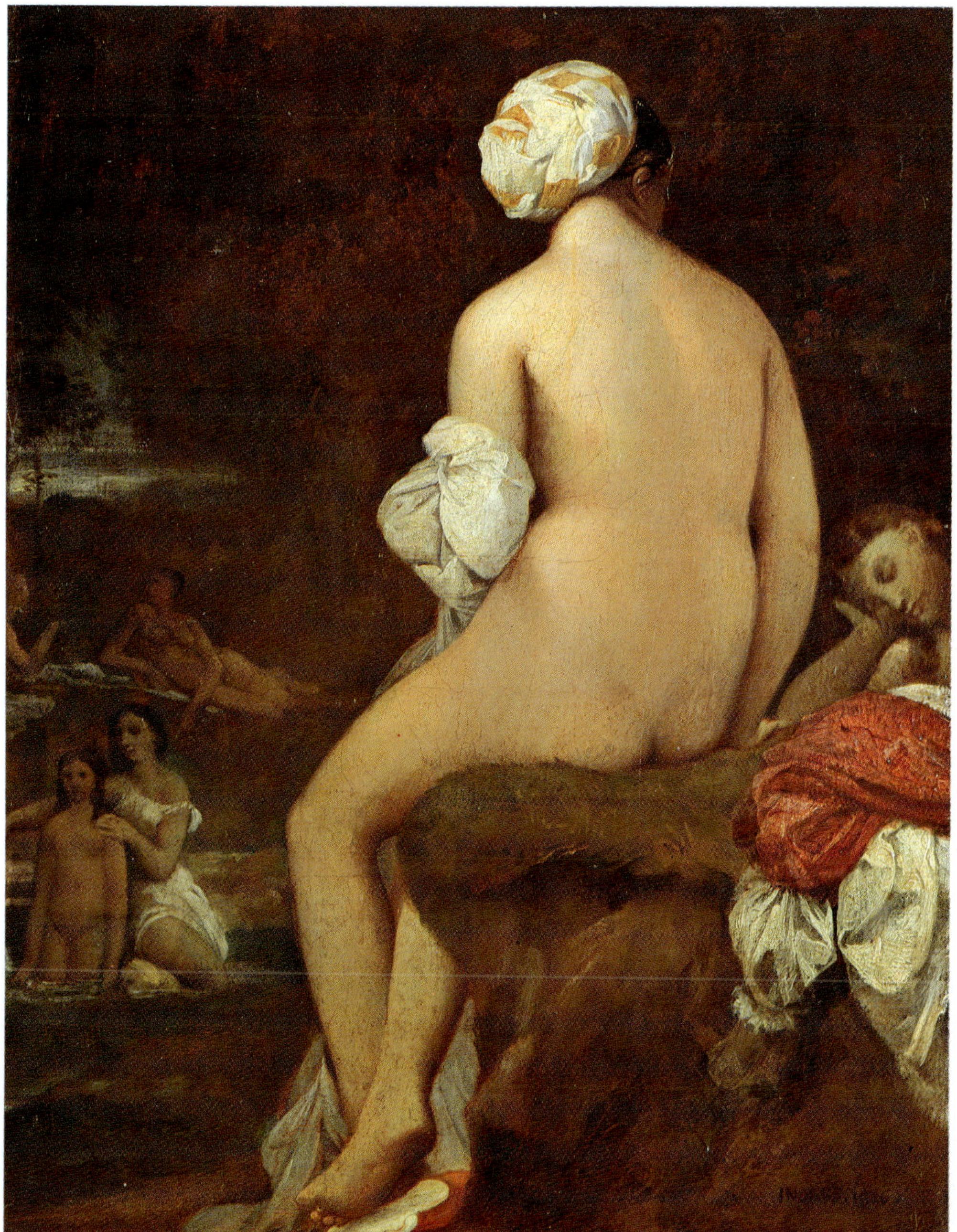

Left *Ingres painted this work,* Bather *(1826), in oil on canvas. Ingres' work shows the attempt to combine landscape backgrounds with figures painted indoors, in the studio. The main figure in particular demonstrates the problems of integrating an indoor lit figure in an invented landscape, for the crisply focused light and sharp, warm shadows could only result from an interior setting. However, the gently diffused light and shade on the back and legs softens the contrast between the nude and her surroundings, and the other bathers appear only in half shadow. This treatment, and the opaque color in the shadows, show how Ingres reacted against the severe tonal contrasts of academic* chiaroscuro. *The main bather had appeared in an earlier work,* The Valpinçon Bather *(1808) and shows Ingres' love of reusing certain poses. This is comparable to Degas' later reworkings of both poses and themes.*

**1860**
**1870**

The 1860s was a decade of dynamic change in painting, a period in which tradition and innovation were fused in the work of major independent, non-academic artists like Edouard Manet (1832–1883) and Edgar Degas (1834–1917), to produce a new style of painting which aptly reflected the modern age. In the next decade, the 1870s, this style was to develop and become established as Impressionism.

### The new face of Paris

Under Louis Napoleon's Second Empire (1852–1870), the very face of Paris itself was transformed. Narrow cobbled medieval streets of houses throughout the city center were razed to make way for the new tree-lined boulevards, designed by Napoleon III's architect Baron Haussmann (1809–1891). Along these broad avenues – like the rue de Rivoli, boulevards St. Germain and St. Michel and avenue de l'Opéra – terrace cafés opened up, and in this environment of light-filled sunny promenades, the life of the Romantic dandy artist, the cool *flâneur* or boulevard stroller, took on new meaning.

The avant-garde Parisian artist was no longer the painter of agricultural life or peasants, but of modern city life – the sophisticated dandy's world of cafés, racetracks, parks, concerts, balls, the opera and the ballet. Backstage, behind Haussmann's elegant, pale stone facades, lay the *demi-monde*, the twilight world which serviced the sophisticated leisured pleasures which characterized the Second Empire's decadent opulence. These city workers – the street musicians, ragpickers, waiters, laundresses, milliners, barmaids, singers, shopgirls, dancers, courtesans, prostitutes in the *maisons closes* – began to dominate the subject matter of Manet and Degas from the early 1860s. But new subjects, a more direct representation of contemporary themes, demanded new techniques. During the 1860s Manet and Degas, among other artists, found alternatives to academic practice which were more suited to their aesthetic needs. The techniques they evolved look forward to Impressionist methods, which began to emerge in the latter part of the decade in the work of Monet, Renoir, Sisley, Pissarro and Cézanne.

### Old versus new techniques

Impressionist painting came into its own in the 1870s. The Impressionist artists rejected the dark transparent shadows, subtle tonal modeling, somber hues and earth colors of academic *chiaroscuro*. Instead, they advocated bright colors, thinly pale-primed canvases and mat, opaque paint surfaces which were uniformly loaded. Developments in the 1860s paved the way for these changes, each of which can be related to the new characteristics of modern painting materials – which differed markedly from those that had made possible the techniques of the Old Masters.

During the nineteenth century, two distinct methods had been widely established for the rendering of light, subtle halftones and shade in studio painting. The first technique, inspired by Flemish oil painters, dominated academic theory and practice in the first two-thirds of the century. It contrasted thin transparent shadows with opaque impasted lights in painting. As these effects became harder to achieve with modern, machine-ground colors, this method was gradually displaced by a more uniformly solid handling, based on Venetian techniques. In this method, both light and shade were rendered in opaque colors, applied with a loaded brush, while the shadows were deepened and enriched only in the final stages by the addition of transparent glazes. This latter method – minus the final glazing – gained wider popularity through Manet's novel approach in the 1860s and was to form the basis for the densely painted surfaces of Impressionist works in the 1870s.

There were clear-cut practical reasons for this change, determined both by developments in the artists' materials trade, and by artists' loss of traditional practical knowledge. Since at least the mid eighteenth century, artists had grown ever more aware that their technical expertise was inadequate to recreate a handling comparable to that of the Old Masters. Further, changes in modern paints due to mass-production made such emulation virtually impossible. In fact, the development of the Impressionists' loaded shadow technique was far from purely aesthetic in inspiration – the mechanical production of colors played a central role in this change from the use of transparent colors. Three factors were of particular importance – mechanical grinding, oil binders, and the additives used to keep paint homogeneous in the new tube containers.

### Mechanical grinding of artists' colors

Traditionally, paint had been ground by hand by skilled workers, using a stone muller on a flat slab made of impermeable stone, such as porphyry. Mechanical grinding first became feasible around 1800, when an Englishman, Rawlinson, published details of a hand-operated, single-roll grinding mill, which was recommended by the influential Royal Society of Arts. Bouvier, the Swiss-French painter and writer on artists' methods, recorded that in 1801 he had first considered the possibility of mechanical grinding, in order to aid the arts and improve the lot of the hand color grinder, who was often obliged to work with poisonous chemicals. In 1833 the Parisian *Annual Commercial Directory* carried an advertisement for the firm of Bonnot & Cerceuil, manufacturers of oil colors for printing wallpapers and for the building trade, which stated that their steam-powered grinding machinery was at the dis-

Below *This wood engraving shows an apprentice or workman grinding artists' color in the 1400s. A smooth slab of impermeable stone such as porphyry was normally used. The stone muller was moved over it, grinding the color with the binder in rhythmical circular movements. Vermilion, the pigment being ground here, requires extensive grinding to produce sufficiently fine particles to give good color. The grinding time and volume of oil binder required varies from pigment to pigment.*

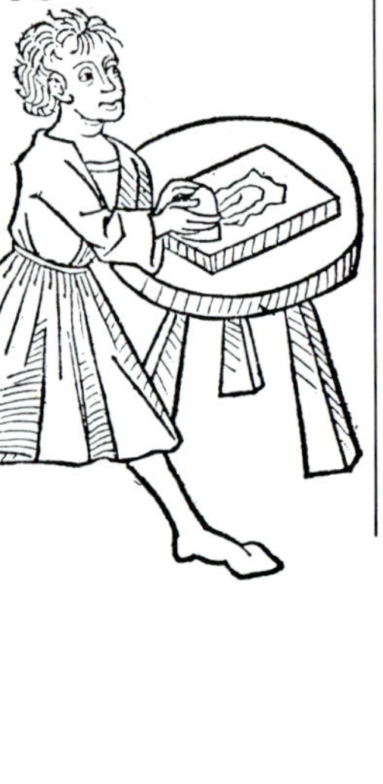

posal of customers for the grinding of all their colors and pigments.

Mechanical grinding was at first considered to produce paints too coarse for artists' colors, which were known as *couleurs fines* to distinguish them from coach or house painting colors. The first color merchant to offer mechanically ground artists' colors was Blot, in the rue St. Honoré, Paris, in 1836.

Although in the early days of mechanical grinding too coarse a substance had been produced for use by artists, growing sophistication soon solved this technical problem, but, instead, overgrinding became a common practice. This meant that the subtle variations required in grinding different pigments to bring out their individual characteristics, were lost. These changes affected what artists could achieve with their colors, making dark transparencies problematic, but encouraging thick opaque painting. When properly ground, oil colors varied greatly in texture. Some tended to be runny, like viridian, ultramarine and vermilion. Others – especially the full-bodied earth colors – were naturally stiffer in consistency and had a coarser grain texture. Dyestuffs, like the red alizarin lakes, may have no discernible particles. When ground correctly, these differences should remain apparent. The distinction in feel of a pigment's qualities, evident to an experienced hand-grinder, were hard to recapture in machine grinding. This, combined with the introduction of additives to create an artificial, uniformly buttery consistency regardless of the properties of individual pigments, resulted in a blandness of paint texture unknown in the old days of hand-grinding to order.

**Oil binders and additives**

Linseed oil was the traditional binder with which powder pigments were ground to make oil colors. However, of all the drying oils used in painting, linseed is the most prone to yellowing. It forms a skin when thickly applied, and thus is best suited to use in thin layers, as in the Old Master techniques, which involved repeated reworkings in thin glazed films. Poppy oil, which came into use only in the seventeenth century, when it was popular with the Dutch, was the most important binder in nineteenth century France. The paint expert Vibert noted that 'today, only poppy oil is used, except for a few dark colors with which the use of linseed oil is accepted.' Unlike linseed oil, which gives the paint surface a smooth, even quality, poppy oil is naturally more buttery in texture. Colors ground in poppy oil retain the mark of the brush, giving a raised textured effect which was exploited by Manet in the 1860s, and which encouraged the development of the textural, descriptive brushwork characteristic of Impressionist techniques. Because it is slow drying, poppy oil was particularly useful where extensive wet-in-wet handling was required, without the repeated reworkings to which it was unsuited.

Artists' colors had traditionally been prepared only as and when they were needed, thus long-term storage presented little problem. However, the rapid expansion of commercial color grinding in the nineteenth century gave rise to a pressing need for an extended shelf-life for the product. There was little point in mass-producing colors which then spoiled during storage in the unpredictable time-lag between manufacture and purchase. As ready ground colors tend to separate from their oil binder when left to stand, and as old oil jellies in the tube, ways had to be found to make sure that paints retained an even consistency, and that the pigment stayed fully dispersed in the oil. Although collapsible tin tubes were only invented in 1840, suitable containers for storing paint had been sought long before then. Bladders for watercolors were in existence in the fifteenth century, and in 1684 the art theorist Roger de Piles mentioned that in Paris some colors, ready ground with their oil binder, were already being sold in pigs' bladders by 'color vendors'. The problems associated with storing oil colors were widely acknowledged by the mid eighteenth century.

Around 1790, an Englishman called Blackman began marketing a new type of ready

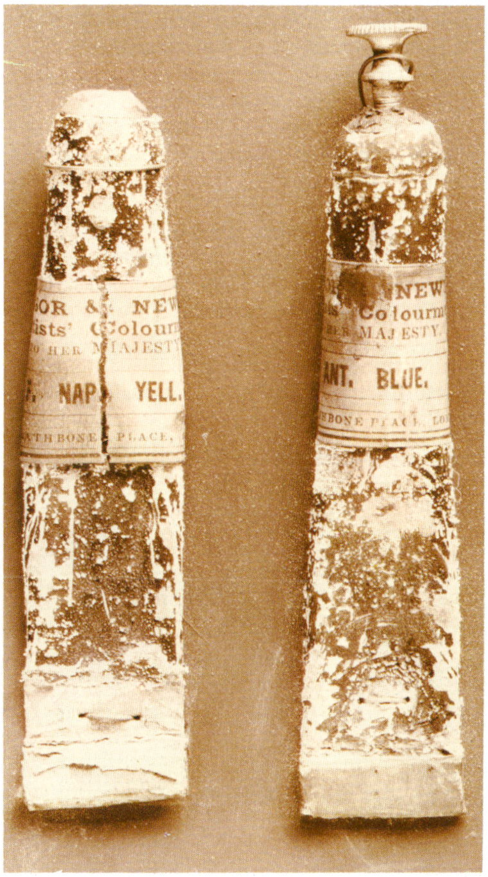

**Left** *This photograph shows two early collapsible tin tubes manufactured by Winsor and Newton around 1841-1842. Collapsible tin tubes were invented, patented and perfected in London by the American artist John Goffe Rand between 1841 and 1843. They improved the handling and portability of oil paints, and solved the problem of airtight storage. Winsor and Newton developed a competitive variant of Goffe Rand's version, which, however, rapidly became the norm. Stoppers are used here instead of screw caps, which Rand promoted. Although tube colors made outdoor oil painting easier, the invention cannot be considered the cause of this practice, since outdoor oil sketching had been popular since the 1780s.*

ground oil color in bladders, which were stiffer in consistency than normal oil colors. He said they were intended to make it easier for landscapists to undertake 'excursions into the country where it might be inconvenient to carry pigments of that kind in the state in which they were usually sold.' To achieve this stiffer paint texture, Blackman added sperm whale oil, or spermaceti – a brittle white fatty substance commonly used in ointments and candles. This addition also involved the inclusion of excesses of oil, for which his colors were soon criticized.

Beef and mutton tallow were other harmful stiffening additives often included in nineteenth century paint manufacture, and these were especially destructive as they never dried. They were thus advantageous only for the color manufacturers, who, as Vibert commented, 'are solely preoccupied with the commercial side of their trade. Their aim is to make colors which retain their freshness in tubes for the longest time possible, and in all climates.'

Wax, especially paraffin wax, was another common additive used in oil colors. While a small proportion of wax – no more than 2 per cent – dissolved in oil of turpentine, improves the consistency of oil colors, and indeed reduces yellowing, excesses are damaging. During this period, up to 30 per cent of wax dissolved in fatty oils was often added, resulting in sticky, dark colors, prone to cracking. Excesses of wax and extra oil went hand in hand. To counteract the fluidity produced by increasing the oil content, which made grinding easier, manufacturers put in more wax to restore the paint's stiffer consistency. This, in turn, permitted them to cut down the amount of pigment required to give a good paint texture. As the pigment was invariably the most costly item in paint manufacture, any reduction increased the color merchants' profits.

By the 1860s color merchants also justified the inclusion of excessive amounts of wax on the grounds that it made the colors more suitable for painting with a palette knife, which had been made popular by Courbet (1819–1877) in paintings like *Deer Haven* (1866). Manet also used knife application of color in the 1860s, particularly for broad background areas. The technique was exploited in this decade and the early 1870s, by some of the younger independent artists, especially Paul Cézanne (1839–1906) and Camille Pissarro (1830–1903). However, knife painting draws the oil binder to the paint surface, and thus aggravates the problem of the yellowing of oil by encouraging it to gather in a surface film. This drawback, together with the Impressionists' growing preference for uneven brush-textured handling, resulted in their abandoning the technique in the later 1870s. It was never adopted by the other members of the Impressionist group, including the major Impressionists, Claude Monet (1840–1926), Pierre Auguste Renoir (1841–1919) or Alfred Sisley (1839–1899).

Unnecessarily large quantities of oil are dangerous, whether in the support priming or in the paints themselves. All oils darken and yellow with age, discoloring and distorting the original color balance and harmonies in a work. Thus, for artists in the 1860s, and particularly the Impressionists later, excessive oils in paints were a serious problem, as their painting required durable bright, light colors. Pale colors were obviously more vulnerable to yellowing and discoloration than dark ones, so, where a luminous effect and subtle color relations were the aim of a painter, special care had to be taken to protect these colors from destruction. Soaking out excess oil by placing colors on blotting paper prior to use, was one precaution adopted by many Impressionist painters.

Every individual pigment has its own optimum level of oil absorption, which it is inadvisable to exceed. This level is the amount of oil required in grinding to achieve both a thorough 'wetting' of each pigment particle, and also the complete dispersal of pigment particles in the oil, to produce an ideal paint consistency. Like the oil absorption level, this ideal

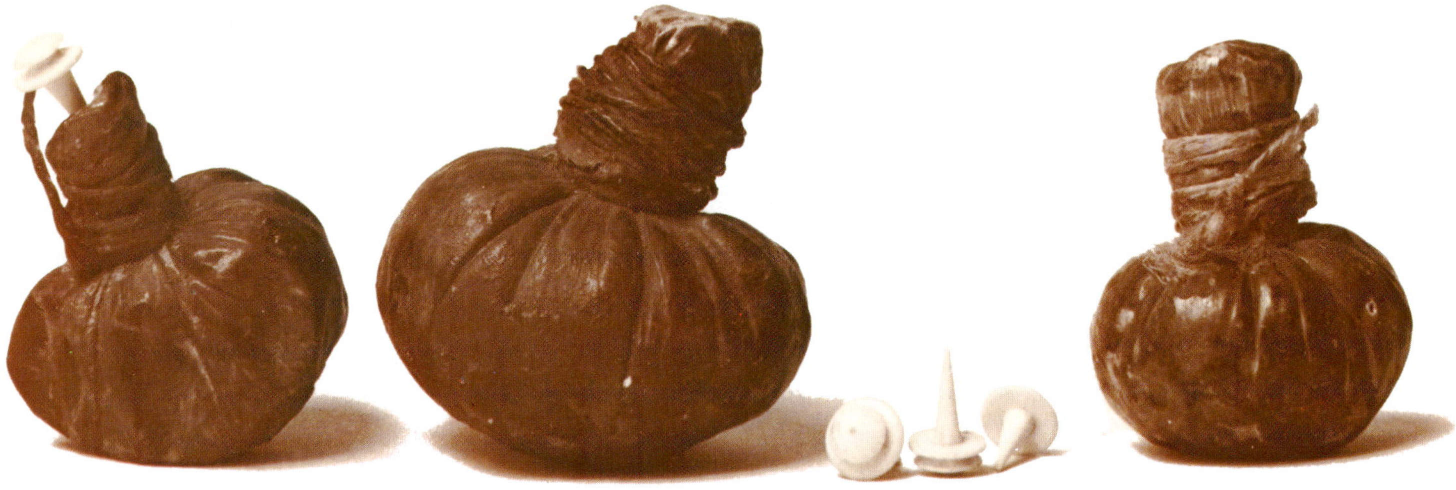

Below *These traditional early nineteenth century oil color containers were pig's bladders, thonged tight and stoppered with ivory tacks, which did not affect the paint chemically. Paints in bladders tended to deteriorate rapidly once they were pierced. In France, collapsible tin tubes only replaced bladders relatively slowly. In 1850, the same volume of color cost 10 centimes more in tubes than in bladders, while in 1855 they still cost 5 centimes extra. The average price of a bladder of paint was then 25 cents, so the difference in cost was considerable.*

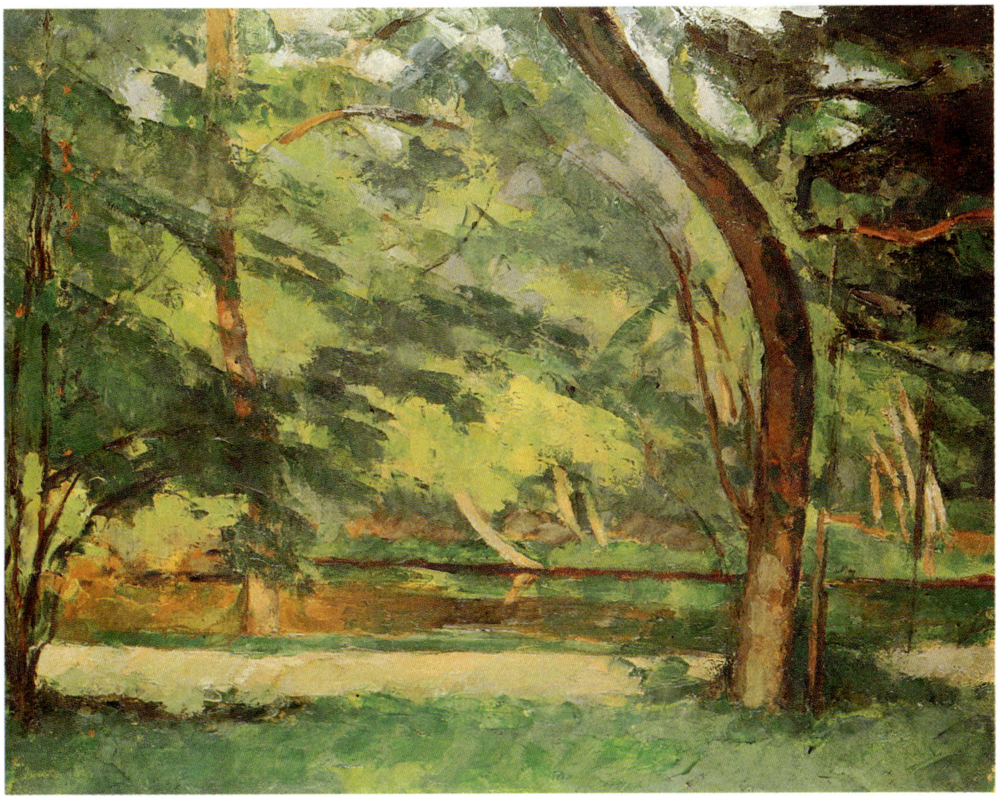

Left *This work,* L'Etang des Soeurs, at Osny, near Pontoise *(1877) by Paul Cézanne shows skilled use of the difficult painting knife technique. The method was popularized by Courbet – and bastardized by less skillful painters, who brought it into ill repute. This technique can be seen in the paint handling, especially in the diagonals which establish rhythms in the foliage. The disadvantage of the technique is its tendency to draw the oil binder to the surface, thus increasing the problems caused by the yellowing of oil.*

consistency varies from pigment to pigment. Some colors, such as raw sienna, naturally absorb high proportions of oil binder, while others, like lead white, require very little oil in grinding. In the long run, pigments which require less oil will result in greater permanency, as these will tend to dry quicker and yellow less.

The homogeneous consistency of modern commercial paints made it difficult for artists to vary their uniformly buttery paint quality – its relative opacity or transparency, stiffness or fluidity – without mixing the colors with harmful thinning vehicles or thickening unctions. Inevitably, any addition to the paint increased its chemical complexity, making its safe usage harder to predict or control. Experts maintained that if only colors were from the outset manufactured with varied viscosity, according to their inherent characteristics and their requisite function on the artist's palette, this further adulteration by the artist could be avoided.

Thus mechanical grinding, poppy oil binder, and waxy additives all combined as factors influencing the texture of mid nineteenth century paints. They no longer possessed the distinctions in texture, that had lent themselves so appropriately to the variations of thin transparency and raised opaques characteristic of Flemish methods, which so many artists continued to seek in their *chiaroscuro* handling. By the 1860s the gradual breakdown of this method, made even more difficult by artists' ignorance of traditional handling techniques, was well under way.

However, rendering the conventional deep, transparent shadows was still a major preoccupation of many artists. For instance, as late as 1867, Manet's teacher, the artist Thomas Couture (1815–1879), described light as mat and shadow as transparent in nature, and noted that the artist's palette was well stocked with sound opaque colors suitable for rendering the lights, but that few good transparent colors were available. Many sound bright transparent colors were on the market then, but traditionalists considered these crass and vulgar, and therefore unsuitable for academic painting. However, it was precisely these colors, usually with the addition of opaque, stable lead white, which were included in the palettes of Manet, Degas and the Impressionists.

**New techniques established**

One of the new techniques which was to be exploited in Impressionist painting was the uniform 'loading' of the paint surface, even in the shadows. Whereas in academic convention, the shadows had been painted thinly and transparently, by the mid nineteenth century many independent artists preferred to paint more solidly, by loading opaque paint in shadow and light areas alike. However, there had been precedents in France for this development. In

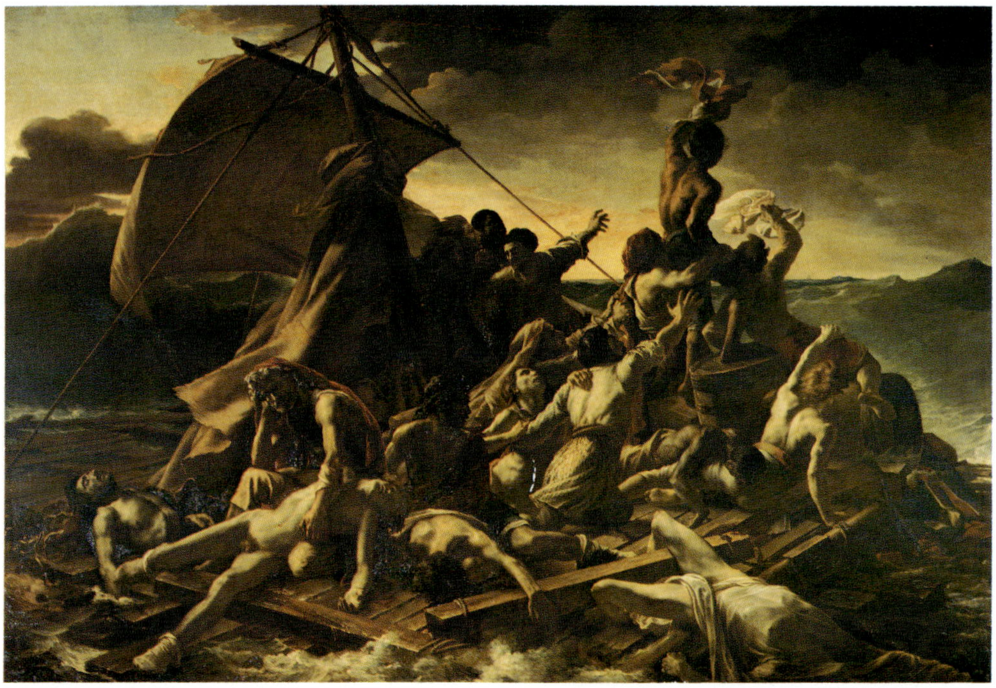

Right The Raft of the Medusa *(1819) by Théodore Géricault was exhibited at the Salon of 1819. The dramatic forms in Géricault's huge contemporary history painting are 'sculpted' by strong contrasts of light and dark. Light falls like a spotlight from the upper left, creating splashes of luminosity which direct the spectator's gaze from lower left up, following the lines and gestures of the figures along the rising diagonal, which ends subtly in the man at the pinnacle of the pyramidical composition. In this way, Géricault combines old and new devices, in depicting this story of modern heroism.*

particular the great eighteenth century painter of domestic scenes Chardin (1699–1779) had used this technique, and his works were much admired by, among others, the artists Paul Cézanne and Camille Pissarro.

In the nineteenth century, Géricault (1791–1824) was the first independent artist to load his shadows, for example in his *Raft of the Medusa* (1819). However, he attempted to retain their transparency by using bitumen – the worst and most dangerous of the glazes, then disparagingly referred to as 'brown sauces', against which painters of the 1860s reacted. When first applied, bitumen gives a seductive, warm transparent brown, apparently ideal for deep shadows. But bitumen is a tarry substance, akin to the asphalt used for surfacing roads today, and, consequently, it never dries completely. Its subsequent cracking and blistering in fluctuating environmental temperatures destroys the paint surface, while the color blackens, losing transparency as it ages.

Géricault's example was followed by the young Delacroix (1798–1863) in the *Barque of Dante* (1822). Such practices, and those of the Romantics, who adopted glutinous brown transparencies, were brought to artists' attention by writers like the famous aesthetician Charles Blanc in the 1860s, who warned of their dangers. Both Courbet and Millet (1814–1875) – whose influence on the younger generation was crucial – also loaded their shadows, although Courbet was more guilty than Millet of the misuse of bitumen. It is significant that all these precedents for richly loaded paint surfaces were among independent artists, painters who were all seeking alternatives to the academic tradition, and whose example was of particular relevance to the younger artists of the 1860s.

Only two artists of the older generation, who trained and worked in an essentially classical tradition, were to prove vital to the younger painters. These were Ingres (1780–1867) and the landscapist Corot (1796–1875). Ingres studiously avoided the use of bitumen in his work, adopting the thinly scumbled opaque shadows taught him by David (1748–1825), which resulted in a shallow pictorial space and a lightness of color which was not found in the work of his academic followers. Corot too, used lead white in his shadows, showing greater concern for depicting the real effects of outdoor light. As a result the overall effect in his landscapes is one of pale silvery luminosity, rather than the somber, toned-down conventional lights and darks of academic studio landscapes, or the heavy darks of Romantic landscapes.

One of the key reasons why Romantics and many Realist painters loaded their shadows, was because they mainly used supports primed with pale grounds, and these needed to be well covered if dark shadows were to be effective. A convincing recession, or turning away of form into shadow, was hard to create on pale grounds. Pale colors tend to advance visually, and dark ones to recede, so dark grounds have an inherent sense of depth which pale grounds lack. In fact, pale grounds have an insistent flatness which resists the most determined efforts to create an illusion of depth on them. Courbet, attempting to persuade the youthful Monet to adopt dark grounds in the early 1860s, was well aware of their advantages when he commented that, on a brown ground 'you can dispose your lights, your colored masses; you immediately see your effect.'

As early as 1750 artists had been aware that the technique of using transparent shadows and thinly applied halftones was vulnerable to the ravages of time. Because the paint layer – the picture itself – becomes increasingly transparent with age, these subtle effects soon disappeared when painted over dark grounds. Even on pale grounds, the overall balance was soon lost, for, as the paint layer grew more transparent, the glazed shadows lost their depth of contrast with the impasted lights. In the long term, pale grounds were safest, as they maintained the overall luminosity of the painting, whereas dark grounds – which darkened further with age – 'rose up' and subdued the hues in the paint layer. It was precisely for these reasons that artists in the 1860s preferred pale grounds.

Isolated examples exist of early works by Cézanne, Monet and Renoir from this decade, executed on dark grounds inspired by Courbet. But, following the example of Manet, they soon adopted pale grounds almost universally because of their brilliance and superior durability. This practice became so common that, in 1865, Pasteur, a professor of geography, physics and chemistry, noted in a lecture at the Ecole des Beaux-Arts that 'nowadays scarcely any but canvases primed white or barely tinted are used.'

In view of the weight of contemporary evidence demonstrating the technical undesirability of chiaroscuresque methods – whether using transparent or loaded shadows – it may seem surprising that so many artists persisted in their use of them. However, not only did these methods have a long and distinguished history, but by the nineteenth century *chiaroscuro* had become more than just a technique.

In the seventeenth century *chiaroscuro* had simply meant either the overall light effect in a composition, or the particular fall of light and shade on each object to give it the necessary relief. By the 1860s, the definition of *chiaroscuro* incorporated a crucial aesthetic ideal too. Its aim, in the words of the important art theorist Charles Blanc, was 'not simply to give relief to the forms, but to correspond to the sentiment that the painter wishes to express, conforming to the conventions of a moral beauty as much as to the laws of natural truth.' Thus the original, practical role of *chiaroscuro* had become overlaid with a new ideological meaning. Chiaroscuresque handling in painting had become synonymous with the academic ideal of elevated moral truth and beauty. Therefore, any rejection of *chiaroscuro* was associated in the minds of the powerful conservative faction, with a rejection of the highest ideals of painting's moral social role, and thus with a rejection of the established conventions of academic art as a whole.

As a result, paintings which failed to exhibit the thin transparent shadows and impasted lights of the approved *chiaroscuro* tradition, were consistently criticized by conservatives for their lack of elevated moral tone. Such paintings were considered deficient in the spiritual, intellectual, refining side of art, which had, since Renaissance times, been thought crucial to the production of great art. A painting which lacked the rational pictorial conventions of *chiaroscuro* was dismissed as raw imitation of nature, banal and unimaginative.

This attitude echoed the traditional split between artist and artisan, between the intellectual and the purely manual in art. For this reason, Impressionist painting was characterized by its critics as exhibiting nothing but manual dexterity. It was even considered seditious. Especially following the Paris Commune of 1871, these artists were often dismissed as communists and anarchists for their flouting of traditional values in art.

**The influence of photography**

Reflecting upon the art of Manet and his followers in the 1860s, the painter and art historian Eugène Fromentin blamed photography for the decline in moral spirituality which he saw in their painting. He felt their work lacked the 'fantasies of the imagination' and the subtle 'mysteries of the palette' which he admired in Dutch and Flemish seventeenth century art. In this period photography had changed artists' vision, particularly their understanding of the effects of light. As a result, with Manet's work in mind, Fromentin observed, 'painting has never been so clear, so explicit, so

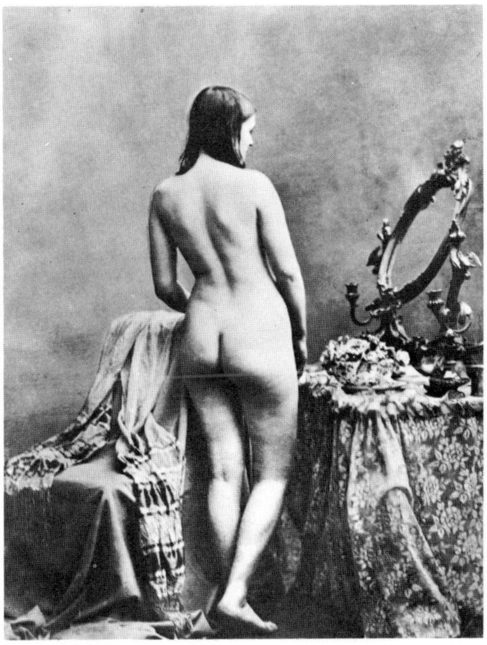

Left *Watson's* Nude Study *of 1856 shows the typical effects of mid nineteenth century photography. Although at first photography was dominated by the aesthetics of painting, technical limitations imposed by the new medium meant that the subtle effects of* chiaroscuro *were impossible to reproduce in a photograph. The lack of sensitivity of early plates or film meant that the delicate gradations of tone from light to dark, so admired by academic painters, were reduced in photographs to simplified blocks of light and dark. Artists like Manet were thus inspired by photography because it suggested an alternative to academic* chiaroscuro *lighting.*

*Below Manet's* Olympia *(1863) was exhibited at the Salon of 1865. The work is close in size to the largest standard canvas format portrait 120, which measures 130 x 194cm (51¼ x 76½ in). Manet's stark full face lighting obliterates tonal gradation. Light and shadow appear as broad, simplified masses or shapes. The directness of the lighting complements the uncompromising presentation of the nude which, as a result, fails to conform to academic conventions.* Olympia *confronts the viewer, who becomes, by implication, her male customer. The artist thus combines new technical as well as aesthetic devices to subvert the traditional depiction of the nude.*

formal, so crude.' The rise of photography from the 1840s, had, for artists, complicated the issue of the illusionistic representation of reality. On the one hand, photography showed them for the first time ever, an 'objective' picture of reality, provoking some artists to attempt an even more fastidiously representational style of painting. On the other hand, for others the very existence of the photographic image was a release from the demands of painstaking representation of the visual world, leaving them free to pursue a more personal recording of nature, like that of the Impressionists. Their method was based on the translation into paint of the individual artist's optical perceptions, a phenomenon beyond the camera's reach. It also freed artists to explore the problems of painting itself.

The lack of sensitivity of early photographic plates or films produced a number of distortions, which were noticed by contemporary critics. In particular, the subtleties of lighting considered so crucial to *chiaroscuro* effects – delicate reflected lights in shadows, and gradated halftones – were destroyed by photography. The resulting exaggeration of darks and lights gave dramatic, simplified areas of strong tonal contrast, which flattened three-dimensional forms into broad, uniform tonal shapes. Thus, artists like Manet, Degas and Fantin Latour (1836–1904), who studied photography in the 1860s, found in its stark contrasts a new way of depicting a simplified, more direct impression of the natural world. Artificial lighting was used in photography from the mid 1850s, created either by electrical batteries or the powerful white flare produced by burning magnesium wire. This resulted in even more extreme oppositions of light and dark. A comparable effect is apparent in Manet's 1863 works *Olympia* and *Luncheon on the Grass*.

**Studios and lighting**

The evolution of new painting technique went hand in hand with changes in studio design and lighting, which were adapted to suit the new aims of the independent artists. The changing layout of the artist's studio reflected the transformation in the organization of pictorial light. The emphasis on a chiaroscuresque handling

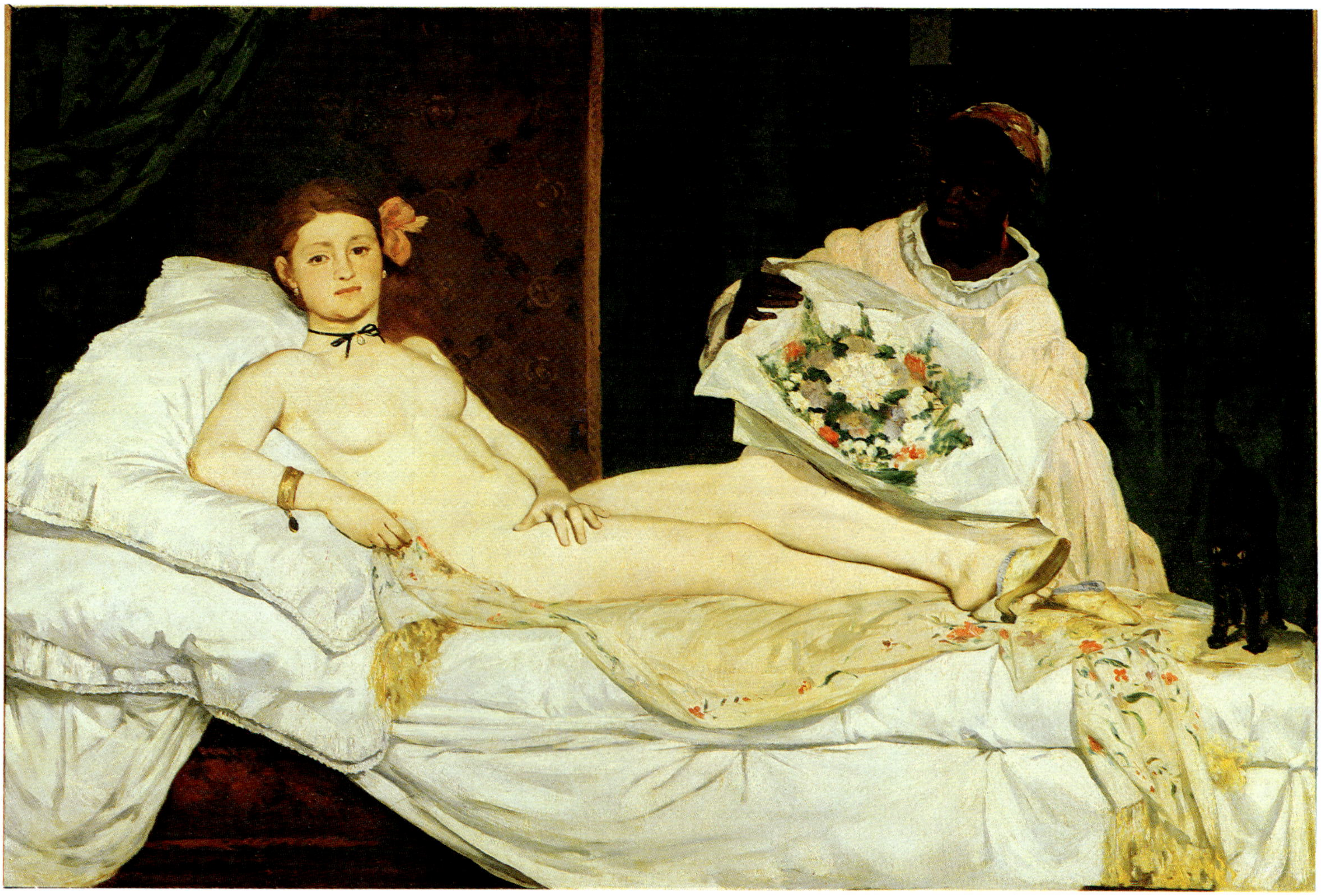

during the century, with its accompanying palette dominated by earth colors and browns, coincided with a studio lighting designed to encourage a tonal pictorial structure. A single high window, giving a controlled light source, was then in common use. This practice gave sharp lights, delicate halftones and deep transparent shadows. All studios normally faced north. This gave a cool, stable light because it was unaffected by the sun's daily passage across the sky, which produced distracting fluctuations in the color of the light and constantly shifting shadows. The academically approved, carefully premeditated, tonal palette layout, with colors gradated from light to dark, and with all the halftones ready mixed by the painter, could only work when painting was done under stringently controlled, steady lighting conditions like these.

A cool northern studio light creates contrasting warm shadows. These were made darker by the restricted volume of light and by the subdued colors with which the walls were generally painted. Thus a tonal palette of somber warm earth colors was perfect for rendering these effects.

The studio environment was therefore constructed to give constant chiaroscuresque lights and shades. Although artists were working from 'nature', it was a nature determined by preconceived ideas of painting, intended only to result in an end-product in which form was depicted through *chiaroscuro*. Multiple light sources and south-facing studios were occasionally recommended by writers criticizing the cool drabness of accepted northern lighting, but they were rarely adopted before the development of Impressionism in the 1870s.

**Landscape painters move outdoors**

As the technical difficulties in *chiaroscuro* painting increased, and dark brown transparent shadows became harder to depict with assured permanency, this form of traditional studio setup gave way to newer environments. The rise of landscape painting was a key factor in this change, for as artists became more committed to an accurate depiction of outdoor sites and lighting, the studio gradually moved outdoors too. At first, in spite of the brilliant sunlight and reflected ambient atmospheric light found outdoors, artists, as it were, took their studio light out with them – they still saw their outdoor environment in terms of *chiaroscuro* and the browns of studio shadows. To some extent this vision was determined by the types of site and lighting preferred in the first half of the century. Dramatic storms, dawns, sunsets, forest or craggy scenes all tend to create strong contrasts of light and shadow, which could be

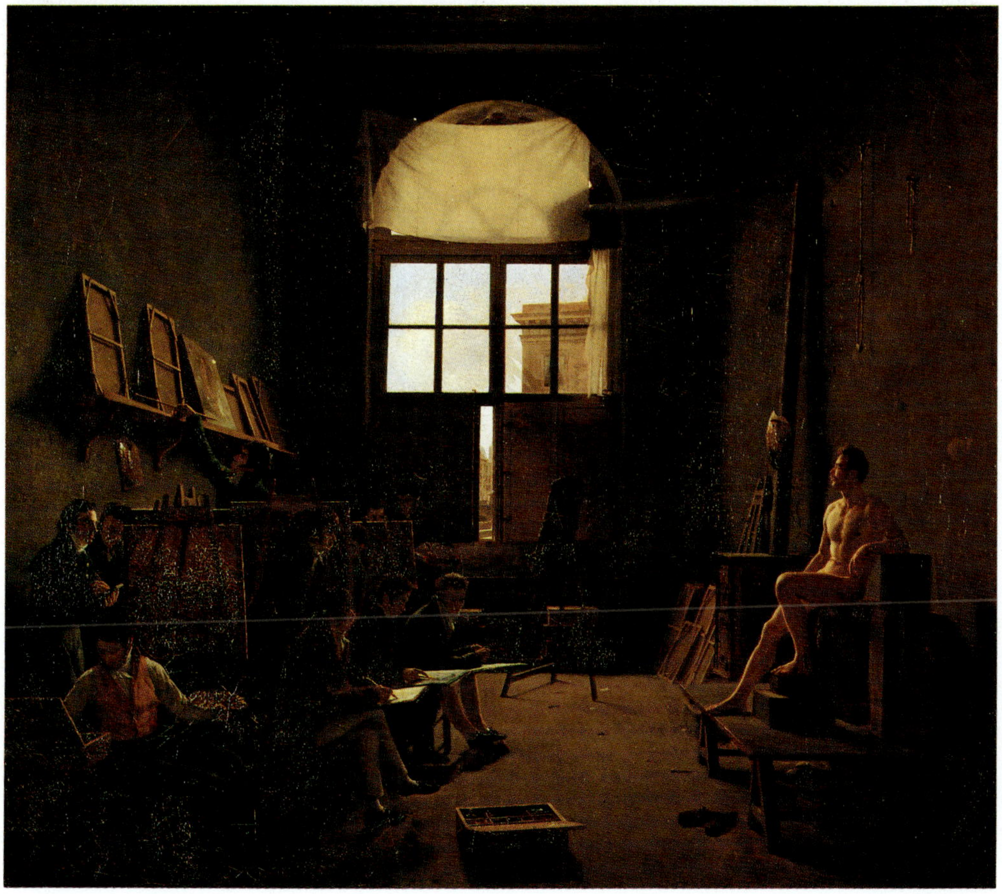

Left *Léon Cochereau's painting of* David's Teaching Atelier *(1814) shows how high windows were used to create a restricted volume of cool northerly daylight, which resulted in a static, controlled fall of light and shade on the model. The lights are bright, as if spot lit, and halftones to make deep warm shadows across the form. The side lighting falling from left to right across the figure enhances the form, emphasizing anatomical detail. A tonal palette is aptly suited to recording these effects. Students are all lined up on the left for, with right-handed painters, light falling from the left onto the work means the artists are not impeded by the shadow cast by their working right arm.*

Right Women in the Garden, *(1866) by Claude Monet was refused by the jury at the Salon show of 1867. Painted in oil on white-primed canvas, this was Monet's first fully successful large-scale figure painting. It shows his commitment to modern life subjects and to creating unified effects of outdoor light in his work. The white dresses provide a neutral base on which to demonstrate the effects of the colored light he observed out of doors. The white is warmed by the yellow sunlight where it falls on the fabric, and, in the shadowed areas, the white is contrastingly modified by cool colors. The violet-blues in the shadows on the foreground dress are composed of the complementary contrast of the yellow light with violet, plus the blue reflected from the sky. The green-striped white dress on the left is tinged by green reflections from the surrounding foliage. Monet has completely rejected the cool light and warm brown of studio modeling, replacing them with contrasts of color.*

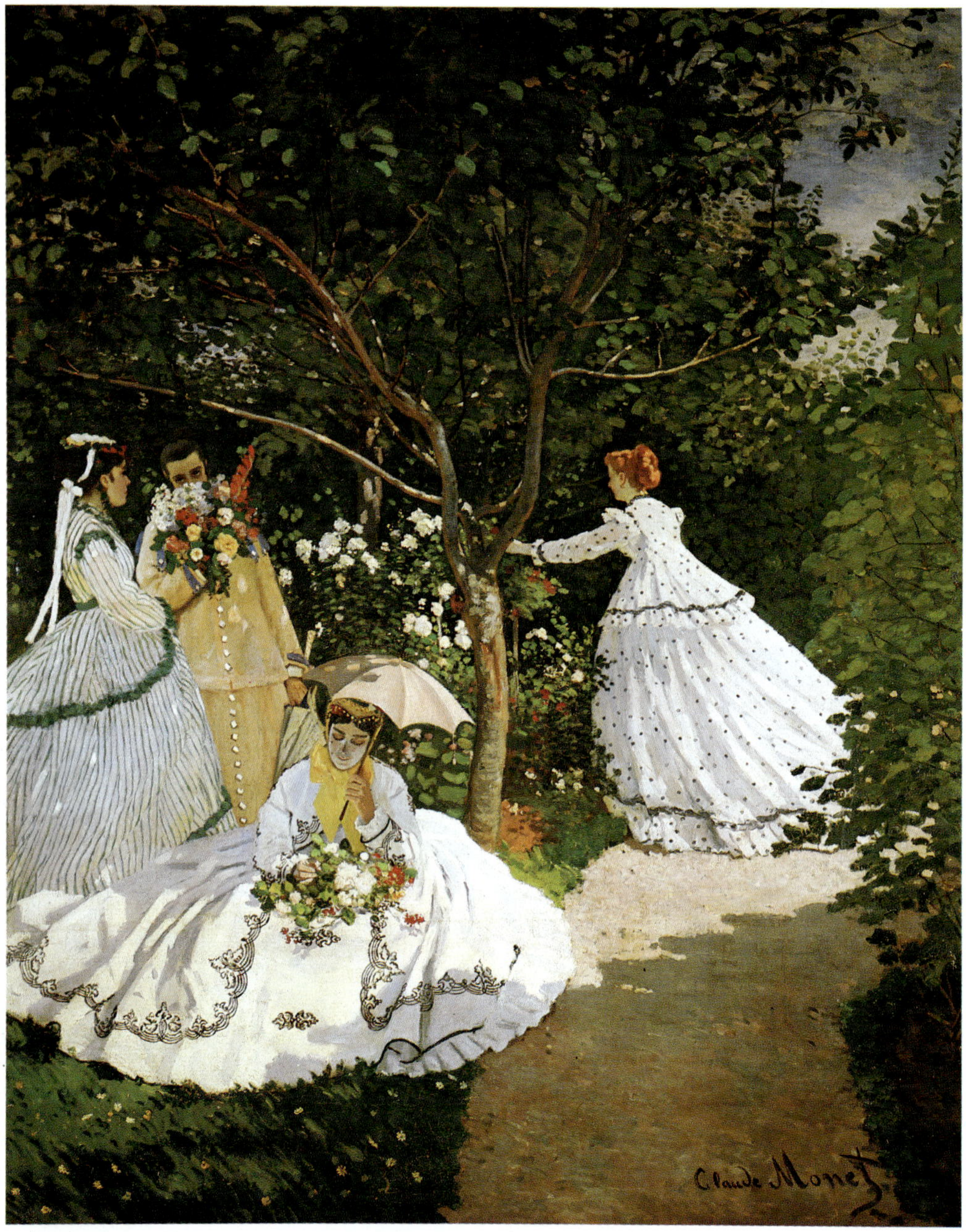


translated in a broadly *chiaroscuro* technique. In any case, many such works, although based on outdoor studies, or even begun outdoors, were normally completed under darker studio conditions.

However, the example of outdoor studies by Corot, with their gold or pale lighting and luminous shadows, provided an important alternative to younger independent painters in the 1860s. Increasingly, artists began to complete their paintings out of doors in order to retain the unity of natural light effects and the impact of the first impression. This renewed determination to capture the quality of light observed *in situ* brought a freeing of artistic vision, which stimulated painters to study brighter, lighter scenery in full daylight.

One of the major problems with studio-executed landscape paintings, especially those including figures, had always been the creation of a convincingly unified lighting. In such paintings, the background lighting was usually quite distinct from that on the figures, which were executed from models under the strictly controlled abrupt lights and darks of the studio. On figures under natural outdoor light, the gradations from light to shade are softer and the shadows more diffused and attenuated, filled with reflected light from the sky. Even in works like Manet's *Luncheon on the Grass*, in which a high academic studio lighting was abandoned, the stark tonal contrasts of interior light are still in evidence. Manet adopted a dramatic frontal light, falling directly onto his figures, which obliterates halftones and reduces shadow to little more than striking black contours. This flattening, full-face light familiar to the artists from contemporary photography, produces broad blocks of light and dark when used indoors. During the 1870s the same full-face light was to be exploited by the Impressionists outdoors, where, by contrast, it suppresses tonal contrasts because shadows fall behind the objects depicted.

**The impact of Japanese prints**

Japanese woodblock color prints, which became widely popular in France from the early 1860s, were an important source of inspiration which offered an alternative to the conventions of European painting. As the critic Théodore Duret remarked in 1878, Japanese prints showed French artists 'the specific appearances of nature by means of bold, new methods of coloring.' These prints used flat areas of bright color, rather than modeling form through a depiction of the fall of light and shade. Form was both implied and denied in their work by evocative contour and by overlapping planes of color. A Western single-point perspective had never been developed independently by Japanese artists. Instead, space was suggested by placing one object behind another. Unusual, often high viewpoints, looking down on a scene were often adopted in Japanese prints, and this emphasized a decorative flatness of form and space by tipping the scene up closer to the surface of the picture. This device was taken over by avant-garde artists from the 1860s on, giving their pictures a spatial and compositional flatness which complemented the new uniform loading of their paint surfaces.

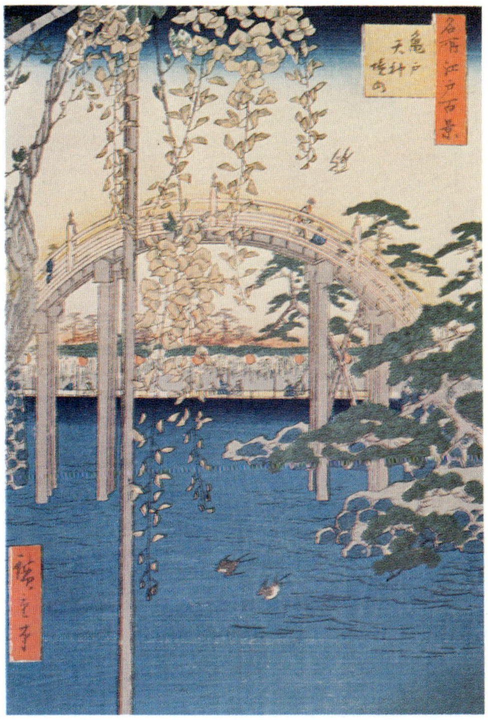

Right *Japanese prints were widely available in France from the early 1860s, and examples of Japanese art were exhibited for the first time on a large scale at the Paris World's Fair of 1867, where the Japanese had a pavilion. This color woodblock print shows* Wisteria Blooms over Water at Kameido *(c1857) by the Japanese artist Hiroshige. The Japanese love of nature, and their pleasure in representing it in their art, attracted French artists' admiration almost as much as their modern life subjects, their unusual compositions and their use of brilliant color. Prints such as this one combine the decorative and naturalistic, and this proved an important example to French artists.*

In Japanese prints, sensual line and blocks of vivid color weave patterns across the picture surface, causing the eye to wander undirected over it instead of forcing the eye to focus on a central point of interest. A comparable phenomenon resulted from the peculiarities of photography, and both proved a timely alternative to academic conventions. The photograph, although no more 'objective' in the strictest sense than the human eye, showed a different picture than that possible with human binocular vision. Within a given depth or field of focus, the camera's monocular lens records every object with equal force and clarity. Human vision is more selective, in that, outside a central focal area, all objects are more or less blurred. A new interest among artists in creating an overall focus of attention in their work was a natural outgrowth of the study of photographs. 'Snapshot' photography, which came in in the early 1860s, succeeded in freezing moving figures. This new vision of accidentally distributed passers-by became a feature of paintings at this time, in which apparently casually placed or cut-off figures gave an air of direct immediacy. The modern city life in Paris could thus be rendered with the sensation of a glimpse of the uninterrupted panorama of teeming activity, a slice of fleeting life, seen most typically in the work of Degas.

Thus, many artists began to avoid a central or single point of focus in their compositions, experimenting instead with designs that had no hierarchy of pictorial interest. This type of leveling process, which failed to direct the spectator's eye into a traditional self-contained, coherent pictorial space and toward a fixed point of interest, left public and critics bewildered. Few understood the aims of this style, and most critics exhorted the independent artists to return to the conventions of traditional academic *chiaroscuro*, which had imposed their own familiar aesthetic order on the painter's subject. The combination of an even, uniform focus, an overall loading of the paint surface, and a flattened pictorial space in the new painting gave no easy clues to the reading and understanding of the pictorial intention. Manet's *Concert in the Tuileries* (1862) and Degas' *Chrysanthemums* (1858–1865), are excellent examples of this.

**Toward Impressionism**

While photography afforded a new and – broadly speaking – more naturalistic vision of light than the conventionalized lighting in *chiaroscuro* painting, it still presented form in

Right Woman with Chrysanthemums *(1858-1865) by Edgar Degas was painted in oil on canvas. It is likely that this work began as a relatively conventional flower study – a testament to Degas' admiration for Delacroix who painted similar subjects. The figure was only added later. The resulting asymmetrical composition probably dates from 1865, when Degas was experimenting with less conventional designs. The off-center placing of the figure shows Degas' active opposition to academic conventions, which dictated a strict hierarchy of composition based on the relative importance of objects depicted.*

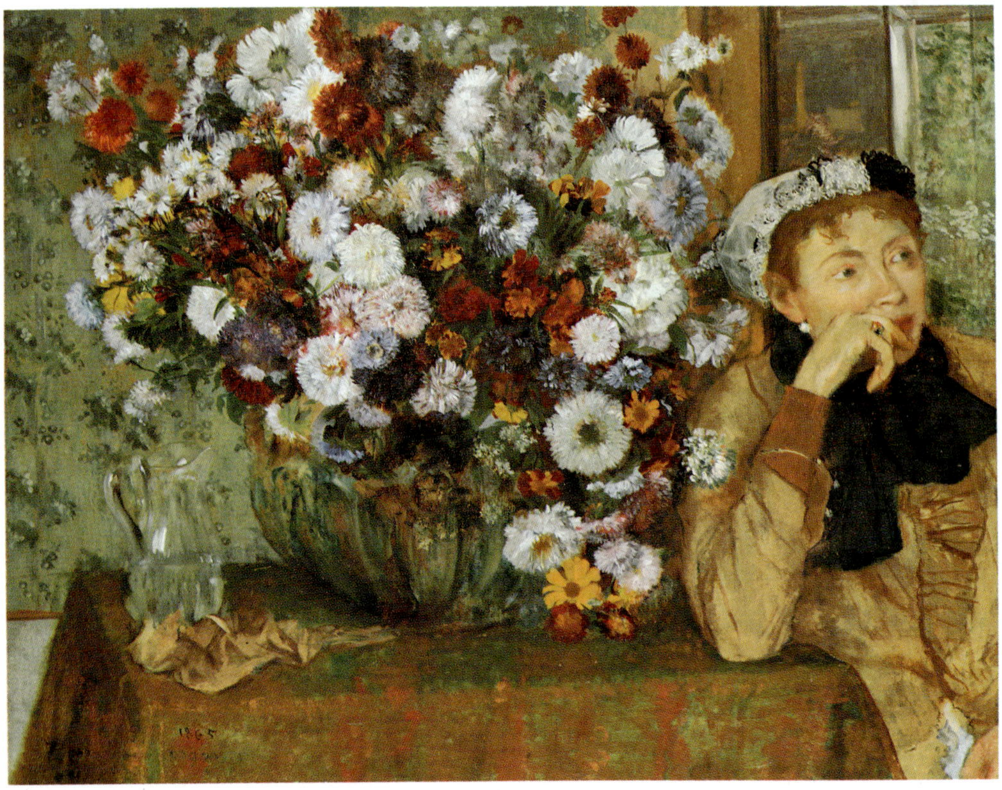

terms of strong tonal lights and darks. Although in their studio-painted studies of interiors the younger independent artists relied greatly on the example of Manet, Degas and Courbet during the 1860s, their landscape work shows them moving away from tonal handling. Thus Monet's reworking of Manet's radical subject of 1863, *Luncheon on the Grass* in 1865 to 1866, of which only fragments survive, attempted a more authentic depiction of outdoor light effects. A more successful painting, Monet's *Women in the Garden* (1866), begun outdoors and finished in the studio, created a new unity between the effects of sunlight on landscape and figures.

In their pre-Impressionist work of the 1860s, artists like Monet and Renoir already gave hints of later developments. The shadows in Monet's *Women in the Garden*, like those in Renoir's *Lise with a Parasol* (1867) and *The Pont des Arts* (1867) were filled with reflected light and cool blue-violet hues picked up from the sky, contrasting with the pervasive warmth of the sunlight. Monet's early experiences in outdoor work with his mentor Eugène Boudin (1824–1898) along the Normandy coast, in the late 1850s and early 1860s, gave him an advantage over Renoir who only began painting outside in 1863. He did this at the instigation of his tutor Charles Gleyre (1806–1874), in whose sympathetic anti-academic teaching studio he had first met Monet, Sisley and Frédéric Bazille (1841–1870) in the autumn of 1862. Since they all worked together regularly, both indoors

Below La Grenouillère *by Renoir dates from 1869. Renoir had gained more experience in figure painting than in work directly from landscape subjects during the 1860s, and his touch shows less confidence and experience than that of Monet. Like Monet, Renoir gave his work a strong underlying structure, with series of vertical and horizontal lines, and recession aided by the foreground boats.*

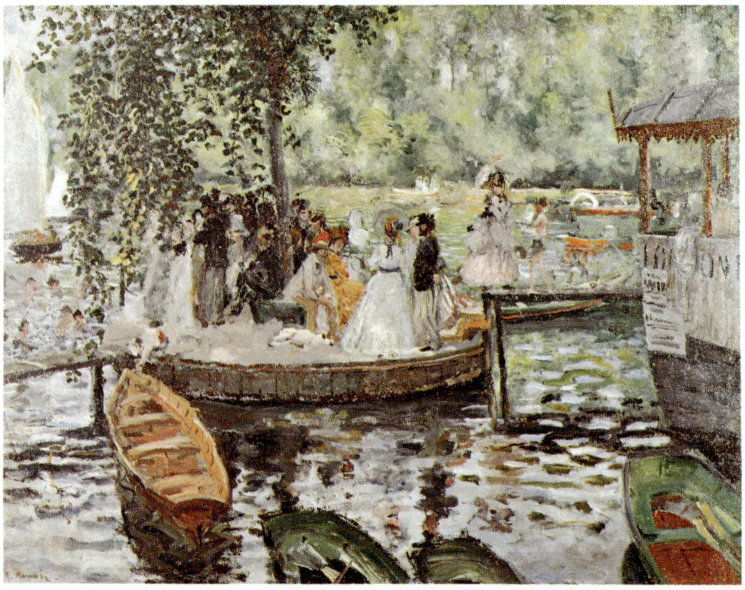

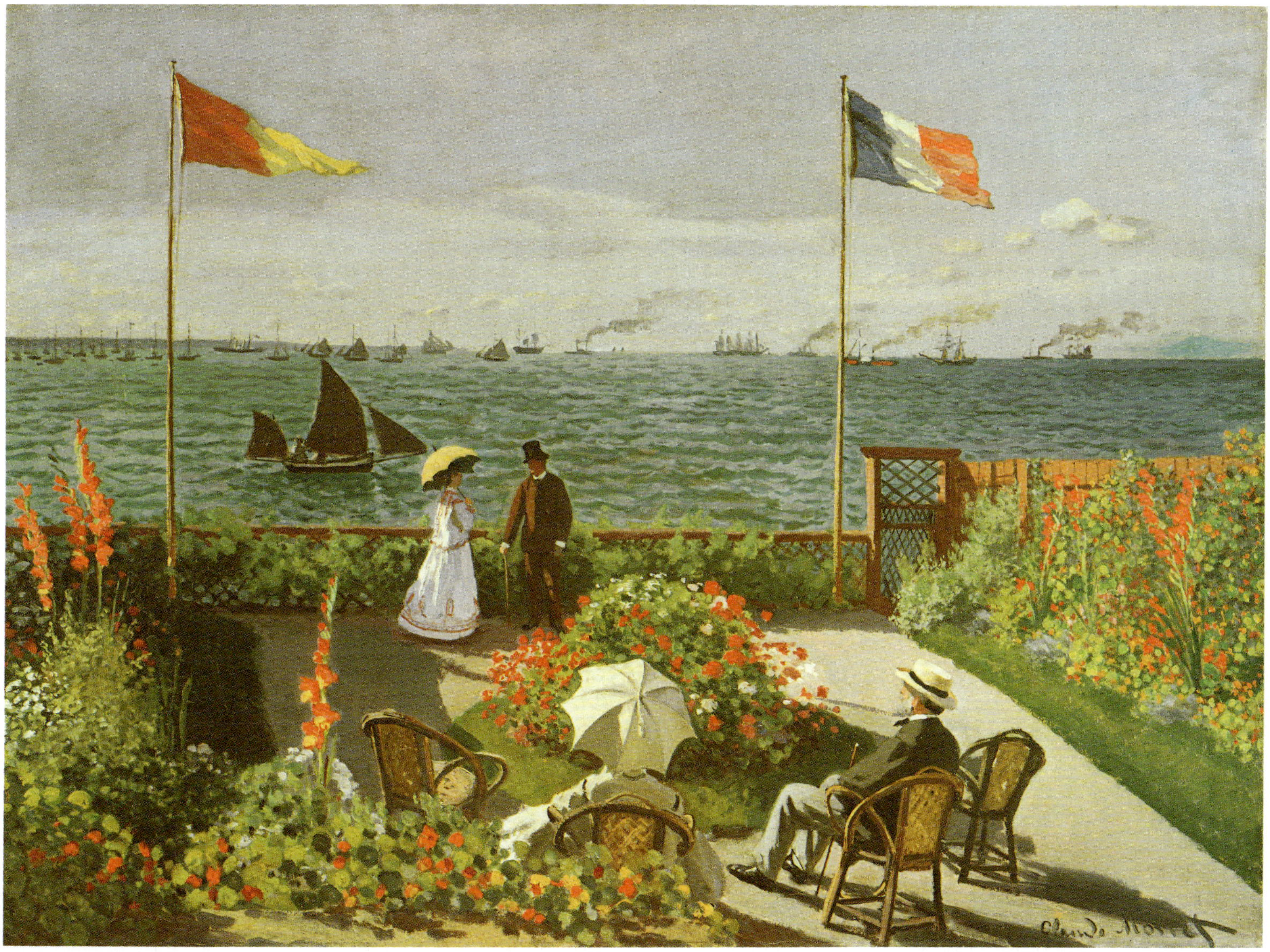

and out in the 1860s and early 1870s, they were able to benefit from each other's growing expertise and competence.

When in Paris, they all joined Manet's gatherings of artistic and literary figures at the Café Guerbois, on one of the new boulevards – now avenue de Clichy – in the Batignolles quarter on the fringe of Montmartre. These discussions often included writers and critics like Emile Zola, Edmond Duranty and Théodore Duret. Artists who joined them included Degas, Cézanne, Renoir, Fantin Latour and Pissarro. Monet later recalled that 'from them we emerged with a firmer will, with our thoughts clearer and more distinct.' As they only painted during daylight hours, in the evenings they were free to meet, argue and exchange the latest ideas. It was during this time that many of these artists began to formulate the project for independent group shows, which would provide an alternative venue to the official Salon exhibition. This idea finally came to fruition in 1874, the year of the first group exhibition, at which a critic coined the name 'Impressionism'.

The year 1869 is now commonly seen as the turning point in the development of the Impressionist style. That summer, Monet and Renoir worked side by side along the banks of the river Seine at La Grenouillère, one of the new leisure spots just outside Paris. With their portable easels and traveling paintboxes, they painted rapid studies in free sketchy brushwork, attempting to capture the fleeting effects of sunlight on mobile water, to note down their impressions before the transitory scene. Although their methods and palette were to change considerably in the following decade, the basis for the new Impressionist techniques was already established.

Above *In* Terrace at Sainte-Adresse *(1867) the afternoon sunlight falls from the left, almost diagonally towards the spectator. Yet stark contrasts of light and shade are kept to a minimum, and used for decorative effect rather than for structuring form or space. Bright colors are concentrated into flat shapes, such as the sky, sea and sunlit terrace. This is reminiscent of Japanese prints. A stark geometric grid of lines also flattens the pictorial space. Sharp contrasts of red and green dominate the lower half of the canvas.*

# EDOUARD MANET

*The Picnic/Déjeuner sur l'herbe* (1863)
Oil on canvas, 208cm × 264cm/82in × 104in

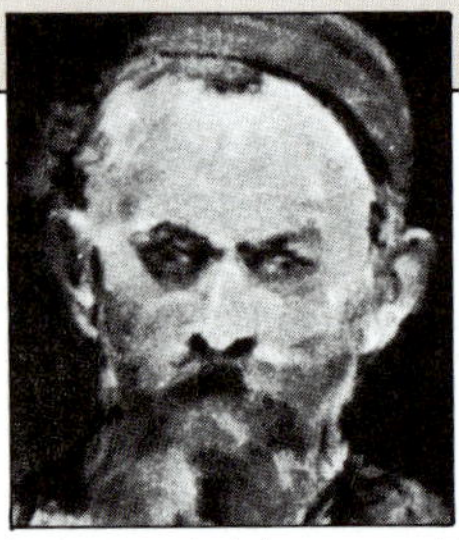

In the course of his career, Manet directed the subject matter of Realist painting away from rural life towards the modern urban life of Paris. Early in his work, Manet developed a slurred, wet-in-wet technique of mixing colors directly on the canvas. He also suppressed middle tones and boldly stressed areas of light and dark. For this, he chose a strong, full-faced light source to eliminate half-tones and create flattened planes of light and shade. Manet's early subjects show the influence of Spanish painting, particularly Velazquez, and reflect an awareness of contemporary, popular prints.

Manet exploited pale grounds, often gray or creamy off-white, for their luminosity and flatness. It is more difficult to create an illusion of depth on a pale ground than a dark one and he used this to advantage in creating a shallow pictorial space. On such a ground, thinly painted areas contrasted with the oil-rich colors in the central motif, drawing attention to the main subject and thus directing the viewer's eye to the more important areas of the painting.

A deliberate and sometimes hesitant artist, Manet sought to disguise his slowness behind an impression of immediacy. Monet said of Manet's *Olympia*: 'He had a laborious, careful method. He always wanted his paintings to have the air of being painted at a single sitting; but often . . . would scrape down what he had executed during the day . . . he kept only the lowest layer, which had great charm and finesse, on which he would begin improvising.'

During the 1860s, Manet used diluted, subdued colors for his underpainting. However, as a result of his contact with Monet, he began to use paler colors, closer to the local colors of his subjects. Observation of outdoor light made Manet abandon his tonal palette and, like the Impressionists, add white in order to brighten his colors.

Manet's early works exhibit the cool light and warm brown shadows of the studio. He was at that time preoccupied with reworking Old Masters' compositions and themes with modern subjects. His painting technique combined traditional and innovative elements. In spite of Manet's contact with Impressionism, he continued to bridge the gap between past and present, and the revolutionary aspects of his technique influenced his successors.

**1.** A pale ground, apparently a creamy off-white, was used to create luminosity and flatness.

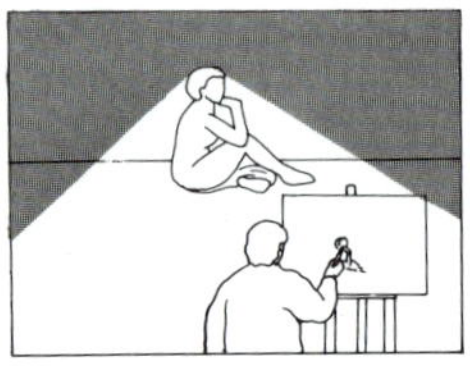

**2.** The lighting was full-faced to eliminate the half-tones in the modelling.

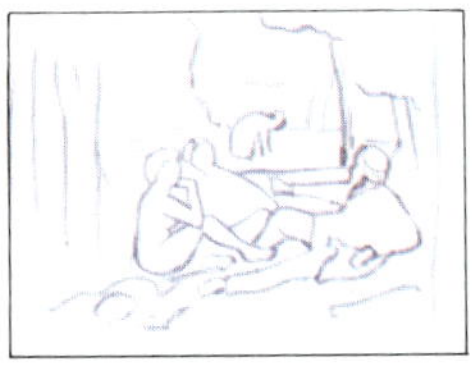

**3.** There is no evidence of underdrawing, and the figures may have been sketched in with a dark fluid umber.

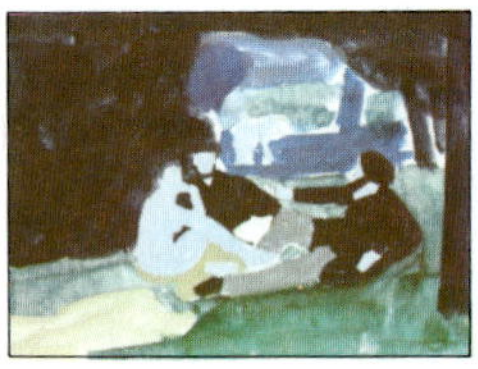

**4.** Scumbles corresponding to the local colours were used to block in the figures and forms.

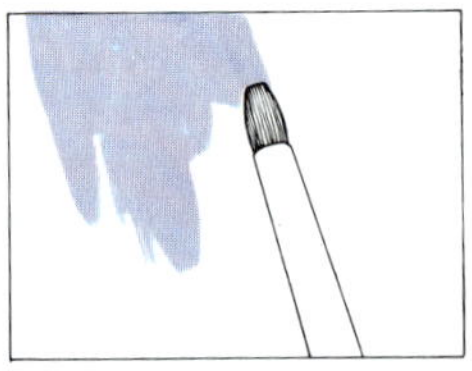

**5.** The build-up of the paint layer was concentrated on the central group of figures using a rich, oily paint.

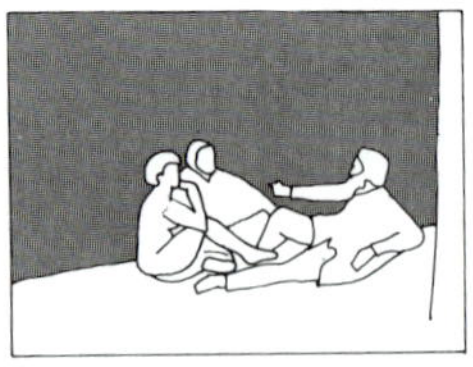

**6.** The background and areas around the figures were reworked in translucent, thinly scumbled paint.

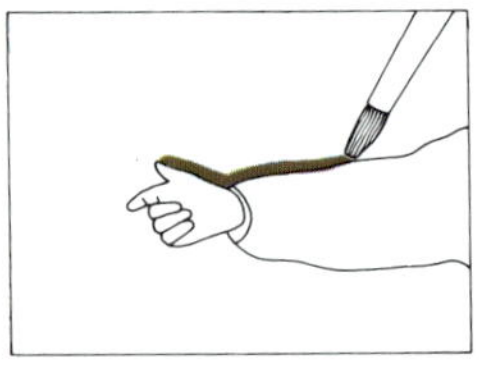

**7.** Curving, flowing brushstrokes were used to define the figures. The grass was painted around the figures after they were completed.

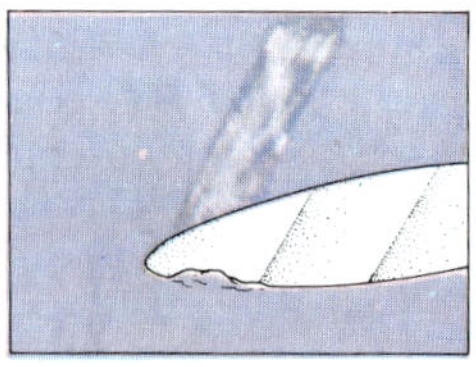

**8.** Manet would often scrape down the thick, impasted areas which he wished to rework. A thin, light varnish was painted over the completed work.

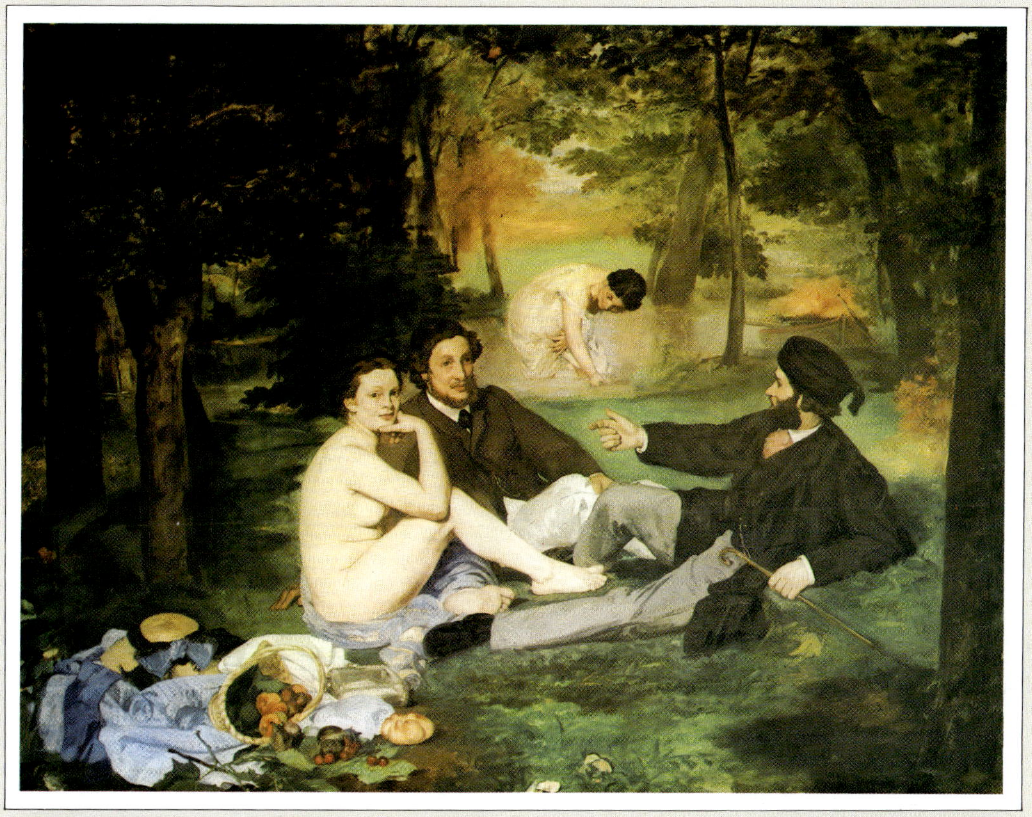

*Manet's underpainting for this studio picture was done more or less according to the local colors of the subject but darker. Focus is concentrated on the central group of figures by the use of dense and opaque paint, as contrasted with the thinly painted or roughly worked areas of the background. The strong light coming from behind the artist exaggerates contrasts of light and shade and suppresses half-tone modelling. The rich oil paint rarely exploits the smooth texture of the canvas but flows with it. The green of the grass is worked up around the finished figures, and the brushwork follows their contours rather than being descriptive of the grass it represents.*

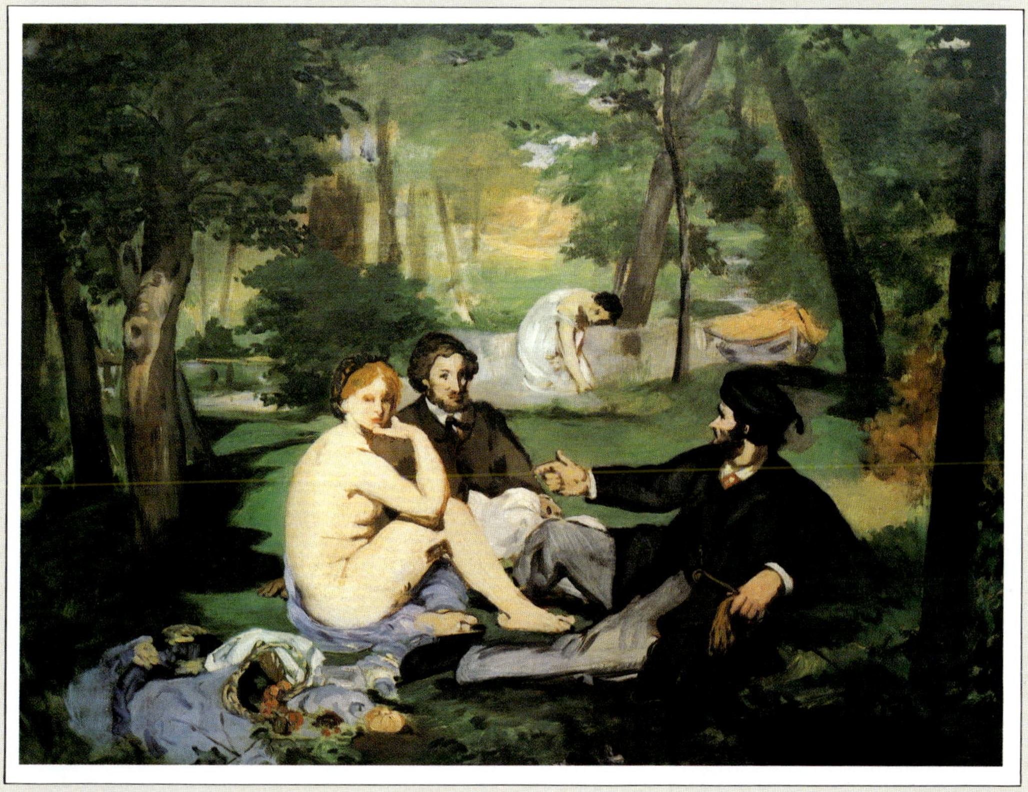

*In this smaller early version of* Déjeuner sur l'herbe, *Manet's unfettered experiments with contrasts and the elimination of half-tones in the modelling are even more uncompromising than in the finished exhibition picture. The main composition is roughly blocked in, the white ground glowing through the mainly fluid transparent colors.*

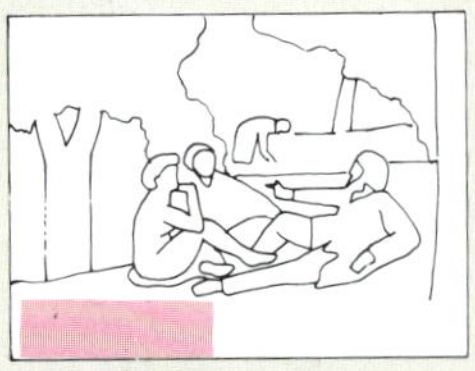

*The boldly evocative handling of the still life motif in the study is here refined by a crisper finish. The picnic and the woman's discarded clothes provide keys to the picture's story.*

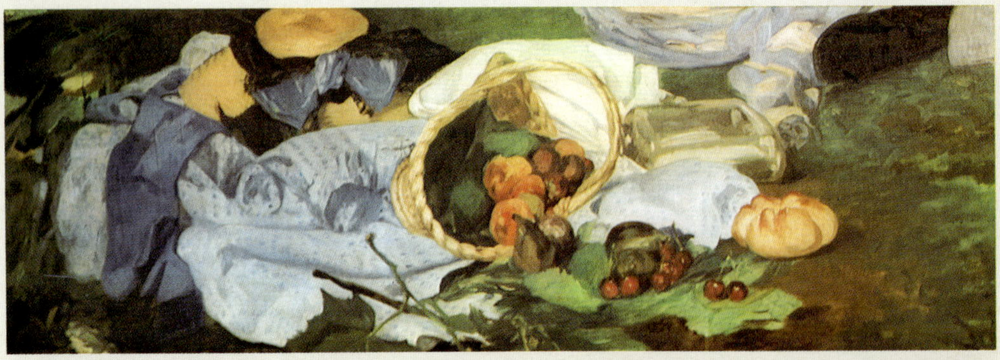

*The duller blue, thin layer in this early version contrasts sharply with rich reds, yellows and greens of the basket, fruit, leaves and bread. The lush paint of the white fabric enhances this overall effect. Although much more freely and sketchily painted, all the essential objects are already depicted, a broad brush defining the forms with remarkable ease and fluency.*

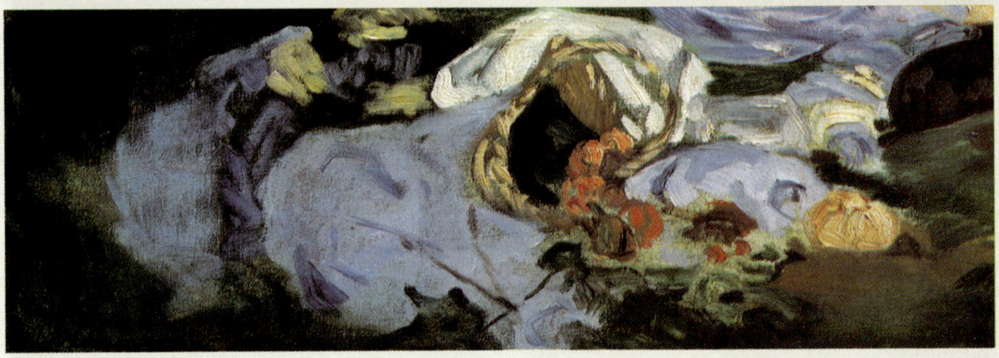

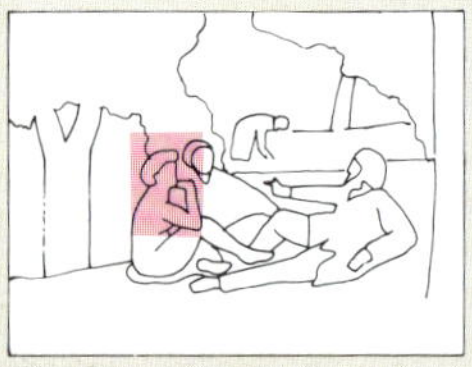

*The strange spatial anomalies, like the overlarge bather, are typical of Manet's compositions, which often disregard the traditional preoccupation with a coherent, three-dimensional illusion. The paint layer on the figures is rich and opaque, with freely painted contours worked wet-in-wet to summarize the forms, the twill canvas weave adding texture to the surface. Brushwork is bold, in places expressively following form to reinforce it, in others swiftly covering the white surface with zig-zag hatched strokes. Manet's varied touch describes the differing surfaces of flesh, grass, and fabric.*

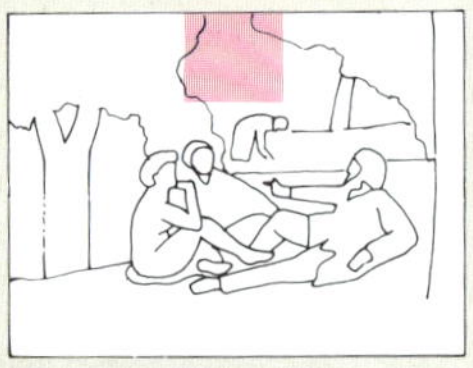

*This area of the background, where the light breaks through and softens the harsh darks of the invented scenery, is the most thinly and fluidly painted part of the picture. The paler, muted washes of color suggesting the distance draw the eye, while dark trees frame the whole scene like theater flats at either side.*

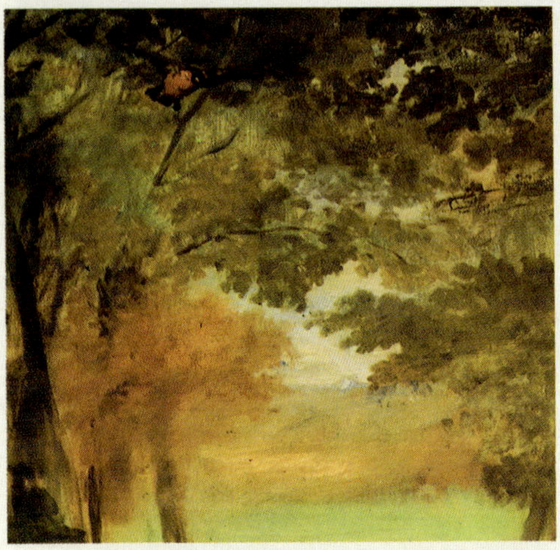

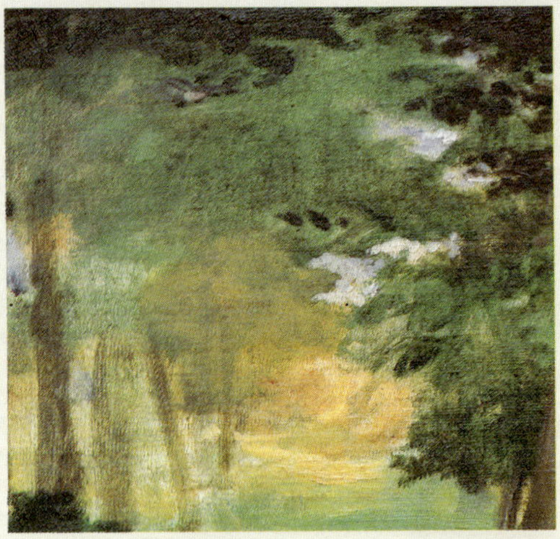

*In the study, the paint is still more diluted, the application giving the most summary hint of the shapes of trees. The initial wash is only reworked and modified in limited areas of the foliage, like the darker greens and the thicker whites. The hovering bullfinch, rapidly delineated here, is more fully detailed in the final version.*

*The raised arm, which was originally longer and thus closer to its position in the study, has been shortened during execution, and moved a couple of inches to the right.*

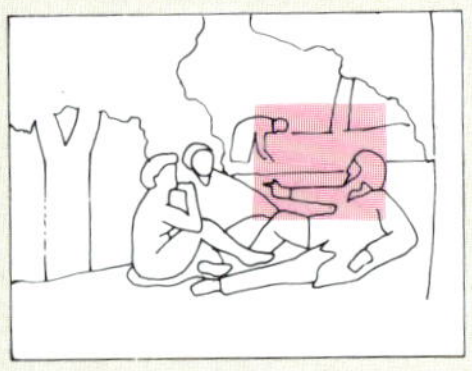

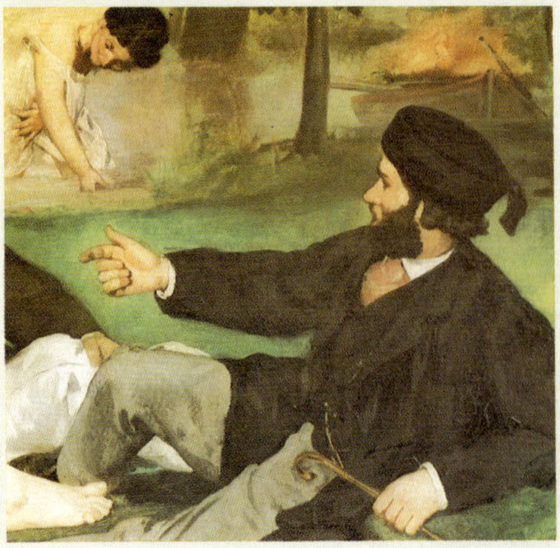

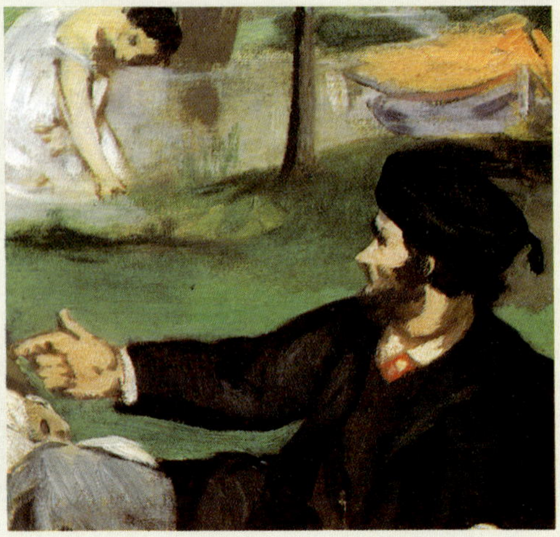

*In both the study and the finished picture the buttery green paint of the grass has been worked around the painted figures, strengthening both their outlines and the flat opacity of the green. In the final version this green obliterates the original position of the hand which, in the study, increases the spatial ambiguity by appearing to touch the other man's sleeve.*

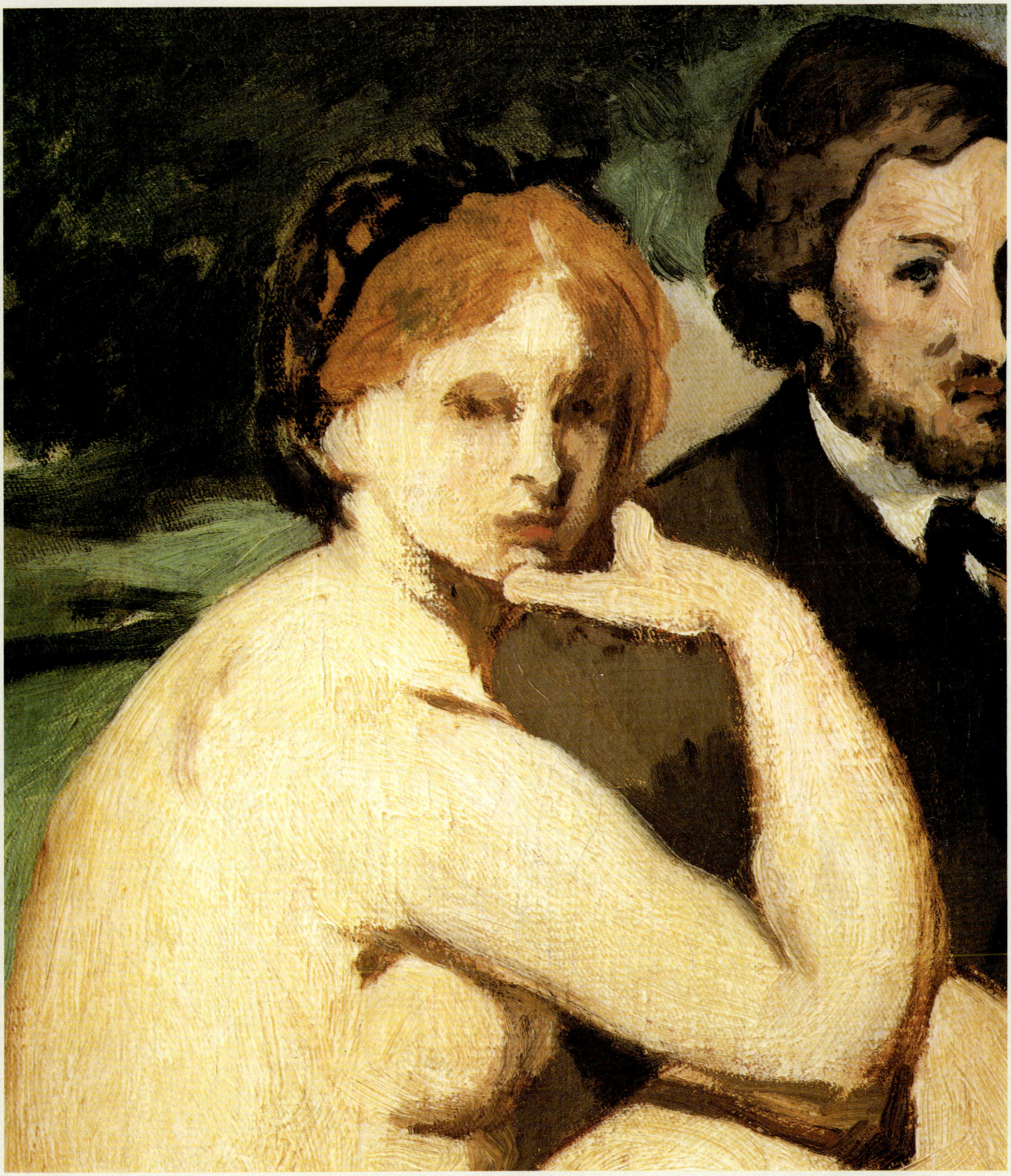

# GUSTAVE COURBET

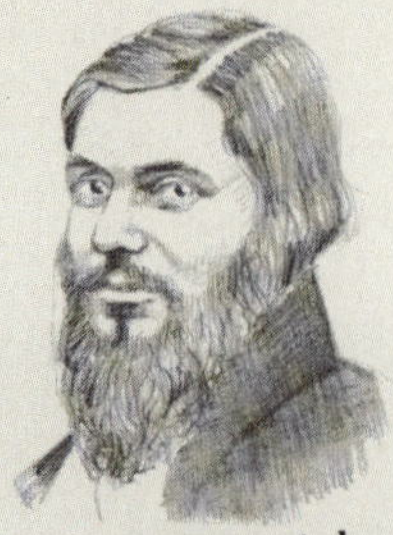

*Deer Haven on the Stream of Plaisir-Fontaine, Doubs/*
*Las Remise de chevreuils au ruisseau de Plaisir-Fontaine*
Oil on reused canvas (1866)
174cm × 209cm/68½in × 82¼in

Gustave Courbet emerged as a force in modern painting around the time of the revolution of 1848. He came from a landowning peasant background in the Jura, the French province close to the Swiss alps, in south-east France. Courbet's father owned land and vineyards scattered on the plateau of Flagey, and property in the towns of Ornans and Flagey. The Flagey farmhouse was simple and unpretentious, while their townhouse was a grander, bourgeois establishment. Courbet's first major canvas, the *Burial at Ornans* (1849–1850), showed his father in his bourgeois clothes and role, while in *Peasants of Flagey Returning from the Fair* (1850–1855) he appears in a peasant's smock and stovepipe hat. Thus, personal experience placed Courbet in a strong position to portray the contradictions and divisions of social class in rural France, because his own family was moving upward socially.

The power of Courbet's direct and uncompromising subjects – unidealized representations on a monumental scale of ordinary rather than heroic figures – was apparent from their problematic reception in the Salon exhibitions. Having gained a second class gold medal at the Salon of 1849 with his *After Dinner at Ornans*, Courbet was automatically exempt from the necessity of submitting his works to the Salon jury. Without this exemption, it is doubtful that his major canvases following *After Dinner*, a relatively traditional subject, would have gained acceptance.

Courbet's Realism took its inspiration from the works of the great seventeenth century masters, such as Rembrandt (1606–1669) and the Dutch, whose work he saw on a visit there in August 1846. The Spaniards Velazquez (1599–1660) and Zurbaran (1598–1664), and Italians Guercino (1591–1666) and Caravaggio (1573–1610) were vital to his development in the 1840s. He also looked at the French seventeenth century realists, the Le Nain brothers, whose work had been rescued from obscurity by the critic Champfleury, a friend who also championed Courbet's painting. Works by the Le Nain brothers were brought to light from the Louvre cellars in 1848, at a time when their depictions of working people had pertinent appeal for radical French artists. Courbet combined these sources with an appreciation of simple, popular images, like those of the crude woodblock color prints, which were widely distributed throughout France. He sought to unite the methods of the Old Master realists with the simple flat compositions of popular prints, to bring a new directness to his art.

Although, like most of the Old Masters to whom he turned, Courbet loaded his shadows, painting them thickly and darkly, his technique was essentially based on the tradition of *chiaroscuro*. He worked from dark to light, seeing himself, as he remarked, as the equivalent of the sun lighting up a dark landscape. With only a few exceptions in his later landscapes, his shadows were usually filled with the browns of the studio setting in which even his outdoor studies were normally completed. He used the problematic, non-drying color, bitumen. In his early years, this was often as a result of financial necessity because bitumen was a cheap color. Courbet's work exhibits a powerful combination of Rembrandtesque *chiaroscuro* with texturally evocative paint handling. Instead of adopting the conventional, smooth academic method for creating an illusion of reality, his application of colors actually imitates natural textures.

Courbet did not always work on a dark ground, building up to the lights. He often

Alley of Chestnut Trees at Celle-St. Cloud *(1867) by Alfred Sisley was influenced by Courbet's forest landscapes. Sisley chose a comparable dark setting and deer motif, but with fewer contrasts of light and shade. Sisley's work has a deeper sense of space, but the recession created by the path is ambiguous. Unlike Courbet, Sisley uses brushwork with less textural differentiation, resulting in a thinner paint layer. The blue of the sky, with much white added, was worked over the greens of the tree foliage.*

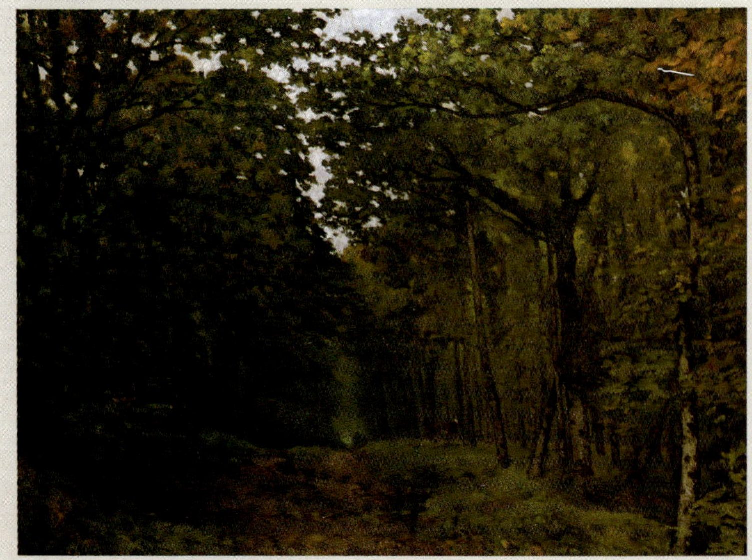

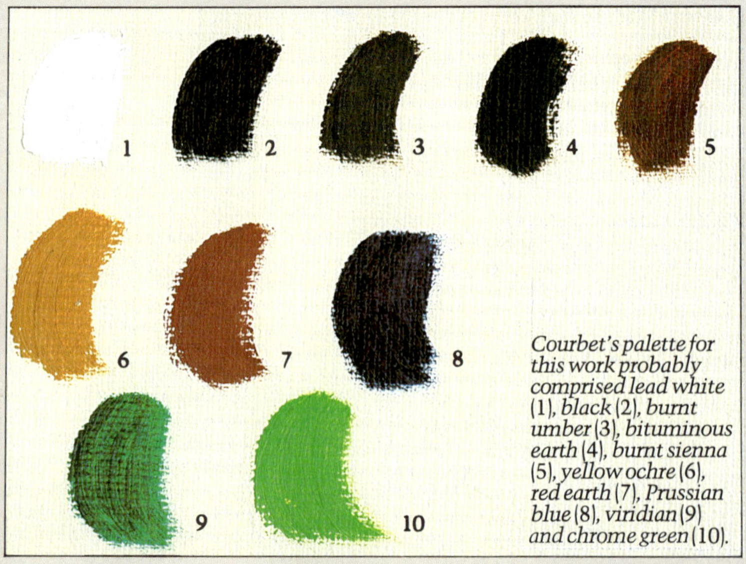


*Courbet's palette for this work probably comprised lead white (1), black (2), burnt umber (3), bituminous earth (4), burnt sienna (5), yellow ochre (6), red earth (7), Prussian blue (8), viridian (9) and chrome green (10).*

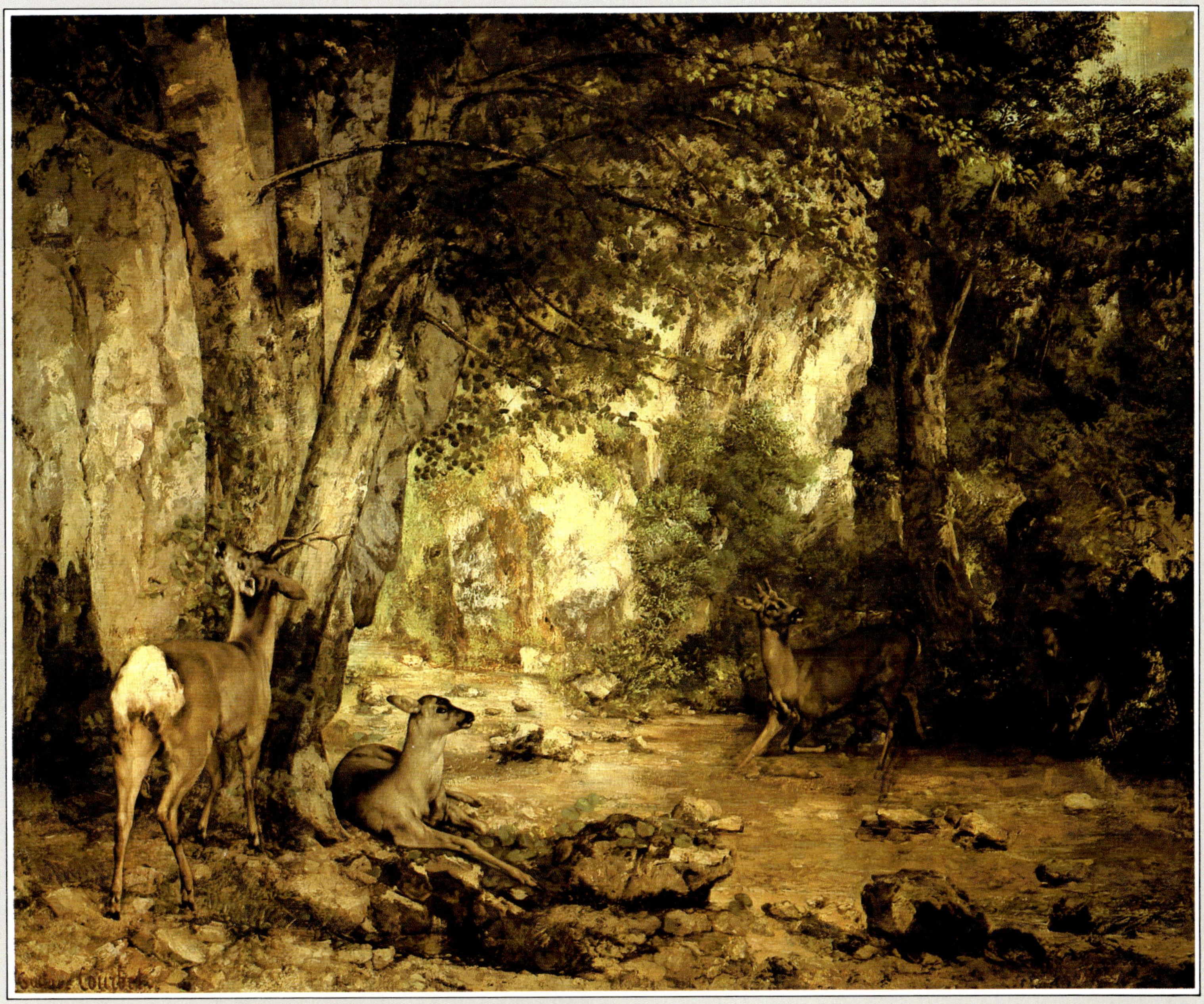

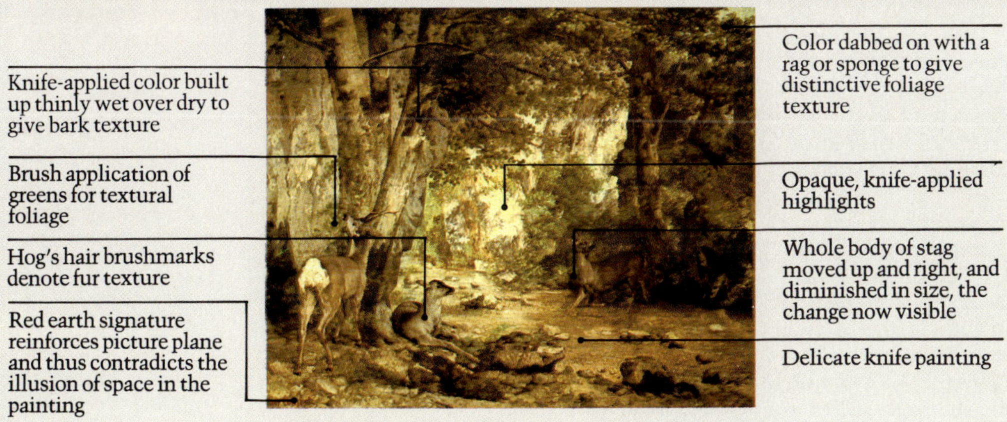


*Works like this finally gained Courbet general acclaim among public and critics in France. Contemporary critics of Impressionism commonly saw Courbet as a direct precursor of the new style, because of his commitment to naturalism. However, a perceptive critic, Henry Houssaye, noted in 1882 that, since Courbet used a good amount of* chiaroscuro *in his painting, he could not really be heralded as a precursor of Impressionism. In opposition to Courbet's approach, the Impressionists avoided extreme contrasts of light and shade. Thus Houssaye was the first critic to define Impressionism in terms of technique rather than purely on stylistic grounds. Courbet built up his painting from dark to light, combining studio work with painting out of doors, in front of his subject.*

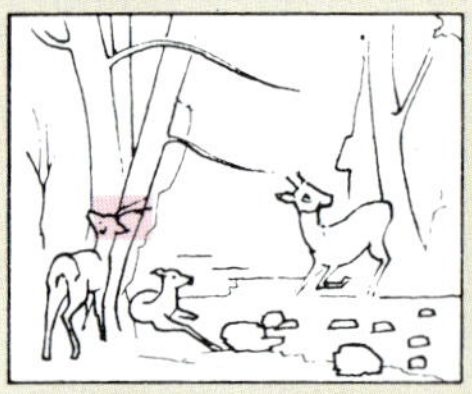

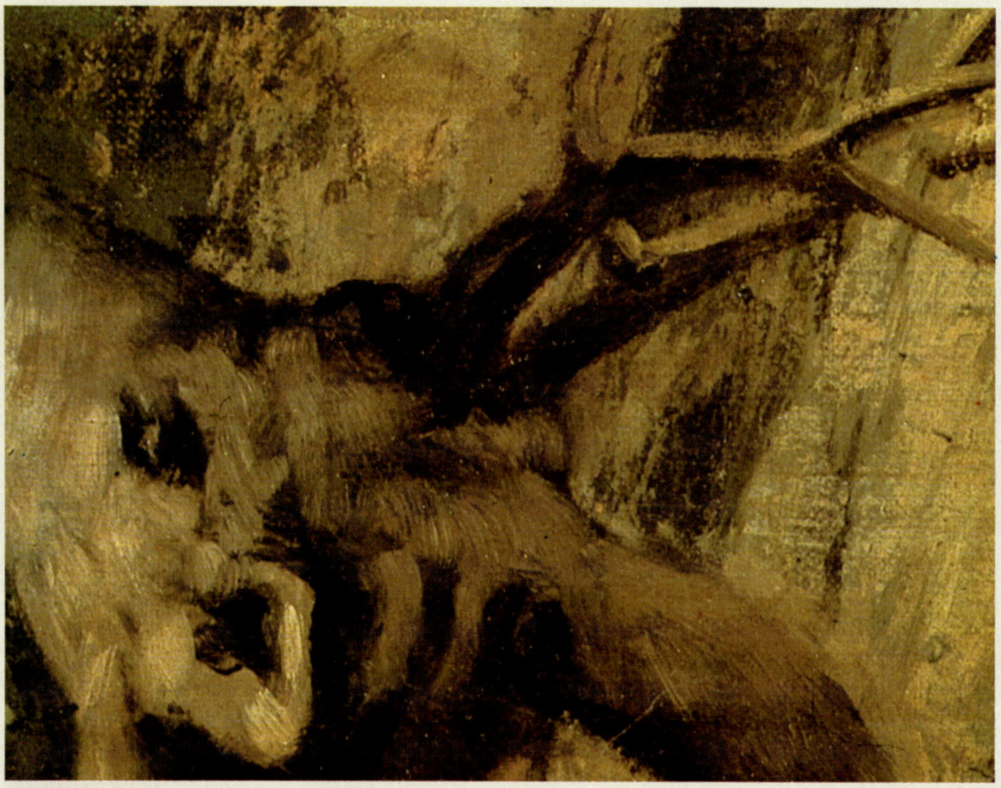

Actual size detail
*A rich paint, probably bound with poppy oil, has retained the marks of the hog's hair brush, permitting the artist to use this effect to describe the animal's hair. The supple movement of the brush also gives an excellent sense of the muscular body of the stag. Adjustments were made here. For instance, the position of the ear has been changed, making it smaller. The break in the paint depicting the antler confirms the fact that the deer were added at a late stage in the composition. The canvas texture is still faintly in evidence in places, and the contrast between brush and knife application of color shows clearly.*

bought ready made, white or tinted primed canvases in standard sizes, and adjusted them to suit his needs. Thus in *Seascape at Palavas* (1854) a white commercial ground was covered by the artist with an opaque red earth ground, before he began to paint his subject. In other works, like the *Flagey Oak* (1864), a white ground has been overlaid with a transparent coat of warm brown paint, to give depth to shadows and a color harmony to the picture.

In *Deer Haven*, which was executed over a previous painting, the ground is no longer visible. However, X-rays of the picture indicate that Courbet applied a thick new ground which obliterated the earlier composition. This second ground probably contained lead white as it is impervious to the X-rays. The present paint layer of *Deer Haven* is covering and, in general, opaque. Courbet's surfaces are in fact deceptive. At a distance they give an appearance of rugged masonry as a result of the broken overworking of colors. Closer inspection, however, shows the superb delicacy of the artist's handling, where thin layers of brushed or knife-applied color give an effect of textural solidity, without excessive bulk.

Courbet used a variety of unconventional methods to create the textural variations in his paintings. He is said to have, on occasions, even added sand to his colors to give an earthy texture. His techniques in *Deer Haven* are no less ingenious. The landscape itself, a well-known spot near Ornans, was mainly painted outdoors, while the deer were added in Courbet's Paris studio during the winter of 1865–1866, when he hired some deer to 'sit' for him. He is also known to have worked from dead deer. Not surprisingly, the landscape and deer are handled quite differently. He used deft touches with palette or painting knife to give substance to rocks, tree trunks and some riverside foliage. The bulk of the foliage is handled with a stiff brush, indicating the individual leaves with precision. Less distinct foliage in the background and top right are applied with color on a rag or sponge, dabbed on to give a feathery effect which contrasts with the more solid handling of brushed foliage and knifework. Finally, the brushwork used on the fur of the deer contrasts with the more vigorous rendering elsewhere. The treatment of the deer is very delicate, and the raised brushmarks left by the hog's hair brush literally recreate the texture of fur. The resulting contrast makes the deer stand out, almost like cardboard cutouts. This was doubtless exaggerated by their being added later.

Courbet painted repeated versions of this theme, which won him enormous acclaim at the Salon of 1866. It brought him, for the first time, widespread acknowledgement for his talent, which had previously been treated with general hostility because of his controversial subject matter. Despite Courbet's importance as an example to the younger artists, his essentially traditional *chiaroscuro* browns meant that they reacted against his handling of light and shade in the later 1860s.

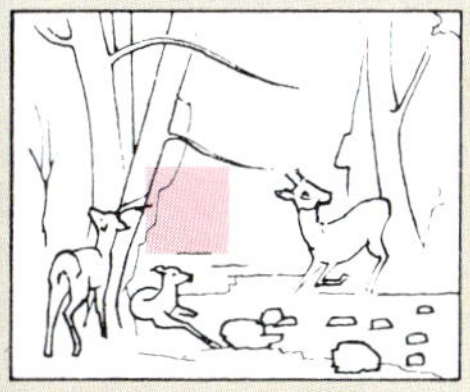

*Knife handling of color gives a broken irregular quality to the paint layer, although the actual paint is remarkably thin and delicate. Creamy-whites have been laid over dark brown, which shows through and strengthens contrasts between light and dark. Quite different are the thinly brushed tendrils of color depicting fine twigs. Thickly applied but basically transparent sienna is visible under rag-dabbed pale greens. The end of a round hog's hair brush was used to apply blobs of dark green, and the bristles give variety to the texture of the different leaves. The brilliant touches of orangey, yellow ochre were probably deftly flecked on with the tip of a supple painting knife.*

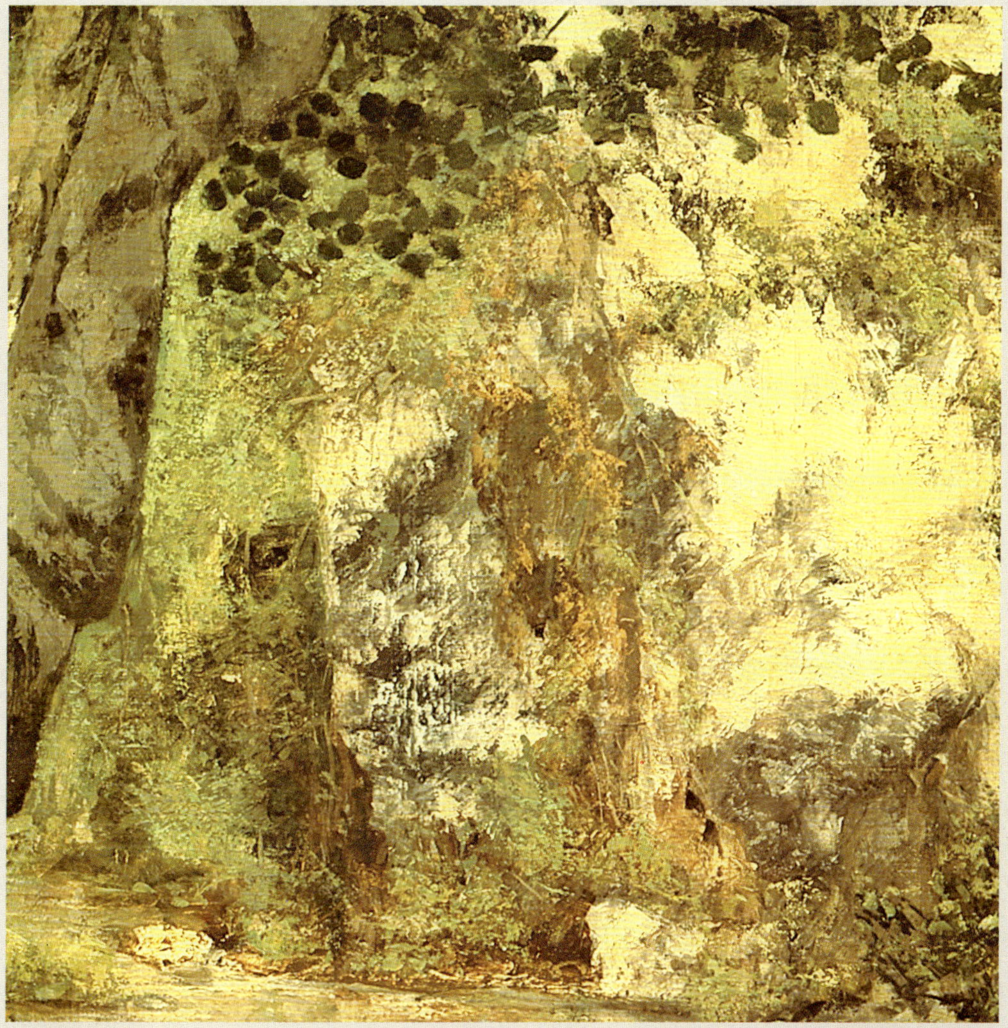

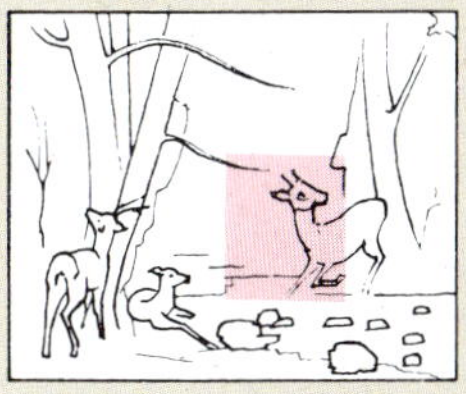

*In this detail changes made by Courbet are apparent. The young stag was originally larger, and placed further down and to the left. The initial ear and neck line can be seen as a ghost-like presence to the left of the current position, and the forelegs were originally below those finally added.*

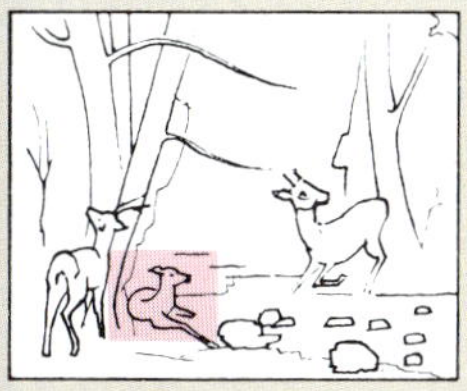

*The lack of shadows cast by the deer and the contrast created by differentiated brush and knife handling, make the deer stand out against the surroundings, so that they almost appear to float. The light and shade on the animal also does not match with the fall of light in the landscape behind.*

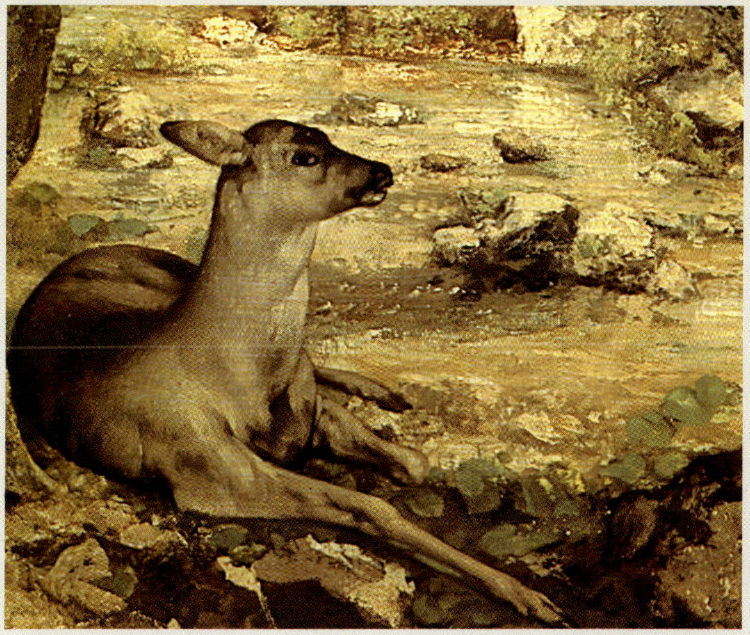

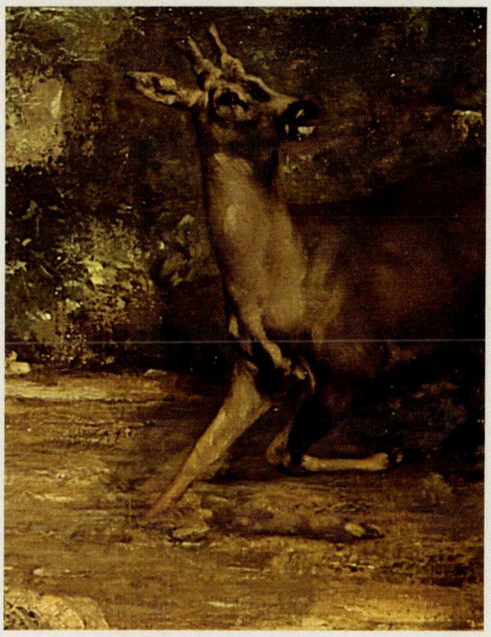

# EDGAR DEGAS

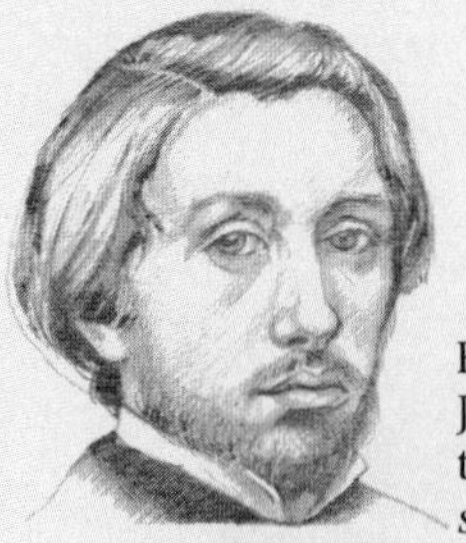

*The Bellilli Family/La Famille Bellilli* (1859-1860)
Oil on pale primed canvas
200cm × 253cm/79in × 99½in

Edgar Degas left France for Italy in June 1856 to make the traditional trip to study the Italian masters *in situ*. However, he had a more personal reason for his trip, since his paternal grandfather had been exiled to Naples, and his father had been born there. At that time, his relatives in Naples, his aunt Laure, his father's sister, and her Baron husband, were themselves in exile in Florence, because the Baron had been involved in the political upheavals of the struggle for the unification of Italy. After visits to cities including Venice, Assisi and Rome, Degas finally arrived in Florence to see his relations in August 1858, only to find his aunt away in Naples, caring for her sick father, Degas' grandfather, who died on 31 August. What was probably intended as a brief stay in the end lasted nine months. During that time, Degas began to plan a large portrait of his relatives, the Bellelli family, making drawn and painted studies which he took back with him to Paris, where the painting was executed in his Paris studio on the rue Madame.

This portrait is Degas' earliest large-scale work, and, while showing his debts to past art, it looks ahead to his innovative mature style. Scholars have likened the work to the portrait of the royal family, *The Maids of Honour* (1656) by the seventeenth century Spanish painter Velazquez (1599–1660). This also uses the subtle device of a background mirror to add depth to the composition. Degas' introduction of an apparently invented red chalk portrait drawing of his recently deceased grandfather, which can be seen on the rear wall behind his aunt's head, places the painting in a long European tradition of portraits which, since the Renaissance, have included a dead member of a family to link past and present. The French Renaissance style, medium and mounting of this drawing seem to confirm the traditional link which Degas intended to suggest. The precision with which he planned the painting included, among numerous preparatory drawings, one projecting how the finished work would look, with even its frame carefully set out in detail.

Old Master sources can be balanced against possible nineteenth century influences on this picture. Degas was a great admirer of Ingres (1780–1867), and had studied with a pupil of his at the Ecole des Beaux-Arts in the mid 1850s. Ingres' delicate group portrait drawings, done mainly in Rome in the 1810s, show a frieze-like distribution of figures across the picture surface in a shallow pictorial space, similar to that in Degas' portrait.

The soft, almost full-face lighting adopted by Degas for this painting is certainly reminiscent of the lighting commonly adopted by Ingres for his painted portraits. However, in a manner typical of Degas, the lighting serves more than just a flattering function in his painting of the Bellelli family. The tensions between the morose and ill-tempered Baron and his wife were common knowledge in the Degás family, and the difficulties could hardly have passed unnoticed by Degas during his prolonged stay with them. The lighting accentuates the division already implied by the composition, separating the father from his wife and two daughters. The fall of light on the three females is clear but gentle, confirming Degas' allegiance to his aunt's side of the family. Documentary evidence suggests Degas had a close and affectionate relationship with her. By contrast, the father, whose back is turned unconventionally towards the spectator, is obscured by shadow, and his features are left ill defined. Mother and daughters are linked not only compositionally and by light, there is also physical contact between them – a protective arm around one daughter, and a merging of black skirts with the other.

The black clothes of the women bear witness to their mourning for the aunt's father, a mark of respect strikingly absent in the casual clothes worn by the Baron. The clear black shapes of mother and daughter form a strong pyramid to the left of the composition, the mother's head being linked directly with the hanging portrait of her father. The crispness, echoed in the rather severe look of sorrow on the mother's face, is in marked contrast to the soft lack of definition surrounding the Baron, who is placed against a complex background. Behind him the geometry of the fireplace gives way to the fuss of ornaments and reflected details in the mirror. Although less taut and unconventional in structure than Degas' later portrait compositions, the germ of his later methods is already clearly present. This can be seen particularly in his use of space and composition not simply to present his sitters, but to suggest the complex emotional and psychological characteristics.

Of particular interest among the preparatory studies for his work is an oil study executed on lightweight *ètude* canvas, made expressly for studies, for the hands of Laure Bellelli which, in the final picture, rests on the table. The paint layer in the final work is remarkably fine and thin, accentuating the classical draftsmanship which underlies the picture. Despite its thinness, the paint is generally opaque and as a result the color of the pale priming cannot be identified with accuracy, as it only glows through the thinly scumbled colors of the paint layer. In the tradition of Ingres, various degrees of finish are used, with a fairly high finish on the important areas and more loosely handled brushwork in wallpaper and carpet.

The painting was in the possession of the Bellelli family until around 1900 when, because it had suffered some damage, Degas brought it back to Paris. Until Degas' death, it remained in his studio, a relatively unknown work despite its importance as a major early canvas.

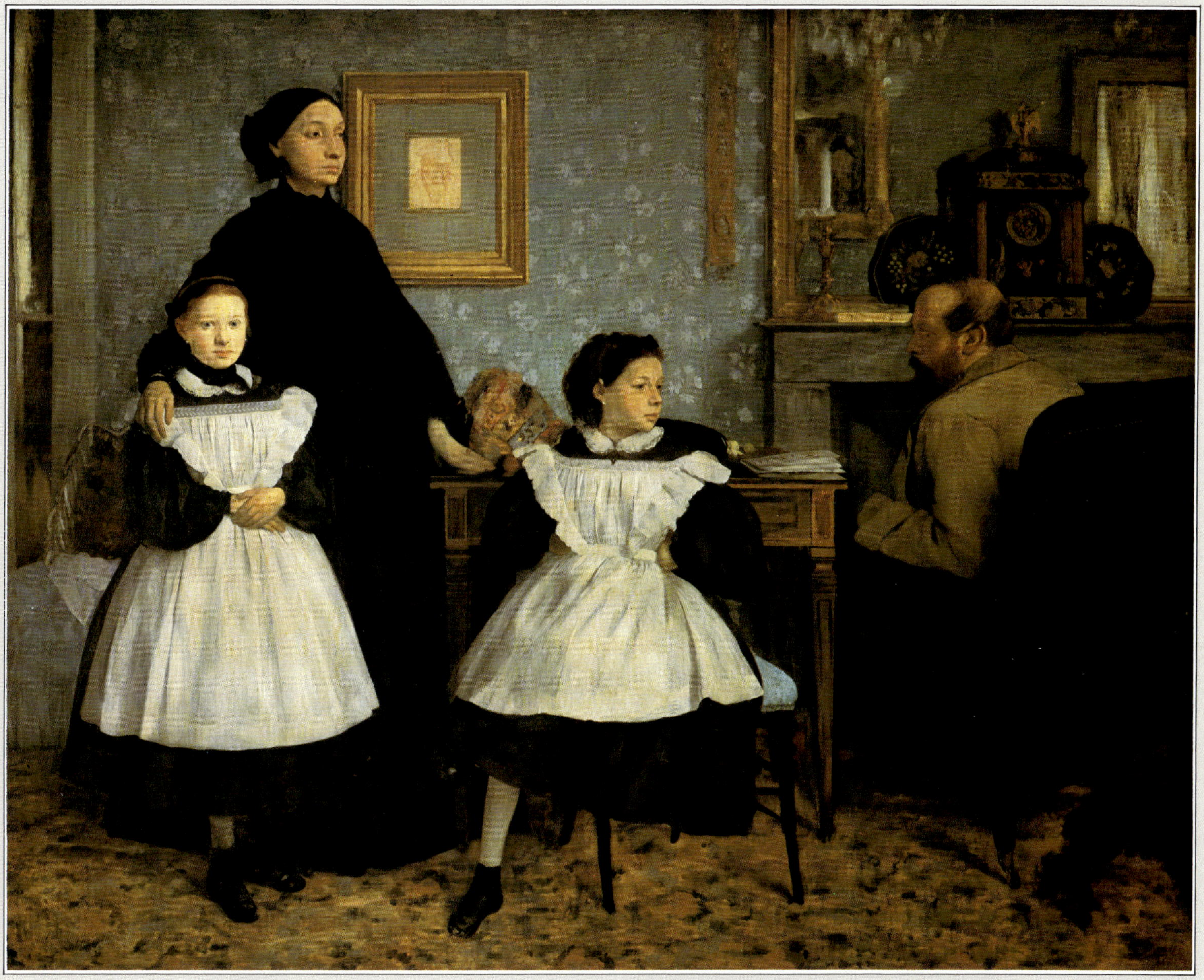

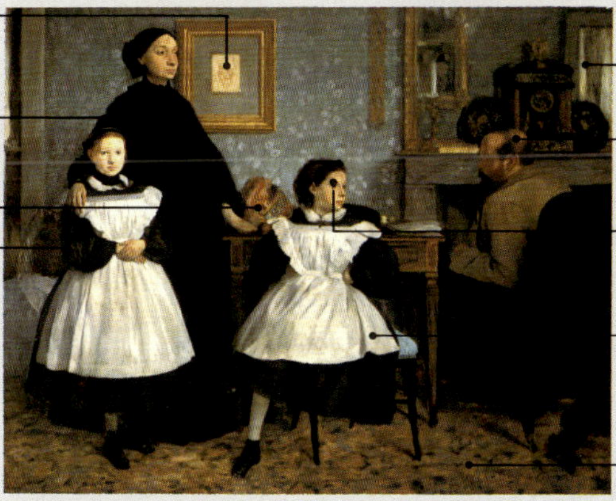


*This extremely large family group portrait is on a scale traditionally reserved for portraits of major political or historical dignitaries. The canvas size is non-standard. Although it can be linked back to compositional precedents, for example the early group portrait drawings of Ingres, Degas' painting contains a novel emphasis upon the deeper psychological aspects of his sitters' characters. Family tensions are echoed and reinforced by artistic devices which create pictorial tension. Thus, even in this early work, Degas' talent for fusing technical and aesthetic elements in his art can already be seen.*

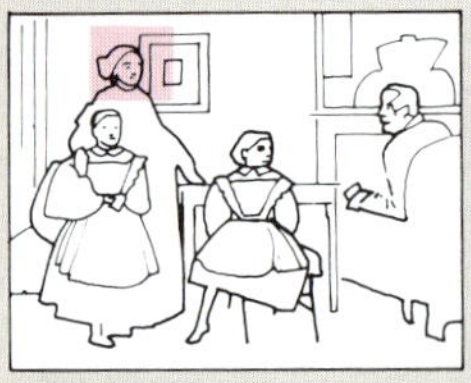

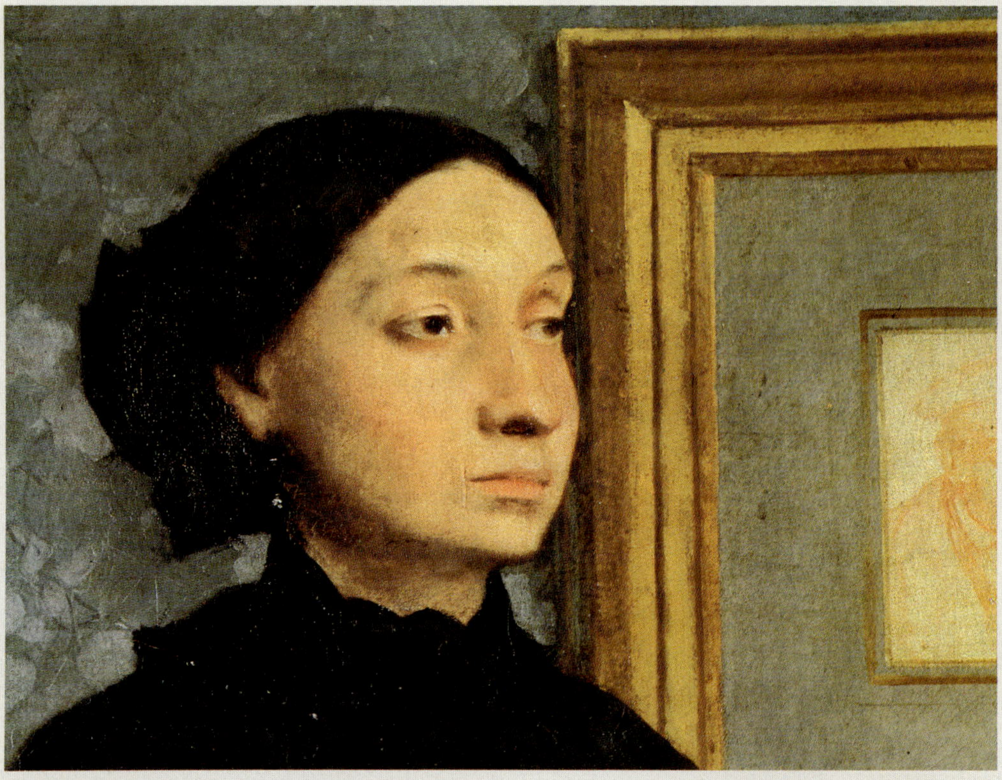

*Here Degas intentionally silhouetted the profile of his aunt against the dark edge of the picture frame behind her, to stress the fine features of his chief sitter. The paint layer, although thin and delicate, is opaque, with smoothly blended flesh painting reminiscent of Ingres. A crack to the left of the mouth results from damage to the canvas. Light is reflected off the varnish especially in the darker parts of the painting, where slight blistering has made the paint surface irregular. The pale parts of the picture, which contain lead white, are more stable and durable.*

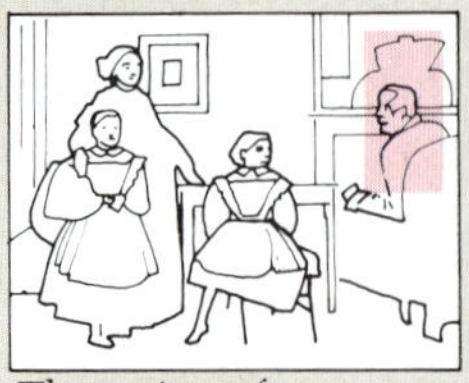

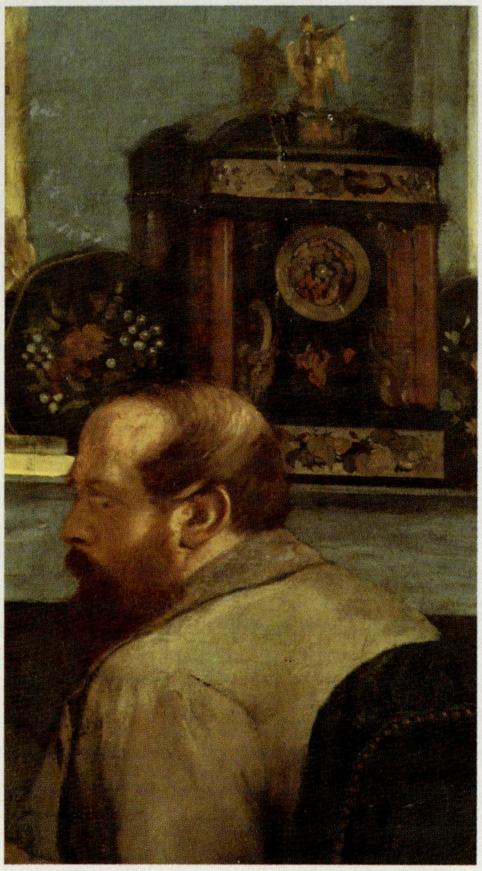

*The variety of brushwork used to evoke texture is evident here. Feathery directional strokes follow the movement of the Baron's hair, not disguising the way it is swept over to hide his balding scalp. Details of decoration on the mantel ornament are picked out either in vermilion or in an earth red which is given comparable brilliance by the surrounding dark hues. Damage to the face has been restored, as has a vertical fissure running across the mantel ornament.*

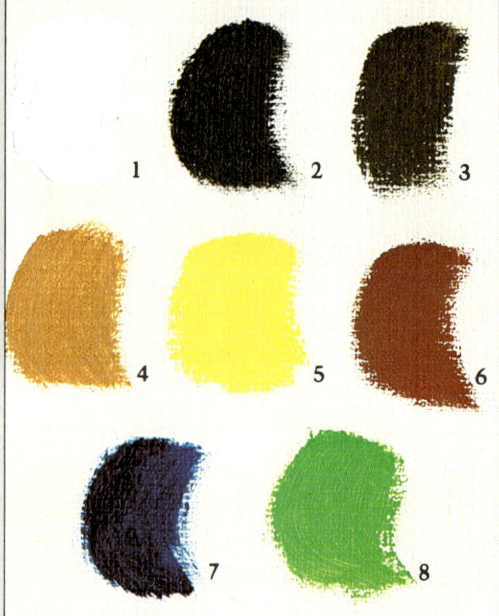


*Degas' palette here probably included lead white (1) and zinc white, black (2), umber (3), yellow ochre (4), lemon yellow (5), red earth (6), Prussian blue (7) and chrome green (8). Vermilion may also have been used.*

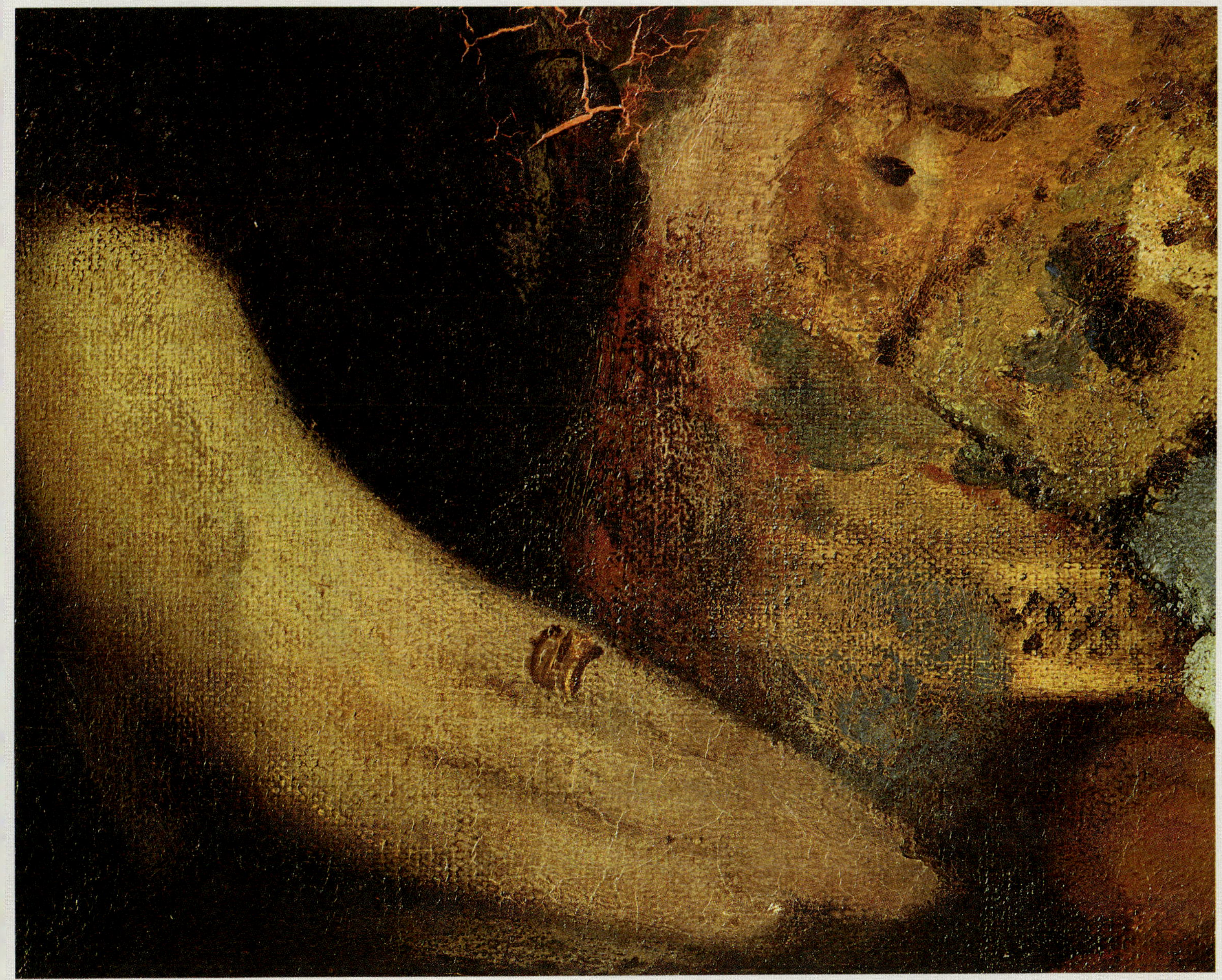

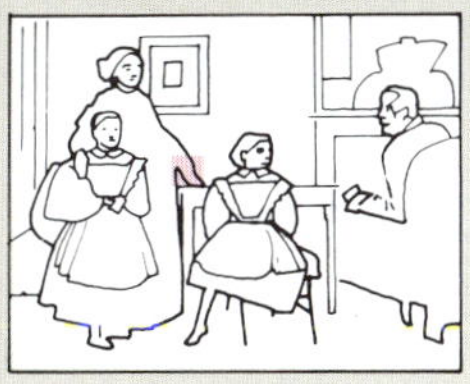

Actual size detail
*Detail in the modeling of the hand is kept to a minimum in the final painting, which nevertheless works perfectly at the correct viewing distance for this large canvas. The paint layer is very thin in the lower area of the decorative fabric, giving a speckled effect where it has caught on the nodes or in the dips of the fine-textured canvas support. The speckled effect on the flesh paint seems to be unintentional. Here, varnish and dirt have darkened the paint in the canvas grooves. There is some surface cracking. This either results from overpainting before the first layer is dry or from working with lean color over a fatty layer, which takes longer to dry. Cracks in the final dark layer now reveal the underlayer of rich pinkish orange color.*

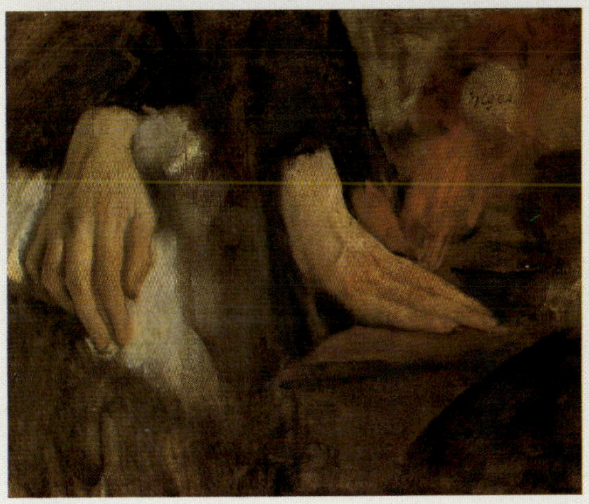

*One of the few extant preparatory works for his portrait, this oil study or* étude *is typical of this stage in the traditional painting procedure. Having established the compositional design, Degas then made these careful studies of his aunt's hands to assist the accurate representation of them in the final work. He made minor changes to their position on the finished canvas. Degas used the special étude weight canvas for this work.*

# EDOUARD MANET

*Concert in the Tuileries/La Musique aux Tuileries* (1862)
Oil on white primed canvas
76cm × 118cm/30in × 46½in

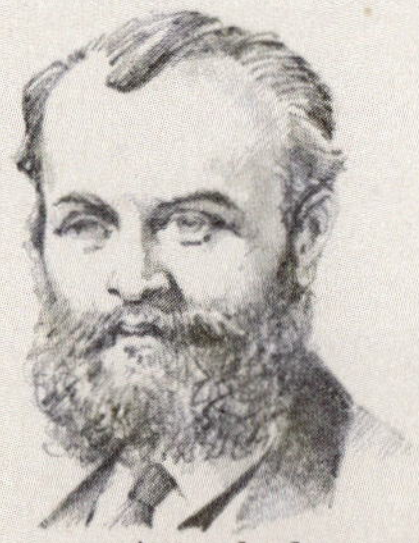

During the 1860s Manet was influenced not only by photography and Japanese prints, but also by the work of several Old Masters, including the seventeenth century Spanish artist Velazquez (1599–1660). In *Concert in the Tuileries*, Manet was reworking the theme of a painting in the Louvre which had at that time been mistakenly attributed to the Spanish master, and which was thought to show Velazquez and his circle of friends. Transferring the idea to modern Parisian bourgeois society and dress, Manet depicted himself – to the extreme left – surrounded by friends including the writers Charles Baudelaire and Théophile Gautier, Manet's brother Eugène, the composer Offenbach, the Realist critic Champfleury, and the artist Fantin Latour. Although scenes from Parisian life were still relatively innovatory as subjects for fine art oil painting, illustrations and popular prints of such subjects had been common since at least the 1790s. More modern prototypes could have been an illustration of a military concert in the Tuileries, published in the magazine *l'Illustration*, or prints from popular mid nineteenth century illustrated books of Parisian life. Thus, in a way typical of his 1860s work, Manet combined influences from the Old Masters with inspiration from contemporary sources and popular imagery.

Reviewing Manet's posthumous exhibition and studio sale in an article published in February 1884, the critic Joseph Péladan forcefully repeated the myth that Manet was incapable of composing a picture. He wrote that Manet was 'merely a painter, and a painter of fragments – devoid of ideas, imagination, emotion, poetry, or powers of draftsmanship.' These were all factors associated with the academic tradition of *chiaroscuro* which Manet rejected. Thus, this critic reinforced the connection, commonly made by conservatives, between modern non-academic methods, and the anti-intellectual tendency in art. Manet's style was considered visually fragmented because it lacked the unifying pictorial coherence which *chiaroscuro* lighting gave to a picture. In some respects, however, Manet was indeed a painter of fragments – fragments of modern life in which he intentionally sought to convey the experiences of such a life more directly than established artistic conventions permitted.

*Concert in the Tuileries*, depicting a segment of the panorama of leisured city life, broke established compositional conventions because the frieze-like distribution of figures across the picture surface gave no central point of focus. The picture was therefore seen by critics as being without *any* composition whatever. In fact, the composition is tightly organized, but in a manner quite novel for its time. There is little spatial recession, and no pictorial hierarchy to subordinate the whole to a main center of action. The spectator is on eye-level with the standing crowd, which reduces recession into depth by stressing the solid horizontal band which the figures form across the canvas. Another device is also used to keep the viewer separate from the scene, for the artist has created a stage-like effect – there are cropped figures only to left and right of the picture and none protrude below the bottom framing edge to 'intrude' into the viewer's space. The picture is a long strip of action, apparently arbitrarily cropped at either side, but very neatly contained by the framing edges top and bottom. The careful positioning of figures or objects right up to the lower edge leaves little open foreground, and this also discourages spectator participation in the scene. Gone are the exaggerated gestures and conventionalized expressions which made academic art eloquent. Instead, the figures whose eyes gaze out, stare blankly and indifferently, with cool, worldly nonchalance.

The line of top hats, the upper extreme of the line of figures, cuts the picture in two just over halfway up the composition. The relatively unmodulated band of green foliage which fills the upper half again emphasizes the picture's flatness. Pillar-like tree trunks punctuate the horizontal rhythm, which moves from left to right – the normal direction for the eye to follow when viewing paintings in Western culture. The trees unite upper and lower halves of the composition. The central foreground tree also links foreground and background, by appearing to sweep up and back. Its ambiguous position in space tends to pull the backdrop of greenery out toward the surface of the picture.

According to his early biographer Antonin Proust, Manet worked outdoors during 1861, making oil studies for this painting every afternoon between two and four o'clock. However, despite this contention, only one or two drawings survive, and the work itself is a studio painting.

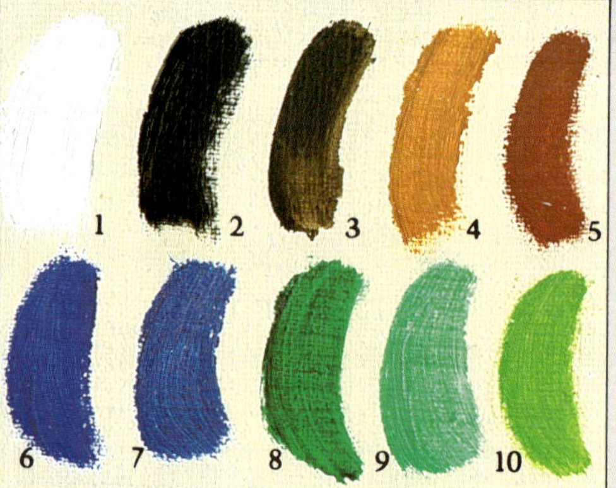


*Manet's palette probably comprised lead (1) and zinc whites, black (2), raw umber (3), yellow ochre (4), red earth (5) or red lead, ultramarine blue (6), cobalt blue (7), viridian green (8), possibly cobalt green (9) and chrome (10) green.*

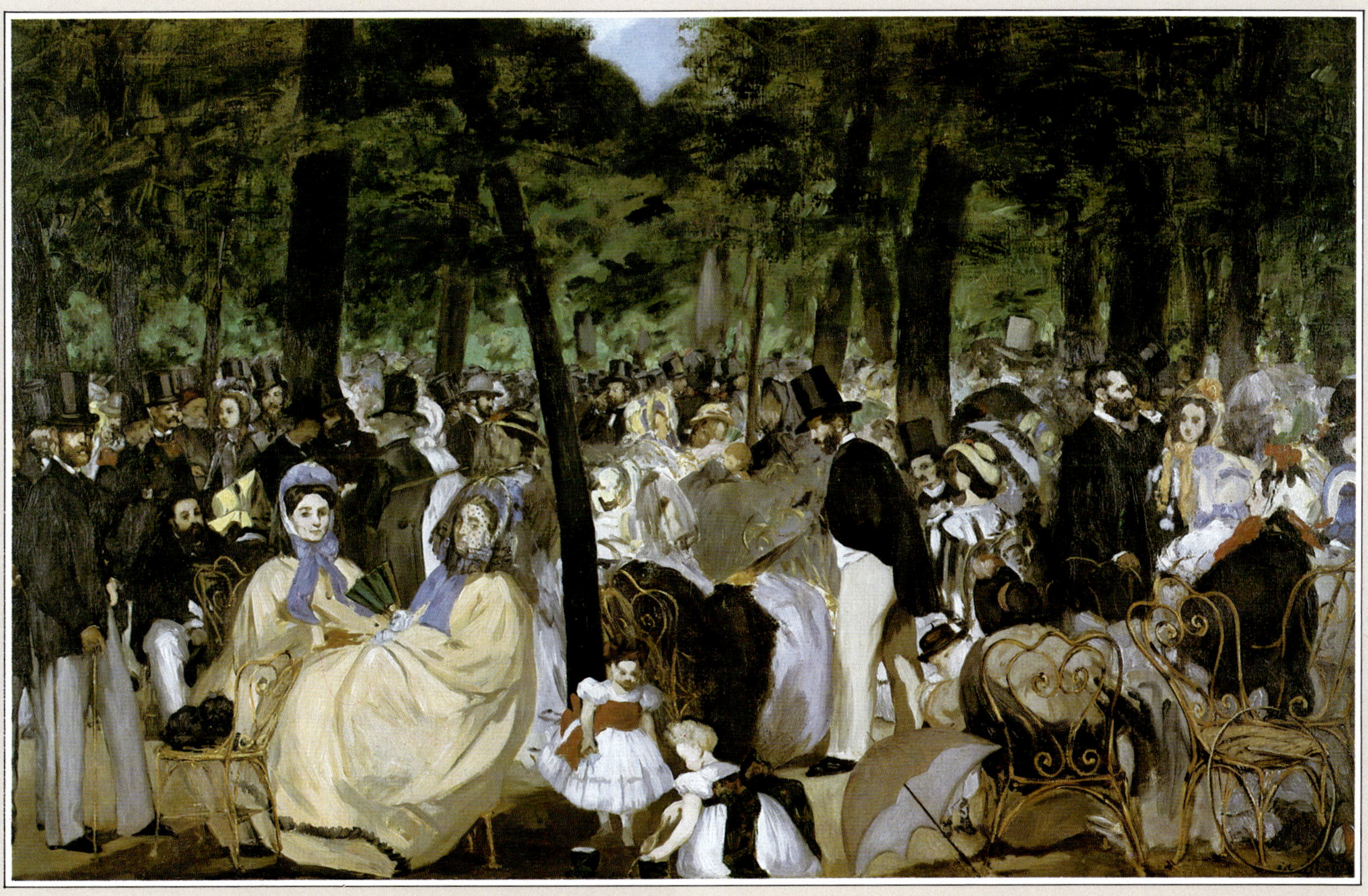

*The poet Baudelaire's plea for artists to treat modern life subjects was first made in his Salon review of 1845, and later extended to form an essay, written in 1859-1860 and published in 1863. Artists like Manet took up the challenge, at the same time seeking a new style and pictorial construction to reflect modern themes. The unbroken parade of figures across the picture surface enhances the sense of immediacy, as does the staccato effect created by alternating blocks of light and dark color. The traditional, careful tonal modeling of form has been abandoned and replaced by strong tonal contrasts punctuated by bright color, which enliven the surface and negate depth. The picture was painted on a non-standard canvas.*

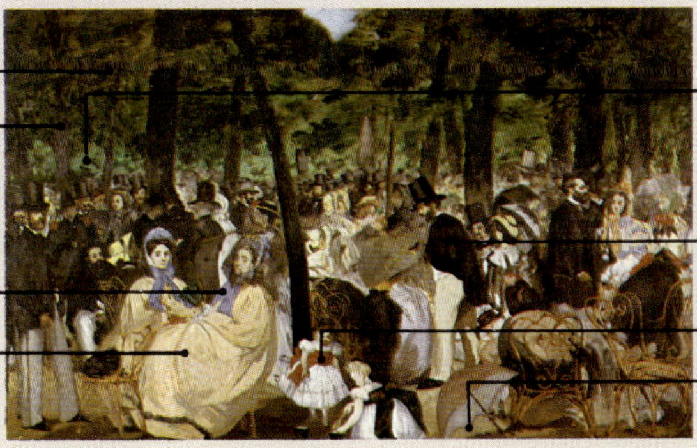

Thin dark transparent underlay, probably raw umber and viridian, applied with a painting knife

Light reflecting off varnish over irregular, loaded paint surface

Probably a mixture of ultramarine and cobalt blues added to white, and slurred on wet into wet

Loaded opaque creamy-whites

Opaque, viridian-based green mixture with white, brushed on over dry transparent green paint

Blue-tinged black paint

Red earth or red lead

Position of parasol altered

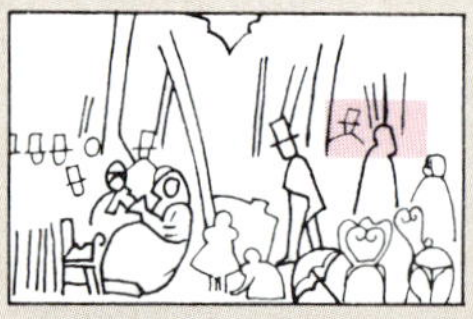

*The figures were worked, with little preparatory underpainting or* ébauche, *directly onto the white ground. The swift wet-in-wet application of colors with a loaded brush contrasts with the thin transparent laying in of the background greens. This device helps the eye to distinguish between foreground and background. The heads are constructed with succinct, lively brushstrokes in simple blocks of light and dark, which gives a vigorous immediacy to the form and captures the quality of the crowded scene. Mixed oranges create a vivid complementary contrast when juxtaposed with the blues of the dress.*

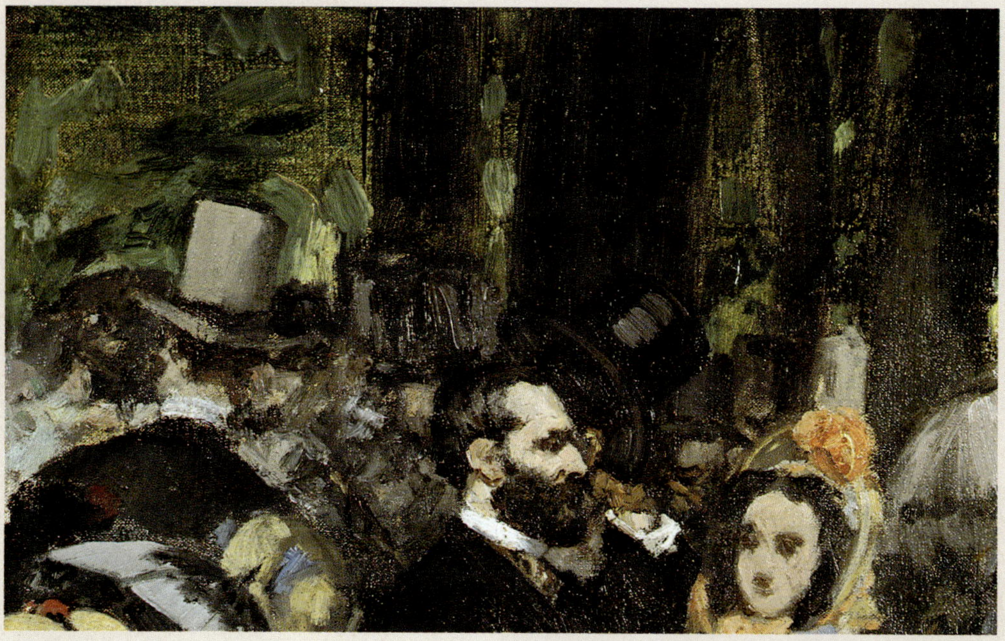

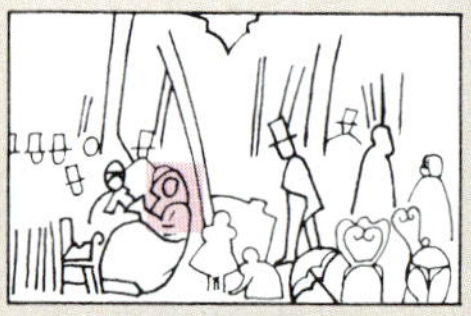

Actual size detail
*The white ground remains uncovered in places. This shows the initial* ébauche *stage was very rudimentary. The disposition of figures is indicated mainly by bold contours. Thinnish opaque yellow ochre underpaint filled in the area of the dress which was then built up wet in wet with paler ochre hues. The black for the veil was dragged lightly through the wet flesh color, and the net motif added in blobs of black applied with the brush tip.*

Although Manet at first adopted the thin brown initial lay-in of colors – the academic *ébauche* recommended by his teacher Couture – he rejected Couture's 'tomb-like' lighting which gave deep dominant shadows. Instead, Manet used strong natural light, falling directly onto his figures, which, as the artist stated, 'presents itself with such unity that a single tone suffices to render it.' His use of white or pale tinted grounds – in this work off-white – strengthened the flat, pale areas in his painting. These contrast with his liberal use of black, to portray the dress of the elegant dandies. Straight black was shunned by academic artists, as its emphatic presence disrupted muted harmonies. Thus, the fragmented feel in Manet's work also stems from his use of color. A jolting effect greets the eye as it moves abruptly over the canvas from white to black shapes, with bold primary hues.

The enclosing canopy of translucent mixed greens was applied mainly with a palette knife. The most opaque, reworked areas of tree are the brighter brushed greens – chiefly viridian and white – which form a pale, emphatic line above the top-hatted heads on the left. The paint layer, although quite thin, is predominantly opaque in the lower half of the picture. Despite the fact, as Monet noted, that Manet 'always wanted his painting to have an air of being painted in a single sitting', he was a slow and cautious artist, often scraping down his canvas at night, to begin again over the first thinly applied layer of color. *Concert in the Tuileries* was acquired from Manet in 1882 by the avid collector Jean-Baptiste Faure, an opera baritone who began buying work by Manet and the Impressionists as early as 1873.

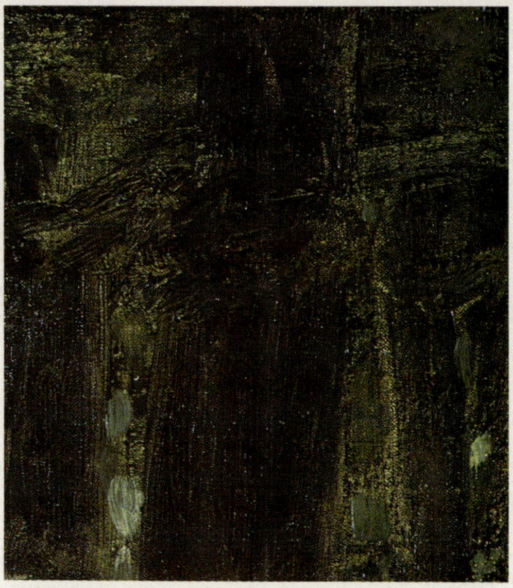

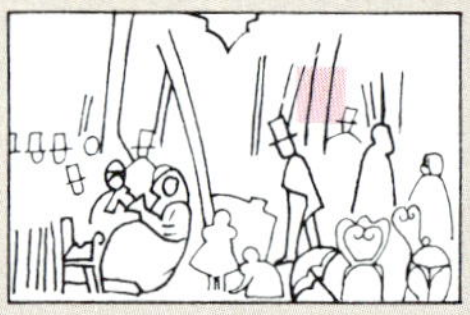

*A fluid transparent viridian green mixture, probably including either raw umber or black, was used for the tree trunks* (left). *These parts are still relatively transparent, although a thicker loading of paint was used than for the foliage. The paler greens were added over the dry background greens, to stand for the foliage. The white ground glows through creating the effect of light filtering through the trees.*

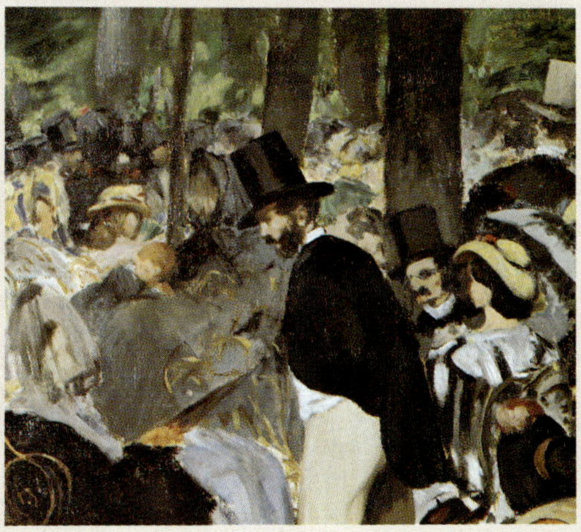

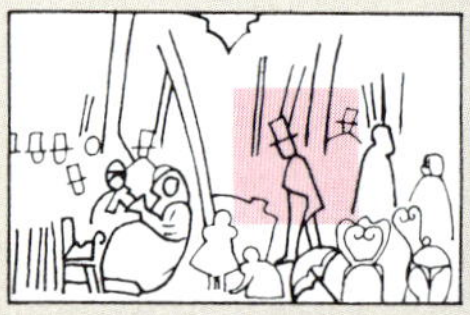

*Unpainted patches of the white ground can be seen among the loosely painted blacks of the skirt of the veiled woman. The grayish blues of the veil were produced by streaking black into the wet paint. The fan is painted with white and viridian green.*

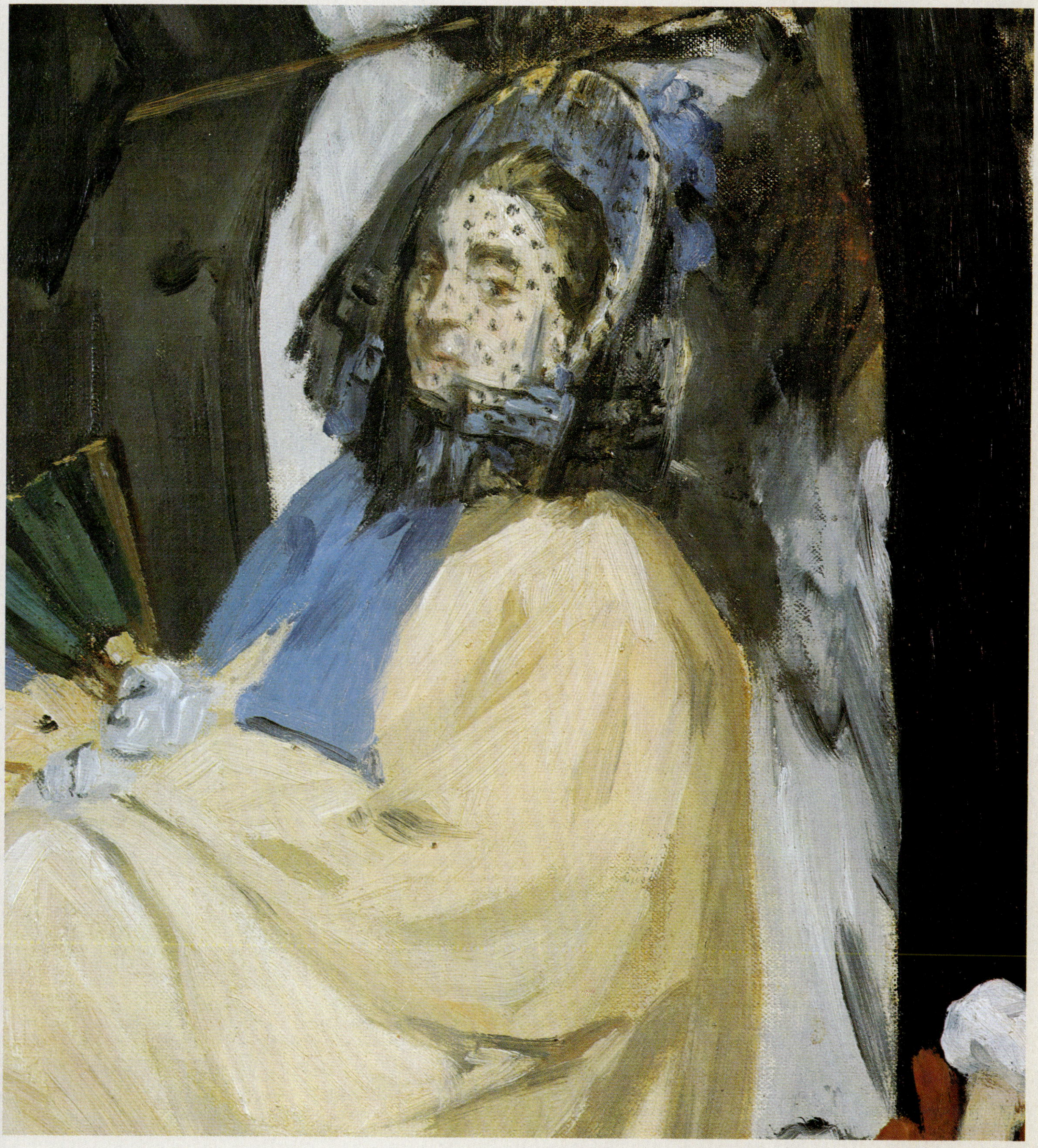

# CAMILLE PISSARRO

*L'Hermitage at Pontoise/L'Hermitage à Pontoise* (1867)
Oil on reused, horizontal chevron twill canvas
91cm × 150.5cm/35$\frac{1}{8}$in × 59$\frac{1}{4}$in

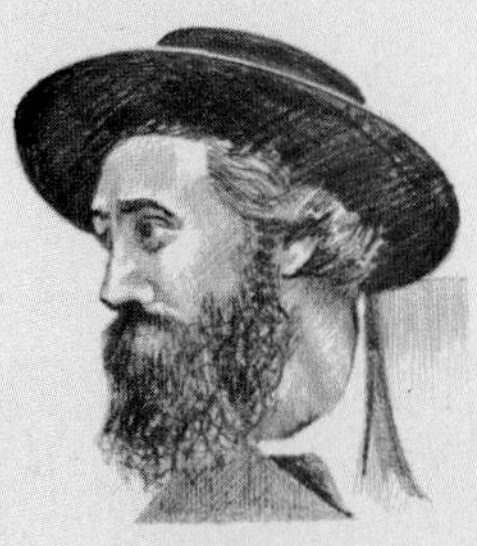

Camille Pissarro lived at L'Hermitage in the north-east part of Pontoise, between 1866 and 1868. He was to return to the area after the upheavals of the Franco-Prussian War and Paris Commune of 1870 and 1871, spending much of his time living and painting there during the 1870s and early 1880s. The work is close in its large scale and elongated format to several other paintings by Pissarro from the mid 1860s, and it is likely that they were intended for showing at the official Paris Salon exhibitions. Although infused with a relatively naturalistic outdoor light and careful observation of natural detail, this was undoubtedly a work executed in the studio. Like his radical compatriots, Pissarro was at this stage of his career still following the traditional procedure of executing studies in the open air, then working up large-scale variants indoors in order to present carefully considered, finished pictures at the Salon. Despite this practice, the painting combines striking elements of prophetically innovatory work with the influence of older artists in the Realist tradition.

The richly painted and varied somber greens are reminiscent of Courbet's forest landscapes, while the panoramic format, broad foreground, punctuated with small-scale toiling figures, and solidly constructed buildings are a reminder of Pissarro's debt to his teacher Corot (1796–1875). While there is a stark contrast between the darks of the landscape and the pale tones of sky and buildings, the light and dark are not used to structure form in a traditional manner. In fact the even, ambient light from the overcast sky eliminates shadows which might strengthen form. Instead, the powerful sense of structure visible in the buildings is created through varied, descriptive brushwork which follows the form and the directions of the planes, and imitates natural surface textures. There are remarkable compositional similarities between Pissarro's picture and that of the same subject from the previous year by Charles Daubigny (1817–1878). Daubigny's vigorously painted landscapes were highly influential in the development of Impressionism. Both artists chose a low viewpoint, close to ground level, and both show a broad open foreground with small, integrated figures, and buildings in the middle distance. In both paintings, the hillside is placed parallel to the picture plane, running horizontally just over halfway up the canvas.

However, Pissarro differs from Daubigny in the extraordinary solidity of his handling of form, and in his lively use of diagonals. The strong foreground horizontals are broken at the bottom right of Pissarro's painting by a diagonal moving in toward the center of the composition. This is taken up, reiterated and reinforced by the diagonal roofs of the buildings and the insistent, flattened stripes of the hillside fields. The hill rises immediately behind the buildings, blocking off distance, and these elements flatten the picture, producing a compact and relatively shallow pictorial space. This lack of deep recession is accentuated by the immediacy of the colors in the background.

Landscape artists frequently used graduated brushwork to indicate increasing distance. In other words, loose broad brushstrokes were used to depict the objects closest to the viewer, while those at a distance were shown with smaller and smaller touches towards the skyline. In Pissarro's painting, however, the size of brushmark remains relatively uniform throughout the landscape, so that his touch tends to contradict the illusion of space, making the spectator very aware of the painted surface.

In *L'Hermitage* Pissarro used an unusual canvas weave, a chevron or herringbone twill, which runs horizontally. However, because this picture was executed over a previous painting, the build-up of paint layers has resulted in the canvas texture being almost completely hidden, except in certain areas, such as the lower edge of the picture, where the paint is less built up. Had there been only a single painting on this support, the canvas texture would doubtless have had a stronger impact.

The paint, which is rich and buttery in consistency, has been applied in separate touches or strokes of a loaded broad bristle brush, building up wet layers over dry with some mixing of color wet into wet on the surface of the painting. The palette is composed predominantly of subdued earth colors and dark greens, with accents of brightish hues restricted to picking out the figures. All the colors are mixed with varying amounts of white to produce a solid, opaque paint layer. This would have been essential in order to obliterate the previous composition.

Spatial ambiguity and the tension between flatness and an illusion of depth are often accentuated rather than eased by the presence of figures in Pissarro's landscapes from this time on. Figures were traditionally incorporated into landscape paintings almost to legitimize the genre as they humanized a scene and gave it a readily identifiable sense of scale. Varied costume and human activity could also locate the picture historically, geographically and socially. Although in this painting there is no direct sunlight to cast shadows and thereby define the precise spatial location of the figures, their relative scale nevertheless helps to establish the spatial relationships in the composition. The bending male worker is carefully placed so that the loss of his feet among the vegetables disguises the uncertainty of his position in space, the vegetable patch almost fulfilling the function of a cast shadow. In later works, for example Pissarro's *Hillside at L'Hermitage* (1873), such guises are abandoned, permitting the artist to exploit such daring spatial complexities to the full.

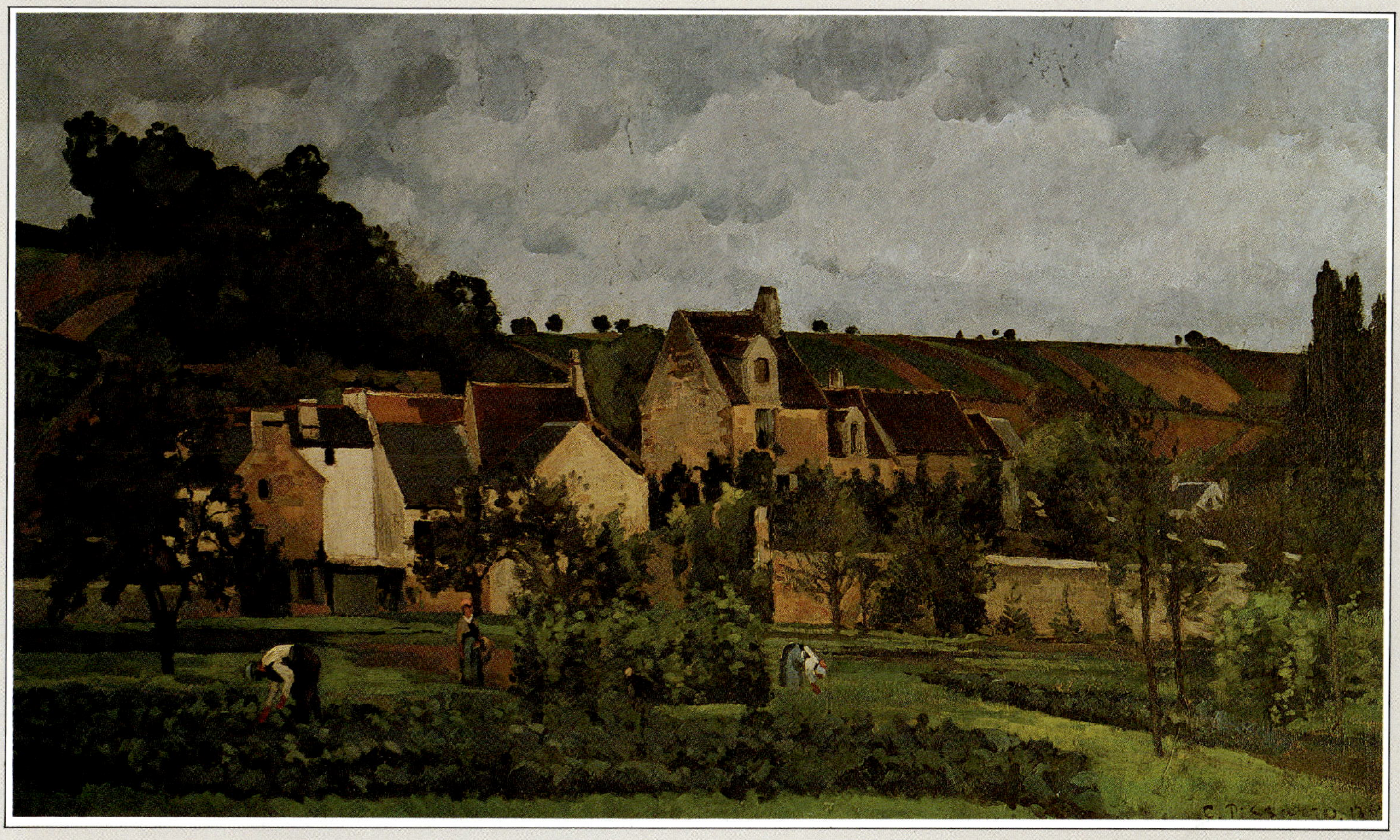

*On his teacher Corot's advice, Pissarro began painting from nature in the summer of 1857, and the unpretentious simplicity of this scene, painted 10 years later, is typical of the type of subject, chosen by Corot. The elongated horizontal format canvas used here by Pissarro is comparable to those generally preferred by Corot, although it is somewhat larger. This canvas is close to the standard format vertical marine 80 (146 x 89 cm/57½ x 35in). Slight variations in commercially manufactured products were common, as were marginal size differences from one color merchant to another. The large scale of this landscape suggests both that it was one of the paintings Pissarro intended for the Salon exhibition, and that it was a composition executed in the studio although based on studies outdoors. The unity of the even, gris clair lighting shows how successfully the artist retained his first impression in the final work.*

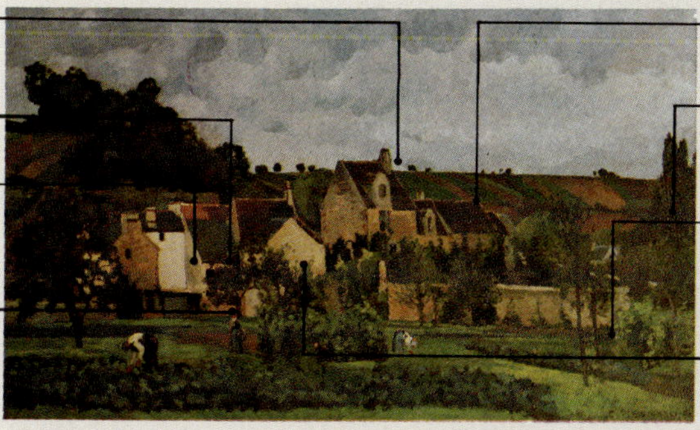

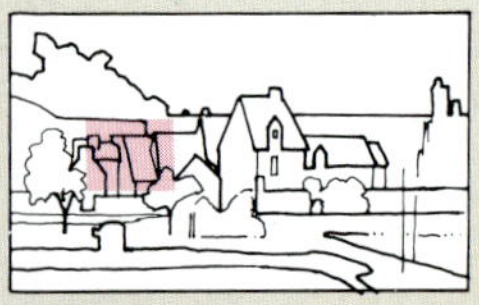

This detail shows white flecks of light bounced off the irregular brush-marks by the thick varnish applied over the paint layer. The paint layer is thick and opaque, the color rich and juicy, loaded on to follow and thus construct the forms of the architecture. In this way, descriptive textural brushmarks replace the form-giving fall of light and shade traditionally used to create structure in painting. The gray-blue of the large roof was laid in with a painting knife, such as those used by Courbet and Daubigny, but most of the paint was applied with hog's hair brushes. Criss-cross, dabbed brushstrokes were used for the foliage, while the contours of the roofs were added later to define the planes.

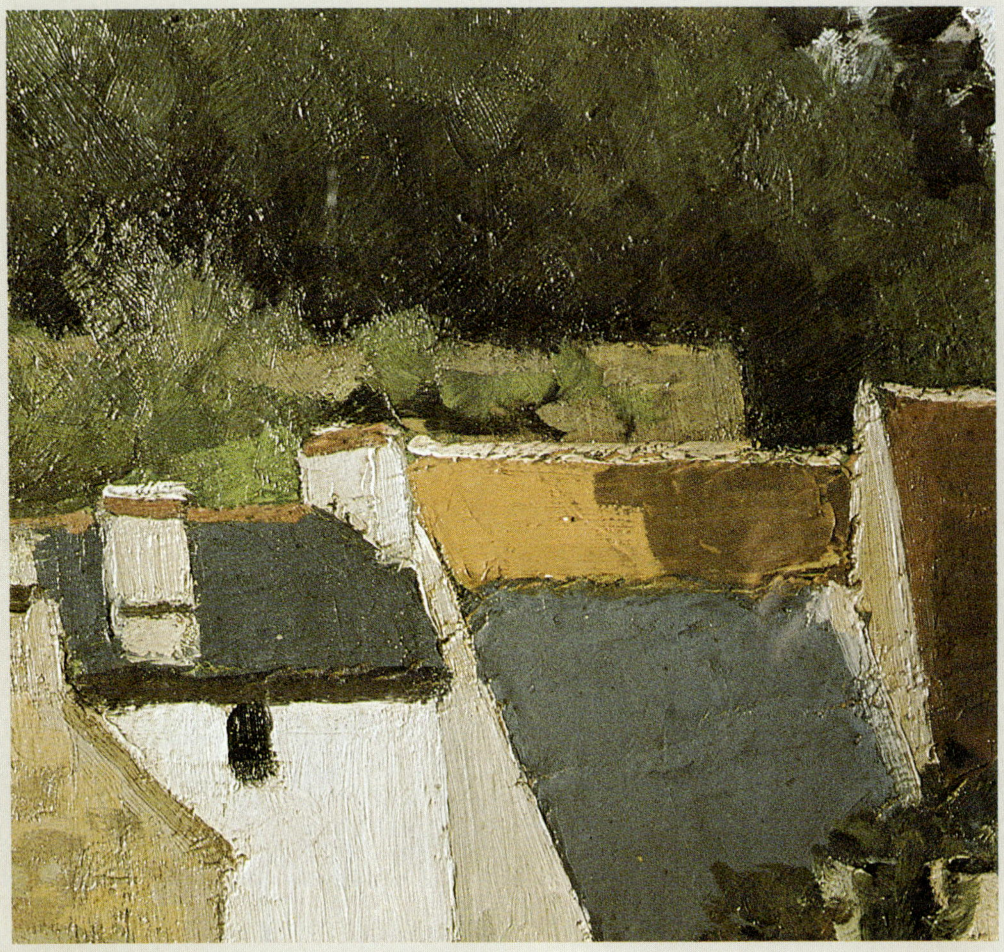

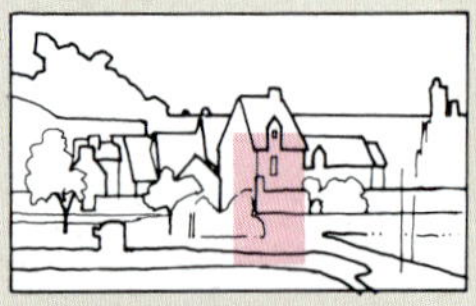

Irregular, dried brushmarks beneath the paint of the wall and the central tree, are remnants of the previous composition over which the present work was executed. The strong horizontal strokes of greens and browns are broken by opposing dry marks from the painting below. Artists often reused canvases as they could not always afford fresh supports. The stooping female figure is summed up with a few deft strokes of rich opaque color applied with a loaded brush.

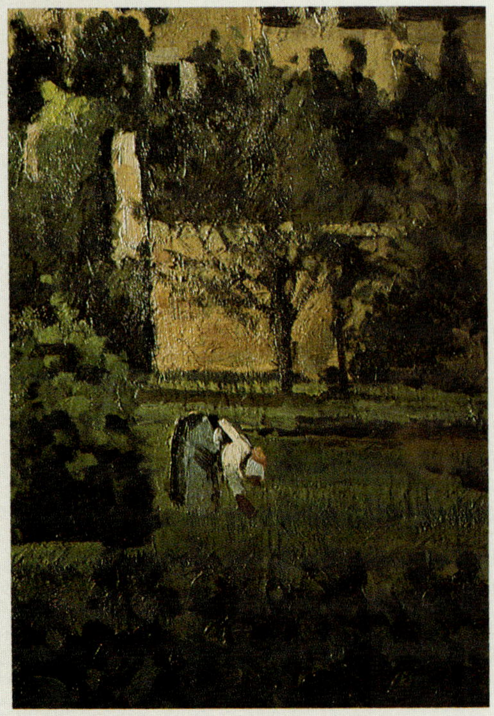

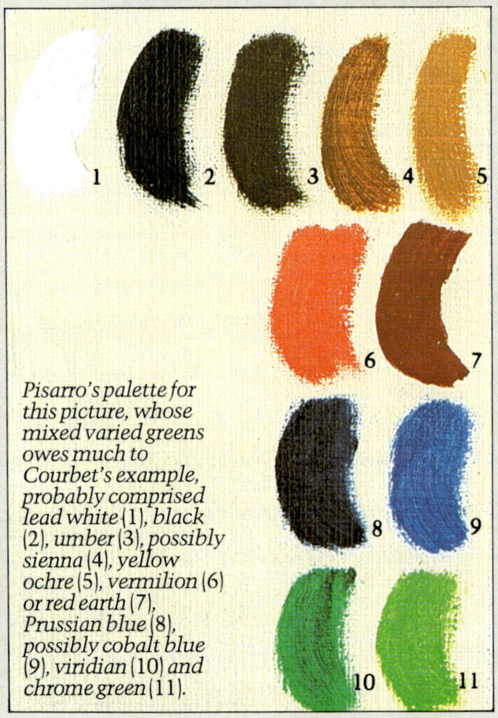


Pisarro's palette for this picture, whose mixed varied greens owes much to Courbet's example, probably comprised lead white (1), black (2), umber (3), possibly sienna (4), yellow ochre (5), vermilion (6) or red earth (7), Prussian blue (8), possibly cobalt blue (9), viridian (10) and chrome green (11).

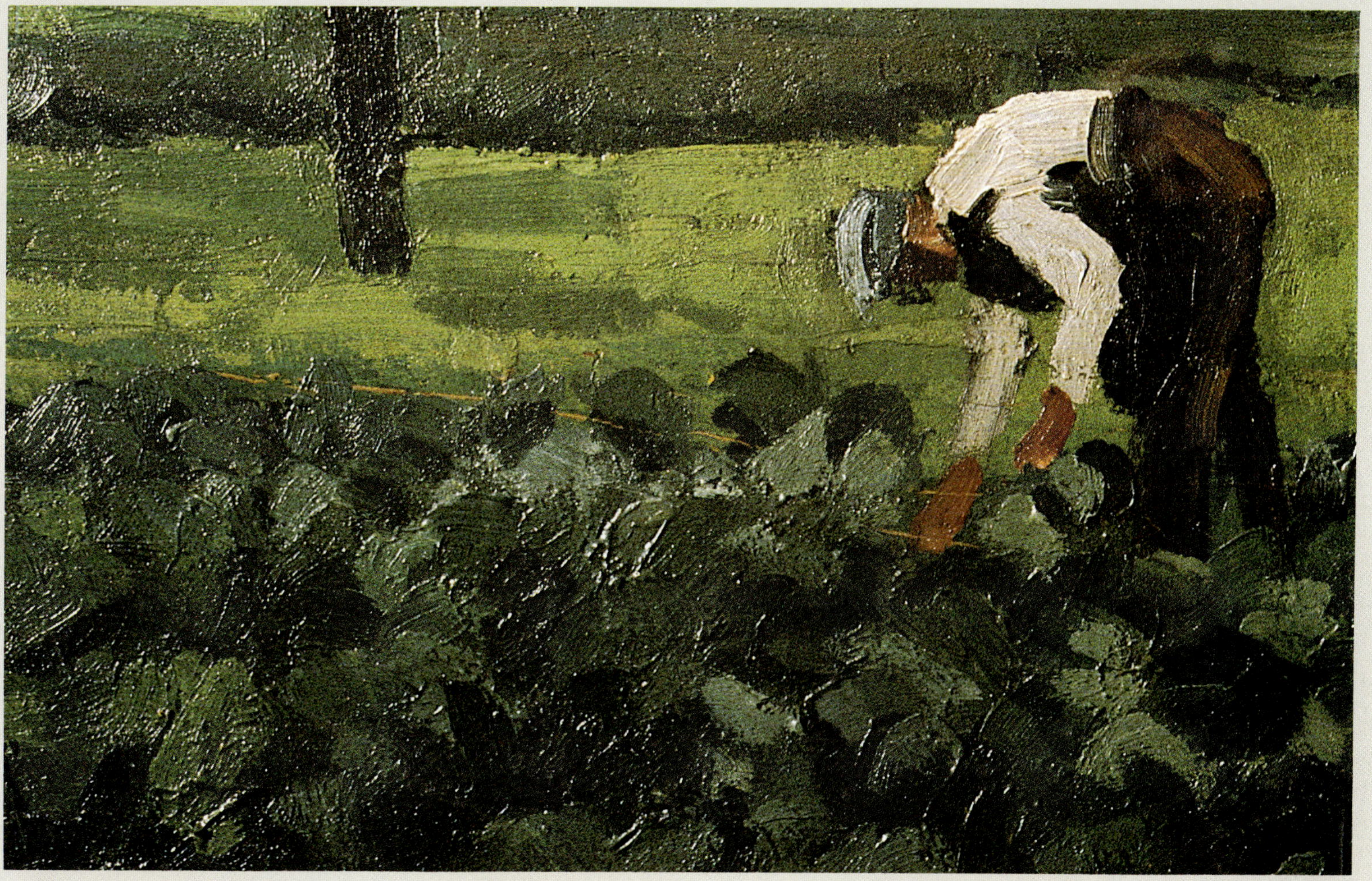

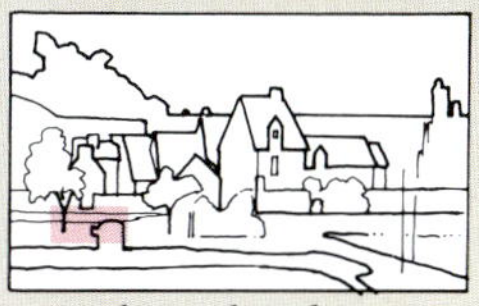

Actual size detail
*The light catching and reflecting off the varnished surface again reveals the brushwork of the previous composition because these brushmarks do not relate to the structure of the present painting. The pale green, possibly a chrome green mixture, at the base of the wall was added after the tree was painted, as the pale green strokes finish short of the colors in the tree trunk. Black, white and umber were juxtaposed for the small figure, with yellow ochre slurred into the black and umber mix to depict the trousers. The position of the figure's head has been moved slightly to the right and up. The colors are mainly broken, mixed both on the palette and* also *worked wet into wet on the paint surface.*

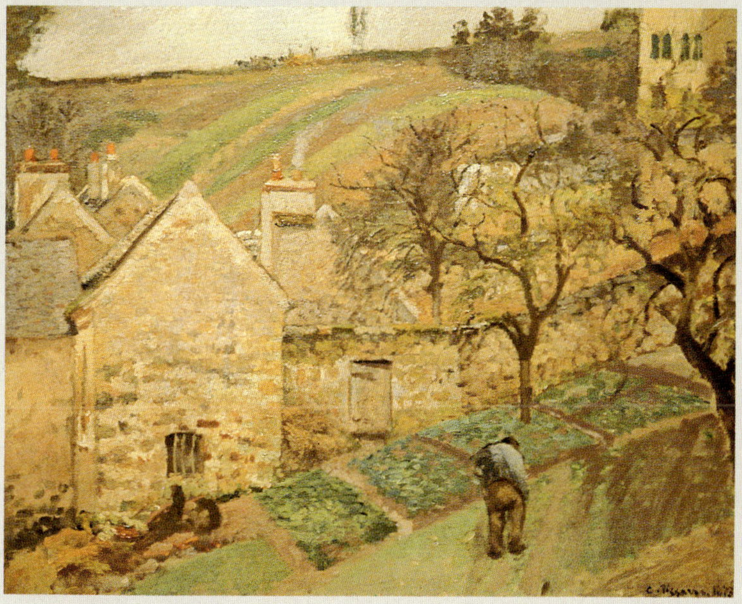

*Pissarro's later work,* Hillside at l'Hermitage *(1873), is on a much squarer, standard figure 20 format canvas (61 x 73cm/24 x 28¾in), and shows a more daring use of light and space. Unlike the earlier work, this painting has a high skyline. Both use diagonal bands of color. This creates a flatness which is enhanced by the even tonality and lighting. The squarish format complements the artist's high viewpoint, emphasizing the chunky interlocking shapes of buildings and land. No direct fall of light and shade structures form, rather, a flat pattern of shapes is created over the picture surface. Pissarro's experiments with flat compositional designs were counterbalanced by the naturalistic descriptive brushwork he used at this time.*

# PIERRE AUGUSTE RENOIR

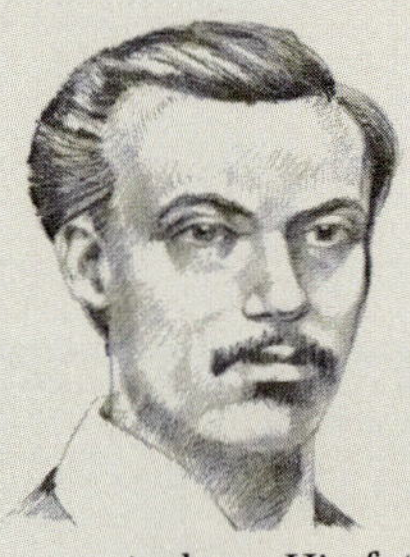

*Portrait of Frédéric Bazille/Frédéric Bazille à son chevalet* (1867)
Oil on pale primed canvas
105cm × 73.5cm/41¾in × 29⅛in

Unlike most of his colleagues, who belonged to the middle or upper classes, Renoir came from the humbler background of the artisan class. His father was a tailor and his mother a seamstress. Thus, it was not surprising that his artistic talent was at first channeled into a career in the crafts. Between 1854 and 1858 he was apprenticed to a firm of porcelain painters, and as a biographer André later remarked 'He retained from his first *métier* of painting on porcelain the taste for light and transparent colors.' When Renoir decided on a career in the fine arts, his respect for tradition led him to enroll for drawing classes at the official Ecole des Beaux-Arts, where he studied from the model each evening for two years from April 1862. Seeking a liberal and yet respected painting master, he signed up with Charles Gleyre, whose name as his teacher appears as early as October 1861, on an application for permission to copy from Renaissance drawings at the Parisian print collection, the Cabinet des Estampes. While most of his friends had independent means or financial support from their families, Renoir had to earn enough money to pay for his tuition before he began training.

Frédéric Bazille (1841–1870), like Cézanne, came from the south of France. His family lived in Montpellier, and were wealthy enough to support Bazille in his wish to become a painter. He too, enrolled at Gleyre's *atelier*, in the autumn of 1862, where he met Renoir, together with Sisley and Monet. Gleyre's studio was closed because of financial difficulties and the master's ill-health in March 1864, thus curtailing the group's artistic training. Renoir and Bazille had a close friendship during the 1860s, up until the latter's untimely death in action during the Franco-Prussian War of 1870. Bazille's position enabled him to help the poorer Renoir, who lived with Bazille in Paris in 1866, and again from autumn 1867, when Renoir and Monet both shared Bazille's Paris studio in the rue Visconti.

It was during this time that the *Portrait of Bazille* was painted. It shows Bazille working on a *Still Life with Heron* which survives today. The still life upon which he was working looks very different in Renoir's version from Bazille's original. While Bazille's work is tight and carefully handled, Renoir's version shows a freer, broader interpretation which does not match the fine sable brushes he has painted in Bazille's hands. Renoir's portrait presents Bazille close up to the picture surface, filling almost the entire picture space. Although he is engrossed in his own work, the sitter's presence is very strong and immediate. Bazille was a very tall, lanky figure, as can be seen by his hunched-over knees and by his appearance in other contemporary portraits.

As in comparable portraits from this period by Degas and especially Manet, the sitter is shown surrounded by the attributes of his profession, which tell the viewer about his character and social life. The large studio easel, known as a *chevalet méchanique* or English easel, indicates that Bazille was well off, as it was an expensive piece of equipment. Designed mainly for very large-scale pictures, it was built on castors and could be moved with ease around the studio. The bar on which the picture rests could be cranked up and down mechanically, and the body of the easel could be shifted forward to change the angle of the painting. It was a complex item of joinery, usually made in solid hardwood.

Other pieces of studio equipment were also included in the portrait. Bazille uses a small, rectangular palette, of the kind usually included in portable paint boxes. It fitted into the box lid where colors left on it were protected from squashing against other objects. Behind Bazille's back, a couple of canvases are turned to face the wall, a trick to prevent the dust gathering on newly painted surfaces. The exposed rear of the stretcher adds to the information which can be gleaned from the picture, by indicating that modern dry-jointed key stretchers were being used by these artists. Key stretchers, invented in France around 1750, were designed to solve the problem of sagging canvases. When canvas sagged on the cheaper, fixed-jointed stretchers, it had to remain loose unless it was restretched and tightened. With dry-jointed key stretchers, the corner keys, visible at one corner in Renoir's painting, could be tapped further in, forcing the stretcher bars out and thus making the canvas tauter. However, care had to be taken not to overdo this, as, while canvas is relatively elastic, the paint layer is rigid, and excessive tightening could cause it to crack.

*This picture shows a typical nineteenth century studio easel, like that used by Bazille in Renoir's picture. This diagram came from a color merchant's catalog, advertising an 'English easel' made in waxed oak, almost 2 meters (6 feet) high.*

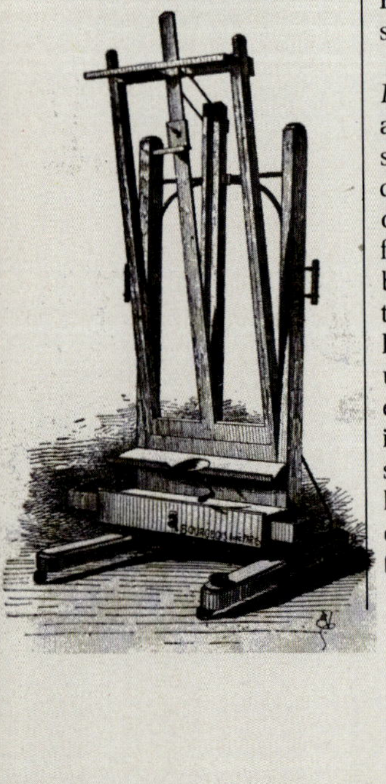

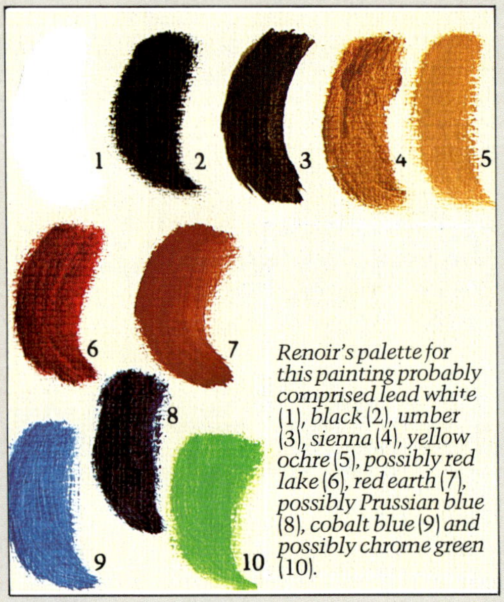


*Renoir's palette for this painting probably comprised lead white (1), black (2), umber (3), sienna (4), yellow ochre (5), possibly red lake (6), red earth (7), possibly Prussian blue (8), cobalt blue (9) and possibly chrome green (10).*

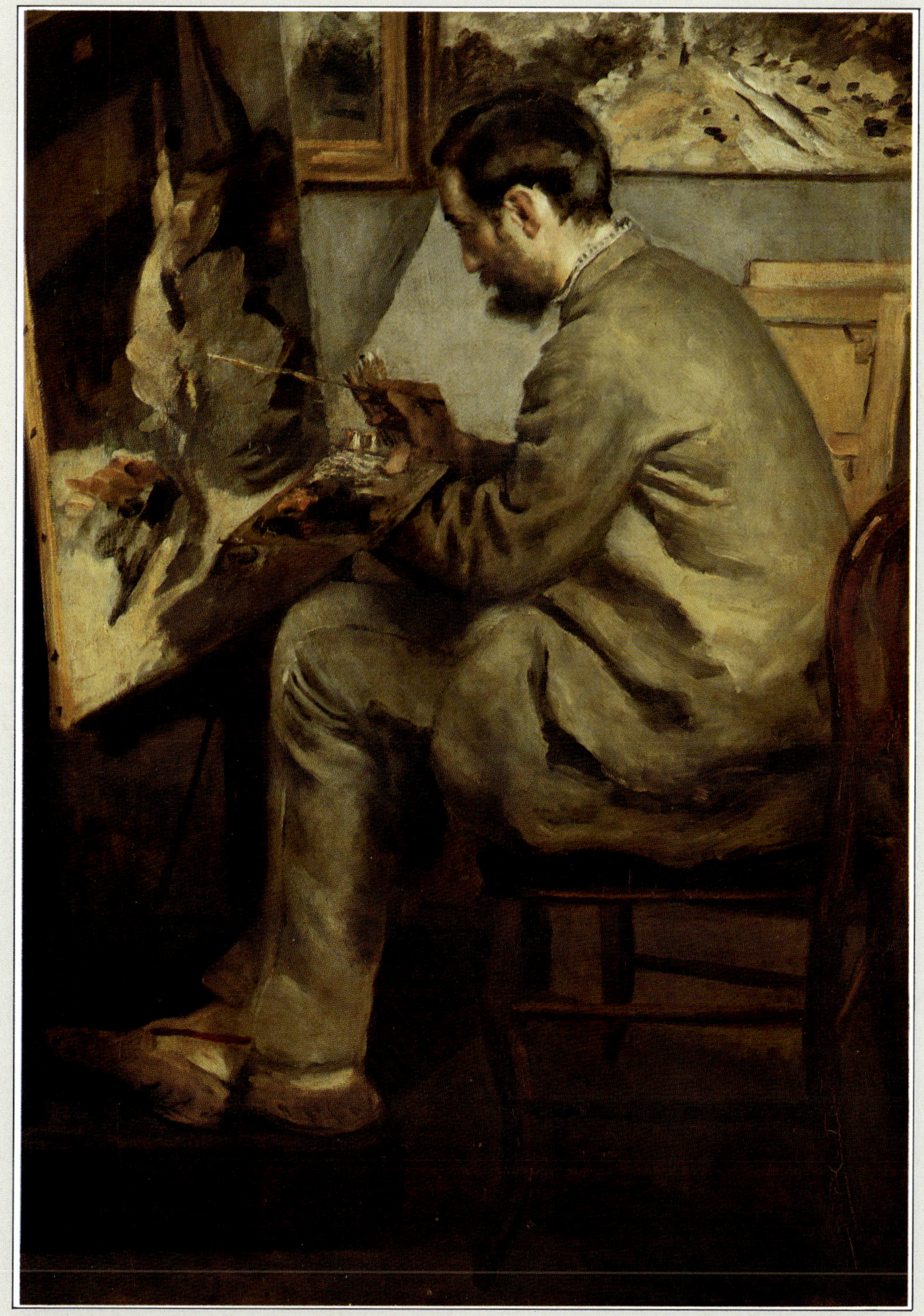

*Nineteenth century portraits and self-portraits of artists provide vital evidence of the social role of artists and image they had of themselves at that time. In this period the social status of the painter was no longer clear, and many artists led a bohemian or dandy life on the fringes of society. In this picture, Renoir has shown Bazille in the role of the craftsman, actively engaged in his work. By contrast, many other pictures of artists show them as thinkers, intellectuals or dreamers, separated from the practical aspects of their trade. This approach echoes the traditional split between craftsman and thinker, artist and artisan, which was so deeply entrenched in European thought. Renoir himself was a very dedicated craftsman, aware of the importance of the careful handling of materials and of the value of sound craft traditions. Renoir's use of black in the shadows is reminiscent of Manet's work, as is his broad, simple modeling of form. The artist's pose is characteristic, with the palette gripped in the left hand, the thumb through the hole in palette. Spare brushes are held bunched in the fingers of the left hand.*

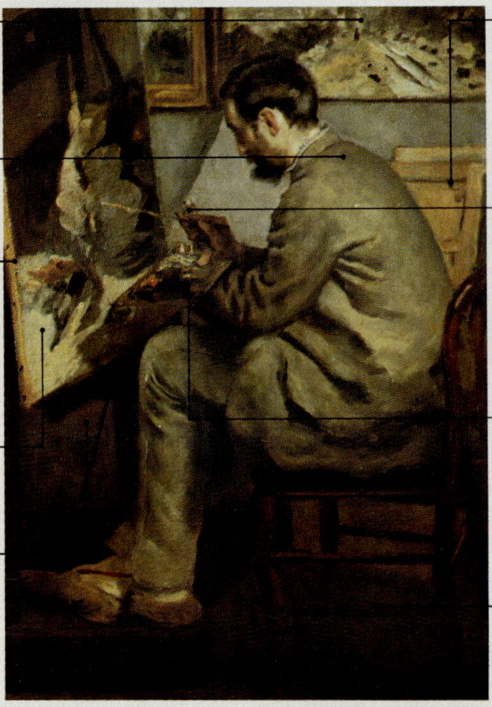


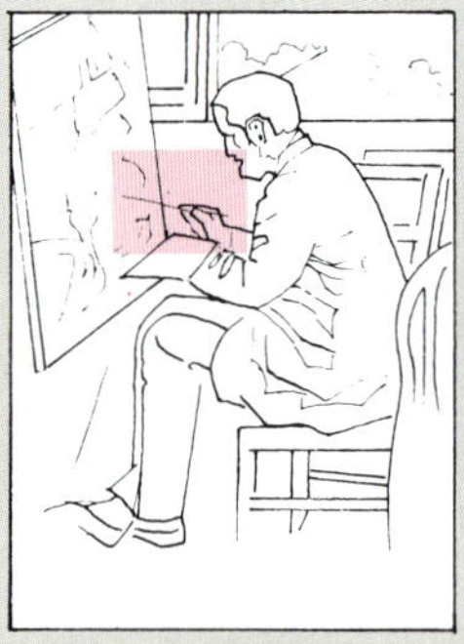

Actual size detail
*The original hues of the painting have been distorted by discolored varnish and dirt in the crevices of the paint, especially in the thickly daubed colors for the palette. Dirt is also visible in the grooves of the canvas grain, giving a speckled effect not intended by the artist. The paint for the hand is deftly worked in rapid confident strokes.*

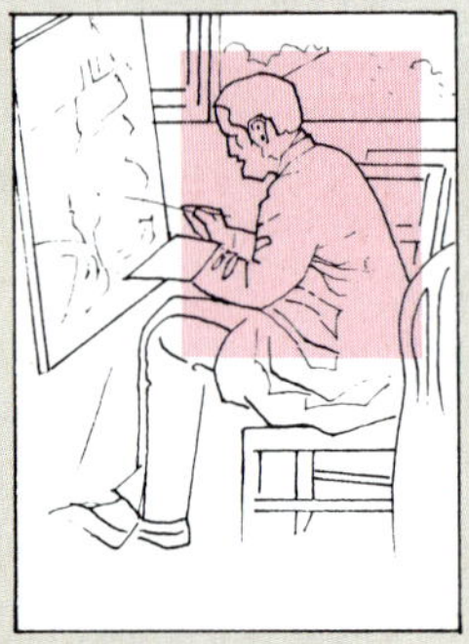

*Opaque gray underpainting was applied over the ground beneath much of the background of the picture, filling in around the edges of the figure. The colors for the stretcher on the right were applied loosely over the dry, gray paint. Gray, usually tinted warm or cool in hue, was commonly used for the walls of studios at this time. A combination of subtle, mixed earth colors, blacks, grays and whites dominates this section of the painting, the colors are thinly but opaquely applied with a delicate, feathery touch which was already characteristic of Renoir.*

Renoir's portrait shows that Bazille is working on a ready primed, commercial canvas, because the exposed edge on the left reveals not the color of raw canvas, but the color of a pale priming which goes around the edge to the back of the stretcher, passing under the securing tacks. A home-primed canvas was normally primed after stretching, so that the ground only appears on the front surface.

In this portrait, Renoir himself probably used ready primed canvas because the ground, although obscured with paint, looks putty-colored on an unpainted strip down the left edge. However, the canvas is not of a standard size. Renoir's portrait shows the influence of Manet in composition, type and in treatment. The figure is broadly handled in relatively flat areas of color, without subtle tonal modeling. Strong contours help to define the form. However, Renoir's application of color already has his individual touch, a feathery, delicate quality Renoir's brushwork was to prove aptly suited to rendering the vibrant, flickering effects of natural light in his Impressionist work. The muted palette colors relate well to the indoor setting here, where the studio walls are painted a conventional dull greenish-gray. The dull ground color corresponds well to the hues of the paint layer. This painting was admired by Manet and became part of his collection. It is not known whether it was a gift from Renoir, or whether Manet bought the work as a gesture of support for the young artist's talent. The subject and purchaser of this work indicate the importance of friendships with other artists to the independent, later Impressionist, painters.

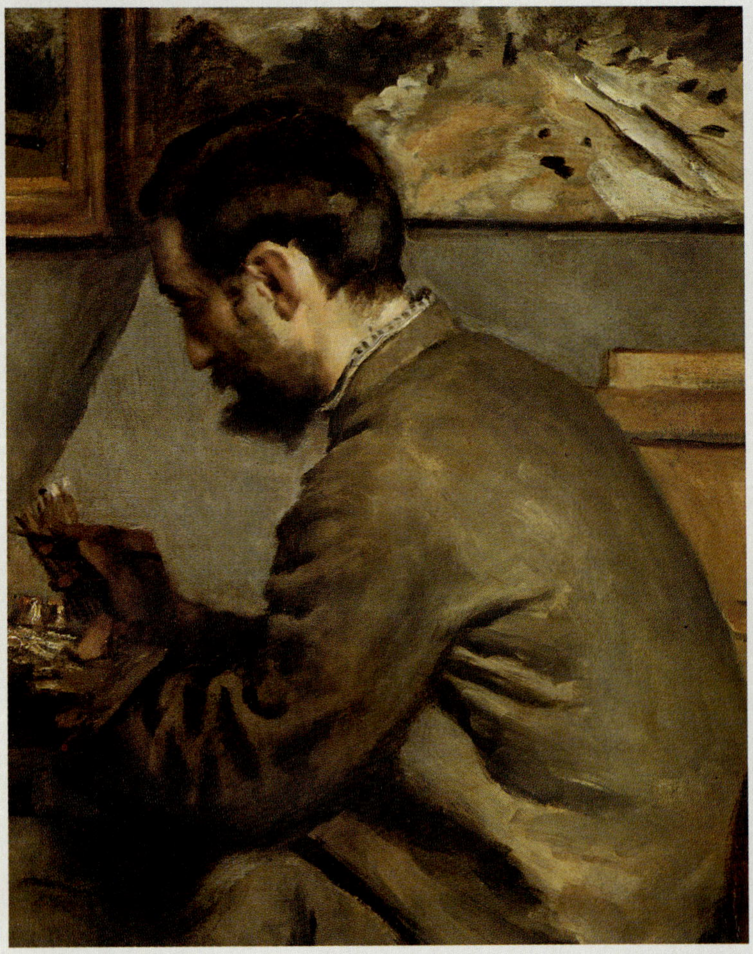

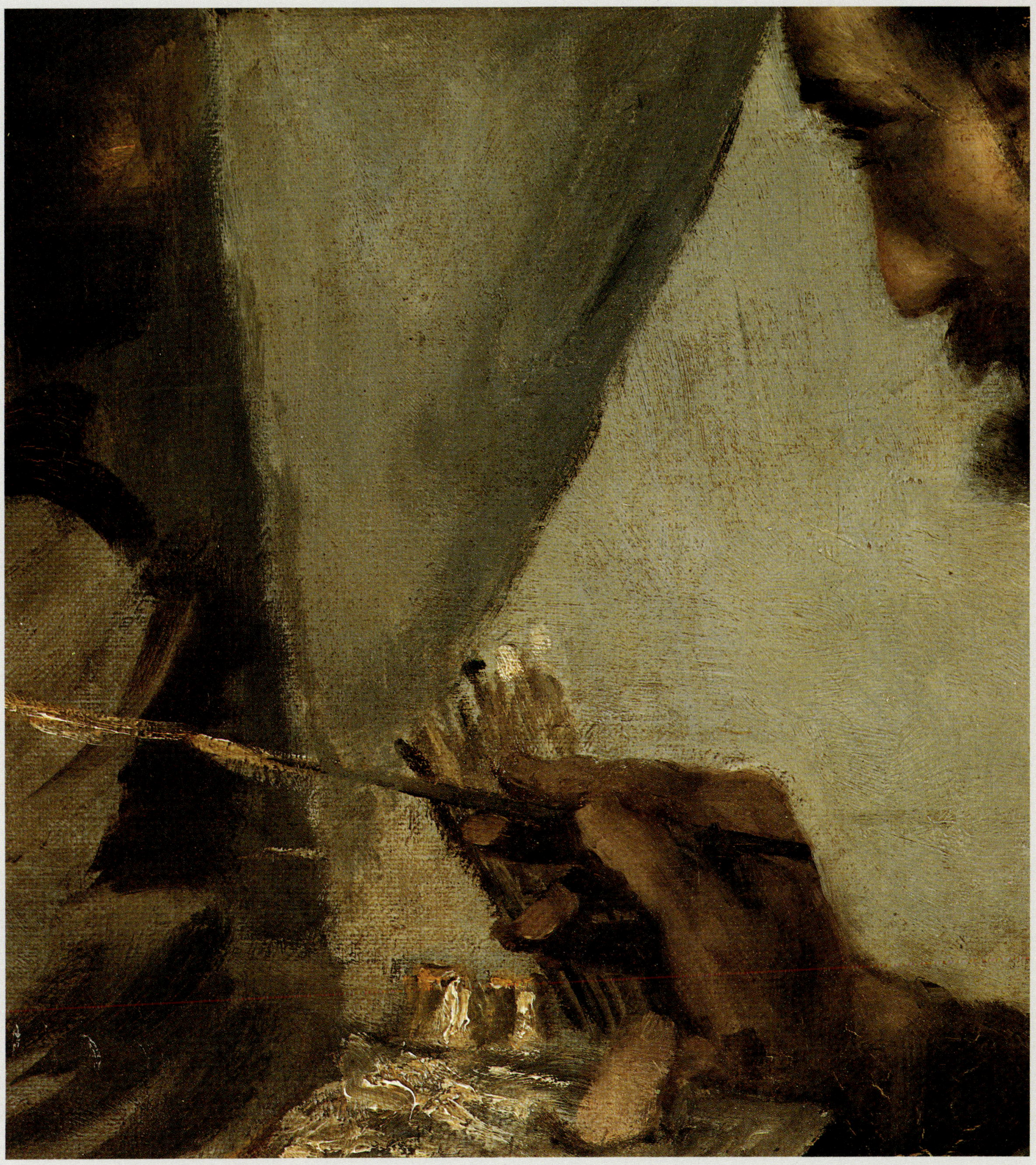

# CLAUDE MONET

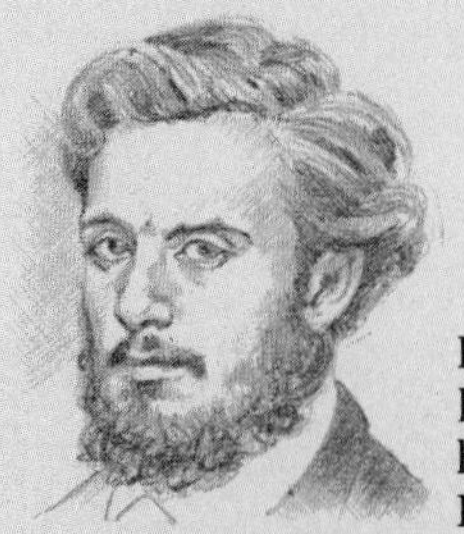

## *Bathing at La Grenouillère/Les Bains de La Grenouillère*
(1869)
Oil on white primed canvas
73cm × 92cm/$28\frac{3}{4}$in × $36\frac{1}{4}$in

During the 1860s, Monet divided his time between his childhood home on the Normandy coast, Paris, and the countryside around the capital. In the earlier part of the decade he had mainly worked near Fontainebleau, southeast of Paris, which was the home of the influential Barbizon school of landscape painters. During that period he came under the influence of older landscapists, like Courbet, who had preferred dark forest settings for their paintings. As his Impressionist style and interests evolved, Monet's love of more open, sunlit scenery, including parks and gardens, gradually emerged, as did the palette which was to complement such scenery. This change in the second half of the decade, was echoed by his growing preference for landscapes to the north and west of Paris, such as Ville d'Avray where *Women in the Garden* was begun in 1866, and Bougival, near where *Bathing at La Grenouillère* was executed three years later.

La Grenouillère was a riverside bathing and boating resort, popular among weekend trippers during the Second Empire (1852–1870) and after. It had a floating restaurant which is seen in another of the paintings executed by Monet during his two-month stay there in the late summer of 1869, and it appears in similar works by Renoir often painted sitting alongside Monet. The resort was situated on the Ile de Croissy, facing the left bank of the Seine.

In Monet's picture, which looks northeasterly, the afternoon light falls from behind the artist – a lighting effect he would have seen in Manet's studio work. However, although this full-face light is used, it is not exploited for the overall brilliance it gives to more open scenery. Monet only turned to this device in the 1870s. Instead, because of the close proximity of dense, overhanging trees, Monet has produced a study with alternating blocks of dark pierced by patches of dazzling sunlight, resulting in contrasts of light and shade reminiscent of Manet's work from the early 1860s. The juicy quality of Monet's paint is also similar to that found in Manet's work of this decade.

Unlike Manet's work, this painting was executed outdoors, and the brushwork is a witness to the speed required to capture the transitory effects which such scenery offered. The paint layer is generally opaque and hides the white ground, except in the most sketchily executed area, the upper right-hand corner. However, the white ground has helped retain the brilliance of the paint layer, which has recently been cleaned. A letter from Monet to his friend, the artist Frédéric Bazille (1841–1870) on 25 September 1869, when he was working at La Grenouillère, makes it clear that Monet was still working in the traditional manner, seeing studies like this as preparatory work for larger, possibly studio executed works.

In this painting, Monet's brushwork is vigorous and the individually distinguishable brushmarks indicate that hog's hair brushes between about 1–2cm ($\frac{2}{5}$–$\frac{4}{5}$in) wide were used. There is little variation between the size of stroke in foreground and background to suggest depth, although more uniformly straight horizontal strokes and pastel shades on the distant water aid the impression of depth and recession. His brushwork is strongly descriptive, catching the character of different forms. Long unbroken strokes outline the boats, short horizontal daubs indicate the foreground water, abrupt jabs are used for flowers and foliage. Monet rejected traditional, smooth brushwork which created an illusion of surface texture; instead, his varied handling helps to evoke the actual natural textures. Monet's talent for summarizing the essential character of his landscapes was already apparent in his early caricatures, which demanded an ability to capture basic features concisely.

Monet's palette for this picture was already fairly limited, moving toward the restricted range of the Impressionists. Black – the absence of light – appears to have been abandoned, confirming his move away from Manet's influence. Most of the colors typically found in Monet's Impressionist palette are already in evidence. Vermilion, one of the few traditional colors used by Monet, has been identified virtually pure in the red flowers on the left, and mixed with other colors elsewhere. The greens were viridian, emerald and chrome, the latter a commercially produced mixture of Prussian blue and chrome yellow widely marketed in the period. All three greens were modern colors. Chrome yellow and lemon yellow mixed, were used in the brightest greens of the background trees. Because of their tendency to blacken in the presence of sulphides, the chrome yellows were abandoned by most of the Impressionists toward the end of the 1870s. Monet replaced them with the more stable cadmium yellows. Cobalt violet, available from 1859, was the first opaque pure violet pigment to appear on the market and was therefore rapidly adopted by artists. It was used here by Monet in mixtures, for example in the foreground water. The early eighteenth century invention, Prussian blue, was used by Monet in the darkest mixtures, such as the swimming costumes, while cobalt blue is the bright blue of the water. Lead white was consistently used by Monet throughout his career, but, as strong contrasts form the basis of this composition, its role in this picture was relatively limited. In his paintings from the 1870s on, lead white was liberally used in most of his color mixtures, bringing with it a new overall brilliance and pale pastel-like quality, as he sought to depict the light tones and minimal light-dark contrasts of full sunlit landscapes. Interestingly, a family of colors commonly used by Monet from the early 1870s, the red

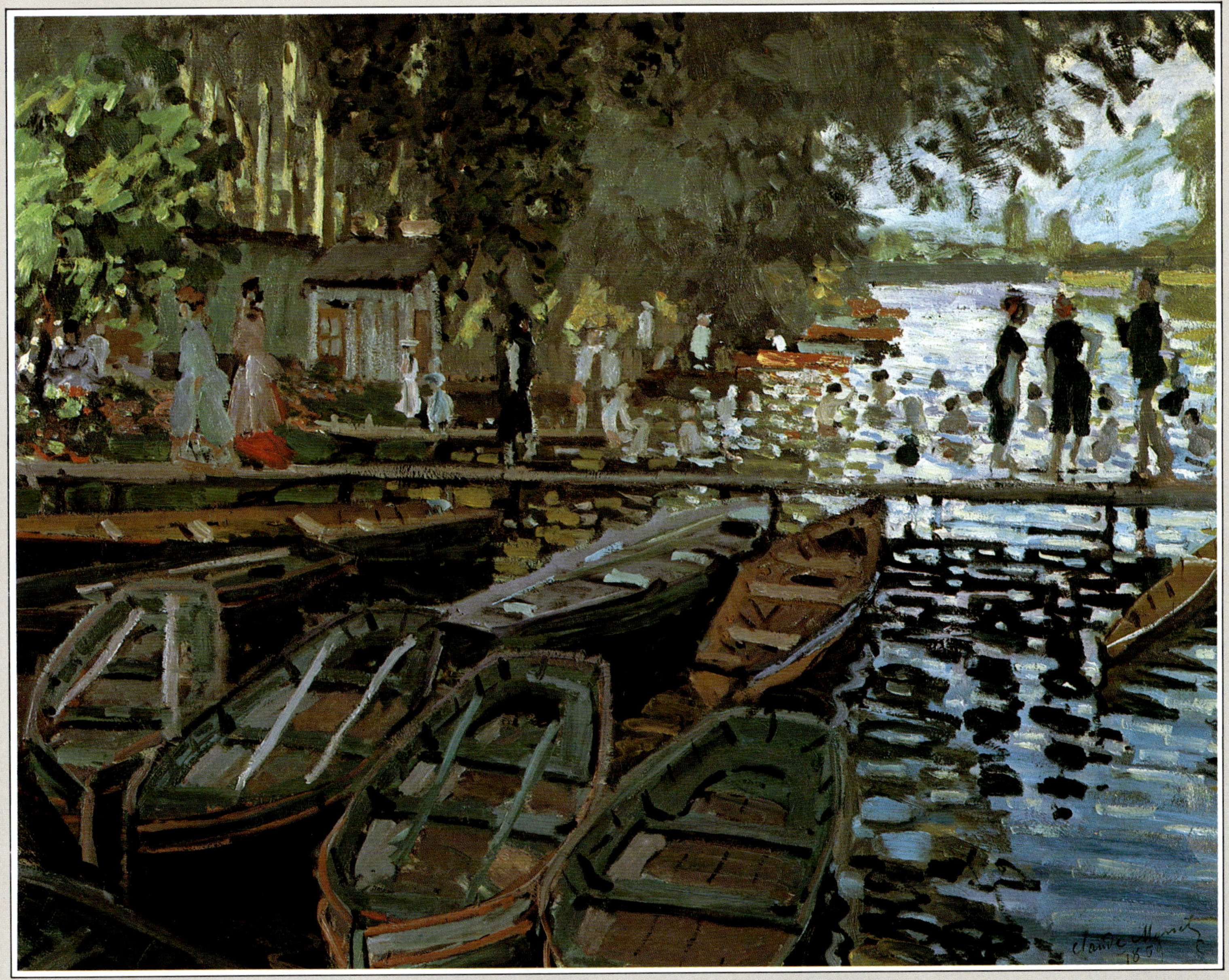

*This leisure scene is animated by Monet's lively brushwork. As well as descriptive of surface textures, the brushmarks, which are almost equal in scale throughout the picture, unify the design. The overall opacity and thickness of the paint consistency add to this effect. The colors are premixed, and also slurred together on the surface. The canvas is a standard, squarish figure 30 format.*

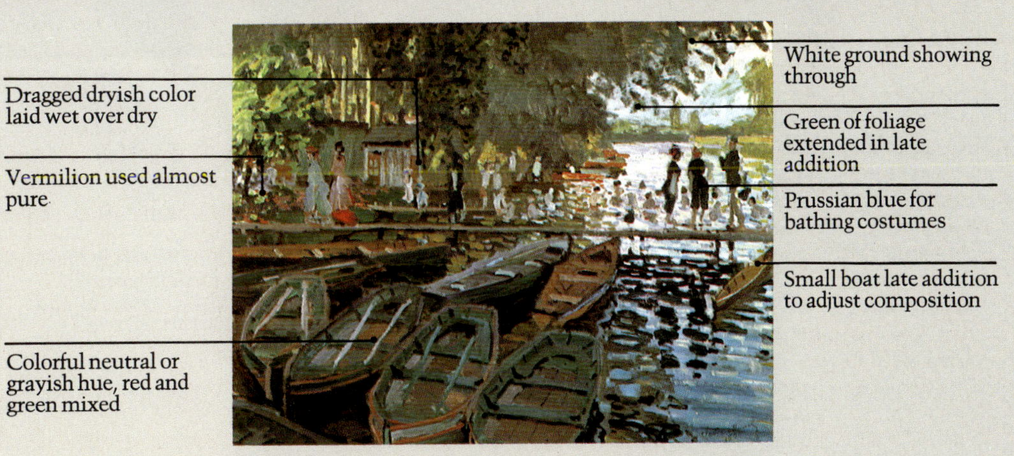

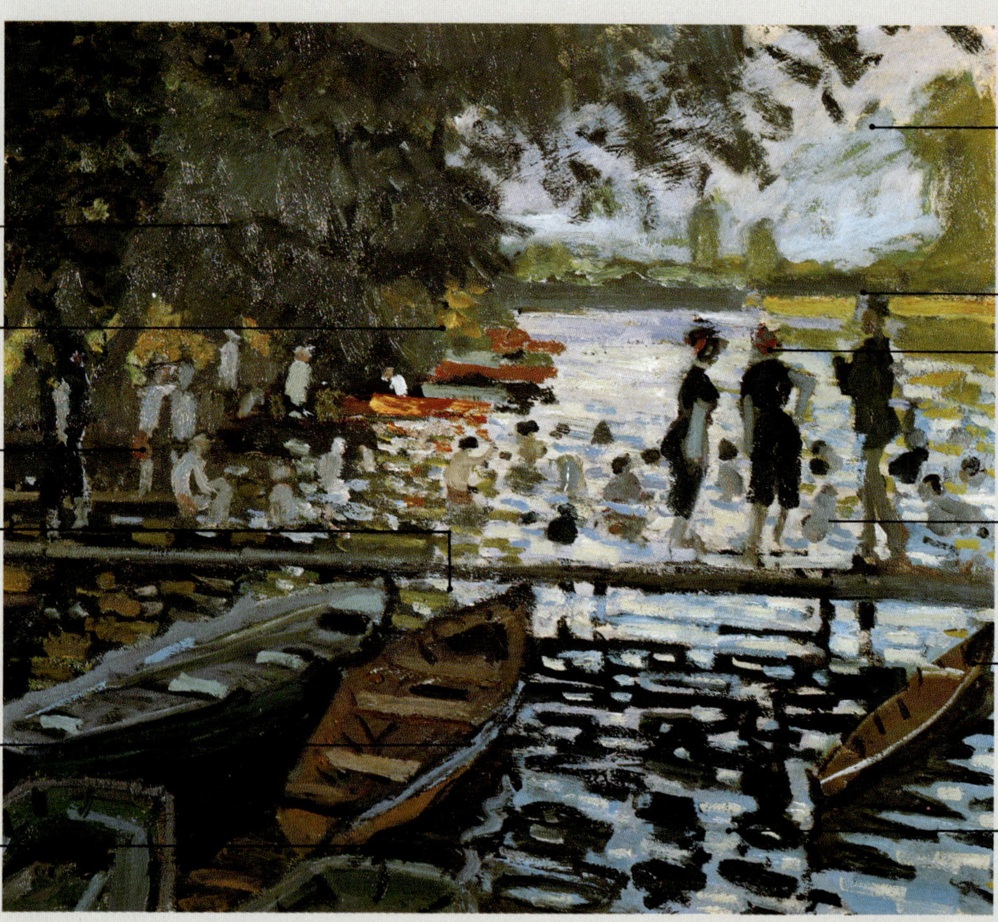


alizarin lakes, has not been identified on this picture. The artificial alizarin, more permanent than the natural organic root derivative madder lake, was only discovered in 1868, which may account for its absence here. Both Prussian blue and probably chrome green were abandoned by Monet during the 1870s. Monet combined slurred wet-in-wet mixing on the canvas with premixed hues. For example, the somber colors on the boats are obtained by mixing complementaries, like red and green, which give darkish neutral hues that are more colorful than those made by sullying a color with black.

The apparently accidental nature of the composition is deceptive. The striking horizontal of the duckboard, which cuts right across the picture surface, is placed almost exactly halfway up the picture. This was an unconventional device at this date. The broad shapes of light and dark above and below that line echo each other, giving a flat decorative unity to the composition which is reinforced by the harmonizing colors and patterned brushwork. Thus, even at this early stage in his career, Monet was already preoccupied with contrasts of naturalistic illusion and flat pattern, which were to become a feature of Impressionism, and to remain with Monet throughout his life.

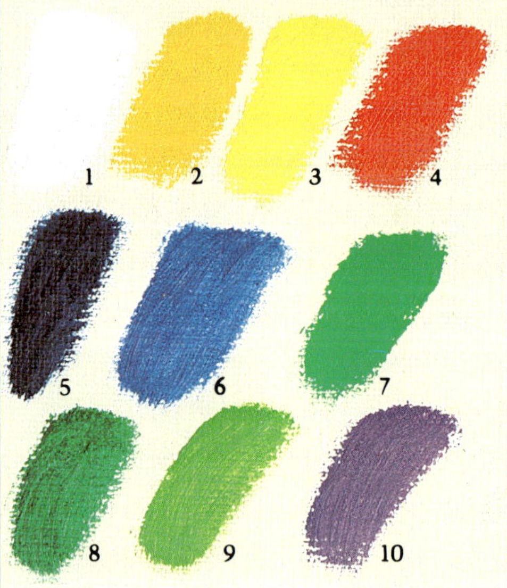


*Monet's palette for this painting, which has been analyzed by the National Gallery, comprised lead white* (1), *chrome yellow* (2), *lemon yellow* (3), *vermilion* (4), *cobalt violet* (10), *Prussian blue* (5), *cobalt blue* (6), *emerald green* (7), *viridian green* (8) *and chrome green* (9).

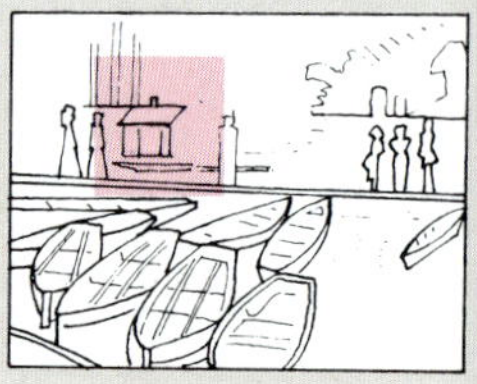

Actual size detail
*The dragged overlaying of the stiffish blue and white paint mixture allows the earlier dry layer of olive green to show through. Such effects add to the vibrant impression of flickering light and color. The colors of the dresses were slurred wet into wet – blue, white and vermilion, or blue, gray and white. Dried, older brushstrokes can be seen cutting across under the present colors, perhaps indicating a previous compositional design. The strong horizontal of the duckboard has been strengthened by dragging dryish, pale pinky-blue over dark, dry paint.*

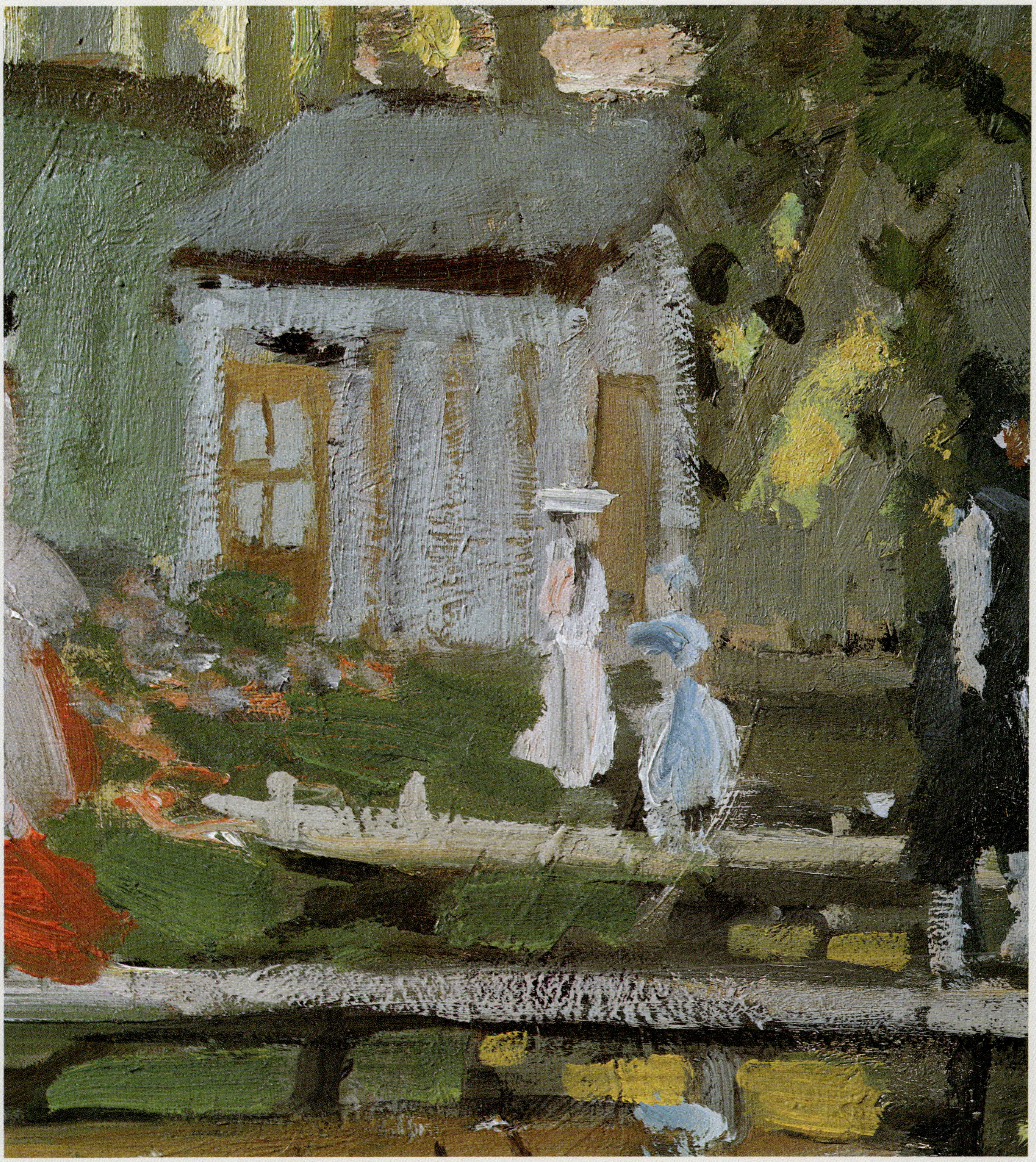

## 1870 1880

The 1870s saw the peak of Impressionism, both as a coherent group movement and as a painting style. During that decade, artists divided their time between landscape painting and studies of Parisian life. The gentle rural landscape along the Seine valley between Paris and Normandy formed the main source of inspiration for Monet, Sisley and Pissarro. Renoir, who regularly worked beside Monet during the first half of the decade, also painted many scenes of interiors, figures and city subjects. Monet and Renoir were joined in Argenteuil by Manet in 1874. In Manet's paintings of this period, figures, as usual, dominated even his outdoor scenes, although he lightened and brightened his palette at this time. During the decade, Degas and Manet continued their emphasis of the 1860s, painting mainly themes of modern Parisian life, such as the boulevards, café scenes, the Opera and the ballet. Gustave Caillebotte (1848–1894) split his allegiance between city life and landscape. The earliest works in the Impressionist style by Mary Cassatt (1845–1926) date from the latter part of the decade, and her subjects included the Opera, indoor and outdoor figure scenes. She often chose themes comparable to those of Berthe Morisot (1841–1895), but their style and handling were quite individual. Pissarro and Cézanne often worked on landscapes together during this period, although Cézanne divided his time between the north and his native Provence.

By the mid 1870s, the artists' period of apprenticeship was over and their ideas, aims and differences firmly established as a result of regular discussions at Paris cafés from the latter half of the 1860s onwards. Indeed, by this time the Impressionists – or independents as they were still called in the early part of the decade – found themselves, with the exception of Manet, sufficiently united in their disagreement with the academic system and its outlet, the Salon exhibitions, to present a united opposition to those institutions. Although their first discussions on the subject in the mid 1860s had come to nothing, by 1874 the members of the Impressionist group finally established their own alternative exhibitions, independent of the official Salon. Their first show took place in April and May 1874, when a critic coined the term 'Impressionist'.

### Basic methods of Impressionism

The brilliant young French Symbolist poet, Jules Laforgue (1860–1887), gave a perceptive and informed description of the Impressionist approach, in an article written in 1883. He said the Impressionist artist was one, who 'forgetting the pictures amassed through centuries in museums, forgetting his optical art school training – line, perspective, color – by dint of living and seeing frankly and primitively in the bright open air, . . . outside his poorly lit studio – has succeeded in remaking for himself a natural eye, and in seeing naturally and painting as simply as he sees.' In seeking to free themselves from the conventional studio vision of line, space and *chiaroscuro*, the Impressionist painters had to re-educate their eyes by careful observation of natural outdoor light effects. They had to learn *not* to see landscape through the artificial eye of European painting.

Photography gave them one alternative vision of the natural world which was not based on painting, and Japanese prints provided another artistic option. The Impressionists' friend and patron Théodore Duret, politician and art critic, noted in an important essay in 1878 'Before Japan it was impossible; the painter always lied. Nature with its frank colors was in plain sight, yet no one ever saw anything on canvas but attenuated colors, drowning in a general halftone.' With their 'piercing colors placed side by side', Japanese artists showed 'new methods for reproducing certain effects of nature which had been neglected or considered impossible to render'. Duret summarized 'After the Impressionists had taken from their immediate predecessors in the French school their forthright manner of painting out of doors from the first impression with vigorous brushwork, and had grasped the bold, new methods of Japanese coloring, they set off from these acquisitions to develop their own originality and to abandon themselves to their personal sensations.'

While their older colleagues, Manet and Degas, remained essentially committed to studio working methods, albeit novel ones, the younger artists, Monet, Renoir, Pissarro, Morisot, Sisley and Cézanne, used outdoor landscape studies as the vehicle for their research into new ways of painting the real world. They abandoned the strongly contrasting lights and darks of Romantic and Realist painting. In particular they rejected the use of the somber earth colors, browns and blacks, which dominated the palettes even of artists like Manet and Degas in the 1860s. Instead they explored the pale colors and close tonal values of studies by Corot (1796–1875), the luminous skies of outdoor seascapes by Boudin (1824–1898), and even the pale opaque shadows which helped flatten pictorial space in works by Ingres (1780–1867). They began to exploit more fully the light-enhancing properties of pale commercial primings, and gradually replaced the traditional brown *ébauche* with a brightly colored initial laying in of paint which related directly to the final colors of the painting. They continued and extended the making of outdoor *études*, adopting this freely executed study stage as their finished work.

### Supports

Although the smooth, dark surface of mahogany panels was often used to advantage by earlier nineteenth century landscapists, the Impressionists preferred the lively give and texture of woven fabric supports. Prepared paper and card were often also used as supports for oil sketching in this period for reasons of economy and their light weight which made them easy to carry. Canvas is a coarse cloth woven usually from flax or cotton, but sometimes from hemp. Its widespread use as a painting support dates from the Italian Renaissance. The rise in importance of fabric supports coincides with the increasing cultivation of flax in Europe from the Middle Ages on. It remained the most important vegetable textile fiber in Europe until the end of the eighteenth century, when cotton began to be imported on a large scale from the United States. Canvas was first used in easel painting merely to provide an underkey for the gesso grounds of medieval panel paintings, and only emerged slowly as an independent painting support. The adoption of canvas went hand in hand with the development of oil painting. Its textured surface stimulated experiments, especially among the Venetian artists, in expressive brush and oil paint handling, which produced emotive effects impossible to obtain with fast drying egg tempera colors on smoothly primed rigid panel supports.

By the early nineteenth century, ready made canvases were being sold in France in a standardized range of sizes for easel painting. The range then available, in a squarish rectangular format designed for portrait and figure work, spanned from a small (No 3) canvas, measuring approximately 6in (15.5cm) by 8in (20.5cm), to the largest, (No 120), measuring approximately 6 feet (1.9 meters) by 4 feet (1.2 meters). At that time the metric scale had not yet been fully established. In the early 1830s a longer 'landscape' format was introduced, together with an even more elongated 'marine' shape. By the 1850s five series were on the market. These were the original portrait, vertical landscape, horizontal landscape, vertical marine, and horizontal marine series. Within these five series, each format number had the same sized shorter side, only the longer side varied in length. The code-numbering of portrait formats probably had its origin in the seventeenth century when the major art theorist Roger de Piles recorded that canvas pieces were sold according to cost – a 'canvas of 20 sous' was of given, commonly accepted dimensions. Thus, for example, a canvas costing 20 sous became canvas size No 20.

Despite the fact that most artists and writers thought that the dimensions of standard formats had been rationally conceived to conform with some aesthetic, harmonious ratio, such as the influential 5:8 proportions of the Golden Section, they were in fact determined purely by economic factors. In order to be able to prepare stretched canvases and picture frames in advance, color merchants found it expedient to use fixed measurements, rather than having to follow the whims of artists by making numerous sizes to order.

Before mechanization in the weaving industry, hand-loom widths for canvas depended upon the distance a shuttle could be thrown through the warp by the weaver. In France this was commonly around 1 meter (3 feet) up to a maximum of 1 meter 40cm (4ft 6in). When standardized sizes are analyzed in relation to the canvas widths available, it is clear that the formats chosen were those which could be cut most economically from the fabric, avoiding undue wastage. For large-scale paintings, like those of historic subjects often shown at the important, annual Salon exhibitions, artists had to order specially made canvases, which were sewn from strips of fabric.

The mechanical spinning and weaving of linen was about 50 years behind developments in the mechanization of the cotton industry, so entirely machine-made linen canvas was not common before the mid nineteenth century. Although large, unbroken widths of canvas made massive pictures simpler as the century progressed, the tendency was, on the contrary, to smaller, easel-scale paintings. This development was prompted by two chief factors – the demands of outdoor painting, which made very large canvases unmanageable, and the neces-

Below *This table shows the main standardized canvas formats. Commercially produced ready primed, ready stretched canvases in a wide range of standard sizes were available off the peg to artists in the nineteenth century. The range shown here of five series from portrait to horizontal marine, were on the market by the mid 1850s, and still sold in the 1890s. This table came from the 1896 catalog of the French color merchant Lefranc. The measurements are in centimeters.*

**TABLE OF STANDARDIZED CANVAS FORMATS**

| NO | PORTRAIT OR FIGURE | LANDSCAPE | | MARINE | |
|---|---|---|---|---|---|
| | | HORIZONTAL | VERTICAL | HORIZONTAL | VERTICAL |
| 1 | 21.5 × 16 | 21.5 × 14 | — | 21.5 × 11.5 | — |
| 2 | 24.5 × 19 | 24.5 × 16 | — | 24.5 × 14 | — |
| 3 | 27 × 21.5 | 27 × 19 | — | 27 × 16 | — |
| 4 | 32.5 × 24.5 | 32.5 × 21.5 | — | 32.5 × 19 | — |
| 5 | 35 × 28.5 | 35 × 27 | 35 × 24 | 35 × 21.5 | 35 × 18.9 |
| 6 | 40.5 × 32.5 | 40.5 × 29.7 | 40.5 × 27 | 40.5 × 24 | 40.5 × 21.5 |
| 8 | 46 × 38 | 46 × 35.1 | 46 × 32.5 | 46 × 29.7 | 46 × 27 |
| 10 | 55 × 46 | 55 × 43.2 | 55 × 38 | 55 × 35.1 | 55 × 32.5 |
| 12 | 61 × 50 | 61 × 45.9 | 61 × 43.2 | 61 × 40.5 | 61 × 38 |
| 15 | 65 × 54 | 65 × 48.5 | 65 × 45.9 | 65 × 43.2 | 65 × 40.5 |
| 20 | 73 × 59.5 | 73 × 56.7 | 73 × 54 | 73 × 51.3 | 73 × 48.5 |
| 25 | 81 × 65 | 81 × 62.1 | 81 × 59 | 81 × 56.7 | 81 × 54 |
| 30 | 92 × 73 | 92 × 70.2 | 92 × 67.5 | 92 × 64.8 | 92 × 62.1 |
| 40 | 100 × 81 | 100 × 73 | — | 100 × 65 | — |
| 50 | 116 × 89 | 116 × 81 | — | 116 × 73 | — |
| 60 | 130 × 97 | 130 × 89 | — | 130 × 81 | — |
| 80 | 146 × 113.4 | 146 × 97 | — | 146 × 89 | — |
| 100 | 162 × 130 | 162 × 113.4 | — | 162 × 97 | — |
| 120 | 194 × 130 | 194 × 113.4 | — | 194 × 97 | — |

sity for artists to produce many, smaller paintings to satisfy the new middle-class market, which called for reasonably priced works which would fit in small city apartments.

Most nineteenth century artists used standardized canvases for their easel-scale works, but the Impressionists and those who followed them found new more appropriate ways of exploiting them. Thus the commercial availability of a product had a direct impact on the most basic level of artistic creation – the initial selection of canvas shape on which to start work. This inevitably influenced compositional design, as this must relate to the canvas edges and overall shape. So an artist planning to tackle a particular subject must choose the most suitable canvas proportions to enhance the projected design. The positioning of the subject on the chosen canvas size and shape is called *mise en page*, and is a crucial, though underestimated, determining factor in Impressionist painting. It shows how self-conscious these artists were, contrary to the currently popular myth of their naive spontaneity.

**Non-standard supports**

Although the majority of their works are on standardized canvases, the Impressionists did not adopt them wholesale. They also experimented with unusual canvas shapes, either to suit particular subjects or to complement innovatory compositions. These would have been made up to order, usually with ready primed canvas. Monet and Degas were among the artists most overtly and consistently experimenting with novel formats and compositions. For example, certain of Monet's studies from the early 1870s of Dutch land- and seascapes, were executed on canvases selected in advance to complement the low-lying panoramic scenery of Holland. These were made-to-order canvases more elongated in shape than even the longest commercial 'marine' format. Artists were also beginning to explore the potential of completely square canvases.

Monet and Degas both began using square canvases in the latter 1870s, and Pissarro then Gauguin followed soon after. Because of the symmetry of their sides, square canvases accentuate an appearance of flatness, making it difficult to create the illusion of reality which a rectangular format can more readily suggest. Therefore square formats were avoided by conservative artists, while they presented the independent painters with an exciting challenge. On square canvases they could more readily wrestle with the problems of compositions in which a balance is created between the illusion of depth and a simultaneous stress on flat surface design.

**Priming**

Standardized canvases were sold not merely ready stretched on their wooden stretchers by nineteenth century color merchants, they were also ready primed for the artist to begin painting directly. Commercial priming was done on large expanses of canvas, which were later cut down to the standard sizes and tacked onto their respective stretchers. It is thus possible to identify commercial preparations by examining the canvas edge, as the priming goes right round to the back of the stretcher. Where canvases are primed by hand *after* stretching, only the face side is covered, and raw canvas remains visible on the overturned edges and around the back.

For priming, the canvas was tacked to huge wooden frames in the workshop and balanced on trestles, the canvas was then primed horizontal. Using tools, like the priming blade which dates back well before the seventeenth century, the first layer of glue size was applied to the fabric. Two skilled men, one either side the flat of canvas, picked up the preparation in ladles and spread it thinly with the blades, working back and forth from the middle out. The size layer sealed the pores of the canvas and made it less absorbent, and therefore less vulnerable to the corrosive effects of the oxides present in the oil of the ground – the next layer. The size dried preventing undue movement in the fabric threads. The surface was then rubbed lightly with a pumice stone to remove fuzz and protruding irregularities in the weave. Then the ground coats, one or two layers of opaque color bound with oil, were applied with the priming blade, ideally allowing thorough drying time between coats. One of the hazards of off-the-peg ready primed supports was that artists had no means of telling when the canvas had been primed, and if it had been left long enough to dry thoroughly. Cracking all over the paint layer could result from a ground which continued to dry long after it had been painted on. Despite this danger, it was rare for artists to take the trouble to prepare their own canvases. As oil grounds could take a year or more to dry, artists were often advised to store them before use to make sure they had a sound base on which to work.

The relatively smooth, two-coated preparation was in general more popular before 1870, but after then Impressionist experiments with canvas texture made the grainy single coat the more sought after. A French color merchant's handbook in 1883 outlined the key differences: 'The texture of the cloth under the prepared ground leaves a good grain, which assists in spreading and laying on the colors, and is useful in giving different textures to the various objects represented. Canvases are prepared with coarse or fine grains, which may be suitable for large or small paintings, or for different styles of working. . . . Canvases may be more or less covered with the prepared ground. The thickly covered is more suitable for small figures and high finish, and the thinly covered is

Right Dancers *(c1880) by Degas was unfinished. This means that the unifying warm hue of the raw canvas shows clearly among the colours. This picture, and the* Portrait of Duranty *(1879), show Degas experimenting with the novel compositional potential of specially made square canvases. Abstract, decorative designs which stress the flatness of the picture plane are easier to create on square formats. Here, geometric shapes are contrasted with the nebulous forms of the tutus which are set against them. The dancers are set in a diagonal which recedes from lower right to upper left, in opposition to the diagonal of the foreground bench. The rectangles in the background, parallel to the picture plane, reinforce it. The unfinished handling provides a softening contrast with the taut composition. The stiff scumbling, seen clearly in the painting of the floor, shows the dragging which is inevitable when working in paint on a relatively absorbent support – this canvas was unprimed but probably sized with glue.*

better adapted to broad and rapid painting.'

A variety of different weights and weaves of canvas fabric were sold commercially for artists' use. Linen was the most common, but cotton and hemp fabrics were also available. Diagonal twill and plain were the two most common weave patterns used for artists' canvas, but odd examples of other more unusual weaves, like the herringbone twill, can also be found. The plain, one-under-one-over simple weave, known as tabby, was sold in a wide choice of weights, ranging from the thin, loose-woven sketching canvas held together by its priming, through to the thickly textured, tightly-woven strong weights. The choice of canvas weight varied according to the size of painting, large ones requiring strong fabric, and to the financial means of the artist. Students often used sketching canvas or the cheapish 'ordinary' weight canvas which was widely sold.

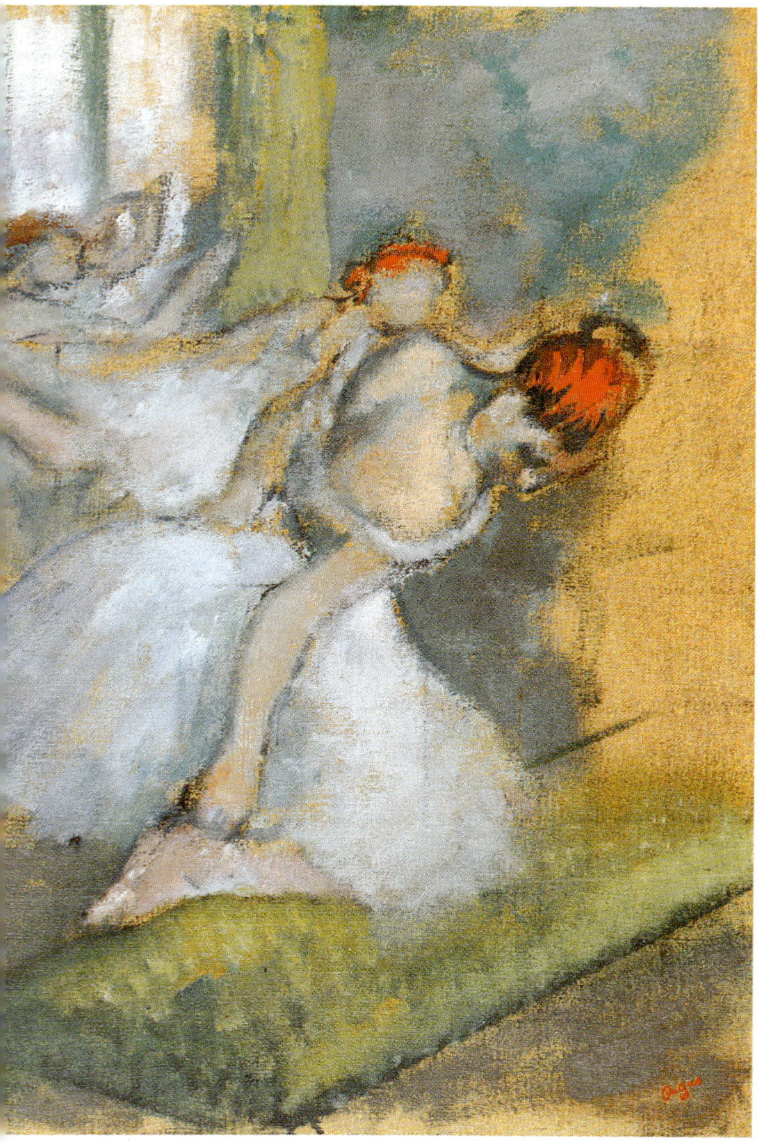

**Supports and paint texture**

Among the Impressionists, Monet and Pissarro both preferred a single-coat primed, grainy texture, which they exploited in combination with a dry, stiffish paint quality. The dragged and often crumbly or crusty colors of the paint layer clung well to the textured key of such canvases, which at the same time served to break the movement of the loaded brush across it. This created a stippled and vibrant web of color through which the ground or previous layers of color could show. When working on smoothly primed canvas or panel, it is possible to build up veiled layers through which earlier colors show. However, the dragged and broken effects in the work of Monet, Pissarro, Sisley, Morisot and Cassatt could only be achieved by combining the properties of stiffish paint applied with a bristle brush on a textured support. This is why panel was almost never used as a support by Impressionist painters.

While white was the most common color for ready primed canvas in the nineteenth century, a wide range of pale tinted preparations were also available on off-the-peg canvas. These included beige, cream, pinkish gray, bluish gray, putty, milk-chocolate brown, and oatmeal. None were darker than a middle tone, and most were considerably paler. One of the main innovations of the Impressionists was that the overall tonal key in their paintings was made lighter and brighter as a result of the concern to represent natural outdoor light. It thus became logical to exploit white and pale tinted primings in the same manner as dark grounds had been used traditionally. A middle to dark colored ground had traditionally been used to speed up execution as it played an active role as a unifying middle tone, which was left to show through the paint layer.

Although, during the 1860s, the all-covering opacity of the paint layer had tended to obliterate the pale grounds used by the independent artists, from about 1870 the ground was increasingly exploited as a color or value in its own right. Patches of white or tinted ground were left bare, to read through the loosely handled web of the colors in the paint layer. By choosing a ground tint appropriate to the particular light effect to be painted, the artist saved precious time in front of the subject, where speed was essential if transient lighting conditions were to be captured.

Incorporating the ground-tint into the final effect side-stepped the necessity for an all-covering paint layer, a necessity which had traditionally been seen as the great disadvantage of pale grounds. A white ground, on which all colors look good, was the perfect base for the technique of the Impressionists who sought to capture subtle color values, minute variations in hue and in warm and cool colors in outdoor light.

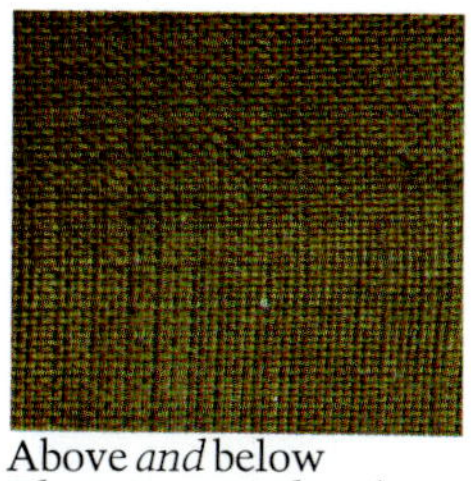

Above *and* below
*These are samples of nineteenth century canvas. Reverse side of primed* étude *weight canvas.*

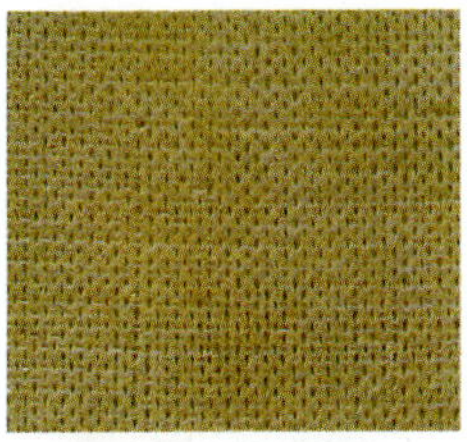

*Face side of* étude *weight canvas, primed with one coat of* ton clair, *a pale yellowish tinted ground.*

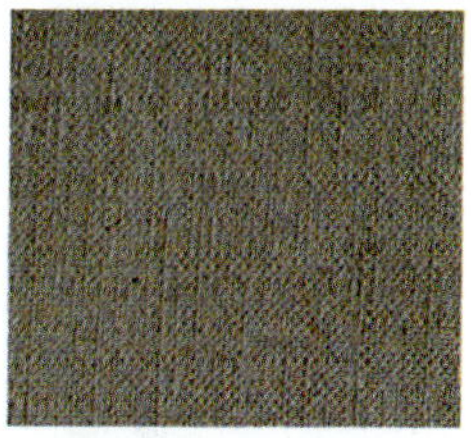

Demi-fine *or half fine weight canvas primed with one coat gray ground to give a grainy or* à grain *face.*

*Half-fine canvas with two coats gray priming to give smooth or* lisse *face.*

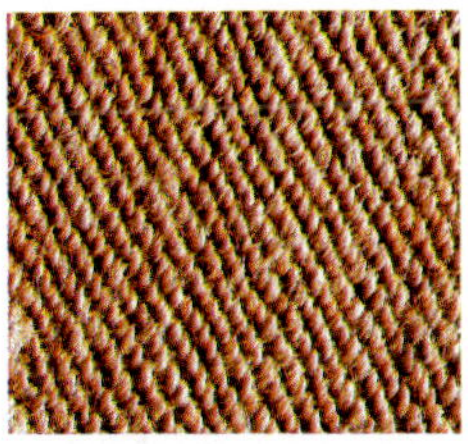

*Unprimed face of twill weave canvas, showing diagonal texture. All these samples date from c1900.*

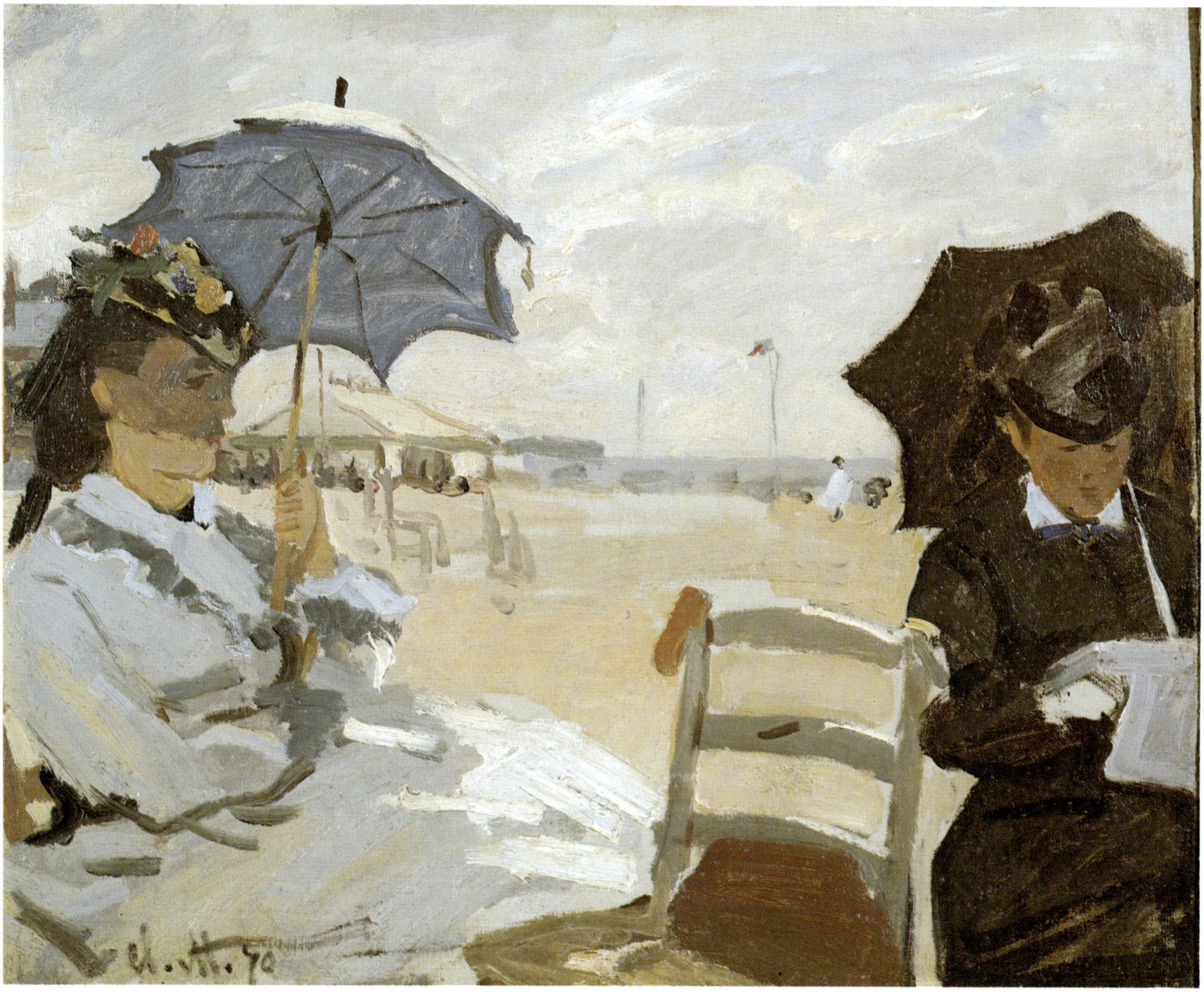

Above The Beach at Trouville *(1870) by Monet has grains of sand on the surface. This was confirmed when the work was cleaned in 1965. This definitely means it was painted* in situ. *The cool gray ground is left to stand among the paint layer colors, on the beach, center, and around the chair. It also unifies these hues and saves painting the entire canvas. The canvas itself is small, measuring 37.5 x 45.7cm (14¾ x 18in).*

**Painting color and light**
The white or pale grounds acted as a luminous unifying field, a visual metaphor for the brilliant light effects portrayed. In purely physical terms, the actual light-reflective properties of white bounces light back into the spectator's eye, enhancing the luminous appearance of the paint surface. The irregular texture of the grainy, single-primed surface exaggerates this effect, because it scatters the reflected light, producing a pale, pastel quality. When Monet, Pissarro, Sisley, Morisot, Cassatt and, to some extent, Cézanne, Manet and Degas used dragged dryish colors mixed with large amounts of light-reflective lead white, these increased the pale, chalky paint surface.

Oil paints derive their richness of color, or glowing transparency, from the oil binder they contain. The glassy quality of oil allows light to penetrate deep amongst the pigment particles, so that when it is finally reflected back to the eye it is rich with color. Inversely, paint with a minimal amount of oil binder appears mat and pale in color, because light is bounced rapidly back to the eye before it has had time to become saturated with color. This is why in nature, wet surfaces appear darker in color than dry surfaces. The Impressionists recognized that the chalky, pastel-like quality produced by paint with only a small amount of oil imitated the effects of pale, reflected light in nature. To exploit this, Monet and Degas – and probably numerous other contemporaries – are recorded as having soaked most of the oil from their colors before use. One way to do this was to leave their colors on blotting paper for several minutes, before using them. Degas then diluted this paste with turpentine and laid it in thin mat washes, while Monet, and the other Impressionists except Cézanne and Renoir, applied it neat, as a dryish chalky paste ideal for abrupt dragged impasto. It is no coincidence that the pale mat surfaces of Millet's large pastel drawings, exhibited in Paris in 1875, were admired at this time.

In Impressionist painting, pale grounds were often used to stand for the lightest tones. Thus unpainted patches of ground left visible among the colors of the paint layer were used instead of applied color as the pale tones in the upper register of the tonal scale. In Cézanne's work in particular, pale cream or white grounds were left to show through as glowing highlights. As their use of this technique and their knowledge of color became more sophisticated, the Impressionists began exploiting the potential of tinted grounds for their color value.

They were aware of the influential color theories of Michel-Eugène Chevreul (1786–1889), and they experimented with the effects of color contrasts. These are strongest when colors opposite each other on the color circle are placed side by side. The artists used such complementary contrasts as a means of enhancing their representation of the atmospheric effects of light and color. Thus a cream ground, showing through a loosely painted blue sky, with roughly scumbled white clouds, resulted in an optical effect of warm, glowing sunlight. The warm cream would be enhanced – made to look warmer and pinker – by the adjacent blue, which would appear correspondingly cooler. Cream showing through the cloud areas would add an airy effect of warmth. This calculated exploitation of color effects produced an ethereal lightness which was impossible to obtain by a more conventional – and deadening – build-up of colors. So, floating veils of translucent, contrasting color or dragging openly worked webs of opaque color over a tinted ground enabled these artists to create a superb impression of natural phenomena. It was realized that color temperature played an important role in the depiction of natural light effects and that the distinction between warm and cool colors made it possible for the eye to distinguish between very subtle nuances of color with imperceptible contrasts of tone.

Color contrasts and juxtapositions of warm and cool colors were also used to evoke form without recourse to conventional tonal modeling. This was possible because warm colors appear to come forward, and cool colors appear to recede. In nature, warm yellow sunlight finds its contrast in the luminous blue-violet reflected light of the shadows. Thus where colors were equivalent in tone but exhibited such warm-cool contrasts, these

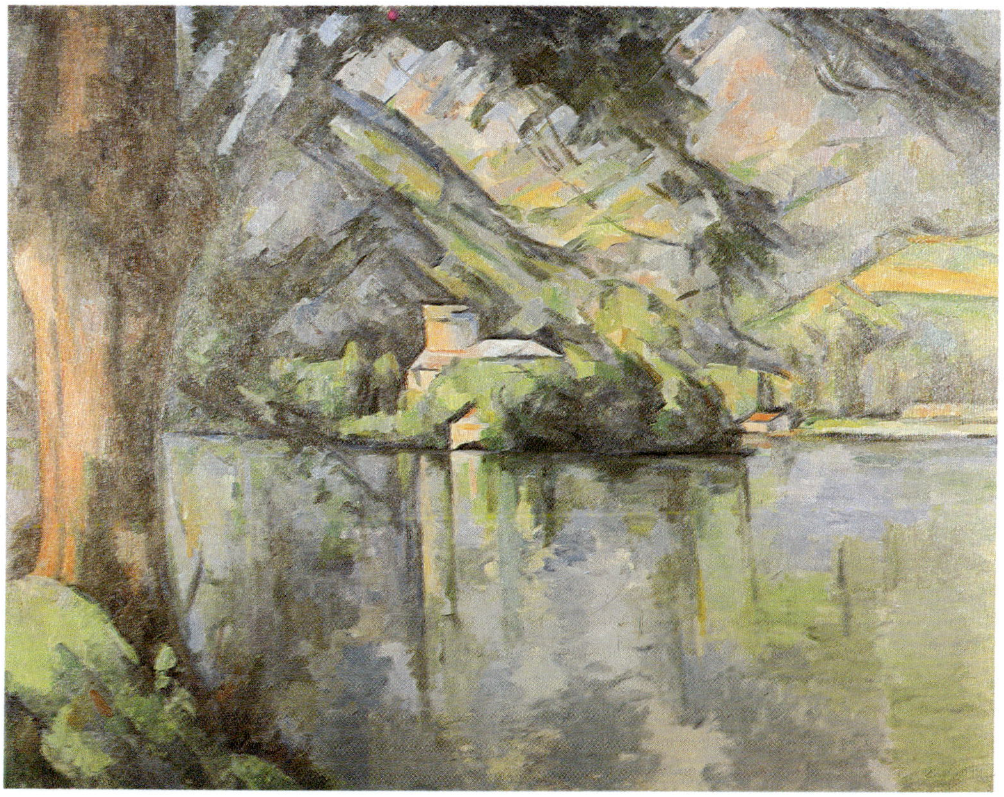

Left *Cézanne painted* The Lake of Annecy *while on a visit to Talloires in July 1896. It shows how contrasts of color temperature – warm and cool colors – can be used instead of purely light-dark tonal contrasts to create a sense of form in space. On the central turret, warm, pinkish-yellow colors indicate the side on which the light falls, from left to right. By contrast, the shadowed side, filled with reflected light from the sky, is tinted blue. The pervasive atmospheric light outdoors means that contrasts of light and shade are minimalized, thus highlights and shadows are close in tonal value, and so distinctions between light and shade are made through warm-cool contrasts.*

Right *Chevreul's* Chromatic Circle of Hues *was first published in 1839. His experiments showed how colors opposite each other on the color circle – complementary colors – are mutually enhancing.*

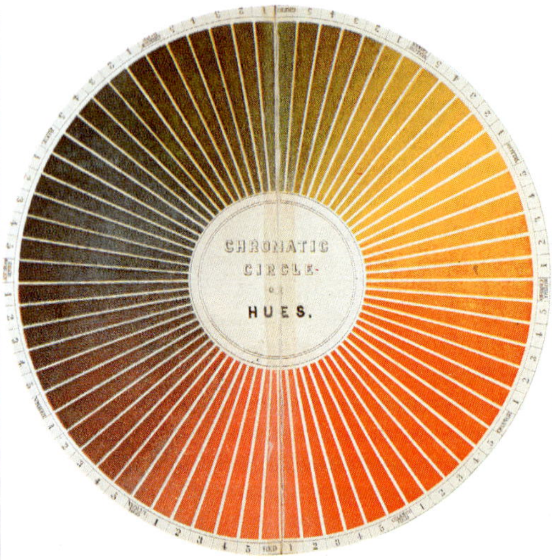


Below *In* The Bridge at Villeneuve-la Garonne *(1872) by Alfred Sisley the midday sun falls full on the scene. All the shadows are suppressed except those in the reflection of the dramatic bridge structure.*

could be used to describe form or movement in space. The inherent tonal differences of colors could also be exploited. Because, in the spectrum, blue is relatively dark in tone compared to, say, a pale yellow, these colors together could provide pure, luminously colored equivalents for traditional dark-light contrasts, giving structure to form.

The Impressionists' protracted study of open-air light effects led them to question the accepted conventions of 'local' color. Local color is the 'actual' colour of objects – the greenness of grass or yellowness of lemons. They noticed that every object's 'local' color appears to the eye modified by reflected colors from surrounding objects and by the colored atmospheric light or sunlight. Rather than painting the colors they had learned objects to be, the Impressionists tried to put down only the colors they actually *saw*.

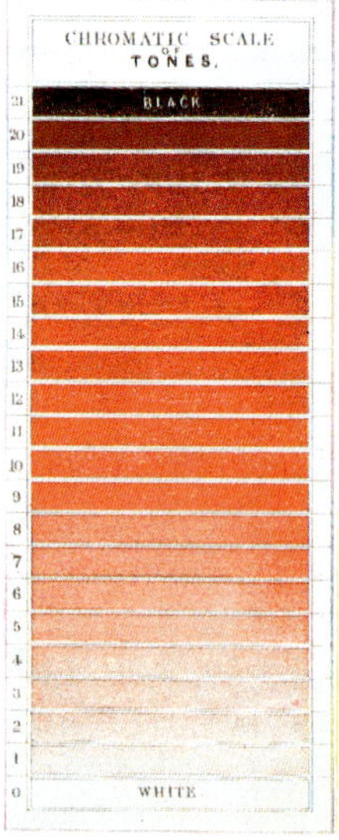


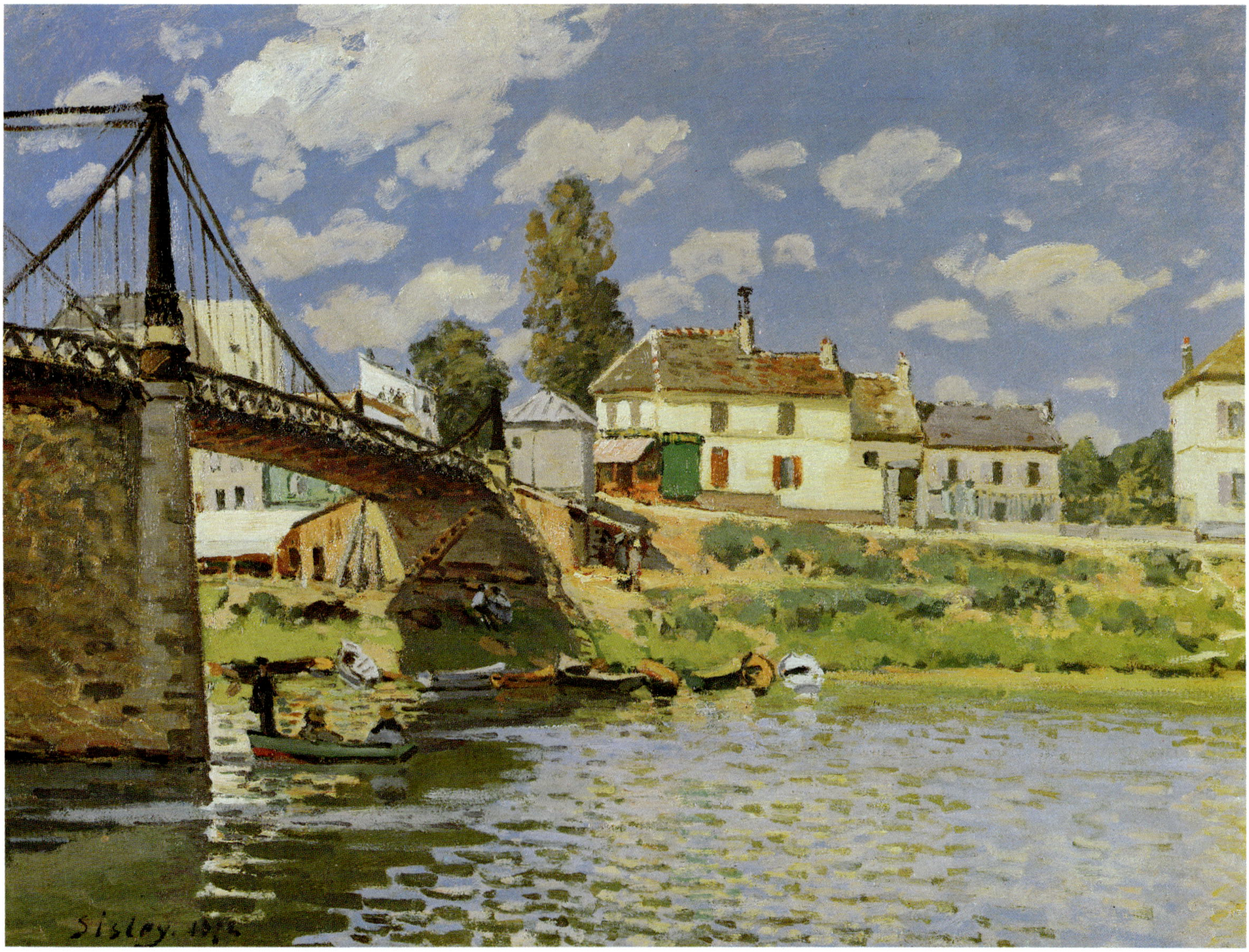

Left *Chevreul's* Chromatic Scale of Tones *shows the gradation of a red from white to black through all variations of tint. Tonal gradations were used by academic painters to create relief on form, but pure color could also be used. As can be seen from the color circle, yellow is pale in tone compared to blue. Such inherent tonal differences between colors were used by Impressionist and Neo-Impressionist painters to structure form through color.*

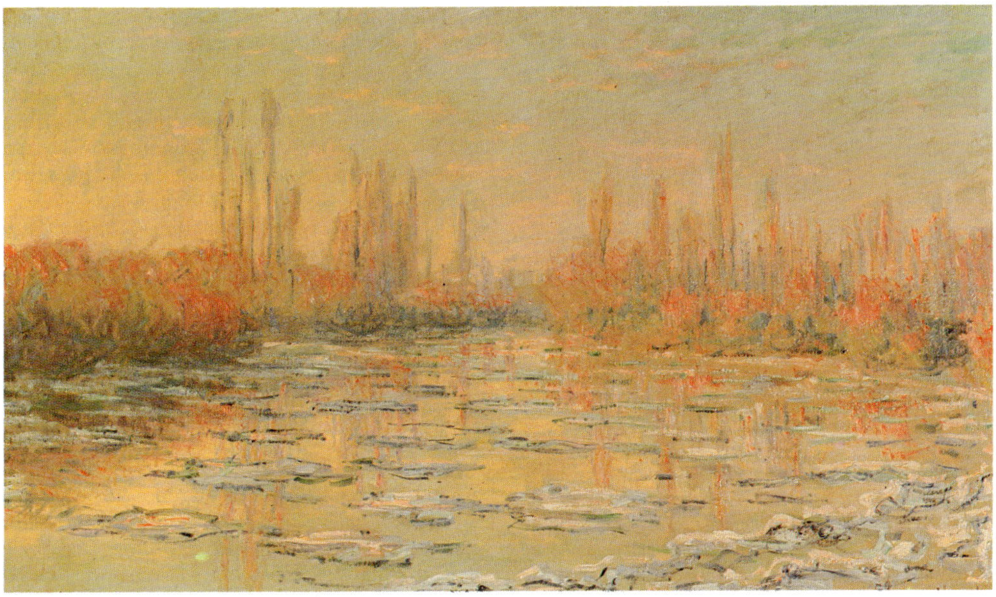

Left *Monet painted* Break up of Ice on the Seine: Ice Floes *in 1880. This dramatic natural event depicted lasted only a few days in early January 1880, yet Monet produced about 17 canvases of it. These included a larger variant of this picture, painted later for the Salon of 1880, where it was refused. Thus he was supplementing outdoor work with studio-painted variations. Snow and ice along with water provided ideal vehicles for the effects of colored light. The unconventional central axis balances the trees and their reflections, while the water surface is defined by the colored ice floes. This canvas is more elongated than the narrowest marine 40 standard format, measuring 60 x 100cm (23¾ x 39½ in).*

**New vistas**

The types of natural lighting the Impressionists chose to depict were selected expressly for the luminous brilliance of their effects, and for their lack of strong tonal contrasts. The Romantics, and Realists like Courbet were, in the words of Edmond Duranty, the critic friend of Degas, 'persuaded that light only existed on condition that it was thoroughly surrounded by shadows. The basement with a ray of light coming through a narrow air hole . . .'. The Impressionists avoided deep dark forest settings, choosing instead open airy scenes, from broad new city boulevards to river- and seascapes. They chose their subjects and viewpoints so that the fall of light produced only minimal shadows. One of the most popular choices was full-face light, which fell directly onto the subject from behind the artist, thus casting any shadows out of sight *behind* the objects in the scene. *Gris clair*, a clear, pale, gray light, is what results from a luminous but overcast sky, leaving a shadowless, even diffusion of light, was also widely exploited. The harsh bleaching effects of midday sun, where shadows are at their shortest, was another type used. Where shadows were included, they were always full of reflected light, and barely darker in tone than the sunlit parts.

Water and snow were, for all but Renoir, studied for their light and color reflective properties. Snow provided a white field, comparable to the white canvas preparation, which showed off all the most delicate varied nuances of warm colored light and shadow. Water was also an excellent vehicle for insubstantial, fluctuating film color, picking up and reflecting light and colors from sky, atmosphere and all surrounding objects. Reflections were also used to structure compositions, for, as mirror-images of real objects, they could strengthen the abstract design qualities in a picture.

The sketchy execution of the picture was essential to the final appearance of immediacy, and to the process of capturing fugitive light effects. Painting had to be a rapid jotting down of visual sensations.

In seeking an appropriate means to render their sensations, the Impressionists looked to the techniques used in earlier landscape studies, and in the freely handled compositional *equisses* common to all art students' training. The Impressionists' use of broken color may in part have its origin in the academic method, where mosaic-like touches of color were used to build up the halftones. However, since the seventeenth century, the use of separate touches of color had been recommended as a means of avoiding sullying the purity of color by overmixing. So, for artists like the Impressionists, who wanted to achieve maximum purity of color, this method made obvious sense, although their touches of color were by no means uniform. Instead of using linear drawing to define form or space, color and brushwork served this purpose in their work. Thus, the varied size, direction or shape of a brushstroke was intentionally eloquent. The foregrounds were often handled in large strokes, distances in small, almost imperceptible touches to give the appearance of depth. Small jerky strokes differentiated foliage from the longer strokes of boughs and tree trunks; objects reflected on water were often described by vertical marks. Reflected light off the water surface was shown in contrasting long, horizontal dashes. Buildings were 'constructed' by solid touches or planes of color which followed and stressed their form.

Below *Renoir painted* Gust of Wind *around 1873. The detail (*right*) shows that Renoir exploited a beige ground to provide a warm color base which shows among the cooler greens of the paint layer. The delicate feathery strokes of yellow-greens, viridian, white and yellow ochre, with touches of vermilion, are floated wet in wet over the beige priming. Where the ground shows through it appears even warmer by contrast to the acid greens. This suggests the dry grasses on the hillside. Thinly applied color for the distances contrasts with impasted touches to evoke foreground textures. Loaded blue-grays and white for the sky and clouds are warmed by the beige ground to suggest sunlight flickering through from behind.*

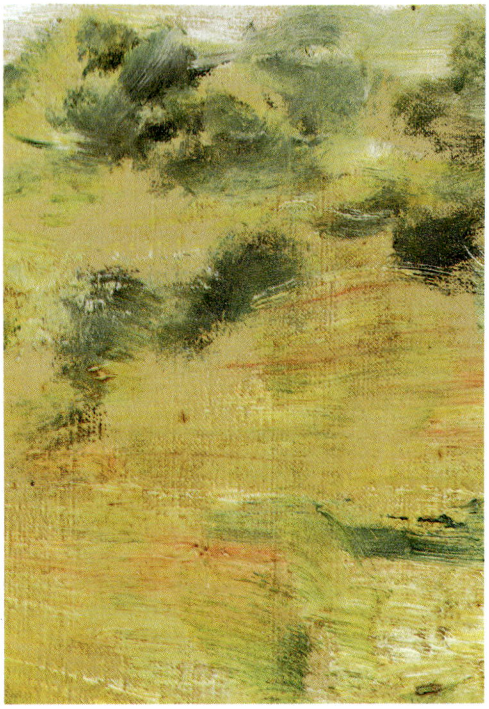

Traditional academic methods of finishing had assumed that one section of the painting would be brought to completion each day. By contrast, Impressionist methods involved making constant adjustments over the entire canvas. This was obviously easier on an easel-size canvas, which the eye could take in complete in a single glance.

A premeditated preparation of colors and tones laid out on the palette, as required by academic practice, was obsolete for the Impressionists, because open-air painting inevitably necessitated a moment to moment evolution of color mixtures on the palette. These had to be adjusted or abandoned as the light effects changed, and the artist took up a new canvas or began a new subject.

The idea of the visual world presenting itself to the eye in colored patches of light, or *sensations*, which was central to the Impressionists' method, derived from contemporary theories about perception. Rejecting the conventional use of abstract lines and edges to give an illusion of form, the Impressionists began to paint light. Their aim was to perceive and record direct optical sense data, or 'visual sensations' as they were called, instead of

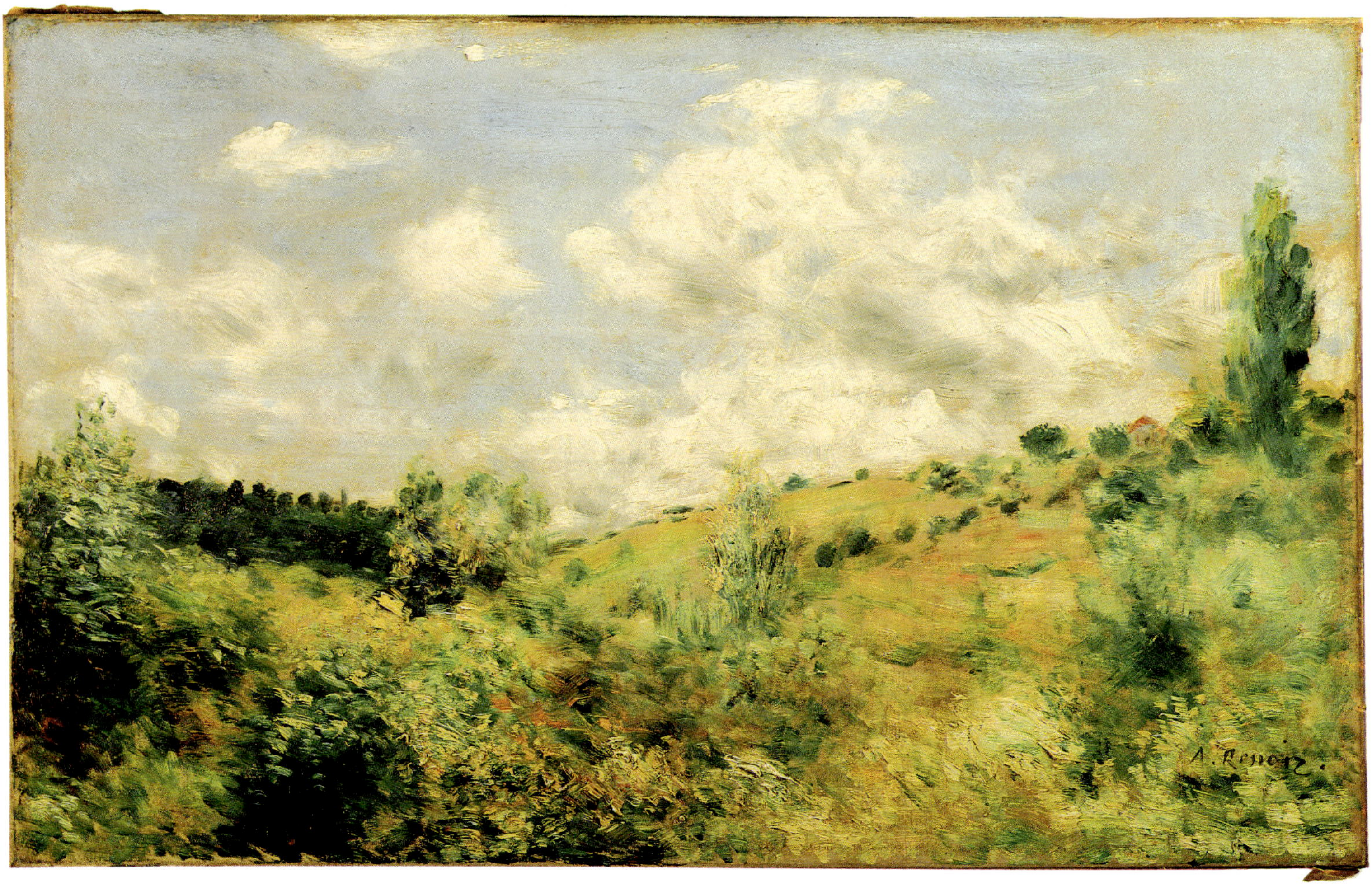

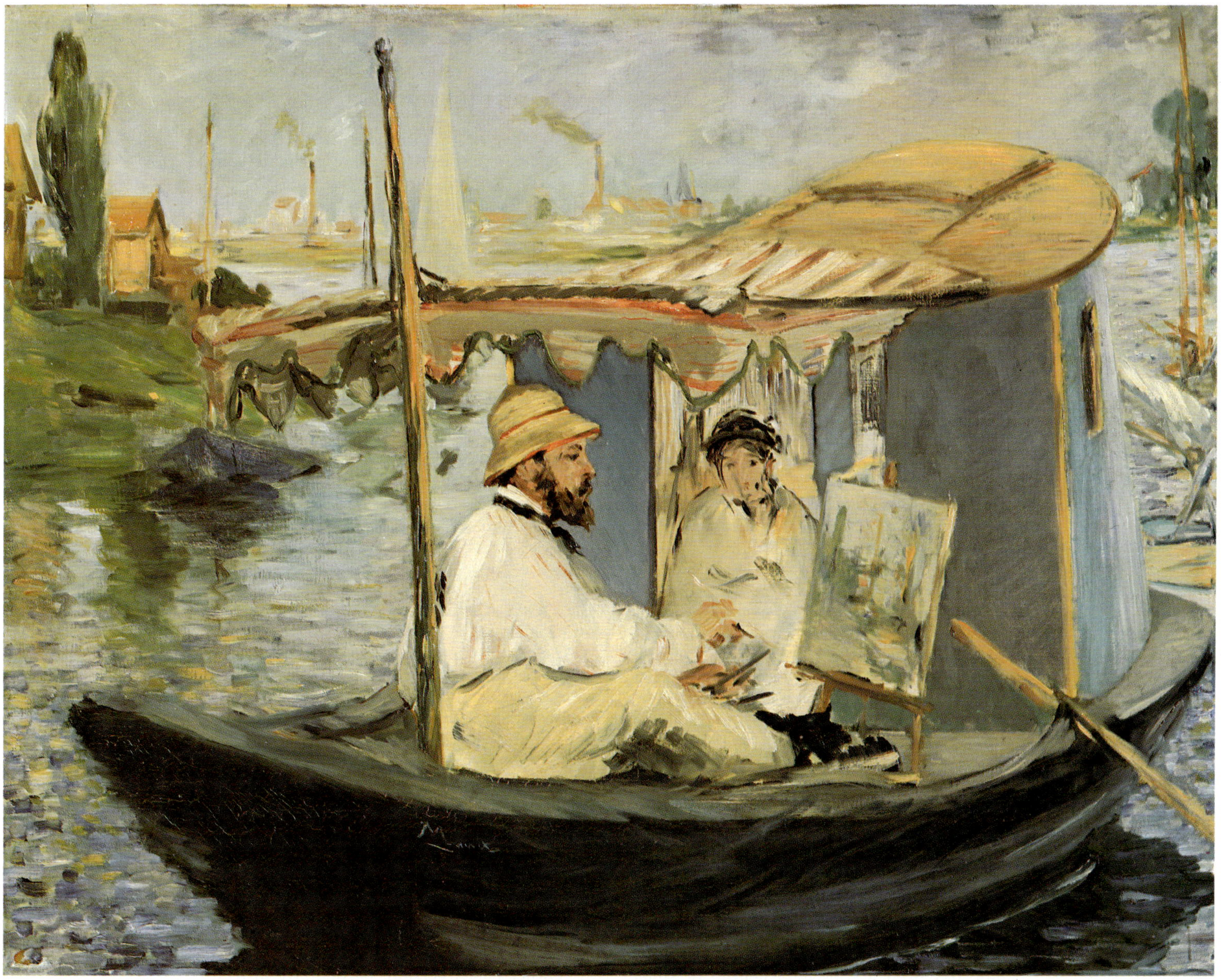

depicting a scene modified and 'corrected' by the intervention of the intellect, which gave only a rationally conceived notion of the real world. This explains references among the Impressionists to the desire for the infant's untutored eye. The Impressionists tried to unlearn their received knowledge of the visual world, and confront its myriad array of colored patches directly. These they translated into touches of paint, which only coalesced into a coherent image as the picture progressed. The importance of depicting visual sensations helps explain why Cézanne described Monet as 'just an eye, but what an eye!'

This search for pictorial equivalents to the artist's perceptions or sensations of light and color outdoors was quite different from the later, more codified and pseudoscientific concerns of the Neo-Impressionists, such as Georges Seurat (1859–1891), in the mid 1880s. Their attempts to create 'optical' color, through the partial fusion on the spectator's retina of colored light emananting from tiny painted dots, has been consistently confused by many critics and art historians, with the 'colored patch' Impressionist technique. No optical fusion was intended or sought in Impressionist painting. The artists simply intended that the colors and brushstrokes should – at an appropriate viewing distance – present the spectator with a coherent equivalent of the painter's visual perceptions.

These methods were developed during the 1870s by Monet, Renoir, Pissarro, Morisot, Cézanne and Sisley. They were carried forward in modified forms during the following years.

Above *Manet painted* Claude Monet and his Wife on his Floating Studio *in 1874. Influenced by Impressionist methods, Manet began painting out of doors in the early 1870s, working with Monet and Renoir in 1874 at Argenteuil, where this work was painted. Manet has lightened his palette and abandoned the harsh contrasts of light and shade and the rich darks of his studio-painted landscapes of the 1860s.*

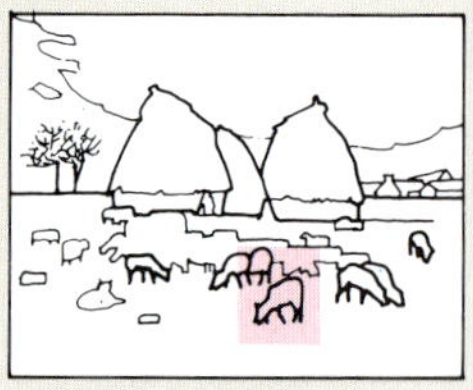

*The black chalk or charcoal underdrawing is strongly in evidence here, showing Millet's talent for swift caricatural lines which capture the characteristic features of the sheep. The lilac pink ground shows through clearly, especially at the contours where the paint is thin or non-existent. The ground color is warmed further by the sharp cool greens of sheep and grass applied over it. Although quite thinly painted in most parts, the colors are mainly opaque.*

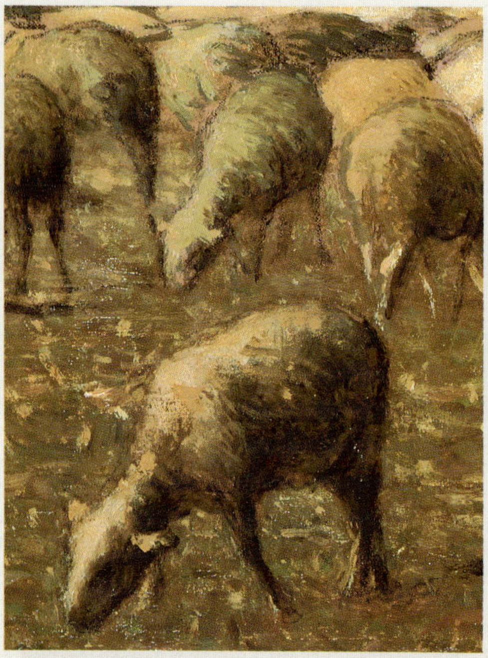

The ground shows through among the sheep, where the artist's preparatory drawing-in of the broad contours of the composition in charcoal or black chalk is strongly in evidence. Millet's touch in pastel and oil is comparable. Although the oil binder inevitably makes the brushstrokes juicier, the use of added white and a dryish paint consistency have enabled Millet to create effects not dissimilar to those in the pastel, especially in the chalky, dragged strokes depicting the spiky, stubbly grass. The greater luminosity of the pastel stems from the absence of oil binder.

The adventurous techniques of these late works show how Millet kept pushing forward with new ideas and methods, which were to have continuing relevance to following generations of painters, from Pissarro and Degas to the later artists Seurat and van Gogh. An important exhibition of Millet's large-scale pastel pictures in 1875 came at an opportune moment for these younger artists, and the publication in 1881 of Sensier's magnificently illustrated biography of the artist, further reinforced Millet's influence on the Impressionists.

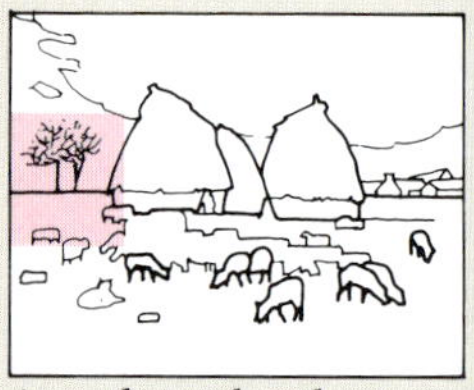

Actual size detail
*Recession into the distance is created both through the use of narrow horizontal bands of color, and by the gradual tonal lightening toward the pale skyline. This technique echoes the natural phenomenon called aerial perspective, where distant views grow hazy and pale blue the further they recede from the eye. Millet used little underpainting or* ébauche. *A thin, transparent greeny-brown wash, unevenly applied, was laid under the opaque greens of the field and worked up to the charcoal contors of the sheep. They were mainly left without underpainting, to allow the warm ground to show through. The sheep in the immediate foreground was firstly indicated with thickish but transparent raw sienna, which was then worked over roughly with opaque palish greens and greeny-blacks for the shadows.*

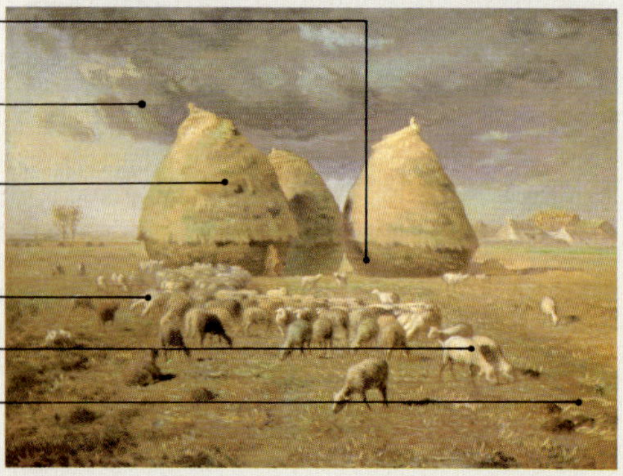

Thin opaque shadows

Pale greens among sky blues

Dragged brush and knifed on dryish, chalky color

Lilac pink ground

Thick opaque lights

Transparent sienna under opaque touches

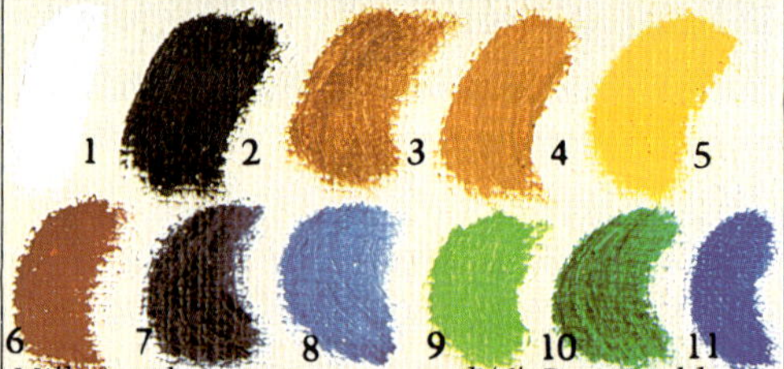


*Millet's palette was probably lead white (1), black (2), sienna (3), yellow ochre (4), probably chrome yellow (5) and a red lake, red earth (6), Prussian blue (7), probably cobalt (8) or ultramarine blue (11). Viridian (10), chrome (9) and emerald greens may also have been used.*

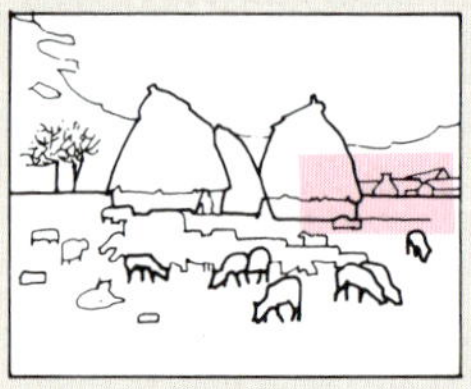

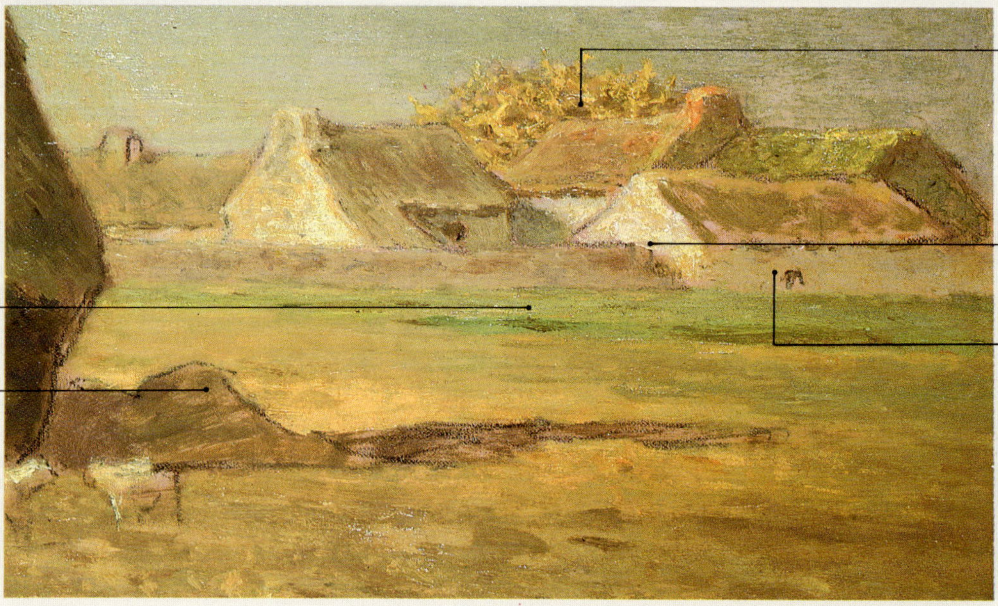

Varied brushwork, foliage depicted in freely daubed strokes of opaque impasted color, contrasting with plane-following brush-strokes for buildings and roofs

Pale tints, much lead white added

Lilac pink ground shows through the thin opaque colors depicting the buildings

Probably emerald green

Thinly scumbled opaque color

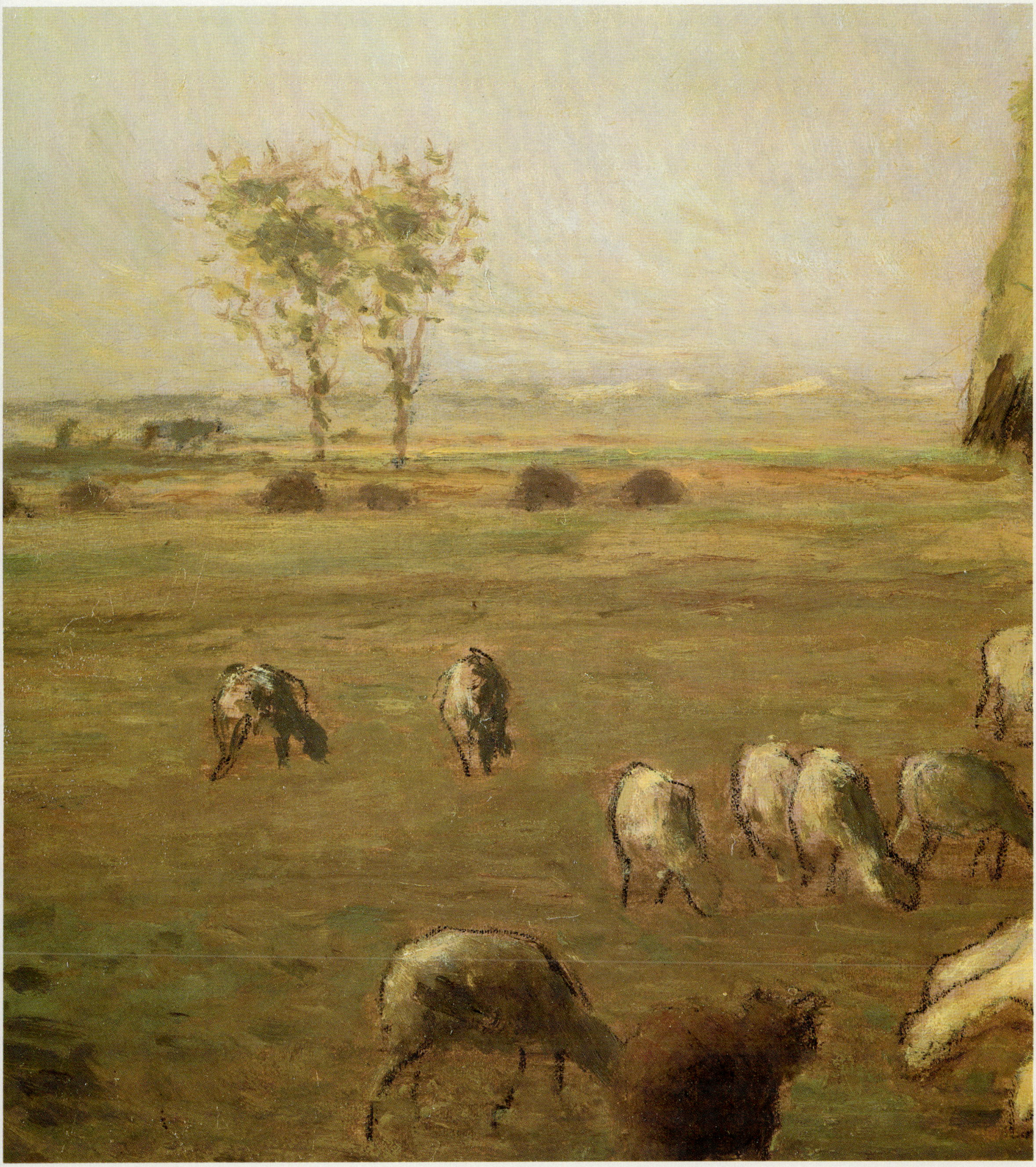

# CLAUDE MONET

*Autumn at Argenteuil/Effet d'Automme à Argenteuil* (1873)
Oil on canvas, 56cm × 75cm/22in × 29in

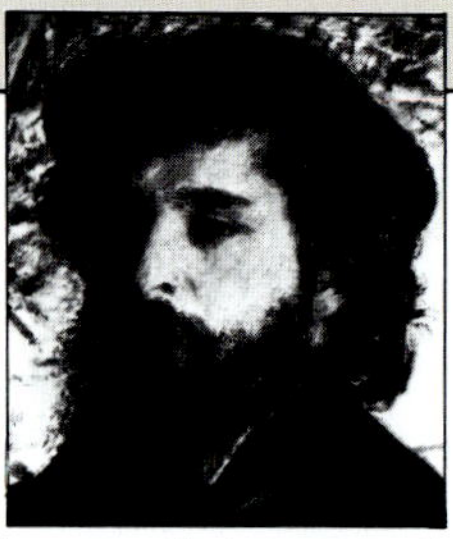

Probably the most typical Impressionist painter, Monet began his career as a caricaturist, summing up his subjects with the same economy he later used in rendering the fleeting effects of light and color in nature. Introduced to open air painting by the French artist Boudin, Monet rapidly developed as a landscape oil painter. His first major figure painting, *Déjeuner sur l'herbe*, painted 1865 to 1866, was a reworking with natural light effects of Manet's painting of the same title. Monet continued to paint figures but they never dominated his work. Monet was also influenced by and appreciated the bright colors, high viewpoint and interlocking, assymmetrical compositions of Japanese prints.

Sincerity and spontaneity in the rendering of nature were crucial ideals of Impressionism and, by the late 1860s, Monet, working with Renoir, was developing the techniques and speed needed to represent fleeting outdoor effects. Few of his paintings were finished in a single sitting; often he got no further than a rough blocking-in before the scene relatively changed, the work then being completed in subsequent sittings. Monet mainly used tinted, pale grounds, particularly grays, cream and beige. He preferred a thin layer of preparation which left the canvas grain exposed. Over this he dragged dry, stiffish paint from which, like Degas, he had first soaked the oil binder, to create ragged vibrant flickerings of color across the surface. His colors, like his ready-prepared canvases, were bought ready made, as the mechanization of paint grinding was commonplace for artists' colors from the 1830s. Collapsible tin tubes, invented in Britain in 1840, had been introduced in France but in 1855 still cost more than the traditional paint bladders. While the lack of tin tubes had not deterred earlier outdoor oil painters, their invention clearly simplified their work.

Monet's pale grounds and opaque paint layer were combined to create a scintillating representation of transient outdoor light. Until the late 1880s, he preferred to paint in full midday light, or shadowless overcast skies, thus avoiding strong shadows and tonal contrasts, so his use of light effects promoted a brilliant two-dimensionality. Monet's painting increasingly concentrated upon capturing colored, atmospheric light and reflections.

1. A pale gray ground was applied to a fine-weave canvas allowing the texture to show through.

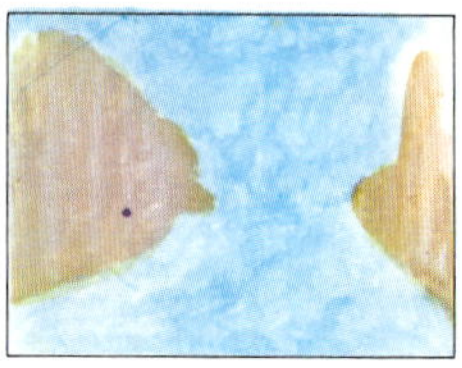

2. Broad areas of local color were blocked in using a thin scumbled paint.

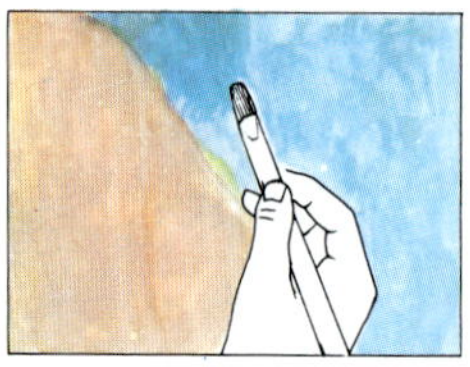

3. The irregular build-up of the opaque paint layer allowed the original blocking-in to remain visible in places.

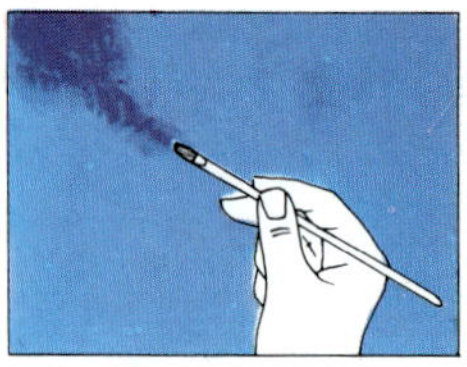

4. Wet paint was applied into wet or over dry to blend the colors.

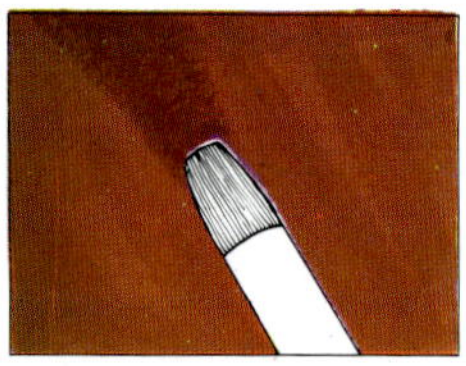

5. Stiff, dry paint was dragged across the surface in broad strokes of wet over dry creating a latticed web of color.

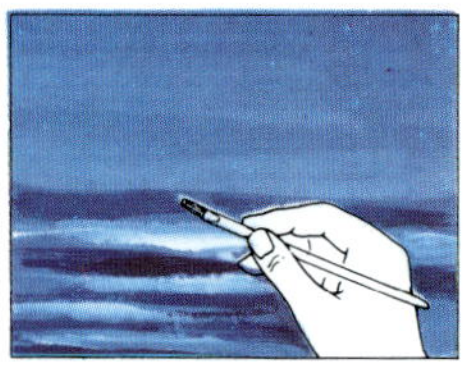

6. Reflections and water were achieved by this same opaque layering technique rather than the more traditional opposition of opaque highlights and transparent glazes.

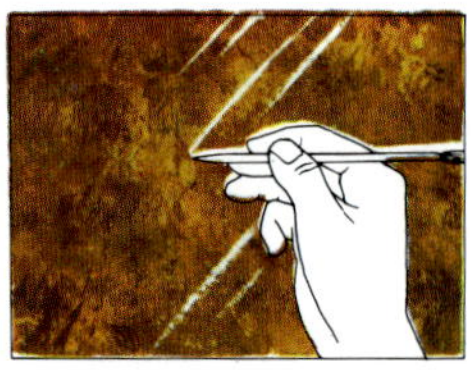

7. Textures were differentiated by varied brushwork. Impasto layers were lightened by scratching through using the wooden end of the brush to expose the pale ground.

*Monet's palette was simple and fairly limited. The blues are ultramarine or cobalt and the cadmium yellows were consistently employed by Monet. Viridian and emerald greens were on his palette but played an unimportant role here. Vermilion and alizarin crimson were his reds and cobalt violet was added from the 1880s. It is important to note that Monet never used colors straight from the tube but all were mixed with lead white in varying degrees to create a pastel-like reflecting luminosity.*

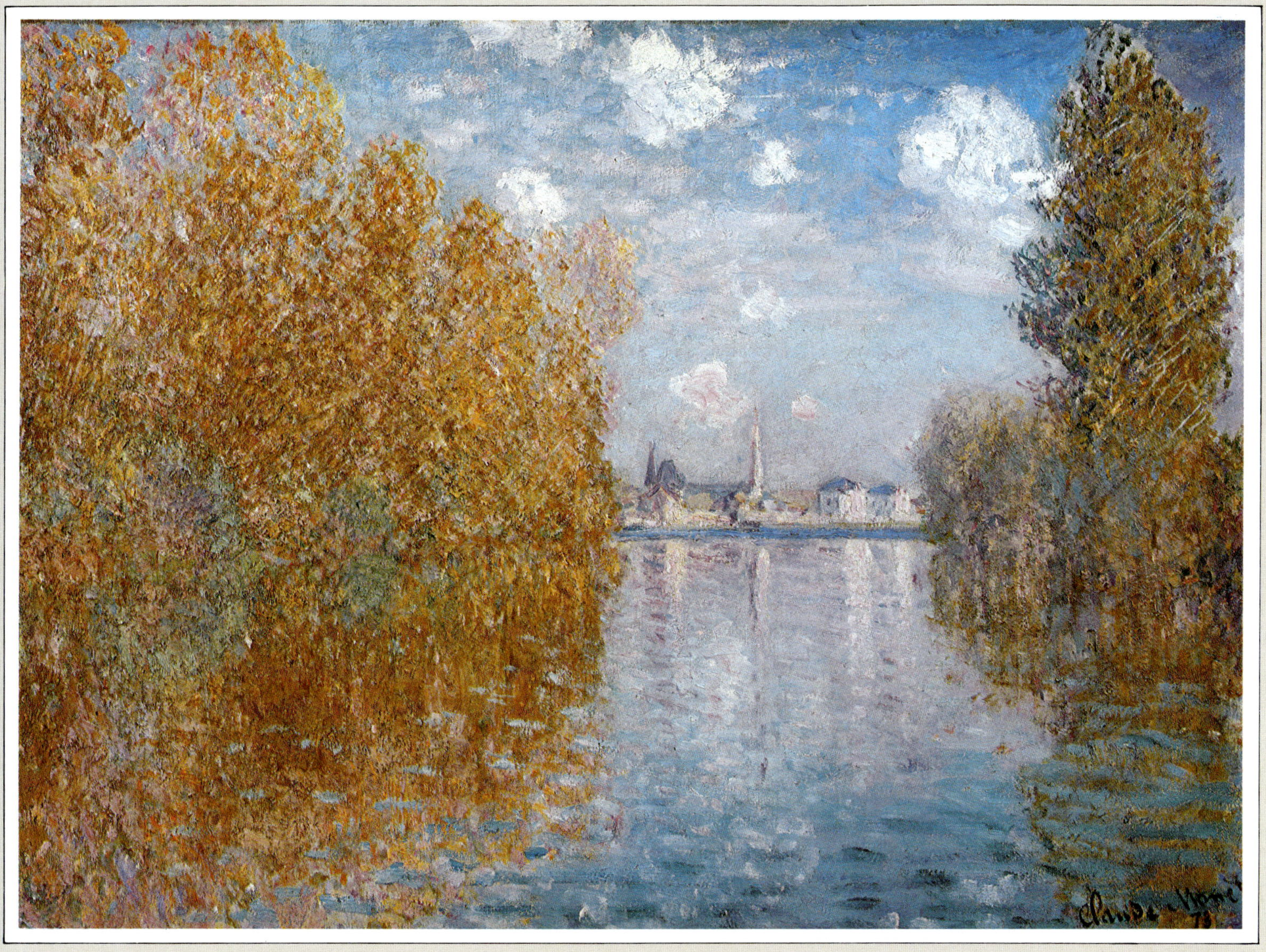

*Monet used a pale gray ground whose luminosity plays a crucial role in creating the illusion of light and sun in this painting. The picture was begun with dilute opaque colors and colors broken with white applied directly to the ground. The paint was built up in increasingly impasted layers creating a web of color through which earlier layers remain partially visible and continue to play an active role. The brushwork and paint consistency are varied to evoke textures and forms. The paint quality is thick, buttery or stiff and often applied by*

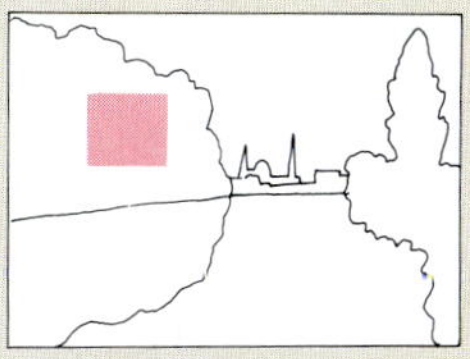

*dragging a stiff hog's hair brush across the surface, giving broken, vibrant effects. Unlike colors which have been mixed in the conventional manner solely on the palette, Monet's colors remain unmuddied.*

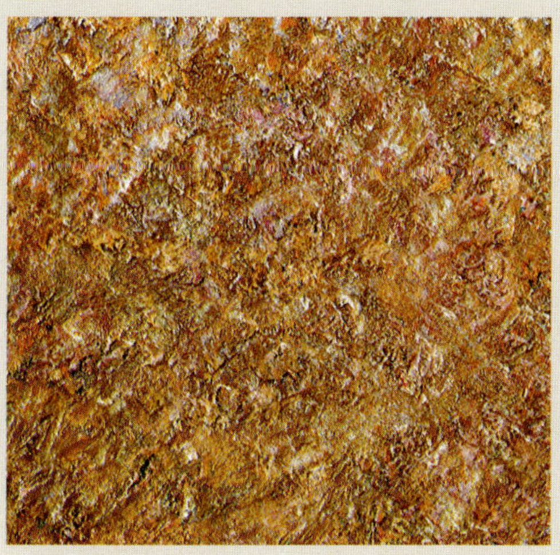

*Monet's brushwork is extremely varied and descriptive of the forms and textures he wished to describe. Rough, crusty strokes are used to depict foliage; longish, horizontal ones for reflections of sky on water, and the sky itself is created with thinner paint and broad strokes. Clouds are represented by churned brushwork with stiff paint used to evoke puffiness, and buildings are created with form-following strokes of thick, smooth paint. Monet's brushwork was also used to create spatial effects as seen in the water which recedes with diminishing touches as it moves into the distance; the sky and water are rendered paler near the skyline to recreate the distant hazy natural scenery. Monet adhered to the basic rule of oil painting: fat over lean. This means that dilute layers are covered by increasingly oil-rich layers. This ensures the durability of the work by preventing inter-layer cracking resulting from placing slow-drying layers beneath faster-drying ones.*

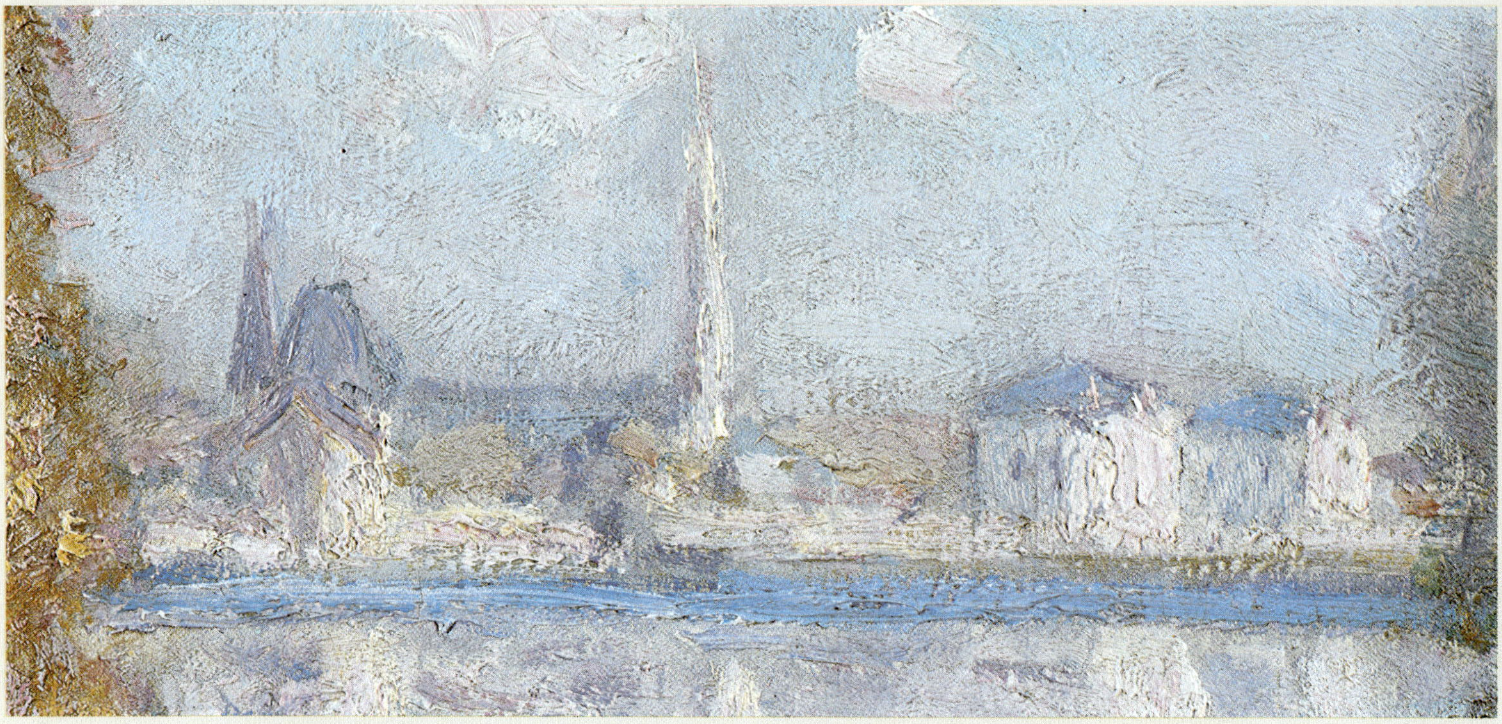

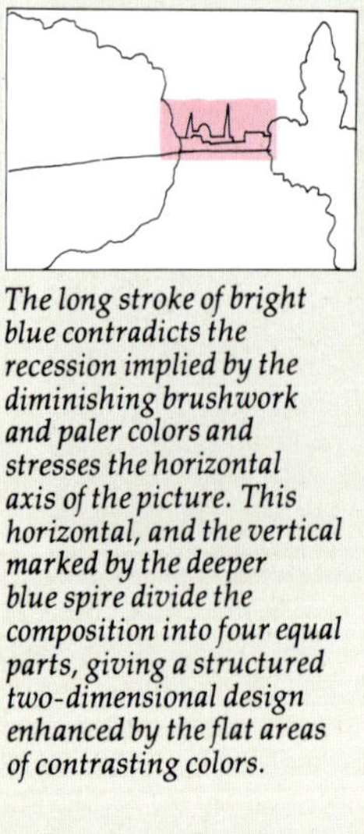

*The long stroke of bright blue contradicts the recession implied by the diminishing brushwork and paler colors and stresses the horizontal axis of the picture. This horizontal, and the vertical marked by the deeper blue spire divide the composition into four equal parts, giving a structured two-dimensional design enhanced by the flat areas of contrasting colors.*

*The thin blocked-in paint is visible beneath the thick vertical strokes of the reflected trees. Wet-over-dry horizontal strokes of stiff blue and white depict reflections from the sky, creating an entirely opaque illusion of water.*

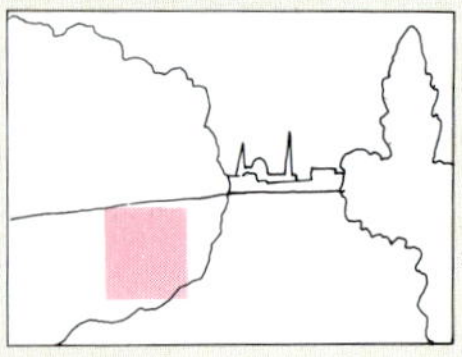

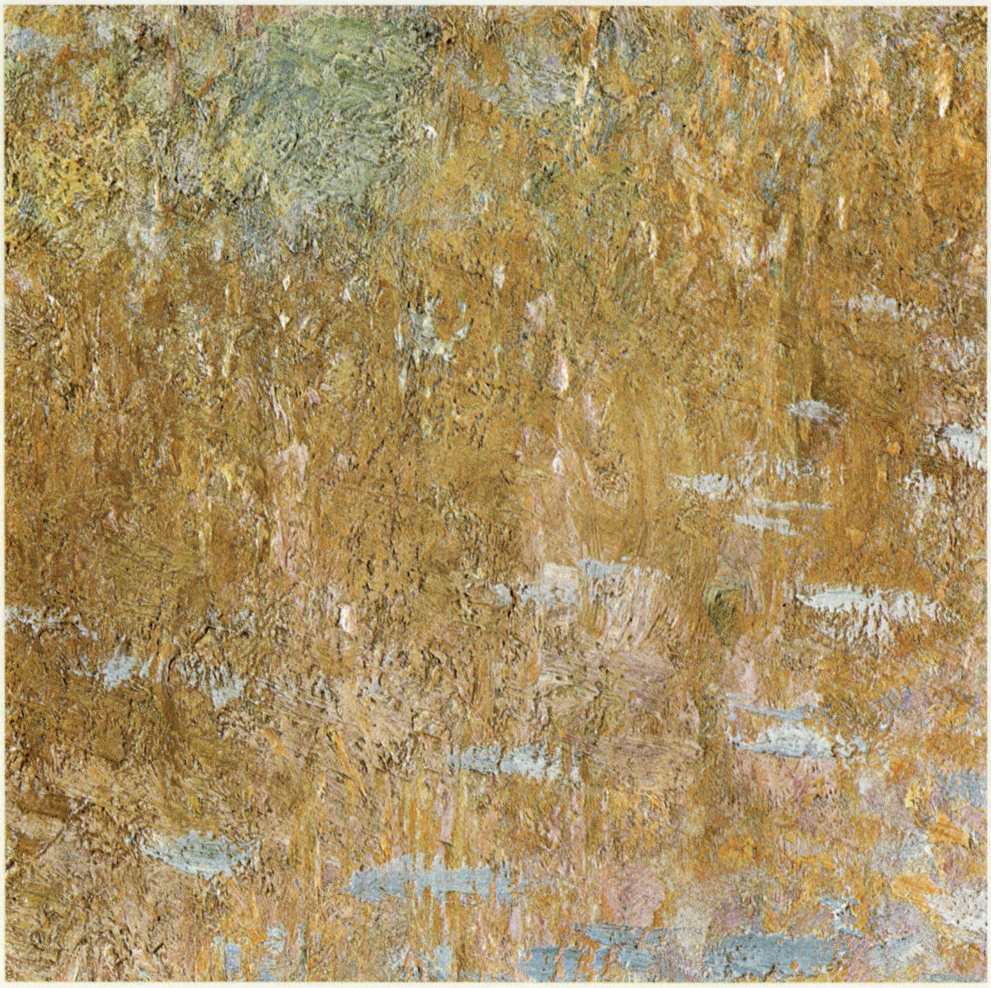

Actual size detail
*Both wet-in-wet and wet-over-dry work can be seen in the paint layer here: whitish clouds were added in stiff opaque colour, slurred over the dry paint of the foliage, upper left, adjusting the silhouette of the trees. To modify the foliage colors and extend the branches out over the sky paint, wet-in-wet colors — blue and white — were slurred together in small touches with a single brushstroke, the fine brush having picked up both colors at once. Alizarin crimson and white were applied in dabs in the same way, both these adjustments being worked over the dry orangey-greens of the foliage. Fine blobbed strokes of mixed white and viridian, and of orangey ochres were added late, over background blues in the foliage.*

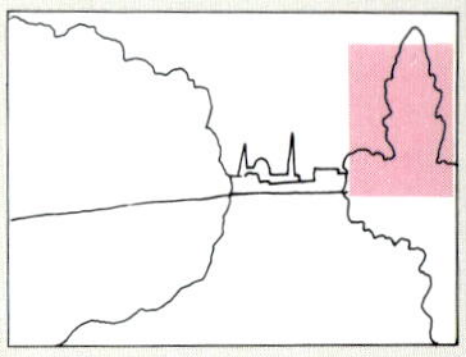

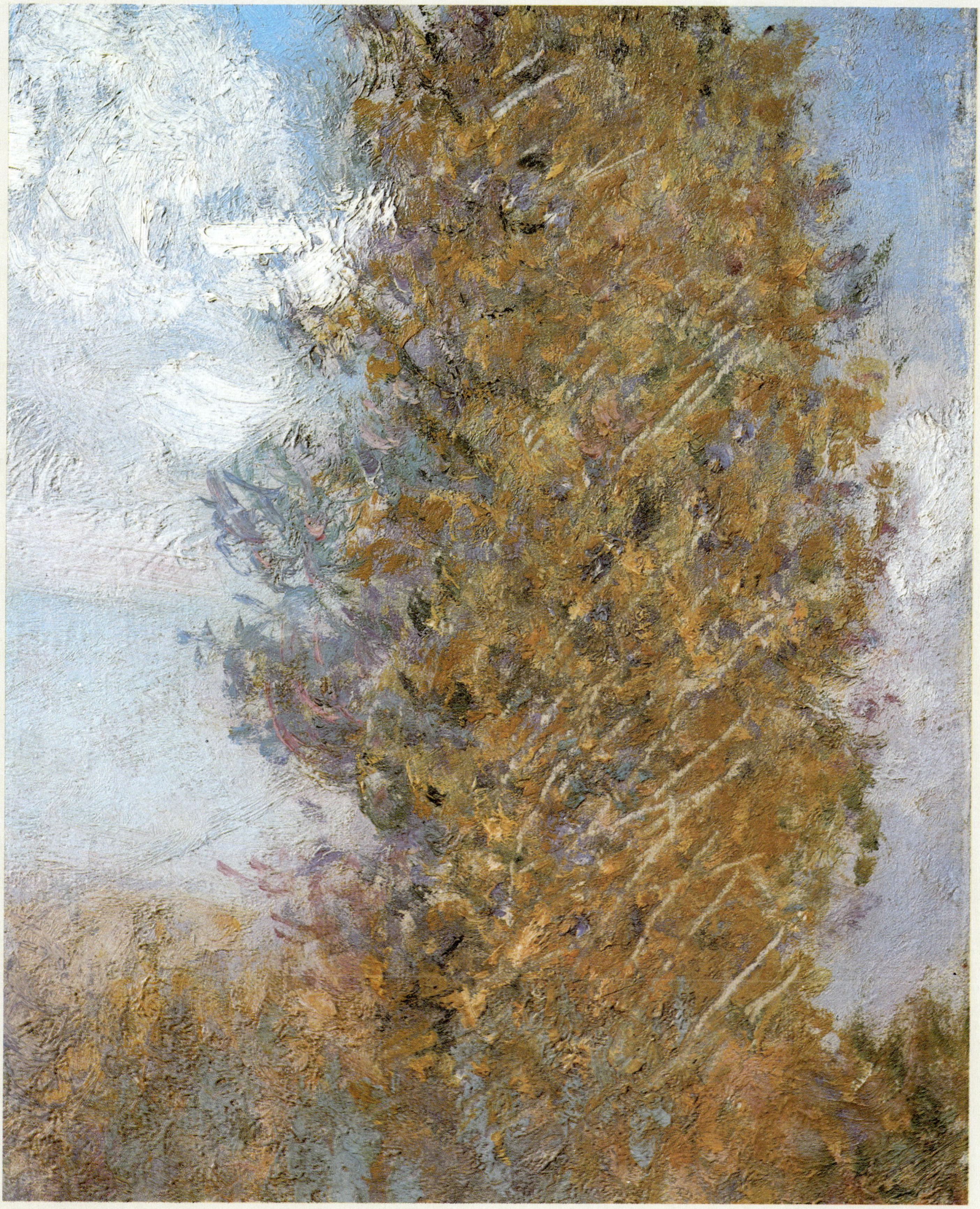

# PAUL CEZANNE

*House of the Hanged Man/La Maison du pendu* (1873)
Oil on pale primed canvas
55cm × 66cm/21½in × 26in

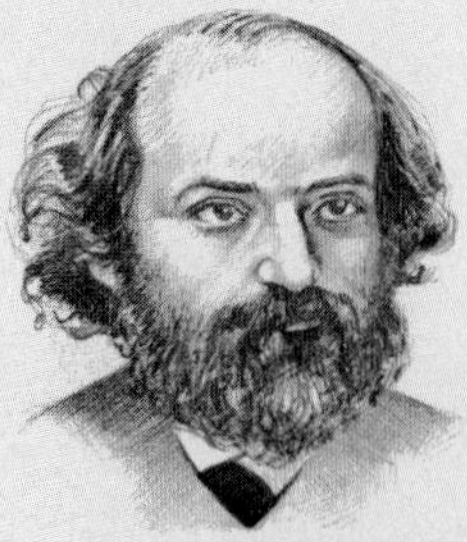

Discouraged by his father, Cézanne's artistic debut was hesitant, but by 1861 he was spending considerable periods in Paris, encouraged by his childhood friend the writer Emile Zola (1840–1902). Failing several attempts to get himself admitted to the Ecole des Beaux-Arts, Cézanne often studied in the life class at the independent Académie Suisse, and copied from Old Masters like the seventeenth century French classical painter Nicolas Poussin (*c*1594–1665) in the Louvre. In 1861 Cézanne met Camille Pissarro at the Academy Suisse, and formed a close friendship which was to be of crucial importance to both artists. Pissarro was older and a more experienced painter than Cézanne. As early as 1857, he had begun painting from nature on the advice of Corot. Cézanne's style of the 1860s was greatly influenced by Old Masters like Rubens, and by Delacroix, whose work remained a source of inspiration. At that time, Cézanne's subjects were Romantic too – passionate scenes of murder and sexual violence were interspersed with more disciplined studies of still lifes, landscapes and portraits. He used thick, juicy paint and expressive brushwork, with a palette dominated by somber colors, especially earths and black. He regularly experimented with palette knife painting.

Although an impassioned abandon often characterized his work of the 1860s, it already contained the germ of his mature style. Strength and vitality, an obsessive dedication, a love of color and the painterly handling of his medium were already apparent. In his drawings, an idiosyncratic, directional hatched structure – which appeared occasionally in his paintings of that decade – was clearly in evidence. Cézanne began working out of doors at Pissarro's instigation, and the tight discipline of such work provided the key to organizing his emotional sensibility. From the early 1870s, he and Pissarro worked regularly together in the countryside around Paris, at Auvers and Pontoise. As a result, Cézanne lightened his palette, and thus began a lifelong research into recording his visual sensations before nature.

*House of the Hanged Man*, a motif from Auvers-sur-Oise, was probably painted in the spring of 1873. It is among the most heavily worked of Cézanne's canvases from this decade, and the rare appearance of a signature, and the fact that – with Cézanne's consent – it was exhibited several times during his lifetime, suggest that it was one of the rare paintings with which he was satisfied. It was executed on a standard portrait 15 format canvas, whose squarish shape complements the composition and the solid block-like shapes within it. The ground, although undoubtedly pale because of the striking luminosity of the picture, is hard to identify with confidence without removing the work from its frame. The ground is effectively obliterated by the dense, thick opaque paint layer, although slight paint losses at the outer edges reveal both raw canvas and what is possibly a pale gray or putty-colored ground.

Repeated reworkings, over almost the entire surface, characterize this painting. Canvas texture is practically irrelevant, but the effects of stiff, crusty paint dragged across previously dried brushstrokes, are fundamental to the grainy appearance of the picture. The tactile quality of natural surfaces, the crumbly limestone walls, roof thatch, and dusty road, are recreated by the built-up paint texture. Stiff hog's hair brushwork is combined with buttery slabs of color applied with a palette knife. In the foreground path this catches on previous brushstrokes, breaking the color to allow earlier colors to show through. This imitates the texture of natural surfaces and creates a vibrant, fragmented paint layer which scatters light, optically enhancing the picture's paleness and luminosity. Dabbed brushmarks of subtly varied colors construct the thatched roof and the grass bank beneath it, on which the movement of the brushstrokes suggests the movement into space. This directs the eye toward the central pivotal point, which is the sunlit patch of ground between the two main houses.

Despite this visual clue, and despite the artist's use of a foreground path which ought, by tradition, to invite the viewer to enter the pictorial space, other devices work against such an interpretation. The flat lighting and solid paint on the foreground path make it ambiguous – it appears as a barrier, blocking off the pictorial space. Similarly, the curve of the path, down toward the central sunlit patch, is obscured from view as it twists out of sight, thus again inhibiting easy visual access. Furthermore, the brightness of the sunlit patch is equivalent to that of the foreground path, and, by association, they appear to be on the same plane, not receding in depth. This is reinforced by a slab of palish ochre color which projects left, from the central sunlit patch of ground. By appearing to eat into, or overlap the left grass bank, this 'bite' of color disrupts the relatively coherent overlapping of identifiable natural phenomena – path, grassy bank, path again – thus stressing instead the activity of painting itself.

The solid forms and monumental shapes in this composition therefore appear stacked up, like a wall, and all are tightly interlocking. Cézanne's high viewpoint encourages this because although a distant vista appears between the houses, it is not made easily accessible, and its strong colors bring it toward the spectator. Thus there is an inherent tension in the painting, between flatness and naturalistic illusion. This was to remain a characteristic feature of Cézanne's art throughout his long and relatively solitary career as an artist.

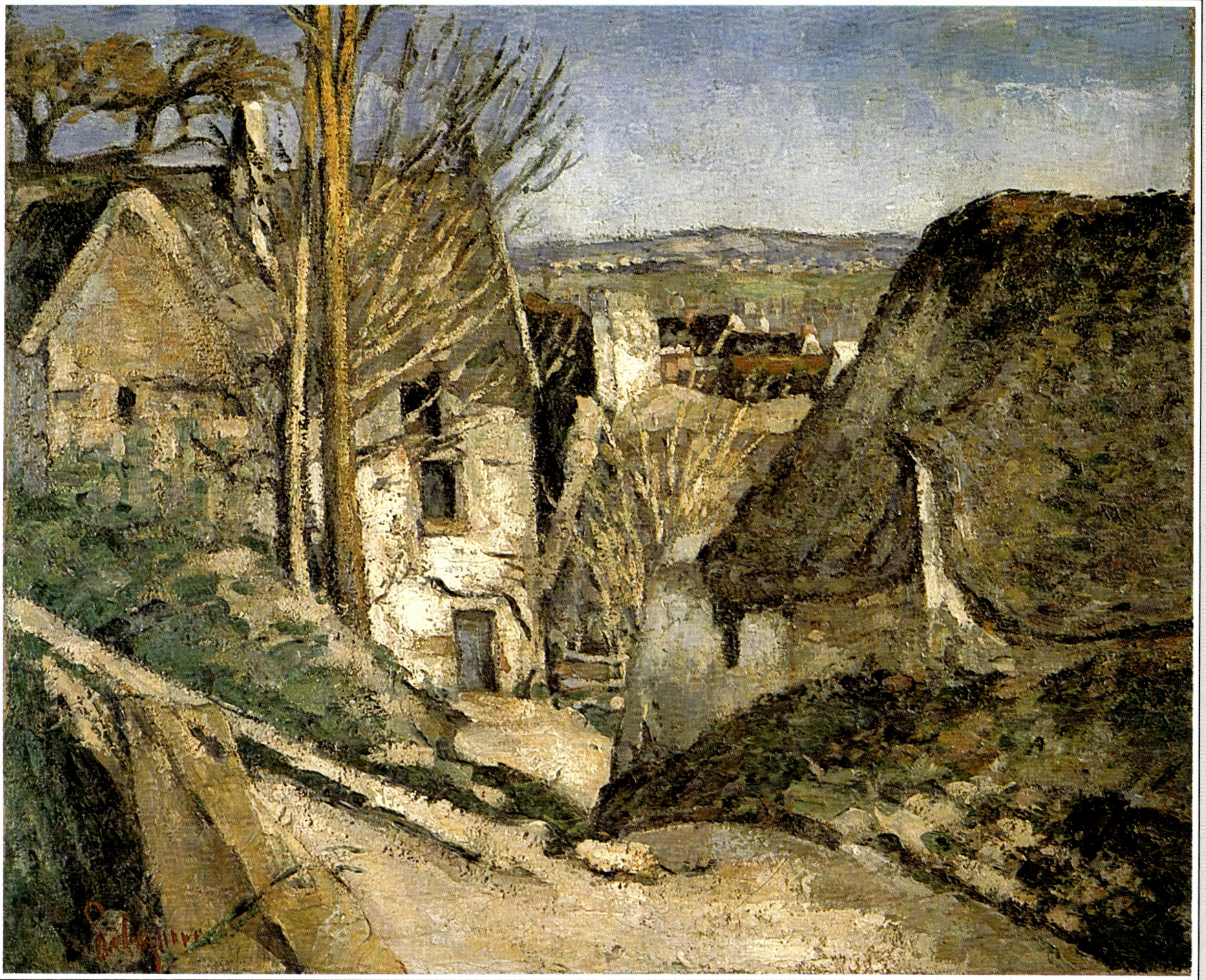

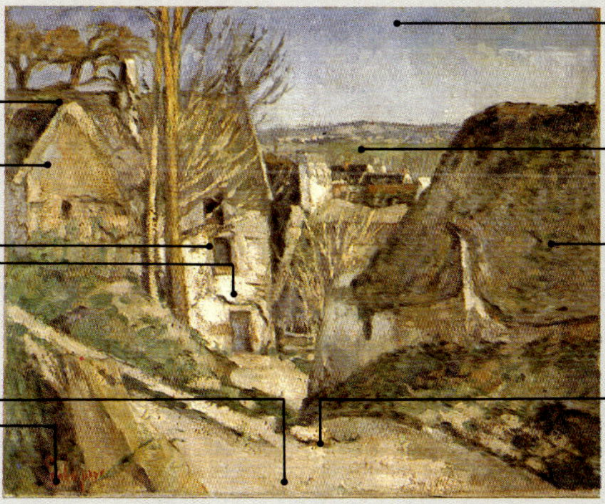


*This painting, which was among the nine works exhibited by Cézanne at the first Impressionist show of 1874, was executed on a squarish, portrait 15 standard canvas. This format admirably suits the high viewpoint and block-like buildings selected by the artist, which can be compared with Pissarro's* Hillside at l'Hermitage *of the same year. The composition fans out in segments from a low central point.*

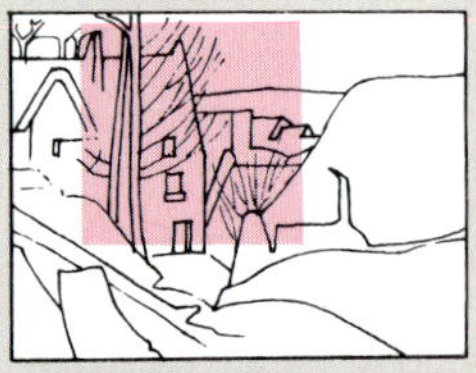

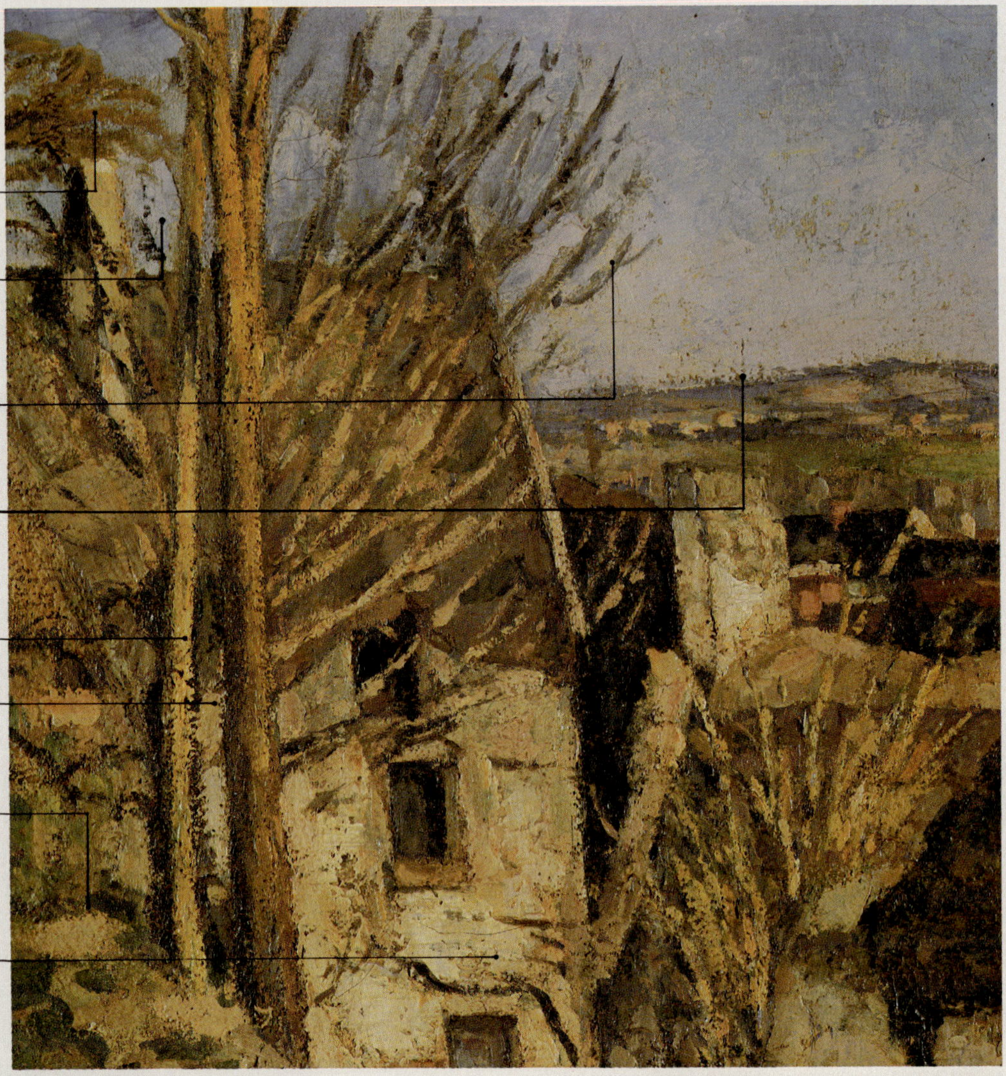

Canvas texture still showing through where paint layer thinnest

Late addition of knife applied blue and white mixture, so thick as to cast a shadow along right edge

More finely brushed color to stand for leafless branches in early spring early spring

Discoloration from dirty varnish in crevices of irregular paint layer

Chalky dragged color for trunks of trees

Added stroke of pale creamy color across to other creams of stone facade

Mixed greens and ochres applied with bristle brush

Knife-applied color describing stone of building

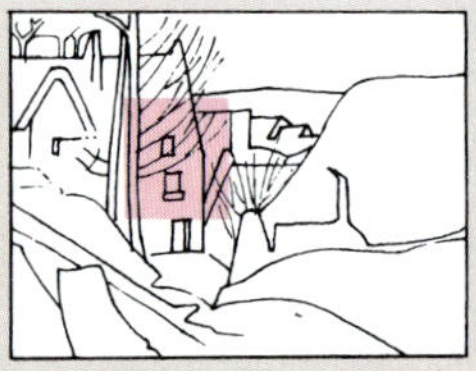

**Actual size detail**
*This is one of the most heavily worked canvases by Cézanne from the 1870s. It exploits varied, descriptive handling in thick, rather chalky, dryish opaque colors. Like most of his fellow painters at this time, Cézanne avoided the use of transparent glazes, which so frequently proved unstable. Instead lead white was added to most of his color mixtures, to increase their luminosity as well as durability. The paint layer was mainly built up wet over dry. However, in the blues of the sky lines the colors are slurred wet-in-wet. The thickness of the paint layer means that the painting must have required much time to execute. Localized fissures have occurred in places as a result of excessive paint thickness. Most of the colors are mixed, thus, despite the results of scientific pigment analysis, the picture appears dominated by earths and green hues.*

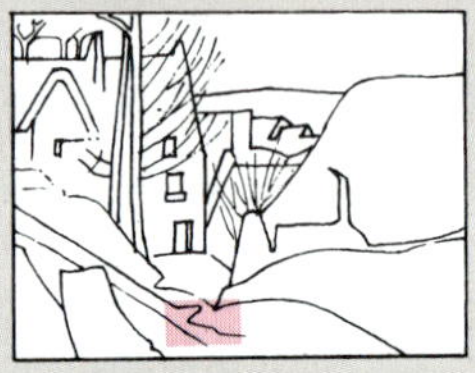

*Varied hues of green are visible, brushed wet into pale ochre tones. Marks of brush and knife are used to enhance the tactile surface quality of the picture, and evoke natural textures. The canvas grain of this cheap-weight support fabric is still visible through the paint layer on the right where the varnish catches the light and reflects it off the surface back to the viewer.*

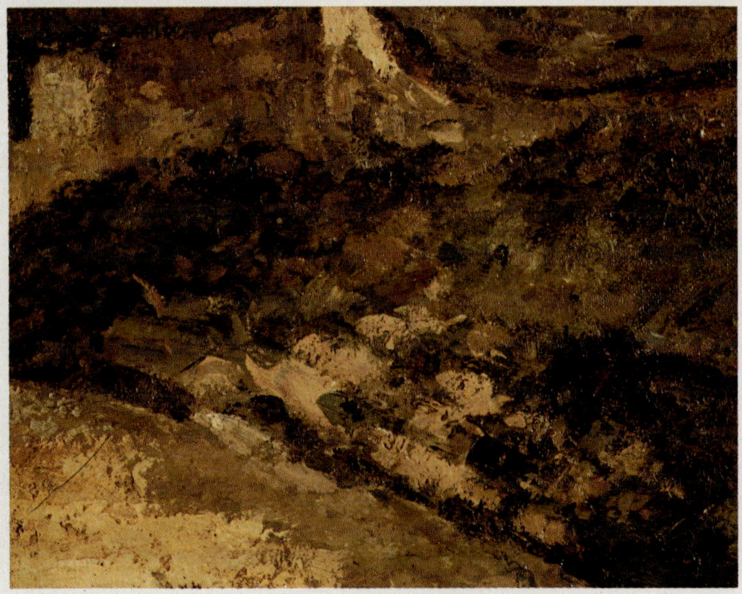

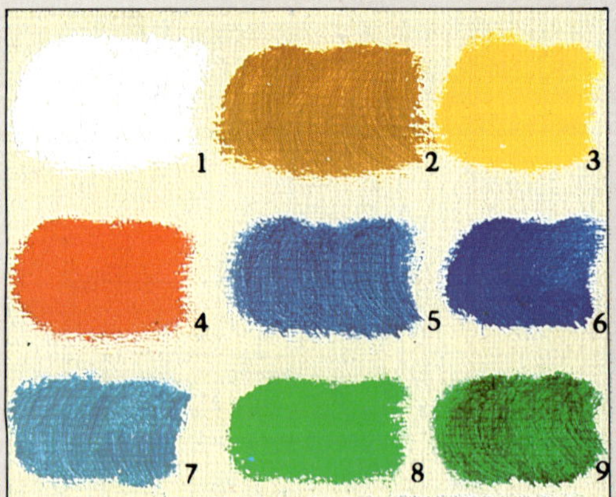


*Cézanne's palette for this painting, which has been analyzed by the Louvre, included lead white (1), zinc white, yellow ochre (2), chrome yellow (3), vermilion (4), cobalt blue (5), ultramarine blue (6), cerulean blue (7), emerald green (8), and possibly viridian green (9). Verdigris was also used.*

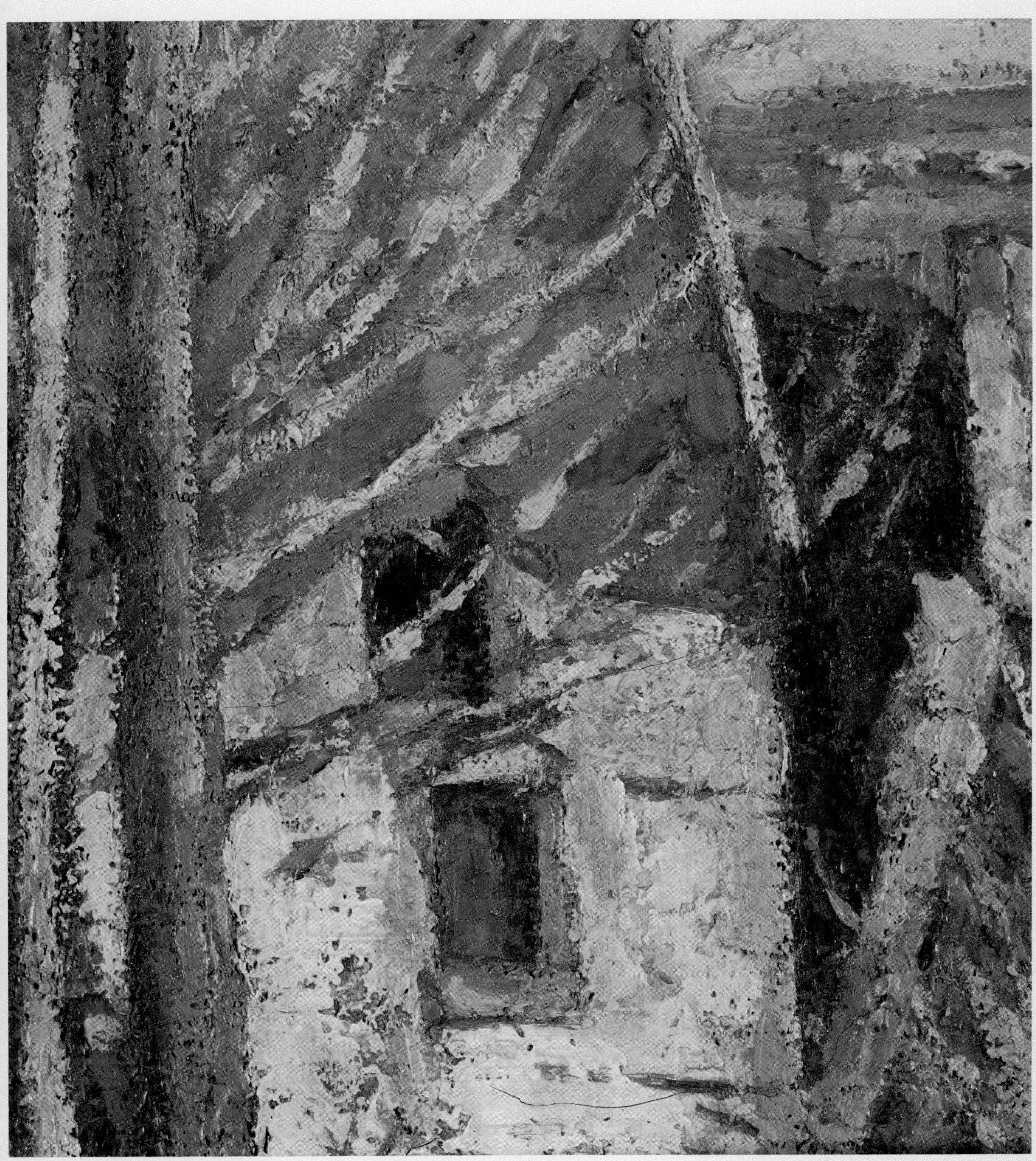

# Pierre Auguste Renoir

*The Parisian/La Parisienne* (1874)
Oil on cream printed canvas
160cm × 106cm/63in × 41¾in

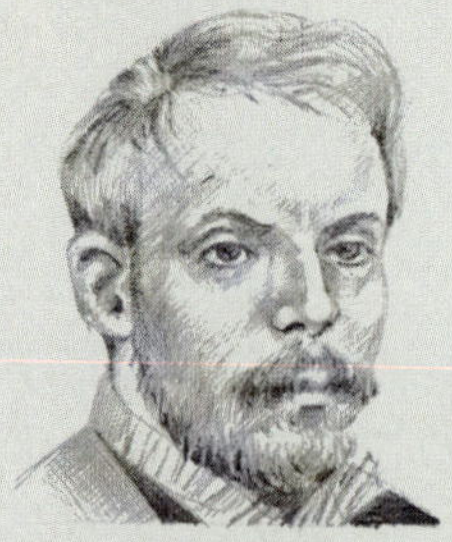

Essentially a Parisian himself by upbringing and allegiance, if not by birth, Renoir spent most of the 1870s working in a large studio on the rue St. Georges – where this painting was doubtless executed. His artisan background and early training as a painter on porcelain gave Renoir a love of eighteenth century French Rococo themes of leisure, and an appreciation of those artists' sumptuous, colorful handling. He infused the pleasurable side of the contemporary modern leisure activities, which he painted, with an idyllic eighteenth century sensuality. During the 1870s, perhaps under the influence of Monet, Renoir painted mainly outdoor scenes, both landscapes and figures, but he also executed many indoor studies of groups or portraits or, as here, of typical Parisian characters. In the 1860s he had attempted one or two winter scenes, but, preferring the warmth and light of summer, he abandoned subjects depicting wintery lights and weather. Even his indoor studies from the 1870s onwards, infused with the knowledge from his observations of outdoor sunlight, gave an effect of pervasive warm light and cool blue-violet shadows.

Renoir's paint surfaces, as in *The Parisian*, were generally much thinner than the stiff textural impastos of the other Impressionists. He usually added a mixture of linseed oil and turpentine to his colors to make them thinner but still juicy. To avoid excessive and thus dangerous overmixing of colors on his palette, he tended to apply them wet into wet directly onto the canvas, slurring them together where necessary. The other Impressionists, especially Monet and Pissarro, achieved light-reflective luminosity in their paint surfaces by using chalky, stiff paint mixtures dominated by lead white, dragged to give opaque, vibrant effects. Renoir, by contrast, used his thin juicy translucent or scumbled colors to allow the brilliance of the ground to show through, reflecting color-enriched light back to the viewer. No dull earth colors tone down the brightness of Renoir's palette here.

*The Parisian* was executed on a non-standard sized canvas format, which had to be made to order. The canvas weave is fine, and the commercial ground is a carefully selected cream color, sufficiently thickly applied to leave the surface fairly smooth. Where the cream ground shows through the thin paint layer, its color is actively exploited among the applied colors of the paint layer. This technique reduces the need for an excessive build-up or reworking of the picture itself. The cream of the ground is very effectively used amongst the blues of the dress. Traditionally, the shadows were the most thinly painted, transparent parts, and highlights were built up in opaque impasto to create an almost physical relief on the paint surface. In Renoir's picture, the highlights are the thinnest parts. By diluting his cobalt blue until translucent and applying it with deft, descriptive brushwork, almost like a wash, he has left the cream ground to glow through the blue and stand for the highlights.

Where shadows were required, helping to structure the form and folds in the dress, Renoir has simply used thicker, undiluted blue, which is thus deeper and more saturated in color. Wet-in-wet smudging of yellow into the blue in the darkest parts, deepens the shadows further without sullying them with black or brown. In places, the sparest touch of lead white was worked into the wet blue to heighten the lights. Slurring the colors gives a more colorful, lively effect than mechanical premixing on the palette. Renoir's overlaying of the cream ground with transparent blue has an optical coloristic effect, too. Warm and cool colors, or colors situated more or less opposite each other on the color circle, enhance each other optically. Thus on the dress in *The Parisian*, the thinly washed blue over cream produces an optical effect of pink so, by contrast, the blue appears cooler, the cream warmer, pinker. Cézanne's *Large Bathers* (*c*1898–1905) exploits similar effects.

In *The Parisian* Renoir's composition is simple and direct, with many precedents, especially in Manet's single-figure studies from the mid 1860s. Like Manet, Renoir used a full-face light, falling almost directly onto his model, but Renoir's lighting is softer, more diffuse than that adopted by Manet which produced strong tonal contrasts. Also, as in Manet's work, the figure is indistinctly located in space – no wall

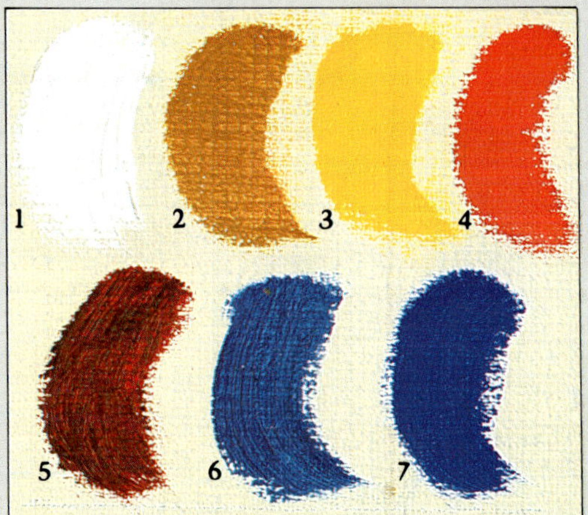


*Renoir's palette for this painting probably comprised lead white* (1), *possibly zinc white, yellow ochre* (2), *chrome yellow* (3), *vermilion* (4), *possibly alizarin red* (5), *cobalt* (6) *or a mixture of ultramarine and cobalt blues* (7).

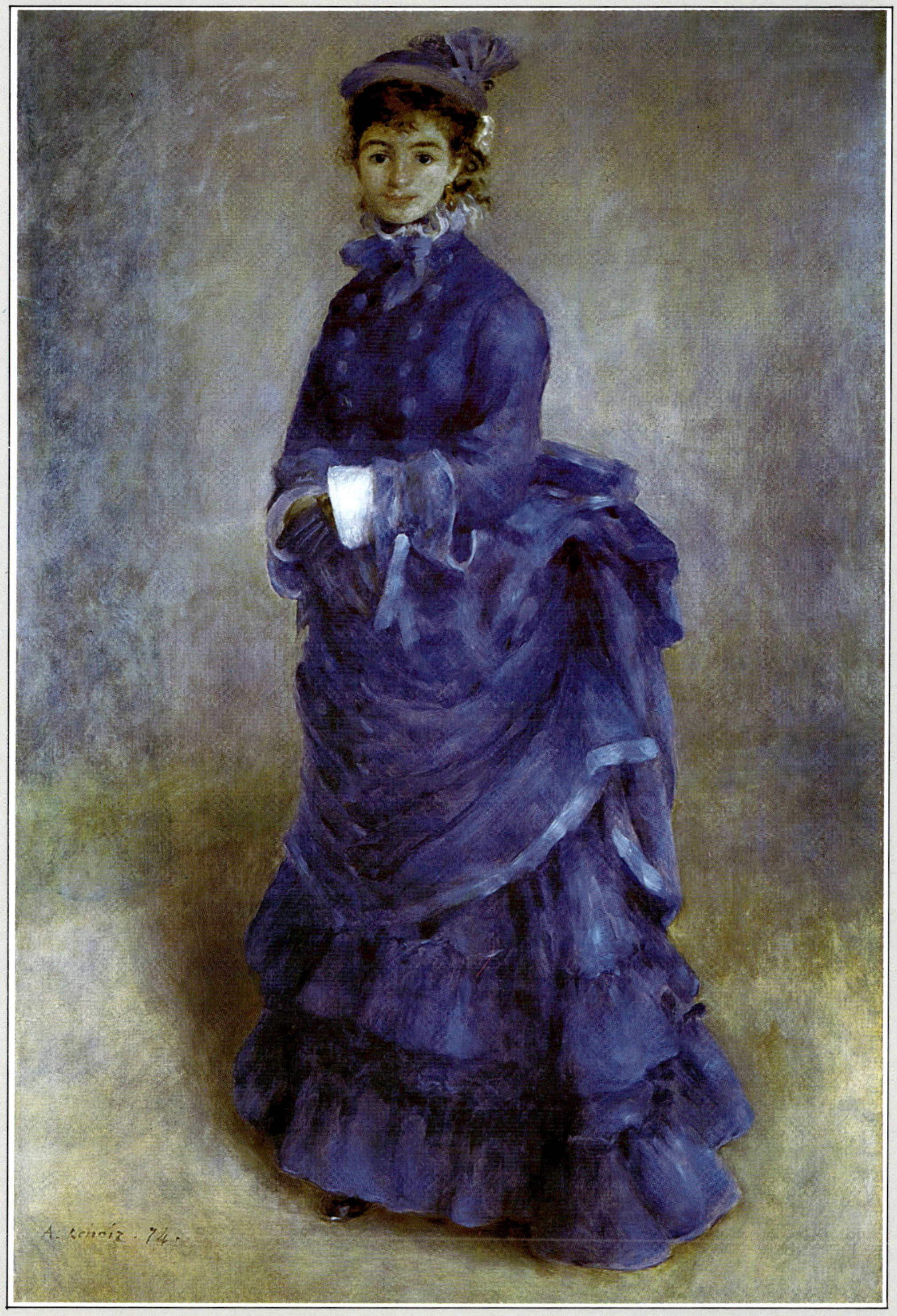


*Unlike Degas' depictions of Parisian women, Renoir's pictures like* The Parisian *show working women at leisure rather than engaged in their trades. The slightly outmoded dress shows this to be a lower class woman sporting her Sunday finery. Renoir's use of a warm, flooding daylight, softly diffused over the figure, unifies the composition and reduces tonal contrasts to a minimum. Instead of lights and darks, warm and cool hues are used to model form, with the cream ground glowing through the thin transparent blues to stand as highlights. The paint layer is thin and varies between fine transparent layers and delicately rubbed or scumbled, opaque veils of color. The stability of Renoir's painting method was confirmed by Signac's observations on the picture when he saw it in 1898. He said 'The dress is blue, an intense and pure blue which, by contrast, makes the flesh yellow, and, by its reflection, green. The tricks of color are admirably recorded. And it is simple, it is beautiful, and it is fresh. One would think that this picture painted 20 years ago had only left the studio today.'*

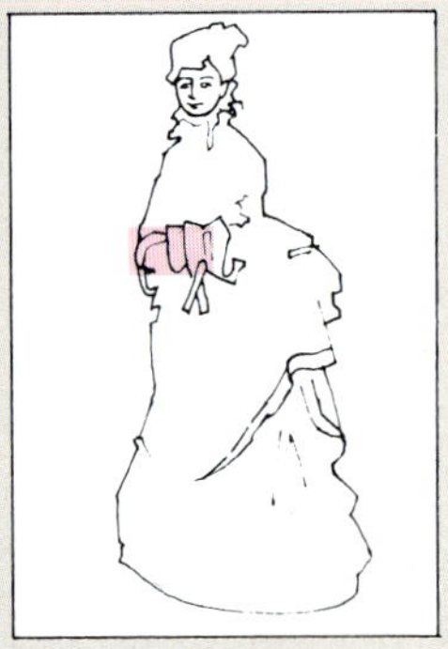

*The thinnest blues are washed transparently over the cream ground, which glows through and appears pink in contrast to the blue. For the palest highlights, white was brushed wet into the blues, but still so thinly that the cream ground generally remains visible. White is used more thickly and is opaque and almost pure for the cuff. Here, brushwork helps to sculpt the form. In the darkest parts, blue is applied undiluted and in its most saturated form, giving a rich deep hue. Slight slurred touches of yellow are laid wet into the blue to tone down and vary the shadows.*

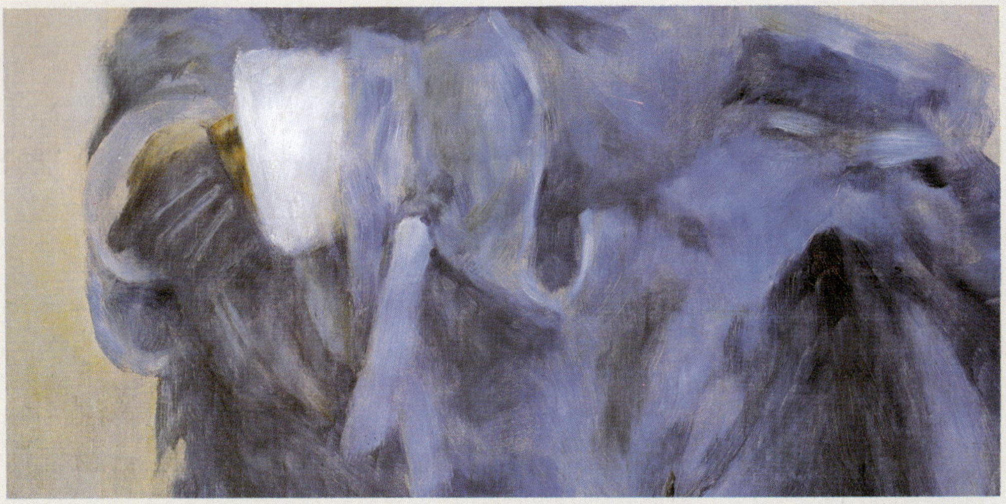

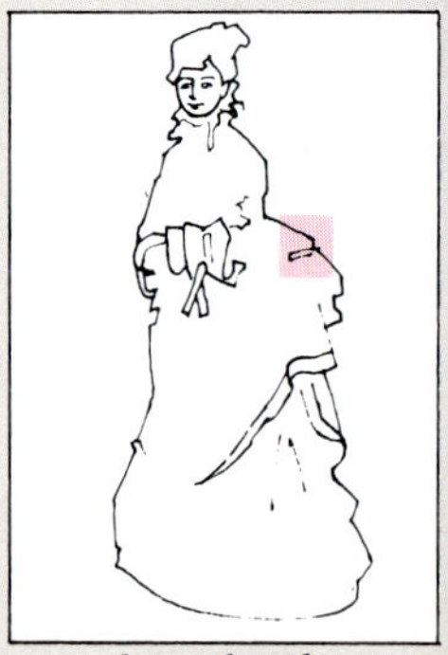

Actual size detail
*The flounces of the woman's bustle are created by lively, descriptive brushstrokes, and the rounded tip of the broad bristle brush can be clearly seen. The blues were applied in varying degrees of dilution, thinnest for the lights allowing the cream ground to show warmly through. Cooler lights are created by slurring deft touches of white into the wet blue paint, making the layer opaque or translucent in those parts, thus covering the cream ground more thoroughly. A hint of yellow, worked wet into the deepest blue, darkens the shadow below the bustle flounce.*

or floor angles define the room, and the figure's cast shadow is minimal. Renoir further simplified his composition during the painting process, obliterating blue drapes which originally hung to either side of the figure, and are now just visible because the thin paint layer has become more transparent with age.

This picture was exhibited by Renoir with six other works at the first Impressionist exhibition, held in the old second floor studio of the famous Parisian photographer Nadar, at 35 boulevard des Capucines. During the month-long show, which opened on 15 April 1874 just prior to the annual Salon exhibition, the criticism received by Renoir was by no means unsympathetic. In fact, it was only when the Impressionist style persisted and spread in popularity in the later 1870s that criticism became more hostile.

Throughout this decade Renoir continued to submit his work to the Salon as well as showing with his Impressionist friends. This earned him the scorn of hardline opponents of the Salon like Degas. Thus, like Manet, he remained committed to seeking official recognition for his work although, unlike Manet, he was also dedicated to independent shows. By the late 1870s, his work was beginning to achieve acceptance and success, at least among discerning private collectors, and the important dealer Paul Durand-Ruel bought his work regularly when finances permitted.

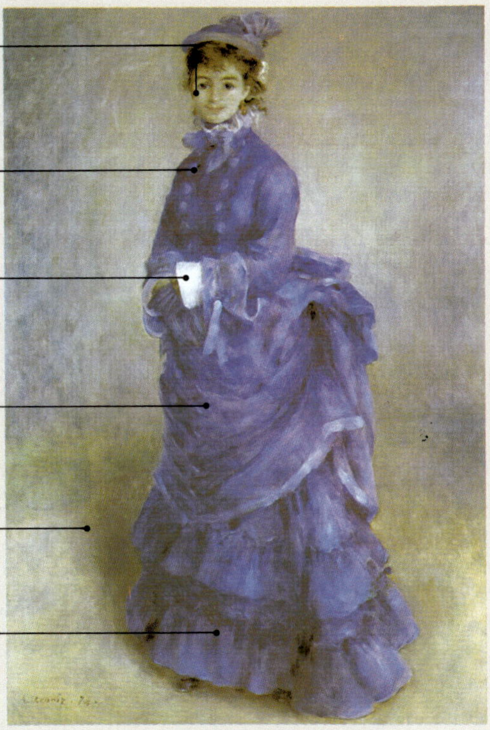

Cream ground actively used for flesh tints among thinly applied colors

Undiluted, saturated blue for darkest parts

White used almost pure for cuff

Cream ground appears pink through transparent blues of dress

Original blue drapes painted out making space ill defined

Vigorous bristle brushmarks convey fabric folds and texture

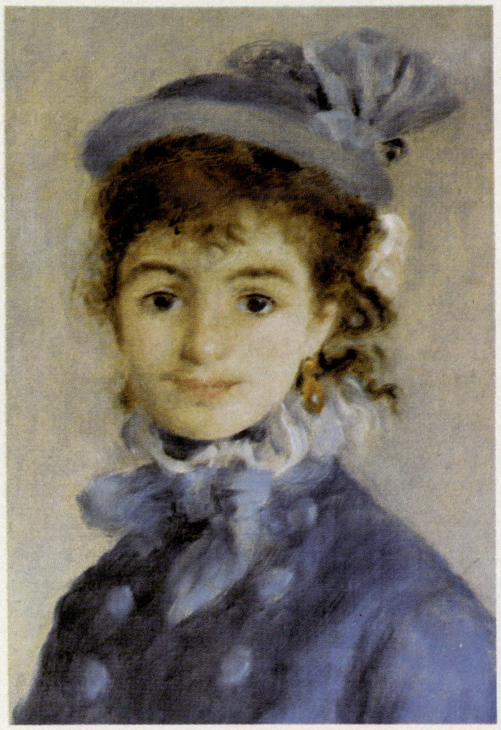

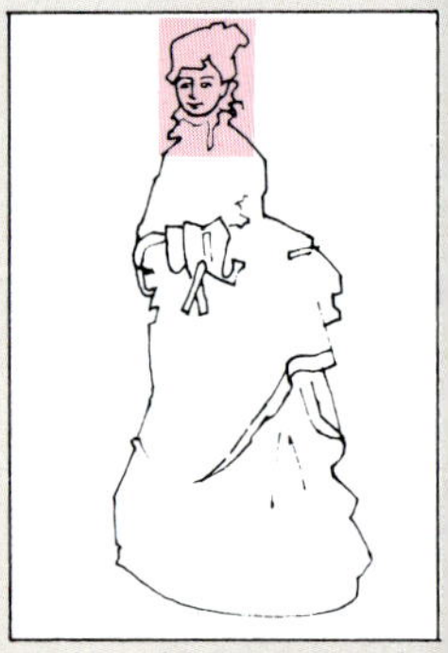

*A thin, dilute sweep of the brush suggests the bonnet brim, while contrasting light feathery touches evoke the hair. The cream ground is left to stand for the cooler flesh tints, and warmer pinks were added for the facial highlights. Thus against warm hues, Renoir made the cream ground appear cooler and greener, while, among the cool blues of the dress, they seem warm.*

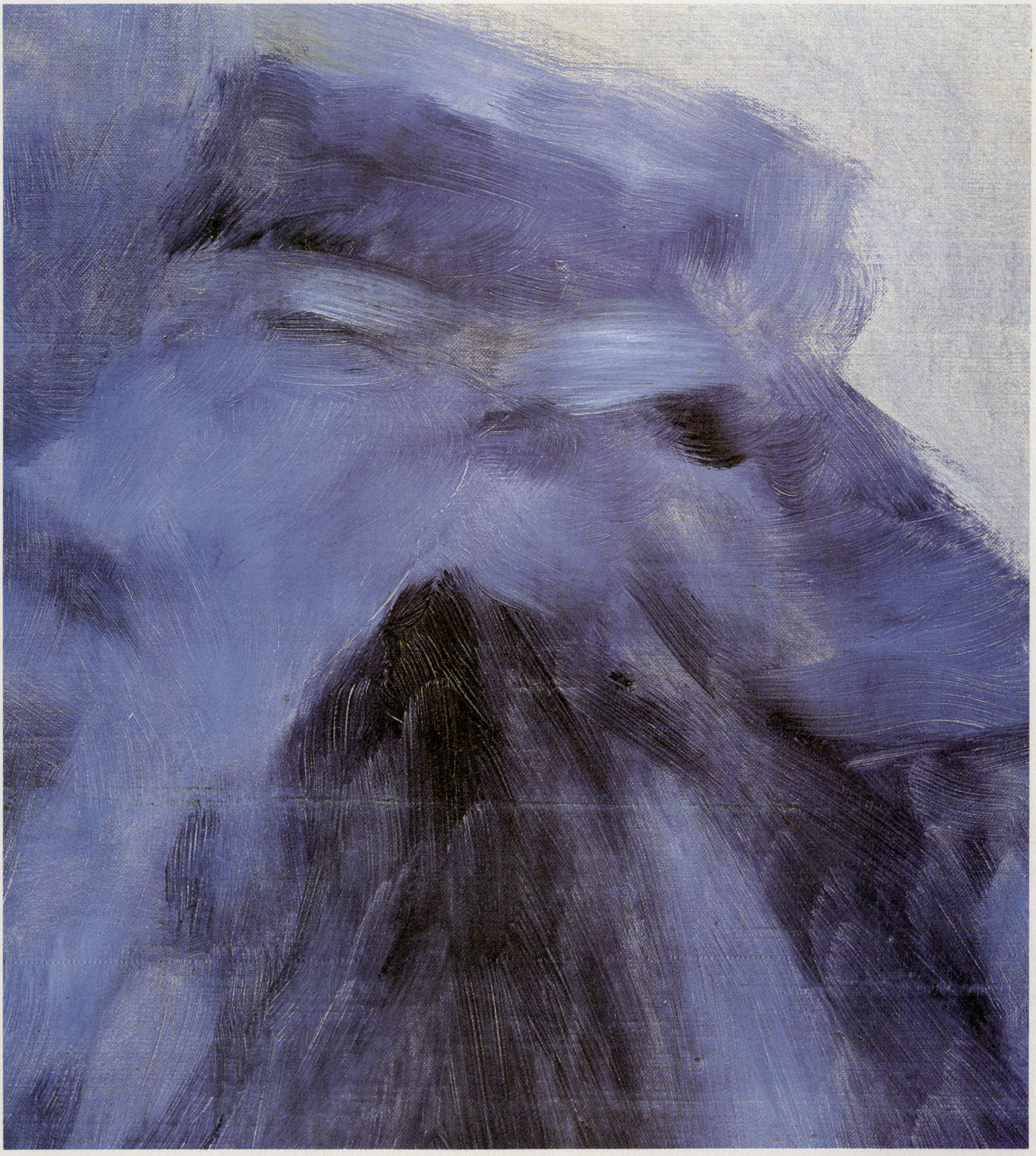

1870
1880

# Pierre Auguste Renoir

*Woman's Torso in Sunlight/Torse de Femme au Soleil* (1875)
Oil on canvas, 81cm × 64.8cm/32in × 25½in

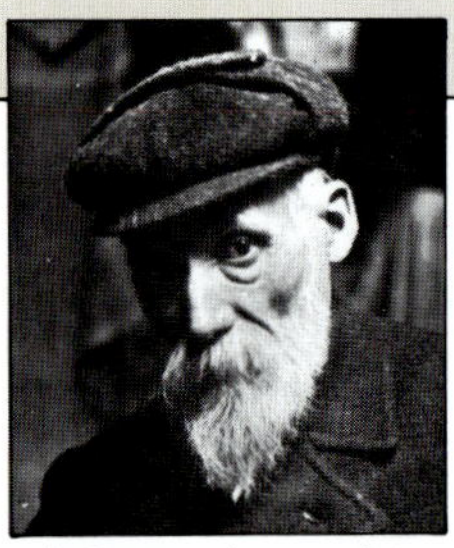

Renoir's youthful experience as a painter on porcelain had a lasting influence on his art, contributing a love of fluid transparencies and introducing him to the eighteenth century Rococo artists. He had a great admiration for Delacroix and, during his formative years, was also influenced by Manet, Courbet, and Corot. Renoir's modern-life figure painting reflected his Parisian artisan background and, while his work with Monet in the late 1860s encouraged him to paint landscapes, he never abandoned his commitment to the human form. Renoir can thus be distinguished from such painters as Monet, Sisley or Pissarro both in the importance he placed on figure painting, particularly the female nude, and by his transparent, rich surfaces, as his fellow artists used impasted opaque paint films.

Renoir preferred pale grounds, using tinted primings in the 1870s and white thereafter. He preferred solid, heavy canvas which he considered more durable, and his paint layer was typically thin, delicate, and diluted with a medium of oil and turpentine which made even opaque colors translucent. The luminosity and brilliance of Renoir's color is thus derived from this use of transparent and translucent color brushed thinly over pale grounds which glow through the paint layer. Renoir applied his color using a wet-in-wet technique, slurring tints in order not to lose their purity by over-mixing. In addition to brushing his colors, Renoir used rubbing and staining to build up form, color and depth.

Renoir was the first artist of his generation to exploit fully the use of warm-cool color contrasts; in one painting of 1874 he used a cream ground in which varied brushstrokes of ultramarine blue created the form and folds of fabric. Where the blue is thin, the cream glows through and appears warm pink by contrast, creating highlights; where it is thickest, the ground is least visible and shadows are evoked by the rich, saturated color.

During the 1880s, Renoir, turned to a more classical and rigorous style and adopted the hatched, constructive strokes of Cézanne, and a tight drawing and modelling technique. Renoir's late style represented a fusion of this with his Impressionism of the 1870s, and resulted in a juicy, succulent handling of figures, reminiscent of Fragonard and Rubens.

1. A fairly fine-weave canvas was bought ready-primed with a single layer of pale, warm gray ground.

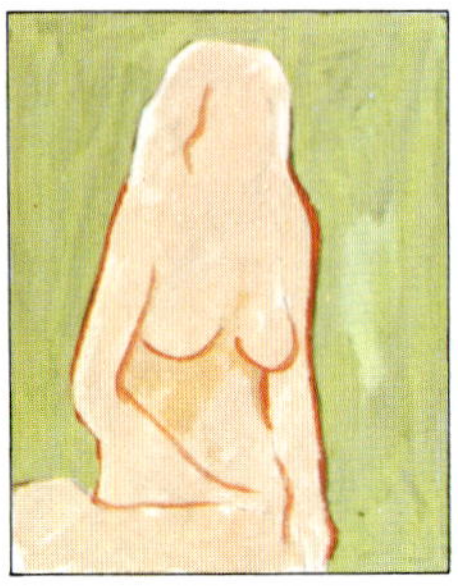

2. Next, thin scumbles were laid down in dilute local colors with warm reds for contours of flesh and the general shaded areas on the figure.

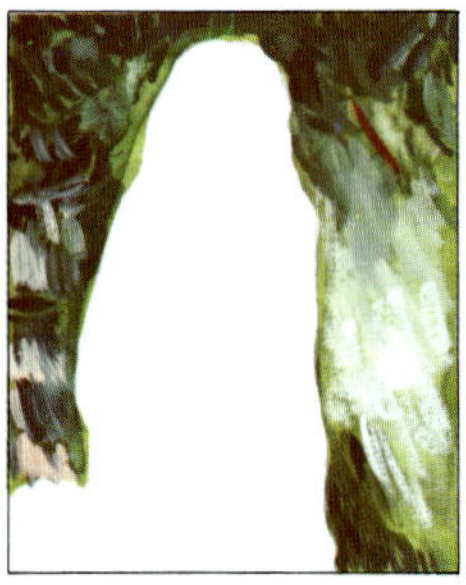

3. The background was rapidly worked wet-in-wet leaving the ground and canvas texture showing through.

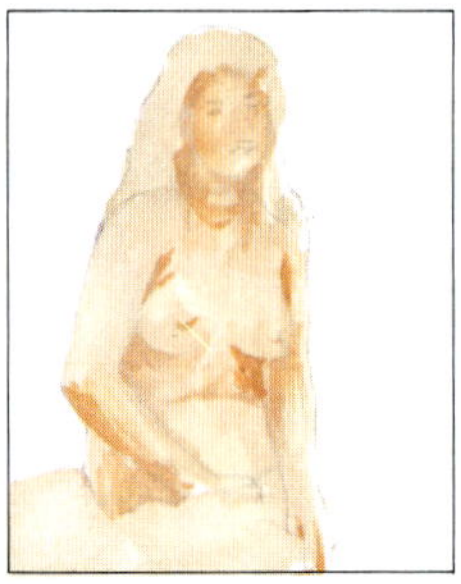

4. The figure was built up slowly working wet-in-wet and then with thin wet-over-dry layers which obscured the canvas texture.

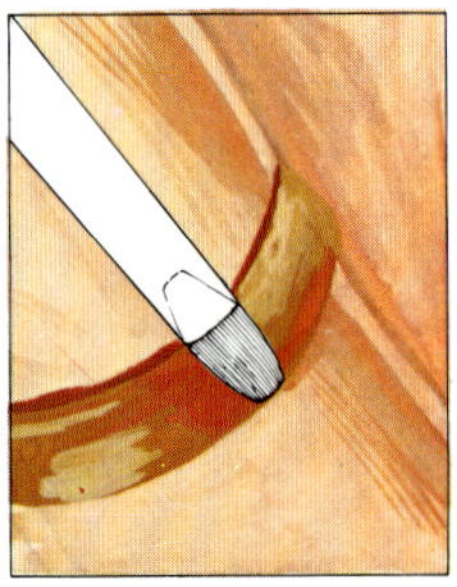

5. Final additions to the figure and foliage such as the jewelry and red stains in the flesh area were made to enrich shadows and cool contrasting complementary colors.

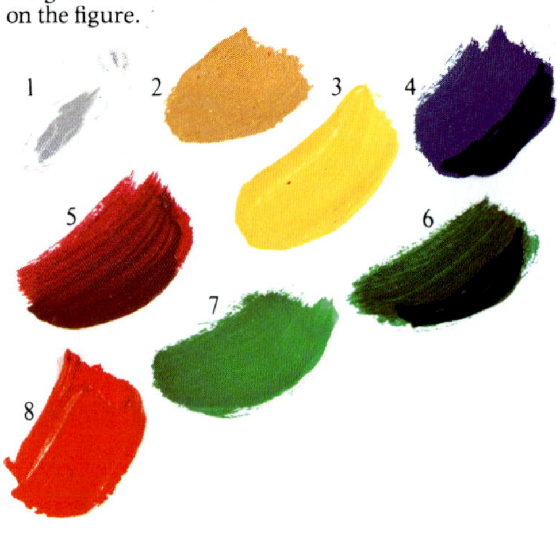


In this work, Renoir used the following colors: flake white (1), Naples yellow (2), chrome yellows (3), cobalt and/or ultramarine blue (4), alizarin red (5), viridian green (6), emerald green (7), vermilion (8).

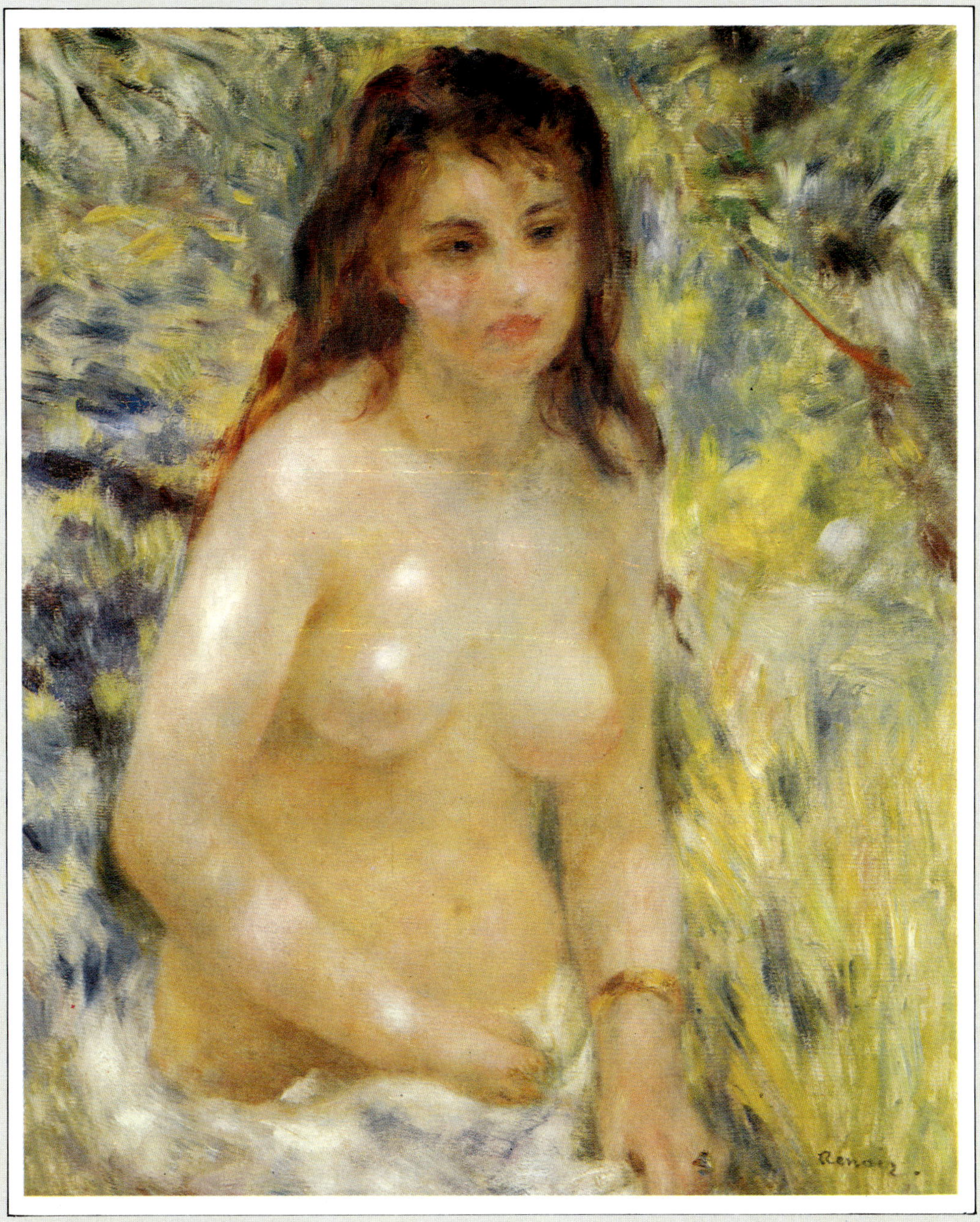

*The painting's overall luminosity is derived from the pale gray ground. Despite the dappled sunlight, the figure never loses its strength of form and solidity, and the foliage is loosely and intentionally blurred to concentrate the viewer's attention on the girl. Renoir's method was traditional, but he used opaque colors for shadows in the flesh and his colors are mixed and broken. There is a superb, confident handling of the wet-in-wet technique, particularly in the foliage, hair, and drapery. Brushwork describes form and texture and is used to increase solidity. Flesh hues exploit subtle warm-cool modulations, with pastel-like blues on the chest depicting the cool reflections of sky and foliage.*

*Several subtle adjustments in the figure were made including obliterating a patch of drapery by extending downwards the area of exposed lower belly. The cobalt blue edging at the woman's left and right elbow stresses the form and separates it from the background. The right shoulder was enlarged and broadened by adding bluish-hued strokes above the patch of sunlight, which were applied over the wet red-yellows of the hair which, in turn, were applied over dry paint.*

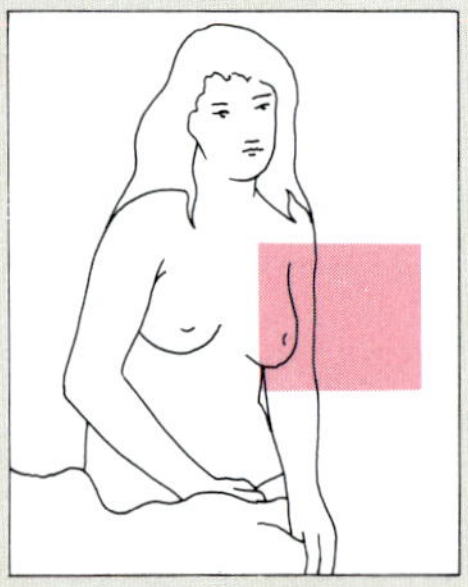

*The woman's left breast has been enlarged during execution. The reddish lower half and a new nipple were added to change the figure's pose to a more classical position. The line of the shoulder, obscured by the fall of hair, remains level. The original, higher position of the under-breast contour is only visible as ridges of dry paint beneath the present opaque layer. The thick opacity of the flesh contrasts with the superb fluid handling of grass, the brushstrokes of which follow the contour of the arm.*

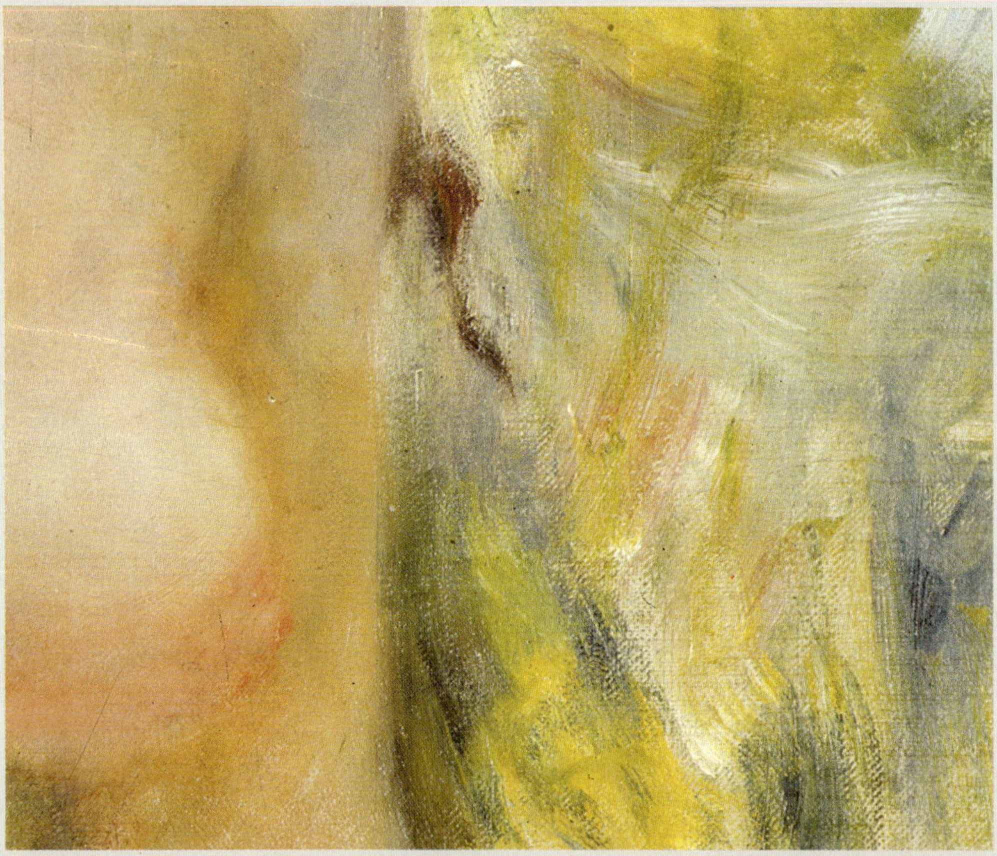

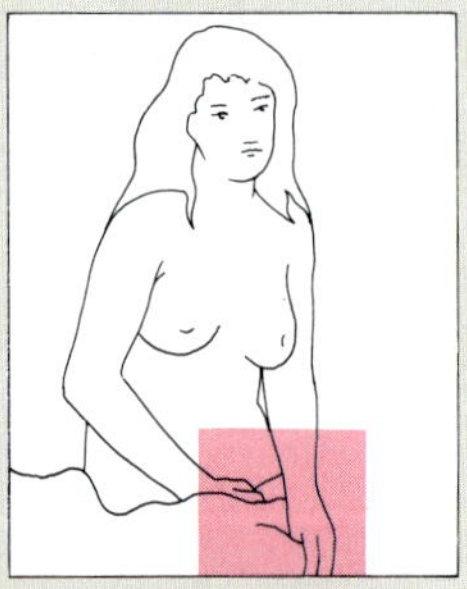

*Renoir's fluent handling follows and builds up the form of the flesh, on which delicate thin layers of opaque color were worked wet into wet. The jewelry was added later when the work was dry, and also, the area of exposed stomach was extended by flesh colors painted over the original marks of drapery. A thin film of transparent blue adds reflected cool tints to the white cloth. Transparent red lakes were stained into the dry flesh paint to give richness and warmth.*

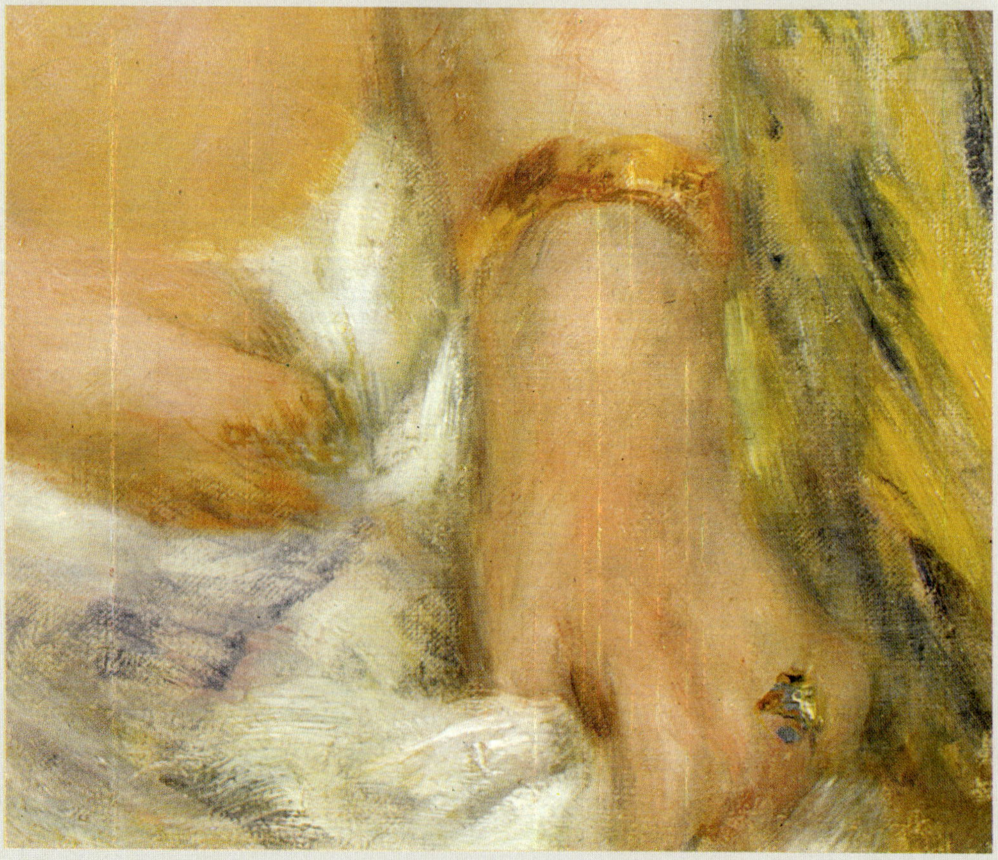

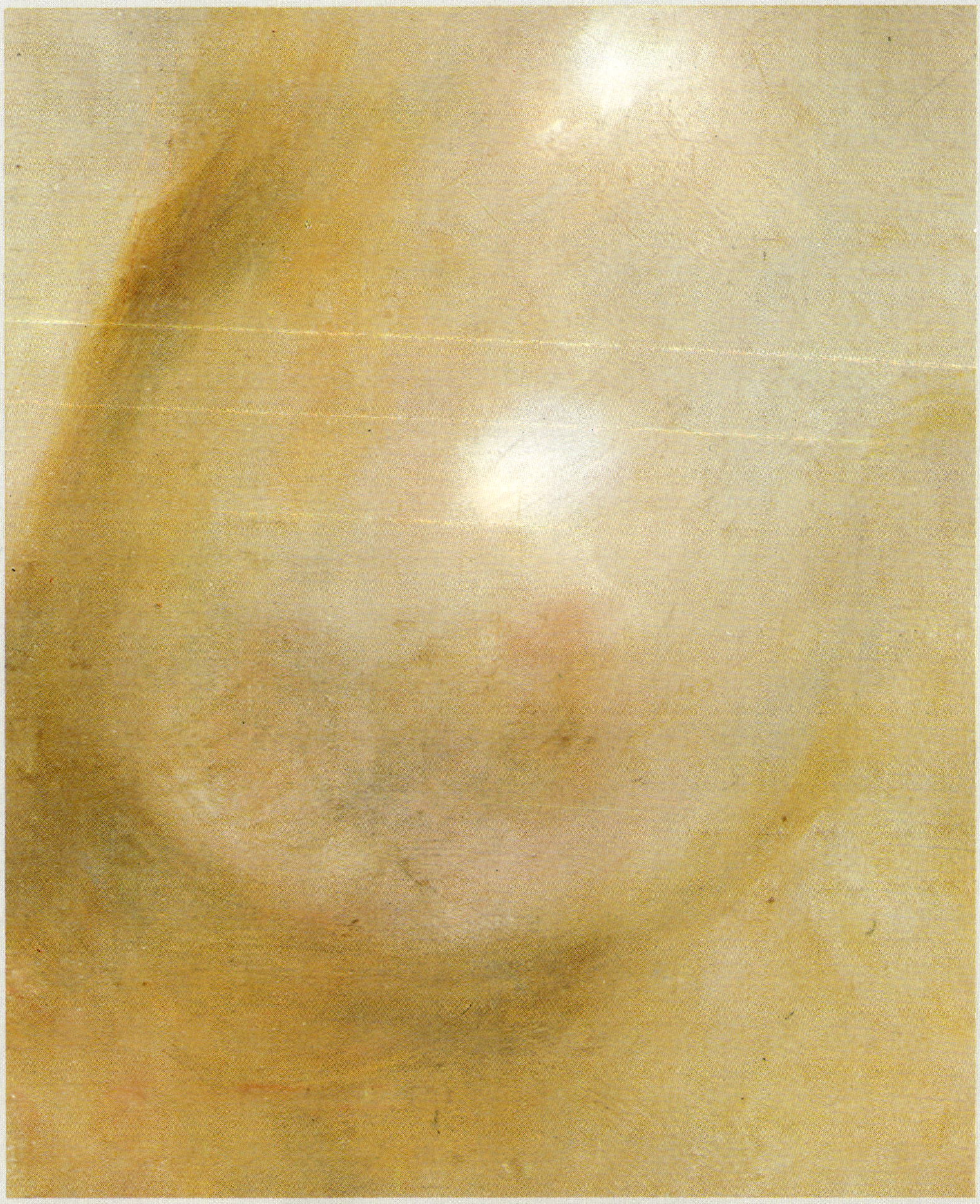

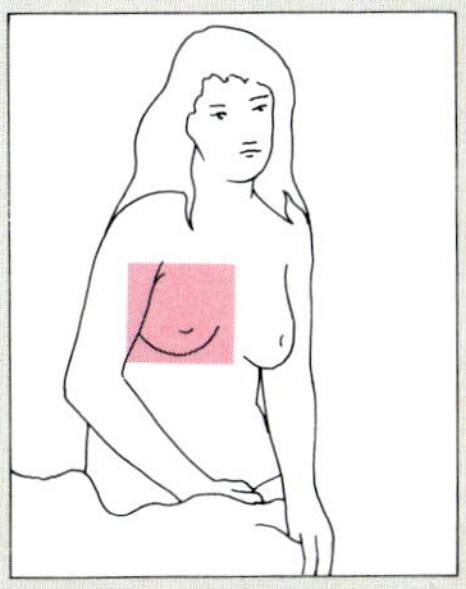

**Actual size detail**
*Color was applied smoothly to obliterate the fine canvas texture and evoke the quality of flesh. When this was dry, the thin opaque highlights and contrasting thin stained red shadows were added in. Fine hatched lines of color, close in tone to the reflected reds of the shadows, were worked over them, following the curves of the breast to stress its form and weight. These light strokes can be seen as parallel touches on the left underside of the breast and, beneath it, longer curved lines following the form of the torso. Similar brushstrokes describe the swell of flesh from the armpit towards the shoulder. The luminous warmth of the shadows contrasts with thin scumbles of pale green-blues indicating the cool reflections from sky and foliage.*

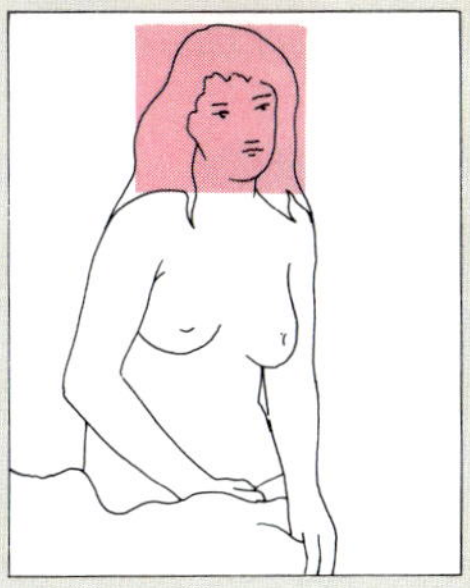

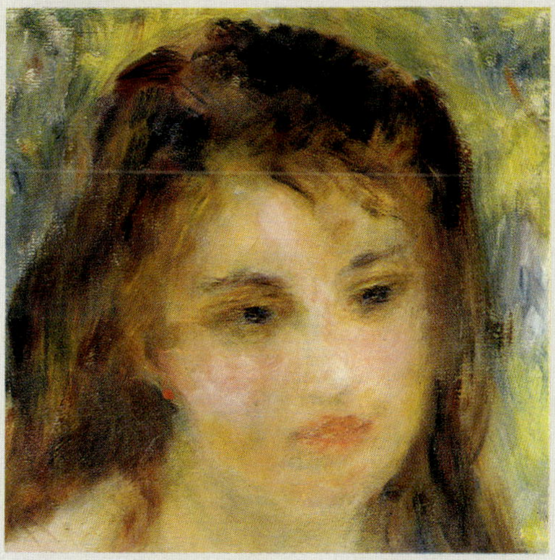

*The form of the face is less strongly defined than that of the body, which serves to concentrate the eye on the woman's torso. The unfocused quality of the wet-in-wet handling of the hair links it to the free brushwork of the background.*

# ALFRED SISLEY

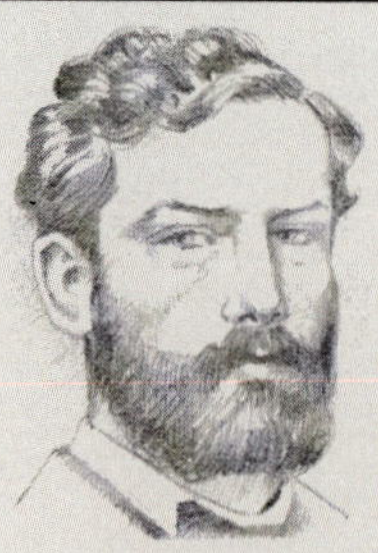

*Boats on the Seine/Bateaux sur la Seine* (*c* 1877)
Oil on pale creamy primed canvas
37cm × 43.5cm/14½in × 17¼in

Sisley was born in Paris of British parents, and although he spent four years of his early maturity in England, he returned to France in 1861 to become an artist and remained based there throughout the rest of his life. In 1862 he entered the studio of Charles Gleyre, where he met Renoir, Monet and Frédéric Bazille (1841–1870), with whom he worked from nature in the Fontainebleau forest in the spring of 1863. Like Monet, Sisley was to concentrate on landscape painting, and he worked regularly on outdoor subjects in the Fontainebleau area during the 1860s, in the company of one or other of the group from Gleyre's studio. Like his colleagues during this decade, Sisley frequently sent paintings to the Salon, exhibiting there in 1866, 1868 and 1870. His father, who worked in commerce, died in 1871, ruined by the Franco-Prussian War, leaving Sisley with no money. For the first time the artist was forced to earn a living from his painting.

Sisley preferred gentle rural scenery in general, landscapes, villages, river views in which the human presence was manifest. During the 1870s he concentrated on subjects found in the countryside to the west of Paris, just north of Versailles, around the villages of Marly-le-Roi, Port-Marly, Celle-St. Cloud and Louveciennes. From there, he was sufficiently close to Paris to maintain easy contact with his artist colleagues and with dealers – like Paul Durand-Ruel and *père* Martin – who bought his work when they could afford to. Perhaps because of closer ties of friendship with the publisher Georges Charpentier, Sisley moved even closer to Paris, to Sèvres, in the later 1870s. Charpentier, whose writers included Zola and Huysmans, published a paper called *La Vie Moderne*. He held small one-man shows by several of the Impressionists, including Monet and Sisley, at his offices in 1880 and 1881. Georges Charpentier's wife, who sat with two of her children for an important portrait by Renoir in 1878, held a regular evening *soirée*, which was an important meeting place for many avant-garde artists and intellectuals.

During the 1880s, Sisley gravitated back to the Fontainebleau area. He concentrated on painting river scenes in particular, around the confluence of the Seine and the Loing rivers, at Marlotte, Moret and St. Mammès. As he was more distant from his colleagues, he saw the other Impressionists less frequently from this time on.

*Boats on the Seine* is painted on a support slightly squarer than the standard portrait 8, measuring 46cm by 38cm (18in by 15in). Sisley, always fairly poor, used an inexpensive, ordinary weight canvas, with a single layer of pale creamy priming which has left a grainy surface texture. In general, Sisley seems to have preferred a rather more bland canvas weave than that popular with Monet and Pissarro, although here, the grain is fairly marked and is used to great effect in combination with dragged, dryish colors in the paint layer. The thin canvas priming is mat, and evidently quite absorbent, for the paint layer has a dull, mat quality and is apparently one of the rare instances where a work has remained unvarnished. Despite the Impressionists' preference for leaving their works unvarnished, to enhance the pale, light-reflective surfaces of their pictures, the habit of dealers and galleries to varnish paintings automatically in order to protect them has meant that few retain their original appearance.

This is one of the rare, truly *alla prima* or 'single sitting' Impressionist paintings. The paint layer is thin and spare, exploiting the cream priming underneath amongst the applied colors, and even the tiny figures in the foreground were added wet in wet before the first colors had dried. The handling of the sky is a superb example of the optical effects which can be achieved by contrasting warm and cool colors. The pinky whites of the clouds brushed loosely over the creamy ground are warmed by it, while the ground shows through amongst the sky blues too. This results in an ethereal, insubstantial quality which aptly evokes the atmospheric effects of the sky. The warm and cool hues enhance each other optically, to give an airy, vibrant effect to the colors, unattainable by conventional overlaying and build-up of paint layers. Sisley's agitated, lively touch in the brushwork aids the impression of fleeting, transient effects.

Sisley's choice of composition and viewpoint varied between the relatively conventional and the daringly adventurous. Often, especially during the 1870s, he used high viewpoints, or visual barriers like a screen of trees, to create a flattened, surface oriented pictorial design, as

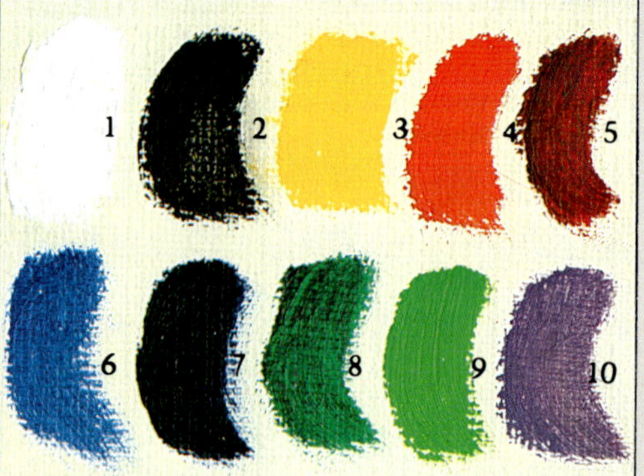


*Sisley's palette for this painting probably comprised lead white (1), possibly black (2), chrome yellow (3), vermilion (4), red alizarin lake (5), cobalt blue (6), possibly Prussian blue (7), viridian green (8), chrome green (9), and cobalt violet (10). Yellow ochre was probably used too.*

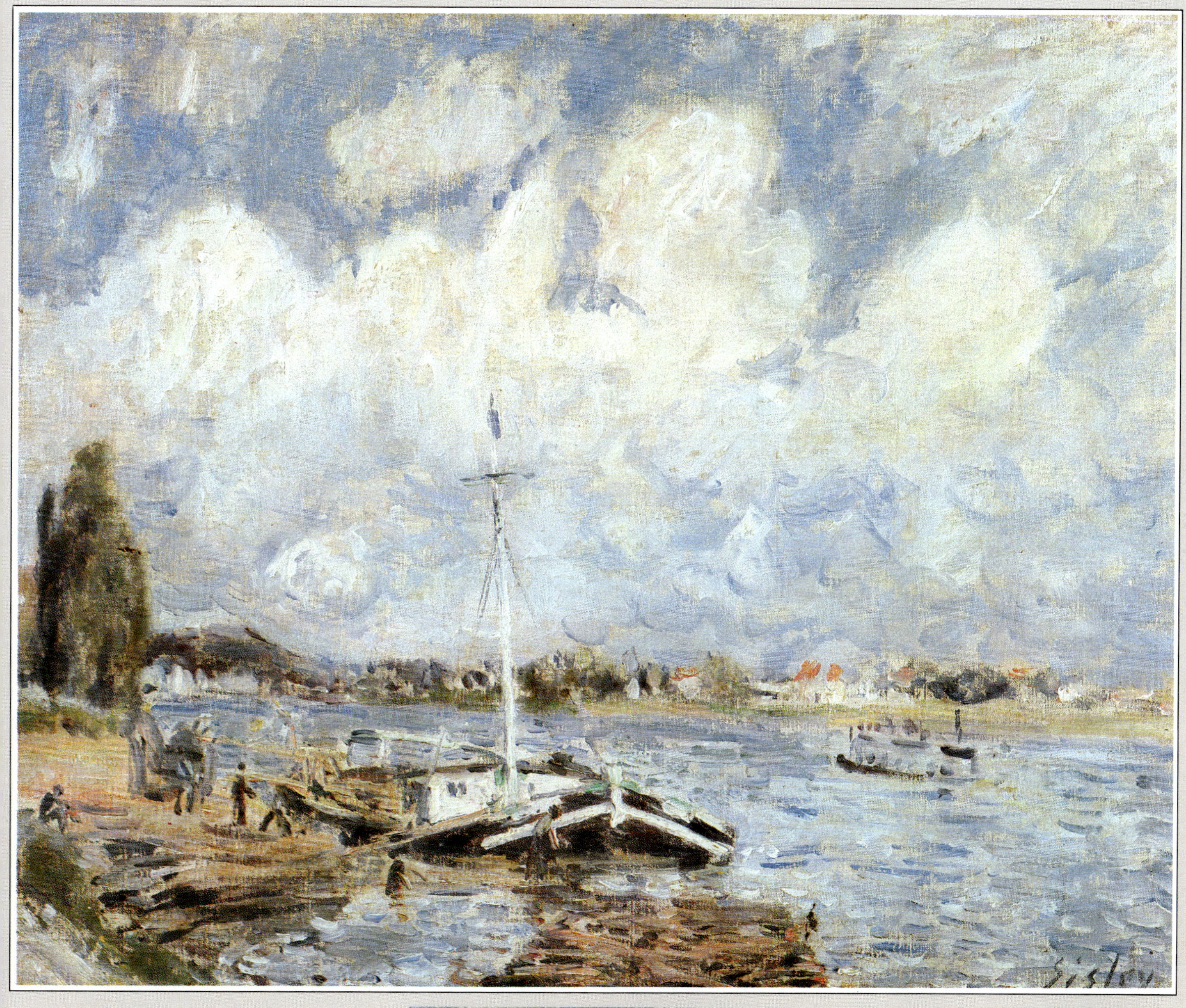

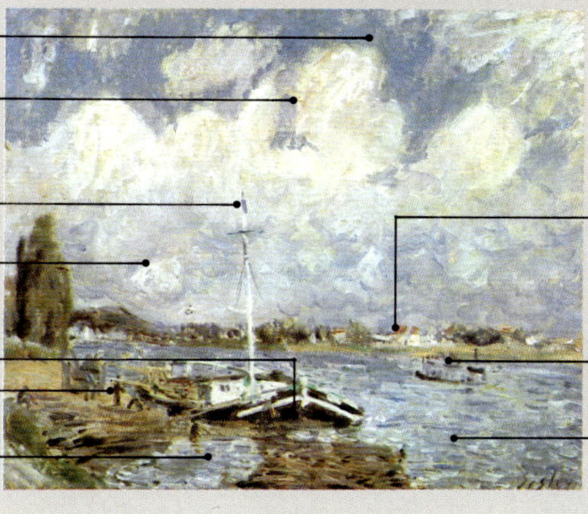


*Few Impressionist works were actually painted* alla prima *or at a single sitting. However, this loosely sketched picture is one example of the method. The pale, creamy ground shows through in many places among the colors of the paint layer, showing that there was no preparatory* ébauche *underneath. Sisley's rapid handling was essential to capture the fleeting effects, and also helps evoke them.*

in *Le Bois des Roches* (1880). At other times his compositions were more traditional, as here, where a low viewpoint and consequently a low horizon give a more conventional, almost panoramic appearance. However, the placing of water in the immediate foreground does serve the role of a visual barrier, discouraging the spectator from viewing the scene as a direct extension of real space, thus reinforcing a sense of the separate, pictorial space.

Sisley's distinctly visible, frenetic brushwork – although essentially form-following and descriptive – also affirms the flatness of the picture surface. His use of color shows both premixing and wet-in-wet slurring on the canvas itself. His palette is fairly limited, with the naturalistic greens and blues dominating in this river scape. Viridian predominates among the green mixtures, and the blue is probably cobalt. Black makes an appearance, broken and therefore made more colorful by the addition of blue, to describe the hull of the river barge. Bright accents of vermilion slurred with yellow attract the eye to the distant bank, bringing it forward visually, and also linking it with the similar red which appears in the left foreground, and amongst the darks of the center foreground jetty. From the size of the figures, Sisley appears to have selected a scene quite distanced from where he set up his easel.

Sisley's retiring nature and relatively isolated existence after 1880 probably contributed to his work remaining less acclaimed during his lifetime than that, for example, of the more aggressively business-like Monet. Sisley's work, Impressionist to the last, continued to be appreciated by a small circle of discerning collectors, although it was only after his death that rises in the price of his paintings began to reflect his abilities.

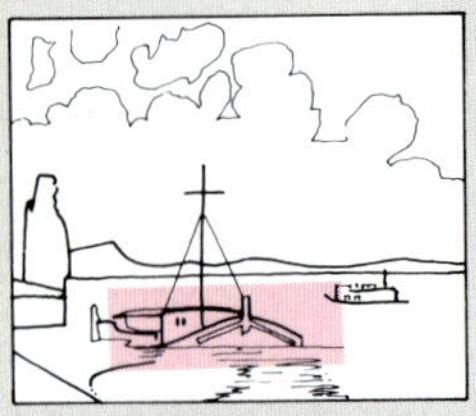

*White was used almost pure on the barge, and the darks may include black, but are more likely a colorful neutral mixture of hues including cobalt violet. The dark brownish hues of jetty and bank are also mixed and include greens and vermilion. The colors were mixed on the palette and added wet in wet on the surface.*

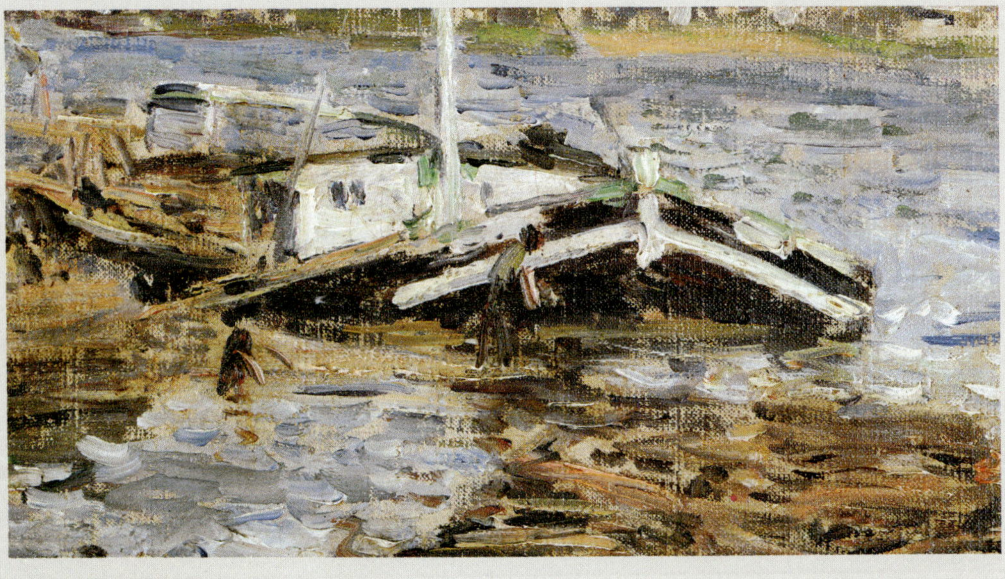

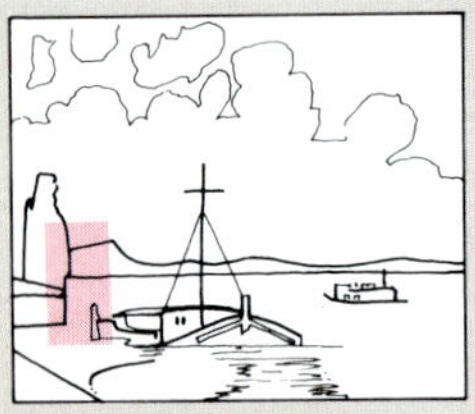

*Yellows, mainly yellow ochre, mixed with white dominate the sandy hues of the bank, with chrome and viridian greens for the foliage. Blue, white, viridian green and cobalt violet were probably mixed for the hill colors. The brushwork is varied, describing the different forms and textures of the objects depicted, adding life and a sense of captured movement.*

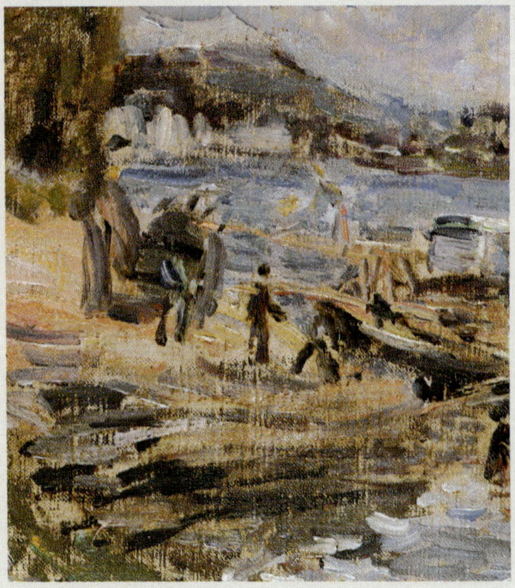

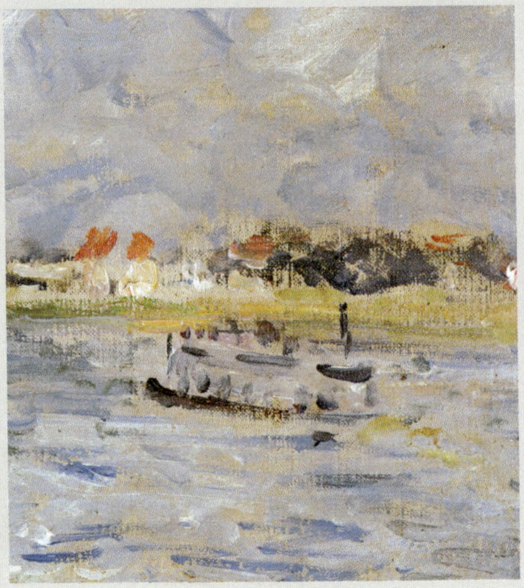

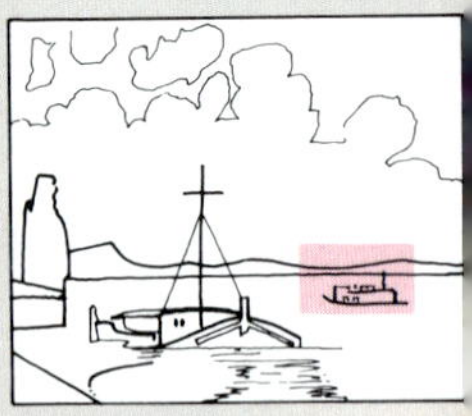

*The distant boat is summarized in a few rapid brushstrokes. Its hull is a single dragged sweep of the brush, which has caught on the grainy canvas texture, exposing the creamy ground below and creating a vibrant interplay between paint and ground. Chrome yellow and vermilion were used almost pure on the far riverbank.*

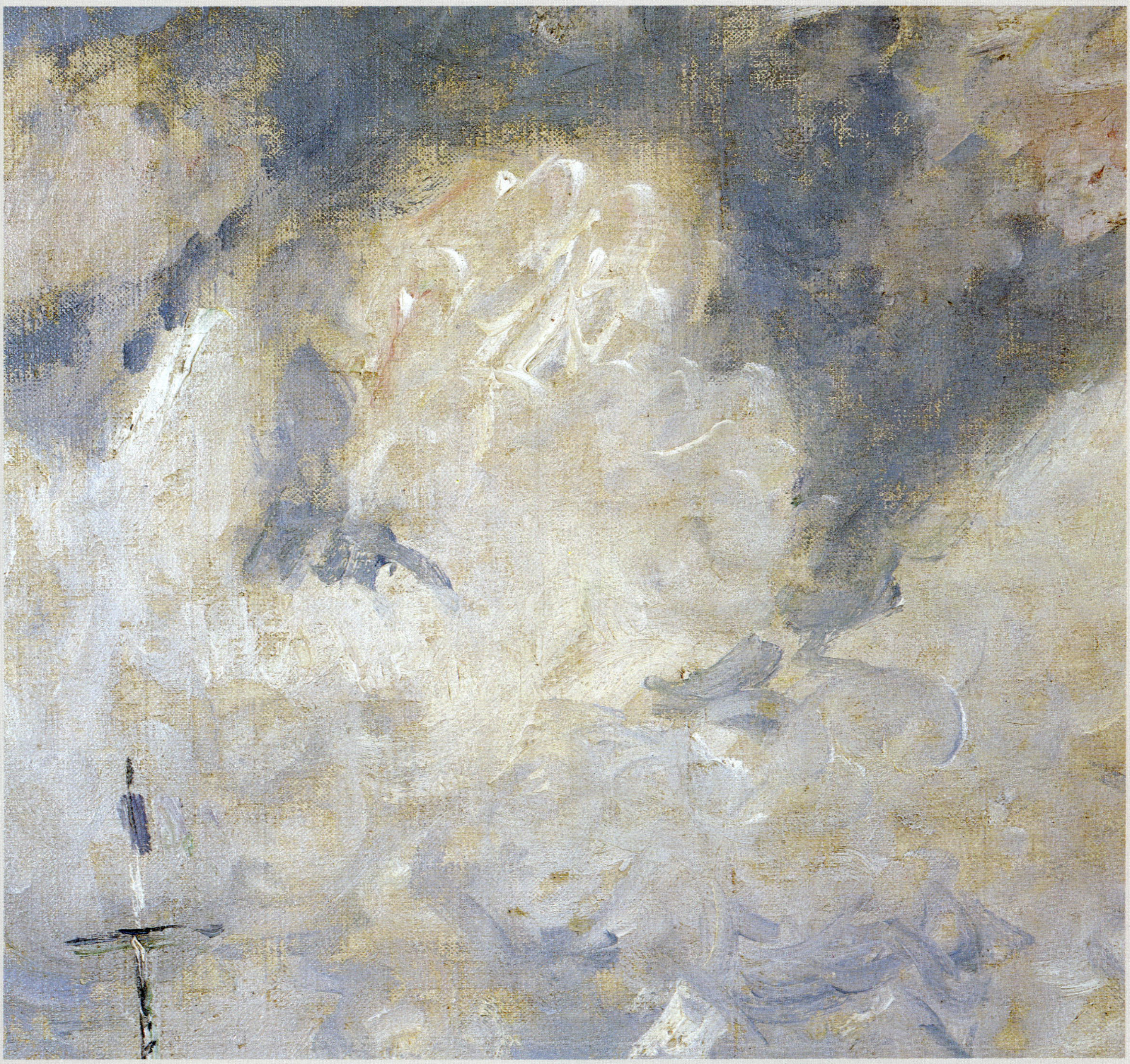

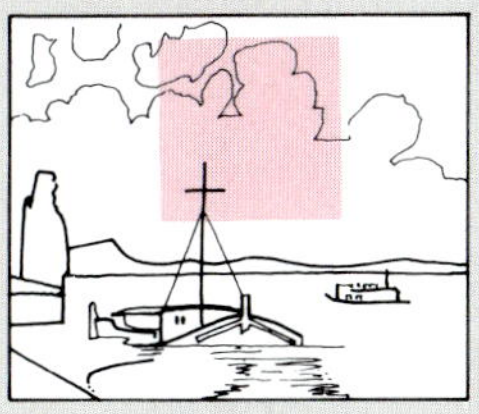

Actual size detail
*The rather dull, mat surface of this painting indicates that it has apparently never been varnished, in line with the preference of the Impressionists. Varnish darkens and eventually discolors the original hues in a painting, and gives an artificial gloss to the surface which many artists disliked. A mat paint surface is closer to the mat, opaque surfaces most often found in nature. A broad bristle brush was used to apply the blues and whites of the sky, over the grainy ordinary weight canvas with its creamy tinted commercial ground. The cream adds warmth which shows through among the blues, and a touch of vermilion was added to the whites to warm them further. The decisive strokes of the mast were added with a finer brush over the wet sky colors.*

# CLAUDE MONET

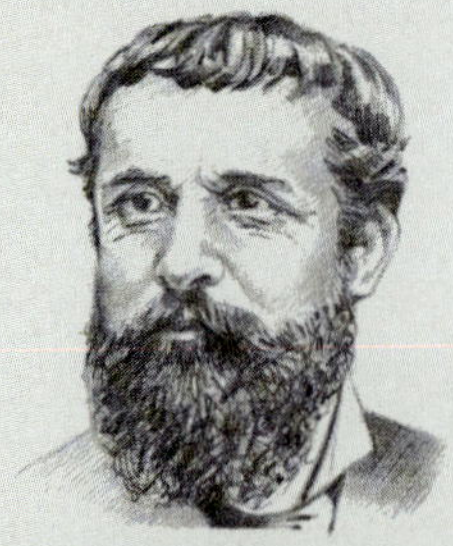

*Saint-Lazare Station/La Gare Saint-Lazare* (1877)
Oil on pale primed canvas
75cm X 104cm/29½in × 41⅓in

In the mid 1870s, Monet worked regularly at Argenteuil, which was close to the Seine and not far from Paris, to the north-west of the city. Alongside Renoir or Manet, or alone, Monet pursued his aims of recording his sensations of light and color in nature, slowly developing his expertise in his chosen method. Although in 1869 he had still been thinking in terms of studies outdoors for larger, possibly even studio-painted pictures, by the mid 1870s his main emphasis was upon works based solely on his visual experience outdoors, in which the unity of natural lighting could be retained.

At the second Impressionist group show of 1876, Monet showed 18 paintings, continuing his commitment with the others to find a viable alternative to the official Salon. The reasons why the Impressionists looked for alternative exhibition space were not just because they opposed the stranglehold of the Academy, but also because the Salon did not offer the kind of environment in which Impressionist paintings could be seen to advantage. The Salon had dark walls and somber lighting, and pictures were hung in rows right up to the ceiling. Most of the traditional Salon paintings were large-scale works and, with their somber light and shade, as well as their heavy, ornate gold frames, looked well in such surroundings. The Impressionists in general disliked the ornate gold frames in which Salon paintings were normally exhibited, and so they began using plain, white or pale tinted frames to set off their pictures more effectively.

Unlike the traditional Salon pieces, Impressionist paintings were generally intimate, and seen at their best in good natural daylight, preferably hung against neutral, pale wall coverings. Since most of their paintings were small in scale, intended to be hung on the walls of modern apartments, they were lost in the huge halls of the Salon.

In the Impressionist group exhibitions and one-man shows at dealers', the rooms were more appropriate in scale and the artists themselves could decide how their works were hung. In the Impressionist shows, no more than two rows of pictures were hung above each other, and the artists began to decorate the walls with colors which enhanced the color harmonies in their pictures.

The theme of the railway was, of course, a modern one in painting, but it had interested artists before the Impressionists. For instance, railway subjects had been suggested to Courbet as early as 1861 by his friend, the critic Champfleury. In 1874, Manet exhibited at the Salon a work called *The Railway*, but the picture showed only the iron railings which screened the street from Saint-Lazare Station below. The emphasis of Manet's composition was the two figures of a woman and child, apparently waiting for a train arrival. The background is obscured by steam rising from engines below. In 1876, Caillebotte chose the bridge over the Saint-Lazare railway tracks as the central theme of his *Pont de l'Europe*. However, the work focused not on the railway itself, but on the bridge with its passers-by, elegant strollers and one or two working people.

When Monet began his series of pictures of Saint-Lazare Station, he dealt not with the travelers or passers-by, but with the modern station itself, an industrial landscape filled with steam and broken sunlight. The cast iron and glass canopy of the station, within which Monet obtained permission to set up his easel, is light and delicate, its new architectural technology permitting a huge span with only thin spindly supports. All its members are fine and elegant, and its symmetrical construction made it perfect as a compositional foil for the light effects Monet portrayed.

Monet began work on this new subject early in 1877, when he was living close by in the rue d'Edimbourg, two minutes west of the station, on the opposite side of the tracks to where Manet lived. He was thus well placed to spend maximum time working in the station below. This work shows the station under full sunlight, the girders of the Pont de l'Europe spanning the middle distance of the composition. The artist faces almost due north, and the midday sunlight from the south bathes the modern apartment buildings which surround the Pont de l'Europe.

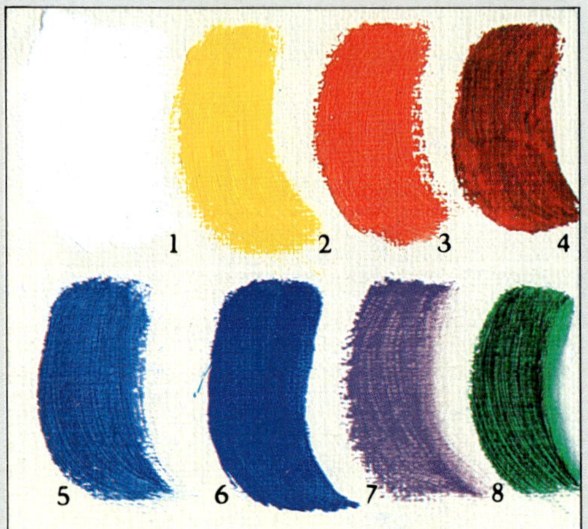


*Monet's palette for this painting probably comprised lead white* (1), *chrome yellows* (2), *vermilion* (3), *red alizarin lake* (4), *cobalt blue* (5), *probably ultramarine blue* (6), *cobalt violet* (7), *and probably viridian green* (8). *Black may also have been used.*

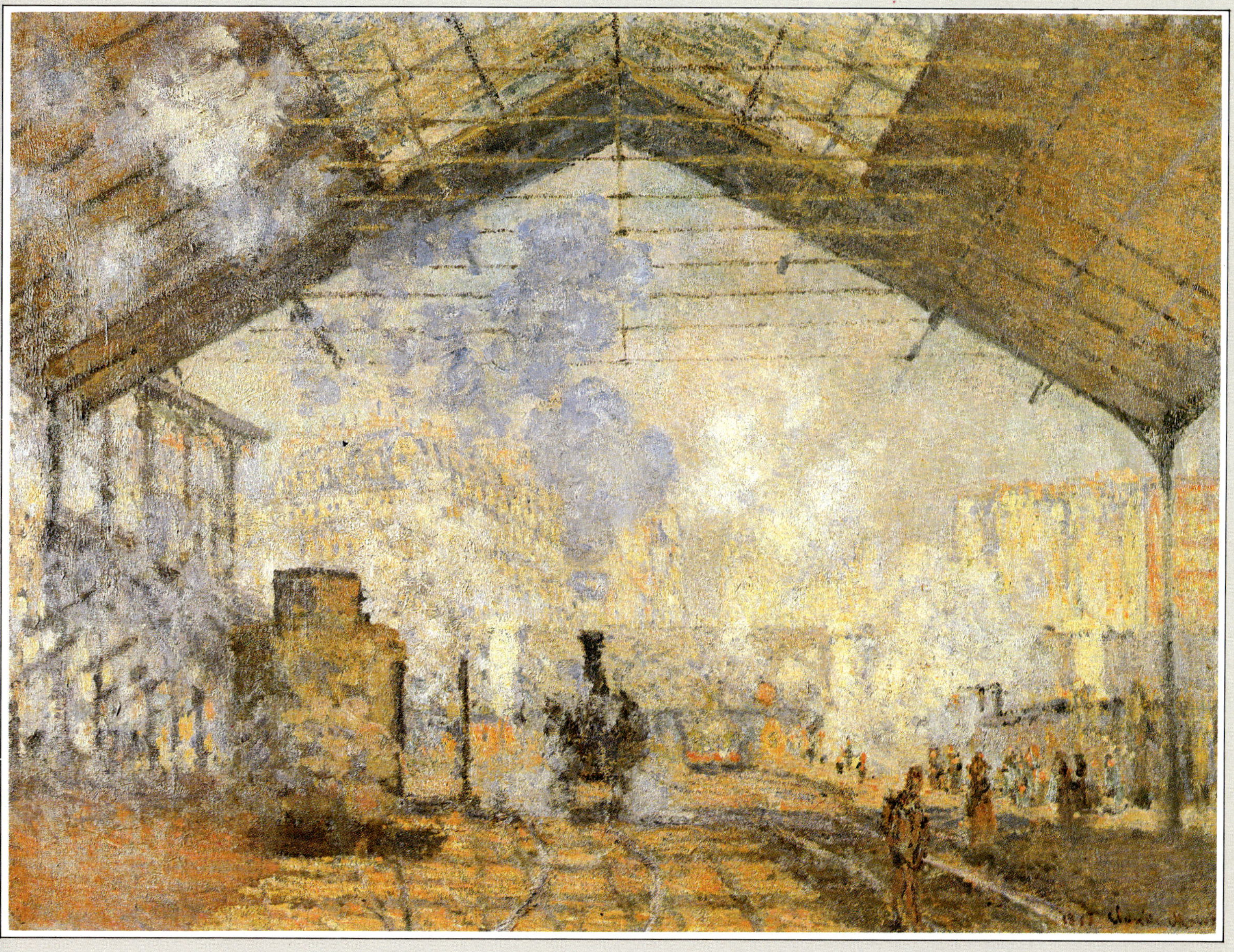

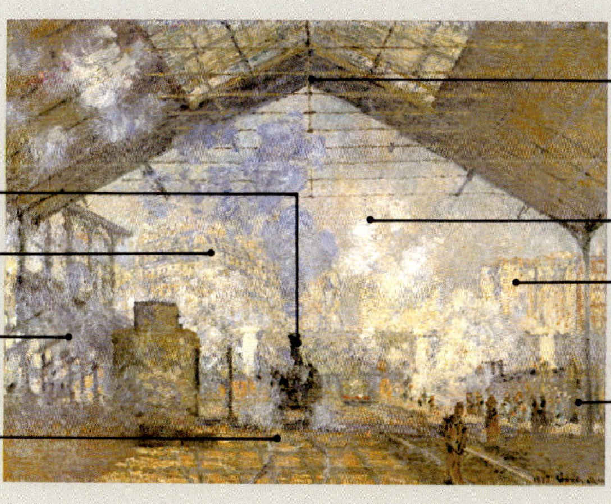


*Like Caillebotte and Manet during this same period, Monet painted several different views of modern Parisian subjects, the best known of which are his scenes of St Lazare station. He gained permission to work in the station itself and made the effects of light and color beneath the steam-filled canopy, the main subject of his paintings. The format of Monet's standard vertical landscape 40 canvas relates well to the grid structure which underlies his composition.*

Monet has set up his easel so that this section of the station canopy balances symmetrically across his composition, creating a strong formal structure. The point of the roof and the middle strut of the retaining grid of iron bars below, are made to coincide, and placed in the dead center of the composition to give a vertical axis to the pictorial structure. The main engine, shown coming towards the spectator, is placed just left of center to avoid overemphasis on the symmetry. The cool light inside the canopy has turned the train's steam a brilliant pale blue by contrast to the warmth of the sunlight outside. But warmth from the sun pouring through the window in the roof, casts golden sunlight on the tracks in the foreground, and that warmth is picked up and mingled with the blues in the shadows to left and right, and under the roof itself.

This half indoor, half outdoor scene thus provides an excellent subject for analyzing the varied effects of sunlight and shadow. The striking contrast between the more subdued hues of the foreground emphasizes the brilliant luminosity of the full-face sunlight seen through the frame of the canopy. Richer, deeper contrasts of warm and cool colors play against the paler, more dazzling tints of the background, producing a harmony of varied tones within the broad color axis blue to orange-yellow.

The paint layer itself is typical of Monet's work. It is exploiting opaque colors, made lighter and more light-scattering by the addition of lead white, and it is liberally applied, forming an almost unbroken skin obscuring the pale ground beneath. As a result the ground color, although evidently pale, is hard to identify with certainty. The ground colors most commonly used by Monet in the 1870s were pale gray, putty, oatmeal and white. The paint consistency is stiff and chalky, with colors mainly applied wet over dry. However, there is some slurring together of colors, such as the blues and white of the central cloud of steam. The effects of colored light on moisture in the atmosphere – whether steam, mist, fog or heat haze – fascinated Monet throughout his life, and provided him with an excellent vehicle for the study of light refraction through the droplets of moisture. Under such conditions the light is often shattered into its component rainbow elements, the drops of moisture serving as myriad prisms filling the atmosphere, and resulting in more colorful, scintillating effects of light.

Monet worked rapidly and enthusiastically on this group of pictures, of which seven were already finished in time for the third Impressionist show in April 1877, where this canvas was exhibited. It was bought by Gustave Caillebotte, who left his collection to the Louvre.

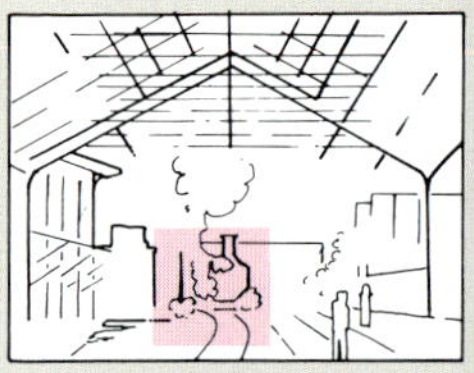

Actual size detail
*Black may have been added to the dark blues to give the engine color, and the paint is mainly built up slowly in layers applied wet over dry. This dragging allows earlier colors to show through, aiding the effects of vibrant, dazzling light and blurring of forms. Vermilion and chrome yellow were mixed for the orange touches. In the dragged creamy whites depicting the stone pillar of the Pont de l'Europe, dirt and discolored varnish have collected in the grooves of the impasto. This indicates the degree of color distortion caused overall by old varnish.*

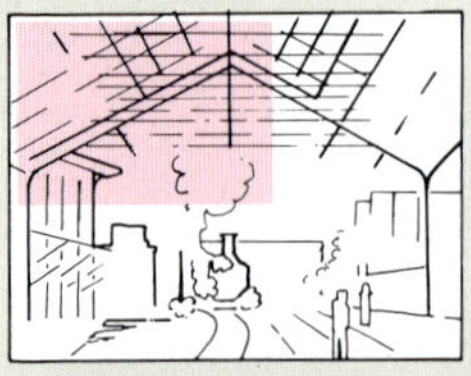

*Caked and loaded dryish colors build up to form a crusty, irregular paint surface. This physically breaks up and scatters the light bouncing off the surface, enhancing the illusion of light represented in the picture. Much of the dragged handling is applied wet over dry. A lively contrast is created between warm and cool hues, and between the stark symmetry of the station canopy and the flamboyant curls depicting the rising steam and smoke. Brushwork mainly echoes form, following planes and describing varied textures in rich paint. Colors are mostly mixed. For example, the blues and yellows were simply mixed with white to give luminous pastel-like tints evoking light.*

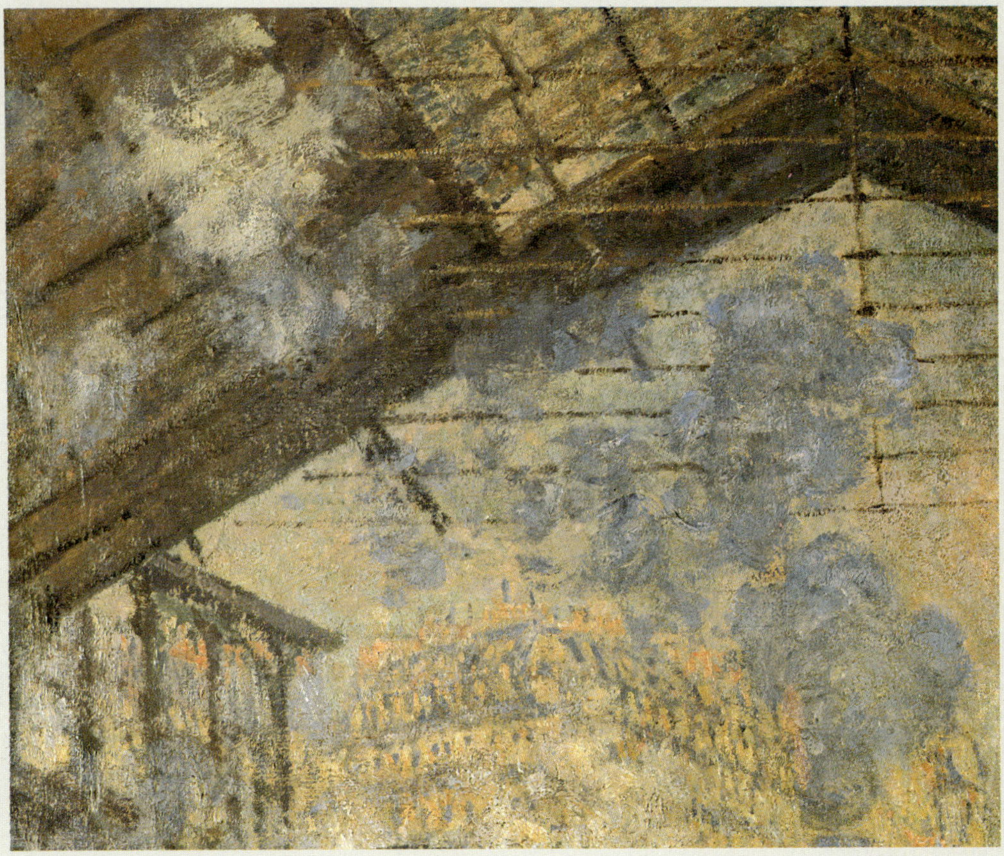

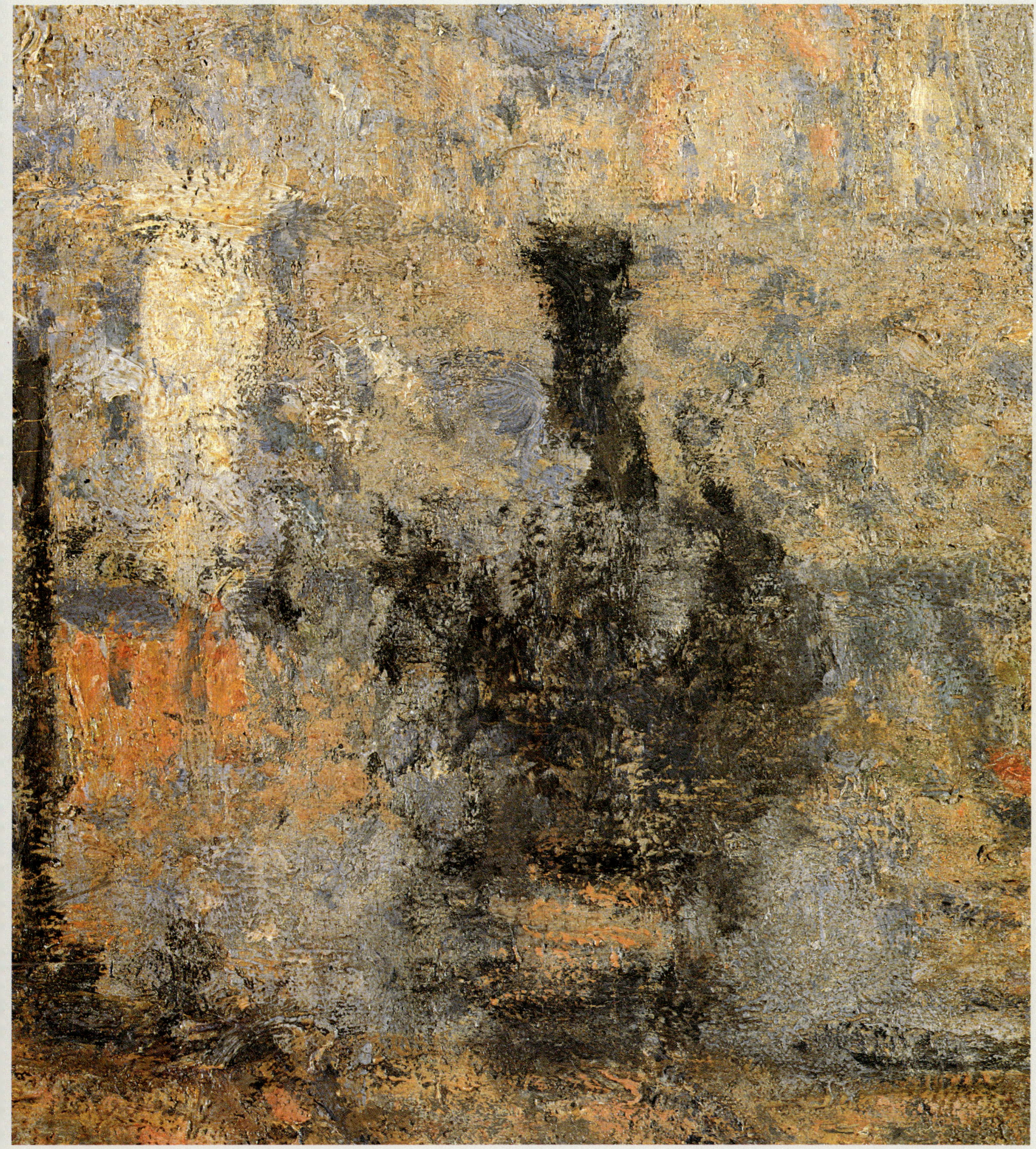

# CAMILLE PISSARRO

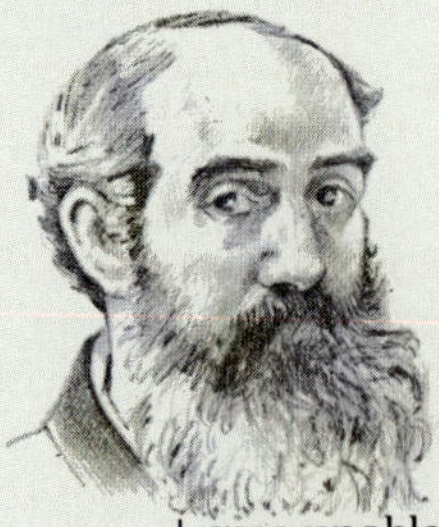

## *Portrait of Madame Pissarro Sewing near a Window/ Portrait de Madame Pissarro cousant* (*c* 1877-1879)
### Oil on twill weave, yellowish-gray primed canvas
### 54cm × 45cm/21¼in × 17¾in

During the Franco-Prussian war of 1870, Pissarro, who was a Danish national, as he had been born in the Danish West Indies, was unable to fight for France. So he fled with his family, first to Brittany, then to London, where they stayed in the suburb of Norwood in Surrey until the end of June 1871. During his stay in London, Pissarro, like Monet, was introduced by the landscapist Charles Daubigny (1817–1879), to the dealer Paul Durand-Ruel. He, like them, was a refugee from the war in France. Thus began the relationship between artist and dealer which was to provide Pissarro, like his colleagues, with vital support during the meager years before Impressionism was widely accepted.

On his return to France, Pissarro discovered that his house in Louveciennes, north of Versailles and to the west of Paris, had been requisitioned by the invading Prussians, and that most of the family's belongings, and the majority of his previous 20 years' artistic production had been destroyed. Only 40 out of approximately 1,500 paintings were saved. For the next 10 years, Pissarro was based north-west of Paris at Pontoise, and, in October 1878, he took the *pied-à-terre* studio at rue des Trois-Frères in Paris where this portrait of Madame Pissarro may have been painted. In November that year, their fourth son, Ludovic-Rodolphe was born in Paris. Although this portrait has traditionally been dated to around 1877, it must date from 1878–1879 if it was executed in the Paris studio, and the style of short, delicate strokes of myriad colors which are close in tone is more characteristic of the later date.

The composition of the portrait is strong and striking. Madame Pissarro's figure is cropped, and placed close to the picture surface, the wall and decorative ironwork of the balcony pushing her close to the viewer. This creates a shallow pictorial space which is not alleviated by the vista through the window, as the curls of the ironwork attract the eye and prevent it penetrating into depth. The outdoor scene is intentionally blurred, and handled with brushstrokes the same size as the interior, which again contradicts depth and recession.

The linear structure of the background is reminiscent of Degas' portrait compositions, in which the figure of the sitter was often anchored tautly within the pictorial space by interlocking horizontals and verticals. Pissarro and Degas worked together making etchings during 1879, and Pissarro used the printing facilities in Degas' studio. In the portrait, Madame Pissarro's head is placed centrally, against the vertical of the window frame which divides the composition into two almost equal halves. The horizontal bar of the balcony rail is echoed by the finer rails of the ironwork below, all of which combine with the strong vertical to create a grid against which the curves of figure are set. The intersections of horizontal and vertical lines are hidden behind the figure, locking it into place in the composition. The rounded forms of her face and hand are echoed in the curving spirals of the ironwork, further strengthening the decorative surface pattern.

The painting was executed on a standard format canvas, a portrait 10, with a single layer of commercial yellowish-gray priming which leaves the canvas texture apparent. The decisive pattern of the twill weave, a diagonal texture which goes from bottom left to top right, is actively exploited among the marks of the brush in the stiffish, chalky paint. The canvas weave is particularly evident at the juncture of blocks of color, and at the contours of forms where the paint is most thinly applied. It builds up more thickly toward the central areas, for example the swelling forms of the face which are the most thickly painted areas, while the paint is thinnest as the form recedes towards the contour lines. This helps suggest round form. The texture of the canvas also enhances the sense of flesh texture, where it is allowed to show through the paint layer.

The pale gray priming, warm in hue, plays an active role harmonizing the broken, muted colors of the paint layer. At the bottom center of the picture, the priming color shows clearly among the loosely added touches of dragged paint. Here the ground stands for the fabric which Madame Pissarro is sewing, and its texture is represented by the texture of the twill weave beneath.

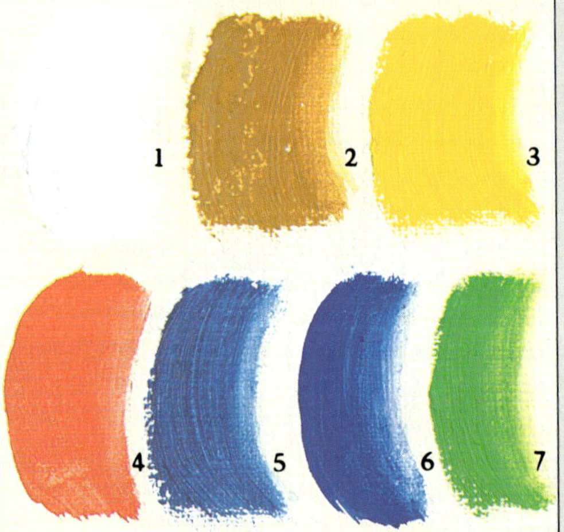


*Pissarro's palette for this work probably included lead white (1), possibly yellow ochre (2), chrome yellows (3), vermilion (4), cobalt (5) or ultramarine blue (6) and probably chrome green (7).*

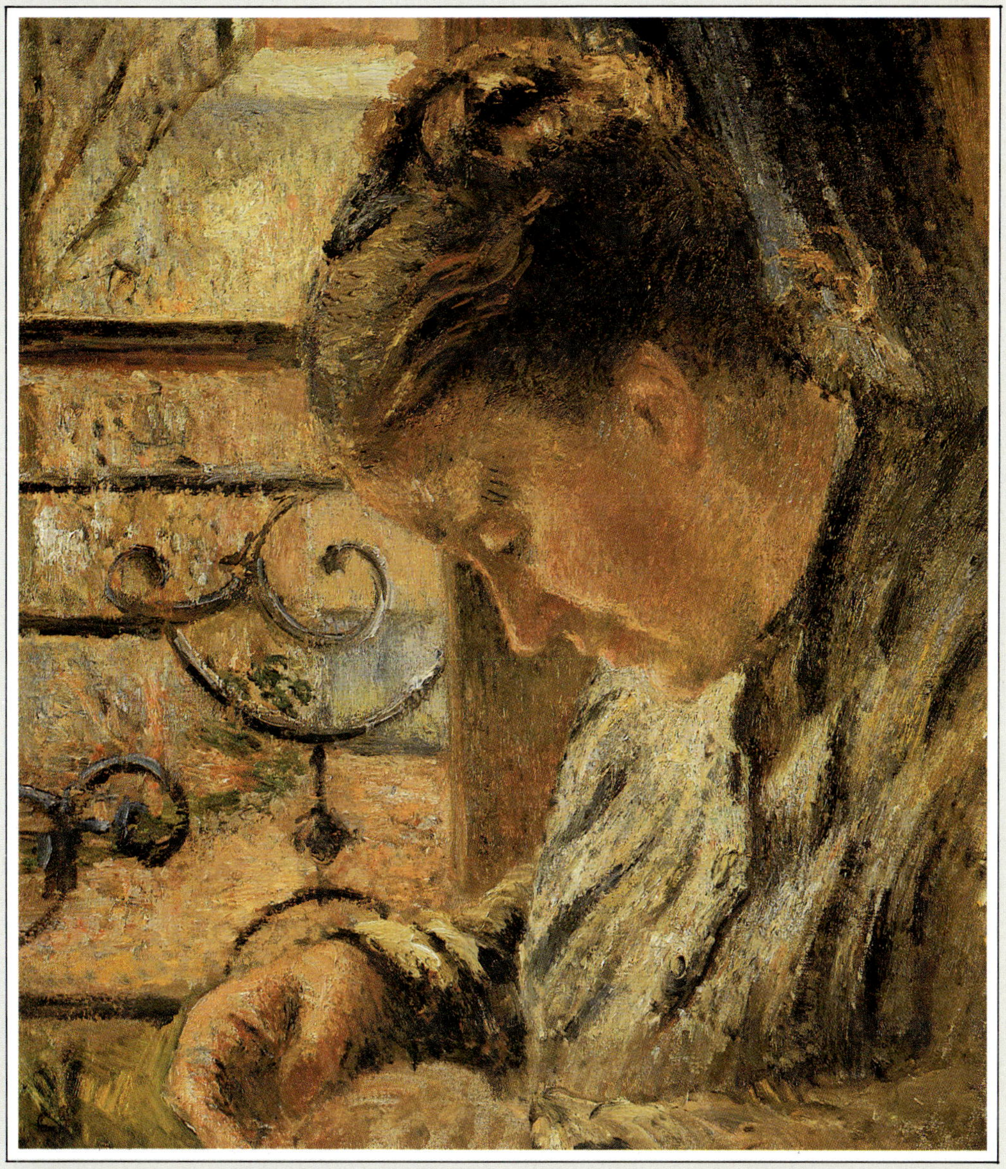

*The quiet intimacy of this portrait of the artist's wife is emphasized both by her total absorption in her domestic work, and by the cropped character of the composition. This gives a close-up view of the sitter, pushing her towards the picture surface. It is a tightly organized compositional design, which relates well to the squarish, portrait 12 canvas format chosen. Like so many of Pissarro's paintings from the early 1870s on, it plays on the tension between pictorial space and flatness. The sensuous curves of the figure are echoed by the curls in the ironwork of the balcony, and both are contained within the broader grid of intersecting vertical and horizontal lines. Pissarro's brushwork has become relatively delicate and regular, often forming into hatched parallel patterns which follow the forms. But the richness of handling and color on the surface tend also to contradict strictly naturalistic qualities. A balance of warm and cool, light and dark colors is achieved here. Light touches pervade the shadow areas, and vice versa. Similarly, warm hues are added to enliven parts dominated by cool hues. This also gives a sense of the pervasive vivacity of the natural light which floods from the nearby window.*

Pissarro regularly used unusual canvas weaves in the 1860s and 1870s, experimenting with the textural and compositional effects they could be used to create. In *Hoar Frost* of 1873, which was exhibited at the first Impressionist exhibition of 1874, Pissarro showed how a twill weave could enhance the impression of rough clods of earth in a landscape painting. In this painting the weave also travels diagonally from bottom left to top right, although the composition is a horizontal rather than a vertical one as in *Madame Pissarro*. The direction of the twill weave, like that of his *Hillside at l'Hermitage*, also of 1873, is used in *Hoar Frost* to stress the lines of the composition, which also move mainly from lower left to upper right. It is evident that Pissarro was pushing further his experiments with flattening compositional designs and surfaces, counterbalanced by naturalistic brushwork, as the decade progressed. In the portrait of Madame Pissarro, the brushwork still follows form and is descriptive, but it has become more uniform in size and texture. This development looks forward to later works like *Apple Picking* of 1886.

Pissarro posed his wife against a window to create a *contrejour* or back lighting. However, the figure is not reduced to a stark silhouette, as in Degas' comparable studies. Contrasts of light and dark are kept to a minimum, and, although the fall of light adds structure to the form, it is nevertheless pervasive and the shadows colorful with reflected light.

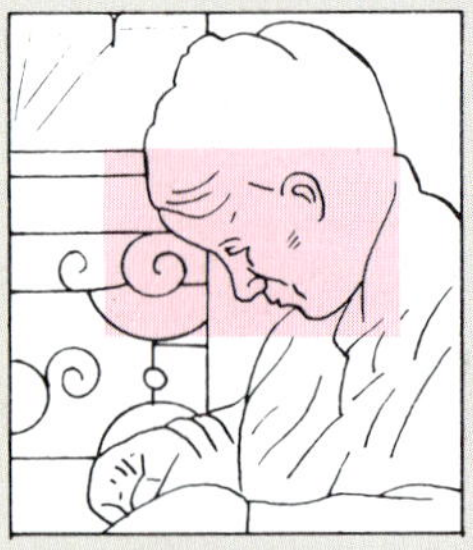

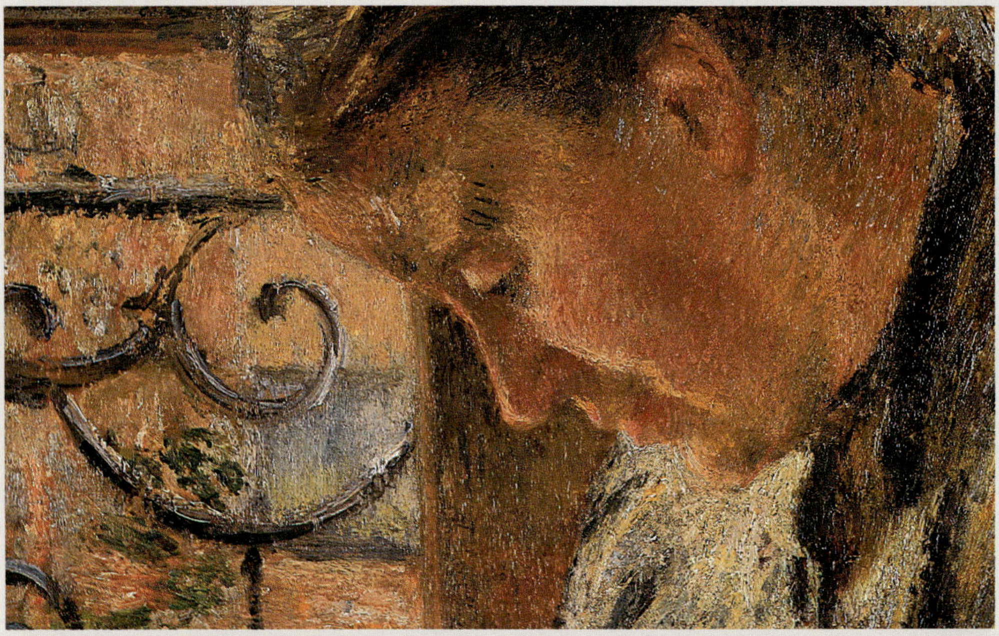

*The decorative texture of the diagonal twill weave shows at the contours, enhancing the textures. The paint on the face is loaded and stiff, built up in tiny, often regular touches with a fine bristle brush. Brushstrokes define form and varied texture. They include long strokes for the railings, and small colored accents on the face, like the dark blueish touches above the eye.*

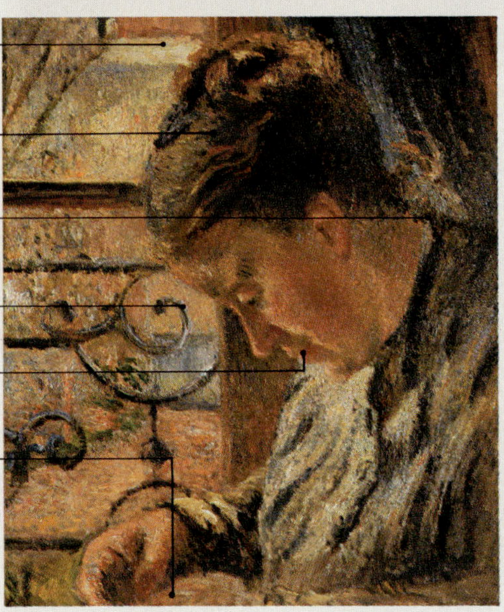

Twill canvas texture exaggerated by dragged color

Fine detailed accents in vermilion, applied wet over dry

Delicate hatched brush strokes

Colors slurred together wet in wet

Twill canvas texture exposed at contours where paint thinnest

Warm gray ground left to stand for linen fabric on which Mme. Pissarro works

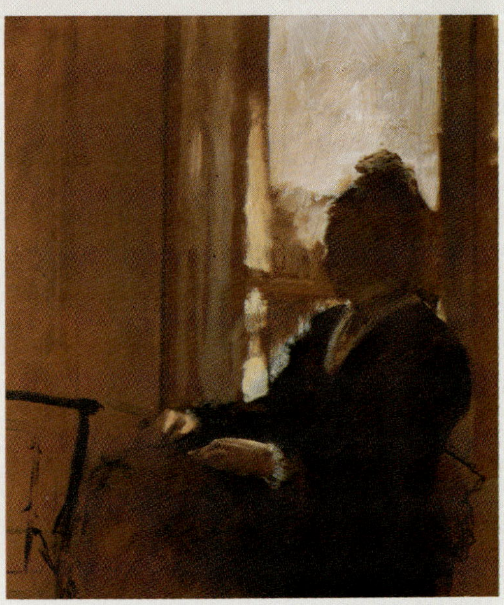

*This detail from Degas' study of a* Woman against a Window *(1871-1872) makes an interesting comparison with Pissarro's portrait. Degas' work is on a specially made support of reddish paper laid down on canvas. This provides a darker, more absorbent and smoother surface than that used by Pissarro. Degas' work is on a standard format vertical landscape 12 support, which relates well to the dominant verticals in his composition. Degas used dilute oils, and strong contrasts of light and shade in an almost monochrome tonal palette.*

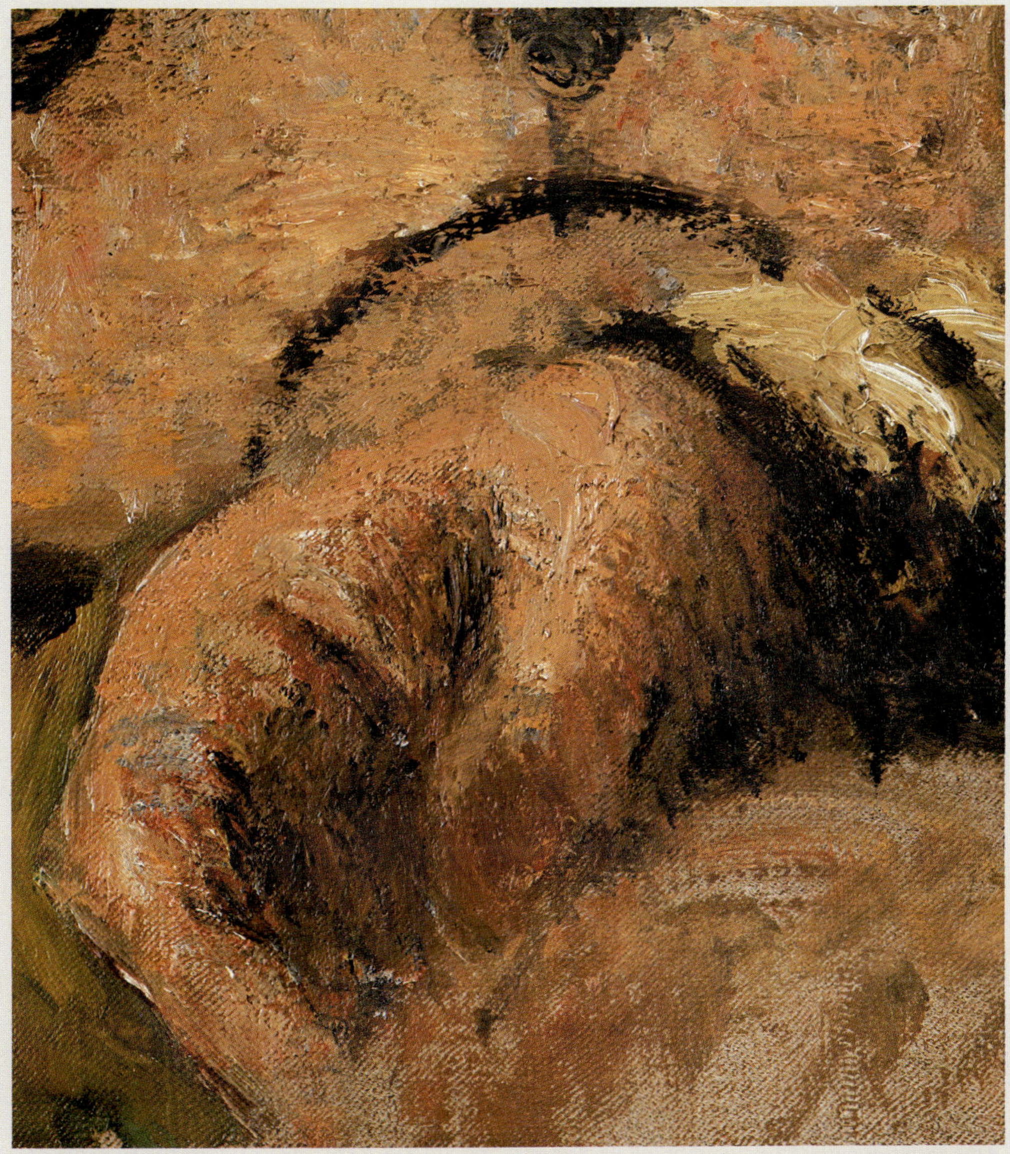

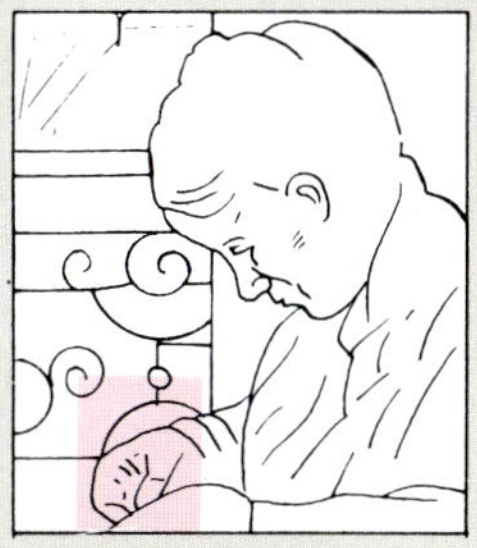

Actual size detail
*The warm, yellowish gray ground is visible here. It is a commercial ground applied in a single thin layer which leaves the texture of the diagonal twill weave exposed. Although the canvas weave has been obliterated over much of this richly loaded surface, it has influenced the paint texture everywhere, as successive layers of stiff dragged color have been built up over it. In this detail, it was left almost uncovered, the pale gray of the priming standing for the dull colored fabric which Mme. Pissarro is sewing. The canvas texture, too, is used to indicate the feel of the fabric represented. Where it is exposed, the ground shows the results of abrasion which has worn the color off the raised canvas nodes, leaving speckles of darker linen support color peppered over the surface. Pissarro has contrasted the fairly richly dragged and slurred colors on the hand with the thin dry rubbed color enlivening the depicted fabric.*

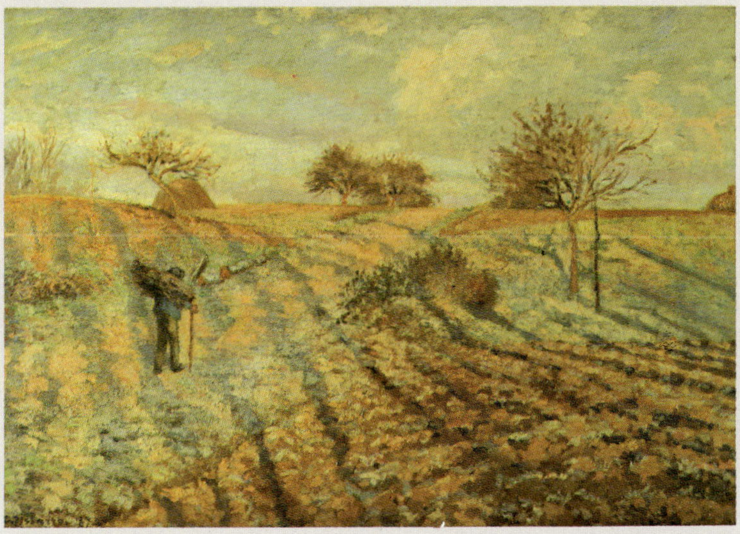

*Pissarro's* Hoar Frost *(1873), exhibited at the first Impressionist show of 1874, shows how the artist used twill canvas in a landscape painting. Executed on an elongated format standard vertical marine 30, the twill texture travels from bottom left to top right, following the diagonal of the pathway. Balancing this diagonal sweep are the lines of cast shadow moving from lower right to upper left. A contemporary critic disapproved of Pissarro's inclusion in his composition of shadows from trees located outside the picture. This novel device shows that the early morning sun was falling full-face onto his subject from behind the artist, and the blueish, light filled shadows were probably cast by leafless poplar trees. The flat light, pattern of crossing diagonals and the high view looking down on the scene create a decorative surface pattern which denies spatial effects.* Hoar Frost *has a dirty layer of yellowed varnish which gives a yellow cast to all the colors.*

# GUSTAVE CAILLEBOTTE

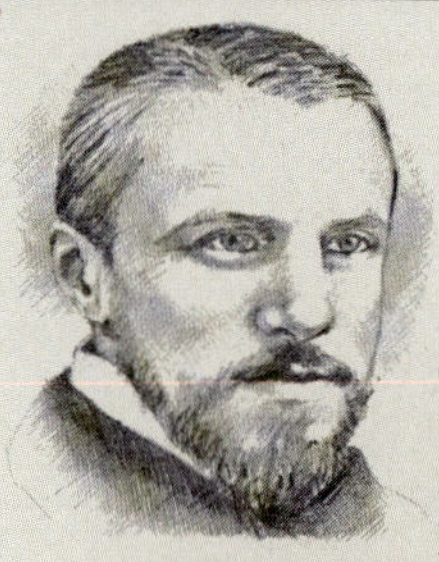

*Paris, A Rainy Day — Intersection of the rue de Turin and the rue de Moscou/Temps de pluies à Paris* (1877)
Oil on white primed canvas (study)
54cm × 65cm/21¼in × 25⅗in

Gustave Caillebotte has unjustly been remembered more as a collector of the works of his Impressionist colleagues than as a painter in his own right. In his late teens, Caillebotte, son of a wealthy textile manufacturer, lived in a modern house which his father had built sometime in the mid 1860s in rue Miromesnil. This was in the new residential quarter of Paris, a few streets west of Saint-Lazare Station, with its huge bridge spanning the railway tracks. The Pont de l'Europe was one of the engineering triumphs of the Second Empire of 1852 to 1870, and six of the streets in the area converged onto it. It was one of the subjects chosen by Caillebotte for his series of major paintings on the theme of the modern city. Caillebotte was therefore depicting subjects within a stone's throw of his family home, which were all new streets, buildings and services constructed within his own lifetime.

Brought up in the aftermath of the 1848 revolution and the upheaval of the transformation of Paris during the Second Empire, Caillebotte trained first as a lawyer. Only after military service during the Franco-Prussian War of 1870 did he turn to painting, training at the Ecole des Beaux-Arts and in the studio of Léon Bonnat (1834–1922), a successful Salon painter who, in 1874, probably introduced him to Degas. This fateful meeting gave Caillebotte access to the whole group of independent artists, with whom he began exhibiting in 1876.

At the third Impressionist exhibition of 1877, Caillebotte showed three major paintings depicting life on the modern streets of the quarter near Saint-Lazare Station. These were *The Pont de l'Europe* (1876), *The House Painters* (1877) and *Paris, Rainy Day*. *Rainy Day* shows the intersection of the rue de Moscou and the rue de Turin, on the rue de Leningrad. This runs from the Saint-Lazare Station at its south-west end to the Place Clichy, painted by Renoir in 1879–1880, at its north-east end. All these early compositions were large in scale, but *Rainy Day* was by far the largest, and most ambitiously monumental, the final canvas measuring over 2 meters (7 feet) long by 3 meters (10 feet) wide. Unlike Degas' earlier city view, *Place de la Concorde* (1873), in which apparently haphazard cropping of figures gives an air of the snapshot, a glimpsed moment in time, Caillebotte's picture has a quality of frozen grandeur that looks forward to Seurat's huge works *Bathing at Asnières* (1883–1884) and *Grand Jatte* (1884–1886).

All three city scapes were based on a linear geometry, and on perspective studies of the sites in question. The linear framework of *Rainy Day* is based on a cross. The central vertical line runs through the lamppost and its reflection, the horizontal cuts through the eye level of the figures and the bases of the buildings, dividing the composition into four equal sections. The framework is less precise in the painted study than in the final oil, for in the study the lamppost is marginally off center, to the right. Thus Caillebotte has adjusted the composition to fit his structural design. The proportions of the study are squarer than the final, specially made canvas, which is more elongated. This provides the extra width needed for the expansion of the right half of the composition necessary to place the lamppost centrally. A number of drawings survive to confirm the calculation Caillebotte brought to this picture, including the complex linear framework which incorporates two sets of proportions – the 1:2 ratio in the cross structure, and also the 5:8 ratio of the classical Golden Section.

Caillebotte's study for *Rainy Day* is closer in style to his more overtly Impressionist work, which dates from after this series of city scapes. The procedures he adopted for the city scapes, with careful preparatory drawings, perspective studies and oil sketches, was characteristic of the methods recommended by the Ecole, where he had so recently trained.

In the later 1870s, he turned away from the rigorous precision which governed the production of these early works. His later freedom of touch and broader, more colorful handling, are already apparent in the *Rainy Day* study. Colors, which became more muted and broken in the final picture, were still fresh and pure in the study. Blues and yellows dominate his palette, the yellow in this case representing not the warmth of sunlight but the sickly colored light from the thundery sky. The blues are the misty blues of rain-obscured distances.

Colors are used relatively pure, or mixed with white to give the pale tints of the background. They are scumbled on thinly in places, such as on the figures, and then worked over in thicker, undiluted paint. Outlines were roughly indicated, the colors varying according to the local colors of the scene. Thus a pale sandy color appears among the wet cobblestones, and darker browns and blue-grays were used to indicate the figures. That

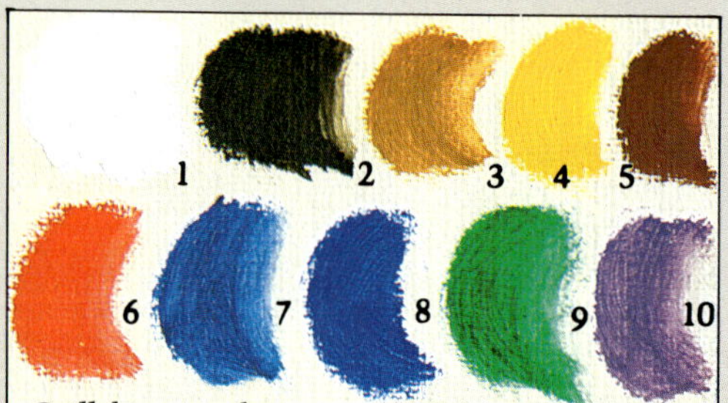


*Caillebotte's palette for this painting probably comprised lead white* (1), *possibly umber* (2), *yellow ochre* (3), *perhaps chrome yellow* (4), *red earth* (5) *or vermilion* (6), *cobalt* (7) *or ultramarine blue* (8), *viridian green* (9), *and probably cobalt violet* (10).

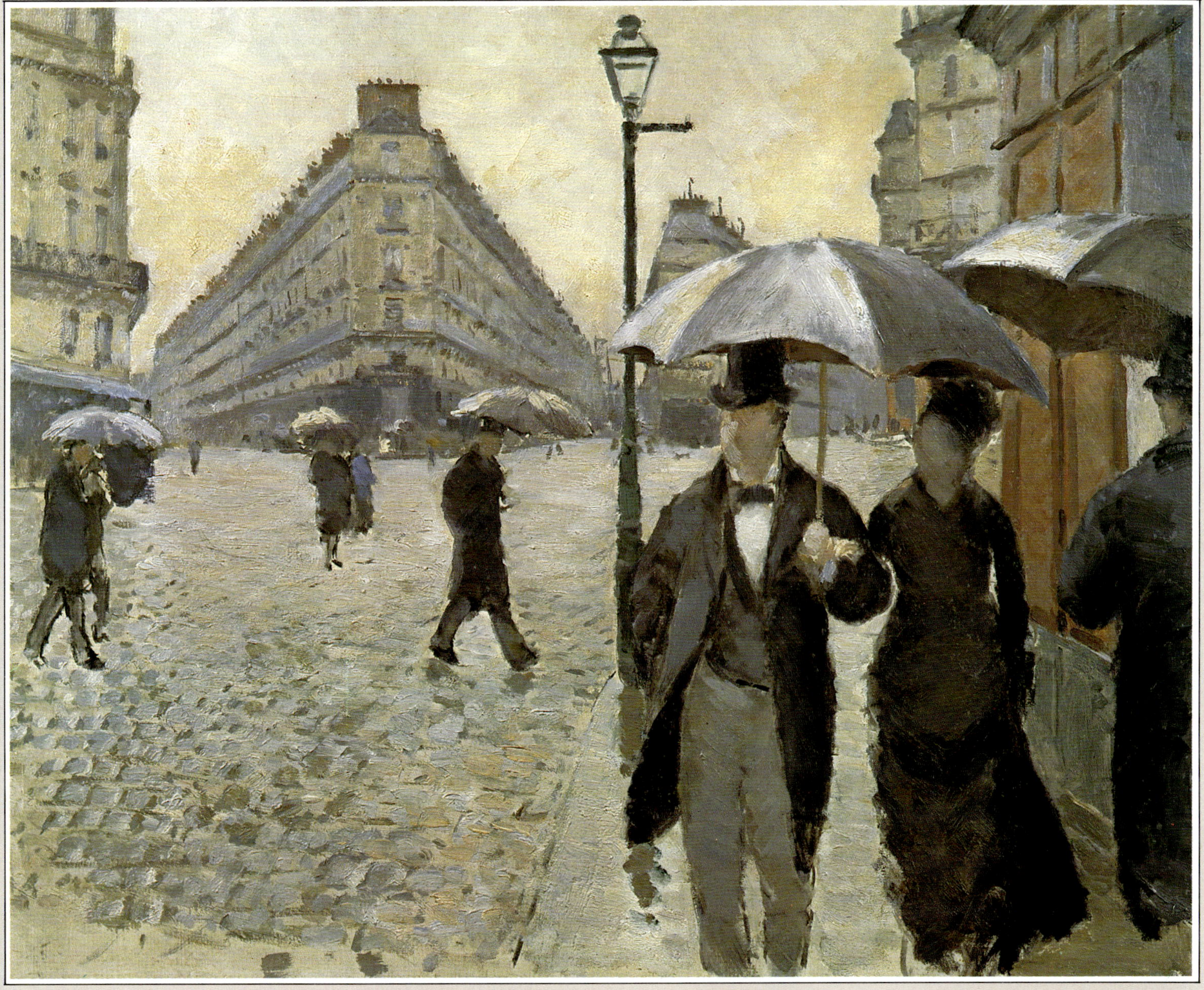

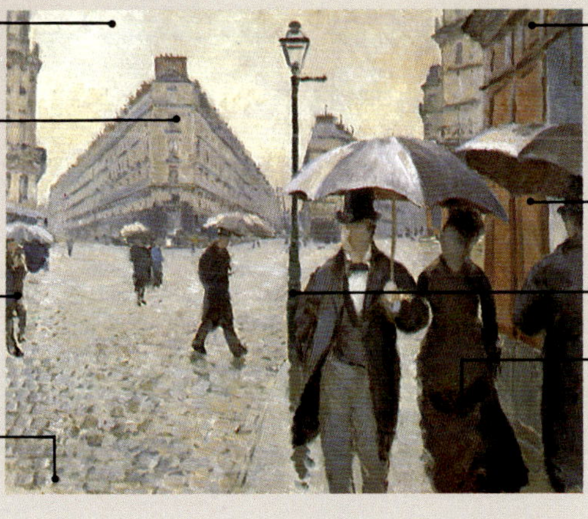


*In this painted sketch, Caillebotte planned the general composition and palette for his final version of the theme. The study may have been done out of doors, but was more likely a studio work composed after drawings and careful studies. Here the palette is fresher and the colors, though mixed, are brighter than in the finished work. The study is appropriately sketchy in its execution, with gaps left unpainted where the pale ground shows through.*

*This is the final work for which the sketch was made. Much larger than the preparatory oil, it measures 209 x 300cm (83¼ x 118½ in). The specially made canvas is more elongated in its proportions than the standard format portrait 15 canvas used for the sketch, allowing the artist to give more breadth to the scene. Elements of the sketch – a strip all around the edge – were cropped from the final version to bring the scene forward and to tighten the carefully calculated compositional design. Several extra figures were added, most notably the two women in the distance to the right of the lamppost. The finish here is much tighter and crisper.*

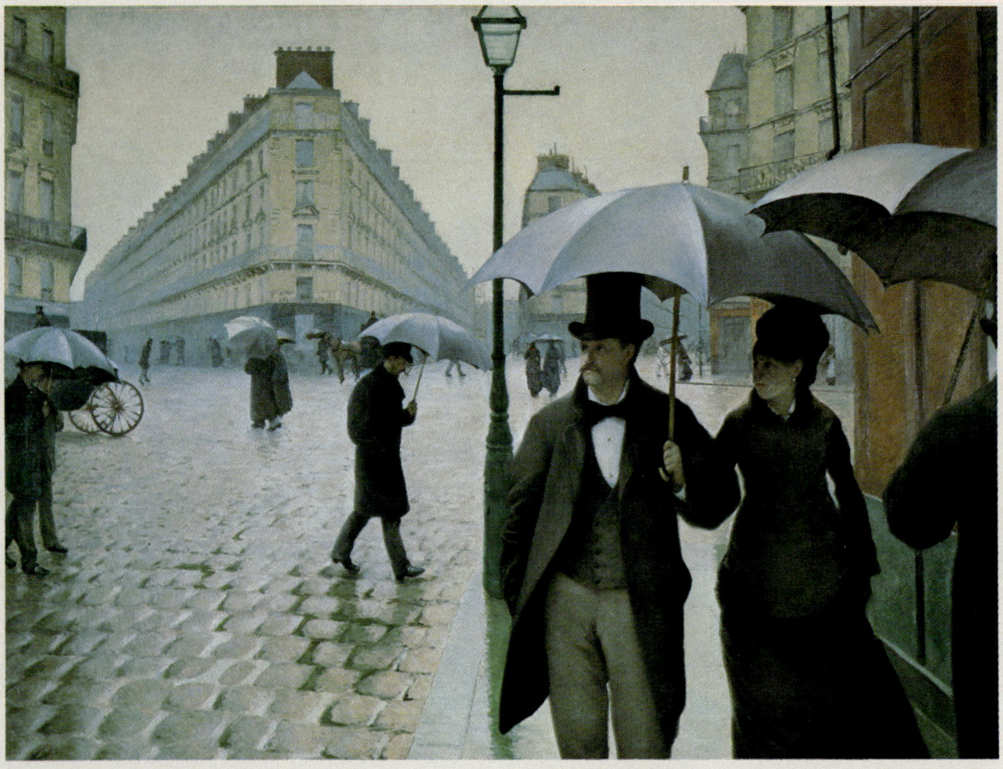

key compositional feature, the modern lamppost, was painted in vivid viridian green, mixed with white to make it brighter and opaque. The overall balance of tints – pale in the left half of the picture, darker and richer in the right – is more striking in the study than in the final composition, which gains in strength, but loses the colorful immediacy of the study.

Caillebotte's work has traditionally been overlooked in preference to that of better known figures like Manet, Degas and Monet. However, his style, until the late 1870s, was perhaps closer to that of Degas and Manet than that of Monet, but has a strength and originality which are unmistakeable. Because of his wealth, and his consequent role as financial supporter of many of his Impressionist friends during the 1870s, Caillebotte's stature as a painter has, until recently, tended to be underestimated. This was probably exacerbated by the fact that, in the early 1880s, after a very active decade of struggle on behalf of the movement in Paris, he retired almost completely from Parisian artistic circles. This move was not dissimilar to that of other painters like Monet and Cézanne at this time. Caillebotte, Degas and Pissarro were the most active in organizing the Impressionist shows during the 1870s. Disillusionment with their lack of success and with disagreements among the group's members may have caused Caillebotte's retreat. However, as a result, his later work was little known outside a small circle of friends and family, although he continued to paint until his death.

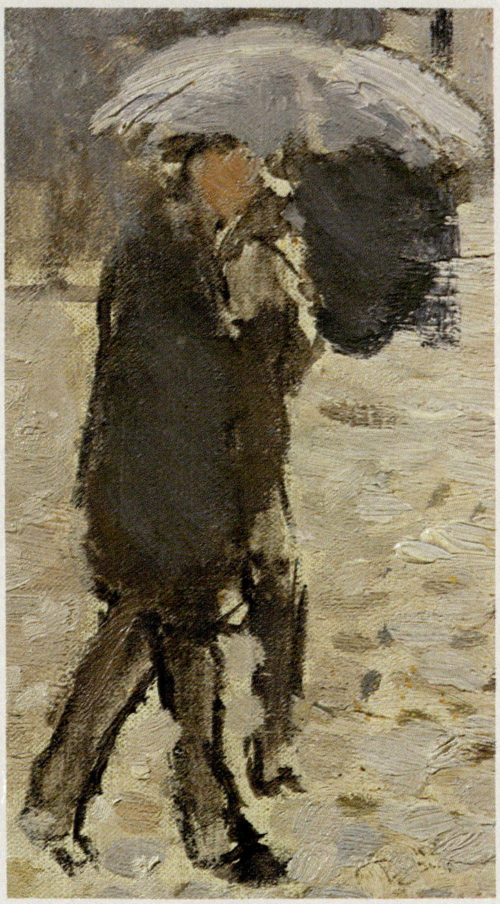

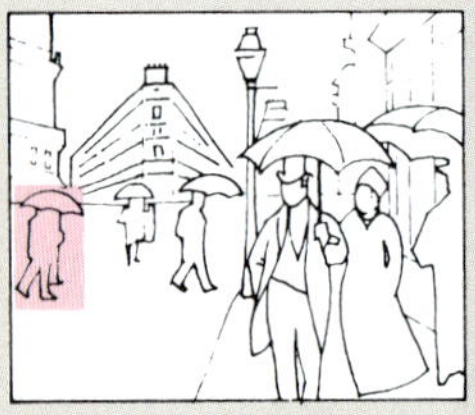

*These two little figures beneath the umbrella are painted with lively simplicity. Dark contours place their forms, which are then broadly filled in with stiffer, more opaque paint. Work on the rendering of the cobblestones was evidently done after the figures, because dabs of the pale color for the cobbles overlaps that on the figures. It also smudges over the line at the base of the distant building. The palette is dominated by varied yellow and blue hues in muted mixtures, but is enlivened by occasional touches of subdued reds. Most colors contain plenty of lead white, to give the effect of scattered atmospheric light.*

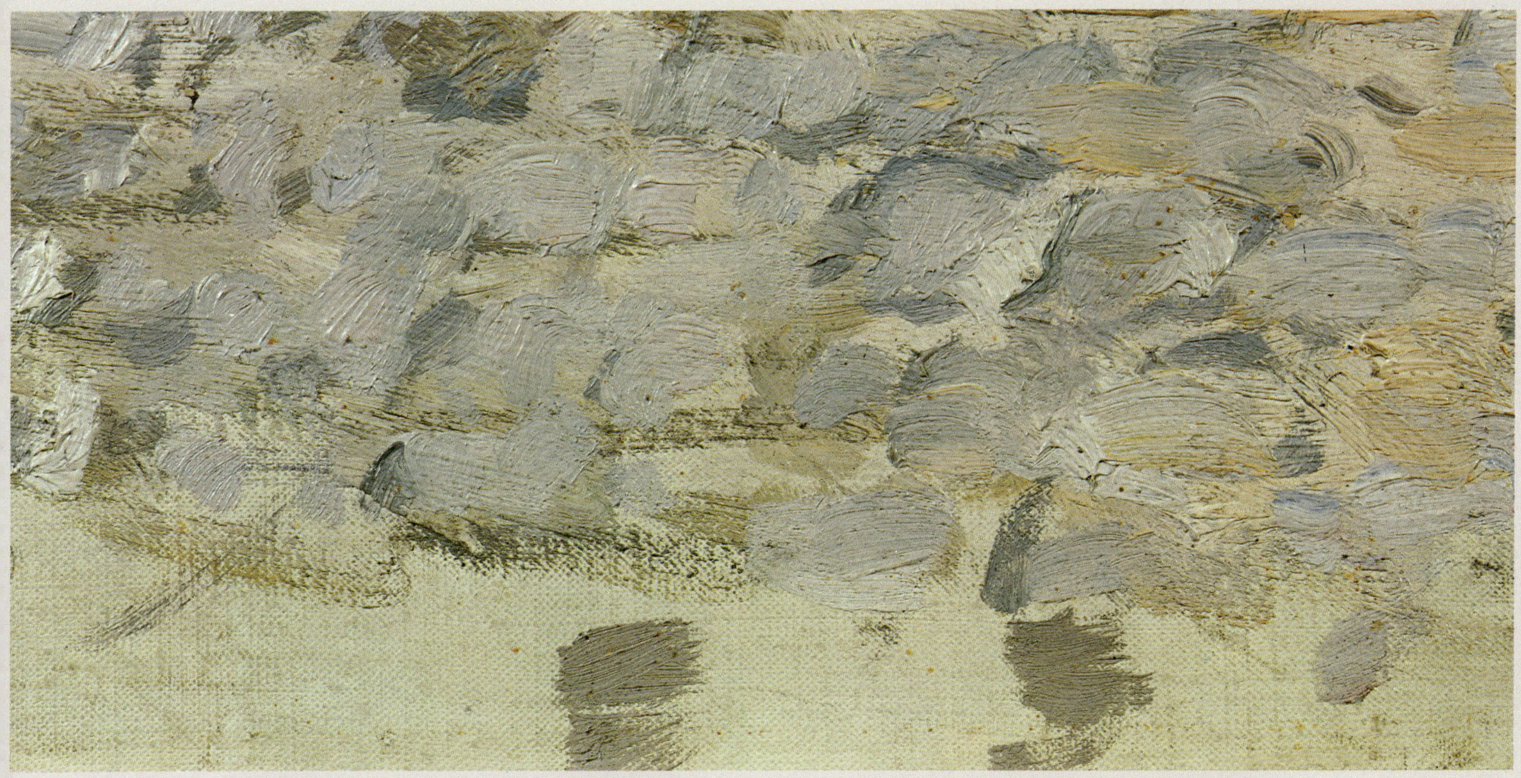

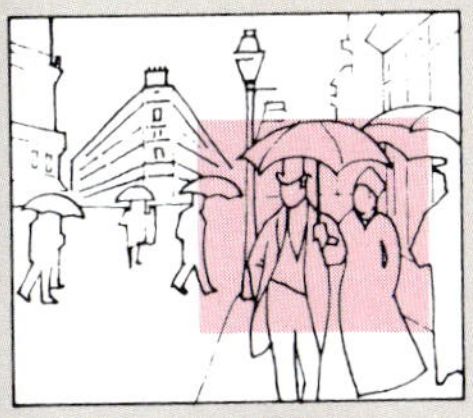

*Fluid lines of dilute browns or blues were thinly brushed in for contours, which were then blocked in by thicker, more opaque paint. A further reworking added weight and form to these figures, so that the resulting subtle modulations of hue and tone give a sense of their bulk. The brushwork helps here too, for, despite its briskness, it follows forms and 'sculpts' the figures. This can also be seen on the umbrellas, where the direction of the brush echoes the swelling forms. Detail is kept to a minimum, as can be seen in the lack of facial features. The final layer of the lightest hues is thickly impasted.*

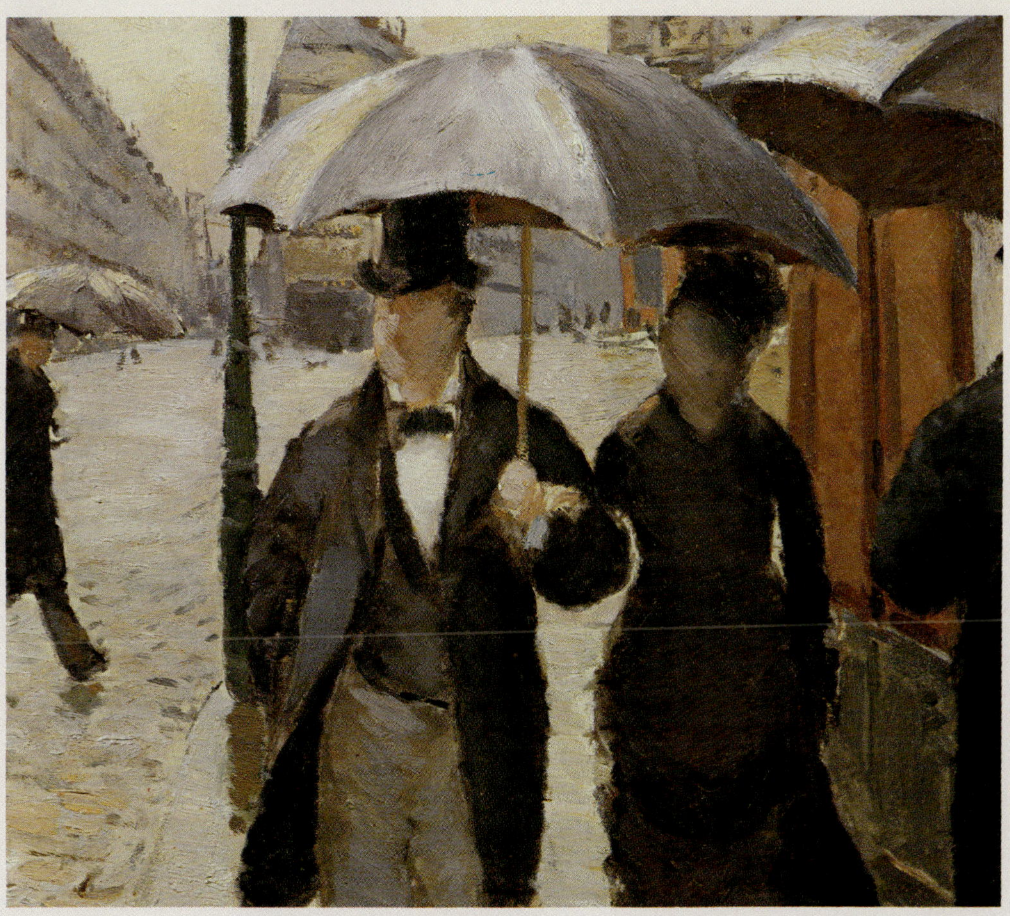

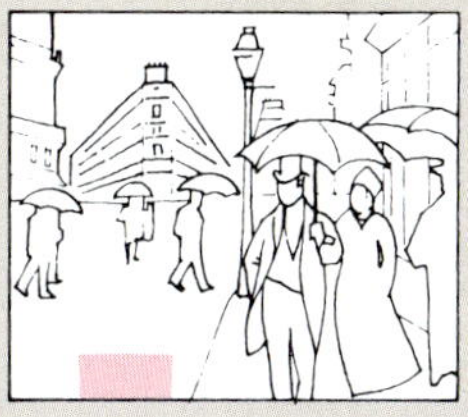

Actual size detail
*Paint was loaded on in thick strokes to evoke the forms of the cobbled street, with a separate slab of color for almost each individual cobblestone. Linear strokes of dragged color define the general grid pattern of the blocks. The pale off-white ground shows through among these colors, which were not preceded by a thin* ébauche *layer. Caillebotte concentrated on the texture of the road, leaving definition of precise detail to the final work. For this reason, he did not bother to cover the entire foreground, but left the extremities of the painting bare. He may already have decided on the compositional cropping which cut these edges in the final work.*

# EDOUARD MANET

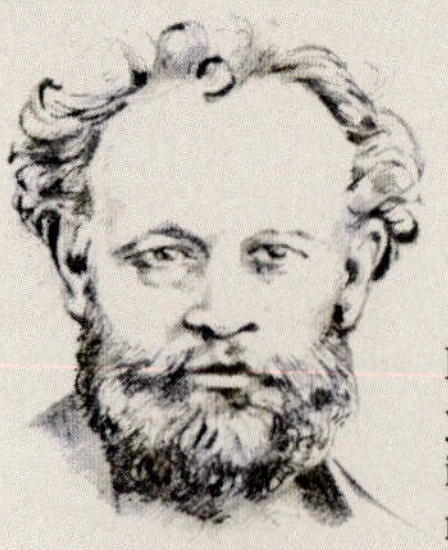

*Roadmenders in the rue de Berne/Paveurs, rue de Berne*
(1878)
Oil on pale gray primed canvas
63cm × 79cm/25in × 31½in

During the middle 1870s, for six years, Manet had a studio on what is now the rue de Leningrad, in a new residential quarter for the middle classes close to, and immediately north of Saint-Lazare Station in Paris' eighth *arrondissement*. From his studio window, Manet could look up the rue Mosnier, now the rue de Berne, onto the view which he depicted in a number of canvases including the present one, just before he left the studio in 1878. The bright palette and new light tonalities evident in this picture show the influence of Impressionist techniques and ideas upon Manet. Although friendly with his younger colleagues and meeting them regularly at cafés and *soirées* in the 1860s, it was only after 1870 that Manet succumbed to their influence. He began making outdoor sketches around 1870 and 1871, and, in 1874, he worked during the summer with Renoir and Monet at Argenteuil, a riverside village on the Seine, close to the north-west side of Paris, where many of the new middle classes were having villas built.

Monet had settled in Argenteuil in 1872, and the area became a popular one for communal landscape painting by the Impressionists during the 1870s. It was sufficiently close to Paris to permit the artists easy access to Paris for exhibitions, materials, social gatherings and meetings with dealers. At the same time, it afforded them a variety of landscape subjects – village, garden and river scenes – all of a gentle, domestic nature. Although Manet was never wholeheartedly committed to Impressionist ideals, he did work directly before nature during the mid 1870s, and continued to do so on occasions. He lightened and brightened his palette as a result of this experience, and, although he did not adopt the limited palette of the Impressionists, continuing to use black and some earth colors, the stark tonal contrasts typical of his work of the 1860s gradually gave way to closer, paler tonal harmonies.

*Roadmenders in the rue de Berne* is a stunning example of Manet's ability to capture open air light effects. It was painted on a canvas slightly smaller than the standard vertical landscape 25, which measures 81cm (32in) by 62.1cm (24½in), but, since standard measurements varied marginally from one color merchant to another, it may have been a standard format. A neutral pale gray ground on extra fine canvas has left the grain of the weave apparent, which is exploited in places by dragged color. The ground color enhances the overall effect of pale luminosity in the painting, uniting the many creamy tints of the paint layer. The paint layer colors are light and pastel-like, with much lead white added to them to increase their light-reflection, and their evocation of sunlit effects.

Looking north-west, up the rue de Berne, the afternoon sun falls from left to right across the street depicted. Its warm yellow color bathes the road and buildings to the right, producing light-filled shadows which are bluey-violet by contrast. No dark shadows or dramatic contrasts of tone break up the unity imposed by the sunlight. The atmospheric blueness at the far end of the receding street is admirably represented here, where Manet has rubbed a thin translucent veil of pale opaque blue over the stone colors, to give a floating insubstantial quality to the reflected light in the shadows. His harsh studio lighting of the 1860s has given way to the natural warm-cool outdoor effects studied by the Impressionists.

The all-pervasive sunlight works with the compositional layout to produce an ambiguity between surface and space in this painting. The unifying light and lack of contrast between depth of hue in foreground and background tend to contradict the illusion of space created by the dramatic recession of the street diving into the distance. The same pale blues of the background are apparent on the nearby buildings and figures, and the gash of brilliant blue sky at the top left further pushes the background forward, toward the picture surface. The rectangular red-brown block of the hoarding in the upper left is the largest block of deep color in the picture, so, because its color is striking and its shape echoes the straight edges of the picture, it sits insistently on the picture surface. This pulls the background forward too. The hoarding's shape also echoes the rectangle of the distant building which blocks the end of the street, and thereby links this shape to the picture surface.

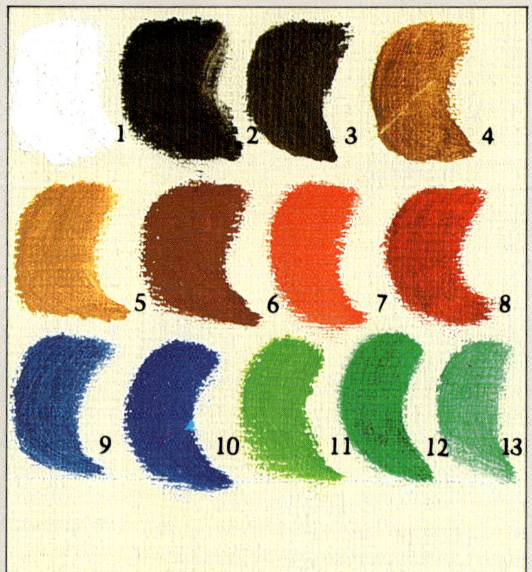


*Manet's palette for this painting probably comprised lead (1) and zinc whites, black (2), possibly umber (3), raw sienna (4), yellow ochre (5), red earth or red lead (6), vermilion (7), probably red alizarin lake (8), cobalt blue (9), ultramarine blue (10), chrome green (11), viridian (12) or cobalt green (13). Cerulean blue may also have been used.*

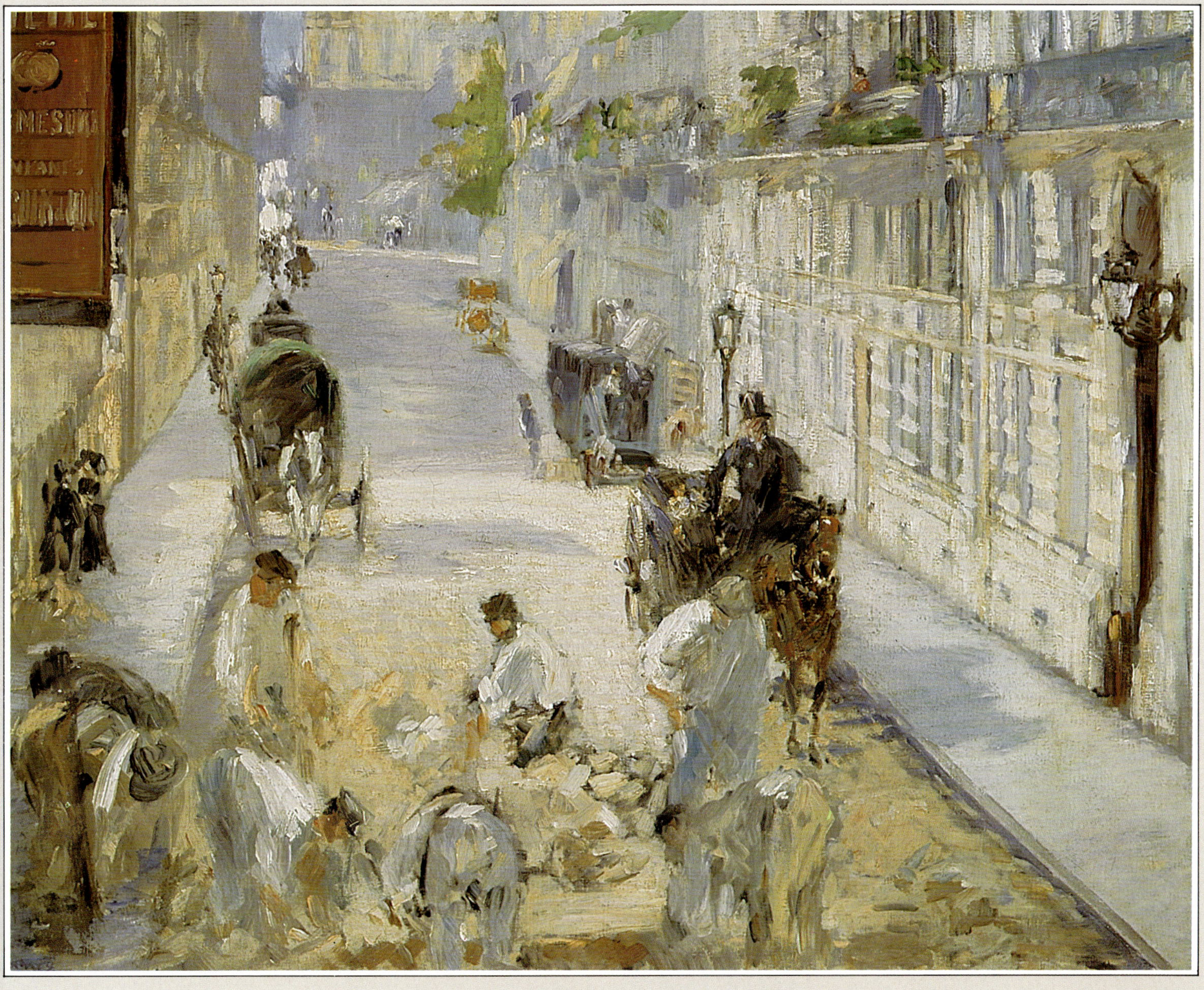

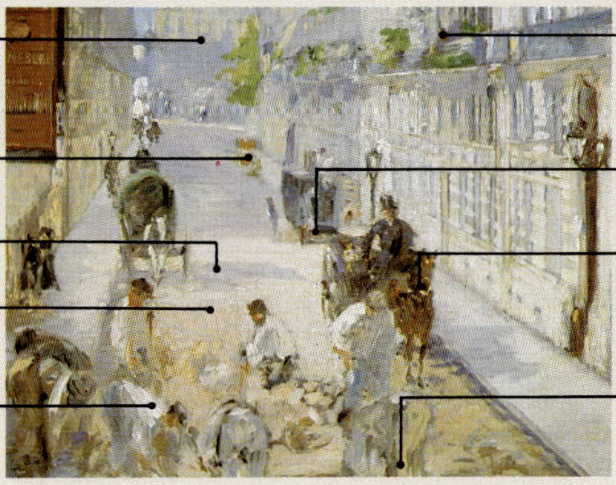


*This painting shows how Manet abandoned the use of dark tonal contrasts and stark juxtapositions of black and white, that had characterized his work during the 1860s. This happened in part under Monet's influence. Here,white has been added to most of the colors, making them pale and pastel-like in tint, and more appropriate for depicting flooding sunlight outdoors.*

The artist's viewpoint, looking down from his studio window onto the scene, tips the street up toward the picture surface, eliminating the skyline, which might have reinforced the recessive features of the picture. Recession is, however, strengthened by the changing scale of brushwork, which is distinct in the foreground and blurred in the background, and by the diminishing scale of figures and the perspectival lines on the buildings on the right. Thus Manet sets up a tension in the painting, a fragile equilibrium between those elements which encourage a naturalistic, spatial reading of the scene, and others which stress the two-dimensional design qualities of the painting.

Manet's brushwork is lively and descriptive, following the forms of figures and buildings, and emphasizing varied surface textures. The men in the foreground are paving this new street with cobblestones, indicating its recent construction. The gap on the left side of the street, behind the wooden palisade, appears still in the process of construction. Like many of his contemporaries, Manet ignored the dark crowded medieval quarters that still survived, and which had been popular with the Romantics, concentrating on depicting the most modern, newly erected parts of the city. These sunny, clean, cobbled streets, with their novel pavements, represented modernity, and, at the same time, offered light-filled settings which appealed to the Impressionist eye.

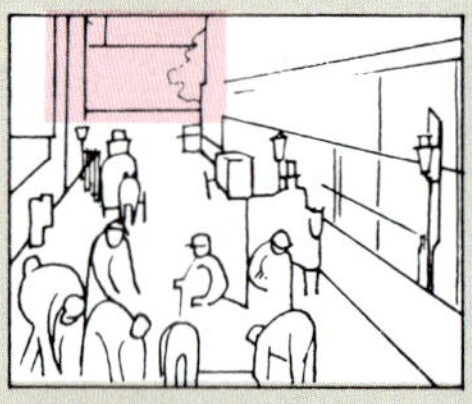

*Delicate, pastel-like creams evoke the sunlit distance, with cool, contrasting blues to give the hazy, light-filled shadows. The addition of large quantities of white enhances the light-reflective properties of the paint layer itself. The pale blues were brushed on thinly but opaquely, and are similar to the blues used in Renoir's* Rocky Crags *(1882). Yellow and chrome greens with added white were used for the foliage. Juicier blue and white paint was flicked on thickly and slurred to create the tiny distant figures.*

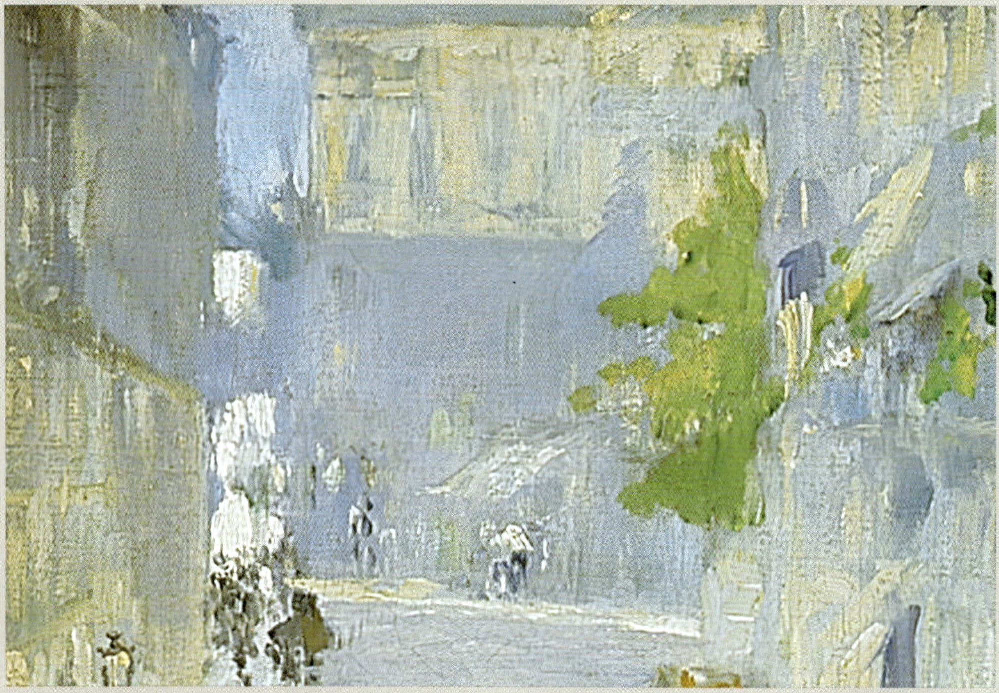

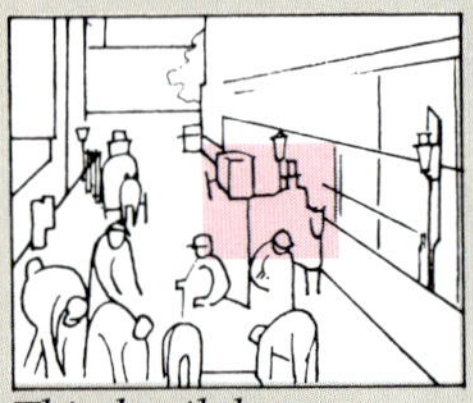

*This detail shows very loose and free brushwork using several colors to each stroke. They are partly slurred together but their separate hues are still often quite distinct. Dragged, the paint allows the ground or earlier dry touches to show through. The palest, greeny-blue may be cerulean blue, the more violet blue is probably ultramarine.*

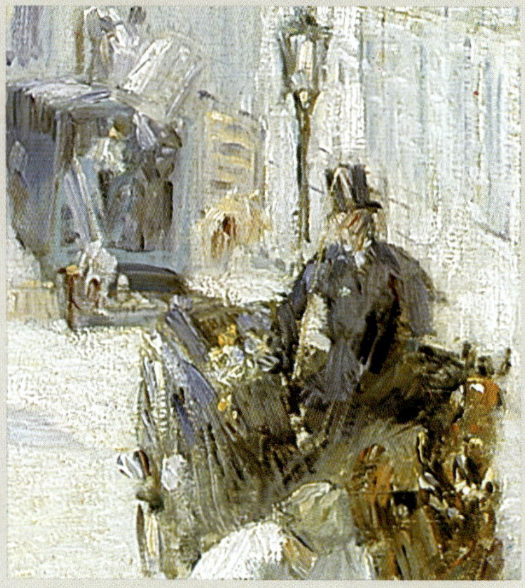

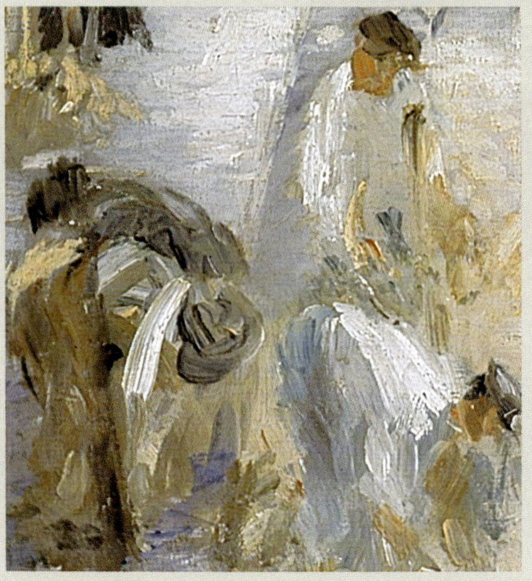

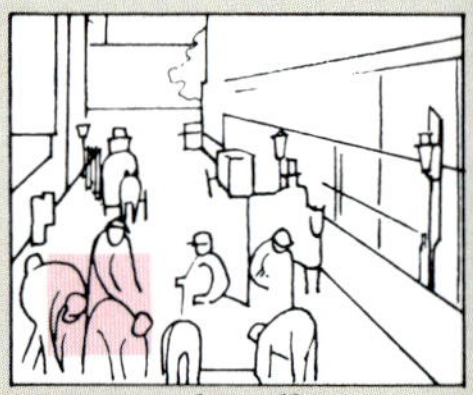

*Vigorous handling combines both wet-in-wet and wet-over-dry work. A fine, grainy canvas texture is evident in places, and the pale gray ground is occasionally revealed too. Touches of mixed orange make a vivid contrast with the lively complementary blues. Manet's loose, unfocused handling adds to the feel of bustling immediacy.*

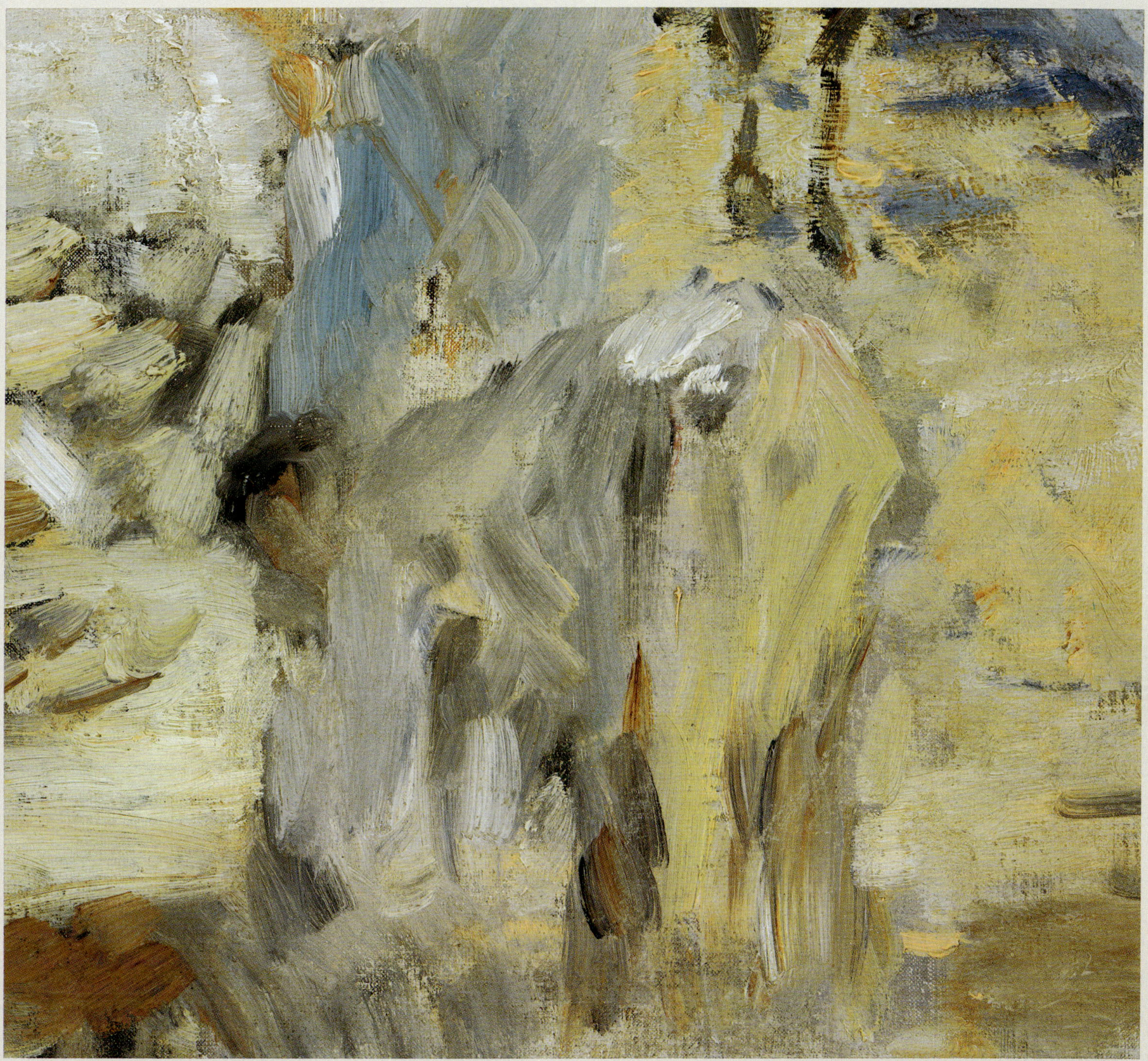

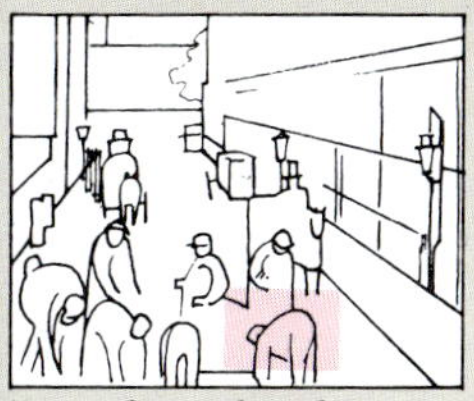

Actual size detail
*A thin transparent black layer underlies the pile of stones on the lower left. This was rubbed or scraped down by the artist, revealing a speckle of pale gray ground at the canvas nodes. Scraping down was a common practice used to eliminate irregularities left by the first* ébauche *layer. The blurred vagueness around the shoulders and head of the bending worker is also evidence of scraping down. Opaque colors were applied both wet in wet and wet over dry over the* ébauche *layer. This loosely and broadly handled color creates a sense of immediacy which reflects the concern for modernity shown in the choice of subject. The colors are mostly broken, pale earthy tints and ochres. Some, such as the blues and yellows, only have large quantities of white added to them. The warm pale yellow may be a mixed hue, or possibly the Naples yellow that Renoir began to use in preference to chrome around this time. The paint is generally quite thin, although mainly opaque, but some areas show loading of the brush leaving raised marks on the surface. The touch of the brush helps to create texture. Hog's hair brushmarks are often left visible as a result, and can be identified. In this work, flat, square and rounded ends are used, in sizes varying from 5mm (¼in) to 1.5cm (⅝in). In the unpainted parts at the bottom edge, the pale gray ground is most obviously revealed. Wear to this edge has rubbed the ground off the raised nodes of the canvas, leaving the darker hue of the linen showing through.*

# EDGAR DEGAS

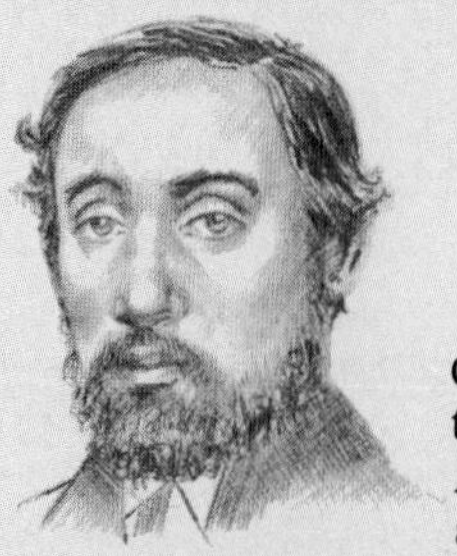

*Portrait of Duranty/Portrait de Duranty*
Distemper and pastel on sized but unprimed canvas
100cm × 100cm/39½in × 39½in

Cool, aloof, intellectual, Degas was the epitome of the Parisian dandy. Abandoning historically inspired academic subjects early in the 1860s, he began a lifelong commitment to rendering the modern life subjects which he saw around him. Influenced by an eclectic appreciation of the art of the Old Masters, and by the great nineteenth century painters, especially Ingres and Delacroix, Degas fused in his art the grand traditions of draftsmanship and coloring. He combined tradition and innovation. He wanted to bring a new emotional subtlety to painting, to rid art of the schematized caricatures of the emotions to which academic artists resorted. His aims were summarized by his friend Edmond Duranty in 1876: 'by means of a back, we want a temperament, an age, a social condition to be revealed.'

Degas met Duranty around 1865, and established a close friendship with this kindred spirit. Duranty had been a staunch supporter of Realism for more than a decade, and had edited a shortlived review *Le Réalisme* in the mid 1850s. An art critic and novelist in the vein of Gustave Flaubert (1821–1880) and Emile Zola (1840–1902), his fame was eclipsed by the success of these writers, leaving him an ironic cynicism akin to that of Degas himself. Duranty was the only writer in his social circle whom Degas portrayed, and he appeared in works other than this portrait.

The *Portrait of Duranty* comes toward the start of the period between 1875 and 1885 which saw Degas' most prolific experiments in artistic techniques. Around this time, artists were increasingly exploiting the matness of modern paints, and here Degas used a combination of opaque non-oil-based mediums. Distemper – a water-based glue-bound medium – provided the basic material of the portrait, which was executed on unprimed canvas. A shine apparent only in areas where the raw canvas is revealed, suggests that the fabric was first sized, with a glue size. The combination of distemper overworked with pastel used here has adhered inadequately to the flexible fabric support, and paint losses are clearly visible in places. The palish beige linen color of the canvas was also intentionally left bare in many parts, and its warmth unifies the overall tonality which, because of subdued canvas tone, results in muted harmony.

The mediums – distemper and pastel – are both mat and opaque, scattering reflected light from the picture surface. The pastel, with its distinct powdery hatched marks, is clearly visible worked over the freely brushed distemper colors. The pastel was used selectively, especially on the figure of Duranty, where it focuses attention on the sitter by strengthening drawing and heightening color. Strokes of a startling violet-blue, used to express reflected light in the shadow, for example on the raised middle finger supporting the sitter's head, have an almost floating, luminous quality. A darker, greener blue pastel was worked into the blue of the jacket, and some black strokes add lines of definition to the form of the figure. Pastel hatching on the face constructs form in terms of modeled color and tone, but, because their direction does not always follow the form, these marks have a life of their own. They contradict the formal structure of the face – even at a relatively distant viewing range – and this results in a striking tension between illusion and surface pattern.

Compositionally, the picture is powerful, and typical of Degas' daring experiments with pictorial construction and space. Influenced by Japanese prints and photography, he sought to express 'the particular note of the modern individual, in his clothing, in the midst of his social habits', as Duranty stated in 1876. Adopting an unusual square format which stresses surface flatness, Degas placed the sitter's head centrally, the midpoint of the canvas coinciding with Duranty's raised fingers pressing against his skull. This was perhaps a humorous reference to the man's intellectual intensity, as well as a typical pose. The figure, thus placed, seems oppressed by the mass of roughly indicated books on the shelves immediately behind him. He appears trapped in a shallow space, completely surrounded by the evidence of his trade, which, in the abrupt slope of his crowded desk, effectively separates him from the spectator – whose gaze he avoids.

Degas' alignment of the bookshelves is also no accident. The second shelf down on the left links with the third down on the right, and together they form a disturbing horizontal which cuts across the picture space, denying recession, and pushing close up to the picture surface. Colors, like the bright blue and the brown beneath it in the foreground left, serve a similar function, linking with comparable colors in the background to flatten the pictorial space. The overall effect of such devices is to emphasize the disquieting tension between abstract design and illusionistic representation, which gives a taut sense of presence and immediacy to the sitter.

Unlike the Impressionists, with whom Degas was associated by friendship and a commitment to alternative, unofficial exhibitions, Degas did not work from nature: 'art is not a sport' he maintained. He always worked in the studio, often from memory and from reworking ideas within his own pictures, preferring the effects of artificial light to outdoor lighting. For him, art was 'falsehood', a picture was 'something which calls for as much cunning, trickery and vice as the perpetration of a crime.' Yet to the casual observer, the final effect was often one of guileless and almost casual immediacy. This result, achieved sensitively in this portrait, is characteristic of many of Degas' works.

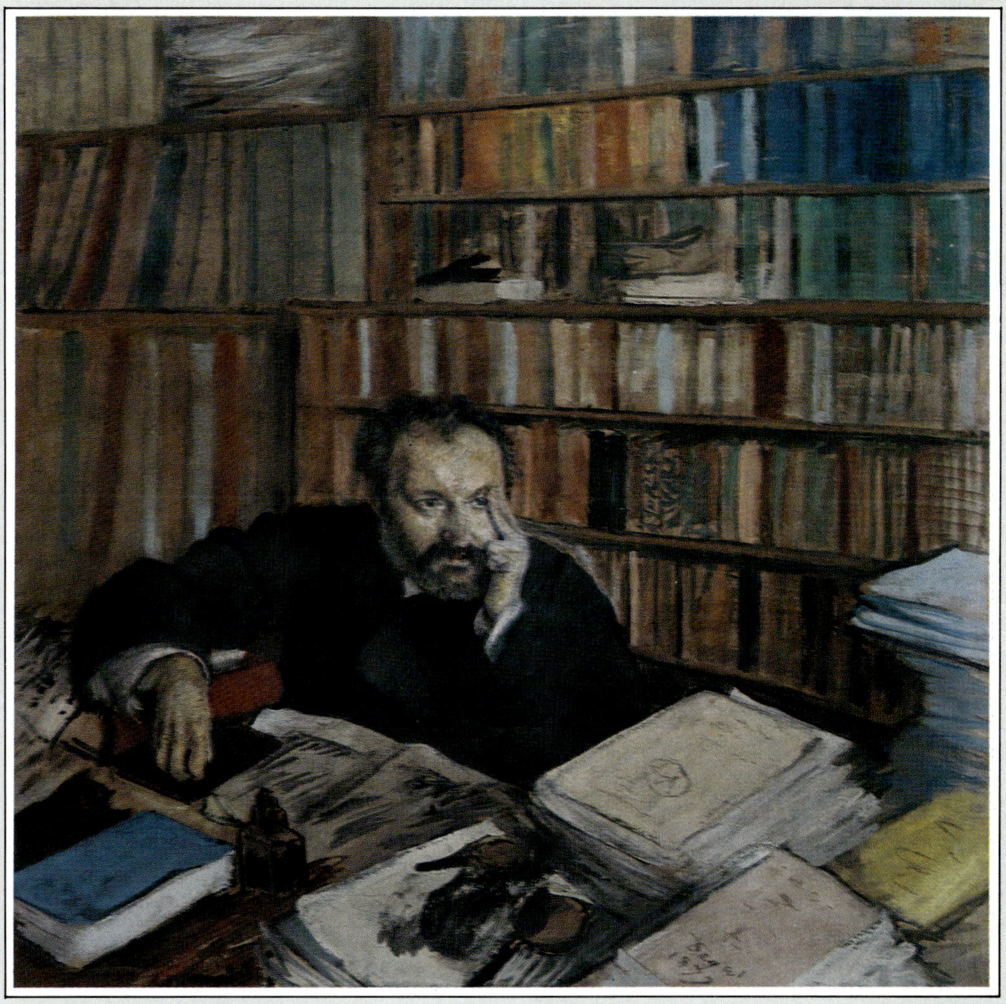

*Like many of his more daring contemporaries, Degas began to experiment with square format canvases during the 1870s. It is likely that his avid experiments with work on paper supports, which were easily cut, altered and added to as need demanded, fed his ideas, permitting him to develop them with great confidence onto the more costly canvas supports. Although Degas only infrequently used oil on unprimed canvas, because it was technically unsound, water-based paints were safe to use with raw canvas. In fact, the dull gloss visible on the unpainted parts of this picture suggests that Degas did give his support limited protection by applying a layer of size glue. At that time canvases could then be bought ready sized, but without a layer of ground color, and Degas may well have used such a product here. Just as Degas was experimenting with fairly binder-free oil colors, applied with turpentine to give dusty, mat effects, so too he used naturally mat media. Here gouache and pastel – the mattest of all media – were combined to give a pale, light-reflective surface.*

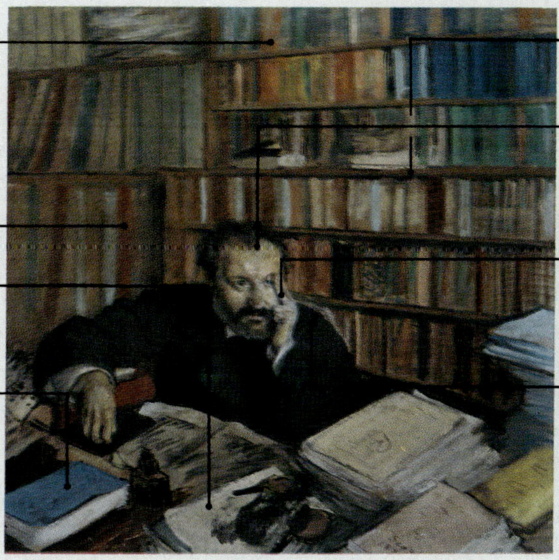

Red earth paint has flaked to reveal unprimed but sized linen canvas

Thinly dragged gouache color

Flaking of gouache which has adhered inadequately to the canvas support

Evenly applied layer of gouache, ultramarine or cobalt blue. Gouache is always opaque because all colors contain added body color, or white

Striking compositional horizontal stresses pictorial flatness

Broadly hatched strokes of pastel define form of head, but create independent, emphatic pattern

Brilliant blue, probably ultramarine, strokes of pastel for reflected light in shadow

Strengthening of contours with black pastel

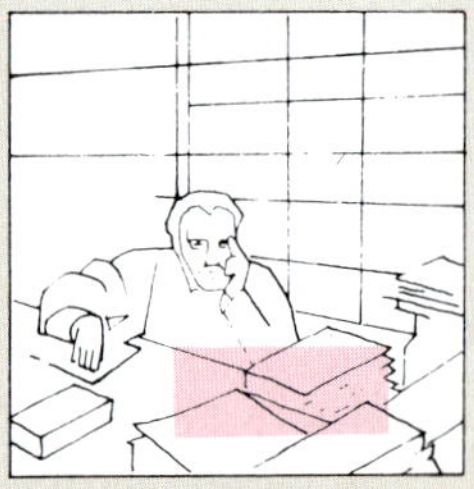

*In places the thinly applied gouache has been strengthened by the addition of black pastel. Degas' signature is ingeniously placed to follow the plane of the pink bookcover so that it appears as part of the printing. Flaking is particularly visible in the off-white gouache.*

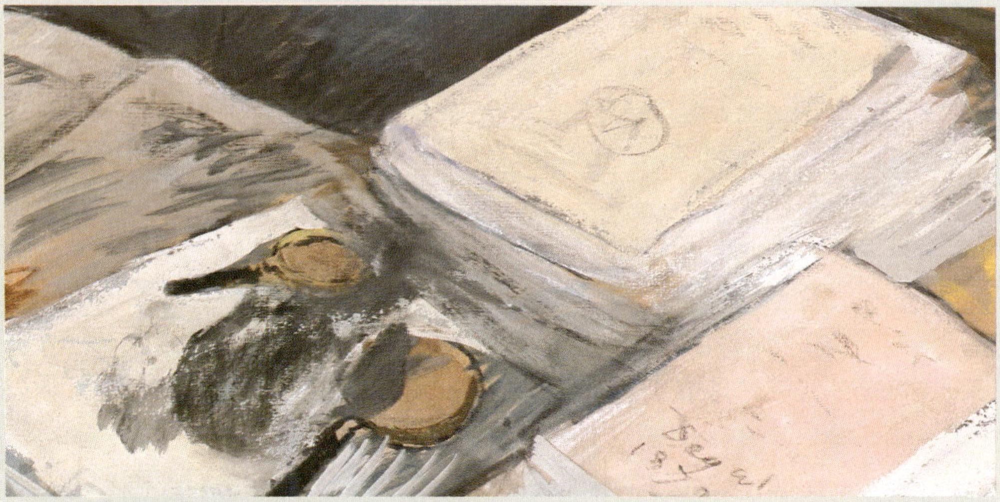

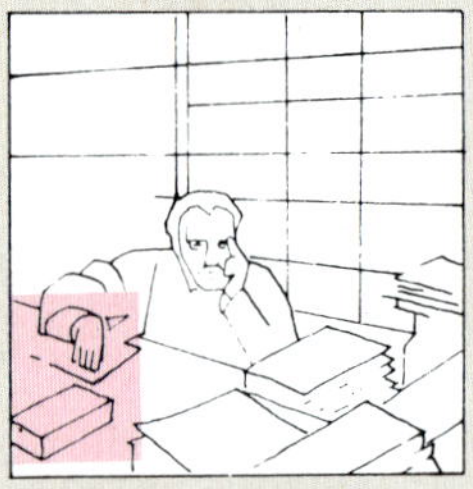

*Free and simplified handling belie the crisp confidence of Degas' draftsmanship. Mainly executed in gouache, the twisting movement of the wrist and hand are superbly captured. Pinks are used for the light parts, with contrasting greens for the shadows. Black gouache was overlaid to strengthen the drawing of the fingers by defining the divisions between them more clearly.*

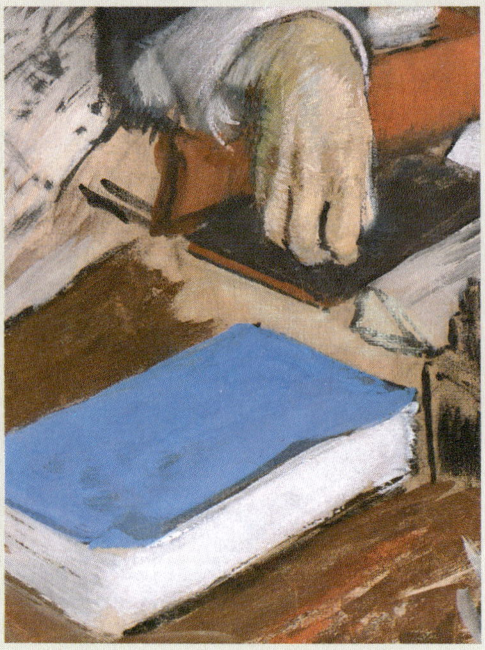

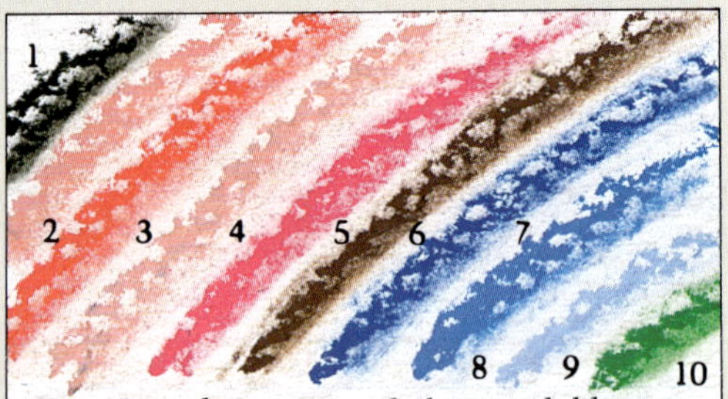


*Degas' pastels included black (1), various shades of pink (2-5), red earth (6), ultramarine blue (7, 9), dark greenish-blue cobalt blue (8) and possibly pale viridian green (10).*

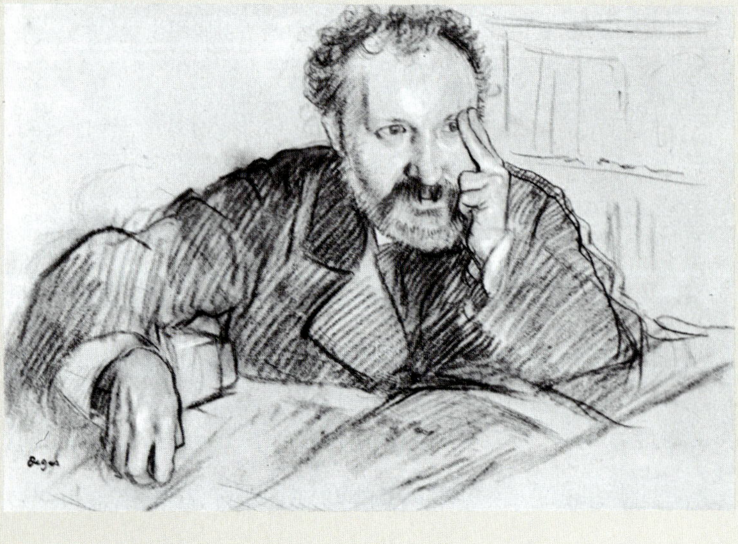

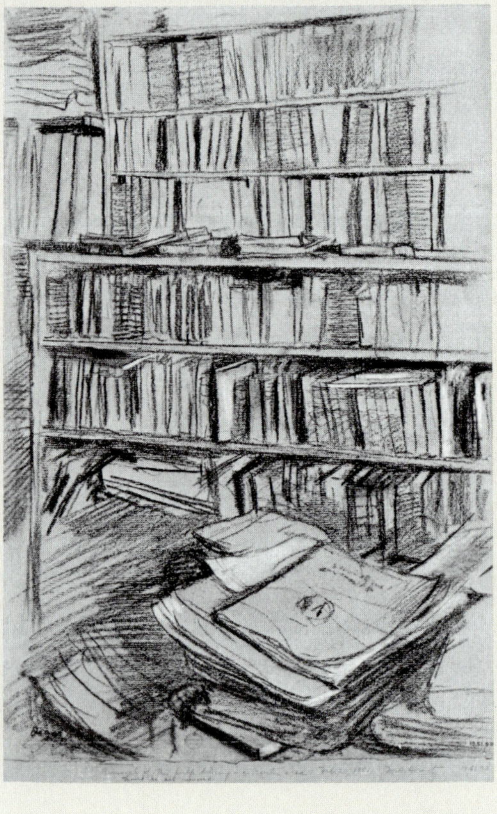

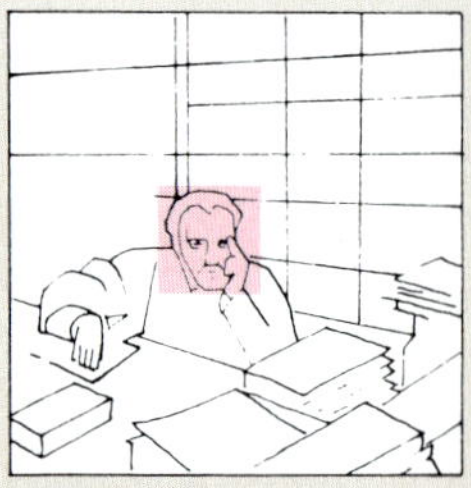

Actual size detail

*The unifying function of the raw sized canvas is apparent here, where it appears as a color and texture among the gouache and pastel. The texture of the canvas is vital, breaking the flow of the colors to give a vibrant effect, where the darker linen shows through the pale hues on top. The horizontal threads of the canvas are evident on the figure's brow, giving the appearance of deep, pensive furrows. The head is emphasized by combining gouache underpainting with pastel overworking, where line is used as color.*

*These two drawn studies show how the artist began his portrait. Only minor changes were made when he transferred the life study of the figure to the canvas. The torso was shifted to stress his raised right shoulder and the modeling of this arm was made more monumental. The new angle of the shoulders was echoed in the more acute angle of the desk, following the sweep of the shelves and seeming to trap the powerful bulk of Duranty among his cluttered papers. The final, striking design of the background shelves, with their strong bisecting horizontal lines, was invented by Degas.*

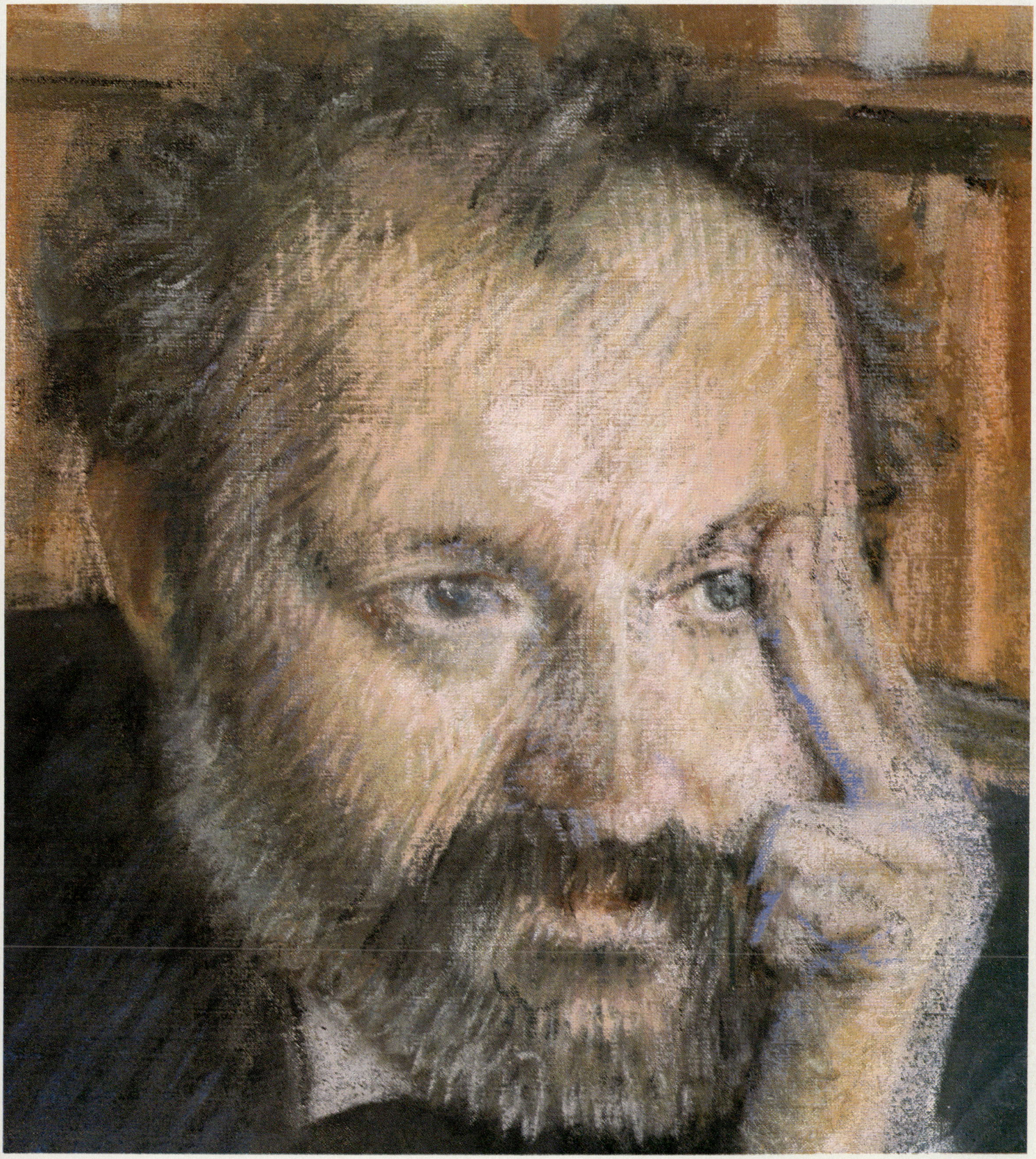

## 1880 1890

During the 1880s, the Impressionists consolidated their technical innovations of the previous decade, while a new generation of artists emerged who began to question Impressionist ideas and adapt their techniques to new ends. From 1879, the cohesion of the original Impressionist group was eroded by the introduction of newcomers. The appearance of Paul Gauguin (1848–1903), and soon after of Georges Seurat (1859–1891) and Paul Signac (1863–1935) at the Impressionist group exhibitions fanned the flames of disagreement which were growing among the older members. Some, like Pissarro, were in favor of moving with the times. Others, like Monet and Renoir, resented the newcomers. Thus, while individual friendships and allegiances were maintained during the 1880s, the overall cohesion of the Impressionist group began to disintegrate early in the decade. Symptomatic of this change was the final Impressionist group show in 1886, which was dominated by the newer artists, the Neo-Impressionists.

**The legacy of the 1870s**

By the late 1870s, most artists in the Impressionist group were beginning to find more tightly organized, structured ways of depicting their visual 'sensations' of nature. Paul Cézanne (1839–1906), early in the second half of that decade, began to adopt what has since been termed his 'directional' brushstroke. This meant that his brushmarks were all generally

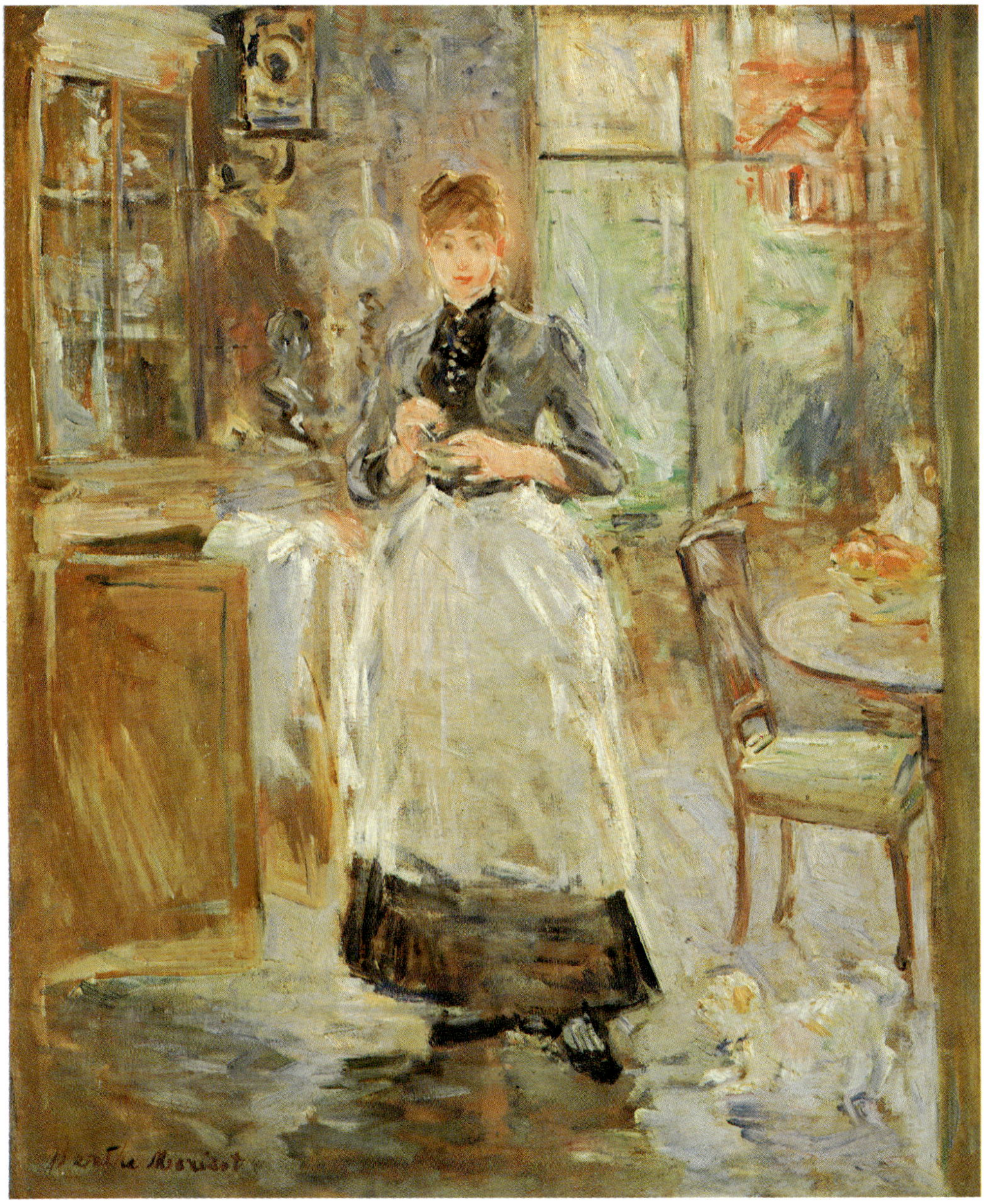

Right *Berthe Morisot's* In the Dining Room *shows the artist's maid in her house, rue de Villejuste, Paris. It was painted in 1884. In the 1880s, like most of her Impressionist colleagues, Morisot continued to make studies of effects of natural light and color on outdoor and interior scenes. Here, daylight floods from the large windows behind the figure, but as in Pissarro's portrait of his wife sewing (1879), harsh contrasts between light and shade are eliminated. Shadows, like that from the maid falling toward the spectator, are filled with reflected light, and the contrasts are between warm and cool hues. Brushwork is lively, dragging the pale opaque colors to create the blurring effect of light dissolving form and contour.*

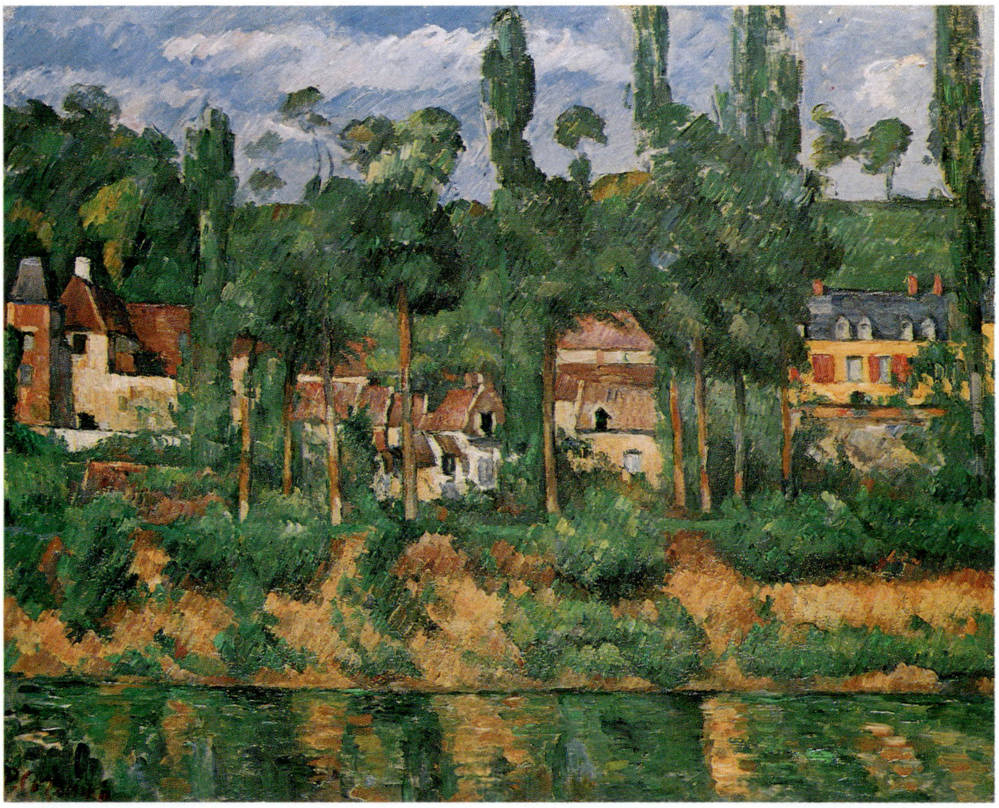

Left *Cézanne's* The Castle of Médan *was probably painted in the summer of 1880, when Cézanne was staying at Médan with his friend the novelist Emile Zola. He owned the small island in the Seine from which the view was painted. Cézanne has aligned the riverbank and the village parallel to the picture plane. A series of bands thus run horizontally, echoing the top and bottom edges of the painting. Combined with the verticals of the trees, they form a strong compositional grid. Hatched strokes of paint are used almost uniformly over the picture, and the color is of almost the same saturation throughout. These devices stress the flatness of the picture surface.*

placed in parallel lines, similar to a hatched drawing technique, usually running from top right to bottom left in his paintings. This particular direction is logical for a right-handed painter. Originally, in more traditional and academic painting, the underlying compositional structure was based on line, on the use of drawing by contour and by edges of forms, on a conventionalized fall of light and shade, to give a linear or tonal skeleton on which color was then laid.

The Impressionists' concentration on color which involved starting their pictorial layout with colored touches which represented the colored patches they perceived in nature, meant that structure evolved as the painting progressed, through a combination of two key elements. The first was the planned, overall compositional design of the subject on the canvas; the second was the build-up of delicate color values and warm-cool contrasts, which slowly cohered into a harmonious unified effect equivalent to the effect afforded by the natural scene. Drawing as a separate, self-contained activity in painting, was abandoned. As Cézanne himself recalled in his later years 'Drawing and color are not separate at all; in so far as you paint, you draw. The more color harmonizes, the more exact the drawing becomes.'

In the first half of the 1870s, the Impressionists had relied on descriptive brushwork – brushwork which echoed and followed forms in their painting – to aid the modeling produced by color values. But during the latter half of the 1870s, brushwork became more independent of form and took on a life of its own. This gradual freeing of touch from its more basic role of describing form had important consequences. It meant that the artist's visual sensations of patches of colored light were more accurately conveyed and also that a greater awareness of flat, plastic qualities in painting were stressed. The size of brushstroke was kept relatively uniform over the entire canvas, and so it no longer aided an illusion of recession, but emphasized the physical surface of the picture. Thus, the artist forced the spectator to remember that the picture confronted was a *painting*, which had its own reality, and was not simply an extension of the spectator's world. The Impressionists were not concerned to produce an art which fooled the eye into believing it saw the 'real' world, but rather to stress to the viewer the individual nature of the artist's perceptions.

By the end of the 1870s, Renoir and Pissarro had both developed their individual equivalents to Cézanne's constructed 'directional' brushwork. It is clearly apparent in Renoir's foreground figure in *Place Clichy* (1879–1880), which sets up a striking contrast with the blurred, rubbed effects which evoke the background bustle of the crowded Parisian street. The tightness of the brushwork on the cut-off female figure acts as a device to focus the viewer's attention on her. Pissarro, who had

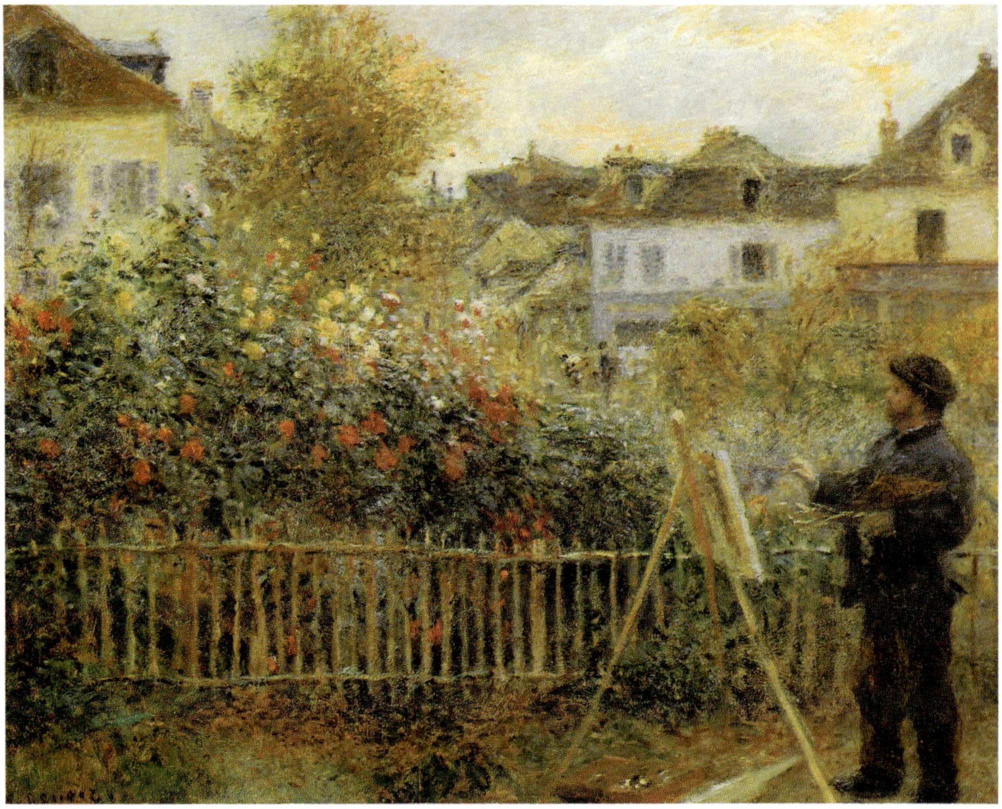

Right *Renoir completed this work,* Monet Painting in his Garden at Argenteuil *around 1874. This shows the artist with his outdoor painting tools in the early 1870s. A three-legged, collapsible easel is used for easy portability and a small paintbox can be seen on the ground below. Nearby is a folded, white painting parasol. This would have been used during bright sunny spells to shade the work and eliminate brilliant reflections off the wet paint surface. An overcast sky here gives bright light but no cast shadows to enhance form. Horizontals and verticals of the fence and buildings run parallel to the picture plane, a geometry softened by the varied brushwork suggesting foliage and flowers. Colors were premixed and worked wet in wet. But this is – for Renoir – quite a heavily loaded surface and paint was also added wet over dry.*

worked regularly beside Cézanne during this decade, used a more controlled, directional touch in works like *The Backwoods of l'Hermitage, Pontoise* (1879), a magnificent, large canvas which can be seen as a summation of his work of the 1870s, and in *Peasants Tending Cows* of 1882. Pissarro's technique was to develop, along with his association with the younger generation of Neo-Impressionist painters, into his pointillist style of the late 1880s. By 1886, this new group of artists, who developed a more scientific approach to Impressionism, were dubbed the Neo-Impressionists. In Renoir's work, the new tightness heralded a return to more traditional painting methods, in which he revived the practice of making preparatory drawings and studies, and did many large-scale studio figure compositions, while remaining committed to Impressionist brilliance of color and luminosity.

**Seurat and the Neo-Impressionists**

The new Impressionist style of ordered brushwork was adopted by the young Georges Seurat (1859–1891), short-lived leader of the Neo-Impressionists, when he first began painting oil studies from nature in the early 1880s. His personal variation was a criss-cross application of hatched strokes which gave his studies a surface uniformity comparable to that found in Impressionist paintings of that date. This technique may in part have originated with Delacroix (1798–1863), who occasionally used it, and in the oil sketching methods which Seurat learned at the Ecole des Beaux-Arts. Like Degas, Seurat trained – if only briefly in the late 1870s – in the *atelier* of one of Ingres' pupils. Like Degas too, Seurat retained from this experience a commitment to drawing, to careful preparatory studies, both drawn and painted, and to a monumental classically harmonious symmetry in his finished studio compositions. In a way, Seurat was a modern classicist, fusing aspects of that tradition, in particular a belief in strong modeling of form, with the Impressionists' dedication to the rendering of natural outdoor light. However, Seurat's novelty lay in his desire to find a systematic, scientific mode of rendering natural atmospheric light which, unlike the approach of the Impressionists, would leave nothing in his paintings to chance. During the first half of his brief career until the mid 1880s, he concentrated upon systematizing the depiction of color and light in his paintings, adopting a variant of the Impressionists' limited palette of bright colors.

Nineteenth century writers on technique had recommended widely accepted, if slightly varied formulae of different combinations of colors for depicting each category of painting – figure, landscape, portrait, genre scenes, and so on. By contrast, the limited palette of the Impressionists – which improved the porta-

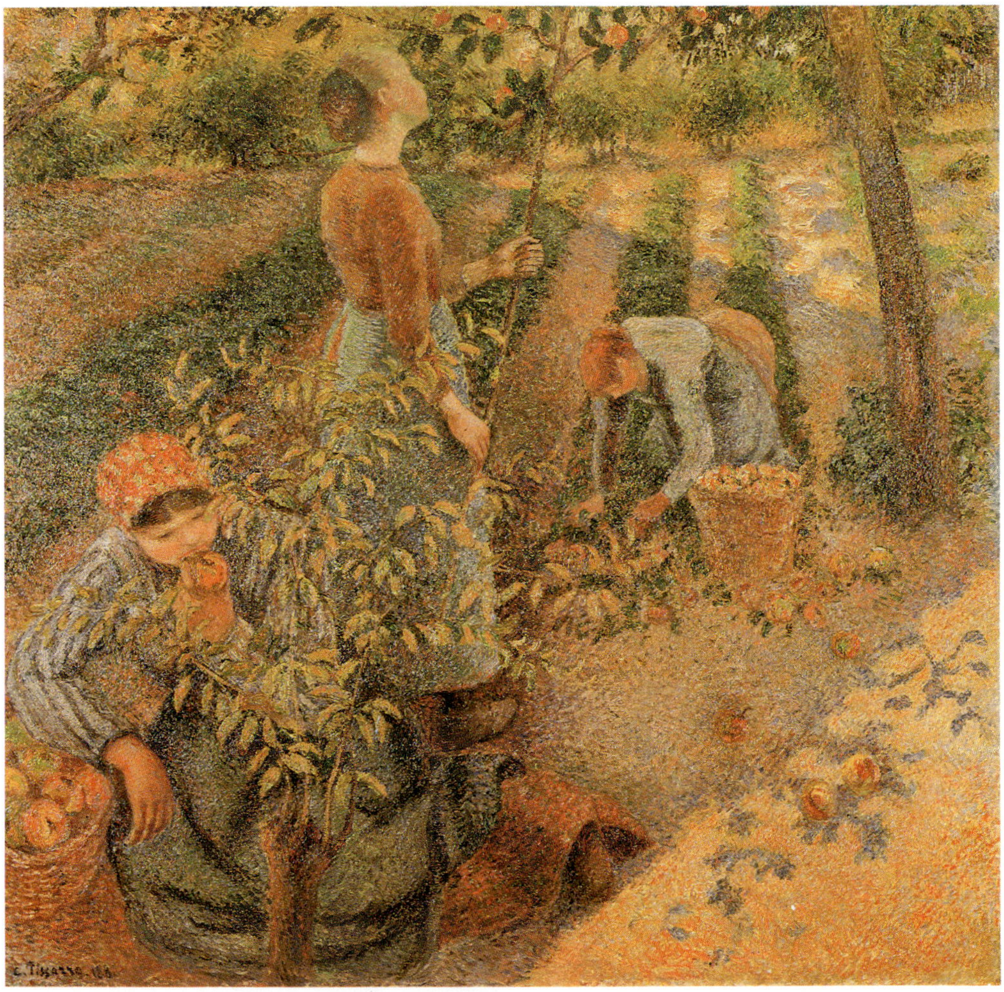

Left *In* Apple Picking *(1886), Pissarro was experimenting with the decorative properties of a square canvas format. A number of preparatory drawings for this major, large-scale work survive. They show the care with which the artist planned the picture. Three figures recede in space. They echo the strong diagonal of the violet shadow, which runs from center bottom to off-center, right. In the upper right, a second triangle of sunlight repeats in reverse that at lower right. The power of these shapes and the shadow, in relation to the square canvas shape, gives the painting a patterned flatness. The brushwork consists of small hatched touches which are, however, not yet Pointillist in size. The brushstrokes create a web of texture which strengthens surface qualities, while also evoking forms. Color is richer and more muted than in the artist's later Pointillist variant of this theme, which dates from 1888.*

bility of their equipment – required of these artists greater versatility and an intimate knowledge of their few colors, to enable them to adapt their palette to suit a wide variety of different subjects and weather conditions.

The Impressionists' palette colors were not strictly speaking 'prismatic'. None conformed precisely to the full, pure chromatic saturation found in the spectrum of colored lights produced by a prism for the simple reason that they were combinations of chemical pigments. What the Impressionists did was to choose pigment colors which approximated most closely to the common notion of the chromatic circle, concentrating on primary colors (red, yellow, blue) and one or two secondary colors (orange, green, violet) which, when mixed, produced a wide range of bright hues. Relative degrees of darkness or colorful neutral tints were made by mixing complementary or near complementary colors. Complementary colors are those colors opposite each other on the color circle – red and green, blue and orange or yellow and violet. This enabled the artists to avoid the sullying effects of adding brown or black to give darker tones. For pale tints, increased amounts of lead white were usually added to the initial mixture.

Documentary evidence and scientific pigment analysis together with visual examination of the paintings can give a reasonably accurate idea of the colors generally used by the Impressionists. The most common colors were lead white, chrome yellows, cadmium yellows, yellow ochre, emerald green, viridian green, cobalt blue, ultramarine blue, red and crimson alizarin lakes, and vermilion. Black virtually disappeared from the palettes of all but Renoir and Cézanne after the mid 1870s, and even they used it only as a color in its own right, and not as a means to darken other colors for tonal shadows. Chrome yellows were in fact abandoned by most of these artists in the late 1870s, when it was realized they tended to blacken in contact with pigments which included sulphides. Renoir commented on this problem, and the change it necessitated in his work, emphasizing one important aspect of coloring. This was that brightness of color depended more upon the relationship of colors within a picture, than on the brilliance of the individual colors. For this reason, he adopted the dull Naples yellow in place of the bright chrome yellows.

In the late 1870s, Monet substituted cadmium yellows for the problematic chromes. He, Pissarro, Alfred Sisley (1839–1899) and Mary Cassatt (1845–1926) all used cobalt violet relatively unmixed from the early 1880s on. This pigment had, however, been used by them much earlier, but only in mixtures. Cézanne and Renoir both used some of the duller – but pale – earth colors, like yellow ochre, raw sienna, green and red earths, and also Naples yellow. Renoir called these 'intermediaries', by which he meant colors which could be obtained by mixing the brighter primary colors and white. However, these artists tried to avoid dangerous overmixing, so the duller tube colors were adopted only as an expedient.

The more colors are mixed together, the darker the resulting hue, because pigments react 'subtractively'. This means that the amount of light they reflect back to the eye diminishes proportionately with each additional color in a mixture. Colored light reacts in the opposite manner, or 'additively', so that adding colors of light together produces an increasingly pale mixture, resulting finally in the pure white light which is a reconstitution of the entire prismatic rainbow. Thus, avoiding overmixing of pigment colors was also a means of retaining the maximum light-reflective power of each individual pigment color, as, for example, Naples yellow direct from the tube would be paler than would a palette mixture.

**The Neo-Impressionist palette**
The Neo-Impressionists were even more rigorous in their attitude toward color mixtures than were the Impressionists. The latter often slurred together or even premixed colors opposite each other on the chromatic circle, because these gave colorful neutral-to-gray hues. The Neo-Impressionists rejected such mixtures as too sullied. Instead they advocated only the mixing of hues next to each other on the chromatic circle, which gave brighter, purer mixtures. Like the Impressionists, they increased the reflective luminosity of their paint surfaces by adding white to most of their colour mixtures. Although as late as 1883 to 1884, when Seurat completed his first major canvas *Bathing, Asnières*, earth colors were included in his palette, after that date he banished them from his color range. His first follower, Paul Signac, recorded the typical Neo-Impressionist palette, which was an extended version of the Impressionist palette, excluding the earth colors. For their yellows they used the cadmiums, from deep through to pale, and the alizarin lakes and vermilion were their reds. Cobalt violet, ultramarine and cobalt blues, and cerulean blue covered the purple to blue range. They used more greens than the Impressionists – viridian green, and two 'composed' greens, probably different hues of chrome green, which was a commercially produced mixture of chrome yellow and Prussian blue.

Since the seventeenth century, the artist's palette had traditionally been laid out in a tonal arrangement, starting with white nearest the thumbhole and moving out around the

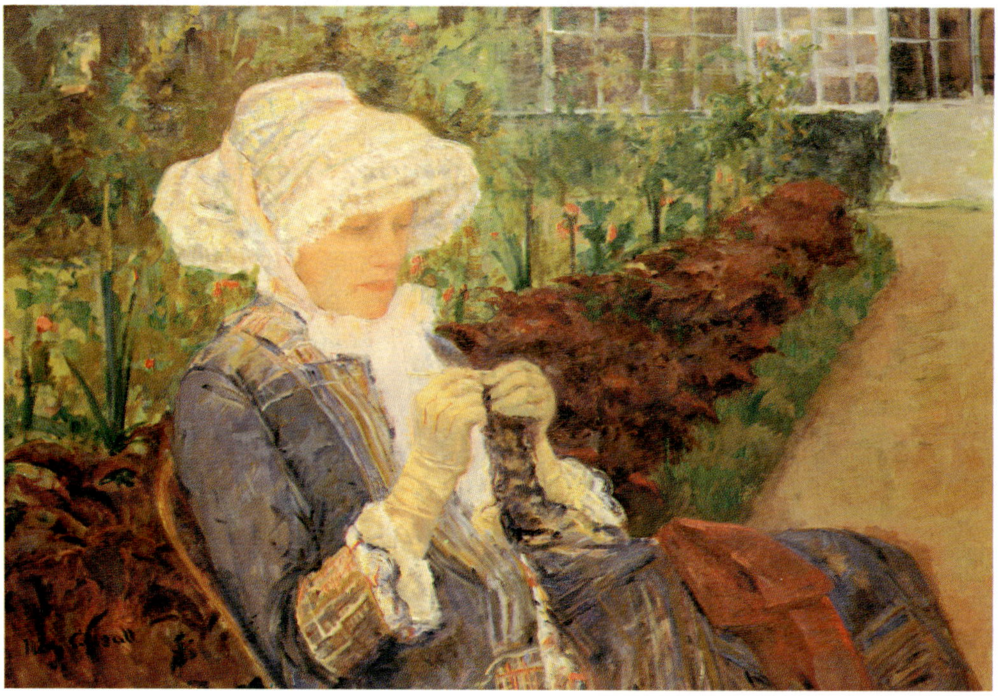

Right *Mary Cassatt's* Lydia Crocheting in the Garden at Marly *(1880) shows the artist's sister Lydia, who was an invalid. It was exhibited at the sixth Impressionist exhibition of 1881, and Degas remarked that it looked well in studio light. The subdued tint of the ground harmonizes with the predominance of middle tonal values of this picture. It was painted in shadowless overcast lighting. The figure is cropped and pushed close to the viewer, against a band of rich, reddish plants. This band seems like a solid slab of color. This produces a flattening effect which is reinforced by the flat color of the path and the grid of windows behind. All of these devices draw attention to the figure.*

Right *Louis Hayet, painter friend of Pissarro and his son Lucien, painted this color circle based on Ogden Rood's color wheel. Such charts aided Neo-Impressionist painters in their choice of hues for their meticulously colored canvases. By contrast to Chevreul's earlier color circle, here there is greater stress on the range of greens. Only colors found adjacent on the circle were premixed by these artists so the colors retained their purity of hue.*

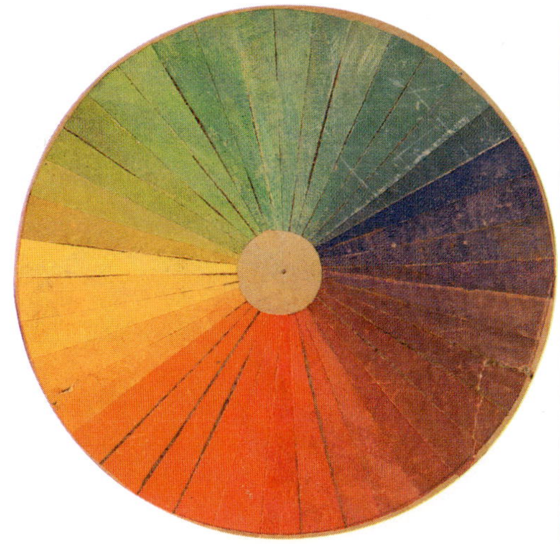

palette edge to end in the black. During the 1870s, the new limited Impressionist palette may well have modified this layout because, by the early 1880s, a new method for arranging the palette seems to have emerged. Unlike previous painters, the Impressionists did not premix and lay out all their tints prior to painting. Their rapid methods of recording fugitive effects of light necessitated constant readjustments in their colors, which were mixed only as and when needed. Their method of merely squeezing out blobs of their tube colors, and mixing or applying them slurred as needed, gave far greater scope for spontaneity during the painting process than had the premeditated mixtures of earlier artists. During the 1870s, it is likely the Impressionists evolved the new prismatic layout for their colors. This meant arranging them according to their position on the chromatic color circle, which was based on the order of the rainbow colors of the prism, rather than tonally, from white to black.

This procedure was tightened up and systematized by the Neo-Impressionists. Since, apart from in their preparatory oil studies from nature, rapid handling to capture fugitive lighting effects was not part of their method, palette layout again became premeditated. Not only were their pure tube colors laid out according to the color circle – yellows, reds, violets, blues, greens and back to yellow – but their tints of these colors with white were also prepared in advance and laid out in a separate row on the artist's palette.

However, the Neo-Impressionists continued to use certain methods developed by the Impressionists. For instance, they, like the Impressionists, were convinced of the advantages of mat paint surfaces and of mixtures with white which gave greater light-reflectiveness and therefore a more luminous, accurate evocation of natural atmospheric light. Similarly, like the Impressionists from the 1870s, the Neo-Impressionists shunned the use of varnish over their finished pictures. Varnish distorted the carefully calculated, delicate color relations, darkened the pale opaque surface effects and destroyed the matness of their paintings. The Neo-Impressionists also adopted the Impressionists' use of relatively oil-free paints because the mat paint surfaces these produced provided a superb visual analogy with the matness of natural surfaces under sunlight. The Neo-Impressionists sought new ways of recreating the effects of vibrant outdoor light. One such method was the adoption of canvases prepared with absorbent grounds.

For oil painting, artists had traditionally preferred relatively non-absorbent, oil-based grounds, because they enhanced the oil colors by leaving the paint layer with the glossy finish and rich colors which were considered desirable. However, absorbent grounds were reintroduced by color merchants in the early nineteenth century. These were similar to the gesso grounds made from chalk and glue which had been used with tempera before the Renaissance. The merchants' motives were purely economic, as absorbent grounds dry more quickly than the oil-based variety. However, absorbent grounds draw oil from the colors, producing a dryer, chalkier paint layer than is possible on oil-based grounds, and this was ideal for the Neo-Impressionists. This mat paint finish, in combination with the white absorbent ground gave a brilliant light-reflective quality which was perfectly suited to creating the visual effects sought by the Neo-Impressionists.

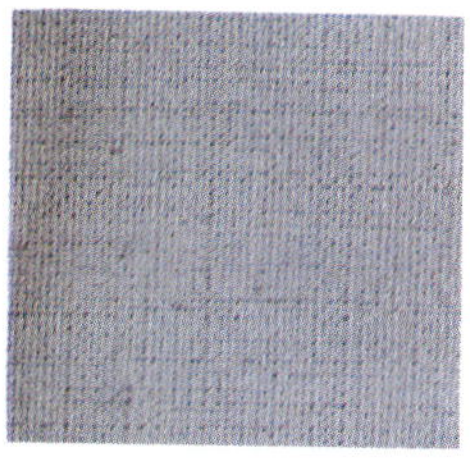

Above *This sample of an ordinary weight canvas dates from about 1900. It has a white 'absorbent' ground of the type preferred by Neo-Impressionist painters. This sample was primed probably with a single coat of glue and chalk based primer, and was widely sold by French color merchants.*

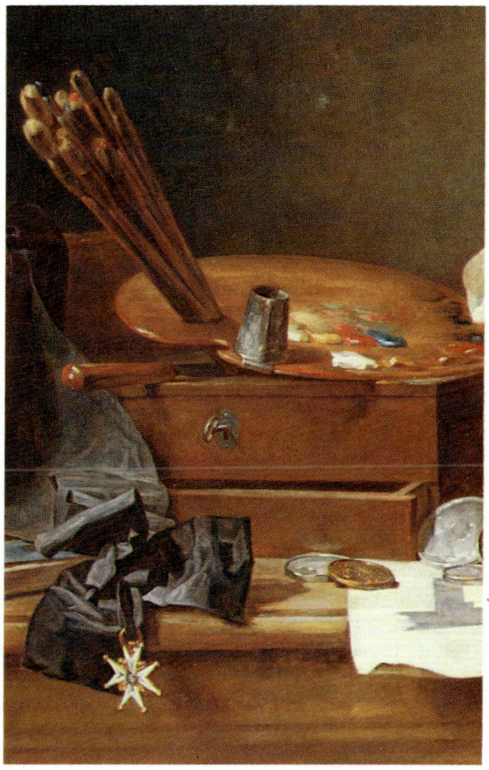

Left *This detail from* The Attributes of the Arts *(1766) by the French artist Chardin (1699-1779) shows a palette, knife, paintbox and brushes. The palette is oval in shape and shows a tonal layout of colors. They are set out in a row, starting with white nearest the thumbhole, working round to the darkest hues. Hog's hair brushes here are attached to their handles with leather thongs. This makes them round in form. With the introduction of tin ferrules, a flat shape could be made. This was popular with the Impressionists. A metal dipper to hold painting medium or diluent is clipped to the edge of the palette. Dark hardwood was usually used for palettes, and this made it difficult for artists painting on light grounds to judge their color values when mixing on the palette.*

Although in his large finished canvases from the first half of the 1880s, Seurat used an opaque paint layer which obliterated most of the white ground, this still adds to the general brilliance and durability of his paint layer. However, in his studies – often from nature – his open criss-cross brushwork often left the ground showing through. It is clear, especially from earlier examples, that he was then also using tinted grounds, particularly gray, in a manner similar to that employed by the Impressionists. On occasions, unlike the Impressionists, he also used small wood panels, usually cigar box lids, which were often left unprimed so that the warm reddish-orange wood played an active role, unifying and complementing the openly applied colors in the paint layer. As in academic practice, these little paintings were either *études*, which served as memory aids, annotating Seurat's first impressions of light and color on the scene, or they were rapidly executed compositional sketches in which he experimented with various alternative compositions for large-scale works. All these elements, together with his careful tonal drawings of individual pictorial components, were finally used as the raw material for his controlled studio pictures.

Seurat's drawing technique, which was adopted by many of his followers, was quite individually distinctive, despite a similarity to the drawing techniques of Millet's late works which clearly inspired them. In the early years of his career, although pursuing his interest in color through reading, and studying masters like Delacroix, Seurat concentrated almost exclusively on developing his drawing technique. This was very much in line with academic practice, yet the resulting images achieved their lucid, timeless classicism with little reference to accepted academic methods. Seurat's preferred drawing medium was black Conté crayon, an artificial chalk so fine as to be almost waxy in feel. He worked on rough hand-made Michallet paper – a famous French brand – which had distinctive paper-mold marks and was commonly called 'Ingres' paper. By varying pressure with the soft chalk on this irregular creamy-white surface, he could achieve great variations of tone. Gentle marks caught only on the protruding ridges or tufts of the paper, leaving the hollows white, while heavy marks crushed the tufts, forcing the crayon into the hollows and resulting in a totally blackened surface. Thus, by varying his touch, Seurat was able to create every possible nuance of tonal gradation, from the white of the paper through to solid velvety blacks. This mature drawing method totally renounced the use of line to create the edges of form, relying completely on subtle tonal modeling instead, enabling Seurat to evolve his strong handling of form through tonal contrast, which he translated in his painting into color modulations and contrasts.

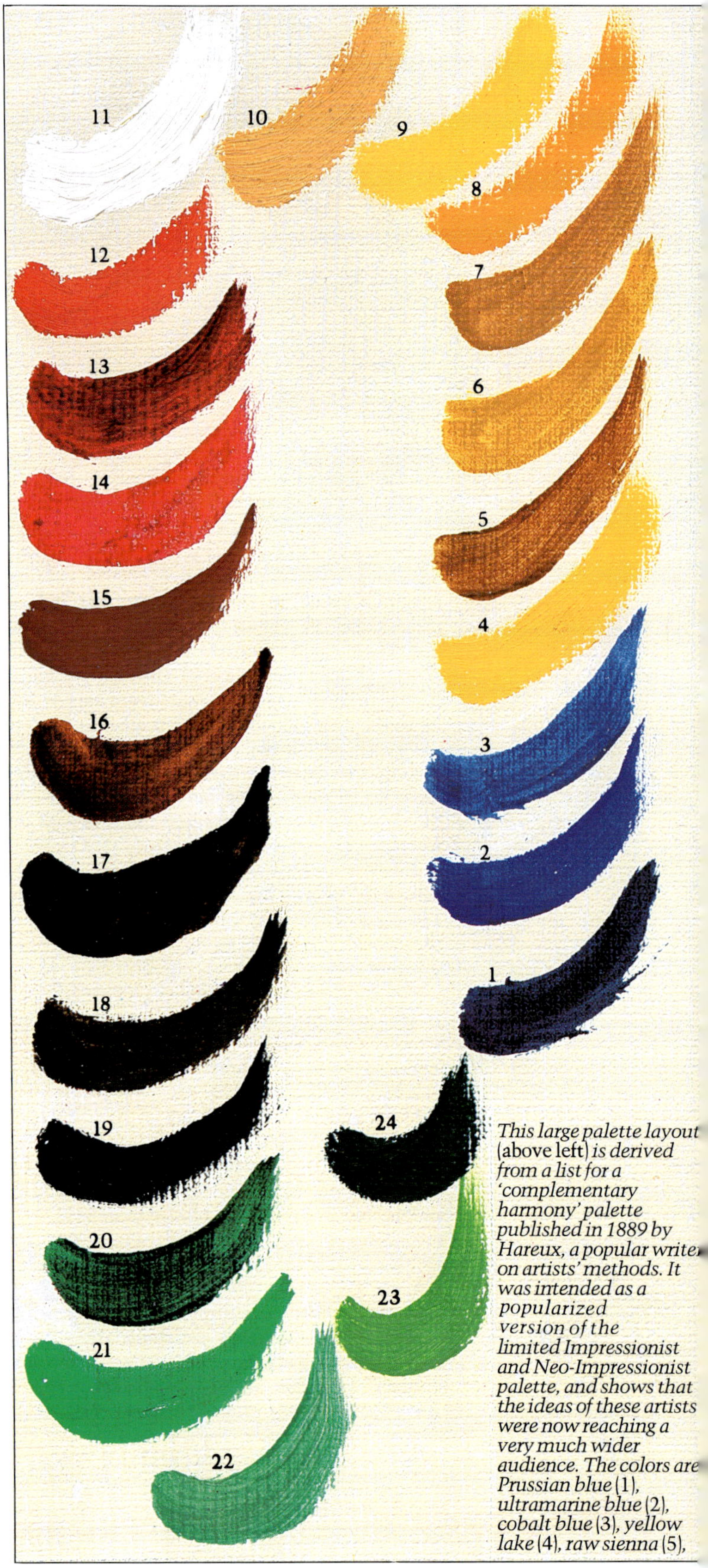


*This large palette layout (above left) is derived from a list for a 'complementary harmony' palette published in 1889 by Hareux, a popular writer on artists' methods. It was intended as a popularized version of the limited Impressionist and Neo-Impressionist palette, and shows that the ideas of these artists were now reaching a very much wider audience. The colors are Prussian blue* (1), *ultramarine blue* (2), *cobalt blue* (3), *yellow lake* (4), *raw sienna* (5),

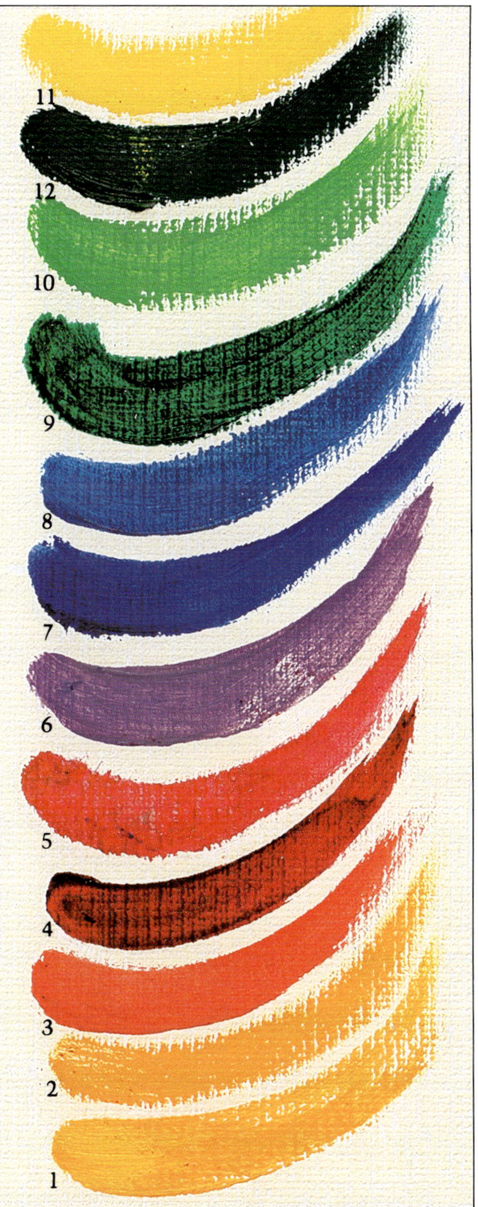


Indian yellow (6), yellow ochre (7), deep cadmium yellow (8), pale cadmium yellow (9), Naples yellow (10), flake white (11), vermilion (12), alizarin crimson (13), rose madder (14), Indian red (red earth) (15), burnt sienna (16), Vandyke brown (17), raw umber (18), ivory black (19), viridian green (20), emerald green (21), cobalt green (22), chrome green (23), and malachite green (24). The smaller palette (above right) shows Signac's prismatic palette layout. The colors were arranged according to the color circle and not in the traditional tonal order. The colors are mid cadmium yellow (1), deep cadmium yellow (2), vermilion (3), alizarin crimson (4), rose madder (5), cobalt violet (6), ultramarine blue (7), cobalt blue (8), cerulean blue, viridian green (9), pale chrome green (10), deep chrome green (11), and pale cadmium yellow (12). Certain of the colors, such as yellow lake, are not available today, so modern equivalents have been shown instead.

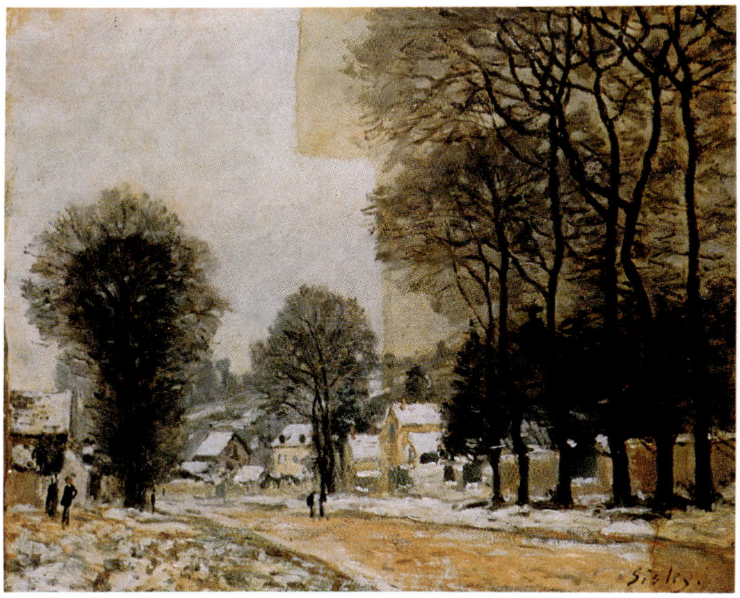

Left *This photograph of Sisley's* Snow at Louveciennes *(c1874) was taken during cleaning by the Courtauld Institute Department of Technology in London. It shows the dramatic effects of dirt and discolored varnish. Yellowed varnish makes the blues appear green, and casts unintended warmth over all color values. To avoid this danger, most Impressionists and Neo-Impressionists preferred unvarnished paintings. They also preferred to leave works unvarnished because they sought mat effects, and varnish not only made the surface glossy, it also darkened the pale tints selected to evoke natural light.*

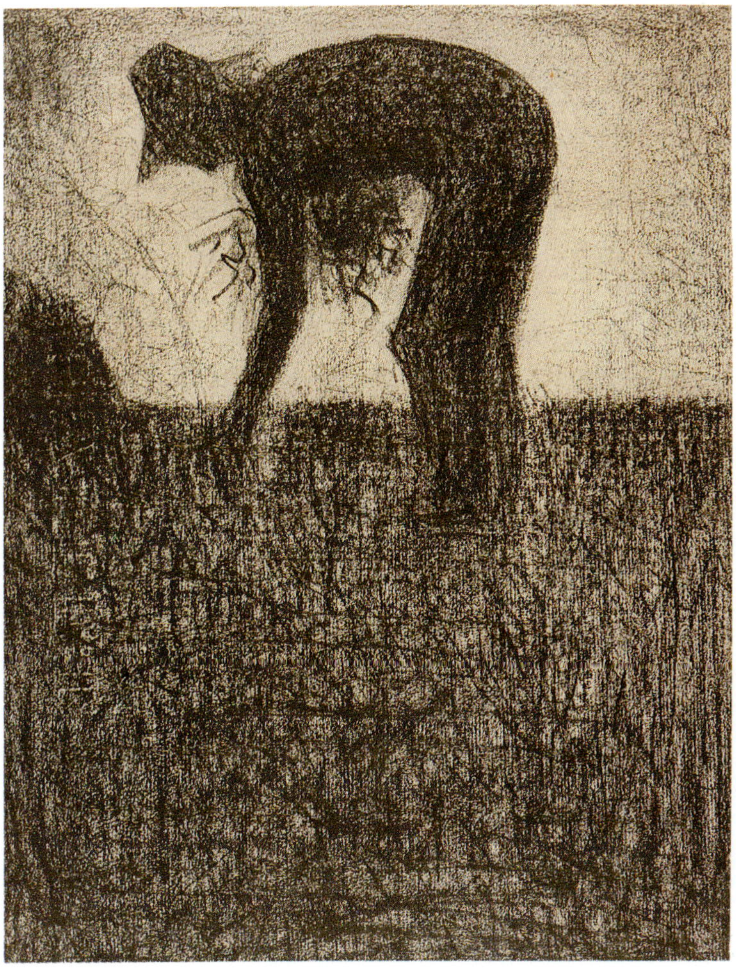

Left The Gleaner *(c1883) by Georges Seurat was drawn in black Conté crayon on Ingres paper. Seurat built up the tonal gradations in his drawing by varying the pressure and the density of the marks. The white of the paper glows through, giving the sensation of light emanating from the drawing itself. Although the criss-cross web of strokes may seem bold and disordered, the technique may in fact have been inspired by the approach for oil sketching taught by his academic tutor Lehmann. Seurat used similar handling in his small oil sketches of this period. Of even greater importance in the formation of Seurat's distinctive drawing style were undoubtedly pastel works by Millet. Seurat's mature drawing, like this one, is completely tonal in style, avoiding hatched lines or contours that contain form. Instead, the forms loom out of the prevailing darks.*

Below *Seurat developed his dot touch during the summer of 1885, when this work,* Le Bec du Hoc at Grandchamp, *was executed. The detail from the center cliff edge (*right*) shows that, despite a reduced size of touch, the shape of mark still varies, subtly differentiating textures and following forms. The dot method enabled Seurat to note minute gradations of tone and changes of hue, giving him great control over his depiction of form and colored light.*

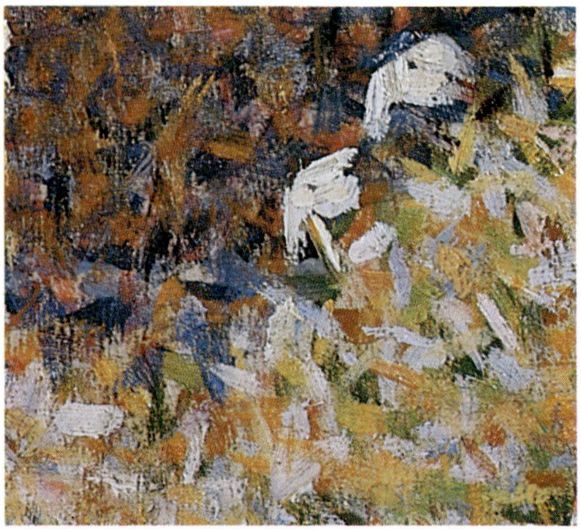

**Pointillism and color theory**

Seurat's mature pointillist technique, in which almost uniform 'mechanical' dots of pure color were built up over the entire paint surface, was already inherent in his work before 1885, although it was handled quite differently. Thus a dotted effect is discernible in his Conté drawings and in a painting technique adopted from the Impressionists. In this, his use of dragged, chalky paint catching on the raised canvas grain or on earlier dried brushstrokes in works like *Bathing* (1883–1884) presents the eye with an erratically speckled effect as broken layers of color reveal previous colors. However, his methodical application of colored dots, developed in works like *Le Bec du Hoc* (1885), was a systematization of previously

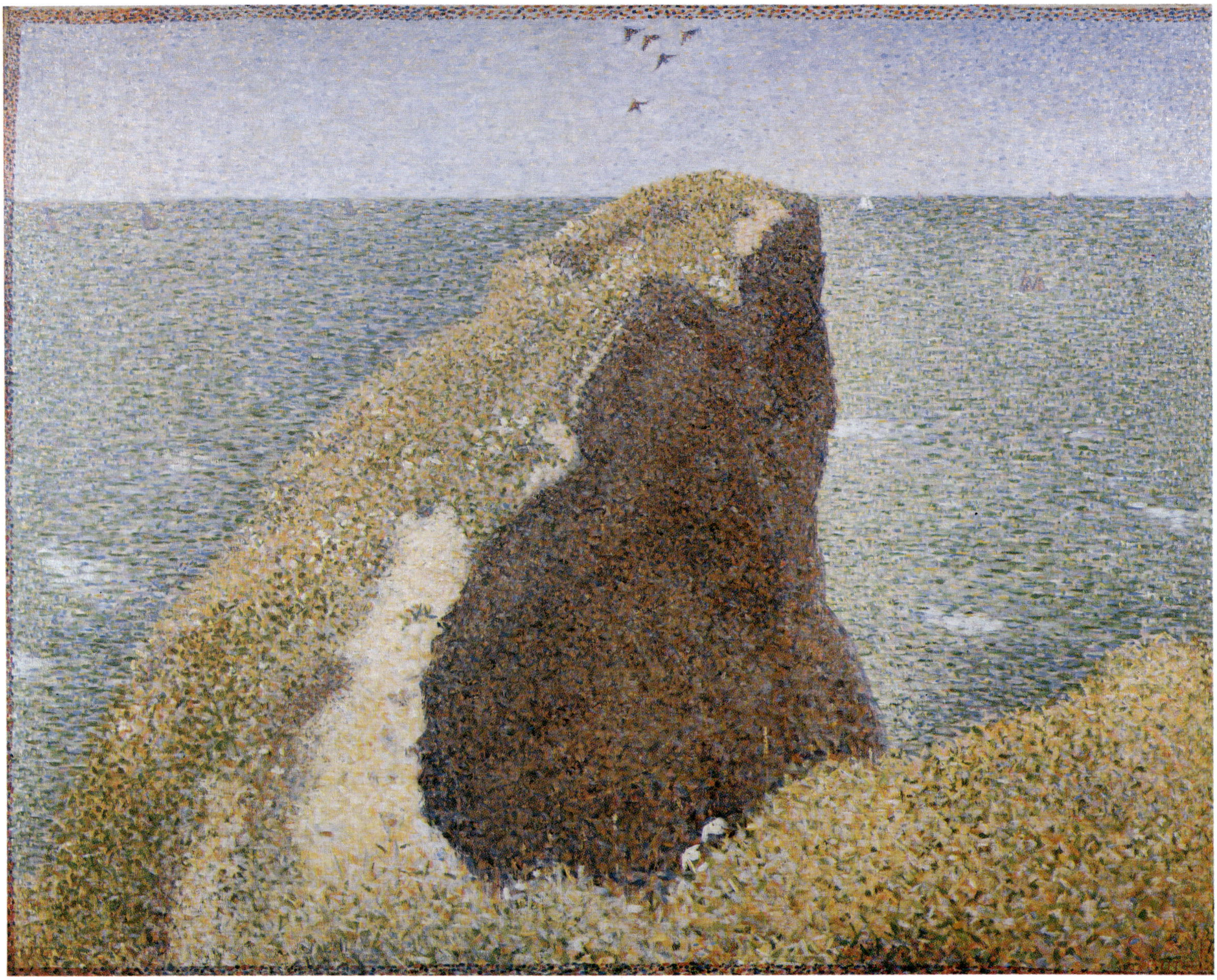

'accidental' effects. Recent scholarship suggests that Seurat's use of the dot technique was inspired by contemporary developments in color printing. Seurat showed great interest in this popular art form, both because of its techniques and its stylized designs. Seurat's radical taste for popular, 'democratic' art forms – which had precedents in the sources used by, for example, Courbet and Manet – and his fascination with modern science and technology, reflected his radical political leanings.

Seurat found the theoretical basis for his use of individual dots of prismatic color to depict the fusion of color and light in nature in the important treatise *Modern Chromatics* written by the American color theorist Ogden Rood and published in 1879. However, these ideas had been prefigured in the writings on color by theorists and critics such as Michel-Eugène Chevreul, Charles Blanc and John Ruskin which Seurat also consulted. Rood maintained that optical mixtures of rays of colored light, reflected from the paint surface and fusing on the spectator's retina, would be far superior in luminosity to the effects afforded by conventional, dull palette mixtures.

In Seurat's painting, the rays of colored light emanating from each separate spot of colored pigment were not intended to result in optical mixtures of greater intensity than their original individual components. They were also not intended to fuse completely on the retina, for the dots were generally too distinct for that. Rather, when seen at the appropriate viewing distance, which was considered to be of three times the length of the pictures' diagonal, the incomplete fusion of colored dots resulted in a flickering optical sensation. This was because, as the influential French Symbolist critic Félix Fénéon perceptively noted in 1886, 'the retina, expecting distinct groups of light rays to act upon it, perceives in very rapid alternation both the disassociated colored elements and their resultant color.' For Seurat, this gave a pictorial equivalent for the shimmering subtleties of transparency and reflected light found often in the halftones and shadows in nature. Seurat's use of small touches of color enabled him to achieve a twofold objective. On the one hand, it lent a limpid atmospheric luminosity to the painting. On the other, it gave a powerful sense of modeled forms. This was because Seurat could create minute variations of tone, from rich saturated color through to the palest tones, by increasing the proportion of white added to his color.

Between 1886 and 1888, Seurat began to extend his desire to systematize painting, searching for methodical means to convey predictable emotional effects in painting through precise combinations of line, color and tone. This new preoccupation was inspired both by the writings of his contemporary, the psychologist and aesthetician Charles Henry, and by the ideas of the literary Symbolists, who were then coming to prominence. In the late 1880s the Symbolist movement in painting grew out of the literary Symbolist movement. Reacting against accepted ideas of naturalism and against modern society and technology, Symbolism emphasized the inner, emotional world of the creator as against the external natural world which had for so long been the chief source of artistic inspiration.

Aspects of Symbolist ideals pervaded most artistic developments during the late 1880s and 1890s, and the movement represented the first widespread repudiation of Impressionist ideas. Despite this reaction, the Impressionists' painting methods continued to provide a rich source of inspiration for many artists. Developments in the 1890s and after, which appear to be reactions against Impressionism, in fact owe much to the lively potential unleashed by Impressionist stylistic and technical innovations.

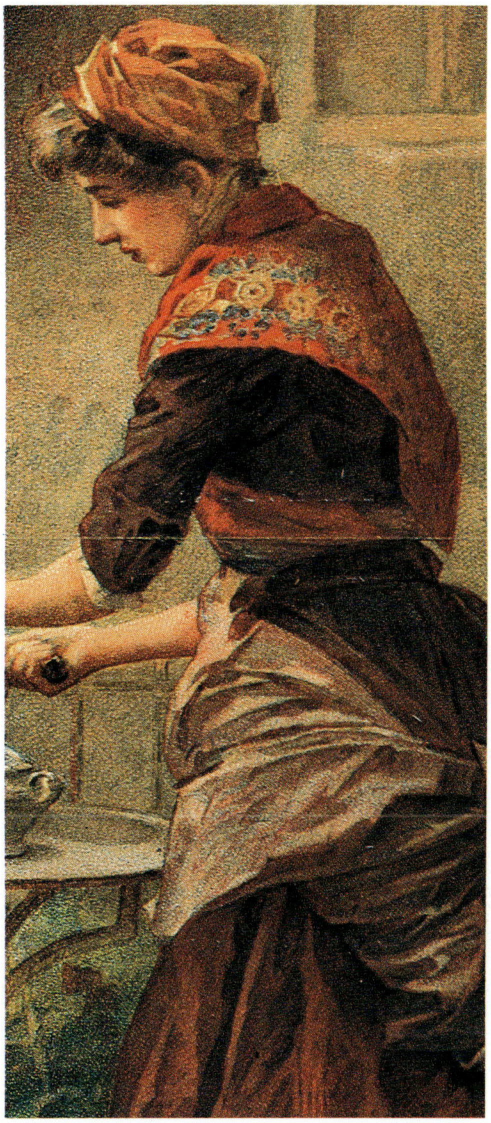

Left *This is an example of a chromotypogravure, published in the magazine* L'Illustration *in December 1885. In this early method of color reproduction, colors were reproduced as a series of dots. This may have inspired Seurat's development of his Pointillist method. He is known to have been fascinated by both modern technology and images derived from popular culture. This detail shows the similarity between Seurat's method, and that used here in color printing.*

# PAUL CEZANNE

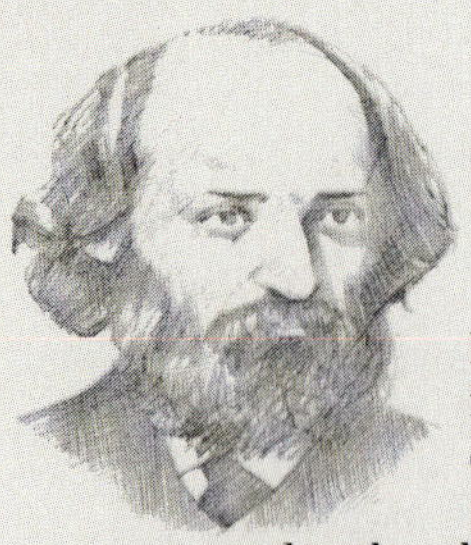

## *Mountains seen from l'Estaque/Montagnes vues de l'Estaque* (*c* 1878-1880)

Oil on cream-prepared paper, mounted later on canvas
53.3cm × 72.4cm/21in × $28\frac{1}{2}$in

Born in Aix-en-Provence, not far from the French Mediterranean coast near where this picture was painted, Cézanne's upbringing under the clear golden light of the south was permanently to influence his vision as a painter. After regular, extended periods in the French capital during the 1860s and 1870s, a dislike of the city, and disillusionment with his lack of success, encouraged Cézanne to return to a more isolated existence in the south. Although visited regularly by friends, like Monet and Renoir in the early 1880s and, later, by the younger generation of artists, Cézanne spent less time in Paris, occasionally staying and working with colleagues in the northern countryside. The generally more stable, good weather, clearer light and purer atmosphere of the south of France provided Cézanne with the best conditions under which to pursue his particular preoccupations in painting from nature.

Cézanne painted slowly and carefully, often working on a single canvas off and on over several years. For this reason, the relatively more stable southern climate worked in his favor, enabling him to return to a motif, or subject, on many successive days and find comparable atmospheric effects. He realized that the effects of sunlight could not be reproduced in painting, but that the artist had to represent light through color. His fastidious concern with finding the precise tone or color value for each brushstroke in a painting, resulted from the need to construct an overall harmony of color – equivalent to that in nature – in which no single note was out of tune with the others. One incorrectly judged value in a painting would thus have necessitated reworking the entire canvas, to make it harmonize with that one jarring note.

*Mountains seen from l'Estaque* is an example of Cézanne's sustained study from nature. As with many eighteenth and early nineteenth century landscape oil sketches, this work was executed on paper. This support may have been chosen by Cézanne for economy and portability, because its large size and the degree of finish suggest that he did not see it simply as a sketch. Another important painting of around 15 years later, *Still Life with Plaster Cupid*, was done on an almost identical support. Cézanne bought the support for *Mountains seen from l'Estaque* ready primed with a cream commercial ground. Prepared paper was sold both in standard canvas size and in the differing standard paper sizes. This support is close in size to the horizontal landscape format 20, which measures 73 × 54cm (29 × 21in), and also to the *demi-grand aigle* prepared paper format measuring 75 × 52cm ($29\frac{1}{2} \times 20\frac{1}{2}$in). Prepared paper was normally sold with a creamy pale tinted priming, available in two different finish textures. The first gave the appearance of canvas fabric, for canvas was pressed into the wet ground and then peeled off to leave its imprint. The second finish had the bubbled appearance of modern emulsion paint applied with a roller; this was the type chosen here by Cézanne. Pinhole marks in the corners of such paper supports are a reminder that they had to be attached to a firm card or wooden backing during painting.

In *Mountains seen from l'Estaque*, as in *Still Life with Plaster Cupid*, Cézanne intentionally allowed the cream ground to show through among the colors in the paint layer, leaving it completely uncovered in places. There it reads as a color in its own right among the applied colors of the paint layer, saving the artist time, or standing for highlights he intended to add in later. Like Renoir, Cézanne exploited the contrasting effects of warm and cool colors in his painting. Where the warm cream ground shows through, it creates vibrant contrasts with the cool colors in the paint layer. Thus, by juxtaposing opaque blues, for example on the skyline, left, against the cream of the ground, they are mutually enhanced. The cool blue appears even bluer and cooler, the cream of the ground is warmed, appearing pinkish against the blues. Because warm colors advance and cool colors recede optically, they can be used to model form and structure spatial recession. Cézanne's limited palette means that subtly modulated mixtures and repeated usages of the same color in different contexts, gives an extraordinary harmony to the work.

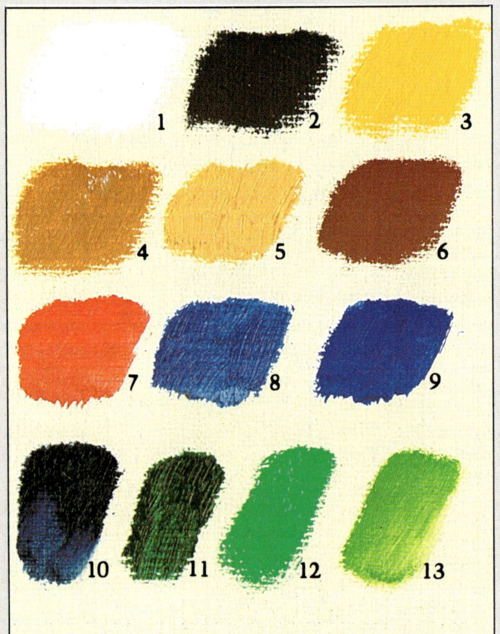


*Cézanne's palette for this work probably comprised lead white (1), zinc white, black (2), chrome yellow (3), yellow ochre (4), red earth (6) or vermilion (7), cobalt blue (8), ultramarine blue (9), viridian green (11) and emerald green (12). Other pigments possibly used were Naples yellow (5), Prussian blue (10) and chrome green (13).*

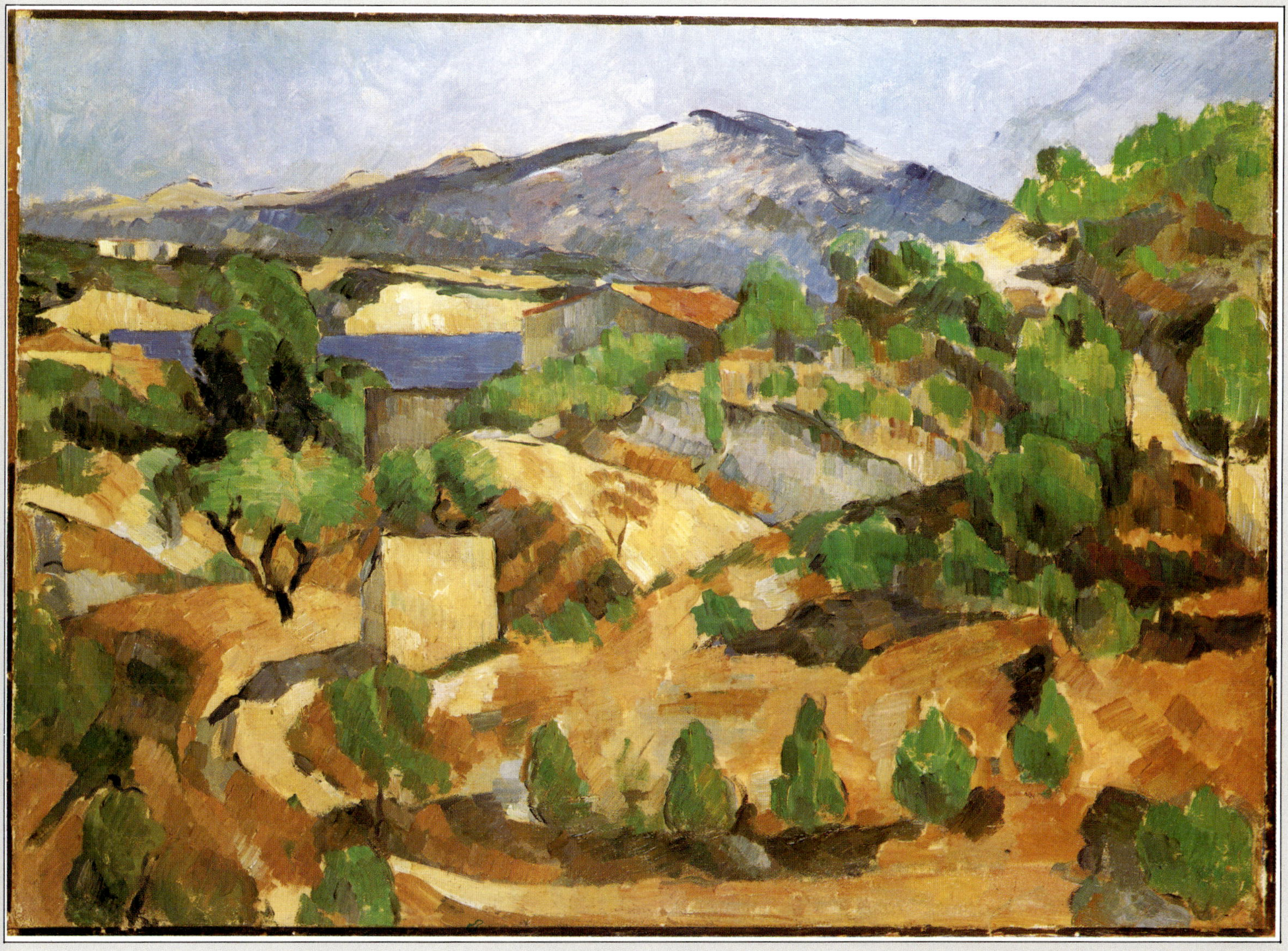

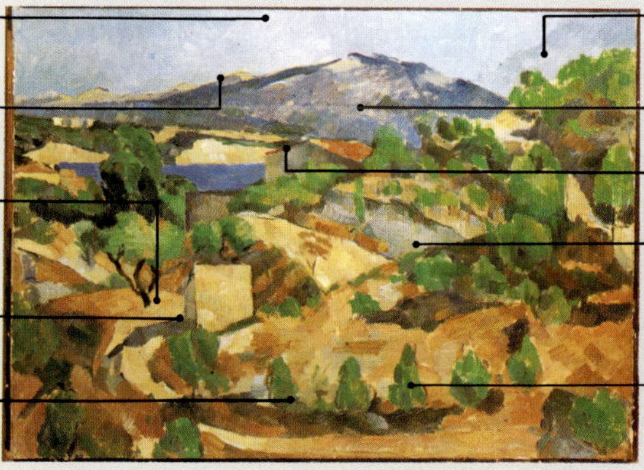


*Cézanne's separate brushstrokes of paint serve both to record his visual sensations of color, and to structure his composition. The touches here vary according to the angle of planes and the direction of forms. The trees in the foreground are depicted with curved strokes which suggest their characteristic form. Local colors are bright in the clear light, modified only by the warm sunlight and cool blue shadows. The fall of light, from right to left across the view, casts shadows which add structure to the composition.*

*Brushstrokes depicting background areas are equal in size to those used in the foreground. This device is contrary to the more conventional use of varied brushstroke size to suggest depth and recession. More traditional landscape painters tended to paint the foreground broadly and diminish the scale of touch for 'distant' objects. Similarly, Cézanne avoided the use of aerial perspective – the lightening of hues toward the sky line to evoke distance. He painted his landscapes with the same degree of color saturation throughout. This tends to flatten the design close to the picture plane, producing tension between the surface pattern and the illusionistic qualities in the work.*

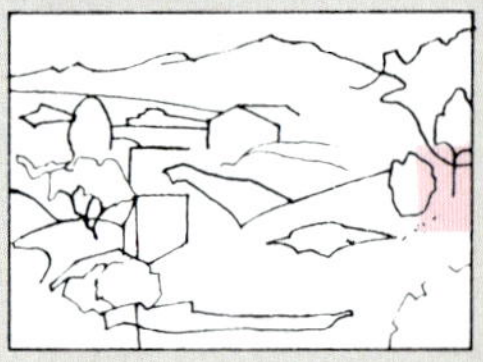

The foreground stone building in Cézanne's picture shows the outdoor effects of warm sunlight. Unlike most of the other Impressionists, he often chose side-lit scenes, and here the rays fall at an angle of about 45° across the landscape, from right to left. The warm yellow sun casts a blueish shadow, picking up reflected light from the clear blue Mediterranean sky. This even shadow adds structure to the composition by 'anchoring' the form which casts it, and defining the ground plane on which the building sits. Alternating planes of warm and cool colors give form and space to the scene, although, by stressing the picture plane, the emphatic brushwork and strong colors tend to work against simple illusion.

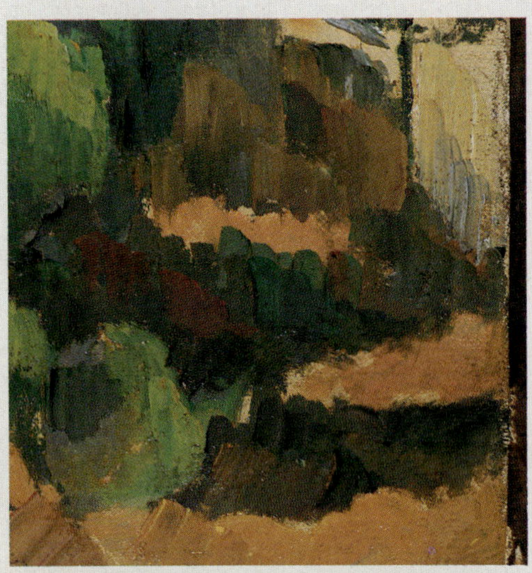

The 'directional' brushwork evolved by Cézanne in the late 1870s can be seen in this picture. In places, for example the more roughly executed mountain in the background, the lack of finish has left the earlier, less organized brushwork exposed, but generally the size and direction of touch is fairly uniform. Sometimes the direction of touch sweeps round, following and emphasizing the separate interlocking folds of the landscape, as in the foreground parts. A high viewpoint, looking down on the scene, was chosen by Cézanne, and this tips the landscape up, flattening it closer to the picture plane and cutting down the sky area.

Cézanne preferred to work outdoors in very clear, crisp lighting conditions, particularly after storms when the air is very pure. In such light, even distant vistas appeared quite close and the phenomenon of aerial perspective – local colors becoming paler and bluer toward the horizon – was at a minimum. This meant that the colors of the landscape were at their most saturated and pure, and distant colors had almost equal strength to those close to. This uniform saturation of color is apparent in this picture, and it contradicts the illusion of space because background colors are as rich as those in the foreground. Cézanne's uniform size of touch, which makes the viewer very aware of surface qualities and textures, has a very similar effect. The contradictions between surface flatness and illusionistic space in Cézanne's painting, like that of Monet and Pissarro, create a characteristic visual tension. This work was first owned by Gauguin, who greatly admired Cézanne's methods.

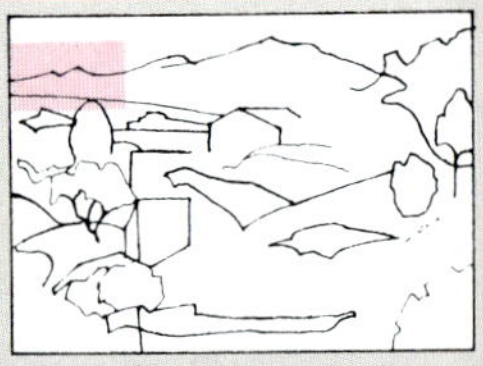

Actual size detail *The cream ground over the paper support is clearly visible here, for it is left uncovered along the line of the mountains. There, the cream color makes the cool blues of sky and hills more intense. The ragged paper edge is visible on the left. For preservation, the work was laid down on canvas, probably when Gauguin owned it in the early 1880s.*

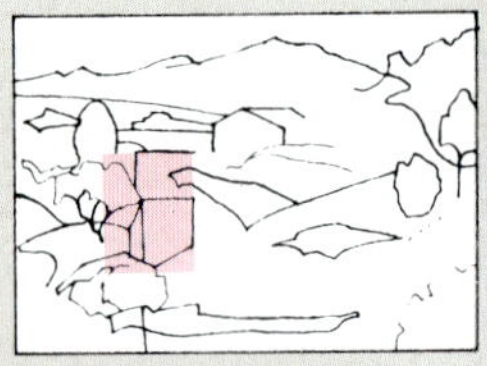

*Vertical, block-like strokes of color help define the form of the building, while the blue light-filled shadow attached to the side wall adds solidity. The shadow cast by the building anchors it in space, defining the ground plane on which it stands. The paint is thick and opaque. Its white hues evoke the quality of sunny southern light, bouncing off pale, dusty surfaces. The flowing rhythms of the parallel brushmarks almost sculpt the changing directions of planes of the landscape terrain.*

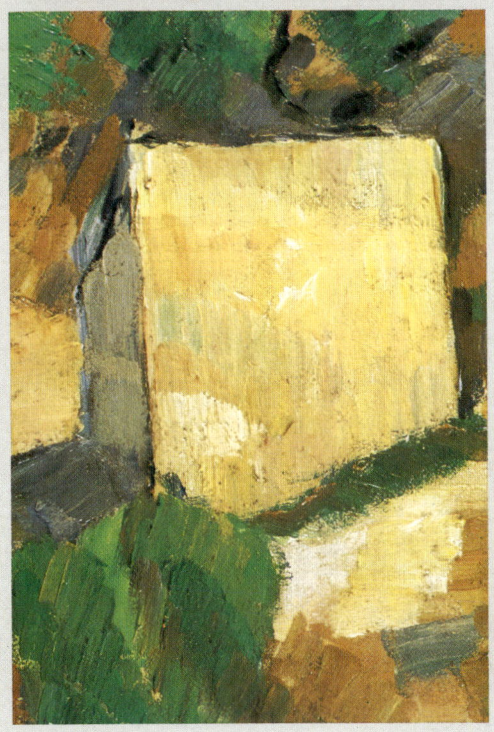

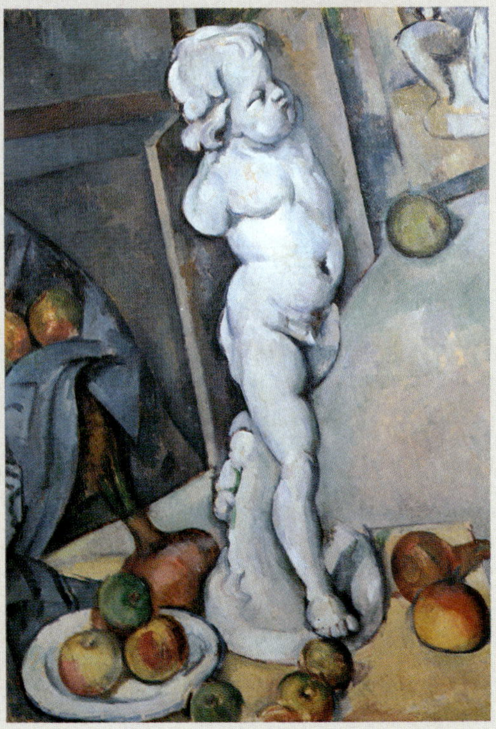

*Cézanne's* Still Life with a Plaster Cupid *from the mid 1890s is painted on a support comparable to that used for* Mountains at l'Estaque. *It too was executed on commercially prepared paper, primed with a cream ground which shows through among the colors. In places, the cream ground was left bare to stand as a hue and tone in its own right, while on the center right, the thinly applied warm and cool colors of the floor area are influenced by the cream of the ground glowing through.*

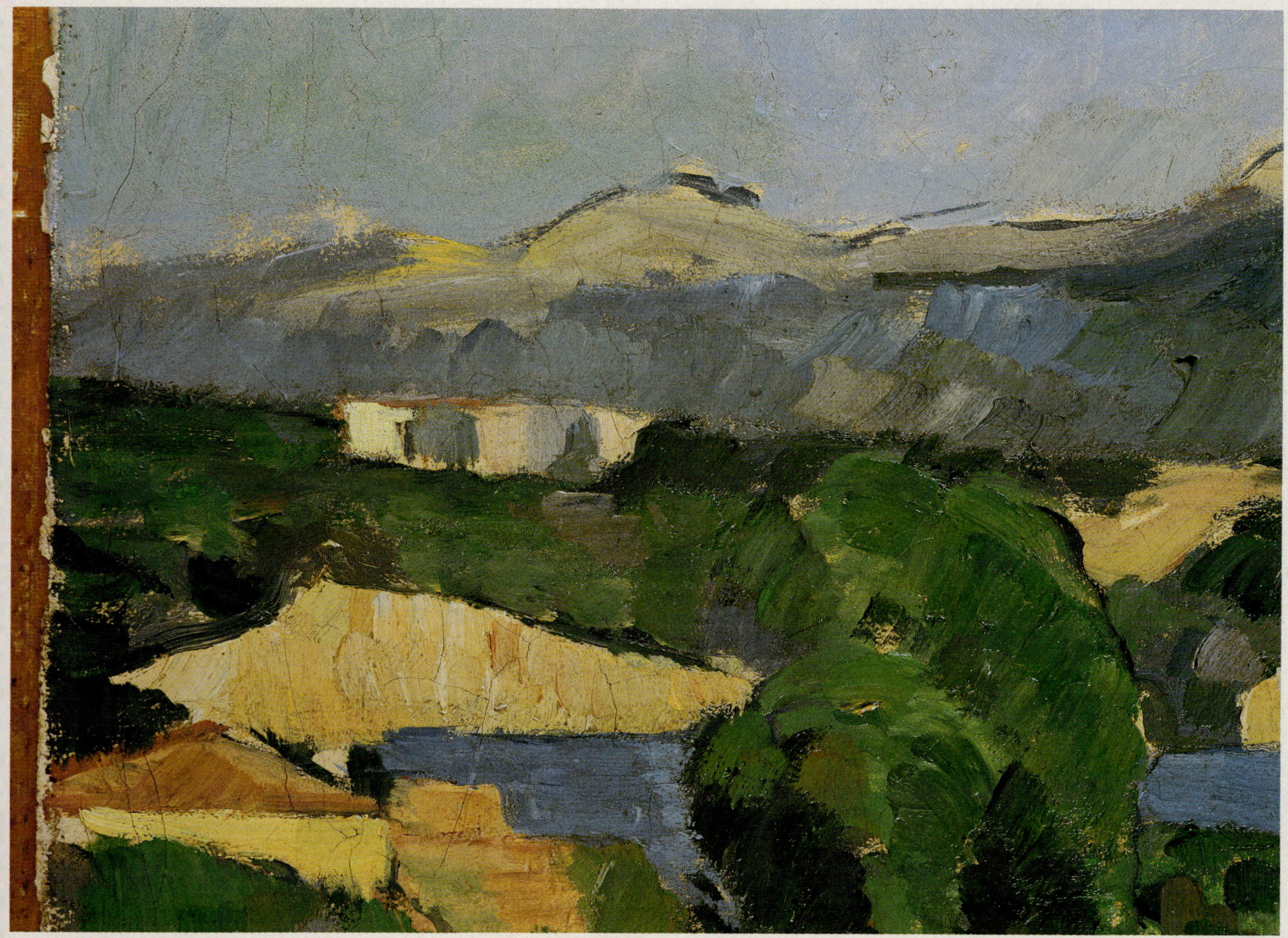

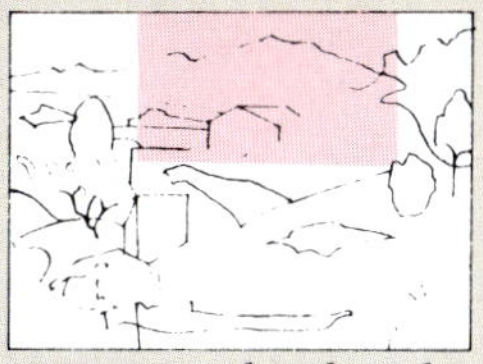

Contrasts in brushwork and paint thickness are visible here. This difference gives distance to the peak. However, this is contradicted by the zigzagged pale blue which overlaps the paint depicting the hillside in the middle distance.

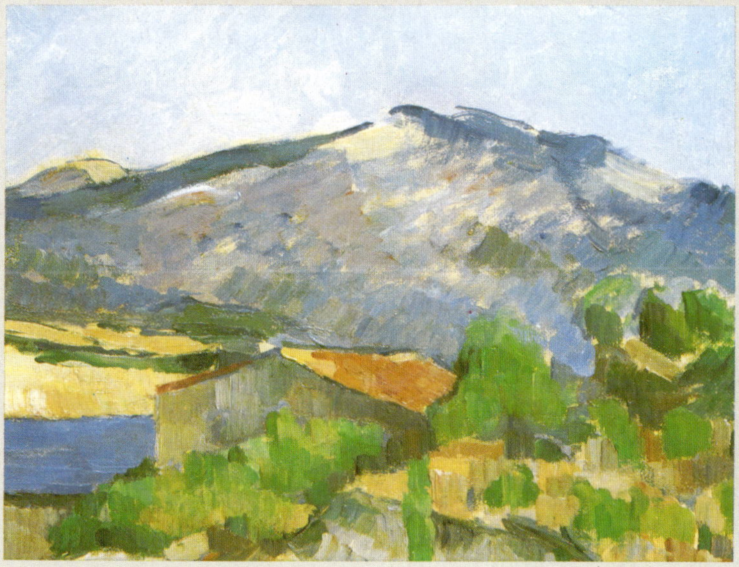

# EDGAR DEGAS

*After the Bath, Woman Drying Herself/Après le Bain, Femme s'Essuyant* (1880)
Pastel on cardboard, 104cm × 98.5cm/40⅞in × 38¾in

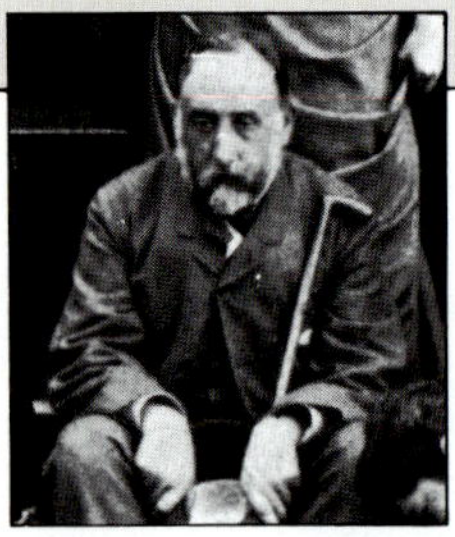

In 1854 Degas abandoned his study of law and began training under Louis Lamothe, a pupil of Ingres. Degas subsequently met Ingres and was encouraged by the master to 'draw lines'. He proceeded to develop as a superb classical draftsman, combining this with his strength as colorist to unite these two conflicting French traditions represented, on the one hand, by Poussin and Rubens in the seventeenth century, and, on the other, by Ingres and Delacroix in the nineteenth.

For Degas, art had a strong intellectual basis, as he himself stated 'What I do is the result of reflection and study, . . . of inspiration, spontaneity, temperament I know nothing.' Unlike most Impressionists, he worked indoors from memory and was not interested in working from nature. Degas' scientific curiosity led him to experiment with many techniques and media.

On canvas, he used a variety of grounds and experimented with raw canvas. He also painted on supports made of colored paper laid on canvas in which the color and absorbency of the paper played a central role. Such works demonstrate Degas' experiments employing a technique of soaking the oil binder from the color on blotting paper prior to diluting it with turpentine to create a fluid, quick-drying, matt medium. The dry, pastel-like film thus created was similar to that of his pastel drawings, and he often combined these techniques adding gouache, drawing materials, and printing ink to his multi-media repertoire.

X-rays of Degas' oil paintings suggest that beneath the precision of his early style lay the economical and blurred studies characteristic of his later work. Unlike Monet and Renoir, Degas' paint film was built up in distinct and fairly regular layers.

Pastels gave Degas an ideal combination of color and line which he built into a web of crossed striations of color each reading through to previous layers. Steaming the pastel surface dissolved the pigment into films of color, which Degas then worked as a paste with a stiff brush or his fingers or, when the mixture was more fluid, spread like a thin scumbled wash. Degas' use of pastel, which made work easier as his eyesight began to fail in the mid-1880s, gave this hitherto relatively underexploited medium a new importance.

**1.** A medium weight, textured cream-colored pastel paper was used.

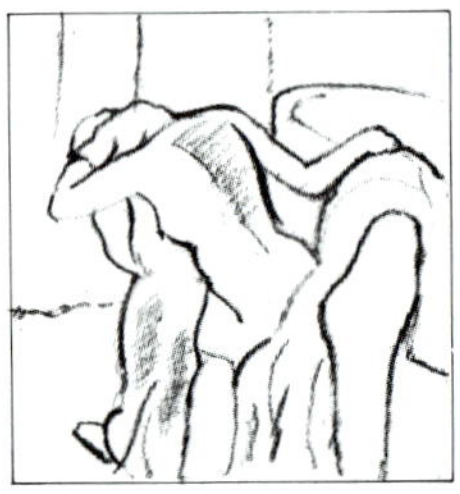

**2.** Charcoal was used for drawing in contours and the gray shadows.

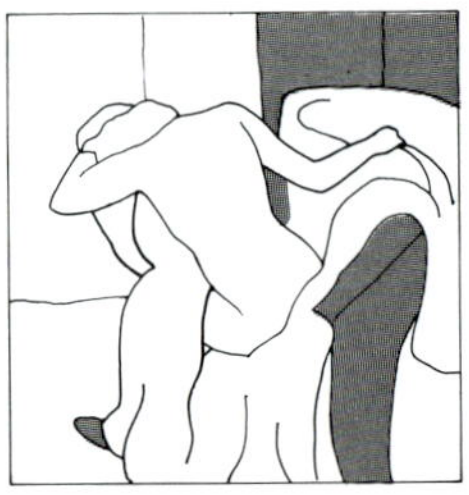

**3.** Colors were built up over the picture simultaneously, the same hue being picked up at different points in the composition and applied with the same intensity.

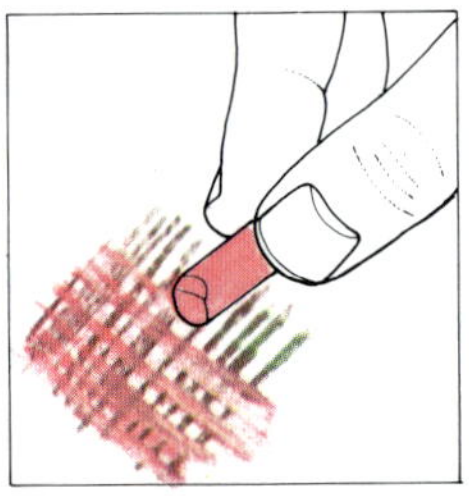

**4.** Colors are worked in open, webbed layers, so that earlier colors read through.

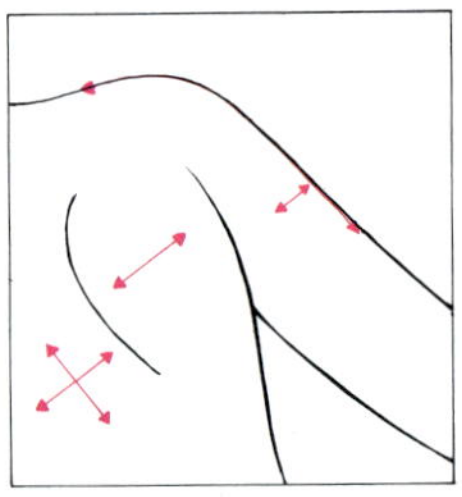

**5.** A variety of strokes was used; some defined the forms and others contradicted it to emphasize the shallow pictorial space.

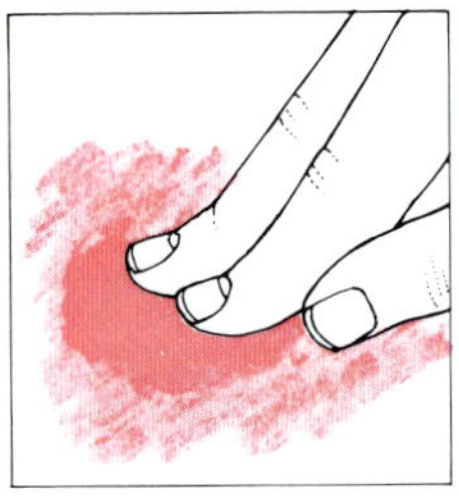

**6.** Sometimes a thin mist of water was sprayed over the surface creating a paste-like consistency which Degas would then work with a stiff brush or his fingers.

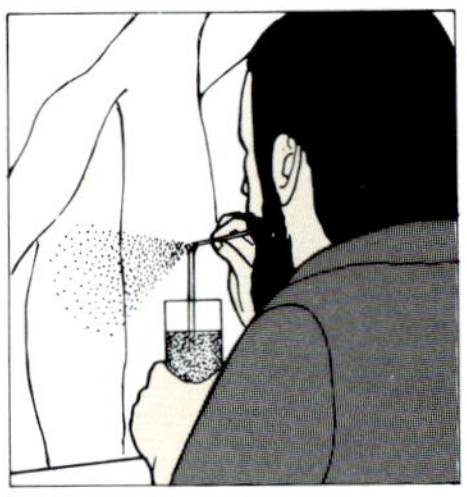

**7.** Degas experimented with different fixatives. A recent innovation, fixatives were generally poor in quality. They tend to darken and muddy colors; artists preferred to have the picture put under glass to protect it.

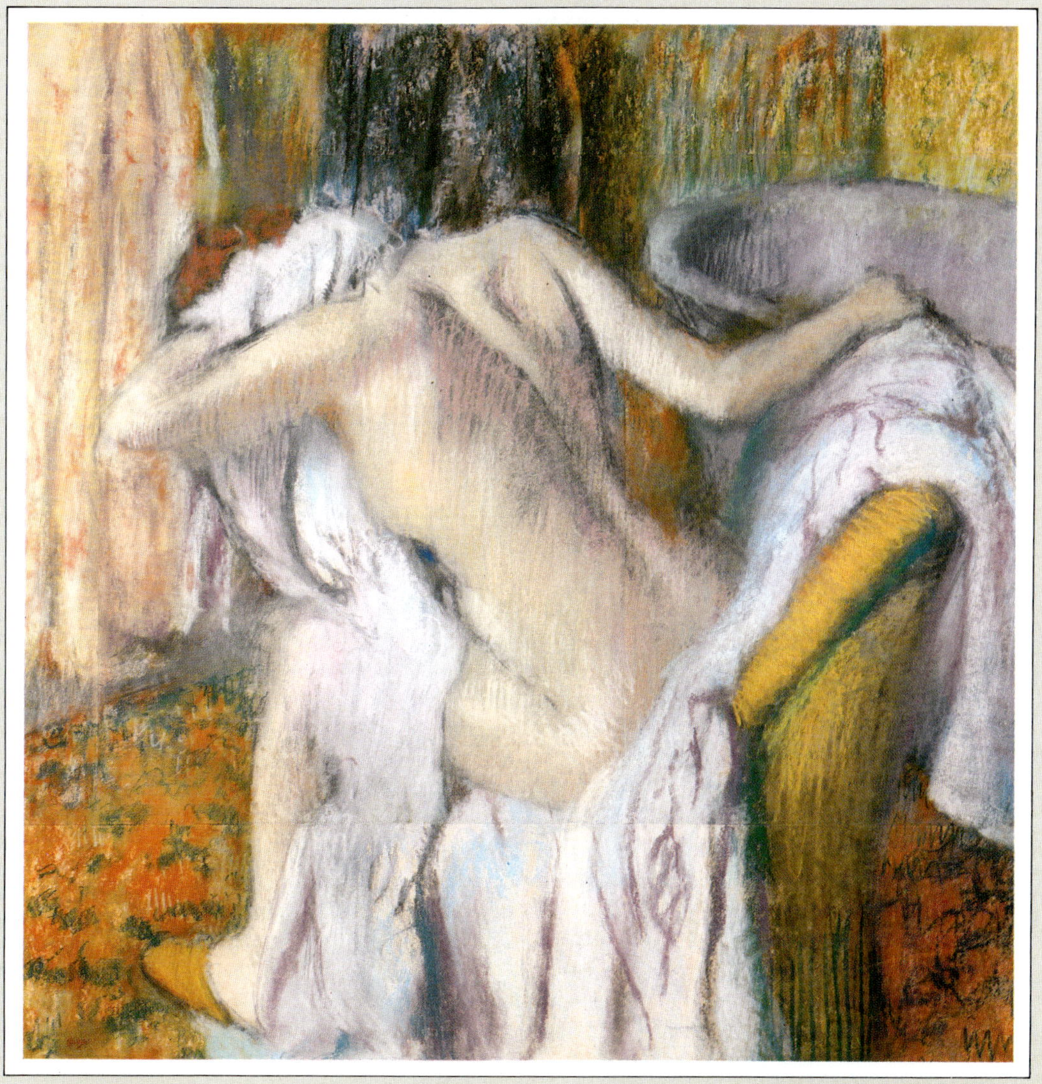

*The squarish format with the figure cramped in the pictorial space is typical of Degas' style. The cream-colored paper adds warmth and provides basic coloristic unity. While the cream color is obliterated in the heavily worked areas of the flesh, chair, and bath, the paper texture remains to break the pastel strokes, giving a flecked surface of interwoven color. The outlines and areas of shading in the torso and towel are established in charcoal. The marks of the pastel evoke texture varying greatly from short, pressured strokes, to longer, sweeping lines. The repetition of color across the picture encourages the eye to move across the surface and make visual links. The woman's pose, with her back flattened parallel to the picture plane stresses the geometry of the composition.*

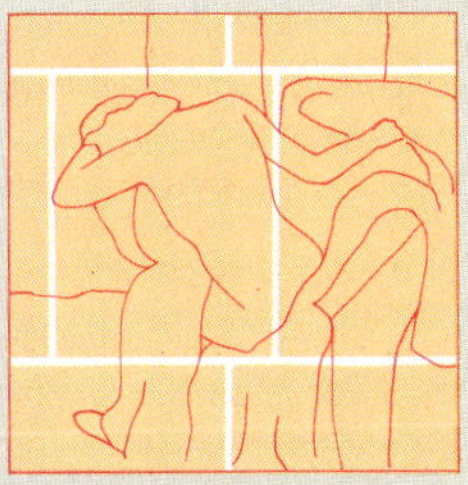

*The picture is on textured, cream non-pressed paper. The central horizontal panel has two vertical joints, one through the outer curve of the woman's waist and one to the left of her projecting elbow. Narrow strips on the top and bottom are divided vertically down the middle. The pieces of paper appear to abut each other and not overlap. The upper and lower strips may be overlapped by the entire central block, as pastel strokes appear to have 'skipped' the seam, and the upper and lower strips seem to be less heavily worked. Faint evidence of a pin-hole may indicate that the central panel was begun before the others.*

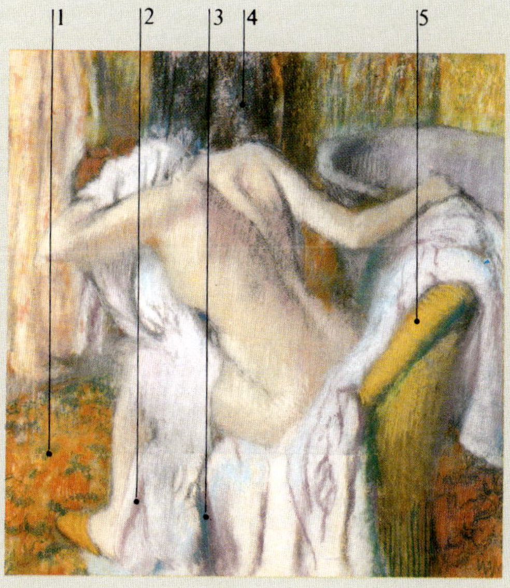


*The pastel marks vary greatly in this picture and are used for both decorative and textural effects. Short, pressured strokes (1) describe the carpet with zig-zags of dark blue-green on top, and longer, sweeping lines of purple (2) give the effect of shadows on the towel; soft, slurred strokes (3) give a bluish reflection on the white fabric. Stabbed, hard touches (4) using the pastel tip give a grayish pattern above the woman's head and neck, and the bright yellow used on the slipper and chair (5) is laid over orange.*

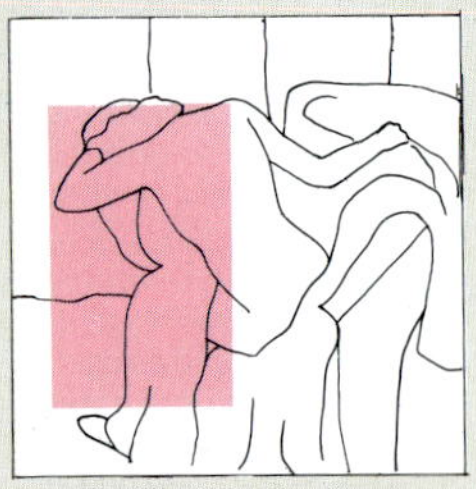

*The artist's hesitation and changes in the position of the figure remain visible. The projecting elbow was shortened as was the thigh, the knee being moved to the right. Adjustments to the upper arm relate to those at the elbow, and neither the arm nor the leg was definitively completed. A late working of orange into the gap between the waist and right arm extends over the hip and may have been due to Degas' failing eyesight. However, it serves to stress the highlight catching the hip and waist to the right of the spine, thus reinforcing the pattern of diagonals and the main axis of the spine.*

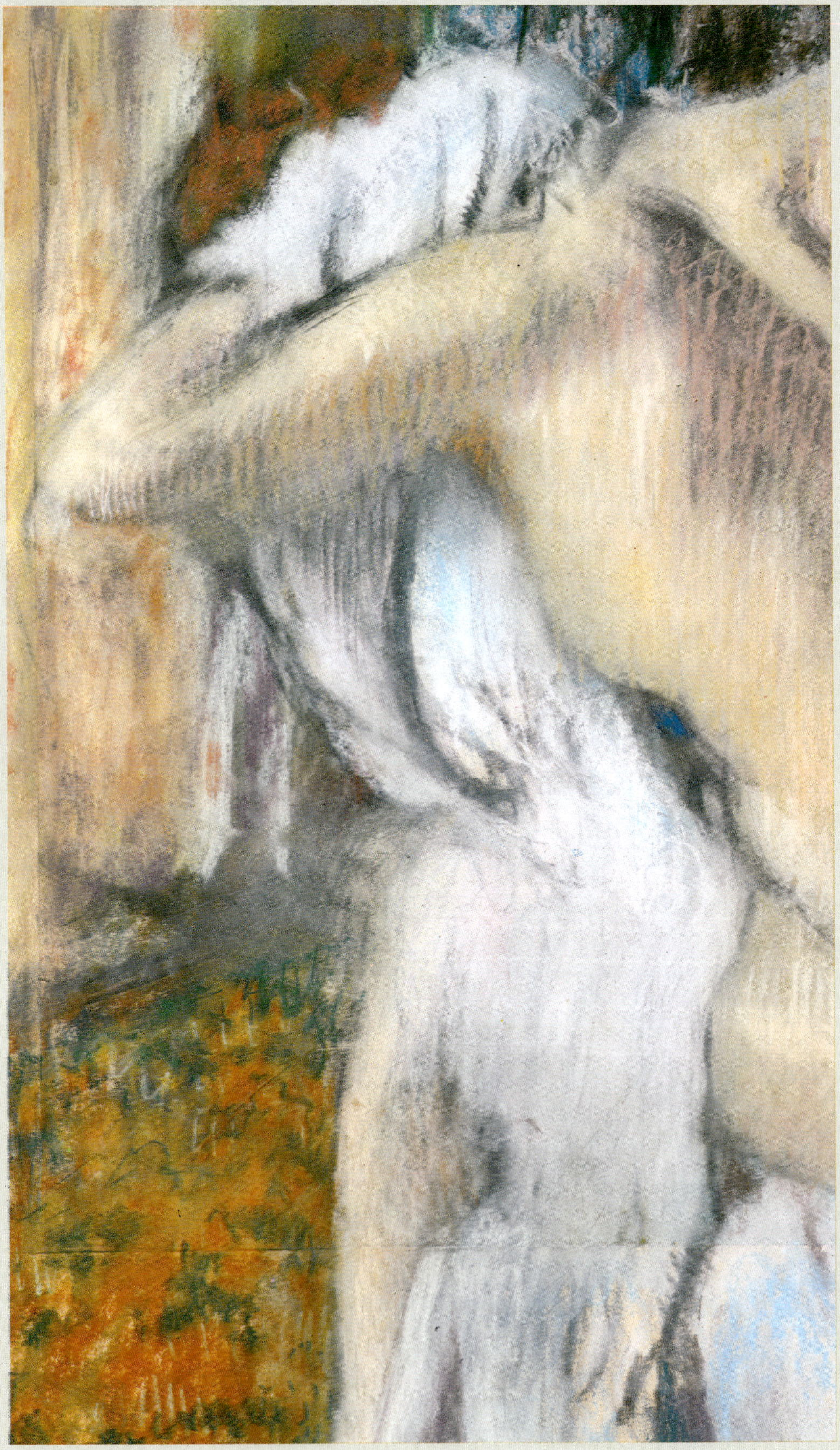

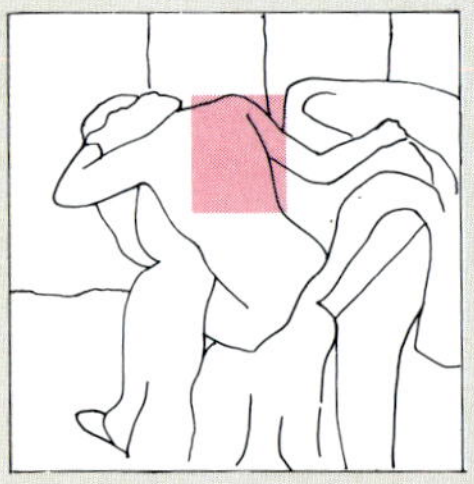

Actual size detail

*The cream-colored paper glows faintly through the smudged charcoal grays of the shoulder blade contour and shadows acting as muted flesh tints. Pale madder pinks and creamy, probably Naples yellow were used, with white on top in strong hatched striations which allow the charcoal grays to show through. Blue pastel is worked into white at the peak of the shoulder, while orange strokes add warmth to the contour of the upper arm. The soft, friable pastel pigment catches on the textured paper creating a stippled flickering effect between the layers of alternate dark and pale color. The dusty opaque dryness typical of pastel surfaces is clearly visible here.*

*Degas used a wide range of pastels, with colors worked into one another on the picture surface to produce additional tints and broken colors. Ultramarine appears in a raw touch just below the breast and in the curtains above the woman's right shoulder. Purple is used on the towel, as are white and pale turquoise. The deep shadows on the towel are dark blue-green which also appears on the chair and carpet. Orange is picked up on the wall under the woman's right arm, the crook of her right elbow, on the wall at top right, and the curtains, top left. Flesh tints are dominated by a grayish yellow and warmed by a variety of pinks. Alizarin is also used in the hair and curtains, and viridian green in the carpet. White is worked into the towel and highlights on the flesh.*

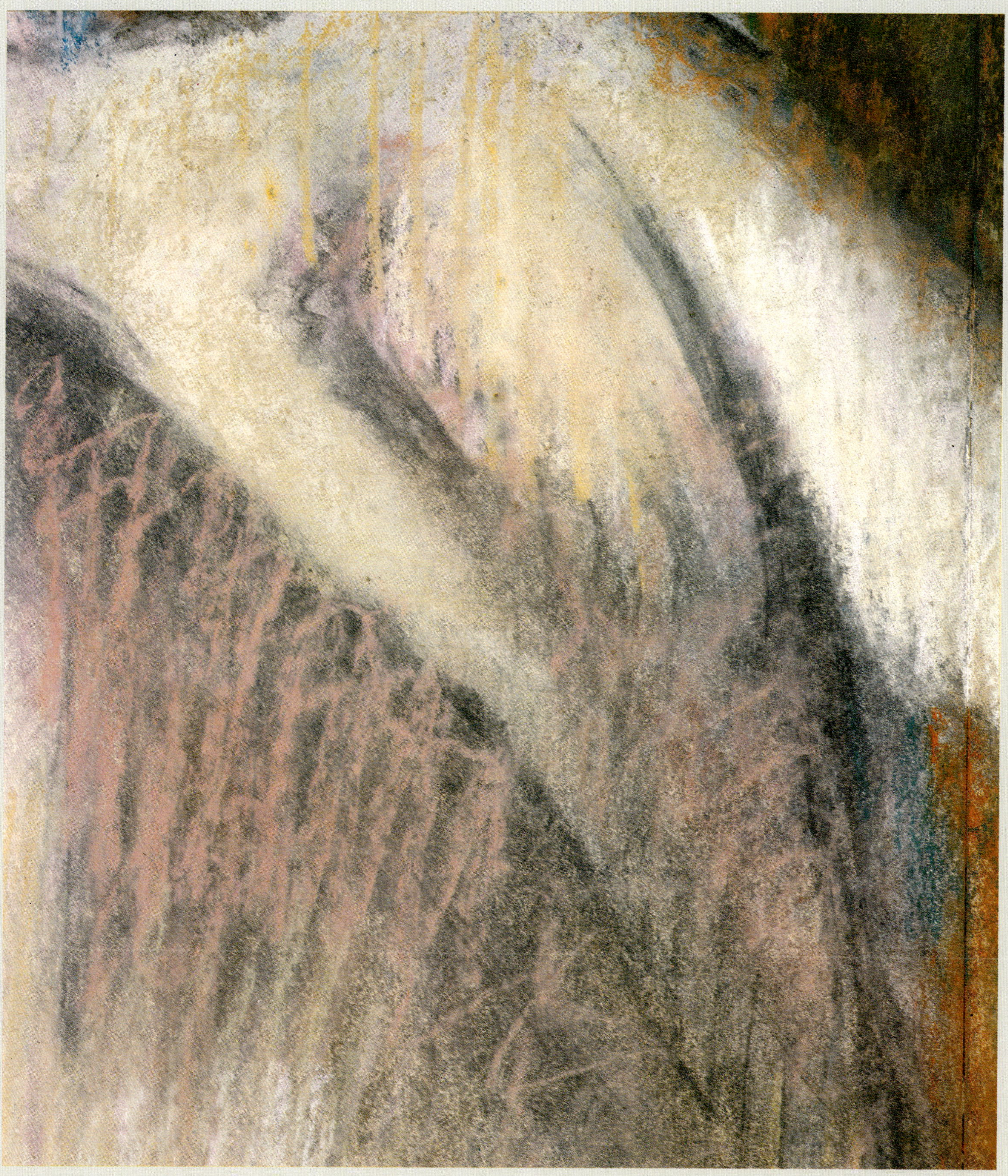

# PIERRE AUGUSTE RENOIR

*Rocky Crags at l'Estaque/Rochers à l'Estaque* (1882)
Oil on white primed canvas
66cm × 80.5cm/26in × 31¾in

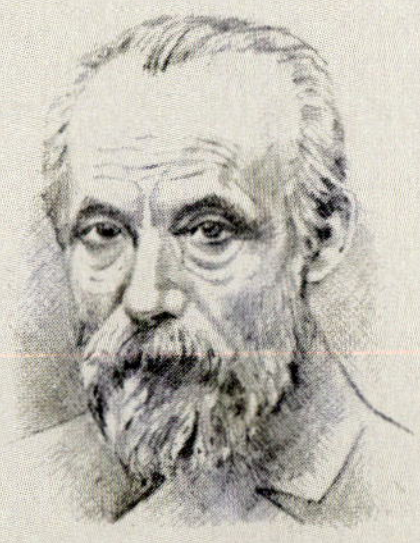

Like Monet, Renoir began the new decade of the 1880s by seeking out new sites for his subjects. In the spring of 1881 he went to North Africa, following in the footsteps of Delacroix (1798–1863), who had made a similar journey almost 50 years earlier. In the winter of 1881 to 1882, Renoir made the traditional pilgrimage to Italy. This journey had earlier been considered essential to artists following the classical tradition in art, but, in the nineteenth century, it had become inextricably associated with the academic monopoly through the Prix de Rome system. Renoir hoped thereby to allay criticism directed at his work, which had in the 1870s classified him as a revolutionary. He was in the process of rejecting what, by this time, he considered the insubstantiality of the Impressionist method, and was seeking to combine the Impressionist vision and palette with a more organized, structured technique.

At this time, he logically turned to Cézanne's example, for that artist had, in the late 1870s, been developing a tighter method for organizing the record of his visual sensations on the canvas. Cezanne's so-called directional brushstroke, visible in works like *Château of Médan* (*c*1880) proved an inspiration to Renoir, whose paintings Cézanne criticized as being formless.

On his return from studying the Raphael frescoes in Rome and the Pompeian frescoes in Naples, Renoir stopped off at L'Estaque to visit Cézanne in early 1882. There he fell ill with pneumonia, and was nursed by Cézanne. *Rocky Crags at l'Estaque* dates from this visit, and it was probably executed while Renoir was working in the company of Cézanne. While Cézanne clearly admired and learned from Renoir's sophisticated use of warm-cool color harmonies, Renoir evidently studied Cézanne's methods for giving greater structure to the arrangement of his compositions.

During the first half of the 1880s, Renoir experimented with thick, smooth white grounds, which obliterated the canvas texture and provided a brilliant base for reflecting maximum light back through the translucent, jewel-like colors of his paint layer. Unlike the smooth, mat absorbent gesso grounds of Italian and Flemish panel painting, Renoir's grounds were oil-based, glossy and relatively non-absorbent. They were applied with a palette knife, presumably by Renoir himself, as a roughness at the edges reveals the marks of the blade. The grounds were usually added over a grainy single coat of white commercial priming, which provided an excellent key for the additional layer. Other examples suggest that the thick, knifed ground was occasionally applied directly on the raw – but presumably sized – canvas. Renoir's son Jean recalls in his memoirs of his father, the ingredients of his later grounds, which were probably not dissimilar to those of this period. Lead white was mixed with one-third linseed oil and two-thirds turpentine spirit. A ground of this type, added over a commercial preparation, is apparent under *Rocky Crags*. Its smooth white surface increases the rich color saturation, especially of the more transparent hues in the paint layer, giving them an effect comparable to light shining through stained glass. Noting Renoir's preference for light and transparent colors, one writer later commented 'the white of the ground today plays the role which the kaolin of his plates once did', referring to the time when Renoir painted on porcelain.

Although in places, stiff, chalky dragged effects of paint are used in *Rocky Crags*, with the addition of opaque lead white, the overriding impression is one of juicy, brilliant color. Some premixing of colors is evident, but most are juxtaposed or slurred together on the paint surface itself. Renoir's mixtures never produce the dull neutrals, which usually result from mixing more than two colors, or from combining two colors directly opposite each other on the color circle. Such neutrals were more colorful than those obtained by adding black or dark earth colors, but they were nevertheless still muddier than those produced by Renoir's method. This involved mixing hues near each other on the color circle – like blue and red, or green and yellow. This method was later to form the basis of Neo-Impressionist color mixtures. Renoir's colors in this picture are so pure and separate as to be relatively easy to pick out. Transparent viridian predominates among the greens, cobalt among the blues. The yellows were cadmiums, and the duller Naples yellow was probably also used. A red alizarin lake, in places slightly browned with age, is used alone and mixed to provide oranges. Lead white appears in many of the pigment mixtures.

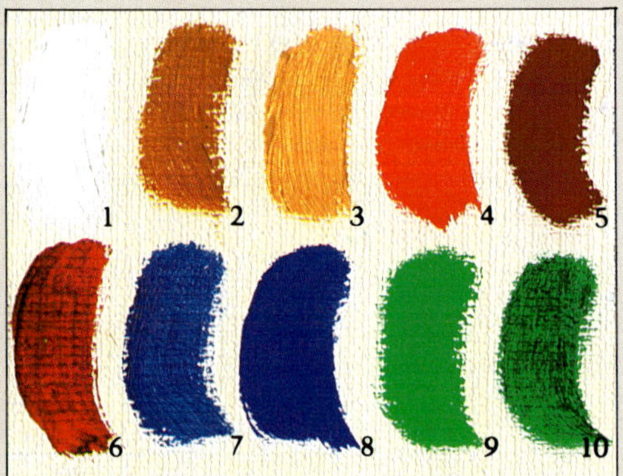


*Renoir's palette for this painting probably comprised lead white (1), yellow ochre (2), Naples yellow (3), vermilion (4) or red earth (5), red alizarin lake (6), cobalt blue (7), possibly ultramarine blue (8), viridian green (10), and possibly emerald (9) or chrome greens.*

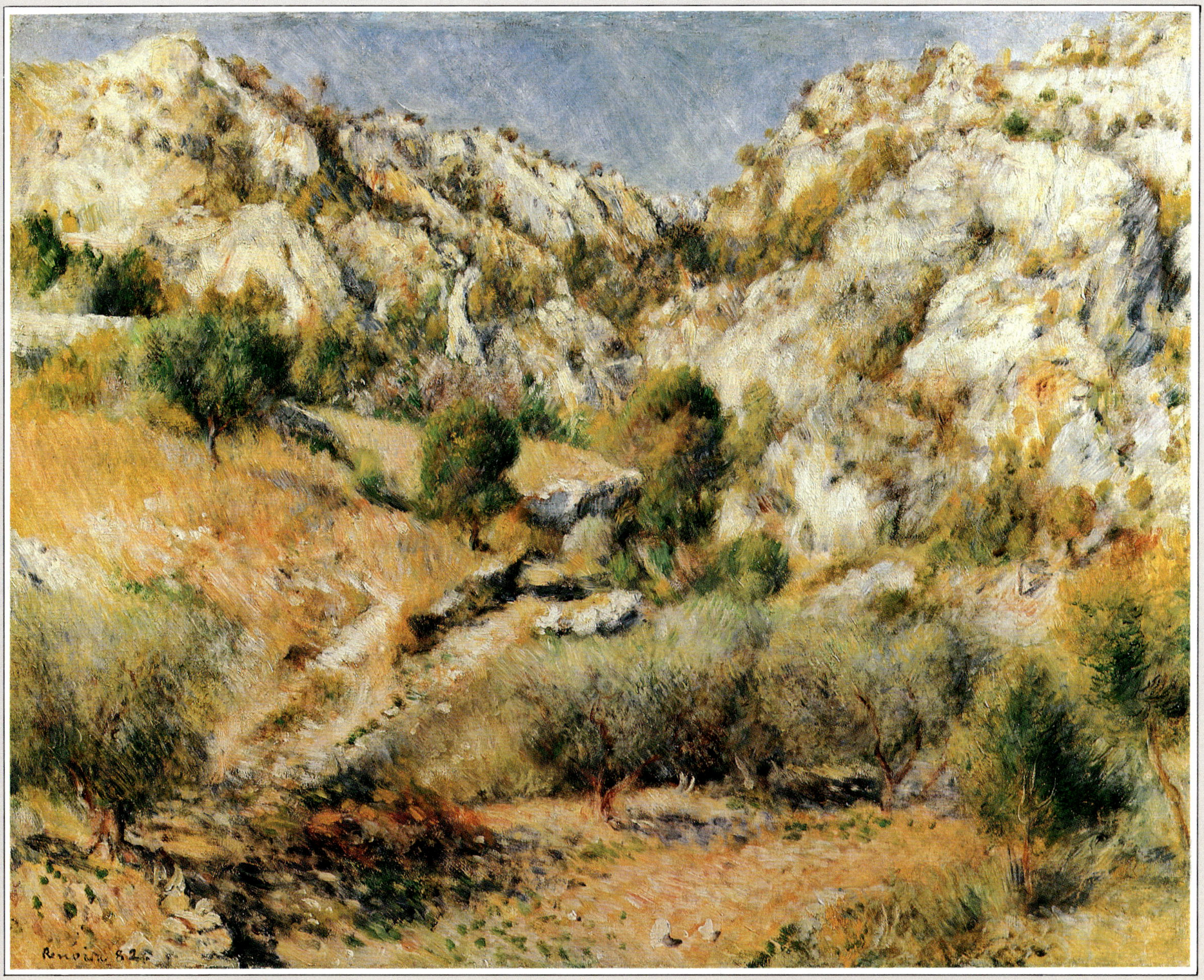

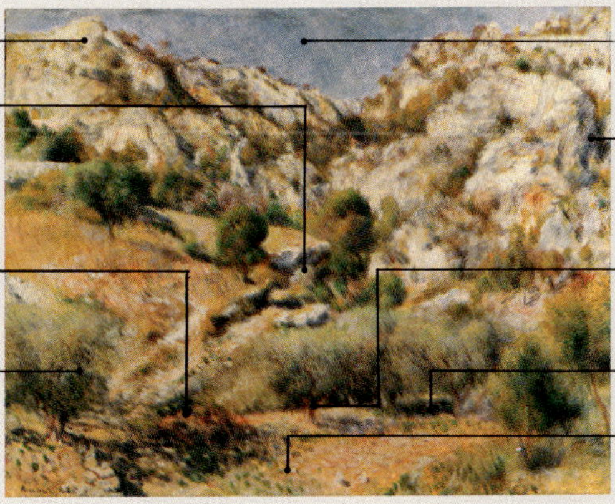


*Though some of Renoir's colors were mixed on the palette, he often combined them on the paint surface itself, delicately blending one hue with another to result in a partial combination of the two. This gives vitality and durability to his colors. The paint layer is fairly thin, with translucent or transparent jewel-like colors applied over thicker opaque colors. A squarish portrait 25 format suits the high tipped-up viewpoint.*

This picture uses a technique with which Renoir had begun experimenting in the mid 1870s. In particular, in the foreground among the trees, the dry paint layer colors have been overlaid with a fine veil of pale opaque blue, which has been rubbed on to enhance shadow areas. This blue veil creates a film of color which appears to float in front of the actual paint layer brushstrokes, giving an effect of the ethereal blue light of the atmosphere. This effect is comparable to that achieved by Manet in the background of his *Roadmenders in the rue de Berne*, 1878. In *Rocky Crags*, the blues are also exploited amongst the shadows of the rocks, which are given form by the contrast of warm sunny colors against the cool blues of the shadows.

Although here Renoir has not yet adopted the directional stroke of Cézanne as universally as he was to in mid 1880s canvases, his touches are nevertheless tending to fall into regular parallel patterns. However, rather than taking on a life of their own, divorced from a descriptive role, Renoir's parallel touches sweep from one angle to another following the movement of land in foreground and rocks, and describing the pattern of foliage in the trees. Thus his brushwork remains personal and basically naturalistic.

The working alliance forged by Cézanne and Renoir during this stay was maintained throughout the 1880s. In 1883, 1888 and 1889 Renoir either visited or worked with Cézanne in the south, and in 1885 Cézanne traveled north and worked with Renoir at La Roche-Guyon, north-west of Paris.

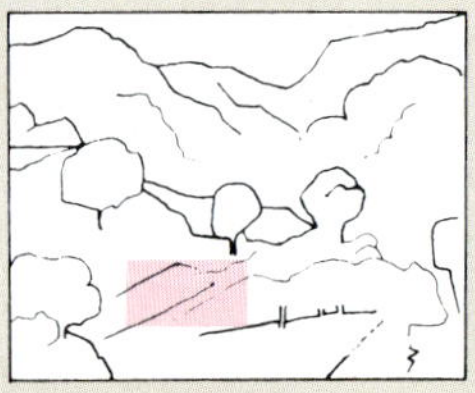

*Like all the darkish areas in Renoir's painting, this is depicted with richly saturated hues. Dark translucent blues were worked fluidly with an oil and turpentine medium added by the artist, and modified by the addition of wet blended colors. Alizarin lake, a rich transparent blueish red, is worked into the blue, and dabs of yellow ochre are added, some over dry and some over wet color below. Touches of viridian green can also be seen in this detail.*

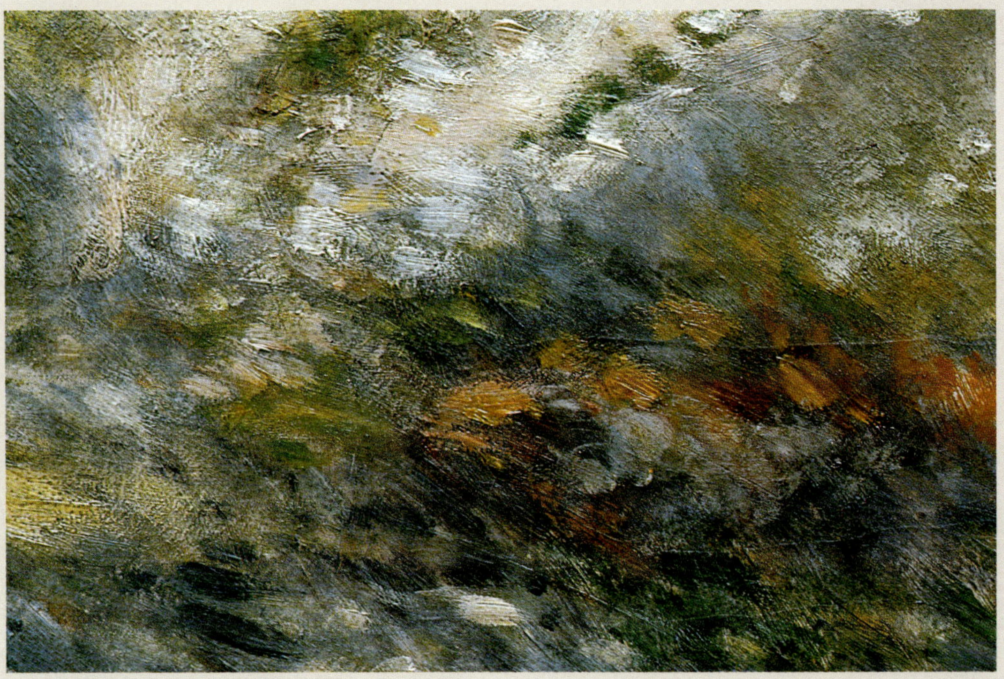

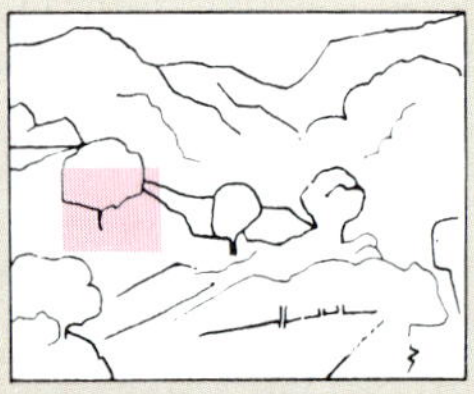

*Here the color is more thickly and opaquely impasted, with chalky creams and yellows to suggest the sunlight of the south on the dusty rocks. Thinner films of color – yellow over blue, green over yellow and pale mauve over blue – were applied lightly and unevenly to modify the colors below without obliterating them.*

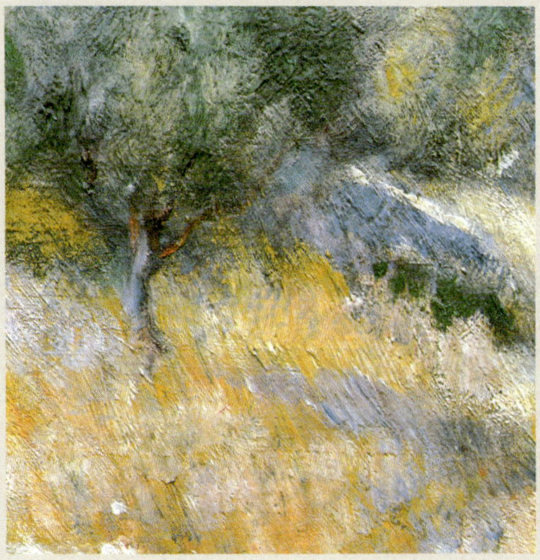

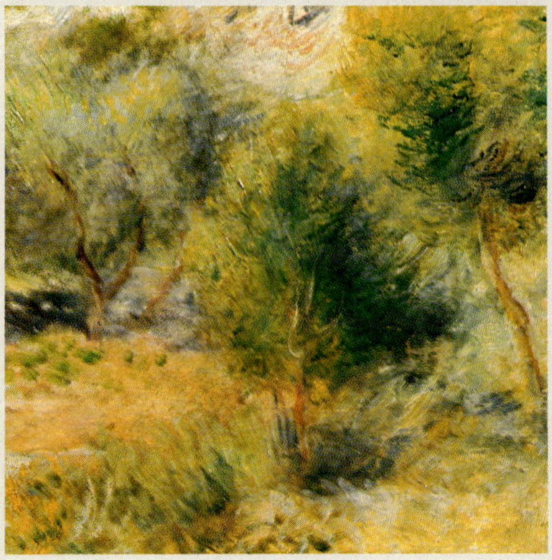

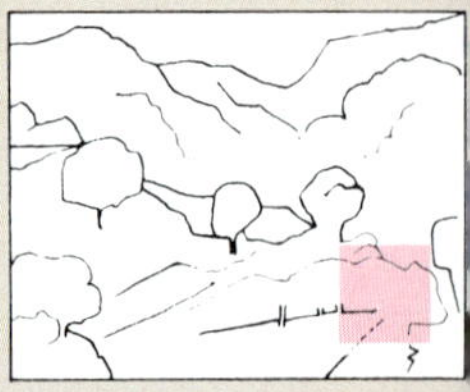

*This larger detail shows the variety of Renoir's touch and its descriptive qualities. Thinly, finely dragged color suggests the foliage, while elongated, fluid strokes of burnt alizarin lake stand for the tree trunks and branches. Dark, saturated blues and greens are slurred together for the shadows.*

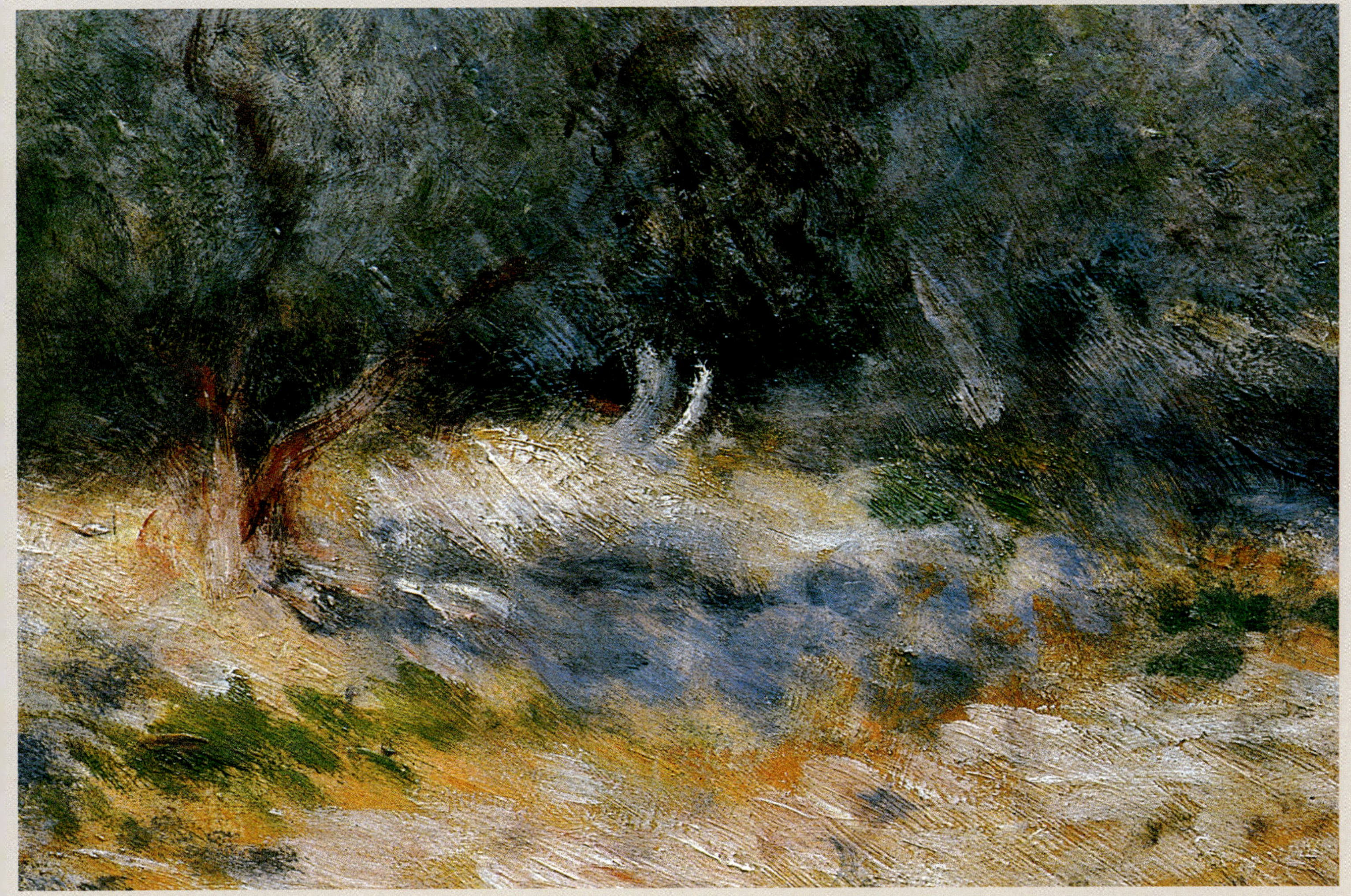

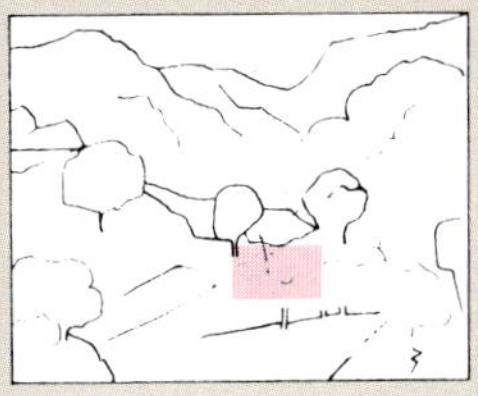

Actual size detail
*Light-reflecting, luminous creamy-whites and yellows evoke the chalky soil where the olive trees grow. The silvery blue-green of their foliage is aptly conveyed by the artist's lightly brushed translucent layers of blue and viridian green. The gnarled tree trunk is suggested by thinly applied red. This may be alizarin red discolored with age, or the intentionally darkened hue of burnt alizarin. The floating, atmospheric blue of the shadow below the tree is an excellent example of Renoir's skill in evoking virtually intangible films of color, by applying a veil of rubbed or brushed color so thinly that it seems to float in front of the colors below. Blue with much white added serves this purpose here.*

# BERTHE MORISOT

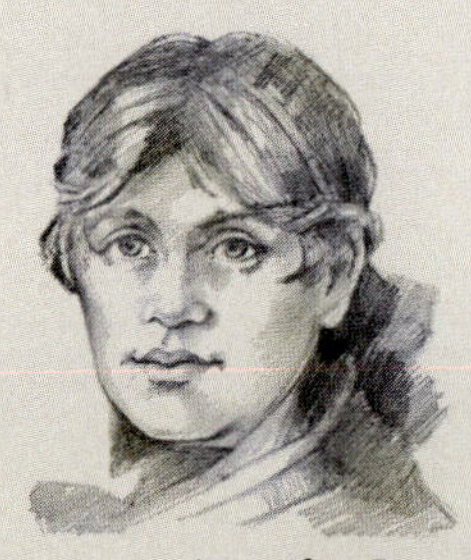

*Woman and Child in the Garden at Bougival/Femme et enfant dans le jardin à Bougival* (1882)
Oil on unprimed canvas
59.6cm × 73cm/24in × 28¾in

Berthe Morisot and her sister Edma both began training for careers in art in the mid 1850s. They made copies after Old Masters in the Louvre, including the Venetian painter Veronese (1528–1588), in the latter years of the decade. From early on in her career Berthe Morisot admired landscape painting, especially that of Corot (1796–1875), and wished to begin working out of doors. In 1861 she was introduced to Corot, with whom she worked on landscape subjects around his home at Ville d'Avray, west of Paris, and she became his pupil. As early as 1864 she exhibited two works at the annual Salon exhibition. Since women were still excluded from life classes, they were effectively prohibited from competing in the history painting category, the height of academic achievement. Thus, the undermining of academic authority through the growing popularity of modern life subjects and landscape painting gave women greater opportunity to achieve renown within the terms defined at that time.

In 1868 Fantin-Latour (1836–1904) introduced Morisot to Manet, who painted her in his *Balcony*, exhibited in the Salon the following year. Manet advised her on her work, to the extent of retouching her painting of the *Artist's Sister Edma and their Mother* (1870), which was shown at the Salon of 1870. A devoted friend and loyal colleague, Morisot exhibited at every group show of the Impressionists, apart from the fourth in 1879 when she was pregnant – she had married Manet's brother Eugène in 1874. True to the Impressionist hard line, she sent no works to the Salon after the first group show in 1874. She also joined in the auction organized with Monet, Renoir and Sisley in 1875 to raise money, although she herself was not in financial need. Her work fetched higher prices than that of the others. In addition to painting in oils, Morisot worked regularly in watercolor and pastels.

Berthe Morisot had a house in Bougival to the west of Paris where, from 1880, she regularly spent her summers painting from nature. This picture, which probably shows her four year old daughter Julie with her maid Paisie, was painted in the garden at Bougival. Morisot's distinctive style and vigorous, nervous brushwork are clearly in evidence here. Her choice of an unprimed support at first seems unusual, for the Impressionists rarely used raw canvas under oil paint because the colors sink and dull, and the oxides in the oil are destructive, corroding the canvas fabric. However, closer examination of the bare canvas, revealed especially at the bottom right-hand corner, suggested that the canvas was indeed primed, but on the reverse side. Removal of the painting from the wall revealed another picture, painted on the original primed face of this standard format portrait 20 canvas, which had proved unsatisfactory and had been abandoned by the artist. Rather than waste the canvas, Morisot simply untacked it from its supporting stretcher, turned it over, and tacked it back on. Few artists primed their own canvases at this time, preferring to buy ready primed canvas directly from the color merchant. Morisot did not prime this new surface, but exploited both its color and its marked texture in her handling of the subject.

The almost orange-brown of the canvas fabric, which may be a linen-cotton mixture, is left most visible among the acid greens of the sunlit grass. Here it adds a warm unifying tint which sharpens those cool green hues. The paint has been built up to its greatest density in the central oval of the composition. This is reminiscent of Corot's technique, for he built up the relief of his pictures toward the central point of interest in his compositions. Yet it is also quite logical here, both because of the centrally placed figures, and because – in accordance with the Impressionist commitment to depict personal visual experience – human binocular vision concentrates upon the central oval field of focus. Many less finished Impressionist paintings betray this unequal distribution of paint, indicating that the four corners of the rectangular canvas were usually the last parts to be fully resolved and tightened. In this work, where the paint is thinnest, it is very dull because its oil binder has sunk rapidly into the absorbent raw canvas. Where it is thickest, the layering of color has gradually sealed the canvas, and the final reworkings have left those parts glossier.

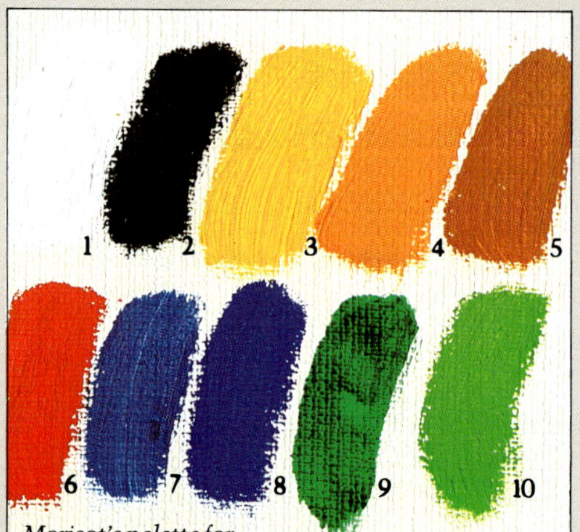


*Morisot's palette for this painting probably comprised lead white (1), black (2), chrome (3) or cadmium (4) yellows, yellow ochre (5), vermilion (6), cobalt (7) or ultramarine (8) blues, viridian green (9), and chrome green (10).*

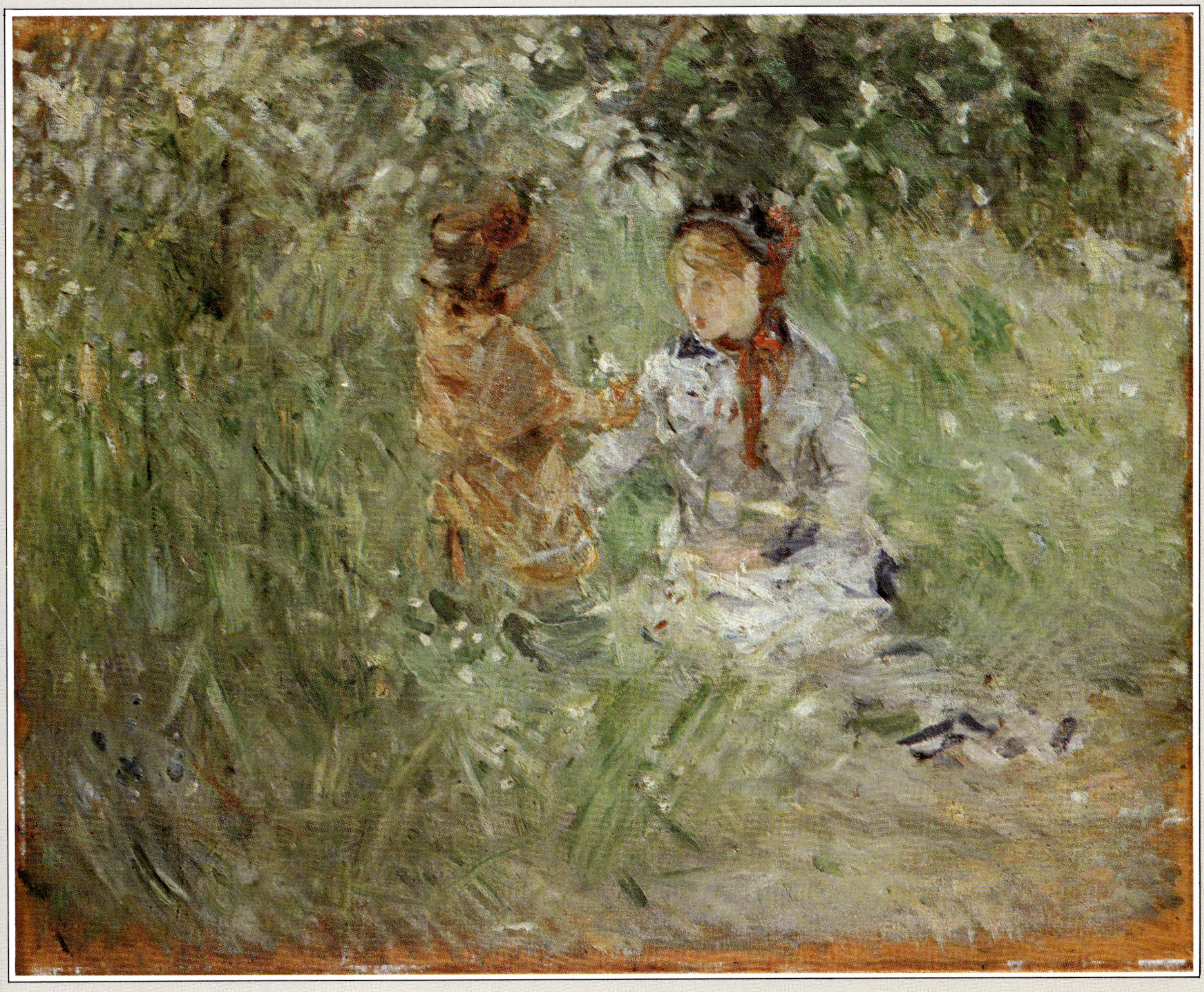

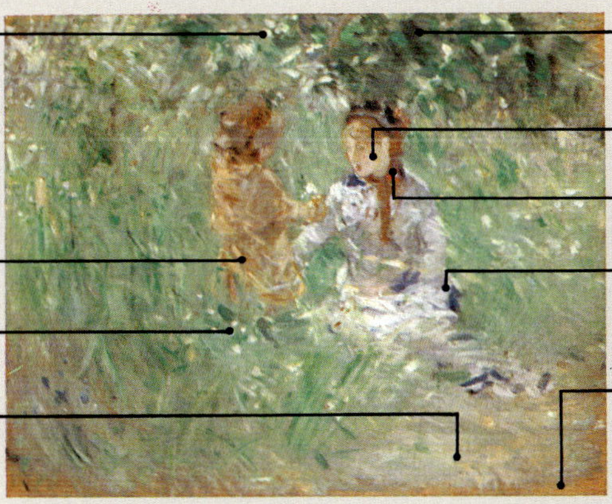


*This is one of the few examples of the use of unprimed raw canvas under oil colors in Impressionist painting. It is a standard format portrait 20 canvas. The ready primed side of the support was turned after an unsuccessful start so the artist could reuse the canvas back. The warm orangey brown of the fabric was exploited by Morisot to unify the paint layer colors and add warmth to the cool greens.*

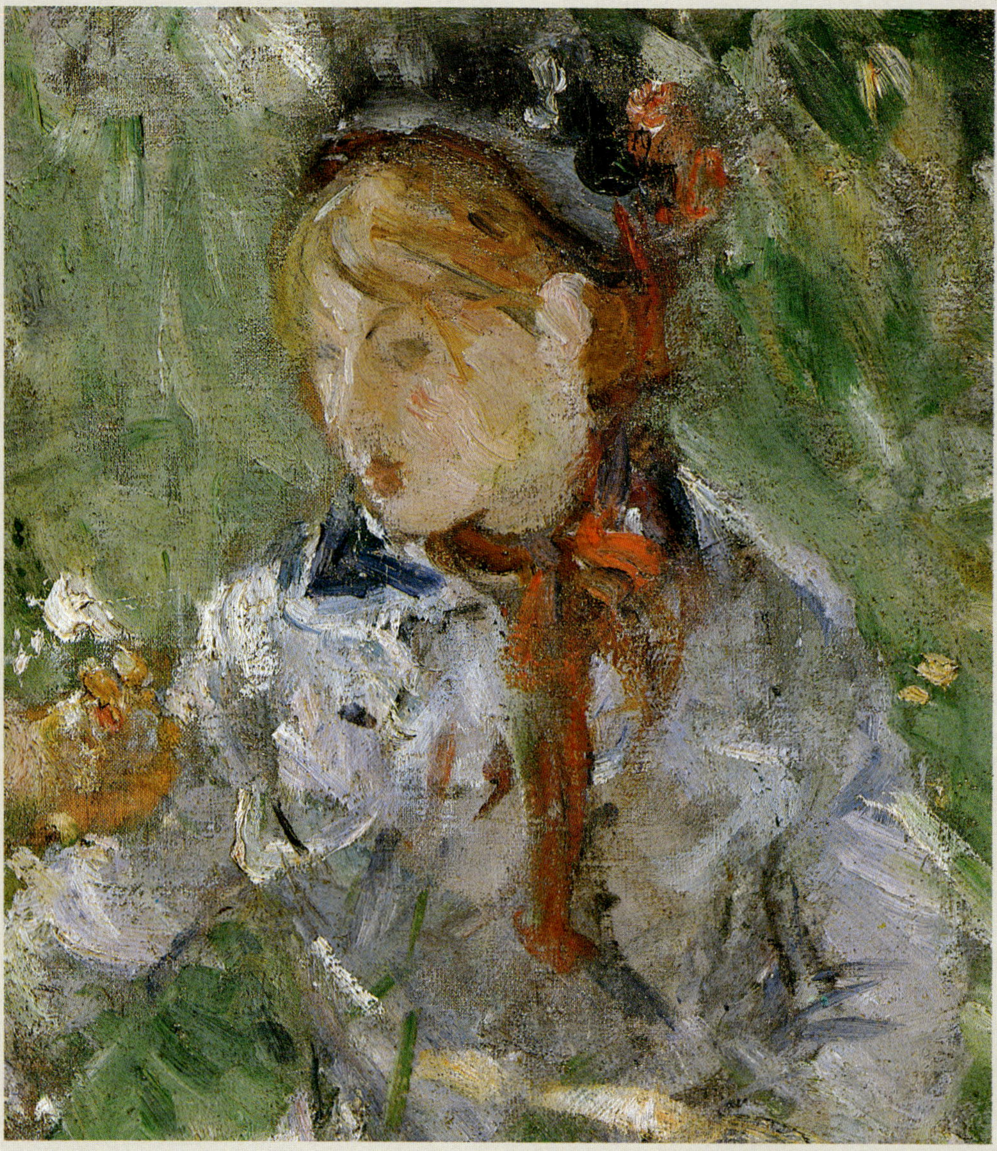

*Morisot's loose, dashing touch is used almost everywhere except for the woman's face. This is more tightly and carefully built up with smoother application of paint, but it is not excessively blended or modeled. In the more shadowed parts, like the neck, cool tints are added to suggest the reflected hues from sky and grass. Elsewhere, the lively dragged, broken and slurred brushwork gives a vital sense of light flickering off and blurring forms, evoking the summer atmosphere. Black may have been used for the color of the woman's hat, and vermilion red was slurred in wet with white for the bonnet ribbon. White was applied almost pure for the highlights on the dress. In the shadowed areas, the white was modified to a colorful neutral hue with pinks, greens and blues.*

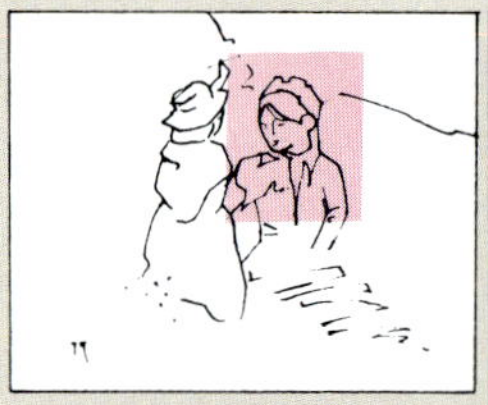

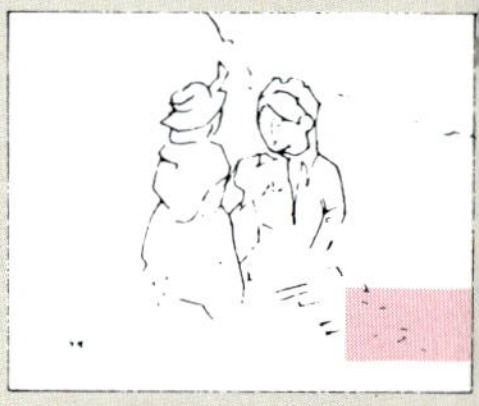

Actual size detail
*In the more thickly painted and reworked central area of the painting the build-up of color has sealed the raw canvas to leave the color glossy. However, in this thinly painted corner even the varnish has become dull and sunk into the absorbent support. The unusually orange hue of the canvas may indicate that it is a cotton rather than a linen-based fabric, a support which gained in popularity during the nineteenth century. As raw canvas is so absorbent, it draws out the oil from the paint, which makes the brush drag as color is laid on. This makes it a difficult surface to work on initially. The use of oil paint on raw canvas was proscribed by technical experts as the oxidizing elements in the oil gradually eat into the unprotected fabric.*

Combined with the upward sweep of brushstrokes depicting tall grass on the left, the lack of excessive reworking particularly in the bottom right corner creates a ground plane, perhaps a path, which gives extraordinary eloquence to the composition despite minimal detail. The composition excludes sky and distance, closing the figures round with an envelope of green, which nevertheless appears to recede back to the right. The darkest green mixtures are above the figures, reversing the traditional method which called for darks in the foreground. The overall tonality of the picture is pale and bright, with much white used in all the color mixtures. The limited palette is dominated by greens, mainly mixed greens incorporating viridian and yellow. A slurred, partly wet-into-wet combination of yellow and vermilion with white was used for the little girl's dress, while a purer vermilion depicts Paisie's bonnet ribbon. Smudges of blue, probably cobalt, appear on her dress, mixed in with some of the greens. Creamy hues dabbed amongst the greens convey reflected light from seeded sun-dried grasses, the whole unified by Morisot's strikingly free brushwork.

During the 1880s, Berthe Morisot's Paris house became a key meeting place for the Impressionists and their friends. From 1886, regular gatherings took place where Monet, Renoir and Degas joined the Symbolist poet Stéphane Mallarmé, Berthe Morisot and Eugène Manet to exchange news and views on artistic developments in Paris. Thus Morisot was a central figure in maintaining contact amongst members of the Impressionist group as their paths diverged geographically. She remained loyal to Impressionist ideals and techniques throughout her career.

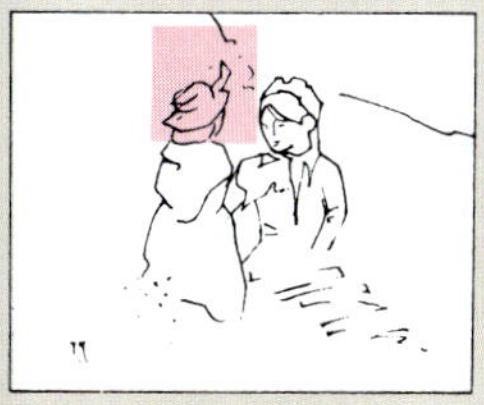

Brushwork for the child's bonnet follows the forms of the hat, helping to give it shape and structure. This contrasts with the freer handling of color for the grass and foliage in the background. Yellow ochre is the basic hue of the hat, which may be darkened by the addition of black, worked wet into the yellow.

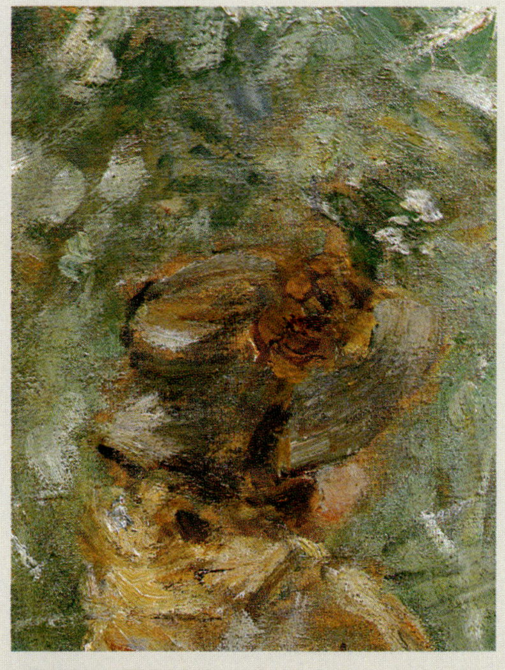

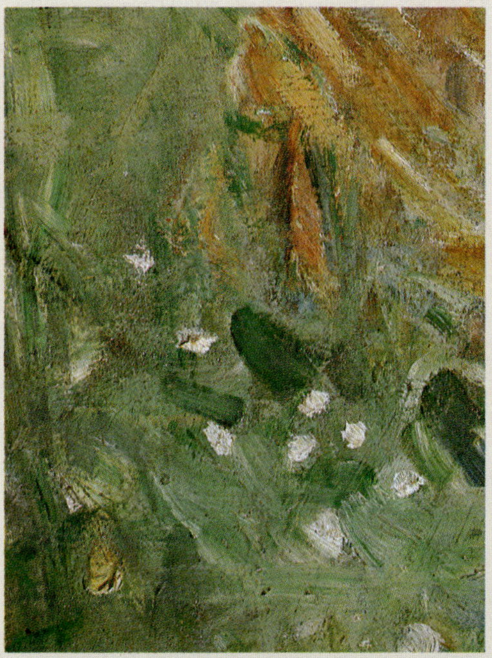

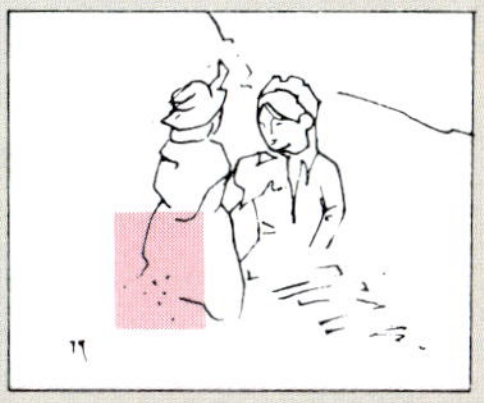

Sweeping, dragged brushstrokes of yellow ochre and mixed greens blend from the dress to the grass, suggesting the ill-defined forms as the child's body disappears among the tall grasses. Touches of almost white paint evoke white flowers.

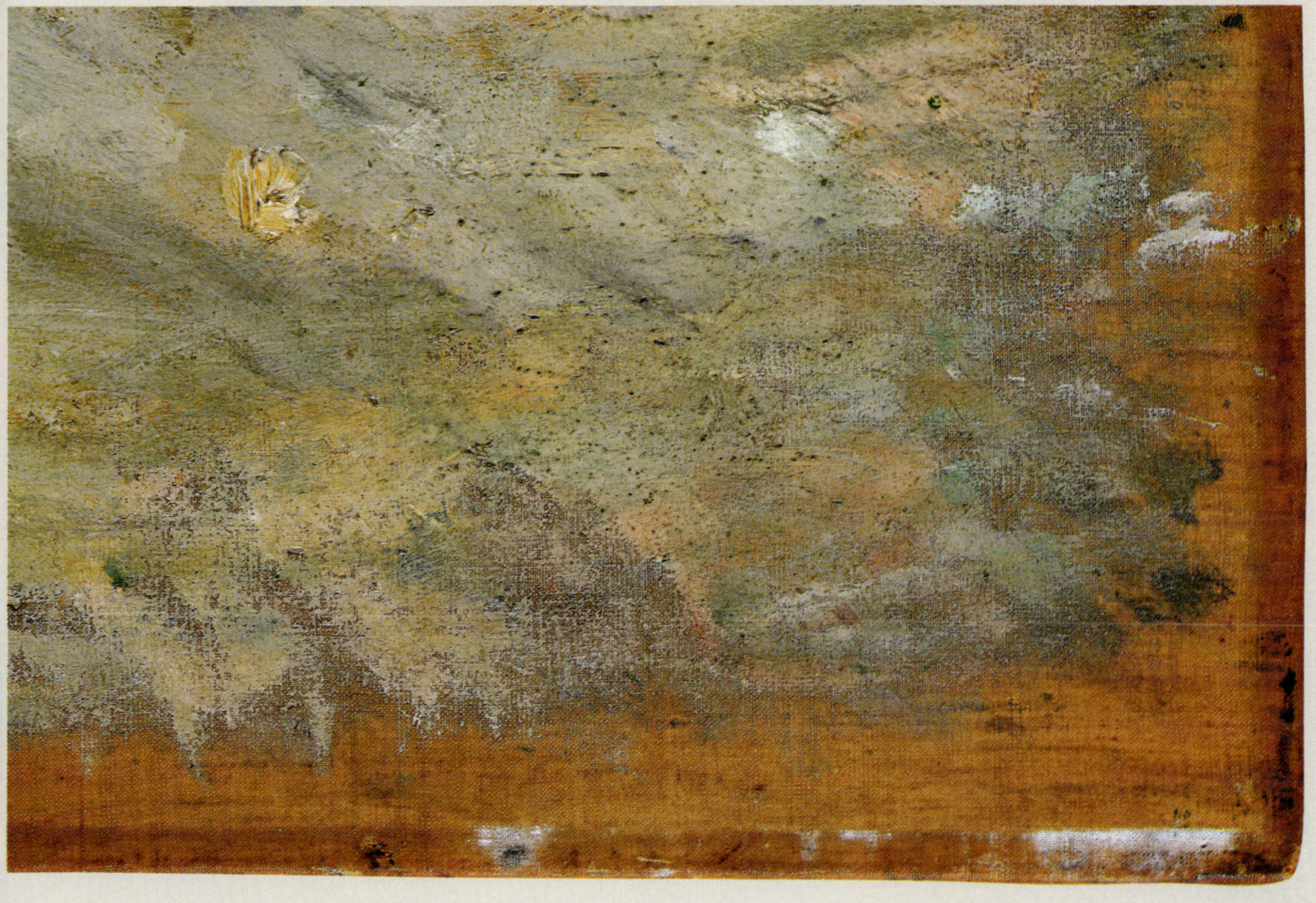

# MARY CASSATT

*Woman in Black/Femme en noir* (*c* 1882)
Oil on pale primed canvas
100.6cm × 74cm/39¾in × 29in

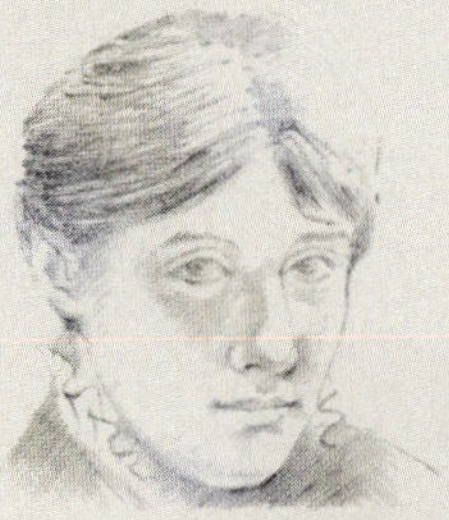

Mary Cassatt came from a wealthy family near Pittsburgh, Pennsylvania, and early on showed her determination to pursue a career in art by enrolling at the Pennsylvania Academy of Fine Arts, Philadelphia, apparently against her father's wishes. It was still unusual, not to say unconventional, for women of middle-class origins to desire or seek a profession at that time, for ladies were not expected to do paid work. If they did, their social status suffered. In Europe, where Cassatt went after four years' study in Pennsylvania, it was easier for a woman to become an artist, as Cassatt herself stressed: 'After all give me France. Women do not have to fight for recognition here if they do serious work.'

Her first travels in Europe from 1866, were to study the Old Masters, for relatively few examples of their works were then available to American students on their own continent. During the Franco-Prussian War and Paris Commune of 1870–1871, Cassatt went back to America, returning to Europe when hostilities ceased. She then went first to Italy, spending eight months studying the work of the proto-Baroque painter Correggio (*c*1489–1534) in Parma. In 1873 she, like Manet earlier, went to Spain to learn from the art of Velazquez in Seville and Madrid. Her earliest entries to the Salon exhibitions, from 1872, show the influence of Manet's 1860s Spanish themes and style. After a visit to Belgium and Holland to study the art of painters like Rubens, she finally settled in Paris.

Her meeting with Degas, and through him the Impressionists, in 1877 meant that, like Gustave Caillebotte, Cassatt was a relative latecomer to the Impressionist group. At Degas' invitation she began exhibiting with them in 1879. Degas had seen her entry to the 1874 Salon, and commented 'There is someone who feels as I do', a remark which gains resonance in view of their lifelong friendship, which evolved from the time of their meeting. Cassatt later recalled 'I already knew who were my true masters. I admired Manet, Courbet and Degas. I hated conventional art. I began to live.' In common with Degas, Cassatt felt that art should be based on a solid study of the Old Masters, on disciplined work from the model, and on complete mastery of line, color and compositional organization.

Unlike Degas, her circumscribed social position as a middle-class woman meant that her range of subject matter was limited. For while men like Degas had unrestricted access not only to teaching studios where the life model was used, they could also hire male or female models to pose nude in their own studios. For women, who were not even permitted to be alone in a room with a man if he were not a relative, work even from clothed male models was unacceptable. Thus Cassatt's chief subjects – domestic interiors, women reading and doing needlework, mothers and children and middle-class leisure activities indoors and out – were determined by what was appropriate for a woman of her class at that time. These restraints resulted in a great awareness in Cassatt of the oppression of women, and she aligned herself openly with the American struggle for women's suffrage.

Her earliest techniques owe much to Spanish art and to Manet. Her palette was then still dominated by somber hues which created a stark fall of light and shade reminiscent of Manet and which reflected the studio environment. Bright colors – reds, blues, greens – sang out in works like *Torero and Young Girl* (1873) against the subdued foil of dark hues and a plain background. Her figures were treated close up to the picture surface, large in scale, dominating the picture space with lively strength. As her style developed, she gradually abandoned the tonal palette for an Impressionist palette of pale tints, bright colors, and colorful rather than brown shadows. As Degas noted around 1890, Cassatt became preoccupied with the 'reflections and shadows on skin and costumes' in her sitters, which she handled with the opaque color mixtures characteristic of Impressionism.

Like Manet, Degas, Renoir and Cézanne, Cassatt never abandoned the use of black, as can be seen from her *Woman in Black*. But, like them, she used it as a color in its own right, not as a substance to tone down and sully pure color, for use in shadows. Her composition here is typically taut and carefully calculated in relation to the canvas edges and shape. The

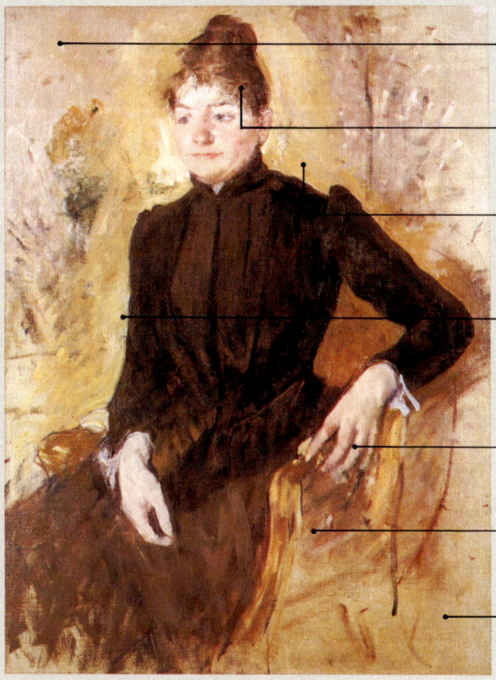

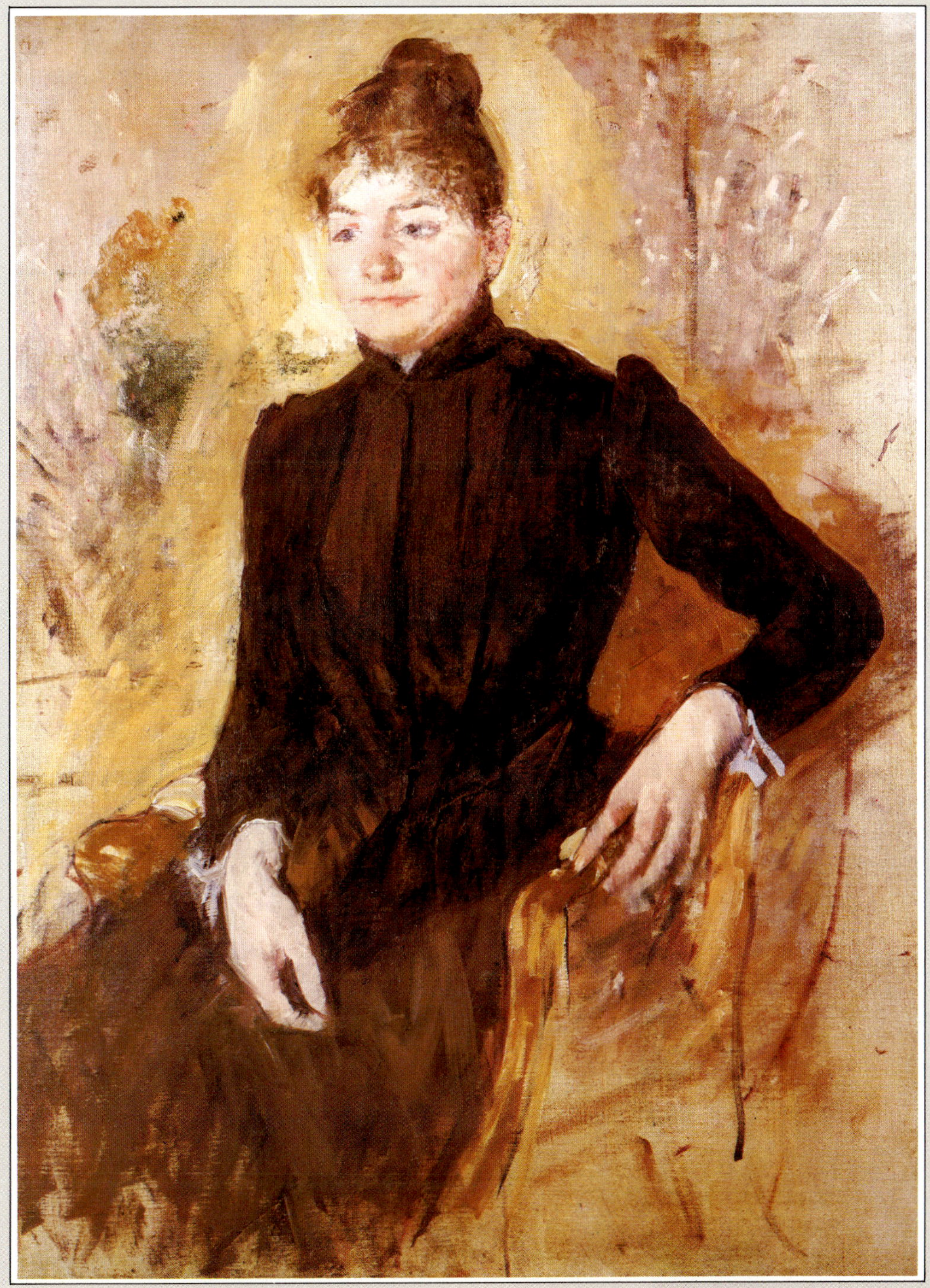

*The unfinished nature of Cassatt's portrait clearly shows her method of working. Contours of the form were laid in and later strengthened with dilute color – probably a mixture of burnt alizarin crimson and black. This same color was used to lay in the masses of the figure's somber costume, but the subtlety of the mixed hue means that undue harshness is avoided. All parts of the figure handled in this first* ébauche *were then left to dry, and certain areas, notably the head, were then scraped down. Some of the scraped areas of the head are still apparent among the incomplete final touches. Parts of the background were sketched in broadly in thicker paint, which has been dragged across the fine but grainy canvas texture. In the upper and lower right of the picture, the oatmeal color of the thin ground remains uncovered. To the left of the head, the background was roughed in with an opaque pinky gray color. Thicker opaque color was also built up on the face, hands and chair. In the flesh areas, Cassatt's characteristic dragging of the wet colors, a personal variant of the old technique of blending, was used to soften and blur the initial vigorous handling of the form. The painting was executed on a standard format vertical landscape 40 canvas.*

figure is pushed close to the canvas surface, filling the space. Her coiled hair is close to the top edge, and her elbow, positioned close to the right edge of the canvas, creates a precise tension. The elongated format of the standard vertical landscape canvas 40 (100x73cm/39½ x29in) aptly suits the tense upright pose of the sitter. This vertical emphasis is strengthened by the position of her right arm, creating a vertical to left of the center of the picture, which ends in the stark contrast of the flesh tints of her hanging hand against the mixed alizarin and black colors of the dress.

The unfinished state of the picture, whose sitter remains unknown, provides ample evidence of Cassatt's working methods. Both dryish and fluid lines, laid rapidly, indicate the contours of the figure and chair, while the rudiments of the interior are loosely summarized, not by broad washes of color, but by chalky, dragged undiluted color scrubbed hastily onto the surface. Logically with a portrait, the bulk of the paint build-up is concentrated on the head and figure, with the face brought to a fair degree of completion.

Cassatt's brushwork is broad and decisive, and the varied width of her brushes, from the fine contour strokes to the wide strokes on the dress, are clearly discernible. Her characteristic handling of flesh, as in the sitter's left hand, where the wet paint has been pulled and blurred across the original contour line, dates from around 1880. It was probably achieved by stroking the wet color with a clean, dry hog's hair brush, so that it smoothed the separate touches of color, blending them together, and adding a softening sense of captured movement to the crisp underdrawing. Cassatt's changes to the left elbow, which are still visible, indicate her concern over the position of the arm, and the foreshortening of the forearm, in relation to the canvas edge. Her awareness of the visual power of the void, the shape created between objects, is clear in her careful structuring of this part of the composition. This relationship between object and void, exploited also by Degas and Cézanne in particular, is apparent in her finished compositions, like *Girl in an Armchair*, (1878).

Mary Cassatt's historical position as an important member of the Impressionist group has suffered because, both as a woman artist and as an American in Paris, her work did not fall into any simple art historical category. However, the strength and originality of her art, which included printmaking and pastels, provide indisputable evidence of her stature as an artist.

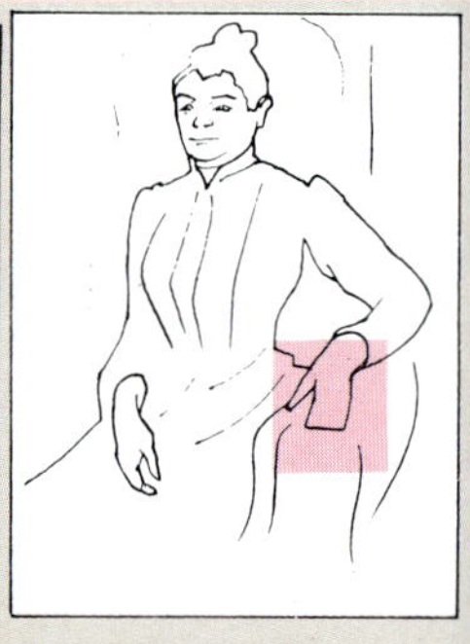

Actual size detail
*Brushwork and paint thickness vary greatly, including slurred wet-into-wet and wet-over-dry handling. The much used mixture of burnt alizarin and black serves for the contours of the fingers. The technique whereby with a dry bristle brush was dragged over wet flesh tints softens the crisp execution of the hand, blurring the pale hues into the darker contour. This gives a feeling of lively movement. The mixed black and burnt alizarin of the dress are visible, and a freely added sweep of cobalt blue mixed with white was added to represent the cuff. In the area below the hand, dryish color was roughly scrubbed on in a thin but opaque layer.*

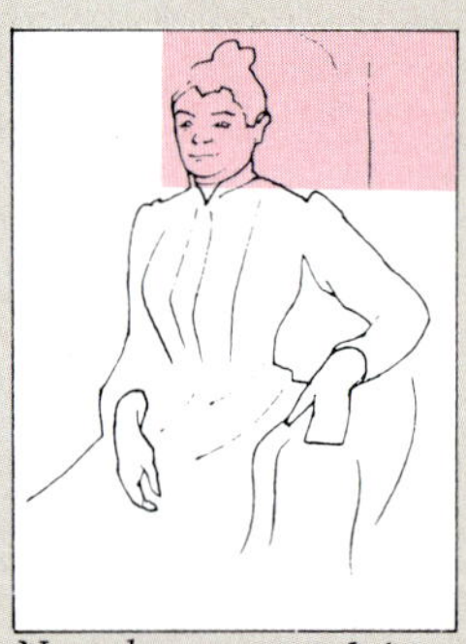

*Near the woman's left eye and ear the ground is worn and specks of raw canvas color show through. This might have been caused by excessive scraping of the* ébauche *layer. Touches of bright vermilion and white can be seen on the face, and red lake on the ear. Yellow ochre dominates the mixture used behind the head. In places it was clearly brushed over the head colors, indicating it was added fairly late. The flesh colors were dragged and slurred wet with a dry hog's hair brush. Thick, stiffish colors were loosely applied for the background on the right where the ground can also be seen.*

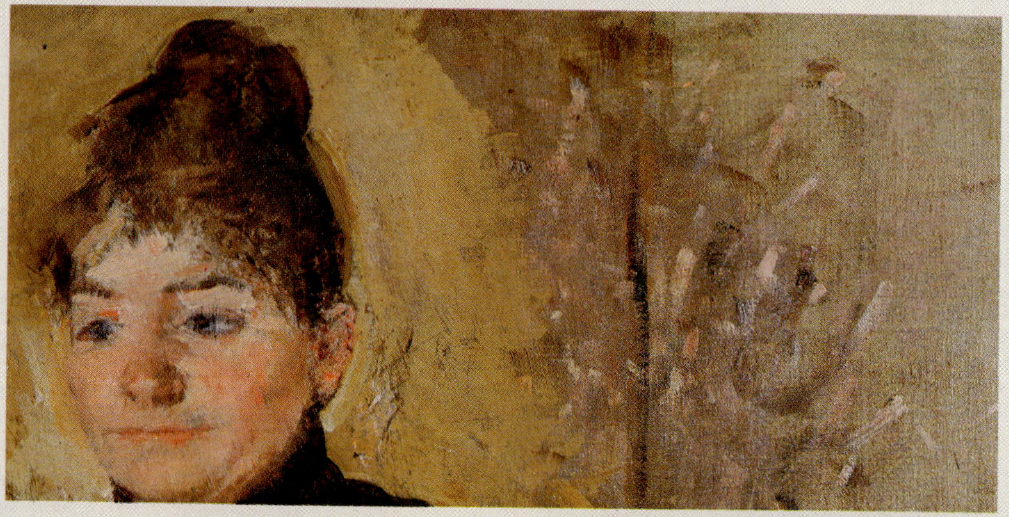

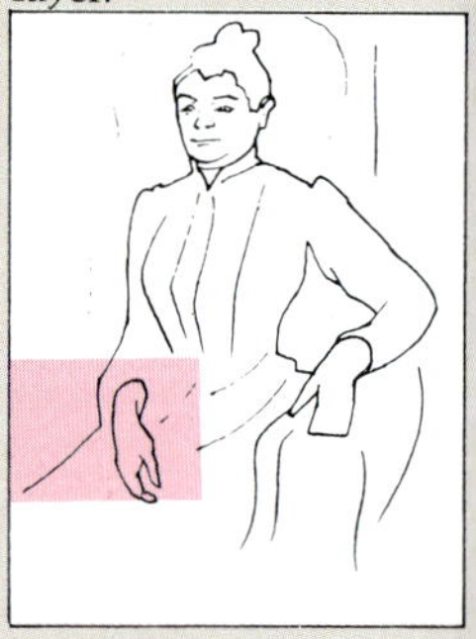

*The chair arm was a late addition, probably added when the woman's right arm was moved in closer to the center to make the pose more three-quarter than full-face. It appears the dress was at first intended to fill the space where the chair arm now is. Outlined in alizarin and black, the chair arm was filled in with a yellow ochre mix, which loosely covers the original design.*

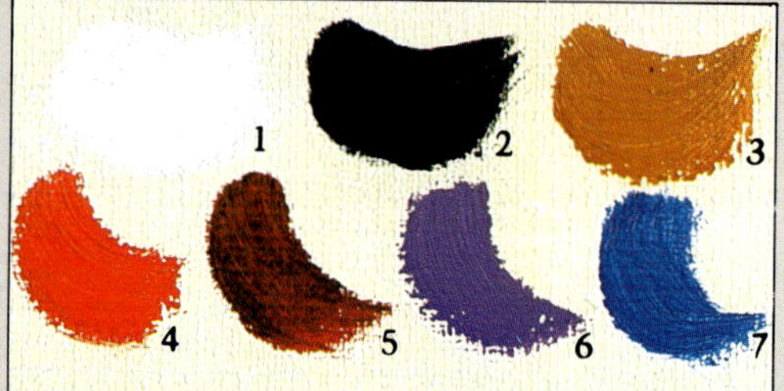


*Cassatt's palette for unfinished work probably included lead white (1), black (2), yellow ochre (3), vermilion (4), burnt alizarin lake (5), cobalt violet (6), and cobalt blue (7).*

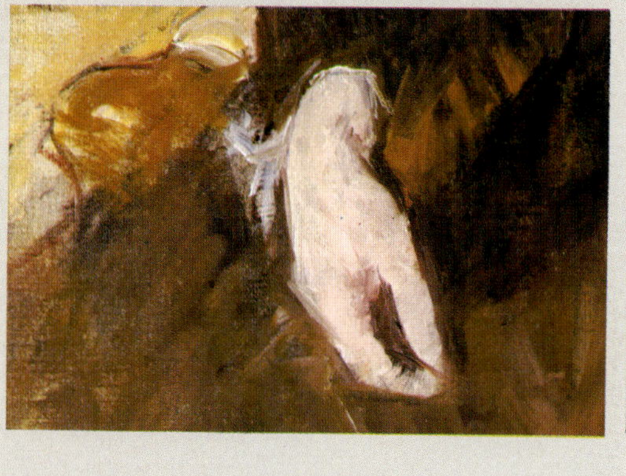

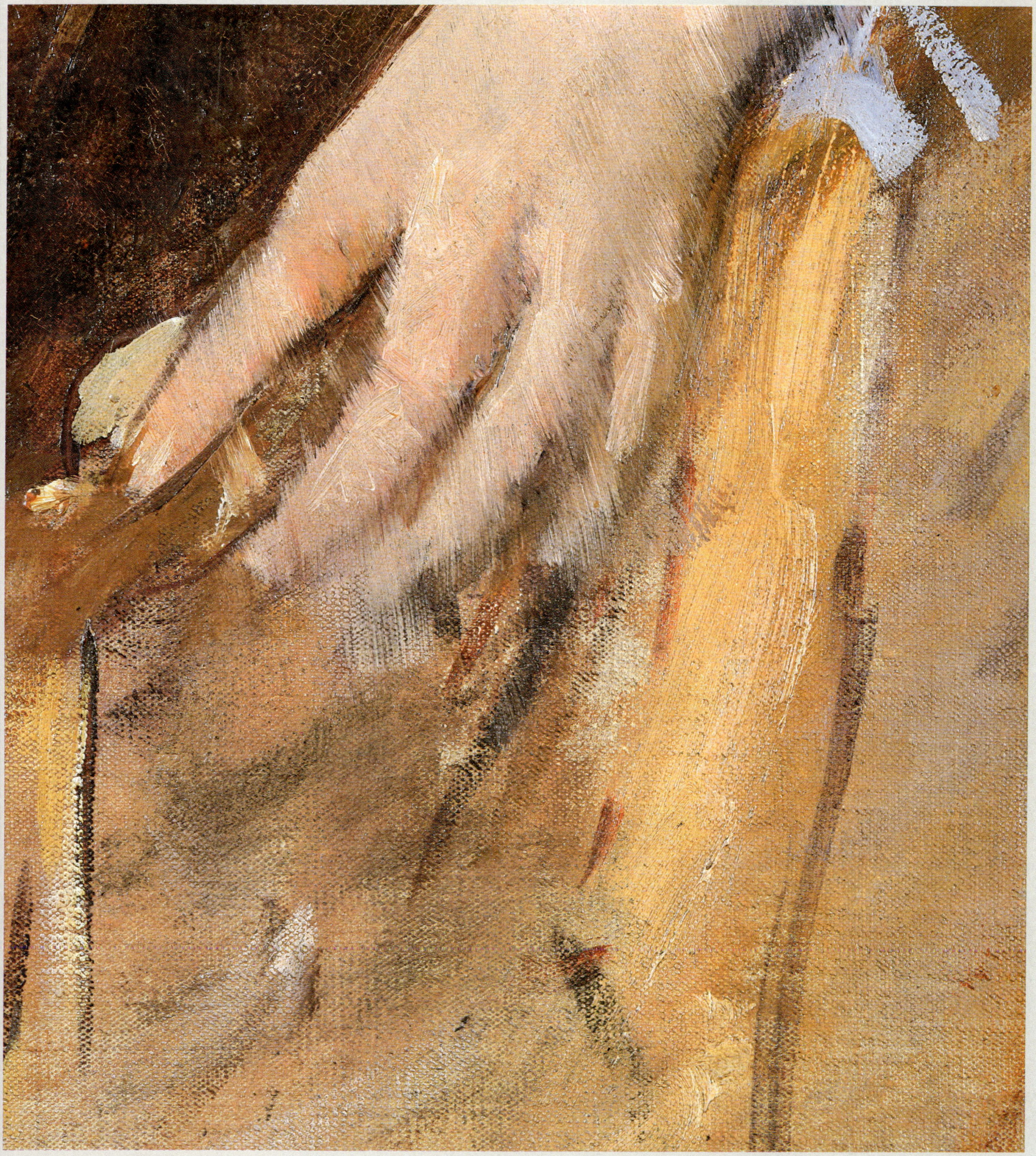

# GEORGES SEURAT

*Bathing, Asnières/Une Baignade, Asnières* (1883-84)
Oil on canvas, 201cm × 301.5cm/79⅛in × 118⅞in

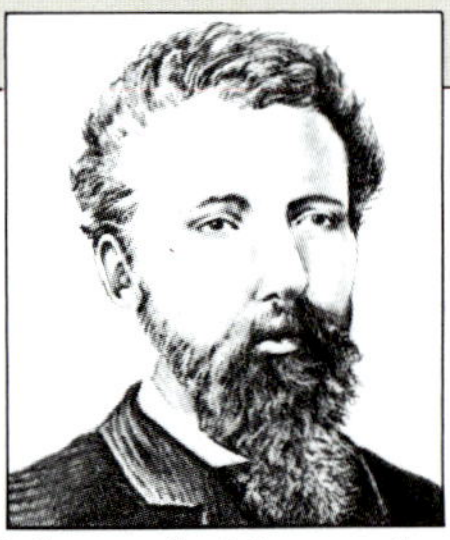

Trained by Lehmann, a pupil of Ingres, Seurat was first and foremost a skilled classical draftsman; and his early drawings, done in the manner of, for example, Holbein, Poussin, and Ingres were crucial in the formation of his mature style. Seurat concentrated on drawing until 1882, evolving a subtle touch and exploring tonal contrasts through the use of soft, Conté crayon on textured paper. The varied pressure and intensity of the black crayon and the fact that it caught on the tufts of the white paper created a varied tonal effect. Seurat's scientific interest in color theory began as early as 1878 and he analyzed the work of Delacroix to understand that artist's use of the law of contrasts.

Seurat began making studies in oil out of doors in the early 1880s. While his drawings express a rigorous analysis of tonal modelling, his early oils reveal an observation of color in nature. While Seurat had been influenced by the work of the Impressionists, his criss-cross hatching of the color was already distinctive and individual.

From 1884 Seurat abandoned earth colors and adopted a 'prismatic' palette consisting of eleven colors chromatically arranged in the order of the spectrum. These comprised the cadmium yellows, vermilion, madder lakes, cobalt violet, ultramarine and cobalt blues, viridian green and two mixed greens. White was crucial for Seurat who, like Monet, mixed it with all his colors thus increasing their reflective powers and better evoking a feeling of natural light. Thus, opacity was important to his surfaces as was a matt finish which was intended to remain unvarnished. Glass was placed over the finished painting as a substitute for the darkening shine of varnish traditionally added for protection.

In 1885 Seurat's descriptive brushwork gave way to the use of the pointillist dot. Using this technique, palette mixtures were limited to hues adjacent on the prismatic circle. Patches of contrasting colors, like orange and blue, enhanced each other when placed side by side, but Seurat's optical mixture, where separate dots of primary colors like blue and yellow were intended to 'fuse' in the eye as green, in fact produced a dull grayish effect, because the colors fused as pigment not as light.

**1.** A strong, heavy canvas with a thin white or off-white ground was used to enhance the paint's luminosity.

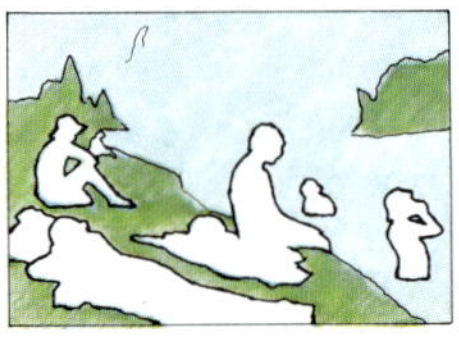

**2.** Broad areas of local color were blocked in. Figures and objects were indicated by thin outlines of paint.

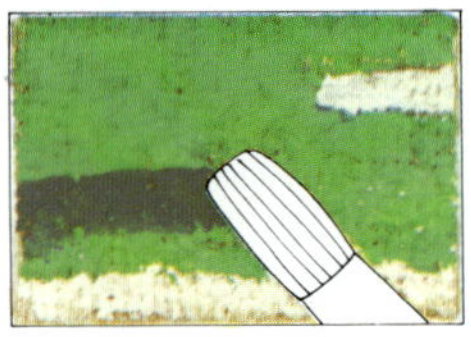

**3.** The paint layer was built up slowly mainly in a wet-over-dry method to retain the purity of the colors.

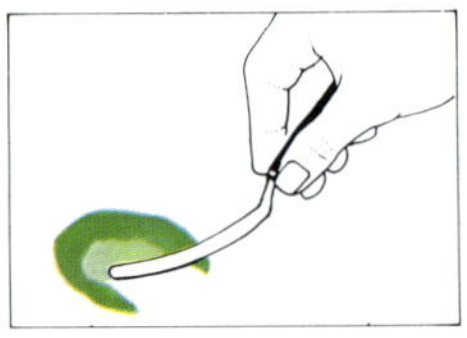

**4.** Dryish paint consistency was used. Colors were mixed with white to add brilliancy.

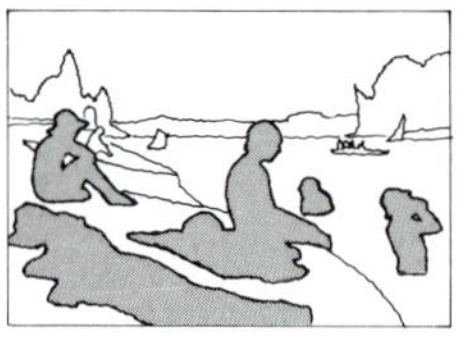

**5.** The figures and garments in the foreground were heavily worked in opaque layers; the background is thinner, paler and softer.

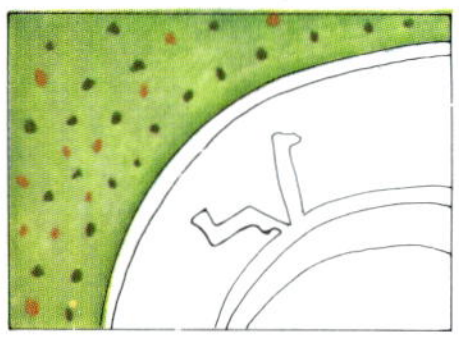

**6.** Pointillist dots were added as contrast in 1887.

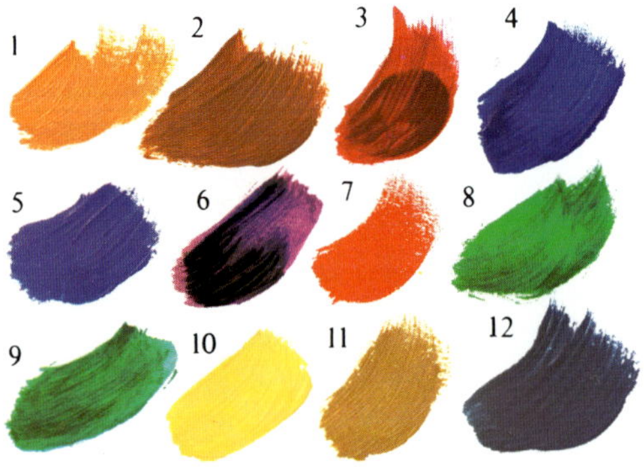


For this painting Seurat's palette included: mixed orange (**1**), raw sienna (**2**), alizarin red (**3**), ultramarine blue (**4**), cobalt blue (**5**), violet (mixed from alizarin red and blue) (**6**), vermilion (**7**), emerald green (**8**), viridian green (**9**), cadmium yellow (**10**), yellow ochre (**11**). Seurat may also have used Cerulean blue (**12**).

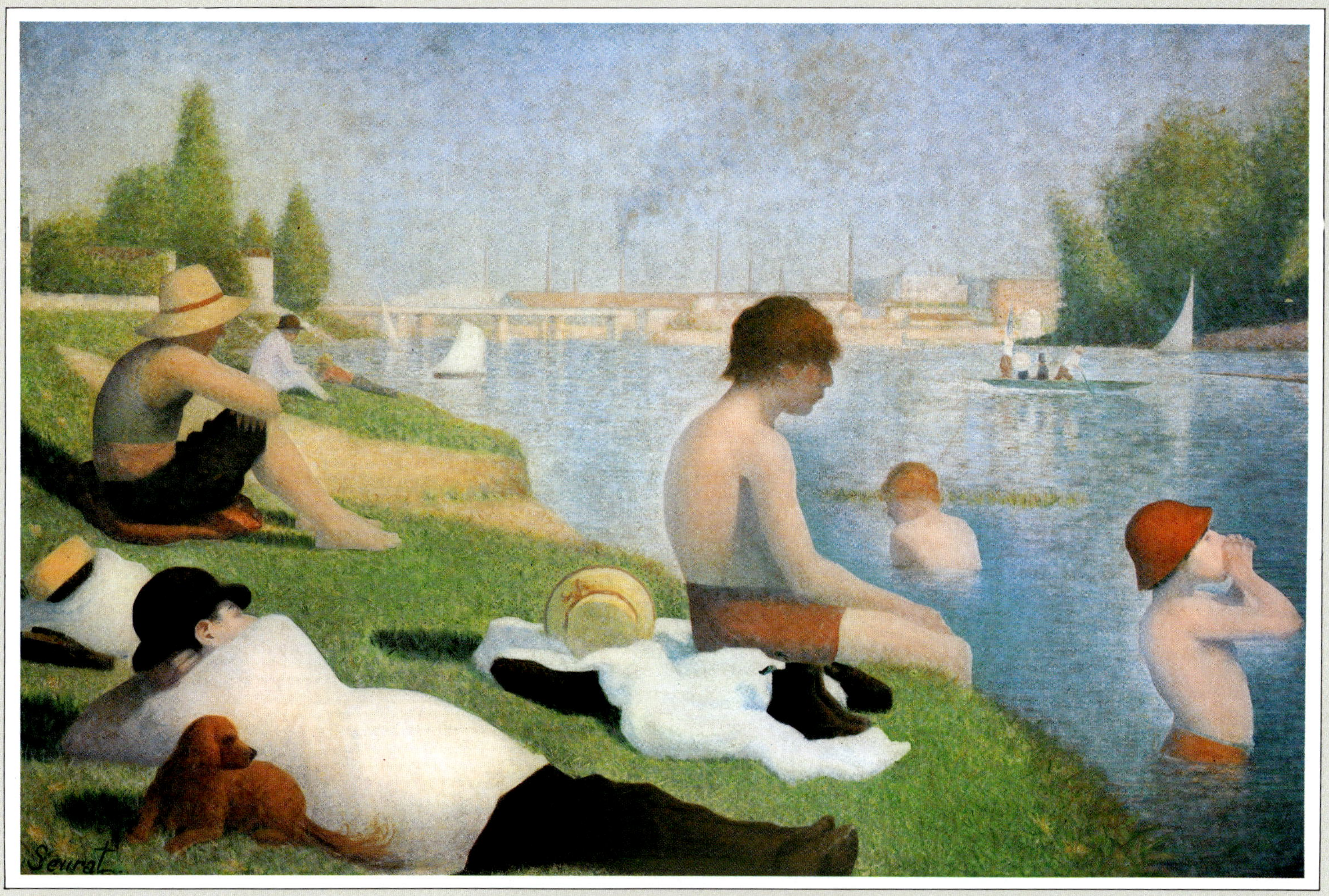


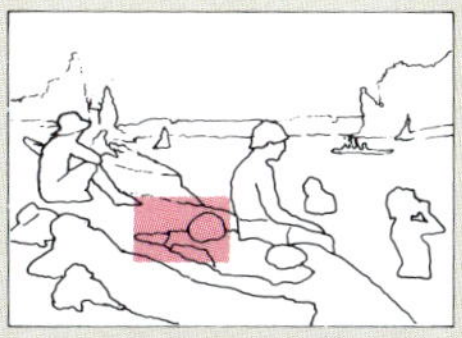

Grass is depicted with dryish, hatched strokes imitating its spiky growth. The clothes are rendered more broadly with sweeping strokes to evoke the weight and texture of fabric. The brushwork follows the folds in the fabric and the curves of the hat. The darks contain transparent colors not found elsewhere in the picture.

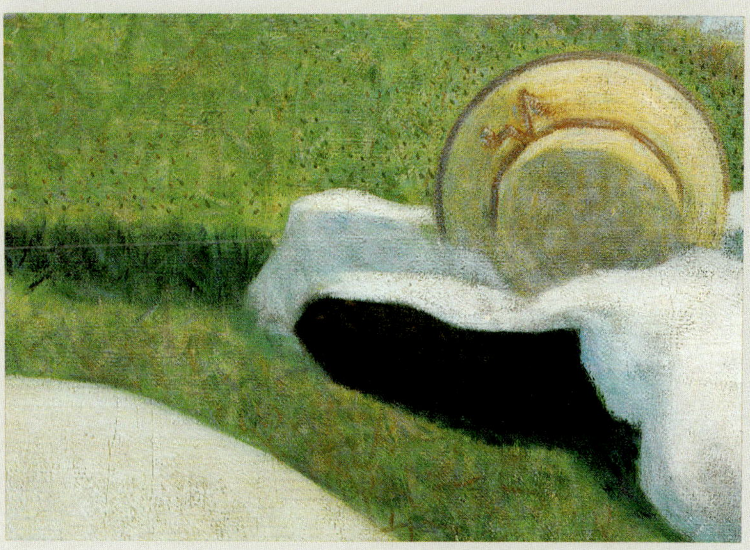

*A strong, heavy-weight canvas with a thin, pale ground has been used and the grain exploited to create a fuzzy, hazy effect evoking the warmth of the atmosphere. The brushwork is varied, descriptively recreating surfaces and textures to help differentiate objects in space. Horizontal strokes are used to define water, and vertical for the grass. Broad, sweeping strokes follow the forms of the figures and evoke the weight and feel of fabric. The mid afternoon sun falls from right to left creating shadows of equal size to the figure and gives a calm stability to the composition. Much of the paint application is wet over dry to retain the purity of the colors. Stiff paint is built up over thin, opaque layers of local color and complementary shades worked in.*

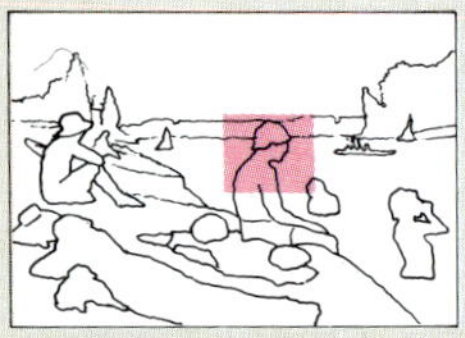

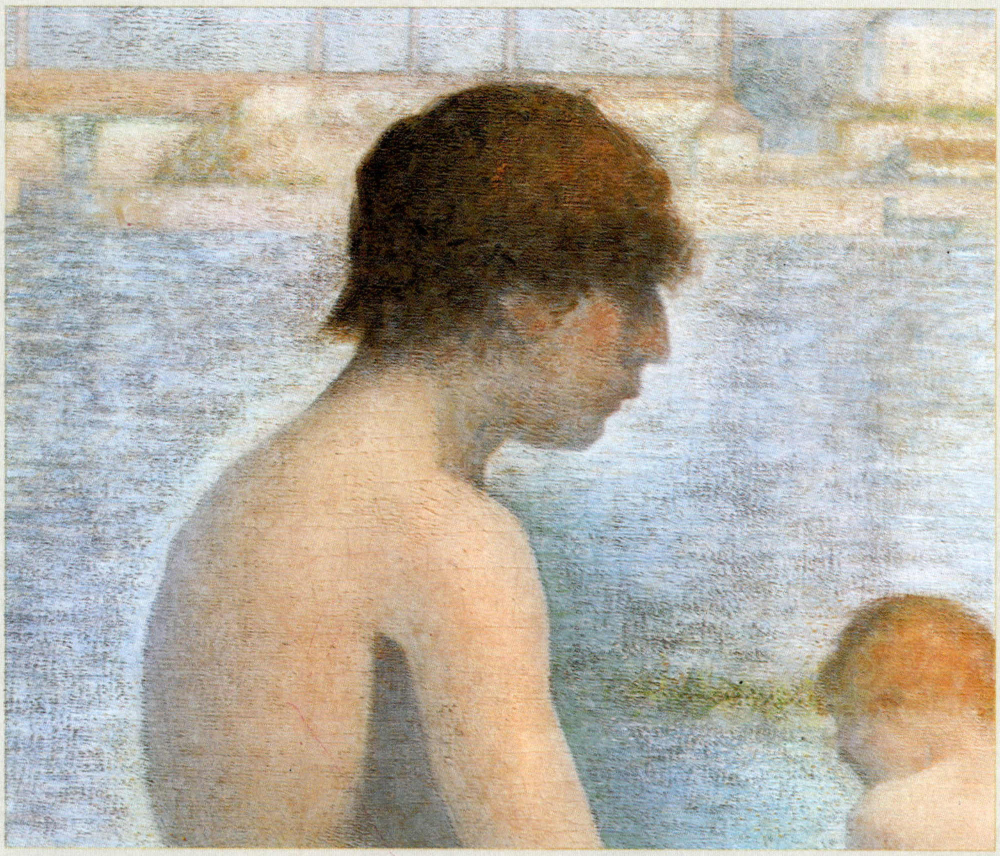

*Here it is evident that Seurat's knowledge of tonal contrasts has come into play. To separate his figures from the background, the natural effects of light and shade have been altered, exaggerating their respective lightness and darkness. This recreates in paint optical laws of tonal contrast with which Seurat was familiar. For example, the pale water is lightened behind the figure's back and the flesh darkened where the two meet, in order to separate them.*

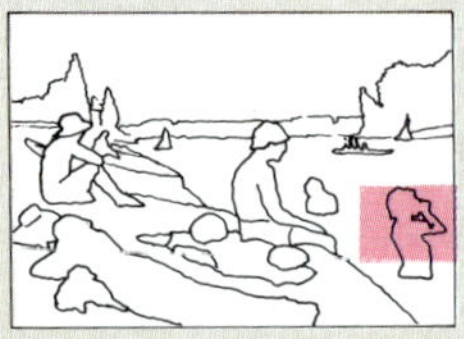

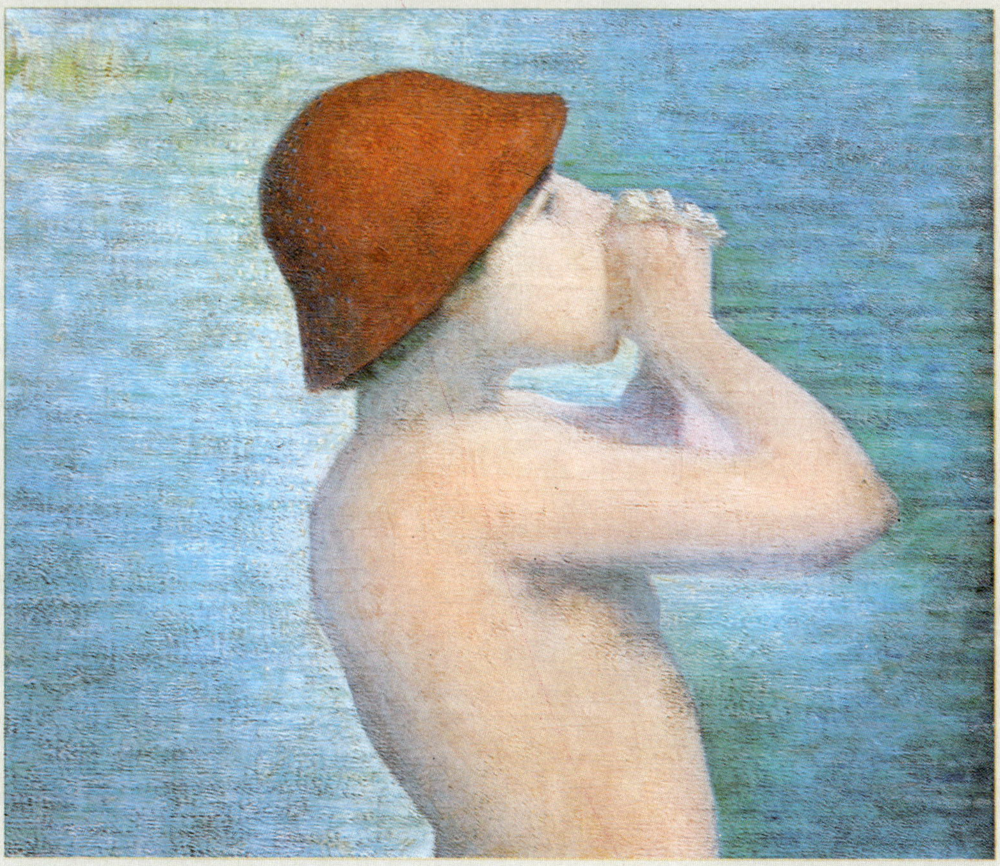

*Here again tonal contrast can be seen. Beneath the figure's chin, shadow darkening the flesh colors is stressed while the water is rendered paler to distinguish the figure from its background. The later addition of pointillist dots can be seen on the hat and in the water.*

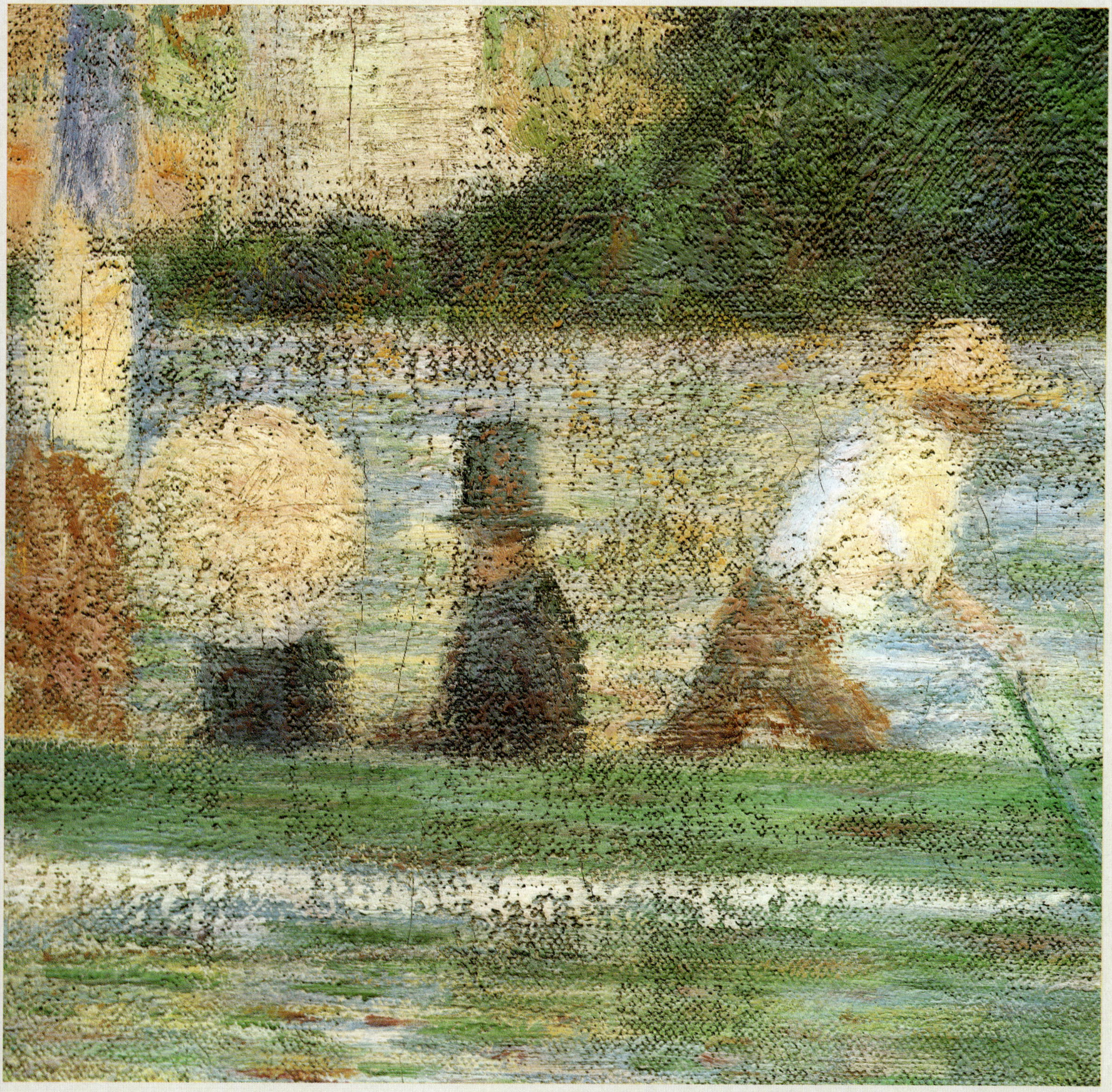

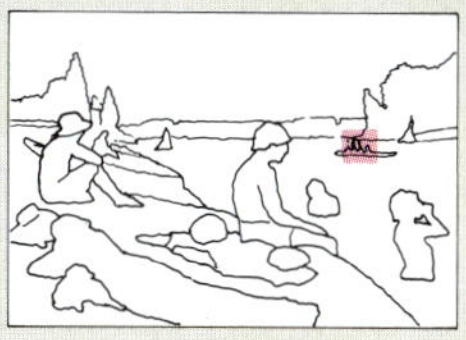

**Actual size detail**
*This detail shows many features typical of Seurat's work. Seurat made changes during the painting process, for example the figure of the boatman was added at a late stage, as can be seen where the blue of the water and the earlier brushstrokes show through. Similarly the reflection was a late addition. The blurred colors of the water were created using a wet-in-wet technique. Seurat may have used a mixture of cobalt blue and white for this. In the top lefthand corner the brushstroke which added a touch of yellow can be clearly seen. This detail also shows the dirt which has accumulated in the crevices of the canvas.*

# EDGAR DEGAS

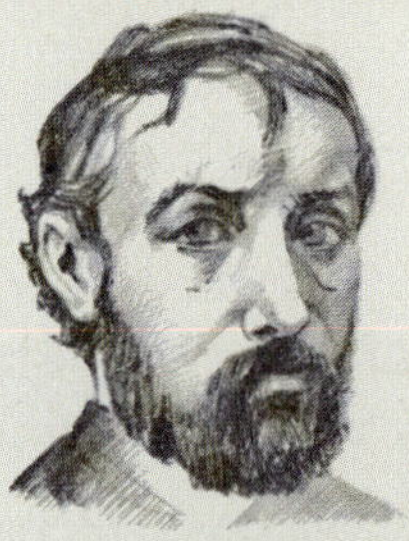

## *Portrait of Mademoiselle Hélène Rouart/Portrait de Mademoiselle Hélène Rouart* (1886)

Oil on putty-color primed canvas
161cm × 120cm/63½in × 47in

During the 1880s Degas' failing eyesight was giving him serious difficulties with his work in general, and with oil painting in particular. This large portrait of Hélène Rouart was one of the last major works in oil attempted by the artist, and his final statement on the theme of the sitter in a characteristic environment, which had preoccupied Degas since the Bellelli family portrait of 1859–1860. Degas had had problems with his eyesight since the early 1870s, and in part as a result of this, he gradually turned to media like pastel, which offered a more direct method of coloring. With oil painting, the artist mixed colors on the palette more than on the support itself, and this extra stage was eliminated by working with pastel, in which the colors are applied and mixed directly on the support.

Degas' friendship with Hélène Rouart's father, Henri Rouart, began in 1870. Rouart was a successful and wealthy industrial engineer, who took up landscape painting and also amassed an impressive art collection, which included Egyptian artefacts, Old Masters and modern painting from works by Corot and Millet to the Impressionists themselves. He owned many works by Degas, whose portrait of his daughter was part of a grander project to portray the entire family, a project curtailed by the death of Mme. Rouart. Henri Rouart was encouraged by Degas to show his work, and apart from regularly lending Impressionist paintings from his collection for exhibition, he also exhibited his own work at almost all the eight Impressionist group shows between 1874 and 1886.

The works from Rouart's collection which surround Hélène's figure in this portrait have been identified. The glass case to the left contains three wooden Egyptian statues, the nearest a funerary figurine. On the wall behind her are, at the top, part of a Chinese silk hanging, and to the right a view of Naples painted by Corot in 1828, possibly included as an allusion to Degas' own familial attachment to that port. Below the Corot is a black crayon drawing of a peasant woman by Millet. Rouart also owned several important pastels by Millet, which may have influenced Degas' development of the medium, late in his life.

Hélène Rouart is thus presented not in an environment which complements or clarifies her own individual character, but one which tells the viewer about her social role as her father's daughter. Indicative of the cloistered, chaperoned life led by most middle- and upper-class unmarried women in this period, this portrayal of Hélène Rouart shows her trapped among her father's belongings, like another of his possessions. The taut precision of Degas' composition, and the shallow, claustrophobic pictorial space aptly convey this.

Degas has placed Hélène Rouart immediately behind the symbol of her absent father, his huge study chair, which dwarfs her physical presence. To her right, she is hemmed in by the free-standing glass case which houses her father's Egyptian statues, the nearest of which – ironically the funerary figurine – echoes her own pose, its head level with hers. This visual pun was perhaps a humorous reference on Degas' part to the stiff formality often imposed on women of her class, by the restraints and expectations of society. However, Degas was not renowned for his sympathy towards women. To her left, she is crowded by the pictures hung on the wall, and their distance from her is made ambiguous to stress the airless feel of the home environment that closes around her. Above, the dark reds of the wall hanging push down and, linking with the same reds of the chair back, squeeze her between them. The blue border at her head level creates a striking horizontal which equates visually with the upper framing edge of the picture, which brings it and the red hanging up toward the picture surface, further diminishing the pictorial space. The blue border meets the frame of the Corot at right-angles, just behind her head, a device which anchors her, tightly immobilized within the composition. Hélène Rouart is completely enclosed in the rigid network of interlocking geometrical shapes and planes that surround her seated figure.

In addition to the chair, the foreground is blocked and dominated by a table piled up with her father's papers, which are a further reference to the implied weighty presence of her father in the painting. The three-dimensional glass structure of the display case could have been used by Degas to open and define a sense of space around his sitter. Instead, its receding

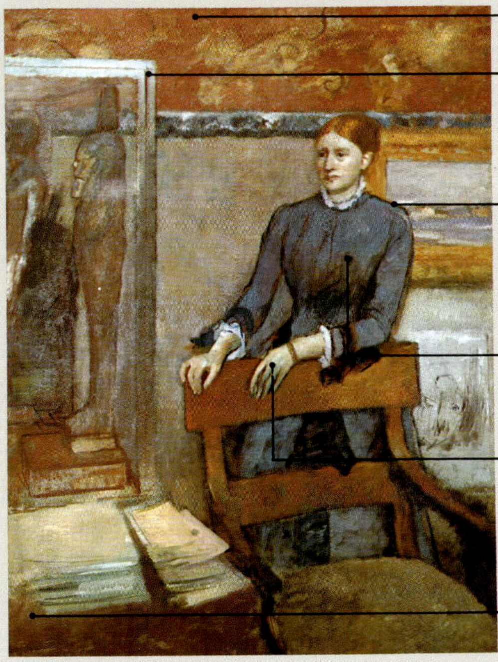

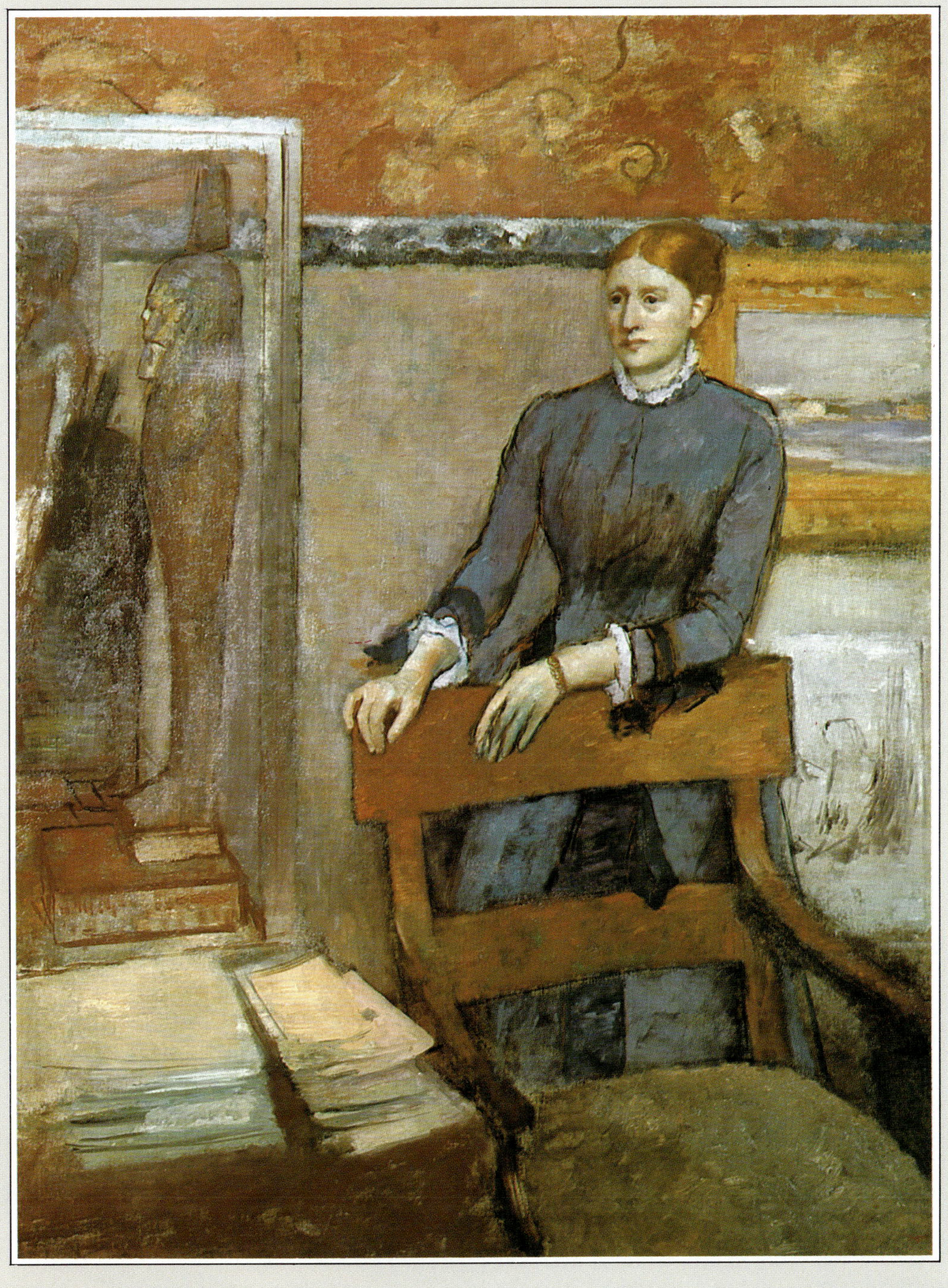

*By the time this work was painted, Degas' eye-sight was becoming poor and his field of vision restricted. This disability may account for the loosely finished state of the picture. However, the artist had lost none of his powers of acute psychological perception and the work lacks nothing in its surety of touch or compositional precision. As ever, Degas was concerned to portray his sitter's persona in its subtlest nuances. Here Degas shows the contradictions faced by middle-class women in late nineteenth century French society. The geometrical grid in which Hélène Rouart is trapped in this composition aptly echoes the formal claustrophobia of her lifestyle. The color range, with it muted, broken hues, reinforces the mood of the picture. This canvas is not a standard format.*

metal frame is barely distinguishable, and the front square edge dominates in its flattening reiteration of the picture edge. Whether or not the portrait was intentionally left incomplete, is not known. In its present state it certainly lacks neither power nor impact, despite idiosyncracies like the hidden or missing little finger of Hélène Rouart's right hand.

Painted on a large standard format, portrait 100 canvas, this work has a monumental quality. Overall, its tone is subdued, the colors mostly broken in mixtures, and earth colors are used. Like in Gauguin's works later, many of which were influenced by Degas, dull harmonies unite the painting, and no strong lights or darks disrupt the middle tone which predominates throughout. A light Indian red earth was used to outline the paler forms and general structure of the composition, over a putty-colored commercial preparation which blends perfectly with tonal and color scheme. For other areas, a darker color, possibly Prussian blue, was used to indicate contours. On the figure, raw umber outlines alternate or are overlaid with dark blue ones. On the hands the two colors are mingled wet in wet. The first *ébauche* layer on the figure was applied in thinly scumbled dilute Indian red, which was left to show through the uneven semi-opaque blue layer on top. The blue is thinnest over her corseted breasts, so the red underlay aids the sense of swelling form. Where the brick red is exposed among the blues it appears, by contrast, to have the brilliance of vermilion. This is typical of the exaggerated brightening of a color which can be achieved either by warm-cool complementary contrast, or by juxtaposing lighter colors, the orange-red, against darker ones, the blue. The insistent use of these two dominant colors in the picture, the warm brick red and the steely blue, which appear repeatedly in modified tints, provide the rich harmony which unifies the composition.

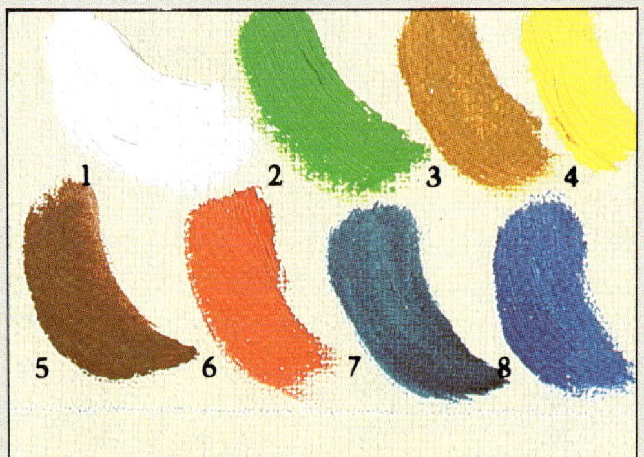


*Degas' palette for this painting probably included lead white (1), zinc white, yellow ochre (3), red earth (5) and Prussian blue (7). Lemon yellow (4), vermilion (6), cobalt blue (8) and chrome green (2) may also have been used.*

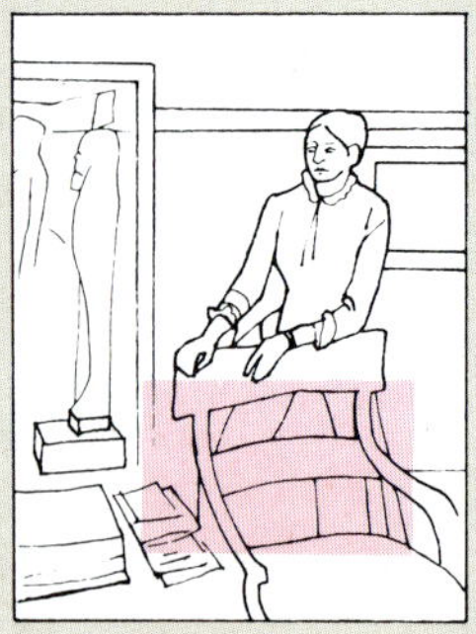

*A transparent umber underlay or ébauche leaves the pale putty colored ground glowing through. Black is used thinly to outline the chair. Opaque, probably Prussian blue and white are 'floated' in thin scumbled veils over the darks below, and appear brilliant by contrast. Indian or earth red, and Prussian blue were both used for outlines on the dress. A flap of blue from the dress was added over the dry paint of the chair bar, to lock the figure more tautly against the chair.*

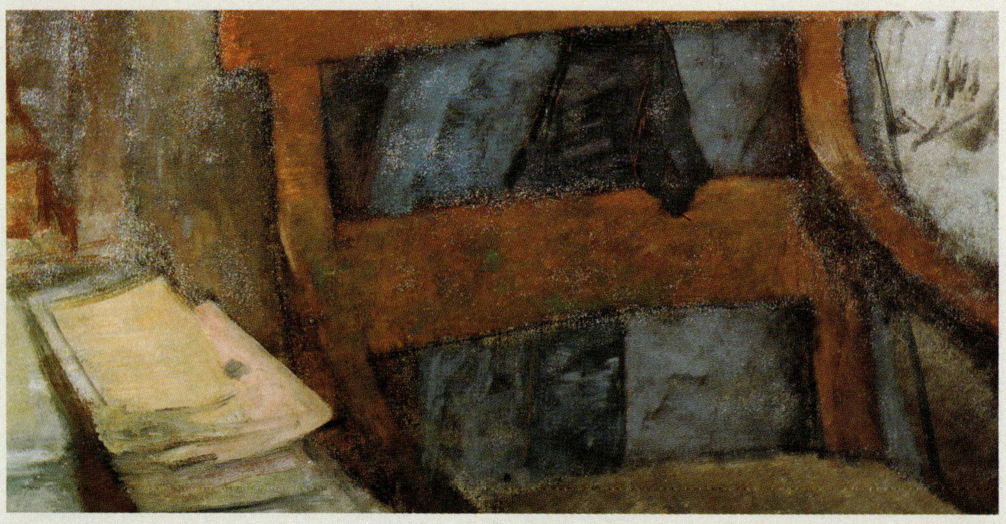

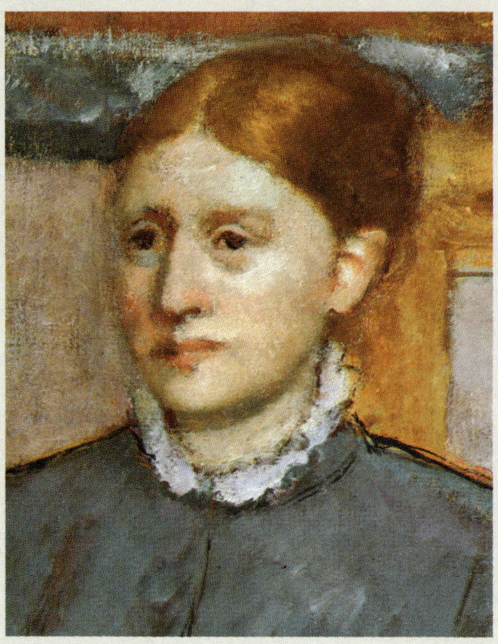

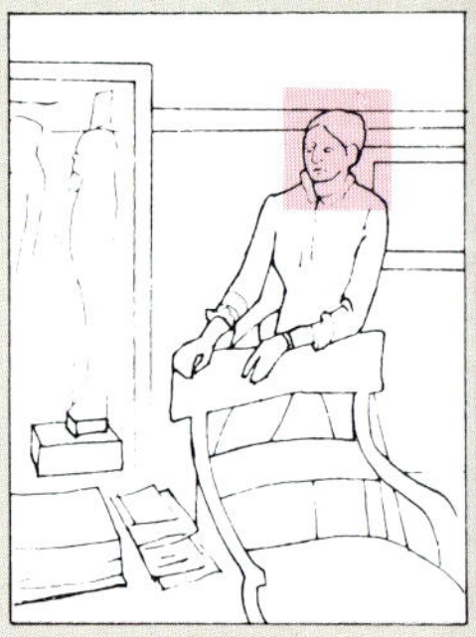

*The contours are washed on in umber, and reworked around the ear with dabs of red. Prussian blue contours were reinforced over red for the dress and neck frill. Delicate warm-cool modulations of varied pinks and greens were used for the flesh colors, which are more impasted than elsewhere. The fine canvas texture is still visible, and can be seen among the dragged and more thinly applied colors. The face coheres well at a distance, although up close it seems very freely handled. The dull pinkish beige of the background wall was laid in vertical strokes which go up to the edge of the face on the left, and over the original counter line, thus changing the shape of the face. The first shoulder line is also still visible.*

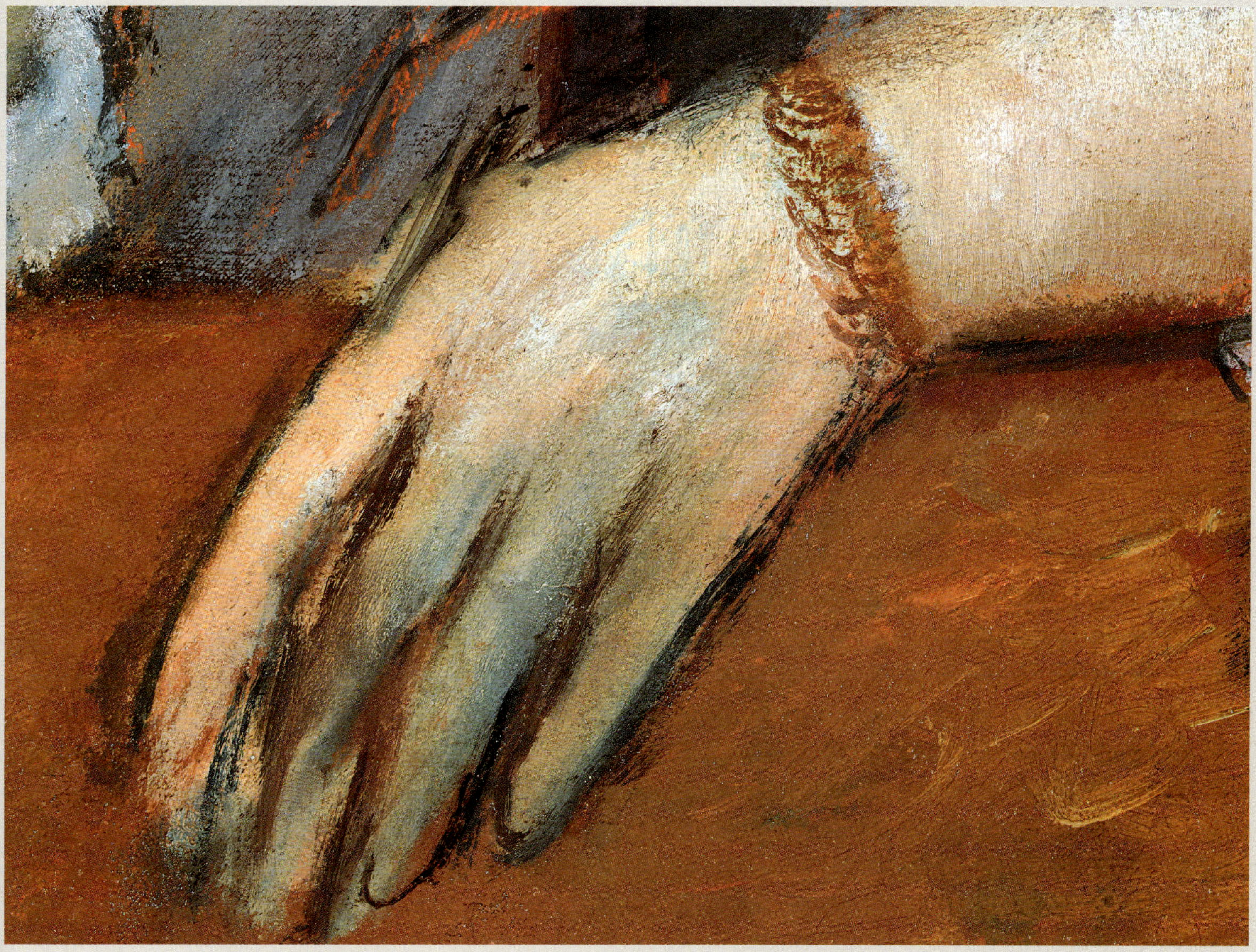

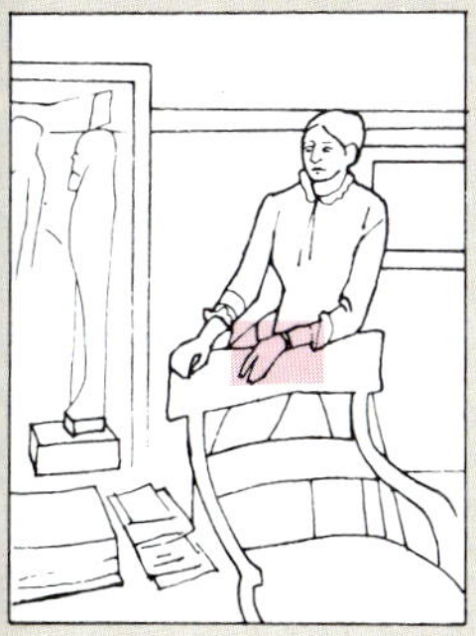

Actual size detail
*Contours of red and blue are intermingled. Red was sometimes laid over Prussian blue, and vice versa. These hues are used both wet over dry and, in places, wet slurred into wet. The red is probably red earth, its hue made more intense and brilliant in contrast to the dark Prussian blue, but it could be vermilion. Umber and Prussian blue outline the fingers, and were slurred together with the wet pink and green flesh tints during the process of adjustment. The handling is direct and immediate.*

# PAUL SIGNAC

*The Dining Room/La Salle à manger* (1886-1887)
Oil on white primed canvas
89cm × 115cm/35in × 45¼in

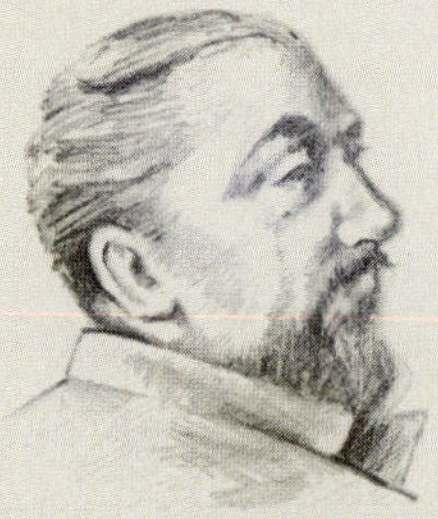

Signac was based in Paris throughout the height of the Neo-Impressionist movement, leaving only in 1892 to settle on the Mediterranean coast at St. Tropez. Virtually self-taught, he based his early techniques on Impressionist painting, until he saw Seurat's *Bathing, Asnières* at the Independents' exhibition in 1884. Signac had been one of the founders of the *Groupe des Artistes Indépendants*, which in 1884 established exhibitions free of awards or juries as an alternative venue to the official Salon exhibitions. In addition to showing their work at the eighth Impressionist exhibition in 1886, the Neo-Impressionists showed regularly with the Independents, and with the Belgian independent artists at their *Les XX* shows also founded in 1884. Although the Belgians had already established links with French art, inviting the Impressionists – like Monet and Renoir in 1886 – to show with them, their closest ties were with the Neo-Impressionists. A number of Belgian artists, like Théo van Rysselberghe (1862–1926) and Henri van de Velde (1863–1957), members of *Les XX*, adopted the Neo-Impressionist style.

The Neo-Impressionists, reacting against the 'romantic' naturalism of Impressionism, and seeking a more scientific method with which to convey their pictorial ideas, found sympathy in the latter half of the 1880s among the Symbolist writers and poets who had begun to displace naturalism in literature in the early 1880s. As their theories extended in the second half of the 1880s, the Neo-Impressionists discovered a kinship between their aims and those of the Symbolist writers like Félix Fénéon, their most astute supporter, Gustave Kahn and Jean Moréas. The Neo-Impressionists no longer sought merely to capture fleeting effects of light and color in nature, as they saw the Impressionists doing, instead they wished to render a more universal and timeless record of contemporary life. Signac was the theoretician of the new movement, explaining its ideas and defending it in his book *From Eugène Delacroix to Neo-Impressionism*, which was published in 1899, in fact long after the movement's peak. Although inevitably written from Signac's personal bias, it reflected the ideals of the Neo-Impressionists, and it has been characterized by the influential modern art historian, Linda Nochlin, as 'an important document of that aesthetic universalism, that attempt to unite and synthesize all human thought and feeling in a symbolic, law-based harmony which animated so many literary and artistic enterprises of the last twenty years of the nineteenth century.'

In 1886, the year in which *The Dining Room* was begun, Signac adopted the 'dot' brushstroke which Seurat had developed in his monumental canvas *Sunday Afternoon on the Ile de la Grande Jatte* painted between 1884 and 1886. In addition to its function in dividing the different color components within a picture, the dot technique enabled the Neo-Impressionists to render minute variations in tonal value. In general, the Impressionists had sought to rid their paintings of tonal modeling, which was still associated with academic painting, and instead to study effects in which contrasts of tone (light and dark) were reduced to a minimum. The flatness this brought to their paintings enabled them to maximize the tensions inherent in painting, between the two-dimensional picture surface, and the illusion of depth. The Neo-Impressionists restored tonal modeling to their pictures, but instead of reverting to the gradations between white and brown characteristic of academic classicism, they explored the means of presenting tonal gradation through the use of juxtapositions of pure color.

In Signac's *Dining Room*, the scene is backlit from a window, giving a dramatic light creating silhouettes and strong contrasts of light and shade. This type of lighting was used occasionally by Degas, but not by the Impressionists, who avoided such extremes of contrast. When sunsets were painted by them, for example certain of Monet's haystack series from 1890–1891, any shadows were brilliant with colored light, reflected from surrounding objects and the sky. In Signac's picture, the back lighting creates a strong sense of form and structure in the composition, a frozen solemnity which may be an ironic criticism of the formal, ritualistic quality of the middle-class life depicted. Form is created by gradations of color from pale tints to full saturation. Thus, the highlighted areas are shown as barely tinted or yellowish whites. These then pass through a series of minute gradations in which increasing amounts ot local color are added until, in the darkest parts, almost pure saturation of the tube colors is reached. To darken the shadow hues

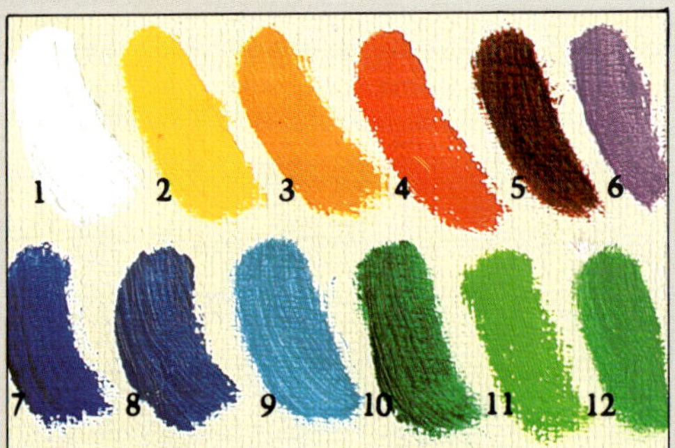


*Signac's limited 'prismatic' palette used here probably comprised lead* (1) *or zinc white, cadmium yellow pale* (2), *cadmium yellow mid and deep* (3), *vermilion* (4), *red alizarin lakes* (5), *cobalt violet* (6), *cobalt blue* (7), *ultramarine blue* (8), *cerulean blue* (9), *viridian green* (10) *and light and dark chrome greens* (11, 12).

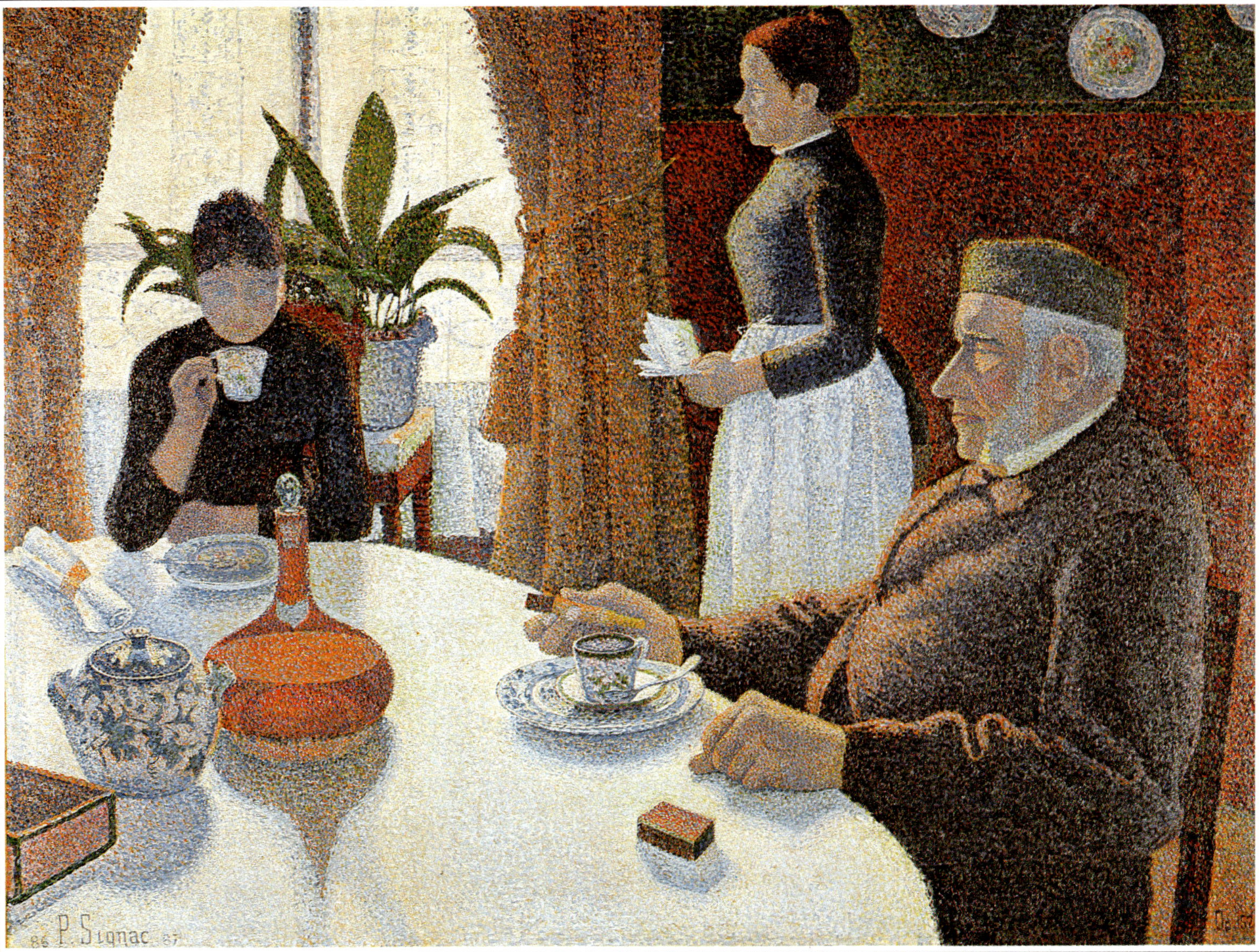


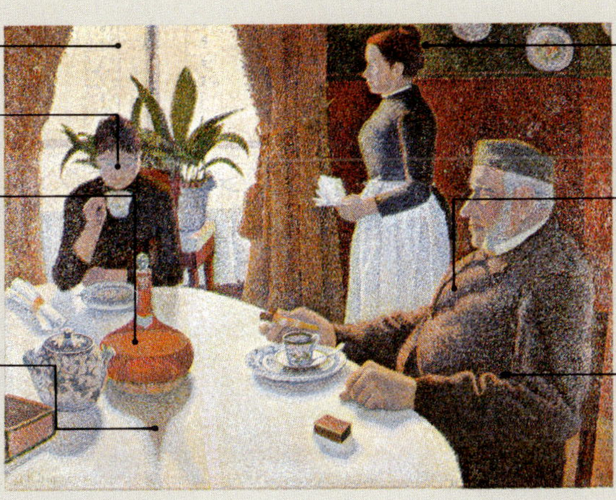


*Signac's use of strong* contrejour *or* back light *exaggerates the stylized starkness of his figures. Their strict profile and full face poses echo those used two years earlier by Seurat in his monumental work,* La Grande Jatte, *and show the influence of stylized ancient Egyptian art on both painters. Like Seurat, Signac did a series of major paintings of modern life themes. Signac's three paintings, all of interiors, were executed in the later 1880s.* Dining Room *was painted on a standard portrait 50 format canvas.*

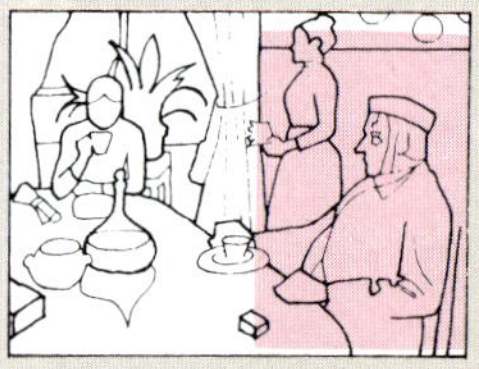

*The monumental stillness of Signac's figures comes from a combination of their static poses with a strong sense of modeled form. While the Impressionists preferred to suppress stark contrasts of light and dark to avoid tonal modeling, the Neo-Impressionists often used dramatic back or side lighting to enhance the sense of form. They replaced the academic modeling of tone in monochrome creams and browns with colorful modeling. This technique exploited the natural lightness or darkness of particular hues, with added white. Thus, pale yellow stands for highlights, with the local colors of the object, say the man's jacket, carefully gradated from that palest hue through to deepest blue.*

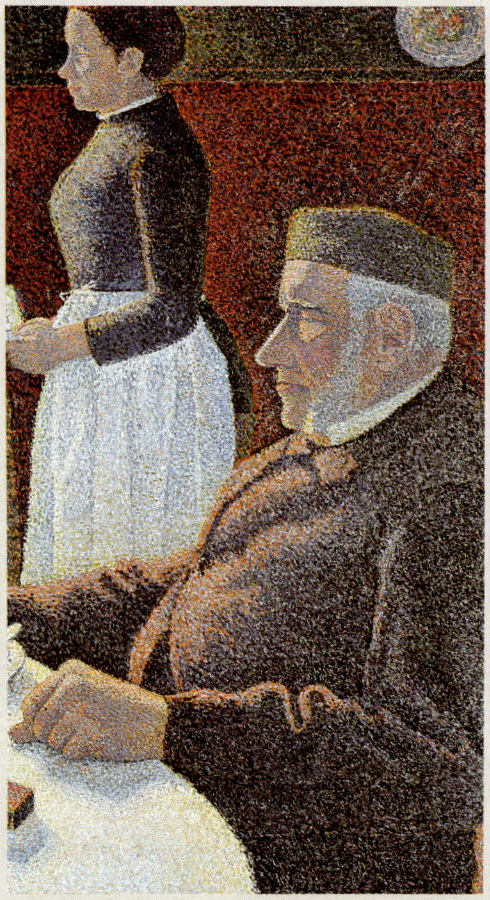

without adding sullying black or earth colors, green and blue are mixed on the palette and juxtaposed next to purer blues. Effects of reflected color among the local colors are represented by additional dots of the appropriate hues. The careful gradation of tones applied in small dots gives a stiff, sculptural artificiality to the composition, whose color scheme is dominated by the complementary colors orange-yellow to blue-violet.

As with Impressionist painting, opaque paint is a crucial feature of the Neo-Impressionist technique. Mat, opaque hues, with white added, have far greater light-reflective luminosity than transparent colors, through which light penetrates before being reflected back to the eye, producing darker, more saturated color. Thus mat, opaque, unvarnished surfaces bounce the maximum amount of tinted light back to the eye to create the effects of partial optical fusion these artists desired. Signac was instrumental in encouraging Seurat to abandon earth colours, such as those used in *Bathing, Asnières* (1883–1884), and to adopt the purer version of the Impressionist palette. He was also influential in van Gogh's lightening of his palette. Signac and Vincent van Gogh worked together at Asnières in 1887, and Signac encouraged the Dutch artist to replace his somber, essentially tonal palette with bright 'prismatic' colors, thus introducing him to a more modern use of complementary contrasts than that which van Gogh had learned through studying Delacroix.

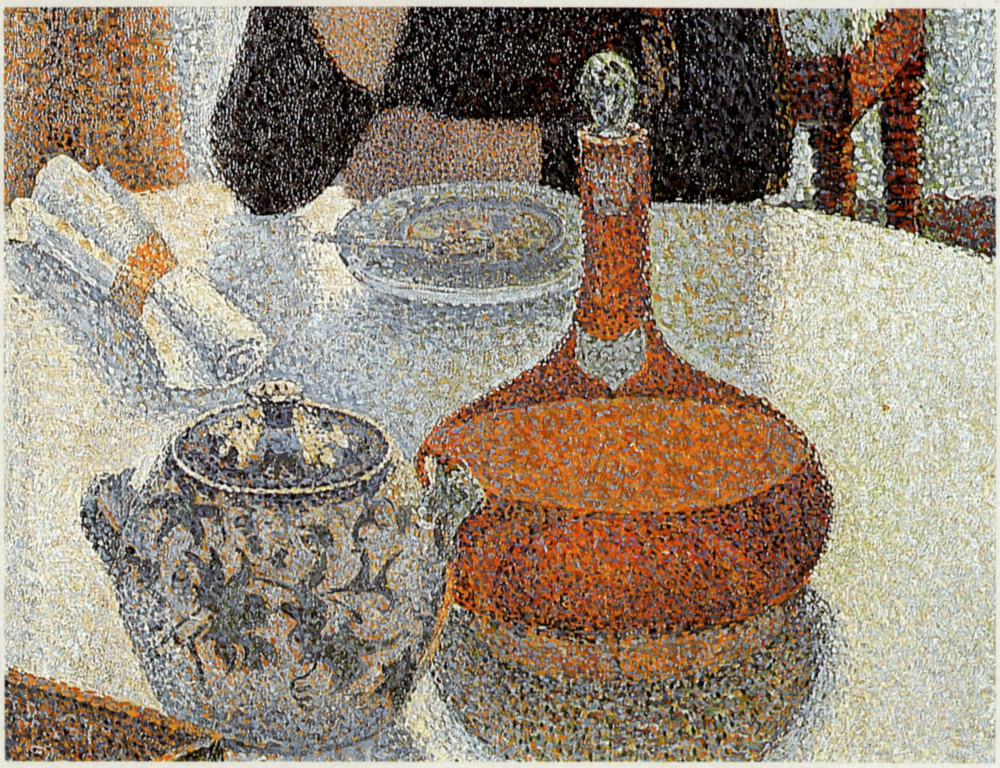

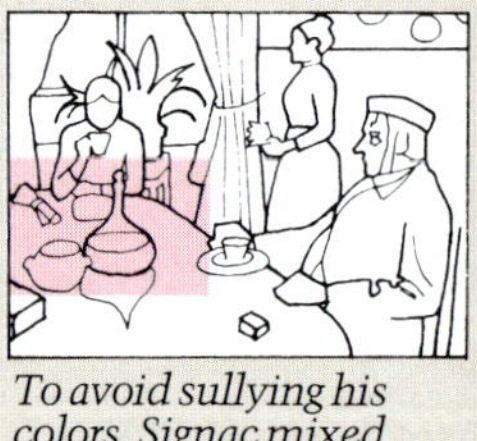

*To avoid sullying his colors, Signac mixed only those hues adjacent to each other on his prismatic palette. The colors were then placed in separate small dots on the picture surface to keep them from blending while wet. He avoided accidental blurring of one color into another by allowing each layer of color or dots to dry before adding more. The dots are too large for any complete fusion of colors on the viewer's retina, but the partial fusion of the dots of color causes some optical vibration. This gives an effect of luminous atmospheric light to the picture.*

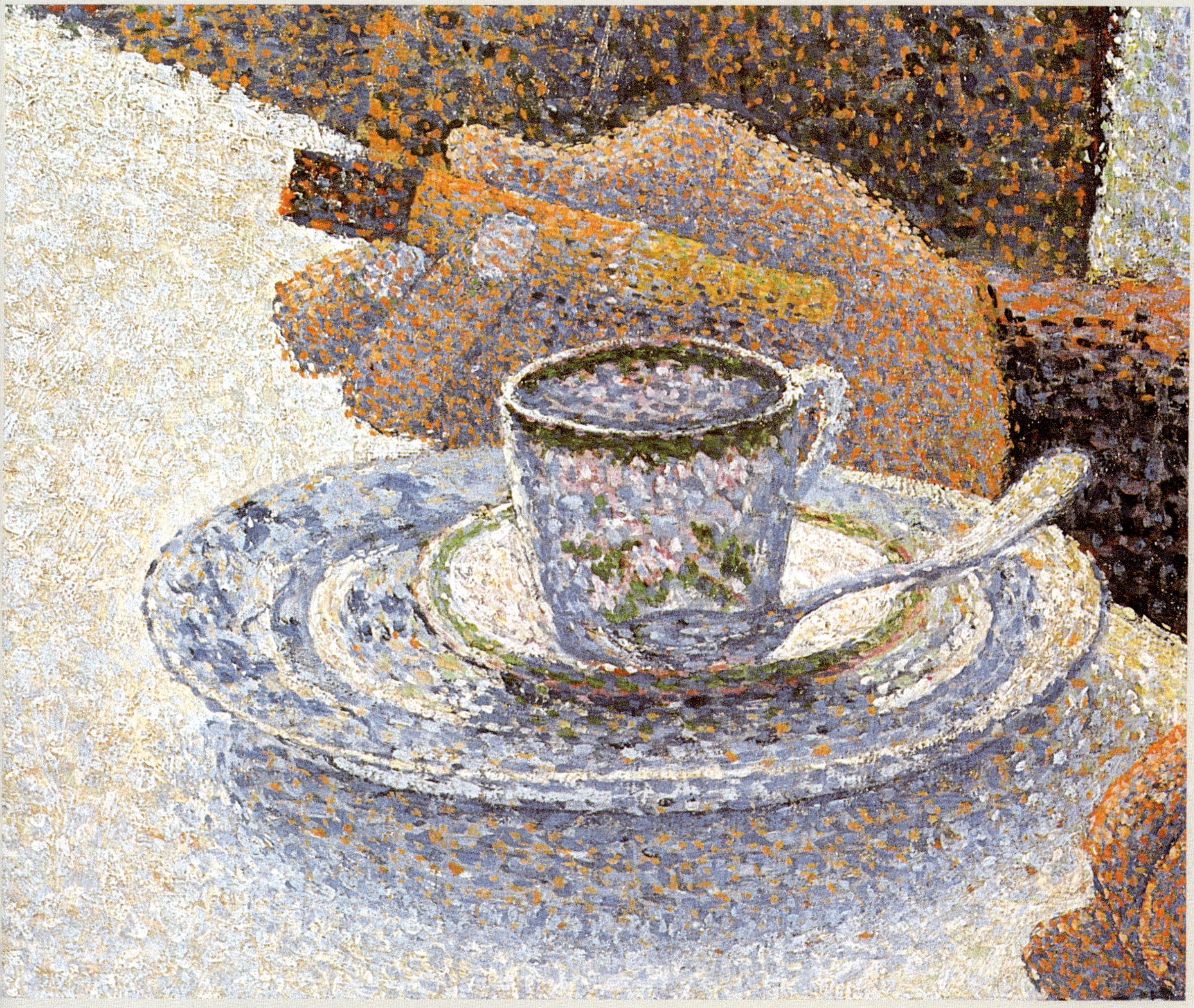

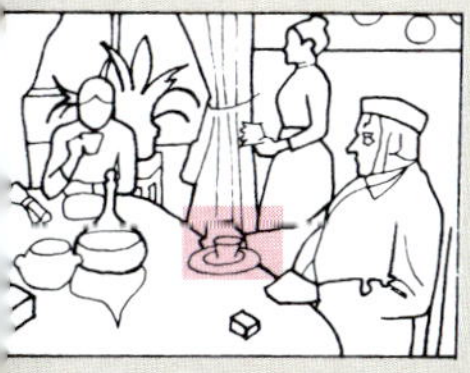

Actual size detail
*The Neo-Impressionist touch was theoretically a uniform dot, but the slight changes of shape almost imperceptible at the correct viewing distance become clear close up. Here, small dots become dashes, which follow the direction of the forms, the edge of the plate, helping to structure form. Among the blues of the shadow, an airy feeling of light is created by the added touches of contrasting orange, which stand for the flecks of warm light penetrating the luminous shadow. In a few instances, the dots turn into fine lines, outlining shapes, like the blue on the spoon and the white highlights on the cup. The deepest shadow, on the cuff, is modified by flecks of paler blue and, close to the highlight, by touches of orange which show the blurred edge between light and shade.*

# Camille Pissarro

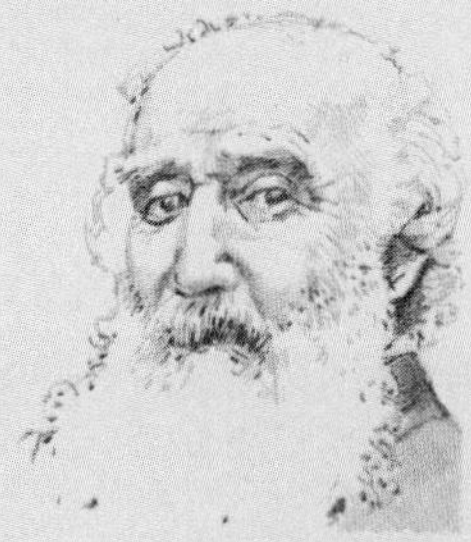

*Apple Picking at Eragny-sur-Epte/La Cueillette de pommes, Eragny-sur-Epte* (1888)
Oil on white primed canvas
60cm × 73cm/23½in X 28¾in

In 1884, Pissarro moved further from Paris to Eragny-sur-Epte, north-west of the city and a few miles east of Giverny, where Monet had settled the previous year. Unlike Renoir, who at this time turned back to inspiration from classical art, Pissarro always remained open to the new ideas of younger artists, and soon adopted the novel Neo-Impressionist style which was emerging in the mid 1880s. He met Seurat and Paul Signac (1863–1935) in autumn 1885, and, acknowledging the importance of the scientific theories evolved by Seurat, began to use the pointillist technique. Pissarro's friendship and allegiance were invaluable to these younger artists, for he argued strongly for their inclusion in the Impressionist group shows, which many of the older members resisted. Apart from their style, they were disliked by some of the group for their commitment to anarchist political principles, which had grown in popularity in France, and which Pissarro himself espoused from the mid 1880s. Any association with radical politics was felt by some of the artists to threaten the cautious acceptance which the Impressionist style had so recently gained among Parisian collectors. Thus at the last group show in 1886, Monet and Renoir were absent because works by Seurat and Signac were included. However, this disagreement did not sour the relations between Pissarro, Monet and Renoir, who at this time were meeting regularly at monthly Impressionist dinners at the Café Riche in Paris.

Pissarro explained the Neo-Impressionist theories to his dealer Durand-Ruel in a letter written towards the end of 1886. He stressed the importance of Seurat's role as inventor of the theory, and described the new function of color, which replaced mechanical mixtures of pigments with optical mixtures, where colors partially fused in the spectator's eye. The component parts of each optical color mixture were to be painted in separate touches so that they retained their color purity. When colors were mixed on the palette, they could only be combined with close neighbors on the color circle, so as to avoid excessive dulling of the hues. Pissarro noted that the great color theorists who had influenced Seurat's thinking were Chevreul, the Scot Maxwell, and the American Ogden Rood. Optical color mixtures, they argued, were more luminous than mixed pigments.

Execution or brushwork was considered unimportant by the Neo-Impressionists, as Pissarro explained: 'originality consists solely in the character of the drawing and the vision of each artist.' The descriptive, individualistic style of touch, associated with Impressionism, was dubbed 'romantic' by the Neo-Impressionists, who sought a more impersonal, mechanical touch to eliminate such gestural individualism from their work. Thus personal originality, which had for so long been linked with a personally distinctive style in brushwork, was rejected in favor of a more restrained and anonymous handling. This aim was in keeping with the cooperative ideals of anarchist politics, and yet, ironically, in practice it caused Seurat much distress. He felt that his 'anonymous' touch – his distinctive handling in effect – was under threat of genuine anonymity, as the numbers of his followers or imitators grew.

The Pointillist dot was considered the ideal vehicle for placing individual myriad touches of bright pigment on the canvas, to obtain the component elements of color without excessive mechanical mixing. Although the dots were too large to be invisible and create full optical fusion of the components on the retina, partial fusion was intended to take place, resulting in a shimmering illusion of atmospheric color. Despite the theory, few of the actual 'dots' are completely round. Frequently, as can be seen in Pissarro's *Apple Picking*, the uniform-sized touches of color are the shape of small brushes, tiny rectangular blocks which build up to form a dense mosaic on the picture surface. They also do not completely avoid a descriptive function. For example, in this picture, and even in Seurat's first major painting in the technique, *Sunday Afternoon on the Ile de la Grande Jatte* (1884–1886), the brushmarks vary in direction, following form and indicating changes of plane, even showing slight variations which echo changes in the texture of surfaces. Thus, the tree trunk in *Apple Picking* is executed with long vertical strokes of color, by contrast to the tiny criss-cross hatching which describes the grass. On Pissarro's figures, too, direction of touch, often curved to follow the form, gives substance to his figures and helps to separate them from their background.

The Neo-Impressionist method was very slow and laborious, for each layer of touches had to dry thoroughly before more dots were added. This was to avoid wet-in-wet slurring, which detracted from the purity of the individual touches of color. The white ground commonly used on Neo-Impressionist canvases provided the most brilliant and light-scattering base possible, enhancing the luminosity of the colors laid on top, and showing through in places with its own stark brightness. Palette colors were more limited than those of the Impressionists, in that no earth colors were used, but more of the brightest tube colors, particularly greens, were added instead. The pervasive effects of outdoor light, especially sunlight, were recorded by the Pointillist technique. Among the shadows on grass, for example, could be found the true greens of the grass, the darker blue and violet colors – the complementary color of the warm sunlight with additional blue reflected from the sky – and also the orange-yellow tinges of sunlight scattered into the shadows. Each of these

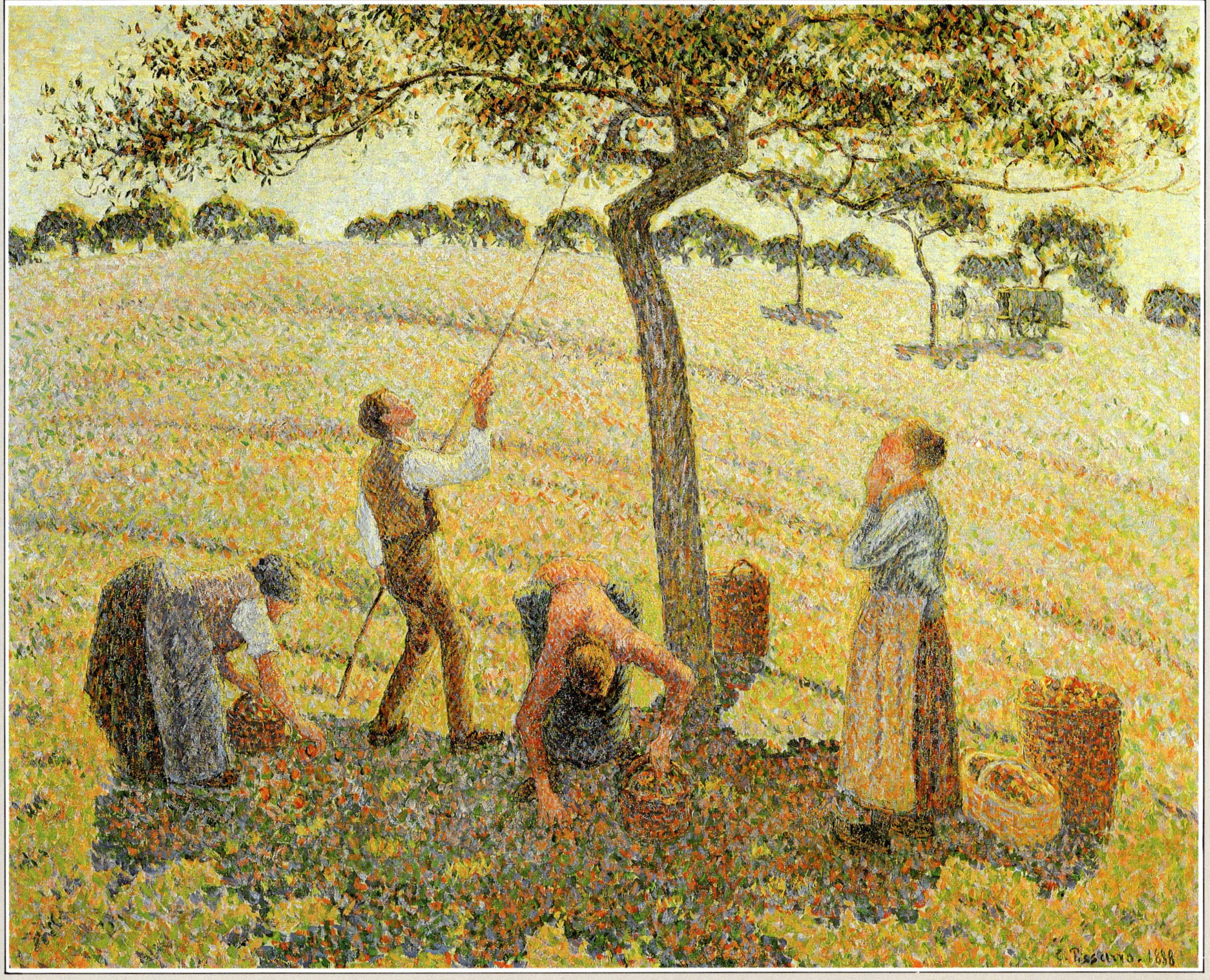

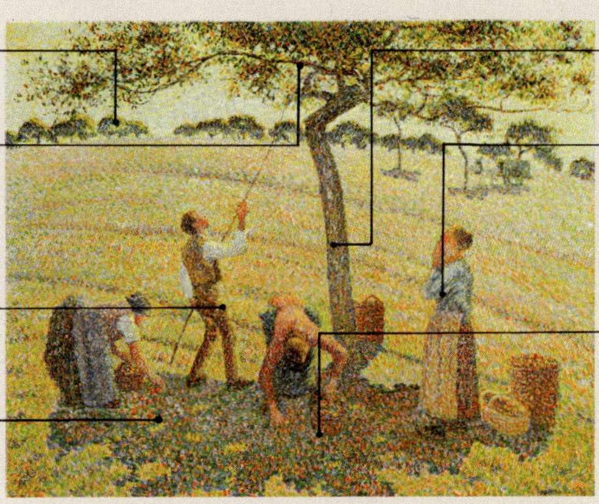


*Pissarro's relative naturalism of the 1870s has given way to a greater degree of formal stylization in the composition, handling and treatment of forms. However, compared to the work of Seurat, whose Pointillist method Pissarro had adopted by this date,* Apple Picking *remains essentially naturalistic. Although his color mixtures are now purer, they still reflect the colors observed in nature. The canvas is a standard format portrait 20.*

features of light and color were recorded in separate dots of the different hues, to result in an overall effect of brilliantly colored atmospheric light.

During the latter half of the 1880s Pissarro adhered to these theories, but, in the end, finding them too slow and inhibiting in terms both of personal expression and of financial necessity, he abandoned Pointillism. The period had caused him even more economic hardship than he experienced previously, for neither his dealer Durand-Ruel, nor the public at large, appreciated his new style. Having begun to establish himself in the early 1880s, many of his most loyal collectors were unable to follow his Pointillist departure, leaving him in quite dire circumstances.

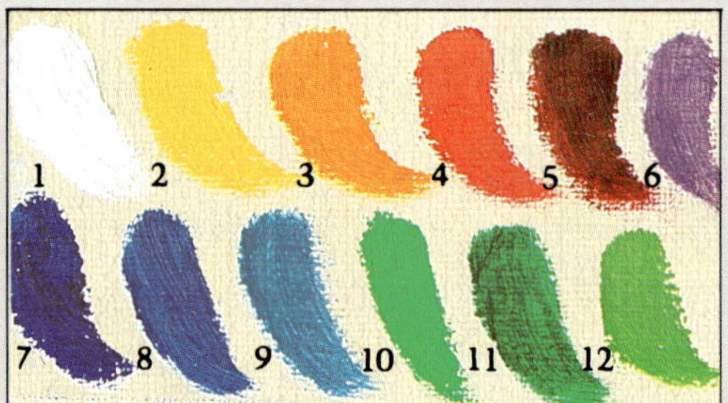


*Pissarro's palette was probably lead (1) or zinc white, cadmium yellows (2, 3), vermilion (4), red alizarin lakes (5), cobalt violet (6), ultramarine (7) and cobalt (8) blues, probably cerulean blue (9), emerald (10), viridian (11) and chrome green (12).*

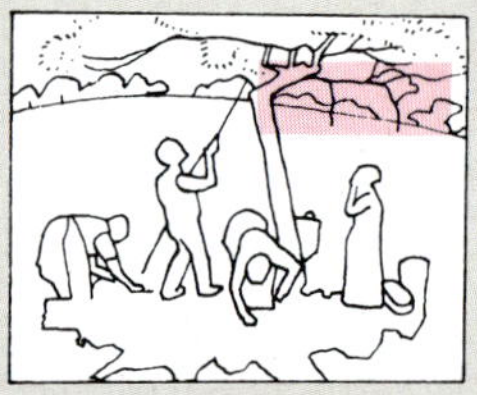

*Pale tints of the colors used in the foreground appear in the background, unifying the painting while aiding the sense of distance through recession. Touch is varied to describe the shape of forms.*

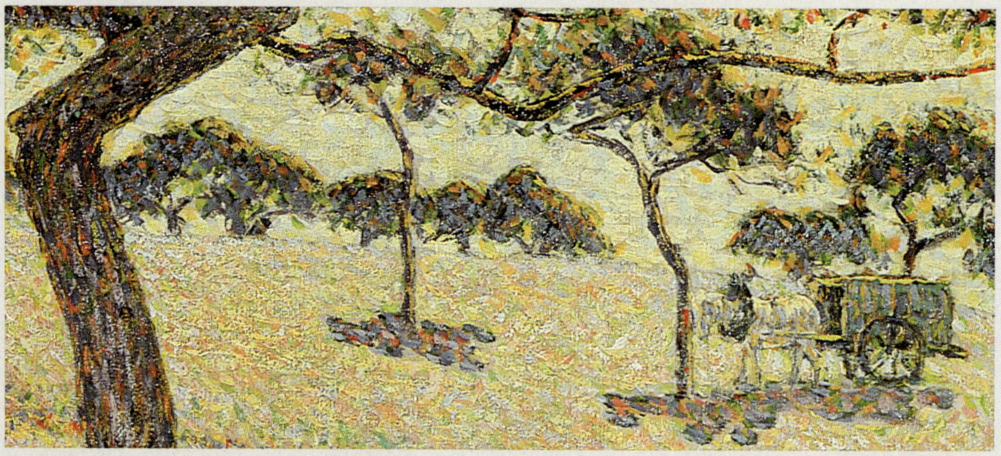

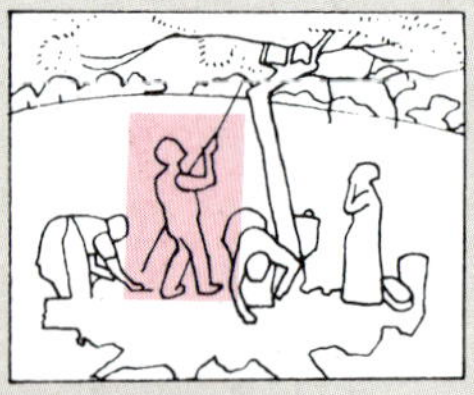

*Color is built up to suggest form. Strokes are hatched or criss-cross, following and evoking form, while the choice of tint and hue serve the same function. The highlighted parts of the figure are depicted in pale glowing yellows, suggesting the fall of sunlight. The shadowed parts, filled with blues reflected from the sky, are painted a correspondingly dark hue, dominated by cool blues. Warm orange-red touches permeate the shadow to suggest reflected rays of sunlight. Delicately painted lines outline the forms.*

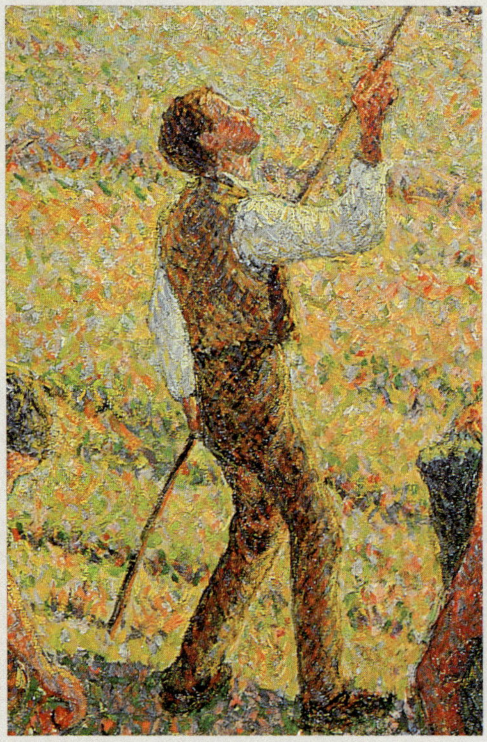

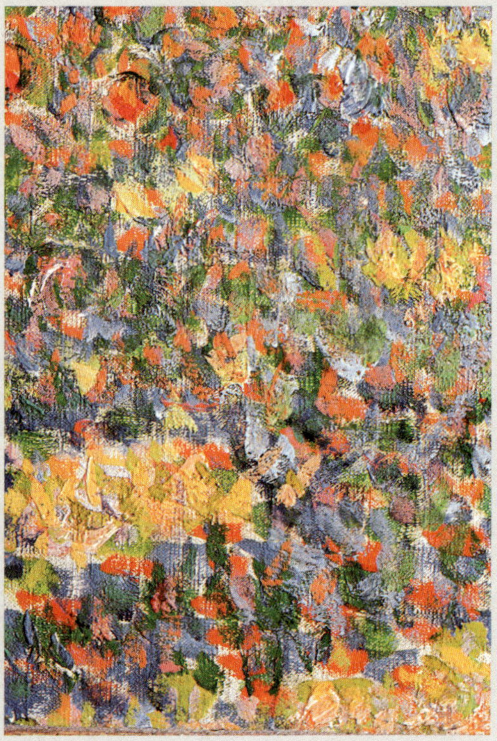

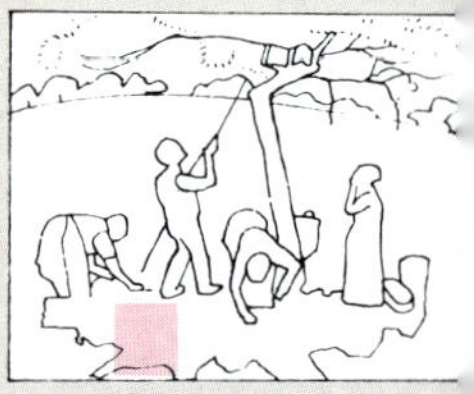

*The Neo-Impressionists preferred canvases primed a brilliant white. They often used chalk and glue rather than oil-based grounds. These were more absorbent and resulted in a matter, more luminous paint surface. The white of Pissarro's ground shows through among the abrupt dabs of color, adding brilliance to the effects of light. Even where it is covered with colors, the white of the ground improves their brightness. Here, Pissarro only mixed colors adjacent on the color circle, retaining maximum purity and avoiding dull neutrals.*

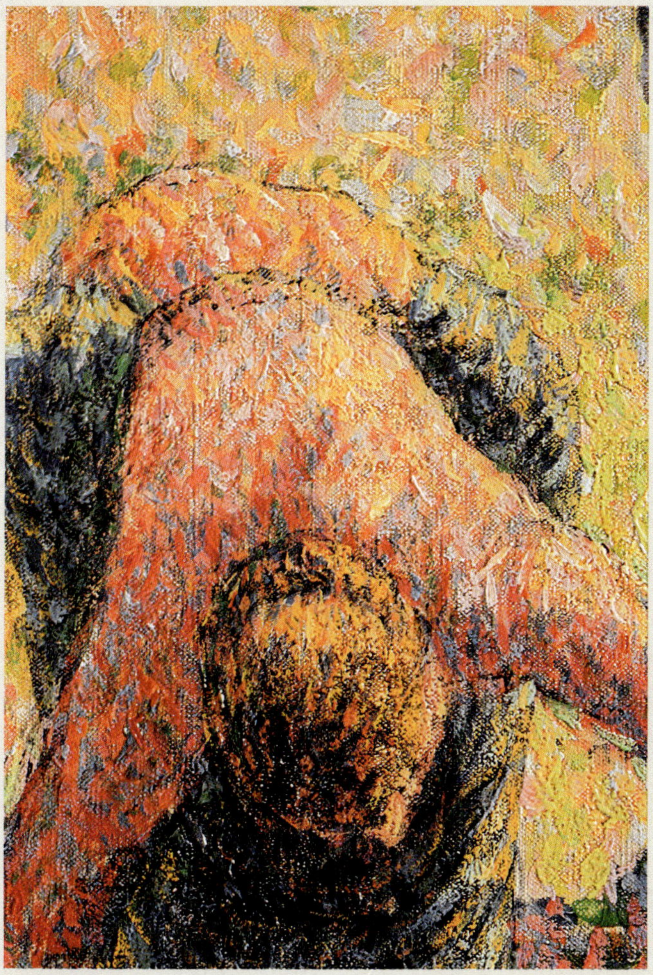

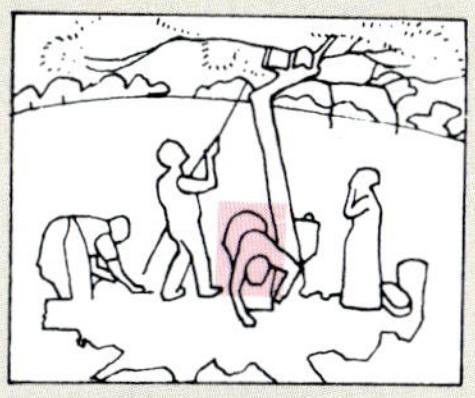

Actual size detail
*Lively reds and blues are the dominant hues on this figure, whose unusual pose has been depicted with grace and simplicity. The theme of work runs throughout Pissarro's art, from the small, toiling figures and distant suburban factories apparent in his work of the 1860s and 1870s, to the more monumental figure compositions, chiefly of female agricultural workers, which date from the early 1880s on. These works echoed Pissarro's belief in cooperative rural labor, an ideal associated with anarchist political thought. The figure is outlined and the form evoked in broad, rounded masses, with a simplicity reminiscent of Millet. Within these masses small directional strokes of individually applied colors construct form through contrasts of warm and cool colors, as well as of pale and saturated tints. Thus the highlighted parts are rendered in pale hues of yellows, oranges and greens, the shaded areas in darker tints of reds, blues, greens and violets. Contours are added to strengthen and contain the forms.*

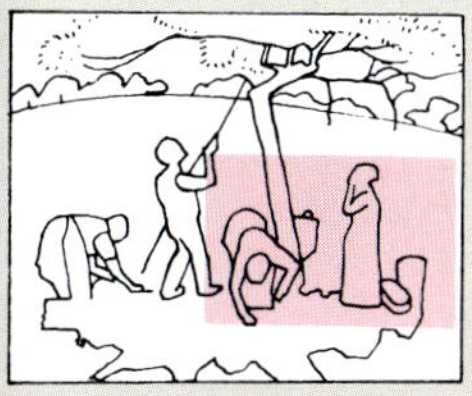

*Pissarro's brushstrokes here are much smaller and closer to the Neo-Impressionist's dot than in the earlier version of this composition painted in 1886. However, they do not conform precisely to a round dot mark. Color is divided into areas of mainly pale, warm hues contrasting with areas in which darker, cool hues predominate. Warm colors – reds, oranges and yellows – are introduced in small, flecked touches in among the cool blues and greens of the shadow areas to suggest reflecting sunlight.*

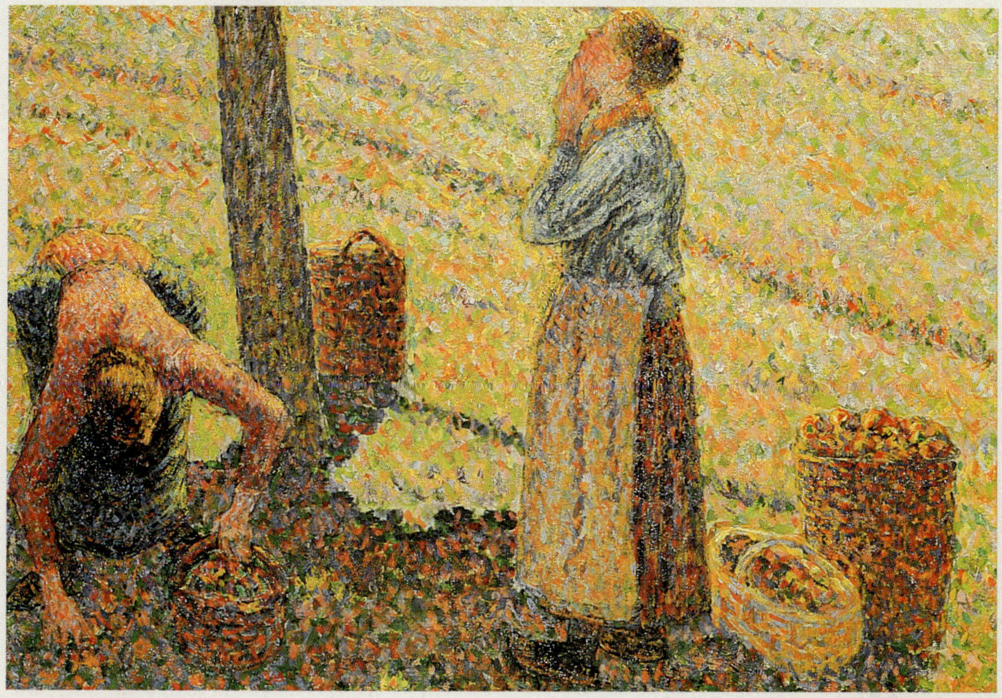

# CLAUDE MONET

*Antibes* (1888)
Oil on pale putty-color primed canvas
65cm × 92cm/25½in × 36¼in

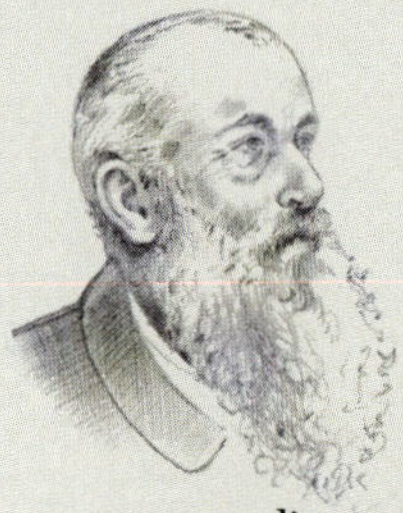

From the late 1870s Monet, having established his methods for depicting fleeting effects in nature, began to explore new, more demanding subjects. In 1878 he settled in Vétheuil, where his first wife Camille died in 1879. During the harsh winter of 1879–1880, he painted the dramatic effects of the break-up of ice on the nearby Seine river. These scenes set the tone for his work on the more elemental side of nature, which he pursued throughout the decade. In 1881 Monet moved to Poissy, again on the Seine, north-west of Paris, but closer to the city than Vétheuil. First this area, then that around Giverny, a short distance west of Vétheuil, where he finally established a home in 1883 which he bought in 1890, provided Monet with a more placid style of subjects to counterpoint the dramatic scenery he sought when traveling during those earlier years. His first major retrospective show, of 56 paintings, was held at Durand-Ruel's gallery in spring 1883.

Monet found his new, challenging subjects scattered the length and breadth of France. In the early 1880s, he maintained his habit of working along the Normandy coast, concentrating on the high, striking white cliffs between Etretat and Pourville. Then, in December 1883, he and Renoir traveled south to the Côte d'Azur and Genoa, a brief trip serving Monet as a scouting tour on which he studied the coast for possible subjects. Monet returned there alone in January 1884, and painted at Bordhigera and Menton around the French-Italian border.

Contrary to his practice in the late 1860s and early 1870s, Monet wished to work alone and kept this visit a secret from Renoir. He remarked in a letter to his dealer, Paul Durand-Ruel, in January 1884, that it would inhibit him working in a twosome, maintaining 'I have always worked better in solitude and after my own impressions'. Renoir had had experience painting in the south in the previous two years, and Monet may have wished to find his feet in the new environment, with its disconcertingly brilliant light and colors, without his friend watching over his shoulder.

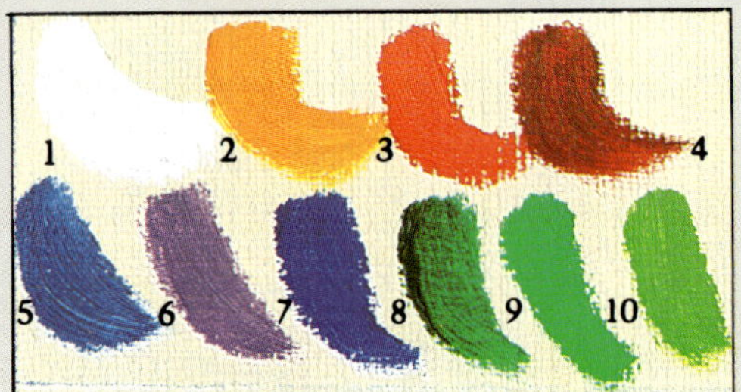


*Monet's palette for this work probably comprised lead white (1), cadmium yellows (2), vermilion (3), red alizarin lake (4), cobalt blue (5), cobalt violet (6) and viridian green (8). Ultramarine blue (7), emerald (8) and chrome (9, 10) greens may have been used.*

Monet evidently found it difficult to pitch his colors and tones high enough to capture even the late winter brilliance he witnessed around him in southern France. He was unable to work in poor weather, stressing it was a landscape which demanded the sun. When the sun did shine, it produced a 'glaring, festive light' and brilliant blues and pinks which he feared would anger those of his critics who had not seen it for themselves, even though he felt his own translations of the tints to be well below their actual brightness. He described the colors he saw as those of the pigeon's throat and of flaming punch – shimmering, evanescent films of colored light. After four years of trips devoted mainly to the wilds of Normandy and especially the rugged Atlantic coast of Brittany around Belle-Ile, in 1888 Monet returned to the south. He was attracted by its total contrasts of landscape, light and color.

It was on this second visit that Monet painted *Antibes*. His subjects in the south were dictated chiefly by information on local beauty spots obtainable from tourist guides, as he was a stranger to that area. This information directed him to sites that were visually interesting, and which would also attract potential collectors, who often preferred to have views of well-known scenes with which they were familiar, rather like high-class postcards. Once more his visit was spread over late winter and early spring and was spent on subjects at Antibes and Juan-les-Pins.

In this painting, Monet's evolution of a brushwork style, where different marks 'stand for' different natural phenomena, is clearly in evidence. There is a sure confidence of touch in his almost calligraphic brushmarks. Flamboyant curving strokes indicate the distant line of hills, against which – with calculated casualness – he emblazons the stark, almost silhouetted arabesque of the tree trunk. The curve of the tree has been adjusted during execution, to exaggerate its rhythmic shape. The emblematic blueness of the water is broken only by the dragged vibrancy of wet-over-dry colors, placed horizontally to indicate the rippling water surface. The lower branches of the tree remain above the level of the horizon, limiting the illusion of distance, which could have resulted from allowing them to overlap the horizon line. The vegetation is rendered by short curled or abrupt dabbed strokes, often blending several colors on a single brushstroke.

The pale tinted priming on this standard vertical marine 30 canvas has been almost entirely obliterated by the opaque paint layer colors. Under both sky and sea, Monet applied a general underlay, perhaps to make the ground more light-reflective and luminous, because it is a brilliant chalky, pinkish-white, lighter in color than the original ground. The fine grain of the canvas is left barely noticeable. Over this underlay, which is in itself visible

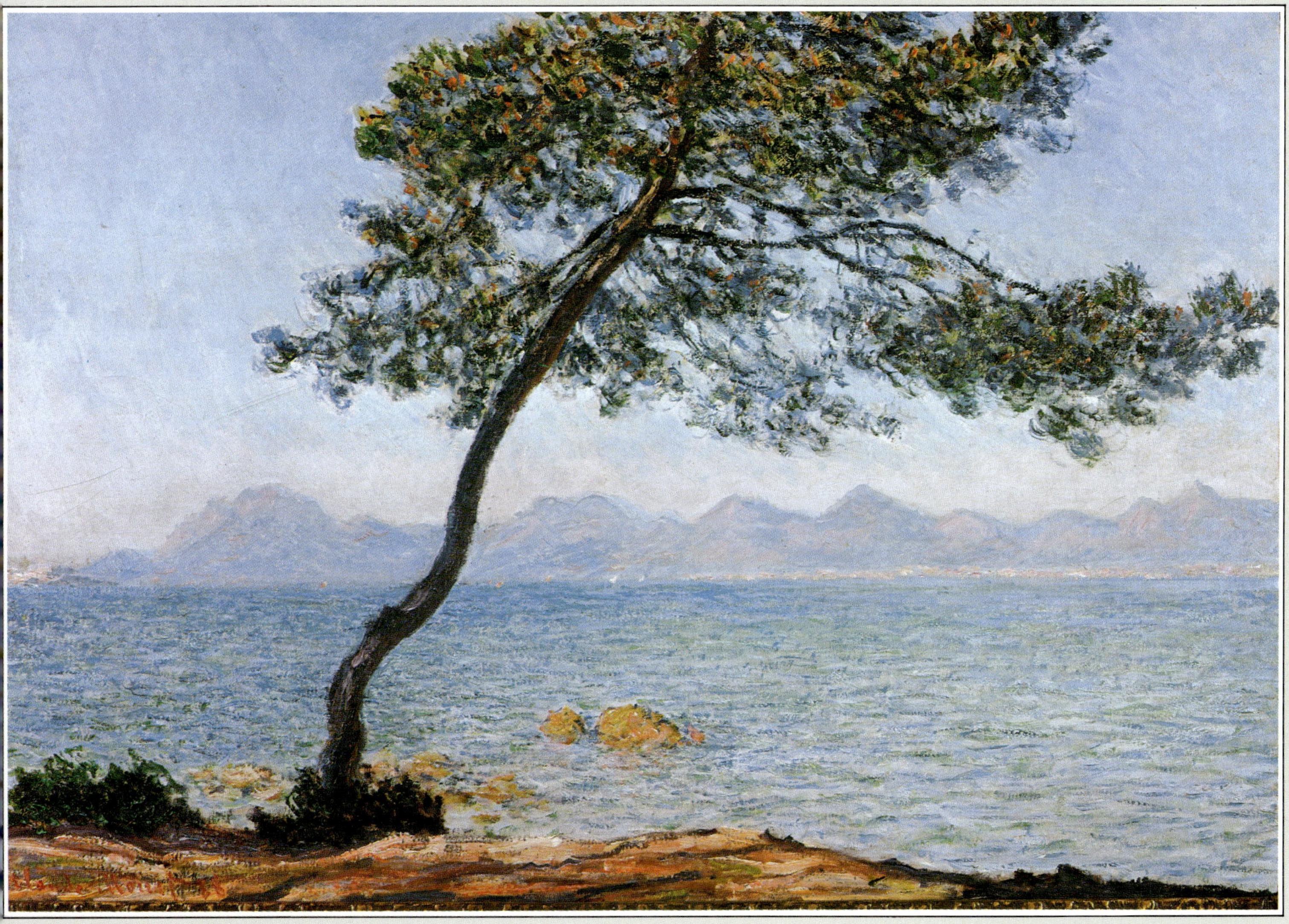

*Like Pissarro in* Apple Picking *which dates from fall 1888, Monet's spring painting of* Antibes *used the device of a dark curving tree set against pale background colors. This composition was of a type popular with Japanese artists. The brilliant pastel blues and pinks of the setting make a superb foil for the darker more severe contrasts in the tree and foreground, where harsh juxtapositions of red and green predominate. The extremes are modified by the appearance of blues among the tree foliage, and the paler reds picked up along the distant waterline. For this painting, Monet used a standard format canvas vertical marine 40.*

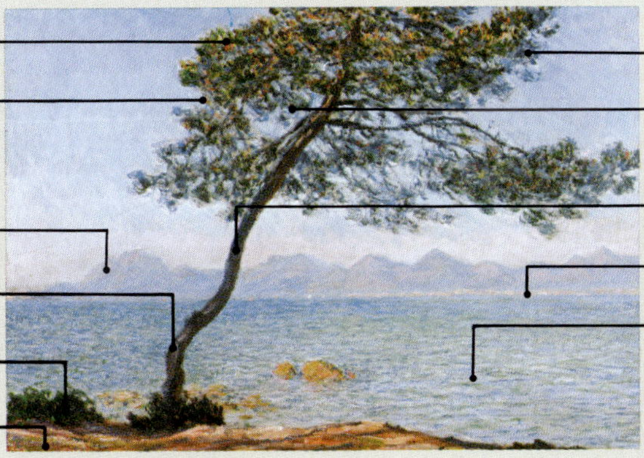

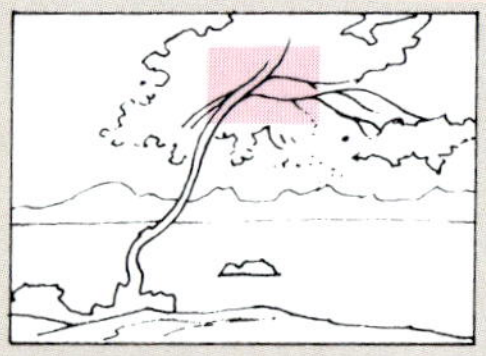

*Gaps in the pale underpainting of the sky, among the foliage, reveal the duller, darker hue of the commercial preparation which is pale putty in color. On the lower left, slurred wet-in-wet blues and white are added thickly, to give more light and break up the dark masses of foliage. Among the impasted, overlaid and slurred blues on the right, the brilliant blueish white tint of the underlay can be seen. Tiny flecks of vermilion enliven the greens.*

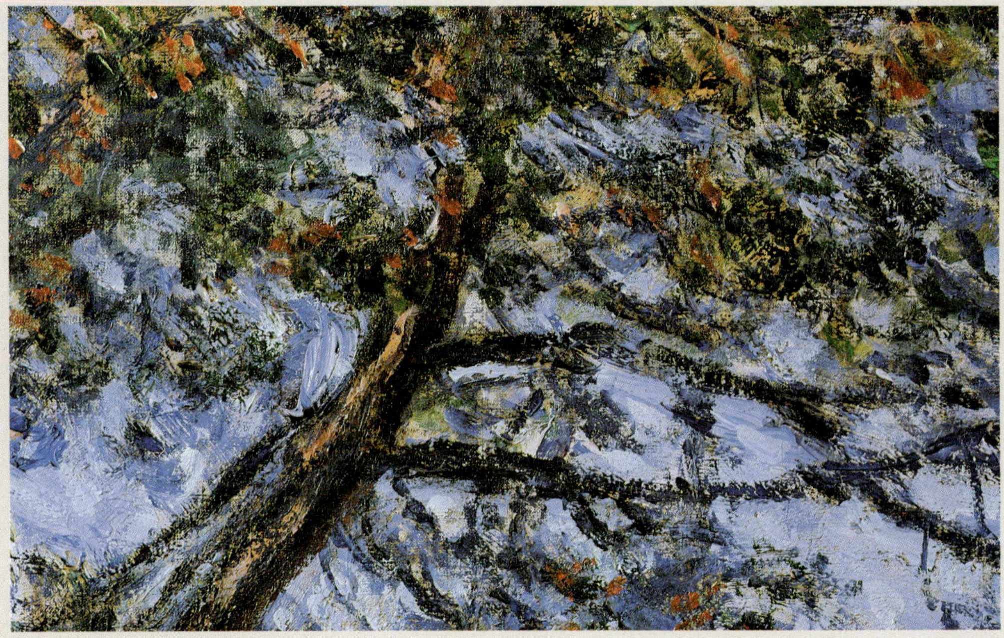

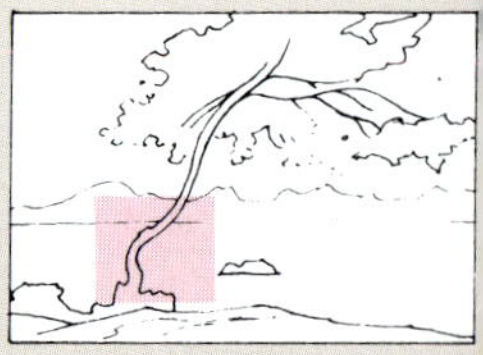

*The flamboyant curve on the tree was exaggerated by Monet. The colors of the sea cut into the concavity of the form on the right, while the tree colors are built up over dry sea paint on the left, convex curve. The vigorous arabesque of the line is echoed on a smaller scale by Monet's brushwork here and along the mountainous skyline. Fluid, sinuous brushmarks are balanced by dryish dragged paint and impasted dabs of color in the foreground leaves. Richly loaded paint in broad strokes of reds and greens give immediacy to the foreground land.*

only in places among the tree foliage and the sea brushstrokes, Monet built up the paint layer in stiff impasted strokes, which are especially vibrant where broken and dragged, allowing the earlier colors to show through.

The sky colors were roughly scumbled in, and worked around the tree, while the sky patches amongst the foliage were mainly worked in over the colors of the branches. The cobalt blue and alizarin crimson hues of the hills were heavily loaded with white, to make them very pale and luminous. Mixed viridian green and white were applied over the darker greens in the immediate foreground, and the same bright green was carried over as small dabs on the water surface, linking these two tonally contrasting areas. A bluer cobalt and white mix was also worked late over the water surface, and picked up by individual blobs of the same hue in the tree foliage. The reds of the foreground, a vermilion-based mixture, were used in the final retouching, again in the tree, and this same color was used for the artist's signature. This is often a clue to the final color touches applied by the artist.

Monet's Antibes paintings were exhibited at Theo van Gogh's gallery in early summer of 1888. Having seen the works, Monet's friend the poet Stéphane Mallarmé (1842–1898) wrote to him 'This is your finest hour'.

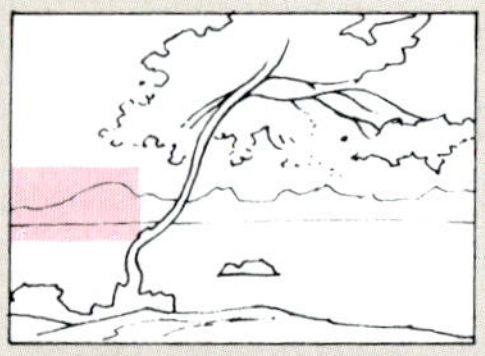

*This detail shows the unpainted canvas edge, where raw linen is visible due to wear and flaking. The dull, pale putty, slightly discolored ground is visible here. The pale blues of the final sky layer go up to and around the upper edge of the mountains, leaving the thin, opaque underpainting exposed. Tiny wet-over-dry strokes of pale vermilion punctuate the softer pastel pink and blue hues.*

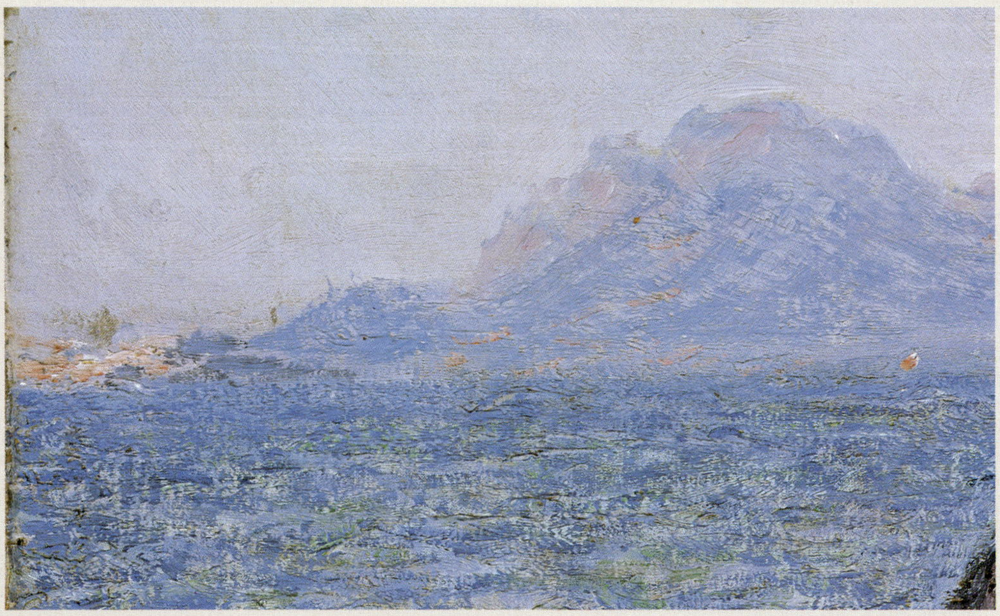

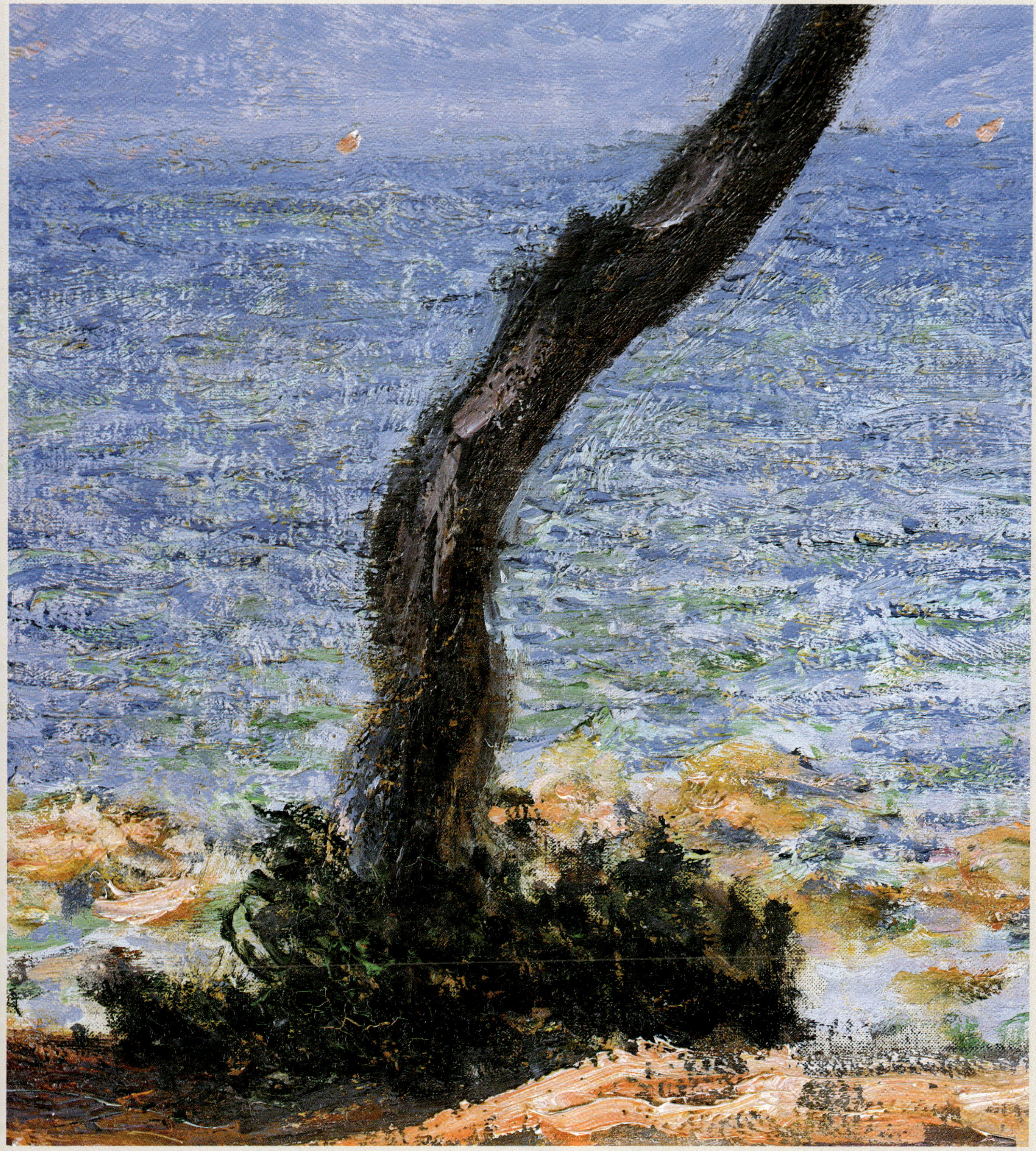

# VINCENT VAN GOGH

*Chair with Pipe* (1889)
Oil on canvas, 92cm × 73cm/36⅛in × 23¾in

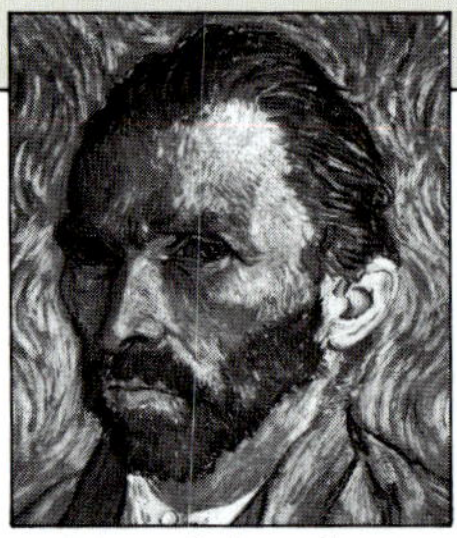

Van Gogh came late to painting after trying his hand in the art trade, teaching, and the church. His earliest influences were from the Dutch Masters and his contemporaries. Widely read, van Gogh first learned about French painting, and especially Delacroix, through books which provided an interpretation of color theory important to van Gogh's own painting. His enthusiasm for French artists lay chiefly with the older generation like Millet and Daumier. During his stay in Paris, a passing interest in Impressionism and Neo-Impressionism encouraged him to lighten his palette and eschew the sombre, tonal renderings of his Dutch period, and he wrote in 1888: 'I should not be surprised if the Impressionists soon find fault with my way of working, for it has been fertilized by the ideas of Delacroix rather than by theirs. Because, instead of trying to reproduce exactly what I have before my eyes, I use color more arbitrarily so as to express myself forcibly.'

Van Gogh was from his earliest years an avid experimenter in new techniques. His work in the early 1880s was predominantly graphic, involving a variety of media. He developed a strength and variation of mark with Japanese reed pens and often used a perspective frame to aid his rendering of space in drawing and painting. He preferred an ordinary weight canvas, and frequently used commercially primed types in a range of pale tints, especially gray and putty. He also experimented with raw, unprimed canvas and heavy sackcloth fabrics. In addition van Gogh liked to use both pink and white grounds.

Unlike the Pont Aven artists, like Gauguin, who stressed the importance of the imagination, van Gogh's work was rooted in the study of nature, and he stated that he retained 'from nature a certain sequence and . . . correctness in placing the tones, I study nature so as not to do foolish things . . . however, I don't mind so much whether my color corresponds exactly, as long as it looks beautiful on my canvas'. Van Gogh used the power of complementary contrasts to make his color emotive, as described in a letter from Arles in 1888: 'to express the love of two lovers by a marriage of two complementary colors, their mingling and their opposition, the mysterious vibrations of kindred tones.'

**1.** A hessian canvas was used, its color a warm, orange-brown.

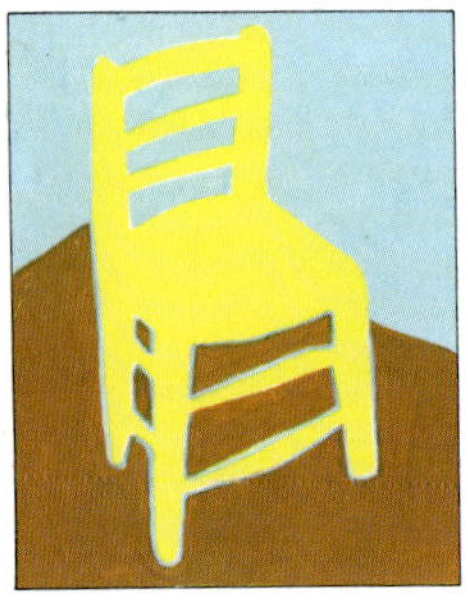

**2.** Opaque paint was applied directly onto the raw hessian and the composition loosely established without underdrawing.

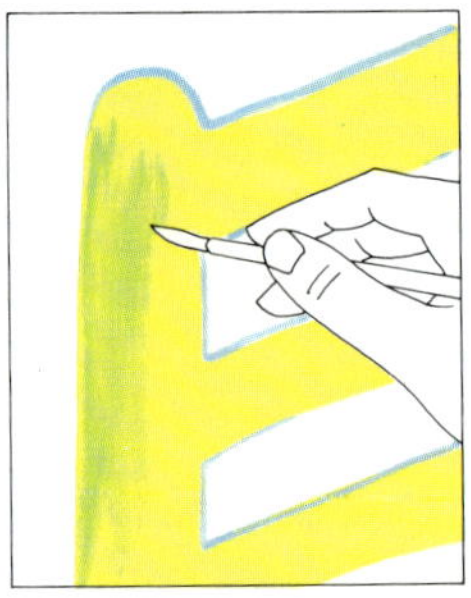

**3.** Separate areas were then reworked and built up using wet-in-wet handling of the paint.

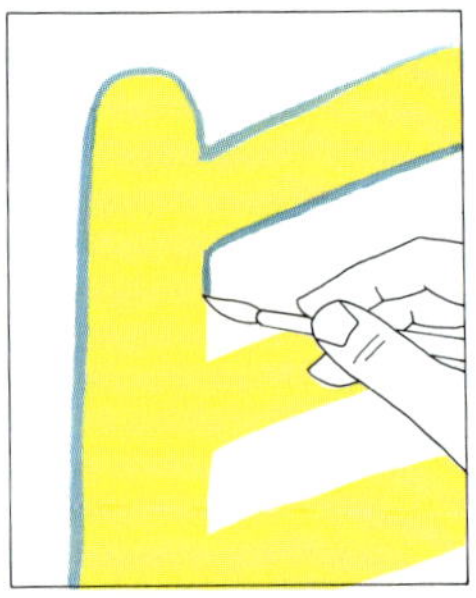

**4.** The outlines were then reinforced with decisive strokes of color into wet paint.

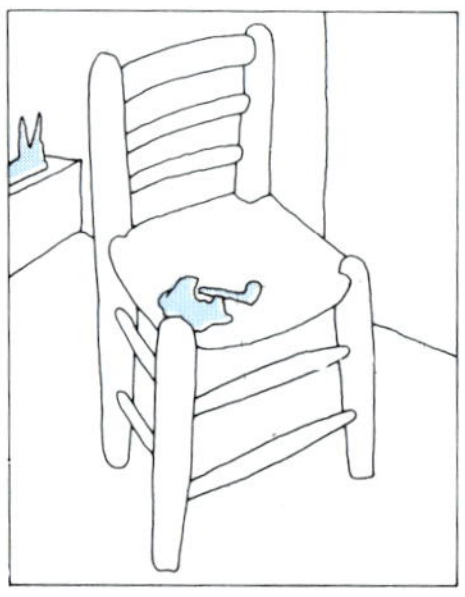

**5.** Still life details were finally added when the picture was dry. Van Gogh preferred matt surfaces, and thus few of his mature paintings were varnished.

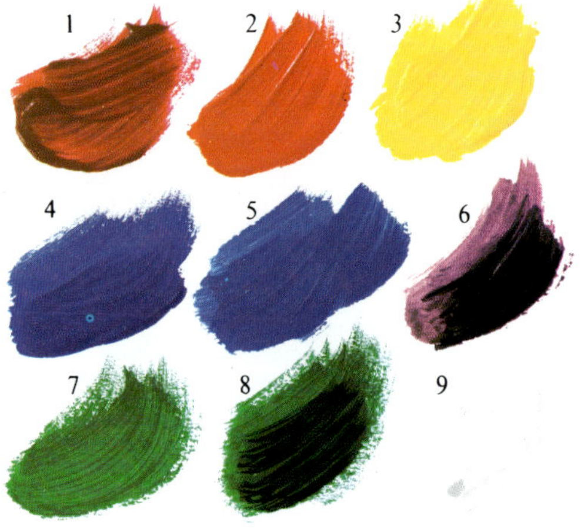


For his mature works, such as *Chair with Pipe*, van Gogh used a palette of: red lake (**1**), vermilion (**2**), cadmium yellow (**3**), ultramarine blue (**4**), cobalt blue (**5**), cobalt violet (**6**), emerald green (**7**), viridian green (**8**), lead white (**9**). In addition he also used some earth colors.

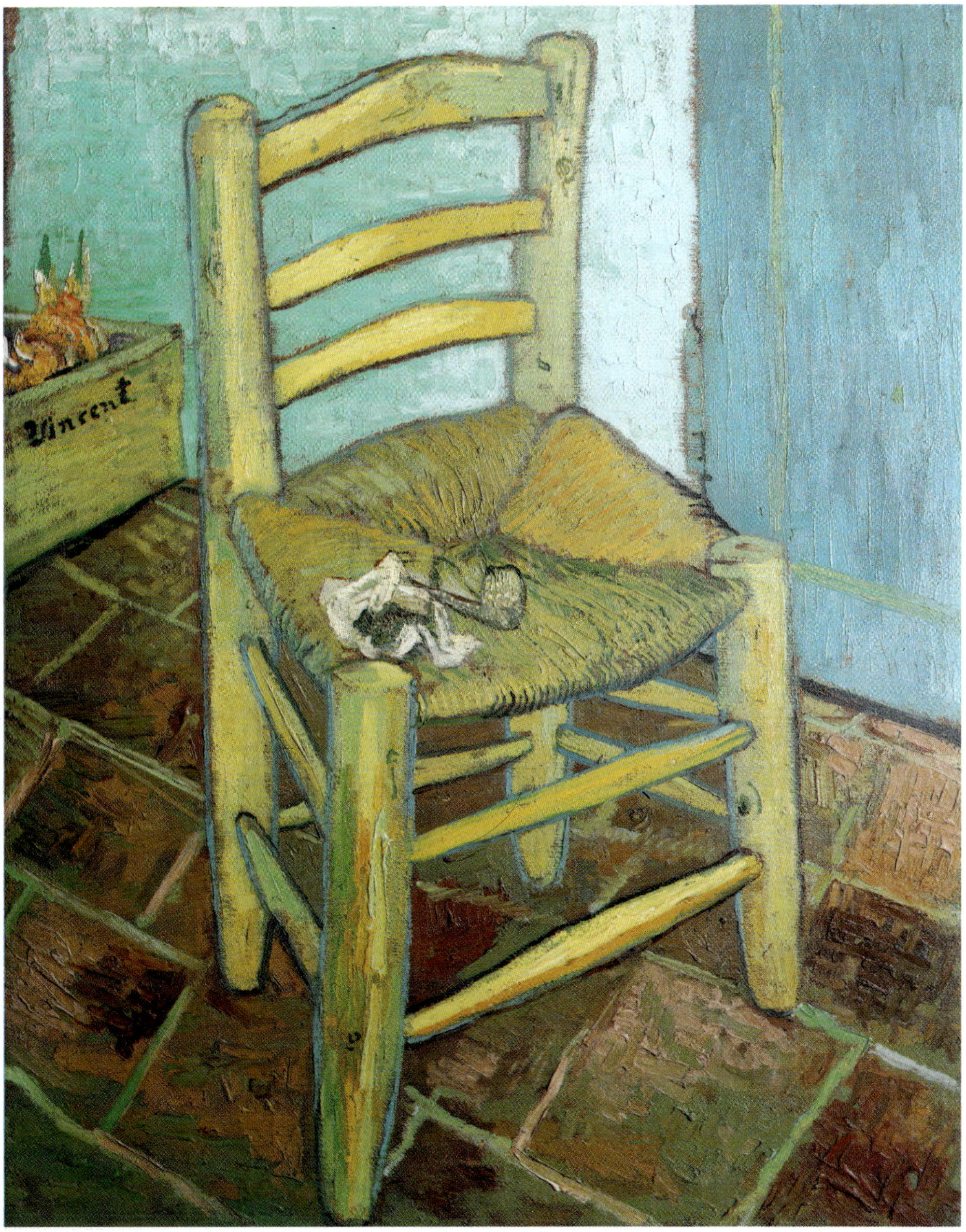


*An unprimed canvas was used and left in places to read as an outline. The basic color areas were established in undiluted paint which, because canvas is absorbent, appears dull and stiffly dragged where not reworked. The brush strokes vary and are worked predominantly wet into wet. The paint quality is rich and buttery where most thickly applied, and this contrasts with a dry, sunken quality where the paint is thinnest near the contours. The tiles are heavily worked with tapestry-like, criss-crossed brush strokes; and the outlines were added into the wet paint with long sweeping strokes. Contrasts of red and green have been slurred together in the floor. Orange-yellow and violet-blue were used in the chair. The pipe and bulbs are late additions over dry paint.*

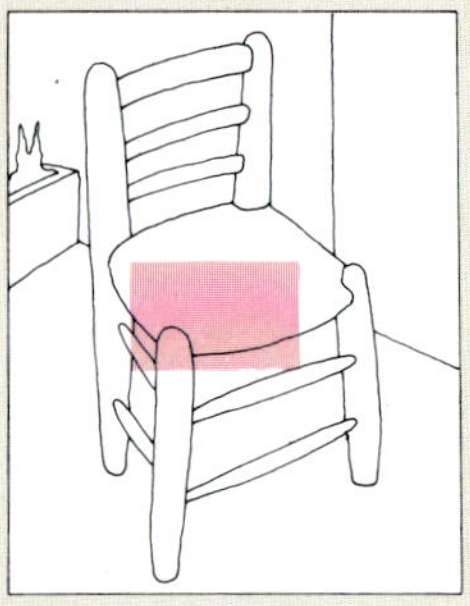

*The autobiographical motif of tobacco and pipe were not apparently conceived as part of the original composition, but were superimposed at a very late stage in the painting. They were added when the paint of the chair was already dry, which, with a surface as impasted as here, would involve considerable delay. Curved, hatched brushstrokes with a narrow brush were used to accentuate the rounded edge of the rush seat.*

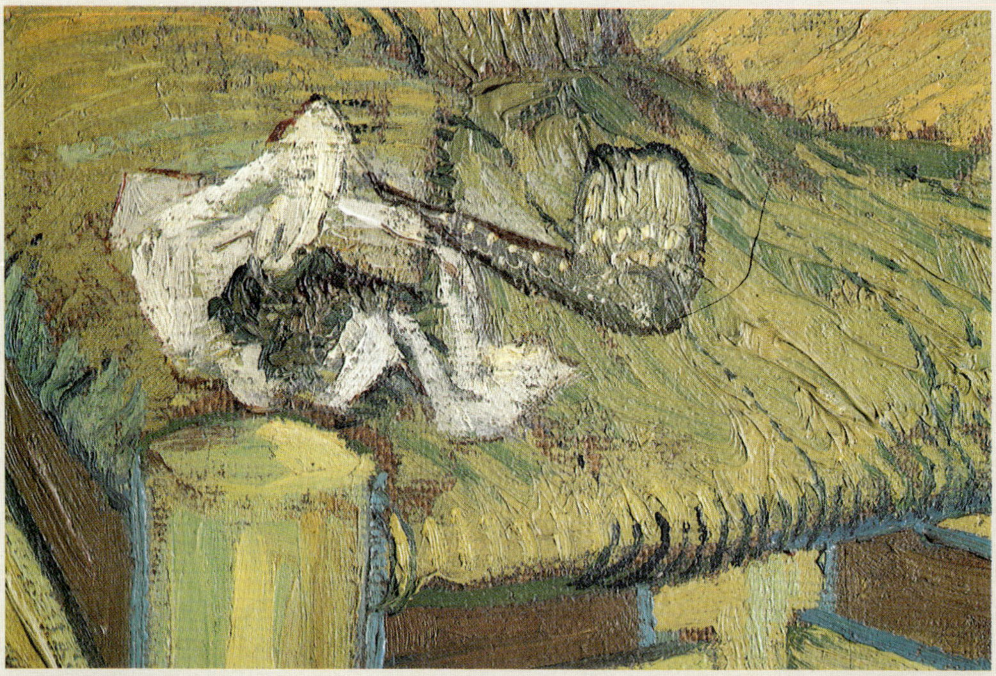

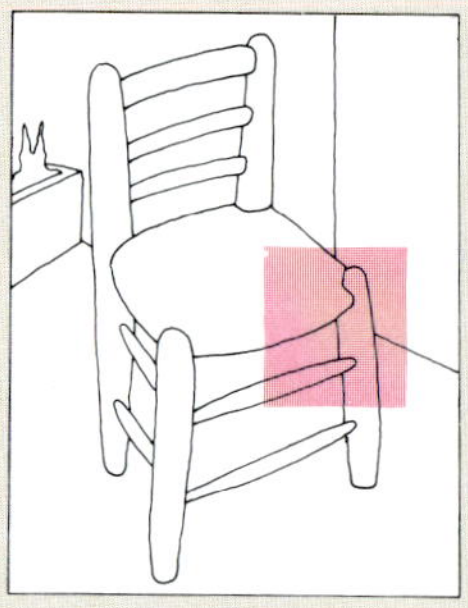

**Actual size detail**
*This detail shows van Gogh's strong brushwork and vibrant use of color contrasts. Both raw hessian canvas and dark blue outlines have been exploited to define and strengthen the forms; the blue lines were laid down with the initial painting and reinforced later on. The paint quality is thick and stiff, especially in the chair, and rich and buttery where more paint has been reworked in the floor.*
*Van Gogh's vigorous brushwork defines form and contour with forceful, hatched strokes. A narrow, stiff-haired brush was used to draw in the chair's rush seat while broader criss-cross strokes enliven the surfaces of wall and floor. Van Gogh's crude contrasting colors can be seen in the blues and yellows of the chair and the complementary red and greens in the floor.*

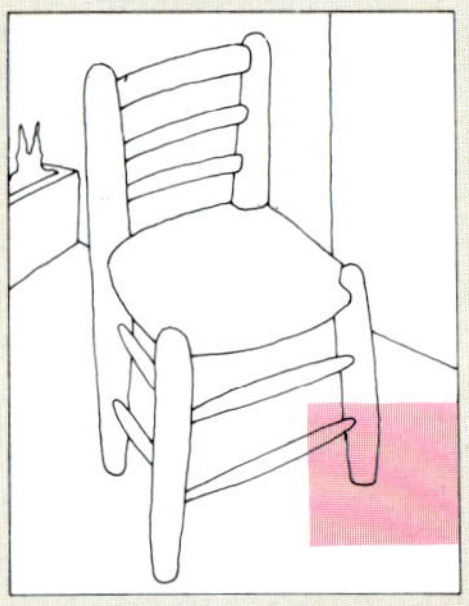

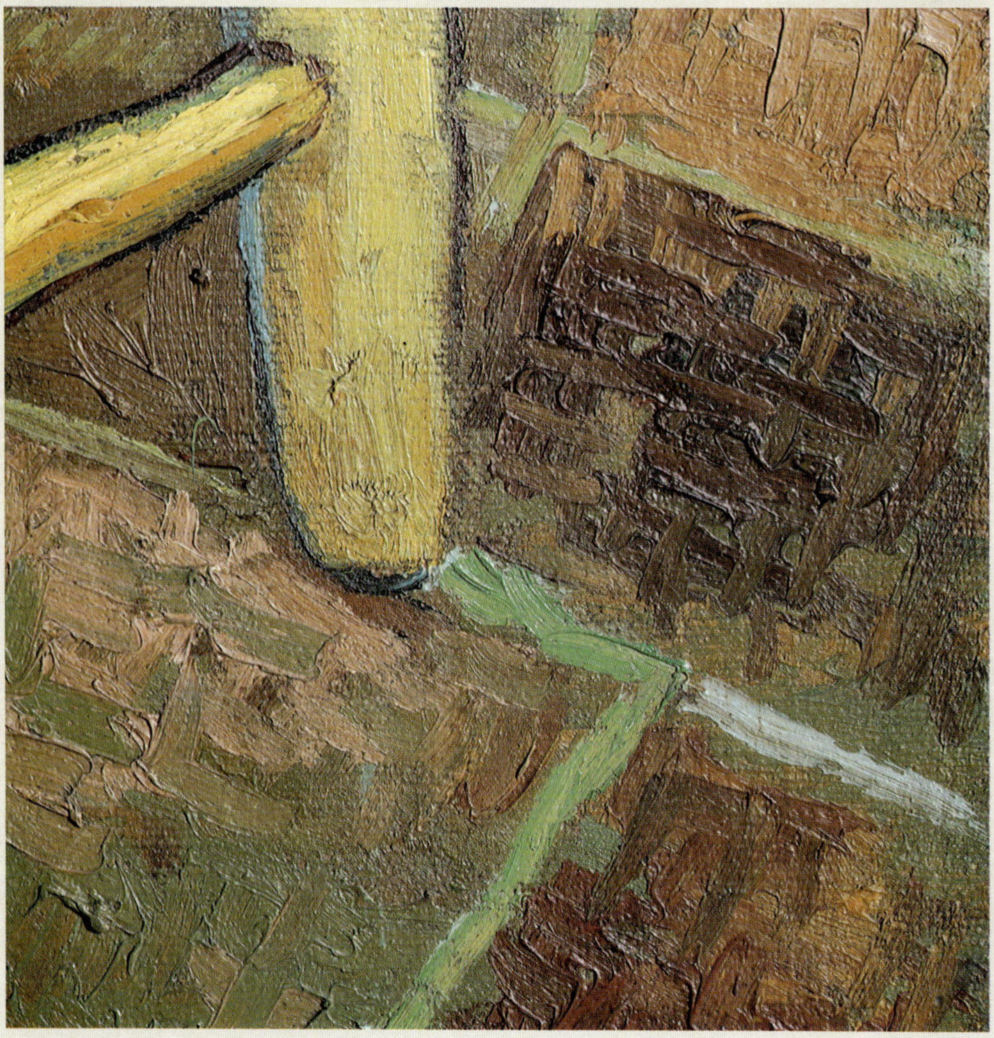

*The reds and greens were worked together with green applied last for the outlines of the tiles. The staggered pattern of the tiles flattens to the rear of the chair leg where the four corners accidently coincide. The irregular shape and recession of the floor tiles are evident, and creates an overall barrel effect with the floor curving up and dipping away almost vertically in the immediate foreground.*

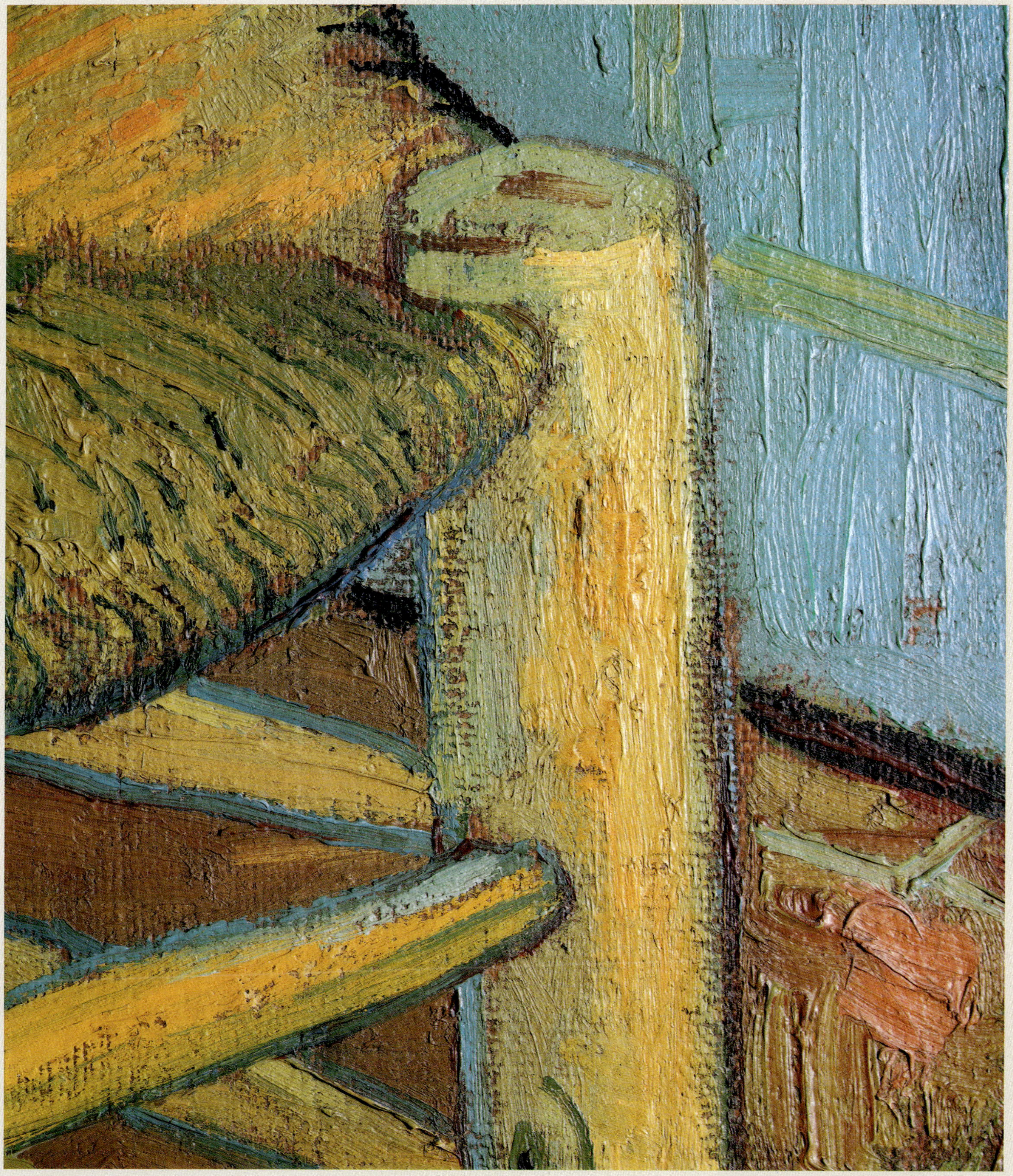

# GEORGES SEURAT

*The Can-Can/Le Chahut* (1889-1890)
Oil on white primed canvas
169cm × 139cm/66½in X 54¾in

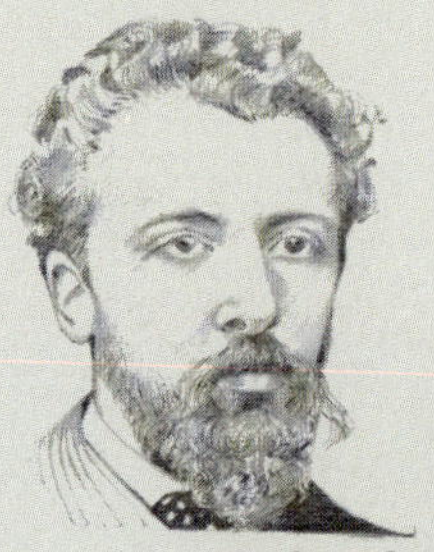

Dissatisfied with the apparently casual, arbitrary methods of the Impressionists, Seurat aimed at a more permanent, monumental record of modern life, an art elevated to the stature of Egyptian or classical art. During the first half of the 1880s, he devoted himself to developing his 'color-and-light' or 'chromo-luminarist' method of scientifically recording the unified effects of light and color in nature. His academic training, albeit relatively brief, gave him a foundation in the classical tradition and in careful draftsmanship which was to remain with him throughout his career. He soon abandoned the more linear emphasis of academic drawing, preferring instead the softer, more tonal approach which had been growing in popularity – particularly among independent artists – and these studies he used to analyze delicate gradations in the fall of light and shade. Seurat's knowledge of the theories of simultaneous, or complementary contrast of tones and colors was gained by thorough reading of Chevreul's theories, and later publications like those of the American Ogden Rood, which appeared in a French edition in 1881. He exploited the phenomenon of simultaneous contrast in his drawings, before he had begun to use color.

In drawings like *Seated Boy with a Straw Hat*, a study, drawn in 1883–1884, for one of the seated figures in *Bathing, Asnières*, the use of simultaneous contrast of tones can be seen. Where a dark block of tone meets a lighter one, the tones are mutually enhanced by contrast. This means that the edge of the dark block will appear optically darker by contrast, and the light edge lighter. In this drawing, Seurat has incorporated this optical effect physically. Thus, he has drawn the background paler behind the boy's back, and the boy's back darker, where the two meet, to exaggerate the contrast and to separate the boy's figure from the background, thereby giving it solidity. Similar handling is visible along the profile of the boy's face. The technique is reversed where the light falls from the right directly on the boy, highlighting his arms and legs. Thus, the light parts on his limbs have been made lighter, and the background darkened, to maximize the contrast and again make the figure stand out from the background.

These effects of tonal contrast are visible in nature, but are not commonly 'painted into' a picture, because they necessitate drastic adjustments to the tone of the background, resulting in an artificial and visually disturbing lightening and darkening of the background. However, for Seurat, these effects were perfect for strengthening structure and modeling in his drawings, and, incorporated in his paintings, they increase the sense of form while introducing an eerie unreality to their atmosphere. Although in his paintings the gradation from black to white of the studies was replaced by gradations from saturated pure color through to white to avoid sullying the hues, the principle remains the same. It can be clearly seen in *Can-Can*, where the planes of the background appear to swell in and out of the picture, as they darken or lighten, depending upon their proximity to the forms in front. For example, the background darkens noticeably in intensity where it adjoins the pale hues of the front dancer's skirt.

In Seurat's painting, contrasts of color replace contrasts of black and white, so that the contrast between light and dark is also one between color complementaries. Thus warm colors, especially dots of orange signifying the gaslighting, pervade the pale creamy-white areas, while darker, cool blues, violets and greens dominate the shaded parts away from the light. The orange-blue complementary pair is the basis for the color harmonies, while dots of orange indicating reflected gaslight are speckled over the entire canvas. The stiff stylization of the composition is far greater than during his earlier phase. This resulted from his study of the recent work of the scientist Charles Henry, with whom Seurat became acquainted in 1886. Henry worked on scientific means to formularize the relationship between line, color and tone and their impact on the emotions. For example, warm orange-reds, such as those which dominate this painting, were considered to denote gaiety. Similarly, lines moving upward, like the legs, arms and facial features of the dancers reinforced the emotion associated with warm color. Seurat's late paintings, based loosely on Henry's theories, were all designed on the basis of the particular emotions evoked by line, tone and color. Thus in these works pale, warm colors signified gaiety and action, while dark cool colors stood for sadness with middle tones and a balance between warm and cool colors in a painting indicating harmony and tranquility.

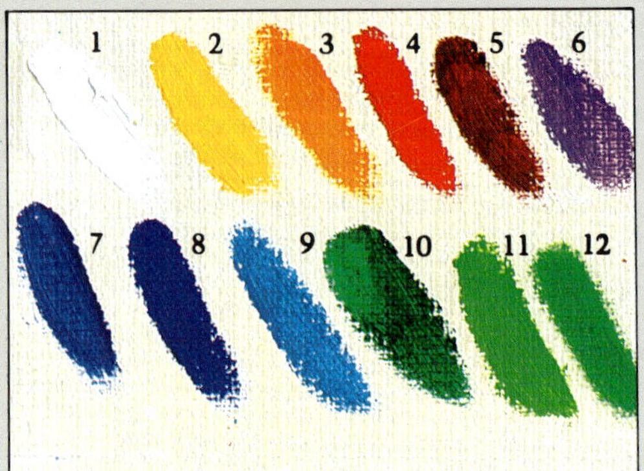


*Seurat's palette probably comprised lead (1) or zinc white, pale cadmium yellow (2), mid or deep cadmium yellow (3), vermilion (4), red alizarin lakes (5), cobalt violet (6), cobalt blue (7), ultramarine blue (8), cerulean blue (9), viridian green (10) and composed chrome greens (11, 12).*

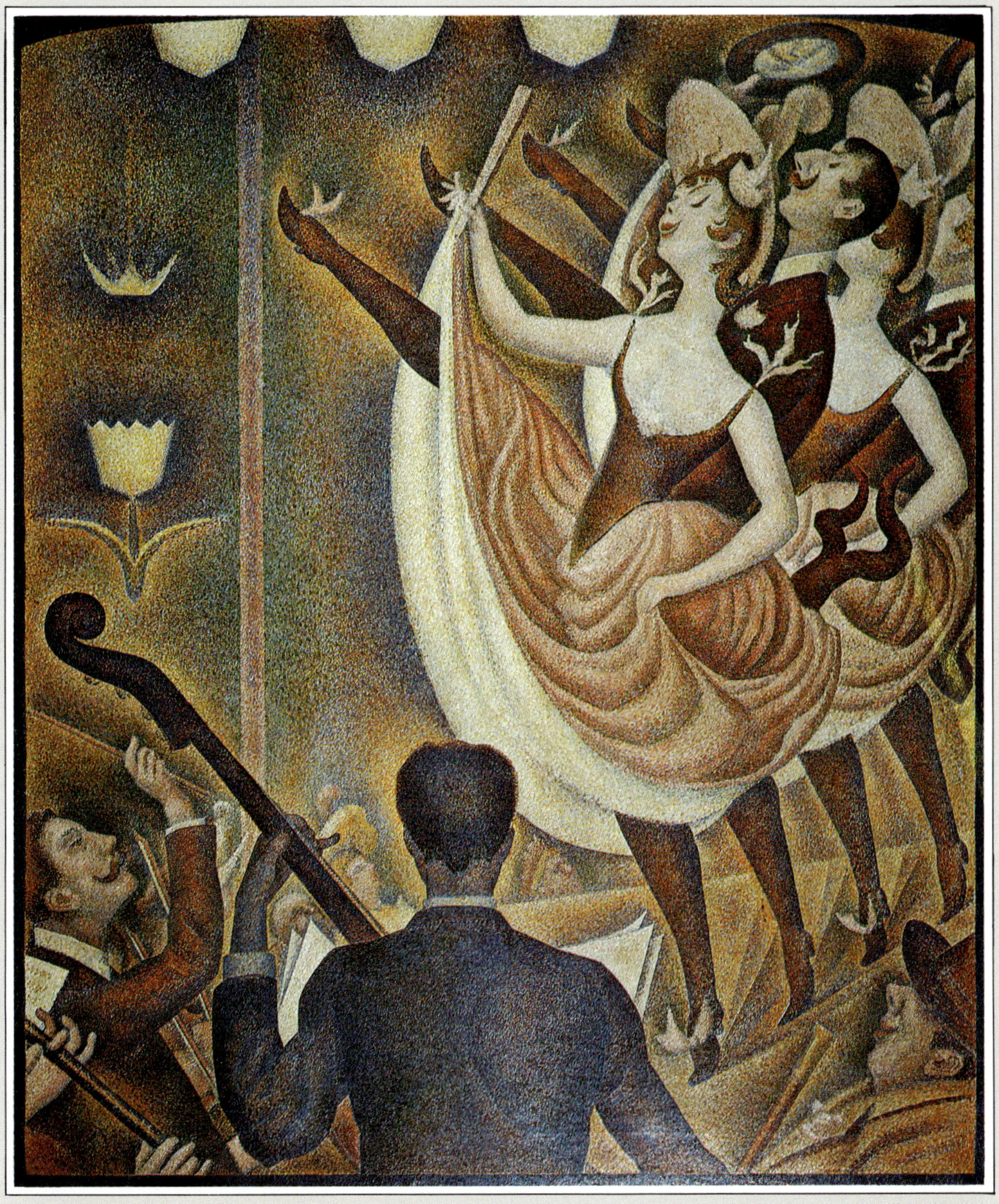

*Within a matter of years of their execution contemporaries began to note the dulling of the brilliant pitch of Seurat's colors. This makes it difficult to assess the impact of the color or its effects in Seurat's work, for it is impossible to know how different they now are. However, Seurat's use of separate touches of pure color in tiny dots in fact resulted in an overall subdued, almost gray tint in his painting, as can be seen here. This is because the color fusion that actually takes place is in fact subtractive – or darkening and graying in effect – in accordance with the laws of pigmental color, as opposed to the additive laws of colored light. In the latter, the mixture of colored lights becomes increasingly lighter, finally resulting in white light. The painting was designed to work on a very large scale – larger than the biggest standard format easel size. The canvas measures 169cm x 139cm (66½in x 54¾ in), and this reproduction is only a few centimeters (inches) high. A comparison with the actual size detail shows how greatly the color is concentrated by this size reduction of the whole picture.*

Lines had a comparable function – upward moving lines expressed joy or gaiety, horizontal and vertical lines indicated tranquil balance, and downward moving lines meant sorrow. It was felt that systematization of these theories could lead to a formula for painting, in which the emotional impact of the picture could be scientifically predetermined. This idea of a universal absolute in the ordered representation of expression in art, is very much in keeping with certain ideas then current in Symbolist theory. However, it also marks a modern alternative to the classical absolutes of truth and beauty, which had become so associated with the constraints of academic dogma in the nineteenth century.

Recent scholarship has suggested that, in his art, Seurat aimed to find a new means of expression by combining the classical with the modern. The famous art historian and theoretician, Charles Blanc, whose book *Grammar of the Arts of Drawing* Seurat consulted in the 1870s, saw the Renaissance as the perfect model for the modern society which sought social and artistic progress through science. Seurat may thus have adapted Blanc's theory which offered the artist a radical way of reconciling in his painting his apparently contradictory admiration for classical harmony and modern technological methods.

Although Seurat remained the undisputed leader of the Neo-Impressionists, his rigorously scientific method was gradually abandoned by his followers after his early death in 1891. They each sought more personal variations of the Pointillist style. Seurat's decorative stylization and his use of classical proportions were much admired by twentieth century artists.

Warm-hued gas lighting provides main light source, depicted as dots of orange throughout

Caricatural upturned features denote gaiety

Background tone and color modified to complement contrasting tones and colors on figures

Solid outlines not entirely suppressed

Colored frame painted on canvas around work complements colors of picture, protects them from influence of colors beyond frame, and reinforces pictorial reality

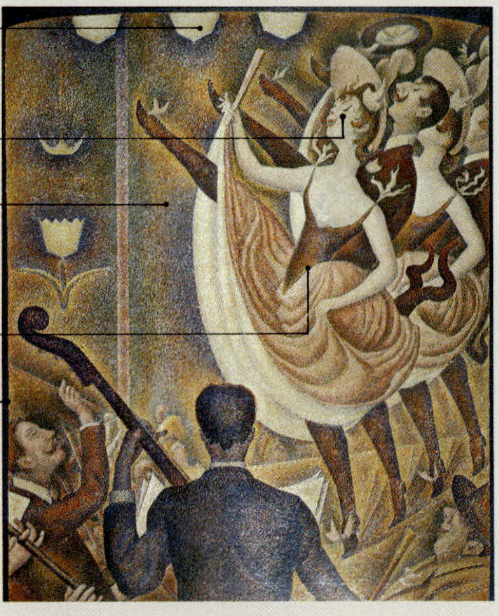

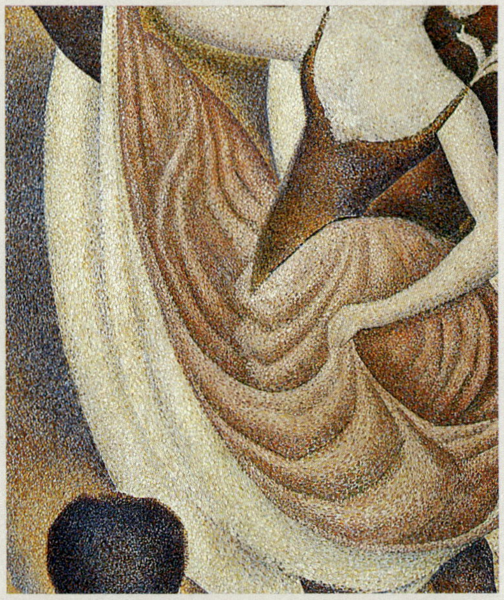

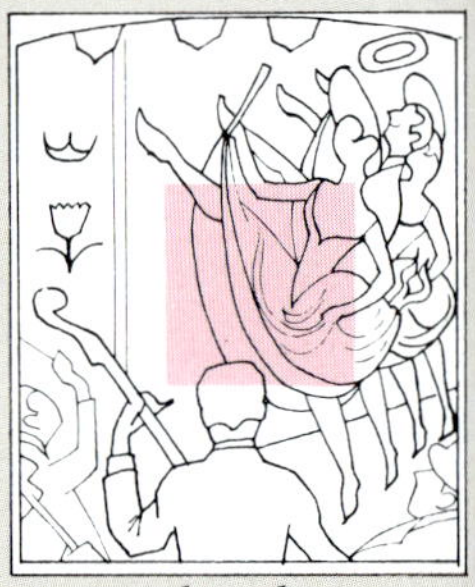

*Against the pale orange-yellow skirt edge, the background is made dark blue by contrast to strengthen the form and separate it from the background. This device also maintains color harmony throughout the painting. Comparable modifications are made all over the canvas.*

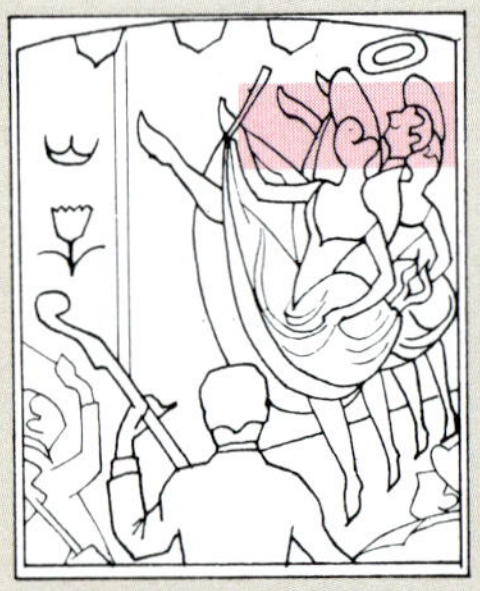

*As in Jules Chéret's poster for the Folies Bergère,* Les Girards, *of 1877, features are stylized and forms are elongated by Seurat. In* Can-Can, *however, the stylization stressed the artificiality of the entertainment world, expressing its brittle gaiety.*

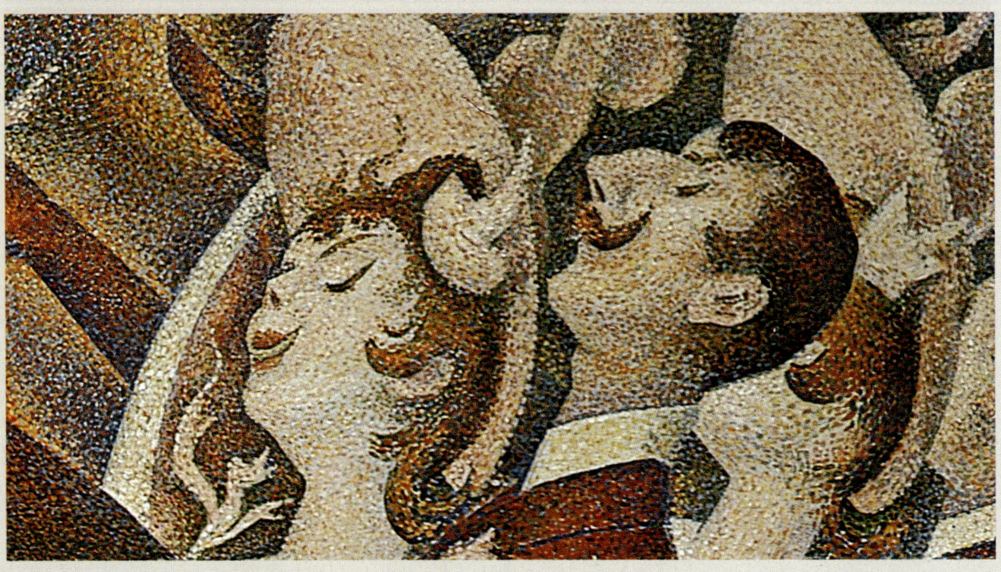

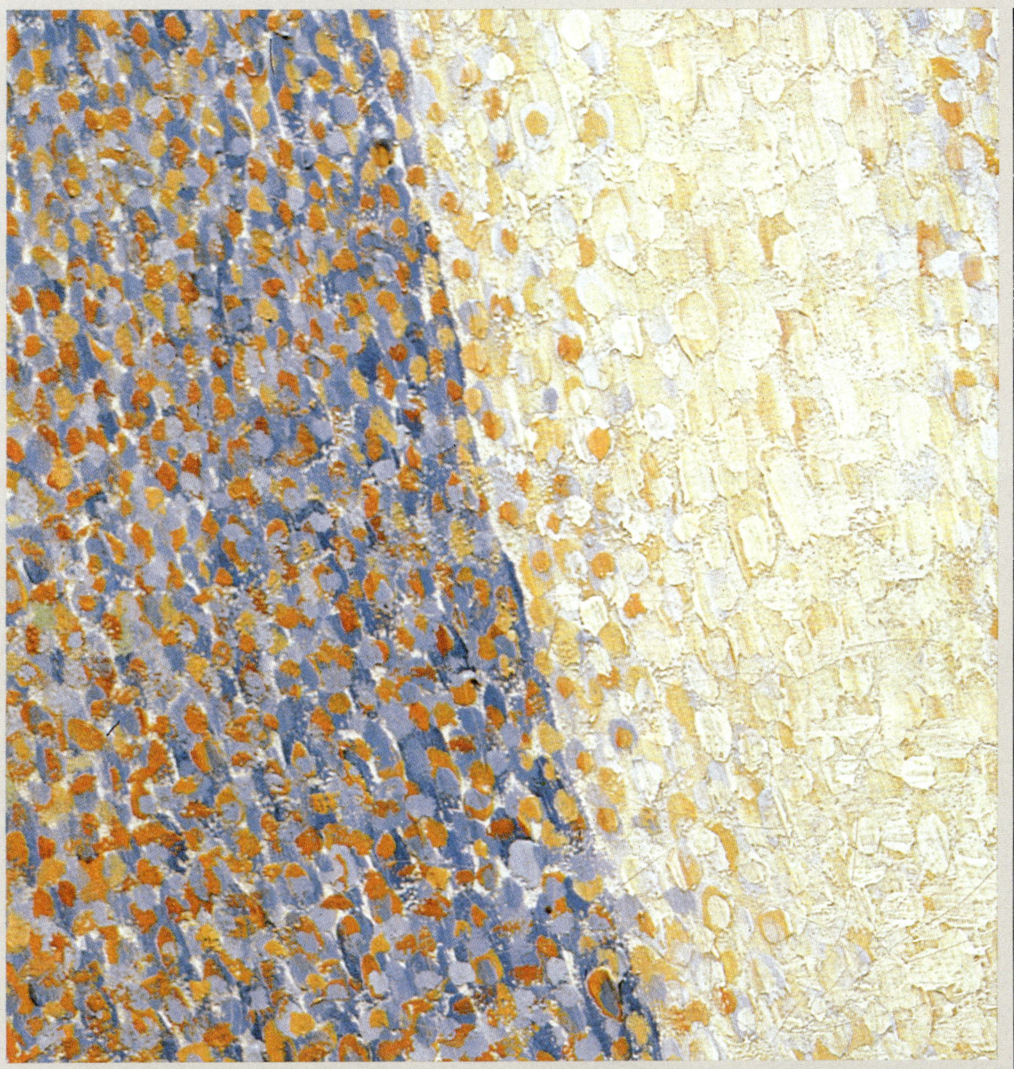

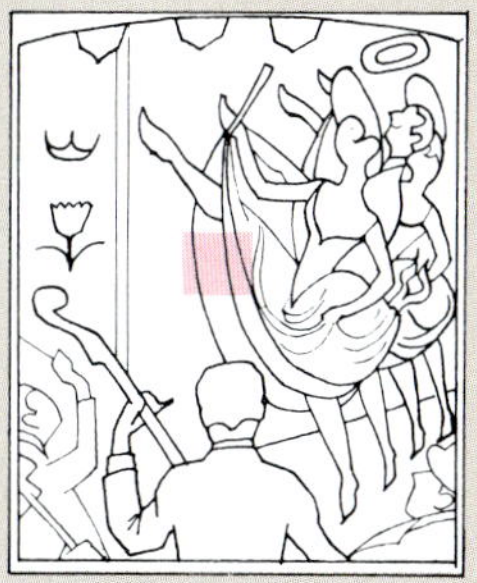

Actual size detail
*This detail comes closest to suggesting how Seurat's surfaces appear in actuality, for his effects are impossible to recreate in book reproductions. The first dots of color, the blues and creamy whites, are in fact elongated dashes which follow the forms, in this case the line of the skirt. Rounder dots in paler blue, orange and pale orange, are all worked over dry color to avoid sullying the purity of the separate hues. So, the dots are not completely uniform in shape or direction, and they set up rhythmic patterns across the picture surface. The orange dots are meant to evoke the pervasive luminosity from the gas lamps. The colors are all opaque to reflect light from the paint surface, but among the blue dots white ground can still be seen.*

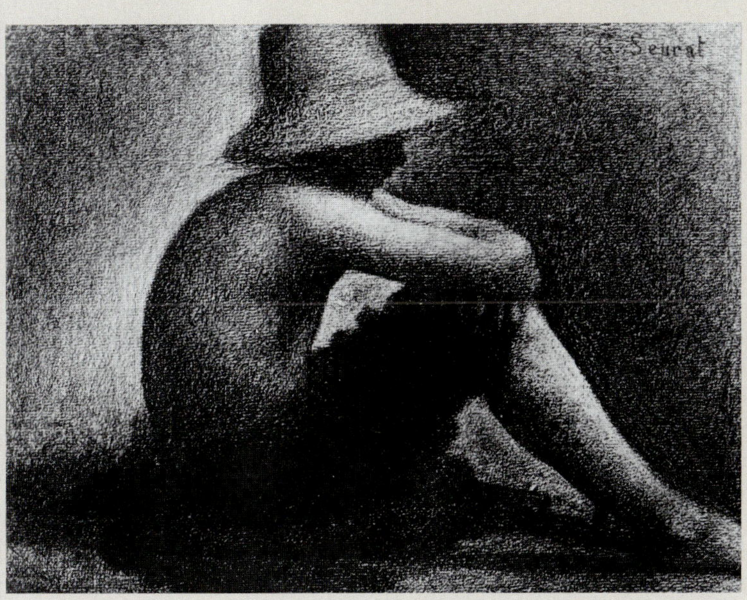

*This detail of Seurat's black Conté crayon drawing on coarse Ingres paper from 1883-1884 shows his mature tonal drawing technique. Precise outline and distinct hatching are entirely suppressed in* Seated Boy with a Straw Hat. *Instead, subtle gradations of tone are achieved by varying the pressure of the soft, dense crayon on the paper. Lightly applied strokes catch only on the paper tufts, leaving the hollows white. Firm marks cover the paper to create deep velvety blacks. These tonal variations sculpt form.*

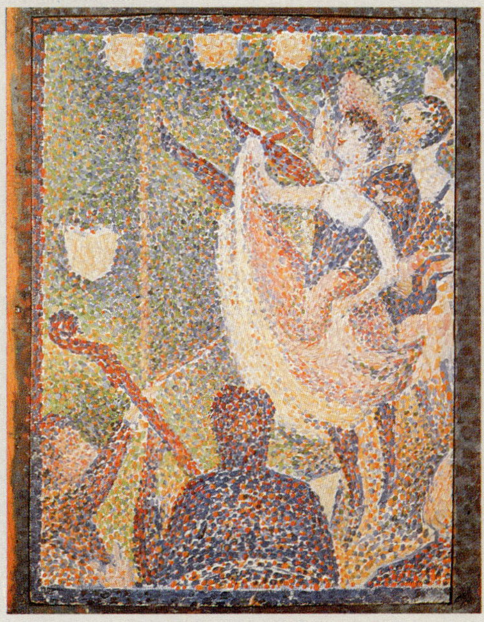

*Seurat's small oil sketch for* Can-Can *is one of several preparatory works for the final picture. His typical working method echoed academic practice, in that he used drawn studies, oil studies, and oil sketches of the composition like this one. It measures only 21.5cm x 16.5cm (8½in x 6½in), and is painted on wood panel, probably a cigar box lid. Seurat often used this type of support for his oil sketches. It is primed with white and has not only a painted frame on three sides, but a painted wooden framing strip was also added.*

## 1890
## 1905

In the 1890s, the public acceptance of the older Impressionists was still only selective. Monet, especially through his 'series' paintings of *Haystacks*, *Poplars* and *Rouen Cathedral*, had achieved widespread success, both critical and financial. Renoir had similar good fortune. However, Sisley, and Pissarro, who had abandoned the Pointillist style, continued to gain only limited recognition. Cézanne, still working in relative isolation from all but close colleagues, remained virtually unknown to the public before his first one-man show at Vollard's Gallery in Paris, in 1895. The ambiguous attitude of the art establishment toward Impressionism can be seen clearly in the reaction to Caillebotte's legacy to the state in 1894 of his superb collection of 65 Impressionist paintings. Only eight of Monet's 16 canvases were accepted, as were a mere seven of Pissarro's 18, six of Renoir's eight, six of Sisley's nine, two each of Manet's four and Cézanne's five pictures. Degas was the only artist to have all his works, a total of seven, in the legacy accepted for entry into the national French collections. From the mid 1880s, other new art styles had begun to emerge and to question the tenets of the Impressionist movement.

**Gauguin and van Gogh**

Both the Dutch artist Vincent van Gogh (1853–1890) and the French artist Paul Gauguin (1848–1903) combined elements of the realist tradition with subjective expression. Gauguin,

Below *John Singer Sargent's work* Monet Painting on the Edge of Wood *was executed around 1890. Sargent was an American, born in Florence, and trained as a painter in Paris. He was friendly with Monet in the later 1880s and visited Giverny several times to see him. This canvas shows Monet's continuing practice of outdoor work which he maintained throughout his life.*

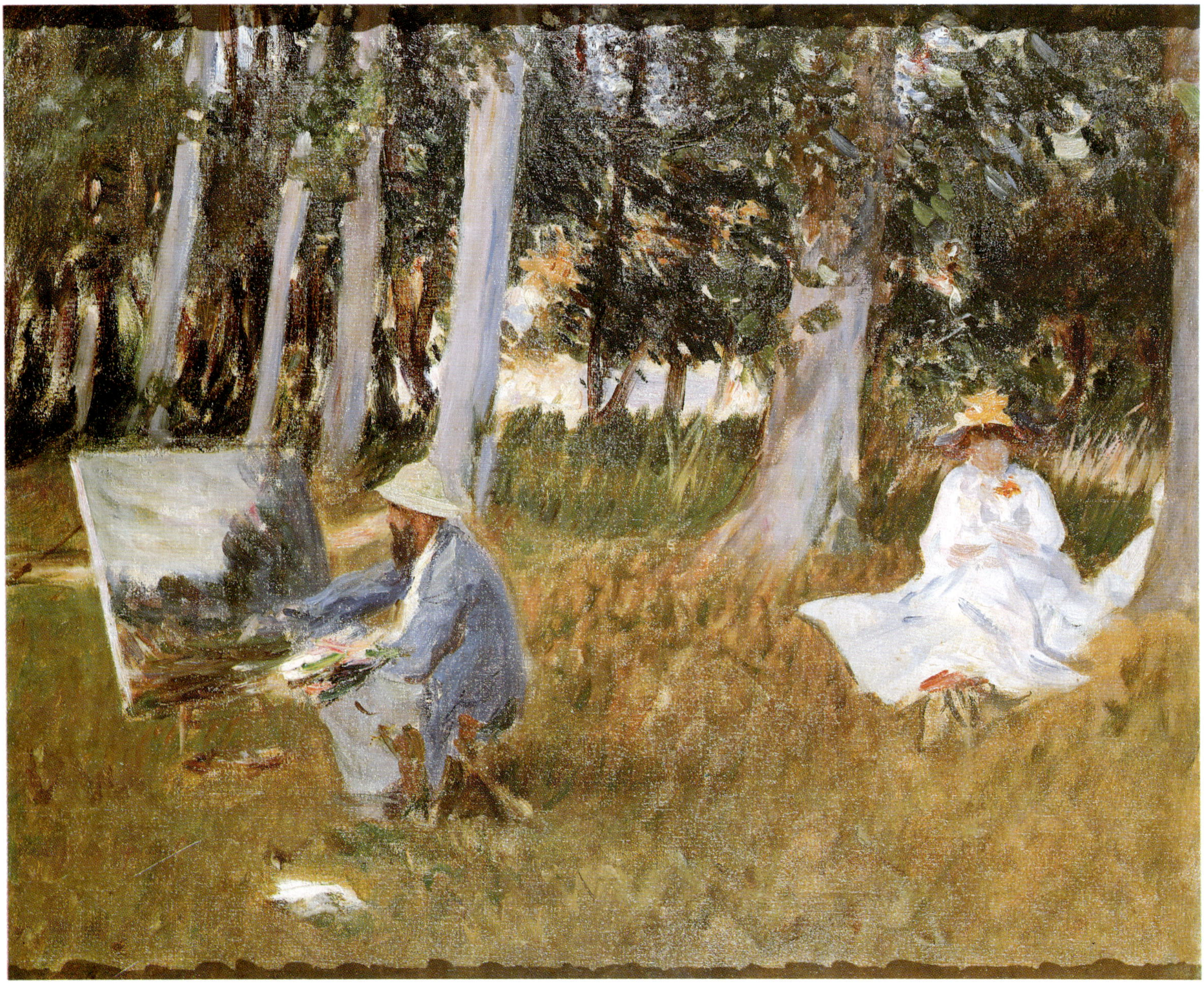

however, came more immediately than van Gogh under the pervading influence of the Impressionist group, whose works he collected in the late 1870s. Van Gogh, by contrast, had been drawing and painting seriously in Holland for almost six years – more than half of his life as a painter – by the time he came to Paris in 1886 and had his first real contact with the works of even the older French masters like Delacroix (1798–1863) and the Barbizon landscapists, let alone with the newest Parisian art. Inevitably, therefore, van Gogh's style was already well formulated before his contact with French art, and it owes more to his Dutch Realist contemporaries and to Dutch Old Masters like Frans Hals (*c*1580–1666) and Rembrandt (1606–1669). Van Gogh's painting style is essentially graphic, as if he drew with color. His mature, post-1887 pictures exhibit a personal, simplified adaption of Chevreul's influential theories on complementary color contrasts, which he exploited for their emotive power, exaggerating the colors he found in nature.

During the first half of the 1880s, Gauguin came particularly under the influence of Degas, Pissarro and Cézanne, and began by working from nature. However, he was soon to abandon Impressionist ideals. In works like *Four Peasant Women* (1886), his debt to Pissarro is clearly apparent. He adopted the short, directional brushstroke characteristic of Pissarro's work of the early 1880s, and his subject is comparable to Pissarro's of that time, except that Gauguin chose to dress his peasant figures in fancy regional Breton costumes rather than ordinary working clothes. This was a feature more commonly found in the paintings of rustic genre scenes fashionable at the Salon exhibitions which rarely showed agricultural laborers actually working. Compositionally, too, there are similarities with Pissarro's art. Gauguin pushed his large-scale figures close up the picture surface, and flattened the pictorial space by eliminating the sky and instead depicting his figures against a modulated green background. Even the slightly stylized anonymity of the women's faces are comparable to the simplified features often found on Pissarro's figures.

However, more strongly non-naturalistic, decorative elements – features of his mature style – are already apparent in this work. The flattened pictorial space itself works decoratively, giving no precise geographical location. Similarly, the frieze-like distribution of the figures across the picture surface, linked by the undulating rhythms of their arms and white collars, stresses abstract pictorial qualities. The rhythm in the figures to the right is echoed and reinforced by the curved tree which, although 'behind' them, appears ambiguously near to the picture surface. Even closer in feeling to this work are Degas' interior scenes of women bathers, of which 10 examples were shown at

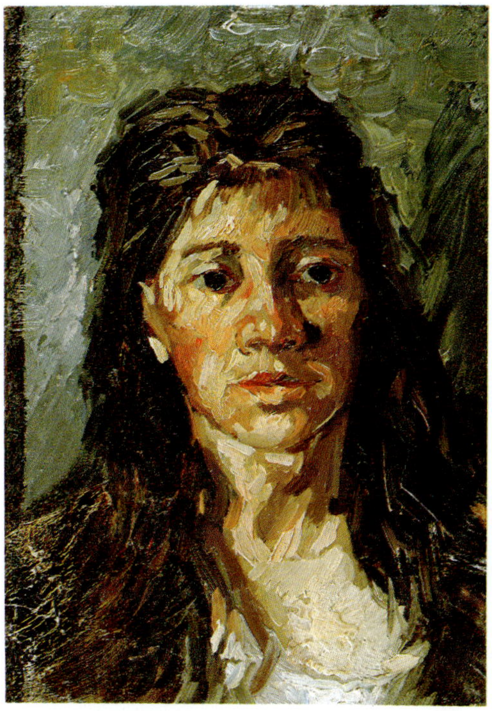

Left *This small oil study,* Head of a Woman, *by Vincent van Gogh shows how formed van Gogh's style was, before he left Holland for Paris. Rich impasted paint was laid on vigorously, in the manner of Frans Hals, one of the seventeenth century Dutch precursors that van Gogh admired. In this work, painted in December 1885, the color is brighter and the paint is more opaque and contains more white than that used for his first large work in oil,* Potato Eaters *of April 1885. Paint is handled wet in wet. The colors are mainly premixed and slurred further into each other on the paint surface. All parts are impasted, but the highlights, like those below the throat, are even more thickly loaded. The modeling of form is still mainly tonal.*

the last Impressionist group exhibition in May 1886. The cramped, claustrophobic space in which Degas commonly located his figures – trapped, as it were, within the tight confines of the four sides of his pictures – is similar to that sought by Gauguin in this exterior, but studio-painted composition. Gauguin was inspired by the simplified form, color and flat compositions of popular prints, and by his experiences of 1886–1887 when he experimented with the simplified techniques of ceramic decoration. He went on to produce far greater symbolic stylization in works like *Vision After the Sermon* which was painted in 1888.

By 1888 at the latest, both Gauguin and van Gogh were experimenting – possibly alone as well as jointly – with oil colors on raw, unprimed canvas, which readily absorbs the oil binder. In Impressionist painting, such technical travesties were rarely found, unprimed canvas normally being used only with non-corrosive and non-oil-based colors like gouache. However, both Gauguin and van Gogh evidently relished the appearance of raw canvas, particularly of rough sacking or hessian, which they exploited from time to time, as in van Gogh's *Chair with Pipe* (1889). Gauguin was more committed to this type of coarse support texture than van Gogh, but even he rarely used its potential in combination with the paint layer colors to full advantage. On the contrary, he avoided the gestural brushwork, characteristic of Impressionism, developing instead evenly painted, flat areas of color where variations in thickness or impasto played little part. The smooth, mat surface and opaque quality of his colors were further enhanced by his addition of extra wax to his paints.

Van Gogh remained more committed than Gauguin to the use of commercially ready primed canvas, which he tended to buy in rolls and stretch up onto stretchers himself. This was marginally cheaper than buying ready stretched canvases. For the ground he preferred gray, putty, white and sometimes, like Millet, a bold pink. He often allowed the color of the ground to show through among the paint layer colors, and take an active role in the final effect alongside his graphic brushmarks. His thickly applied colors and buttery impasted brushstrokes evoked varied textures, while following and strengthening the sense of form in his subjects. He sought and exaggerated the natural shapes and rhythmic lines in the objects he depicted, but remained consistent in his commitment to study and work from nature. In some paintings a compositional ambiguity suggests van Gogh's interest in the Impressionists' novel approach to pictorial structure and space. Like many other artists at the time, he too, collected Japanese prints. However van Gogh's continued concern to achieve a satisfactory depiction of depth in his landscapes with the aid of a perspective frame, are a reminder of his debt and allegiance to the art of the Old Masters.

Van Gogh's paint surfaces, like those of the Impressionists, show the mark of the artist's hand, creating textures which reinforce awareness of the paint surface. Both the bold strokes of van Gogh's brush and his exaggerated color, proved important sources of inspiration in the evolution of the Fauve style in the early twentieth century.

**The Fauves – Matisse and Derain**

The two main Fauve artists, Henri Matisse (1869–1954) and André Derain (1880–1954), worked together at Collioure in the south of France in the summer of 1905, in a productive partnership not dissimilar to that of Monet and Renoir in 1869. There they evolved their own distinctive contributions to the vibrant style, which subsequently earned them the title 'Wild Beasts' from critics later that year.

Aspects of their new approach were also already present in the work of the Neo-Impressionists, particularly the mature works of Signac, and in the anti-naturalistic paintings of Gauguin. In 1888, Gauguin told his followers in Brittany to intensify the colors found in nature in order to stress their essential characteristics and to abandon 'imitative' color. These views were remarkably close to Matisse's ideas. Yet Gauguin's advice departed from his practice, in which he developed a personal symbolic art almost exclusively derived from his imagination and eclectic borrowings from the earlier art of many cultures.

Matisse, by contrast, sought neither symbolic color nor imitative color, but color in its own right, subject only to the harmonious relationships established within the painting.

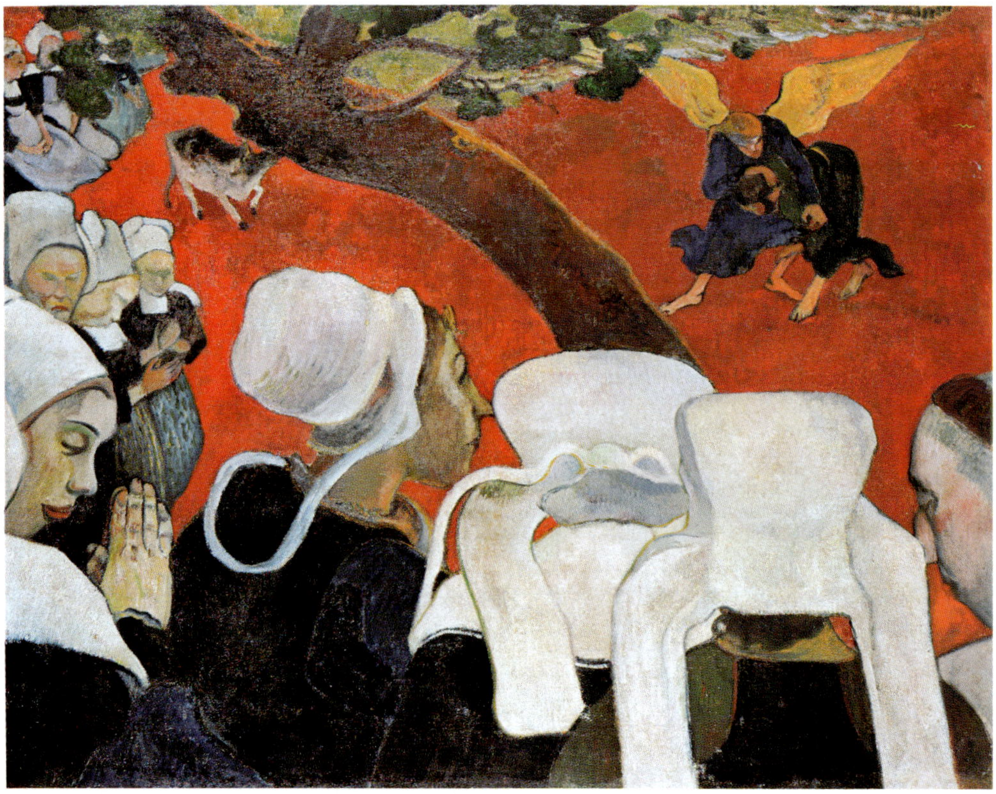

Right *Paul Gauguin painted* Vision after the Sermon, Jacob wrestling with the Angel *at Pont Aven in 1888. As its name suggests, Gauguin's work was concerned with inner rather than external truth. He combined stylized images of Breton figures in a shallow pictorial space with a 'vision' in the top right corner. Thus the 'real' and 'imagined' worlds depicted, are separated by the strong, diagonal of the tree, which was inspired by Japanese prints. Like the Impressionists, Gauguin studied Japanese prints and even adopted their use of bold, flat areas of solid color. The figures are distributed unconventionally, cut off and framing the canvas edge at the left and in the foreground. No identifiable source of light is used, a device which, looks forward to developments in Fauvism.*

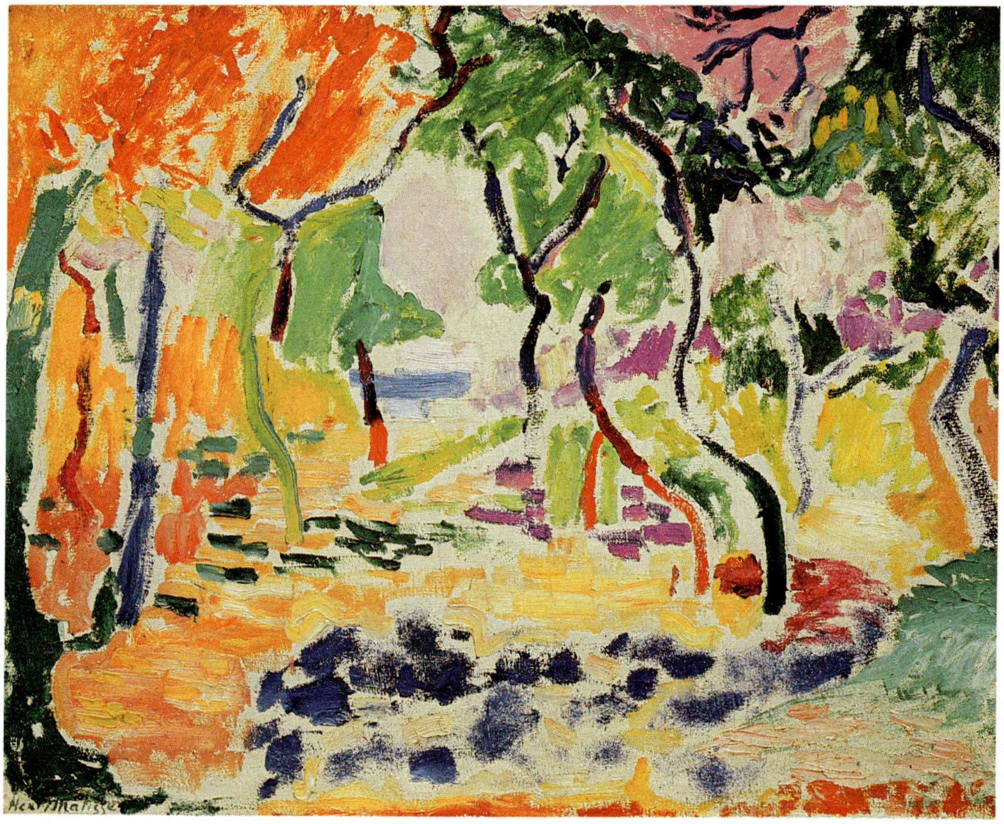

Left *Matisse's* Landscape at Collioure *dates from the summer of 1905. This landscape was painted on the French coast near the Spanish border. It was painted* alla prima, *wet into wet, the colors kept as pure and bright as possible by placing them side by side rather than slurring them. However, the broad strokes, solid areas of color and long sinuous lines show Matisse moving away from the influence of Signac, whose Neo-Impressionist methods had dominated his work the previous year. Light is suggested, not directly depicted by the juxtaposition of vivid colors.*

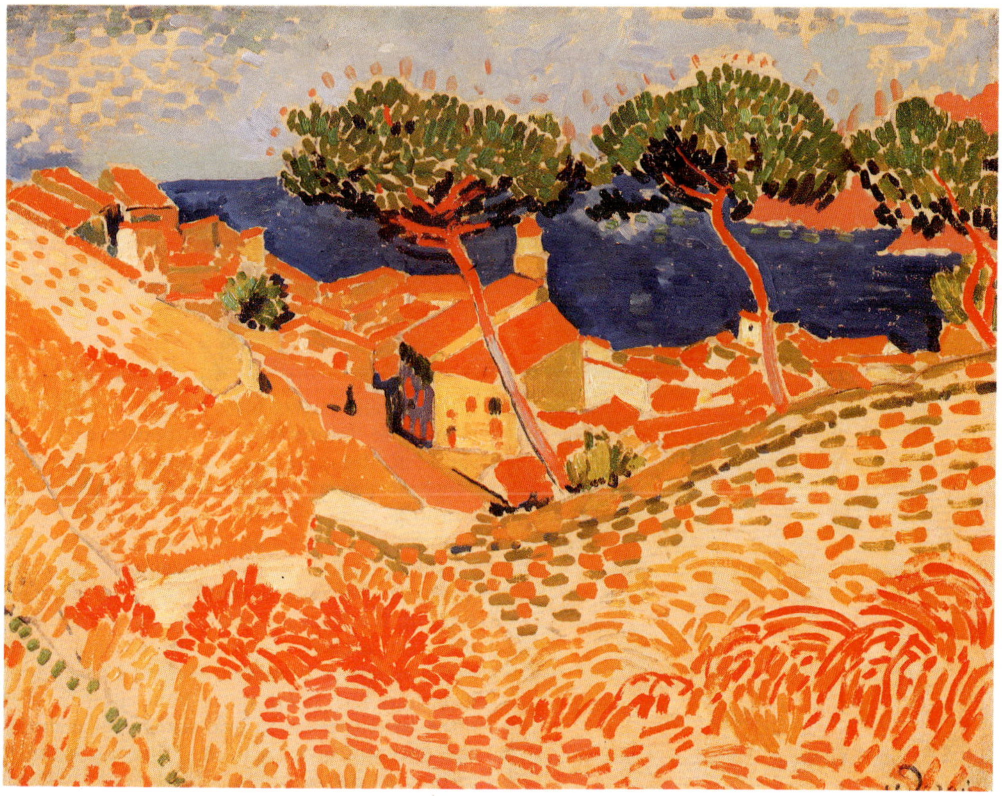

*André Derain's* Collioure *was, like Matisse's landscape* (above), *painted in 1905. Derain's landscape combines dashes of color, derived from the Neo-Impressionist method, with more broadly brushed areas of flat bright hues. He wrote from the south that 'the light here is very strong, the shadows very luminous. The shadow is a whole world of clarity and luminosity which contrasts with the light of the sun – this is what is known as reflections.' His words might have come from an Impressionist, although his color is breaking away from strictly naturalistic depiction. The white ground gave added luminosity to the colors.*

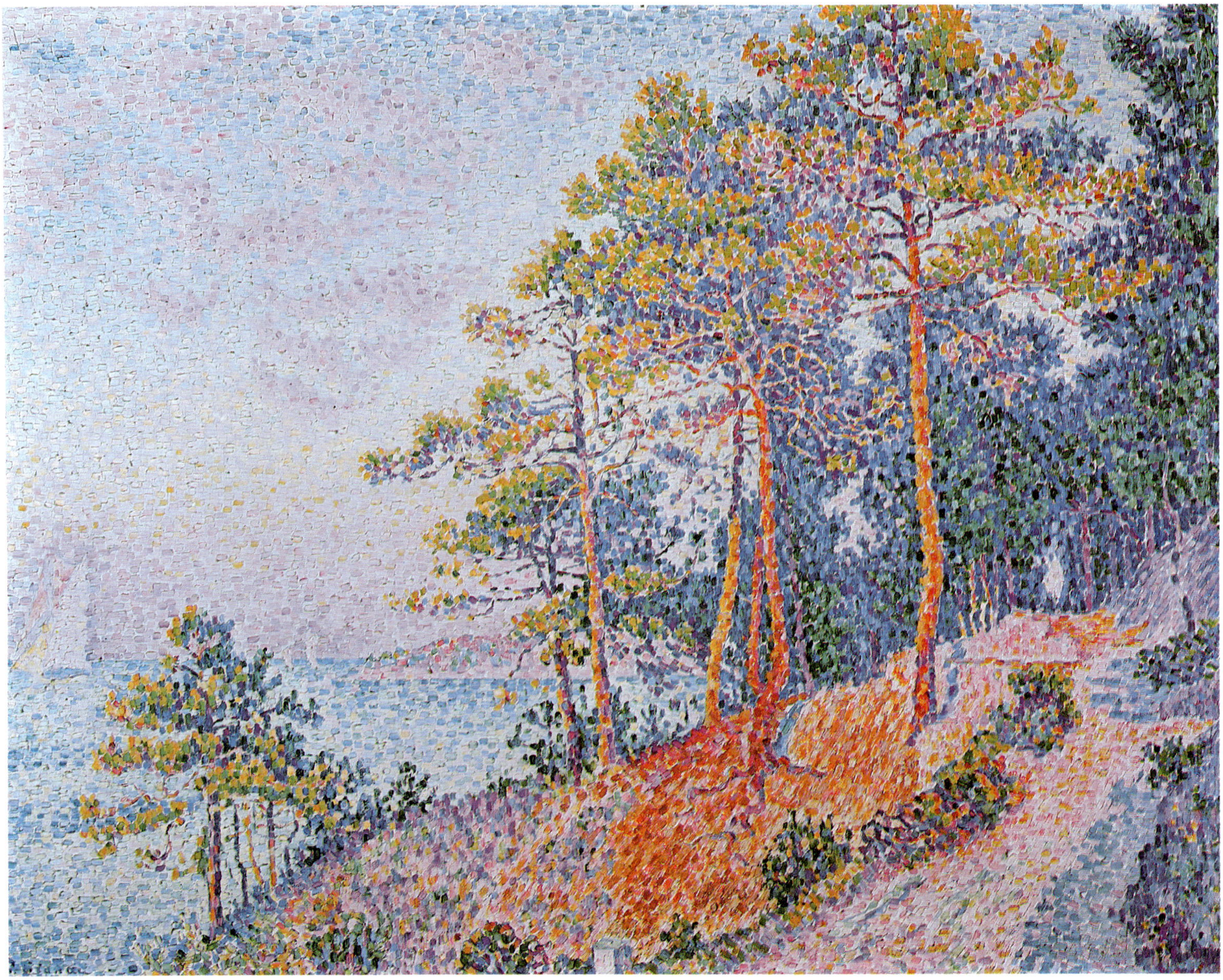

Above Saint-Tropez, the Customs House Pathway *by Paul Signac was painted in 1905. Signac's style in the 1900s was freer than his work in the late 1880s and shows a less rigorous touch. The detail (right) shows the mosaic-like application of blocks of color, which vary in hue and tone to build up the formal structure of the subject. This method was abandoned by the Fauve painters.*

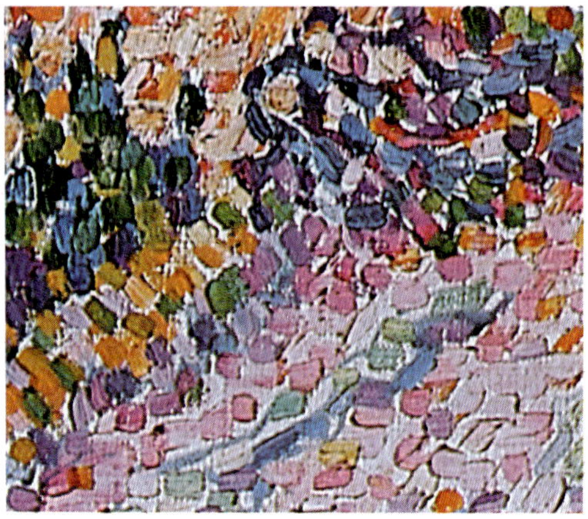

He stated in 1908 'It is impossible for me to make servile copies from nature, which I am obliged to interpret and subordinate to the spirit of the painting.' Matisse's inspiration came more from what he discovered in his own painting than directly from nature. Unlike Gauguin's synthesizing approach, Matisse's art was both analytical and conceptual, as he emphasized 'For me, everything is in the conception. It is thus necessary to have, right from the start, a clear vision of the whole.' Despite this conviction, however, Matisse's paintings – especially the color correspondences – were often heavily worked and transformed during the painting process itself. Thus, as with the Impressionists, the final appearance of directness and spontaneity in his work was frequently in contradiction to the laborious care of his execution. Matisse found the methodical application of color theory in the work of the Neo-Impressionists too restricting. His approach to the use of contrasting and complementary colors was more intuitive and instinctive.

The Fauve painters generally adopted the brilliant white canvas preparations preferred by both Impressionists and Neo-Impressionists in the 1880s. Like the Impressionists, the Fauves appreciated the textured, grainy single priming. This luminous and light-scattering base was often left partially uncovered by their loose, open paint handling. For Matisse in particular it often served to separate areas of contrasting color, assisting in the vibrant activation of such juxtaposed blocks. While the Impressionist use of color contrasts had concentrated mainly on the complementary yellow and violet-blue pair, because these most aptly imitated the effects of sunlight and shadow in nature, Matisse shifted to the red-green complementaries. This pair creates the greatest optical vibration when juxtaposed because the two colors are the closest in tone of any on the color circle. As the eye tires of reading, say, the red as dominant, the green at once appears to come forward and dominate. This vacillation of the eye between the two colors vying for dominance sets up an optical vibration, which enhances the color properties of each simultaneously. By focusing upon the red-green pair – which Matisse often biased towards pink-turquoise – he avoided the emphasis on the naturalistic representation associated with the Impressionists' use of color. It was also a pair which, again because of tonal equivalence, affirmed the flatness of the picture surface by negating the illusion of depth.

All the Fauve painting techniques and devices stressed the activity of painting itself above all else. Although remaining figurative in subject matter, brushwork, color and drawing were all finally freed in their painting from the restrictions of naturalistic representation.

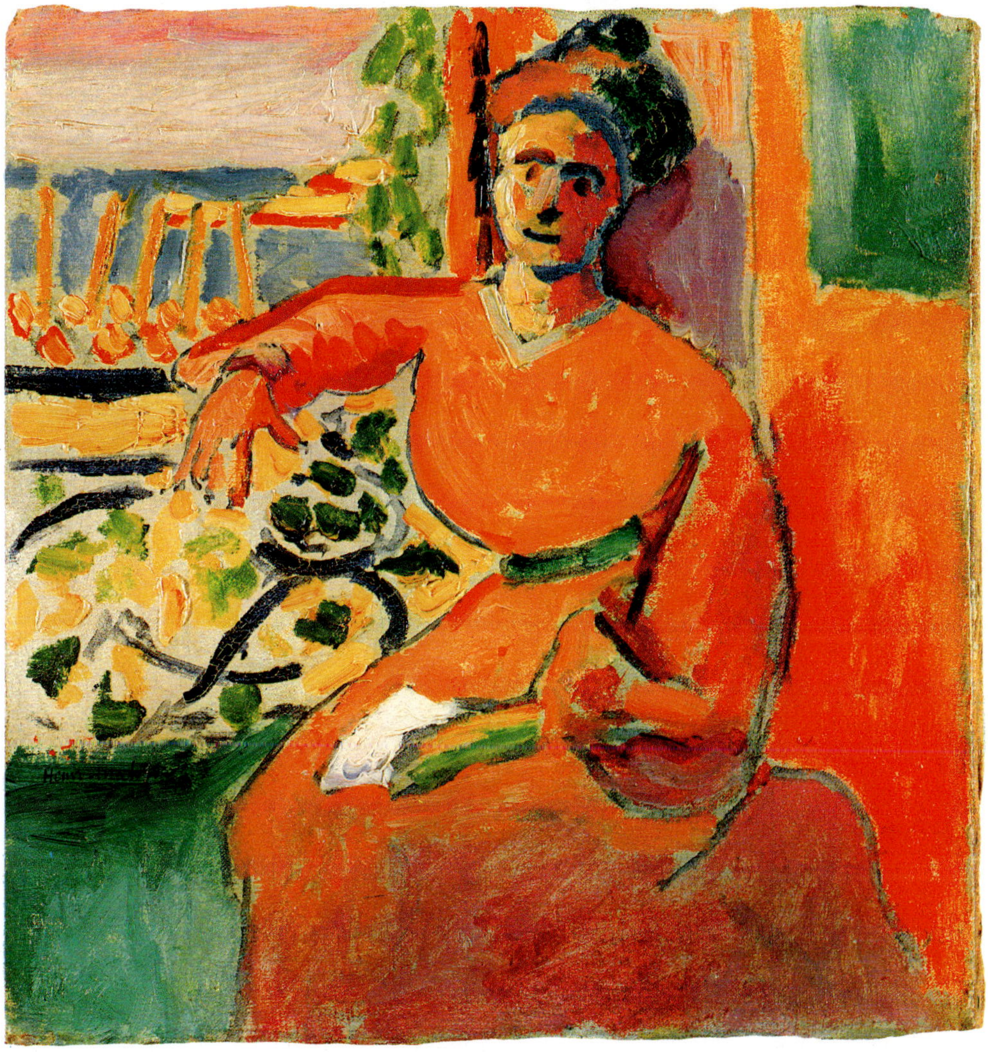

Left Woman in Front of a Window *(1905) by Matisse is a tiny, non-standard size canvas, almost square in shape. The white ground shows among the broken touches of color for the window and bay beyond. The handling here contrasts with that for the interior. Broad areas of flat bright color are applied quite thinly but opaquely. They fill in fluid blue lines which surround the form. A fall of light appears to be depicted on the face alone, but it does not in fact conform to any naturalistic effects. It simply divides the face into two separate areas of color. Colors in the composition are already being adjusted by Matisse to evoke light by contrasts and hue, rather than by imitation of actual colors perceived. Color balance – like the greens in the top right and bottom left across the reds, oranges and yellows – is more important than direct representation. Thus internal pictorial needs determine color structure.*

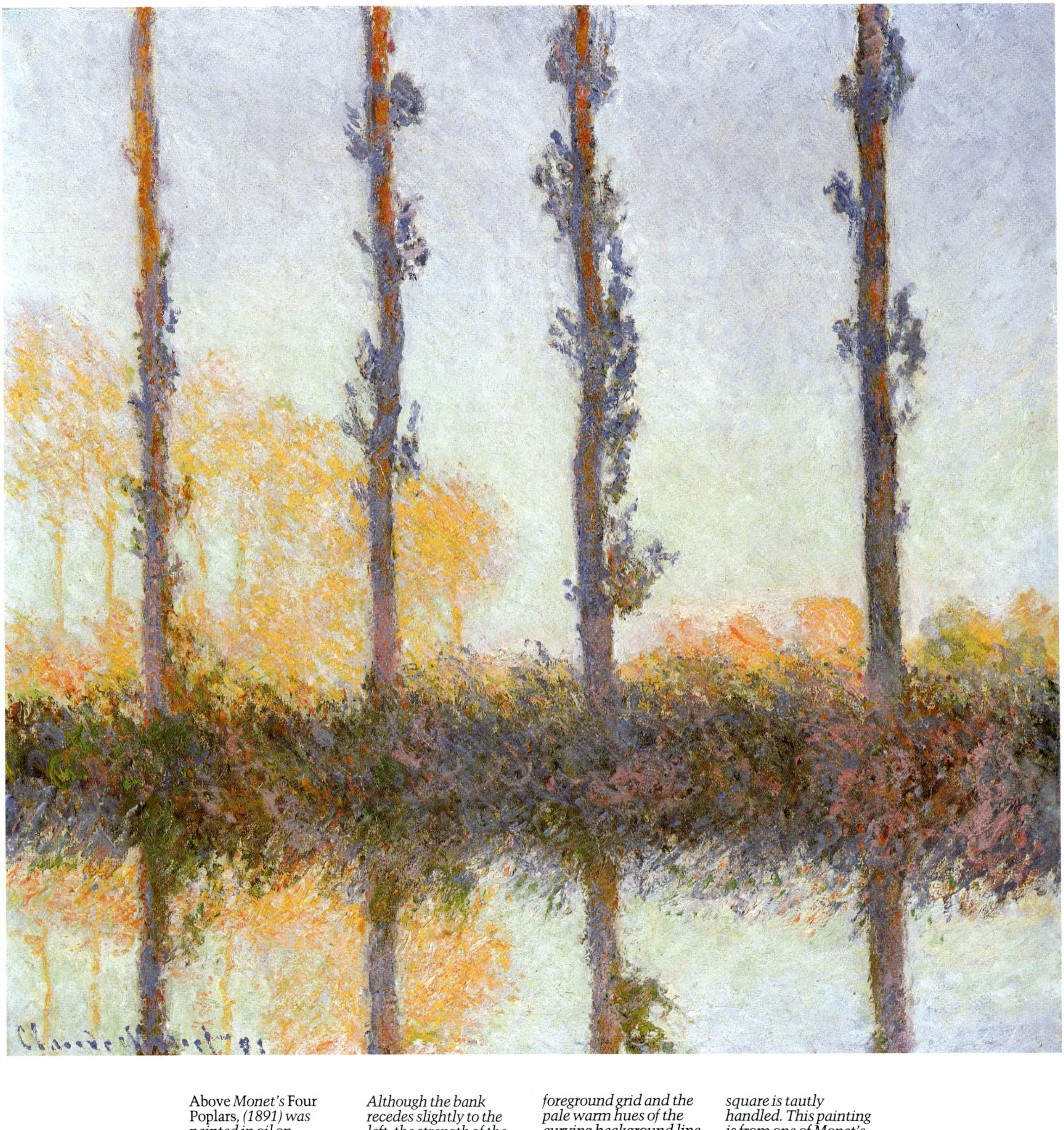

Above *Monet's* Four Poplars, *(1891) was painted in oil on pale-primed canvas. Monet's sensational use of the square canvas format is obvious here. Although the bank recedes slightly to the left, the strength of the geometric grid structure emphasizes the picture plane. The play between the dark, cool foreground grid and the pale warm hues of the curving background line of trees animates the painting further. The relationship of these elements to the overall square is tautly handled. This painting is from one of Monet's 'series', an approach to subjects in varying lights, which he perfected in the 1890s.*

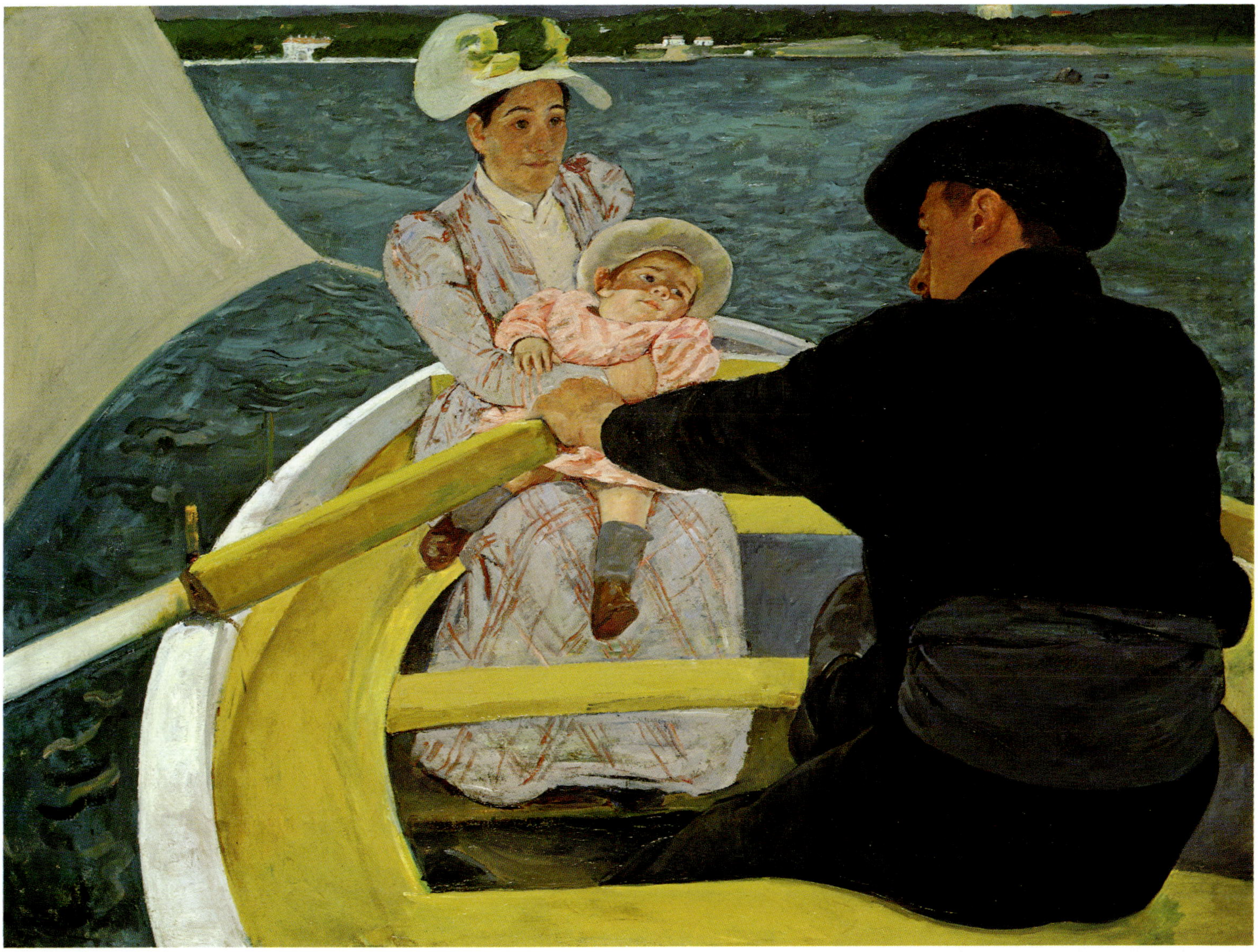

### The legacy of Impressionism

Impressionism had freed painting from the conventions of tonal *chiaroscuro*, giving new emphasis to color, pure bright luminous spectral color. It had offered new approaches to space and to composition, which liberated art from the window-on-the-world illusionism dominant since the Renaissance. It had freed brushwork from its purely illusionistic or descriptive role, pointing the way both to greater emphasis on abstract, formal qualities in painting, and to a greater expressive potential in touch.

The Impressionists had fused line and color, drawing and painting, resolving the centuries-long dichotomy between these two elements of art. They had found new, more appropriate techniques with which to exploit the full potential of modern materials. Yet, still faithful to the nineteenth century natural philosophy, they all remained more or less committed to a depiction of the natural world.

It was in his transformation of their ideas that Seurat, in his late paintings, suggested a new, more stylized and non-naturalistic art-form, which Gauguin, in his entirely different way, pursued in his Symbolist Tahitian paintings. With the Fauves, and Matisse in particular, the final legacy of Impressionist naturalism was overthrown, as color was freed from its imitative function, paving the way for the twentieth century abstraction already implicit in the avant-garde art of the 1860s and 1870s. Thus, until 1907 and the advent of Cubism, the radical approach and techniques of Impressionism remained a powerful force with which successive generations had to come to terms.

Above *Mary Cassatt painted* The Boating Party *in 1893/1894. A high viewpoint tips up the plane of the blue Mediterranean water, and reduces the sky to a thin bright blue line. All the blues are rich and saturated, linking across the surface to stress the spatial ambiguities created by the strong curved shapes, such as the sail and boat. Within these broad flat shapes, the figures of woman and child are handled with contrasting delicacy of tone and touch.*

# VINCENT VAN GOGH

*Peach Trees in Blossom/La Crau d'Arles: pêchers en fleurs*
Oil on canvas (1889)
65.5cm × 81.5cm/$25\frac{3}{4}$in × 32in

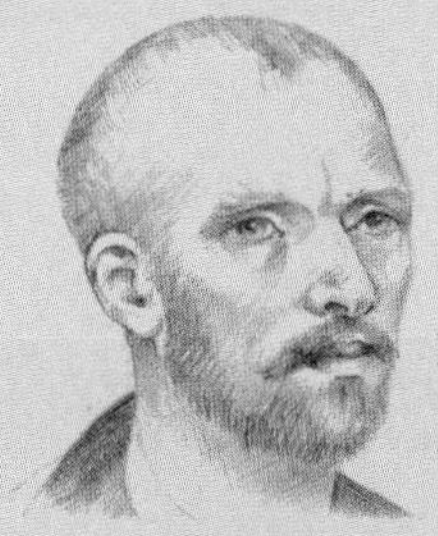

Following a turbulent early career which included work in the picture dealing trade, teaching, and religious missionary work, van Gogh finally turned to painting in his late twenties, around 1880. The first five years of his career as a painter were spent in his home country, Holland, where he studied briefly in the Hague in 1883, and in Antwerp in the winter of 1885 to 1886. In keeping with academic practice, van Gogh concentrated at first solely upon drawing, but he experimented with a variety of unusual media, including waxy black lithographic chalk, and carpenters' broad graphite pencils. These enabled him to produce harsh contrasts of light and dark, with powerful line and modeling, features which characterized his early Dutch style, and which were retained in his later work where color contrasts were substituted for contrasts of tone. He was greatly influenced by the Dutch Old Masters, and by his contemporary Dutch realist painter friends.

He went to France in March 1886, knowing little of the complex trends in modern painting that would greet him on his arrival. He had studied and read about earlier French painters, like Delacroix, Millet and the Barbizon School of landscapists while in Holland, and on his visits to England and France in the early to mid 1870s. In Paris, where he remained until February 1888, he lived with his brother Theo in Montmartre. They had a close but often difficult lifelong friendship, and Theo's work as an art dealer with the firm of Boussod & Valadon provided the financial support Vincent needed to survive as a painter. Their correspondence is an invaluable source of information on the artist's life and work.

Although at first van Gogh's work showed no real influence from his move to Paris, he soon met many of the new generation of artists. He worked for a time in the *atelier* of Frédéric Cormon (1845–1924), where he met Toulouse Lautrec and Emile Bernard (1868–1941). Bernard was, with Gauguin, one of the founders of the school of artists based at Pont Aven in Brittany. In the fall of 1886 van Gogh met Gauguin himself, and, through Theo, became acquainted with Degas, Pissarro, and the Neo-Impressionists Signac and Seurat. Van Gogh worked regularly outdoors at Asnières, painting landscapes alongside both Bernard and Signac in 1887, and, through Signac in particular, he learned to lighten his palette and use bright complementary color contrasts. Although he briefly adopted a broken touch akin to that of the Neo-Impressionists, he in fact remained only superficially influenced by the Neo-Impressionists and Impressionists.

Toward the end of his time in Holland, he had already been evolving a more colorful, free handling, influenced by what he read of Delacroix's techniques and by his own study of the bold painting of Dutch artists like Frans Hals (*c*1580–1666). The impact of the complexities of modern French art on van Gogh paled to insignificance beside his admiration for artists who exploited color like Delacroix and the Provençal painter Adolphe Monticelli (1824–1886). Like many of his contemporaries, van Gogh was greatly attracted to Japanese prints, which he began to collect in earnest from late 1886, even organizing an exhibition of them in the Parisian Café Tambourin in March 1887. But, unlike his contemporaries, van Gogh was not interested in the novel pictorial qualities of Japanese prints, instead delighting in their bold color and their representation of nature.

Disturbed by the unfamiliar bustle and excitement of Paris, and seeking the color and light he perceived in Japanese prints, van Gogh set off for the south of France in February 1888. He settled in Arles, in Provence, where *Peach Trees* was painted the following year. After a brief flirtation with Gauguin's Symbolist style, during that artist's visit to van Gogh between October and December 1888, van Gogh returned to his first love, to finding in his art a modern idiom which situated man in nature. Unlike Gauguin, van Gogh disliked working from his imagination, preferring to have subjects in nature to refer to for his inspiration. *Peach Trees* was one of six studies of spring done in 1889, and he complained to Theo of the problems in painting the shortlived effects of blossom. In fact, in this picture, the paint of the blossom lies over earlier dry paint in many places, suggesting that this is one of those which van Gogh reworked from memory in July 1889, after his move to Saint-Rémy.

*Peach Trees* was executed on an inexpensive study or ordinary weight canvas, primed a yellowish off-white, which the artist may himself have stretched up onto a standard portrait 25(65.5× 81.5cm/ $25\frac{3}{4}$× 32 in) stretcher. The thin layer of priming has left a grainy canvas texture, which is apparent in the more thinly worked parts between the bold impasted brushstrokes. Underpainting is present only in the area of the sky, where thin mat colors were broadly laid in. For this, muted colors were used, white barely tinted with pale blue for the upper part of the sky, and with a pinkish-gray for the lower half. This was worked over with short horizontal strokes of brighter color, cool sharp blues and pale greens, probably cobalt or malachite. As with the Impressionist technique, van Gogh's colors included white in most of his mixtures, and the paint layer is covering and opaque. Only an alizarin lake – possibly a burnt alizarin – was used in its original transparent state, in order to denote the trunks of the peach trees.

Van Gogh's brushwork is vigorously descriptive, echoing the textures and forms in his subject. Although the impasted build-up of

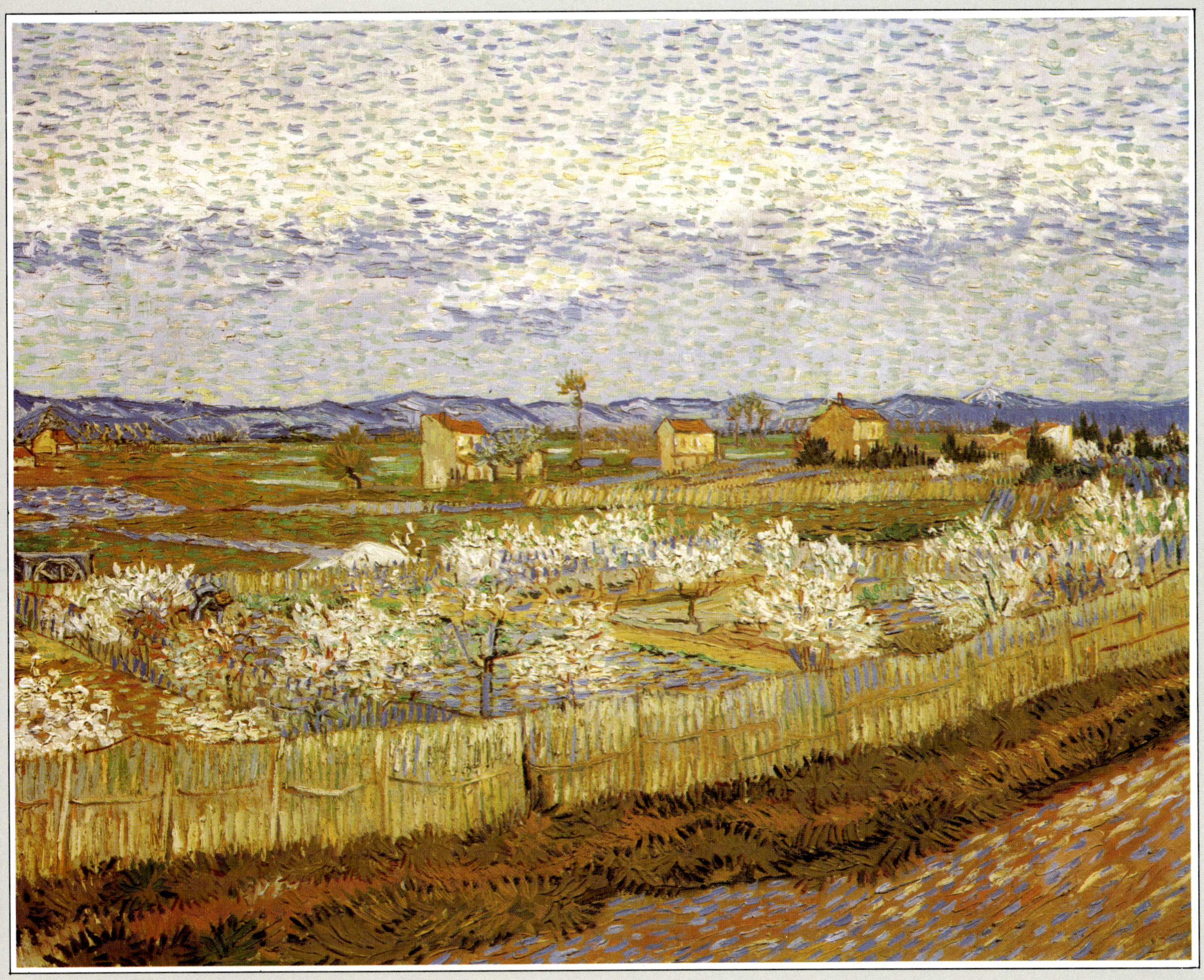

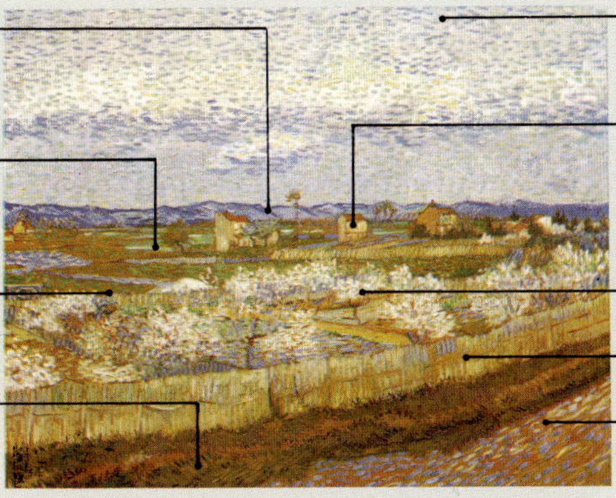


*The essentially descriptive quality of van Gogh's brushwork here becomes more abstracted from the natural subject in the handling of sky and foreground. The blue, pale yellow and green dashes of color in the sky are taken up and reiterated, following movement of the path in the foreground. The colors are heightened, but still naturalistic, and the creation of recession and space is carefully organized.*

paint tends to emphasize the patterned surface of the picture, his careful concern with establishing a strong sense of space and perspective through the receding fields and changing scale of objects, confirms his commitment to traditional Dutch landscape painting.

While this picture is brilliant and luminous, its more subdued hues, for example in the foreground, look forward to his work at Saint-Rémy between May 1889 and May 1890. During that period, his nostalgia for the somber hues of the Dutch countryside led him to use less brilliant colors than those which characterized his stay in Arles. In May 1890, van Gogh returned to the north, but not to Holland. He settled in Auvers-sur-Oise, an old haunt of the Impressionists, north-east of Paris, where he died at the end of July 1890.

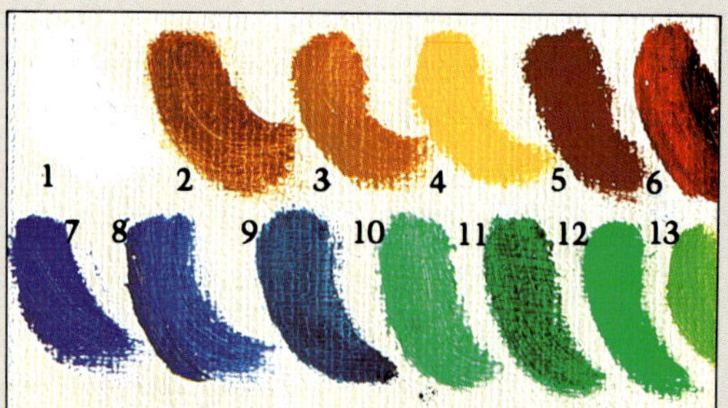


*Van Gogh's palette probably comprised zinc white (1), raw sienna (2), yellow ochre (3), chrome yellows (4), red alizarin lakes (6), ultramarine (7) or cobalt (8) blues, Prussian blue (9), cobalt green (10) and viridian green (11). Red earth (5), and emerald (12) and chrome (13) greens may have been used.*

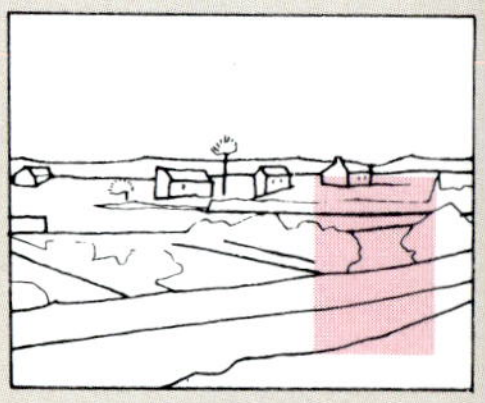

Actual size detail
*The texture of the canvas, thinly primed with off-white, can still be seen between the more impasted strokes with which the surface is loaded. Even though it is often obliterated, the pale ground remains a stable luminous tint that helps maintain the overall brilliance of the colors used. The opaque colors, often loaded with white, have a similar effect, because they bounce light back to the eye. The addition of extra color for the blossom suggests this picture was reworked later. Van Gogh executed six paintings of spring blossom that year, and is known to have completed some of them later in the year, after the brief season of blossom was over. Brilliant touches of what are probably red earth, cobalt blue and cobalt green enliven the more muted earth colors and the pale blossom.*

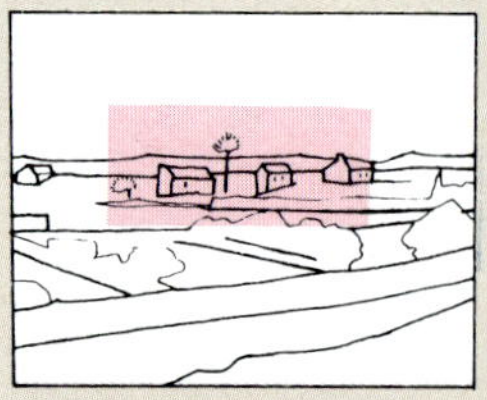

*Van Gogh constructed the sense of recession using finer handling for the distances. Varied forms and textures are characterized by changes in brushwork. Thin horizontal strokes suggest the receding fields in alternating blues, greens and creamy hues. Paint is worked mainly wet over dry in unblended dabs.*

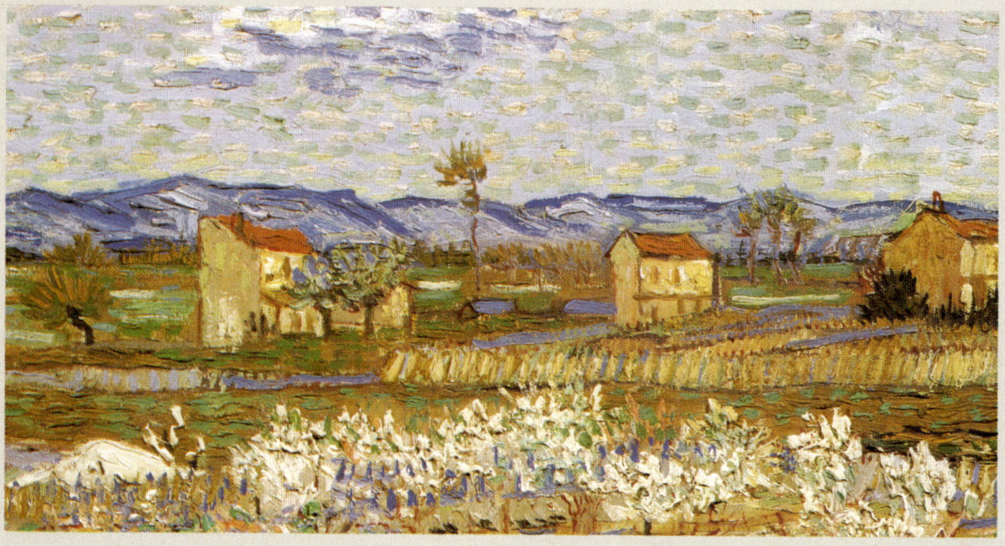

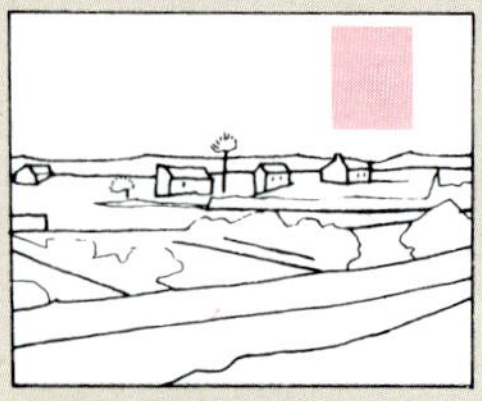

*Thin, opaque layers of pale tinted color – pale green in places, pale blue in others – were applied and allowed to dry before the artist added short horizontal strokes of brighter, more saturated color. These wet-over-dry patches animate the sky in a relatively unnaturalistic way in comparison to the more naturalistic handling which dominates the rest of the painting. The paint is chalky, thick and full of white pigment even in the quite saturated hues.*

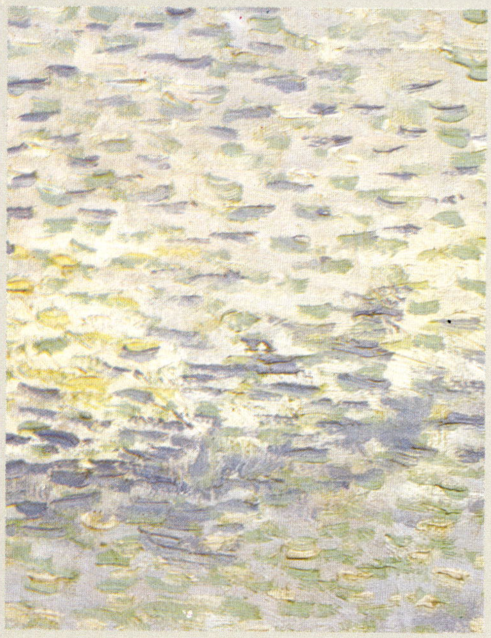

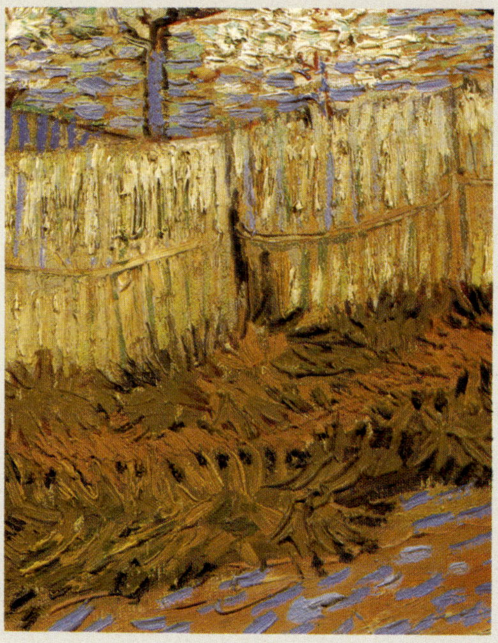

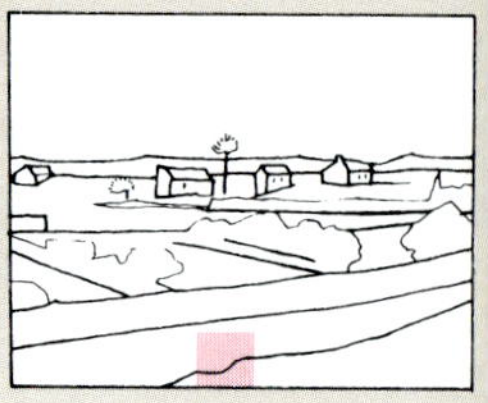

*The paint layer colors are almost entirely opaque and densely loaded, the mark of the bristle brush remaining apparent in the raised paint. Wet-in-wet slurring is visible among the colors denoting the grasses, while wet-over-dry dragged paint used for the fence creates a stippled, vibrant effect. Colors are mainly mixed and broken, but the green and blue are relatively 'pure'.*

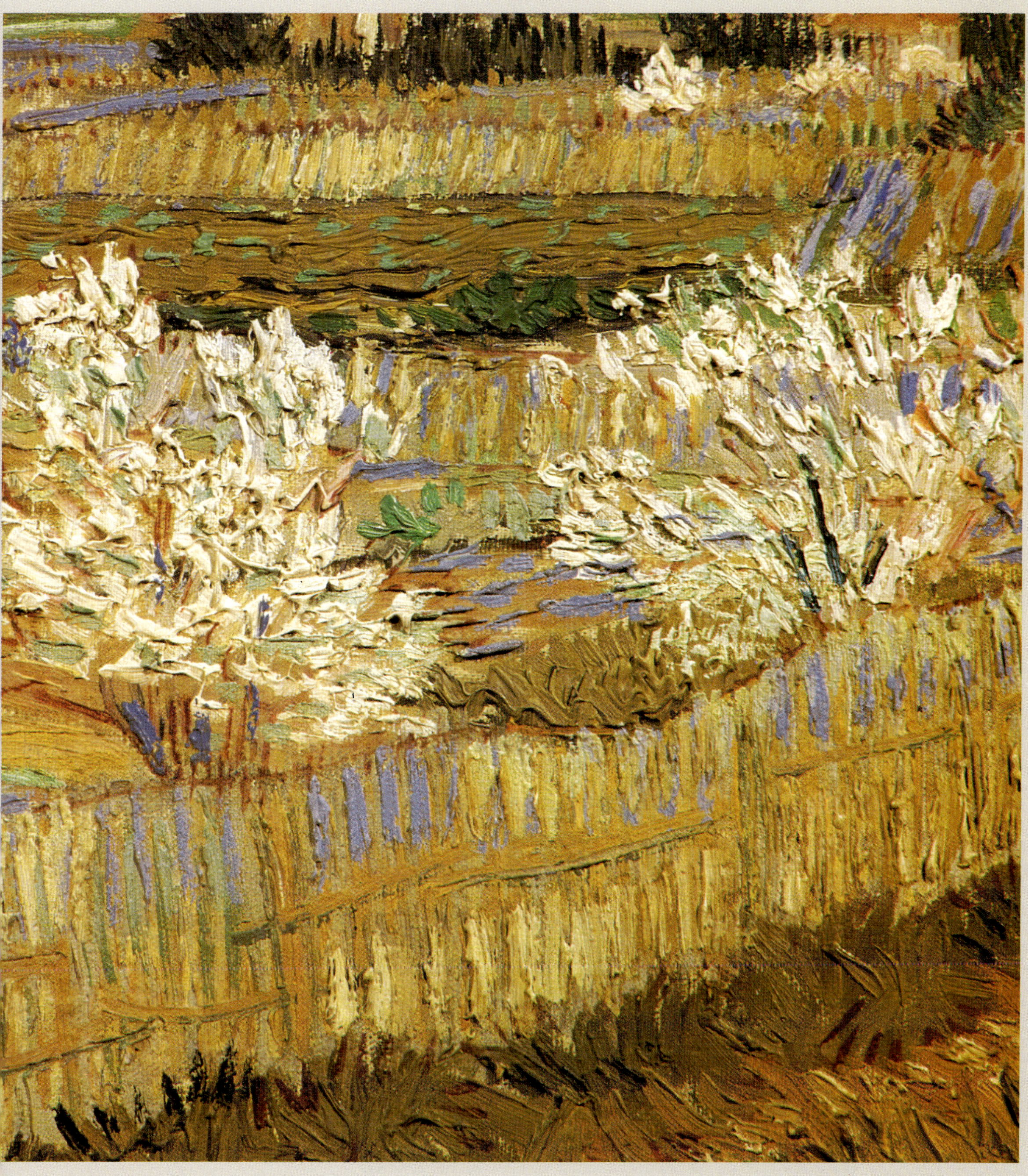

# EDVARD MUNCH

*Jealousy* (1895)
Oil on canvas, 67cm × 100cm/26in × 39in

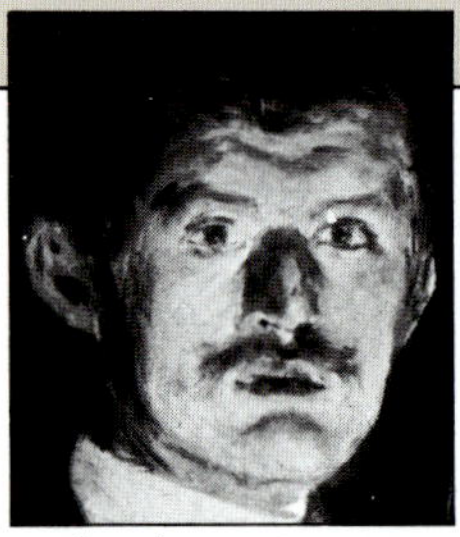

Edvard Munch, Norway's greatest painter and one of the major precursors of Expressionism, is remembered above all for a thematically related group of paintings executed in the 1890s which he called, after 1918, his *Frieze of Life*. Munch's *oeuvre* was concerned with conveying passion and emotion. For example, he wrote of the *Frieze of Life* 'These paintings are the moods, impressions of the life of the soul, that at the same time form a development in the battle between men and women that is called love.' *Jealousy*, painted in Berlin in 1895 as part of the series, is an outstanding example of Munch's genius for creating unforgettable images endowed with universal appeal and meaning out of autobiographical subject matter, and for conveying complex and conflicting mental states and ideas through the subtleties of his technique.

On 9 March 1893 Munch introduced a young Norwegian music student, called Dagny Juell, into his Berlin circle of friends. Juell immediately acted as a catalyst in the break-up of the group because seven of them, including the dramatists August Strindberg and Stanislaw Pryzybyszewski, the principal protagonist in the painting, fell in love with her. However much the group may have advocated free love, their mutual jealousy turned the affection of close friends into hate. Przybyszewski eventually married Dagny on 24 September 1893. As if to have practical confirmation of his medical theories on the power of subconscious emotions over the intellect, he allowed Dagny to continue to have affairs with other men, including Munch himself. Munch and Dagny are seen together as Adam and Eve in the background of the painting. The painting universalizes these events into a modern allegory on the destructive power of love and its regenerative potential to triumph over death.

It is difficult to generalize about Munch's technique because the emotional content of the painting dictated his approach to the painting. Munch's approach was also highly symbolic. For instance, the crimson lily on the left of the picture in the foreground is apparently Munch's symbol for art. Although Munch's approach may look spontaneous and unplanned, the organization of the canvas was carefully rehearsed in preliminary drawing which was carried out on the canvas itself.

**1.** The close-grained linen canvas was sized to give an overall warm mid-tone. In the finished work, the ground can be seen in the face in the foreground and on either side of the tree.

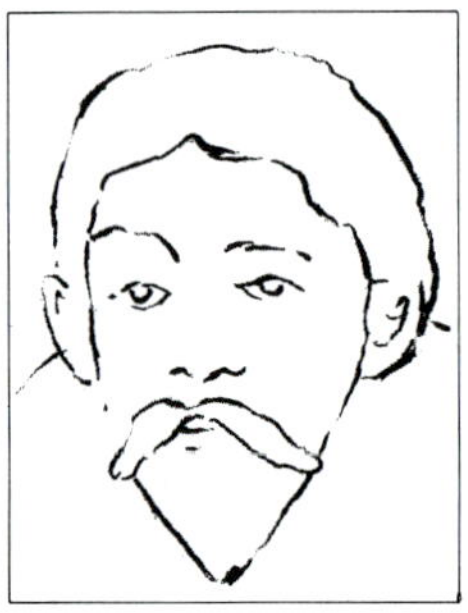

**2.** The charcoal underdrawing was next applied to the canvas. It was evidently detailed and remains clearly visible in the face.

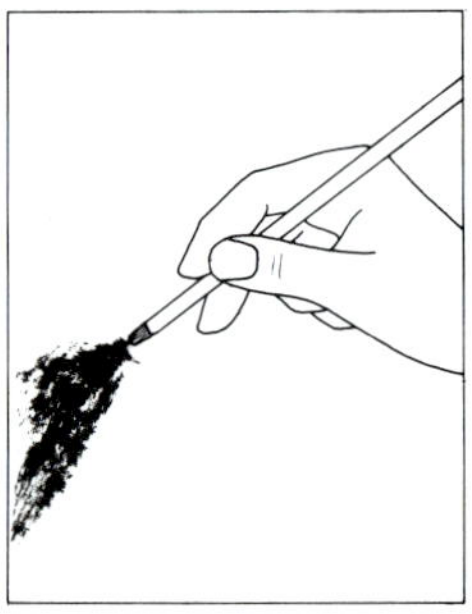

**3.** Munch used a wide variety of techniques to apply the paint. These included turpentine washes, scumbling, overdrawing and scratching into the paint surface with a dry, bright hog's hair brush.

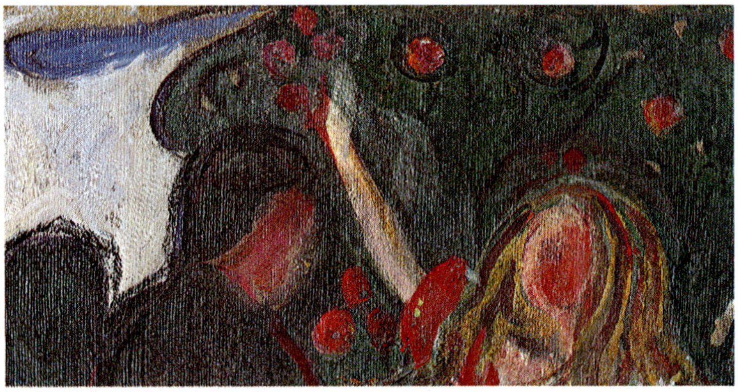

*Here the green and red juxtaposition which characterizes the whole work can be clearly seen. The paint has been applied in a crude way in order to convey the passion which was the work's subject. For Munch, changes in technique were related to the emotional content of the work. The crudity of the technique here is evident in the clear alteration to the position of the woman's arm and the overlapping of the thick blue and white of the sky.*

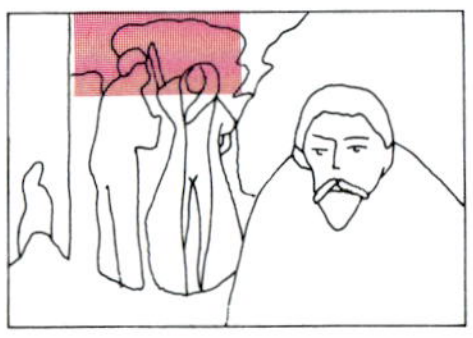

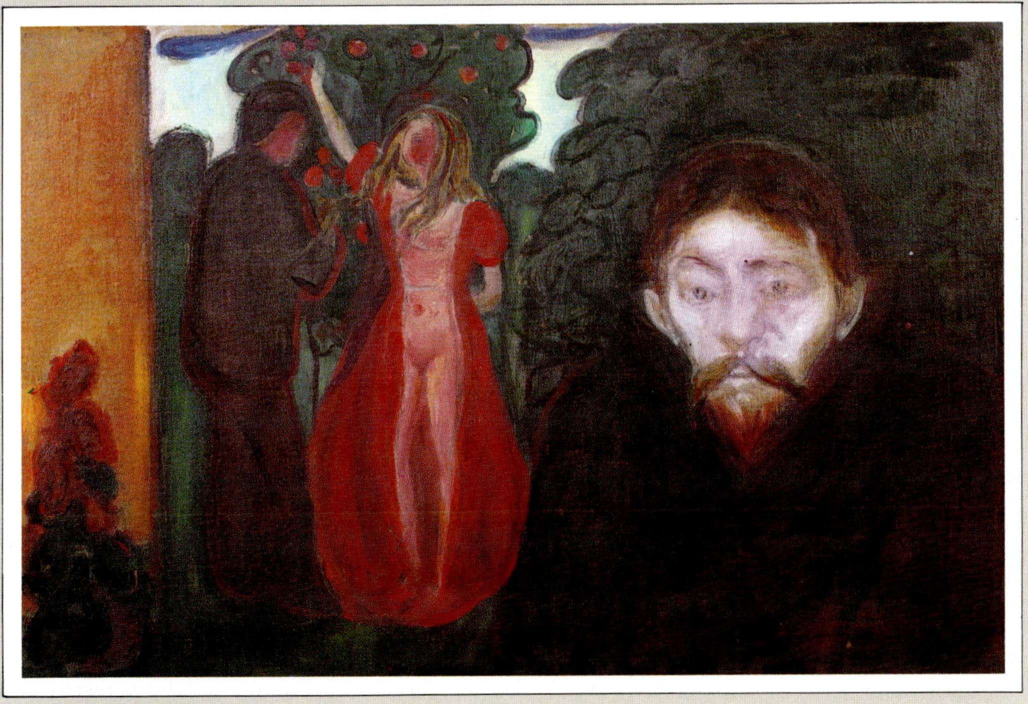

*In* Jealousy, *psychological contrasts are expressed through contrasts of color and technique. The picture is divided into two halves, one light and one dark; red is shown against green, and thin washes against thick opaque paint. Przbyszewski's disembodied presence is indicated in washes of paint and his face, drained of color, is juxtaposed against the thick opaque vermilion of the woman's red robe. The three figures are connected by red — the red of the woman's robe links up with the red contours around the two male figures. Despite the apparent freedom in the application of the paint, there are no major changes in the painting's composition, indicating that Munch worked with absolute assurance. Munch used a wide variety of techniques varying from turpentine washes to scumbles and from scratching into the paint layer with a dry brush to overdrawing. For example, the deep claret red washes on Przybyszewski's smock were applied in such a liquid state that they have, in places, run down the canvas.*

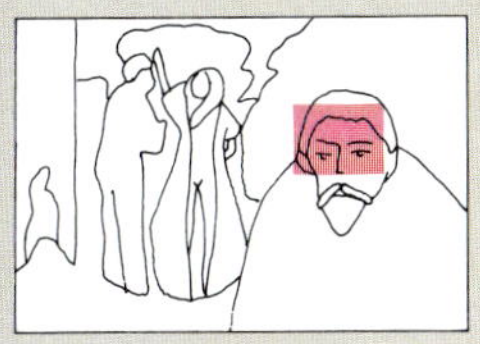

**Actual size detail**
*The face which dominates the foreground of the painting shows the important part played in the final depiction of form by the charcoal underdrawing which shows through clearly in the eye on the right. Munch also uses the warm mid-tone of the ground as part of the local color of the face. The paint is applied with great sensitivity. For example, the opaque white is subtly differentiated on the eyebrows by the addition of touches of red, and, on the eyes, with tinges of blue. The white is applied thickly to the forehead area and cheeks where a little additional yellow lends an almost ghostly pallor to the whole countenance.*

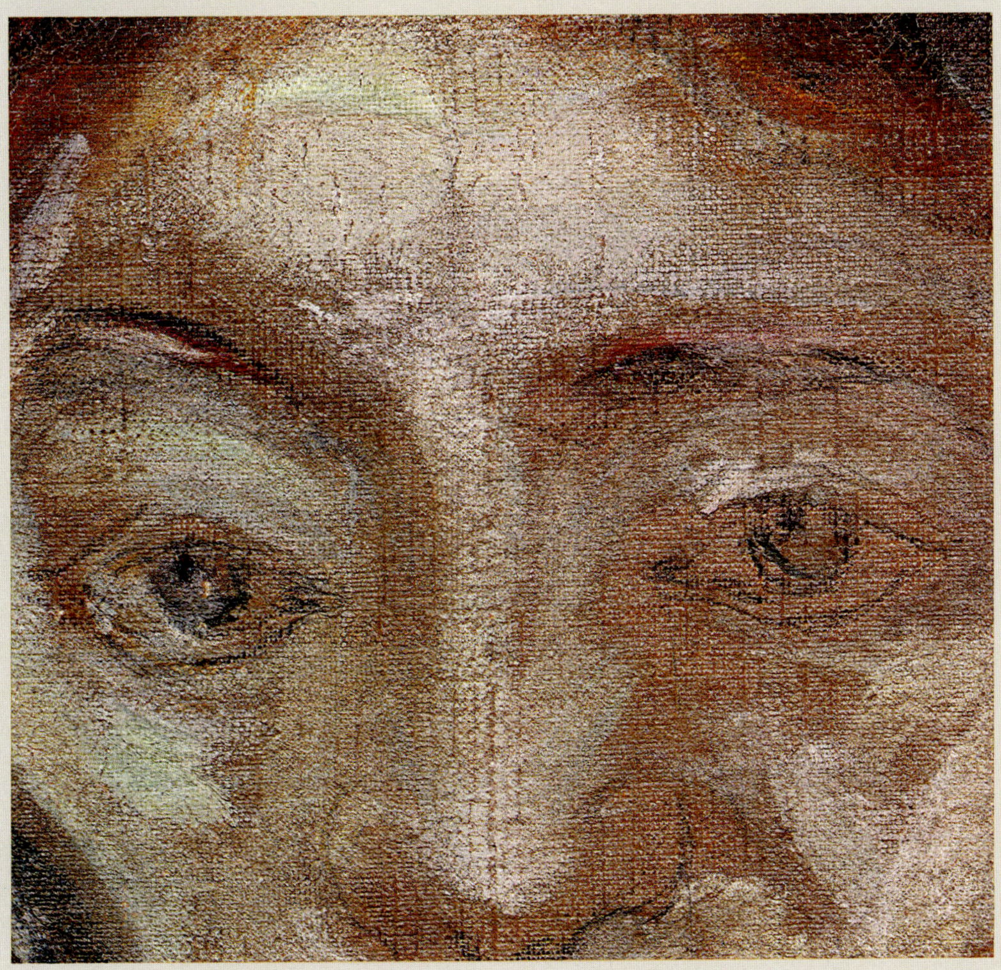

1890
1905

# PAUL CEZANNE

*Still Life with Plaster Cupid/Nature Morte avec l'Amour en Plâtre* (1895)
Oil on paper mounted on panel, 70cm × 57cm/27½in × 22½in

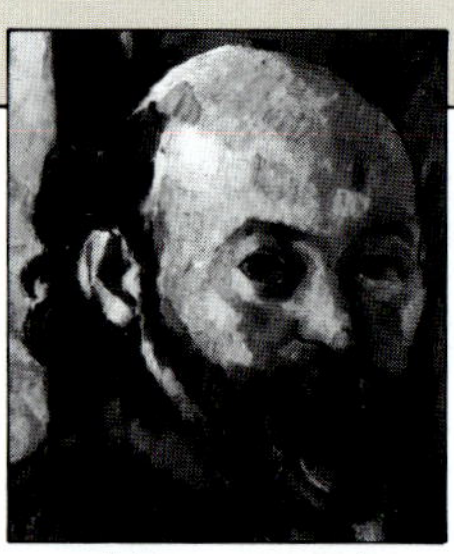

Cézanne spent much of his life between his birthplace, Aix-en-Provence, and the environs of Paris. He first arrived in Paris in 1861 where he met and worked with the artist Pissarro, who introduced him to open air landscape painting. Thanks to Pissarro, Cézanne lightened his palette, and his passionate subject matter gave way to more tender and imaginative scenes which culminated in his later monumental studies of bathers.

Using the Impressionist ideals of color and a commitment to nature, and wishing to imbue his work with a sense of permanence and monumentality, Cézanne developed his 'constructive' brushwork, in which separate, parallel strokes often with a diagonal bias were used to create structural solidity. To this end, he chose a neutral gray light which gave the truest impression of color, or a diagonal sunlight as seen in mid-morning or mid-afternoon, which gave landscapes a calm stability.

Cézanne used pale grounds, visible through gaps in the paint layer. As in Renoir's work, cream grounds were enhanced and warmed by the adjacent placing of cooler tints. Particularly in the later landscapes and wooded scenes, Cézanne used these pale grounds to create the lights, thus obviating the need to overload the surface with paint. Thin, translucent paint films frequently appear in Cézanne's mature works and his experiments with overlaid transparent watercolor were incorporated into a number of his oil paintings. By contrast, other works in oil were heavily built up with layers of paint standing out in relief from the canvas surface. The densest paint follows the contours of the form, and the thinner applications, often revealing the ground, were used for form and contours. Cool colors, mainly blues, were used for the shadowy areas, while warmer pinks, reds, and yellows appear to create the roundness of the forms.

Cézanne used interlocking planes of subtly modulated, contrasting colors to create the complex spatial arrangements of his paintings. His slow, methodical way of painting meant that he often spent years on a work, returning to and adjusting it many times over. When reworking a painting Cézanne often worked from a different viewpoint. His revised perceptions of the subject would often be incorporated into the picture making it more complex.

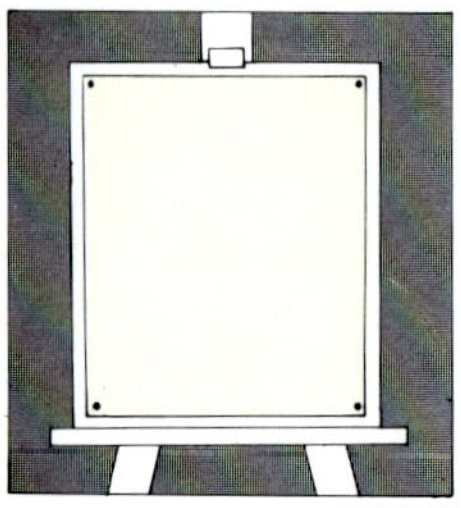

**1.** Paper was bought commercially primed with a cream-colored ground. This was pinned to a rigid support.

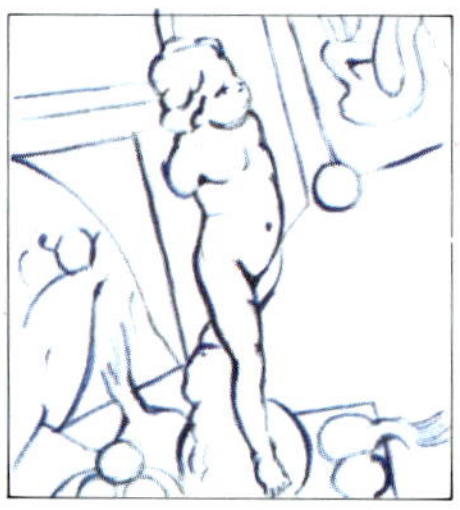

**2.** Original outlines were drawn in graphite and overlaid with a dilute blue paint, possibly ultramarine.

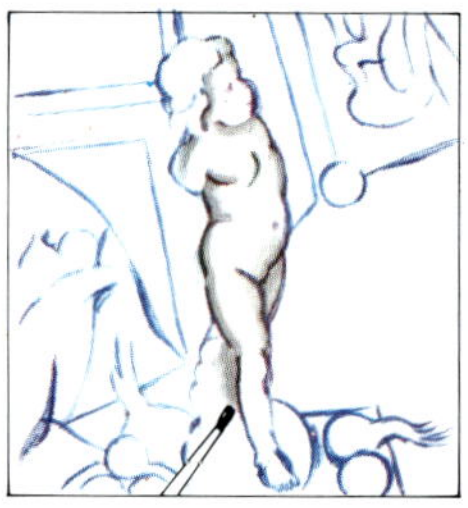

**3.** Wet-in-wet application of paint was begun before the outlines were dry, and reworking and adjustments took place continuously throughout the painting process.

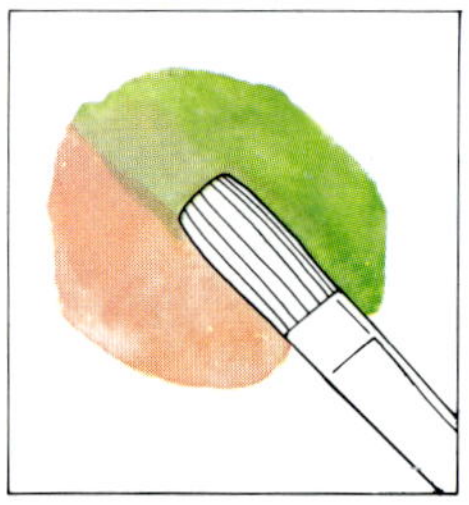

**4.** Brushstrokes of thin opaque color were applied following the contours of the form and modelled with contrasting warm and cool tones.

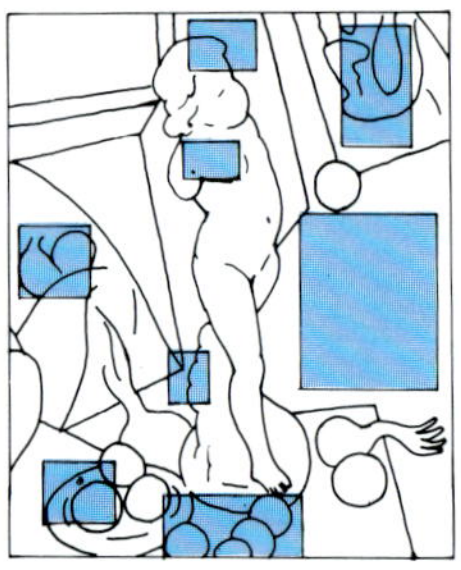

**5.** The ground was often left uncovered and used to define highlights.
The painting was not varnished.

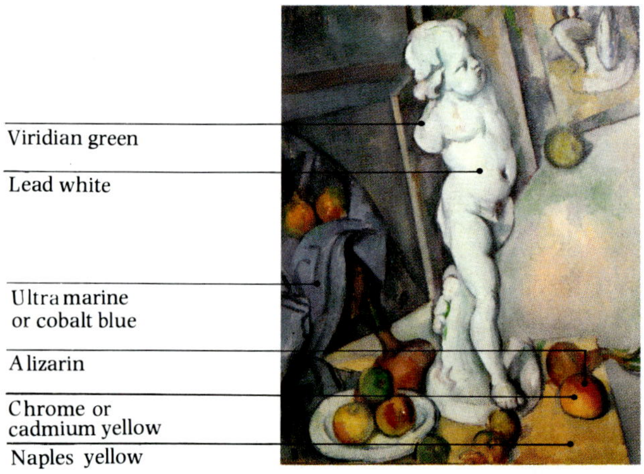

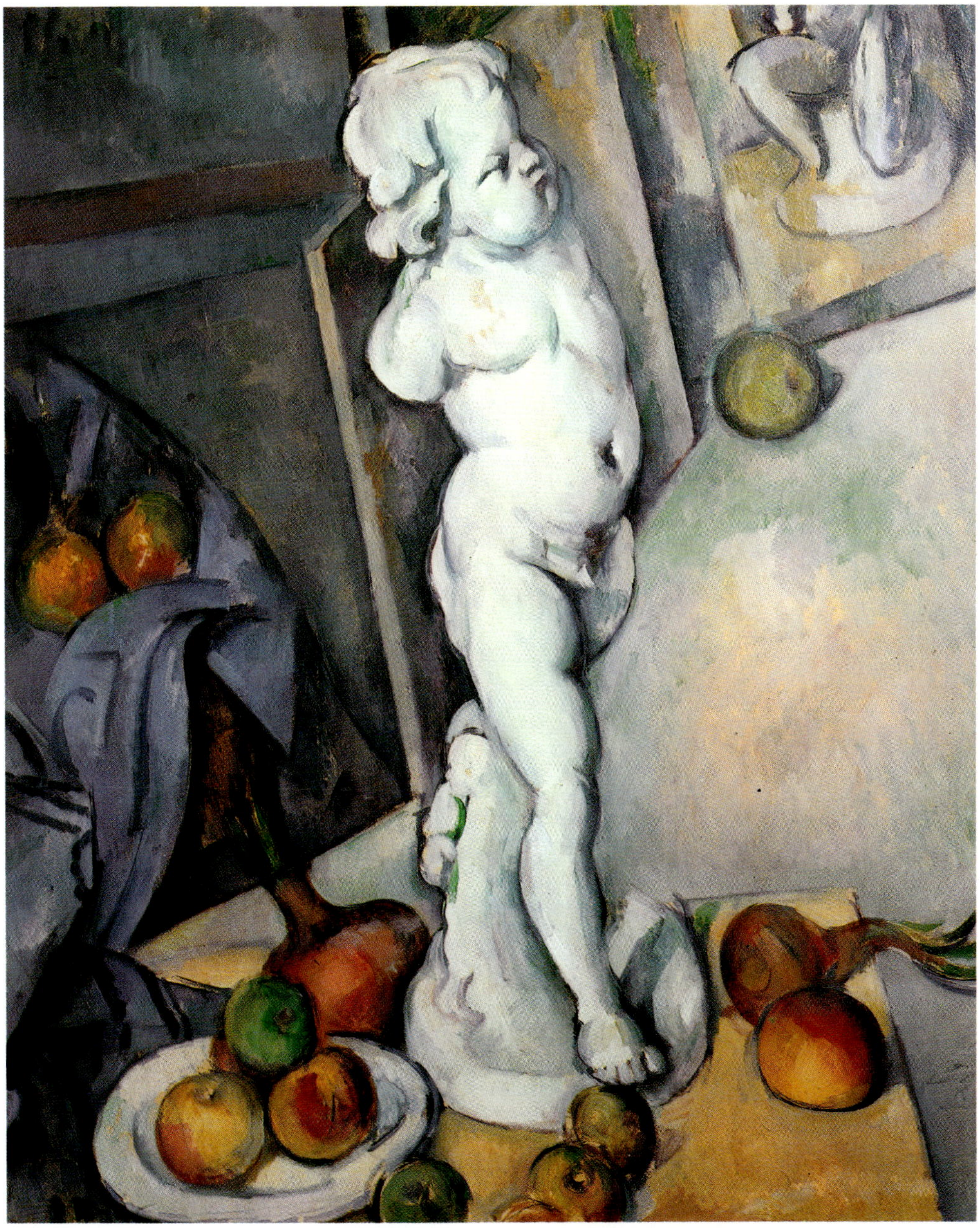

*The high viewpoint and enlarged proportions of the cupid suggest this work was done with the subject very close to the painter. The paint layer is remarkably thin with the cream ground showing through in a number of places. The basic outlines were drawn in a fluid blue paint. The painting was begun before the outline was dry, as witnessed in the blue dragged into adjacent colors. The painting is not heavily worked and has an immediacy and surety which often eluded Cézanne. The palette is simple and included ultramarine or cobalt blue, emerald and viridian greens and vermilion. Naples and chrome yellows, lead white and alizarin crimson. Cézanne has used many sophisticated techniques to create this spatially complex picture. The left wall is lined with pictures placed to direct the viewer's eye into the pictorial space. The placing in the background of an apple which is the same size as those in the foreground has the effect of halting the recession and flattening the surface. These two effects vie for the viewer's attention, and the tilting plane of the floor changes to accommodate both. The painted still life in the canvas on the left is both separate from the 'real' still life and indistinguishable from it. The onion on the table has shoots which extend into the painted still life, while the apples and blue fabric on the table reappear, with no apparent disjunction, in the painted still life.*

*This detail shows the growth of the onion on the table 'into' the painted still life of the canvas to the left. Although the shoots belong to this onion they also merge with the picture; a line describing the lower edge of this canvas disconcertingly cuts the onion shoot just as it changes to green, compounding the ambiguity of the illusion which plays on our notion of 'real' and 'painted' realities. The bottom of the statue is here separated from the similarly pale hues of the floor by strong dark outlines.*

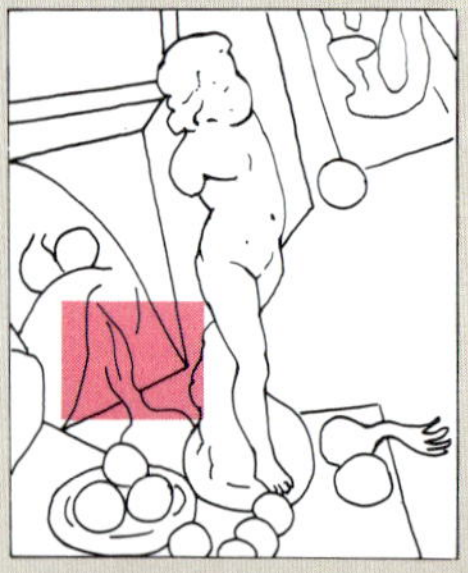

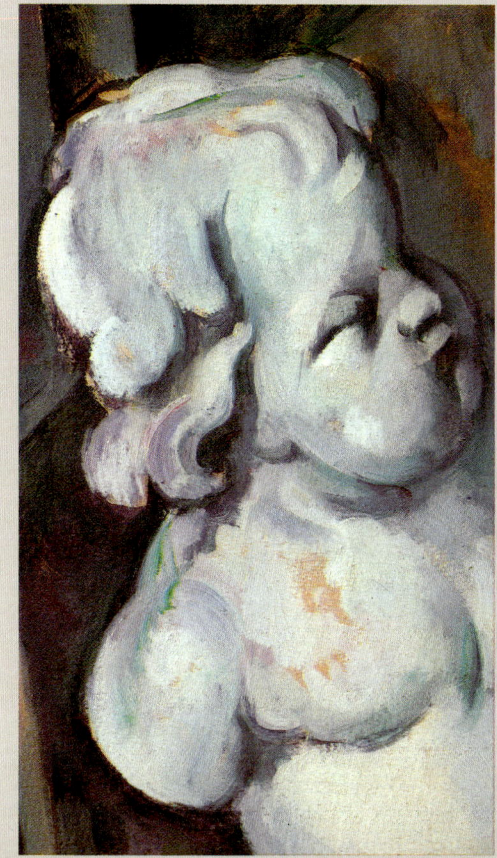

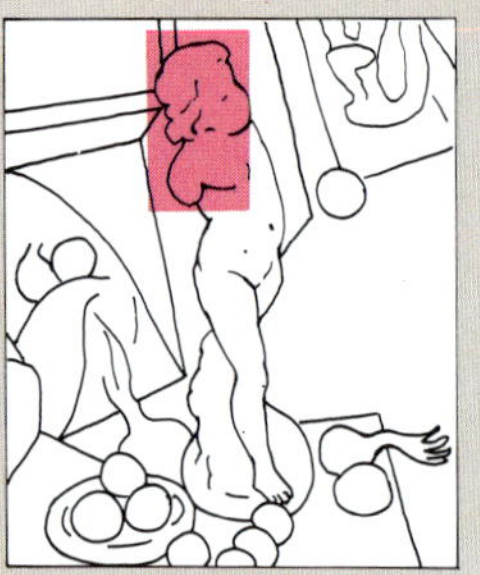

*The plaster cupid, which survives today in Cézanne's studio in Aix, is in reality much smaller than it appears in this painting; its actual height is 18 in (46 cm), while the painted cupid measures 24 in (61 cm). Cézanne's deft handling of the opaque, subtly colored grays sculpts the form in broad hog's hair brushstrokes which follow and describe features such as the hair. Shadows are mainly attenuated with diffused light, but, where deep, are treated simply and opaquely. Delicate, separate but blended patches of color build up close-toned hues on the chest, which appear cool against the exposed cream ground.*

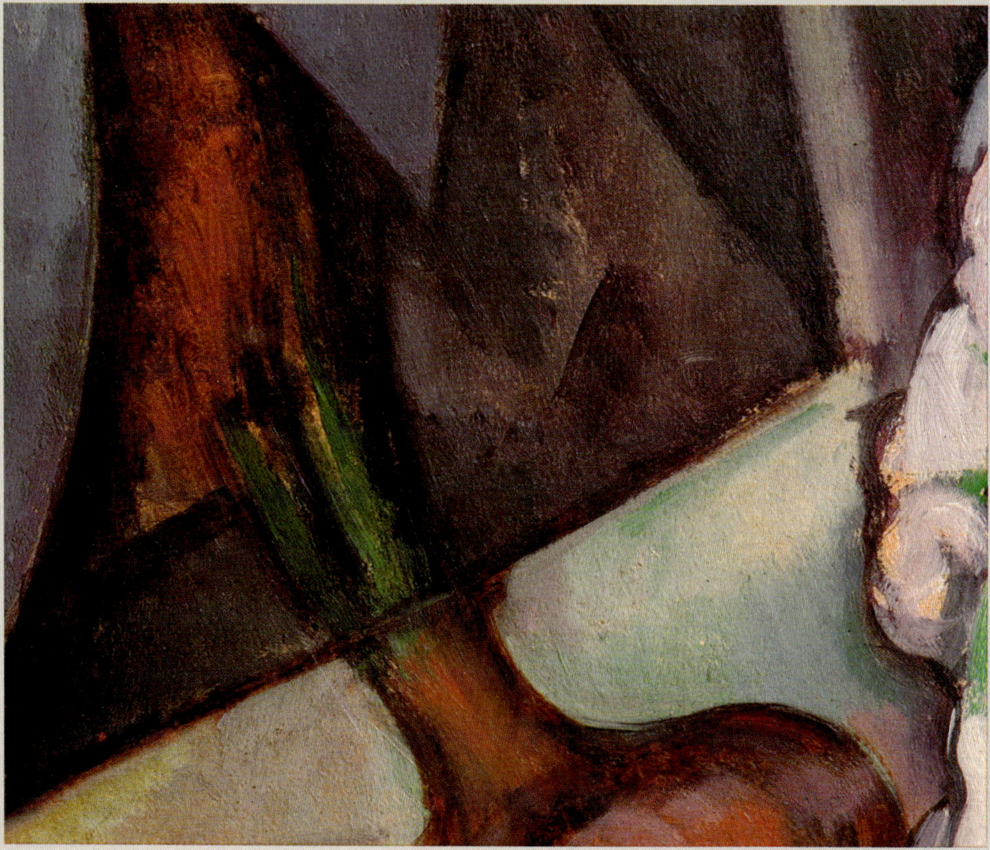

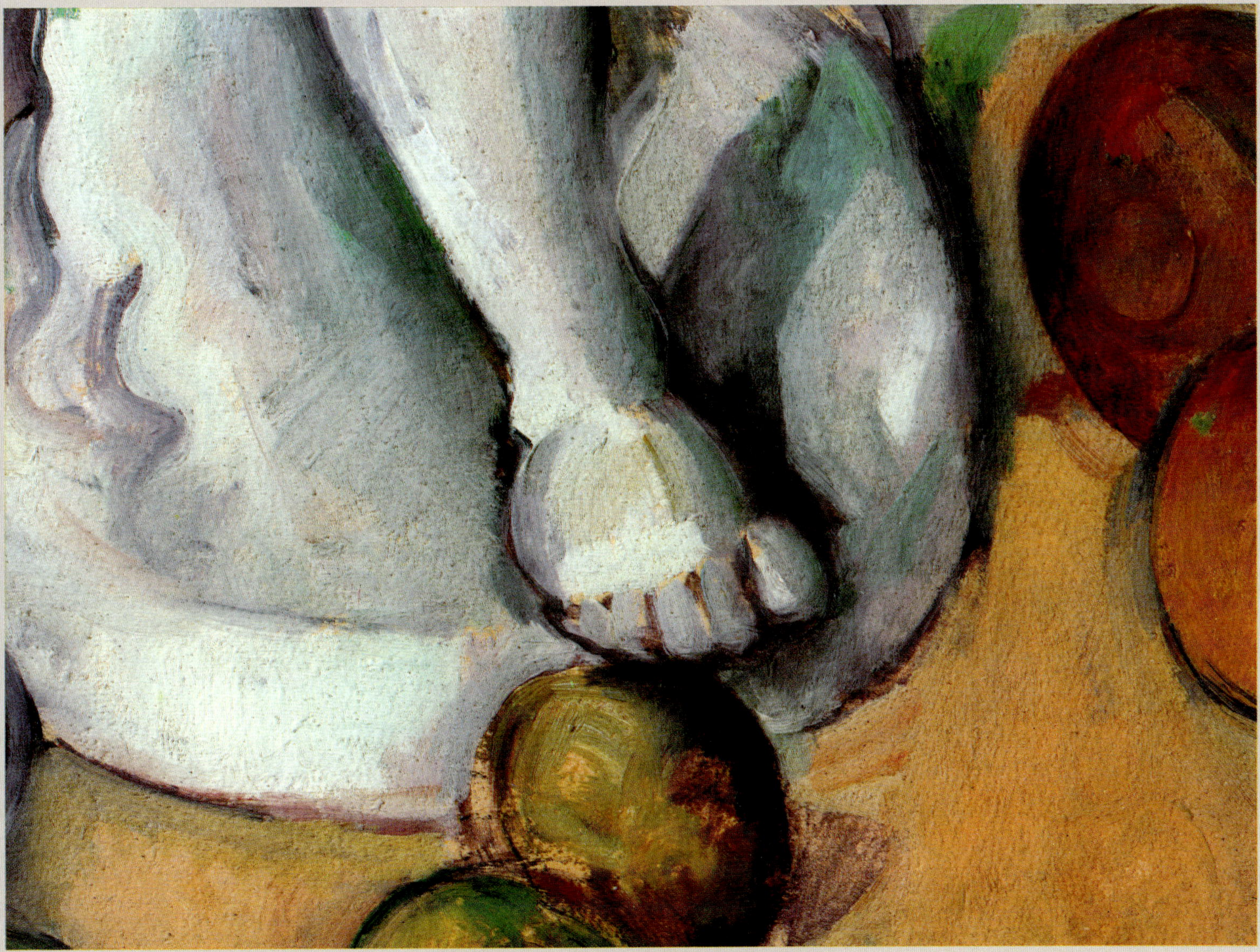

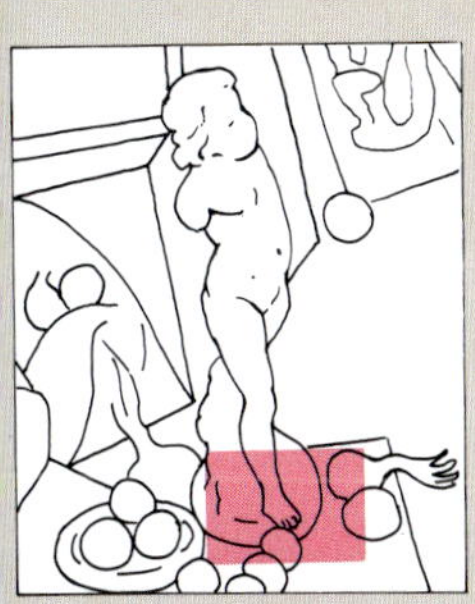

*Cézanne was known to work with meticulous care. The brushwork and fluid color in the apples is particularly interesting and reminiscent of Cézanne's watercolors.*

**Actual size detail**
*This detail reveals how Cézanne used both color contrasts and a variety of brushstrokes to describe objects in space. This gives his work an overall solidarity and monumentality. Although the painting appears to have been executed quickly and with confidence.*

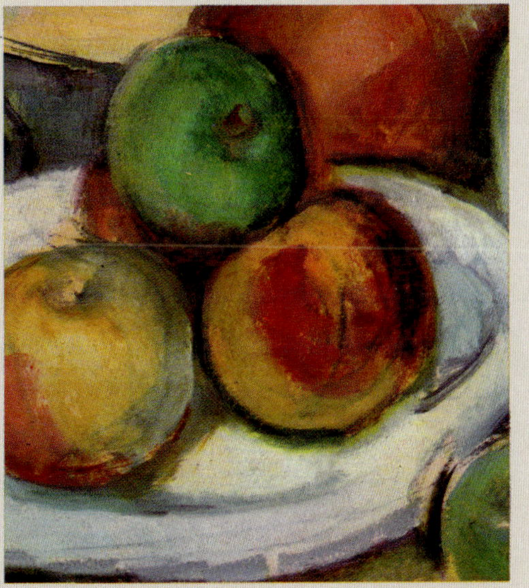

*Cézanne's characteristically reiterated contours are visible here, especially in the apple to the right of the plate, where exposed ground and fine graphite lines can also be seen. The irregular oval of the plate shows that Cézanne preferred to respond to visual sensation rather than simply depicting objectively the actual shapes of everyday objects. A red lake glaze on the righthand red apple has darkened and coagulated with age.*

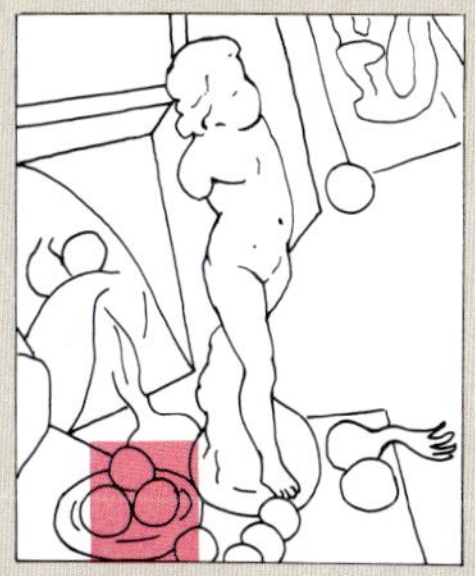

# PAUL GAUGUIN

*Christmas Night or The Blessing of the Oxen* (c. 1896)
Oil on canvas, 72cm × 83cm/28¼in × 32¾in

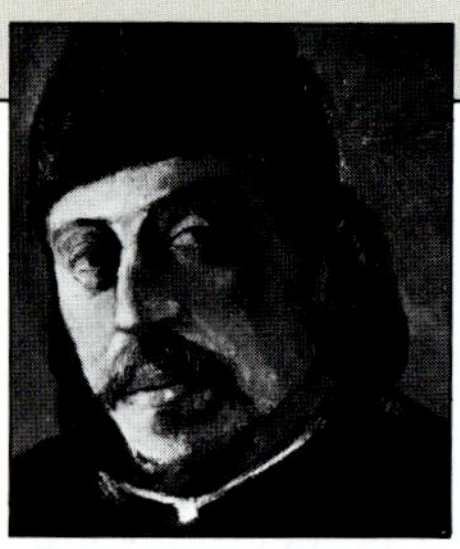

Gauguin began painting in 1873 while still working in the Paris Stock Exchange and only began as a professional when he lost his post there in the slump of 1883. His childhood in Peru and subsequent travels in the Navy gave him a taste for the exotic and primitive cultures; after visiting Martinique, from 1890 he lived mostly in the South Seas. Highly eclectic, Gauguin's sources of inspiration ranged from the art of Degas, Manet, Cézanne, and Pissarro to the Buddhist art of Java, Japanese art, and Oceanic mythology. The French mural painter Puvis de Chavannes, with his simplified, majestic treatment of the human form and flat planes of color, was another strong influence in Gauguin's painting style.

In the late 1880s, with other artists in Brittany, Gauguin evolved his personal symbolist style which involved a simplification and exaggeration of form, line, and color to express anti-naturalistic spirituality. Gauguin was also experimenting with other media like woodcarving and ceramics, and these influenced his painting. These and his work with lithography encouraged a use of simple, strong contours and flat planes of color.

Gauguin often used unprimed, heavy sackcloth-like fabrics, exploiting both their ability to produce dull, matt surfaces and their texture, which he allowed to read through a thin but opaque paint layer. When he used primed canvas, the layer was thin and pale. Gauguin also felt that the use of absorbent grounds was important as these gave a sunken and dull appearance to the paint which was similar to unprimed cloth.

Although Gauguin's paint was chiefly brushed on – sometimes as stiff color and sometimes as scumbles – on some occasions he used a palette knife. He also added wax to his paint to stiffen and make it more matt. The commercial addition of wax to artists' colors was common at this time, to stabilize the paint and reduce the amount of pigment required. During the 1880s, Gauguin bought minimally hand-ground colors. These had a granular texture very different from the smooth quality of machine-made pigments.

His palette included the cadmium and chrome yellows, yellow ochre, viridian and emerald greens, ultramarine and cobalt blues, cobalt violet, red lakes, vermilion and white.

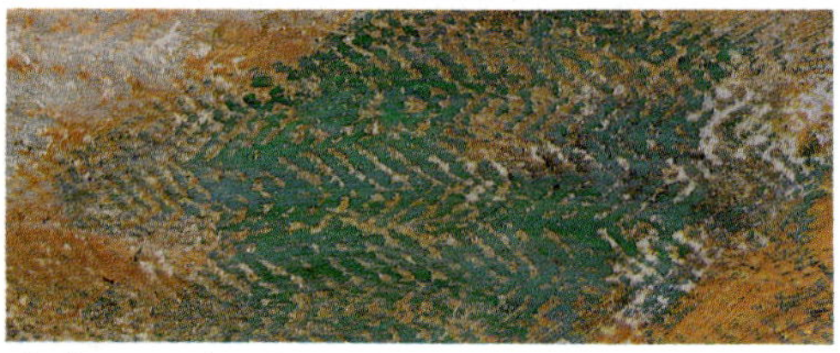

**1.** A strong, herring-bone twill canvas was used which plays an important role in the painting.

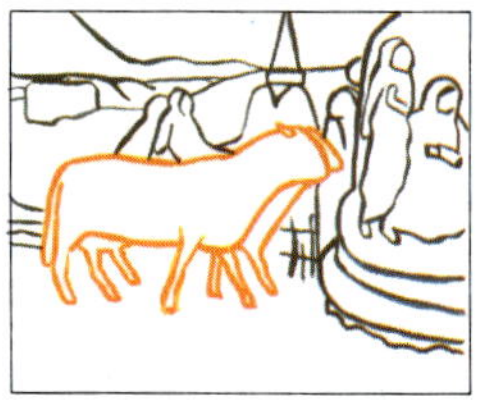

**2.** The contours were outlined directly on the primed canvas in vermilion and dark ultramarine or Prussian blue paint.

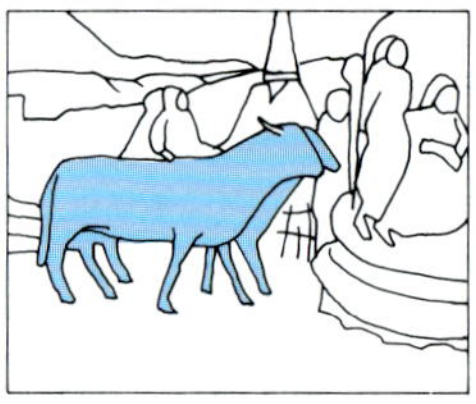

**3.** The modelling was built up in flat areas of contrasts with outlines and contours reinforced. Within the broad color areas the tones were unified with blues.

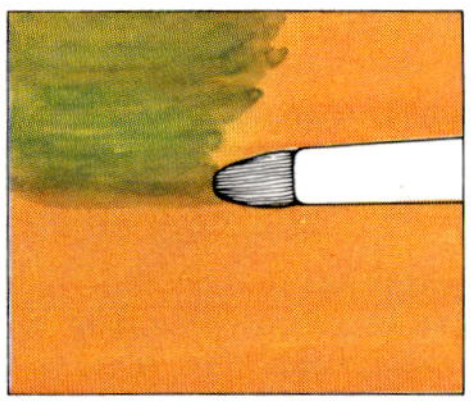

**4.** The color was applied wet over dry to exploit the texture of the canvas by dragging layers of opaque color over one another and allowing previous colors to show through.

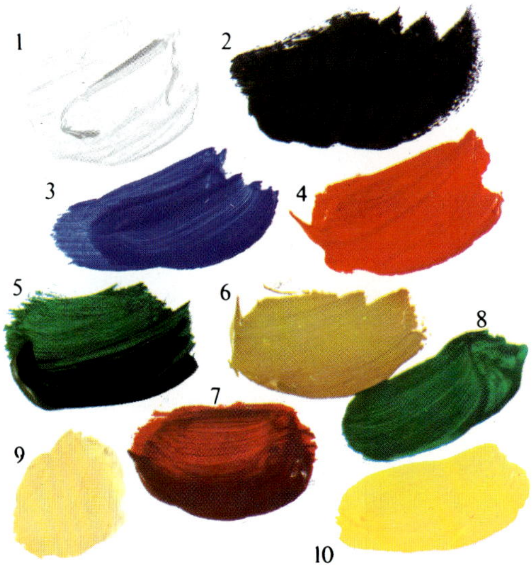


Gauguin's palette for this work included: white, possibly zinc white (**1**), Prussian blue (**2**), ultramarine or cobalt blue (**3**), vermilion (**4**), viridian green (**5**), yellow ochre (**6**), alizarin red (**7**), mixed greens, or emerald or cobalt green (**8**), Naples yellow (**9**), and perhaps cadmium yellow (**10**).

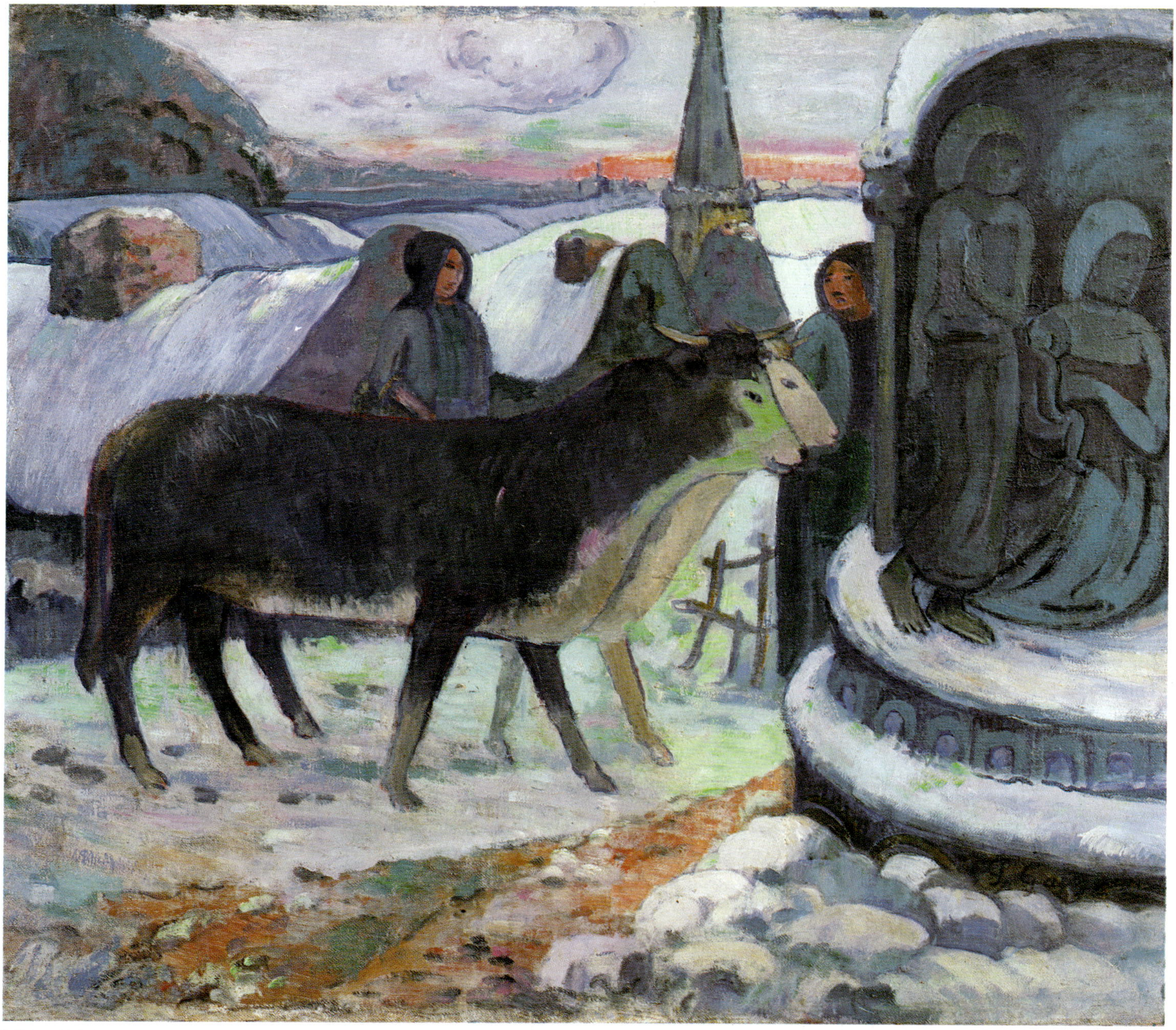

*Both the unusual shape and fabric of this canvas suggest that the picture was done in the South Seas rather than Brittany. A thin ground has left the canvas weave in evidence, and Gauguin has used this by applying a thin paint layer and dragging stiffish paint across the textured surface. The subject was apparently sketched in without preliminaries in muted vermilion and dark, probably Prussian, blue. Both lights and shades are flat and opaque; no glazing and little scumbling are apparent. The handling of the paint is lively and varied with subtly modulated overlays of color, with wet over dry predominating. The brushwork is texturally evocative with the figures sculpted with color and brushstrokes.*

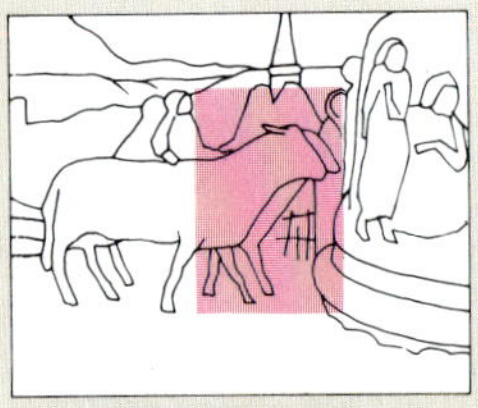

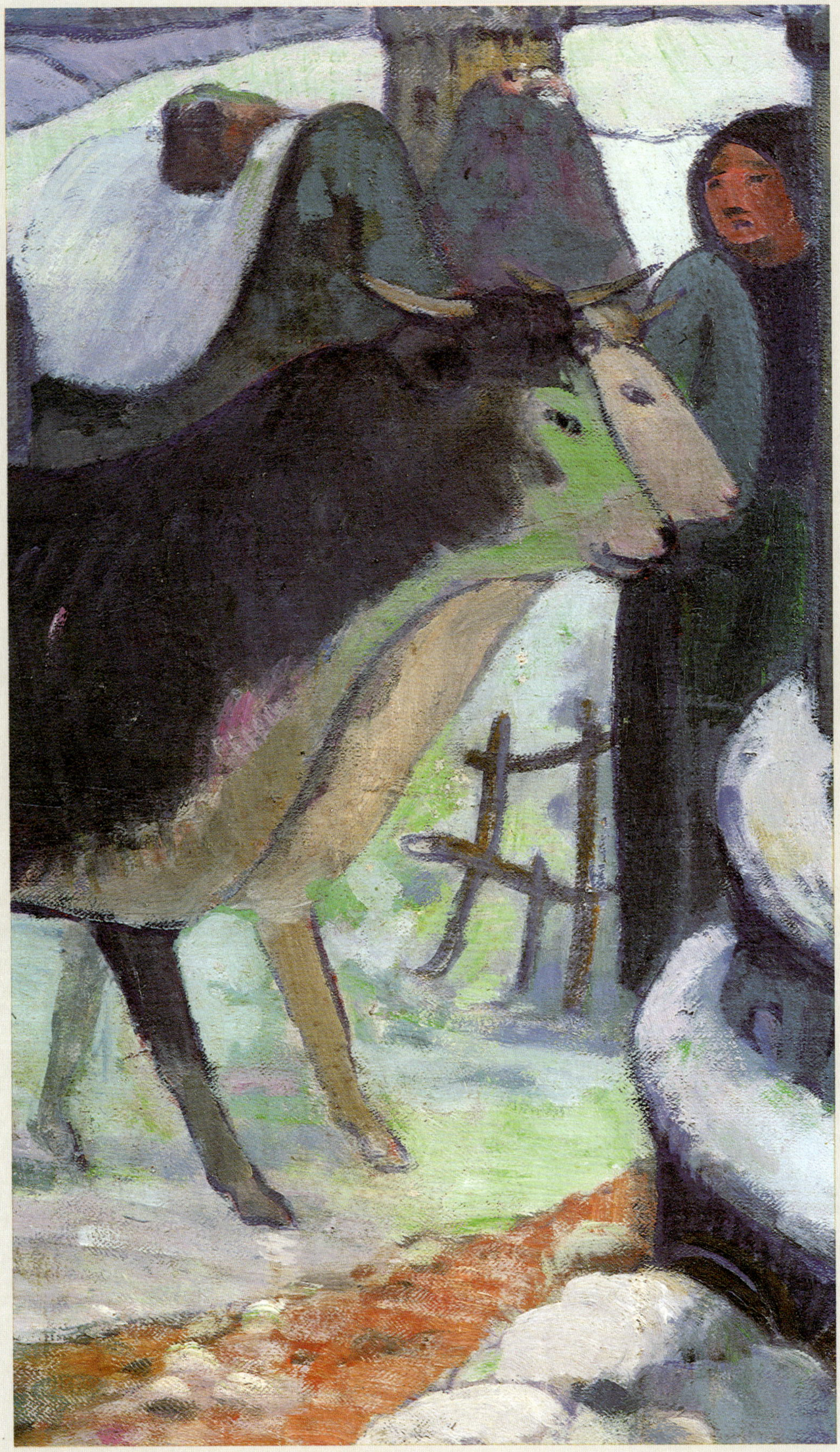

*The dark outlines of the oxen's heads have been filled in, and partially overlapped, with the wet-in-wet colors representing their faces. On both muzzles, a hint of vermilion appears among the blue lines. The pale snowy background was worked in around the figures, obscuring one horn and obliterating the outline at the near ox's chin. Where the paint is thinnest, the tapestry-like canvas texture broke the movement of the brush, producing decorative irregularities and stressing the two-dimensionality of the picture surface. The faces were treated as flat stylized types, the clothes as simple shapes of little modulated color. The original and reinforcing contours outlining the oxen remain discernible, and the snowy ground was clearly filled in around them. The unifying blues in the picture are enhanced by contrasting areas of pale pinks and greens — alizarin crimson, vermilion and viridian green, each mixed with a generous amount of zinc white.*

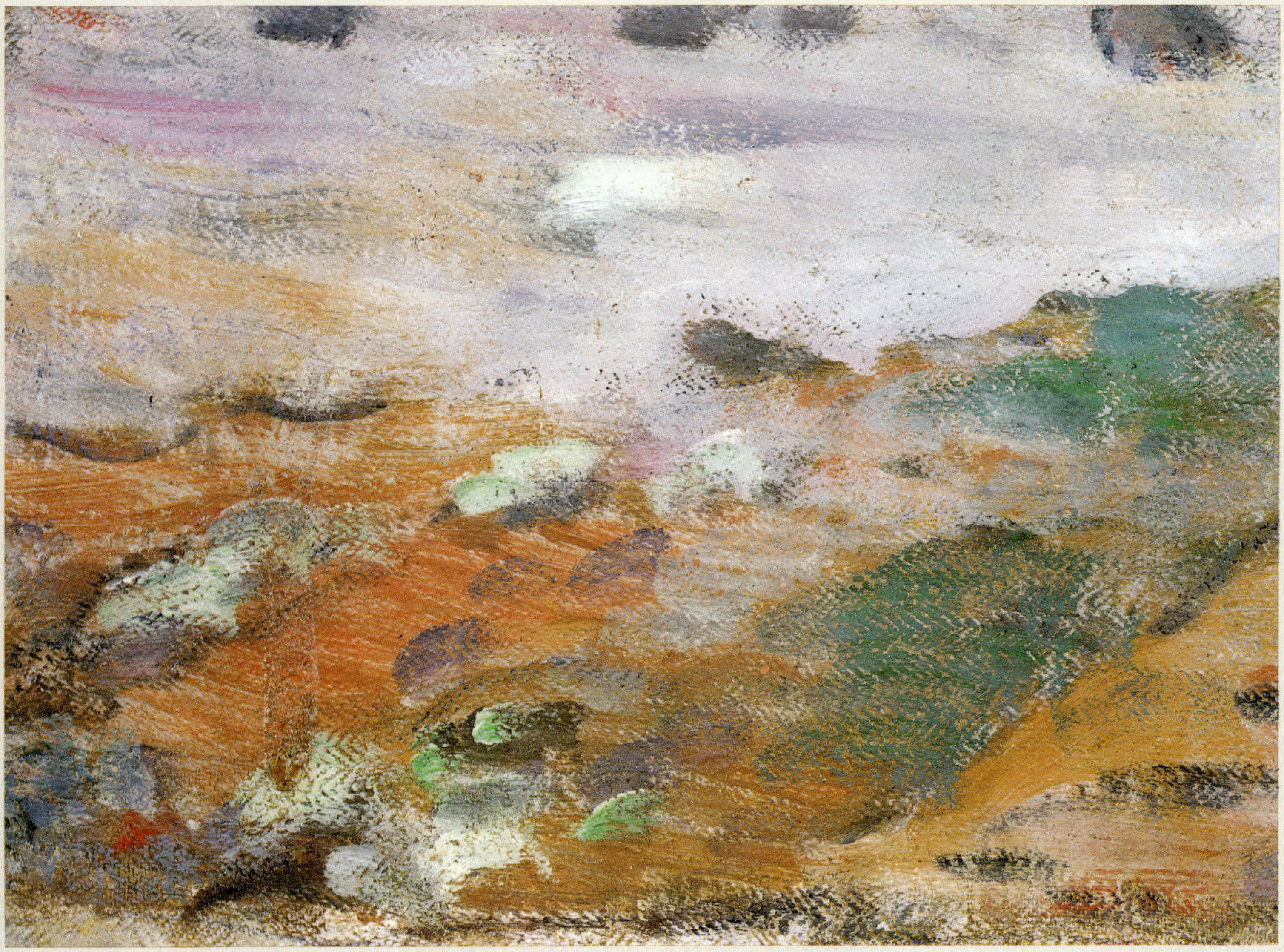

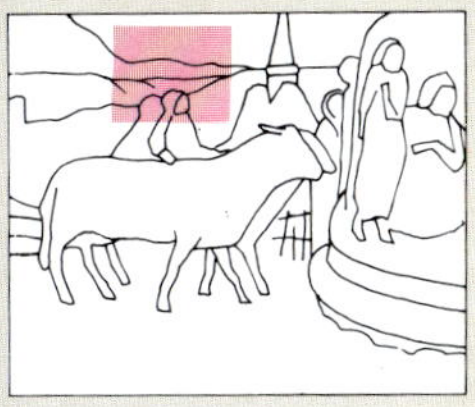

*Blue and green are streaked wet-in-wet to depict the snow-covered roofs, and the skyline softens in blurred hazy deeper blues. Alizarin crimson, vermilion and green worked with white indicate the sky colored by the sunset. The clouds are decoratively outlined in pale blue.*

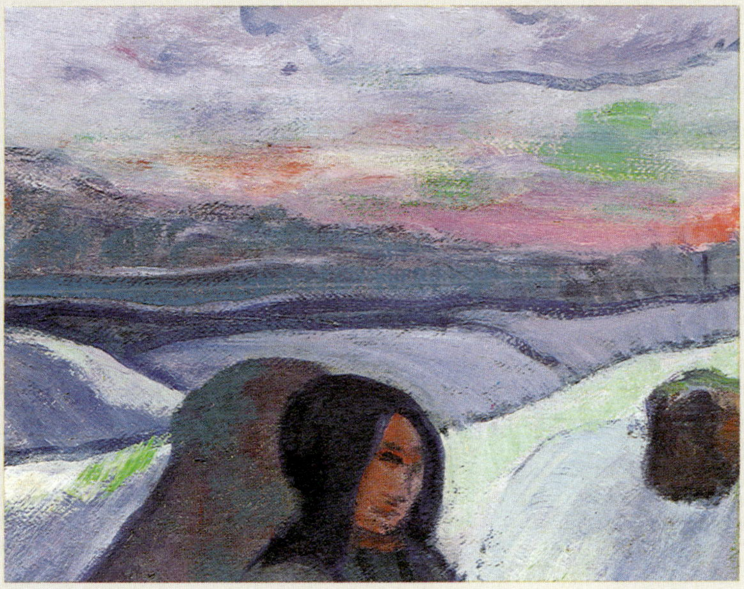

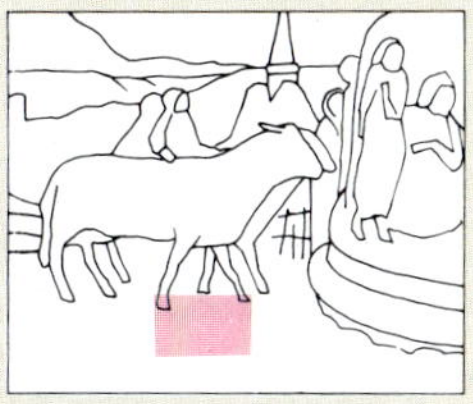

**Actual size detail**
*In this detail, the herringbone texture of the canvas is apparent and exploited by the thin paint layer and dabs of stiffish paint which catch on the irregular surface. Along the bottom edge, the ground appears as a warm gray or dirty white which suits the dull winter atmosphere. There is a delicate overlaying of paint in the path with some wet-in-wet work seen in the blue-whites of the snow, which overlaps the dry ochers and greens. The paint layer is flat and opaque, with individual, brush-shaped marks of whitened viridian, blue, vermilion and orange adding texture to the rocky foreground.*

# PAUL GAUGUIN

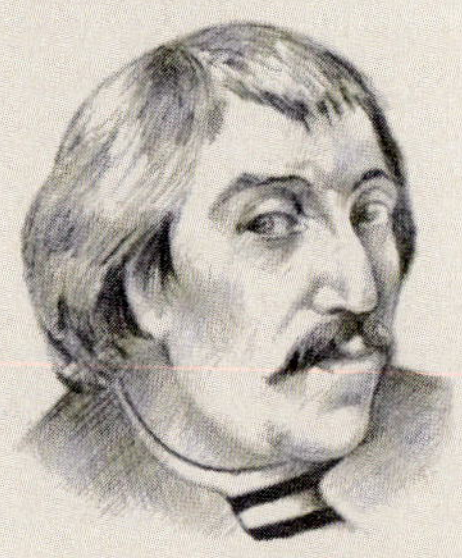

*Te Reroia* (1897)
Oil on unprimed hessian
95cm × 130cm/37½in × 51¼in

Gauguin lived in Tahiti for two periods from 1891 to 1893, and 1895 to 1901, so *Te Reroia* was executed around the middle of his second stay. Although born in Paris, much of Gauguin's early life, from 1849–1855, had been spent in Peru, and, later, traveling extensively first as a merchant seaman and then with the navy between 1865 and 1871. His early travels gave him both a taste for the exotic, and a restlessness which he never overcame. During the 1870s he worked on the Paris stock exchange, losing his job during the financial slump of 1883.

He had taken up painting as an amateur in 1873, but by 1879 was already exhibiting with the Impressionist group, albeit against the wishes of some of the members. Through his guardian Gustave Arosa, Gauguin met the Impressionists, and from 1879 he occasionally painted with Pissarro, whose style and approach had a marked influence on his early development. Gauguin also worked with Cézanne in 1881, but his enthusiasm for discovering what he thought to be Cézanne's 'secret' method made Cézanne both angry and resentful. Despite Gauguin's consistent argument that the younger generation of Symbolist painters were all dependent on his totally innovatory style, he himself was highly eclectic, using sources as widely disparate as Far Eastern Buddhist and Asiatic art, the Greek Parthenon frieze and Manet's *Olympia* (1863). He had photographs from these and other sources with him in Tahiti, and wrote of them that 'when marbles or wood engravings draw a head for you, it is so tempting to steal it.' Gauguin clearly had the feeling that such borrowings were in some way wrong, making his art less original or casting doubt on his own creative abilities. However, such practice was common, and all his borrowings were transformed in his work, resulting in a completely personal style.

Gauguin's rejection of decadent Western society, and turning to what he considered the more genuine, naive simplicity of life in the South Seas, was symptomatic of a broader cultural disillusionment in Europe at that time. The Symbolist movement in art and literature can in general be seen as a reaction against the ills of the industrial society, which artists saw growing up around them, and an urge for a more introspective, contemplative ideal. Neither Gauguin himself, who was a sophisticated European intellectual, nor his art, can be considered primitive as such. Yet, by choosing to live among so-called primitive peoples, and by embuing his art with emblems and meaning derived from various non-European and non-Christian sources, Gauguin sought to express his belief in the importance of natural innocence and simplicity. With pessimistic horror he watched Western civilization spread, relentlessly imposing its own ideas and destroying original civilizations wherever it went. The primitive life that Gauguin hoped to find in Tahiti, and had read about in idealized guidebooks before he left, had long disappeared from the French colony by the time he arrived there. Gauguin's understanding of Polynesian culture and rituals came from historical textbooks taken out with him, because Christian missionaries had already destroyed the indigenous culture. The reflective melancholy of Gauguin's art represents both his own mood, and a pessimistic view of the times in which he lived.

Early in Gauguin's career, the critic Félix Fénéon, reviewing the last Impressionist exhibition in 1886, had remarked upon the 'dull harmony' of his paintings, which resulted from the muted close tones of his colors. The unnatural, almost dream-like quality produced by his colors, is apparent in *Te Reroia*, painted 11 years later in Tahiti. They give to the painting the quality suggested by the title, which means 'Daydreaming'. On 12 March 1897, Gauguin wrote to his friend Daniel de Monfried about this painting, saying 'Everything about this picture is dreamlike: is it the dream of the child, the mother, the horseman on the track, or, better still, is it the painter's dream?' Unlike the Impressionists, Gauguin did not seek to represent the surface appearance of things in his painting. Instead, like the French Symbolist poet Stéphane Mallarmé, Gauguin sought the essence of reality in his art, the individual's experience of the object, rather than its external characteristics. Gauguin's painting was anti-naturalistic because he tried to depict his conception of the world, not simply his perception of it.

Gauguin's technique was often dictated in part by external factors. He was frequently short of money, and had to use whatever materials came cheaply to hand. His paint surfaces – often deliberately meager – were sometimes thin because he had inadequate supplies of paint. He had already begun to experiment with rough, coarse canvases, which could express a rugged primitive or ethnic quality, with van Gogh in 1888. However, in Tahiti, his use of hessian fabric was sometimes the result of financial hardship. The unprimed sacking support in *Te Reroia* adds to the so-called barbaric qualities Gauguin admired, its hairy surface is distinctly visible among the delicate colors of the paint layer.

Gauguin reacted against what he considered to be the self-conscious virtuosity of Impressionist handling, preferring to apply his colors with little gestural inflection, in broad areas of subtly modulated hues. He often added wax to his paints, to increase their matness and the smoothness of his surfaces. It would have been easier to handle wax-filled colors in the warm Tahitian climate, where they would remain malleable, whereas they would become too stiff to paint with in the colder environment of

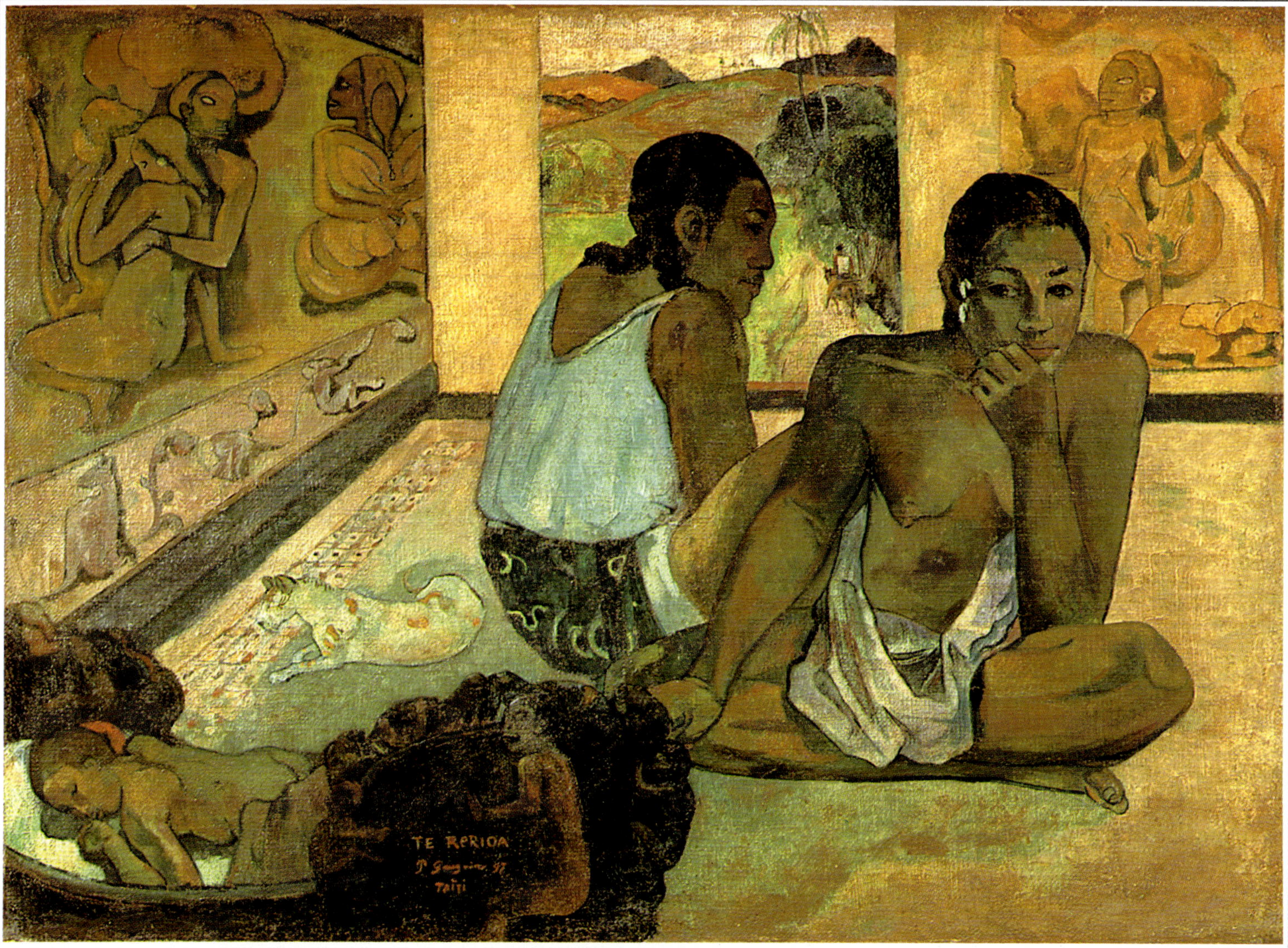


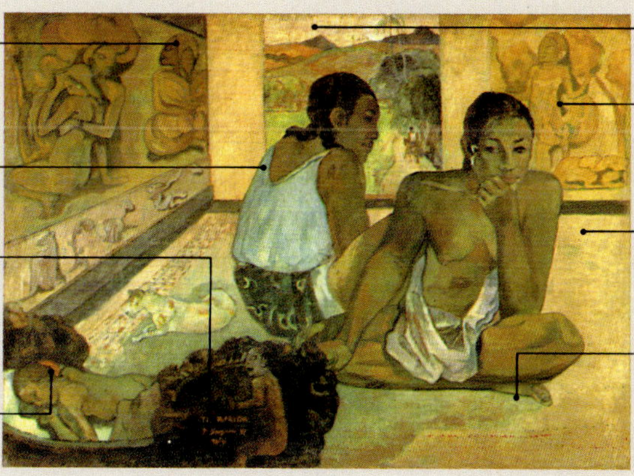


*This work, executed by Gauguin in Tahiti in March 1897 six years before his death, has a brooding melancholy which is evident both in the muted, broken colors and the strange, unreal light. The external world through the door appears as a picture on the wall, distinguished by its brighter hues. The figures are treated as simplified, statuesque forms, the one to the fore especially Buddha-like in both pose and enigmatic gaze. The dark sinister symbolism of the murals and the carvings on the cot evoke the dream world suggested in the title.*

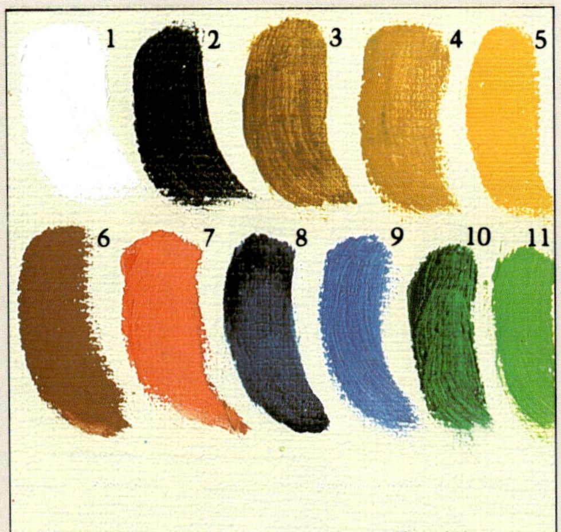


*Gauguin's palette probably comprised lead white (1), black (2), sienna (3), yellow ochre (4), cadmium yellows (5), red earth (6), vermilion (7), Prussian blue (8), viridian (10) and chrome (11) greens. Cobalt blue (9) may also have been used.*

northern Europe. The paint is thinnest at the contours, where dark Prussian blue or dark earth red was used to outline the initial compositional structure. These lines were in places reworked and reinforced later, after the forms had been built up. Thus it is at the contours too that the rough canvas shows through most strongly, although it gives a tapestry-like effect to the entire picture.

Parts of the background, such as the right half of the floor, were applied first with a palette knife, giving a surface flatness, then overworked in thin translucent color with a brush. The somber tones of the interior contrast with the view through the door, executed in more brilliant hues which enhance the dream-like atmosphere of the room.

Gauguin's final years were spent on the Marquesas Islands in the Pacific. Although his work was greatly admired by fellow artists during his lifetime, it was only after his death that he finally achieved the widespread fame he had coveted so strongly.

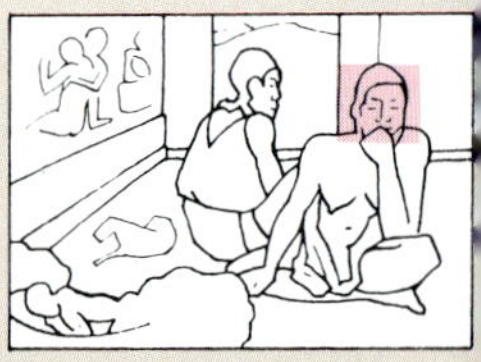

Actual size detail
*The monumental simplicity of Gauguin's handling of this head belies the sophistication required to achieve it. Forms are reduced to smooth planes of subtly modulated hues, which give the appearance of sculpture. The greenish-bronze cast to the flesh tints reinforces this association. Echoing the other head, this one is also placed against a pale background, the yellow ochre tints being picked up and repeated as accents suggesting light on nose and brow. The flesh areas tend to be the most loaded parts, but still the rough weave of the hessian support remains visible. It was unprimed, and the resulting absorbency of the fabric has dulled the oil colors. The addition of wax to the colors may have increased this effect, which has definitely been enhanced by the dark color of the raw fabric. Fibrous hairs which protrude from this hemp cloth have been 'glued' flat by the paint. No identifiable light source illumines the figure, instead, an eery luminosity seems to come from within.*

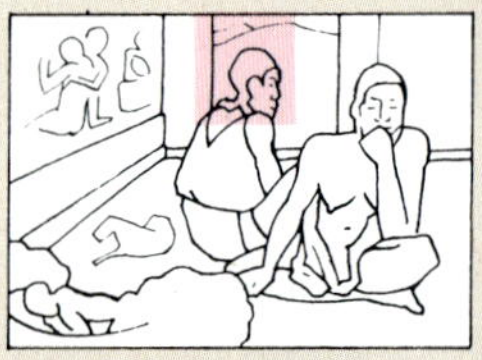

*The unlit head of the woman in profile is starkly silhouetted against the pale acid hues of the landscape beyond. These sharp greens pick up the green cast of the flesh hues, accentuating them rather than making them warmer by contrast. The artist plays on the air of unreality in the work by avoiding any clear link between the interior and exterior scenes. The thin walls of the hut have no bulk, giving no hint of perspective to the door jambs. No compositional devices link the floor to the distant pathway, and so there is no coherent middle distance connecting foreground to background. This emphasizes the introspective nature of the subject. The more richly loaded paint on the head helps detach it from the background, which is broader and thinner in its color application.*

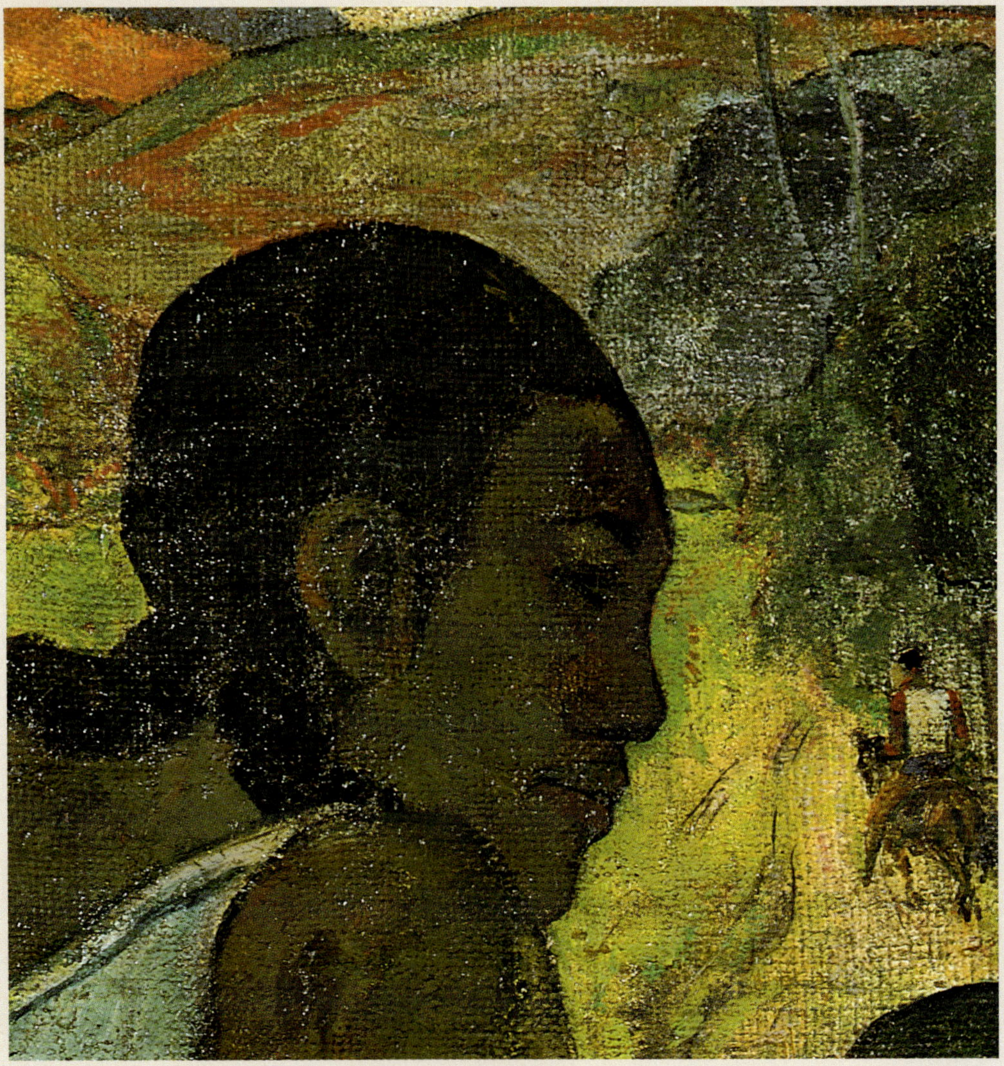

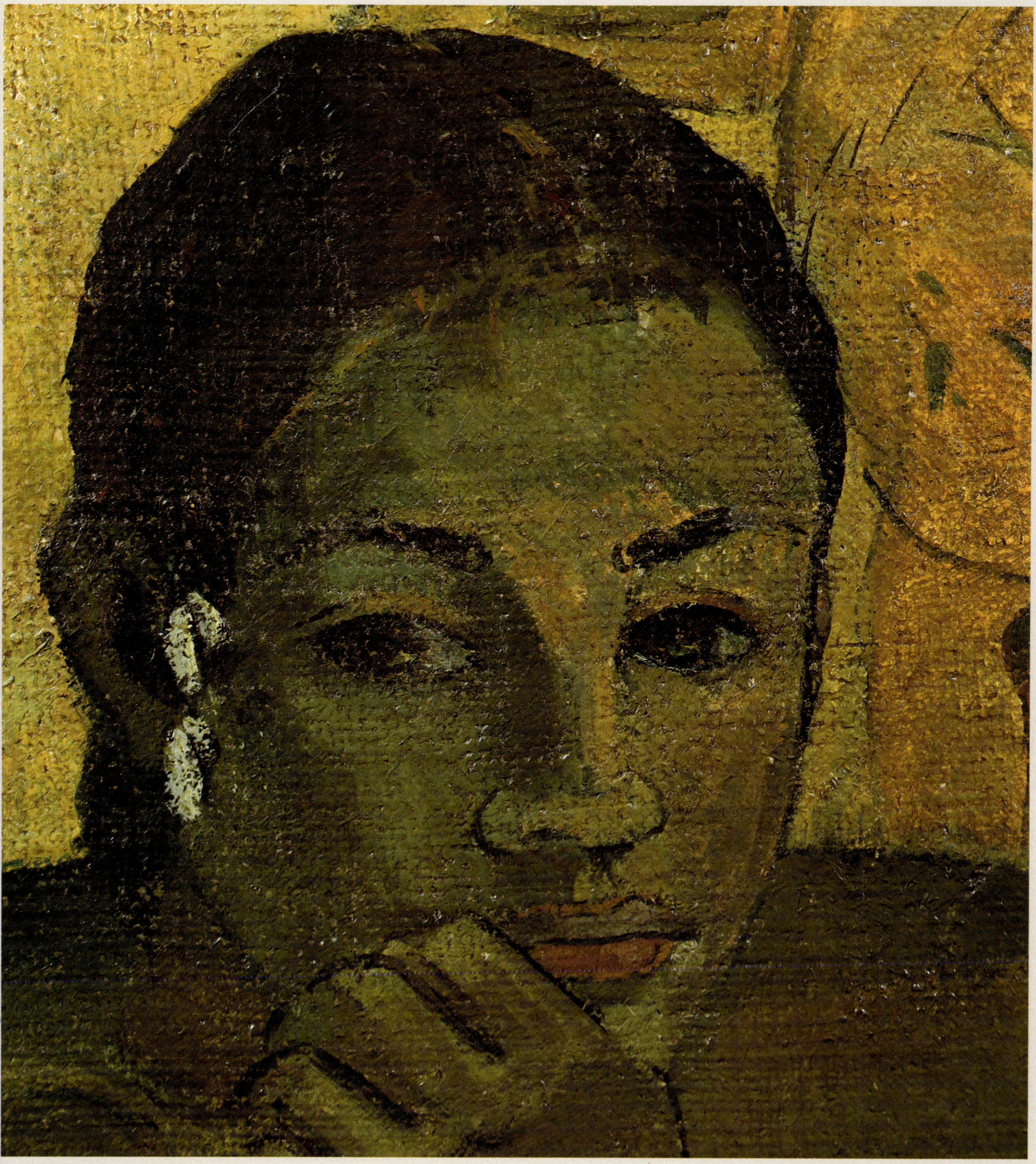

# HENRI DE TOULOUSE-LAUTREC

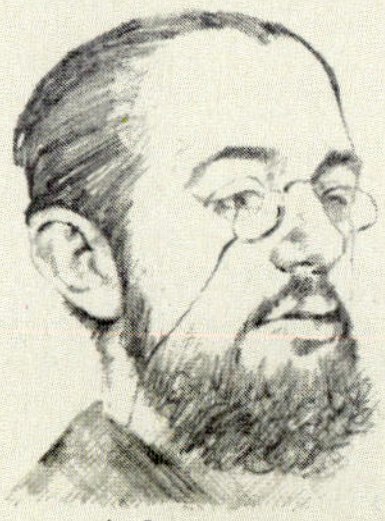

## *The Tête-à-tête Supper/En Cabinet particulier* (1899)'
Oil on pale primed canvas
55cm × 45cm/21½in × 17¾in

In 1884, Toulouse-Lautrec moved into a studio in Montmartre, which formed his base for the following 13 years. Lautrec found his main subjects in Montmartre with its popular, fashionable nightlife. He had trained in the studio of Léon Bonnat (1834–1922), from 1882, then in the studio of Frédéric Cormon (1845–1924), where in 1886 he met van Gogh, and also the artist Louis Anquetin (1861–1932). Although Lautrec had met the singer and café proprietor Aristide Bruant in 1885, the artist's meeting with Anquetin introduced him to the latter's brilliant circle which frequented Bruant's café-cabaret Le Mirliton in Montmartre. From this time, Lautrec regularly worked in Montmartre's cafés, sketching its characters and entertainers from life. He also painted courtesans and prostitutes. Indeed, the central figure in *Tête-à-tête Supper* was the famous *demi-mondaine* Lucy Jourdan, eating in a private cubicle at the then famous restaurant, the Rat Mort, in the rue Pigalle.

Lautrec's earliest painting style was derived from the Impressionists, more especially the hatched brushwork used by Pissarro in the late 1870s and early 1880s. Lautrec exploited the decorative, surface effect created by this type of patterned brushwork. This mid 1880s to 1890 handling was later replaced by a freer, more open technique, where fluid, graphic contours outlined blocks of more uniform color, applied with rapid, bold sweeps of the brush. He often varied his touch – dots, short lines and zigzag strokes – to create a decorative equivalent for different surface textures, in a manner similar to, but less naturalistic than, that found in van Gogh's pen drawings.

Lautrec was greatly influenced by the techniques, style and subject matter of Degas, who was a close neighbor between 1887 and 1891. Lautrec's art, however, has a more immediately accessible feel to it than Degas' more intellectual style. Like Degas, Lautrec experimented with painting with turpentine which was called *peinture à l'essence*. In Degas' method, oil was drawn out of his colors by placing them on blotting paper. Then the chalky paint was diluted with turpentine and applied like a wash to his support. Because the turpentine spirit evaporated quickly, the colors dried rapidly, so that the paint surface could be reworked and built up without enormous delays. Unlike paint applied thinly in glazes, with this technique the color dries mat, and has a chalky surface only thinly and sparely colored. Similarly, as in Degas' *Portrait of Hélène Rouart* (1886), Lautrec preferred dull muted ground colors, and a palette of broken rather than pure bright hues. These colors suited the indoor nightlighting that he, like Degas, so frequently depicted. Lautrec also experimented with the dulling, absorbent effects of unprimed canvas, and with using unconventional supports like brown cardboard.

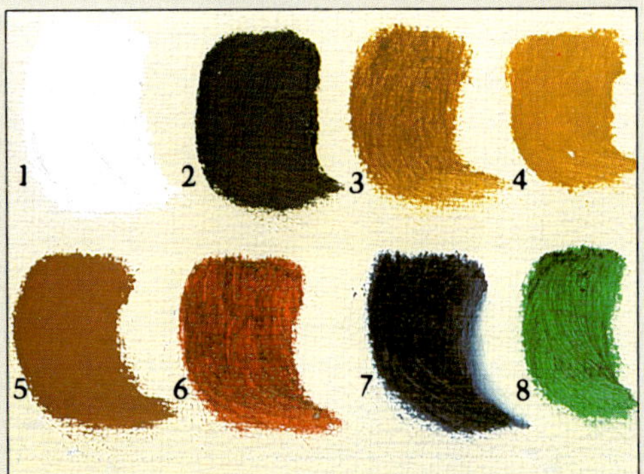


*The palette for this work probably consisted of lead white (1), black (2), yellow ochre (4), red earth (5), Prussian blue (7) and viridian green (8). Sienna (3) and red alizarin lake (6) may also have been used.*

*Tête-à-tête Supper* was a late painting, executed on a primed, squarish, standard format canvas. Although the paint layer is thin, it is all-covering and this makes it hard to identify the ground color accurately. It is undoubtedly pale, because its luminosity lights up the dark translucent colors laid on top. It may be a pale putty or oatmeal color. The canvas is fine in weave, relatively smooth in texture, and suited to Lautrec's fluid application of color. The light in the picture is theatrical, and does not conform to a specific source of lighting, but is arranged arbitrarily to shine from below onto the central figure's face, exaggerating and caricaturing her features. Like the graphic art of the painter and caricaturist Honoré Daumier (1808–1879), Lautrec's drawing summarizes the essential features of his subjects, adding only as much detail as is needed to capture the important elements of personality and environment. This facility with caricature is an important feature of his style, which was also necessary in his lithographic work. In the posters, which he began to produce in 1890, visual simplicity and direct impact were demanded both by the technique and by the commercial function of the image. His experiments in color lithography made it one of the most important and exciting media in late nineteenth century art.

The composition in *Tête-à-tête Supper* is strong and direct, giving an effect of immediacy through the abrupt cropping of the seated gentleman which creates an impression of a fleeting encounter. Yet – as in Degas' works – the appearance of immediacy is deceptive, for the picture is carefully structured and balanced. The background is sketchy and simple, with only the gas lamps on the left to punctuate its yellow-green blandness. Beneath, a solid block of dull loosely brushed Indian red, suggests the red plush seating, which forms a strong horizontal where it meets the greenish hues above. At the center point of this horizontal rises the

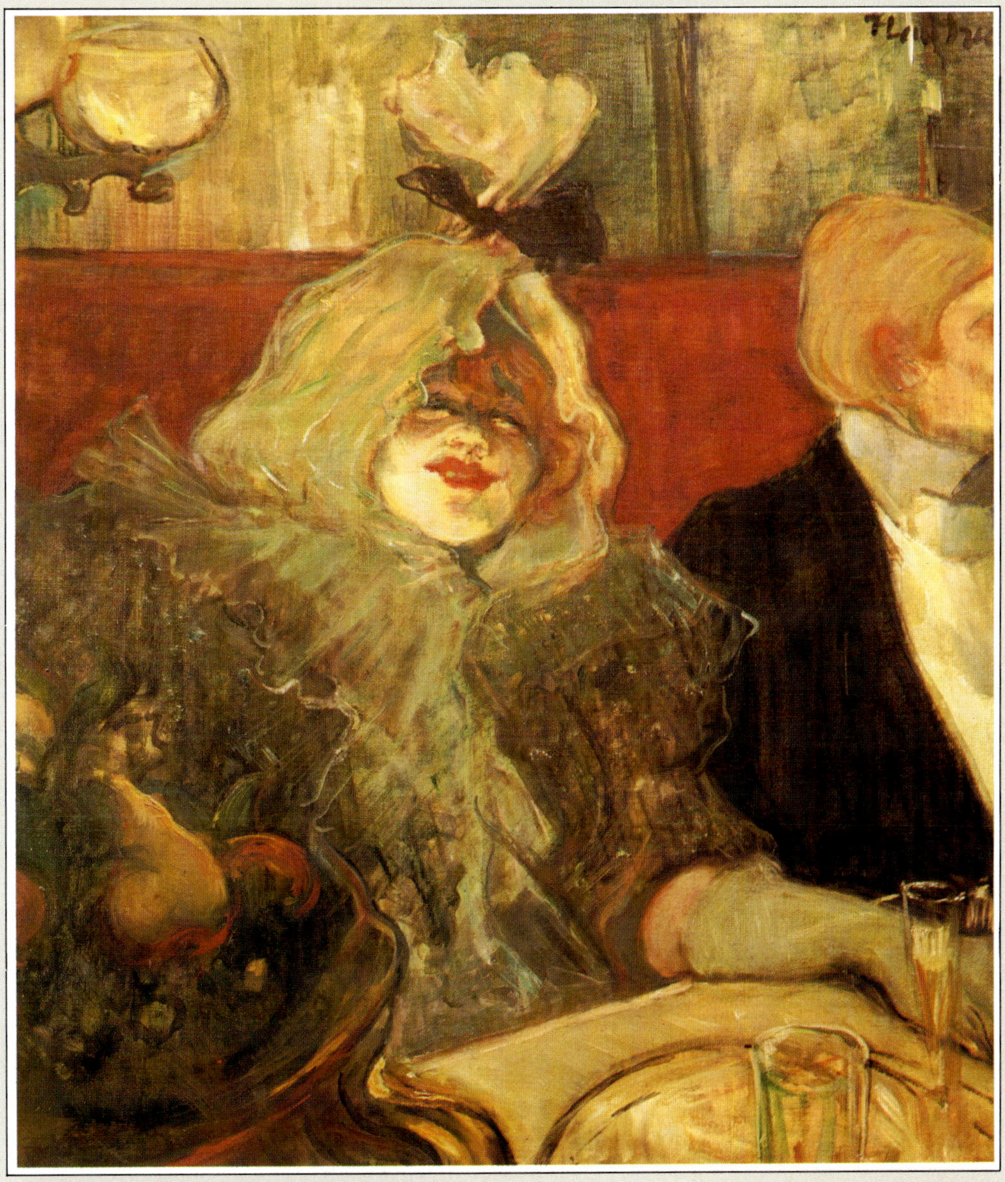

*Lautrec's characteristic thinly worked paint layer is apparent here. His technique, like his fascination with experimentation, seems to derive mainly from Degas. He also used colors diluted with turpentine to make them wash-like and mat. This was a very rapid handling method, which allowed for reworking after only a short drying time. Lautrec's reworkings are in color which is only slightly thicker and more opaque. This gave a final effect of immediacy and capturing a fleeting encounter. However, unlike the other Impressionists, both Lautrec and Degas preferred to study the effects of artificial light rather than full daylight. Lautrec used a standard format portrait 10 canvas for this painting, and its squarish proportions are well suited to the compositional design.*

flamboyant beribboned hairstyle of Lucy Jourdan. Her yellowish blonde hair is streaked with green reflections. The vigorous brushwork, its lively energy echoing the sitter's personality, changes to a drab reluctant touch when describing the partial figure of her escort.

The tabletop, which the viewer appears to look down on, as if standing engaged in conversation with the sitter, supplies evidence of the event's location. Glasses and dishes form the after-dinner debris, while a luscious dish of fruit almost lurches out of the frame toward the viewer. The analogy between the ripe lushness of his sitter and the full fruits beside her, is a stereotypical image in European painting. Lautrec's spare, thin paint surface, in which there is virtually no impasto, nevertheless creates a surprising richness of surface textures. The surface is relatively uniformly covered, with fluid translucent washes overlaid with delicate opaque scumbles. For example, the ruffles of her dress almost appear to float. The pictorial space is shallow, confined by the visual barrier of the table and fruit dish in the foreground, and cut off at the back by the wall of greenish hues, emphasizing the claustrophic artificiality of the life-style depicted. Lautrec was at this time already suffering from the effects of alcoholism from which he died two years later.

Strongly graphic, dark contours define shape

Thinly applied opaque reds appear translucent

Thickly applied opaques for highlight

Palish opaque whites and greens thinly scumbled over washed black layer create optical grays

Transparent black wash over paler underlay

Cropped composition on side and bottom edges pushes figures forward to enhance impression of immediacy

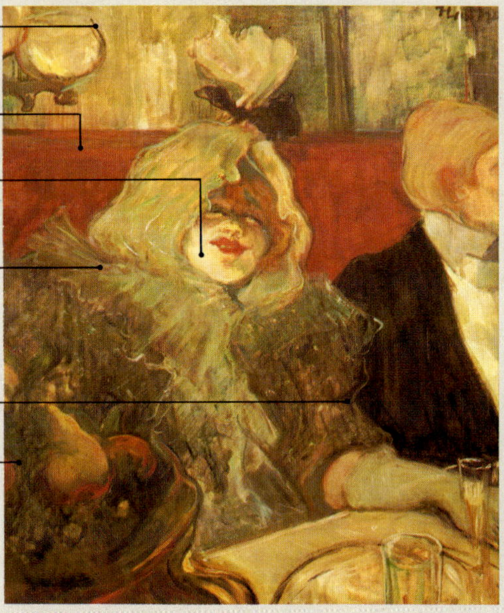

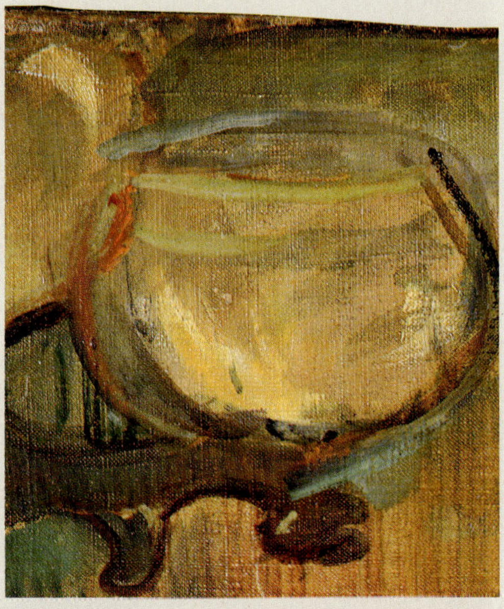

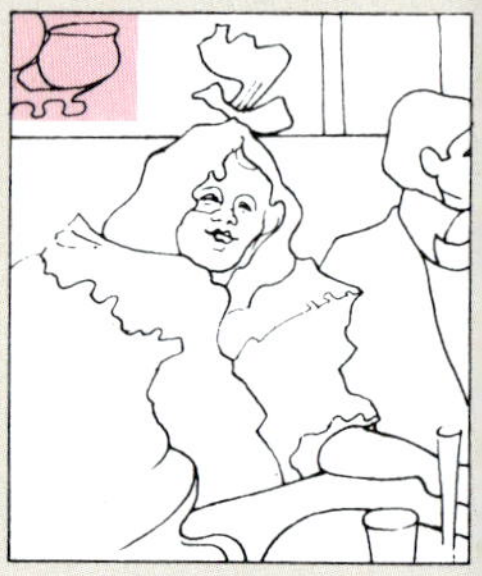

*The decorative form of the gas lamps adds pictorial interest to the flatly placed and painted back wall. They are thinly washed with translucent paint, outlined with vigorous, dark brushstrokes. A splash of opaque yellowish-white stands for the flame within. The gas lamps do not provide the light source which falls on the main subject. The woman is strikingly lit from below, producing an almost unflattering raking fall of harsh lights and shadows on her face. It would seem that a light is hidden behind the fruit bowl, projecting up onto her face like a spotlight. However, such a light would in fact have more effect on the garments she wears. Thus Lautrec creates an arbitrary lighting for purely dramatic, compositional reasons.*

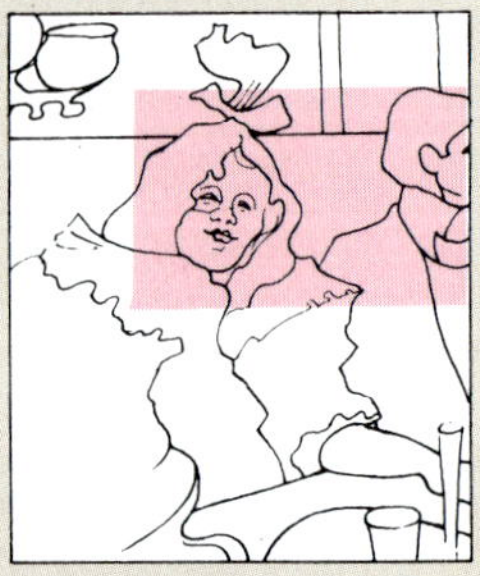

*The inclusion of two heads underplays the portrait function of the picture. The woman's blonde hair is streaked with vivid but pale viridian green with white, adding to her flamboyance and to the drama of the light. Lautrec's method makes the shapes between the forms, in this case the red seating, as active forms themselves.*

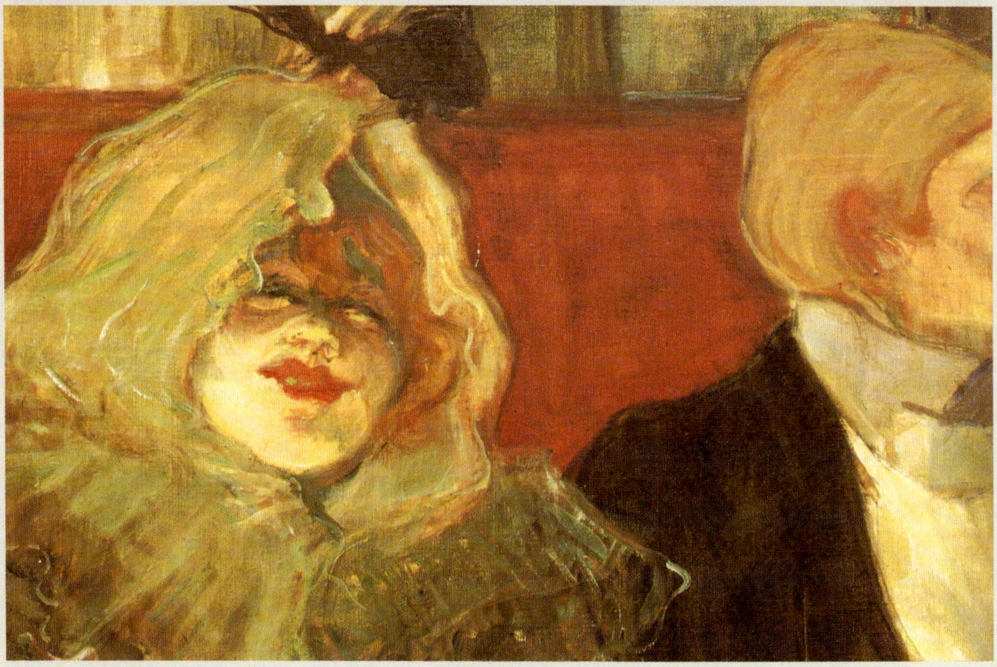

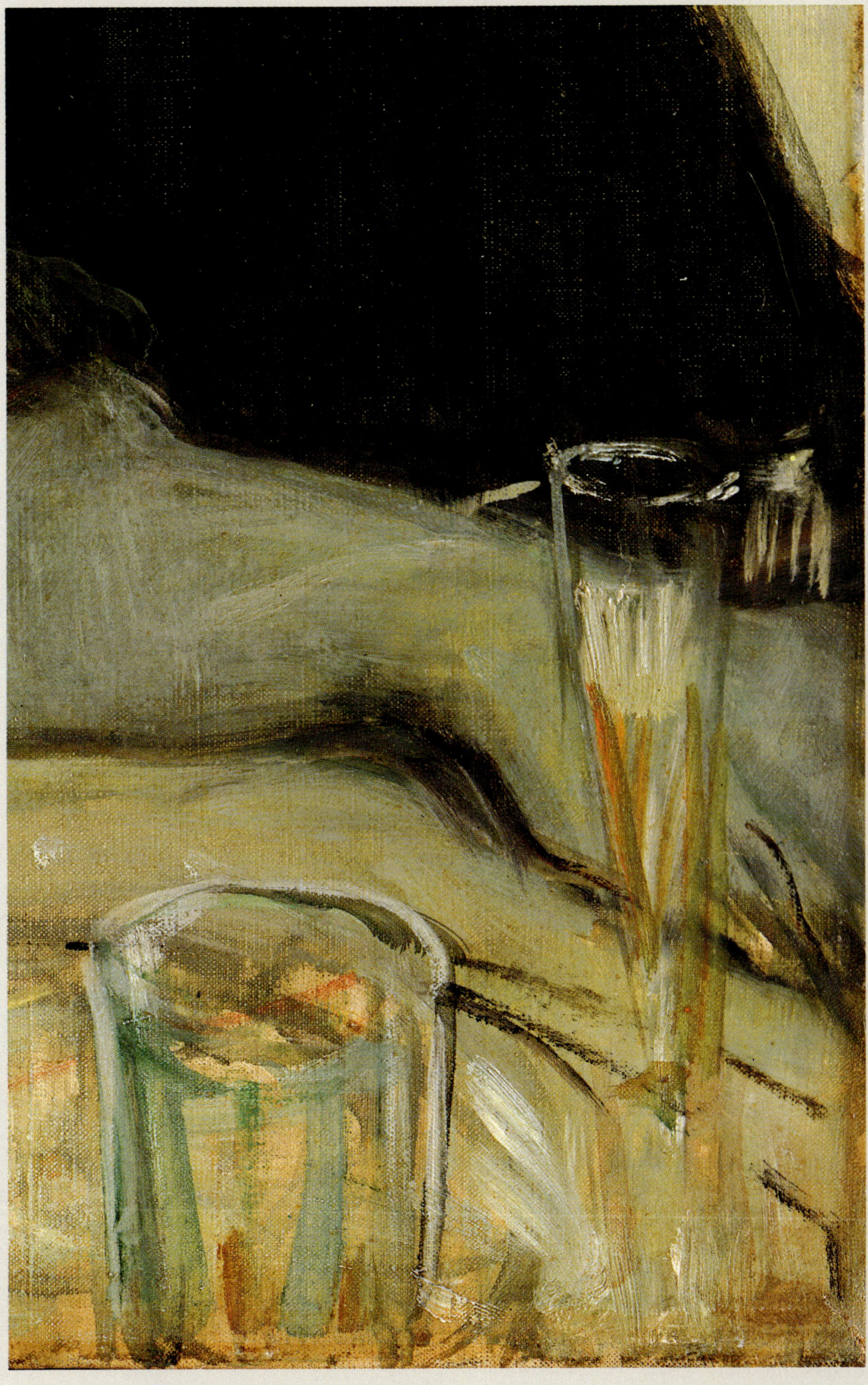

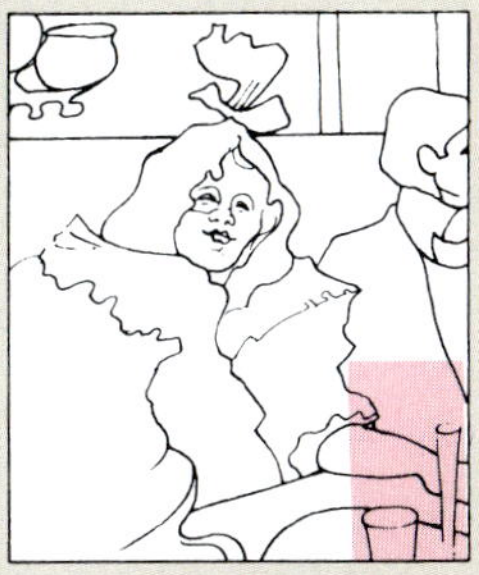

Actual size detail
*The lively, fluid handling of the still life on the table in the foreground is typical of Lautrec's skilled but sketchy technique. The paint is very thinly applied, washed on color diluted with considerable quantities of turpentine spirit. The rapid drying promoted by the evaporation of the spirit allows for speedy reworking, like the addition of further thin layers here, and of accents like the green strokes which give substance to the glass. The fine canvas has a thin commercial priming, in a pale tint. This may be an oatmeal or off-white hue. It is hard to identify this with certainty because its tint is modified by the thinly washed colors of the paint layer. Thus the paint layer, although often translucent or even transparent in places, is sufficiently colored to disguise the ground color.*

# PAUL CEZANNE

*Large Bathers/Les grandes Baigneuses* (*c* 1898-1905)
Oil on creamy white primed canvas
136cm × 196cm/53½in × 77⅛in

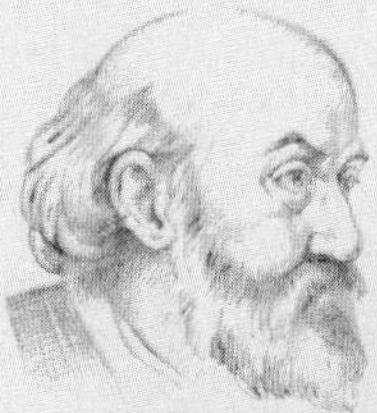

Cézanne has frequently been placed under the broad and uninformative Post-Impressionist banner, although, like Monet, he remained true to the essentially naturalist tenets of Impressionism throughout his career. That label seemed appropriate when his aims were considered more monumentally structural and suggestive of permanence, in contrast to the notion of Impressionist painting as transient and unstructured. However, when Cézanne's painting is seen in terms of techniques and painting methods, it is far closer to that of the Impressionists than to the anti-naturalist art – like that of Gauguin – normally labeled Post-Impressionist. Recent researchers into Impressionist painting have begun to question these accepted ideas, for so long taken at simple face value, about the 'spontaneous immediacy' of Impressionist practice, to demonstrate just how careful and calculated was their approach to painting. Within this context, Cézanne's work after the 1870s does not appear in opposition to the aims of the Impressionists. His commitment to recording his visual sensations remained with him throughout his life, as did his use of an Impressionist palette and basic Impressionist working methods. His late, large figure compositions done from the imagination, like the *Large Bathers*, were no more or less unrealistic than the bather compositions he executed in the 1870s, nor is his color in them any less naturalistic than that of Renoir's Impressionist interiors, like *The Parisian* (1874). Both used their observation and understanding of the effects of outdoor light, to give comparable luminosity to pictures which were in fact executed in the studio.

During the final 10 years of his life, Cézanne worked, among other things, on three major compositions of women bathers set in landscape surroundings. Studies of their chronology suggest that this version was the second begun by Cézanne, but that all three overlapped in time of execution, for they were worked on over many years. The theme of nudes in a landscape has a long and distinguished history in European painting, and many artists in the latter half of the nineteenth century took up the challenge it offered as a subject. Such paintings had, of necessity, to be worked from the imagination, because posing nude figures out of doors was unacceptable at that time. Matisse, early this century, was the first artist to paint nudes posed outdoors. Cézanne in particular, was an artist of exceptional reticence where it came to using live models, rarely doing so in his Aix-en-Provence studios for fear of the suspicious prudery of his provincial neighbors. In fact, only once during the period when he executed his large bather compositions is he known to have worked directly from a model. This was in Paris, in 1898–1899. Thus his sources for his figures tended to be from past art, either his own student studies, or his studies after the Old Masters.

The rich blues, which dominate the color harmonies of this version of the *Bathers*, evoke the atmospheric blue which saturates the Mediterranean countryside, without depicting a specific landscape. The figures are modeled through contrasts of warm and cool colors, blues for the receding contours of the figures, as their limbs turn out of sight, and warm pinks, oranges and yellows for the flesh as it comes out toward the viewer. No particular fall of light is used to sculpt the form, although a sense of light is created through the appearance of shadows cast by the limbs of the two main seated figures to the foreground right and left. Instead, as with color, form is suggested by the way in which the tone is modified over the forms, pale in the fleshy parts that swell out toward the viewer, and darker as the forms turn away. As in Renoir's *Parisian* the highlights, or rather, in the Cézanne, the parts closest to the spectator, are the most thinly painted, leaving the off-white ground glowing through. The 'shadows' or parts furthest away, are the most thickly painted. When the picture is lit with a light raking across it from the side, the density of built up paint in those areas is visible. The intense blues of the contours are like tramlines, ridges of layered color following the outlines of the figures, creating a physical structure or relief which contradicts recession, but creating an illusion which has the effect of enhancing it.

The academic method advocated painting the lights thickly and the shadows, or edges of forms, thinly, to produce a relief which imitated the actual relief of the subject. Thus Cézanne's method, like that of Renoir, is in opposition to traditional means. It is closer to pre-Renaissance methods of representing form, when – before actual light and shade had been copied by artists – the parts of the form nearest the viewer were painted pale, and the receding parts were painted as becoming progressively darker. This is one of the reasons why independent artists, who broke away from *chiaroscuro* techniques, were denigrated as 'primitives'. This was referring to the so-called primitive painters in pre-Renaissance Italy. The work of these latter artists was then generally considered flat and lacking satisfactory illusionism. They also, like the Impressionists, avoided the use of black for shadows, because it sullied the purity of their colors. Instead, the Italian primitives gradated their tempera colors from white through to full color saturation to suggest form. Cézanne's method also has parallels with this use of color, although medium and handling are, of course, quite different.

Cézanne's composition for *Large Bathers* has been called architectural in feeling, because it evokes an architectural solidity both in the monumental simplicity of the individual figures,

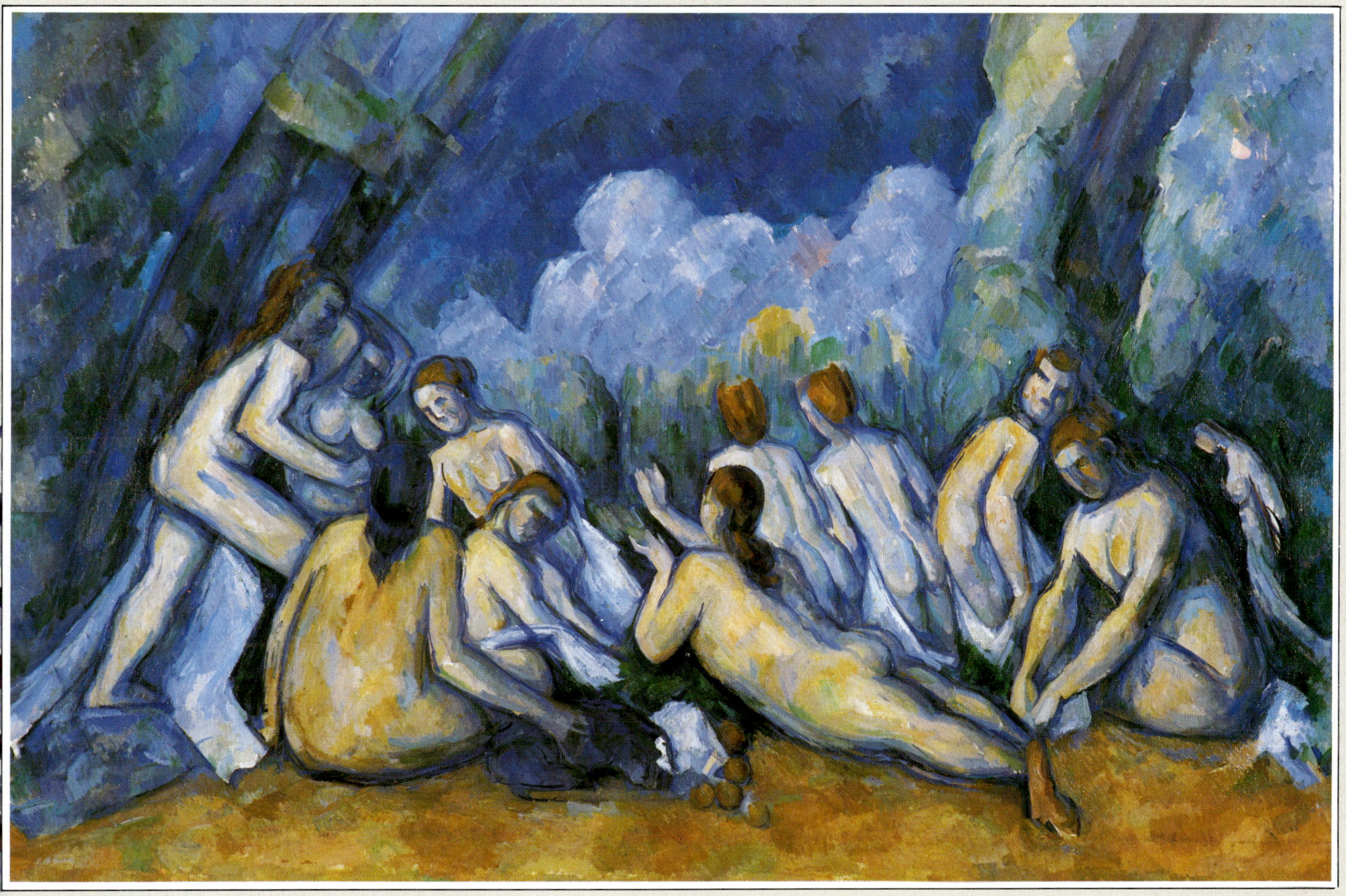

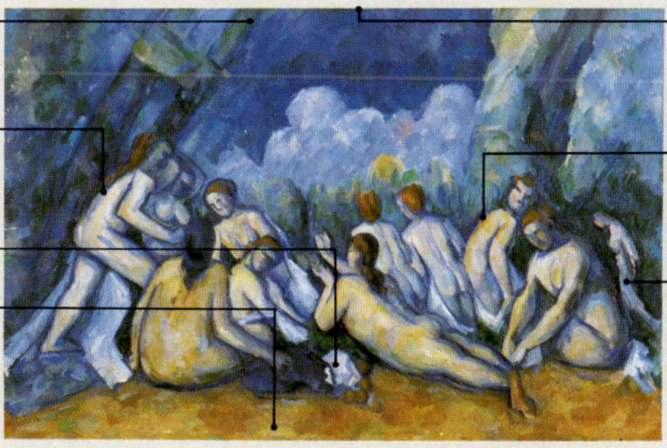


*Cézanne's group of partially draped female nudes is treated with monumental grandeur reminiscent of the classical tradition, although his handling of the subject breaks with tradition. In effect, he is restating that tradition in contemporary terms. His knowledge of light, color and the atmospheric blues of the Provençal landscape have influenced his studio compositions of imaginative subjects. The figures are disposed in a frieze-like band parallel to the picture plane. Warm colors dominate in the foreground, but are modified by the blues which permeate the entire painting. The forms closest to the spectator are painted most thinly.*

and in their overall relationship to each other and to the huge pillar-like forms of the trees. Cézanne modified his composition, progressively adding 7.5cm (3in) to the bottom of the picture, on canvas that had been turned over the base of the stretcher. Similarly, he reduced the height of the picture, along the top of which is a strip of about 7.5cm (3in) where the paint is thinner and less worked. This is usually hidden by the frame. This adjustment enabled Cézanne to extend the open foreground separating the audience from the figures, and to reduce the expanse of sky above them. The canvas proportions chosen for this and the other two large bather pictures, seem to confirm the chronology put forward for the three *Large Bather* pictures. The earliest canvas is elongated in format, the second, the present *Large Bathers*, is less elongated, and the final variant is the squarest in its proportions.

From the mid 1880s, following his father's death, Cézanne's financial freedom enabled him to pursue his artistic interests without the pressure to sell to a generally unsympathetic public. His first major retrospective exhibition was only to take place at Vollard's gallery in Paris in 1895.

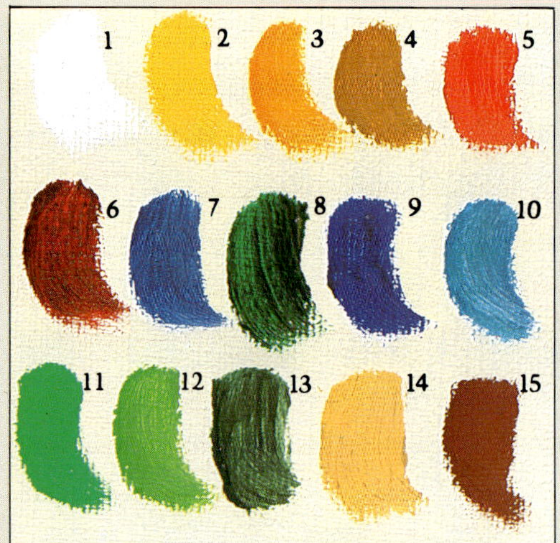


*Cézanne's palette for this work probably comprised lead white (1), chrome (2) or cadmium yellows (3), yellow ochre (4), vermilion (5), red alizarin lakes (6), cobalt blue (7), viridian green (8) ultramarine blue (9), emerald green (11), green earth (terre verte) (13). Naples yellow (14), red earth (15), cerulean blue (10) and chrome green (12) may also have been used.*

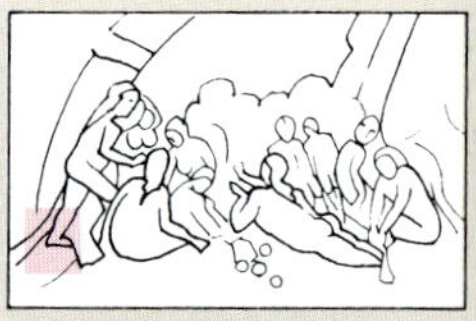

Actual size detail
*Cézanne's painstaking, slow method of painting can be seen here. The proportions of the figure have been changed as the painting progressed, and this leg has clearly been shortened. The calf is now thinner, and the foot about 3.75cm (1½ in) further up. The original position is apparent from the ridges of dry paint over which the final colors were opaquely applied. Light catches and bounces off the varnished surface at these points. At the bottom edge of the drapery in the lower left the white ground shows bare among the strokes of varied blue and green. It serves as the palest tonal value. Thickness of paint application varies considerably. The top and bottom left areas are thinly worked in opaque paint, as is the drapery. The reworked parts are inevitably more loaded, but the contours and the wedge shape between the heel and drape are built up most. The successive layering of rich blues for the contours are evidence of Cézanne's concern to create the effect of roundness in the forms.*

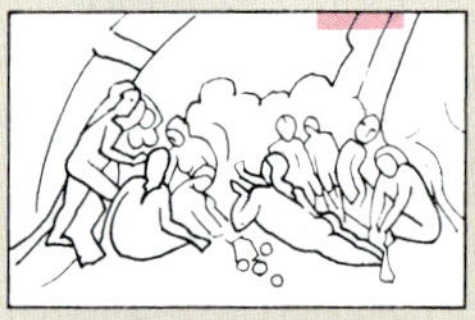

*Above this upper line remains about 7.5cm (3in) of partially painted canvas which the artist decided to exclude from the composition. It is hidden beneath the frame when exhibited. The white ground glows through the more thinly applied areas of color, as here.*

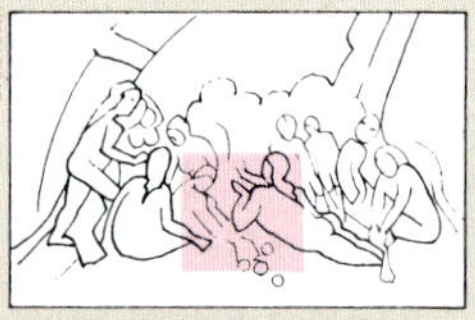

*The incomplete form of a dog, caressed by an unfinished hand, dominates the middle foreground, beside a still life of fruit which harks back to Manet's* Luncheon on the Grass *(1863) and to Cézanne's own numerous studies of fruit. Above the dog, further alterations had been made.*

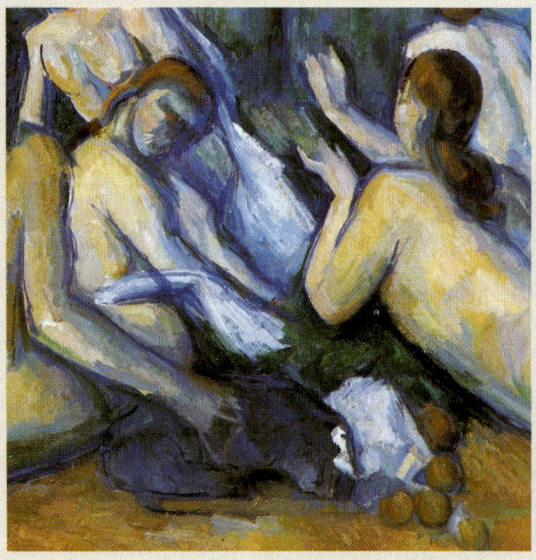

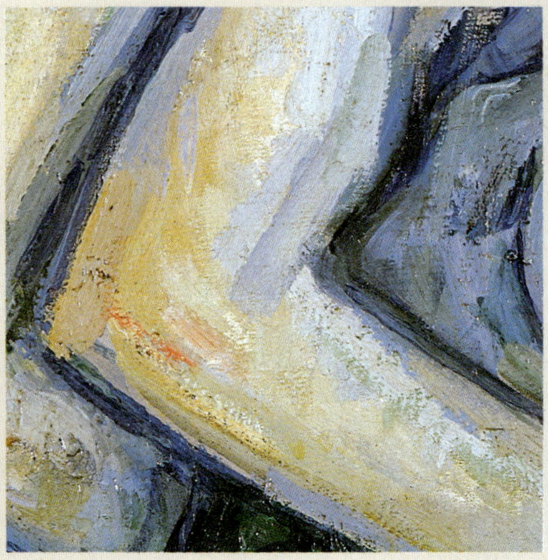

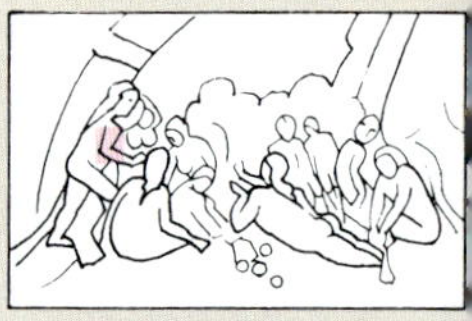

*In the thinly painted parts, the ground still shows, adding luminosity to the rich hues of the paint layer. Variations in the paint application are apparent. The dark areas show repeated reworkings which contrast with the thinly worked pale hues. Oppositions between opacity and translucency are also exploited.*

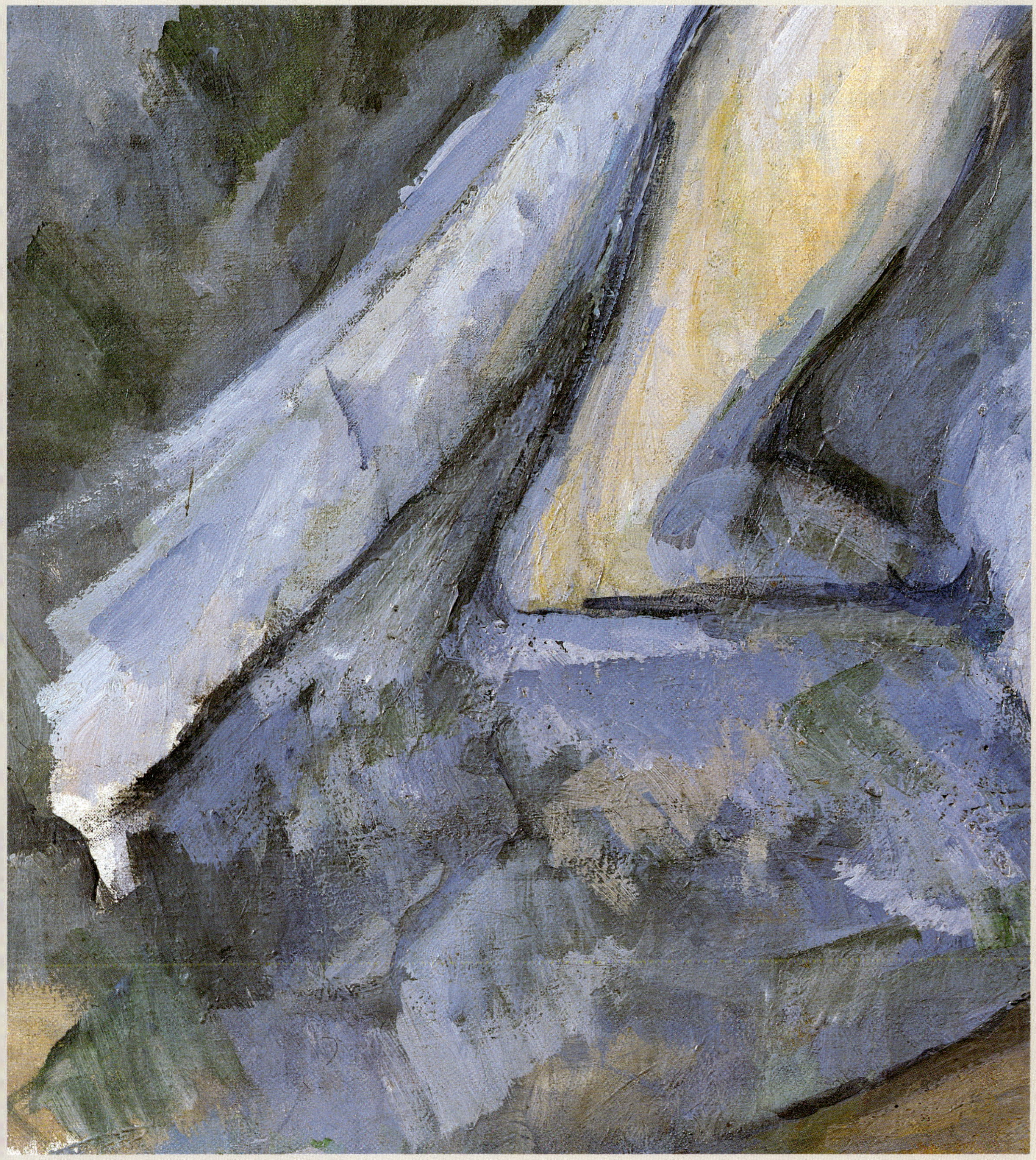

# CHRONOLOGY

KEY
- Important dates in the lives of featured artists
- Featured paintings
- Important paintings
- Important dates or events in the lives of other artists
- Other artistic events and exhibitions
- Technical developments
- Historical events

1840 1841 1842 1843 1844 1845 1846 1847 1848 1849

**Gustave Courbet** 1844 1st Salon exhibit 184
1819 born in Ornans; 1839 leaves Ornans for Paris

**Edgar Degas** 1845 enters Lycée Louis-le-Grand
1834 born in Paris

**Edouard Manet**
1832 born in Paris

**Camille Pissarro** 1842 attends boarding school in suburbs of Paris
1830 born in Virgin Islands, Danish West Indies 1847 returns to join

**Pierre Auguste Renoir** 1844 family moves to Paris
1840 born in Limoges

**Claude Monet**
1840 born in Paris; brought up in Le Havre on Normandy coast

**Jean-Francois Millet** 1844-46 early florid style 1848 *Winno*
1814 born in Gruchy, Normandy 18

**Paul Cézanne**
1839 born in Aix-en-Provence

**Alfred Sisley**
1839 born in Paris

**Gustave Ca**
1848 born in

**Berthe Morisot**
1841 born in Bourges, France

**Mary Cassatt**
1844 born in Allegheny, Pennsylvania, USA

**Paul Gaugu**
1848 born in

1841 **Frédéric Bazille** French Realist artist, influenced by Manet, friend
1844 Eugène Boudin meets several of the Barb
18
1847 Couture *Roma*
1840 **Emile Zola** French novelist born 1845 Balzac *Les Paysans* 18
1842 Chevreul's course in the contrast of color advertised at Sa
1843 **Henry James** American novelist, lives and work

1844 wood pulp paper invented by F.G. Kelle
1840 Viridian green becomes available commercially
Early 1840s cadmium yellows commercially availab
1841 collapsible tin tubes first patented by American painter John Goff

1848 revol
1848 Marx
1844 Treaty of Tangiers ends French war in M
1843 world's first night club *Le Bal des Anglais* opens

1851 1852 1853 1854 1855 1856 1857 1858 1859 1860 1861 1862 1863 1864 1865 1866 1867 1868 1869

on – 3rd class gold medal for *After Dinner at Ornans* · 1860 works in Honfleur · 1866 *Deer Haven at Plaisir Fontaine, Doubs*
9-50 *Burial at Ornans* · 1855 *Studio* painted and exhibited with other pictures · 1862 opens a teaching studio

1853 begins copying in Louvre; studies law briefly · 1859-60 paints *Portrait of Bellelli Family*
1855-56 trains briefly at Ecole des Beaux-Arts · 1862 meets Manet · 1865 exhibits race scene at Salon

50 pupil of Couture at Ecole des Beaux-Arts · 1856 makes copies of Old Masters at the Louvre · 1862 *Concert in the Tuileries*
1859 *The Absinthe Drinker* rejected at the Salon · 1865 *Olympia* shown at Salon

1852-54 lives in Venezuela · 1856-60 works regularly around Paris · 1861 meets Cézanne at Académie Suisse · 1867 *L'Hermitage at Pontoise*
iness, Virgin Islands · 1855 arrives back in Paris · 1859 exhibits landscape at the Salon; meets Monet at Académie Suisse

1856-57 apprentice porcelain painter · 1862 enters Ecole des Beaux-Arts · 1867 *Portrait of Bazille*
1864 works with Monet, Bazille and Sisley

1856-57 draws caricatures · 1860 works at Académie Suisse · 1865 works with Courbet at Trouville
1858 meets landscapist Boudin · 1862 enters Gleyre's studio · *La Grenouillère* 1869

of first major peasant subjects, shown at Salon · 1857 *Gleaners* exhibited at Salon · 1868 pastel version *Autumn, The Haystacks*
ves Paris for Barbizon · 1859 *Angelus*, not shown until 1865 · completed; oil version begun

1855 attends college in Aix · 1861 stops studying law, goes to Paris; meets Pissarro at Académie Suisse
1858-59 studies law but wants to become a painter

1857 sent to London to prepare for commercial career · 1866 shows first works at Salon
1862 enters studio of Charles Gleyre in Paris

military service and law studies 1868
Bachelor of Law 1869

1855 lives in Paris · 1861 works with Corot · 1864 2 landscapes at Salon
1856-57 studies with pupil of Ingres and Delacroix · meets Manet; friendship with Degas 1868

1851 family moves to Europe, settling in Paris · 1861-65 attends Pennsylvania Academy of the Fine Arts
1855 visits Paris World Fair · 1866-70 in Europe

**Paul Signac**
1863 born in Paris

**George Seurat**
1859 born in Paris

**Vincent van Gogh**
1853 born in North Brabant, Holland · 1857 brother Theo born · joins Hague branch of art dealers Goupil & Cie 1869

1856 school in Orléans · 1865 becomes merchant seaman
s in Lima, Peru · seaman with French navy 1868

**Henri de Toulouse-Lautrec**
1864 born in Albi

**Henri Matisse** 1869 born

pressionists born · **Emile Bernard** artist friend of Gauguin and van Gogh, founder member of Pont-Aven group in Brittany born 1868
ists · 1852 Corot exhibits first open-air painting of a French site · 1862 Sarah Bernhardt's debut in Paris at Comédie Française
rot exhibits first open-air painting · 1855 Whistler arrives in Paris · 1861 Wagner *Tannhauser*, a scandal in Paris
*Decadence* chief Salon attraction · 1857 Baudelaire *Fleurs du Mal* · 1862 **Claude Debussy** French composer born
éodore Rousseau's first work accepted by Salon since 1836 wins 1st class medal · 1862 International Exhibition, London; Hugo *Les Misérables*
50 **Guy de Maupassant** French writer born · 1857 Daubigny awarded Legion of Honor and also criticized for painting 'impression' of nature
rope born · 1854 **Arthur Rimbaud** French Symbolist poet born · 1861 Charles Garnier designs Paris Opera
1856-57 Flaubert *Madame Bovary* · 1863 Baudelaire *Peintre de la vie moderne* published
1856-57 Duranty publishes periodical *Le Réalisme* · 1863 Ingres *Turkish Bath*
1851 Great Exhibition, London · abortive plan by Monet and friends for alternative to Salon show 1867
1855 Paris World Fair including works by Ingres, Delacroix, Rousseau; Courbet exhibits independently in his *Pavillion du réalism*
1856 magenta introduced · Early 1860s snapshot photography developed
50 cobalt green available · 1850s magnesium flare and battery give artificial light for photography
95 · 1856 aniline (coal tar) dyes developed · alizarin crimson (synthetic madder) introduced 1868
Mid 1850s stereoscopic viewers popular · 1862 green oxide of chromium available as artists' pigment
50 collapsible tin tubes still cost 10 centimes extra in France · 1859 cobalt violet introduced · 1863 *Salon des Refusés* exhibition
ndon · 1854 zinc white oil paint manufactured · 1860 cerulean blue
1852 2nd Empire begins · 1860 Abraham Lincoln elected US President · 1867 Maxmilian executed in Mexico
1853 Baron Haussmann begins reconstruction of Paris · 1862 Nobel uses nitro-glycerin as explosive
is and elsewhere in Europe · 1856 **Sigmund Freud** Austrian, founder of psycho-analysis born
gels *Communist Manifesto* · 1859 Charles Darwin (1809-1882) *Origin of Species* · 1867 Zola *Thérèse Racquin*
1853 Crimean War · 1856 Americans make first Western treaty with Japan · 1863 French capture Mexico City
1852 Louis Napoleon proclaims himself Emperor Napoleon III · 1861-65 American civil war · 1865 Lincoln assassinated

1870 1871 1872 1873 1874 1875 1876 1877 1878 1879 1880 1881 1882 1883 1884 1885 1886 1887 1888 1889

**Gustave Courbet** 1872 in exile in Switzerland dies 1877
1871 President of Commune Art Commission

**Edgar Degas** 1872 visits New Orleans 1876 24 works in 2nd Impressionist group show 1885 meets Gauguin at Dieppe
1870 discovers sight in right eye poor 1879 *Portrait of Duranty* 1886 Durand-Ruel exhibits

**Edouard Manet** 1873 sells 29 paintings to Durand-Ruel 1878 *Road Menders on the rue de Berne* 1884 memorial exhibition and studio sale, Pa
1870 joins National Guard 1874 works at Argenteuil with Monet and Renoir dies 1883

**Camille Pissarro** 1872-73 works with Cézanne at Pontoise and Auvers 1879 *Mme Pissarro Sewing* 1886 adopts Pointillist techn
1870 flees to London with family because of war 1883 one-man show at Durand-Ruel gallery 1888 A

**Pierre Auguste Renoir** 1874 *La Parisienne* one of 7 works at 1st Impressionist group show 1882 *Rocky Crags at l'Estaque* painted while working with Céz
1881 travels to Algiers and Italy 1887 *Large Bathers*

**Claude Monet** 1872 settles in Argenteuil 1877 begins *St Lazare Station* paintings 1883 settles in Giverny
1870-71 visits London and Holland 1875 works sold at Impressionist group auction 1881 moves to Poissy 1884 works in south of France 1888 *Antib*

**Jean-Francois Millet** dies 1875 1881 Sensier's influential biography published

**Paul Cézanne** 1873 *House of the Hanged Man* 1878-79 *Mountains seen from l'Estaque* 1886 Zola's novel *The Maste*
1874 3 works at Impressionist group show 1882 works at La Roche Guyon with Renoir

**Alfred Sisley** 1872 Durand-Ruel begins buying paintings c1877 *Boats on the Seine* 1881 one-man show at *La Vie Moderne*
1875 settles at Marly-le-Roi 1880-82 lives in Veneux-Nadon near Moret-sur-Loing 18

**Gustave Caillebotte** 1872-73 trains at Ecole des Beaux-Arts 1879 25 works at 4th Impressionist group show 1886 *Garden at Petit-Genne*
1870 called up for active service 1874 meets Degas 1877 study for *Paris, Rainy Day* 1883 retreats from Parisian art world to his home nea

**Berthe Morisot** 1872 visits Spain 1876 joins 2nd Impressionist group show 1882 *Woman and Child in the Garden at Bougival* 1887 participates in
1874 9 works in 1st Impressionist group show 1885 visits Holland

**Mary Cassatt** 1872-73 travels and studies in Europe; finally settles in Paris 1882 *Woman in Black* 1886 exhibits at the 8th (and Impressionist group show
1870 returns to Philadelphia 1877 Degas invites her to join the Impressionists group

**Paul Signac** Early 1880s working under influence of Impressionists 18
1884 co-founder of Independents; meets Seu

**George Seurat** 1874 first drawings 1877-79 attends Ecole des Beaux Arts 1883-84 *Bathing, Asnières*, first major oil compositi
1875 Municipal Art School – 1876; reads Blanc's *Grammar of the Arts of Drawing* 1886 *La Grande Jatte*

**Vincent van Gogh** 1873 transfers to London Branch of firm 1880 begins career as painter 1885 paints *Potato Eaters*
1875 transfers to main Paris office 1876 dismissed, returns to England as teacher and lay preacher *Peach Trees in Blossom* 1889

**Paul Gauguin** 1871-72 works for Paris stockbroker; part-time painter 1879 sculpture in 4th Impressionist group show 1885 meets and quarrels with Degas
1876 begins buying Impressionist works 1881 8 works in 6th Impressionist group show 1888 Britta

**Henri de Toulouse-Lautrec** 1884 lives and works in Montmartre
1886 attends Cormon's stu

**André Derain**
1880 born at Chatou, near Paris

**Henri Matisse** 1887-89 studies law

1871 **Paul Valéry** French poet born 1876 **Maurice de Vlaminck** French co-founder of Fauvism born 1886 Moréas *Symbolist ma*
1870 Fantin-Latour *Batignolles Studio* 1876 Philadelphia World Fair 1881 **Pablo Picasso** Spanish artist, co-founder of Cubism born
1872 Whistler *The Artist's Mother* 1876 2nd Impressionist group show 1882 **Georges Braque** French painter co-founder of Cubism bor
1871-93 Zola *Les Rougon-Macquart* series of novels 1878 Paris World Fair 1881 Durand-Ruel resumes purchase of Impressionist works
1873 Durand-Ruel begins buying Impressionist paintings 1880 Maupassant *Contes* 1883 Amsterdam World Fair 1888 Gust
1870 **Bazille** dies 1875 Impressionist auction includes works by Monet, Renoir, Morisot, Sisley 1886 Rimbaud *Les Illumina*
1874 1st Impressionist group show, Paris 1879 Ibsen *A Doll's House* 1883 **Wagner** dies 1886 Durand-Ruel shows
1876 Debussy *L'Après-midi d'une Faune* 1881 *Chat Noir*, first cabaret, founded in Paris by Rodolphe Salis 18
1877 3rd Impressionist group show 1881 6th Impressionist group show 1886 8th and last Impressio
1879 4th Impressionist group show 1884 Independents' exhibitions founded
1880 5th Impressionist group show 1885 Impressionist dinners institute
Early 1870s first experiments with color photography 1882 7th Impressionist group show
1873 first color photographs successful 1886 George Eastman devel
1879 Ogden Rood *Modern Chromatics* 18
Early 1880s glass instead of varnish becomes popular for paintings
Late 1880s Eadweard Muy
1873 Germans leave France 1880 France has about 26,000 km (16,200 miles) of railways 1888 Geor
1871 Germany united by Bismarck 1880 French Socialist Party founded 1887 M.W. Goodwi
1879 **Albert Einstein** German physicist born 18
1871 revolt in Paris, 3rd Republic proclaimed; siege of Paris by Prussians; Paris commune – rules Paris 2 months to May
1874-80 economic crisis affects picture dealing, hence artists 1883 France gains control of Tunis
1870-1 Franco-Prussian War; Napoleon capitulates at Sedan 1880 France annexes Tahiti
1881 population of Paris 2,200,000 1886 Bonaparte and Orléans

1891 1892 1893 1894 1895 1896 1897 1898 1899 1900 1901 1902 1903 1904 1905 1906 1907 1908 1909

1892 exhibition at Durand-Ruel gallery
York; *Portrait of Hélène Rouart* 1895-1905 makes pastel studies of Russian dancers
**Edgar Degas** dies 1917

)0 abandons Pointillist method 1896 January-March and September-November in Rouen
of paintings still only 500 francs; *Apple Picking* 1898 offered studio by Matisse dies 1903

1896 *The Renoir Family* 1900 increasingly paralyzed by rheumatism
1903 moves to Cagnes in south
**Pierre Auguste Renoir** dies 1919

0 first 'series' paintings – *Haystacks* followed by *Poplars* 1898 61 paintings shown at Petit gallery 1903 new series of *Waterlilies*
1892 begins *Rouen Cathedral* series difficulties with eyesight; visits Venice 1908
**Claude Monet** dies 1926

es split in their friendship; October – inherits fortune after father's death 1898-1904 paints *Large Bathers*
0 exhibits with *Les XX* in Brussels 1895 on Pissarro's advice Vollard shows 150 paintings dies 1906

es to Moret 1893 show at Theo van Gogh's gallery, Paris; paints *Church at Moret* series dies 1899

*Roses* **Gustave Caillebotte**
nteuil dies 1894

nal Exhibition **Berthe Morisot**
t Petit gallery dies 1895

1893 show at Durand-Ruel gallery 1898 first visit to America since 1871 1904 awarded Legion of Honor by the French government
)0 visits exhibition of Japanese prints at the Ecole des Beaux-Arts in Paris 1901 visit to Italy
**Mary Cassatt** dies 1926

Gogh at Arles 1893 buys house in St Tropez; town becomes famous for artists as a result
0 visits Italy; elected member of Belgian *Les XX*
**Paul Signac** dies 1935

ies
891

1891-93 lives in Tahiti 1894 back in Paris 1897 paints *Te Reroia* 1901-03 lives in Marquesas Islands until his death
s with van Gogh 1895-1901 lives in Tahiti

1891 first music hall posters for Moulin Rouge dies 1901
1892 first color lithographs *Tête-à-tête Supper* 1899

0 intends to become engineer 1899 meets Matisse while studying under Carrière 1905 *Portrait of Matisse*
1900 meets Vlaminck 1904-05 works with Vlaminck
**André Derain** dies 1954

0on takes up painting; studies at Academy Julian 1901 on exhibits with Independents 1905 *Portrait of Derain*
1895-97 studies at Ecole des Beaux-Arts coins term 'Cubism' 1908
**Henri Matisse** dies 1954

1893 **Maupassant** dies
1893 Art Nouveau spread in Europe
1893 Chicago World Fair
-1923) designs Eiffel Tower
essionist paintings in New York
d Fair – Eiffel Tower opened
show
1891 **Rimbaud** dies
1896 **Verlaine** dies
1896 **Boudin** dies
1896 **Goncourt** dies
1895 first public film show, Paris
1898 **Moreau** dies
1898 **Mallarmé** dies
1900 Paris World Fair
1900 Freud *Interpretation of Dreams*
1900 **Nietsche** dies
first daily comic strip in San Francisco Chronicle 1907
1902-05 Picasso Blue Period
1903 Henry James *The Ambassadors*
Stravinsky *Firebird* ballet performed in Paris 1909
1904 **Fantin-Latour** dies
1903 **Whistler** dies
1903 **Chekhov** dies
Kandinsky first abstract paintings 1909
1905-06 Picasso Rose Period
1905 'Fauves' named at Autumn Salon
1905 Marinetti *Futurist Manifesto*
**Tolstoy** dies 1910

1894 Louis Lumière invents cinematograph
d photo paper
reul dies
1896 new evidence on innocence of Alfred Dreyfus suppressed
1892 anarchist violence in Paris
Louis Lumière develops process for colour photography using 3-colour screen 1907
shes photographs of moving figures
nan perfects Kodak camera
cadmium red available 1910
ts celluloid film 1893 trial in Paris over Panama Canal corruption
1906 Dreyfus rehabilitated
Day celebrations, Paris
1898 Zola writes *J'Accuse* in defence of Dreyfus
1904 Church and State separated in France
1895 Freud *Study on Hysteria* 1899-1902 Boer War
1903 King Edward VII visits France to establish Entente Cordiale
1898 Paris metro opened
hed from France 1894 Dreyfus trial begins, anti-Semitism rife in France 1901 Queen Victoria dies Louis Blériot flies across Channel 1909

# SECTION 3
# MODERN MASTERS
# 1905-1980

This book is an introduction to the vast subject of twentieth-century art, from the important perspective of the painters' techniques; a perspective that art historians, until very recently, have tended to ignore. Since the work of modern artists is almost inexhaustibly varied – in terms of vision, concept, style, form, content, materials and tools – this approach may seem at first to be unnecessarily limited. But, on closer examination, it proves a fruitful way of examining the changes that have characterized the art of this century.

In this age of artistic freedom and experiment, it might be expected that easel painting, for centuries the most important of all the artist's means of expression, would have been almost completely abandoned. Surprisingly, it survives, partly, at least, because it *is* a convention – the convention of the flat surface or rectangle. As such, it provides the type of limitations which often spur rather than inhibit creative activity.

Technique goes beyond mechanical and manual processes; it is a useful standpoint from which to view artists' overall intentions. This is not just because choice of materials and working methods reveals crucial attitudes, but has more to do with the way in which modern artists have redefined not only the object of their creativity, but also the process by which it is produced. Indeed, an important contribution of artists in this century has been to emphasize the critical mental aspects of technique, as opposed to the merely physical application of paint, for example, to a support.

**Painting and its opponents**

No book on twentieth-century painters (as opposed to twentieth-century painting) can or should avoid at least touching on methods and materials outside the scope of painting. On a mundane level, many painters have also been sculptors and vice versa – Henri Matisse (1869-1954), Pablo Picasso (1881-1973), Alberto Giacometti (1901-1966). For others, however, choice of materials goes beyond a desire to experiment with different media. Marcel Duchamp (1887-1968), having achieved fame and success as a painter, virtually gave up conventional painting in 1913 at the age of 26, the same year his *Nude Descending a Staircase* (1912) took New York by storm at the Armory Show.

For Duchamp, the idea of the artist as a sort of magician was much more important than the notion of the artist as mere painter. By abandoning painting so abruptly after so much success, both as a conventional and as an avant-garde painter, he demonstrated his doubt about the validity of painting as a modern art medium.

From 1913 on, Duchamp made a series of devastating attacks on the notion (among others) that the artist needed to have a technique at all. All the artist had to do was to appropriate the techniques of mass production by, for example, setting a *Bicycle Wheel* (1913) upon a stool and exhibiting it as art. In the same spirit Duchamp purchased a *Bottle Rack* (1914), in his own words, '... as a means of solving an artistic problem without the usual means or processes ...', and a 'ready-made' *Fountain* (urinal) (1917). This last was turned on its back, signed 'R. Mutt' and sent into the 'Salon des Indépendants' exhibition. It was refused. In response to the criticisms Duchamp wrote: 'Whether Mr Mutt with his own hands made the fountain or not has no importance. He chose it. He took an ordinary article of life, placed it so that its useful significance disappeared under the new title and point of view – created a new thought for that object.'

It could be said that Duchamp wanted to prove that, in theory, an artist's technique could be 100 percent a mental technique. The hands were not necessary; the eye and the brain would manage without them. Duchamp was in a strong position to attack painting: he had already demonstrated his proficiency in the medium during the period from 1902 to 1913. He was also in a strong position to attack manual technique because between 1915 and 1923 he produced one of the twentieth century's most technically elaborate works of art, *The Bride Stripped Bare by Her Bachelors, Even (The Large Glass)*; a work which cannot be properly described as a painting, nor as a sculpture.

Marcel Duchamp is not the only major exponent of easel painting to envisage its demise. Piet Mondrian (1872-1944), a theosophist, an idealist and the creator of geometrical abstract painting, looked forward to the day when society as a whole would show more creative visual attitude – that pioneered by the De Stijl group of artists and architects of which he was a member – and would transform the environment, making easel painting redundant.

Recently, various artists have criticized the art object, including easel painting, on the grounds that it is a 'bourgeois' form. They have social and political objections to the way paintings have been used for purposes unintended by the artist; in other words as investments or speculations. Sol LeWitt (b 1928) a key figure in both the Minimal Art and Conceptual Art movements, neatly sidesteps such problems by producing temporary wall drawing. A small design on paper by LeWitt is magnified onto a wall. It can be viewed by people near and far, and any transport costs are reduced to postage. Like Duchamp, LeWitt has more or less delegated 'technique'.

In the face of such wide-ranging attacks it is a wonder that easel painting has survived at all. But it has more than survived. Not only is it still the stock-in-trade of the academic artist and the purveyor of boardroom portraits, it has also contained and conditioned a high

RIGHT *Larry Rivers (b 1923) took up painting in 1945, and studied with Hans Hofmann from 1947-1948. His work is pitched squarely between Pop Art, of which he is held an important precursor, and Abstract Expressionism, whose loose, improvised brushstrokes he put to his own original use.* Parts of the Face *(1961) was painted in Paris and represents the artist's wife, Clarice, whom he had recently married. It has its source in a labeled language school drawing and the painting here is one of an intermittent series which varies both in length, pose and identity of sitter, as well as the languages used for labeling (English, Italian, Polish and Persian). Technically, Rivers has worked up a partially realistic head which is surrounded by thickly brushed swathes of color — yellow, green, white and black — which have been allowed to run and scuff over the surface. A commercial stencil (recalling the Cubists) and ruled lines have been used to itemize the head's parts. The painted area also extends around the sides of the stretcher, a technique used by Jackson Pollock.*

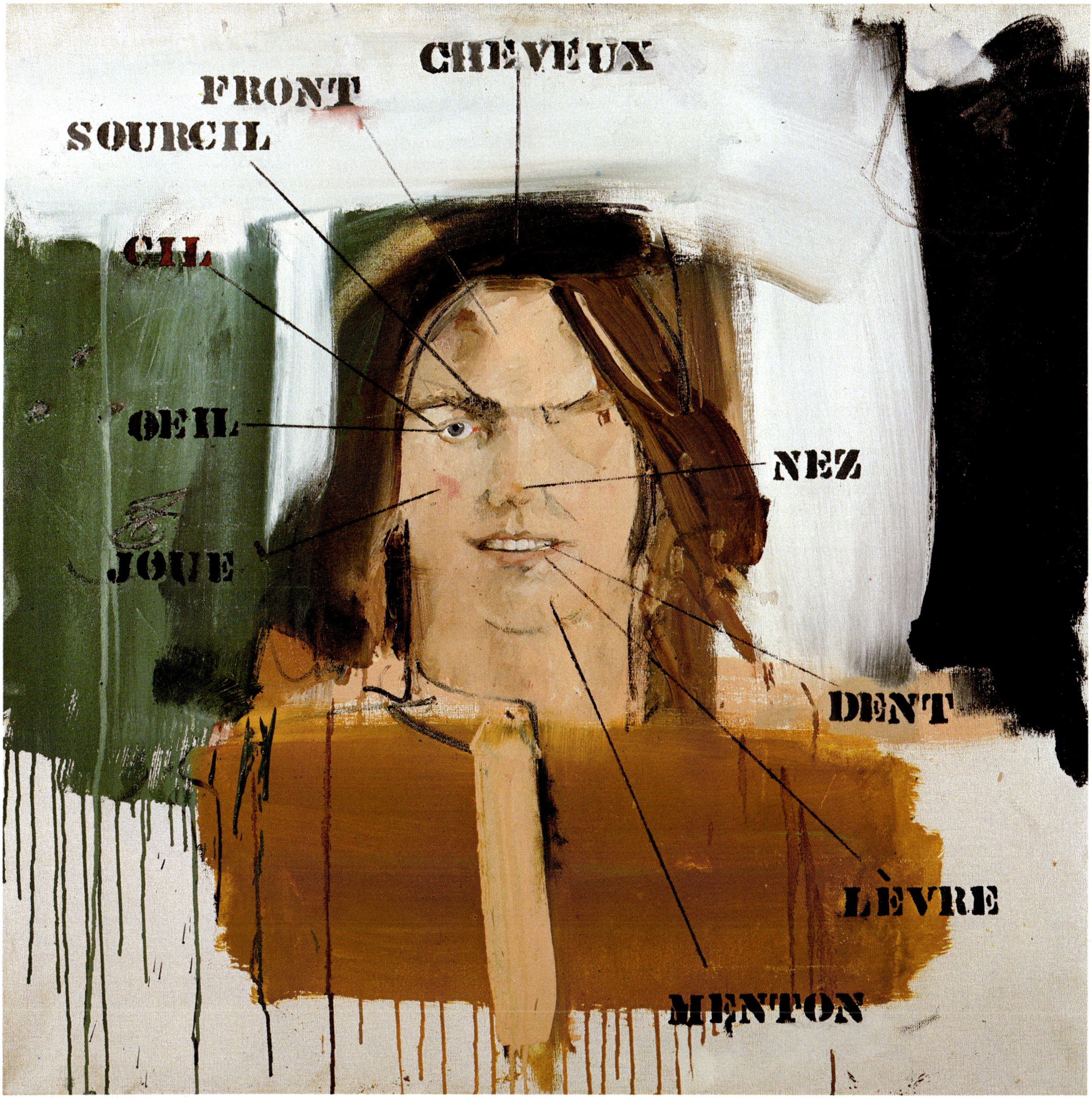
CHEVEUX
FRONT
SOURCIL
CIL
OEIL
NEZ
JOUE
DENT
LÈVRE
MENTON

*BELOW Stuart Davis (1894-1964) was born in Philadelphia, USA. After studying with Robert Henri he became a member of the so-called 'Ash Can School' of American-scene realism which championed the depiction of low-life social subject matter. The Armory Show of international modern art in 1913 made a tremendous impact on the young artist, who was captivated by the technical and tonal innovations of Post-Impressionism, Fauvism and Cubism.* House and Street *(1931) is one of a number of 'stereoscopic' paintings which portray different views of a similar area. There is a complex (modernist) interaction here between technical decisions and subject-matter which can be found, for example, in Edward Hopper's series.*

proportion of the major statements of the modern movement in art, including Picasso's *Les demoiselles d'Avignon* (1907) and Matisse's *The Red Studio* (1907). Many of the works discussed in this book go beyond a literal or pedantic definition of easel painting. Pierre Bonnard (1867-1947) preferred to pin his canvases to the wall while painting and Jackson Pollock (1912-1956) put his large canvases on the floor. The results belong to the same class of object.

The reasons for the survival of such painting techniques are in part historical, social and economic and in part aesthetic.

When easel painting came into existence during the Renaissance, oil paint and canvas were beginning to be used in place of tempera and panel. Easel painting was supplanting the church fresco and reflected the rise of the secular patron, an individualist who wanted an easily transportable image, often a portrait, and who could easily afford to pay for it at a time of advancing prosperity. The Renaissance patron was often a passionate participator in the creation of art. The twentieth-century patron has tended, rightly or wrongly, to insist on the absolute freedom of the artist. But easel painting continues to survive, partly because it still satisfies the same sort of demand that was established during the Renaissance.

Perhaps the 'aesthetic' reason for the survival of easel painting in an age of almost complete artistic freedom is that it provides a constraint. Its basic characteristics provide the sort of limitations that often stimulate rather than hinder artistic endeavor. These characteristics are so elementary that their special qualities are easily underrated or forgotten. They condition the modern artist just as the cave wall conditioned the prehistoric artist. The easel picture has a flat surface and it is usually rectangular. In other words, easel painting stands for the convention of the flat surface and the rectangle.

Although increasingly since the nineteenth century, a premium has been set on originality and the modern artist is supposed to abhor convention, 'originality' is only a relative term. When Frank Stella (b 1935) breaks the rectangle with his shaped canvas, or Richard Smith (b 1931) contradicts the notion of flatness by his sloping canvas, they are playing their role in what the critic Harold Rosenberg has called 'the tradition of the new'. If the spectator did not continue to carry the notion of the flat rectangle in his or her head, such

*RIGHT Juan Gris has been described as the most 'refined and classical' of the four Cubist masters (with Picasso, Braque and Léger). Certainly he reintroduced color into the analytical experiments of Picasso and Braque from 1910-1912.* Still life (The Violin) *(1913) is painted entirely in oils, so that we notice at once the technical imitation of wood paneling, of the wood of the violin, of the white 'chalk' lines which continue the instrument and of the pink patterned wall-paper. This imitation is more suggestive than eye-fooling, and alternates with the thickly painted monochrome or undetailed areas. Vertical and diagonal plane lines, disrupt and silhouette the still-life elements.*

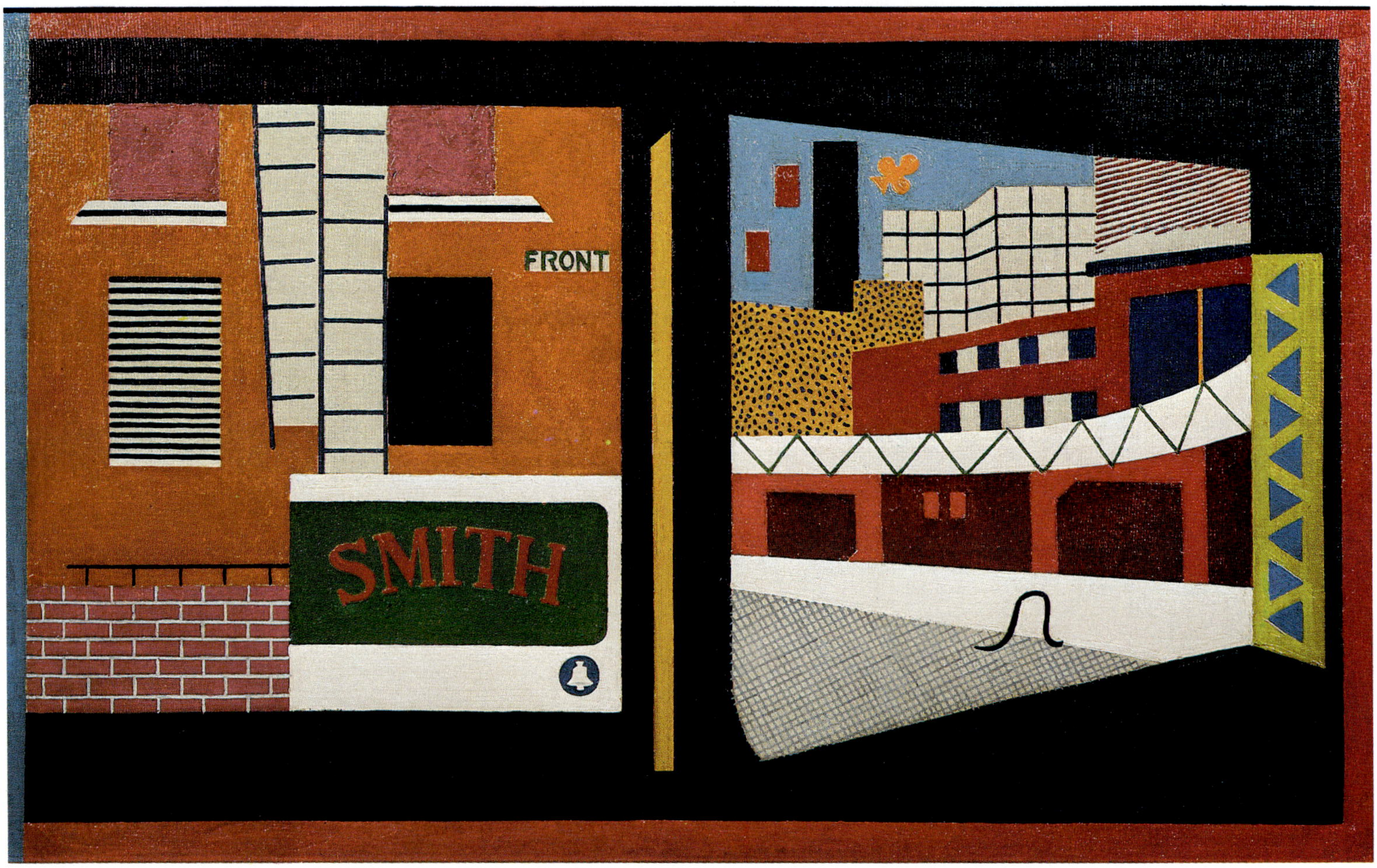

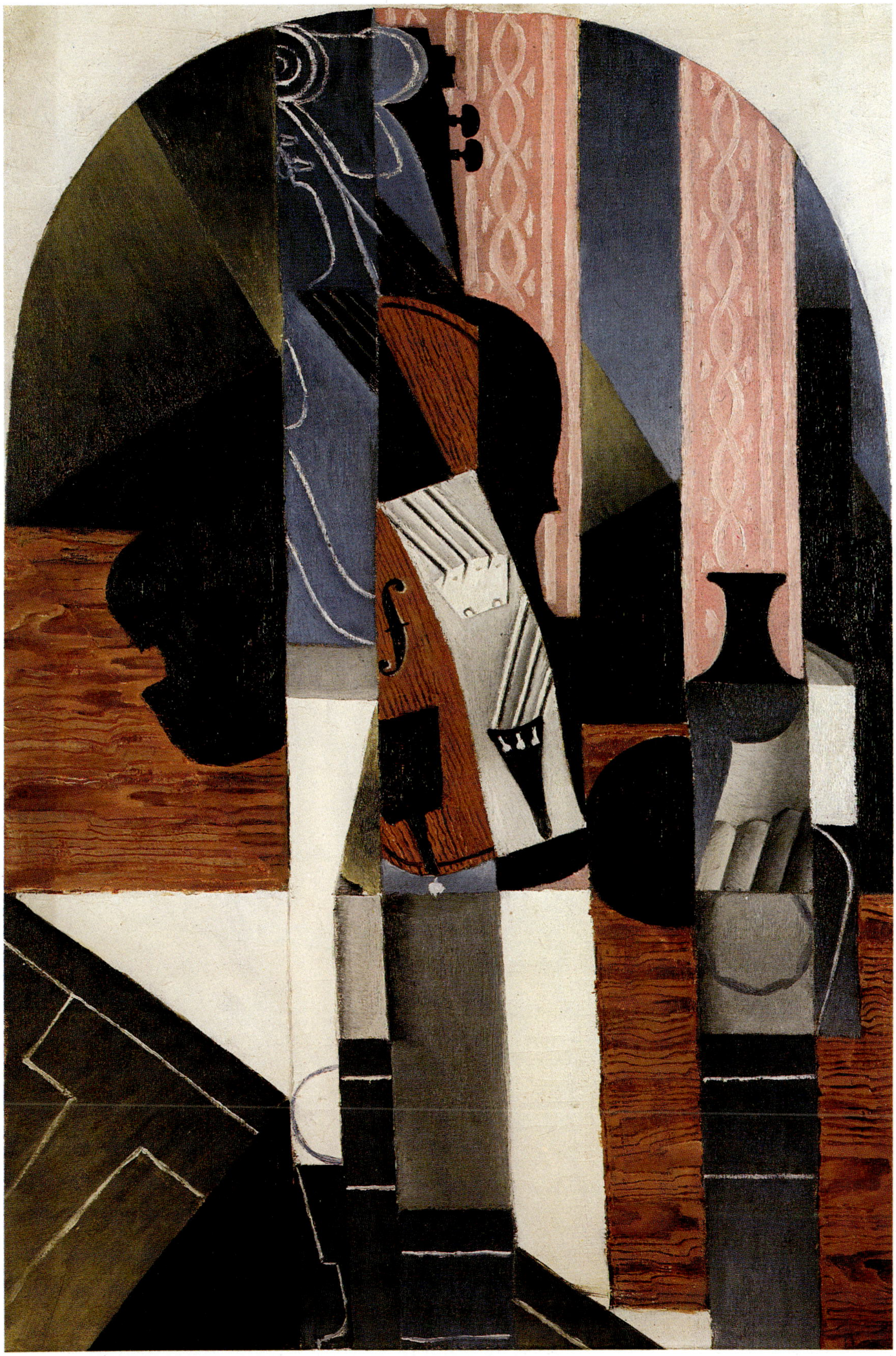

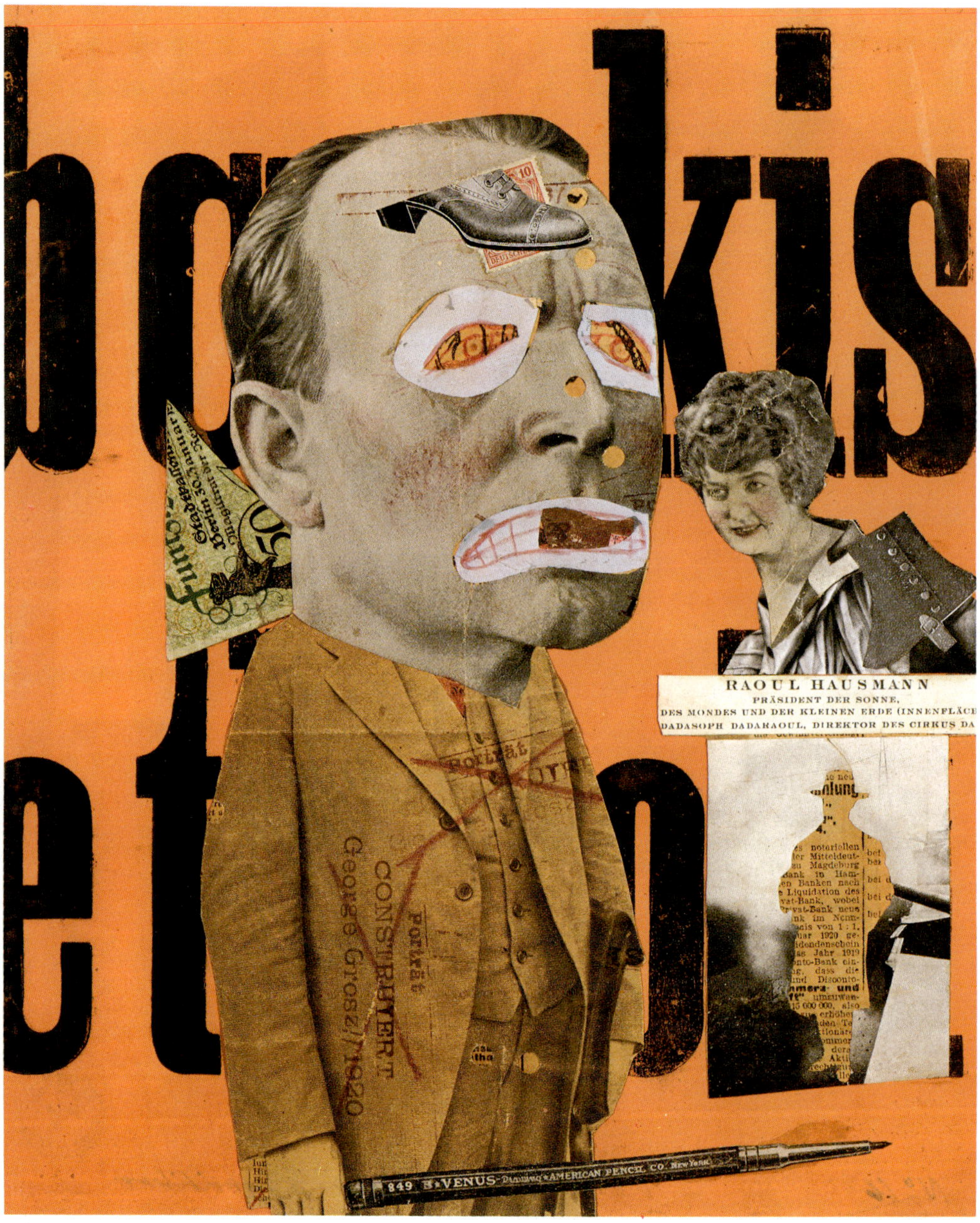


*RIGHT Raoul Hausmann (1886-1971) was the co-founder of the Berlin Dada movement in 1917, and the creator of photomontage in the following year. Photomontage is the art of arranging and glueing photographs or other found illustrative material onto a surface. Strictly speaking it is a type of collage, and it is included here because it is a process of selection, placement and sometimes embellishment, which sets it apart from photographic record, no matter how much this 'record' is distorted by the photographic apparatus or by subsequent techniques of developing. Hausmann actually gave up painting in 1923 and became more interested in various experimental photographic procedures. In* The Art Critic *(1919-1920) the orange-brick background is probably from one of Hausmann's phonetic poem-posters intended to be stuck on walls all over Berlin. The figure with giant head and pen is stamped* Portrait — constructed — of George Grosz 1920, *and is probably a magazine photograph of Hausmann's colleague, Grosz.*

'originality' would be meaningless. While no artist is obliged to paint easel pictures, easel painting may well have survived and flourished precisely because artists have instinctively needed order and tradition at a time of violent conflict in the visual arts.

**Technique**

One of the central problems which arises out of any discussion of artists' techniques is the difficulty of establishing exactly what is meant by the term itself. The work of twentieth-century painters is immensely varied and, consequently, the part played by technique is different for each artist. While to know an artist's materials is to know something of his or her technique, a complete understanding could never be achieved by cataloguing equipment and media. The manual and mechanical processes by which artists employ their materials is also implied by the term but, as Duchamp demonstrated, mental processes or intentions cannot be ignored when discussing methods of execution. What must be established in the case of each artist, therefore, is the nature of the relationship between the three elements: the raw materials; the manual and mechanical processes, and the intention.

A striking portrait of the painter Derain by Balthus (b 1908) provides a useful starting point for a discussion on the definition of technique. The subject of the picture is an

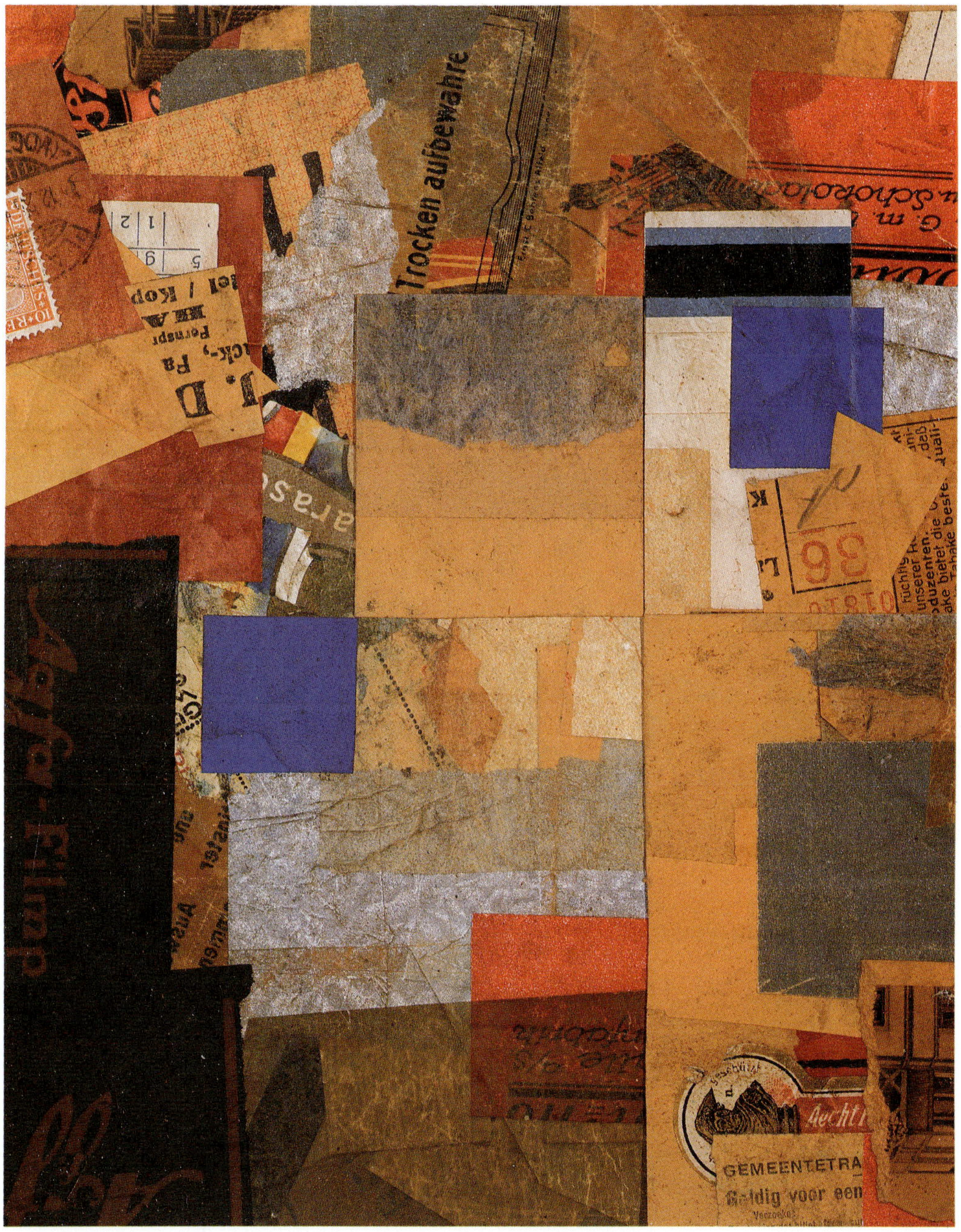


*LEFT After the First World War, Kurt Schwitters (1887-1948) took up the Cubist's technique of collage and made it the basis of his life's work. Like so many of his generation, he moved through a succession of painting styles from Academic to Expressionist, Cubist and Abstract before, in 1910, he created the first of his MERZ-pictures. In the artist's words those consisted of 'disparate elements merged into a work of art, with the help of nails and glue, paper and rags, hammers and oil paint, parts of machinery and bits of lace'. Schwitters also produced MERZ-writing based on the same principle as his painting, where extracts and snatches from a wide variety of printed material were assembled together.* Fernspr *(1926) is a fine example of the minute craftsmanship and original sense of design that Schwitters brought to his work of collage. A miscellany of printed and other paper material is disposed on a cardboard base and articulated in relation to more definite regular cut-out shapes, to produce a dense and original abstract composition.*

artist, portrayed in his studio, with canvases leaning against a wall and a model sitting on a chair: the artist is placed where he belongs, at the center of the stage.

Albert Camus, referring to the technique of Balthus, wrote that it was the distinction of painters to be able to pin down fleeting images glimpsed briefly on a journey upstream towards forgotten springs. For Camus, the true painters were those who, like the great Italians, conveyed the impression that this act of 'pinning down' had just taken place, just as if an aeroplane had stopped in mid-air. All the *figures* in great painting made Camus feel, as he put it, 'that they have only just stopped moving and that, through the miracle of art, they go on living and yet are no longer perishable'.

What does Camus mean by the word 'technique' here? If we substitute for 'technique', 'method of execution' (*Webster's* definition), the sentence barely makes sense. To substitute the word 'achievement' makes better sense but something is lost. Assuming that the word was chosen carefully, it seems likely that Camus uses 'technique' because of the nuance it has of what he calls, 'the miracle of art'. A painting lives in two different worlds – the mental or spiritual, and the physical – at one and the same time. The patient approach of

Balthus, the slow painstaking realization of the image in paint is the result of a long study of masters such as Piero della Francesca (*c* 1410/20-1492) and Nicolas Poussin (*c* 1594-1665). Camus' use of 'technique' points to the intellectual intention of Balthus at least as much as to the materials he uses, or to his 'method of execution'.

The American critic, Clement Greenberg defines Modernism in painting as 'the use of the characteristic methods of a discipline to criticize the discipline itself ... to entrench it more firmly in its area of competence'. These 'methods' can only be considered part of the painter's technique. For Greenberg, Modernist painting is that which not only acknowledges its physical constraints but regards them as distinguishing virtues: flat surface, properties of pigments and shape of support are much more than just the grammar or substructure of art. In certain cases, for example the action painting of Jackson Pollock, the painter's subject and the only discernible *content* of his or her work is the act of painting itself.

The painter Frank Stella said in 1964: 'My painting is based on the fact that only what can be seen there *is* there. It really is an object ... What you see is what you see ... I don't know what else there is. It's really something if you can get a visual sensation that is pleasurable.' Stella's statement leads, of course, to certain difficulties. Mondrian, the inventor of modern geometrical abstraction, sometimes known as Concrete Art, pointed out that even a blank square or circle is an *image* of something. Jean-Paul Sartre, in *L'imaginaire* (1940) demonstrated convincingly that an abstract painting is an *imagined* object, rather than a real one, its aesthetic life being *feigned* by the pigments just as a representational picture feigns reality.

Stella is implying that art and technique are indistinguishable, virtually one and the same thing. It is reasonable to assume that Stella paints instinctively without knowing the sources of his inspiration. Whatever the motive force, his work demonstrates what painting can do that no other art-form can compete with, at a time when cinema has taken over the role of the history painting, the photograph is a substitute for certain types of naturalistic painting and so on.

Certainly introspective tendencies have been exhibited by all the arts, including drama in both theater and film. Sir Charles Eastlake, in the preface to his pioneering work *Materials for a History of Oil Painting* (1847), wrote that 'the author trusts that details relating to the careful processes which were familiar in the best ages of painting will not lead the inexperienced to mistake the means for the end; but only teach them not to disdain the mechanical operations which have contributed to confer durability on the productions of the greatest masters.' In the twentieth century, with some artists, the *durability* has been deliberately disdained and the *mechanical* operations have grown enormously in significance. It is clear in this context that 'technique' is much more than a 'method of execution'.

*A Dictionary of Art Terms* by Reginald S. Haggar (1962) defines technique as a 'complex of manual and mechanical operations that act upon the raw material to organize, shape and mould it according to specific artistic intentions'. If we give this meaning to the word 'technique' in the passage on Balthus by Camus, the sentence makes sense. It furnishes a working definition for technique with respect to the art in the past and art now.

As far as intention is concerned, in many cases not even the artist can describe what actually took place inch by inch, minute by minute, precisely because the process (however much it may rely on experience) is largely instinctive. A picture may have been conceived and painted very rapidly in a state of high emotion or trance. The general intention may be remembered, but the order each area was painted, each brushmark made, is likely to have been forgotten. The intention may have changed as the artist proceeded.

Francis Bacon (b 1909) said that, especially as he got older, '... all painting ... is accident. So I foresee it in my mind ... and yet I hardly ever carry it out as I foresee it. It transforms itself by the actual paint. I use very large brushes, and ... I don't in fact know very often what the paint will do ...'

'In painting, you know, there is not a single process that can be made into a formula', Pierre Auguste Renoir (1841-1919) once told the dealer Ambrose Vollard. 'For instance I once attempted to fix the quantity of oil that I add to the paint on my palette. I couldn't do it. Each time I have to add my oil at a guess.'

The modern artist tends to start with ideas and feelings and has to come down to the mundanities of craft in order to express them. Some artists start as craftsmen – for example Renoir (who painted figures on porcelain) and Georges Braque (1882-1963) – and move on to the realm of ideas and feelings.

**Art or craft?**

The notion of the 'craftsman' is intimately connected with the artist's methods and materials. It also raises the problem of the social role of the artist in a given society; a role which has changed from period to period and from place to place. Some societies have created or assigned a definite place for both artist and artisan, or regarded them as one and the same.

The intention of the cave artists is thought to have been one of magic. By drawing a beast of prey, a bison or a deer pierced by an arrow, psychological power was gained for the purpose of hunting. Since hunting meant sur-

*RIGHT Patrick Caulfield was born in 1936, and his work from the mid-1960s constitutes an individual contribution to British Pop Art. His familiar procedure evolved from about 1968-1970, during which time, like other artists before him, he changed from working in oil paint to acrylic paints, which promote greater flatness and color contrast and whose solubility can make changes and revisions invisible.* After Lunch *(1975) represents the interior of a restaurant done up in a 'Swiss' style. The design was transferred and enlarged by means of a grid from an initial drawing onto polythene which was placed onto the bare canvas. After the canvas had been covered with a ground color the design was traced onto it with bold, black lines. Touches of color or infill were then added where necessary, the waiter's bow-tie or the orange goldfish, for example. The photo-mural of the Château of Chillon was originally intended to be glued into the picture directly onto the canvas. When this proved technically impossible, the artist decided to execute a minutely exact copy of the original photo-mural, again using the grid-transfer method. The result is a striking confluence of modernist style, and illustrates the technical competence and resourcefulness of some recent painting.*

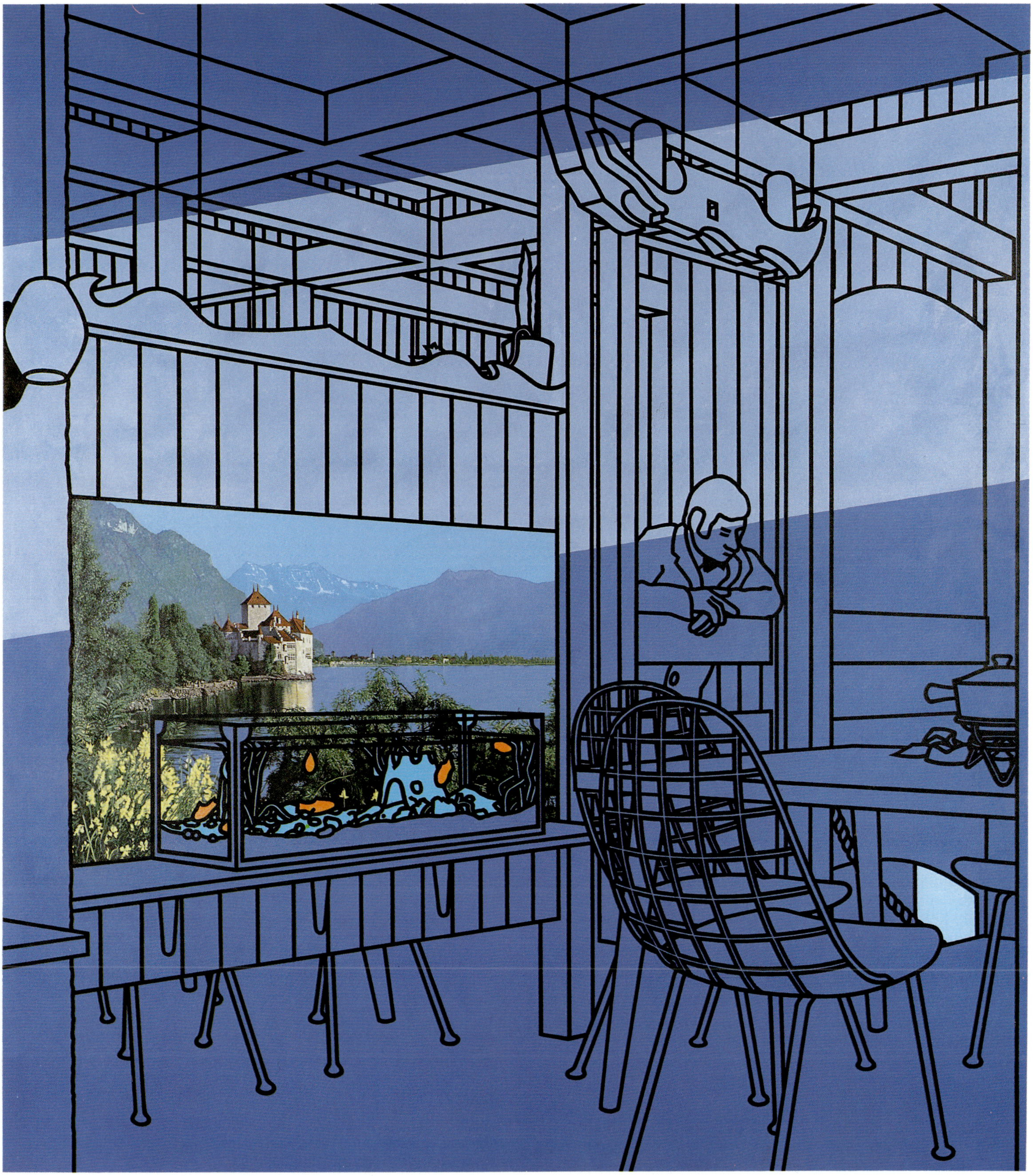

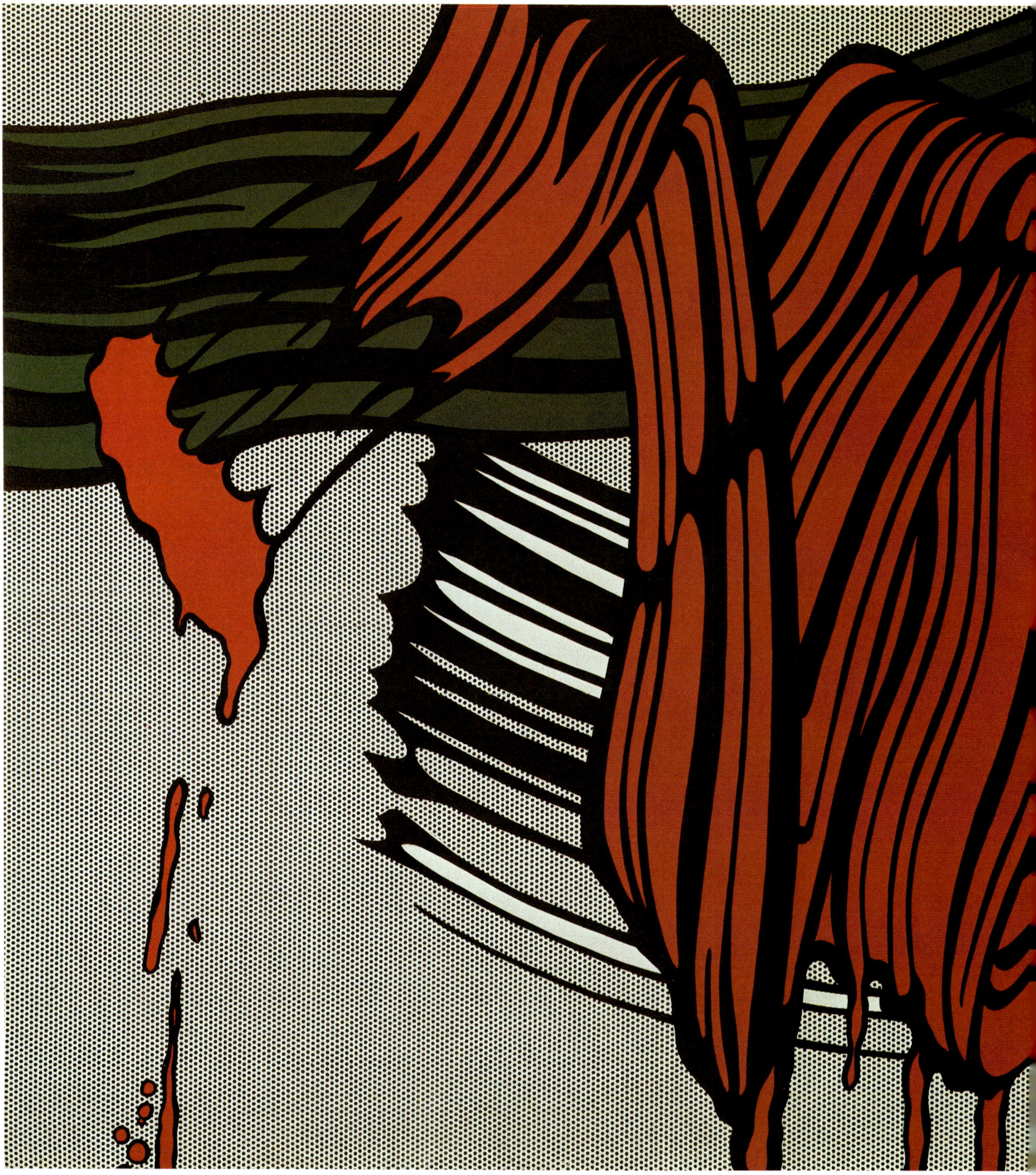

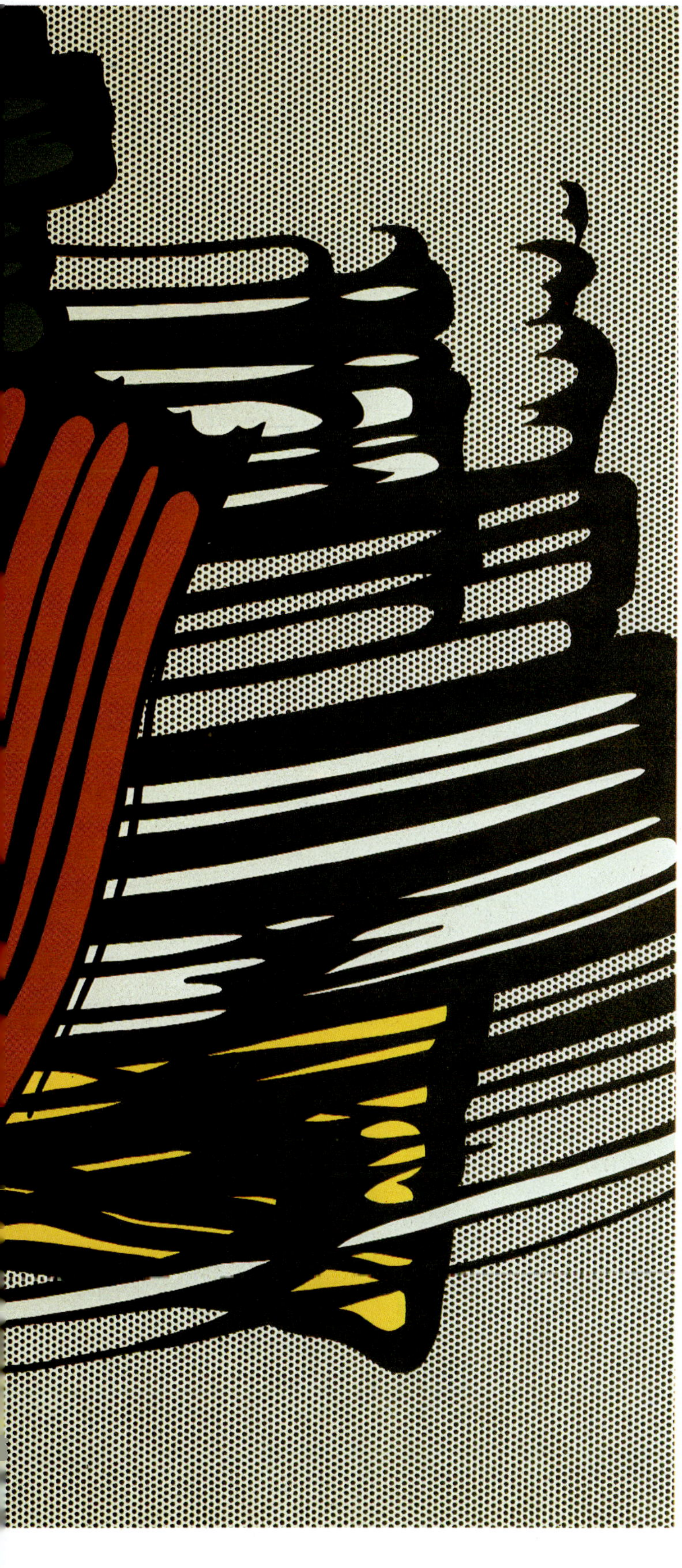

vival, the artist's role must have been closer to the witch doctor than the craftsman. The role of the artist in prehistoric times seems to have been more fundamental to the life of the group than that of the artisan in modern times. Perhaps this is why certain artists of the twentieth century, especially Duchamp and the Surrealists, have tried to recapture a magical role for the artist.

By way of extreme contrast, in fourth century BC Athens, Plato in *The Republic* seems to have considered a painter of pictures as inferior in certain ways to a carpenter. This idea is reinforced by the Greek language: the word *teuxy* meant an 'art' and it was akin to *tekton*, a carpenter. According to Plato, a carpenter produced something useful like a table which was an honest copy of the idea of an (idealized) table. (The whole of the physical world, according to Platonic philosophy, was a kind of shadow of an ideal world.) The painter portraying that table was only making a copy of a copy of the idea of a table. Such a painter was a mere purveyor of illusions. Plato also believed that the artist was inclined to be socially disruptive, however admirable individually, and had the potential to inspire fear among a society's authorities.

In the Middle Ages, the artist was generally thought of as a sort of craftsman. In addition, from the seventh to the twelfth centuries, the clergy guarded the technical secrets of painting as they guarded the secrets of medicine. In the thirteenth century, artisans' guilds were formed and technical knowledge became more widely accessible. In about 1390 Cennino Cennini, a somewhat obscure artist himself, wrote his famous treatise, *Il Libro dell'Arte (The Craftsman's Handbook)* which gives an account of the tempera technique of the school of Giotto (*c* 1266-1337). Cennini noted that there are two attitudes among those entering what he calls 'the profession': some enter it through poverty and domestic need, or for profit; others, whose 'intellect will take delight in drawing' are moved by 'the impulse of a lofty spirit'. His words already reflect the difference that was being discerned between the artist and artisan (and perhaps the artist and the commercial artist of today). It was the difference between the everyday world and that of the intellect and the senses.

During the High Renaissance, the position of the artist changed, strongly influenced by humanism and individualism. Some artists were also intellectuals; Piero della Francesca was a mathematician as well as a painter. And clearly Michelangelo (1475-1564) and Leonardo da Vinci (1452-1519) were two of the great minds of the time: manifestly superior to a simple craftsman from some medieval artisans' guild. Interestingly, Antonio Pollaiuolo (1431-1498), Andrea Verrocchio (1435-1488), Sandro Botticelli (1445-1510) and Domenico

LEFT Big Painting No 6 *(1965) is one of a number of large-scale works representing brushstrokes that Lichtenstein executed in the mid-1960s. By isolating and amplifying a single or a small number of brushstrokes the artist is drawing attention to the basic unit of most painting techniques, as well as casting an ironic glance back at the methods of the Abstract Expressionists. The irony is augmented by the fastidious technical procedure that Lichtenstein engineered in order to paint these works on such a scale. 'The images were arrived at by applying loaded brushstrokes of black Magna color upon acetate, allowing the paint to shrink on the repellent surface and to dry, and then overlapping the sheets to find a suitable image, which was finally projected onto a canvas and redrawn.'*

Ghirlandaio (1449-1494) all started their careers as goldsmiths.

The Renaissance view of the artist had a profound and lasting effect on technique in painting. The enquiring mind of the Renaissance extended to technical experimentation. Hilaire Hiler, in his *Notes on the Technique of Painting* (1934), took a pessimistic view of the results: 'It [the Renaissance] was a great period of experiment, and technically the rush of revolutionary ideas crying for expression made painters seek for new techniques fitted to express them. In spite of the prodigies performed by individuals whose very names have come to be normalities in the history of art, such fame did these *tours de force* bring them, it must be considered from a standpoint of material technique as a period of decadence. Technically speaking, we are still in it.'

Hiler's points are as relevant to this century as to the fifteenth and sixteenth. He is not questioning the right of the artist to experiment but lamenting some of the results from the point of view of durability. Leonardo da Vinci's *Last Supper* (1495-1497) is a notorious example of a great fresco which began to disintegrate shortly after it had been painted. The wall in Milan on which it was painted was first covered with a mixture of resin, mastic, gesso and other materials. This coating proved insufficient for an unusually damp wall in an area prone to flooding. But Leonardo more than compensated for his unfortunate technical error. Sir Charles Eastlake (in *Materials for a History of Oil Painting*) credits him with introducing the following changes in the practice of oil painting:' i) The exclusion of the light ground by a solid preparatory painting. ii) The use of essential oils together with nut oil in that preparation. iii) The practice of thinly painting and ultimately scumbling and glazing over the carefully prepared dead color, as opposed to the simpler and more decided processes, or sometimes the single *alla prima* operation of the Flemish masters. iv) The reservation of thick resinous vehicles (when employed to cover the lights) for fixed operation, so as to avoid as much as possible a glossy surface during the earlier stages of the work. v) The use of essential oil varnishes.'

This list gives us an insight into how a great innovatory artist proceeds with the practicalities of his work. Leonardo's pictorial achievement was literally to create a new way of seeing, by inventing or perfecting *chiaroscuro* (light and shade to produce an effect of modeling), *sfumato* (the subtle blending of colors into a misty effect) and aerial perspective, which gives an illusion of distance by grading tones and subtle color relationships.

Increasingly, the artist was being thought of as a scholar and a gentleman. This coincided with the foundation of academies where painting could be studied, not primarily as a craft but as a branch of learning like mathematics, literature or philosophy. The Académie Royale de Peinture et de Sculpture was founded in Paris in 1648, the Royal Academy of Arts in London in 1768. The use of line, which is an abstraction, was thought to be more intellectual than the use of color, which is more obviously present in nature and more sensual. Students were taught to concentrate on the human figure and to idealize it. In the middle of the eighteenth century when excavations at Herculaneum and Pompeii dramatically underlined the interest that the Italian Renaissance had shown in the ancient civilizations of Greece and Rome, the Neo-Classical Movement gathered strength. Neo-Classicism boosted not only classical style and subject matter but also the influence of the academies; as late as the end of last century, art students learnt to draw by copying plaster casts of antique statuary before graduating to the live nude.

There is little doubt that during the early nineteenth century the cause of craftsmanship suffered greatly. Jacques Louis David (1748-1825), whose ideas dominated art education from 1790 into the early decades of this century, spurned the traditional expertise of crafts and guilds and in the cause of Neo-Classicism discouraged his students from studying the Baroque and Rococo styles or methods. The tradition of revolt, which is inimical to the passing on of technical knowledge, had begun to get under way. In addition, the preparation of artists' materials was done outside the studio. As soon as the artist stopped grinding and preparing colors according to proven recipes, he or she became the dupe of the color merchants.

There was a general resentment on the part of artists such as Eugène Delacroix (1798-1863) that the technical secrets of the great late medieval and early Renaissance oil painters, whose work has proved so astonishingly durable, had been lost forever. Even seventeenth- and eighteenth-century practices were not handed on to succeeding generations. To take one example, the nineteenth-century use of bitumen in underpainting, a purpose for which it is not suited, has been responsible for damage to innumerable pictures. Its poor drying power has tended to crack the layers above, causing the asphaltum to press through. In the seventeenth century, bitumen was correctly used as a glaze – by Rembrandt (1606-1669) for example – and it did no damage. Fortunately, as has been seen in Leonardo da Vinci's *Last Supper* in Milan, it takes more than one technical error to spell disaster.

At the end of the nineteenth century, the debate about the status of the artist was resurrected. William Morris (1834-1896), the English poet, artist and socialist, wanted to return to the medieval view of the artist as artisan. He refused to accept the Industrial

RIGHT *Marcel Duchamp (1887-1968) was one of the most technically inventive of modern artists. But unlike Picasso, for example, he was not dedicated to the procedures, however innovative, of the fine art tradition. By 1913 he had abandoned conventional media such as oil on canvas, for experiments in three-dimensions, ready-made, constructions and 'machines'. After 1923 he virtually gave up work as an artist altogether.* Nude Descending a Staircase No 2 *(Jan 1912) caused a sensation at the Armory Show in America (1913), and has been claimed as 'one of the watersheds of twentieth-century art'. Duchamp admitted the influence of chronophotography (figures, animals and objects recorded photographically in motion), and white points in the area of the hands recall the dots in chronophotographs which resulted from torches carried by the protagonists to aid the recording of their movement. But so complex are the sources for this work and its place in the chain of Duchamp's activity up to the early 1920s, that the viewer is constantly aware of the crucial interface between technique, form and the world of ideas.*

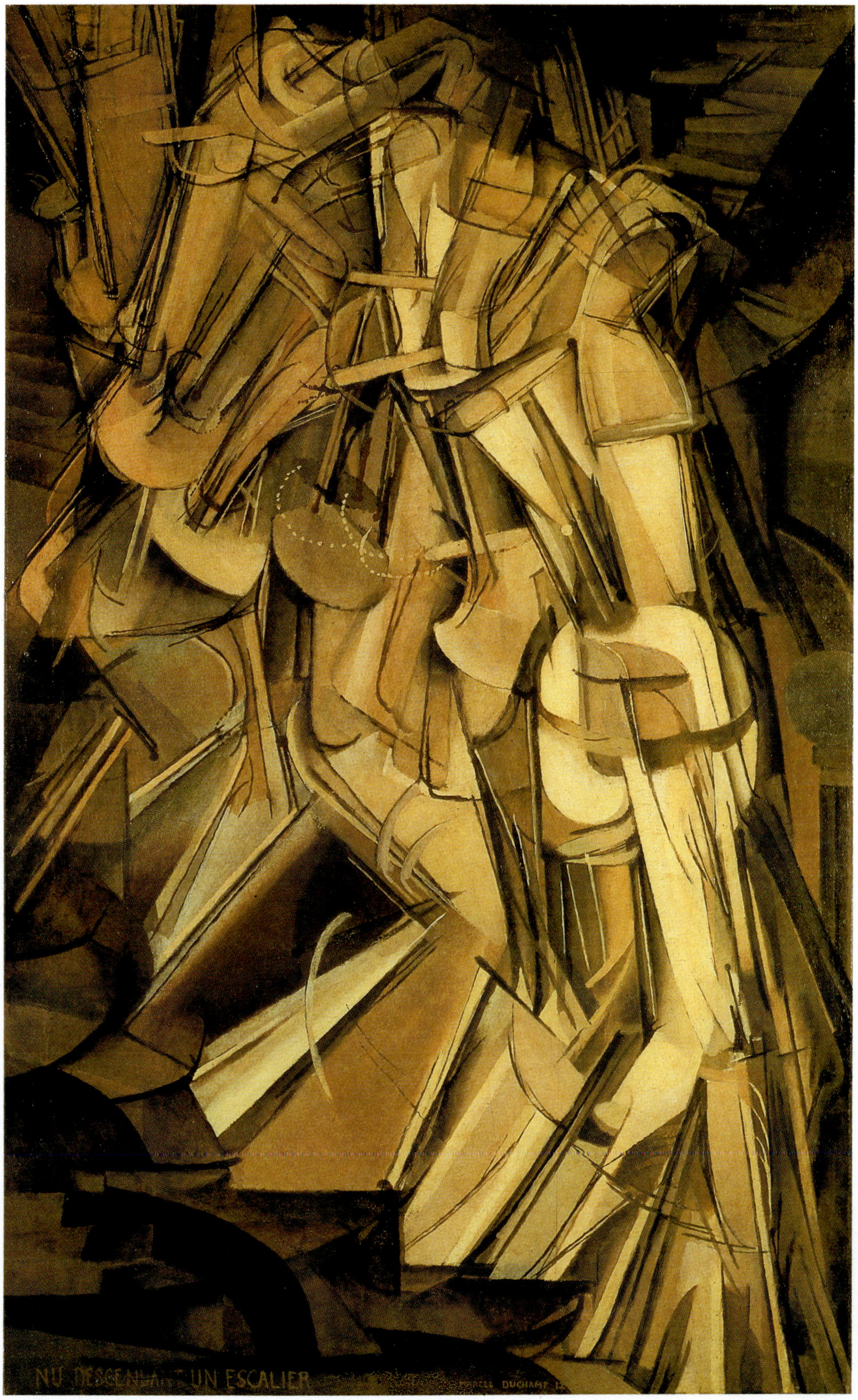
NU DESCENDANT UN ESCALIER
MARCEL DUCHAMP

*BELOW* The Conservationist *(1978) by Boyd Webb (b 1947) is a recent example of the kind of challenge issued to painting by other media, but notably by the photographic image, either still or moving. Boyd has arranged a scene, a tableau, and then recorded the information at a crucial moment; here before the painter (decorator) reduces the interior to blankness.*

Revolution and advance of technology and dreamed of reviving the handcrafts of weaving, pottery and furniture making. In 1862 he started a designing and furnishing business and used his private printing press, the Kelmscott Press, for artistic productions. If society were to restyle the artist as craftsman, Morris felt, there would be a welcome relief from the pressure to be an individualist, an intellectual living up to a Michelangelo or aspiring to the Romantic notion of the passionate genius.

Morris had a great influence on late Victorian art and decoration in both England and on the continent, and his idealism continues to provoke discussion today. But he was not himself a painter of any importance, unlike the Pre-Raphaelite painters Dante Gabriel Rossetti (1828-1882) and Edward Burne-Jones (1833-1898) (an artist who at one point influenced Picasso); and he was in no position to change society radically. Possibly when describing the artist as craftsman, he was merely describing himself.

**The twentieth century**

Another art and craft movement, more successful and enduring than Morris's, was the Bauhaus Movement of the 1920s. It, too, took inspiration from the Middle Ages, wanting to fuse art and craftsmanship and lead art back into daily life. But its methods and style were essentially modern. The painters Paul Klee

*RIGHT Lucio Fontana (1899-1968), in his* Manifesto Bianco *(1946), developed a theory known as Spazialismo (Spatialism).* Spatial Concept 'Waiting' *(1960) is a work where the natural canvas has been slit. This mode of working grew out of his attempt to repudiate the illusory space of conventional painting and propose, in his own words, 'a new dimension beyond the canvas, time and space'.*

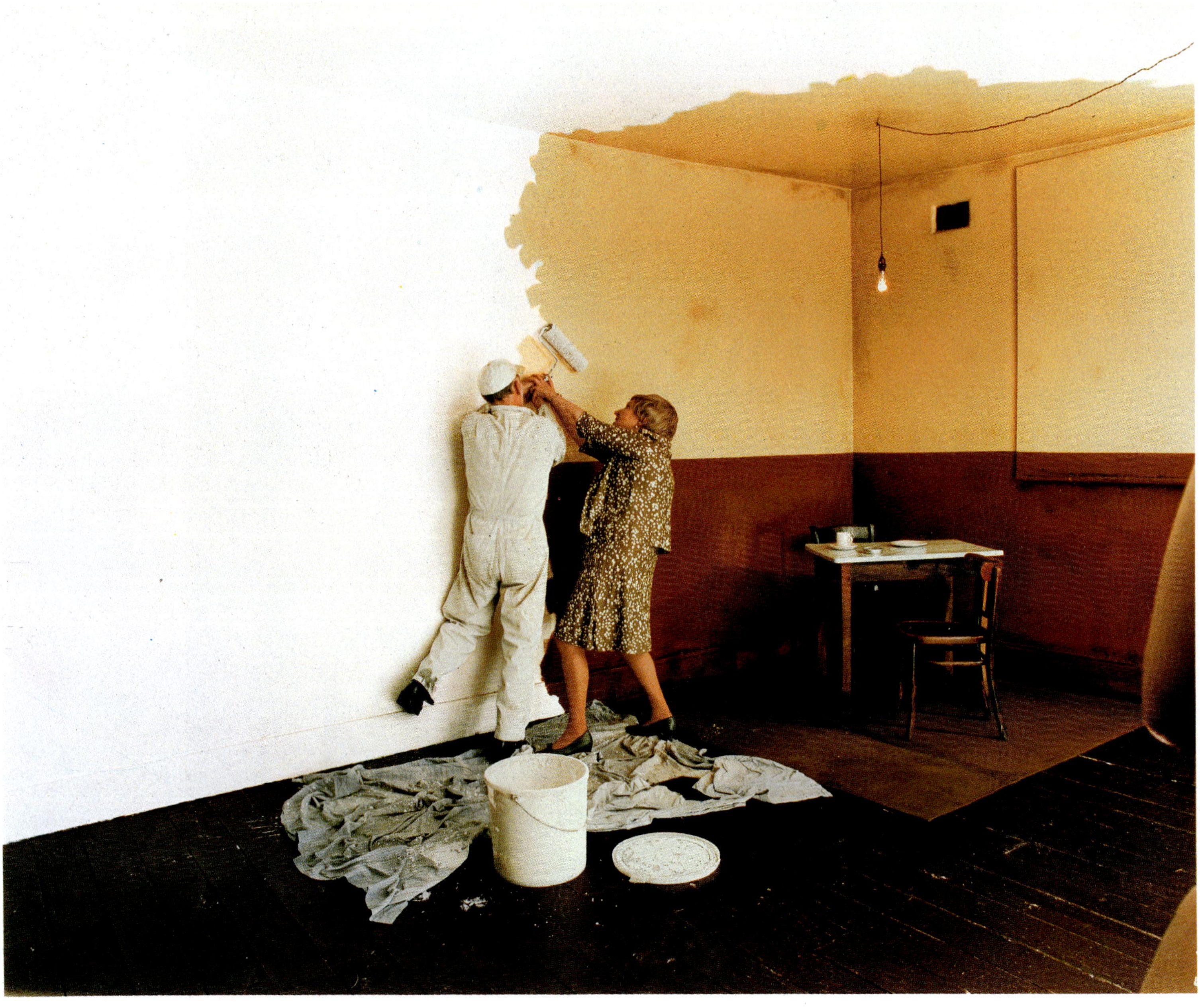

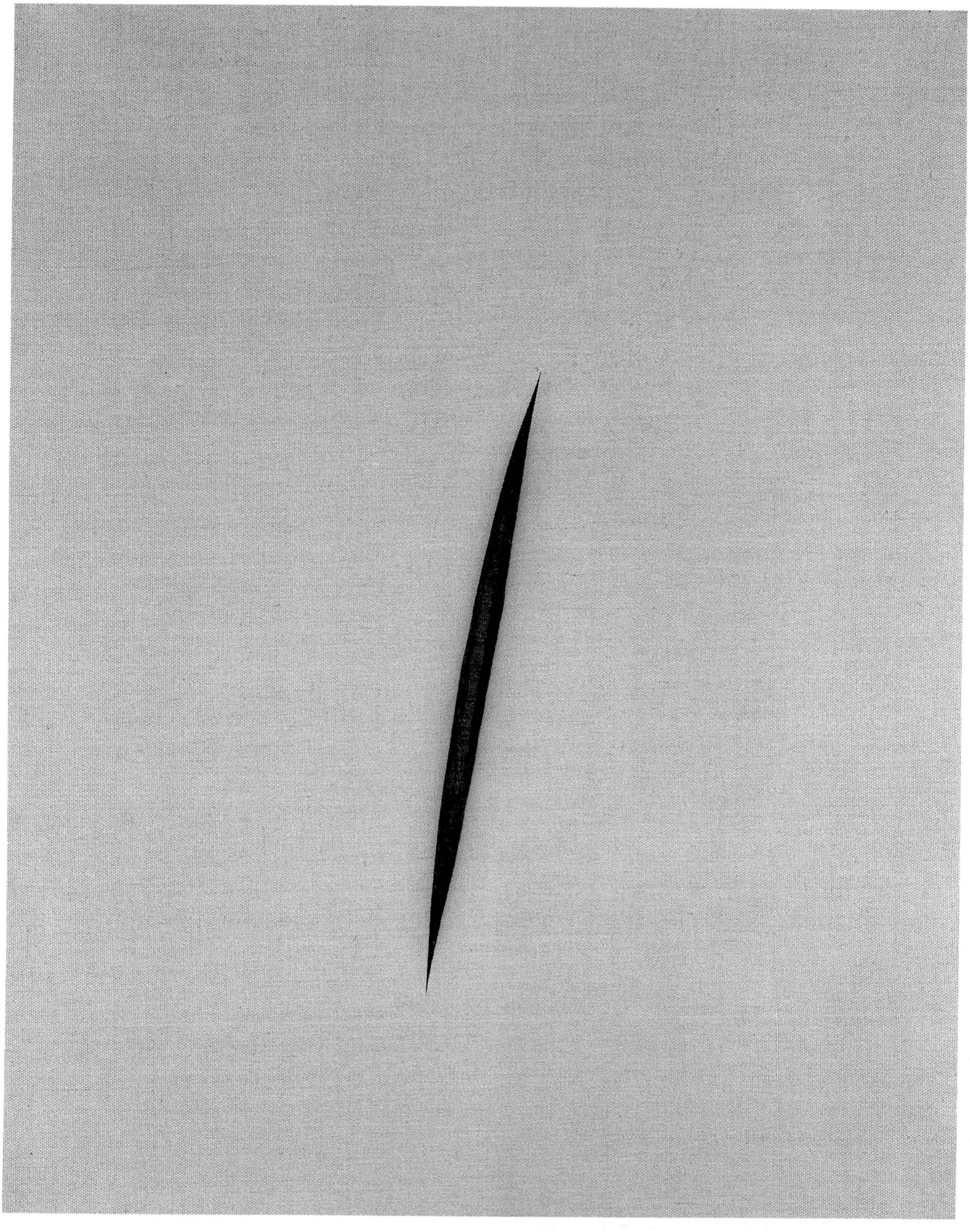

*BELOW Henri Matisse (1869-1964) produced* The Painter and his Model *(1916-1917) at the end of his own 'period of experiment', and suggests that for him 'painting was ultimately life-painting, recording an instinctive reaction of the living model posing in the studio.' Passages of densely worked black and white are relieved by the decorative Baroque mirror, but the work is deeply reflective, too, on the complex relation between artist, model and picture, and between the interior and exterior worlds represented.*

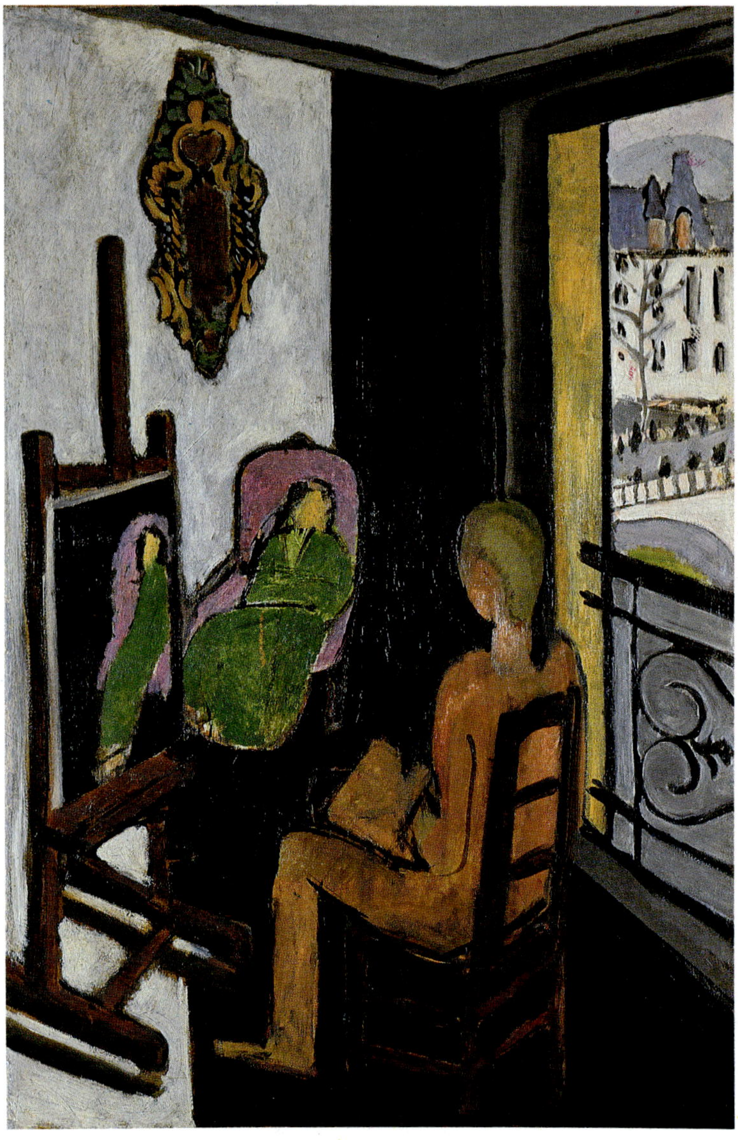

(1879-1940), Wassily Kandinsky (1866-1944) and Piet Mondrian were all involved in the Bauhaus, which still influences art.

The Bauhaus school placed its notions of art and craft firmly in the context of contemporary life, while Morris had a romanticized view of the medieval artist,which was misleading. Interestingly it is Plato's view of the artist that turns out to have been prophetic. Plato's *Republic*, his Utopian, closed society, could not tolerate the disruptive individualism of the artist. The same has proved true of the closed societies of this century. In Nazi Germany in the 1930s the Expressionists were declared decadent, and persecuted. In Russia immediately after the 1917 Revolution artists, many of whom had backed the revolutionaries, were accepted or at least tolerated. As soon as the Bolsheviks were in full control, they stamped out what Lenin called the 'puerilities of the leftists' and the works of pioneering artists such as Kasimir Malevich (1878-1935) was virtually censored. Some artists fled; Kandinsky went to Germany. The official art approved by the authorities, Socialist Realism, became more like propaganda than art. Extolling the virtues of work in field and factory, Socialist Realism to this day often bears an uncanny resemblance to the art Hitler admired, in which healthy blond youths play the part of the workers.

Fortunately for the development of modern art, a significant number of important artists escaped the closed societies engendered by the Stalinists in Russia and by Nazism in Europe. Many ended up in America during the 1940s, giving an impetus to the modern movement of art which had begun to grow there since the Armory Show of 1913.

A painter in the twentieth century has a highly individualistic approach to technique and to craftsmanship. It is instructive to compare Picasso and Braque in this respect, since at one point in the creation of Cubism, their work was so close. Braque is often referred to as a good craftsman. 'I make the background of my canvases with the greatest care', he wrote in 1954, 'because it is the ground that supports the rest; it is like the foundations of a house. I am always very occupied and preoccupied with the material because there is as much sensibility in the technique as in the rest of the painting. I prepare my own colors, I do the pulverizing . . . I work with the materials, not with ideas.' Braque, like his father and grandfather, was employed as a house painter as a young man, and certain principles and practices of the craft stayed with him. He developed a *sound* technique patiently. Picasso was often a good craftsman too but it does not seem to have been one of his primary concerns; he was more interested in ideas and the company of poets than painters. Restlessly inventive in the area of technique, Picasso was gifted with an instinctive knowledge of how to handle all kinds of materials. If sometimes his craftsmanship was less sound than Braque's, it is a small price to pay for his protean inventiveness. Highly visible cracks have developed in the left center area of Picasso's painting *The Three Dancers* (1925), due to the contraction of the thick top layer of paint over the years. 'The paint is solid enough and will not flake off', Picasso commented. 'Some people might want to touch them [the cracks] out but I think they add to the painting. On the face you see how they reveal the eye that was painted underneath.'

For Picasso, vitality was the measure of art. For him a 'finished' painting, in the sense of being highly finished like nineteenth-century glossy varnished Salon paintings, was a dead painting. In fact, the technical difference between Picasso and Braque, although seeming extreme, involves only a shift of emphasis.

It may be concluded therefore that for both

philosophical and historical reasons the craftsmanship of a craftsman is unlike the technique of a painter in important ways. A major distinction between the artist and craftsman is that we expect the artist, whose aims are more ambitious and complicated, to be more experimental in terms of technique.

The issue of craftsmanship boils down to two main elements: the problem of durability or permanence, and the problem of facility with materials. Commonsense decrees that a painter should build a painting to last as long as possible; but the history of twentieth-century art is not the history of commonsense. One of the characteristics of the consumer society is that of inbuilt obsolescence in goods such as cars and even apparently in houses, in blocks of flats and offices. A number of modern artists have reflected this irony and have borrowed from it, deliberately stressing the impermanence of their own work. Obsolescence featured in the historic 'This is Tomorrow' exhibition at the Whitechapel Art Gallery, London, 1956, which showed the artists Richard Hamilton (b 1922) and Eduardo Paolozzi (b 1924) as the precursors of Pop Art. The German artist, Diter Rot (b 1930), later made works of art out of substances such as cheese and chocolate.

Such *advertising* of obsolescence cannot be criticized on the grounds of dishonesty. It may be a perfectly valid comment for an artist to incorporate into a work and when the work itself disintegrates, a photograph preserves its memory. Such work must be valid as far as it corresponds with the intention of the artist.

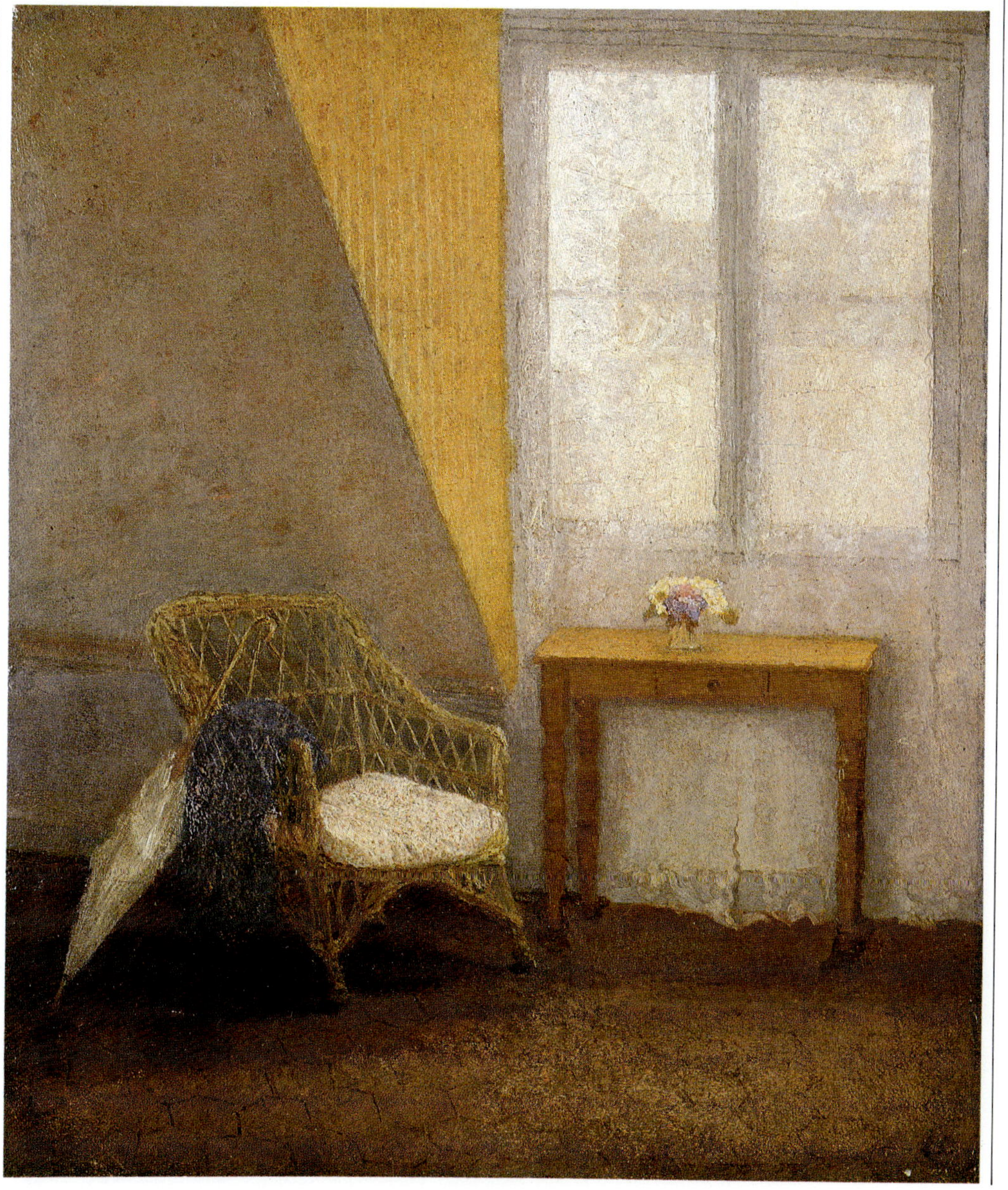

LEFT A Corner of the Artist's Room in Paris *(1907-1910) by Gwen John (1876-1939) reveals the strong influence of the American James Whistler (1834-1903) with whom she studied in Paris. John's work consists mainly of figure paintings and landscapes executed in a simple retiring style, which display an almost neurotic sensibility.*

# 1900 1920

## Influence

The crucial years for the modern movement in painting are from 1905 to 1914. It is more straightforward to analyze the whole first half of the nineteenth century in terms of movements, styles and techniques than these early years of this century. But the twentieth century only rejected the values of the nineteenth when it had received as much stimulus as it could take.

From 1800 to 1850 in France the three outstanding styles were the Neo-Classicism of Jacques Louis David (1748-1825) and Jean-Dominique Ingres (1780-1867) which, from a technical viewpoint, invariably reveals a smooth paint surface beneath the glossy varnish and a look of high finish; the Romanticism of Théodore Géricault (1791-1824) and Eugène Delacroix (1798-1863) which generated a more imaginative and expressive use of oil paint; and finally the Realism of Gustave Courbet (1819-1877) in which paint was ap-

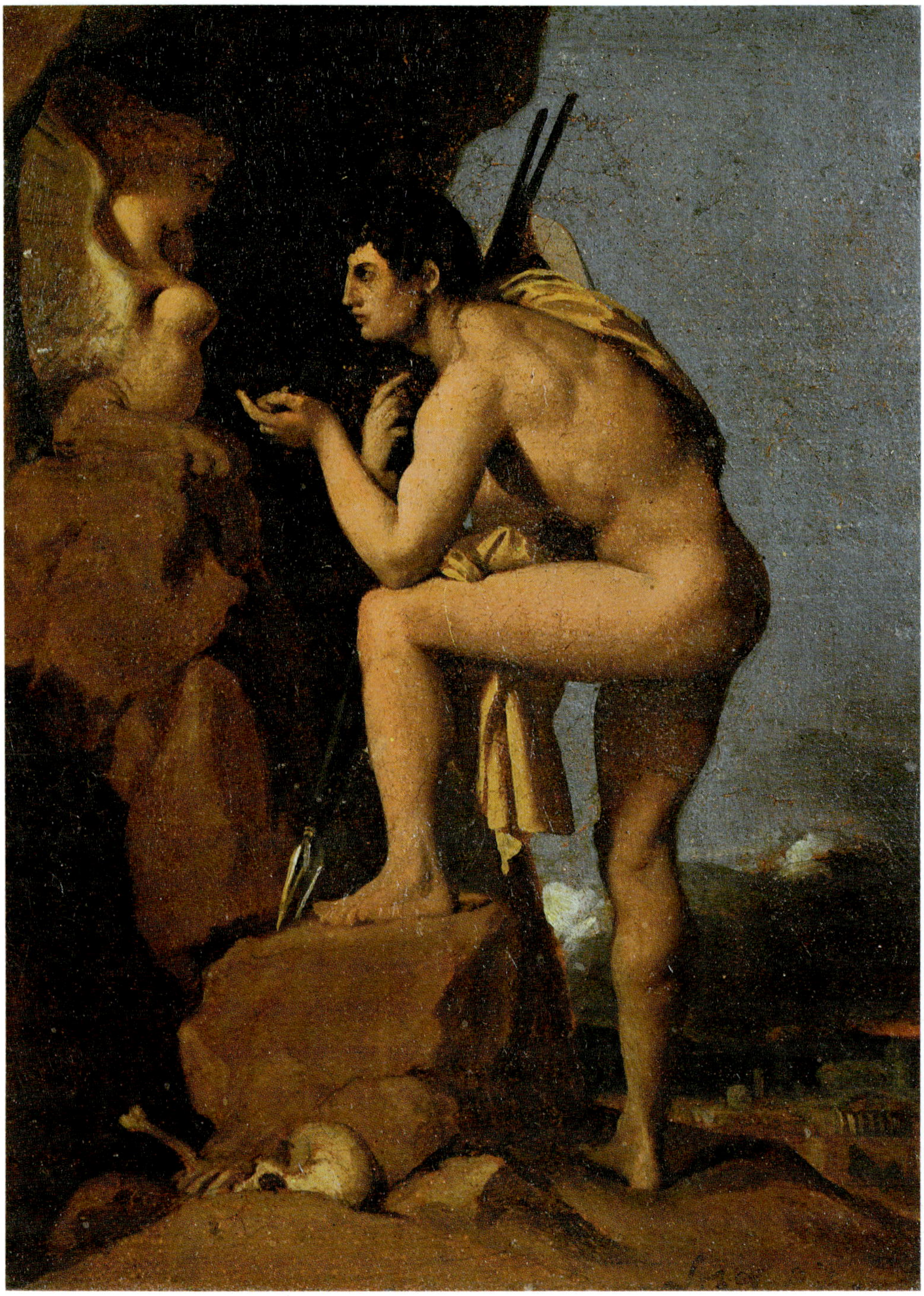

LEFT *Ingres created a personal, sensual style that moved away from the grand manner of late eighteenth-century Neo-Classicists, using line with a new expressiveness and replacing the dramatic cross-lighting with soft, full-face light and opaque shadows (which used non-traditional white). The exposed canvas texture in* Oedipus and the Sphinx *(1828) was an Ingres innovation; it was unconventional among the Neo-Classicists who preferred a smooth finish.*

plied thickly in a straightforward, direct way. As the century progressed, many artists felt less and less need to build a painting up in successive layers according to the methods of the late medieval and early Renaissance masters.

Neo-Classicism continued to influence the teaching methods of the academies and the practice of academic artists. Very few non-academic modern artists have imitated the smooth, highly finished surface of Neo-Classicism. The masters of twentieth-century painting have tended to reject or ignore such methods and practices. A few, including Henri Rousseau (1844-1910), Max Ernst (1891-1976) and Yves Tanguy (1900-1955), did not even attend art academies or schools. On the other hand, an older more potent tradition of classical art, which stresses form rather than subject matter and is represented in seventeenth-century France by Nicolas Poussin (*c* 1594-1665), embedded itself in the modern movement in a new guise with Paul Cézanne (1839-1906), who insisted on structure in painting. At least one art historian, R. H. Wilenski, writing in 1927, regarded Cézanne and the modern movement as fundamentally classical. But Cézanne cannot be summed up by the word 'classical' and the highly eclectic modern movement owes more to Romantic painters.

The aim of Romanticism was the expression of emotion directly and subjectively through color and the actual handling of paint; an idea which Fauvism and German Expressionism brought to twentieth-century painting. The Romantic Movement also led by a different path, that of the imagination and literature, in the direction of Surrealism.

The idea behind Courbet's realism, the shockingly novel idea that art should be concerned with what is before the eyes and should be contemporaneous, found a twentieth-century counterpart, in a less legible stylistic form, in Cubism (a fundamentally realist form with classical and Romantic affinities). But the way that Courbet applied paint was almost heavy-handed in its directness.

The second half of the nineteenth century in France is a much more complex period. There was an acceleration in the pace of stylistic change; styles and techniques began to multiply. The vocabulary of art criticism and art history responded with terms such as 'Impressionism', 'Post-Impressionism', 'Expressionism', 'Symbolism' and 'Neo-Impressionism' which tend to oversimplify what happened.

Year by year, painter by painter, the Impressionists modified their aims and techniques. In the area of brushwork the densely applied brushstrokes of Claude Monet (1840-1926) (in whose work Impressionism reached its highest point) have gained new signifi-

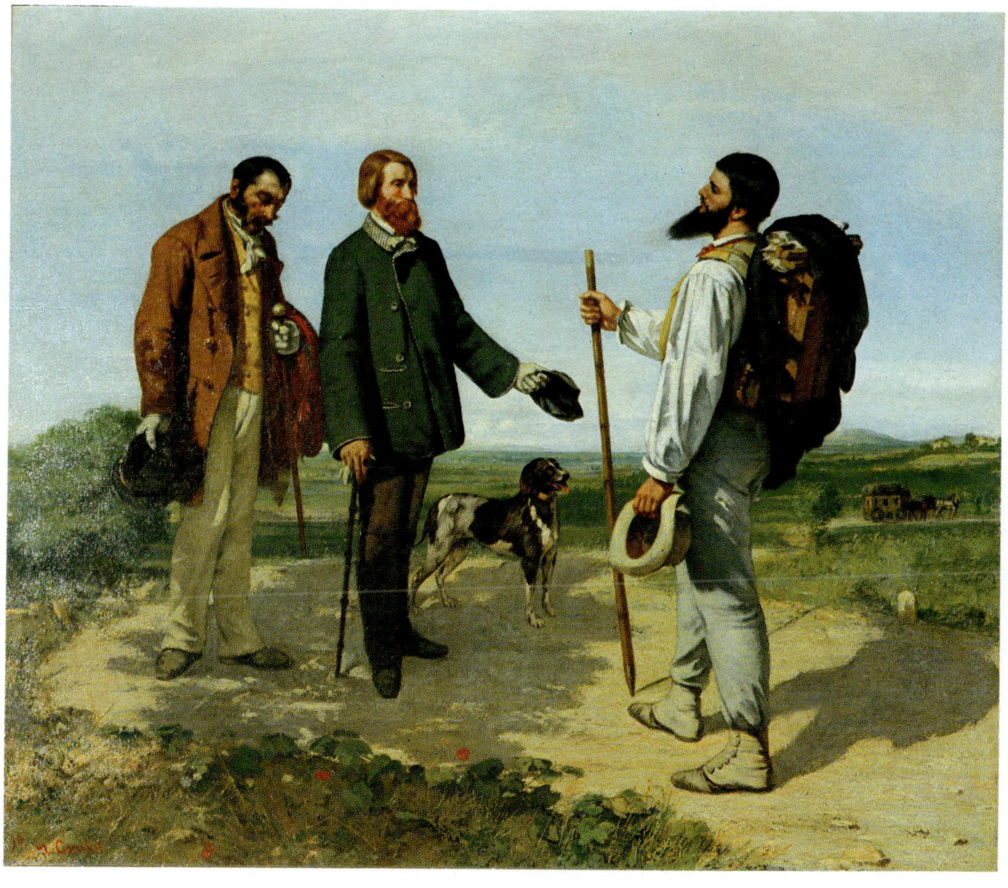

LEFT *Gustave Courbet, the most influential Realist painter, chose subjects alien to both public and critics — middle- and working-class provincial people and rural themes — and employed a lively and uncompromising painting technique which was highly innovative. In* La Rencontre, *painted in 1854, Courbet has omitted his normal practices of laying in a dark ground over the pale commercial priming, in order to convey the luminosity of the bright light of southern France. Courbet's paint surfaces were robust and he painted his shadows thickly and darkly. But his technique was based on the tradition of* chiaroscuro. *He worked from dark to light; as a painter, he was, he remarked, the equivalent of the sun lighting up a dark landscape.*

cance in the light of American Abstract Expressionist procedures of the 1940s. In the field of color, by lightening the palette, dismissing muddy and murky tones in favor of an array of clear, bright pigments, the Impressionists opened up immense color possibilities. These were exploited in different ways by four great painters reacting against the naturalistic aims of Impressionism – namely Cézanne, Vincent van Gogh (1853-1890), Paul Gauguin (1848-1903) and Georges Seurat (1859-1891). Cézanne turned Impressionism into something solid, monumental and profound which provided a basis for the Cubist revolution of 1907-1914. Impressionism drew van Gogh into a passionately expressive style which was highly influential on the Fauvist bombshell of 1905. Gauguin, by exploring the symbolic possibilities of color, was a precursor of the Symbolists.

The Symbolist painters, Pierre Puvis de Chavannes (1824-1898), Odilon Redon (1840-1916), Gustave Moreau (1826-1898) and their followers, aimed to express literary ideas by associations of form and color. They foreshadowed the dream images of Surrealism. Gustave Moreau, whose own technique was idiosyncratic and prophetic of Surrealist procedures, encouraged an individualistic and experimental attitude in his *atelier* among pupils such as Henri Matisse (1869-1954) and Georges Rouault (1871-1958). In 1891 Symbolist Maurice Denis (1870-1943) wrote, 'It must be recalled that a painting, before it is a war horse, a nude or some anecdote, is essentially a flat surface covered by color assembled in a certain order.' The importance of this often-quoted doctrine cannot be overestimated. A flat surface means a support. Color means paint. By focusing attention on the painter's materials and support, the statement contributed both to the theory and practice of modern painting. It provided a theoretical justification of so-called 'abstract art'; in the absence of a figurative image, a painter is almost bound to explore the properties of materials with intensity.

The Neo-Impressionists or Divisionists, Seurat and Paul Signac (1863-1935), reacting against what they considered the Romantic element in Impressionist naturalism, developed the more scientific technique of Pointillism, in which color was applied to the canvas in separate dabs or dots of color. From the strictly technical point of view this method of applying oil paint to canvas was the most radical departure of all in the nineteenth century; more radical than Fauvism to which it helped give birth. The procedure had as much in common with the method of the mosaic artist as with traditional oil painting. Seurat's use of the dot technique was probably inspired by such contemporary developments in color printing as the chromotypogravure.

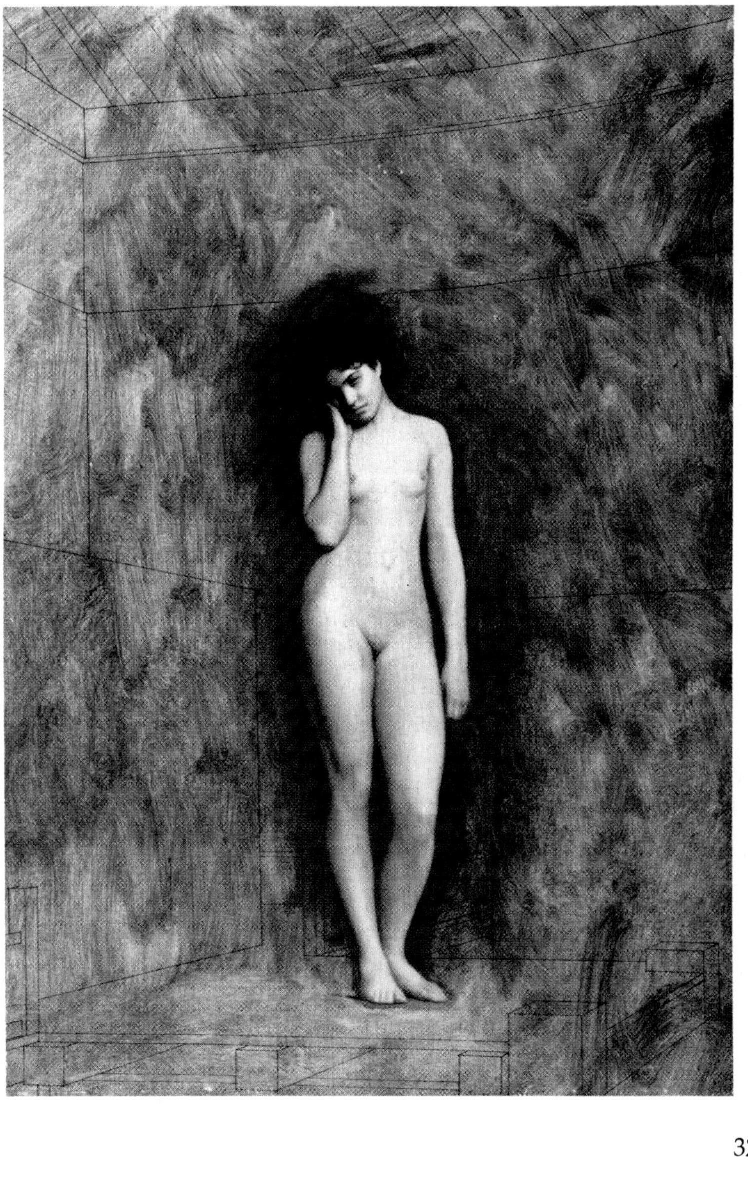

BELOW Greek Slave *(c 1896) by the French academist, Jean Léon Gérôme. As a young man, Henri Rousseau was impressed by Gérôme's work, and he gave every inch of his canvases the same punctilious attention and loving execution. This example of* ébauche *in oil on canvas, displays Gérôme's excellent draftsmanship and his careful establishment approach to art.*

### The Fauve explosion

Fauvism was the first major shock to be administered by painters to the twentieth-century public. The 1905 Salon d'Automne exhibition of work by Maurice de Vlaminck (1876-1958), André Derain (1880-1954), Matisse and their followers was dubbed an 'orgy of pure colors' by critic Louis Vauxcelles, who went on to name the group Fauves (wild beasts) when he described a restrained sculpture of the torso of a child as 'Donatello among the *fauves*'.

The Fauves were a loose association of painters: Matisse, Albert Marquet (1875-1947), Charles Camoin (1879-1965) and Henri Manguin (1874-1949) worked in the studio of Gustave Moreau; Georges Braque (1882-1963), Raoul Dufy (1877-1953) and Othon Friesz (1879-1949) were from Le Havre; Derain and Vlaminck were from Chatou; Kees van Dongen (1877-1968) came from Rotterdam; Jean Puy (1876-1960), a relatively tame Fauve had met Matisse at the Académie Carrière in 1899. Fauvism's later influence was international, affecting Expressionism in Germany and such artists as Alfred Maurer (1868-1932) in America, and the English painters Augustus John (1878-1961) and Matthew Smith (1879-1959).

The various individual styles and techniques of the Fauves reflected a common aim, the subjective expressiveness of color. Fauvism can be seen not only as an attack on the official art of the academies, but also as yet another reaction against Impressionism in the wake of a series of Paris exhibitions of the great Post-Impressionist painters in the early 1900s. Although considered revolutionary, Fauvism was little more than a combination of the culminating elements in the work of Cézanne, van Gogh, Gauguin and Seurat. No new subject matter was introduced and the subjects – landscape, portrait or still life – remained legible despite the nondescriptive liberties that were taken with color. Like Impressionism, Fauvism was largely a matter of oil on canvas, the whiteness of the primed canvas often being allowed to enhance the intensity and consequent drama of color.

This color was not used for symbolic purposes, nor was it used arbitrarily; it was used in response to pictorial demands such as the construction of space. Representational demands continued to be set and Fauve paintings often retained a rough tonal accuracy in relation to naturalistic vision, an accuracy that is easily apparent when Fauve paintings are reproduced in black and white. Although Matisse, the leader of the Fauves, did sculpture during this period, the term Fauvist is not used to describe sculpture, because color *not* form was the instrument of Fauvism.

Derain, who introduced Vlaminck to Matisse, looked back on Fauvism as in part a violent response to the challenge of photography. It was, according to the critic and poet Guillaume Apollinaire (1880-1918), the period of Derain's 'youthful truculence'. The intention of the Fauves was to use color like 'sticks of dynamite' (to use Derain's own words); to express the joy of life (*Joie de Vivre* [1905-6] was the title of one of Matisse's early paintings);

*BELOW By the time he painted* Large Bathers *(1898-1905), Cézanne had broken down everything he painted — a landscape, a still life, the human figure — into a series of facets in order to express the relationship between three-dimensional reality and two-dimensional representation. Each facet expressed the object's color, the effect of light and shade on it, and molded it so that it had a realistic feel. As well, each facet imposed a certain order on a fundamentally abstract structure.*

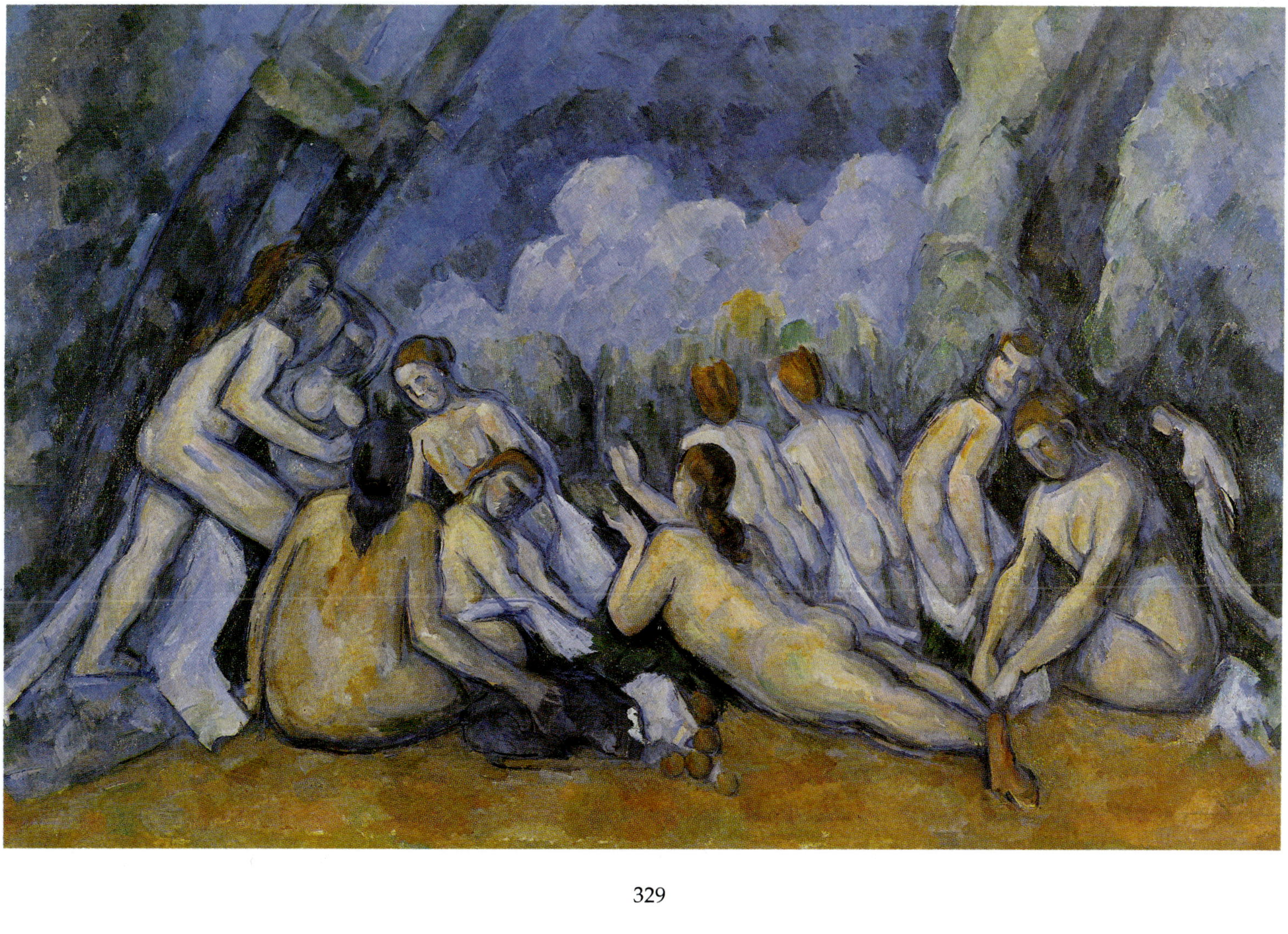

and to prove a dictum of Matisse's that 'exactitude is not truth'.

**The emergence of Cubism**

A radically new vision tends to produce a new style and a new technique. Cubism, as it came to be known, has been the outstanding revolution of vision and style in this century. It rejected the monocular perspective that had dominated Western art since the Renaissance and created a new kind of pictorial space.

Cubism was the invention of two men, Pablo Picasso (1881-1973) and Georges Braque. A third important figure, Juan Gris (1887-1927) joined them in 1911, about four years after Cubism began.Thereafter, the list of painters in Paris and abroad who either became overt Cubists or were influenced by the movement up until 1920 becomes enormous. Cubism was a movement that developed dynamically from painting to painting.

**Early Cubism**

Historians have divided the Cubist revolution into three main phases. To the early phase belong two oil paintings: Picasso's *Les demoiselles d'Avignon* (1907) and a famous Braque *Nude* (1907). These paintings show the influence of Cézanne in the analysis and simplification of form. In *Les demoiselles d'Avignon* there are other more 'primitive' aspects which can be traced back to an Iberian sculpture and North African masks. Such primitive and exotic sculpture combined a strong conceptual (as opposed to a perceptual) element, with the expressive power exerted by magic. *Les demoiselles d'Avignon* is a figurative work showing five nudes in a room in a brothel. The painting underwent numerous changes in progress. Originally there was to have been a sailor seated among the nude women and a man carrying a skull symbolizing death. The pictorial space remains shallow. The color is less explosive than in Fauvism, but is not so far from Gauguin. Having completed this exploratory and expressive painting, Picasso put it away and it remained unseen for years.

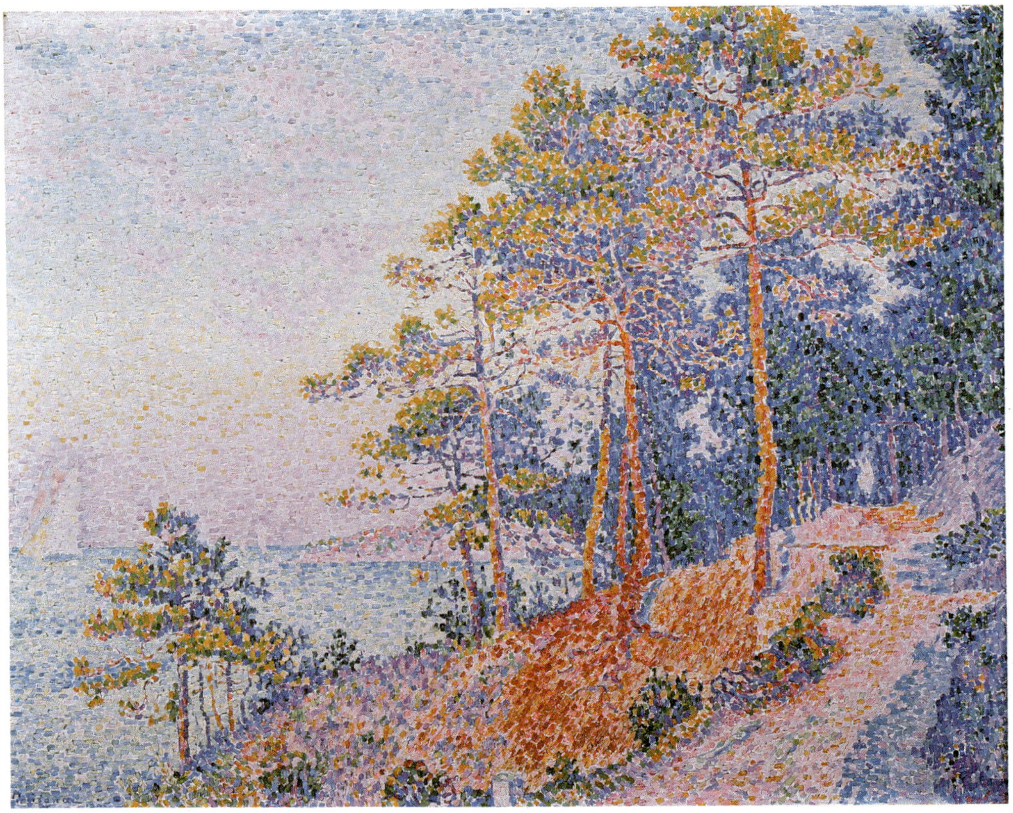

*RIGHT By 1905 when Paul Signac painted* Saint-Tropez, the Customs House Pathway, *he had been much influenced by the work of his friend Georges Seurat. Like Seurat and the other Neo-Impressionists, Signac displayed a scientific approach to painting. Because light penetrates transparent colors before being reflected back to the eye, matt opaque hues were used to obtain far greater light-reflective luminosity. Signac applied mosaic-like blocks of color, varying in tone and hue, which built up the formal structure of the subject. The object was to obtain brighter and clearer secondary colors.*

*RIGHT Gauguin painted* Girl Holding a Fan *in 1903, the year he died in the Marquesas Islands in the Pacific. He was disillusioned with the Western world and its relentless destruction of other civilizations in order to impose its own ideas. He conveyed this deep-seated pessimism in his paintings, where other artists, confronted with the same subjects, would have seen only the romantic and the exotic. The brooding, inert figure in* Girl Holding a Fan *is painted in the pure expressive colors typical of Gauguin, and later seen in the work of the Fauvists.*

In the second phase of Cubism (the first phase perhaps of Cubism proper), known as Analytical Cubism, the use of color was restrained as Picasso and Braque concentrated on form. In 1908 Braque went to L'Estaque, near Marseilles and the landscapes he produced show, in a less dramatic way than Picasso's *Les demoiselles d'Avignon*, the combined influences of Cézanne's analytical method and the force of African sculpture.

The jury of the Salon d'Automne, which included Matisse, rejected these landscapes. Matisse mentioned to Louis Vauxcelles that Braque had sent in paintings with 'little cubes'. Vauxcelles referred to them as *bizarreries antiques* (cubical oddities) and the movement was soon christened Cubism.

By 1908 Picasso's still lifes had reached a point near to Braque's landscapes, and the two

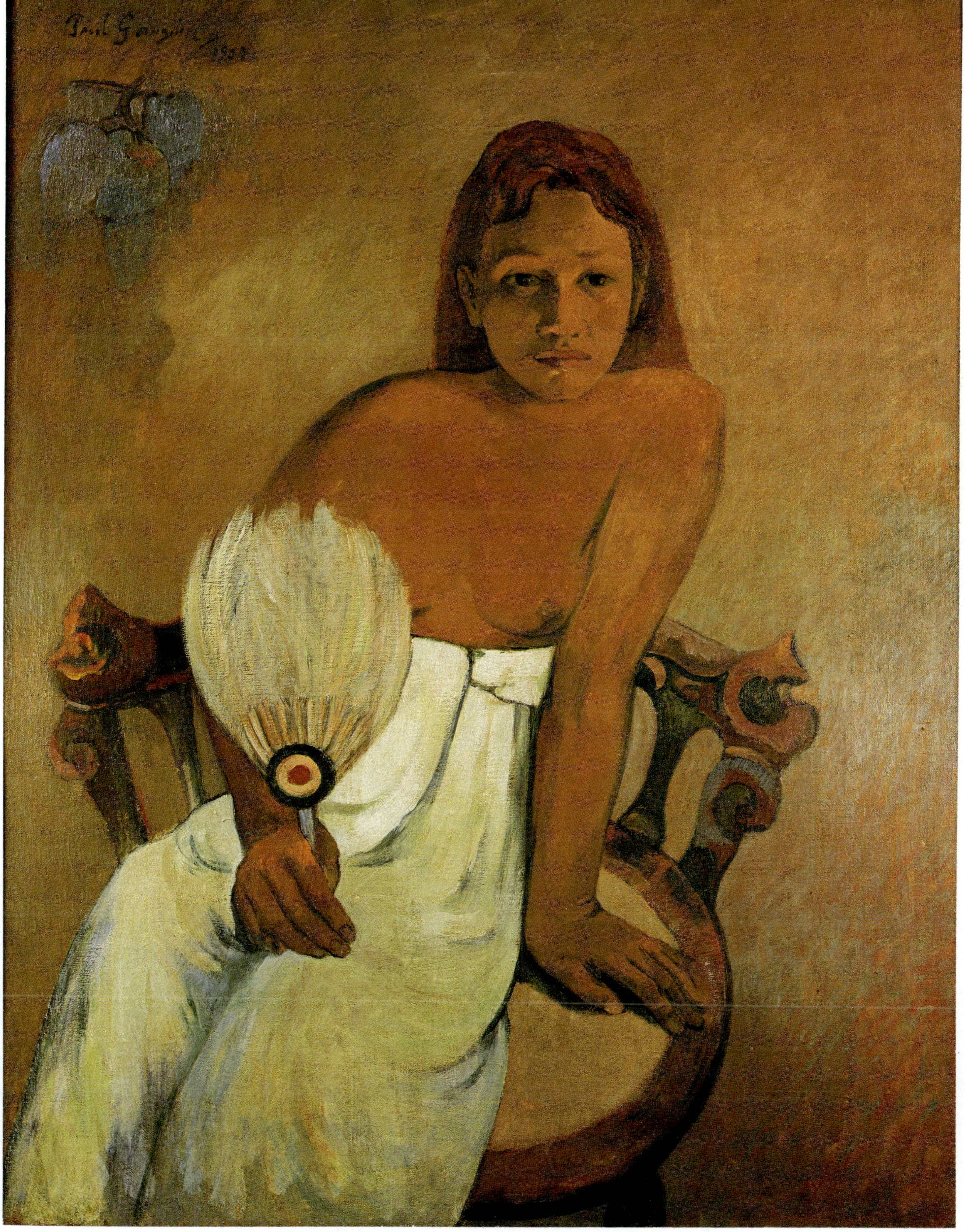

painters began to work closely together in a spirit of friendship and creative rivalry. The austere, at times almost monochromatic, element in Analytical Cubism, the restriction of the palette to black and white, subdued ochres, greys and greens was a revolt against the sensuous appeal of the Expressionist styles current, including the Fauves.

**Analytical Cubism**

Analytical Cubism was concerned with representing nature in the sense of taking a given subject to pieces then reconstructing it again. From various viewpoints it took elements from a still life and then rearranged them in a new order. In the process, a whole new pictorial architecture of interlocking planes was created. This new code for reality included elements of precision and Picasso boldly challenged the Renaissance with his work and the words: 'It is impossible to ascertain the distance from the tip of the nose to the mouth in Raphael. I should like to paint pictures in which that would be possible.'

In 1911 Braque began to introduce letters into pictures. A letter belongs to another information code system. At the same time printed words are very much a part of ordinary visible life casually observed in a café window or a newspaper headline. From here it was a small step to include a real object in the picture.

**Cubist collage and Synthetic Cubism**

The second, or synthetic phase of Cubism evolved out of the new technique of *papier collé*

*BELOW AND RIGHT This detail of Seurat's* Seated Boy with a Straw Hat *(1883-1884), was a study for one of the seated figures in* Bathing, Asnières. *The black crayon drawing on coarse paper shows his rigorous tonal modeling technique. Instead of precise outline and distinct hatching, there are subtle gradations of tone, achieved by varying the pressure of the soft, dense crayon.*

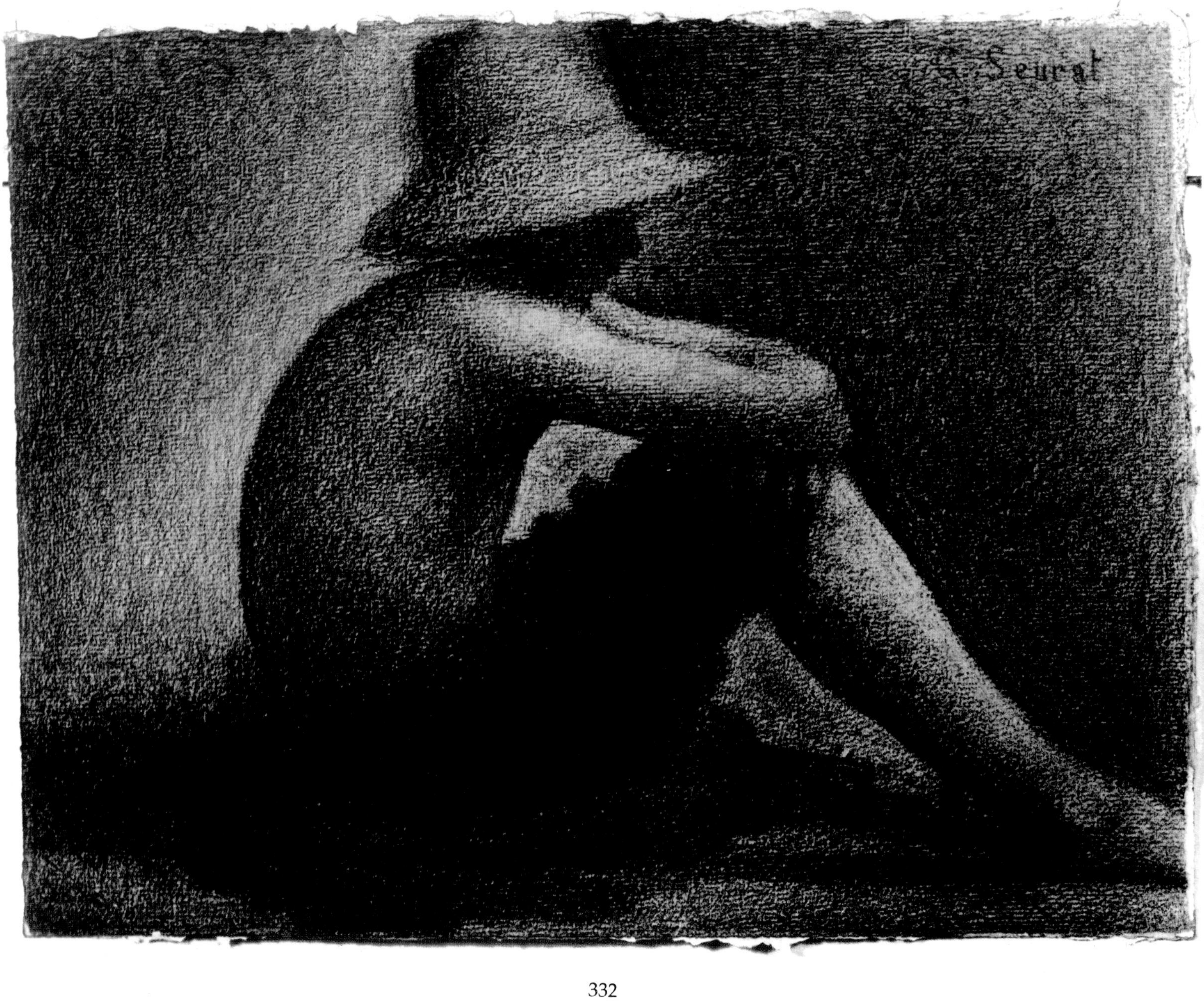

*While Seurat's drawings concentrate on sculpting tonal form, his early oils such as* Bathing, Asnières *(1883-1884) celebrate colors in nature. Seurat used his already distinctive and individualistic cross-hatching of color. This detail shows how Seurat worked the foreground figures and garments heavily in opaque layers, while the background is thinner and paler.*

(*colle* means glue) begun by Braque in 1912. Newspaper was a favorite early ingredient, and wallpaper, oil cloth, matchboxes and programs followed. Picasso added other elements such as plaster. Braque combined the new materials with drawing in charcoal or pencil, while Picasso and Gris combined them with oil painting. The almost monochromatic color soon gave way to bright colors.

Gradually pictorial composition became more important than representation, although Cubism was always a realist movement. The physical objects used in the paintings were real in themselves, rather than merely a coded imitation (image). An important later development was the ambiguous game the artists played when they returned to painting in oil: they *simulated* the *papiers collés* or collages. Here the interaction of technique and style reaches a climax. A further development was the thickening of pigment with sand and other materials.

From 1918 onwards, Braque began to explore the expressive textural qualities of his materials, but by 1920 – although still influential over half a century later – the movement of Cubism itself had run its course.

**Futurism**

On first investigation the possibility of giving a summary account of the techniques of the Futuristic movement in painting looks promising. On 11 April 1910 the Futurists Umberto Boccioni (1882-1916), Giacomo Balla (1871-1958), Luigi Russolo (1885-1947) and Gino Severini (1883-1966), published the *Technical*

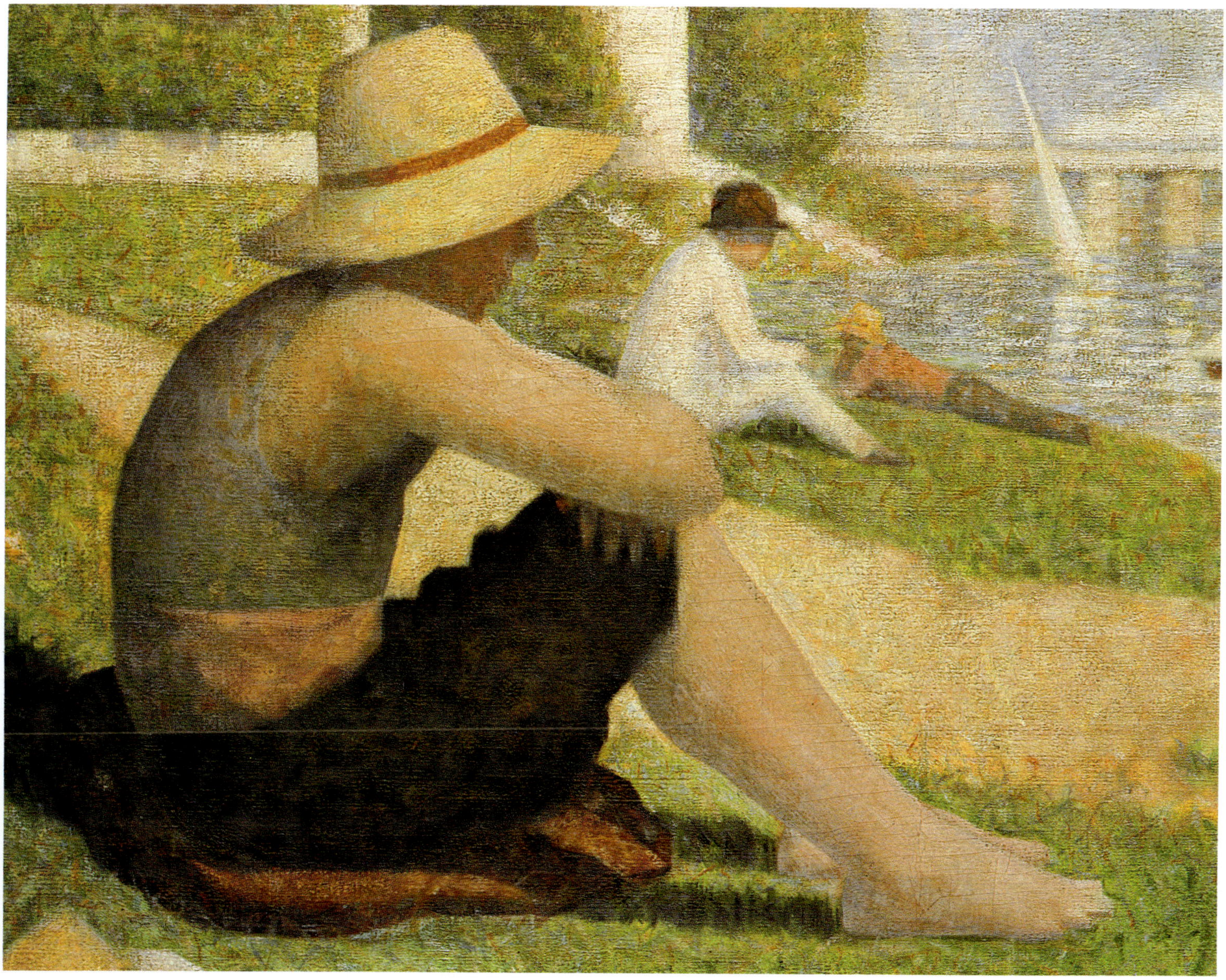

*Manifesto of Futurist Painting*. Unfortunately for present purposes there is nothing technical in the practical sense about this manifesto. The closest it gets to expressing plastic aims are in such phrases as: 'The gesture for us will no longer be a *fixed moment* of universal dynamism: it will be decisively the dynamic sensation made eternal ... a galloping horse has not four legs, but twenty and their movements are triangular ... a portrait in order to be a work of art cannot and must not resemble the sitter ... To paint a figure you must not paint it: you must paint the atmosphere around it.' These phrases are a clue to the styles of Futurism painting, but to understand the absence of practicality or rhetorical tone, it is necessary to know the origins of Futurism.

Both Fauvism and Cubism, though very different, were movements rooted in the visual arts. In contrast, Futurism was a polemic explosion, an attack on Italy's cultural stagnation initiated by a poet and propagandist. F. T. Marinetti (1876-1944) published his first Futurist manifesto on 20 February 1909 in the newspaper *Le Figaro*. It applauded speed, the machine and violence, including war, and scorned traditional social values. Professors, archeologists and antiquarians were especial targets. Marinetti declared that: 'A racing motor, its frame adorned with great pipes, like snakes with explosive breath ... which seems to run on shrapnel, is more beautiful than the Victory of Samothrace'. The 1914-18 war was to put an end to the movement. While it lasted, Futurism took many outward forms including a hybrid form of writing; painting such as *Free-word Painting* (1915) by the Neopolitan poet Francesco Canguillo; and the sculpture of Boccioni, whose *Unique Form of Continuity in Space* (1913) is widely regarded as Futurism's outstanding work of art. The movement extended into theater and cinema, music and architecture. The architecture of Antonio Sant'Elia (1888-1916) never left the drawing board, but its concepts influenced the artists of the Russian avant-garde. Sant'Elia envisaged a modern city where, he said, 'the houses will last for a briefer period of time than ourselves. Each generation will have to build its own city.'

Futurist painting was stylistically diverse, too diverse to permit useful generalizations. In the realm of technique, but buried beneath the rhetoric and bombast of the *Technical Manifesto*, was at least one original plastic aim, which distinguished Futurist painting from rival styles or 'isms'. This aim was to represent actual movement by repetition of the image in a given painting, aided by an Italian version of Seurat's Divisionism. Interestingly, the Futurist painters denied that they had been influenced in their depiction of movement by the photographs of Eadweard Muybridge (1830-1904) and E. J. Marey (1830-1904).

If the Futurist contribution to the techniques of painting is slight, their achievement in the sphere of techniques of propaganda is more assured. Futurism was speedily internationalized. Its repercussions were felt in Russia, in England and in France; it has even been claimed that Futurist ideas gave a fillip to the development of Synthetic Cubism. Certainly, Futurist painting was an attempt to bring art up to date with what the movement considered to be modern life.

### Other movements in Paris and Munich

Only when Fauvism (expressive color), Cubism (form) and Futurism (movement) have been understood is it possible to appreciate the many subsequent developments in style and technique during the first two decades of the twentieth century. Every subsequent movement has points of contact with these three styles, particularly Cubism.

In Paris, Guillaume Apollinaire coined the term Orphism to describe the paintings of Robert Delaunay (1885-1941),exhibited at the Section d'Or in 1912, which he saw as an offshoot of Cubism and moving in the direction of non-representational color abstraction. However, Delaunay himself saw his interpenetrating and revolving areas of pure color as originating more in the Neo-Impressionism of Seurat than in Cubism. Sonia Delaunay (1885-1979), Francis Picabia (1878-1953), Duchamp, Fernand Léger (1881-1955) and Frank Kupka (1871-1957) were also associated with the movement.

### German Expressionism

Stylistically, German Expressionism has much in common with Fauvism, including an interest in Neo-Impressionism and van Gogh,

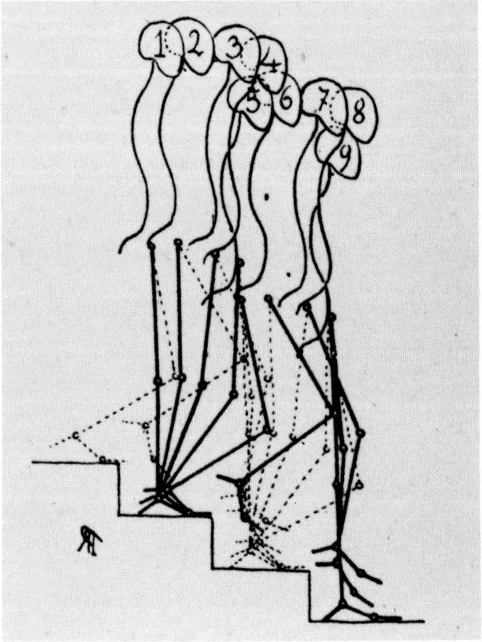


LEFT *Marcel Duchamp used various references when working on* Nude Descending a Staircase *(1912), in which the segmented figure is reduced to simple geometrical forms, and the fragmented nude is multiplied and elaborated to suggest spiraling movement. Preliminary studies and the painting itself clearly show the influence of the work of Etienne Marey, Paul Richer and Eadweard Muybridge. Richer published his* Physiologie artistique l'homme en mouvement *in 1895. The drawing,* Figure Descending a Staircase, *based on chronophotographs from the book, reveals how influential such work was to Duchamp.*

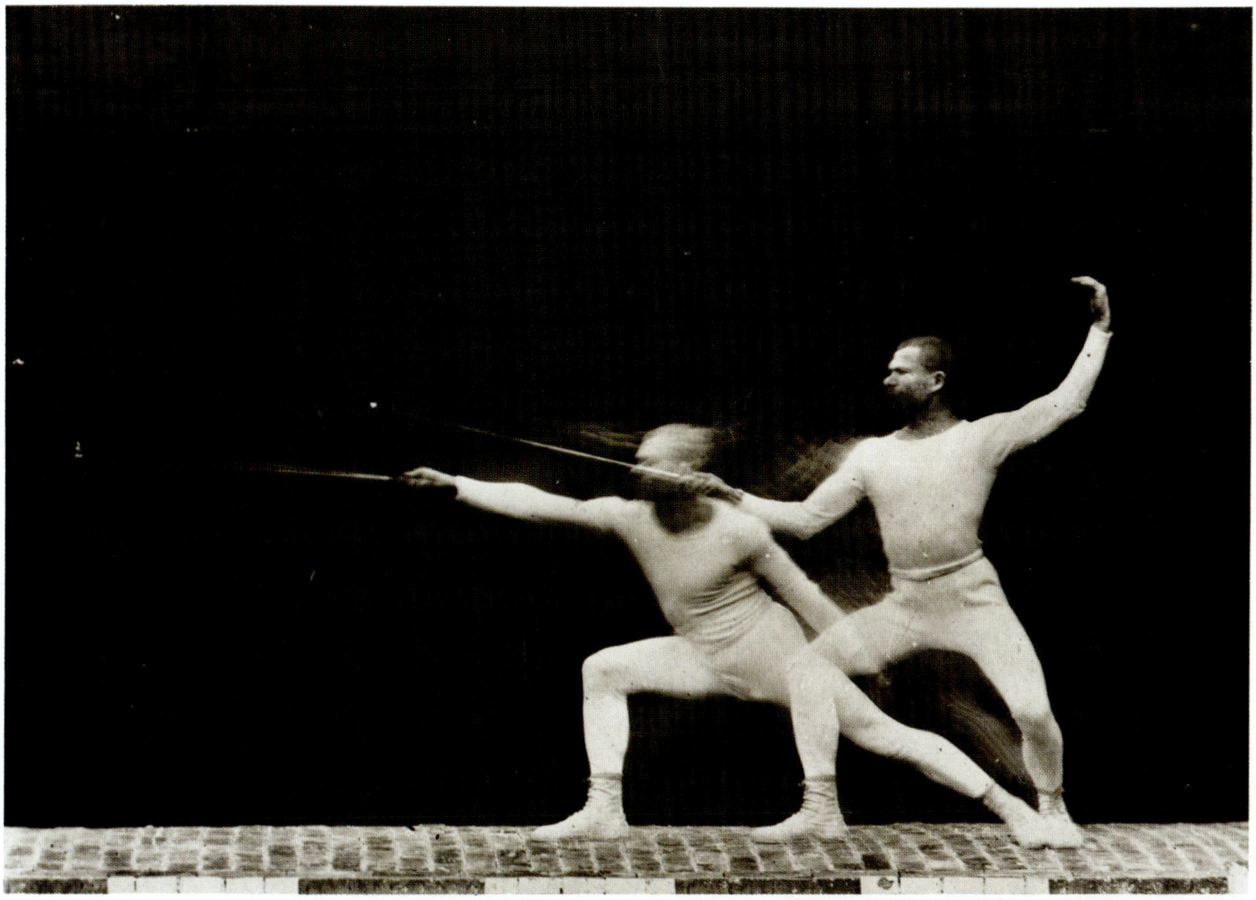

*LEFT This image,* Chronophotographie d'un escrimeur *(1891), is by the French photographer Etienne Marey who developed the technique of chronophotography. It is a method of producing multiple images on a single plate which made it possible to record the movements of a man boxing, a bird in flight, or a child jumping. Marey drew graphs tracing the patterns and rhythms of movement recorded on the chronophotographs. These became the source of inspiration for a number of artists. Duchamp made no secret of the fact that Marey's chronophotographs and subsequent diagrams provided the initial impetus for the paintings he produced which attempted to record movement, and also the passage of time.*

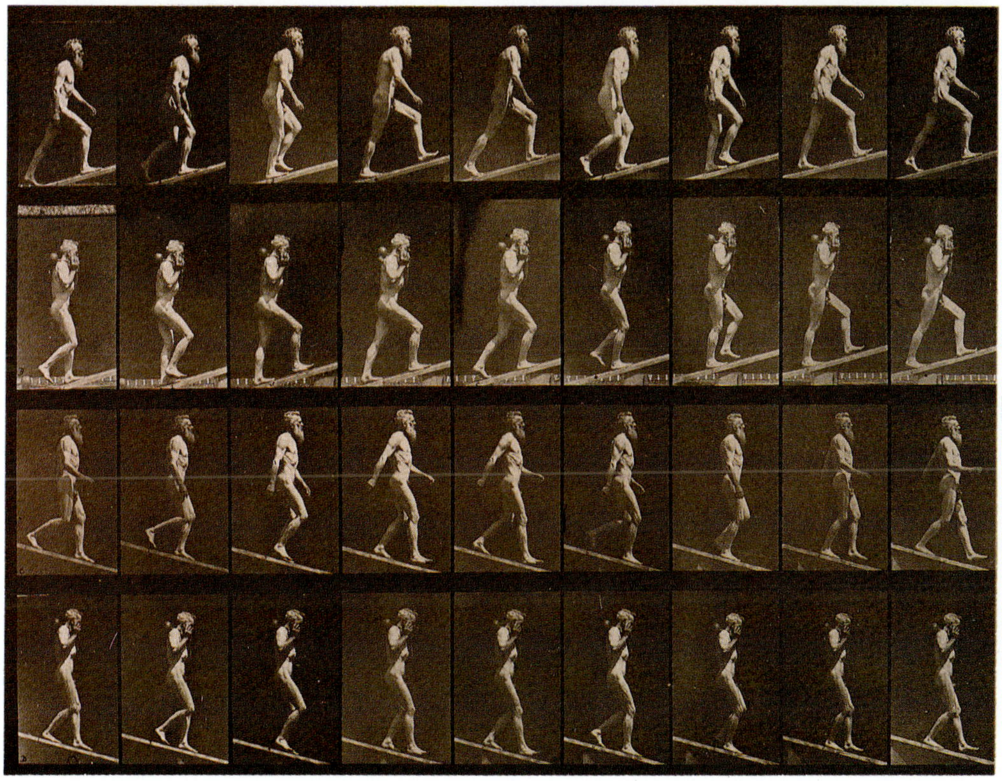

*RIGHT* Man walking down an inclined plane *by Eadweard Muybridge, the photographer who pioneered the recording of movement. His first experiments, published in 1878 and 1879, analyzed the locomotion of a galloping horse in a series of consecutive photographs. He then went on to record the movements of humans and animals involved in various everyday activities.*

although the artists of Die Brücke, an association established in Dresden in 1905, were as much influenced by the great Norwegian Expressionist painter, Edvard Munch (1863-1944). The founder members of this group included Ernst Ludwig Kirchner (1880-1938), Erich Heckel (1883-1970) and Karl Schmidt-Rottluff (1884-1976), three architecture students who turned to painting, lithography and woodcuts. With the exception of Kirchner they were self-taught as artists and they were later joined by Emil Nolde (1867-1956).

The German Expressionist Movement reached a high point in Munich in 1911 on the formation of the Blaue Reiter group. The principal artists were the Russian emigré Wassily Kandinsky (1866-1944), Franz Marc (1880-1916), Gabriele Münter (1877-1962), August Macke (1887-1914) and the Swiss artist Paul Klee (1879-1940). Marc and Macke died during World War I and the group disintegrated.

BELOW Auguste Forel *(1910) was painted in oils on canvas by Oskar Kokoschka (1886-1980). Although the artist was only 24 when he completed this portrait, it is a surprisingly intimate study of the old man. Later in life, Kokoschka's aims altered quite dramatically: using bright, even luminous colors, he developed an Expressionist style, and before the outbreak of the Second World War produced some imaginative political allegories.*

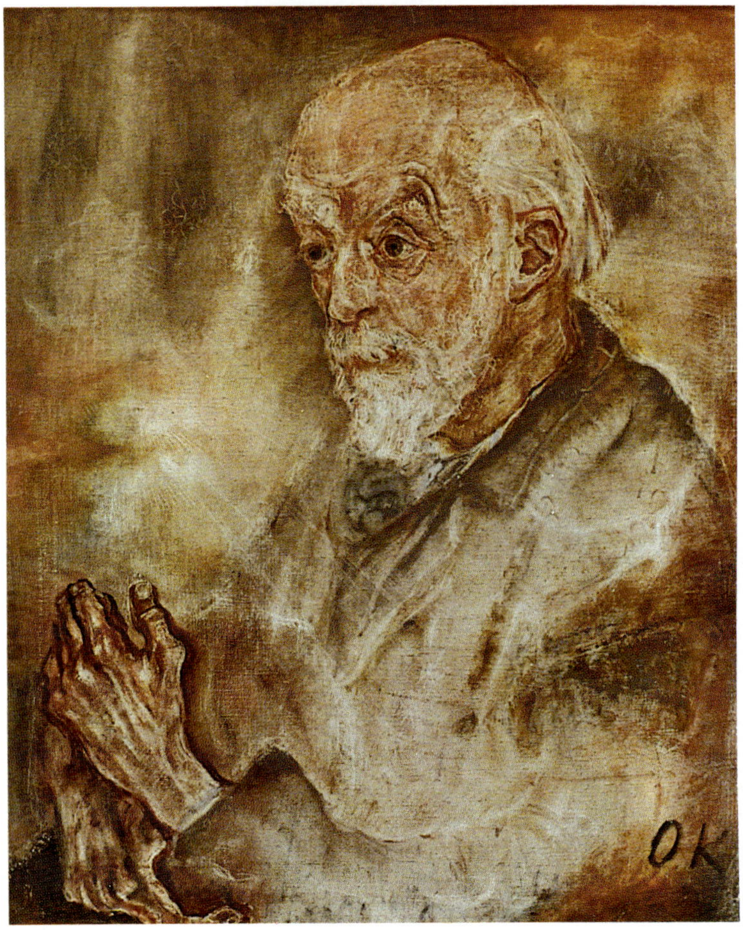


### Vorticism

Vorticism in England, like Futurism in Italy, was an attack on local cultural apathy. It was similar in tone to Futurism in some of its verbal manifestations, such as the thick combative magazine with a red cover, *Blast! A Review of the Great English Vortex* known as the 'Puce Monster', which was edited by writer and painter Wyndham Lewis (1882-1957).

Vorticism developed a characteristic painting style in which the diagonal was stressed rather like an imaginary plastic equivalent of a vortex. It was a style that took much from Cubism and Futurism.

The artists involved included Wyndham Lewis, Edward Wadsworth (1889-1949), Frederick Etchells (1886-1973), David Bomberg (1890-1957), William Roberts (1895-1980) and in sculpture, Henri Gaudier-Brzeska (1891-1915) and Jacob Epstein (1880-1959). A high proportion of the Vorticists' oil paintings, gouache and watercolors have been lost or destroyed, but virtually all Wadsworth's black and white and colored woodcuts survive.

### Developments in pre-Revolutionary Russia

Rayonnism was the style practiced by Mikhail Larionor (1881-1964) and Natalia Gontcharavo (1881-1962) from 1912 to 1914. It aimed to be a synthesis of Cubism, Futurism and Orphism.

In 1915 Suprematism was launched by Kasimir Malevich (1878-1935), who believed that the expression of pure artistic feeling was all that was of value in art. Social and political events and representation were thought to be outside its sphere. Malevich acknowledged a debt to Cubism and Futurism but concentrated on elementary geometric shapes in his paintings – the purest of which he considered to be the square. Between 1913 and 1919 he graduated from using black and white to a series of white on white paintings. The white square can only be distinguished from its white ground by the different textures created by the brushstrokes.

Another Russian movement, Constructivism, can be seen as having grown out of Cubist collage. Vladimir Tatlin (1885-1953), the founder of the movement, was familiar with developments in painting in Western Europe. Tatlin used a variety of materials such as wood, plaster, tin and glass in order to do away with pictorial illusion. He developed a doctrine of the 'culture of materials'. The two other important Russian Constructivist artists were Antoine Pevsner (1886-1962) and his brother Naum Gabo (1890-1977). They too took their cue from Cubism but supported the Futurist emphasis on movement in space rather than volume, and favored transparent materials such as perspex. By 1922 the Constructivist Movement lost its place as the dominant style in post-Revolutionary Russia.

### Abstraction

Many artists and commentators have stated that there is no such thing as pure abstraction in art: a picture must be based on something in the visible world. Another argument is that all good art (given that art depends partly on formal qualities) is abstract. The major and characteristic difference between ancient non-figurative decorative painting and twentieth-century art has been non-figurative abstraction. It is useful to divide this sort of abstraction into two parts: the Expressive or Expressionist, and the Geometrical.

Expressive Abstract can trace its origins back to late nineteenth-century ideas, but Wassily Kandinsky in about 1911 is generally credited with being the most important artist to produce a consciously abstract work, a work which in the artist's view is freed from landscape or figure or still life – the usual subject matter of painting. For Kandinsky such a work approached the condition of music.

Geometrical Abstraction originated in Russian Suprematism and Constructivism, and found its greatest figure in the Neo-Plasticism of Piet Mondrian (1872-1944). From the technical point of view, there are as many ways of applying paint to a surface as there are abstract painters; abstract art before 1920 produced no technical change as radical as that of Cubist collage.

**Dada, Duchamp and Metaphysical painting**
Marcel Duchamp, a leading force in Dada, has often been called a one-man movement. Dada originated before 1920 but it is more convenient to discuss it in relation to Surrealism. Metaphysical painting (Pittura Metafisica) dates from 1916 when Giorgio de Chirico (1888-1978), perhaps the greatest single non-Surrealist influence on Surrealist painting, met Carlo Carrà (1881-1966) in the military hospital at Ferrara.

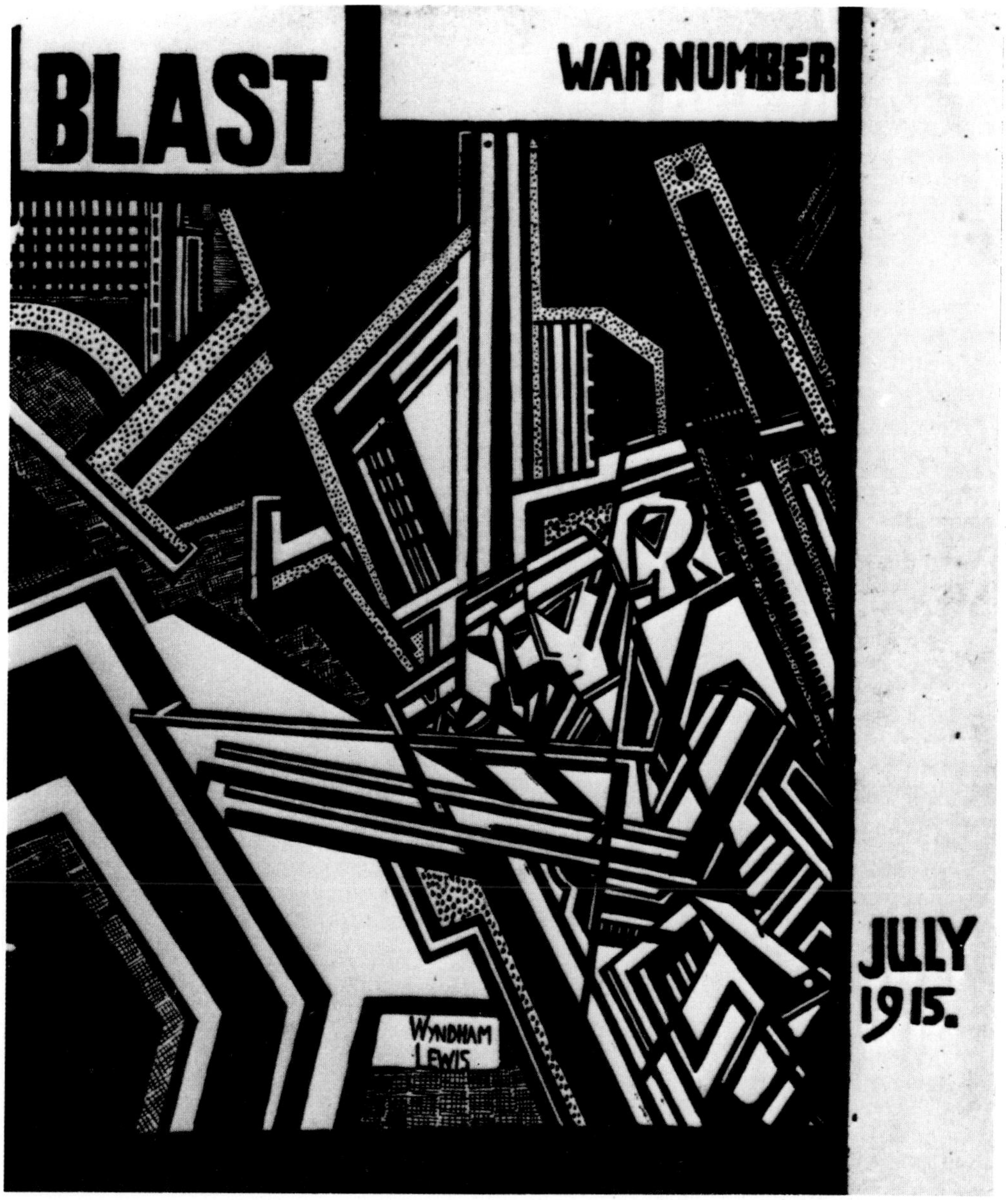


*LEFT Wyndham Lewis's cover for the second and last issue of the Vorticists' magazine* Blast!, *which he edited. Stimulated partly by exhibitions of Italian Futurists in 1912 and 1913, and the personal appearance of Marinetti in London, the British Vorticist movement was short-lived. Its name came from a statement of Boccioni, that all artistic creation must originate in an emotional vortex.*

# PAUL CEZANNE

*Still Life: Apples, Bottle and Chairback (1902-1906)*
Pencil and watercolour
44.3cm × 59cm/17½in × 23¼in

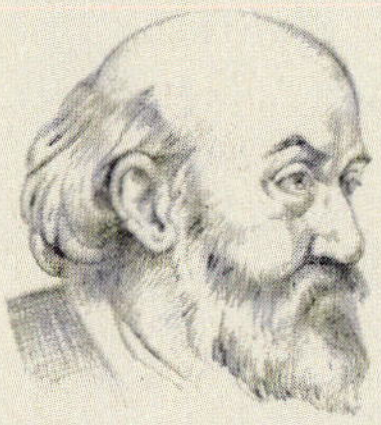

Cézanne's painting provides a link, possibly the most vital link, between the naturalism of the nineteenth century and the conceptualism of the twentieth. Largely because his work pointed in the direction of Cubism and, in the opinion of some observers, in the direction of Abstraction, Cézanne has earned the title 'the father of modern painting'.

Cézanne was born at Aix-en-Provence in 1839, the son of a local banker. He was the schoolfriend of the novelist Emile Zola (1840-1902) and in 1861 he went to Paris to study painting. Influenced by Delacroix, Honoré Daumier (1808-1879), Courbet and Edouard Manet (1833-1883), Cézanne's early paintings in oil, unlike his late works, are often dark in color, and violent in both subject matter and the handling of paint which he plastered on thickly. It was not until the 1870s that he began to find his own direction. In 1872 he joined Camille Pissarro (1830-1903) at Pontoise, later moving to Auvers. Here he learnt the principles and practices of the Impressionists, aided by Pissarro, although he applied them to different ends. Above all, he learnt the importance of pure color and the study of nature. He later remarked that the Louvre was 'a good book but only a means to an end' and that he wished to 'do Poussin over again after nature'. Nature was the obsession and the key.

Dissatisfied with the fleeting atmospheric effects of the Impressionists, Cézanne was interested in rendering the volume and the solidity of objects, using planes translated into color. This feeling for form expressed in his work and in his much quoted advice to see objects in nature in terms of 'the cone, the cylinder and the sphere' was matched by an equally strong sense of the structure of the painting itself.

Cézanne passed much of his life working in isolation at Aix-en-Provence. Although he was moderately successful in his lifetime, it was a retrospective exhibition held in Paris in 1907 which had a profound, immediate and lasting impact. In the first place, it influenced Picasso and Braque who were struggling to work out a way of painting which would represent visible reality in a new way, namely Cubism. Secondly, Matisse was very interested in Cézanne; he purchased *Three Bathers* (1879-1882) which was to remain a long-lasting inspiration to him.

Cézanne worked mainly in oil on canvas or in watercolor on paper. For Cézanne, the spontaneity required by the medium of watercolor seemed at first to be a relaxation from producing works in oil, what he considered the painter's great vocational responsibility: 'The picture is not going badly but the days seem long,' he wrote to Zola on 30 June 1866. 'I must buy a box of watercolors so that I can paint when I am not working on my picture.' Lionello Venturi ends his book on Cézanne watercolors, *Cézanne: Son Art, Son Oeuvre* (1936), with the words 'And to those who love Cézanne, his watercolors are the dearest creations of his imagination.' In them the artist is caught at his most intimate.

'To read nature is to see it, as if through a veil, in terms of an interpretation in patches of color following one another according to a law of harmony. These major hues are thus analyzed through modulations. Painting is classifying one's sensations of color,' Cézanne wrote at about the time he painted *Still Life: Apples, Bottle and Chairback*.

This work belongs to the artist's last and mature period. The subject, a still life with apples, was a favorite one; although, paradoxically, the specific subject was probably of little importance to Cézanne, despite his obsession with nature. The still life was painted at the beginning of the twentieth century which has witnessed a great exploration of the visual and emotional effects of color. Cézanne's sense of color was impeccable and often discreet, but in this particularly rich painting the two primary colors, blue and red, are used with boldness. A distinctive technique of Cézanne's, which was considered a daring innovation at the time, was leaving part of the paper blank: here, the warm-toned paper indicating those areas of the apples which catch the most light. In this way the artist suggests volume while representing light. Such a device was part of Cézanne's struggle to break away from what he considered to be the insubstantial atmospheric effects of the Impressionists.

The picture exemplifies another important aspect of Cézanne's vision, style and technique. When the viewer tries to join up the right and lefthand rims of the apple bowl, he or she discovers that Cézanne has been looking at and rendering the scene in front of him from more than one angle, thereby breaking with the typically monocular vision of Renaissance perspective. More important, this shifting of viewpoint may be seen as a step in the direction of Cubism.

The brushstrokes vary in size more considerably than in Cézanne's oil paintings. The marks which complement and emphasize the pencil contour round the apples are literally drawn with a brush – a small sable brush or perhaps the tip of a large one. Cézanne did not lay on washes successively covering whole areas of the paper. He placed large and small planes of pure color in a manner that keeps the forms open. The transparent watercolor has been laid on in a way that keeps the whole pictorial architecture in a state of pleasurable continuity.

The painting is, as it were, complete at every stage. Aware of the potency of suggestion, Cézanne always stopped long before the paper looked overworked.

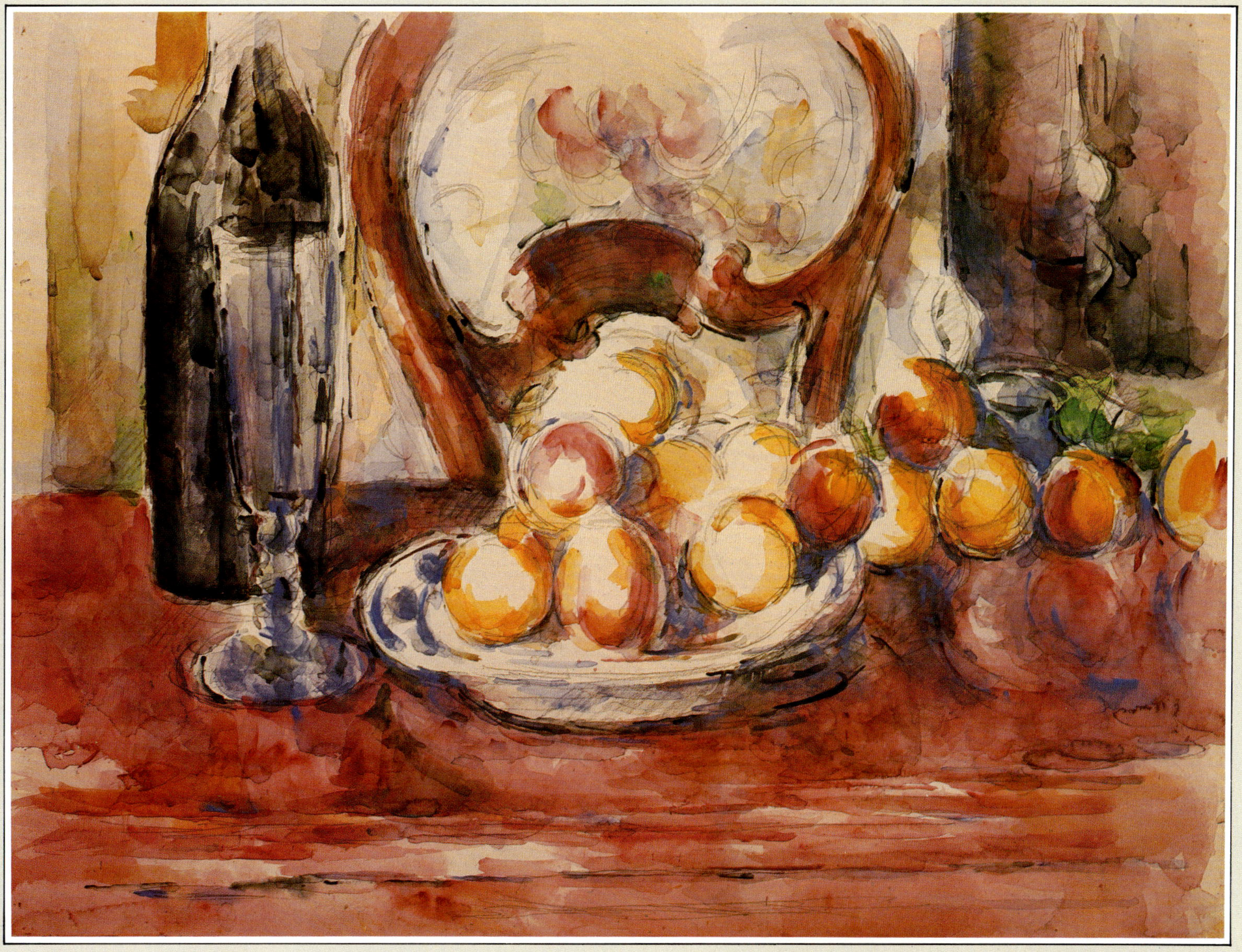

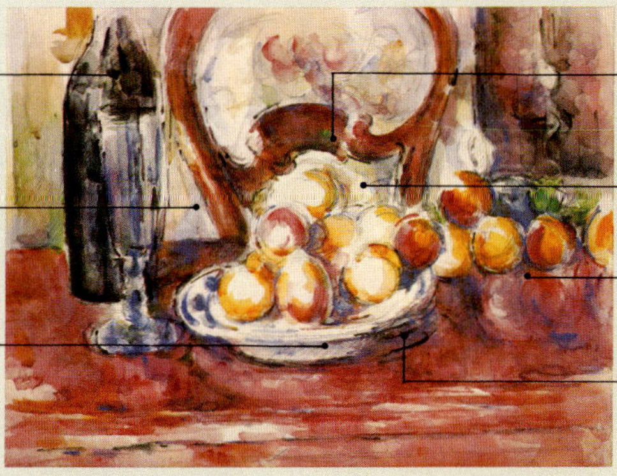


*Cézanne's scrupulous but exciting sense of design, his obsession with the relation between forms on a flat surface and in the round, produces in this late work a remarkable confrontation between the swirls and flurries of pencil marks, the painstakingly worked translucent touches of watercolor, and the gaps, cracks and open spaces between these two modes.*

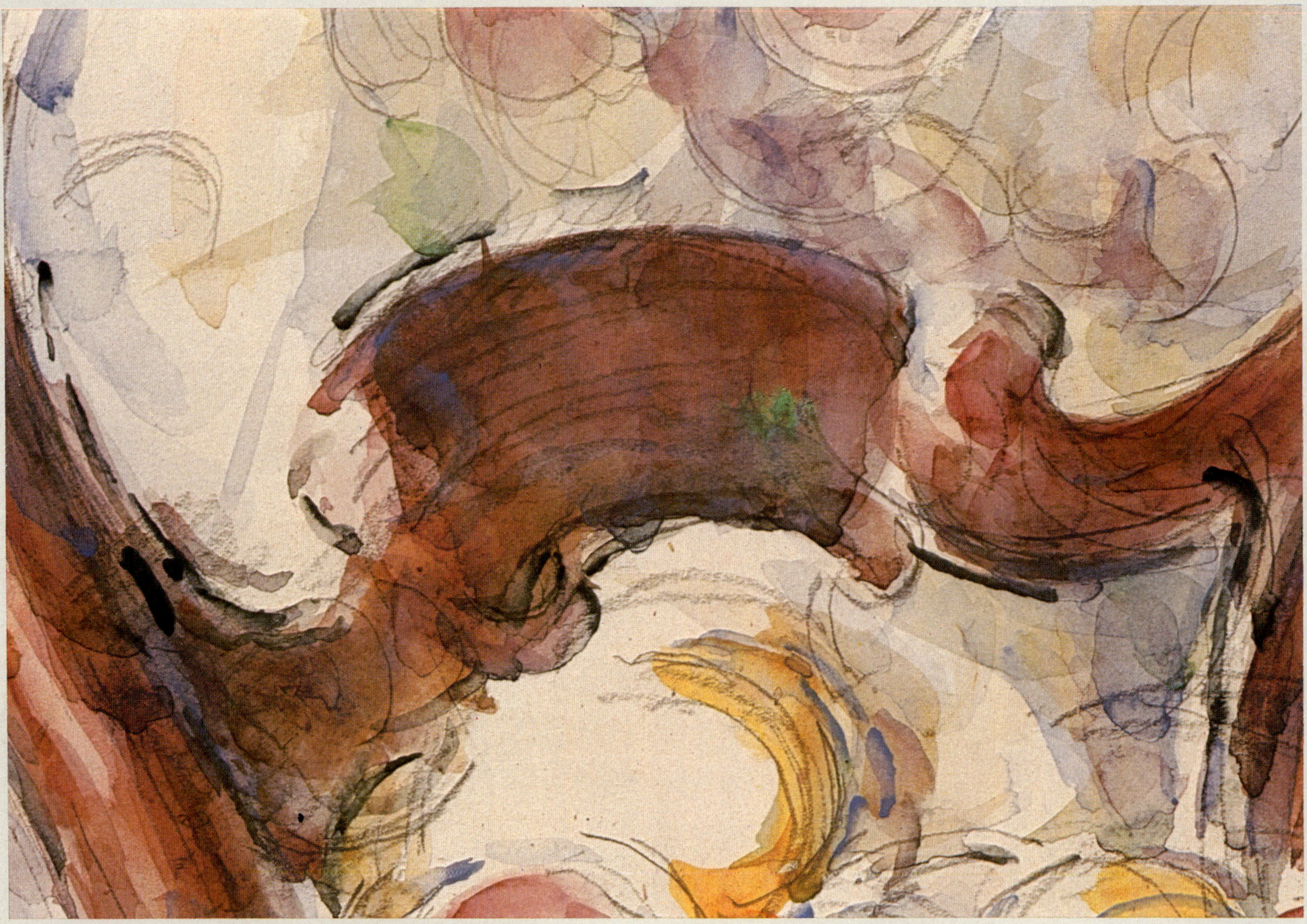

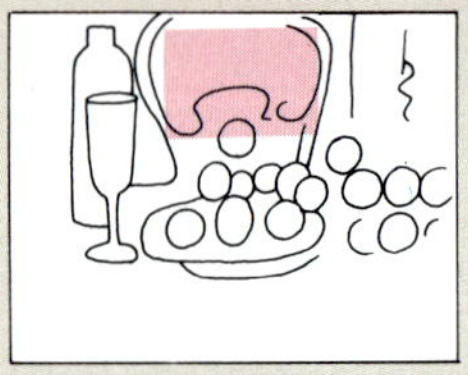

ACTUAL SIZE DETAIL
*Cézanne focused on the central area of interest in this composition with intensity. The sinuous forms in the chair are pursued in a series of loosely parallel curvilinear pencil lines, while a flux of marks and color dabs echo these in the space on either side of the wooden frame.*

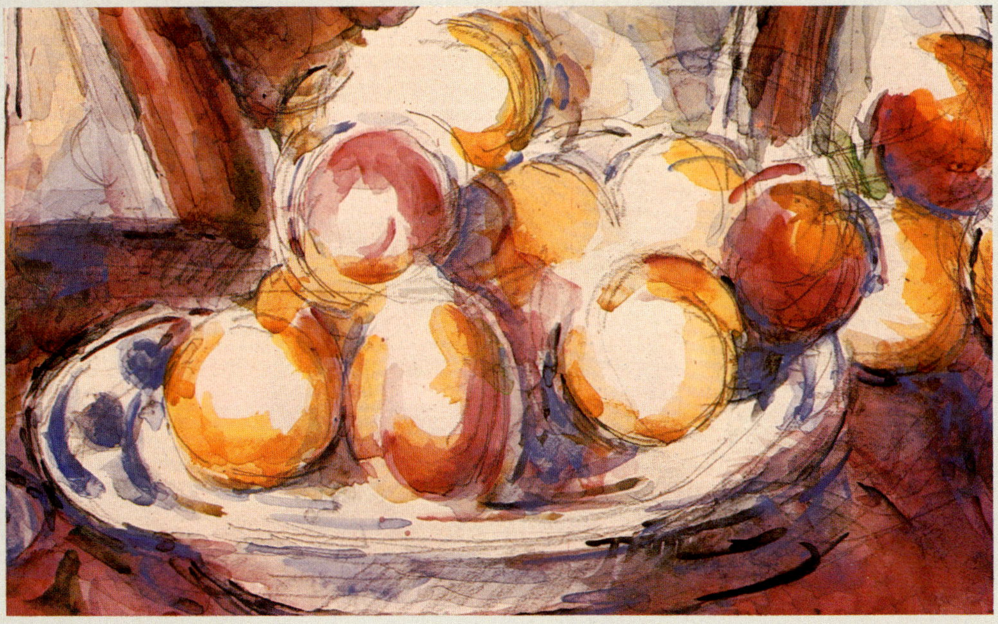

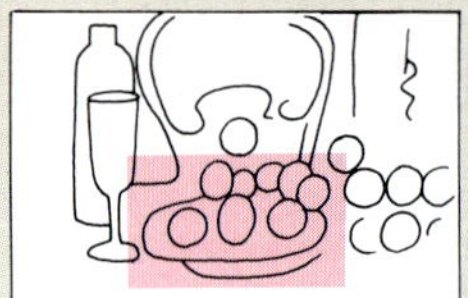

LEFT *The treatment of the bowl of fruit itself illustrates the effectiveness of Cézanne's technique of 'incompletion'. The pattern of the bowl is initiated on the left, but relinquished as the angle of vision makes only the lip visible, and hides the rim. The apples, too, are in various states of finish, their forms exhilarated by the penumbra of ghosting pencil curves.*

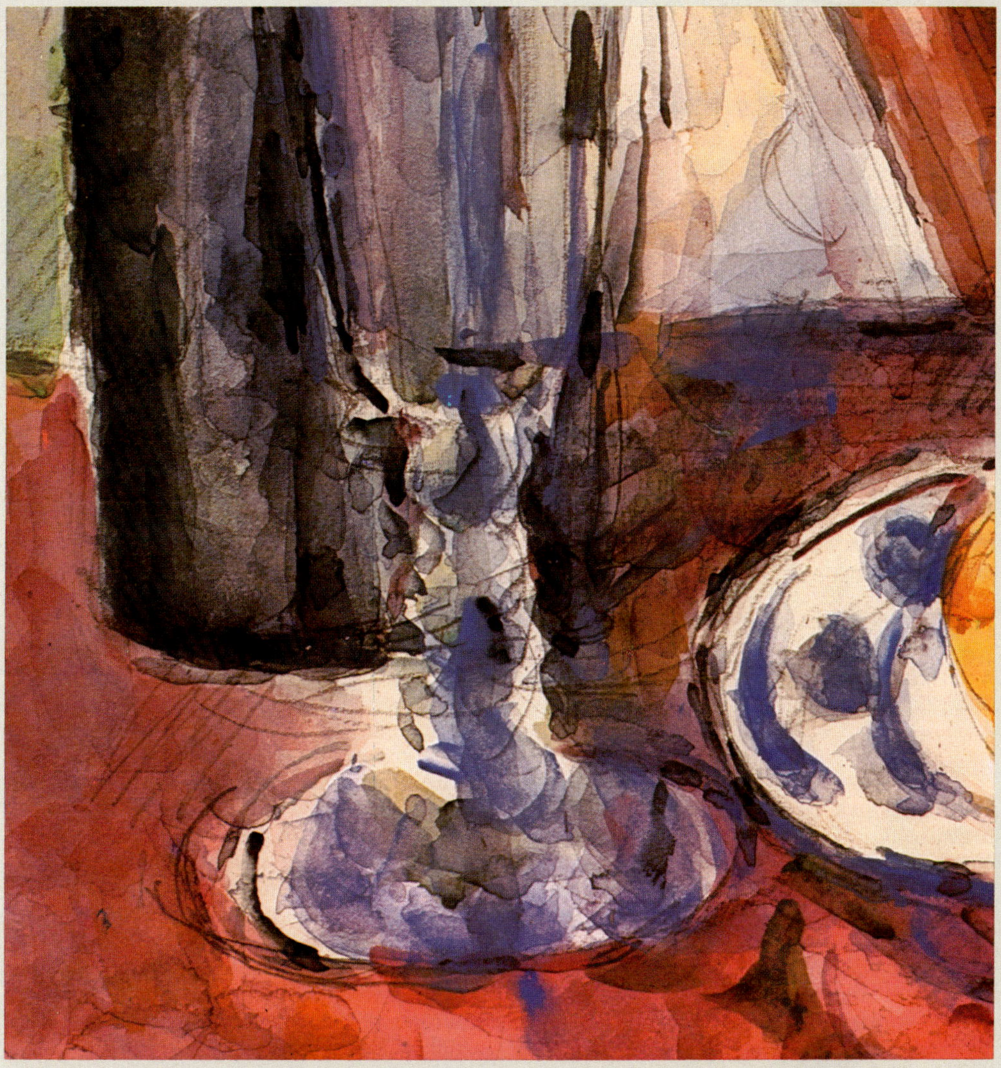

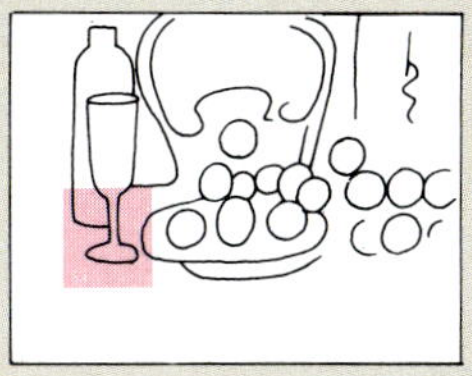

LEFT More intense than the reflections on wood, and on the fruit, the sheen of bottle and glass is worked up in vertically aligned brushstrokes which hug the contours of the two containers and which oppose the diagonal and horizontal penciling. Particularly effective is the discrete treatment of the globes of glass in the stem with appropriate knobs and curls of watercolor, which fan out below to produce the shallow disc-like base. There is especially intense working in the area of spatial uncertainty between the edges of the glass, bottle, chair and dish.

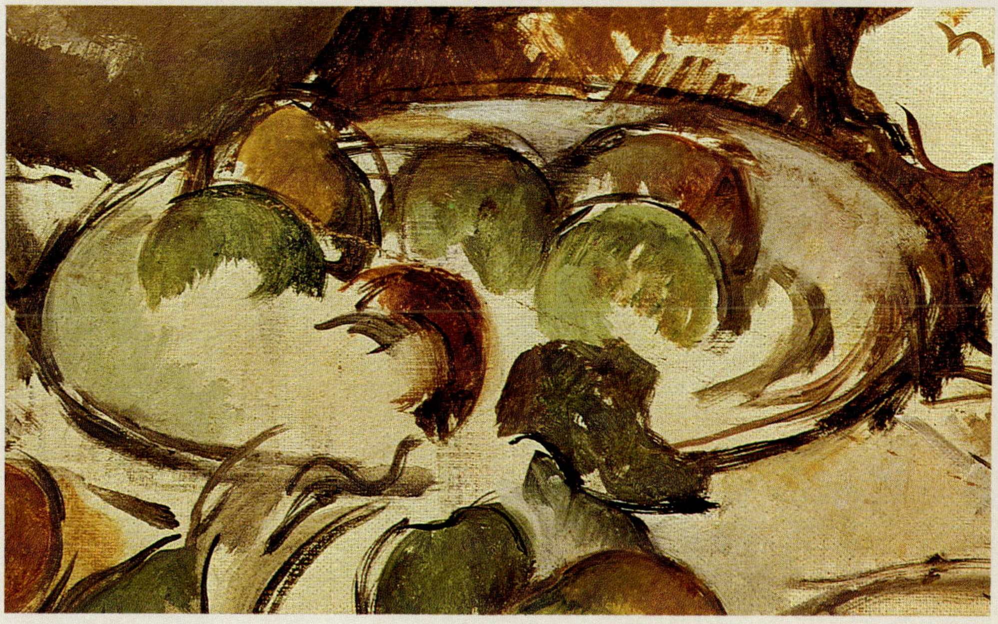

LEFT Cézanne's treatment of a similar subject in oil paint reveals an exaggeration of many of the effects handled with such delicacy of touch in the watercolor. The material thickness of the oil imparts a greater sense of volume to the apples but at the cost of a luminous color range and the substitution of bolder painted black lines for the animated buzz of pencil marks.

# ANDRE DERAIN

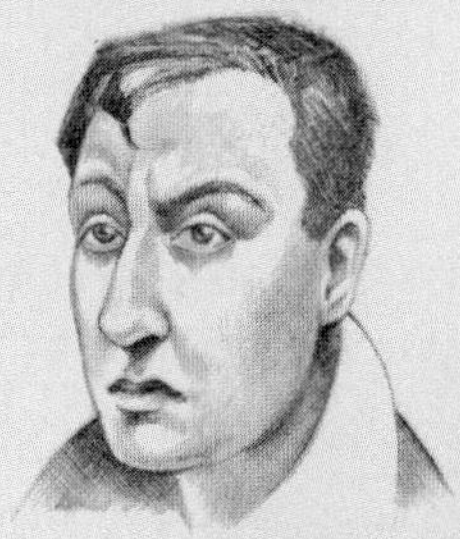

*Portrait of Matisse/Portrait de Matisse* (1905)
Oil on pale coffee-color primed canvas, primed on front face only
46cm × 35cm/18⅛in × 13¾in

Born in 1880 at Chatou, one of the old Impressionist haunts near Bougival, west of Paris, André Derain began painting at the age of 15. In 1898, he attended life classes at the independent Académie Camillo in Paris, where the Symbolist painter Eugène Carrière (1849–1906) taught regularly, and met two of the future Fauve painters, Henri Matisse and Jean Puy (1876–1960). In June 1900, on a suburban train, Derain met Maurice de Vlaminck (1876–1958), a neighbor from Chatou with whom he established an immediate friendship, and the two young artists set up a communal studio. Vlaminck was also to become a Fauve painter. In 1901, at the important exhibition of paintings by van Gogh – who was a great influence on the Fauves – Derain introduced Vlaminck to Matisse. From late 1901 to late 1904, Derain's career was brought to a halt by his military service, but he returned to Chatou and to painting in September 1904.

1905 was the crucial year in the development of the Fauve style, and it was at the historic September exhibition of independent artists, called the Autumn Salon, that the title 'Fauve' was coined. During that summer, Matisse and Derain worked together in the south of France at Collioure, the Mediterranean port that had been 'discovered' by Signac in 1887. The Fauve style is usually defined in terms of liberated bright color, but – unlike the earlier Neo-Impressionist, or the later Cubist styles – its exponents had no specific platform of theories, nor did they form a distinct movement. Fauvism, which was a comparatively short-lived style concentrated in the years 1905 to 1907, was more the product of friendships and artistic contacts. Its artists had very different styles of painting, but they held a common concern for using bright, non-descriptive color.

The partnership between Derain and Matisse is celebrated in this pair of portraits from their campaign of 1905, portraits which also highlight the differences between the styles and aims of the two artists. In his study of Matisse Derain's brushwork shows his debt to van Gogh, whom he greatly admired. Derain wrote of van Gogh in 1902, a year after seeing the Dutch artist's exhibition: 'Van Gogh offers not so much total cohesion as a unity of spirit.' Derain's touch is reminiscent of van Gogh's parallel hatched brushstrokes, particularly in the handling of Matisse's beard.

In his color, however, Derain's allegiance is to Gauguin, whose work had again been forcefully brought to his notice that summer when he and Matisse visited Daniel de Monfried to see his collection of Gauguin's paintings. The burnt golds, sharp greens and brick reds of Gauguin's later Tahitian paintings are the basis for Derain's palette in his portrait of Matisse. With the exception of the cobalt blue and white of the shirt, all his colors are mixed hues, achieved by combining two or more colors. These result in a muted harmony which is comparable to that found in Gauguin's pictures. Within the broad areas of color, Derain's hues are varied and modified, but overall, the picture appears as a series of blocks of flattish color. Although Gauguin's brushwork had more delicacy and finesse than Derain's vigorous touch, there are remarkable technical similarities between Derain's result here, and Gauguin's work.

It even seems that Derain was encouraging the analogy with Gauguin by his choice of a canvas with a grainy texture, albeit one much less coarse than Gauguin's typical hessian. The Fauve artist chose a coffee-colored preparation, which must have been applied by Derain himself, for it is less solidly opaque than the usual commercial grounds, and it only covers the face side of the canvas indicating that it was primed after stretching. This ground, which protects the canvas while simultaneously giving it the color of unprimed canvas, is also a reminder of Gauguin's use of raw canvas surfaces. Its color unifies the colors in the paint layer, making them more subdued in tone to complement their muted Gauguinesque hues. The mixed, broken colors, the predominantly middle tones, and darkish ground of Derain's picture, are in marked contrast to the brilliant luminosity of Matisse's portrait of Derain. Derain's head also has a descriptive solidity which is lacking in Matisse's painting.

Derain's fairly smooth, flat application of solid color – orange-yellows and yellowish greens – in the background of the composition, pushes Matisse's head, which inclines toward the spectator, further forward. Its texture separates it from the figure of Matisse, all of which is handled with more open, block-like strokes of color. This gives the bust a sense of form, which is further enhanced by the use of light. The depiction of an identifiable fall of light, in colors which still approximate to natural light and shade, make the Derain less truly Fauve than the Matisse. In the Derain, the light falls from the right, giving a powerful highlit effect to the right two-thirds of the face and the neck. The contrasting, predominantly viridian green and white shadowed side of the face, is a complement to the pinkish-oranges of the lit side. Thus, in addition to producing a startling interplay of colors, there remains a powerful sense of form sculpted by a specific light and shade.

The first outlines and contours of the form were laid in dark, probably Prussian, blue, diluted with turpentine and applied fluidly with a sable hair brush. The execution is then *alla prima*, with wet-in-wet reworking where necessary, and Derain has left the individual marks of the brush clearly visible. Hog's hair brushes were used, with color applied thickly and, in general, opaquely. The dark viridian

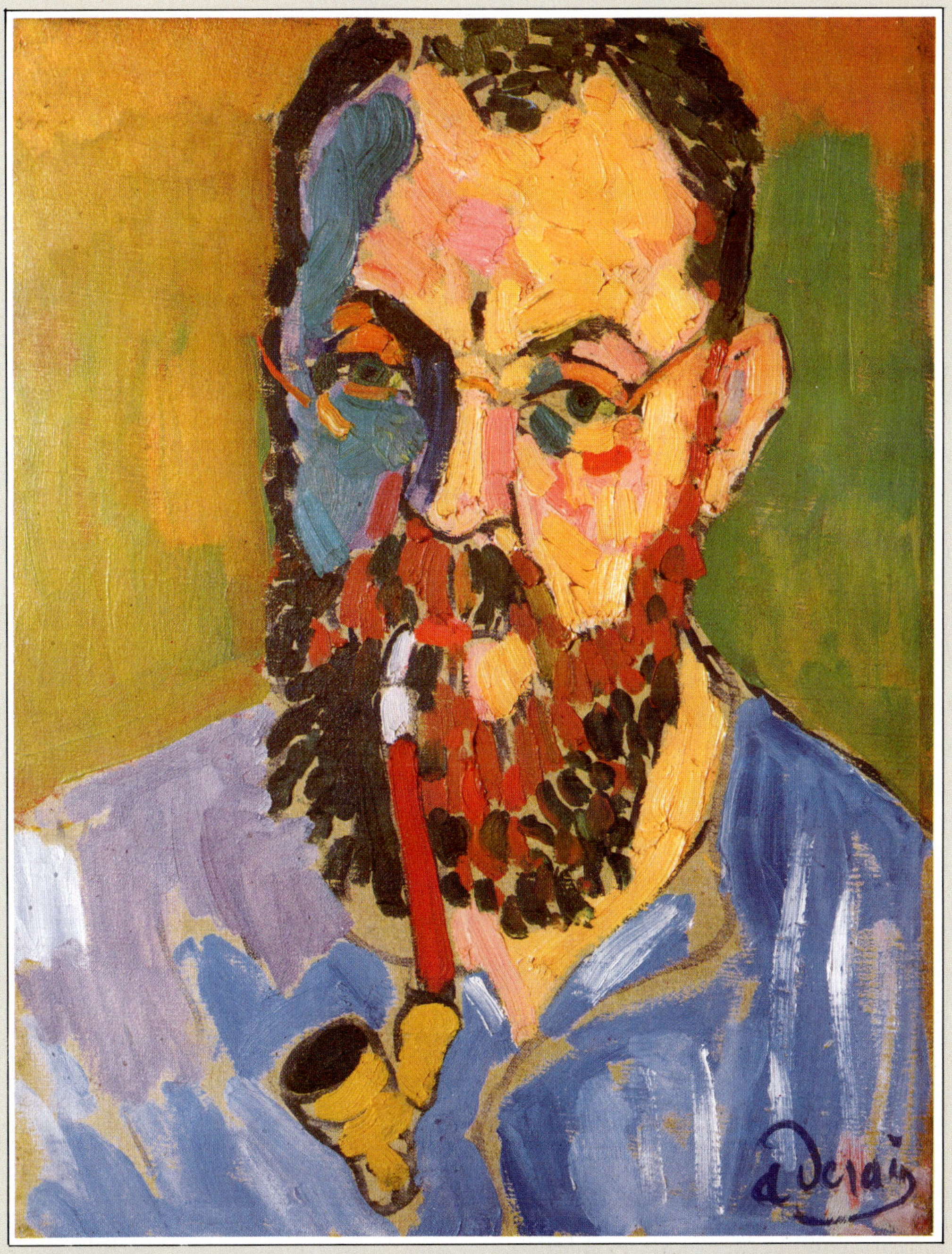


*Derain and Matisse worked together at Collioure in the summer of 1905, when this and Matisse's portrait of Derain were both painted. Matisse appears intensely introspective in this dynamic study. His gaze is directed outwards but not focused upon the spectator. The angle of his head, pitched forward slightly and positioned high up on the canvas, emphasizes this mood. A lively fall of strong light and shade accentuates the strong forms of the head. The lights are handled in warm orange pinks, the darks in cool greens. The painting is* alla prima, *boldly and rapidly executed in large, loaded brushstrokes with the coffee-colored ground showing actively among the broken colors which dominate the painting. The elongated form of Matisse's head and beard relate well to the standard format vertical landscape 8 canvas chosen by Derain.*

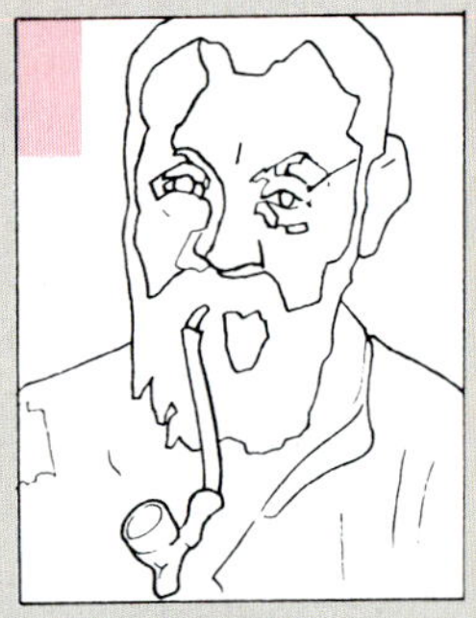

*The background is handled with distinctive brushwork, which helps to make the head stand out. It is more smoothly and evenly laid, with wet-in-wet blending of orange yellows and yellow greens brushed directly over the muted ground color. The middle tone of the ground subdues the luminosity of the colors while unifying them. The grainy canvas texture remains apparent through the more thinly applied areas and also where stiffer colors are dragged over the surface. A painting medium, such as oil and turpentine mixed, may have been added to the background colors to make them more fluid.*

green and cobalt blue mixture used for the shadow side of the beard is the only area where the color is translucent. Other palette colors here include vermilion, red lake, and yellows, probably the sounder cadmiums, all in mixtures. A 2.5cm (1in) stroke of cobalt violet mixed with white is placed, as a livid contrast to the surrounding greens, to the left of the sitter's nostril. The brush sizes used are easy to identify from the individual touches of applied color. They are mainly round-ended, all flat, varying in width from 6mm ( $\frac{1}{4}$in ) in the beard, to 1.25cm ( $\frac{1}{2}$in ) or even 1.9cm ( $\frac{3}{4}$in ) width in the shirt and background.

By 1907, Derain had begun to abandon the brilliant colors of Fauvism, and, later, under the influence of Cubism, he returned to a somber tonal palette, dominated by earth colors. Derain met the poet Guillaume Apollinaire (1880–1918) in 1904. The poet later described the Fauve period of Derain's style as 'youthful truculence', stressing the sobriety of his post-Fauve work, and his passionate study of the Old Masters.

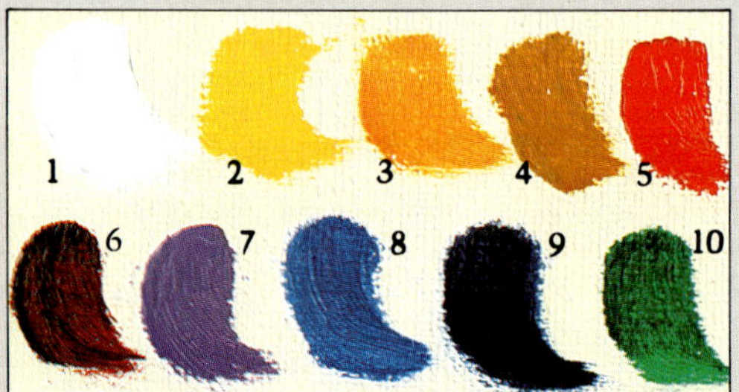


*Derain's palette was lead white (1), chrome (2) or cadmium yellows (3), vermilion (5), red alizarin lakes (6), cobalt violet (7) and blue (8), Prussian blue (9) and viridian (10). Yellow ochre (4) may have been used.*

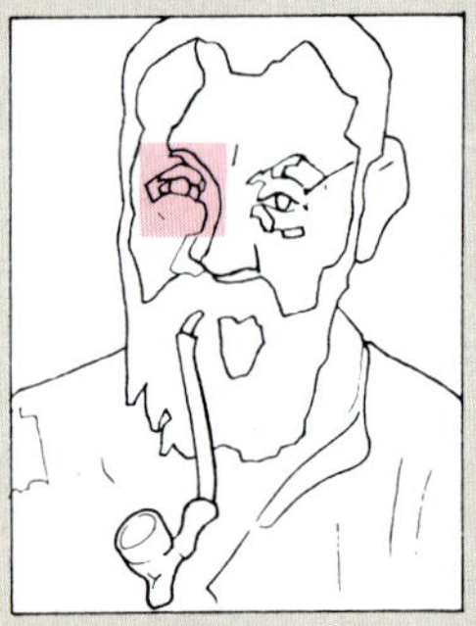

*The features of the face are reduced to simplified blocks of tone and color. Broad single strokes are used for the eyelids, brow and nose. The spectacles are merely suggested by an orange stroke or two, and left to the spectator to 'complete'. Pink-orange and green-blue provide the key colors as well as tonal contrasts.*

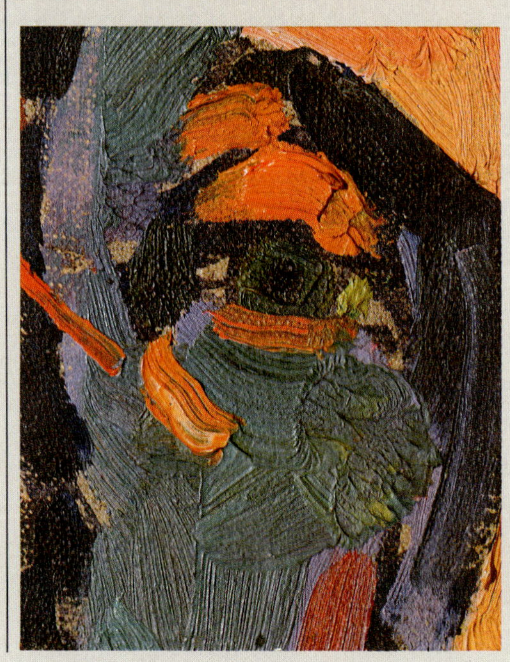

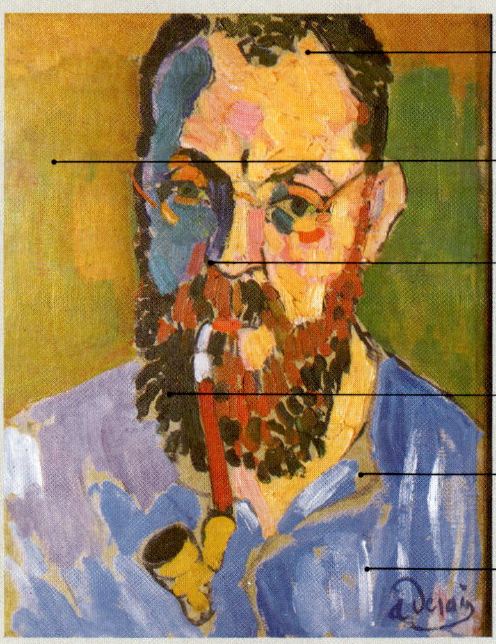

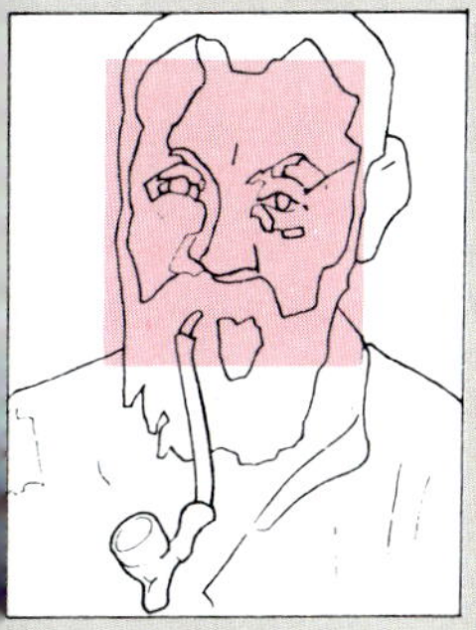

Actual size detail
*The paint layer colors are almost entirely used opaque, mainly with the addition of white to give a subtle luminosity. Thinly dilute contours were applied to establish the figure, and this was then painted directly, with no underpainting, in thickly loaded brushstrokes. Although the brushwork has a lively, almost separate existence in places, such the beard, in general it is still descriptive, following and sculpting the forms of the face. A mixture mainly of viridian green and white describes the shadows, applied over wet to modify a bluer tint below on the left side. Pinks and oranges, mixed with white, record the light side of the face, with a brilliant touch of vermilion beneath the eye. The colors are all worked wet into wet.*

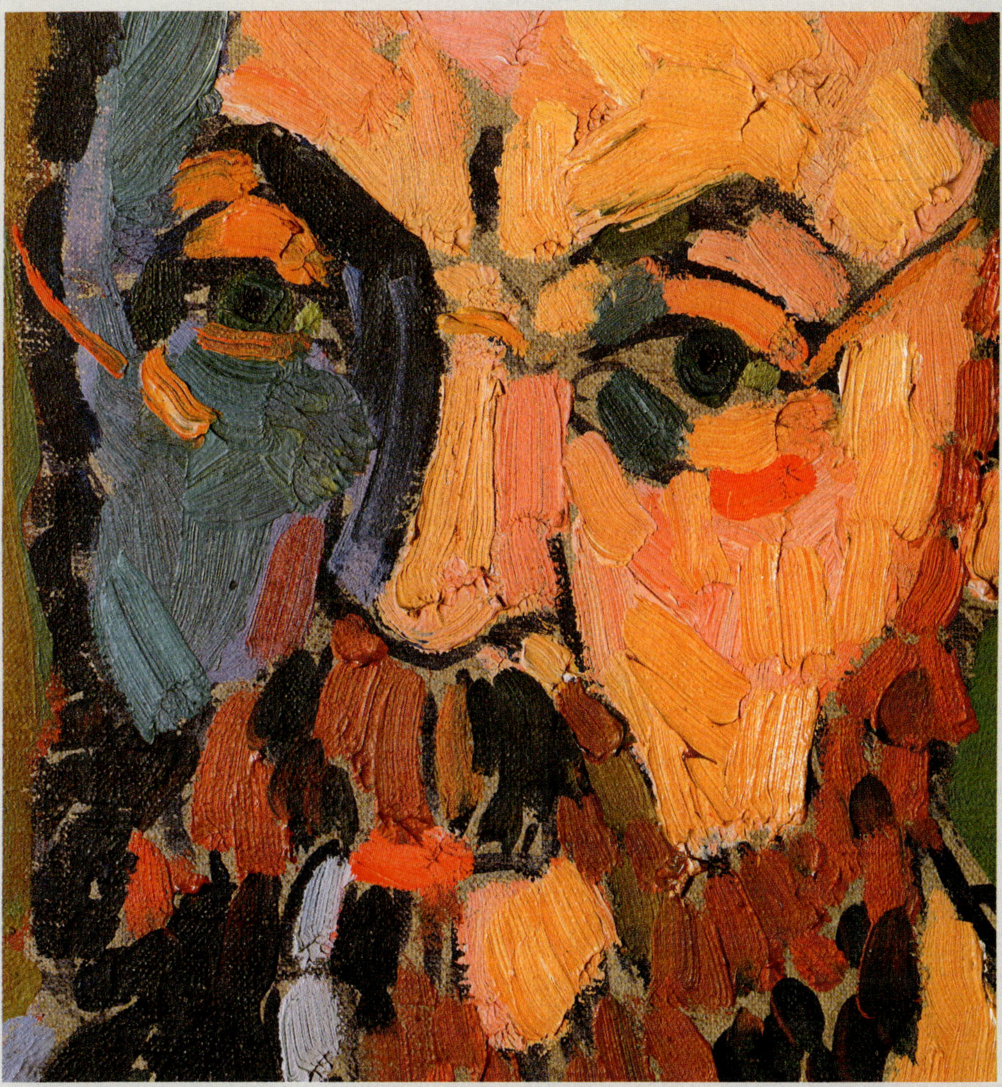

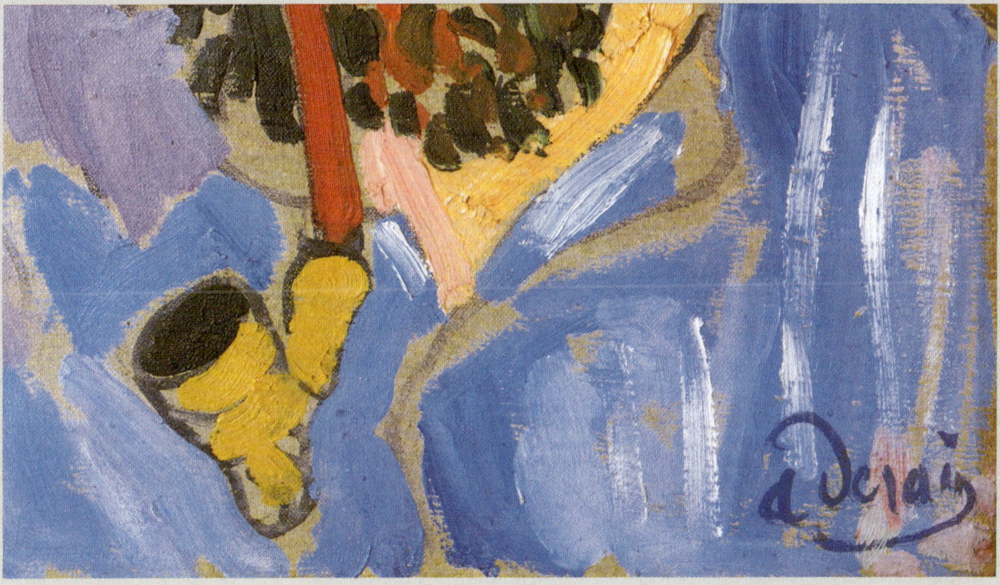

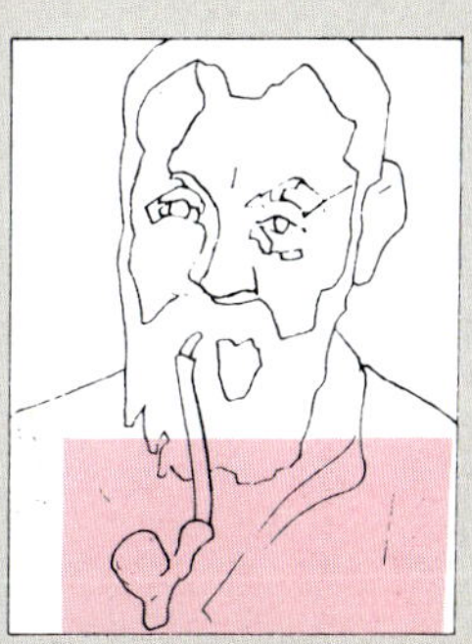

*A single sweep of red provides the pipe stem. The bowl is worked in bright, probably chrome, yellow. The pale blues of the shirt are applied in strokes which follow and outline the shape of the pipe. The coffee color of the ground shows through the blocked in colors.*

# HENRI MATISSE

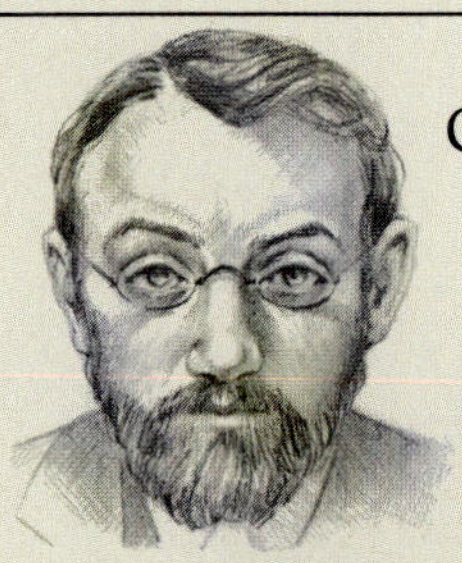

*Portrait of Derain/Portrait de Derain* (1905)
Oil on white primed canvas, primed on front face only
39.3cm × 28.8cm/15½in × 11½in

Henri Matisse was born in Picardy, in northern France. He came to painting late, in 1890, having first trained as a lawyer. Between 1895 and 1897, he studied in the *atelier* of Gustave Moreau (1826–1898), the Symbolist painter whose love of color had an important influence on Matisse. When Moreau died, Matisse left the *atelier*, which was taken over by a less sympathetic master. He journeyed in the south of France in 1898, and in 1899 worked in an independent studio under the Symbolist painter Eugène Carrière (1849–1906), where he met Derain. In 1904 he began his regular periods of working in the south of France, painting that year with Signac, who lived at St.Tropez. Matisse's early career as painter was characterized by daring innovatory steps, followed by longer periods of careful reassessment and consolidation. His apprenticeship, as he saw it, continued for many years beyond what was typical at the period, only really ending with his first major imaginative composition *Luxury, Calm and Voluptuousness*. This was painted in 1904–1905 in a style derived from Signac's late Pointillism, and exhibited at the Independents' Salon in Spring 1905, where it was bought by Signac.

Unlike the essentially naturalistic color oppositions of yellow-blue/violet which characterized Impressionist color, Matisse began to exploit the more abstract, and at the same time more vibrant, oppositions of red-green. Because red and green colors are the closest in tone of all the complementary color pairs, they set up a dazzling sensation which gives its own light and brilliance, without any direct imitation of natural effects of light. Thus the properties of color itself, and the interactions of color with their power to create light, instead of reproducing the effect of light, were the basis of Matisse's mature art. Color no longer stood for, or symbolized, anything external to painting itself; it was color as color.

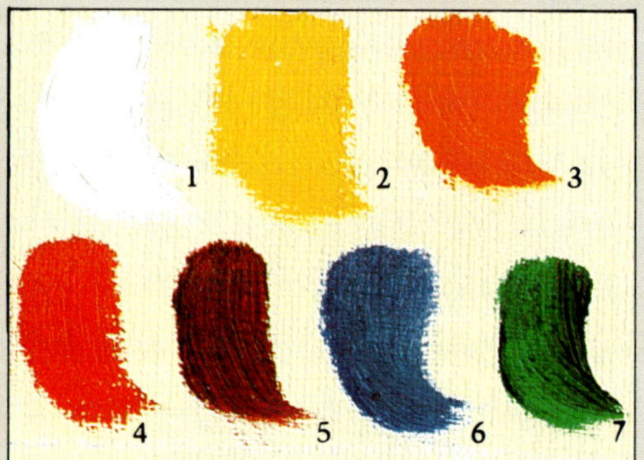


*The palette for this work comprised lead white (1), chrome yellow (2), cadmium orange (3), vermilion (4), scarlet alizarin lake (5), cobalt blue (6) and viridian green (7).*

By the time Matisse painted his portrait of Derain, he had rejected the mosaic-like pointillist touch of Signac. The restraint of this imposed systematic method had served its purpose for Matisse, in opening the way to a more directly pictorial handling of pure color. When broken touches of color appear among larger, flat areas of color in Matisse's Fauvist work, they do so in order to enhance intuitive color correspondences, not to fit in with a preconceived color system.

The thin white ground, applied only on the face side of his fairly fine, ordinary-weight canvas, was already degraded as a result of surface abrasion before Matisse began work on it. This was possibly because it had rubbed against other canvases while being transported. Thus the white finish of the canvas is broken by tiny dark dashes and dots, where the somber linen color of the canvas has appeared through the worn ground. This marginally reduces the luminosity of the surface, where it shows through among the colors of the paint layer. However, the white of the ground still increases the overall luminosity of the picture, and the flatness it gives enhances the pictorial flatness.

Matisse's brushwork in the handling of the shirt, with its radiating parallel marks, is reminiscent of the brushwork of van Gogh. However, it remains much less ostentatious and lacks the emotional charge inherent in the latter's handling. Elsewhere in the picture, Matisse's brushwork has an unselfconscious awkwardness. Its directness is such that it avoids the comparatively tasteful descriptiveness in Derain's *Portrait of Matisse*. Thus Matisse's brushwork stands for itself, instead of playing an illusionistic role. In the background, a hasty scrubbing application is used, while on the head, abrupt strokes of thick impasto vie with longer, flowing lines – as in the sweeping application of premixed red lake and white on Derain's hat. Matisse's unconventional brushwork gives an air of excitement and urgency to the picture.

No identifiable light source falls on the figure, which is treated in broadly complementary pairs of colors contrasting with the background. Orange-red on the face contrasts with the cobalt blue and white of the background on the right, while the viridian green and white mixture of the left side contrasts with the red lake and white mixture, which probably also contains a touch of vermilion, for the hat. This red also contrasts with the pure viridian of the hair, and the viridian tint beside the ear and on the neck.

The pale yellow yoke of the shirt creates the lower third of the green-blue-yellow outer color ring. However, except for the cobalt violet monogram, there is no contrasting violet counterpart for the yellow, which acts as a subtle foil for the scintillating hues of the upper half of the painting, drawing attention

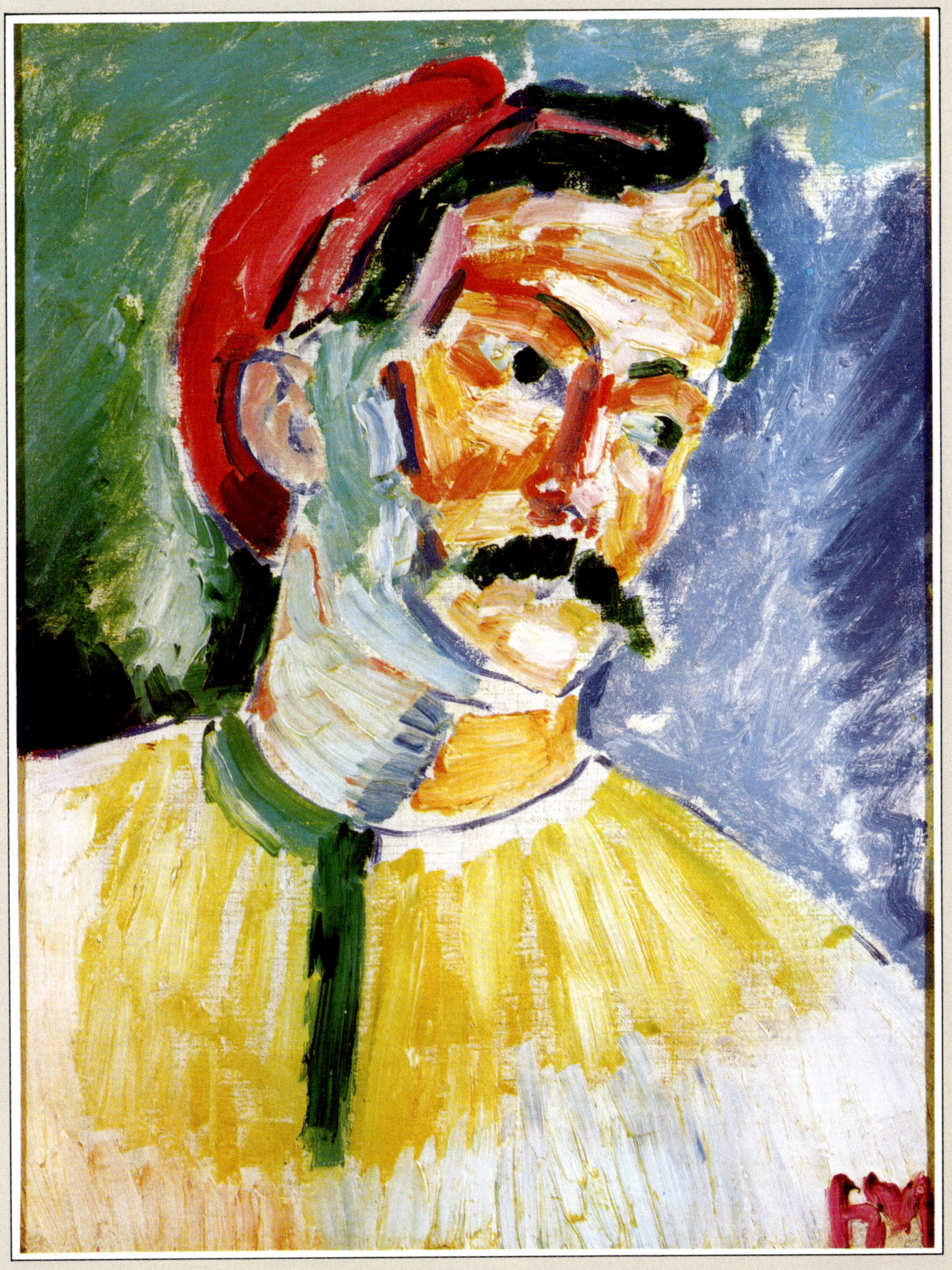

*Matisse's head of Derain is more adventurous than Derain's portrait of Matisse in color, light and handling. Instead of a subdued ground color, Matisse chose a brilliant white, which was thinly laid and slightly abraded from wear or rubbing, perhaps even before he began work. This was doubtless accidental. The white enhances the glowing luminosity of the colors, and is often left to show among them. The palette is severely limited, exploiting colors which are almost unmixed except with white, and are in complementary pairs. There is no specific fall of light, but light seems to glow from within because of the mutually enhancing effect of the complementary colors. The blueish viridian green, used for the background on the left and for the hair, the left side of the face and the shirt band, contrasts with the blueish red of the scarlet lake on the hat. The orange-reds on the face are made livelier by the cobalt blue and white mix used for fluid contours and for the background, right. Matisse's brushwork shows an exuberant irreverance for traditionally accepted modes of paint handling. The sitter's backward tilt creates a distance effect, cutting him off from the spectator.*

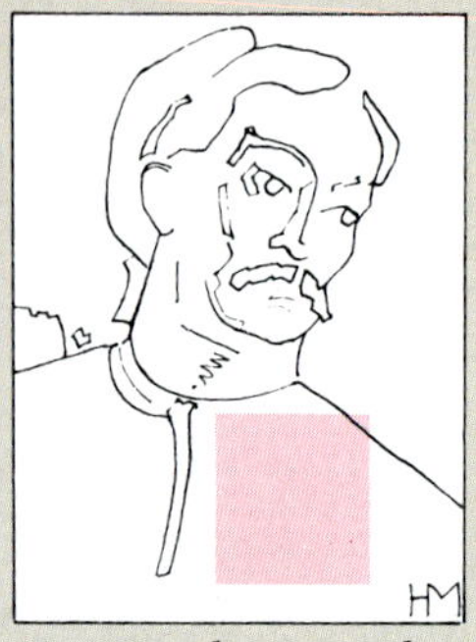

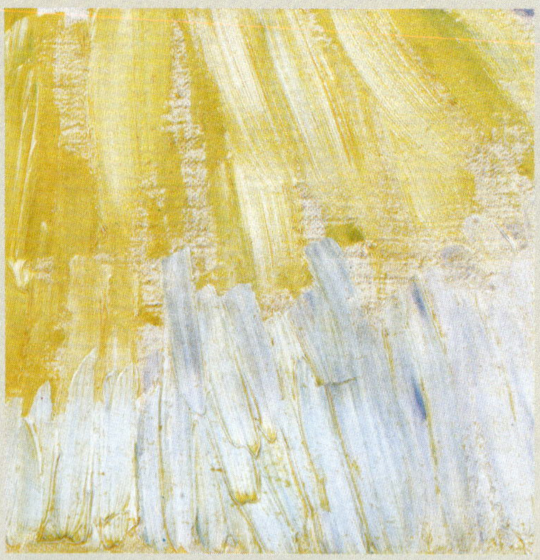

Strong, radiating strokes of chrome yellow and white, and white with a touch of blue, denote the shirt yoke and suggest the form below. The speckled, abraded white ground is seen among the brushstrokes.

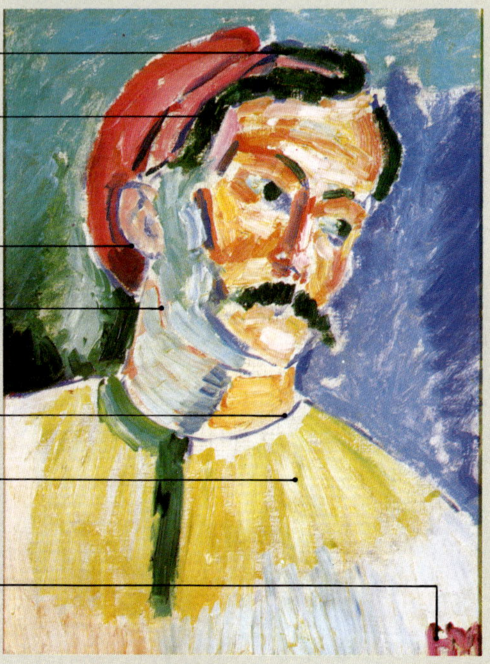


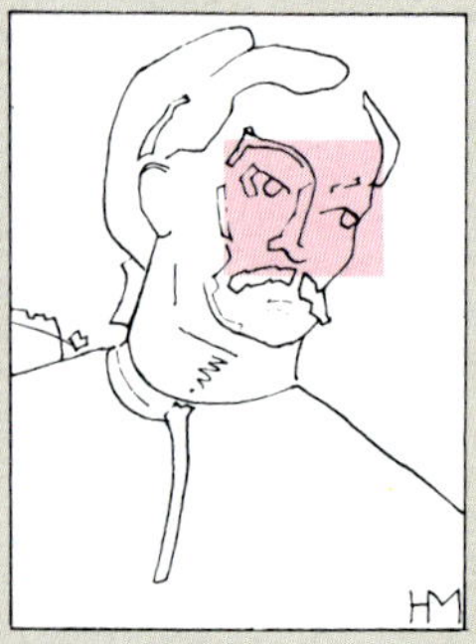

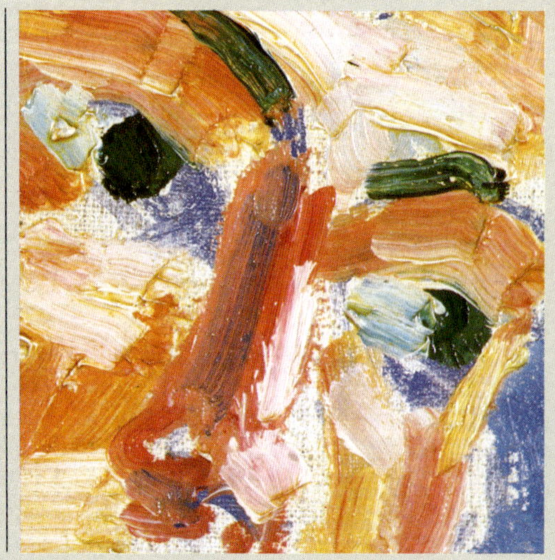

*The colors are both premixed and blended wet in wet on the canvas surface, over the initial, limited indications of the figure which were painted in fluid cobalt blue and white.*

to the main subject, the head. The solid stroke of green that follows the curve of the neck and dips vertically down the shirt, gives an ambiguous sense of form to the figure, and anchors the head to the shoulders. The contours of the figure were applied fluidly with a sable hair brush, in a light cobalt blue close to the color of the right background. The blue on the chin and neck links across the contrasting orange-red to the blue background, just as the saturated viridian green of mustache and hair link across to the green of the left background. The light in Matisse's painting comes from within, from his carefully calculated oppositions of brilliant, pure color.

The picture was painted *alla prima*, the reworkings painted directly over and mingling with the wet paint below. The pink hues first used for the left side of the neck were then adjusted to their complementary opposite, green – a change resulting not from the demands of naturalism – the colors Matisse saw in the sitter – but from internal pictorial necessity. This type of alteration, where adjustments were made to the colors during the painting process, to shift or correct their corresponding harmonies or contrasts, is typical of Matisse's work.

The evolution of a painting by Matisse is thus a dialectical process, in which the individual component colors are constantly adjusted, in relation to each other and to the whole, until a satisfactory internal pictorial coherence is reached. By the time his Fauve style had evolved, during the summer and the ensuing months of 1905, Matisse had stated the basic artistic problems which were to preoccupy him throughout his long career.

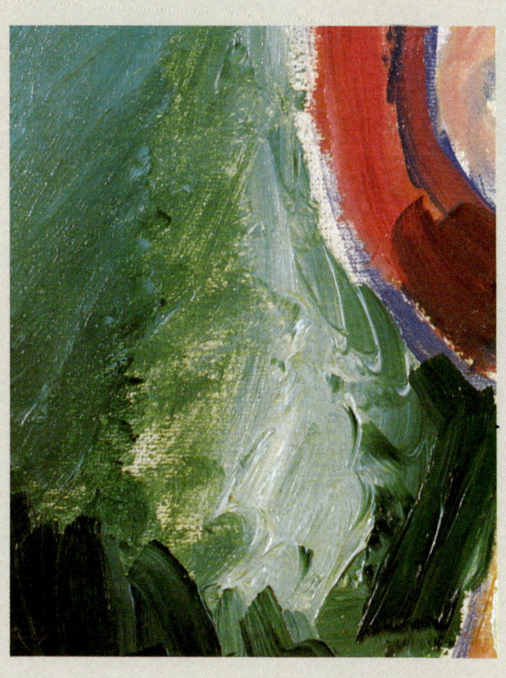

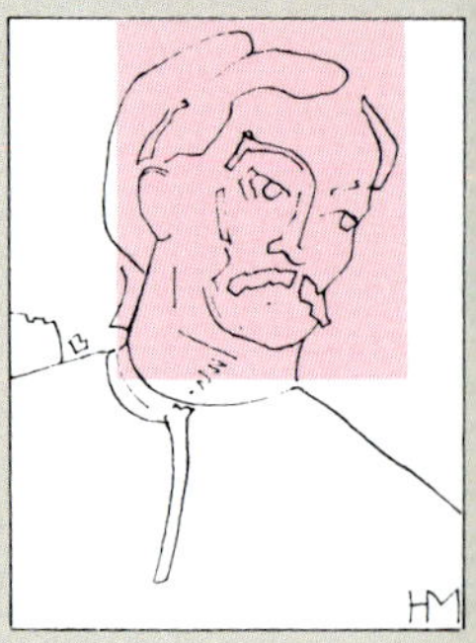

Actual size detail
*Wet-in-wet slurring is seen here, as is the rich impasto on the face. Dirt and yellowing of varnish is apparent close to the ridges in the paint, in the eye-whites, neck and forehead highlights.*

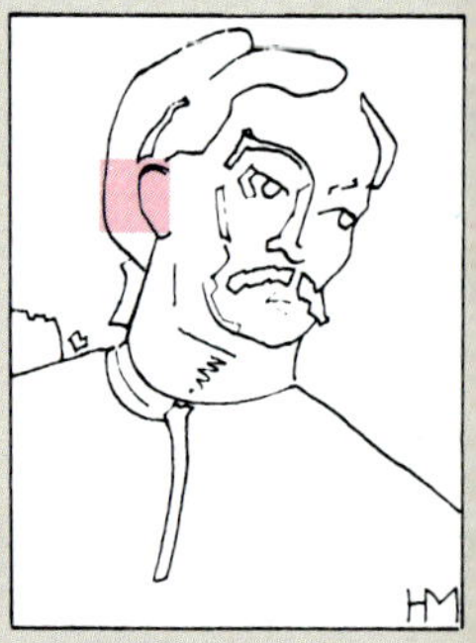

*Over the white ground a dilute cobalt blue and white mix was applied for the contours, and viridian green and premixed white was loosely scrubbed to fill the background. Reds and pinks block in the hat and ear. Viridian green and white were then slurred wet in wet for the richer, thicker parts.*

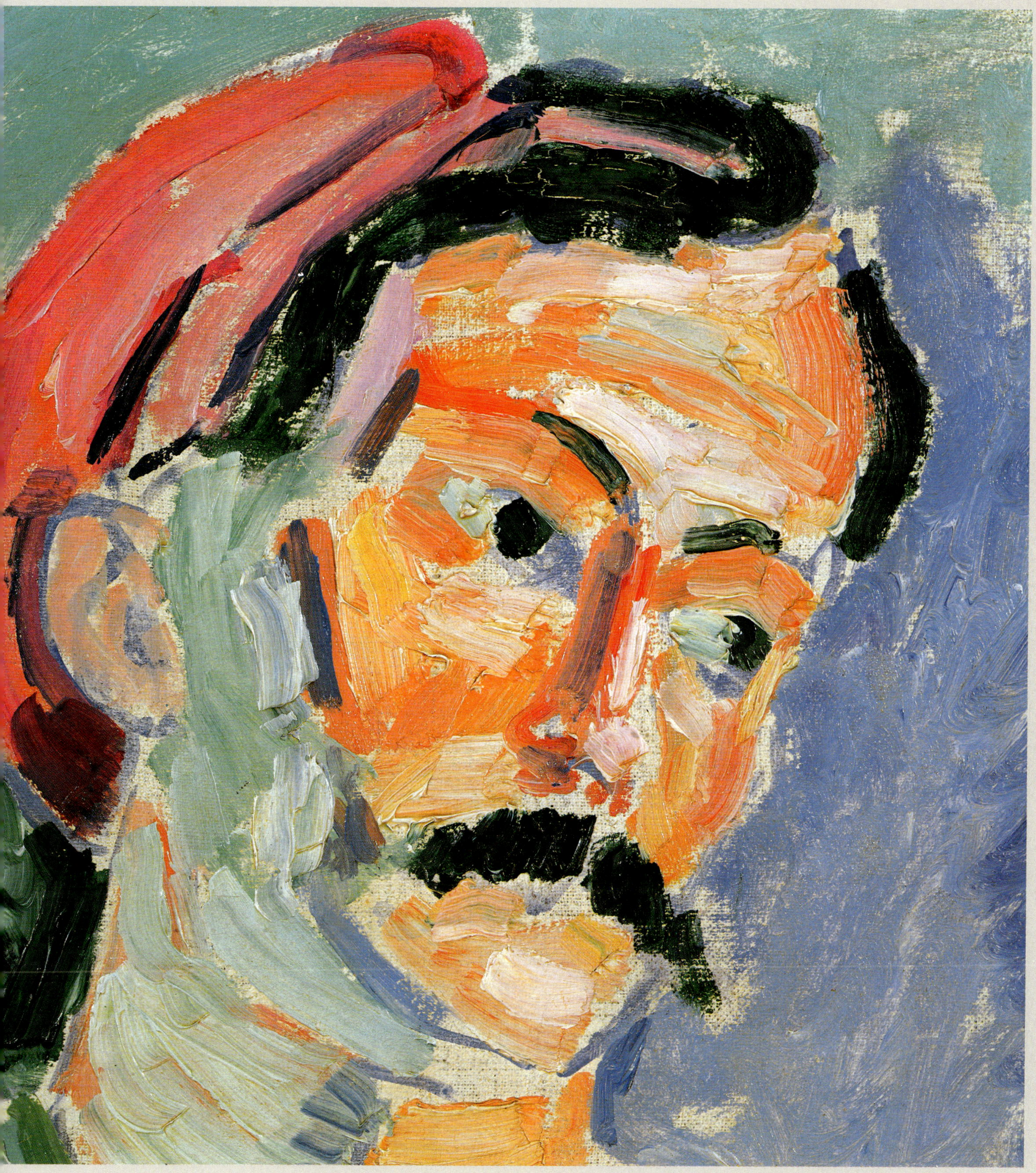

# ANDRE DERAIN

*The Pool of London (1906)*
Oil on canvas
65.7cm × 99.1cm/26in × 39in

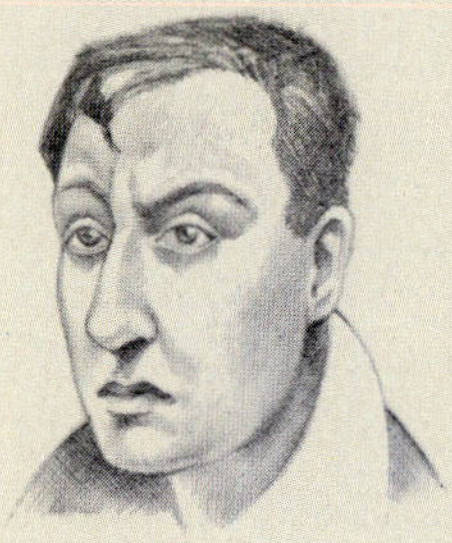

With Matisse and Vlaminck, André Derain was one of the three prime movers of the loose group of Parisian artists who became known as the Fauves ('wild beasts'). The high moment of Fauvism was during the years 1905 and 1906; a period which saw exhibitions at the Salon d'Automne and the Salon des Indépendants and, also, the crucial collaboration between Matisse and Derain at Collioure on the French south coast in the summer of 1906. While Matisse has been celebrated as one of the foremost artists of the twentieth century, his work often seems to evade certain of the defining characteristics of Fauvism. Vlaminck, similarly, has been seen as Fauvist more through the impetuous force of his wayward and anarchistic personality than his actual painting. It is therefore to Derain that we should turn for typical Fauvism.

Derain was born in June 1880 at Chatou on the Seine, a few miles to the west of Paris. He was sent to Paris to become an engineer but he was more interested in painting which he had taken up in his middle teens. He drifted in and out of Symbolist circles meeting both writers and painters, including Matisse whom he encountered at the Académie Camillo. Of more immediate significance was a chance meeting with Maurice de Vlaminck in a derailed suburban train. They had a fascinating attraction for one another which spawned an intense collaboration called the School of Chatou. The period 1904 to 1907 was one of animated discussion and experiment among the Fauves who painted in various permutations.

When Derain turned to figure painting in early 1907 the coloristic exuberance of Fauvism was already draining from his work; and while from about 1908 to 1910 he seemed to pursue a sort of classical realism based on an advanced and individual interpretation of Cézanne, thereafter his painting steadily bypassed the innovations of Cubism. His later work, uneven in quality, was painted in the nineteenth-century French academic style.

Both technically and historically Fauvism as a movement, and the work of Derain in particular, may be regarded as a summation of Post-Impressionism. The techniques and triumphs of Seurat, van Gogh, Gauguin and Cézanne were rehearsed and exaggerated by the Fauves in virtuoso displays of the potent expressiveness of oil on canvas. The Neo-Impressionism of Seurat and Signac prompted Matisse's experiments with smallish dabs of pure color disposed over the whole canvas surface, as well as the 'broken-touch' Fauvism which characterized the earlier work of Derain, Matisse and Braque. Gauguin's 'flat-color' technique dominated Fauvism from about 1905 to 1906, though many paintings exhibit a combination of these methods (called 'mixed-technique' Fauvism). The influence of Cézanne cut across these divisions to a certain extent, but when it became pervasive in 1906 to 1907 Fauvism lost its coherence.

Color and expression monopolized the conversations of the Fauves and filled their pictures: Derain and Matisse debated Vlaminck's injunction to paint 'with pure cobalts, pure vermilions, pure veronese'; Derain wrote to Vlaminck in July 1905 of his 'new conception of light consisting of this: the negation of shadows', of the need to 'eradicate everything involved with the division of tones', and of his new concern with 'things which owe their expression to deliberate disharmonies'.

Painted during Derain's second visit to London in 1906, *The Pool of London* was 'one of the high points of his Fauve career', according to art historian John Elderfield. The whole series of his London works manifests a considerable variety of techniques and subject matters, ranging from the Divisionist-derived pyrotechnic display in *Big Ben* (1905), to the suave almost anecdotal whimsy of *Hyde Park* (1906), the vigorous bustle of *Regent Street* (1906) and the more loosely brushed 'mixed-technique' of *Charing Cross Bridge* (1906) with its complementary paint flecks in the water and diluted color patches in the sky.

*The Pool of London* shares with many of the London paintings, including three of those mentioned above, the same horizontal dimension, 99.1 cm (39 in); the vertical measures 65.7 cm (26 in ). The slight lateral emphasis promotes Derain's interest in wide-angled effects and accentuates the bold, diagonal intrusion of the carrier boat from the bottom right into the center of the work; it was a formal device which he exploited frequently in opposition to well-managed up and down lines, and to subtly disposed subsidiary diagonals.

As often with the Fauves, the employment of certain techniques of paint application is directed by recognizable contingencies of subject matter. The surface of the water, for example, with its natural tendency to scatter and reflect light becomes the main arena for broken touches and dabs of greens and yellows, while the complexity of equipment and cargo on the boat suggests a more block-like mosaic patterning of bright, pure hues.

Elsewhere, variously shaped patches of color are spread fairly evenly to define continuous surfaces such as the sides of the main vessel and portions of the barges and tugs which surround it. Color intensity is focused on the foreground areas, and the lefthand and top margins of the canvas are more loosely brushed in paler, vibrant shades. This murkiness of the distant scene is promoted, naturalistically and symbolically, by smoke rising in three places in the upper third of the work. Dominating the whole is the potent clash between sharp reds and deep blues which in many ways was the essential coloristic contribution of the Fauvist enterprise.

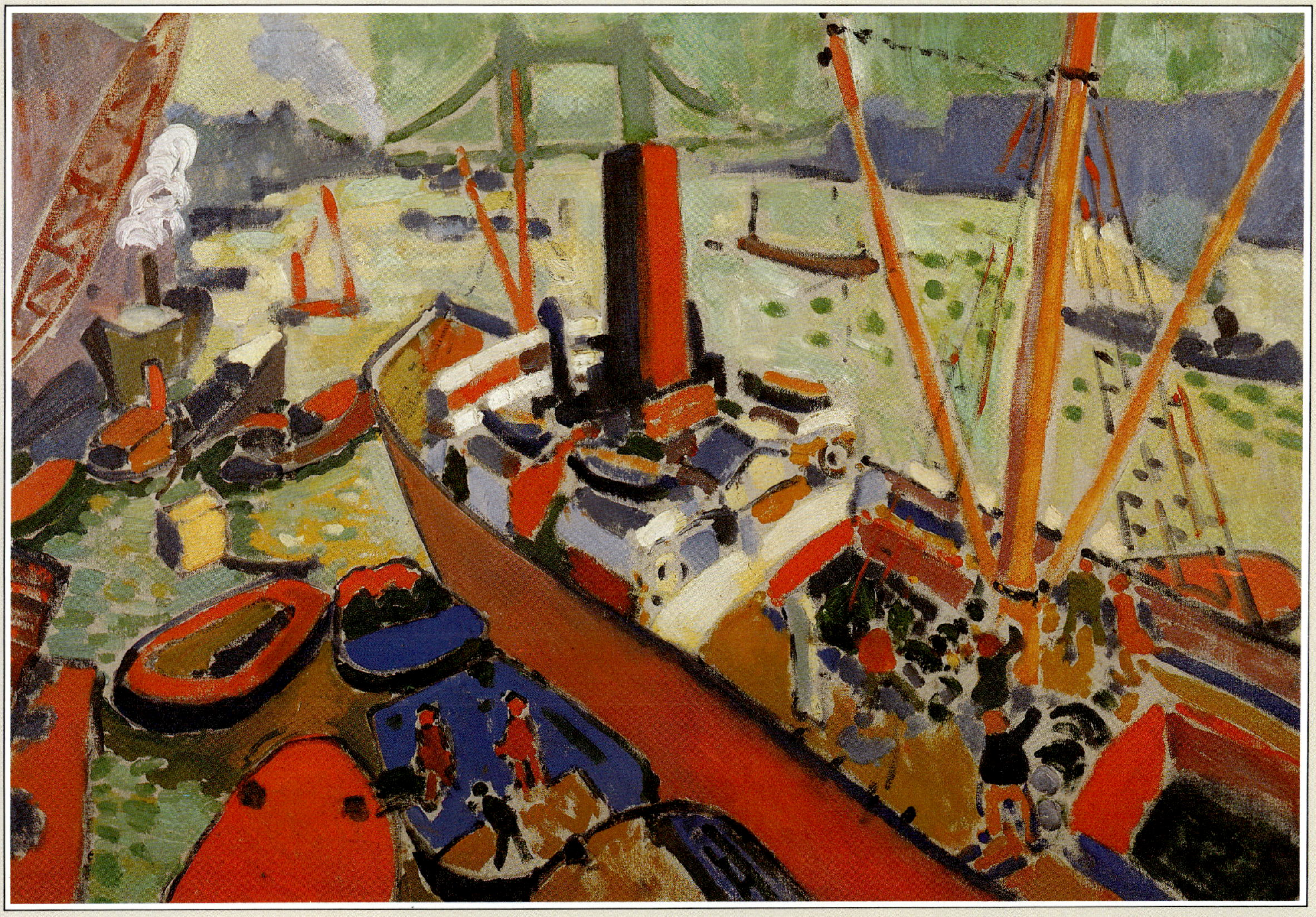

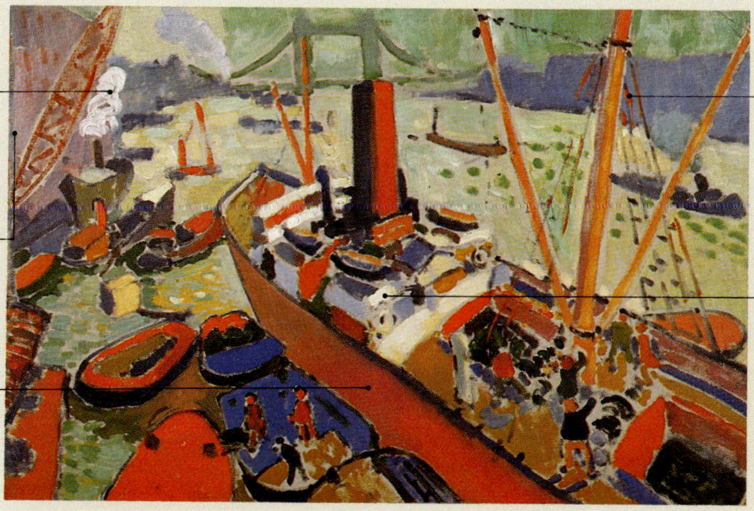


*Derain's* The Pool of London *(1906) exemplifies the chromatic exuberance which is the defining characteristic of Fauvist painting. Shape, volume, depth and design are subordinated to the foreground of complementary color patches. Ample flashes of the white ground indicate the typical Fauvist combination of haste, accident and control from which the compositional shape of the work evolves. More than with Cézanne's 'constructive' brushstroke or the Neo-Impressionist color spot, our attention is arrested by the variety of individual paint marks and the vibrancy with which they cohere and collide over the canvas surface.*

*RIGHT* *Monet's* The Houses of Parliament *(1903) is an exploration of atmospheric conditions in paint. The canvas has a kind of 'all-over' unity of paint application not sought by the Fauves in most of their works. Monet has blended, smudged and slurred his paint touches to present a pale, nuanced surface in which forms are dissolved by the remorseless saturation of light as well as by the intervention of patchy fog. The colors are muted and often worked up in layers inch by inch, to produce complex tonal gradations.*

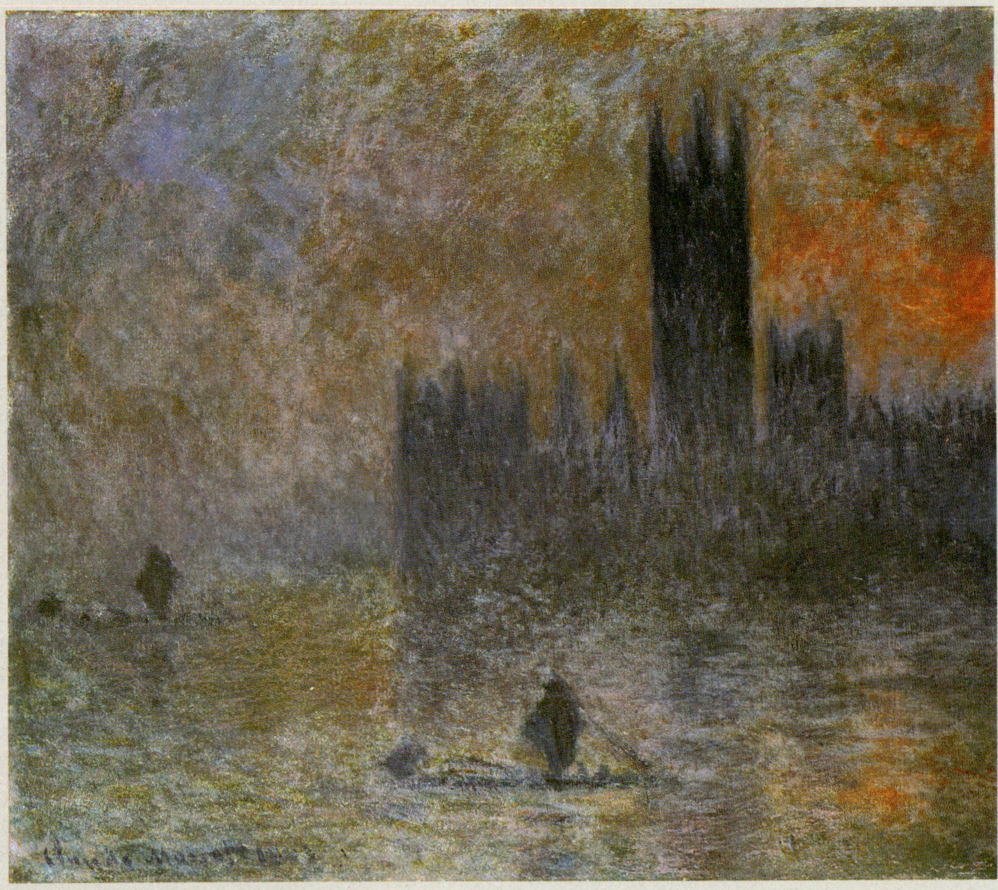

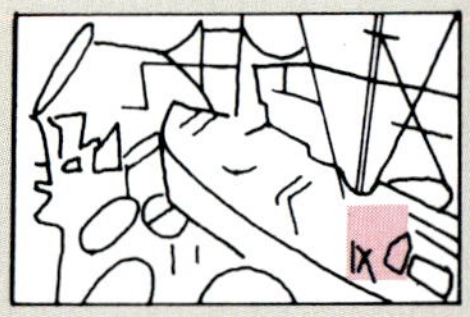

*ACTUAL SIZE DETAIL*
*This striking detail illustrates the tension between figurative and coloristic impulses. Brushstrokes are remarkably thinned and unladen for Derain; there are random impasto ridges, and only a small proportion of the painted areas in this detail indicate the direction of brush movements. The pinhead nodes of the canvas weave are almost constantly visible. Virtually the full spectrum of Derain's palette is employed here, mostly in discrete patches, as if in response to the naturalistic complexity of at least five men striking attitudes of work amid a welter of deck machinery and items of cargo.*

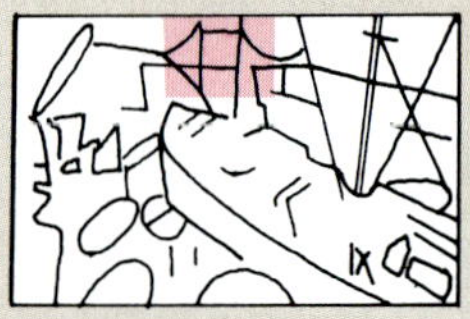

*RIGHT Derain has worked up effects of distance at the top extremity of his composition, featuring the symbolic geometry of Tower Bridge, through the skilful dilution of viridian green in a succession of pale and creamy 'sub-tones' vigorously brushed, and, in general, less yellow with distance. In addition, certain of the more structural concerns of the artist can be appreciated in the calculated vertical alignment of the central funnel and the right bridge turret, and the prow masts and the left turret, the subsidiary mast striking a complementary angle to the bridge support.*

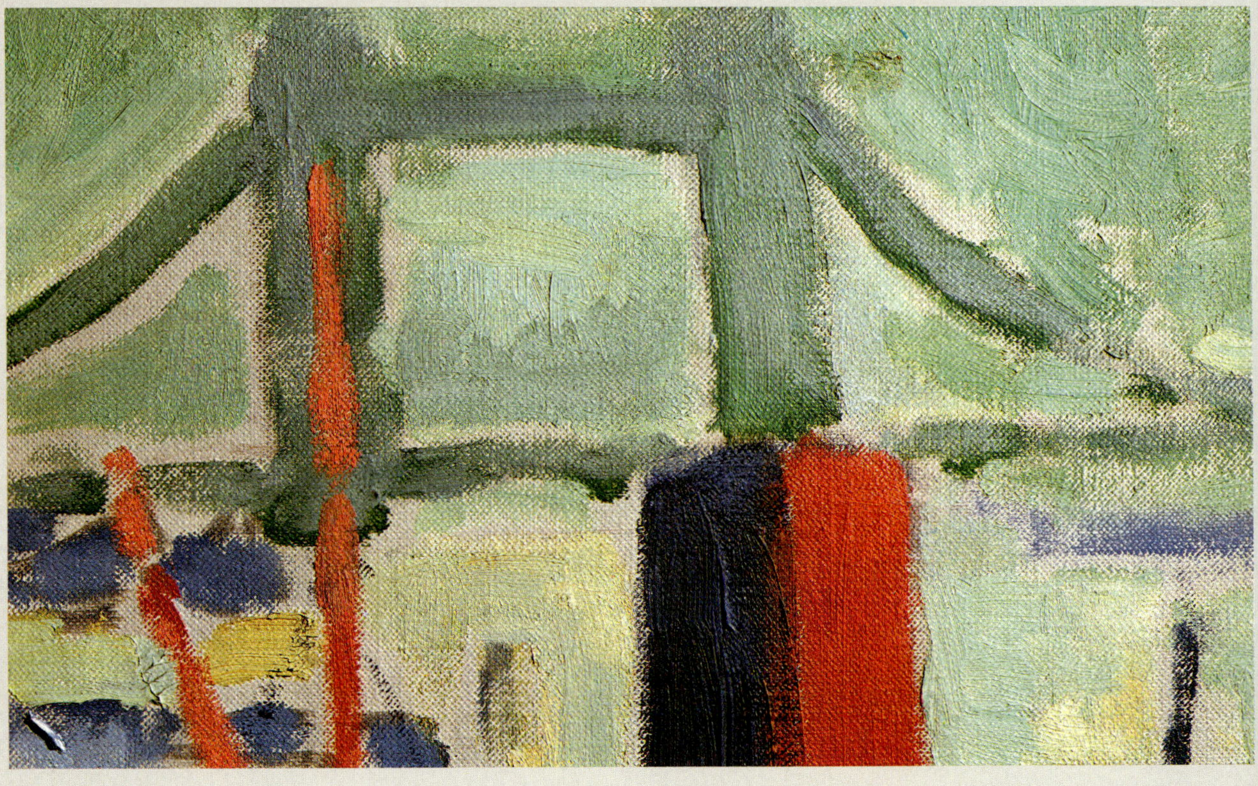

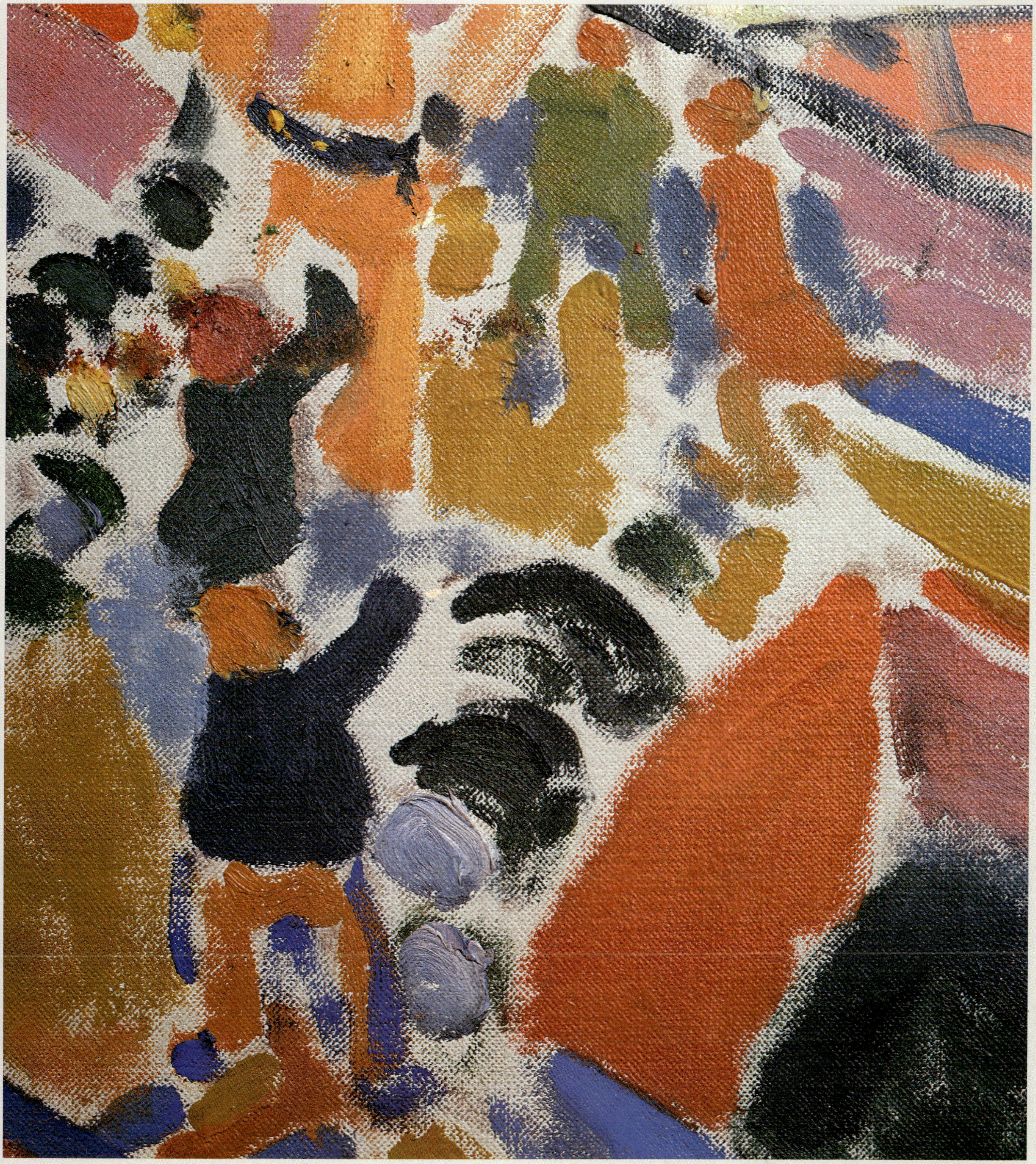

# HENRI ROUSSEAU

*The Dream (1910)*
Oil on canvas
204.5cm × 299cm/79½in × 117¾in

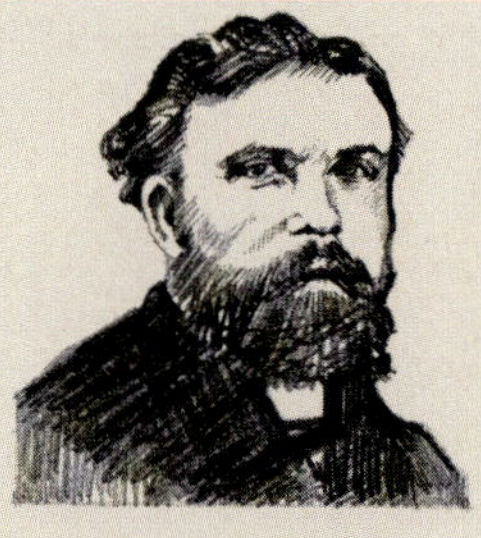

*The Dream* was one of Henri Rousseau's last paintings, and certainly the last he sent for exhibition. The final months of his life were marred by an unrequited love affair. He had fallen in love with a woman 12 years his junior, the daughter of one of his former colleagues and she did not return his affection. It has been proposed that the subject matter of *The Dream,* a naked woman stretching out her hand, reflects the confused emotional state which Rousseau was suffering at the time. However, all the elements in the painting can be discovered in works of previous years. When it was sent for exhibition in March 1910, a poem was attached to its frame: 'Yadwigha in a beautiful dream/While sleeping peacefully,/Heard the notes of a pipe/Played by a thoughtful snake charmer./While the moon casts its light/On the flowers and verdant trees/The wild snakes listen/To the gay tunes of the instrument.'

Rousseau was born in Laval in 1844, the fourth child of a tinsmith, and as a youth he won prizes at school for both art and music. Because his family was poor, he was unable to attend an art school; he worked as a solicitor's clerk and also joined the army. His main career was that of a second-class toll-collector in the Municipal Customs Service in Paris. Determined to become a professional artist, Rousseau retired in 1885 on a tiny pension and set himself a disciplined course of action. Self-taught, he drew and painted 'alone with only nature as a teacher and some advice received from Gérôme, and Clément.' Clément (1826-1888) was an academic painter, director of Fine Arts at the Ecole de Lyon, who exhibited at the official French Salon, and who introduced Rousseau to his colleagues – Gérôme (1826-1904), Cabanel (1823-1889) and Bouguereau (1825-1905). Gérôme, an important teacher at the Ecole des Beaux-Arts, upheld the value of technical ability of the highest standard, and exhorted his students to render exactly and clearly even the smallest details in their canvases.Brushmarks were not to be apparent.

Rousseau believed Egyptian art was supreme. He is reported to have told Picasso 'We are the two great painters of the age, you in the Egyptian style, I in the modern style', which must have accorded some kind of compliment towards Picasso's art. He thought less of Cézanne, venturing the memorable comment at the 1907 Cézanne memorial exhibition – 'You know, I could have finished all these pictures.'

Finish is most certainly one of the qualities of *The Dream.* A painting of this scale would have taken Rousseau up to three months to execute, and he is known to have worked in his studio seven days a week, from morning till night. He always began at the top of his canvas, and slowly and carefully worked his way down to the bottom. Ardengo Soffici (1879-1964), an Italian painter who watched him paint and who wrote an article about his work in 1910, recalled how Rousseau would work with one color at a time and fill in all those areas where he wished it to occur, and only then would he turn to the next color. Usually he began with the greens: there are over 50 variations of green alone in *The Dream,* which indicates the application needed to produce such a large work.

Judging from a photograph which shows him at work on a canvas of 1909, *The Muse Inspiring the Poet,* Rousseau completed the background foliage before he began on the two figures in that work. The area they were to occupy was simply drawn in, probably with a paint brush, with only their smooth external contours evident, and it is quite probable that he adopted the same method for *The Dream.* The naked woman and the sofa have a hard edge and give the impression of being a cut-out, so much do they stand out from the rest of the composition. The strong contrast in tonal values between the light flesh of the nude and the dark red of the sofa help to create this impression – they are also reminiscent of the stark tonal contrasts in Edouard Manet's *Olympia* (1863). Rousseau gave this explanation: 'The sleeping woman on the sofa dreams that she is transported into the forest, hearing the music of the snake charmer. This explains why the sofa is in the picture.'

Certainly, the positioning of the sofa with its sensuous passenger near the edge of the canvas and behind a somewhat *coulisse*-like plane of dense luxuriant foliage, gives a slight impression of a theatrical tableau or stage set. Invisible and silent stage hands have just sidled the sofa into the picture.

However dreamlike or theatrical the painting may appear, its motifs are taken from life. Rousseau liked to refer to his paintings with dense luxuriant foliage populated by wild beasts and brightly colored birds as his 'Mexican' pictures, and he initiated a legend about spending part of his army service in Mexico. But the luxuriant foliage was the result of many hours spent studying exotic plants in the conservatories of the Jardin des Plantes in Paris, and most of the animals and birds were directly observed at the zoo.

Only Yadwigha is new, and it is impossible to say whether a real-life nude model was the source, or a photograph or print in a popular journal, material from which Rousseau regularly drew inspiration. Rousseau told critic André Salmon that 'The sofa is there only because of its glowing red color.' Thus the painter offered two reasons for the inclusion of the sofa, one lyrical and the other formal.

In *The Dream* Rousseau contrives a magical balance between form and content, between complementary colors, and between detail and the evenness in the composition.

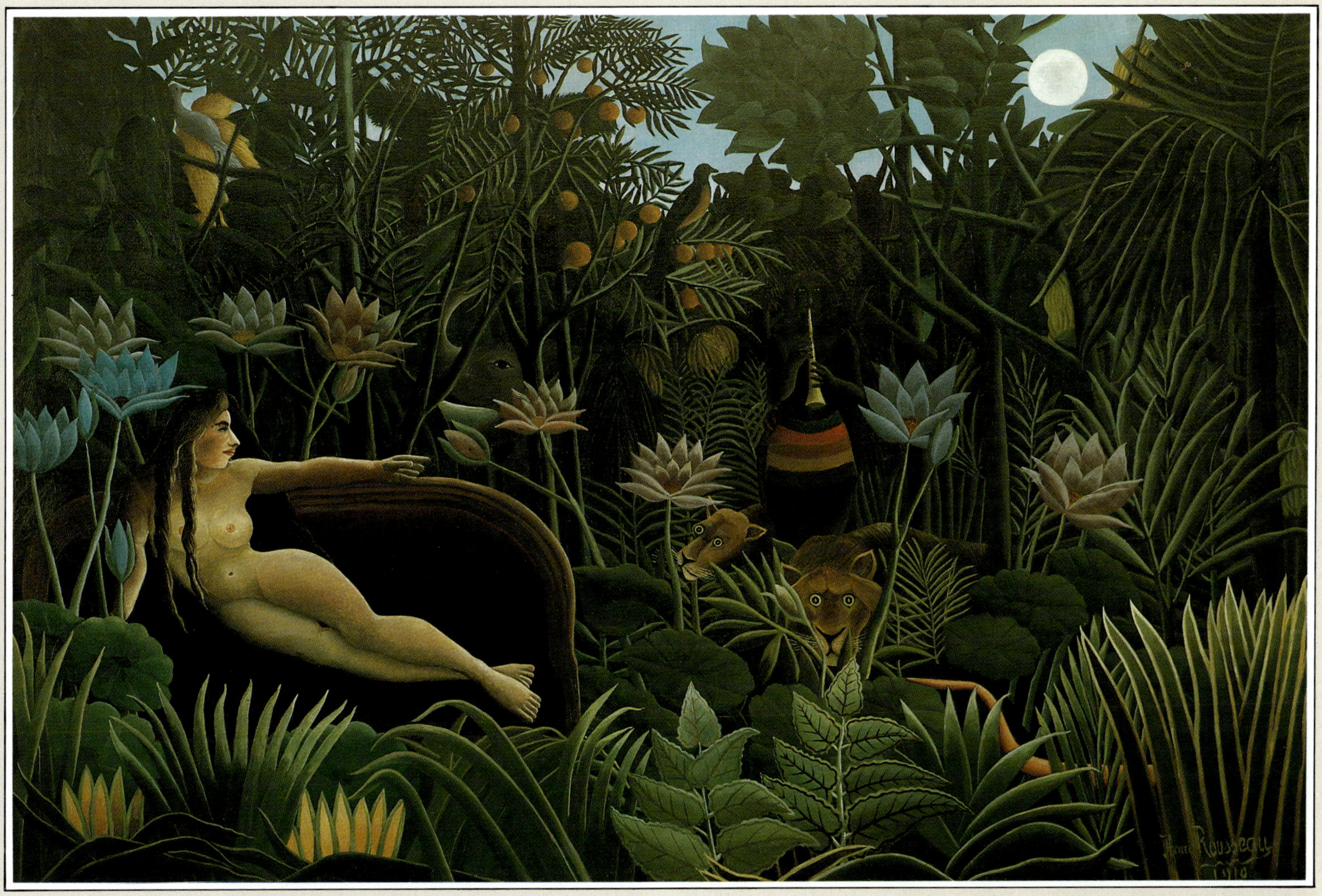

*The first example of Rousseau's use of exotic subject matter was his* Storm in the Jungle *of 1891.* The Dream, *the largest of all his exotic 'Mexican' works, was the culmination of this series. The composition contains elements which had appeared before on their own.*

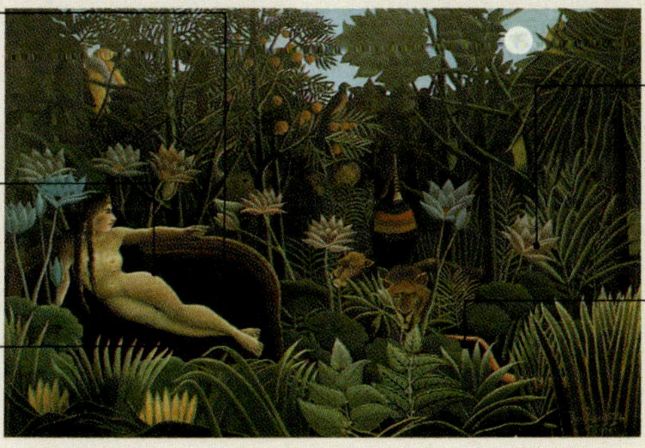

Sofa no longer 'glowing red', due to fugitive quality of the red pigment used

Area of maximum tonal opposition which serves to highlight the nude figure

Line visible showing alteration in lower contour of right leg

Pink waterlily-like flower painted on top of green plant, a variant on Rousseau's usual method of working

Pure black used for snake; Gauguin admired Rousseau for his use of blacks

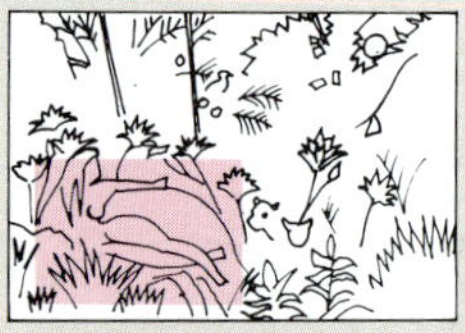

RIGHT *White is mixed with the fleshtones to produce an area of reflected moonlight on the lower thigh; it is applied unmixed as a single brushstroke line along her profile.*

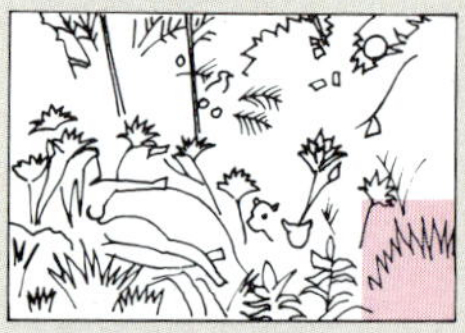

BELOW *These leaves are given a flat coat of paint, the color having been mixed in quantity on the palette, and the brushmarks are hardly visible.*

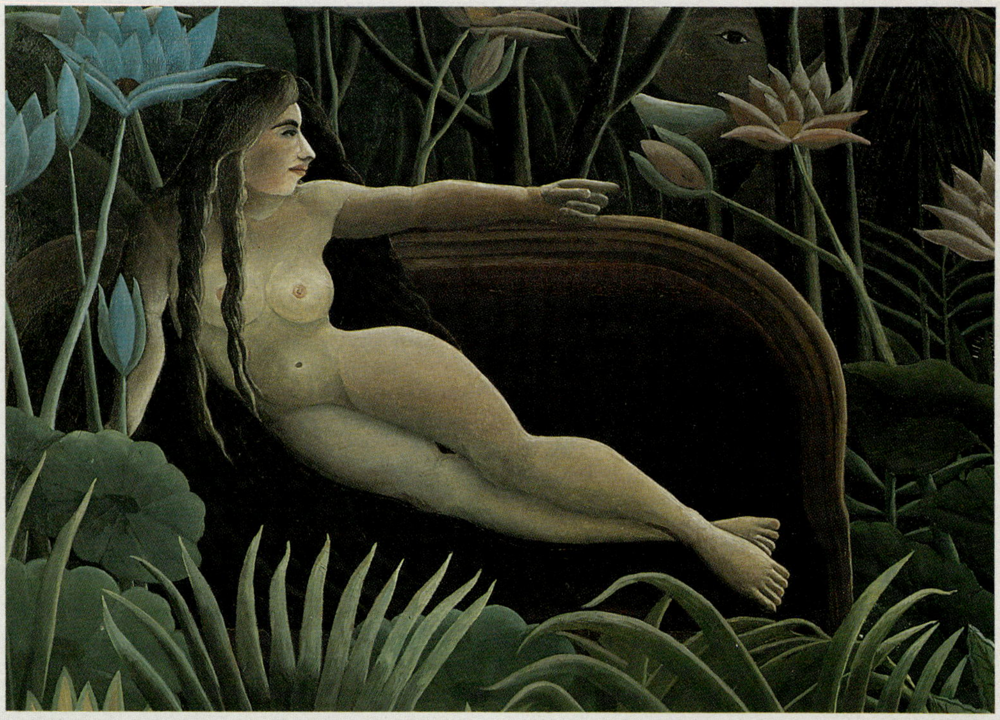

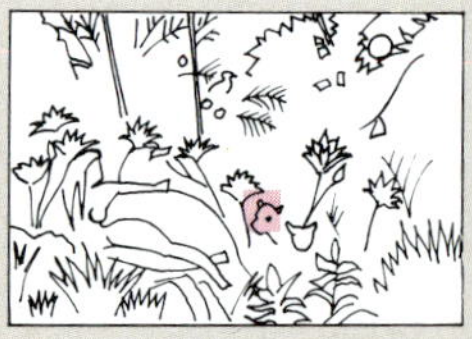

ACTUAL SIZE DETAIL *The entire area of the animal's head has first been given a layer of umber mixed with white, then the highlights and shadows have been laid on top. The paint is applied quite thinly, and a sense of volume is built up from the hatched brushstrokes, particularly below the animal's left eye, where the paler ground shows through in part.*

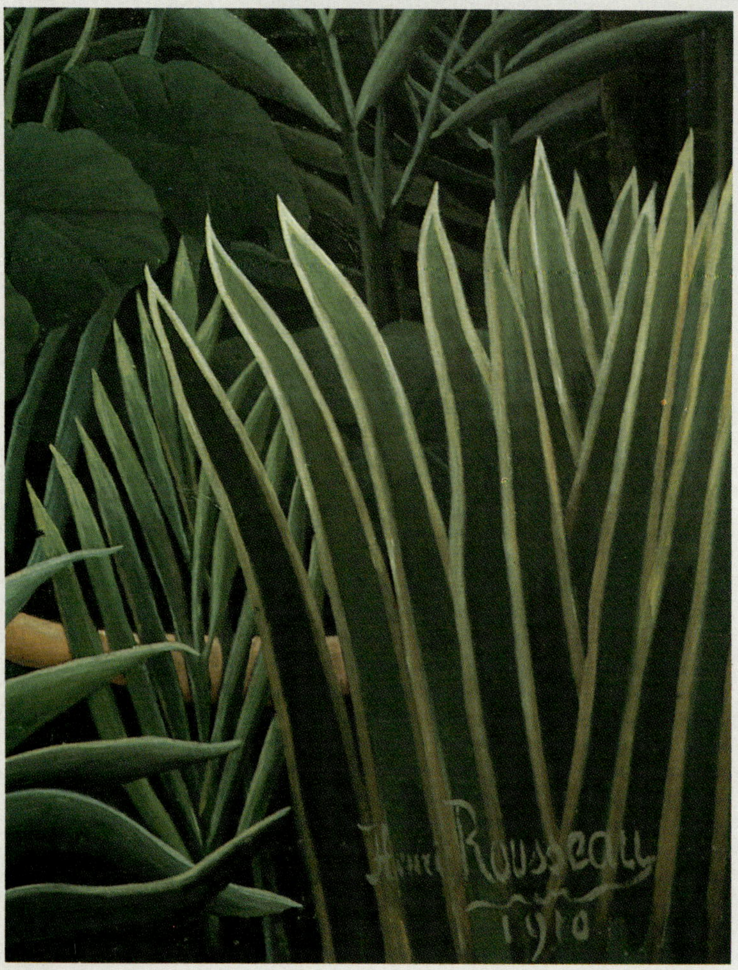

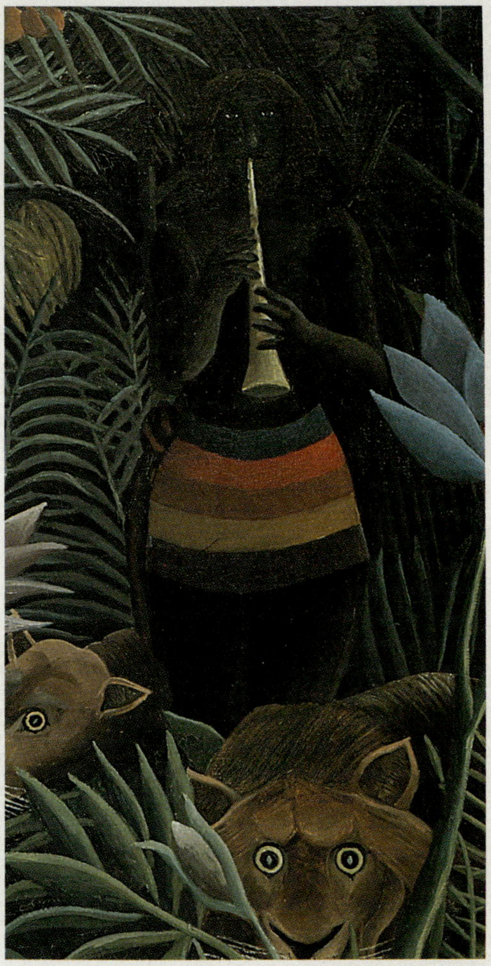

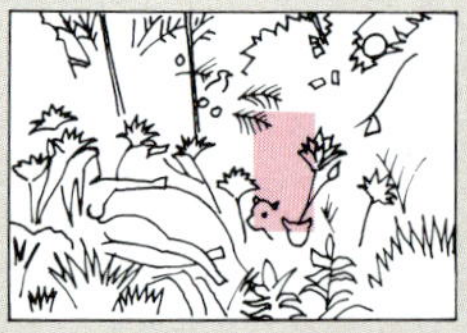

LEFT *The snake charmer is brought into prominence by tonal and coloristic contrasts. In a 1907 painting entitled* The Snake Charmer *Rousseau paints him with only an umber flute as a prop. As if to enrich his presence in* The Dream, *Rousseau gives him a yellow-green clarinet and a multi-striped loincloth, the vermilion stripe being the hottest color note in the whole painting. Although most of the motifs were taken from life or from printed illustrations, that of the snake charmer arose from Rousseau's imagination, sparked by Robert Delaunay's mother's reminiscences of India.*

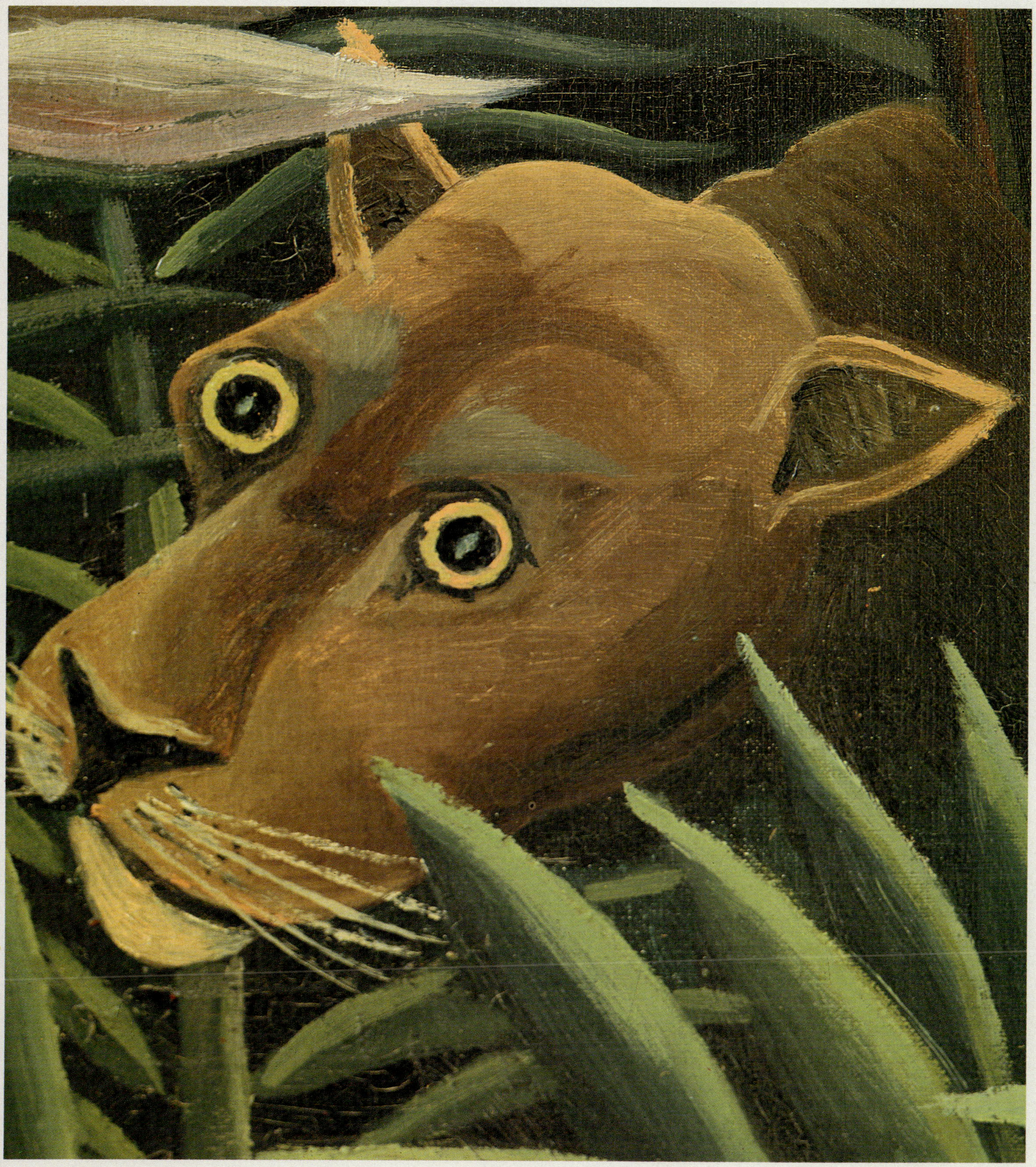

# PABLO PICASSO

*Still Life with Chair Caning* (1912)
Oil and oilcloth on canvas, 27cm × 35cm/$10^3/_4$in × $13^5/_8$in

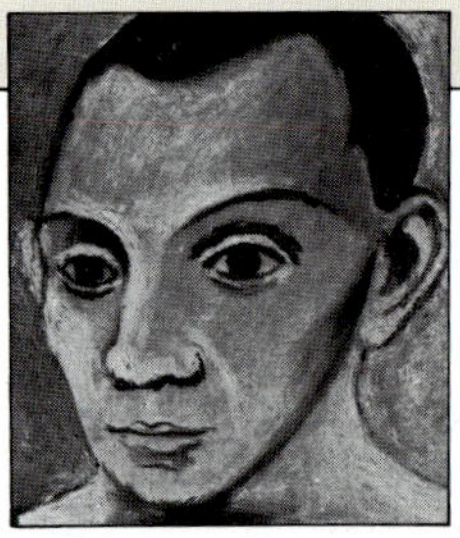

Picasso's great technical contribution to painting came with his and Braque's development of Cubism in the early years of this century. Cubism, which Picasso described as 'an art dealing primarily with forms', sought to dislocate space, eliminate perspective and split forms up in order to relate each one to an overall pattern in new ways. The Cubists did this, for example, by depicting several planes or surfaces of an object rather than portraying it from a single viewpoint. Picasso summed up his view of the goal of Cubism as 'To paint and nothing more. And to paint seeking a new expression, divested of useless realism, with a method linked only to my thought – without enslaving myself or associating myself with objective reality.'

However, *Still Life with Chair Caning* introduced another major Cubist development – collage. Indeed, Picasso's inclusion of an actual piece of oilcloth patterned with wickerwork chair caning amongst the painted objects on a café table can perhaps be regarded as the major technical innovation in painting of this century. This new technique, called collage from the French verb *coller* meaning 'to glue', broke with the traditional integrity of the oil medium and the notion of beauty associated with the skilful counterfeit of photographic realism. It set a challenge for painters to explore new techniques and to use any materials available in the achievement of their ends. The technique of collage evolved from Picasso and Braque using lettering as an integral part of the construction of a painting. In this work, for example, the letters 'JOU' from the word for newspaper, *journal*, are used to indicate the picture plane, while also hinting at the French word for play, *jouer*. Similarly the oilcloth with its wickerwork pattern has several functions in the painting. It suggests either a seat or some wallpaper; it is something 'real', taken from life, and yet it is only a printed illusion of a piece of wickerwork. Collage became a versatile and influential technique.

*Still Life with Chair Caning* was one of a sequence of oval still lifes painted in Spring 1912. Like another in the series, it was placed by the artist in a frame made of rope. Picasso described his working methods thus: 'I usually work on a number of canvases at a time. . . . I like to work in the afternoons, but best of all at night.'

1. Picasso used an off-white ground on a fine-grained canvas to lend the work its overall light tone.

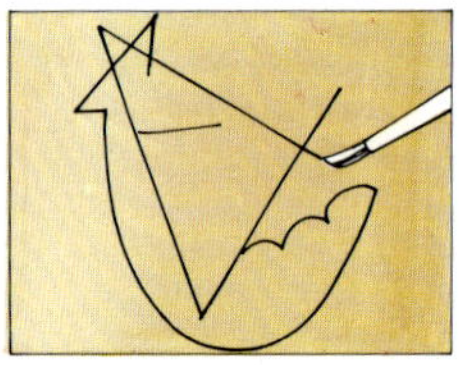

2. The paint surface was built up in layers worked wet into wet. Forms such as the shell were achieved by applying moulded impasto over an initial layer of ochre and then overdrawing in black with a brush to represent the scallop.

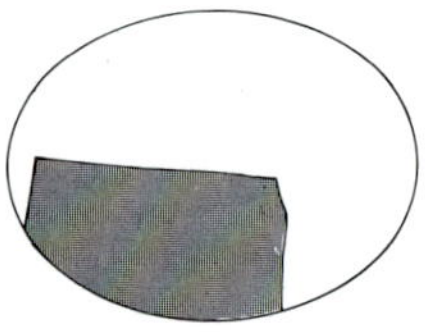

3. The oilcloth was attached to the canvas with fixative and brought into the general paint surface by the large brushstrokes applied across it.

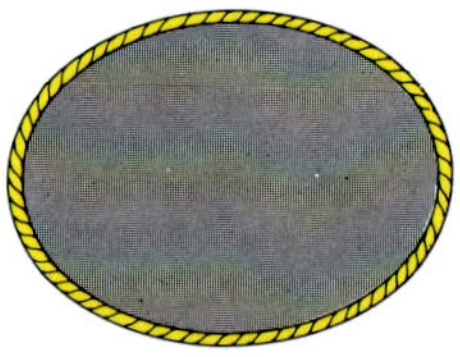

4. The picture was framed with rope, which forms an integral part of the finished work.

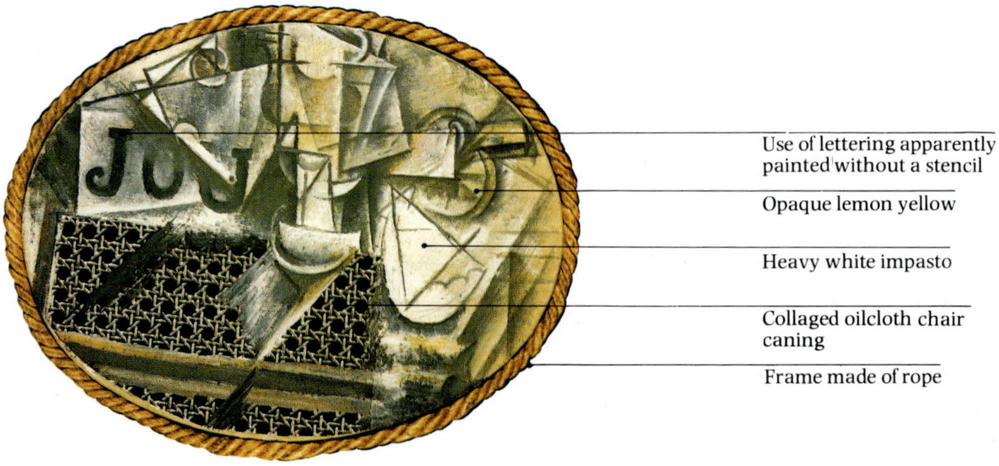

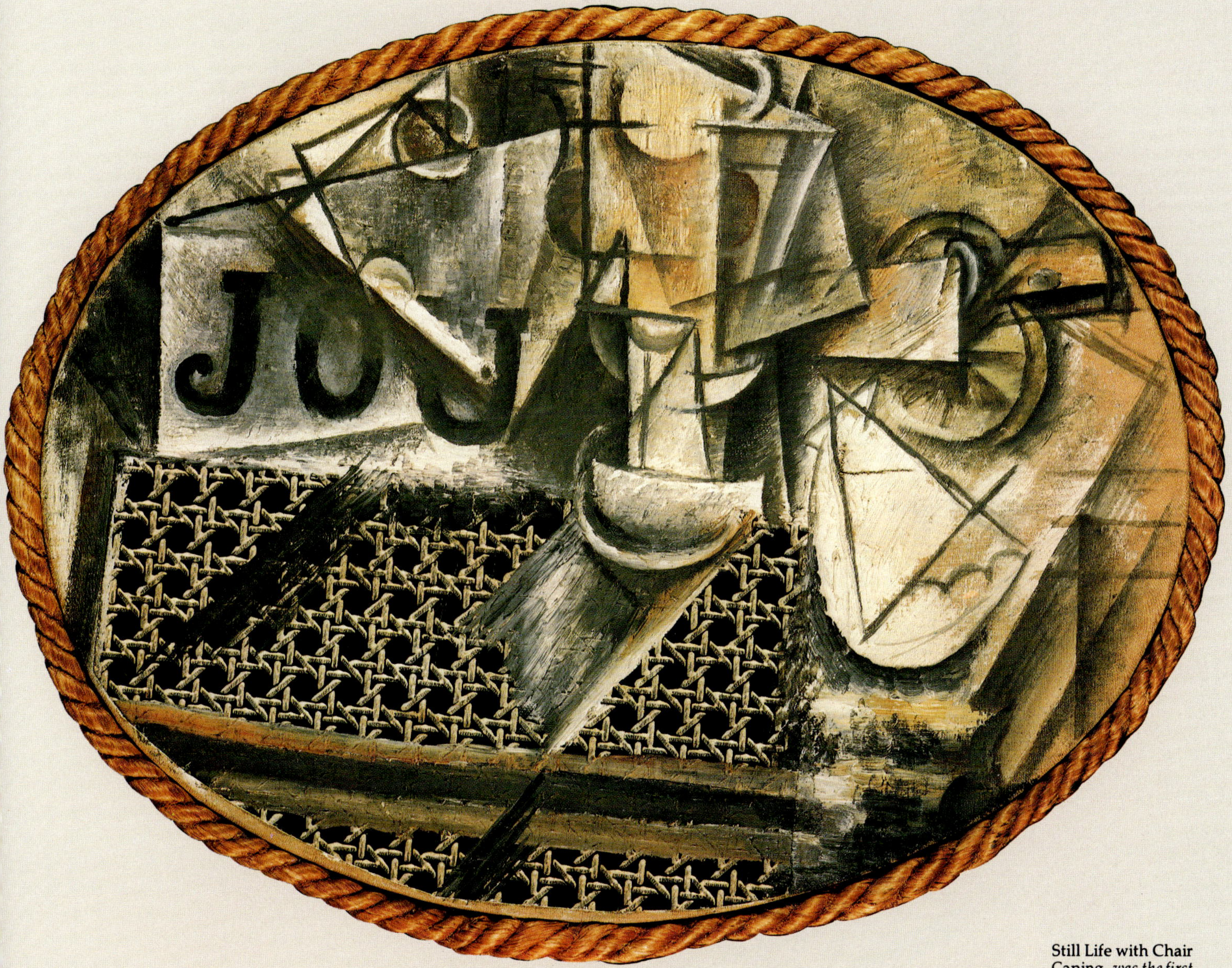


Still Life with Chair Caning *was the first picture to use collage. The pallette, with the exception of the opaque touches of lemon yellow to represent the sliced lemon, is restricted to a range of ochres and siennas. The collaged element, the oilcloth chair caning, is integrated into the overall image by the paint applied to it. The rope framing the oval emphasizes the fact that the painting is a constructed object, and perhaps is making reference to a raised edge around a café table. The oval shape itself also suggests a circular plane seen in perspective.*

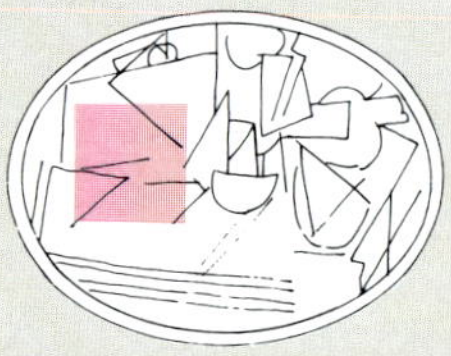

*Among the innovatory features of this work are the piece of oilcloth chair caning which was the first use of collage in a painting, and the lettering. The letters 'JOU' spell the beginning of the French word for newspaper,* journal, *and also of the French word for play,* jouer. *The lettering and the oilcloth are integrated into the overall image by the broad brushstrokes across them, which possibly signify shadows.*

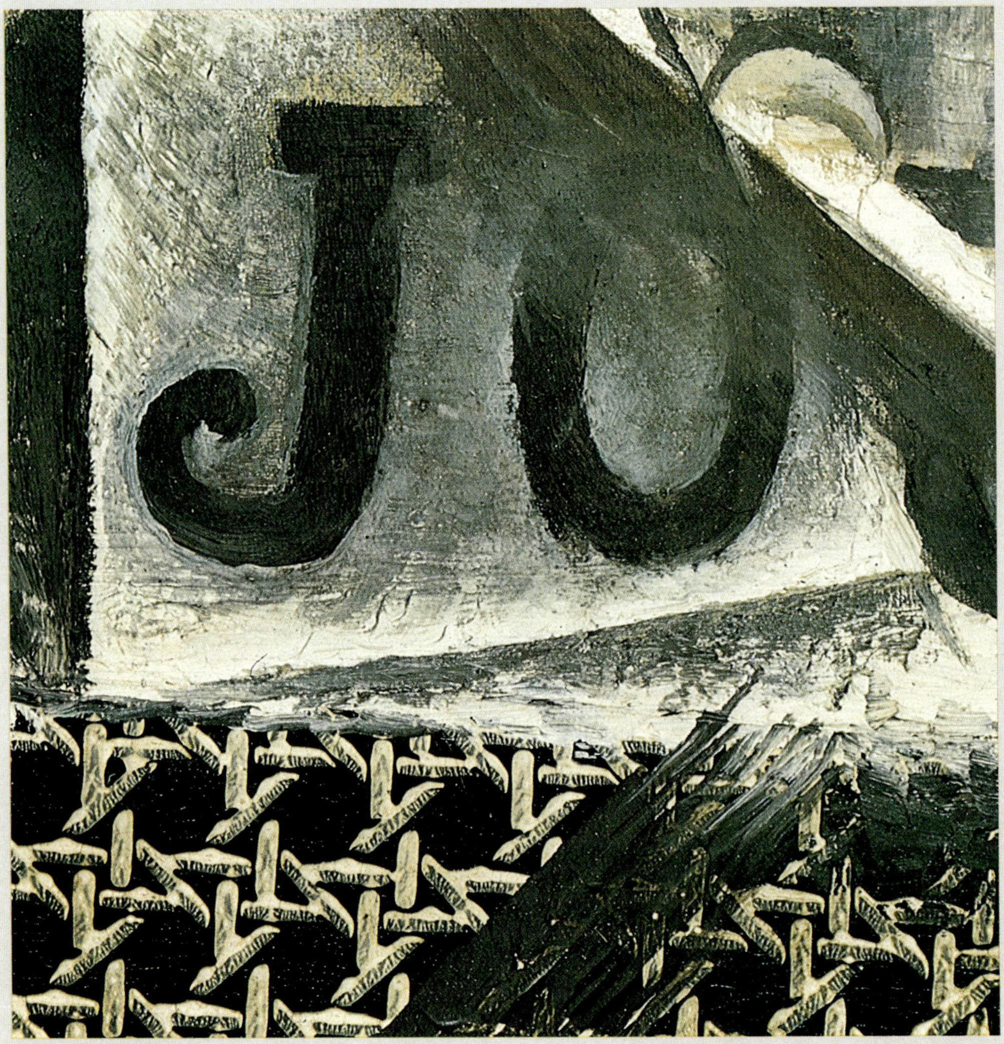

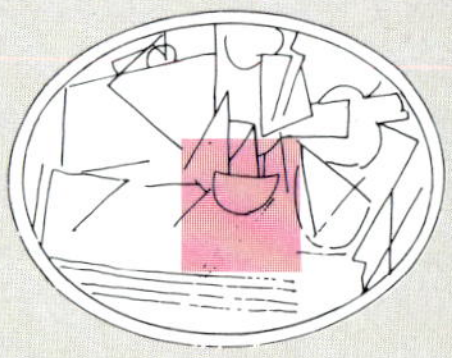

Actual size detail
*The wickerwork-patterned oilcloth, which was the first collaged element to be included in a painting, is absorbed back into the overall image by the exaggerated horizontal brushstrokes across it, which perhaps indicate the edge of the café table, and by the base and shadow of the wineglass placed across it.*

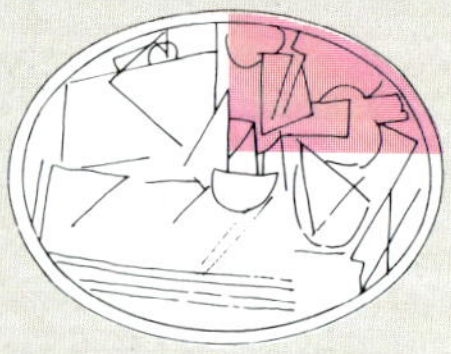

Still Life with Chair Caning *was one of a series of still lifes which Picasso painted in 1912. He framed the work in a piece of rope. When looking at a picture in an art gallery, for example, it is easy to assume that the artist selected the frame to suit the picture. However, in very many instances, the pictures are framed by the gallery. In the case of this Picasso work, the unusual material and its texture form an integral part of the picture and its overall effect.*

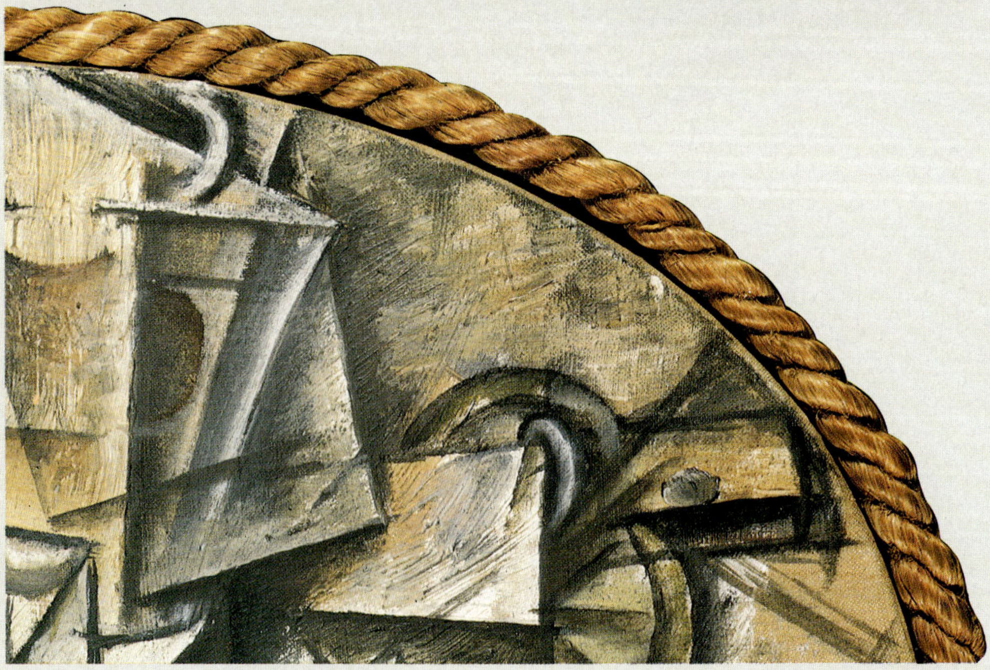

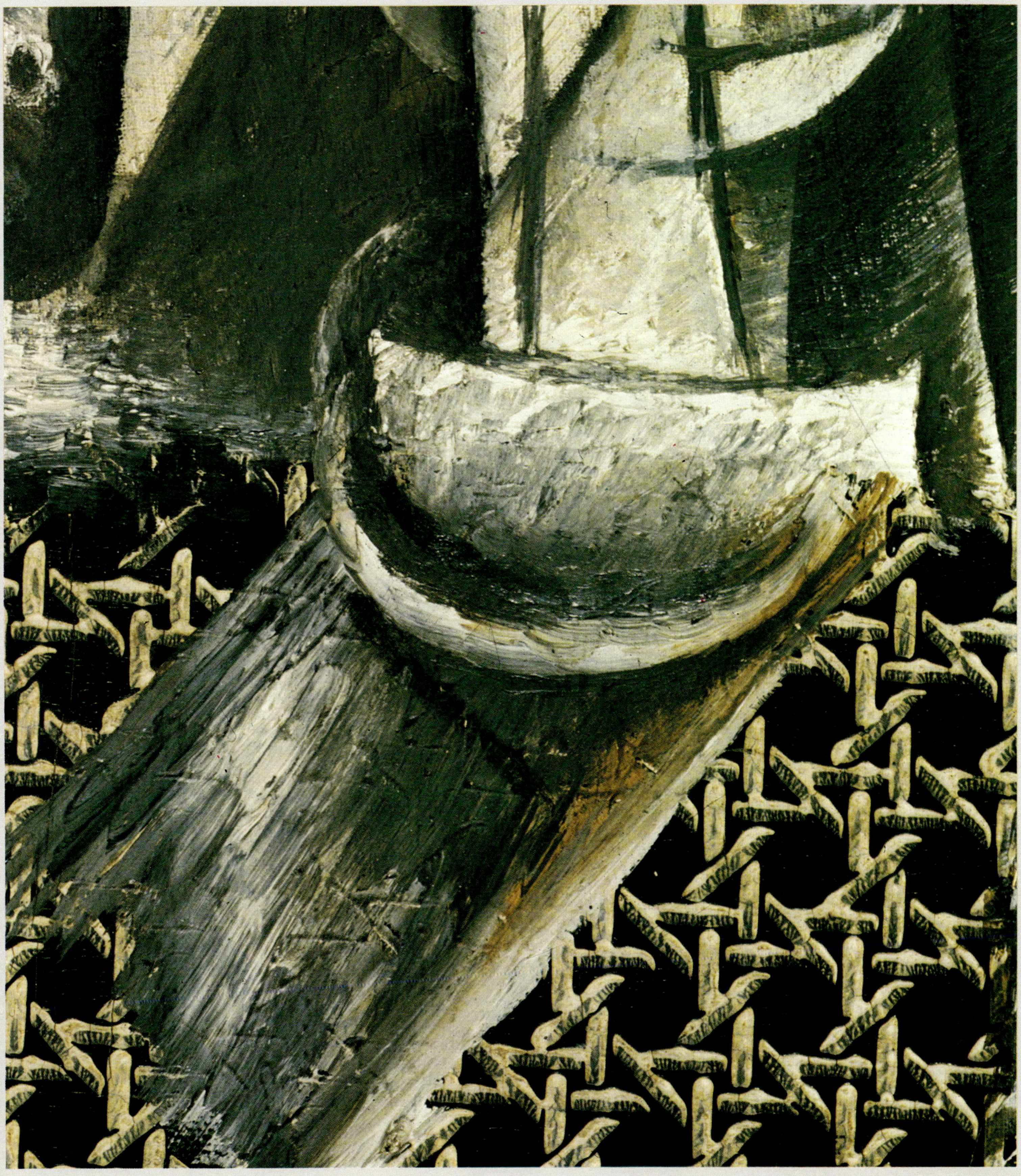

# WASSILY KANDINSKY

*With Black Arch* (1912)
Oil on canvas, 186cm × 193.3cm/73in × 76in

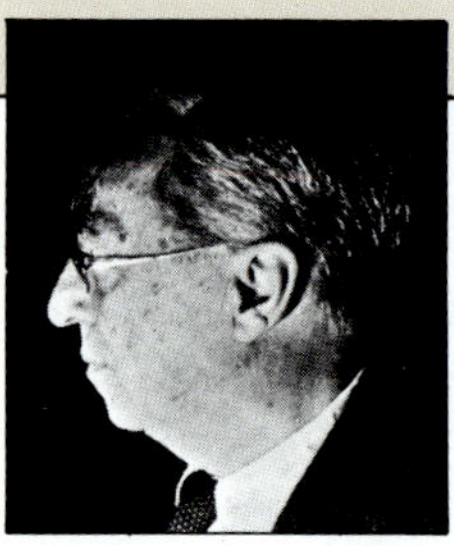

At the age of 30, Kandinsky abandoned a career in law in order to study art in Munich. From 1909 onwards he struggled to achieve an abstract art of emotional and spiritual intensity derived from the mingling of forms and colors. It is worth emphasizing Kandinsky's Russian origins because his mystical conception of art as a spiritual presence acting as a link with a higher plane of reality has more in common with his native tradition of religious icon painting than with the European tradition of naturalistic representation. Kandinsky equated naturalism with materialism, and believed that it was the mission of the artist to instil a consciousness of the soul of man and of the hidden laws of the universe into a materialistic society which was doomed to destruction. *With Black Arch*, painted in 1912, can thus be seen as the expression of an inner spiritual struggle.

Kandinsky's principal artistic problem was how far he could reduce the representation of objects without lapsing into mere decorative pattern making. To achieve this, he developed a technique characterized by bold brushstrokes and areas of color which were inspired by such sources as icon painting and Bavarian peasant glass paintings. It was Kandinsky's hope that the public could be educated to experience his new language of abstract art in the same direct way as music. In 1912 he wrote that music was devoted 'not to the reproduction of natural phenomena but to the expression of the artist's soul and to the creation of an autonomous life of musical sound'. Kandinsky wished to apply this approach to his own art.

Kandinsky described his working methods in the most general and metaphysical of terms 'Each work arises technically in a way similar to that in which the cosmos arose – through catastrophes, which from the chaotic roaring of instruments, finally create a symphony, the music of the spheres'. For his major compositions, Kandinsky did preliminary paintings, watercolors and drawings. However, these are self-contained stages in the process of making the image abstract, rather than studies in the usual sense. The main objective of Kandinsky's approach was to maintain the identity and impact of the pictorial elements. Throughout his long career, Kandinsky was associated with a number of artistic movements including the 'Blue Rider' group.

1. An off-white ground was applied to a large format canvas.

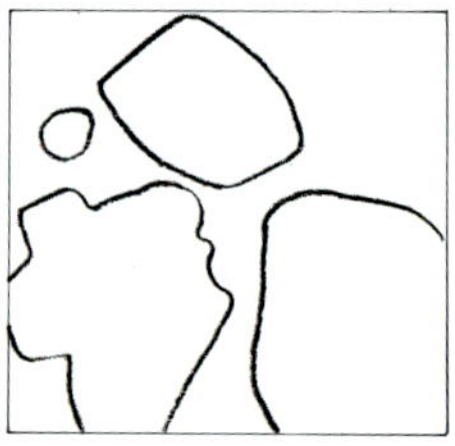

2. A charcoal outline of the forms was then drawn in.

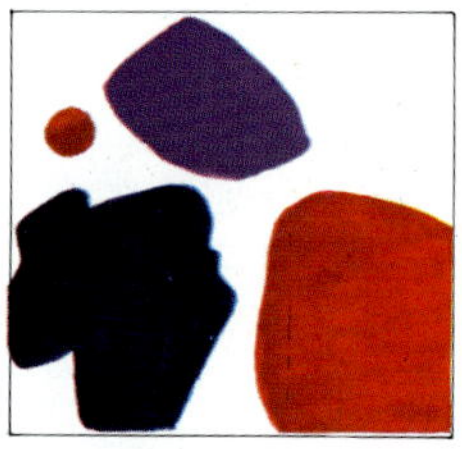

3. Kandinsky next blocked in the main color areas.

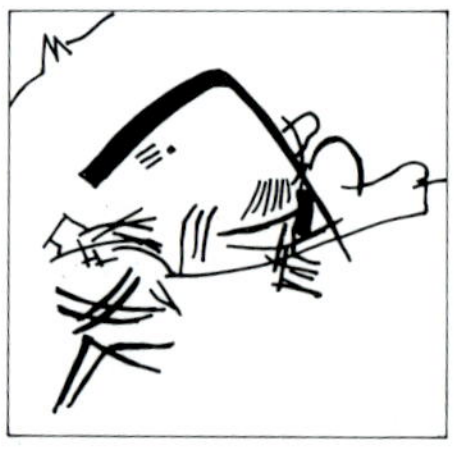

4. The linear structure was then drawn in.

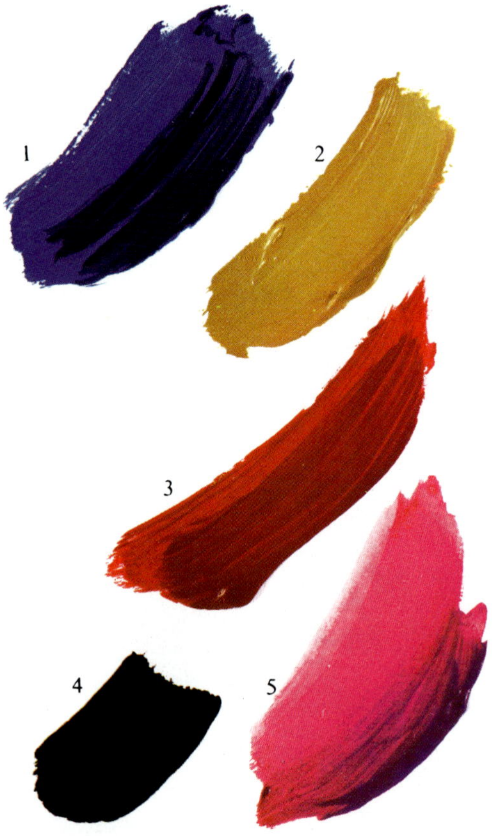


In this work Kandinsky used the following pigments: Prussian blue (1), yellow ochre (2), madder (3), black (4) and madder lake (5).

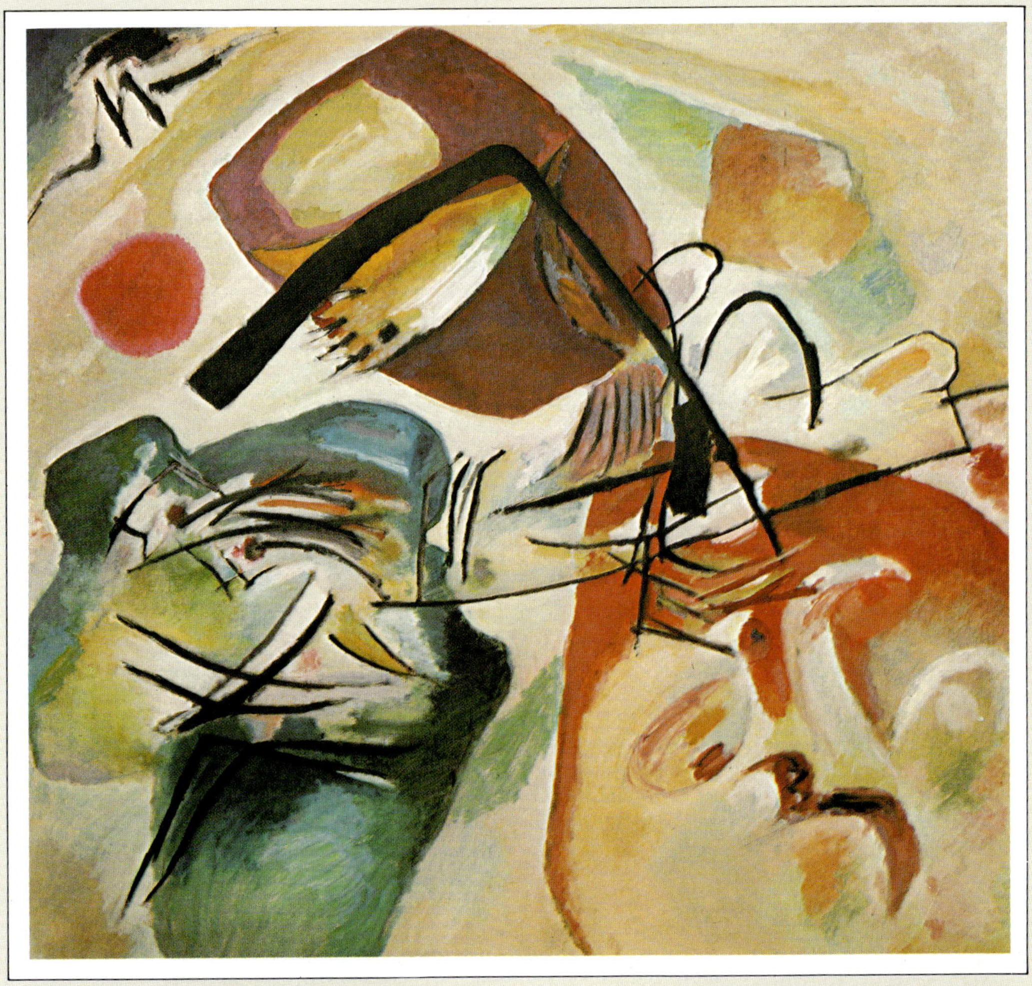

*The scale of the picture is large, so that the viewer can experience to the full the 'spiritual vibration' of the colors and forms, as Kandinsky put it. Important use is made of the off-white ground which covers the canvas giving vibrancy and impact to the colors. Kandinsky felt that the abstract forms painted in opaque black denoted negative forces. The movement of the painting is concentrated towards the center and the illusion of speed is suggested by the technique of leaving the wake of a passing color in a pale glaze and by the scumbled passages of white. The shapes in the painting cannot be identified with any degree of certainty. Similarly, it is impossible to tell exactly what order the painting was done in.*

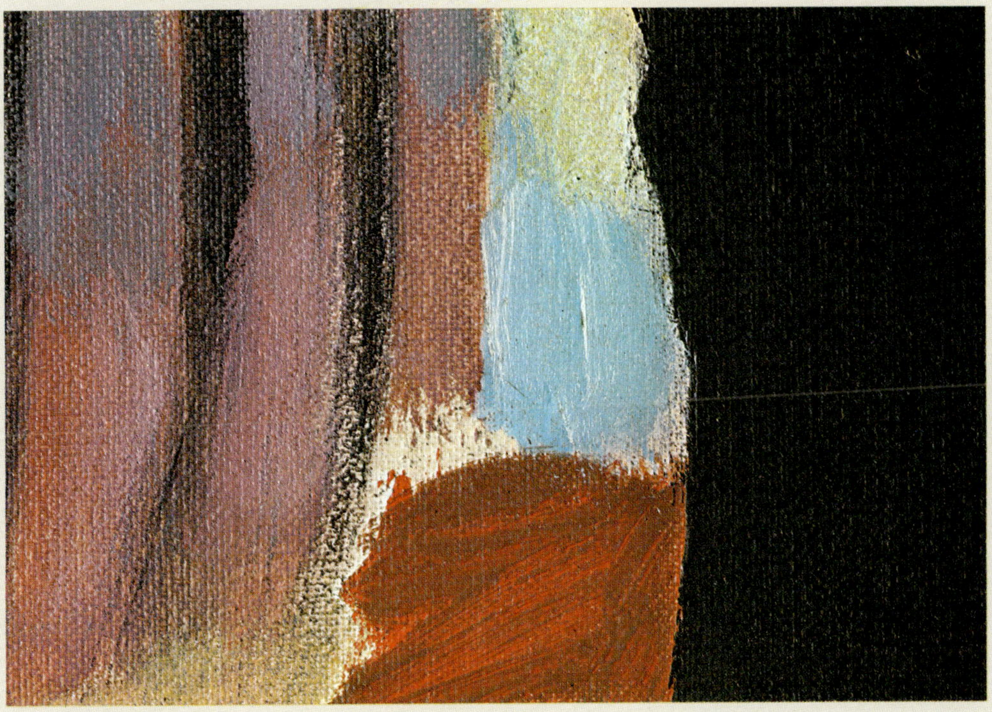

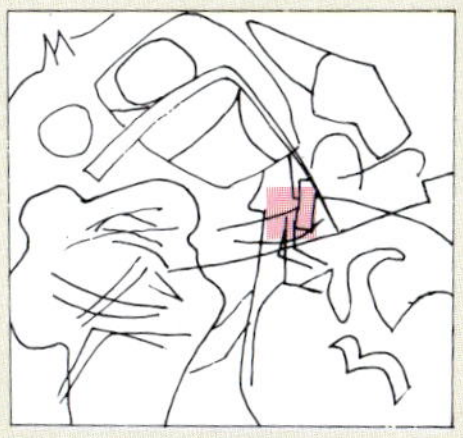

**Actual size detail**
*The off-white ground can be clearly seen in this detail. Kandinsky's colors are mostly flat and evenly brushed. The paint was modified with subtle movements of the brush. The black lines were not added at the end, as can be seen where the colors overlap. The picture was built up with precise and controlled brushwork.*

# GEORGES BRAQUE

*Clarinet and Bottle of Rum on a Mantelpiece (1913)*
Oil on canvas
81cm × 60cm/31⅞in × 23⅝in

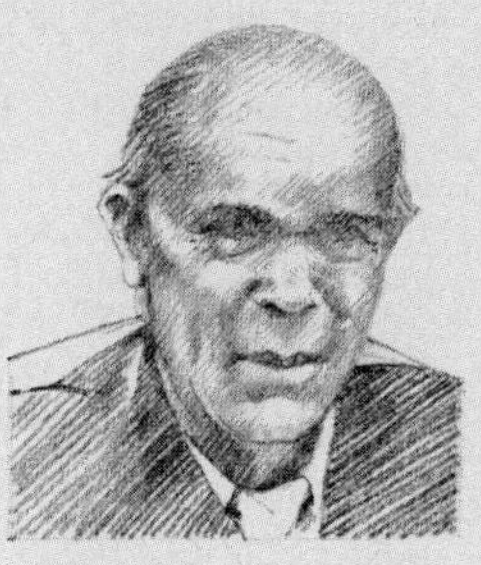

Georges Braque had not the protean sensibility or the Expressionistic urgency of his friend and colleague Pablo Picasso; yet he may be considered as the most important and innovative painter of still life in this century. His dedication to the 'pictorial fact' led him to explore, more fully perhaps than any other artist, the environment immediate to his practice.

Braque was born in May 1882 at Argenteuil on the Seine near Paris, but his family moved eight years later to Le Havre on the north coast, where his father started a domestic painting business. Braque himself began an apprenticeship in this trade while studying at the Ecole des Beaux-Arts in Le Havre. He established a long friendship with the Dufy brothers, Raoul (1877-1953) and Gaston, at this time. His move to Paris in 1900 was interrupted by military service from 1901 to 1904. Back in the capital, Braque spent the next two years at the Académie Humbert and at the Ecole des Beaux-Arts, often painting with the Le Havrais artists Othon Friesz and Raoul Dufy. In 1906 and 1907 his painting embraced a stylized Fauve manner, before his crucial encounter with Picasso and Picasso's recent painting *Les demoiselles d'Avignon* in 1907. The history of the association of these two great painters *is* the early history of Cubism; until 1914 they worked intensely to co-produce the most revolutionary visual style since Renaissance perspective.

Unlike Picasso, for whom the 1920s and 1930s were decades of prolific eclecticism, Braque grafted and consolidated his previous ideas. In the last years of his life (he died in 1963), Braque produced two astonishing series, *Ateliers* (1948-1955) and *Oiseaux* (1950-1958); and he was fêted ceremonially as the grand master of French twentieth-century painting. The dominant influences on Braque's early career were Cézanne and Picasso. (Braque's metaphor for his relationship to Picasso at this time is revealing: he spoke of them as roped together like 'mountain climbers'.) Having rejected Impressionism and his own decorative, curvilinear version of Fauvism, Braque moved away from coloristic excess, in pursuit of greater structural coherence across the picture surface.

The impact of Braque's painting on younger generations has, of course, been immense. Juan Gris, Fernand Léger (1881-1955) and the 'Salon Cubists' attempted to imitate, often directly, the Analytic and Synthetic periods of Braque and Picasso. But the stylistic influence of the years 1909 to 1914 became more diffuse.

During the first part of Braque's career – up to 1920 – he worked almost exclusively as a painter and producer of collages. But the formative significance of his early interior decorating work, possibly the major impetus behind the incorporation of pasted paper and other materials on to the canvas surface, appears to have fueled his appetite for technical experiment. He tested different materials and processes in periodic bursts of activity, which recurred throughout his later career. In 1920 he produced his first real piece of sculpture, *Standing Nude* in plaster, and woodcuts for *Piége de Mèduse* by the composer Erik Satie (1866-1925).

Braque has been credited with many of the most important technical 'inventions' of Cubism during the movement's early years, 1907 to 1914. He was the first to introduce lettering; to make use of a paint comb; to introduce passages of imitation wood graining and marbling; to vary the texture of paint by mixing with sand and other ingredients, and finally to discover the technique of *papier collé*. During this period Braque's commitment to intense pictorial experiment was considerable.

*Clarinet and Bottle of Rum on a Mantelpiece* is a fully convincing, mature example of the style of Analytical Cubism which Picasso and Braque developed between 1909 and 1912. Analytic Cubism is so called because of the division (or analysis) of the work's subject (usually still life, as here, or portrait) and the space which surrounds it, into a series of angular planes (or facets), which record various types of information as the motifs are seen from more than one point of view.

There are several phases of Analytical Cubism, and *Clarinet and Bottle* – almost certainly painted in the summer of 1911 in Cèret in the Pyrenees where both Braque and Picasso were staying – comes in the last and most complex of these, appropriately called 'Hermetic' Cubism, where the subject becomes often very hard to identify, but never fully disappears. In this work, for example, the clarinet and glimpses of sheet music can be readily discerned; as well as a nail or pin and its shadow; a variety of 'scroll-like corbets'; and several letters stenciled onto the surface, 'VALSE' being the only complete word.

The canvas used is linen and is of a simple weave. It has been primed in grey primary oil, and worked over with brushstrokes ranging in direction and register. The overall configuration of the objects and the dominant diagonally orientated facet marks were probably mapped on to the canvas first, possibly from a sketch, followed by the versatile 'stippling' technique with the brush, which is typical of works from this period and produces a mottled effect that can act both as a kind of shading device, and a mode of partial coloring in.

Braque's palette is characteristically reduced to white, black, raw sienna, with a touch of lemon and a stroke of red in the bottom right. These pigments are laid on fairly densely in places, with some quite considerable gradients of impasto. As a final touch Braque appears to have added a few slim lines in charcoal, perhaps structural afterthoughts.

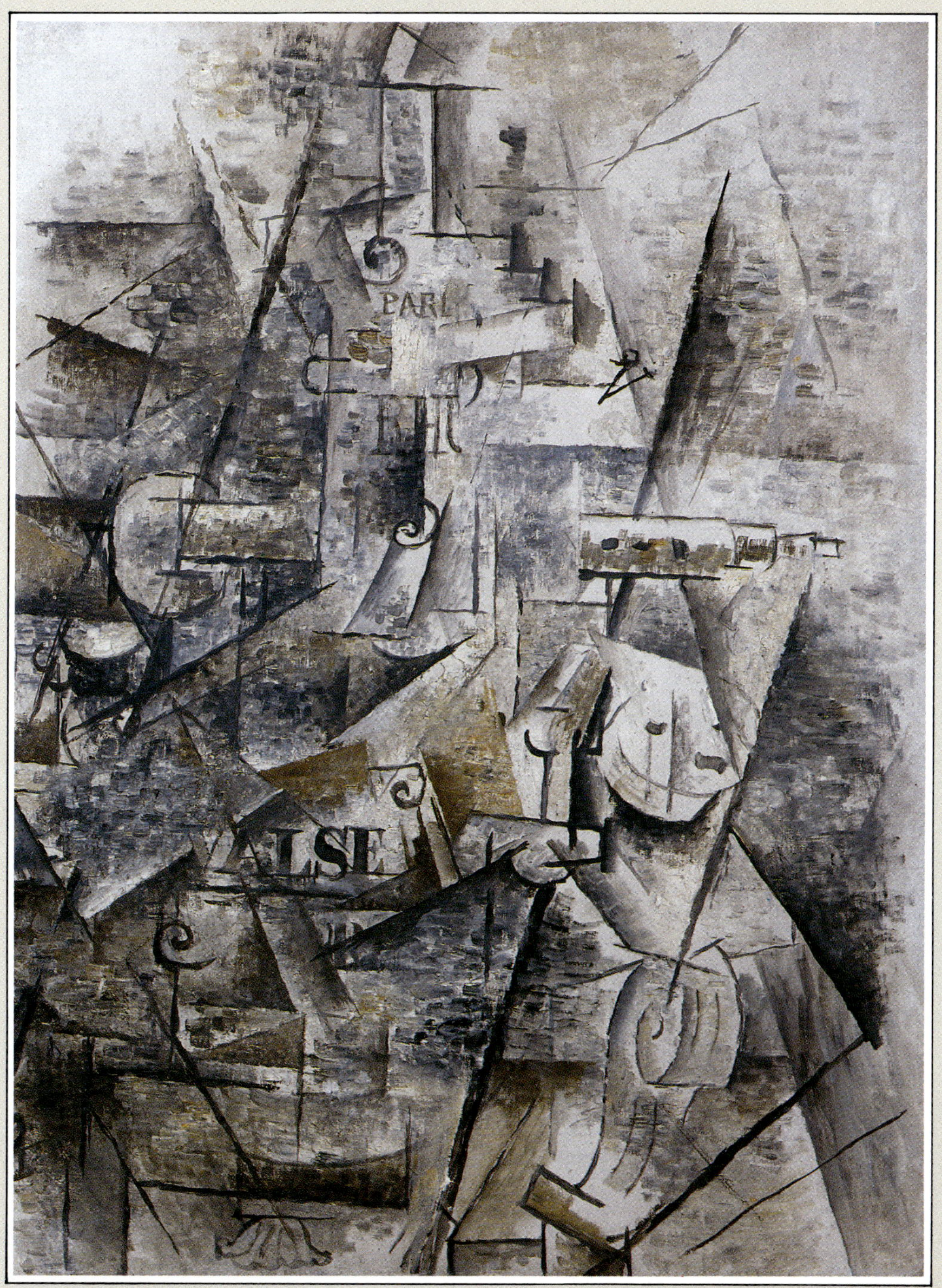


*The subject matter here is ostensibly a still life, but, taking his lead from Cézanne, Braque gives such priority to an abstract and intellectual analysis of the spatial structure of the mantelpiece, clarinet and bottle of rum which is his motif, that both style and technique are dominated by this informing logic. In comparison with other Analytic Cubist works of the same period* Clarinet and Bottle of Rum *is less densely worked and its ochre patches flatter and more sparse.*

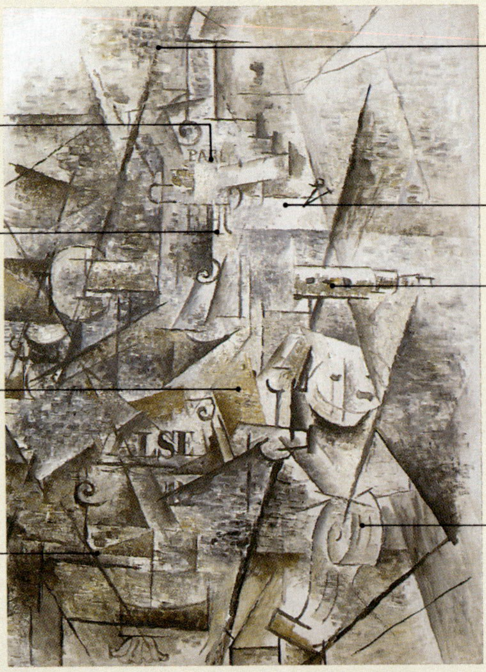


Lines deliberately extended beyond the limits of surface areas produce a kind of grid or scaffolding system

Lettering probably done without stencil

Unpainted surface showing ground

Stenciled lettering RHU(M) — 'rum', the bottle label

Clarinet realistically represented

Sienna unevenly scumbled over a black/white slurring

Stone bracket or corbel probably supporting the mantelpiece

Black 'triangulation' line of varying thickness

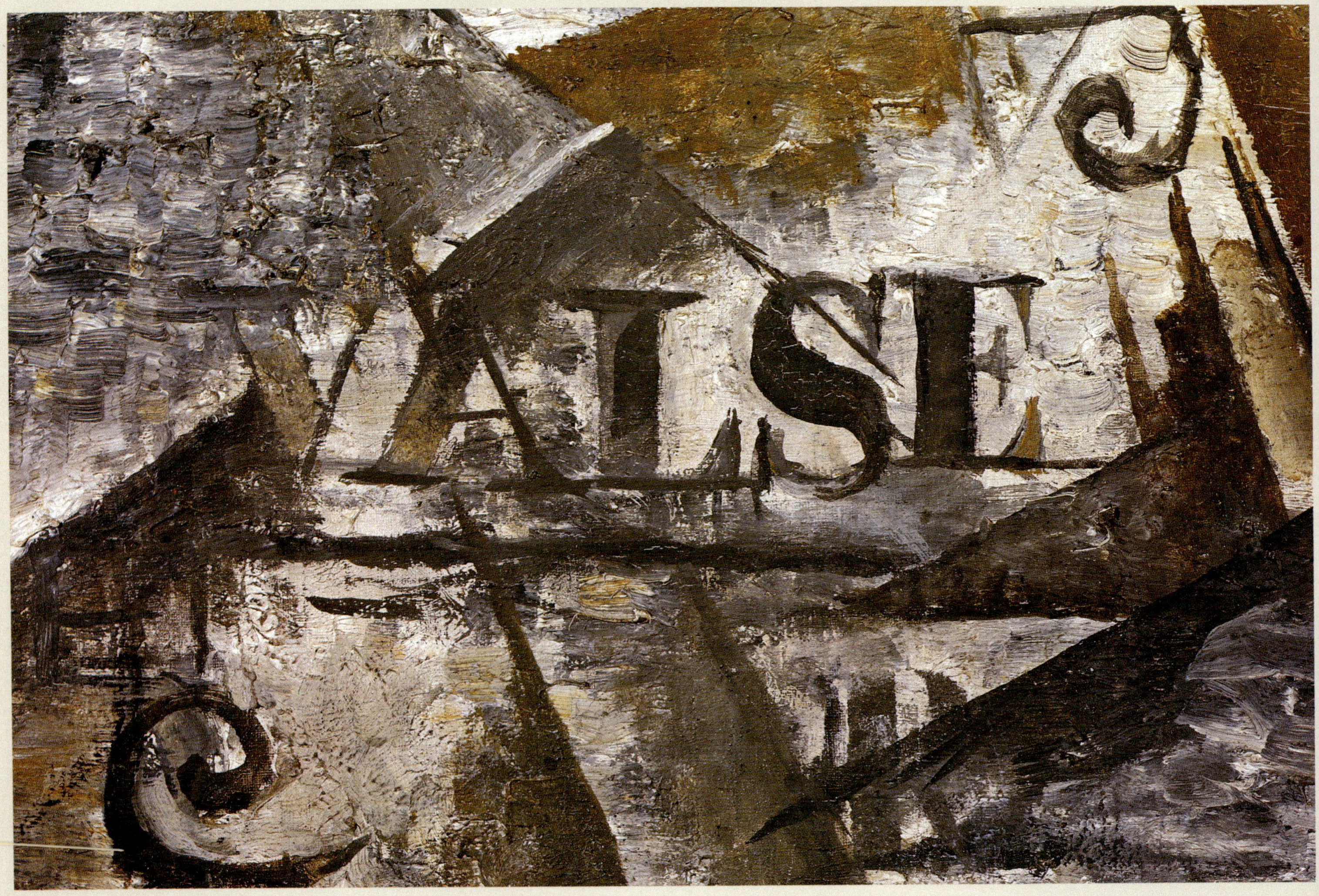

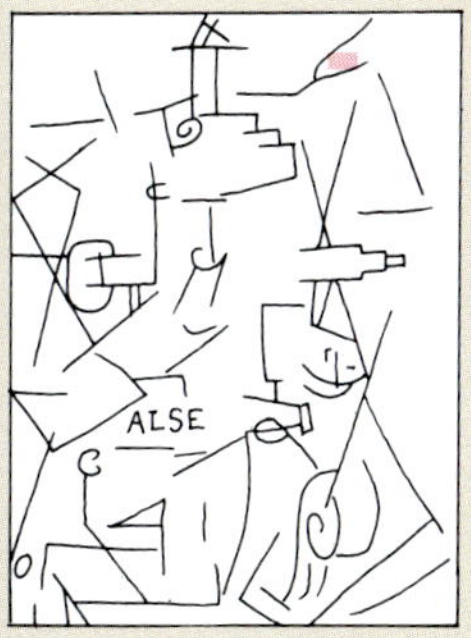


RIGHT This section from the top right extremity illustrates the thinness and uncertainty of touch which often characterizes the peripheries of Cubist compositions. The fragile linear geometry seems on the threshold of dissolving into the canvas priming itself.

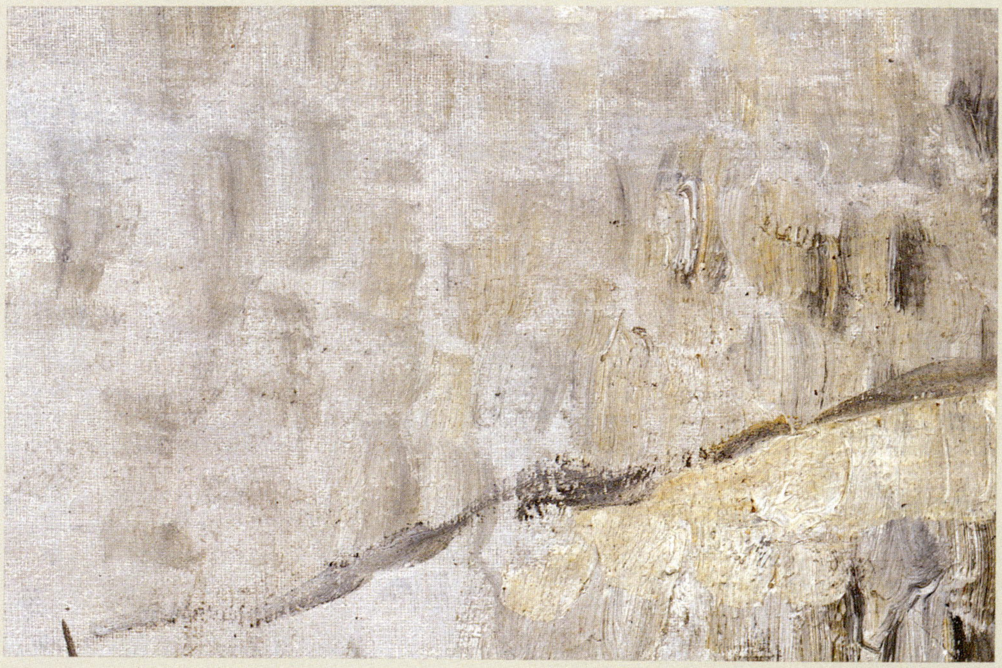

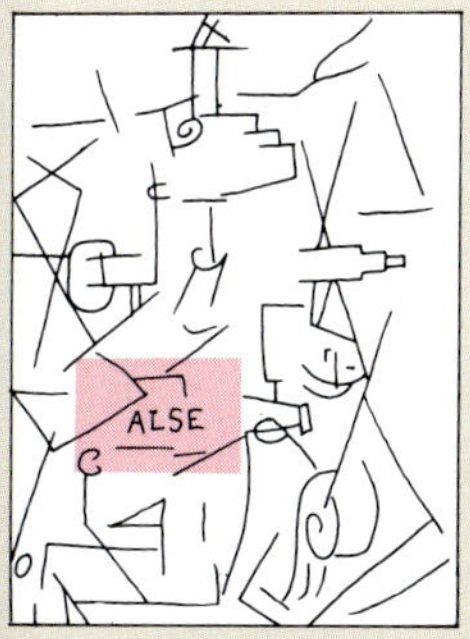


LEFT The French word 'VALSE' (waltz) has been written onto the canvas surface, probably using a commercial stencil. This instantly recognizable word is surrounded by a field of merging and intersecting planes with straight, definite boundaries, and framed by two clef-like spirals. There is wealth of minutely adjusted brushwork, often wet on wet, which forms the texture of the planes, but which appears to have no real descriptive reference. Lead white is used effectively to enliven the muted greys and browns. Above and to the left of the 'V' are thick clumps of impasto.

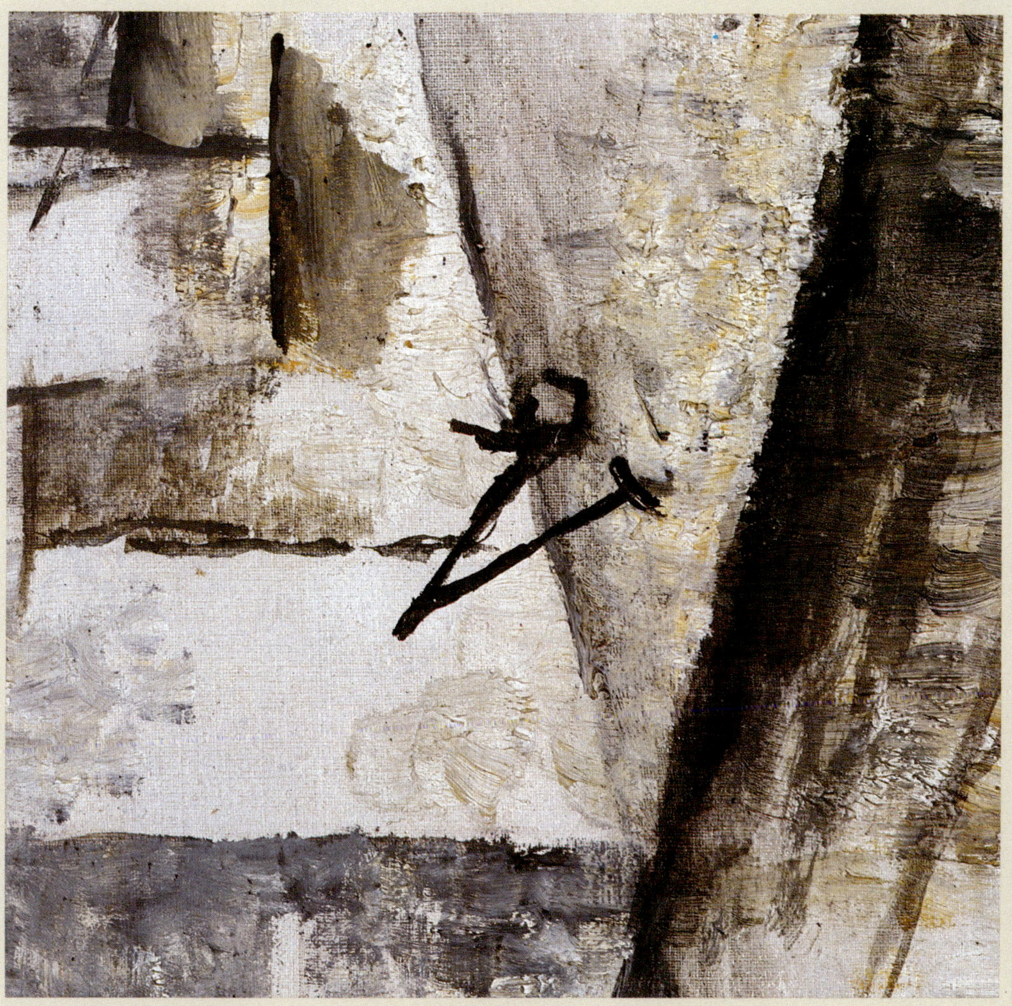

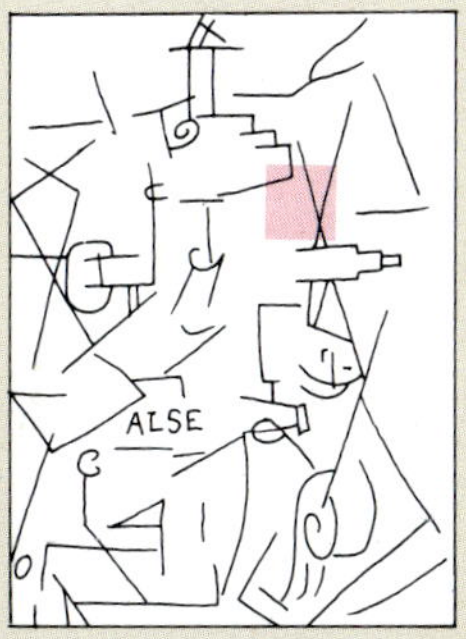


ACTUAL SIZE DETAIL The boldly painted nail with its cast shadow is an obvious but important manifestation of the visual wit and inventiveness of the Cubists. The illusionism of this motif probably inspired the eventual use of real materials in Cubist collage. The implication of a light source may have led to the thickening and blurring of the black boundary line to the right. The lightly brushed line slightly above the beginning of the nail, is discontinuous and irregular, showing that Braque was not interested in flawless geometric precision, but rather in an accurate disposition of lines and marks with an expressive purpose.

# Pablo Picasso

*Guitar (1913)*

Collage (charcoal, wax, crayon, ink and pasted paper)

67cm × 49cm/26½in × 19½in

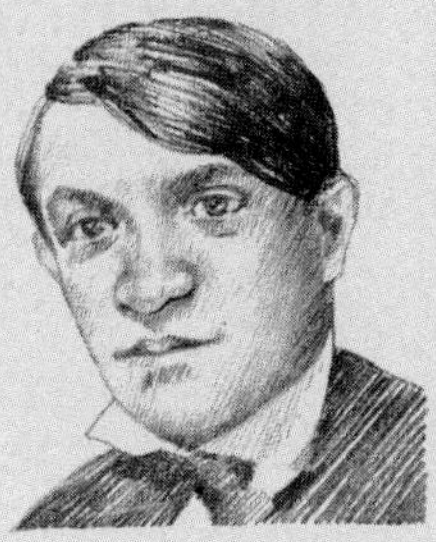

Pablo Picasso is the most important, most celebrated and the most productive artist of the twentieth century. He was born in October 1881 at Malaga in southern Spain and began to draw and paint when he was only seven years old, under the eye of his father, Don José Ruiz, a teacher of painting. During the late 1890s Picasso studied and painted in Barcelona. In 1900 he made his first visit to Paris, and for the next few years commuted between Paris, Madrid and Barcelona.

By 1901, the beginning of his so-called 'Blue Period', Picasso's work had become fully convincing and mature and from 1904 he was established in the Bateau Lavoir area of Montmartre and consorted with the leaders of the Parisian avant-garde. For the next two decades, Picasso was the driving force of the visual avant-garde. He exhibited, for example, in the first Surrealist exhibition at the Gallery Pierre in Paris in 1925, but was never fully comfortable with the spirit and aims of Surrealism. Instead his work manifests a remarkable stylistic originality, whether in the naturalistic portraits he painted after the First World War, in the Neo-Classicism of the early 1920s or in the savage pictures of women, which preoccupied him in the early 1930s.

From about 1940, however, while there is constant vigor and renewal, Picasso's extraordinary capacity as a draftsman, together with his uncanny talent for convincing formal experiment and his life-long resistance to fully abstract tendencies, had become the core of his contribution to modern art. But the majority of his technical excursions postdate Picasso's most revolutionary visual achievement – the Cubism he created with Georges Braque. But as art historian Pierre Daix put it, 'He forged an immense critical vocabulary out of the whole heritage that Classical art had rejected: pre-Hellenic and pre-Roman art from the Mediterranean, medieval, African and South Sea Island [art]. Of the recent Post-Impressionists he only borrowed consistently from Cézanne.'

The innovations in form and style perpetrated by Cubism changed in proportion, as the technical pressure which fragmented and faceted the canvas surface became too great for oil on canvas alone. 'I want to get to the stage where nobody can tell how a picture of mine is done,' Picasso commented in 1923. 'What's the point of that? Simply that I want nothing but emotion given off by it.'

Collage, developed in the period of Synthetic Cubism (*c* 1912 to 1914), is the incorporation of ready-made objects and images into the picture plane. *Papier collé* is a variety of collage and specifies the addition of 'pasted paper'.

Picasso's *Still Life with Chair Caning* (May? 1912) was probably the first collage by virtue of the piece of oil cloth glued to the surface. But Braque seems to have initiated *papier collé* in early September 1912. Typically, Picasso immediately took up the new idea with gusto and his most intense period of work in *papier collé* lasted until May 1913 while he was in a studio in the boulevard Raspail, Paris. His early efforts (for example, *Man with a Hat* [1912-1913]) were more severe than *Guitar*, often on a white or off-white ground, with quite heavy charcoal outlines and a minimum of collage.

*Guitar* dates from the Spring of 1913 and has been described as one of the most majestic and sumptuous of Picasso's *papiers collés*. His way of working for these compositions appears to have been based on preliminary drawings. There is a photograph of Picasso's studio, showing numbered drawing schemes for forthcoming *papiers collés*; one sketch relates closely to the finished *Violin* (1912-1913), and indicates that Picasso predetermined his outline and then sought appropriate shapes and textures with which to amplify the design.

The procedure for *Guitar* appears to have been slightly different, but is analogous. Here the black charcoal lines were probably the first marks on the translucent blue paper. Some of these would have been masked off by the pasted paper strips, then reinstated with a white wax crayon, probably the last medium to be used. These white lines also produce new structural suggestions towards the edges of the composition.

The material units of this work can be isolated: a roughly edged rectangle of blue transparent paper; a series of black charcoal lines; two approximately equal rectangles of black ink; pasted paper, and a series of white wax crayon lines. The pasted papers can be further divided into categories: two areas decorated with an acanthus-like pattern; five various shapes of ivory-colored paper with an intermittent square based geometrical design; a sharply white area, sensitively edged with charcoal; an ochre-colored area more boldly edged; and three pieces of newspaper. Two constitute the front page of the Barcelona *El Diluvo*, the third stands for the guitar's sound hole.

Listed in such a way these elements seem banal, but the two skills which animate them – selection and arrangement – are uniquely synthesized and encourage a volume of speculation on the significance of the finished composition. Picasso had the ability to build humor and irony into his work and he delighted in turning a blind eye to even the most far fetched of these speculations. In *Guitar* the rhythmical oppositions between the 'male' and 'female' elements of the instrument are managed with wit and dexterity. But there is possibly a more wicked humor in a newspaper fragment that includes notices for two medical practitioners, Dr Casasa, a specialist in venereal diseases, and Dr Dolcet, an oculist!

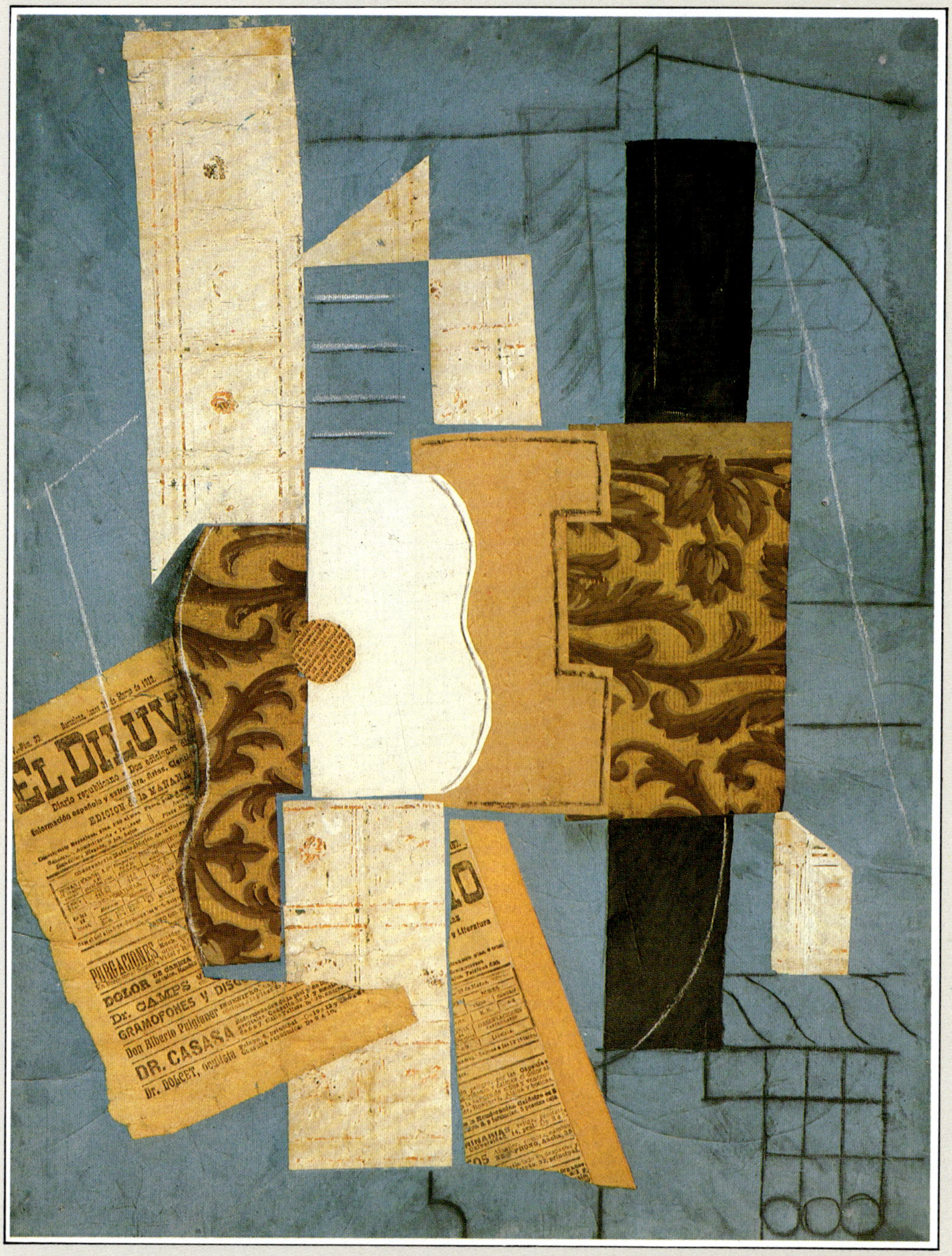


*The ramifying shapes of the guitar are the organizing theme of many works by Picasso and by Braque in both the Analytic and Synthetic styles of Cubism. Picasso in particular was alive to both the formal possibilities of the subject and to any scope for wit and visual punning. All these contingencies were admirably serviced by the innovative technical means that both artists brought to the picture surface.* Guitar *is a colorful* papier collé *producing a vibrant union of technique and expression.*

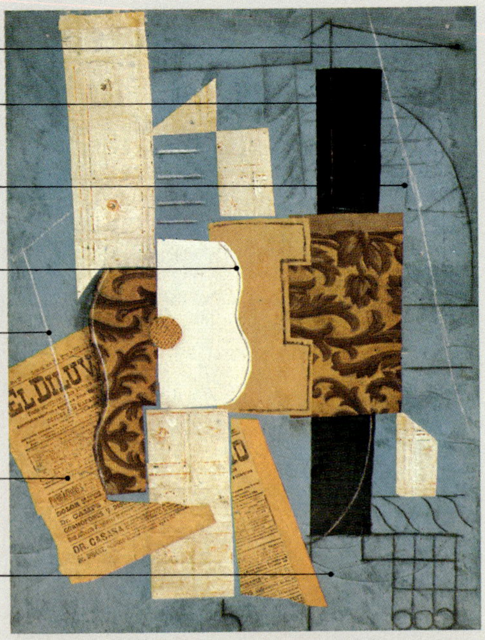


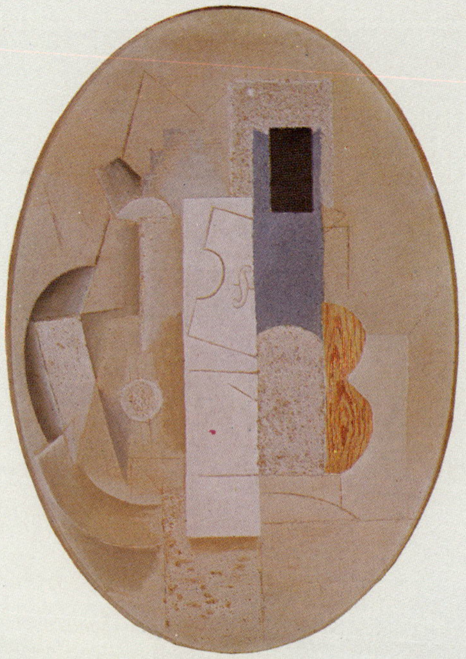

LEFT *Violin and Guitar was produced in the same year as Guitar and obviously shares a similar subject matter. Here, however, as if in response to the pairing of musical instruments, the composition is arranged in an oval format to allow the freer play of a double set of sinuously curved surfaces. In addition, Picasso has used a different set of materials, pasted cloth, oil, pencil and plaster, which conveys a drier less sensuous, less coloristic effect, particularly in the abrasive, pock-marked plastered areas.*

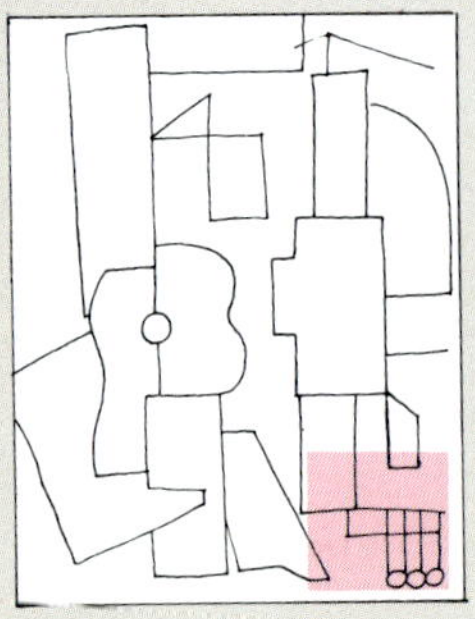

RIGHT *The unruled charcoal grid probably represents the tassels or braiding of a chair (or tablecloth). But all hints of volume are suppressed by the inevitable flatness of the handling and by the common tendency for line to be extended beyond what is expected to be the limits of objects. In the middle, left of the extract, the black arc of charcoal procedes into the inked area and is effortlessly continued in white wax crayon. This peripheral unit then introduces an element of context to the analysis of forms which occupies the center of the composition.*

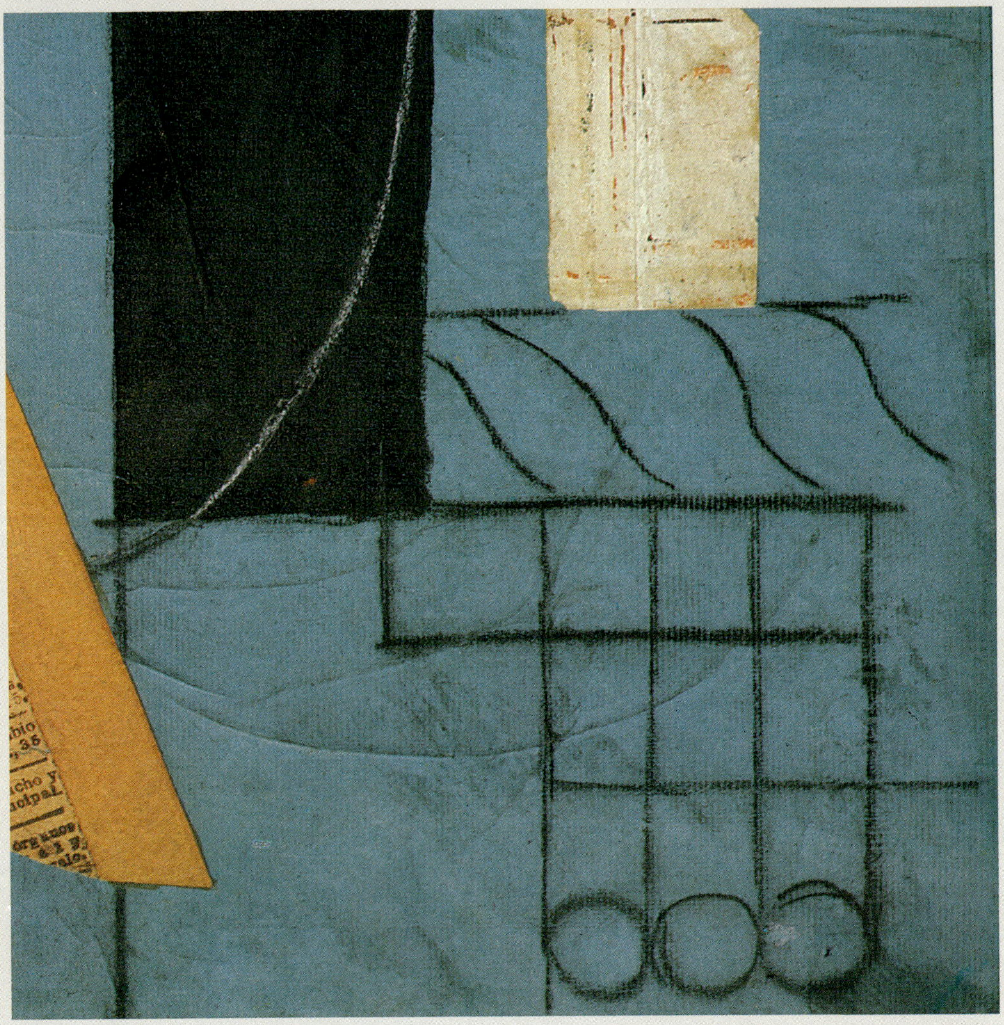

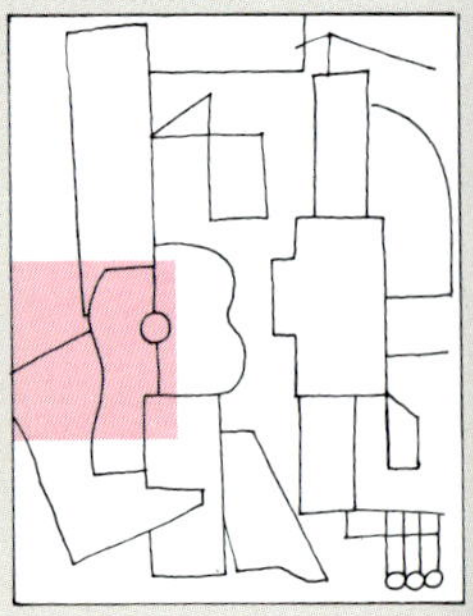

ACTUAL SIZE DETAIL
*Picasso's play of depth and layering is readily apparent here, exploited by the smudged shading to the left of patterned paper area, by the intrusion and termination of the white line in the newspaper page, and by glimpses of the blue paper ground in the bottom right. The five or six types of pasted paper, then, set up an effective counterpoint in terms of structure and of pattern. The torn and cut-out nature of these collaged elements is not effaced, but rather foregrounded, especially under the sound hole of the guitar where there is a slightly inset snip line.*

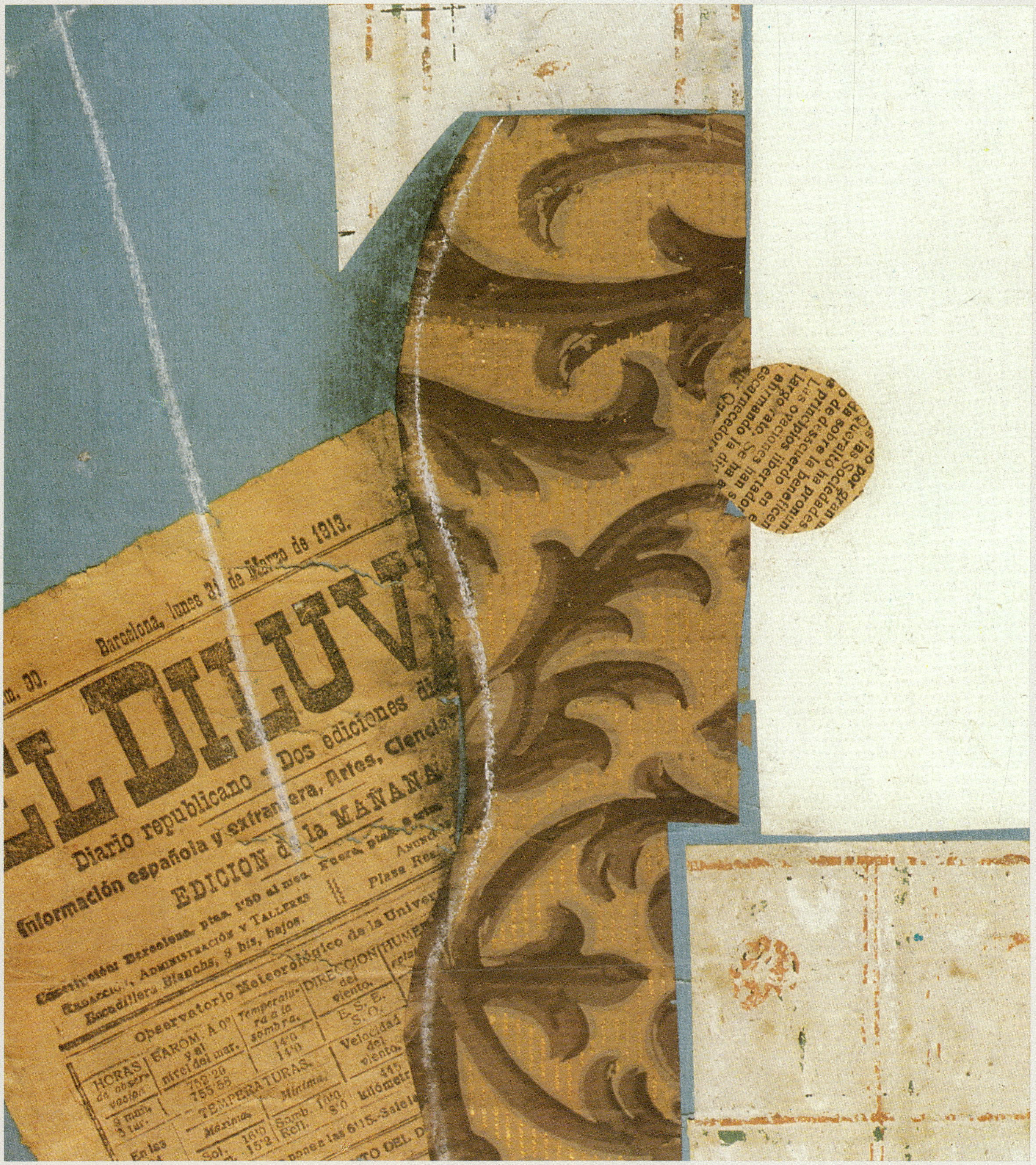
Barcelona, lunes 31 de Marzo de 1913.
EL DILUV
Diario republicano · Dos ediciones di
Información española y extranjera, Artes, Ciencia
EDICION de la MAÑANA
Observatorio Meteorológico de la Univer

# Wassily Kandinsky

*Small Pleasures (1913)*
Oil on canvas
110cm × 120.6cm/43¼in × 47¼in

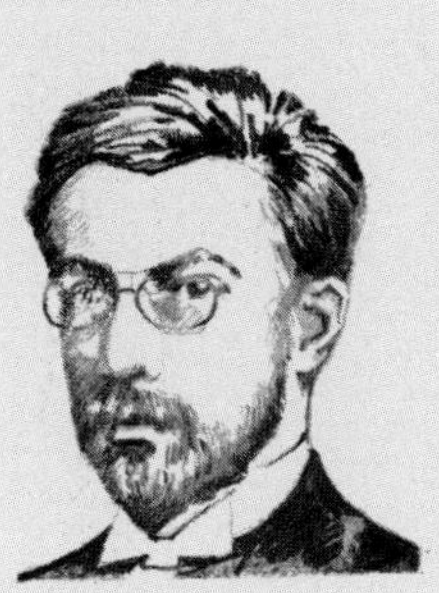

Kandinsky was probably the first, the most important and, in the end, the most influential of the pioneers of abstract art. He was the focal point for the converging forces of German Expressionism, and the measure of its achievement against a Paris-centered avant-garde.

Wassily Kandinsky was born in Moscow on 4 December 1866. He received a classical education at school in Odessa and went on to study law and economics at the University of Moscow. After this scholarly beginning, Kandinsky moved to Munich in 1896 where he studied art under Anton Azbé and later Franz von Stuck. But he maintained crucial links with his mother-country and retained a constant, if residual faith in the Russian Orthodox Church. In 1901 he co-founded the artists' association Phalanx and spent the next two years organizing, traveling, painting and writing while based in Munich. In 1911 he formed Blaue Reiter with Franz Marc, and in the following year published his key text *On the Spiritual in Art* and had his first one-man show. During the first years of the Great War he traveled in Scandanavia, before settling in Moscow from 1917 to 1921 where he was active in the artistic debates of the Russian state. He became an influential teacher at the Bauhaus school in 1922, and continued working there until it closed in 1933. Kandinsky spent the last years of his life in Paris. He died in 1944.

Kandinsky's painting falls into two notable periods of activity, but it is in the first of these – an explosive series of works from about 1909 to 1914, precisely the epic years of Cubism – that he sought to liberate line and color from the imposing weight of representation. These paintings are often pushed to the limits of disorganization and amorphousness, their calligraphy darting across color patches.

Paradoxically, in many ways, the pictorial rationalization of his language which ensued in the later works during his Bauhaus years was its undoing: line shape and color were straightened, geometricized and smoothed as if some semantic magnet had pulled them into psychological order. It was Kandinsky's textual and pedagogic activity that became his most important contribution to the modern movement in the 1920s.

The influences on Kandinsky's 'impulse to abstraction' are notoriously difficult to assess. There is no doubt that the Munich *milieu* was crucially formative, but even during collaboration on the Blaue Reiter project, there is always the impression that Kandinsky is working out his ideas, a view confirmed by a lack of continuity with Marc's work of the same period. Apart from textual influences, only Paul Klee had a direct visual impact on Kandinsky.

Having decided to become a painter relatively late in life, Kandinsky gave most of his energies to this particular medium. There is a problem involved in any consideration of his oil technique, a problem which he himself drew attention to in a letter of 1937: 'I have listed six hundred and forty-five "oil-paintings" and five hundred and eight-four "watercolors". ... this division is a conventional one because in the case of oil there are often other media at work (eg tempera, watercolors, gouache, indian ink) and equally so with watercolors.'

It is extremely difficult to tell exactly how and when Kandinsky mixed his various media, but many of the great range of effects that he managed to achieve in his work from 1909 to 1914 seem in part attributable to the dilutions, combinations and 'impurities' which he conjured from his palette.

*Small Pleasures* was preceded by a number of studies and related works, the earliest of which, *With Sun* (oil and tempera? on glass) appears to date from about 1910. The composition of *Small Pleasures* is centered round two hills, each crowned by a citadel. On the right-hand side is a boat with three oars which is riding a storm under a forbidding black cloud. To the bottom left it is possible to make out a couple at a steep angle to the hill, and above them three horsemen arrested in full gallop. A fiery sun flashes out wheels of color.

The actual interpretation of these elements has been the subject of much controversy; especially since the recent discovery of an unpublished essay on the painting written by Kandinsky in June 1913. This document appears to discourage the irony which some have read into an imagined discrepancy between the title and the actual work, and reduces the heavy apocalyptic signification of the imagery. Indeed Kandinsky writes of the 'joyfulness' of execution. It is legitimate then, to see the work as a celebration of Kandinsky's style during this period, as affirming the spiritual and practical pleasures he manifestly derived from painting; he speaks of 'pouring a lot of small pleasures on to the canvas'.

While giving the impression of heavenly chaos, *Small Pleasures* is obviously not the product of pure spontaneity. The various modes of paint application, and the complexity of pigment selection and mixing are enormous. The way colors are washed and blurred together, and seldom contained by bounding lines is typical of Kandinsky's work at this time. The predominantly curvilinear aspect of the work, however, is undermined by the angular geometry of the citadel, perhaps presaging Kandinsky's Bauhaus style. There are few monochrome patches in the composition, underlining the local scale of execution, and part of Kandinsky's pleasure in the work was his reflection on a number of minor technical achievements. He wrote of the 'fine, very fine lines' scrupulously worked in with an extra-thin brush, and of his successful suppression of 'lustre' from the gold and silver areas.

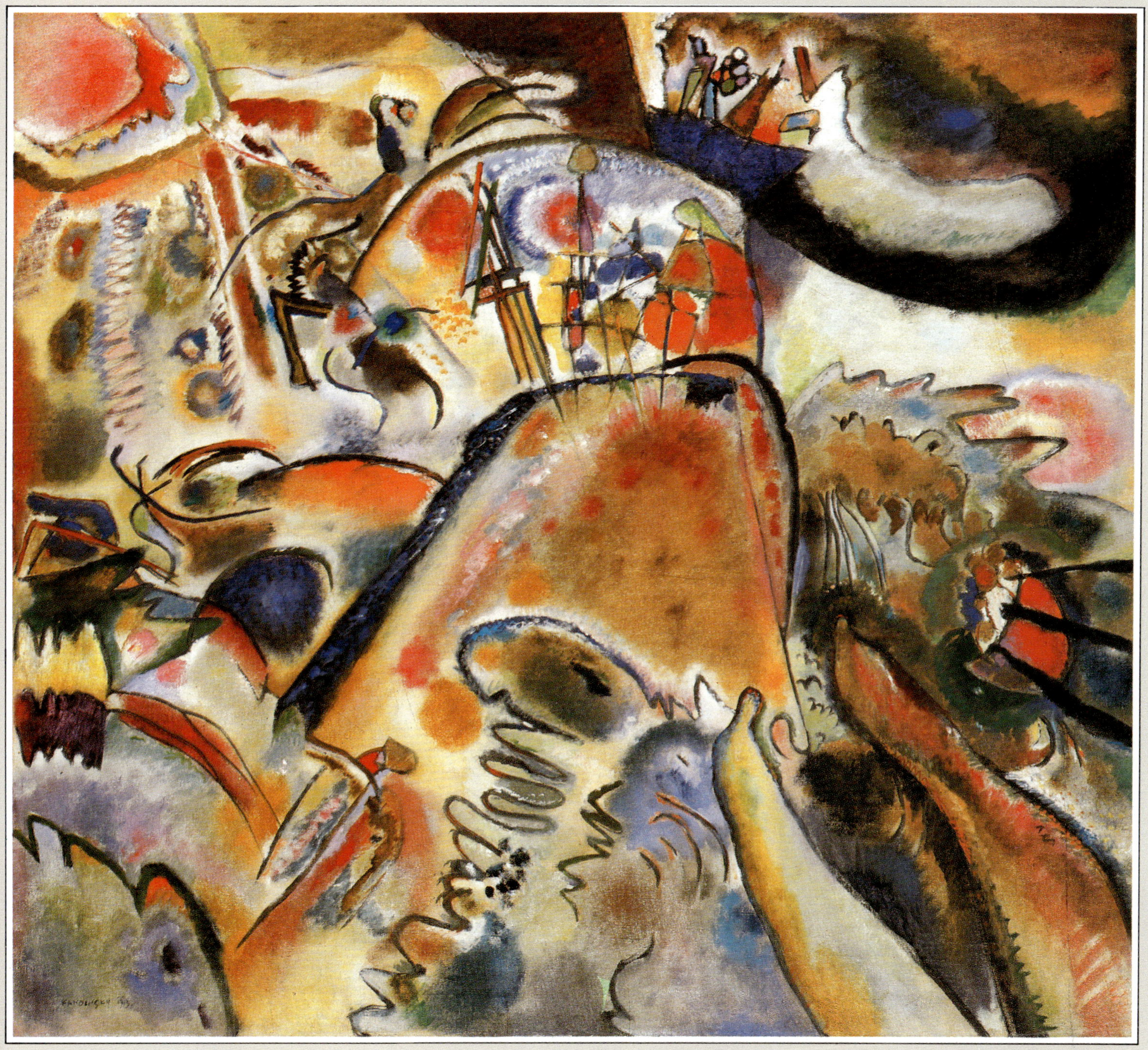

*At first sight* Small Pleasures *seems like an abstract but exuberant polychromatic display. In fact color, line and other formal components are expressive agents in the service of a highly charged apocalyptic imagery, which is revealed unevenly across the picture surface. Some of these symbols are identified in the text.*

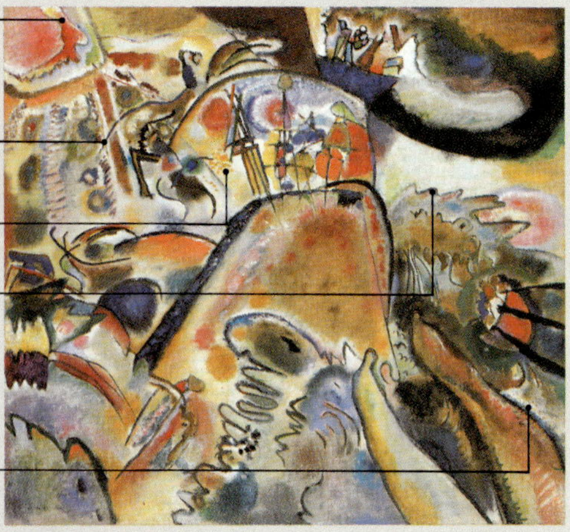


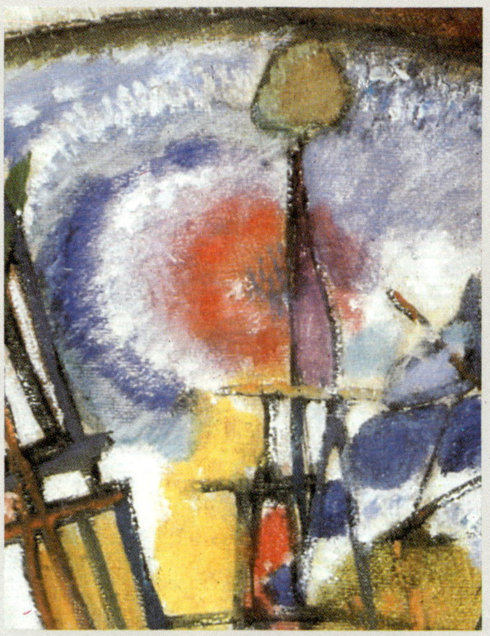

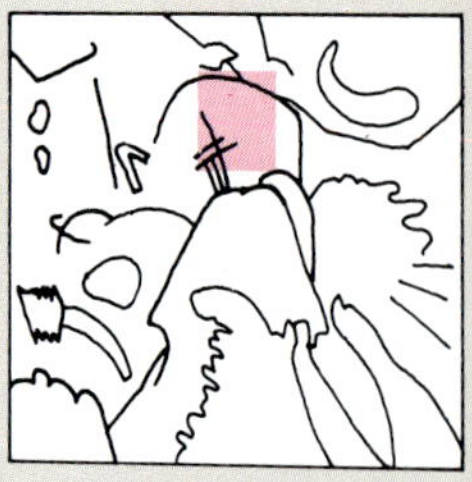

*LEFT The straight-line construction of the buildings on the hill is conspicuously out of phase with the apparent formal and colorist anarchy of the rest of the composition. They are an attempt to reduce the features of the walled town to a geometric skeleton which yet contains its essential signifying features. The relation of color to this structure, however, suggests that Kandinsky was not interested in rigid infilling or strict equivalence; it is not applied subordinately and describes its own shape and forms.*

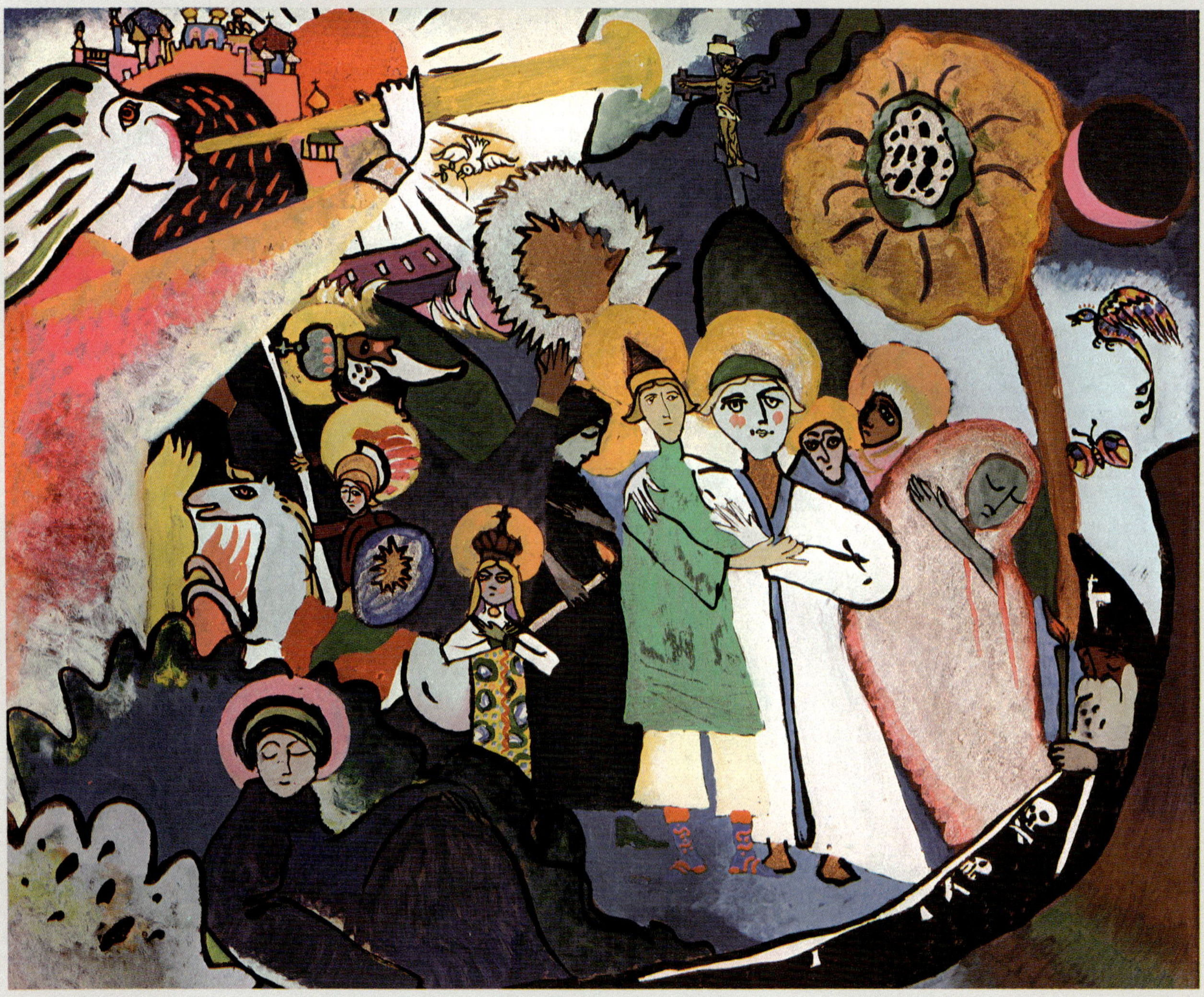

*LEFT Painting on glass was still a flourishing folk art in some of the villages around Munich and Kandinsky was evidently inspired by this technique. In many respects,* All Saints I *(1911) and* Small Pleasures *represent complementary poles of Kandinsky's activity 1910-1914. There is a bold, almost humorous realism in* All Saints*, matched by the use of relatively unmixed clear color patches. This work is a pool of images and motifs which Kandinsky abstracted and abbreviated in his later work, the trumpeting angel, St George on horseback, and other saints.* Small Pleasures *too has a Kremlin on a hill, and the fiery red sun, but two years later these motifs are veiled behind a frenzy of expressive painting devices.*

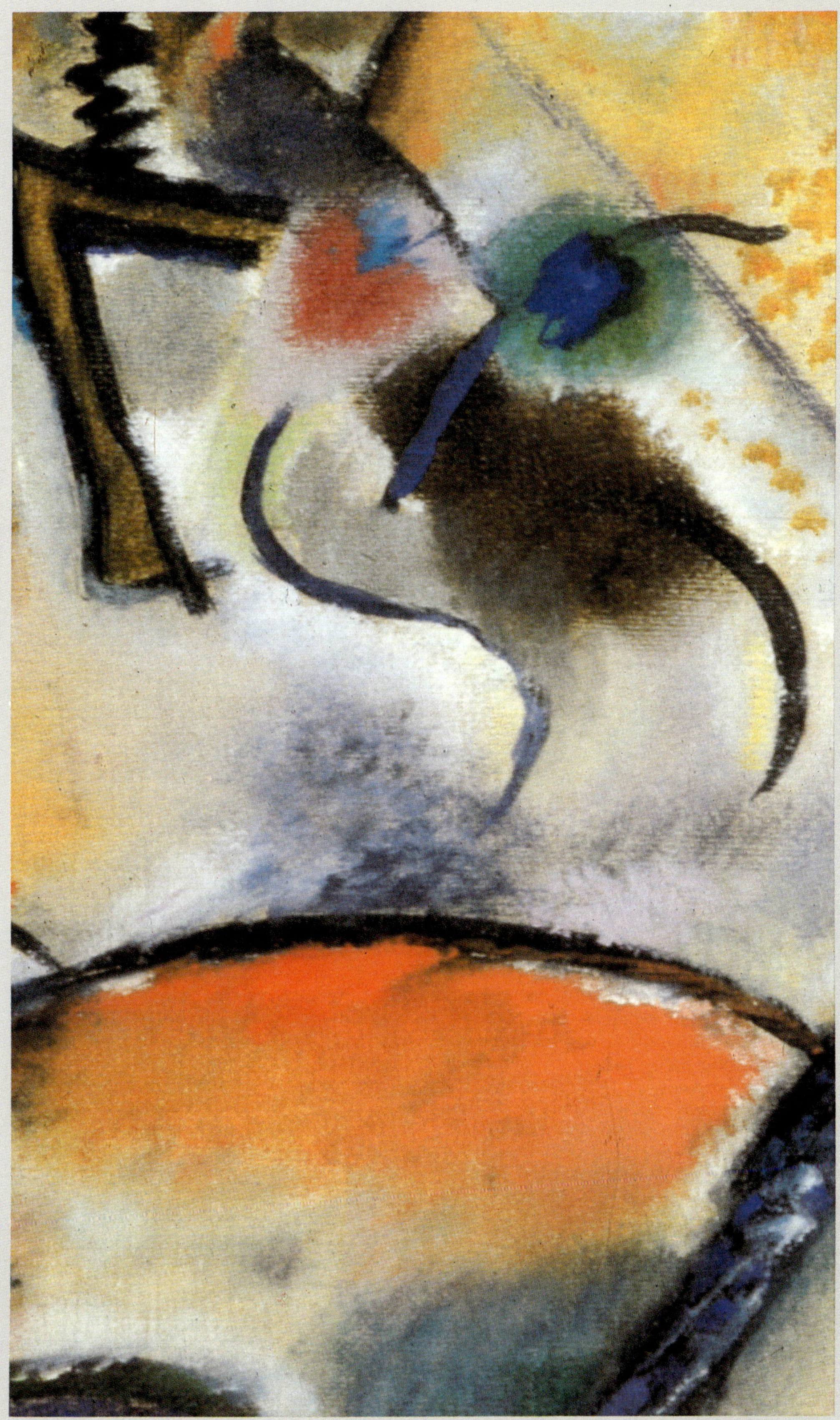

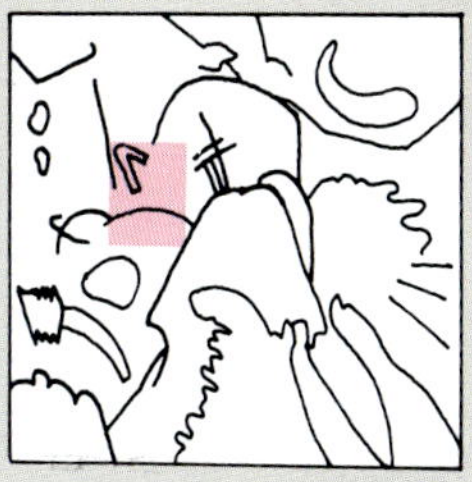

ACTUAL SIZE DETAIL
*The horse and rider featured here is probably Kandinsky's leading motif in his pre-1914 work. It can be traced through a multitude of technical and stylistic transitions from the heavily textured* The Blue Rider *(1903), the jeweled and romantic* Couple on Horseback *(1906), to the archer on horseback in 1909 and the exquisite brevity of* Lyrical *(1910).*

# GINO SEVERINI

*Centrifugal Expansion of Light (1914)*
Oil on canvas
69cm × 49.6cm/27½in × 19¾in

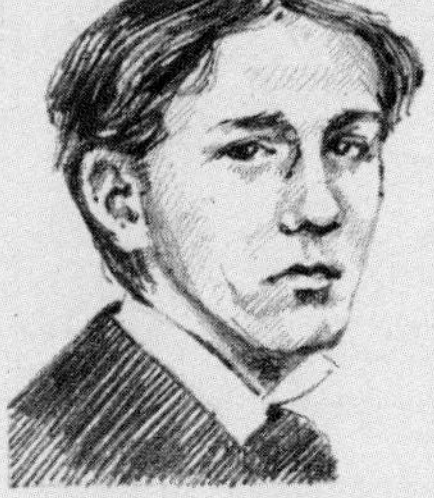

Gino Severini was one of the leading painters of the Futurist Movement, which supplied much of the inspiration and theoretical stimulation that sustained his output.

Born at Cortona on 7 April 1883, Severini began his artistic studies in Rome where he became a close friend of the young Umberto Boccioni, who was to be instrumental in the formulation of the first Futurist painters' manifesto in 1910. Like his friend, Severini found himself drawn to the art of Giacomo Balla, which he felt was a new exciting way of painting the modern world. These connections placed him at the center of the *milieu* in which Futurism was germinating, but he left Italy for Paris in 1905, missing the movement's birth.

Paris became Severini's adopted city and he absorbed himself in the recent major developments in the visual arts there, producing, firstly, canvases in the Neo-Impressionist style, and then, through acquaintance with the avant-garde circle of Picasso, Max Jacob and Guillaume Apollinaire, experimented with the discoveries of Cubism.

Temperamentally more suited to formalist investigations than many of his literary-inclined colleagues in Italy, Severini found the rigorous grid-like structure and shifting viewpoints of Cubism attractive and, moreover, extremely useful as a disciplined compositional technique: within it he could pursue the Futurist interest in portraying the speed, vigor, color and bustle of modern life. He tightened the fragmented jaggedness of Analytical Cubism into a more straightforward geometric mosaic of movement. The result was both persuasive and forceful. The showpiece of this technique is the *Dance of the Pan-Pan at the Monico* (1910-1912), which Apollinaire described as 'the most important work painted up to now by a Futurist brush'. But the pursuit of a more lyrical luminosity of color led him away from Cubism to the influence of the Orphists.

Severini was the first to introduce the peculiar strain of Futurist excitement and verve to Paris. More importantly, he was instrumental in bringing the Italian artists to the French capital to see the new styles of painting.

Severini worked predominantly in oil, but to produce looser, freer brushwork he occasionally used gouache. His contact with the Cubists, and more especially Apollinaire, encouraged him to experiment briefly with *papier collé* and collage. More significant, however, was his use of multi-colored sequins, metallic dust and a sheet of painted aluminium as part of the exploration of light, color and movement.

In the 1920s Severini produced a series of frescoes for the decoration of the Sitwells' castle at Montegufoni in Tuscany in which the nostalgic subject matter of the *Commedia dell' Arte* (a type of theater production developed in sixteenth-century Italy by traveling actors), treated in a monumental manner, complemented the use of a traditional medium. More frescoes followed, mostly in the apses of churches; they display an increasing interest in Byzantine and Early Christian art, which was to provide an important stimulus to the mosaics Severini produced in the 1930s.

The *Centrifugal Expansion of Light* was painted at the height of Severini's involvement with the formalist experiments of Parisian art during 1913 to 1914. This was when he produced his first abstract works, clearly influenced by Apollinaire's enthusiasm for Orphism, and more particularly by the pioneering *Fenêtres simultanées prismatiques* series (1912) of Robert Delaunay (1885-1941). Like the *Fenêtres,* this piece has been worked on the canvas itself without any involved preparation, and of necessity its color relationships grow one from another across the surface. The genesis of the work owes much to Severini's own idea of 'plastic analogies of dynamism', made concrete in *Sea = Dancer and a Vase of Flowers* (1913) where the abstract pattern of light on the sea's surface suggested to him the rhythm of dance and the title. *Centrifugal Expansion of Light* is another product of the same period spent by the sea at Anzio.

Describing his technique at this time, Severini wrote of: '... colors which were as pure as possible and applied to the canvas with great concentration on nuances and contrasts of tone ... The typical characteristic of my way of working consisted in the carrying to the extreme limits the independence of Neo-Impressionism in relation to exterior reality. I did not wish the *mélange optique* to be realized either close to, or at a distance from the observer; I wanted the colors, instead, to remain orchestrated and colored modulations. With this technique I stabilized the successive series of movements . . . architecturally arranged and chosen by me with the aim of obtaining an overall harmonic effect.'

Within the confines of the complicated surface structure, ultimately Cubist in origin, the Divisionist brushstrokes are applied with freedom and varying degrees of sparsity, in order to allow the foundations of white or, in the case of the darker pigments, the plain ground alone to breathe through and increase the impression of lightness and movement between the dabs of color. Towards the edges, the plain ground is increasingly evident as an effective *diminuendo* to the central core of the most vibrant hues and thickly applied paint.

Complex modulations of tone are also manipulated within each form, where clearly discernible second layers of the brushwork 'mesh' have been applied, both allowing the base to shine through, if not actually to comingle, and often effecting a definite mix on the canvas with the undried pigment beneath.

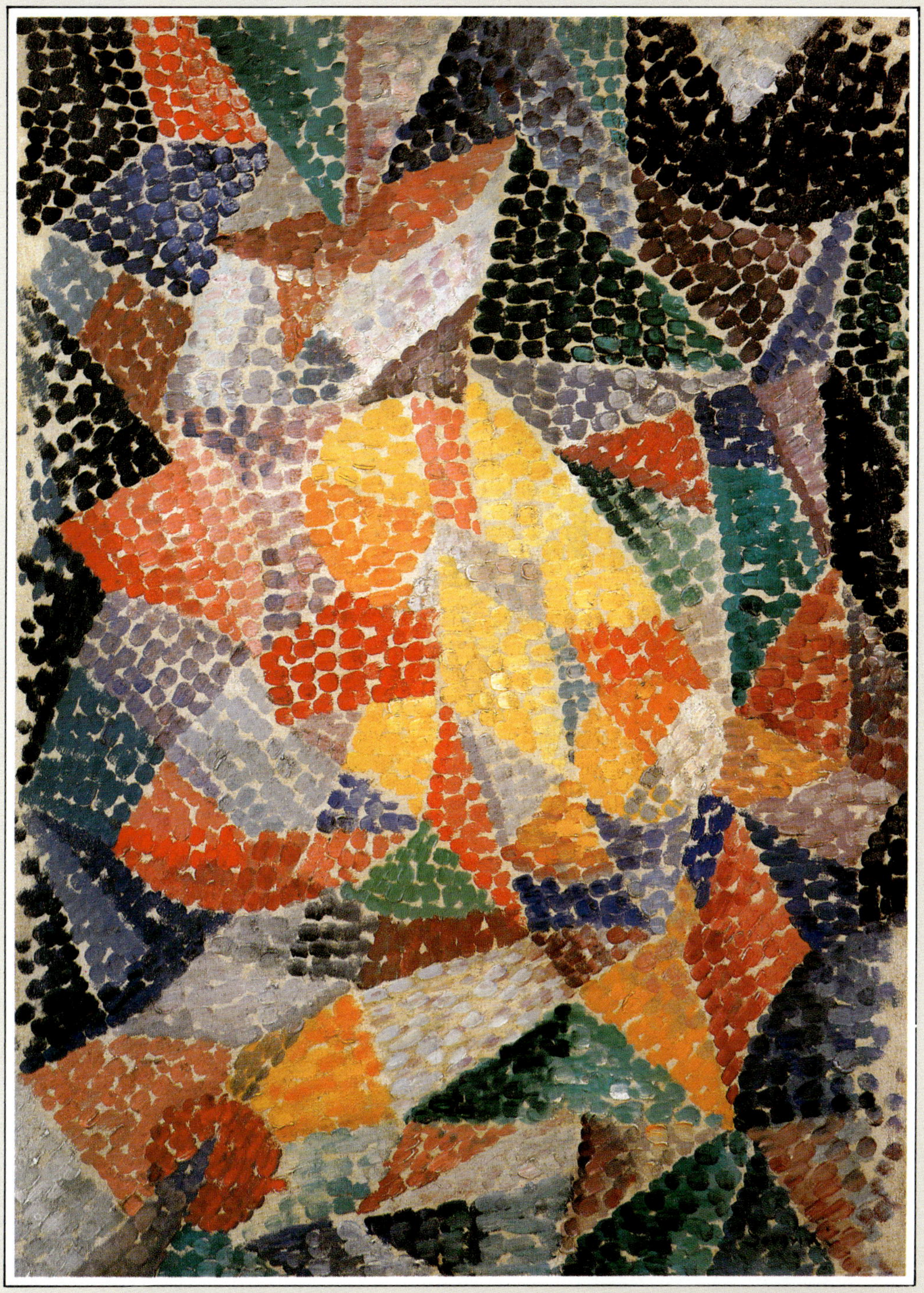

*The tessellation of colored forms — triangles, pentangles, diamonds, rhomboids and irregular and curved shapes — achieves a surface cohesion through the use of exaggerated dots. A dynamic expansion of light is envisaged from the center of the work to the peripheries which are inhabited by black and other darker tones.*

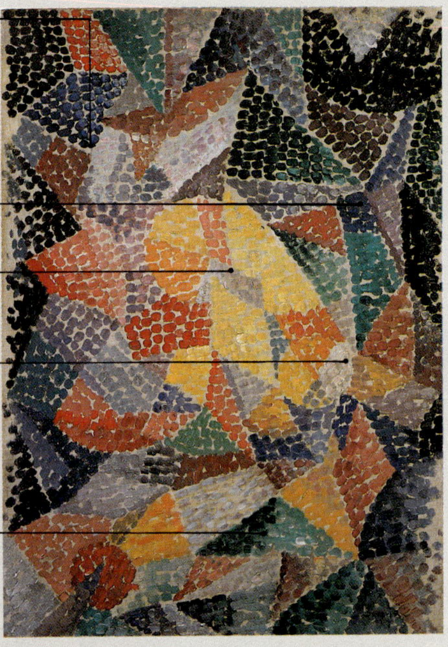


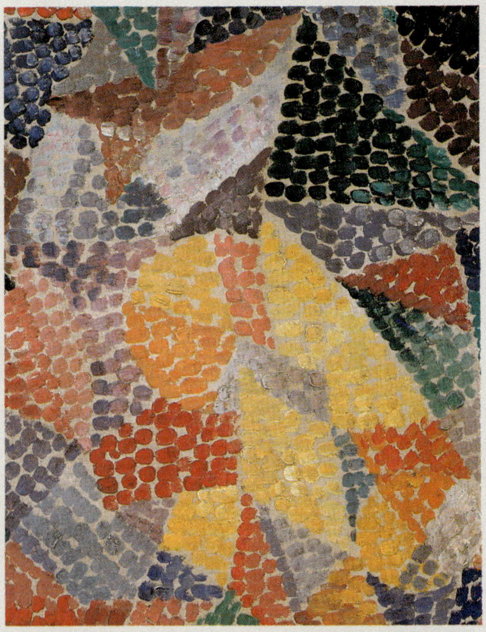

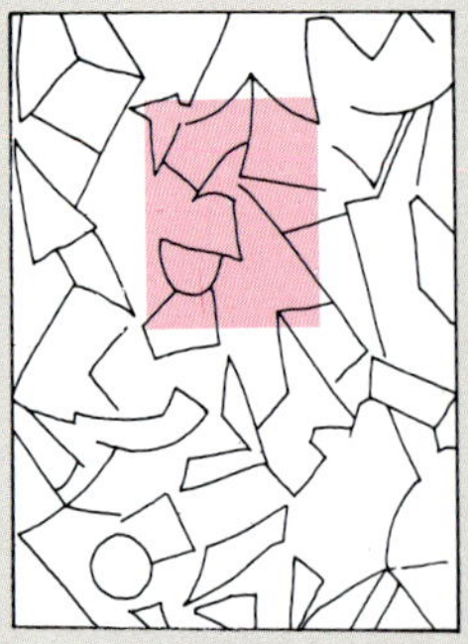

*LEFT The center of the composition is occupied by a diamond-shaped lozenge whose position and shape suggest the prismatic scattering of light. There is a cluster of yellow dots around this diamond whose hues are darkened into orange.*

*RIGHT Severini, an enthusiastic dancer himself, found in the dance theme an exemplary motif for the exploration of movement and rhythm.* The Dynamic Hieroglyph of Bal Tabarin *(1912) is crowded with incident and anecdote, but the individual items are reduced and abstracted into 'hieroglyphs' structurally dependent on the luminosity and faceting of Analytic Cubism. As Picasso and Braque began to add foreign material to their canvas producing the first collage in 1912, so Severini here affixes sequins to the swirling dresses which glamorize the pulsing jamboree of form and color.*

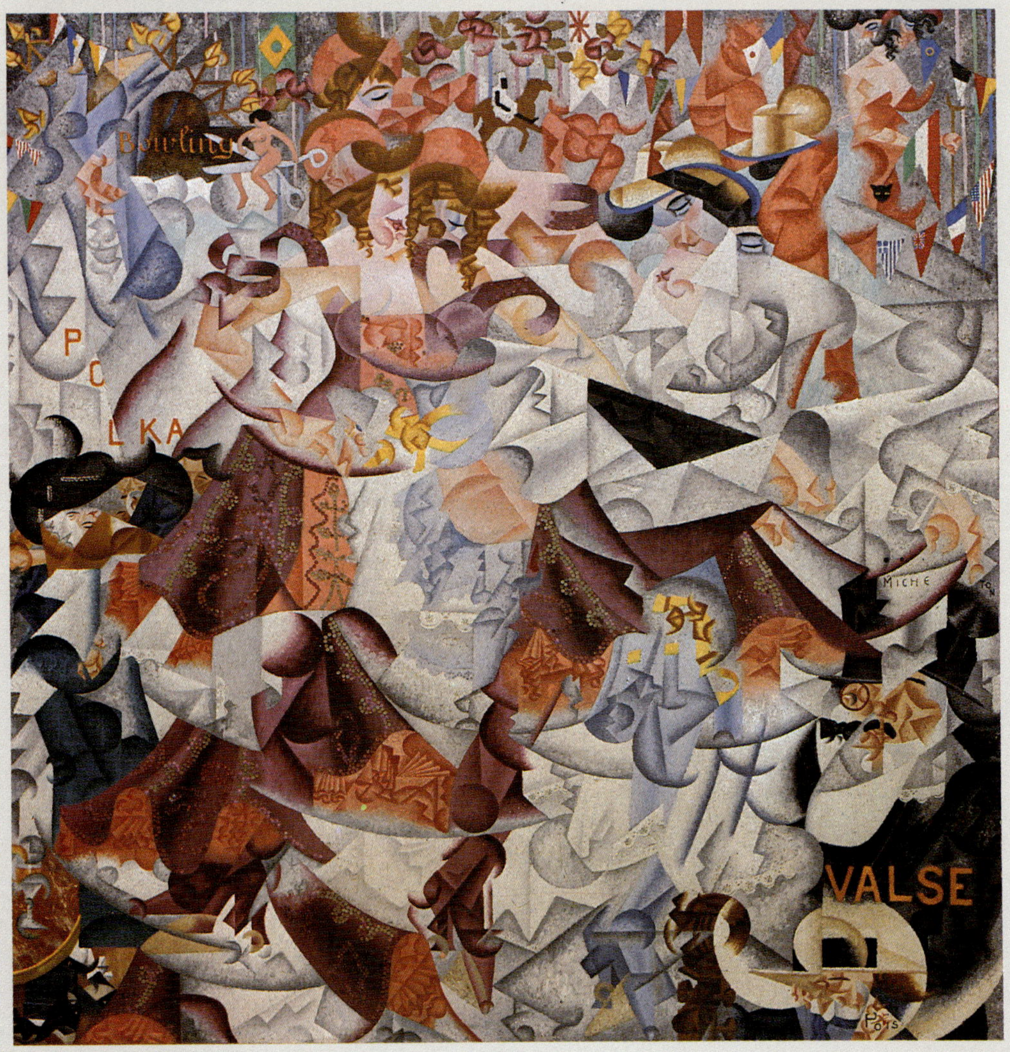


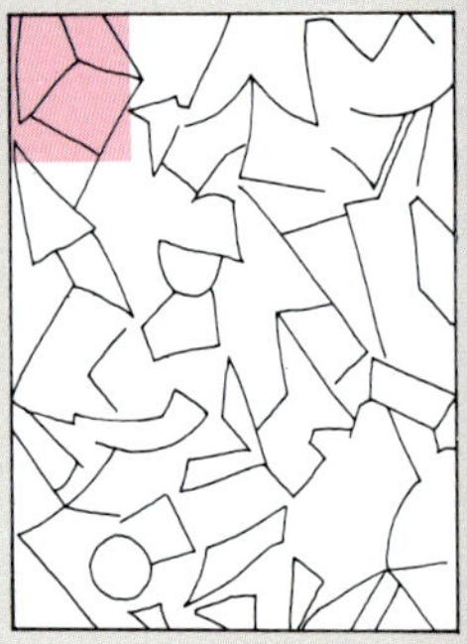

*ACTUAL SIZE DETAIL This detail demonstrates the coarseness of finish of an area along the margins of the work. The thick off-white ground on the extreme left does not reach the edge of the canvas. The top left sector is occupied by a battery of black dots, through which the ground is occasionally glimpsed, and on which are a few hints of blue and green, probably carried over from nearby dot clusters. Elsewhere the color patches are not so discretely handled: they either merge together with impasto ridges, as in the smeared turquoise-green area, are creamed with white in the red and blue zones, or are mixed wet into wet as in the paler colors.*

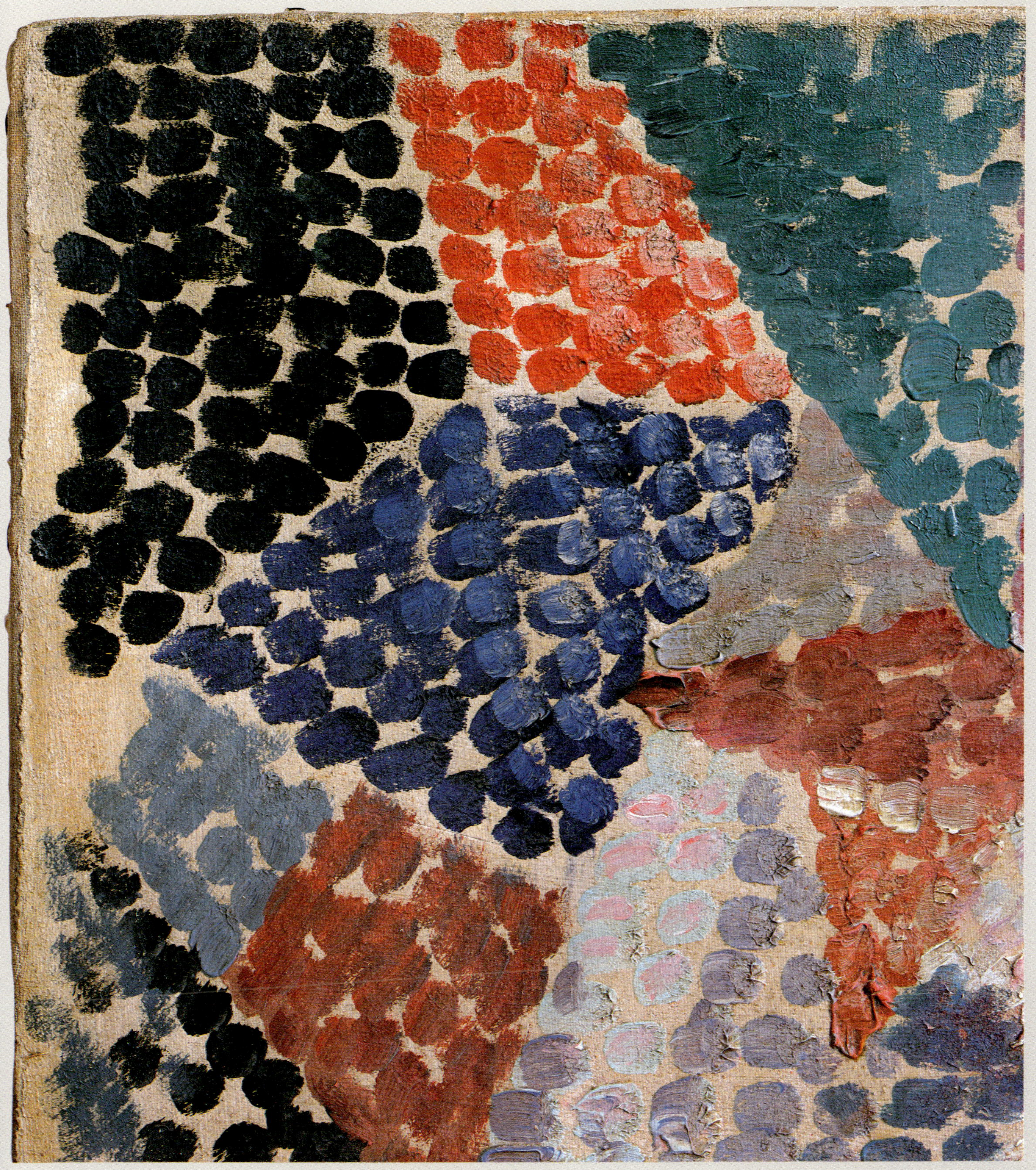

# MARCEL DUCHAMP

*The Bride Stripped Bare by Her Bachelors, Even (1915-1923)*
*Reconstruction* Richard Hamilton *(1965-1966)*
*Oil, varnish, lead wire, lead foil and dust on two glass panels*
*277.5cm × 175.8cm/109¼in × 69¼in*

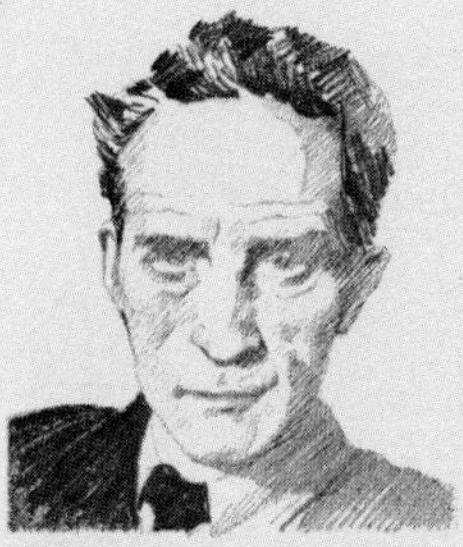

Marcel Duchamp began planning *The Bride Stripped Bare by her Bachelors, Even,* or *The Large Glass* for short, in the summer of 1912, and made numerous notes, and drawings concerning its iconography and its execution. The notes, which are even more complicated than the physical work, were considered by Duchamp to be an equal work of art. A facsimile edition of these notes from 1912 to 1923 were published as *The Green Box* in 1934.

Marcel Duchamp was born near Blainville in 1887. At school he showed intellectual promise in a number of fields, including mathematics. His grandfather was a painter; two brothers and a sister were artists. When he was 15 he showed precocious accomplishment as a painter with the oil on canvas, *Landscape at Blainville* (1902). Duchamp studied painting at the Académie Julian from 1904 to 1905 where he worked in the manner of the Neo-Impressionists, Fauvists and Cézanne.

In 1911 he began to absorb and experiment with some of the very recent developments of Cubism and Futurism, producing the painting *Nude Descending a Staircase* (1912), which was the first successful attempt in painting to depict movement and the passing of time on a static flat canvas. In 1913 he turned his back on conventional painting in order to concentrate on the conceptual aspects of art. He wanted to recognize and initiate art that was a product of the mind rather than a formal sensual manipulation and even wastage of standard artistic materials.

The scenario for *The Large Glass,* although complicated, can be condensed. The Bachelors in the guise of nine Malic (Duchamp's own word) molds or uniforms emit a gas which passes along tubes and through the cone-like Sieves, becoming a liquid which must then be imagined to be directed upwards into the Bride's domain. The horizontal dividing line between the two panels is the area which Duchamp designated as the Bride's garments and the gilled cooler. This area cools the ardor of the Bachelors and they fail in their attempt to win the Bride. The Bride – the stick insect-like configuration at the left of the top panel – has meanwhile issued her commands, threefold, in the form of a 'blossoming' semaphore at the very top of her panel. The purpose of the large Chocolate Grinder, to the right of the center of the Bachelors panel, is to occupy the Bachelors grinding their own chocolate and thus temper their disappointment.

He used glass as a support and, with its utter receptive transparency, would provide its own background ready-made from its immediate environment. *The Large Glass* was to have a back and a front however. Because Duchamp worried about the impermanence of the oil medium, he conceived the notion of trapping oil pigment between the glass support and a sealing layer of lead foil pressed on to the wet paint, to prevent oxidization. But, of course, an observer looking at *The Large Glass* from the side on which the paint and its cover of lead foil was applied would be unable to see the oil pigment. Also this process did not arrest deterioration since the lead of the foil reacted with the lead in the white paint, and the color of the Malic molds, for example, has darkened considerably.

To paint the glass, Duchamp fixed a full-scale working drawing to one side of it. Lead wire (in fact contemporary fuse wire) was then bent on the other side to mark the contours of the areas to be filled. The lead wire was stuck to the surface of the glass with mastic varnish.

The only shapes to look the same color from both sides are the seven Sieves, which describe an arc in the center of the Bachelors panel. Since a sieve is permeable in real life, Duchamp decided that they should be permeable in his artistic system too. But with the logic that was his art, the Sieves are represented by a non-porous material. He chose dust. He mapped out the contours of the Sieves with lead wire, let the dust of three months settle within the area (the glass was lying flat to allow him to work on it), and then fixed the dust with varnish.

As the working notes reveal, Duchamp wanted to use different techniques in the Bride panel. He tried to fix the image of the Bride upon the glass by projecting a negative of a previous oil painting of the Bride onto an area prepared with photographic emulsion, but the result was unsatisfactory. He had to return to the lead wire and foil process, but he introduced shading by tone and by hue instead of laying the paint on as a flat color field, which was the method of the Bachelor panel. The painting of the Bride and her 'blossoming' is quite sensual in its handling.

The three Oculist Witnesses, situated to the right of the Bachelor panel, were the last forms to be completed. This was an area of the work which was meant to dazzle the efforts of the Bachelors and to encourage the close inspection by the viewer. Duchamp used technical and optical means to achieve this. The three shapes were copied from charts used by French opticians and Duchamp prepared careful perspectival drawings which were then traced on to a silvered area of the glass. The silver was then scraped away.

Finally the nine holes or Shots, at the extreme right of the Bride panel, were achieved by firing matches dipped in paint from a toy cannon aimed at the glass. Where the matches struck, a hole was then bored through. The Shots are the only attempt by the Bachelors to impose their mark upon the panel of the Bride.

Duchamp's *Large Glass* is a work of vital importance in twentieth-century art, with its immense technical, philosophical and iconographical implications.

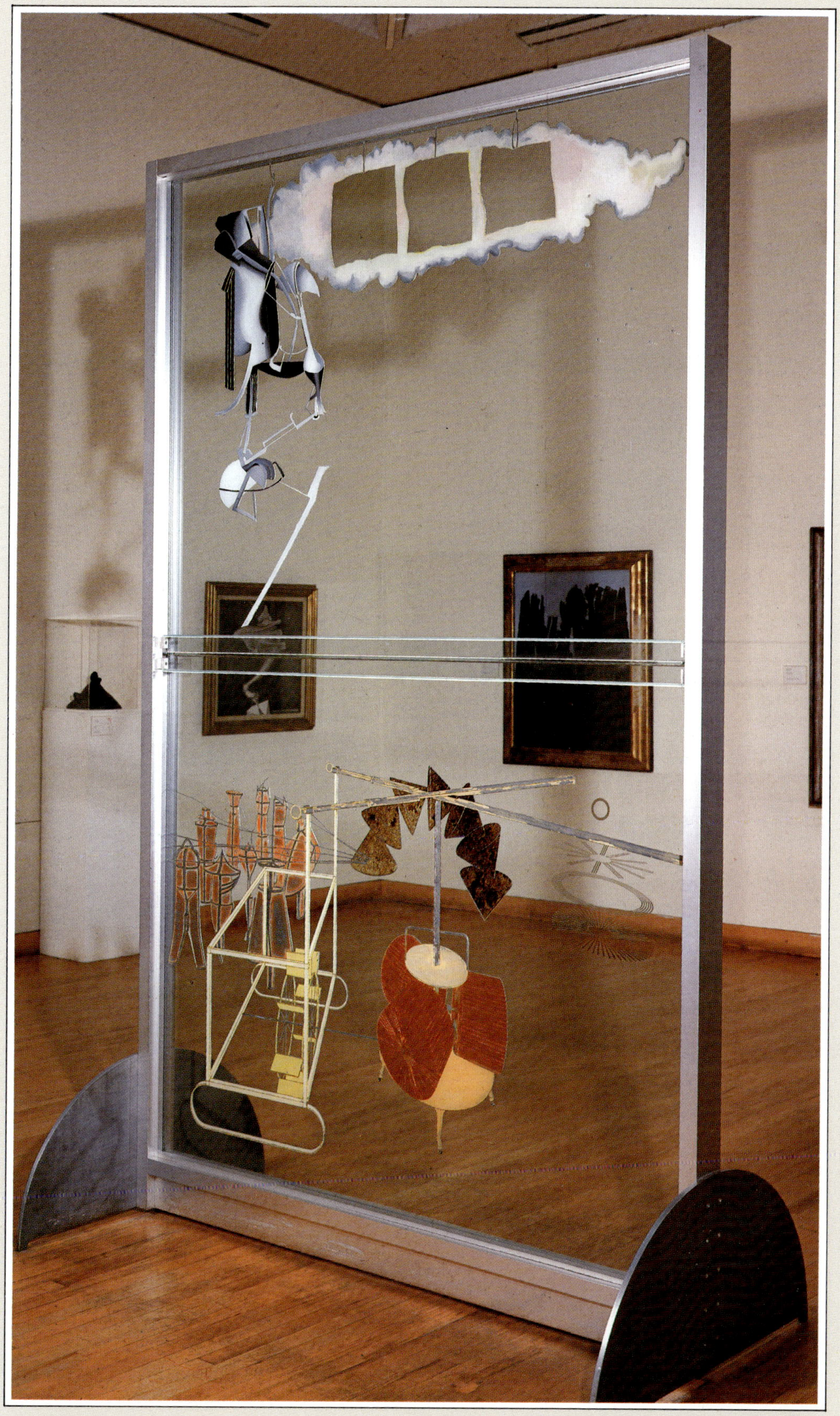

*After the initial shock of the complete transparency of the glass support, which in this situation allows a Max Ernst painting to be viewed at the same time,* The Large Glass *settles into some kind of solidity and normality with the forms dispersed over its bipartite structure. Although the support is transparent the work does have a front and a back because of Duchamp's unique technical procedures which only allow the pigment to show through on one side, the front. Renaissance artists who developed the system of one-point perspective thought of the picture planes as a transparent window and Duchamp here ironically takes this notion to its logical but unexpected conclusion. The lower section, the realm of the Bachelors, contains all sorts of illusory perspectival constructions, whereas the upper section, The Bride, appears much flatter.*

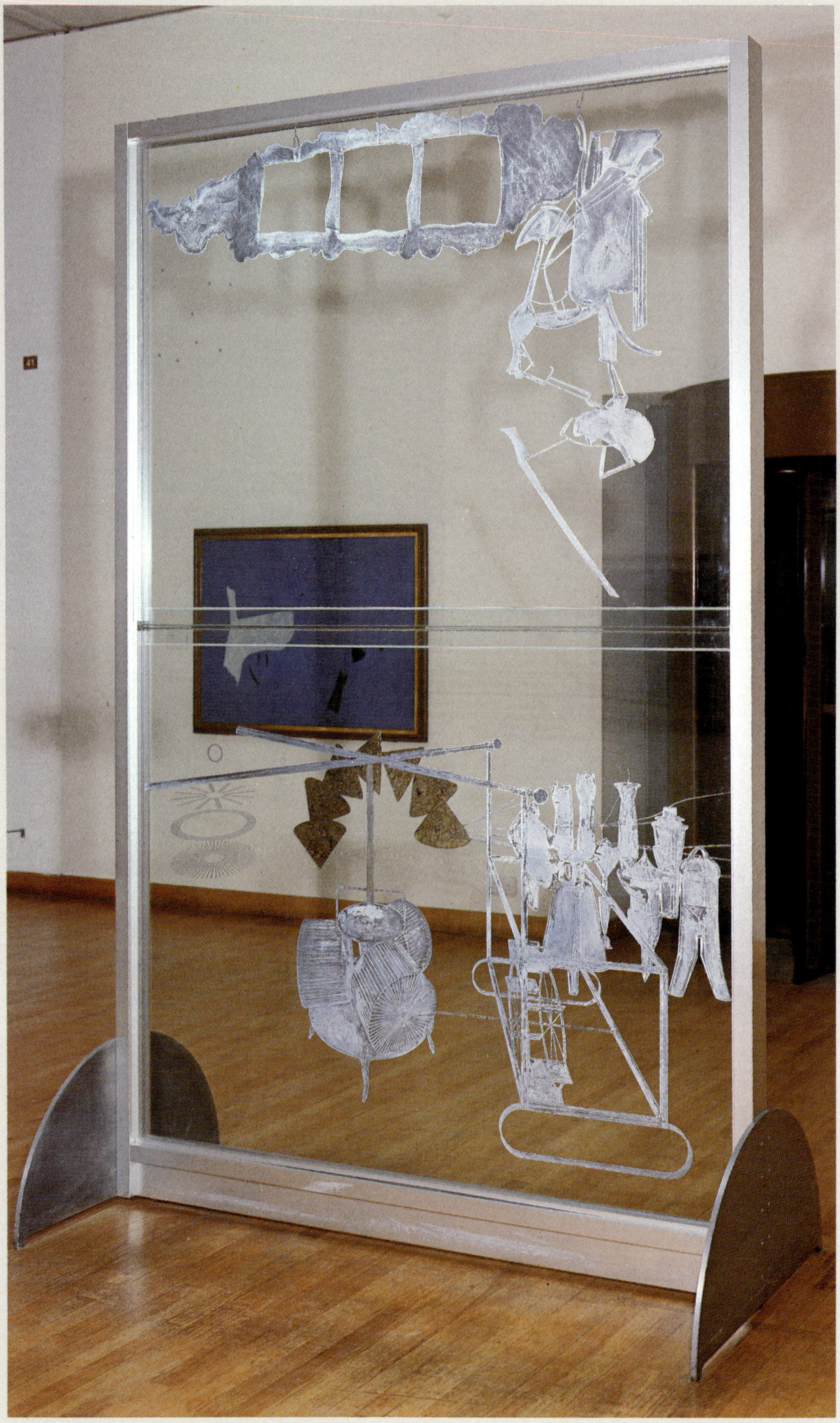

RIGHT *Seen from the back,* The Large Glass *appears to have an almost ghostly presence. This is due to the uneven silvery finish of the lead foil with which Richard Hamilton, following Duchamp's method, covered the oil paint in the hope of keeping it in a permanently stable state. The lead foil, when seen in conjunction with the aluminium frame, gives the work the air of being a strange machine, with a hermetic, slightly sinister purpose. In the Bachelor section, on the shape known as the necktie, Duchamp autographed and authenticated this version of* The Large Glass, *adding Richard Hamilton's name along with his own.*

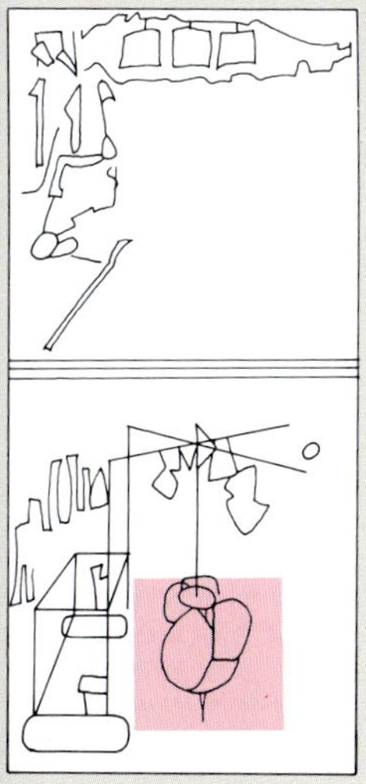

BELOW This, the Chocolate Grinder, is the most prominent machine in the Bachelor section. It comprises three rollers, with a flat disc christened the 'necktie' above, and a 'Louis XV nickeled chassis' below. The metal chassis and the Louis XV legs are given a sumptuous peach hue which countermands their iron strength, whereas the three rollers are painted a burnt sienna which does come closer to the idea of milk chocolate.

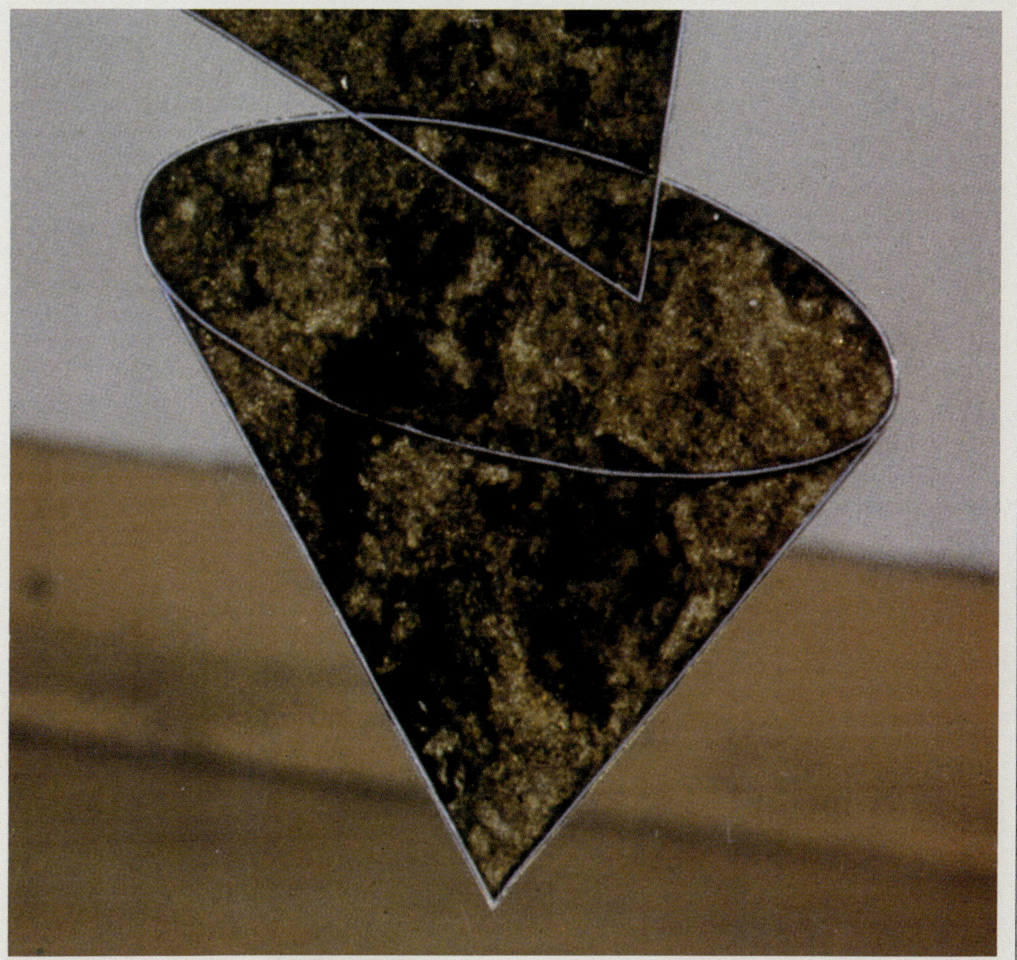

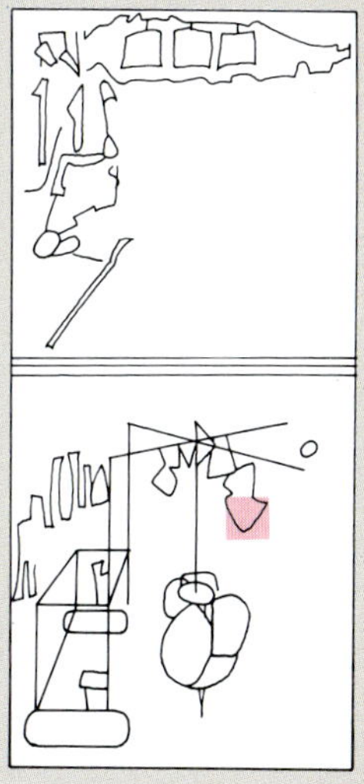

ACTUAL SIZE DETAIL Duchamp organized a dust breeding process in his studio, which helped to raise the dust necessary for the coloring matter for the seven Sieves. This is the last of the Sieves, which get progressively darker from left to right. Duchamp wanted the dust to be 'a kind of color (transparent pastel)', and the combination of dust fixed by mastic varnish produces a rich umber pigment.

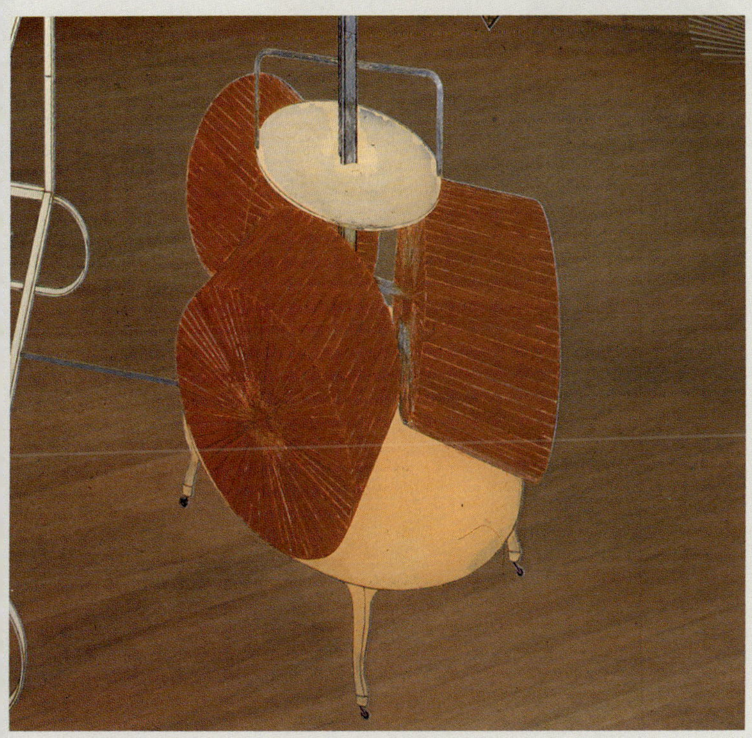

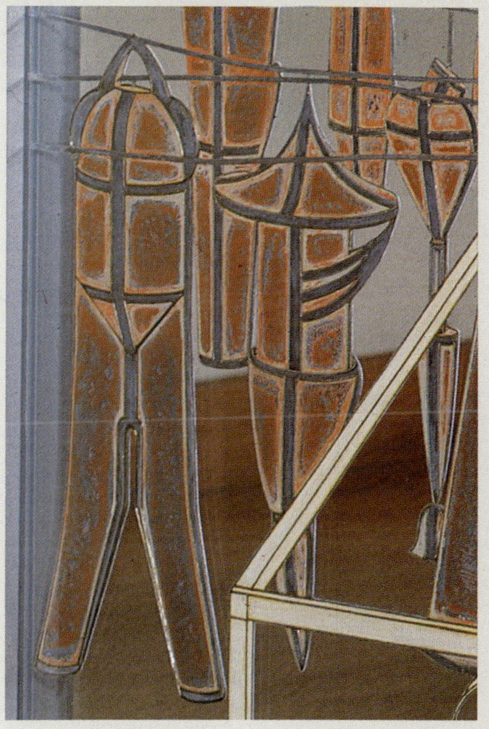

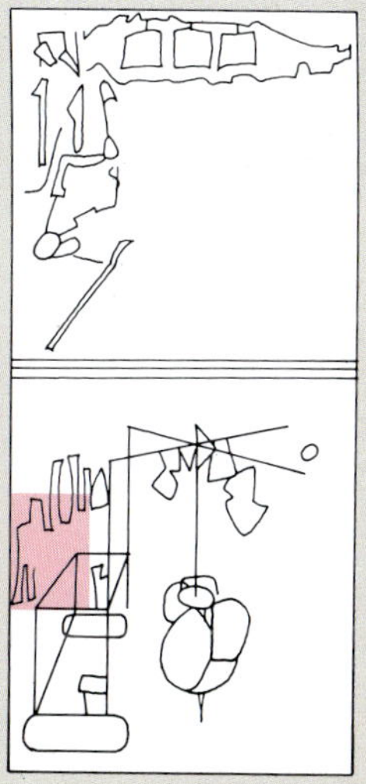

LEFT This shows five of the nine Malic Molds, different categories of Bachelor identifiable as, reading from left to right, Priest, Delivery boy, Gendarme, Cavalryman and Policeman.

# PIERRE BONNARD

*Interior at Antibes* (1920)
Oil on canvas, 116.2cm × 121.6cm/46in × 47½in

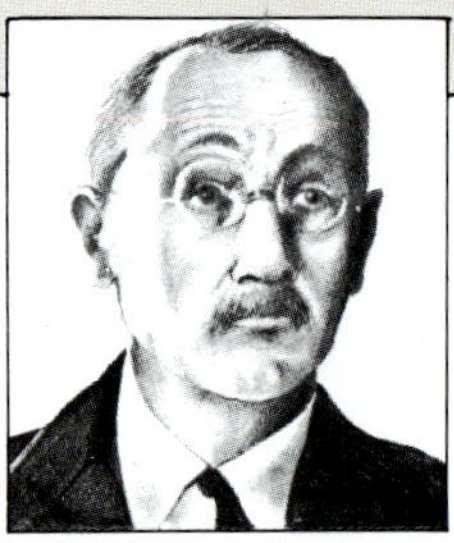

Bonnard is an outstanding example of a painter whose art evolved through a study of the nineteenth century French painting tradition into something significantly new. Thus, to see Bonnard's work as an eclectic synthesis of Degas' subject matter and compositional methods, Gauguin's imaginative color and Monet's modified *alla prima* technique would be to underestimate his achievement in conveying the seen world onto the whole canvas surface with vitality and immediacy. He saw technical control as the basis of expression and defined technique as 'the experience of centuries to guard against errors by the knowledge of the means employed'.

Bonnard did not paint directly from life. Memory and preliminary drawings together formed the starting point of a painting in the studio. He apparently never made any sketches in color, although he did occasionally note on a drawing the intensity of the color to be used. Any available room served as his studio, and his working methods were equally unconstrained by studio props and a fixed routine. A contemporary description makes this clear 'He had no easel; his only equipment was a little bamboo table on which were strewn the paintbrushes and a chipped plate on which he set out his colors. His canvases, fixed to the wall with thumbtacks, he sometimes left for months without finishing, then one day added to them a little color smeared with his finger. On more than one occasion, visiting friends, he touched up a canvas sold to them perhaps ten years earlier'. Bonnard sometimes painted several pictures at once on a large piece of canvas tacked to the wall. Intuition dictated the final format and he would, if necessary, cut a strip from the canvas or add one on. His working methods were guided by what he described as the wish 'to show all one sees upon entering a room. . . . What the eye takes in at the first glance'. He further noted that 'To begin a picture there must be an empty space in the center' and that the artist should 'work a fragment hiding the rest'. However, Bonnard also cautioned that it was necessary to know in advance the effect of the work seen from a distance. Like his working methods, Bonnard's color scheme relied on personal experience rather than on any predetermined system which might prove too inflexible in practice.

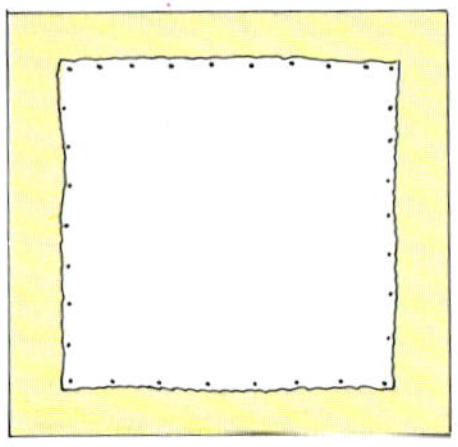

**1.** Bonnard did not use a standard format canvas he let the painting assume its own dimensions on a large piece of canvas tacked to the wall. He used a finely-grained, closely-woven canvas with a commercially-prepared white ground.

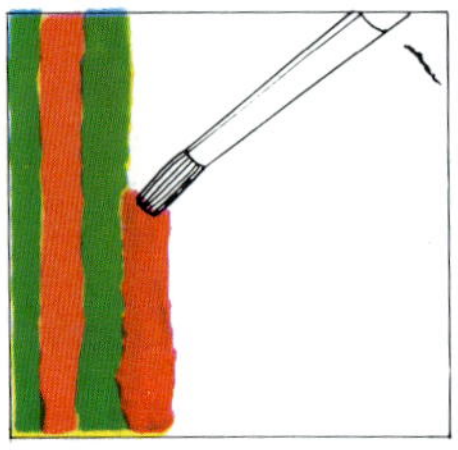

**2.** Some areas were built up in several thin layers.

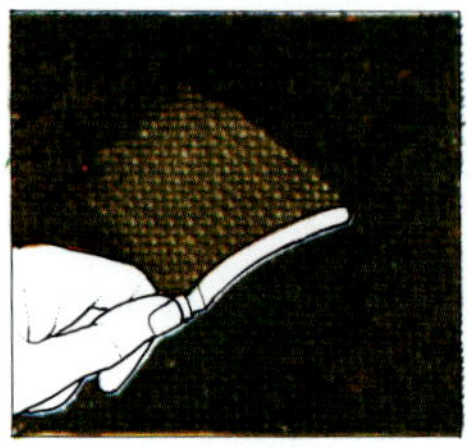

**3.** Others were painted in thicker layers with emphatic brushwork and some impasto.

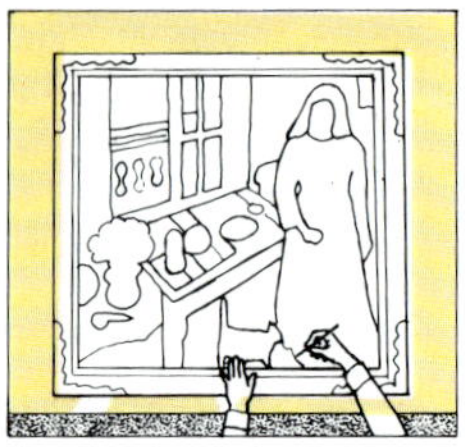

**4.** The finishing touches were added to the painting after it had been stretched and placed in its gold frame.

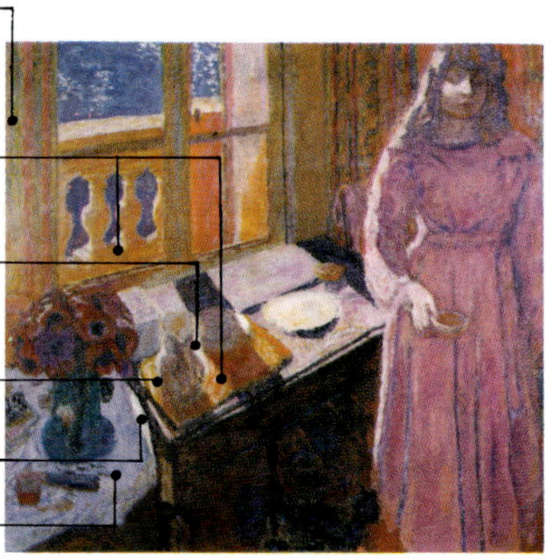

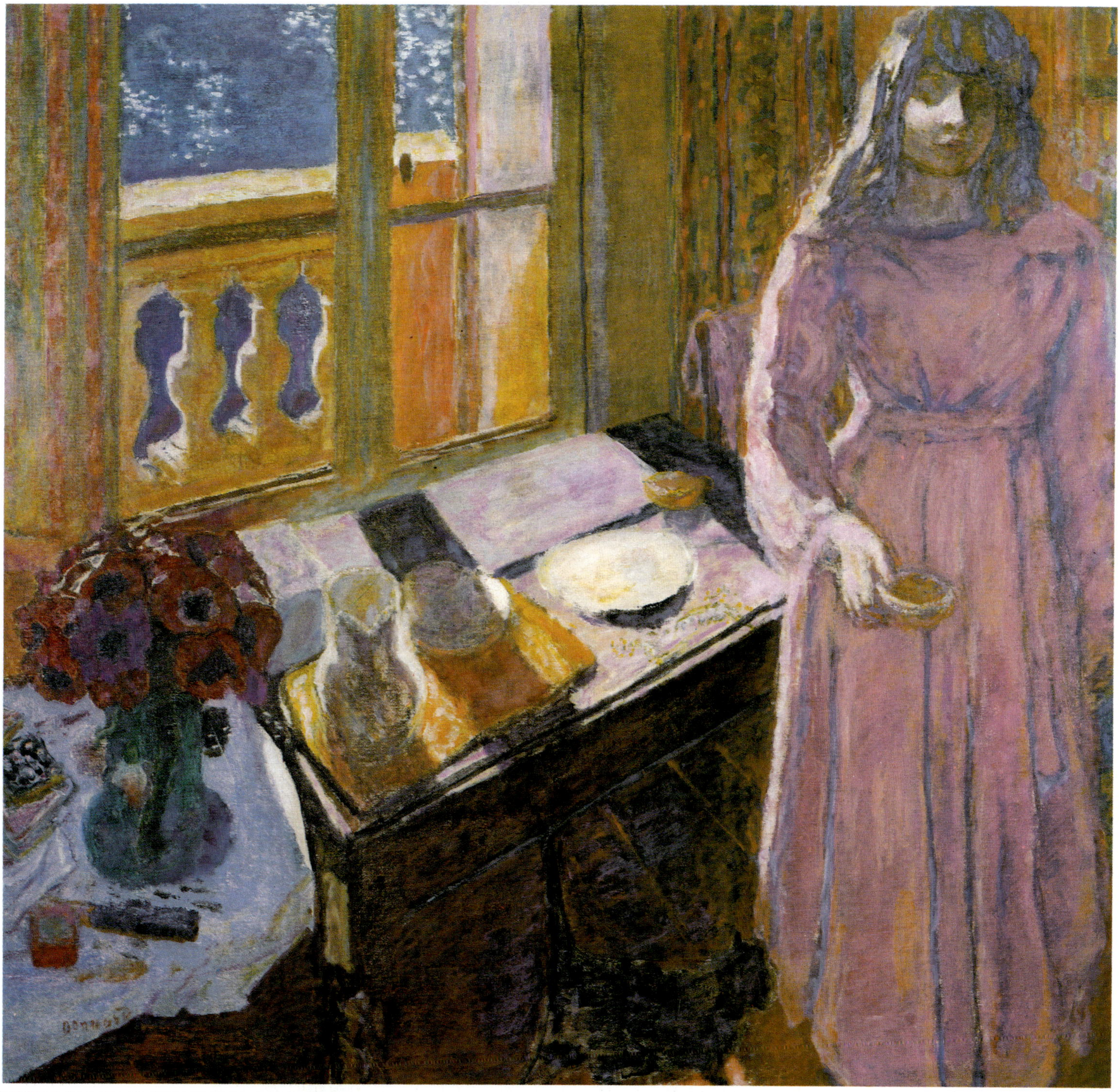

*Bonnard's technique is very varied. Some areas are built up in thin layers, while others show thicker layers with emphatic brushwork and some impasto. For example, on the left of the window, the pattern is created by touches of vermilion red and scarlet lake worked wet-in-wet into chrome yellow and a composite middle green. The jug, and cup and saucer in the center of the painting, on the other hand, are scraped down with a palette knife and then built up to a white impasto. The woman's right hand and sleeve are painted in crusty scumbles of dry paint on the exposed white ground.*

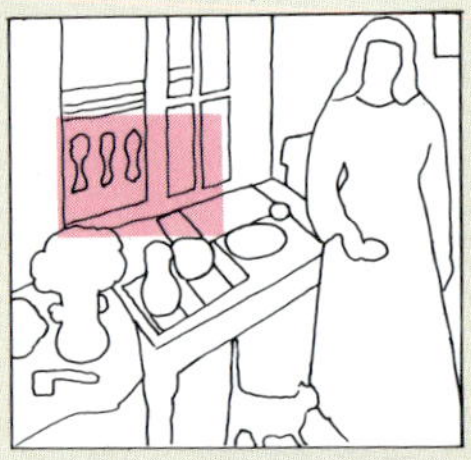

*On the left of the window the impression of cascading light is created by touches of vermilion and scarlet lake worked wet-in-wet into chrome yellow and a composite mid green.*

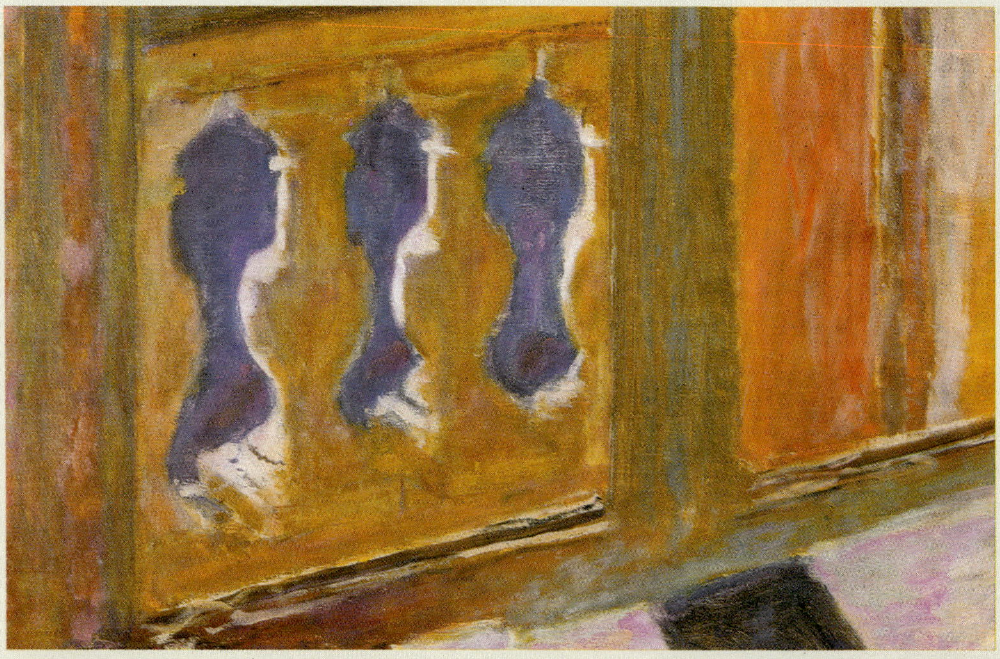

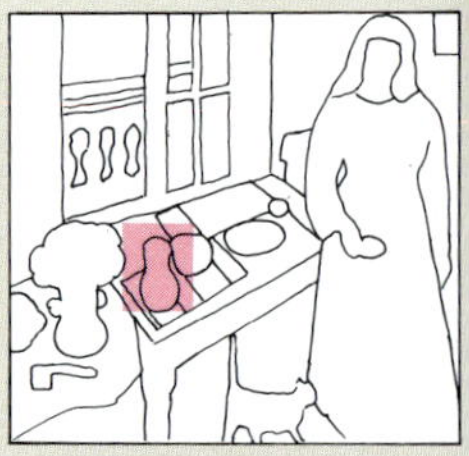

Actual size detail
*This detail shows the full range of Bonnard's technique. The righthand side of the jug was built up and then scraped away with a palette knife. The blue to the right of the jug was built up using dry paint scrubbed over the surface using a dry hog's hair brush. In the top area the violet was rubbed on over the blue-green paint when it was dry. The main area of the jug was painted in a reddish-violet, overpainted in black, and then the color was scraped back, so that the canvas threads showed through.*

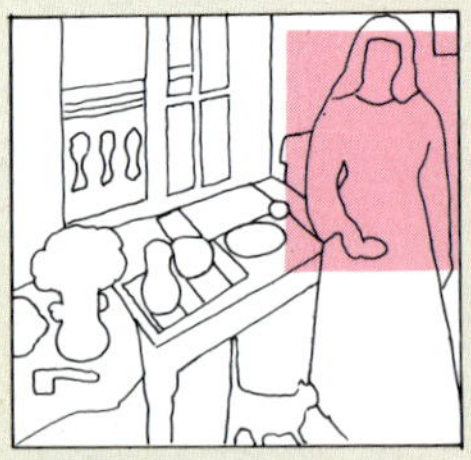

*The basic color is provided by the white canvas ground. Bonnard would work by applying layers of color and then scraping them down and reworking with paint, so that the residual layers became part of the content of the painting. In this area he worked wet-into-wet, applying a cool red such as scarlet lake and cooling the tone by applying further layers of blue-violet in the shadow areas particularly. Nowhere is Bonnard's approach programmatic.*

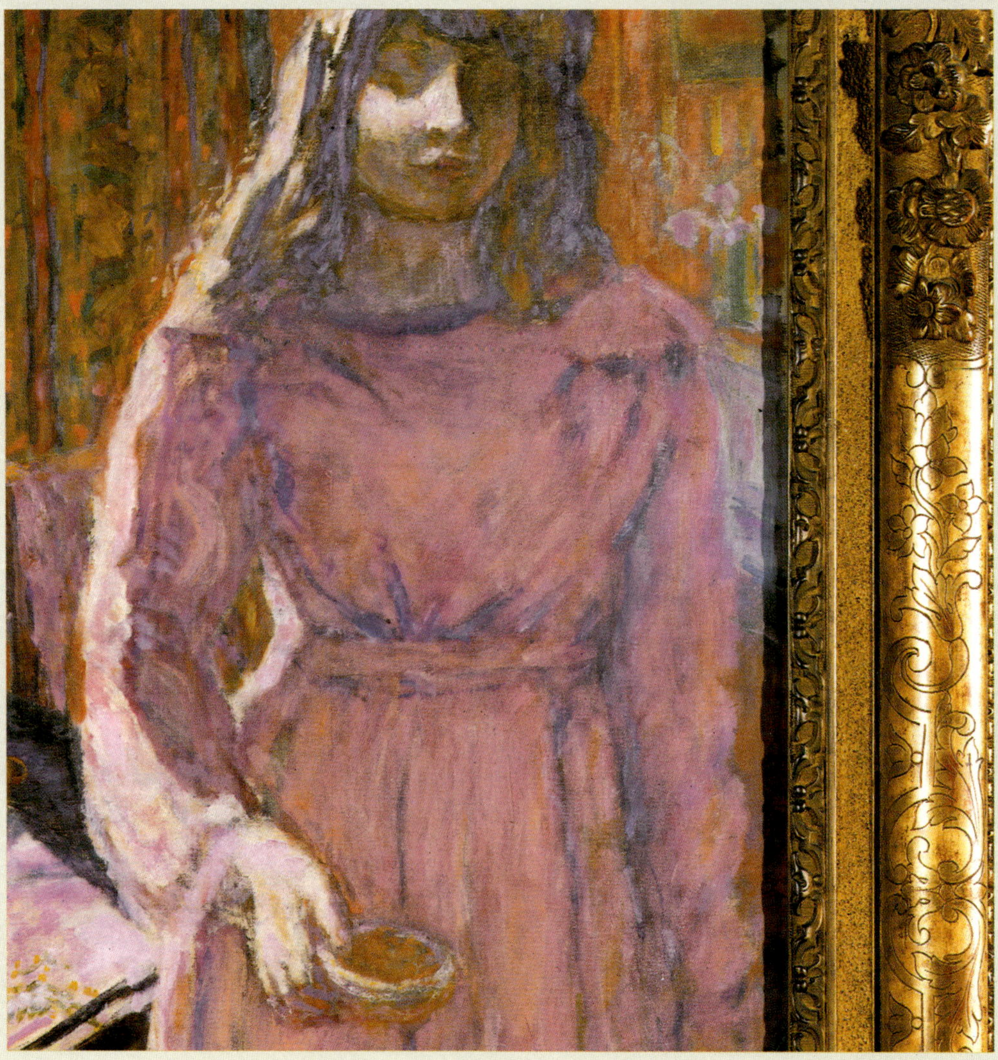

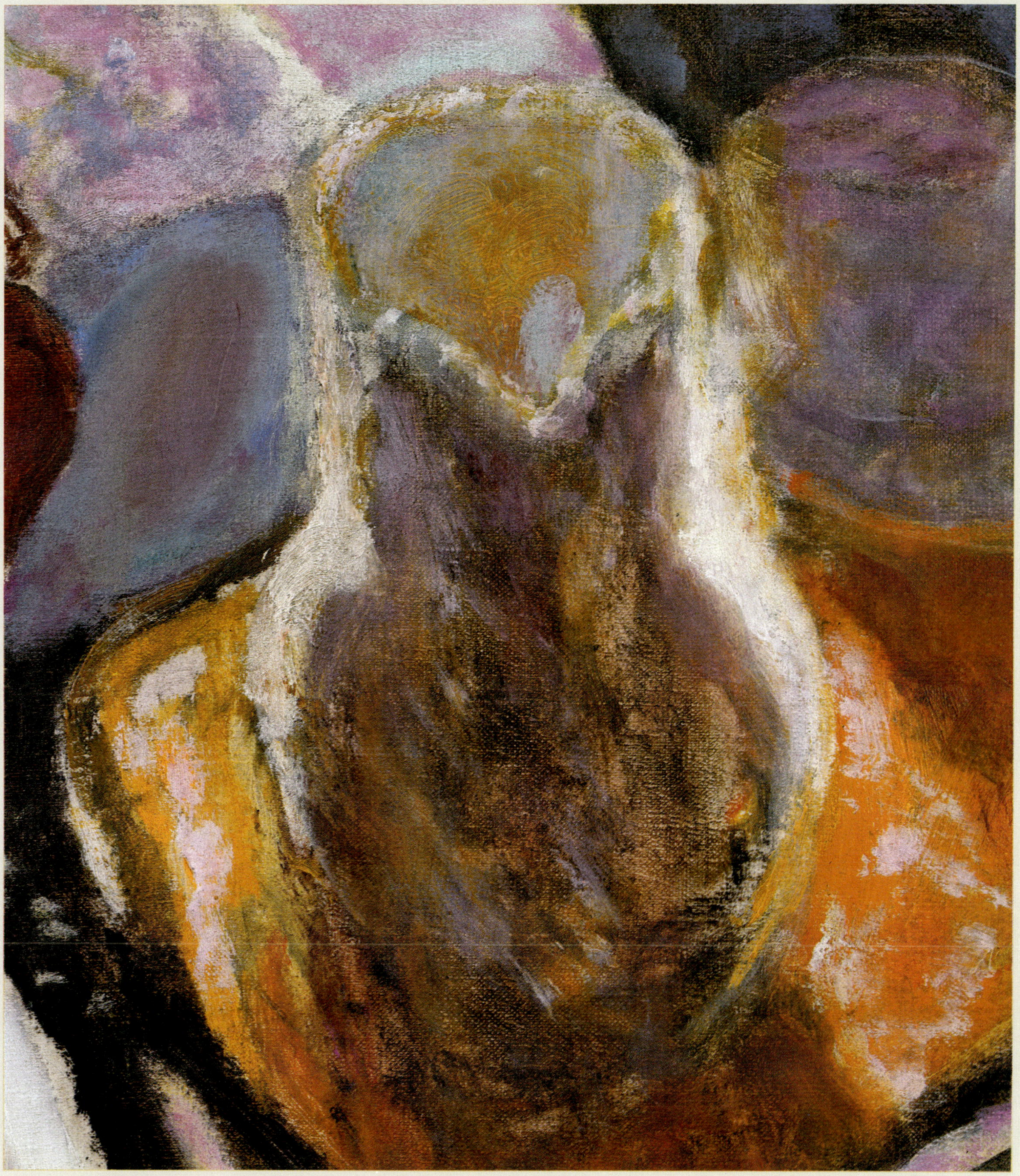

# 1921
# 1940

**Dada and Surrealism**

The Dada-Surrealist Movement is now part of art history more in spite of, than because of, its initial aims. Dada began as an anti-art movement or, at least, a movement against the way art was appreciated by what considered itself the civilized world; Surrealism was much more than an art movement and it thrust home Dada's subversive attack on rational and 'civilized' standards. Whether people are aware of it or not, the Dada and Surrealist revolt has helped to change modern consciousness.

Dada had no formal aesthetic, virtually disregarding easel painting, but the Dadaists shared a nihilistic ethic. The word 'Dada', ambiguously denoting both 'hobby-horse' and 'father', was arrived at by chance and gained immediate acceptance by its suitably childish and nonsensical ring. An international movement originating in Zürich and New York at the height of the First World War, it quickly spread to Berlin, Cologne, Hanover, Paris and, to some extent, Russia.

This revolt was against the senseless barbarities of war. It pinpointed the hypocrisy of those who felt that art created spiritual values. Civilization – despite Christianity, despite museums – had indeed broken down when thousands of grown men shelled each other day after day, from muddy trenches. It was no use for the person 'of sensibility', one of Dada's early targets, to take refuge in beauty.

The first step was to make negative gestures; to attack the icons of the old culture. It was in this iconoclastic spirit that in 1917 Marcel Duchamp put a moustache and beard in black crayon on a colored reproduction of Leonardo da Vinci's *Mona Lisa* (*c* 1502).

'The Dadaist', said the German poet Richard Huelsenbeck (1892-1974),'is a man of reality who loves wine, women and advertising.' The Berlin Dadaists, such as Raoul Hausmann (1886-1971), particularly liked the technique of photomontage, using illustrations and advertisements cut out of popular magazines. The Dadaists adapted the Cubist idea of collage to new purpose, that of making puzzling or strikingly incongruous juxtapositions of images and letters. The collages of Kurt Schwitters (1887-1948) in Hanover were subversive because they were made of litter – bus tickets, sweet wrappings and other scraps. Duchamp's 'ready-mades' likewise tended to start life as objects of unmitigated ordinariness: the snow shovel, urinal and hat rack.

Other significant artists connected with the Dada Movement are Man Ray (1890-1976), whose basic tool was the camera and who invented the rayograph (an object placed on photographic paper was briefly exposed), Francis Picabia (1878-1953), an eclectic artist; Jean Arp (1887-1966), a poet and a sculptor, and Max Ernst (1891-1976) a collagist who was to become one of the great Surrealist painters. Writers and poets, such as Hugo Ball (1886-1927) and Tristan Tzara (1896-1963), were at least as prominent as the artists. Dada gave much to the Surrealist Movement and was finally absorbed by it in Paris in the mid-1920s.

Surrealism probably had more influence on twentieth-century art than any other movement except Cubism. It began as a literary movement, involving a special philosophy and lifestyle for its members and has been compared to religion in its aim and practices. It lost no opportunity to attack the Pope as a symbol of the restrictive authority of the established order, and it replaced him with one of its own, the poet André Breton (1896-1966) who was capable of 'excommunicating' those he thought misguided or recalcitrant: Salvador Dali was expelled in 1937. Breton developed a political program for the improvement of society but in practice, because politics invariably involve compromise, this proved incompatible with the major Surrealist aim of exploring and liberating the creative powers of the unconscious mind.

In 1924 Breton published his first *Manifeste du surréalisme* defining the movement 'once and for all' as he put it: 'SURREALISM , noun, masc. Pure psychic automatism by which it is intended to express either verbally or in writing, the true function of thought. Thought dictated in the absence of all control exerted by reason, and outside all aesthetic or more preoccupations. ENCYCL. Philos. Surrealism is based on the belief in the superior reality of certain forms of associations heretofore neglected, in the omnipotence of the dream and in the disinterested play of thought. It leads to the permanent destruction of all other psychic mechanisms and to the substitution for them in the solution of the principal problems of life.'

At this stage, in 1924, there was no mention of painting but under the aegis of Breton, the Surrealists developed pronounced likes and dislikes in both the literature and the art of past and present. Breton liked pre-Freudian demonstrations of the 'unconscious', such as the eighteenth-century English gothic novel and the nonsense writings of Lewis Carroll (1832-1898) and Edward Lear (1812-1888).

Admiring the primitive mystery suggested by Gauguin's work in Tahiti, the Surrealists wanted an art to wonder and marvel at, not an art of reason and balance but something miraculous and mystical. They were great collectors of the products of 'primitive' cultures such as Oceanic sculpture. (The Fauves and the Cubists had already 'discovered' African sculpture.) In European painting they looked behind the classical tradition for obsessions and eccentricities of vision and imagination: for example, the views of hell with its hybrid monsters by Hieronymous Bosch (1453-1516);

the bizarre results of the obsession of Paolo Uccello (1396/7-1475) with perspective; the fantastic and menacing prisons of Giovanni Piranesi (1720-1778), nightmares of Henri Fuseli (1741-1825) and the black period of Francisco de Goya (1746-1828). In the nineteenth century, they found Impressionism too naturalistic, too rational. They preferred Pre-Raphaelite and Symbolist dreamlike images. Scorning fashion, Breton was a devotee of the visionary paintings of Gustave Moreau (1828-1898), and at a time when art nouveau was disregarded by the *cognoscenti*, the Surrealists marveled at its wrought iron plants as though the transformation of natural organic forms into metal was a sort of alchemy. They found Cubism too rational, too logical (although an exception was made for Picasso's totemic proto-Cubist painting *Les demoiselles d'Avignon*. Picasso himself was also a special case, being held in awe as a phenomenon and a sort of unordained priest of Surrealism.) The Surrealists preferred the 'primitive' vision of Henri Rousseau (1844-1910). They rejected Futurism, preferring the Metaphysical painters, especially the haunting enigmas of Giorgio de Chirico (b 1888).

André Breton's phrase 'pure psychic automatism' was intended to apply to the process of writing and Breton even gave practical

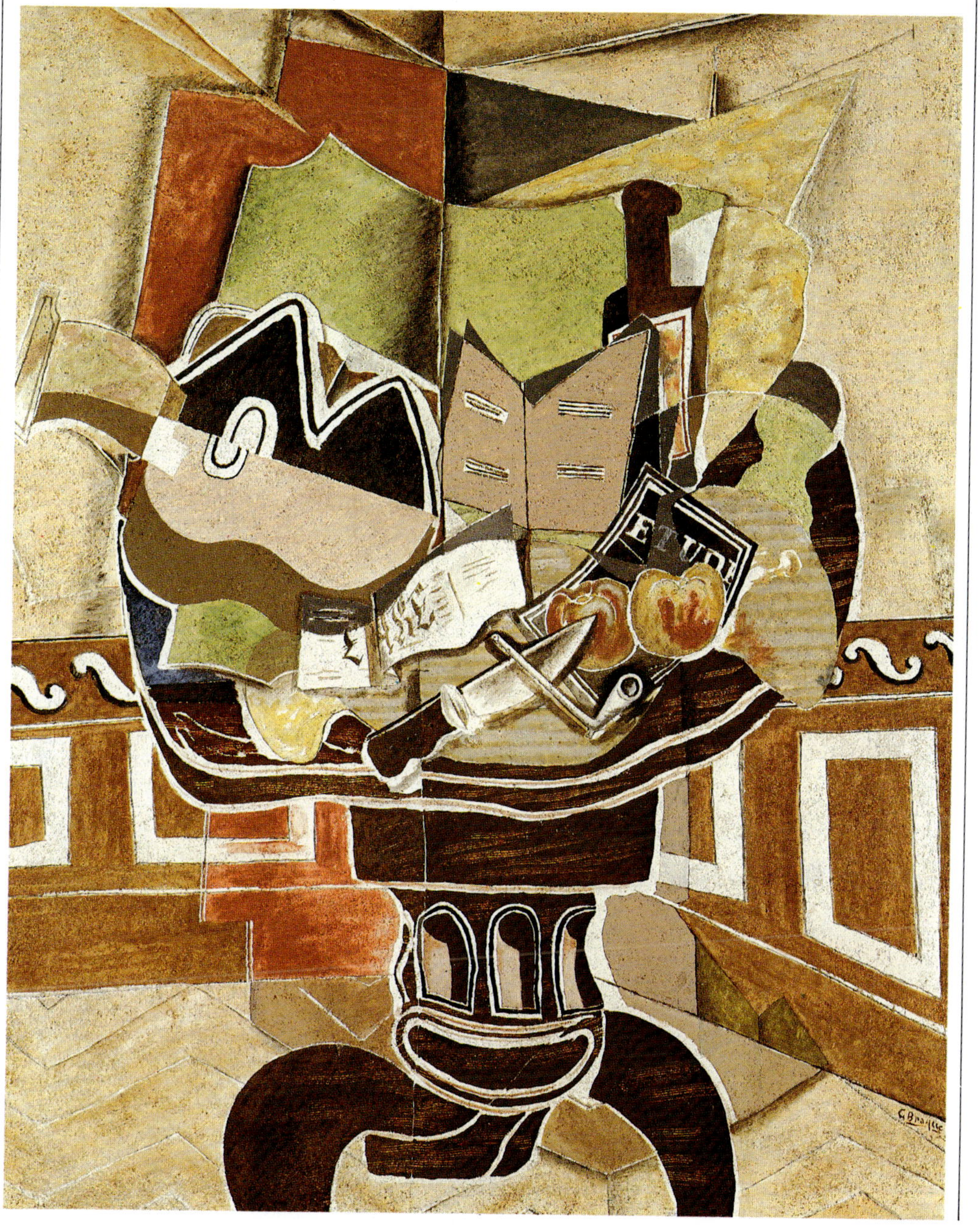

LEFT *At the time Braque painted* The Round Table *(1929), as well as executing nudes and landscapes, he was also concentrating on still lifes in the French classical tradition. Strongly emphasizing structure, Braque's treatment of form had become more realistic and his very restricted palette had become very rich.*

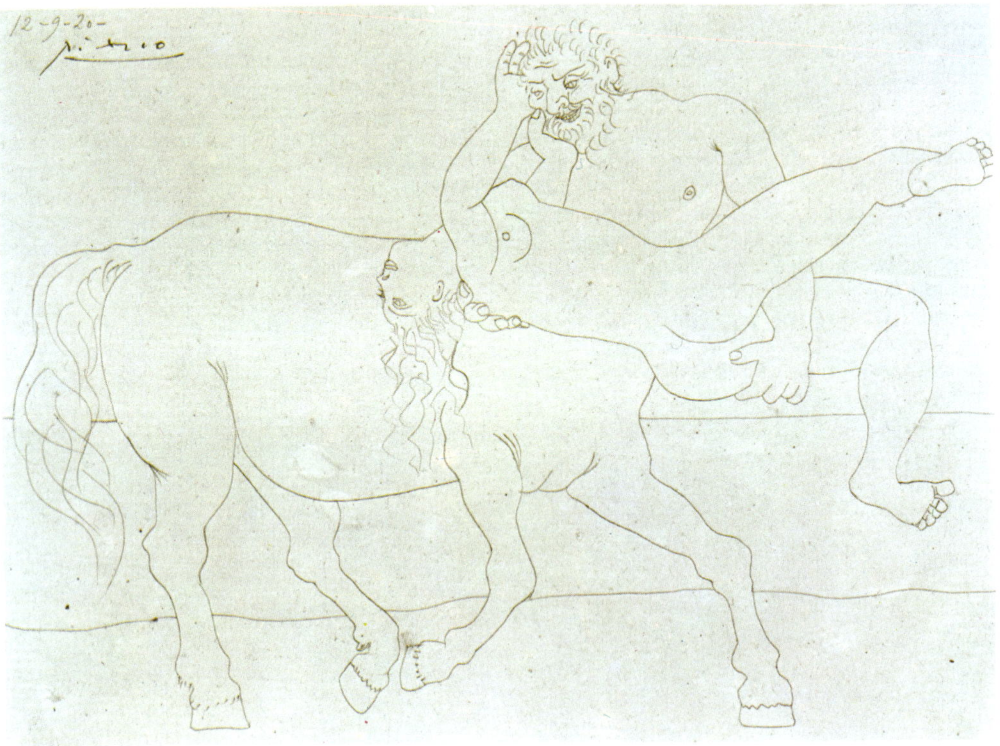


*RIGHT Picasso drew* Nessus and Dejanira *in 1920, while he was developing what finally evolved into a classical drawing style, which had a volumetric quality and, at the same time, was subject to the Cubist experiment.*

hints on how to do it. In 1930 he published his second *Manifeste du surréalisme* in which he defined 'surreality' as the reconciliation of the reality of dreams with the reality of everyday life into a higher synthesis.

Underlying the interest in automatism and dream lay the Surrealist notion of what was called 'objective chance'. They believed that the existence of coincidences (events for which there were no rational explanations) was evidence and that true reality was not ordered or logical. Access to reality could only be gained through the unconscious mind.

**Surrealist painting**

Three painters too great to be contained by Surrealism – Picasso, Klee and Miró – produced Surrealist work, while remaining somewhat aloof from the group. Miró and Picasso created improvisatory images and techniques that were ambiguous and suggestive rather than figurative. *The Three Dancers,* painted by Picasso in 1925, is a brilliant example of this kind of painting. Klee's 'poetry of the heart', was a deceptively simple attempt to transcend the gulf between people and nature, and is at once abstract and representational.

There is no dominant painting style in Surrealism. Considered from the point of view of technique it exhibited three main tendencies. The first tendency (which proved in the short term to be the most innovatory in terms of physical working methods) was that of discovering imagery by mechanical techniques where chance was exploited. The purpose was to 'irritate' the vision, to stimulate the imagination and to force inspiration.

*Frottage* (rubbing), developed by Ernst and described by him in *Beyond Painting* (1948), comes into this category: 'On 10 August 1925, finding myself one rainy evening in a seaside inn, I was struck by the obsession that showed to my excited gaze the floor-boards upon which a thousand scrubbings had deepened the grooves. I decided then to investigate the symbolism of this obsession and, in order to aid my meditative and hallucinatory faculties, I made from the boards a series of drawings by placing on them, at random, sheets of paper which I undertook to rub with black lead. In gazing attentively at the drawings thus obtained, the dark passages and those of a gently lighted penumbra, I was surprised by the sudden identification of my visionary capacities and by the hallucinatory succession of contradictory images superimposed, one upon the other, with the persistence and rapidity characteristic of amorous memories.'

Surrealist painting dates from the invention of *frottage,* although Ernst had used collage in a similarly 'psycho-technical' fashion. He brought together scientific images,'... elements of figuration so remote that the sheer absurdity of that collection provoked a sudden intensification of the visionary faculties in me and brought forth an hallucinatory succession of contradictory signs... These visions themselves called for new planes, for their meeting in a new unknown... It was enough then to add to these catalog pages, in painting or drawing, and thereby obediently reproducing only *that which was to be seen within me*, a color, a pencil mark, a landscape foreign to the represented objects, the desert, a tempest, a geological cross-section, a floor, a single straight line signifying the horizon, to obtain a faithful fixed image of my hallucination...'. A list of the techniques or psycho-techniques of the Surrealists, therefore, is no more than a list of aids to vision in which the spiritual overwhelms the technical.

By the technique of *grattage* (scraping) Ernst transferred *frottage* from drawing to oil painting. In *decalcomania* (transferring) the image was obtained by laying arbitrary patches of color on a piece of paper. A clean piece was then rubbed gently on top. When separated, strange grottos, exotic vegetation and underwater scenes suggested themselves to the imagination. A picture was made by chance.

*Fumage* (smoking) was a technique of automatism invented by Wolfgang Paalen (1907-1959) in the late 1930s. Here the chance imagery was provoked. by moving a candle under a sheet of paper; and random areas of soot would develop from which the mind could form images. All these techniques depend for their application upon the hallucinatory mind of the artist.

**Dali and the Veristic Surrealists**

The second tendency of Surrealist painting, sometimes called Veristic Surrealism, was to depict with meticulous clarity and often in great detail a world analogous to the dream world. Before responding to the Metaphysical painting of de Chirico and being brought into the Surrealist Movement in 1929, Salvador Dali had admired the command of detail in artists such as Ernest Meissonier (1815-1891) and the Pre-Raphaelites; his physical technique continued to reflect this admiration. Dali's importance for Surrealism was that he invented his own 'psycho-technique', a method he called 'critical paranoia'. He deliberately cultivated delusions similar to those of paranoiacs in the cause of wresting hallucinatory images from his conscious mind. Dali's images – his bent watches, his figures, half-human, half chest of drawers – have made him the most famous of all Surrealist painters. But when he changed to a more academic style in 1937 Breton expelled him from the Movement.

The Surrealist paintings of René Magritte (1898-1967) combine convincing descriptions of people and objects in bizarre juxtapositions with a competent but pedestrian physical painting technique. The results question everyday reality, stand it on its head and present a new surreality. These odd juxtapositions were explored by the English painter Edward Wadsworth, who used tempera to achieve a dreamlike clarity in his work. Surrealists approved of *desire* in its attack on reason and the Veristic Surrealism of Paul Delvaux (b 1897), in which women appear in the cool surroundings of noble architecture and exude an hallucinatory eroticism.

Veristic Surrealism subdivides into a second main type in the work of Yves Tanguy. The dreamlike visions that Tanguy produced from the unconscious layers of the mind contain meticulously described yet imaginary objects. There are no bizarre juxtapositions. His is a self-consistent world that convinces on its own terms as in a dream. In the work of the Veristic Surrealists, the surface of the painting tends to be flat and glossy: the viewer is reminded as little as possible that the illusion is composed of paint and the hallucinatory effect is thereby enhanced.

**'Automatic' techniques**

The third main Surrealist tendency drew more attention to the materials used by the artist. This tendency survived the break-up of the Surrealist movement during the Second World War. It began with the 'automatic' drawing technique practiced by Miró, Paul Klee and André Masson (b 1896). The line of the pen or other instrument was allowed to rove at will without any conscious planning. Masson tried to achieve the same sort of result in painting, by drawing a mass of lines in an adhesive substance on the canvas, adding color by coatings of different colored sand. After the end of the Surrealist epoch, this approach was carried into painting in New York by Arshile Gorky (1904-1948), the 'white writing' paintings of Mark Tobey (1890-1976) and, above all, the vast abstractions of Jackson Pollock which contain a strong element of drawing with paint while the artist was in an ecstatic trance.

**Contrasts: Mondrian and Bonnard**

Piet Mondrian developed his Geometrical Abstractionism from Cubism and Fauvism. His early work – for example, *The Red Tree* (1908) – shows a Fauvist color influence. The form, although derived from, and much influenced by, Cubism, had been refined and ordered. Mondrian eventually reduced the representational elements and the pictorial construction into relationships of form and rhythms.

The Post-Impressionist Pierre Bonnard occupies a relatively isolated position in the art of the 1920s and 1930s, and his work appears out-of-step with contemporary developments. But Bonnard's rich luminous palette and his flexible and expressive style (in fact, meticulously painted) was a reminder of the more pictorial possibilities of painting.

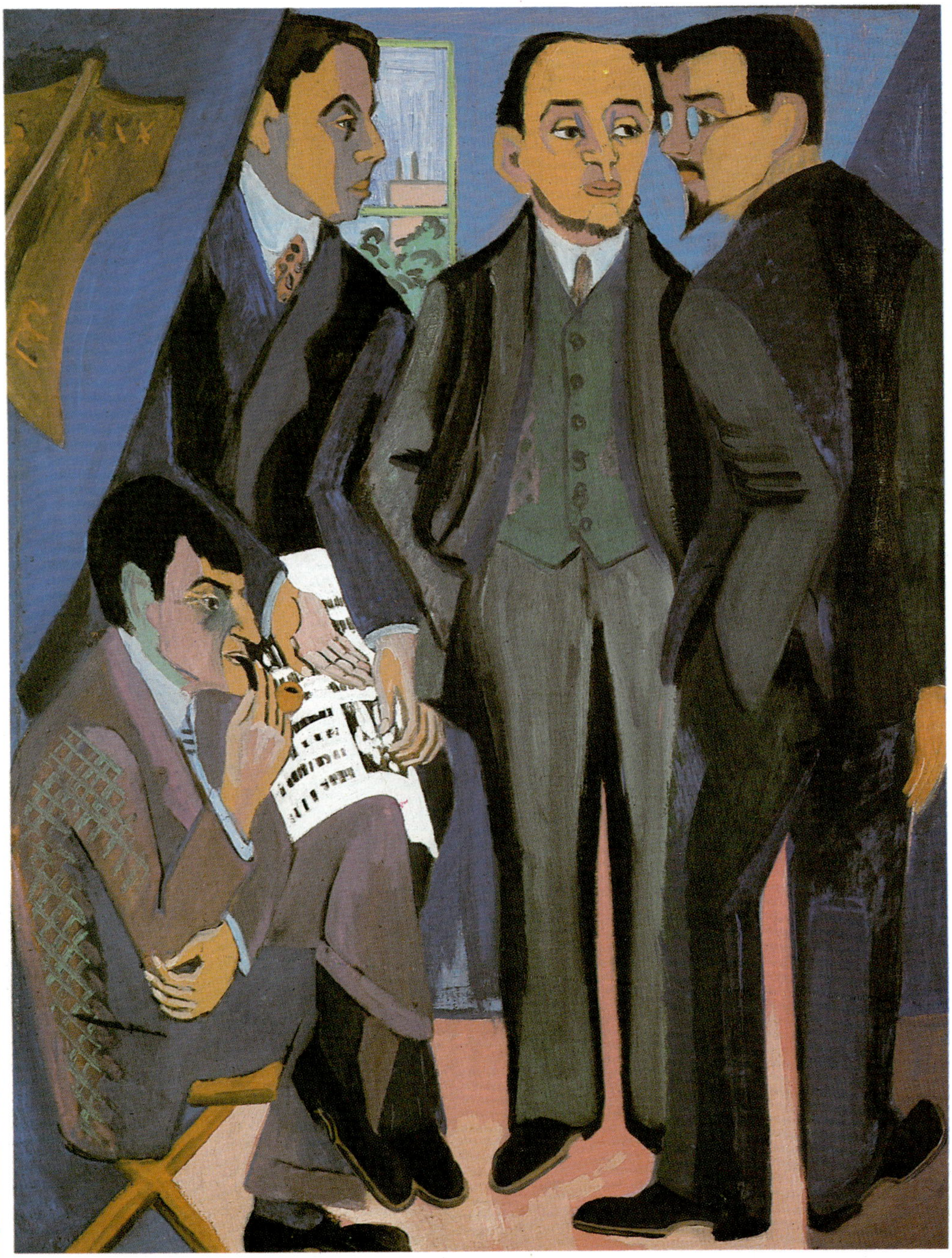

*RIGHT Ernst Kirchner's* Artists of the Brücke *(1925). Kirchner was the most gifted, sensitive and vulnerable of the Brücke artists, who met in 1903 in Dresden. Influenced by Munch and Oceanic and other primitive art, they evolved a rather wild, archaic German version of Expressionism. They attempted to express psychologically and symbolically a vaguely conceived creative urge and a sense of revolt against the established order. Kirchner wrote: 'We accept all the colors which, directly or indirectly, reproduce the pure creative impulse.' By the time Kirchner painted this work, the members of the Brücke had long been following divergent paths and the group style had disappeared. It was painted at a time when he was recovering from a mental breakdown; he was becoming more and more engrossed in purely painterly problems.*

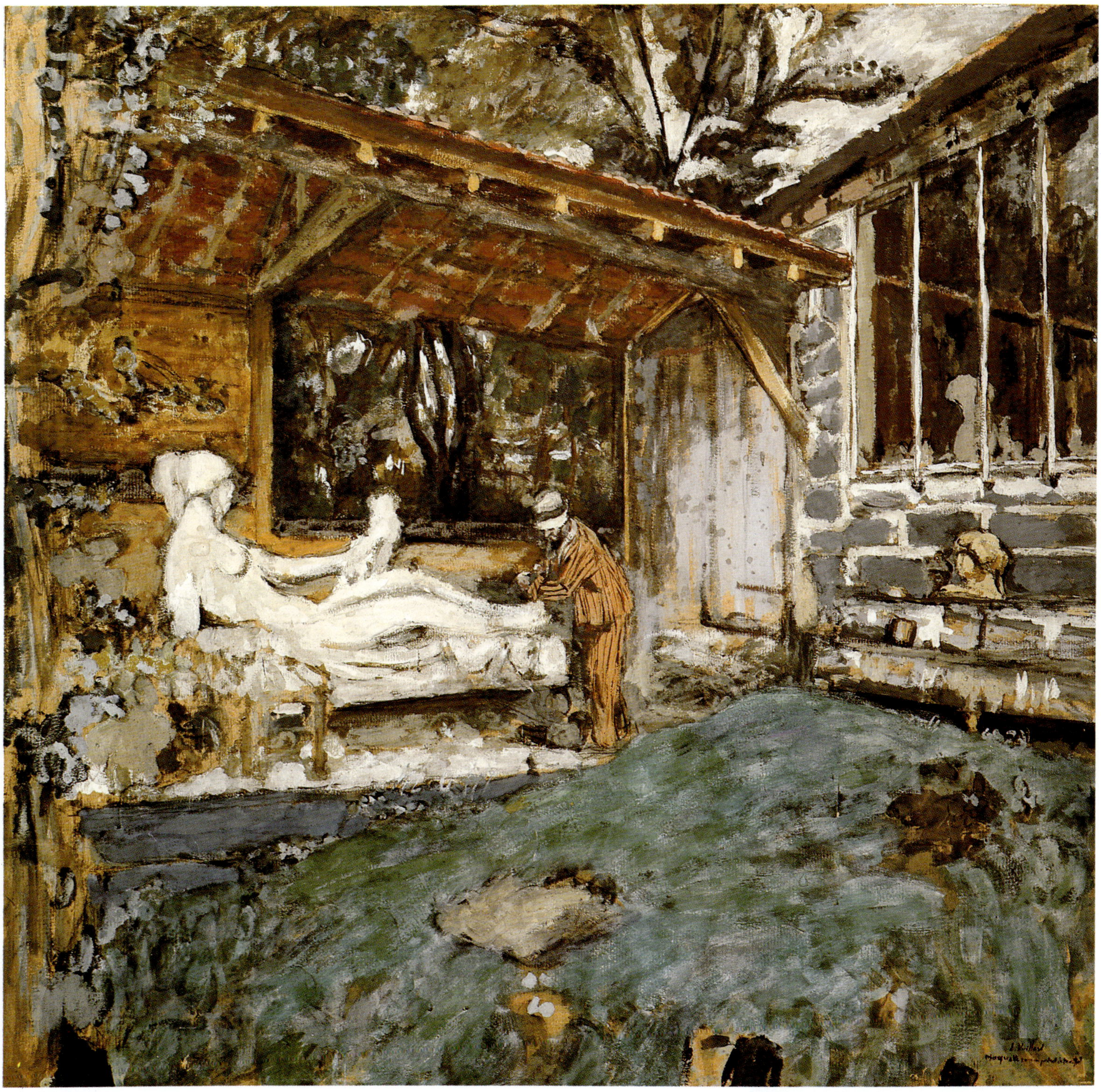

ABOVE *A painter paints a sculptor's homage to a dead painter —* Edouard Vuillard's Maillol at Work on the Cézanne Memorial *(c 1930). It was left to Vuillard and Bonnard to preserve the lyrical pictorial qualities of nineteenth-century painting during a period of technical experimentation. They both concentrated on the quiet intimacy of their immediate environment.*

# FERNAND LEGER

*Still Life with a Beer Mug* (1921)
Oil on canvas, 92.1cm × 60cm/36in × $23\frac{1}{2}$in

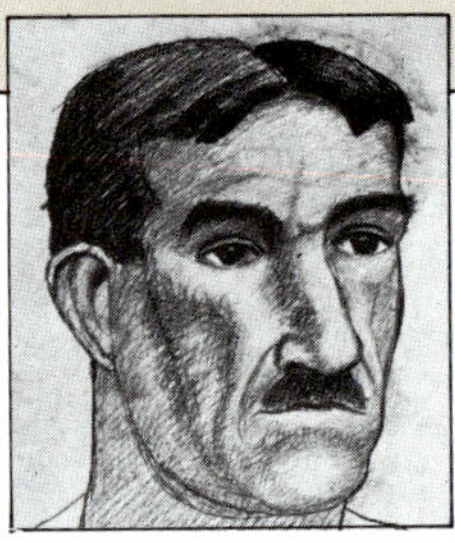

Léger wanted to develop the ideas about Cubism into an artistic vocabulary commensurate with the machine age. He saw modern life as characterized by dissonance, dynamism and movement, which he felt could only be expressed in painting through contrasts of color, line and form. In the various works which Léger completed in Paris before 1914, movement meant fragmentation, but after the war, he began to reconcile traditional subjects with his new feeling for the beauty of some manufactured, every-day objects, which were seen in terms of flat planes of bright, contrasting colors. In *Still Life with a Beer Mug*, which was painted during 1921 and 1922, the shaded modelling of the curtain, objects on the table and the interior view of the mug contrasts with the flatly painted geometric shapes and the patterned rendering of other forms. This illustrates Léger's preoccupation with plastic contrasts, which he described as follows in 1923: 'I group contrary values together; flat surfaces opposed to modelled surfaces; volumetric figures opposed to the flat facades of houses . . .; pure flat tones opposed to grey, modulated tones, or the reverse'. Léger did not want simply to copy a manufactured object, but felt that its clean, precise beauty should be accepted as a challenging starting point which would, if necessary, be distorted to achieve the final desired result.

Léger found his source material in what he described as 'the lower-class environment, with its aspects of crudeness and harshness, of tragedy and comedy, always hyperactive'. Léger's work can thus be seen as a response to a view of the world as being in flux and opposition on which, through its being rendered in art, order is imposed through the methodical preparation and execution of the work. The canvas of *Still Life with a Beer Mug* was divided into 24 squares, some of which can still be seen on the canvas. Léger's rather aggressive statements about his work should not obscure the fact that *Still Life with a Beer Mug* is an outstanding example of sensitive and subtle handling of the oil painting medium. Léger took vast pains to achieve exactly the result he wanted. In this work slight adjustments were made in the final paint layer even after the work had been photographed at the Galérie Simon in Paris.

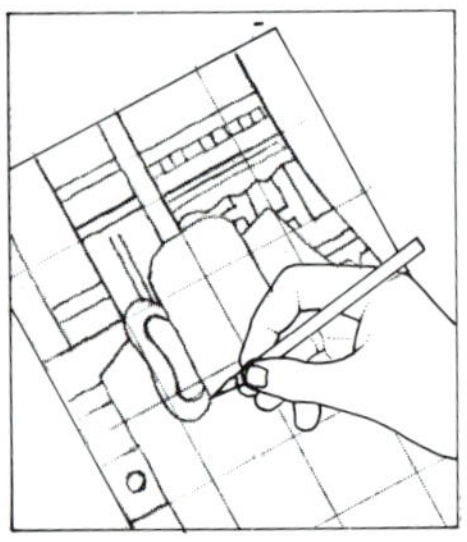

**1.** Léger began by doing a detailed drawing in pencil, which he squared up preparatory to transferring the design.

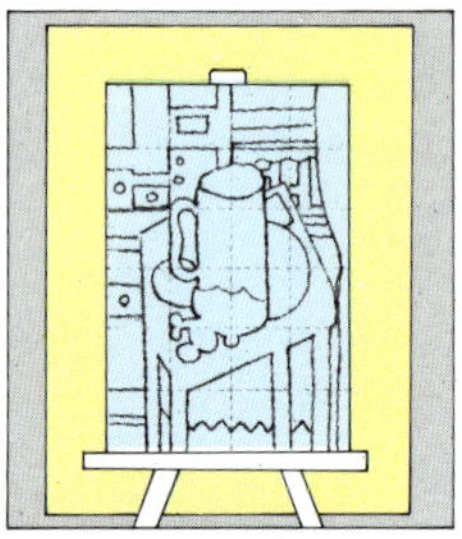

**2.** He prepared a preliminary painting, for which he used a squared-up grid. This was in a different format to the final version, measuring 65 × 46 cm (26 × 18 in).

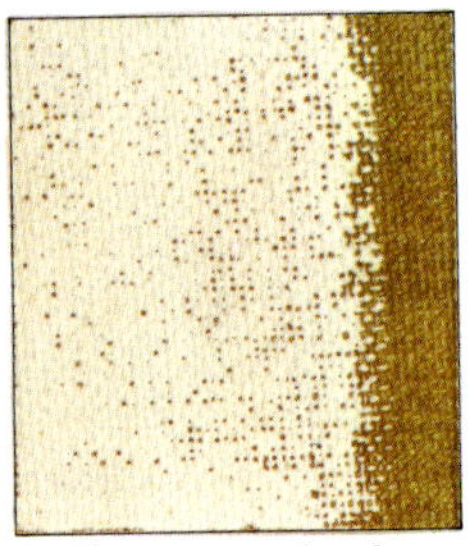

**3.** The support for the final version is an open simple weave, linen canvas. It was heavily sized before the off-white ground was applied thinly and evenly all over the canvas.

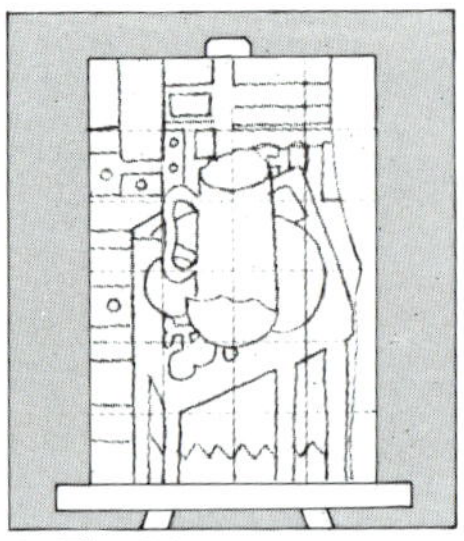

**4.** The 24 squares were executed in pencil and the design was then also sketched in. The moderately rich oil paint was applied fairly thickly, but without impasto and with little brushmarking.

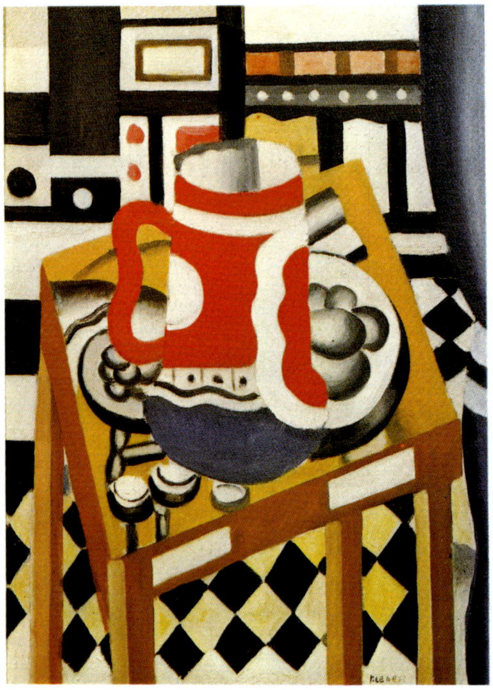

This preliminary study shows how Léger's conception of the work changed in the final painting. In the study, the background tends to draw the viewer's eye away from the central image of the beer mug, while in the final picture, contrasts were added and strengthened.

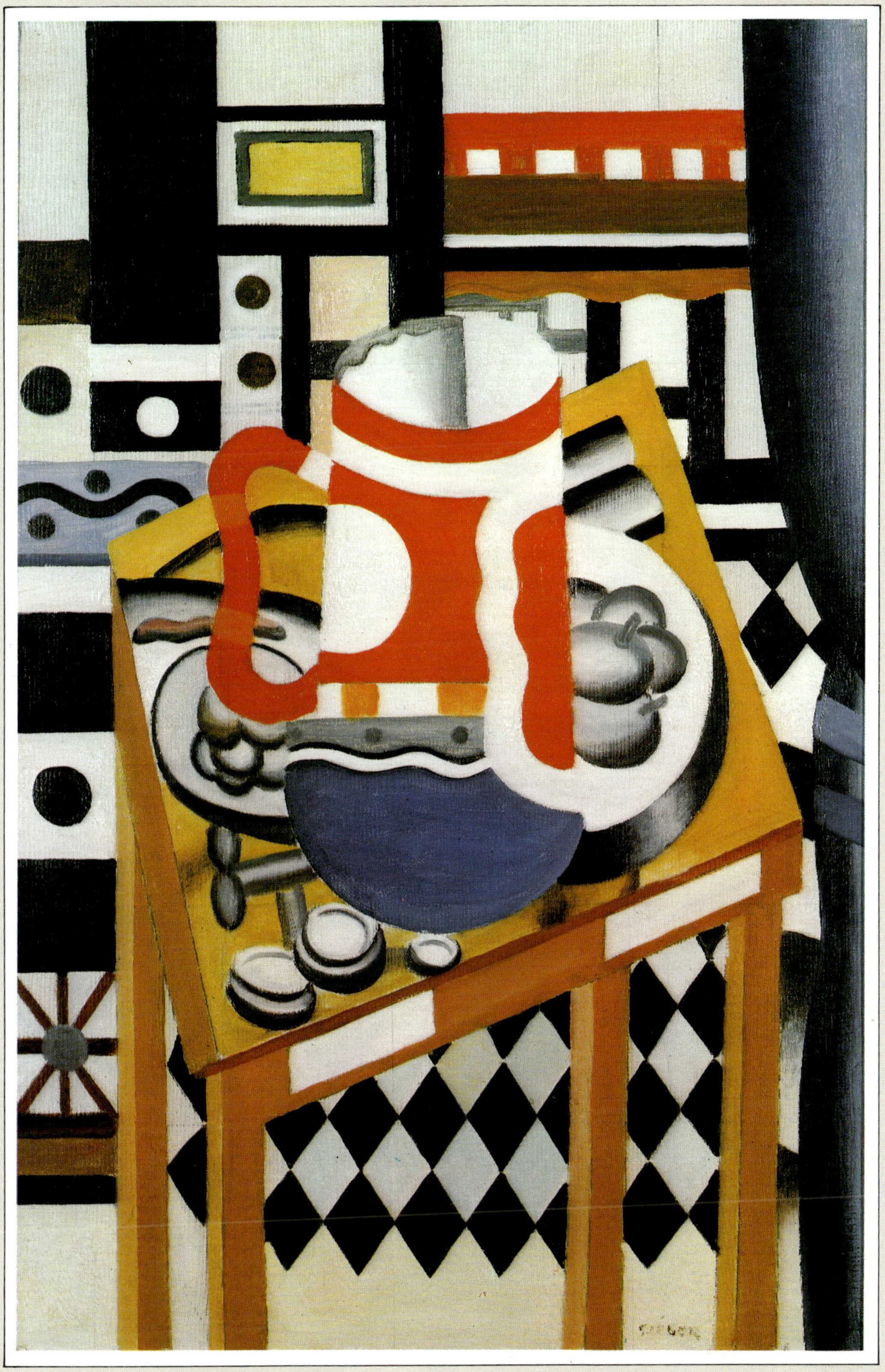

Still Life with a Beer Mug *shows an extremely subtle handling of oils. The strong color contrasts show a range of carefully worked tones. The black tones are played against white. The warm colors, vermilion, cadmium orange and yellow, are played against the cool tints and shades of Prussian blue, and these intense areas are relieved by the delicate interaction of almost creamy washes of pale lemon yellow and pale blue-green in the diamond pattern below the table. The picture retains the fine but emphatic canvas pattern which shows through the ground. Indeed, the ground itself makes up much of the white background.*

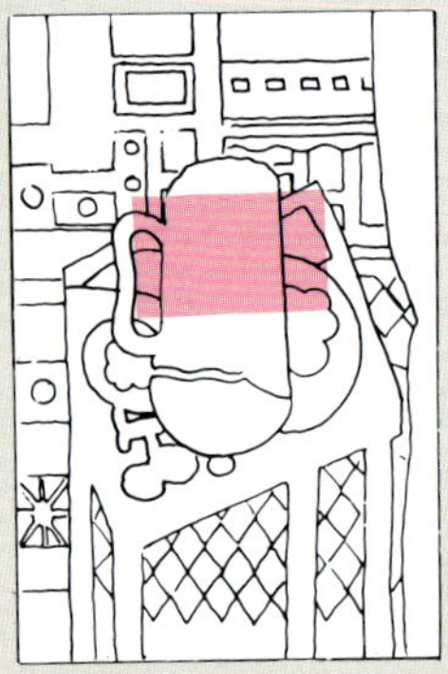

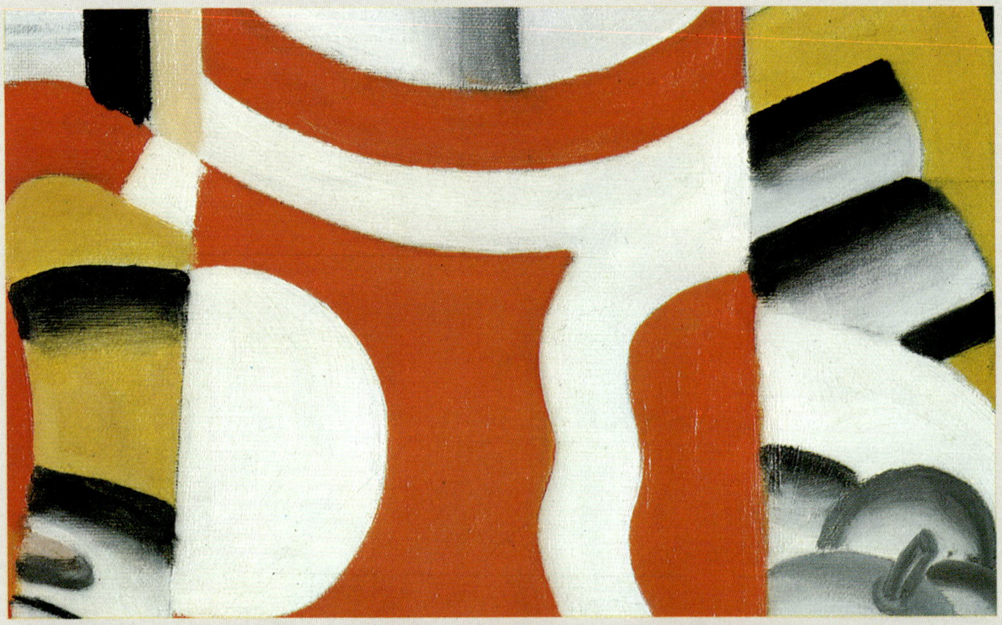

*The strong tonal contrasts which are characteristic of Léger's work can be clearly seen in this detail. The brushstrokes on the beer mug and plate are also typical. The pencil underdrawing can be detected around the mug and plate.*

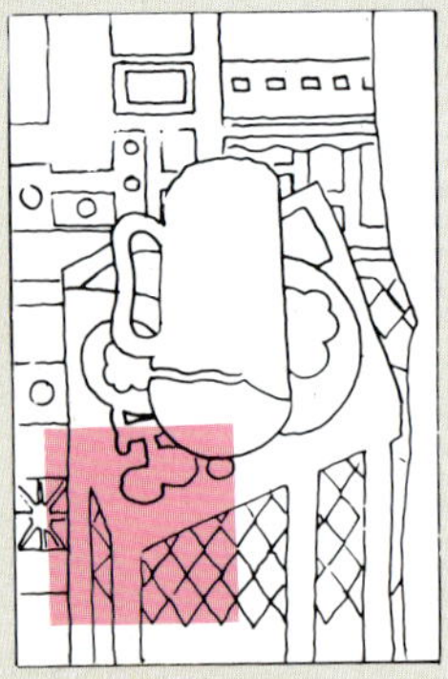

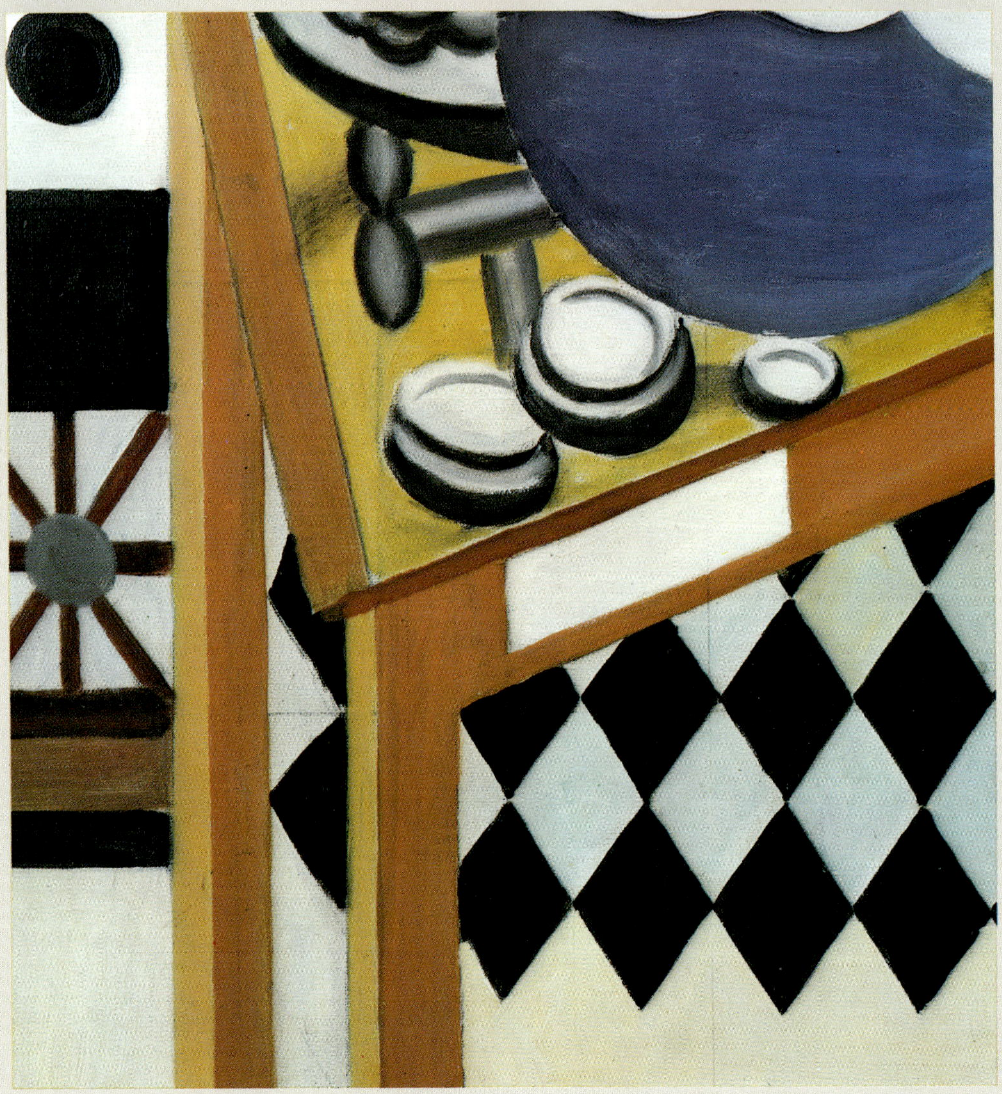

*Léger's subtle tonal variations which contrast so effectively with the strong colors are shown in this detail. The apparently black and white floor under the table is, in fact, a mixture of pale gray and cream tones which changes from square to square. Similarly the grays in the objects on the table also consist of a careful blend of tones ranging from black to white.*

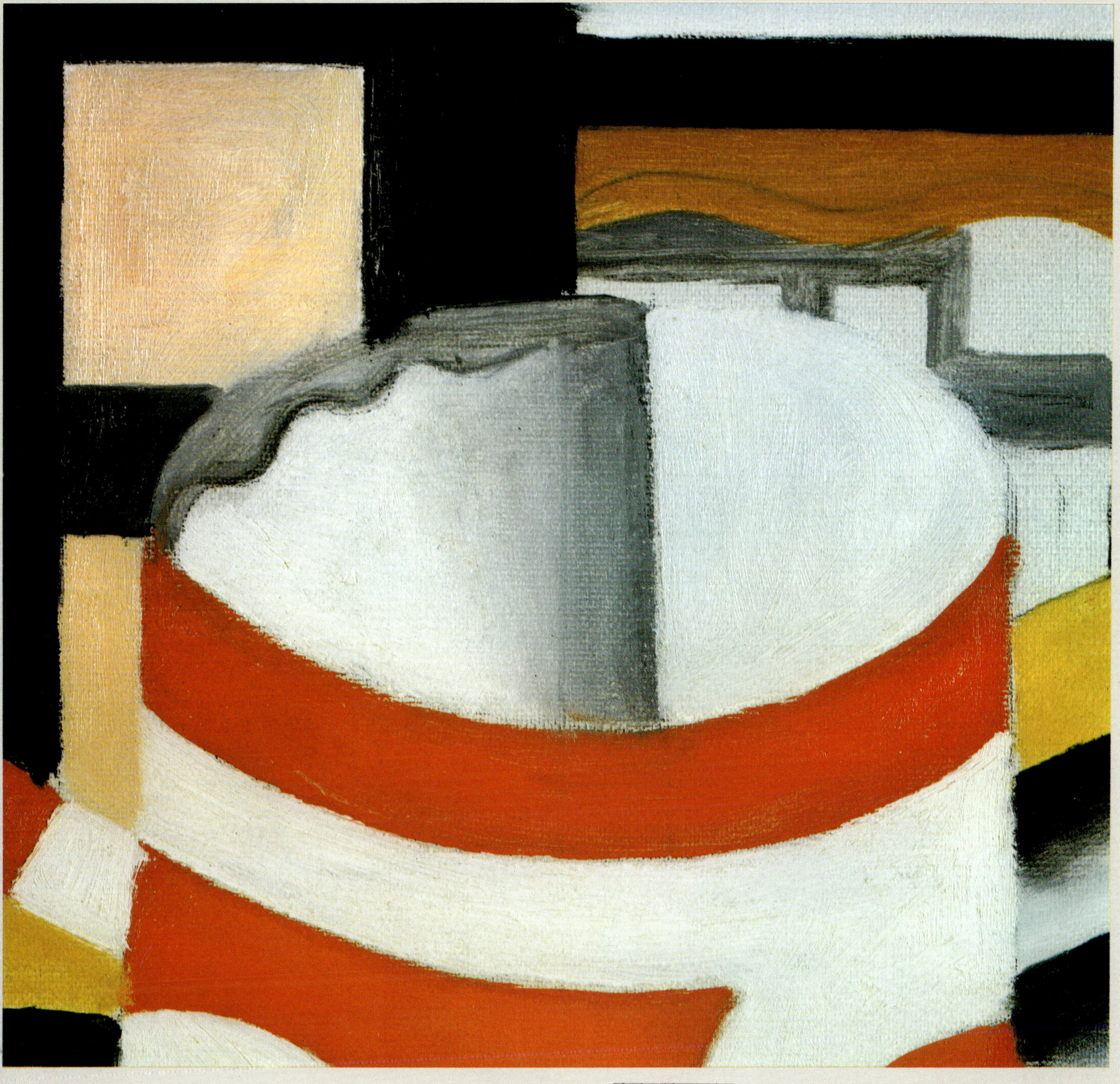

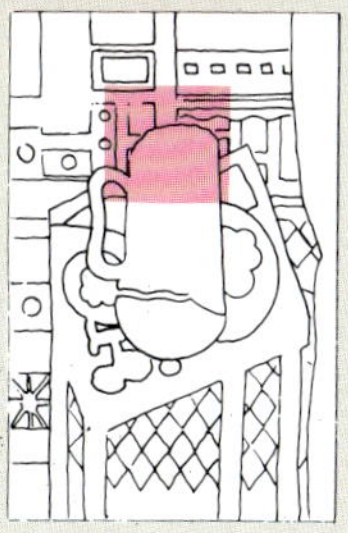

**Actual size detail**
*Léger's brushwork can be clearly seen in this detail. On the right, the ground shows through. The change in position of the orange line can also be detected — Léger made many such changes in order to achieve precisely the effect he desired. The inside of the beer mug is executed using gray shading on one side and leaving heavily brushed white on the other. The grays on the shaded side are much less thickly applied and the canvas texture shows through.*

# EDWARD HOPPER

*House by the Railroad* (1925)
Oil on canvas, 60.9cm × 73.6cm/24in × 29in

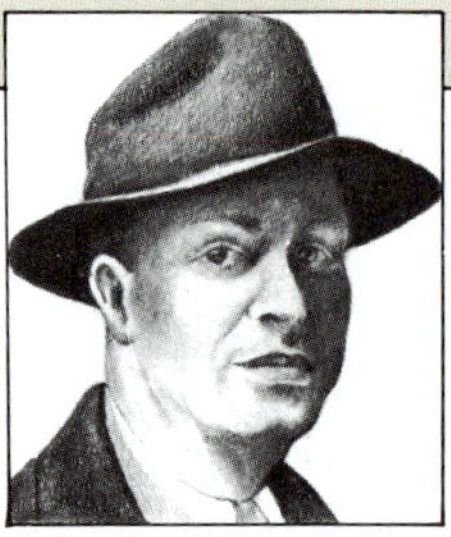

Edward Hopper is best known for his oil paintings, but they did not generally bring him critical or financial success until he was in his late forties. During the first fifteen years of his career, Hopper was only able to paint in his leisure time and, until 1924, when an exhibition of his watercolors in New York sold out, he had to support himself as a commercial artist and illustrator. He also made over 50 etchings between about 1915 and 1924.

In 1955, Hopper remarked that: 'After I took up etching, my paintings seemed to crystallize'. During the early 1920s, he found a satisfactory way of expressing his ideas in oil and, in particular, concentrated on the effects of bright light on solid forms, which may have stemmed from his use of strong tonal contrasts in etching.

In the early 1920s Hopper made few oil paintings, but, after his initial success in 1924, he began to produce and exhibit several oils each year. In 1960 Hopper, who rarely made any statements about his work, commented on his painting technique: 'I have a very simple method of painting. It's to paint directly on the canvas without any funny business . . . I use almost pure turpentine to start with, adding oil as I go along until the medium becomes pure oil. I use as little oil as I possibly can. It's very simple'. In his early years, Hopper made extensive use of free brush-work and applied paint in a thick impasto. Gradually, however, he suppressed any tendency towards technical display and the surface of his paintings became more evenly textured. In his later work, Hopper created a transparent surface by building up the paint surface in thin layers and scraping down and repainting.

Hopper frequently used a straight, horizontal motif, usually a road or railroad track, to construct the space within the picture and to emphasize the division between the picture space and the viewer's world. Indeed, the more the viewer tries to penetrate the depths of a Hopper painting, the more impenetrable it becomes. What holds the viewer is that the artist's vision seems under control and yet, on closer inspection, the viewer realizes that the visible surface is a tissue of improbabilities and unreadable shifts in space. Hopper's view that nature and the contemporary world were incoherent contributed to his artistic vision.

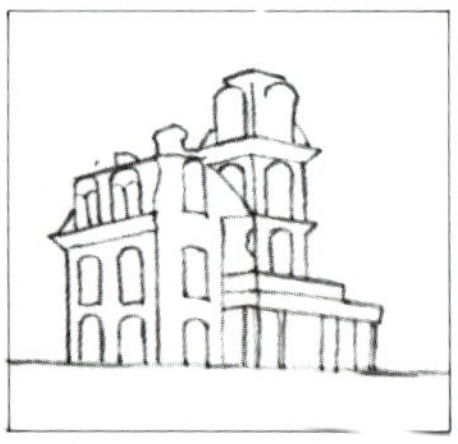

**1.** Indications of the structure of the house were brushed in with a minimum of black paint in a turpentine mixture. The columns and windows on the right shadowed side of the house clearly show this.

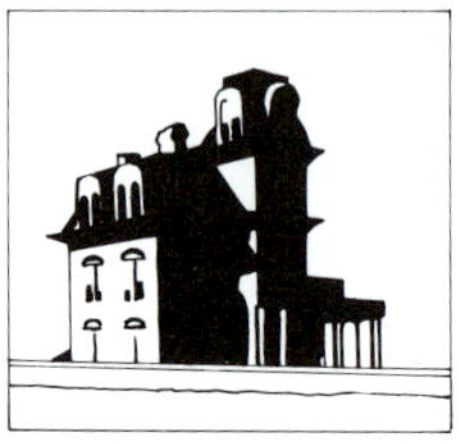

**2.** The house was then painted from dark to light; Hopper gradually added more oil paint to the turpentine and built up the forms with free, often diagonal brush-work.

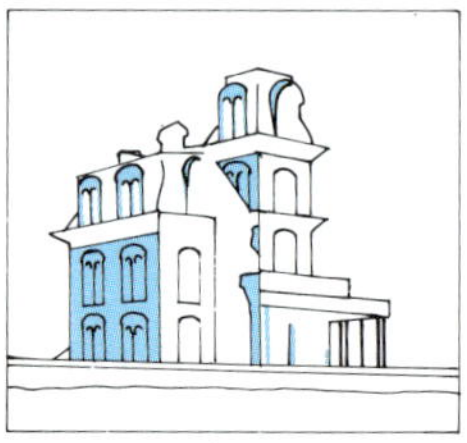

**3.** The side of the house in bright sunlight was executed less freely with transparent darks and opaque lights. Lines of blue were added after the opaque white to define forms.

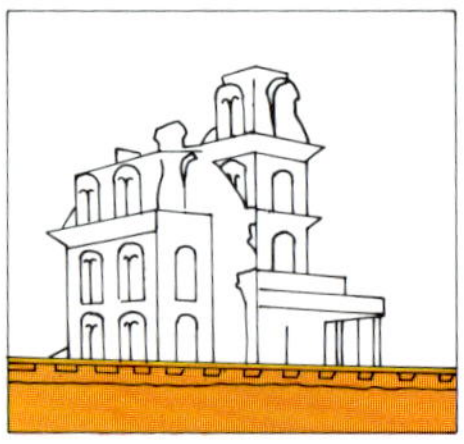

**4.** The railway line and embankment were also executed from dark to light. The orange and ochres on the bed of the track are virtually impasto with short brushstrokes applied in various directions.

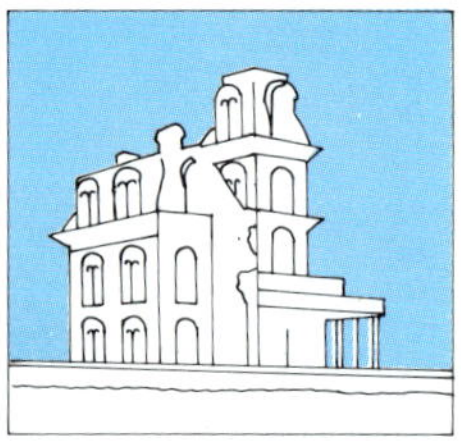

**5.** Although the sky may well have been indicated from the start of the painting, it appears to have been brushed around the form of the house and may have been the final part of Hopper's painting procedure. In the blue areas,the paint is thin with the grain of the canvas clearly visible. White areas were applied more thickly, but not as thick as those of the house, and brushstrokes are visible.

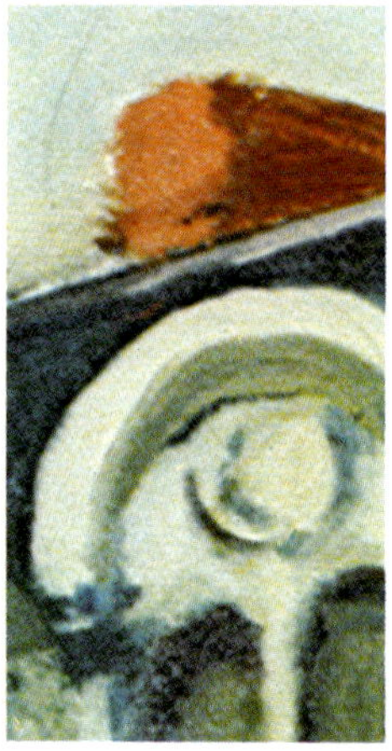

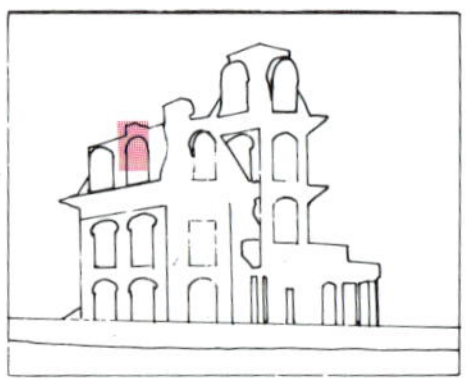

Actual size detail
*The painting was executed working from light to dark and this detail, taken from the bright sunlit side of the house was painted with less freely worked brushstrokes.*

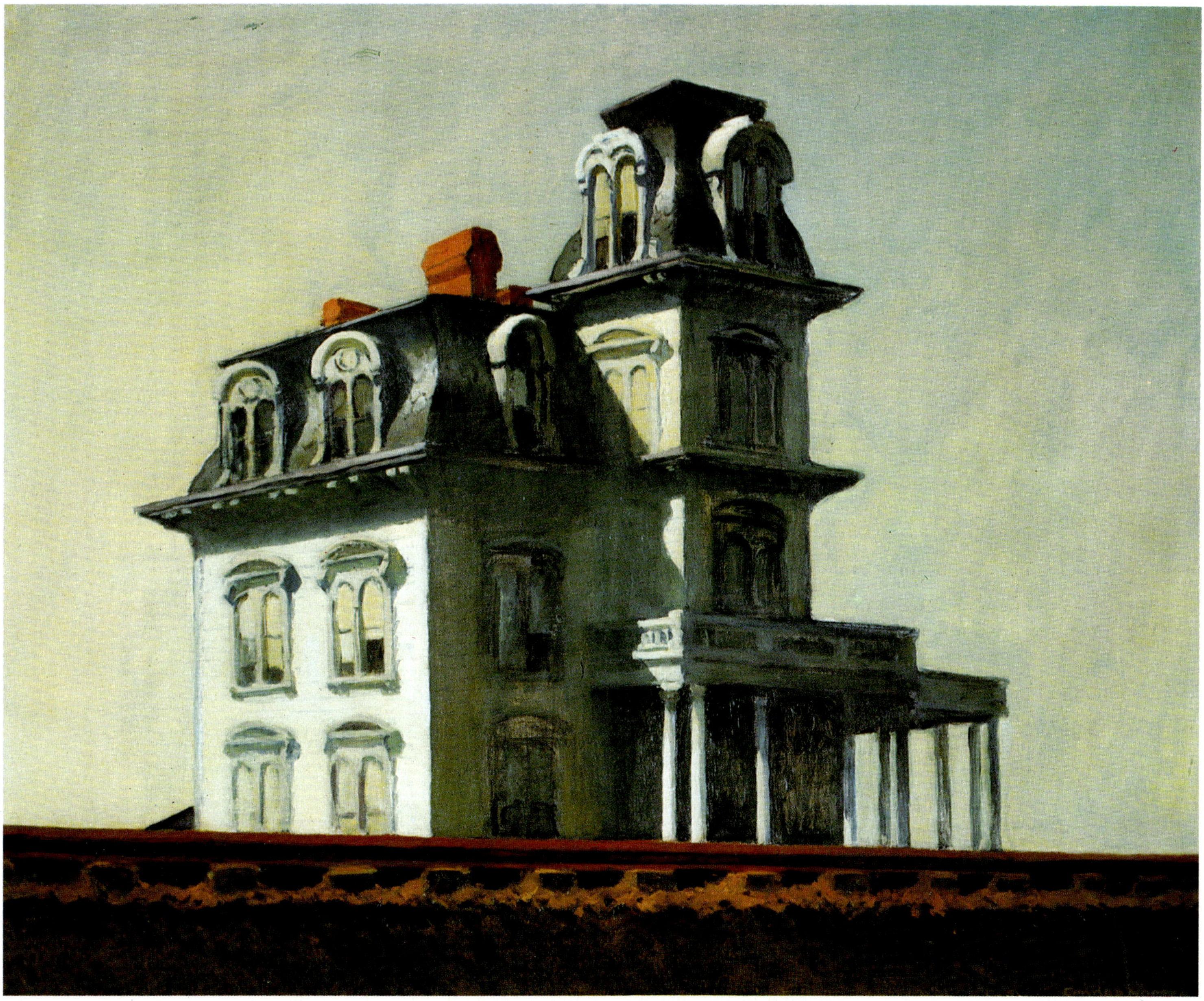

House by the Railroad, *painted in 1925, is Hopper's first painting to represent successfully forms defined and modelled in light. In this painting, a solitary Victorian house and railroad track are represented in a way more expressive of Hopper's imagination than of the real world — most of Hopper's paintings are composites with the subject matter derived from several sources. The observer's viewpoint is not indicated and the track which sweeps across and beyond the edges of the canvas serve to disconnect the house from the ground and the observer's side of the railroad. It is also Hopper's method, which drew from, but did not specifically represent, the American scene which contributes to the strange and slightly disturbing effect of the painting.*

House by the Railroad *has been interpreted as being satirical in intention and it was generally felt that the Victorian houses which Hopper often painted did not provide a serious subject. To this, however, Hopper commented that 'the great realists of European painting have never been too fastidious to depict the architecture of their native lands.' It is clear that Hopper regarded the often grotesque forms of late nineteenth century American architecture as particularly suited to a serious transcription of his vision.*

# JOAN MIRO

*Personage Throwing a Stone at a Bird (1926)*
Oil on canvas
73.7cm × 92.1cm/29in × $36^1/_4$in

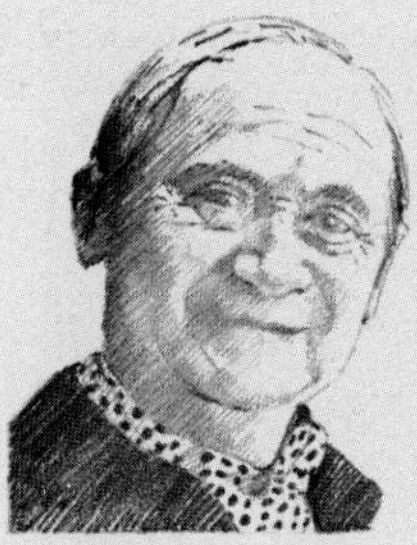

Within the two dominant types of Surrealist painting, Joan Miró must be counted as the master of the 'abstract' and 'automatic' tendency, while Dali and Magritte dispute pre-eminence in the 'illusionist' style. André Breton, the so-called 'high priest' of Surrealism, was immediately impressed by what he called Miró's 'tumultuous entrance' into the Paris scene in 1924, and by 1925 was lauding him as 'the most Surrealist of us all'. Breton's partisan claims notwithstanding, temperamentally Miró was naturally given to emphasize those aspects of drawing and painting which are promoted by unconscious activity. Over a long career he produced a body of work which constitutes an unparalleled contribution of this kind, but which seems to evade the stylist categories that characterize the period.

Like Dali and Picasso, Miró came from Spain, and gravitated to Paris, the center of the international avant-garde. He was born in Barcelona in April 1893, and showed an aptitude for painting early. Miró was encouraged by the gallery-owner Dalman, and he visited exhibitions of work by the Impressionists, Fauves and Cubists.

In 1919 Miró made his first visit to Paris, where he called on Picasso, and was warmly received. From 1920 he spent his summers in Montroig where his parents had property, and wintered in Paris, rapidly making the acquaintance of the now famous *dramatis-personae* who created the Dada and Surrealist Movements. He was closest of all to André Masson who moved to the studio next door.

In 1925 Miró had his own show at the Gallery Pierre, and also took part in the first Surrealist Exhibition at the same venue, which included the work of Arp, de Chirico, Ernst, Klee, Man Ray, Masson and Picasso. Thereafter he played a prominent, if distinctly individual, part in Visual Surrealism, maintaining his own style in the face of the challenge of photographic realism. He continued to exhibit in the International Surrealist Exhibitions of the 1930s and 1940s, and there were a number of important retrospectives and traveling shows all over the world.

A highly imaginative man, Miró was very influenced by the landscape and environment which surrounded him; whether the hot, dry farming community at Montroig which inspired his early detailist masterpieces, or the devastating Spanish Civil War which moved him to paint the most realist of his mature works *Still Life with an Old Shoe* (1937). But this is not to deny the importance of his contact with individual Surrealists and their ideas.

Having established himself exclusively as a painter, Miró was drawn, like other Surrealists, to experiment with a much wider range of materials and techniques from the late 1920s. He incorporated sand and rope into his paintings, and turned also to lithography and *papiers collés*. Just before the Second World War Miró started working on a much larger scale than he had done before, and for the rest of his career he took up occasional commissions for murals and for wall-scale decorations.

*Personage Throwing a Stone at a Bird* (1926) was painted at a time when Miró was working at an intense pitch and in a variety of original and persuasive styles.

By 1926 Miró had moved definitely towards calculation and even anecdote. *Personage* is much more deliberate and posed. Indeed, on one level the work seems to be all about balances and oppositions. The figure throwing the stone, which writer William Rubin aptly characterized as an 'amoeboid biomorph with a cyclopean eye and giant foot', combines the organic contours of its 'body' with the strict linearity of the long straight line that designates its arms. There is a wry enjoyment of the very specific fulcrum in the person's body section, from which the arms lurch in the effort of throwing and which topples the body backwards, drawing attention to the spread-eagled stability of the out-sized foot.

The color and linear components of the picture operate in localized areas to suggest oppositions of space and scale. The tail feathers of the bird 'invert' the sky and foreground hues, as if to signify the bird as an adept of both media; its chromatic head and crest are strikingly complementary, and this is faintly echoed in the eye of the figure.

Miró demonstrates here enormous technical skill in the management and disposition of the paint in both the larger color 'fields' and in the minute bands and ribbons of color. The whole of the green sky area, for example, is deliberately given a scrubby appearance with small, strong brushstrokes aligned predominantly along the diagonal axis described by the 'arms' of the person, but more densely worked in places. This is particularly apparent around the contours of the figure and of the stone, and has the effect of projecting the figure slightly from the surface and of giving it a kind of mock three-dimensionality.

Clearly visible behind this textured area are a series of faint lines, suggesting the original grid from which Miró tended to construct his work. The thin black arm-line terminates precisely against one of these grid markers. Notable also is the miniature signature and date, near the 'wing' of the bird, which stand out against the yellow ground rather like the color that highlights the mini-cliffs and peaks of the shoreline.

In this work, Miró has allied the skills of the detailist to the larger sweep of Surrealist biomorphism with its continuous curves and contours, and he sets the two within abstract-looking color fields and geometries. *Personage* is one of the most remarkable syntheses in inter-war painting.

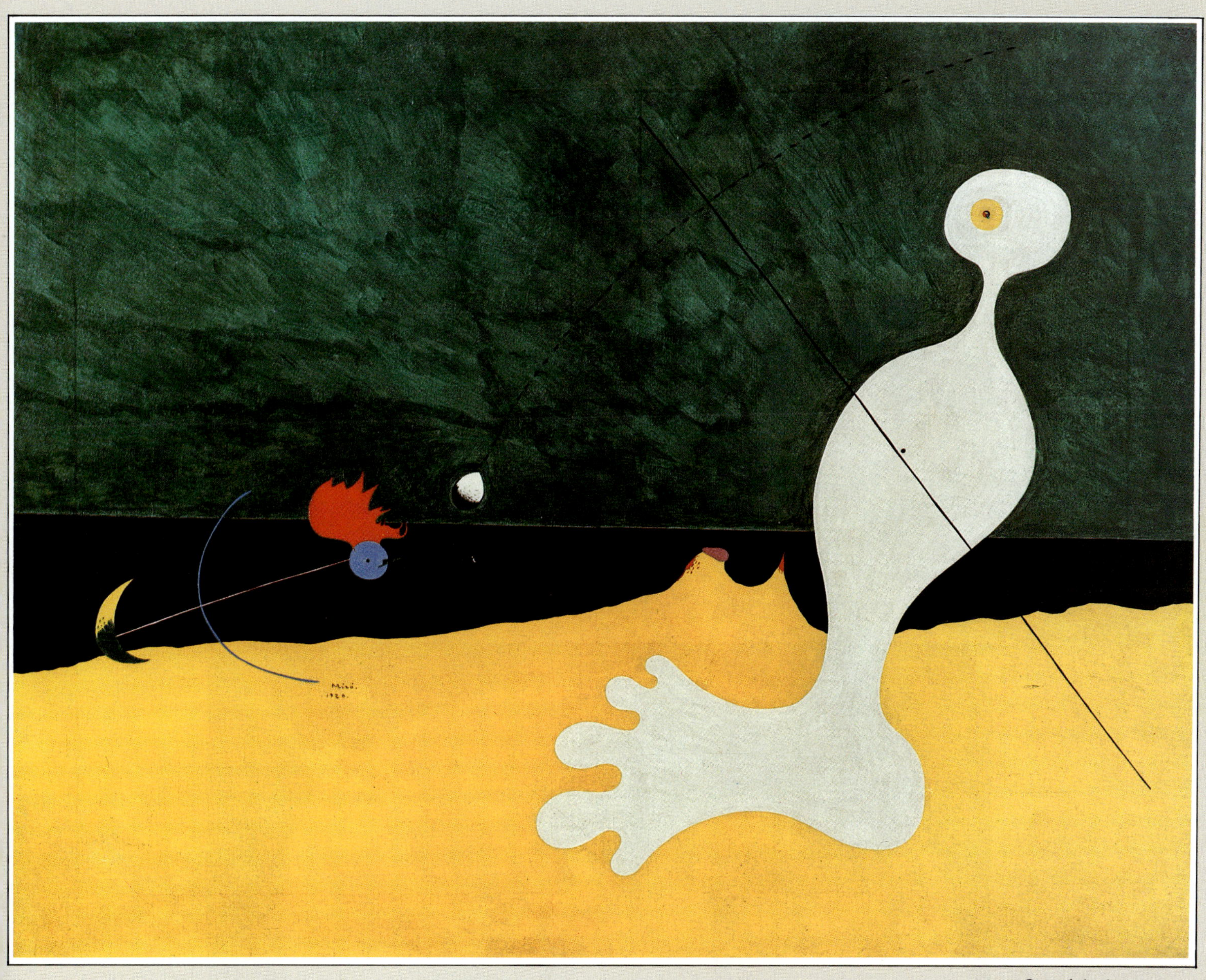

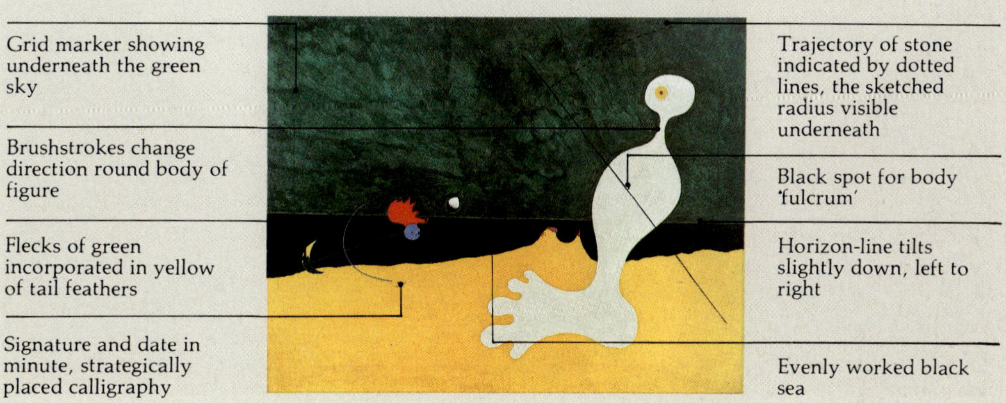


*One of the fascinating series of 'Personage' paintings by various Parisian-based artists in the later 1920s and 1930s, this is divided into three zones — sky, sea and sand — each worked in a different way. There is a delicious visual wit in the articulation of the activity in process, that of 'throwing' which takes place on the shore. A series of very fine touches enhances the poise, balance and placement of the scene.*

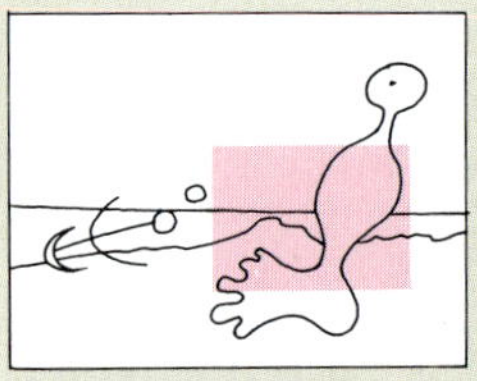

*RIGHT* *The body of the Personage is brushed with visible, greying white strokes, their directions mostly following the figure's contours. All descriptive reference is reduced, the torso swelling in a bulbous shape, and flowing into the disproportionate foot. Arms are signified by a trim black line which is momentarily 'lost' passing through the similar black of the sea. The horizon line behind the colored peaks of the shore is flared with white. Slight traces of blue are blurred into the green above and to the right of the purple 'crater'.*

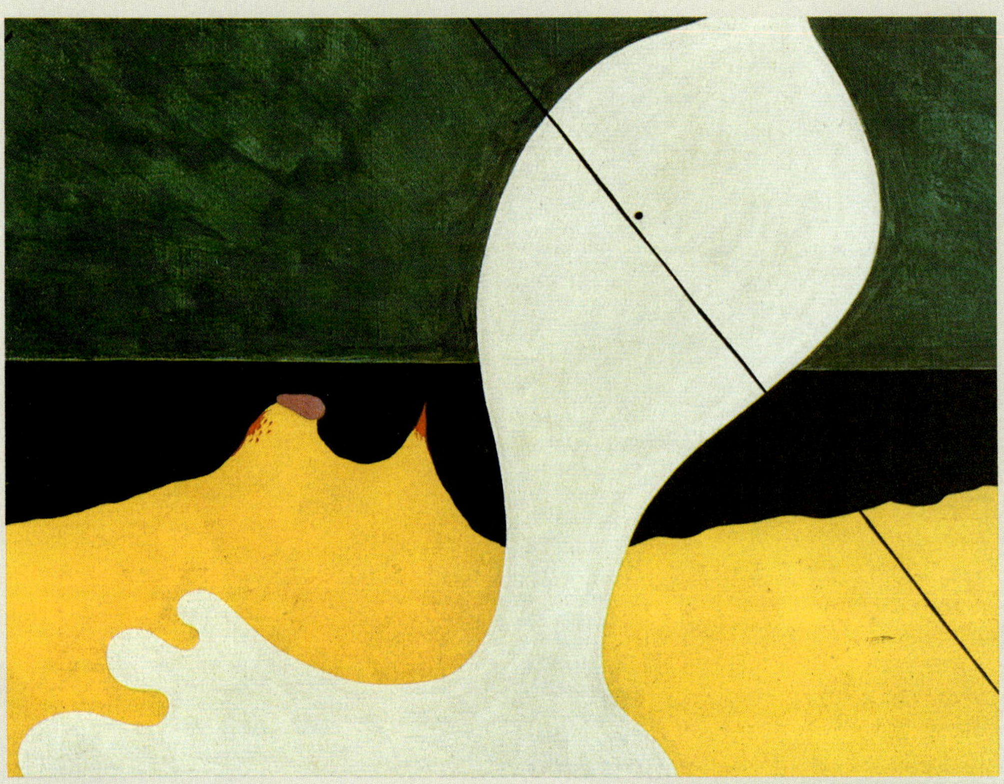

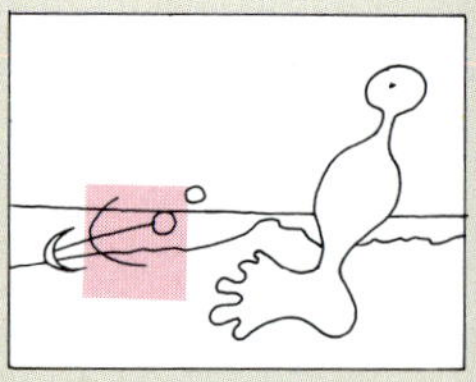

*ACTUAL SIZE DETAIL* *Like the Personage itself, the bird is an amalgam of abbreviated signs, reinforced by an appropriate color system. Its body section is a pencil-thin shaft of white, the wings, an arc of light blue which cuts through the sky, sea and land zones. This blue is concentrated into the circular head with its eye and beak, while the red crest is skilfully designed as a sweeping curve on the left and a succession of fiery peaks on the right, which actually incorporate strands of sea-black where the two colors intersect.*

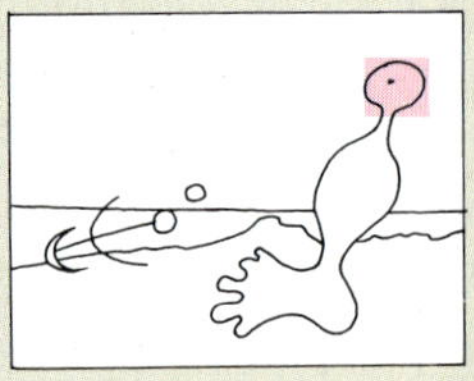

*RIGHT* *The head of the Personage is devoid of particularizing features, except for the off-center eye. Miró has deliberately chosen to echo the dominant hues of the eye work in miniature here, so that the 'white' of the eye, as it were, is the same yellow as the sand, and the inner eye combines the red of the bird's crest with the sky — green and a touch of white in the center. As elsewhere in the figure, brushstrokes are aligned in accordance with the external form and hug the internal features; here they rotate around the eye and funnel down the neck.*

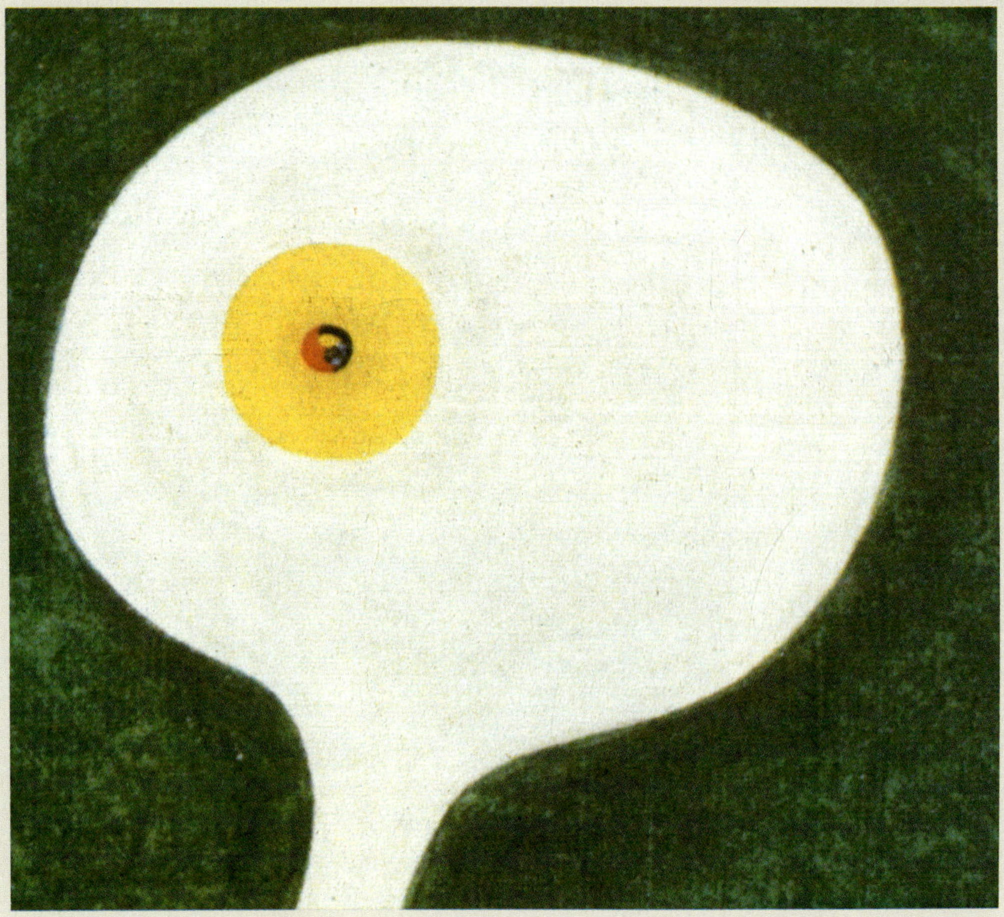

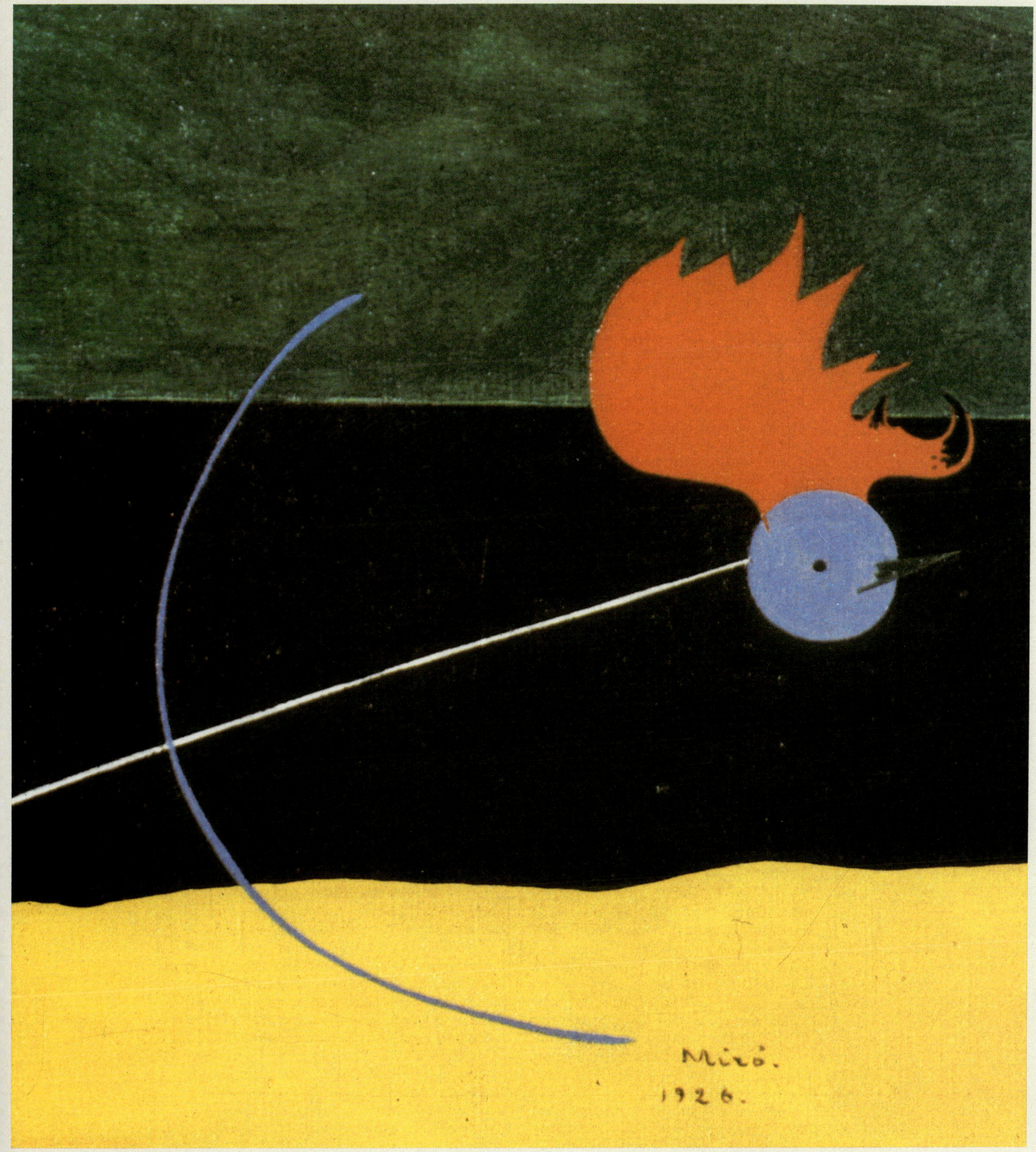
Miró.
1926.

# PIET MONDRIAN

*Composition with Red, Yellow and Blue (1921)*
Oil on canvas
39cm × 35cm/15½in × 13¾in

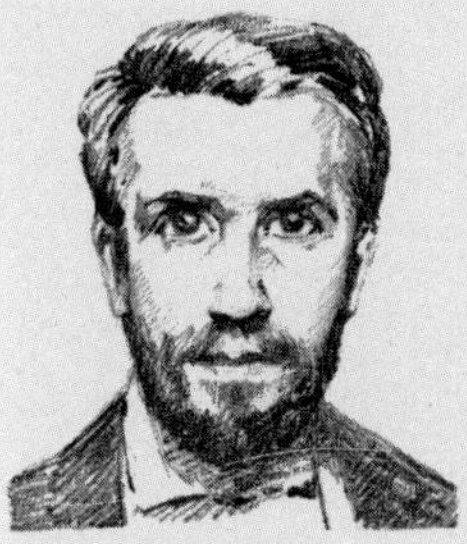

Mondrian is the twentieth century's greatest exponent of Geometric Abstraction; the model or frame of reference for most, if not all, subsequent activity in this area. His dedication and purity of vision have become legendary; the sequence of his works in a mature career of some 35 years constitutes the most scrupulous evolutionary progression, within the tightest margins of trial and error, of probably any Western artist in the history of painting. His aims were lofty and spiritual: he fought constantly against materialism, and he was determined that the world would benefit from the creation of purely 'abstract environments'; his paintings were just a starting point – red, yellow and blueprints for a new mode of living.

Piet Mondrian was born in March 1872 in Amersfoort, in the central Netherlands, into a strict Calvinist family. He attended a teacher's training course in drawing at the National Academy of Art in Amsterdam, and then spent most of the 1890s learning and painting influenced by the seventeenth-century Hague school realism. His work for the next 10 years was mainly in landscapes; the River Gein was his favorite scene. From 1908 he made formative visits to Domberg in Zeeland and painted briefly in the style of Dutch Luminists such as Rembrandt and Jan Vermeer (1632-1675) and later in his own version of Fauvism.

As with many important non-French artists in the first half of the twentieth century, his visit to Paris (in 1912) was crucial. He quickly responded to the Cubist painters and was noticed by Apollinaire when he exhibited at the Salon des Indépendants in 1913. Forced to return to The Netherlands in 1914, he made contacts with the theosophist Dr M. H. J. Schoenmaekers, the painter Bart van der Leck (1876-1958) and the ambitious critic and artist Theo van Doesburg (1883-1931). This led to the publication in 1917 of the magazine *De Stijl* (*The Style*) and to the launch of the movement of the same name.

But at virtually the first opportunity, Mondrian returned to Paris, where, from 1919, he lived an isolated and occasionally poverty-stricken existence throughout the 1920s. In 1920 a summary of his theoretical ideas was published by Léonce Rosenberg; he moved to London in 1938, and spent the last four years of his life (1940 to 1944) in New York, where his work developed remarkably.

As well as being affected by the major modern movements of the 1900s and 1910s, Mondrian was peculiarly susceptible to ideological influences, particularly from theosophists. For him, the opposition of vertical and horizontal lines represented the quintessence of the life-rhythm. Mondrian spent a lifetime exploring this relationship.

But Mondrian was subject to many other important stimuli. His fondness and sympathy for modern music is reflected in an essay he wrote in 1927, *Jazz and Neo-Plasticism;* and the culminating role which he assigned to architecture indicates his visionary, Utopian nature: 'At present Neo-Plasticism manifests in painting what will one day surround us in the form of sculpture and architecture.' Mondrian's own influence has been enormous, and embraces areas such as architecture, design and advertising.

Piet Mondrian was essentially a painter and a perfectionist. He moved fairly rapidly through a large variety of methods of paint application in his earlier works; the heavily textured impasto work of *Dusk* (1890), Neo-Impressionist dots and splashes in 1908, and slightly later Fauve color patches. As he tightened his pictorial structure and reduced his color under the influence of Cubism between 1912 and 1914, the technical effort of adjustment, concentration and refinement is often visible on the canvas surface as *pentimenti* or erasure scars. This is visible evidence of experiment and uncertainty, and the practice continued even into the 1920s when he had finally established the basic relational units of his composition as the straight line, the right angle and the three primary colors (red, yellow and blue) and non-colors (white, black and grey).

Late 1921 has been seen as the great threshold in Mondrian's career; the year in which his elementary triad of colors was first organized with confidence and deliberateness, and his lattice-work of lines became thicker and more certain. Other factors were so reduced that his art had become one of placement, balance and equilibrium.

Mondrian's working method is difficult to reconstruct precisely, but there are a number of first-hand accounts of his famous Paris studio with its bright white walls and mobile color rectangles. He favored canvas formats which approached squareness, but seldom had sides of exact equivalence. *Composition with Red, Yellow and Blue* is small in comparison to the bulk of his Paris production. He often worked from small preparatory drawings, and transposed and amplified the system of lines on to the sized canvas with charcoal. The artist and critic Michel Seuphor (b 1901) noted that Mondrian used a ruler and 'ribbons of transparent paper' as his only tools. His biographer J. J. Sweeney embellishes this account: 'How did he approach the picture? Well, I found that he approached it by using collage frequently, pasting papers on the canvas,changing the colors around, organizing them that way, not just in his mind only but also on the canvas.'

'He built his paintings as if they were marquetry', noted one critic. Especially in the 'classical' Neo-Plastic works, color choices were normally made at a fairly late stage, and may have been quite arbitrary; they were certainly subordinate to the painting's structure.

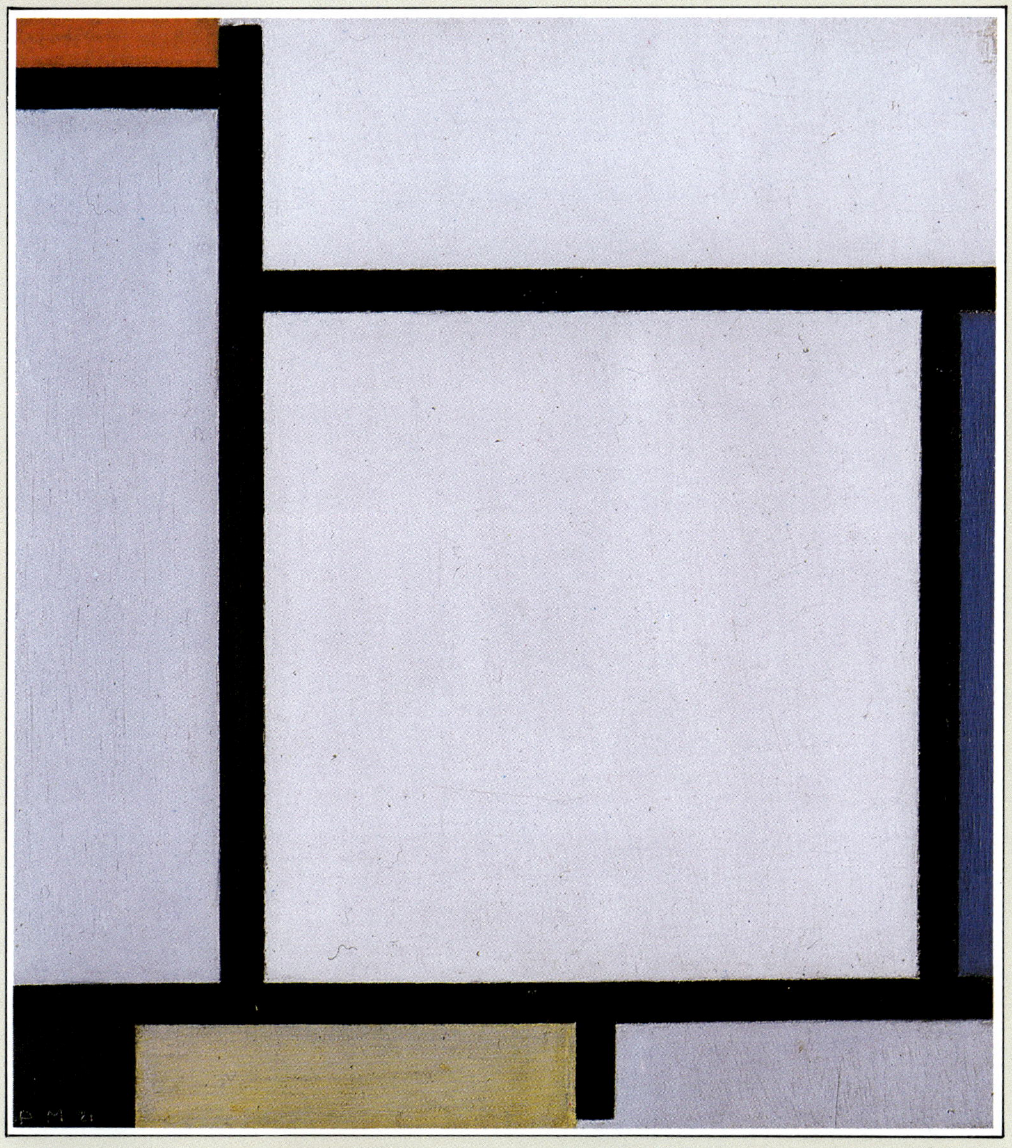

*In the first two years of the 1920s, Mondrian finally resolved his compositional structure and the dialog of colors which was to animate it. But close examination of this painting's surface reveals that fineness of finish is entirely subordinated to the effect of the design; placement is vaunted over neatness of paint application. This may be related to the reduced circumstances in which the artist found himself in Paris, but more important is his passionate assertion of the priority of ideas and spiritual values over the material means of painting.*

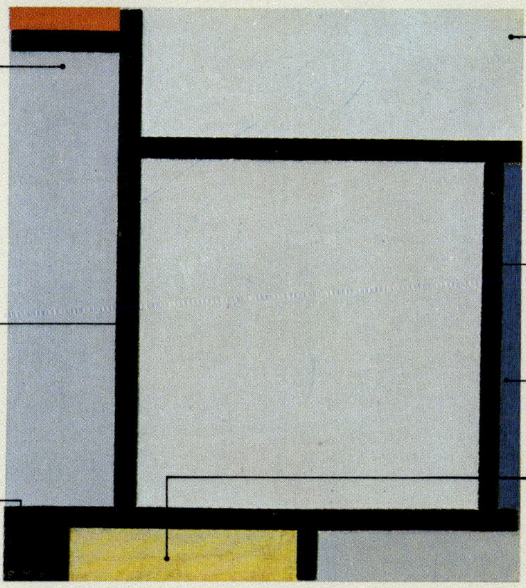

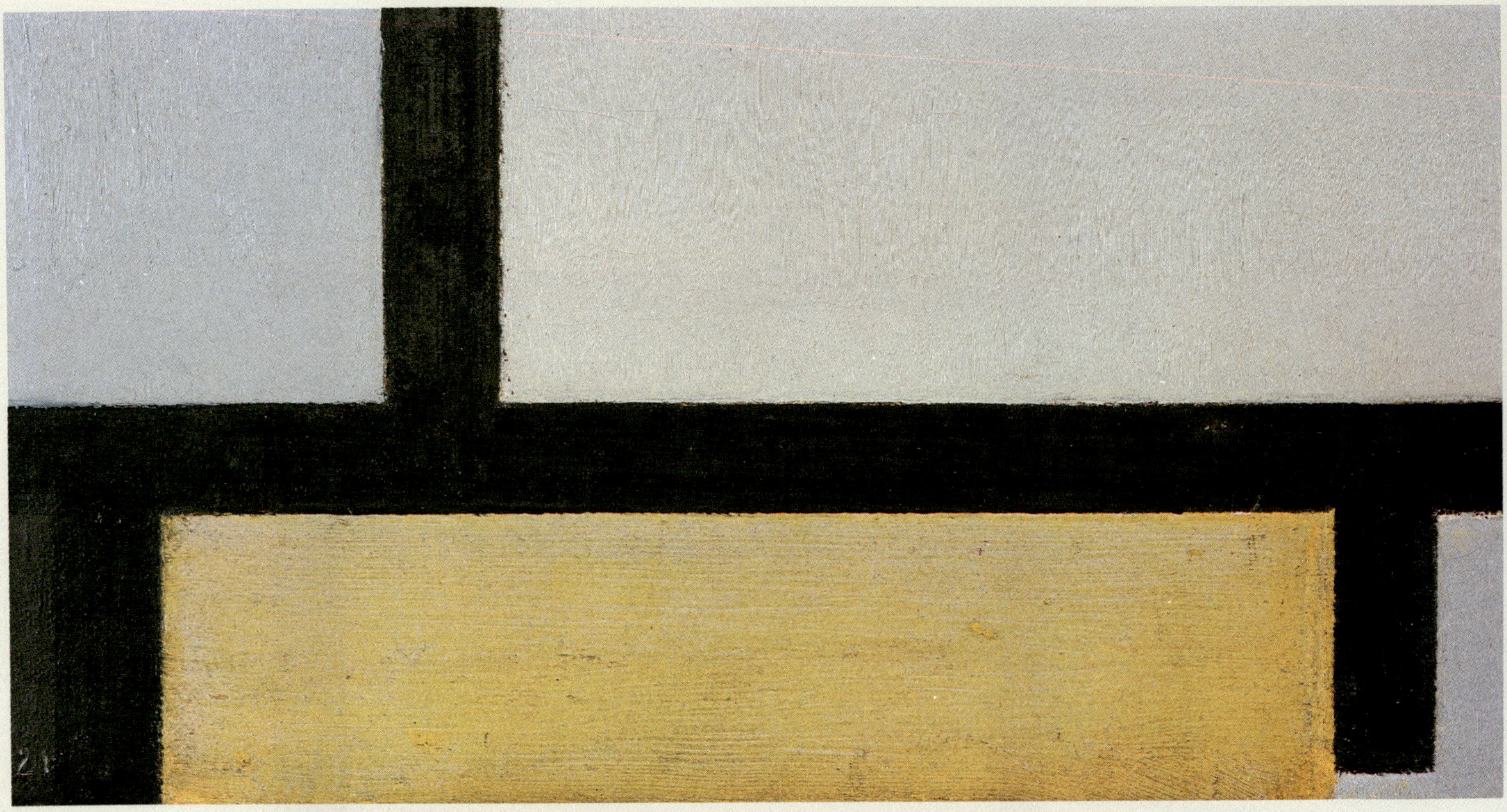

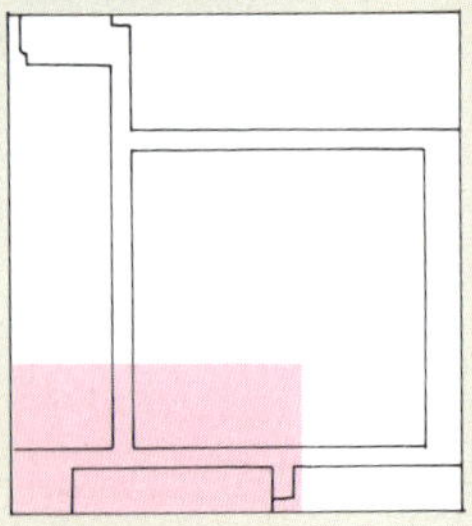

ACTUAL SIZE DETAIL *The coarsely painted frame is set back from the edge of the canvas, its white spilling into the picture on the left, and sections of brown wood visible along its outer edge. The yellow rectangle is unevenly filled in, with a discontinuous band of denser pigment round the perimeter and small deposits of impasto in the bottom corners and in the interior. Elsewhere, the brush has furrowed the paint in yellow bands alternating with white ribbons where the ground is visible. Minor flecks and incursions are evident along the black/color boundaries.*

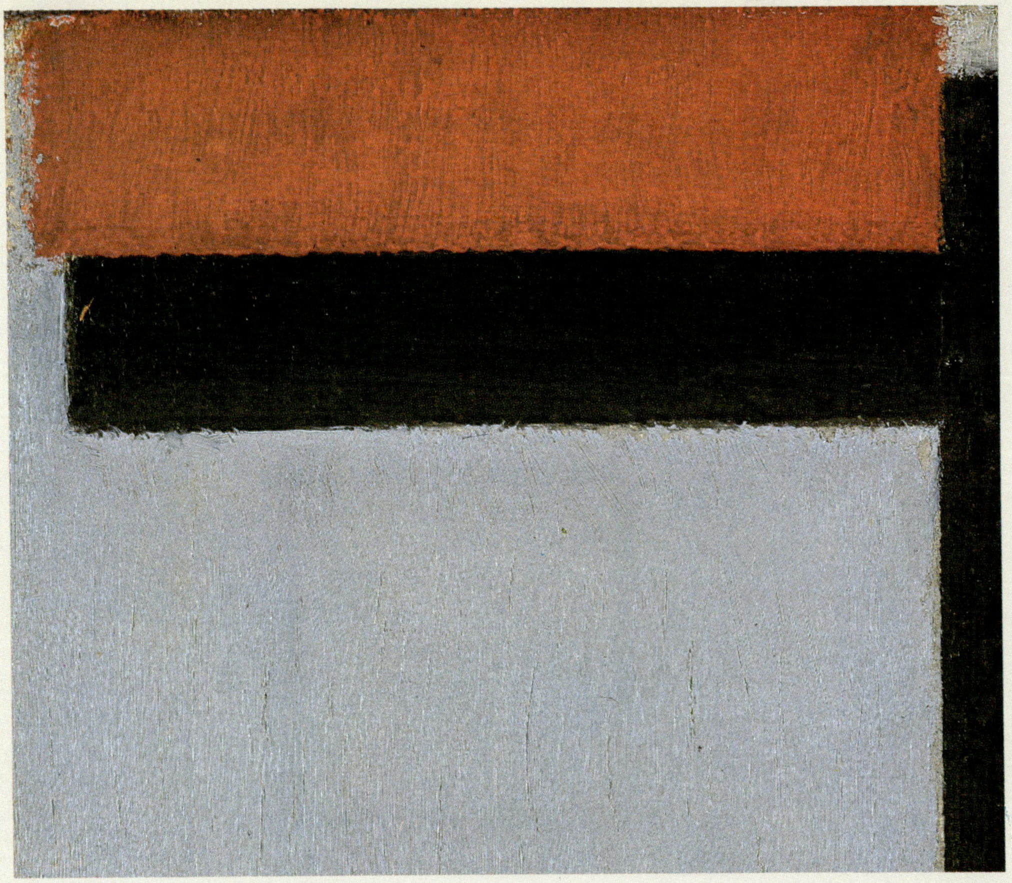

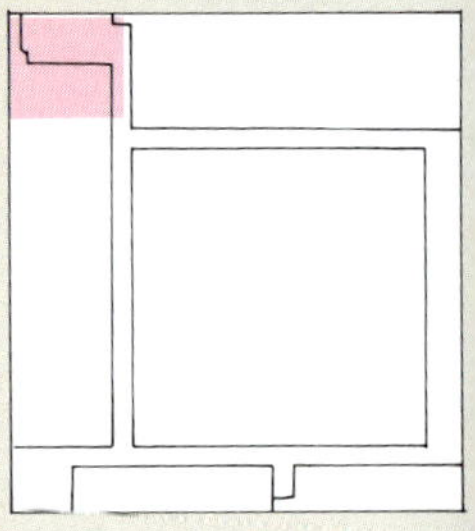

LEFT *All the colored rectangles at the peripheries of the composition are zones of painterly complexity and irregularity, but the red area here is blitzed with uncertain dabs. In three places, Mondrian has deliberately resisted the termination of black lines and of the red rectangle flush with the canvas edge. This disencourages the viewer's imaginary construction of a tessellated continuation of the design. It removes the work from the world of mere pattern and asserts it as a statement in paint about balance and equilibrium, bounded by a painted frame.*

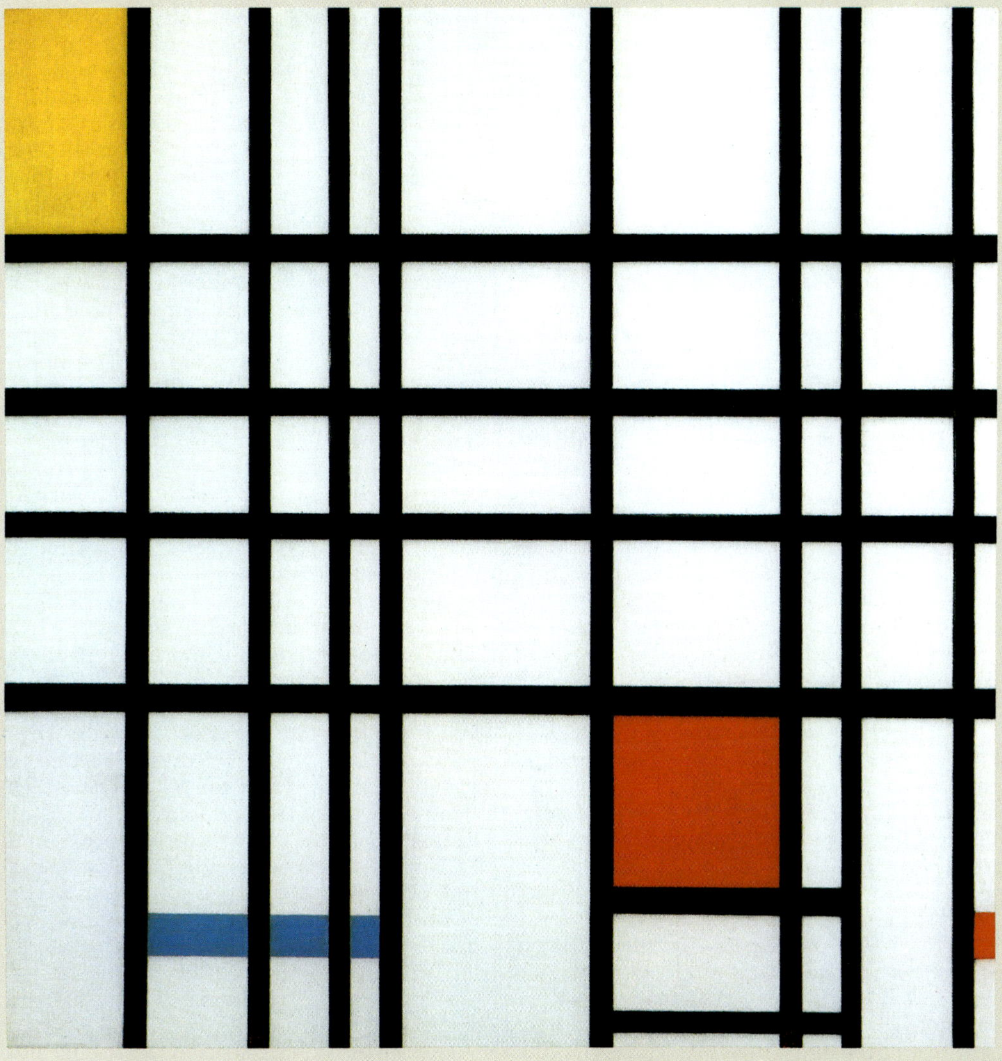

*ABOVE* Composition with Red, Yellow and Blue *was begun in 1937 and worked intermittently until 1942, by which time Mondrian had moved to New York. The lattice-work of lines has been complicated considerably so that eight unevenly spaced vertical black bars mesh with four horizontals and two partial lines. As in the earlier painting of 1921 color zones inhabit the center, but one important modification is the use here of unbounded edges for the long sides of the blue and red rectangle. The blue thus becomes neither color patch nor line. Technically the finish of this work is more rigorous and definite than the earlier one, but still is in no way mechanical or completely 'hard-edged'.*

# EDWARD WADSWORTH

*L'avant port, Marseilles (1924)*
Tempera on linen laid on a wooden panel
61cm × 89cm/25in × 35in

Edward Wadsworth's wife recalled how her husband loved to read books about art; indeed he read almost constantly 'on painting, and most of all, books on the technique of painting. As for Cennino Cennini's treatise [*Il Libro dell'Arte*] he read it again and again – he was always reading it.' Cennini was a Florentine painter who wrote a treatise in about 1390 as a technical textbook for those who wished to enter the profession of artist. It contains, among much else, detailed practical information on tempera techniques. Wadsworth, a painter who cared passionately about technique and craftsmanship, abandoned oil painting in favor of tempera in mid career, and he could not have turned to a better technical guide.

Right from the beginning of his artistic career in 1908, Edward Wadsworth, who was born in Yorkshire in 1889, favored a style which was precise, ordered and mathematical. He liked to portray subjects with a definite shape and recognizable function. He had studied engineering which he gave up to become a painter. After studying at Bradford School of Art and the Slade, he flirted briefly with Post-Impressionism, and for a time was associated with Wyndham Lewis's Vorticism.

Wadsworth had a deep love of the sea and ships. His first recorded oil painting in 1908 was a view of Le Havre; in 1919 he produced an oil painting of *Dazzle Ships in Drydock at Liverpool*, and he made copperplate engravings, which he then hand-colored, for a 1926 publication entitled *Sailing Ships and Barges of the Western Mediterranean and the Adriatic Seas.*

1926 was also the year in which he exhibited *L'avant port, Marseilles* at the Leicester Galleries in London. Five years earlier, on the death of his father, Wadsworth had inherited a fortune. He spent most of his time from then on in the south of France, and several paintings exist with the same subject matter: the port of Marseilles. Wadsworth is known to have planned a series of paintings of the principal ports of Britain but this seems to have been abandoned with his growing interest in France.

Tempera is a medium peculiarly suitable for depicting decorative and detailed forms seen in the clear open-air light, as in *L'avant port, Marseilles.* Although Wadsworth loved the sea and ships, the sea, in his art, was always seen in a subordinate role: he portrayed it in perfect calm as a still support for the complicated and detailed vessels which traverse its surface.

*L'avant port, Marseilles* is painted in tempera on a plywood panel. The plywood has a fine layer of linen canvas stretched over it to provide a base for a thick layer of gesso ground. To temper means to mix with powder pigments a binder or medium, usually the yolk of an egg mixed with a small amount of water, and acetic acid, such as lemon juice (which prolongs the life of the yolk).

The most important aspect of tempera is the rapid drying of the pigment once it comes into contact with the gesso support. This means that the color has to be built up gradually by laying one thin coat over another, or that transitions of tone or color have to be made by hatched strokes. Both approaches can be seen in *L'avant port, Marseilles.* The cool blue of the sky is laid on so that the white of the gesso ground textured by the linen layer shows through in parts. It also appears to have been rubbed, bringing up white highlights in the sky. (This rubbed quality cannot be due to wear and tear, since the painting seems to be in its original frame behind glass.) The hatching technique is apparent in the shadows, especially in the shaded areas of the three hulls. Wadsworth began work on the panel by drawing his composition in pencil upon the gesso ground. He had a preliminary sketch as a model, and he used the squaring up method to transfer the original sketch, done in front of the motif, into the design for the painting.

The clarity of the composition and the intricate detailing of some of its parts are due in a large measure to the amount of preparation which preceded the actual painting. The art critic S. Kennedy North, who wrote the preface for Wadsworth's first exhibition of tempera paintings at the Leicester Galleries in March 1923, noted that the oil painter 'could think once and draw six times', whereas the tempera painter 'must think six times and draw once'. Some of the finest lines in *L'avant port, Marseilles* have not only been drawn in before painting, they have also been scored into the gesso ground so as to give Wadsworth the clearest possible guide for his loaded brush. His signature and date have also been scored into the ground.

The range of colors used is subtle and harmonious, with a gamut of earth colors relieved by sharp accents of viridian and ultramarine. Unlike in oil painting, the tempera artist cannot rely upon thick impasto, or upon the texture of the pigment for effect, nor can one color be fused into another.

For a few months in 1938 and 1939 Wadsworth experimented with Seurat's Pointillist technique in tempera. (A stippling technique – laying colors in by means of dots of paint – was an accepted tempera technique.) Wadsworth's experiment was short-lived, but it did produce *Honfleur: Entrance to Harbour* (1930). This painting is dependent for its choice of subject matter and its composition on Seurat's canvas *Entrée du port à Honfleur* of 1886.

But *L'avant port, Marseilles* is an example of the technique which dominated Wadsworth's work until his death in 1949. Surrealism was a strong influence and from it he developed his distinctive painting style – notable for its dreamlike clarity and the oddities of scale and juxtaposition of familiar seaside objects.

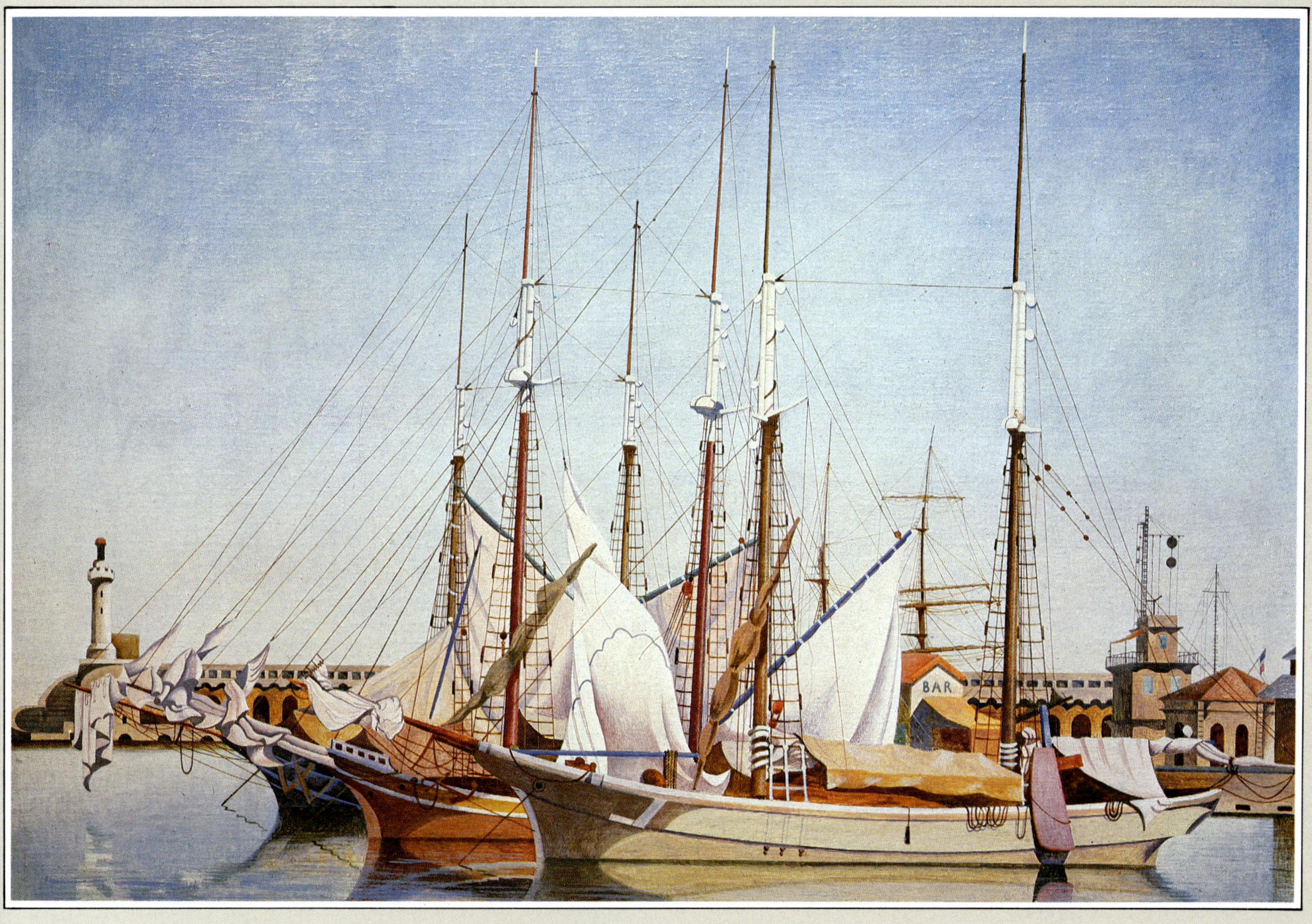

*Tempera is an ideal medium with which to portray a bright sunlit scene, and Wadsworth proves he is a virtuoso in the handling of it, setting himself a subject with a wealth of minute detail.*

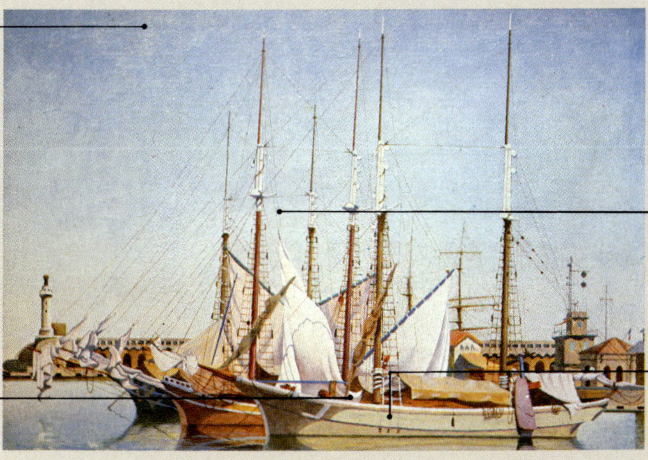

Sanded surface showing gesso ground through the paint layer

Fine lines of rigging drawn and painted with the aid of a ruler

Hatched brushstrokes create the shadows

Preliminary squaring-up of ground with pencil still visible

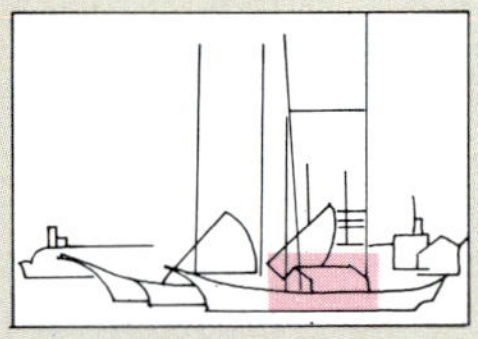

*RIGHT The main color accent, ultramarine, is used equally for the mast in sunlight and the building in shadow. For the plane in shadow it is applied over a layer of terre-verte. The word BAR thrusts itself forward onto the picture plane.*

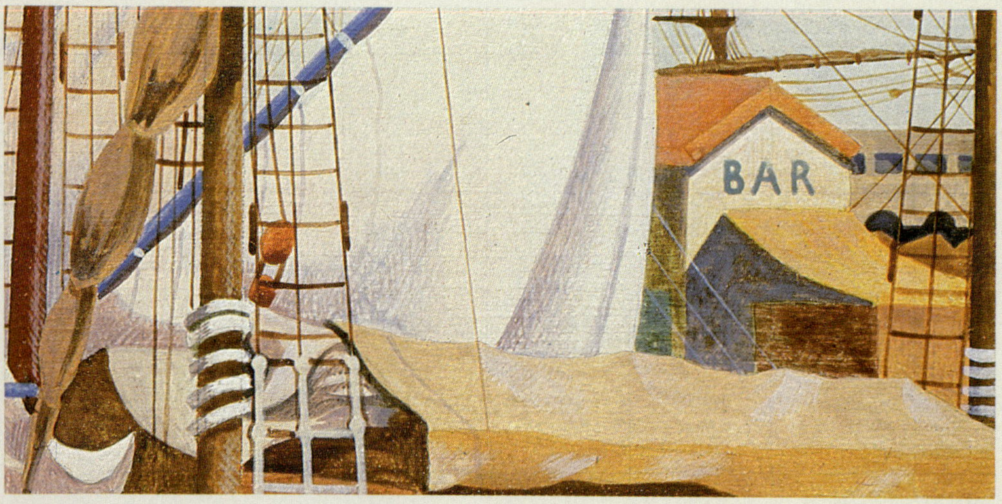


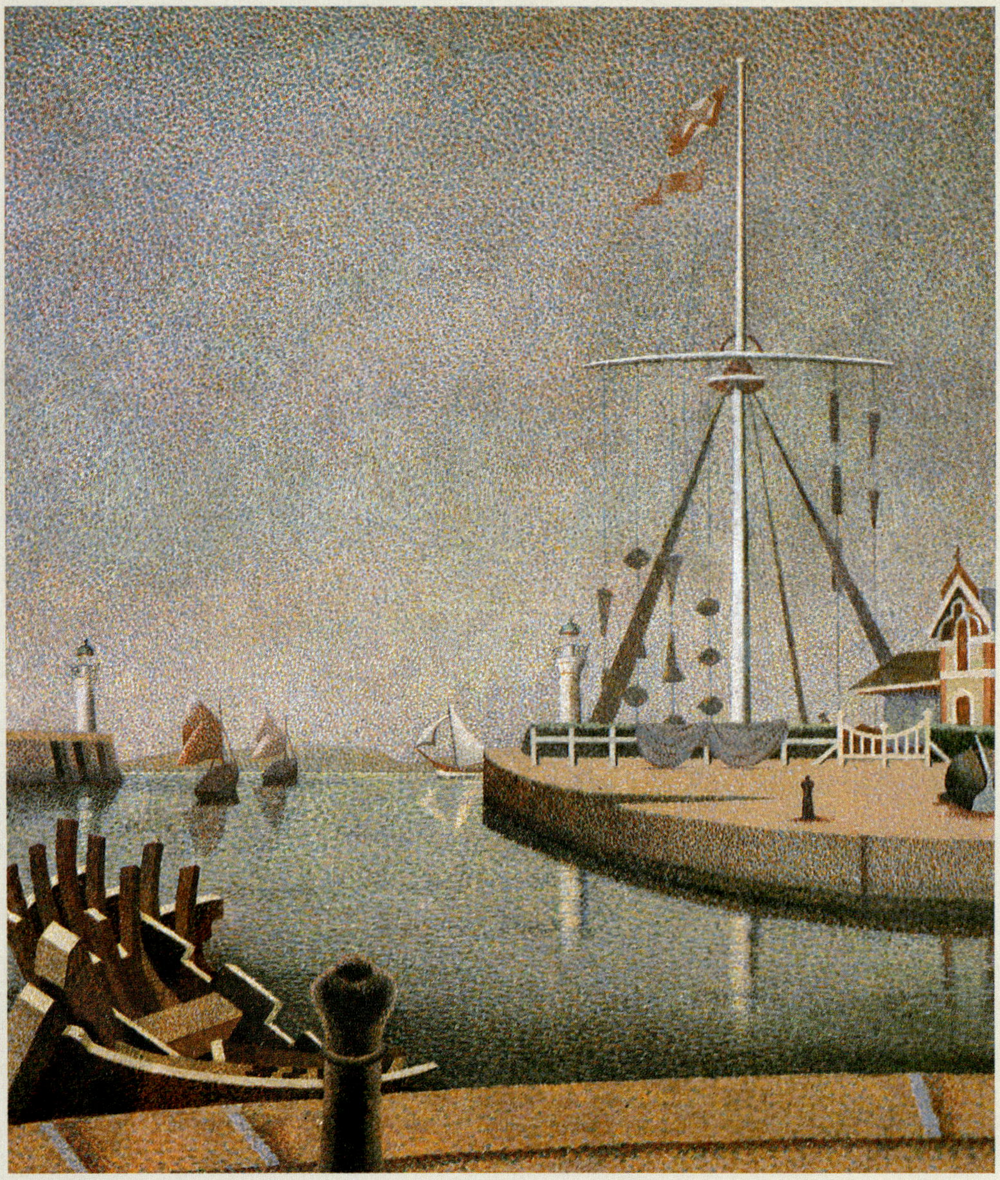

*RIGHT: In* Honfleur: Entrance to Harbour *(1939) Wadsworth does not rely upon the effect of luminosity which a white gesso ground can provide. He has covered the whole panel with a thick weave of Pointillist dots and dashes, the largest brushmarks being at the bottom of the composition. Stippling, or Pointillism was not a technique he employed in* L'avant port, *and he was only to pursue it for a short period.*

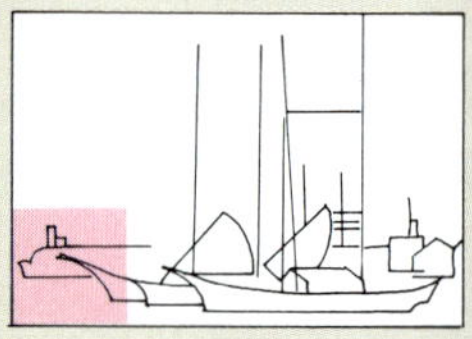

*ACTUAL SIZE DETAIL The nails with which Wadsworth attached the plywood panel to its backing, a strong wooden frame, are visible at intervals along its edge. At the very edge some flaking of the gesso ground can be seen, and also air bubbles caused by the application of thick pigment. The light areas of the composition, the sails, the sunlit lighthouse and sea, are the most thickly painted and become opaque in quality, preventing the white gesso ground from showing through. In contrast, the areas of dark shadow, the water under the hulls, have more diluted paint and rely upon transparency. The original pencil drawing marking out the contours shows throughout, and Wadsworth has preserved those contours by carefully painting his colors up to their edges.*

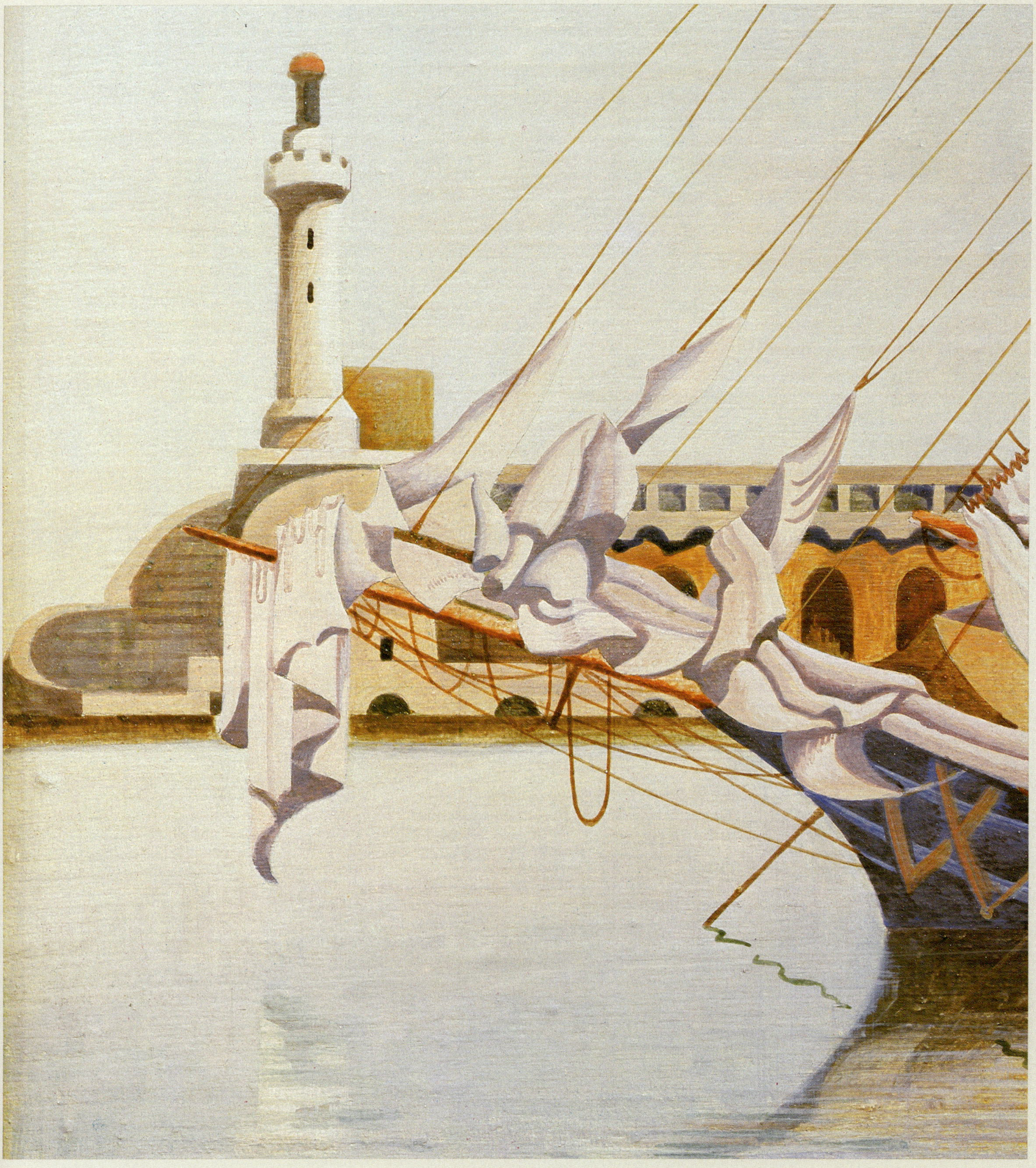

# PIERRE BONNARD

*La fenêtre (1925)*
Oil on canvas
108.6cm × 88.6cm/42¾in × 34⅞in

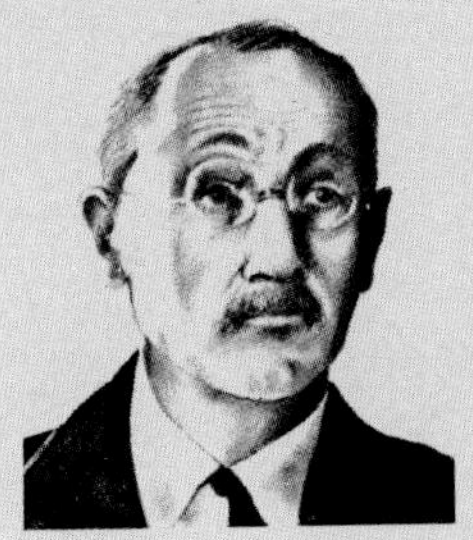

An acute observer of light values, though a rather conservative painter by twentieth-century standards, the Post-Impressionist Pierre Bonnard was born in 1867 in Fontenay-aux-Roses. As a young man he first studied law, and then painting at the Ecole des Beaux-Arts and Académie Julian. He joined a group of artists associated with Gauguin who were called Nabis (a Hebrew word meaning 'Prophets'). His first success was a poster *France – Champagne* (1891).

Bonnard's early career covered many aspects of design including furniture, poster and theater commissions and many important book illustrations, in particular for the novel *Marie* by Peter Nansen, which was published in *La Revue Blanche* in 1898 (and which appears on the table in *La fenêtre*). These lithographs were singled out for praise by Renoir. From about 1905 Bonnard concentrated increasingly on painting in the Post-Impressionist tradition, uninvolved with the avant-garde.

In 1925 Bonnard moved to Le Cannet near Cannes. *La fenêtre* is a view from the window of his house Le Bosquet, where he died in 1947. Bonnard required the white priming in this canvas to act in two ways: firstly, left uncovered, it is used as a tone or shade of white in several parts of the picture, such as some house sides; secondly, it gives the colors additional radiance, if they are applied thinly enough, just as watercolors gain their brilliance from the whiteness of the paper.

Bonnard's technique was also linked to his instinctive discipline for color which came from his experience of poster and printmaking, especially lithography: 'I have learned much about painting proper from making lithographs in color, when one has to establish relations between tones by ringing the changes on only four or five colors, superimposed or juxtaposed, one makes a host of discoveries.'

Henri de Toulouse Lautrec (1864-1901) had been a strong influence on Bonnard's lithographic work. The two painters, like many others including Monet, were fascinated by Japanese prints with their powerful compositions and purity of color. In *La fenêtre* this influence can be seen in the almost flat diamond pattern of the tablecloth, and the abstract rhythm of the green shutter slats which have a tendency to flatten out the perspective of the composition and make the distant colors jump forward with surprising strength.

Bonnard used a palette of about eight high-quality colors which he applied, for the most part, very thinly. They were made to perform a great number of functions. A scarlet vermilion was applied pure, speckled beneath the green window bar. Bonnard often mixed it with a Venetian red which appears in the cover of the portfolio on the table. Mixed together they make a warm pink (with the addition of zinc white). An expensive cobalt violet produced a near rose pink when mixed with the vermilion and white in the writing box at left, and a cool brown when combined with the colors of the window frame at the top left of the picture. This same violet adds a coldness to the sky next to a cerulean blue, and is a powerful dark when touched into the hair of the woman.

Only two blues were used. The cerulean can be seen pure in the distant hills running in from the left and in dashes on the right of the window frame. There are only small amounts of the cobalt blue, often applied with a finger to add a particular depth, such as in the tiny area between the chin and arm of the figure.

Two yellows are discernible. A lemon cadmium appears with rare impasto over some foreground roofs and thinned with white for glazes in the foreground cloth. Yellow ochre complements the lemon to provide some drawing around the red book. Vermilion and lemon were put side by side to color the rooftops 'orange'; a common Divisionist device.

Bonnard used viridian to great effect. He thinned it with zinc white to create the transparent acid green of the shutters and in the angled window bar. It was also used in the heavy green of the clumps of woodland.

White is one of the keys to an understanding of Bonnard's technique in *La fenêtre*. A flake white was used in the thickly applied pure white sheet offered to view, which then calls across to the pure whites and primed canvas of the houses, creating a set of optical stepping stones into the distance.

Bonnard also employed a black in a similar way. It was applied very pure, not to darken any of the colors artificially. This was a practice inherited from Monet. Ivory black can be found in the ink pot and in the dark areas of trees which draw the eye into and across the distance; like opening a Japanese fan.

Bonnard's planning of this painting is complex, and would have taken a long time in order to record color and light precisely while, at the same time, sacrificing nothing of its transparency and depth. There is evidence of the meticulous brushwork which achieves such results in places such as the grid of the tablecloth, and in the house roofs and in the verticals at right. The only area which is truly opaque is the rectangle of sky. Much of the painting was applied with rags rather than brushes. This technique creates an unfocused appearance yet allows a strong sculptural quality in the 'architecture' of the painting.

Bonnard's slow, planned application of color next to color or superimposed one on the other, forces the viewer to actually do the color mixing and see the world in skilfully contrived contrasts. The result is a sophisticated color 'mechanism' which convinces with painterly deception, as Bonnard himself confessed: 'Il faut mentir' (one must lie).

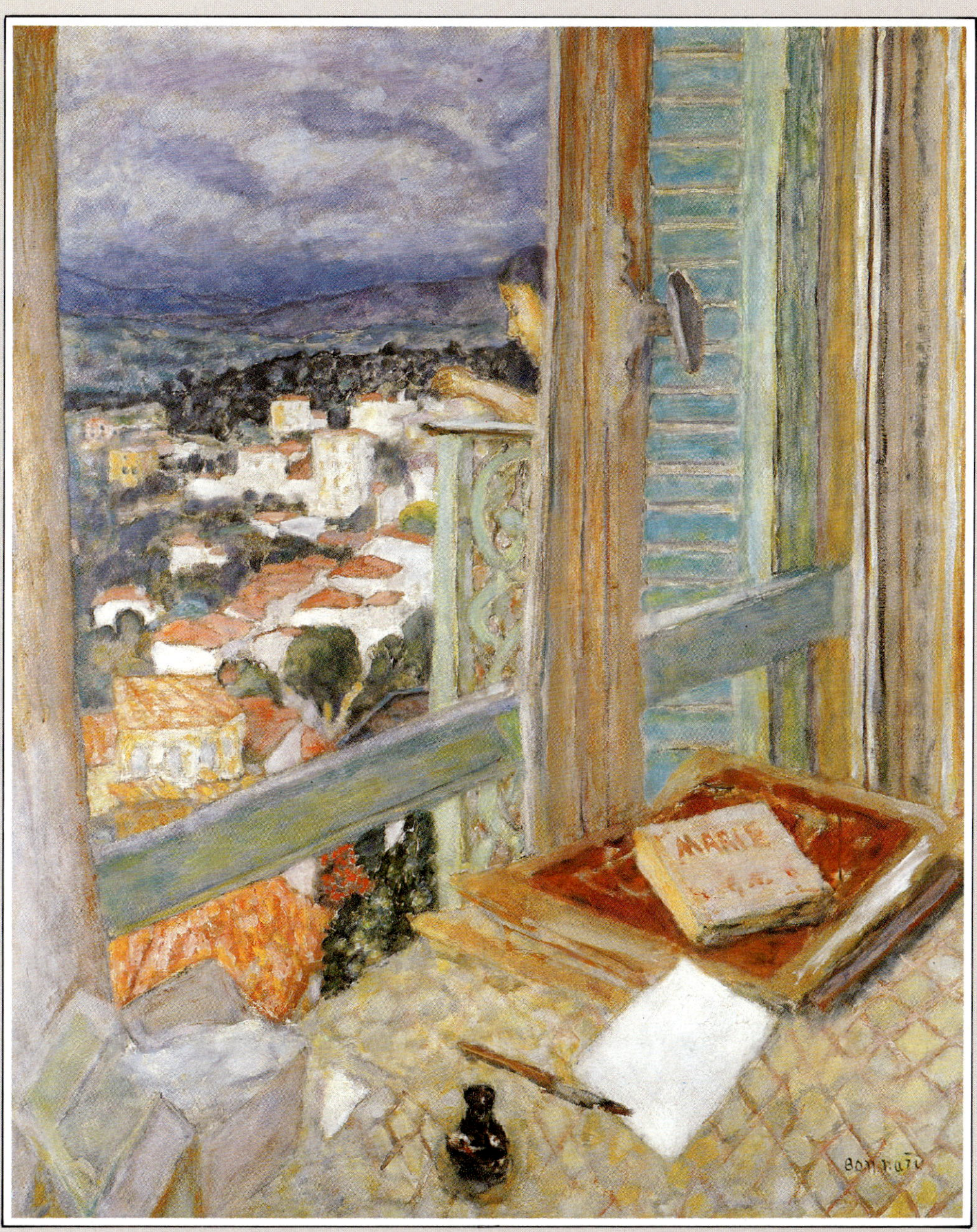


*Bonnard is best known for his 'intimist' paintings. In* La fenêtre *he has made the randomly placed articles on a desk top echo the pattern of the village below. These mundane elements are elevated by Bonnard's slow and meticulous assembly of brushed and wiped color and glazes to bring out a compelling mesh of abstract color relationships.*

The white primed canvas was allowed to break through in places, especially in the sides of the houses

Some touches of pure vermilion or cadmium red are put in to vibrate against the emerald green window frame

Areas of quite thick impasto create the texture and color of some foreground roofs

A fine brush was used to mark in areas of drawing with greater emphasis, such as the tablecloth or verticals of the window frame

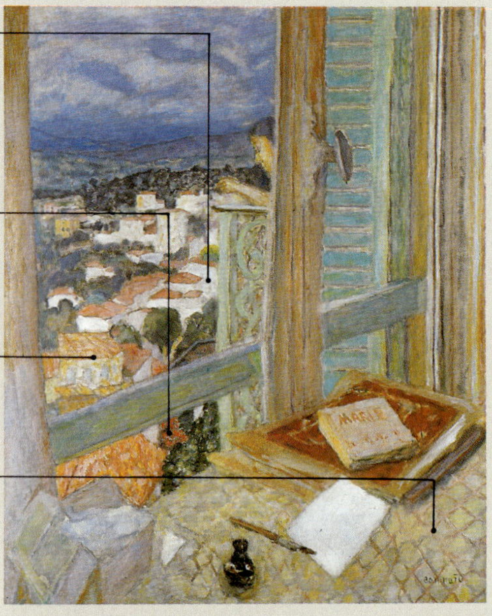

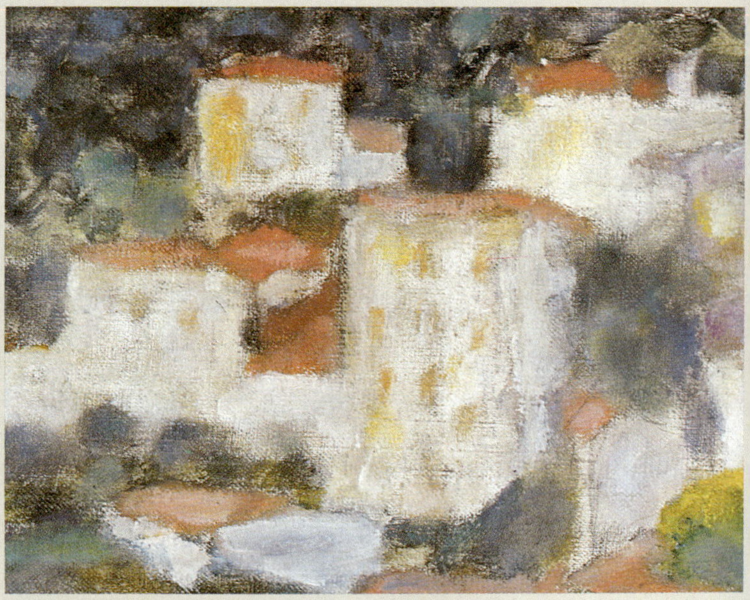

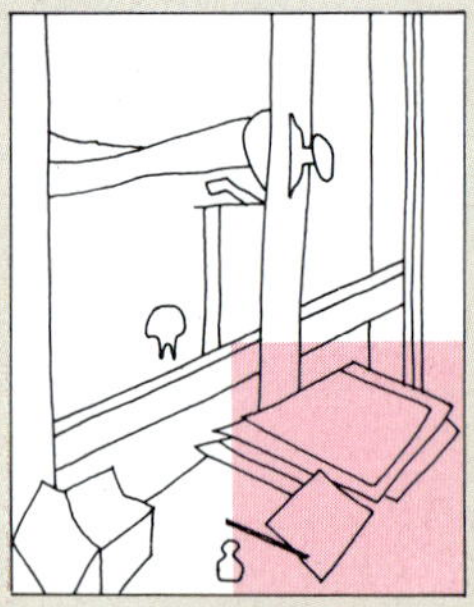

*RIGHT In 1897, some 28 years earlier than* La fenêtre *Bonnard had made a set of lithographic illustrations for Peter Nansen's novel* Marie *which Renoir admired and was a triumph that is wittily referred to. Bonnard was noted for a great sense of humor. His interest in Japanese prints is evident in the flattening out of the foreground perspective to emphasize its pattern-like qualities. The blank sheet, probably another piece of pictorial wit is brushed in with an impasto of flake white as is the pen handle. In contrast the tablecloth was built up slowly from a series of transparent glazes to create a translucent mosaic of pastel tones.*

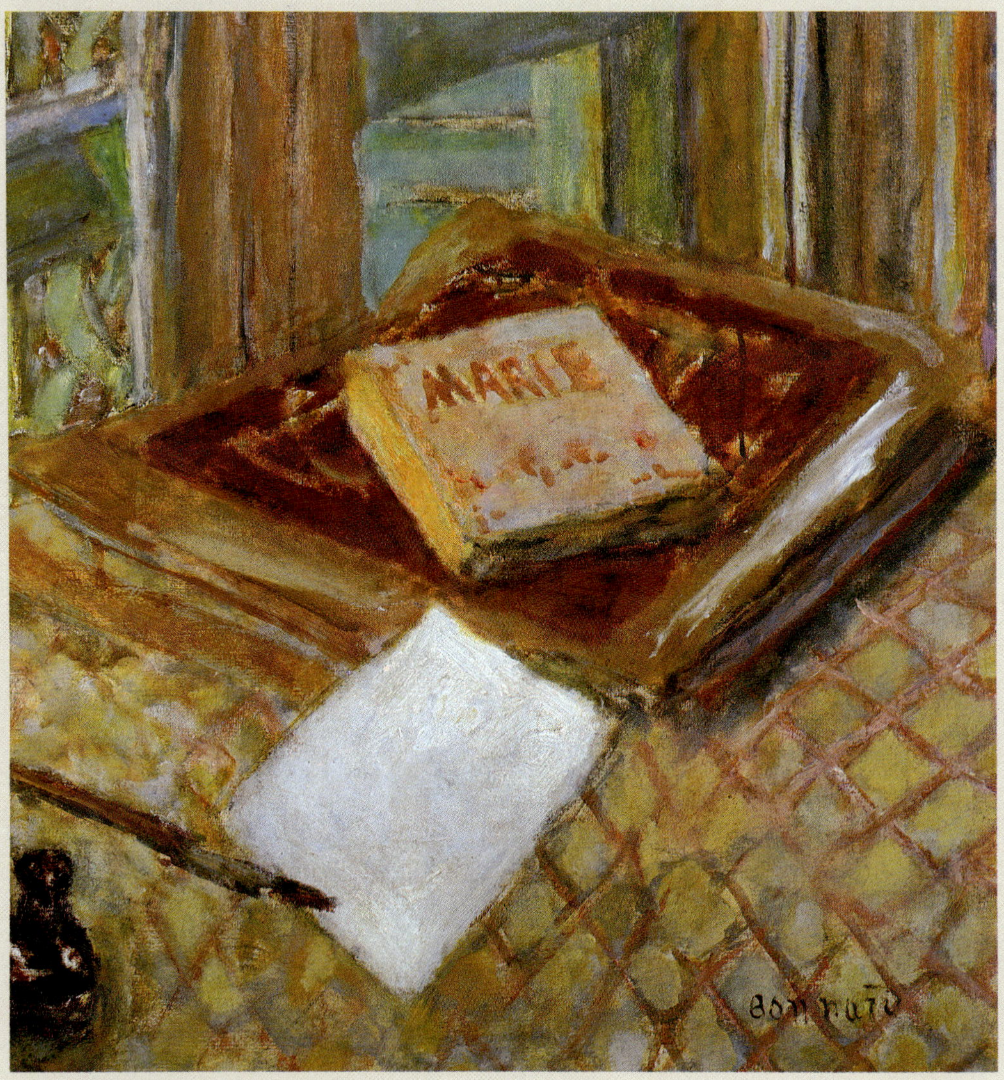


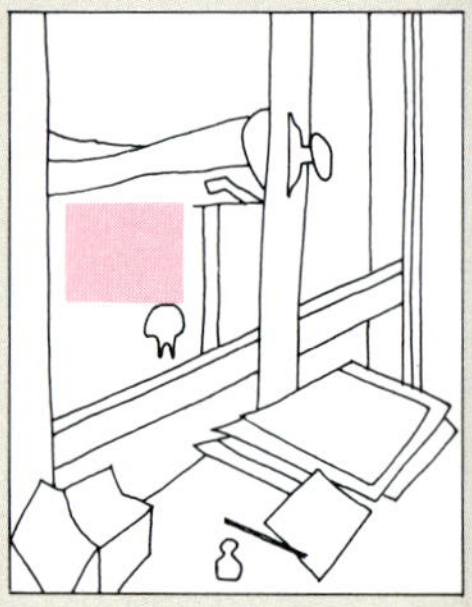

*ABOVE Bonnard had worked with Monet for a while and inherited an Impressionist approach to landscape that did not prevent him rendering visual facts with a level of accuracy. The whites of the houses are a combination of flake white and the white canvas priming. These tones harmonize with the pure white sheet on the table, just as the pink and yellow ochre brushmarks in the roofs and windows find their equivalents in the tablecloth pattern.*

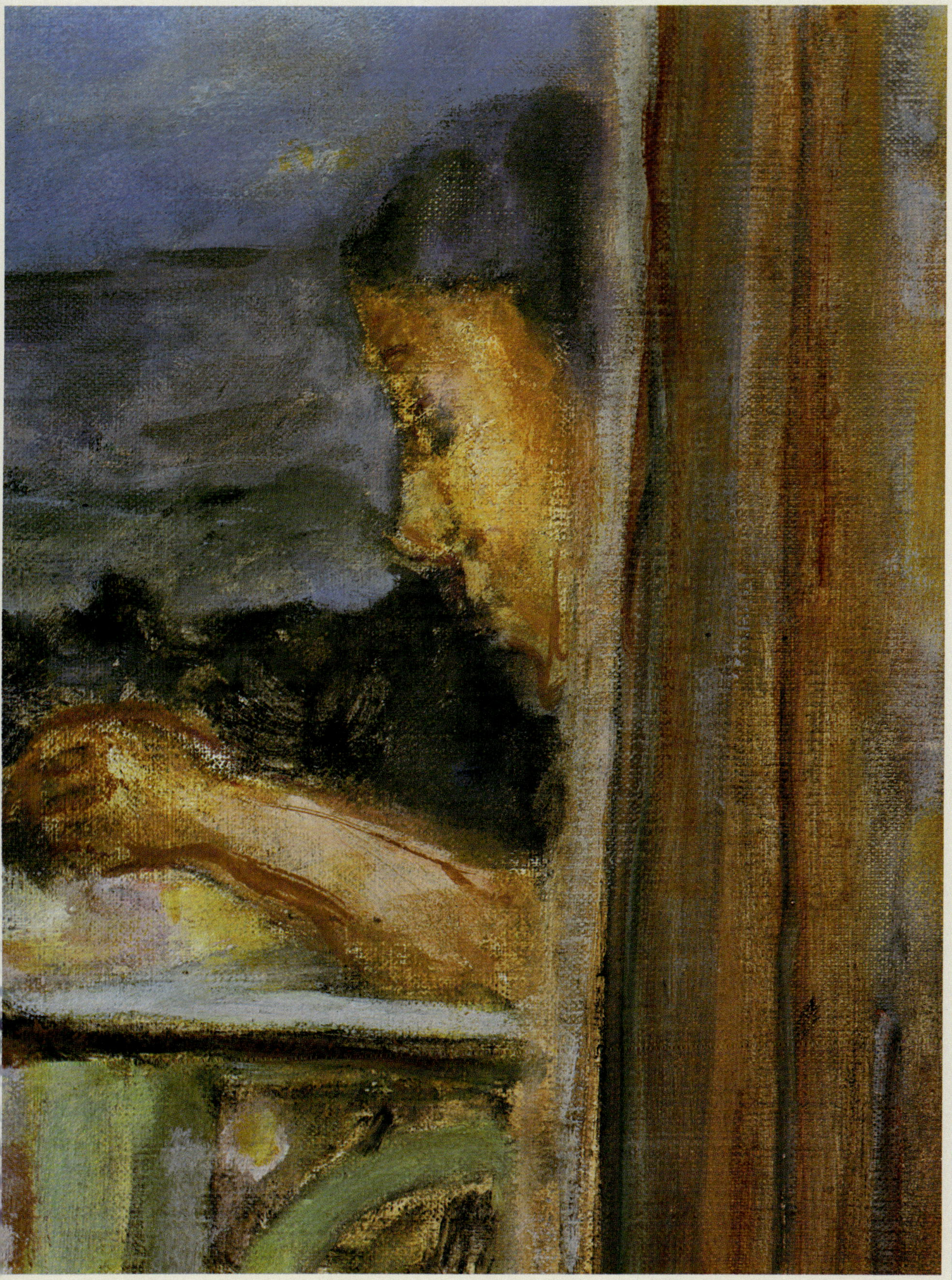

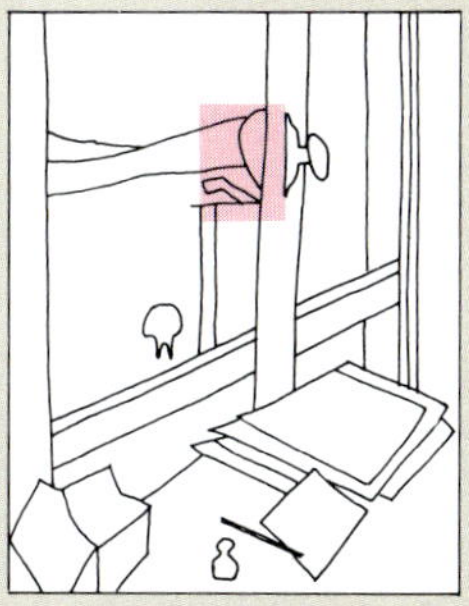

ACTUAL SIZE DETAIL *In 1925 Bonnard moved to this small house called 'Le Bosquet' at Le Cannet, near Cannes after marrying Maria Boursin who preferred to be known as Marthe de Moligny. She had lived with him for about 30 years previously and had been a model in many interior and bath tub paintings. She is also included in still lifes and interiors as if she had strayed into view. Bonnard rarely painted from life but made sketches and worked on his paintings over a long period in his studio. This method involved the application of thin veils of paint which would be left to dry before they could be reworked, using brushes, fingers and pieces of rag. His choice of color is Impressionistic and emotional, rather than realistic. He uses a favorite cadmium yellow deep and yellow ochre for Marthe's face with the complementary purple applied to the hair, mostly with a finger. He made full use of the color and texture of the primed white canvas to give strength to the thinly applied colors. It breaks through in the cheek of the figure and in the balcony. The sky is the most opaque passage in the painting. This creates depth in contrast to the open handling of the foreground elements.*

# PAUL KLEE

*Refuge (1930)*

Oil and watercolour on plaster-coated gauze, on paper-faced board
56.8cm × 38.1m/22⅜in × 15in

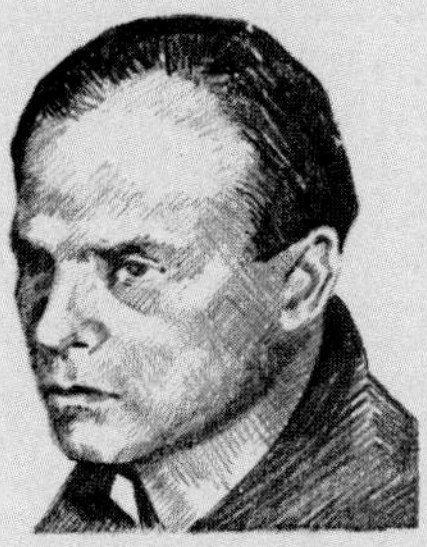

The fact that *Refuge* has a packed sentence describing its medium indicates that Paul Klee enjoyed producing works with a complicated technical development. He liked art that grew and developed in just the same way that the natural world worked: a many-layered and rich process.

Klee was born in Switzerland in 1879, into a family of musicians. He was as gifted musically as he was artistically, but he chose painting as a career because of the two 'it seemed to be lagging behind'.

Klee was also an inspiring teacher, and was appointed by Kandinsky to the Bauhaus in 1920; he taught there for 10 years. From 1931 to 1933 he taught painting at the Düsseldorf State Academy, then gave up teaching and devoted himself entirely to his own creative progress. By 1933 the political situation in Germany appeared threatening and unconducive to artistic freedom, so he returned to his native Switzerland, where he died seven years later.

Alongside his codification of the various factors such as line, tone and color which make up a work of art, Klee devoted much attention to the technical side of painting. His belief that technique should be the artist's servant, not master, led him to take great care in the use of his materials, and to consider the soundness and durability of his work. He was a great experimenter in the field of painting techniques and materials, and appears to have undertaken his technical experiments in a scientific guise. He recorded the stages involved in a work so that he could use them again for reference, or as an indication of what did not work well to his satisfaction.

*Refuge* is inscribed on the reverse, in Klee's hand, with the nine stages used in its execution. The inscription reads: '1, cardboard, 2, white oil-enamel pigment, 3, when 2 has become tacky gauze and plaster, 4, watercolored red-brown as undertone, 5, tempera Neisch [a brand name?] zinc white with linseed mixture, 6, delicate drawing and brush-stroked hatching with watercolor, 7, lightly anchored with oil-painting varnish [turpentine thinner], 8, partly illuminated with zinc white oil paint, 9, covered with oil grey-blue washed with oil madder lake.' The painting is basically a color field made up from oil and watercolor, onto which, at stage six, the lines and the hatched shading which define the figure and the shape above were drawn.

*Refuge* is a fascinating combination of fragility and strength: the fragility is invoked by the tender frailty of line, and the strength by the effort and material involved in creating the base for it. The support is board which was given a layer of white pigment to prime it and to provide a sticky base, onto which Klee pressed a layer of thin gauze. The loose weave of this gauze shows through in patches all over the surface, and the warp and weft of the fabric are cleverly echoed by the painted texture of the hatching. Most of the gauze, however, has been overlaid and impregnated by a thin layer of white plaster, applied with a flat implement – probably a palette knife. The scooped edge of several sweeps of wet plaster is clearly visible. Klee would not have wished to rub his plaster flat, since the visible evidence of the making of the work was important to him.

Klee usually thought up a title for a work after he had completed it: the experimental nature of its genesis totally occupied him and only when it was finished could he stand back, take stock and fully reflect on the nature of its content. *Refuge* was painted in 1930; the year before Klee left the Bauhaus and took up his post in Düsseldorf. It is tempting to speculate whether *Refuge* refers to Klee's own position, torn between holding influential social positions, and yet wanting to create poetic lyrical fantasy works in the quietude of his studio.

Stages one to five of *Refuge* laid in the texture and color of the ground, the space or void, onto which the form was drawn. *Refuge* has a strong vertical axis; the straight line of the creature's nose, if continued upwards, would pass through all four apexes of the curtain-like structure at the top. Since the ground, with its texture and light tonal value, shows through the forms of creature and curtains, it imparts to them a great sense of transparency; and it is difficult to determine whether the formations at the top are to be read as four curtains held back from a central point which recede into space as they descend, or four mountain peaks which recede into depth as they ascend.

This ambiguity is continued in the subject matter. Does the creature wish to seek refuge in the structure at the top of the panel, or is it fleeing away from there, or even from the viewer who completes the picture? The only opaque area of the painting is the dark grey stain, the amorphous shape placed significantly between figure and structure. Reference to other works by Klee, especially *Mixed Weather* (1929), indicates that this opaque shape can be assumed to be a heavy and ominous thundercloud. Since it threatens to discharge matter, and is dense and brimming with material, Klee has wittily made it the only area of the canvas in which the gentle patina of the ground is overridden. Also, when he came to stage nine in his execution, he concentrated the grey-blue and madder lake pigments in their greatest density around this cloud.

Three further washes of various media lie on top of the figures and their hatched shadows. These final layers reinforce the idea of the plane, of the flatness of the painting which may have been in danger of disruption.

*Refuge*, although formally very simple, repays close study since its rich and complicated technical development contains the painting's main statement.

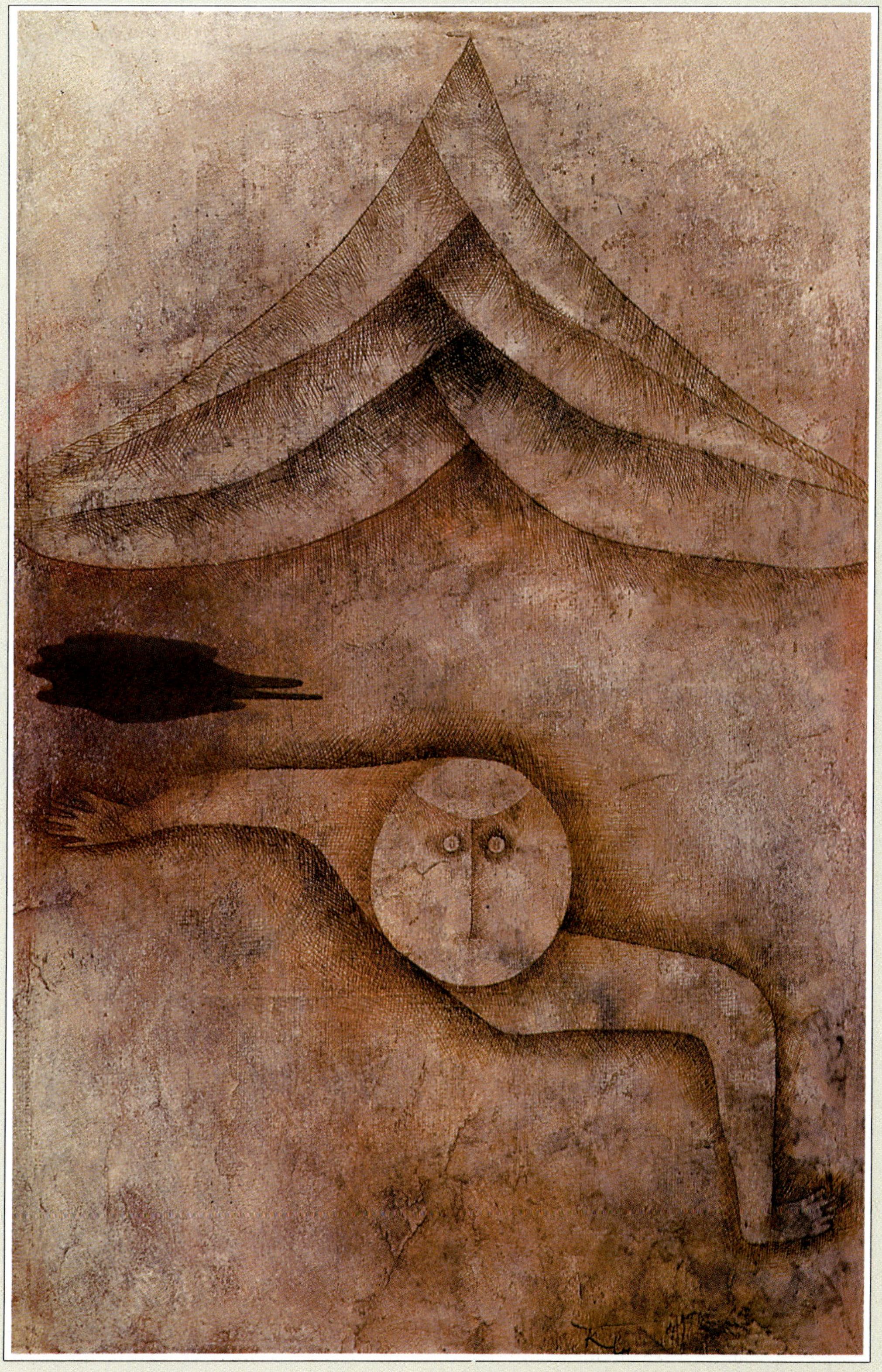

*Paul Klee began his artistic career by cultivating his youthful dexterity as a draftsman. His early works are drawings, engravings and some watercolors. Color gradually came to assume great importance for him, and he took up oil painting around 1919. This work combines an interest in line with an interest in the permeating qualities of color. Klee was always experimenting with technique, and he liked to undertake work in the spirit of a scientific enquiry. The nine processes by which* Refuge *reached its final state are written on the back of the board in the spirit of a speculative theory.*

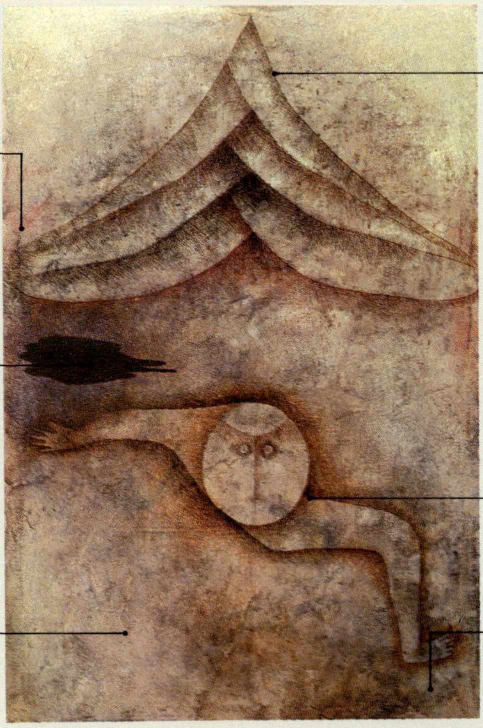


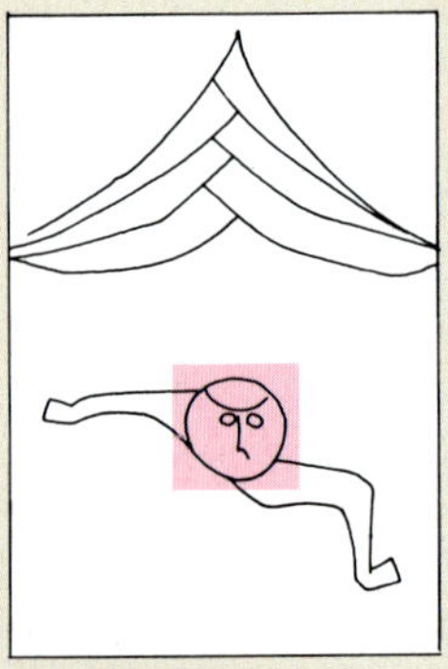

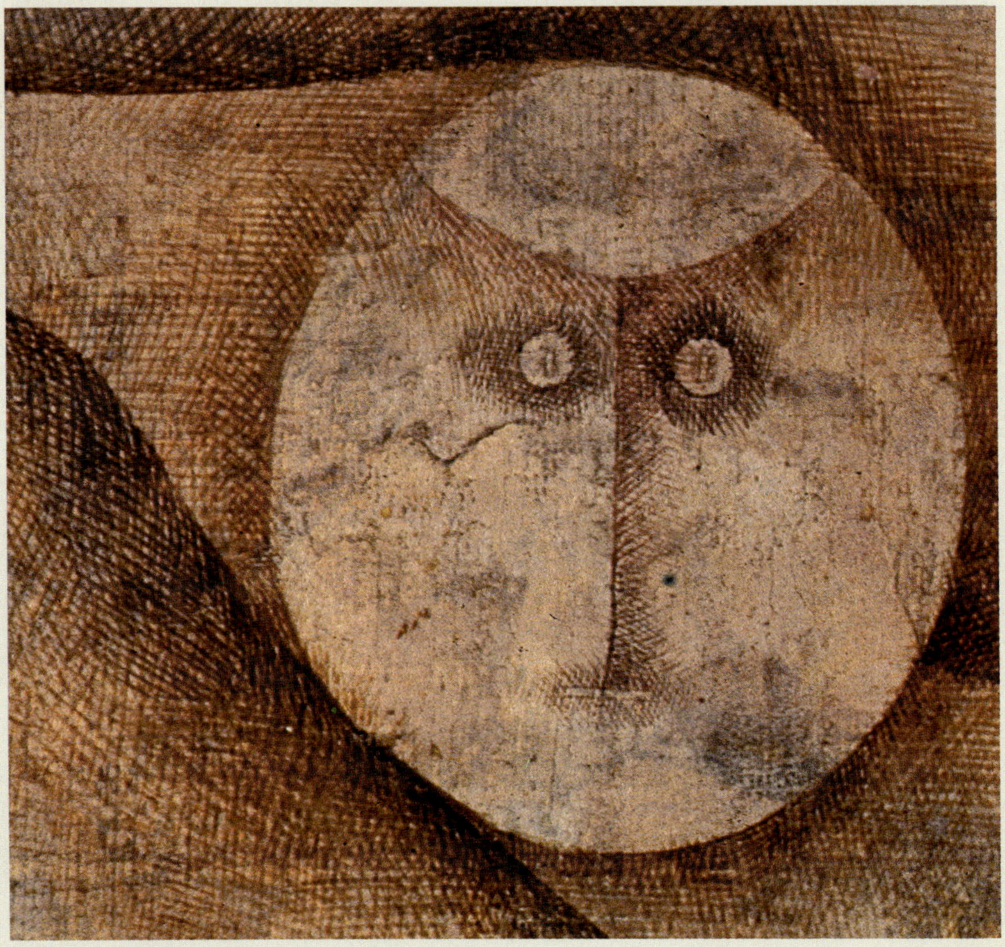

*ACTUAL SIZE DETAIL*
*The figurative element, this creature and its environment, only emerged at the sixth stage in the technical programme of* Refuge. *The regular weave of the gauze stuck on to the cardboard support shows through clearly in the area designated as the creature's hair. The gauze can be seen uncovered at the lower edge of the curve of its right cheek. The mottled ground serves as flesh tone, while the delicate hatched watercolor brushstrokes provide a sense of volume, and serve to distinguish the creature from its background.*

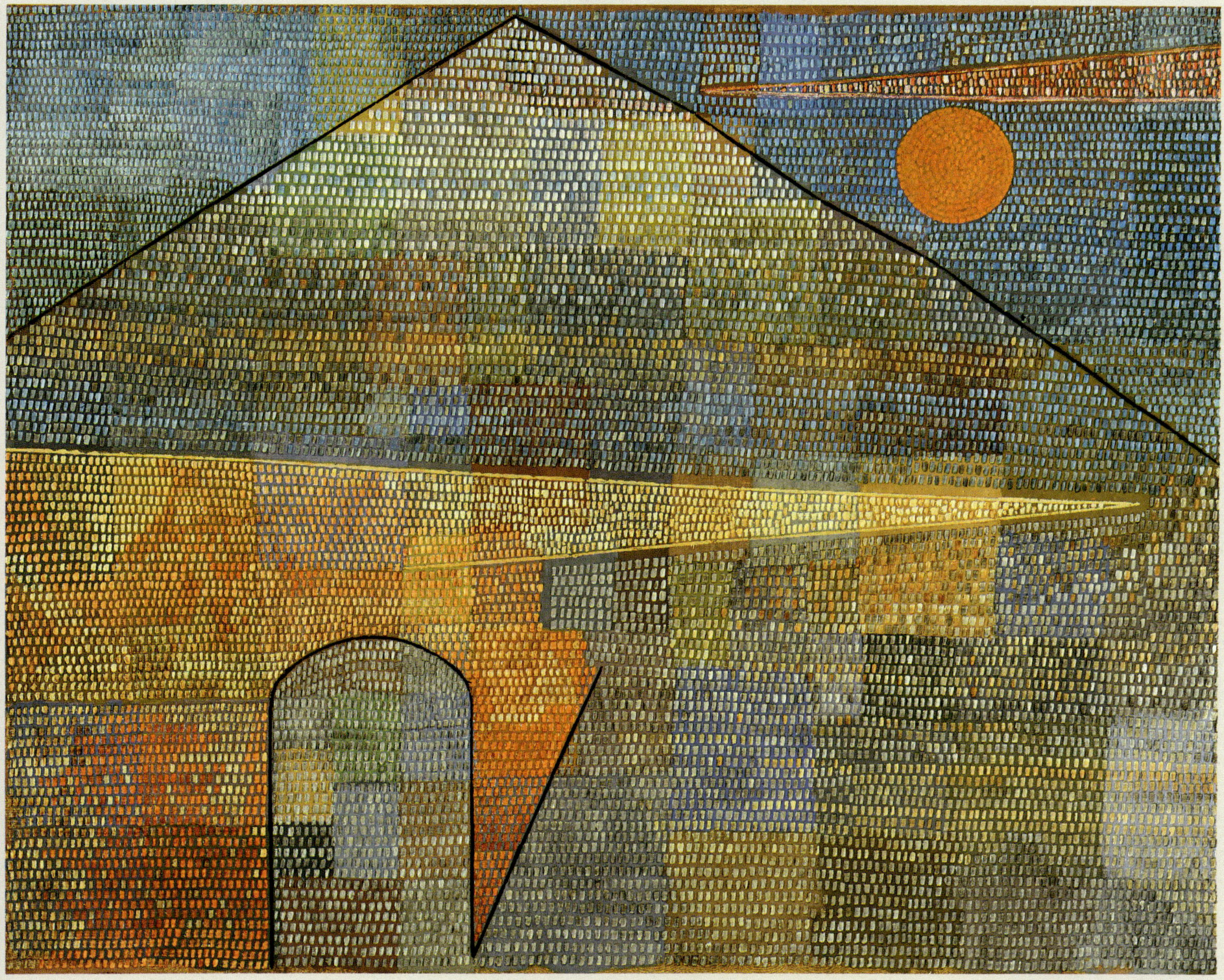

*ABOVE Klee liked to draw musical analogies with painting; if* Refuge *were to be likened to a Scarlatti harpsichord sonata, then* Ad Parnassum, *painted two years later, could compare with a Brahms symphony.* Refuge *is dominated by a single, central motif, while* Ad Parnassum *relies upon the repetition and orchestration of shapes, which are organized into warm-cool, and light-dark oppositions. It uses the traditional materials of oil paint and canvas to achieve this.*

# Salvador Dali

*The Persistence of Memory* (1931)
Oil on canvas, 24.1cm × 33cm/9⅖in × 13in

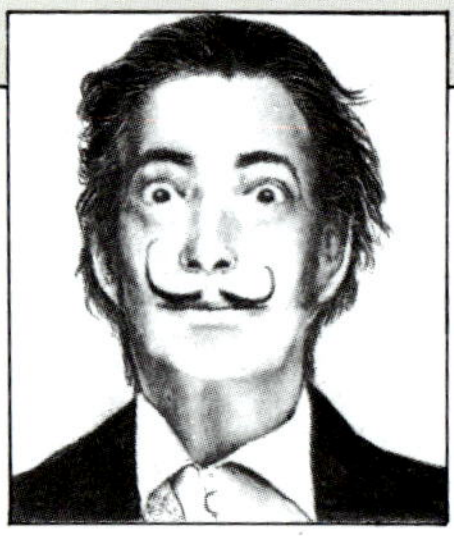

Salvador Dali was born on 11 May 1904 at Figueras on the Spanish coast not far from Cadaquès where he now lives. 'I have adored this region since my childhood with a quasi-fanatic fidelity', Dali states with the hyperbole which characterizes most of his utterances. He joined the Surrealist movement in Paris in 1929 and evolved an art and lifestyle which have come to personify Surrealism in the eyes of the general public.

Dali developed the deep illusionistic space of the twentieth century metaphysical painter Giorgio de Chirico into a setting for paintings of a dream-like and almost paranoiac quality, and from 1929 to 1932, Dali painted a series of small works of almost unequalled hallucinatory intensity. *The Persistence of Memory*, one of the most celebrated paintings in this series, shows a beach near Port Lligat with the distant rocks lit by the transparent light of the end of the day.

Dali described the appearance of the floppy watches in the painting as 'Like fillets of sole, they are destined to be swallowed by the sharks of time'. He found his inspiration for the image after eating a runny camembert cheese. Dali's work is characterized by disturbing and recurring images. For example, the limp, womb-like creature straddled over the rock in the foreground was an obsessional image for him at the time. Dali's technique sought to duplicate the appearance of touched-up photographs to the point where it became impossible to tell what he called his 'handmade photograph' from a collaged fragment of an actual photograph. In doing this, he was using a technique which people had grown accustomed to accepting as a confirmation of reality, as a means of undermining that reality. Dali's revival of photographic illusionism in the late 1920s and 1930s was seen at the time as an attack on the very notion of art. This challenge appeared to question the basis and status of art – if it was impossible to tell the technique of a painting from that of a photograph, how could the painting be called art? However, in recent years, thanks partly to the re-awakening of interest in Realist painting of the nineteenth century and the growth of such movements as photorealism, Dali's technique is now acknowledged to have made a major contribution to the history of twentieth century painting.

**1.** Dali used a small French standard format canvas with a closely woven texture.

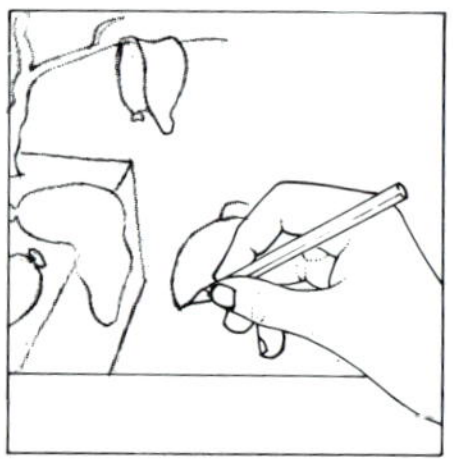

**2.** Dali carried out careful preliminary drawings, which were essential for this type of painting.

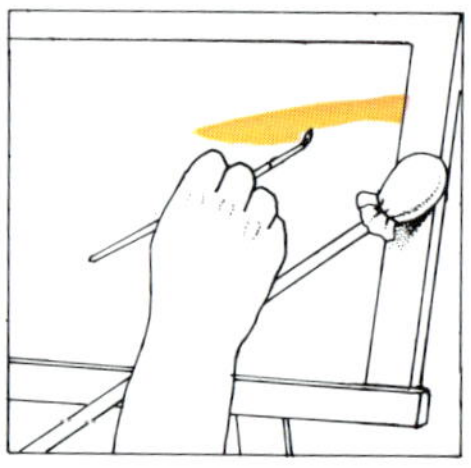

**3.** He used small, round sable brushes to build up the surface in opaque color. He rested his painting arm on a mahl stick. For very close work he used a jeweller's glass to examine the work in progress.

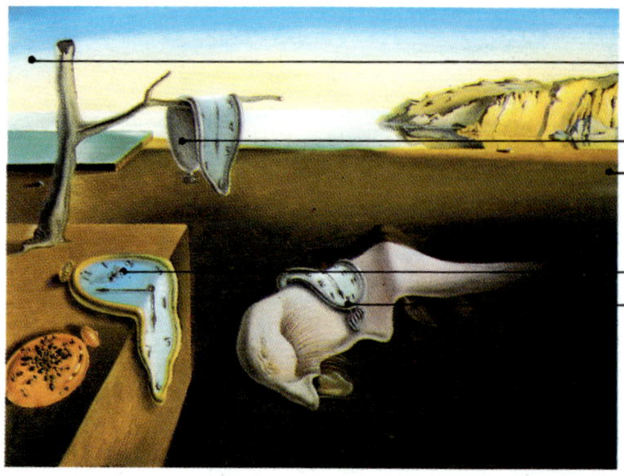

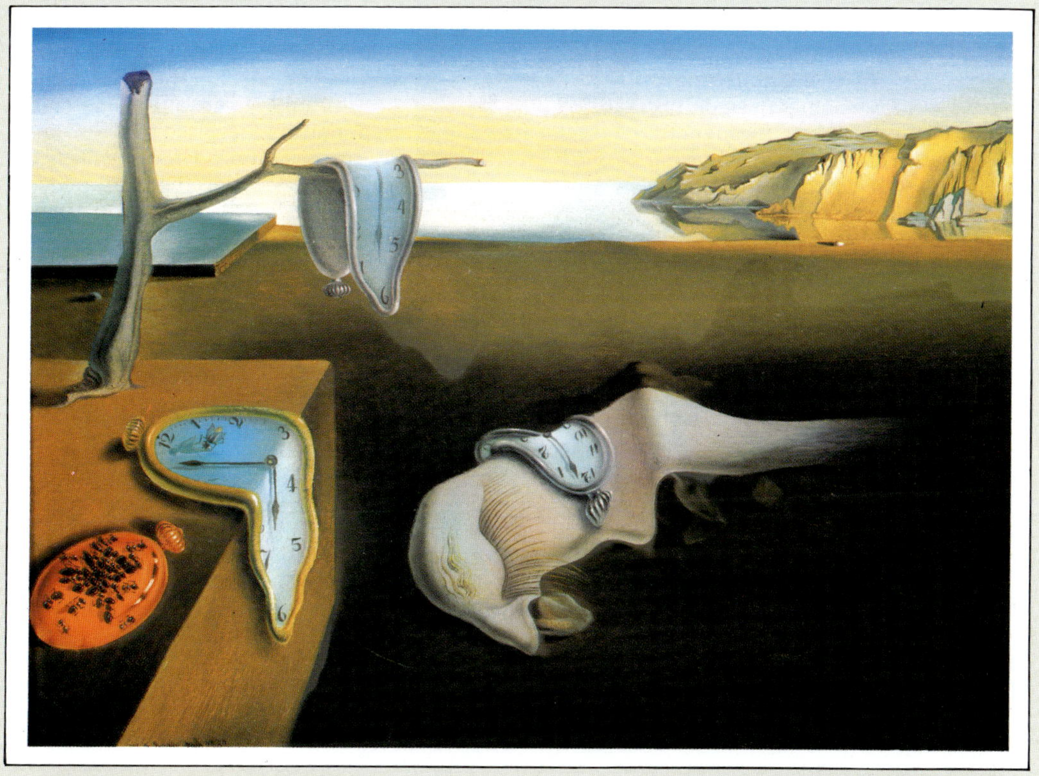

*The jewel-like intensity of the image is achieved due to the application of the paint. The luminosity of the work is conveyed by the careful tonal gradation of the paint layers from the dark foreground to the yellow glow of the fading light in the background. Dali's delicate brushwork and painstakingly careful building-up of the paint mark a reaction against the ideas of the autonomy of color and brushstroke which occupied artists who were contemporaries of Dali. In many ways, Dali's technique looks back to those of the nineteenth-century academic painters, or even to Vermeer. Dali combined realistic technique and surrealistic images to portray a credible image of reality, and, simultaneously, to undermine conventional ideas on that reality. For example, soft objects become hard and hard objects soft, and the relative scale of objects is often changed.*

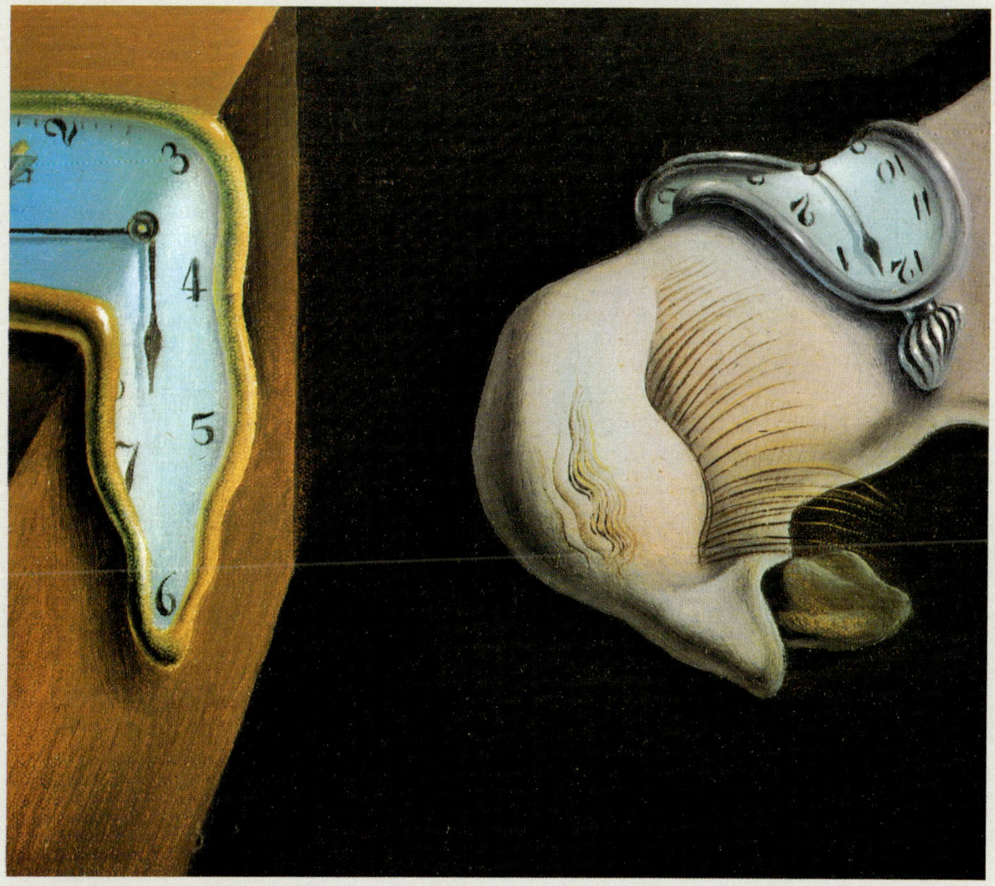

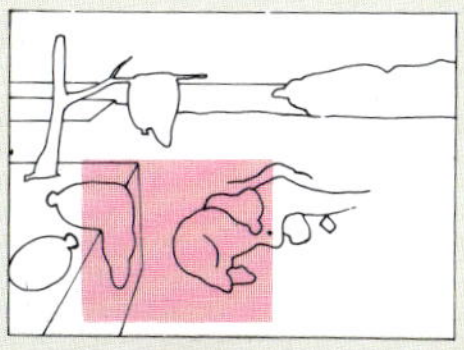

Actual size detail
*The paint surface was built up meticulously in opaque paint. In order to achieve the precise counterfeit of 'naturalistic' appearance, Dali used small, round sable brushes and paint of a liquid consistency. He also used a maulstick and, for particularly close work, a jeweller's glass. Careful preliminary drawings were essential for work of this nature.*

# PAUL KLEE

*Ad Parnassum* (1932)
Oil on canvas, 100cm × 126cm/39in × 49in

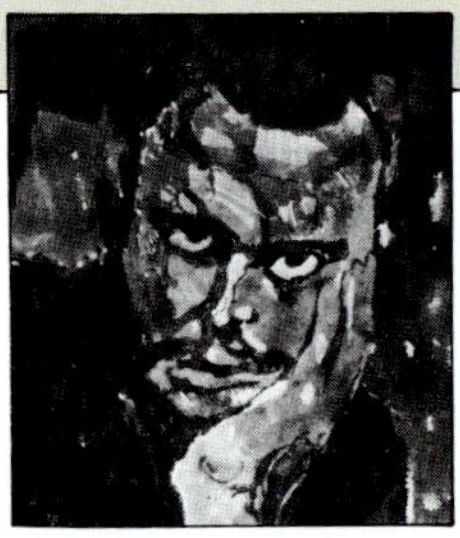

Paul Klee was undoubtedly one of painting's most inventive technicians. He was an astonishingly prolific artist; photographs of his various studios, taken throughout Klee's career, reveal a virtual forest of easels with dozens of works at various stages of development being executed in a wide variety of media. These included, for example, oil on cardboard mounted on wood, oil on plaster-coated gauze on cardboard, oil on canvas mounted on cardboard, oil on canvas coated with white tempera mounted on wood, and even pastel, watercolor and oil on cotton, damask and silk mounted on cardboard. This astonishing technical variety can be explained by Klee's stated belief that a painting should grow like a living organism – 'Art', he wrote, 'is a simile of Creation', and its function 'is to reveal the reality that is behind things'.

Klee's studies in the related fields of natural history, comparative anatomy and anthropology had brought Klee to the belief that nature was characterized by the permutation and movement of fundamental units of construction. He wanted to achieve an equivalent way of working in painting. In addition to his interest in the natural world, Klee also turned to theories of both color and music. As he worked on the basis of units of construction taken from nature, Klee tried to create linear improvisations which he likened to the melody of the work. Klee evolved a system of color organization in which all the colors of the spectrum were conceived of as moving around a central axis dominated by the three pigmentary colors – red, yellow and blue.

From 1923 Klee created a series of imaginative color constructions which he called 'magic squares' in which he applied his theories. This series came to a conclusion in 1932 with *Ad Parnassum*. Klee likened each element in the painting to a theme in a polyphonic composition. He defined polyphony as 'the simultaneity of several independent themes'. In addition, each artistic element in *Ad Parnassum* is itself a distillation of several ideas and personal experiences. For example, the graphic element illustrates the gate to Mount Parnassus, the home of Apollo and the Muses, and also may refer to the Pyramids which Klee saw in 1928, and to a mountain near Klee's home.

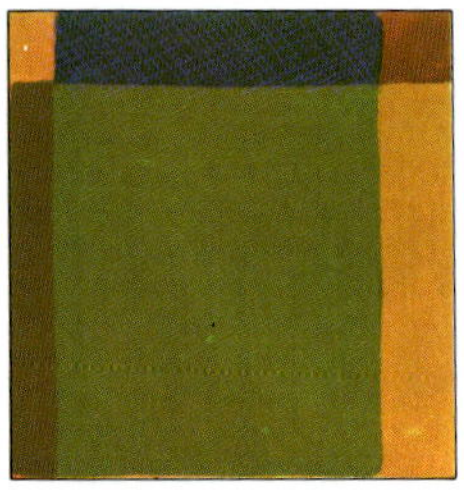

1. On a traditional canvas with a white ground. Klee painted in a grid of flat squares in muted casein-based pigments. Casein is a milk-based medium which gives a subtle, slightly opaque effect. The colors were arranged according to Klee's ideas on color disposition.

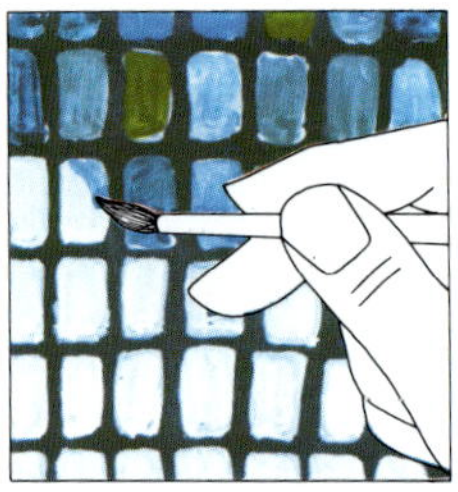

2. The mosaic-like dots were organized in smaller units. Each individual fragment was built up with successive translucent glazes on a preliminary white base.

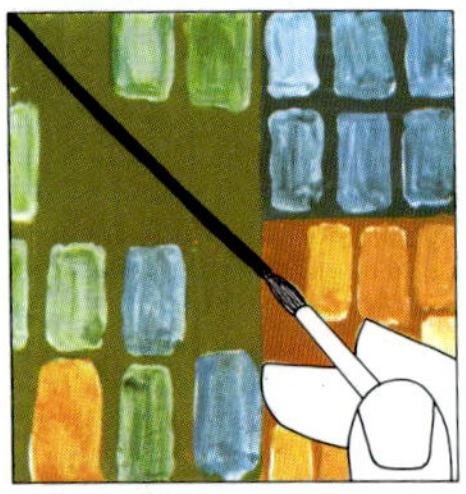

3. Finally the linear element, the 'melody', was painted in in bold lines drawn with a pointed sable brush.

*In* Ad Parnassum, *the colors become stronger towards the top right-hand corner, so in the lower detail the colors are fairly muted. The underlying grid can be seen clearly and the superimposed tones are less crisp and sharp than in the upper areas; indeed this section appears almost shadowy.*

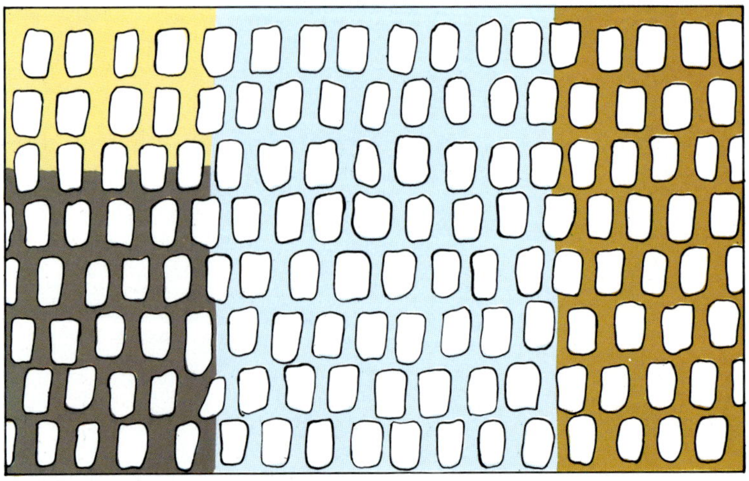

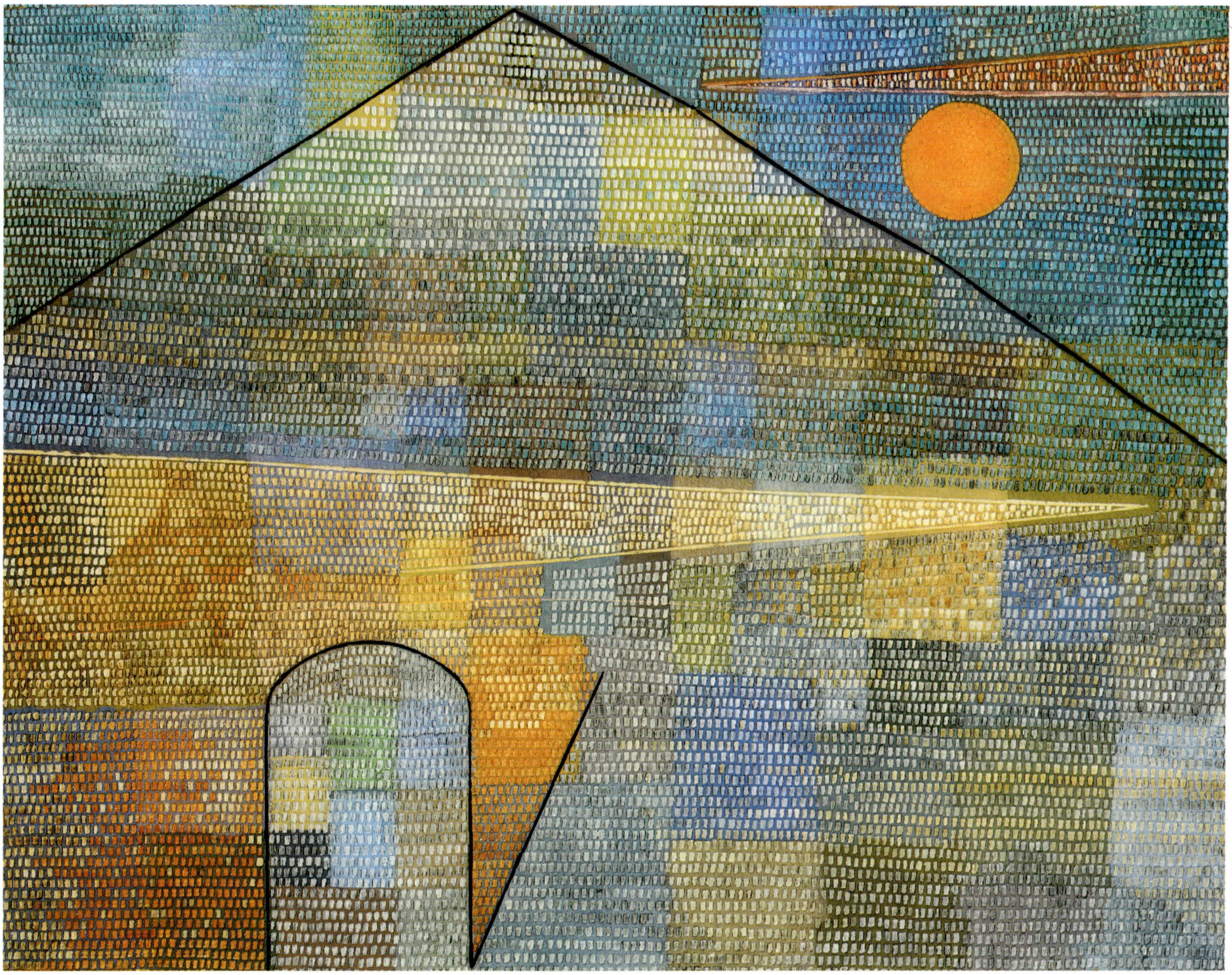

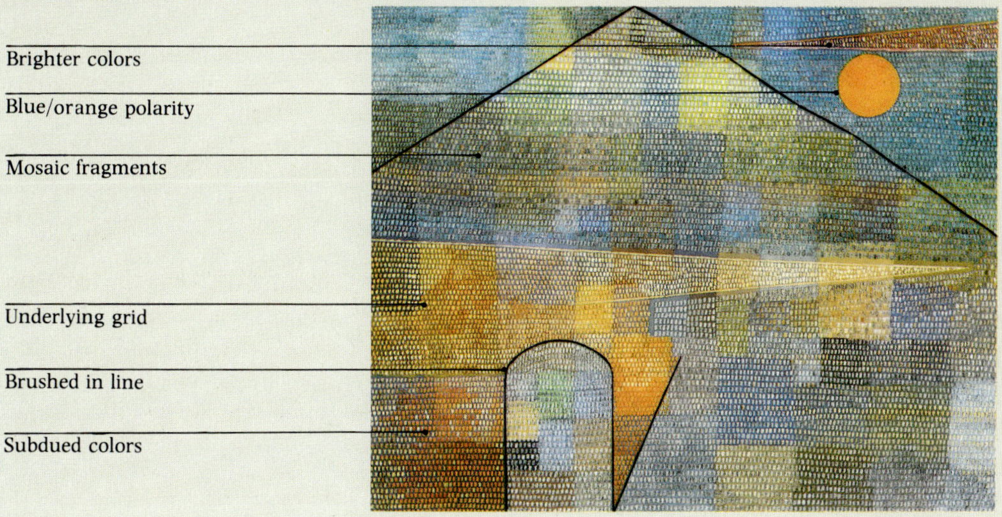


Ad Parnassum *is by far the largest work which Klee painted before 1937, and, in many ways, it sums up his previous achievements. The color scheme moves between poles of light and dark, between orange and blue in two distinct layers. There are three main elements in the painting — the grid of muted colors which was laid first, the superimposed layer of mosaic-like shapes, each individually painted in, and the linear element which was painted in last.*

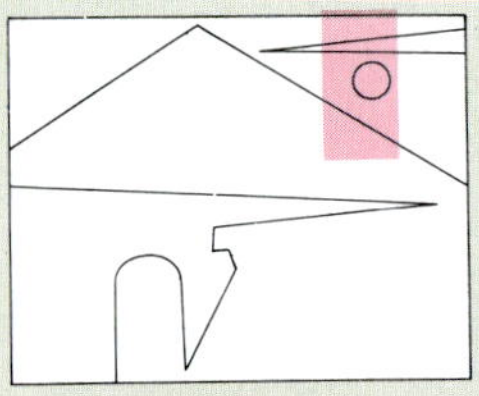

*In* Ad Parnassum *the colors increase in intensity towards the top righthand corner. The brightest part of the work is the orange circle. This is a vital element in the work. It is the culmination of the structural movement of the painting from rectangle to circle through rotation around a central axis. It also marks the conclusion of the color progression from blue to orange and from the bottom lefthand to the top righthand corner.*

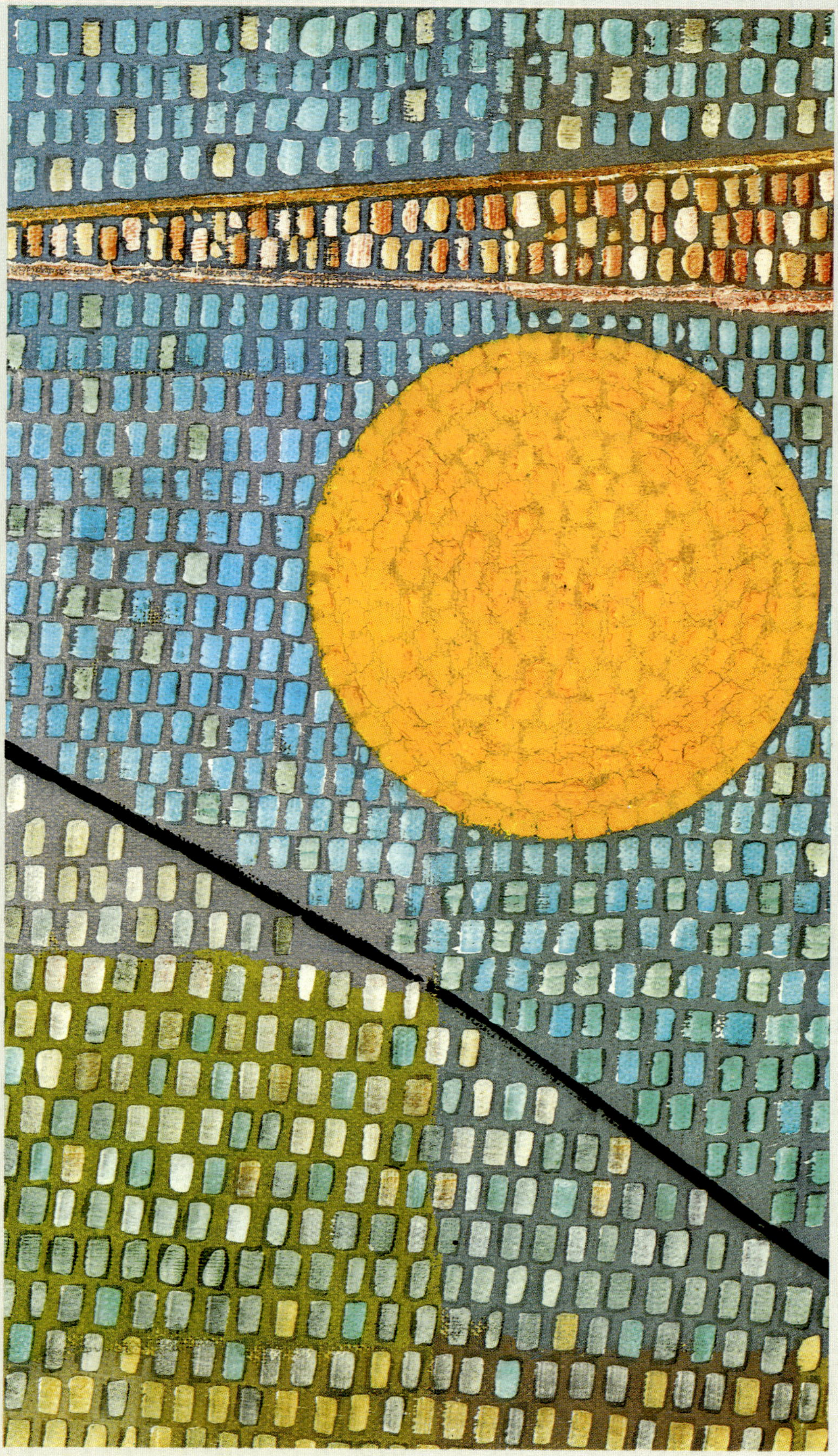

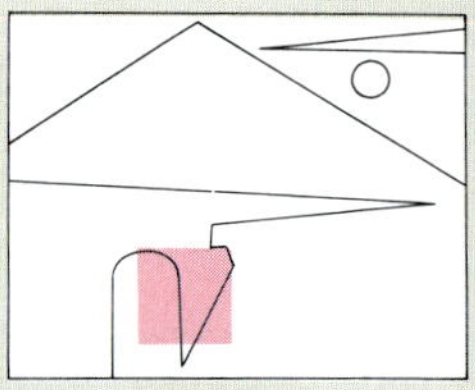

Actual size detail
*This detail shows the artist's working method clearly. The painting was developed from the underlying grid framework, which was painted in muted tones of olive green, blue and violet through to the superimposed grid of mosaic-like fragments, or* tesserae, *in luminous tints. These contrast and counterpoint the underlying grid. The black line was added last. Klee's technique of building up the color in each of the sections allowed him to intensify the color gradually until he achieved the right relationship with the color of the underlying grid.*

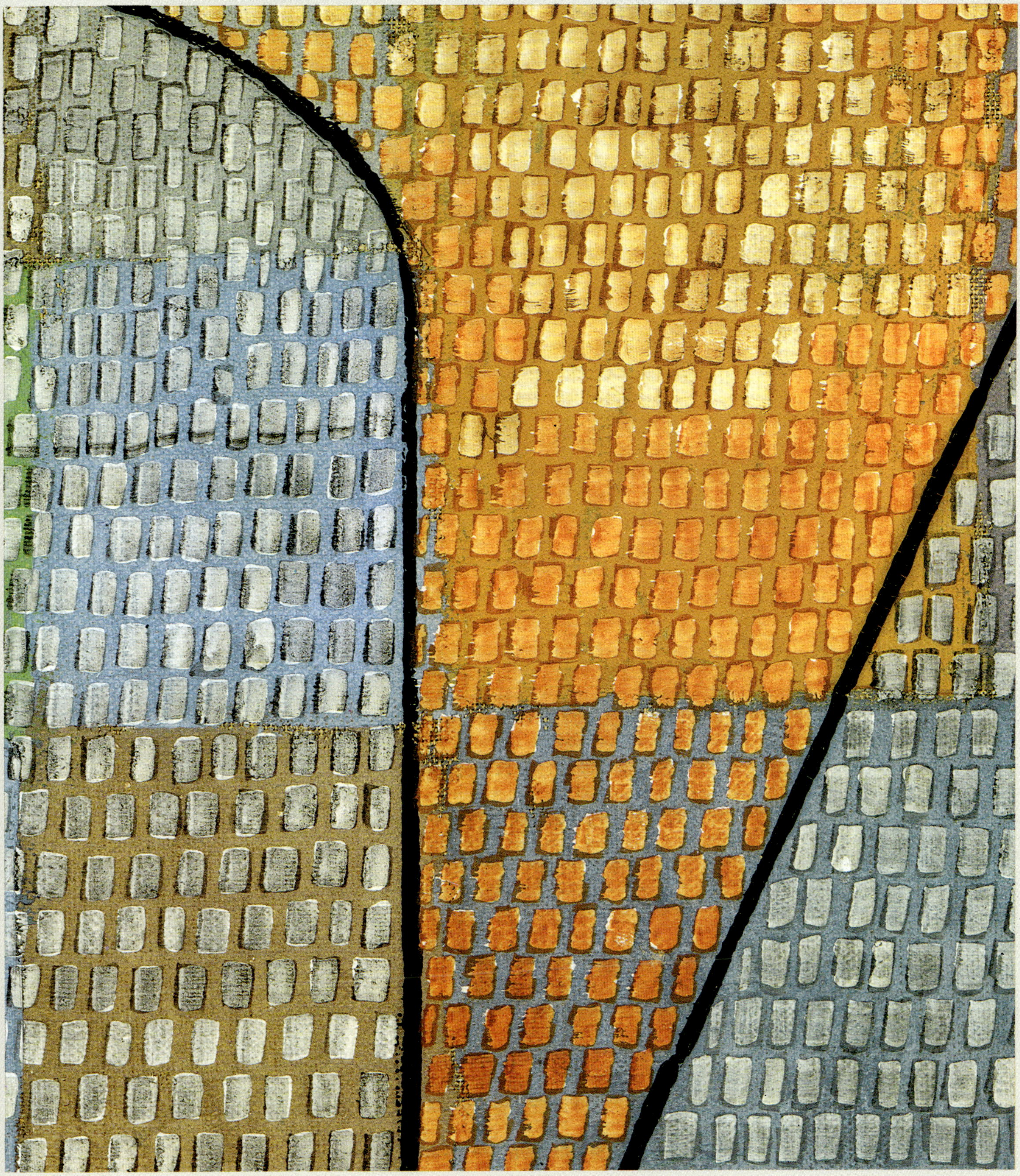

# MAX ERNST

*The Petrified City: Le Puy, near Auch, Gers (1933)*
Oil on paper
50.3cm × 60.9cm/$19^{7}/_{8}$in × 24in

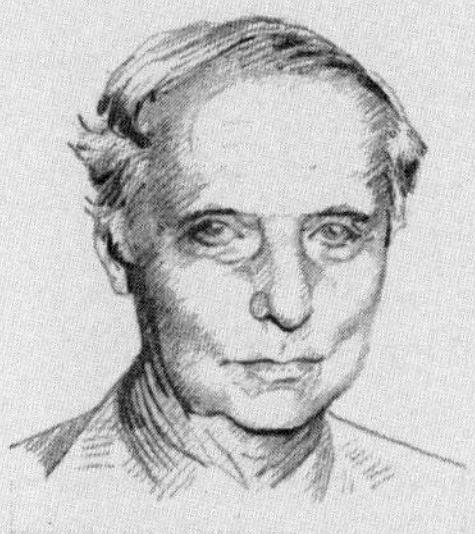

Between the two wars Max Ernst established himself as a major figure in Surrealism and was one of the few artists who survived all the vicissitudes of the movement with his reputation enhanced. Prior to his arrival in Paris in 1922 he had almost single-handedly fired Dada in Cologne and he was one of the few painters who effected the transition from the anarchic effusions of Dada to the more programmatic concerns of Surrealism.

Born in 1891 at Bruehl, in Germany, Ernst always stressed the importance to his art and imagination of nearby Cologne and the formative influence of his childhood there. In this way he conformed to a typical Surrealist notion, that of the creation of a personal myth; but the 'myth' does draw attention to the importance of his provincial background in a city of Catholic legends, magic and relics, set, so he suggests, at no great distance from the primeval Germanic *wald.* The German tradition of painting, particularly the fantastic, unkempt forest world of Albrecht Altdorfer (1480-1538) and the calm but disturbing inner visions of Caspar David Friedrich (1774-1840), was important to Ernst's Surrealist work. He was also inspired by literature – both the romantic poetry of his own country and a select pantheon of French writers, particularly Alfred Jarry (1873-1907).

Ernst had a conventional academic education at the University of Bonn, where he acquired a thorough knowledge of psychiatry and psycho-analysis; knowledge that lay behind his apparently instinctive ability to summon up deep fears and desires in his work. It was at this stage, too, that he became involved with modern painting, meeting Macke in Bonn in 1909, attending the second Blaue Reiter and Sonderbund exhibitions in Cologne and gaining familiarity with a large range of avant-garde work.

Ernst had already achieved a certain cult status in Paris through his 1920 exhibition there before he actually settled in the city. Thus he was already a figure of authority to the young Surrealist group; his influence was enhanced by his nationality, which provided the Parisians with a genuine flavor of the fantastic German tradition they so admired.

Ernst's great importance at this point was as the pioneer and virtual inventor of Surrealist painting. His erudition and his friendship with the poet Paul Eluard (1895-1952) helped him to gain acceptance into what was still a firmly literary circle. Its leader, André Breton, still possessed doubts about the possibility of a visual equivalent of the written work that he hoped would express the character of Surrealism. Ernst's exploration of the Surrealist energy of de Chirico's work (who, like Ernst, was familiar with German poetry and philosophy) produced the celebrated work *Celebes* (1921), in which the use of factual, realistic elements, reassembled with the mysterious logic of the dream, created the technique used in most subsequent Surrealist paintings.

In this crucial respect, Ernst's work was enormously influential and his technique of drily applied oil paint, which he derived from de Chirico, became a medium favored by the Surrealists, its studied conventionality acting as the perfect foil for the unnerving juxtaposition of images.

Ernst had used oils before the war but, like most Dadaists, rejected them in favor of alternatives less associated with a discredited, self-absorbed aestheticism. Thus in Cologne he had turned to collage, cannibalizing technical manuals, medical handbooks and mail order catalogs to create subversive anthropomorphic machinery and sinister, animated little organisms moving in pen, pencil and watercolor landscapes that were the precursors of the arid, hallucinatory plains of Surrealism. Actual machine parts were used in a rudimentary form of printing to leave their inked impression on the paper. Photomontage, too, gave the opportunity for manipulating familiar imagery until it lost the assurance of its factual associations.

Ernst was a considerable technical innovator in his own right. *Frottage* – the process of producing rubbings through paper from the surface of wood, leaves, fabric or anything with textural pattern – produced the 1926 set of drawings *Histoire Naturelle,* an alternative handbook of Surrealist fauna inspired by the natural materials that lent themselves to the technique.

From *frottage* it was an easy step to *grattage,* which Ernst used in *The Petrified City,* painted in 1933. A painted canvas was pressed down on a surface, necessarily of a less fragile nature than those used in *frottage*; often metal grids were used, producing a harder, more linear form, and then the paint was scraped back to reveal a negative image of the texture beneath.

*The Petrified City* is a fine example of a subject that was to appear in many versions during Ernst's work of this decade. These lost citadels rise up from the tangled forest world that he had developed in his earlier work, and suggest the ruins of a lost civilization, now overcome by the dark, dense power of nature. Often he removed the central core of the 'moon' to create a mysterious 'ringed' planet which reveals more clearly the idea of parallel natural world upon another planet.

Besides the Surrealist concern for the creation of a new world, recognizable yet also disconcertingly apart from our own, the melancholy and menace of this work suggests too the prophetic quality that Ernst was often capable of creating. An image such as this can be seen as a vision of future desolation and a response to the darkening skies of Europe before the war.

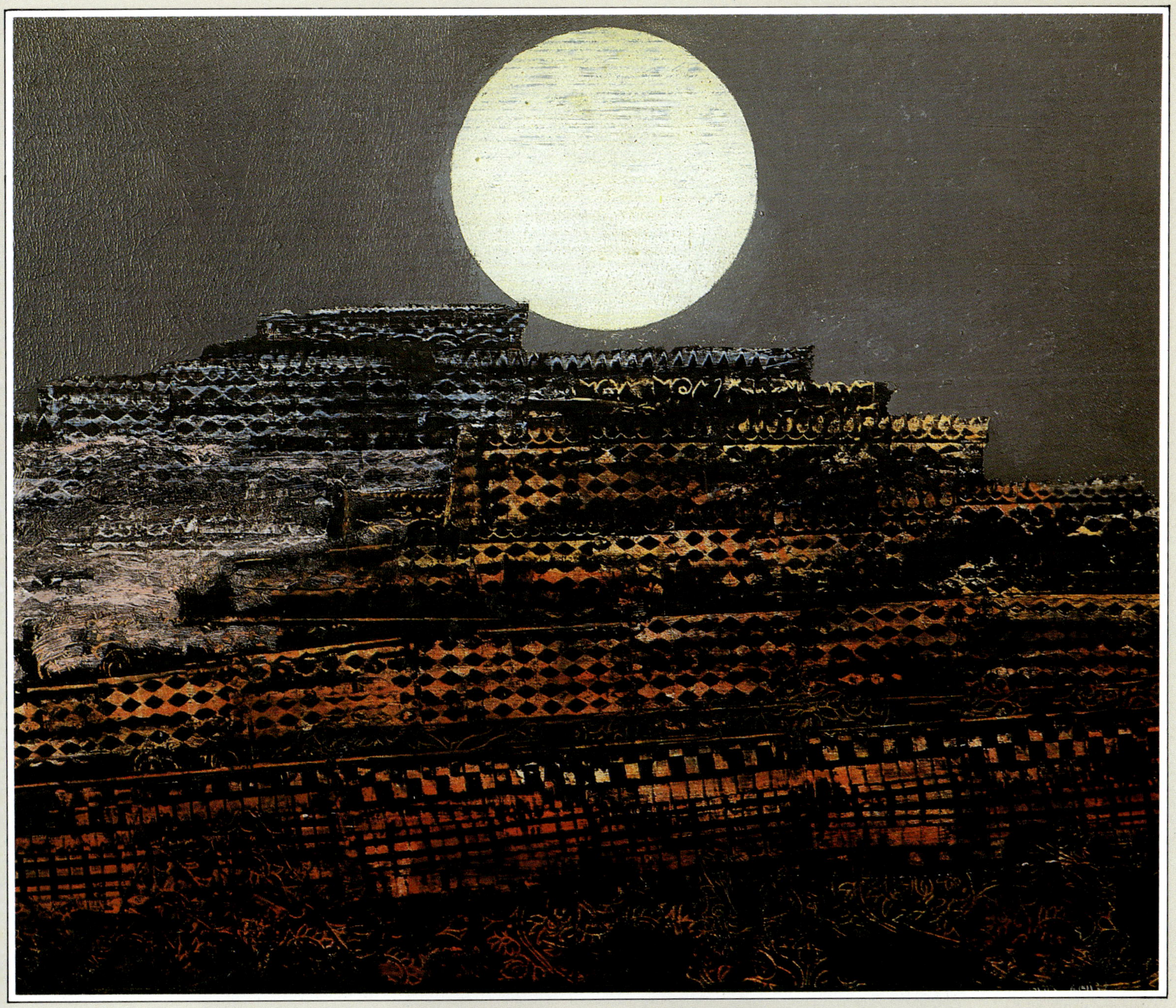

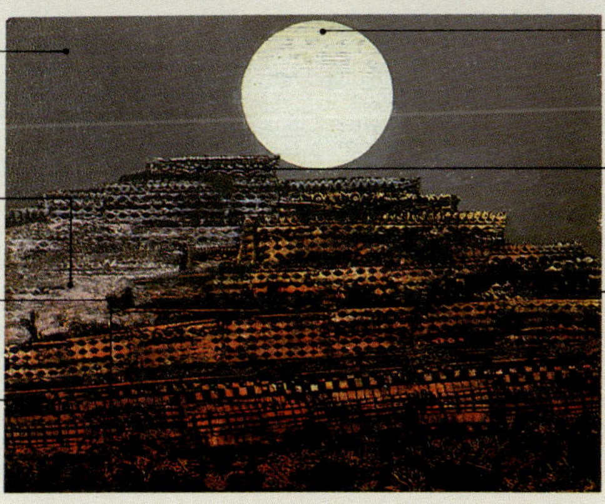


*Typically with Ernst, while the entire look of* Petrified City *derives from the technique of* grattage, *he has used his original method for highly expressive ends. Eschewing traditional modes of paint application and representation he has created a hallucinatory, other-worldly image which is registered instantly, and which works itself out more through our powers of imaginative projection, than of close scrutiny.*

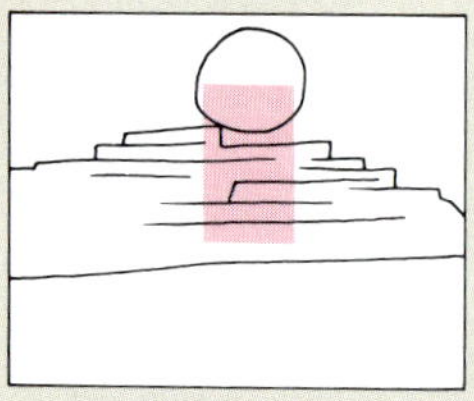

*RIGHT To the left, the blue background has been loosely overpainted wet onto dry, the brushmarks at the point flecking the surface of the 'moon'. Pale blue points and ribs are visible across this moon, and the yellow paint has blistered into small bubbles and patches. Conversely, to the right, spots of yellow are visible through the blue. The crowning level of the 'city' overlaps the moon-disc a fraction, but there is a suggestion that this corner 'battlement' was added at a later stage. The dog-tooth and scroll-like patterns deriving from the spread of paint across a similarly designed surface are reddened with a sunset-like glow towards the bottom, smeared with a lighter blue in the top, and enlivened with touches of pink on the left. Black lozenges and blacked-out areas everywhere complement these brighter hues, while the whole grattaged surface has a kind of deep textural unity made possible only by Ernst's infinite technical finesse.*

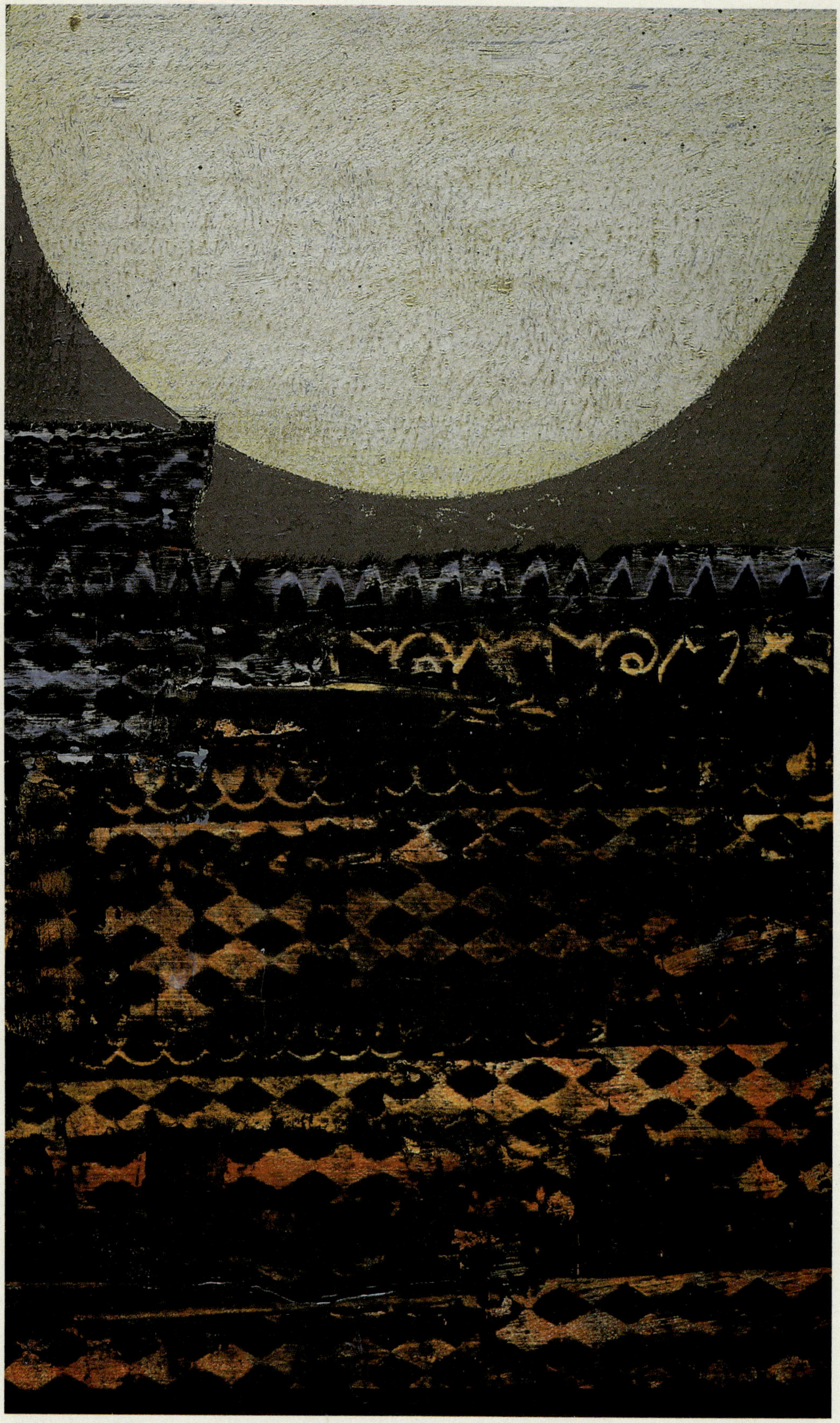

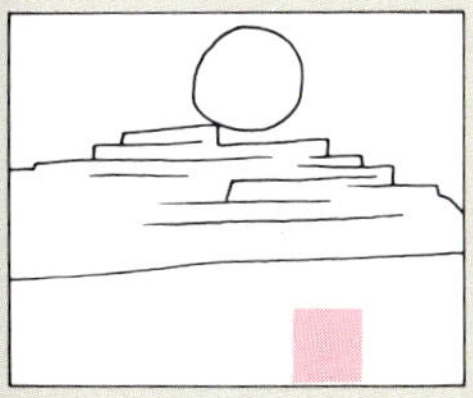

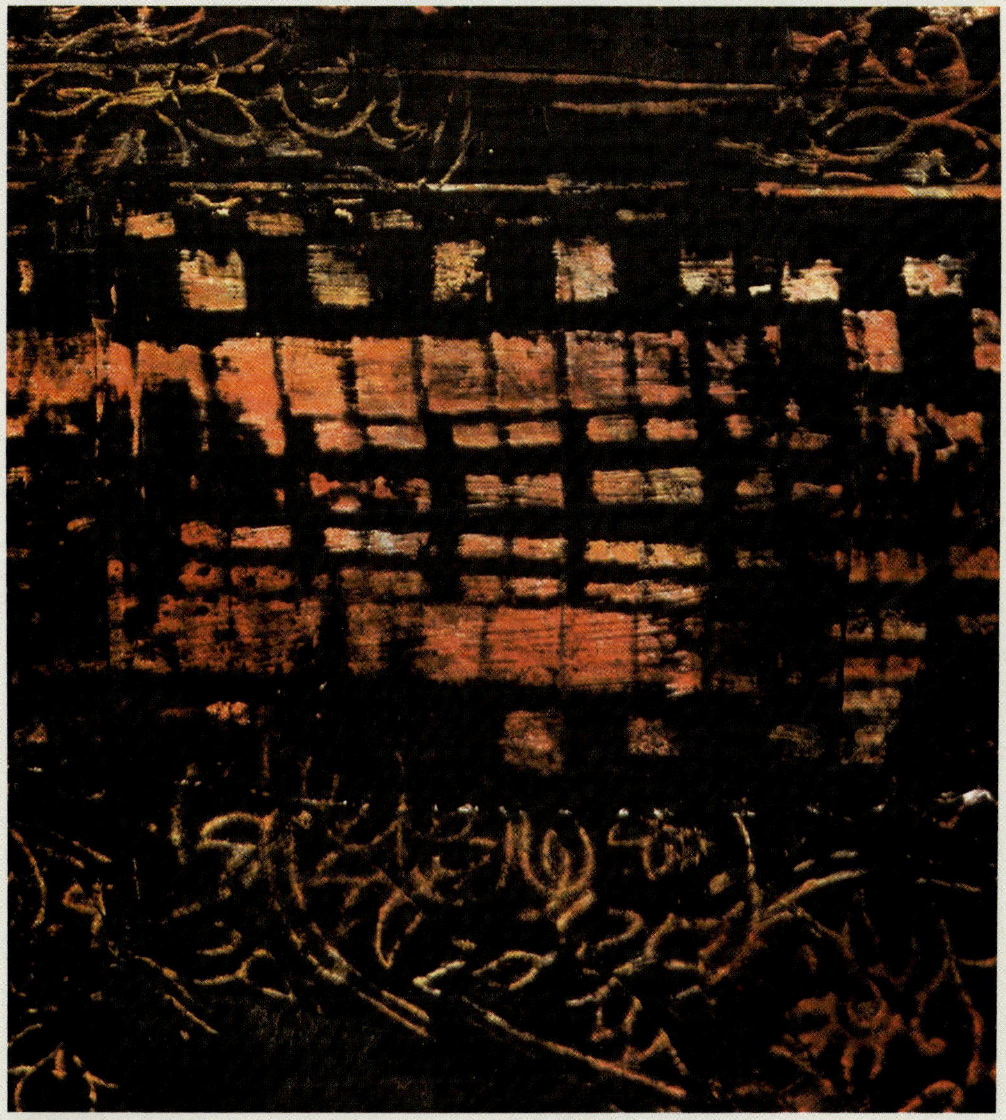

*ACTUAL SIZE DETAIL*
*This section through a grattaged layer shows the main alignment, rather like a band of film with heavy black checks and a thinner, irregular grid underneath. The grid is interrupted by the intermittent acanthus-like motifs below, which appear ghosted-through the thick black paint, taking on miscellaneous roseate hues. The fineness of lines in this pattern and the coarseness of application behind it, is a subtle juxtaposition, typical of the grattage technique itself.*

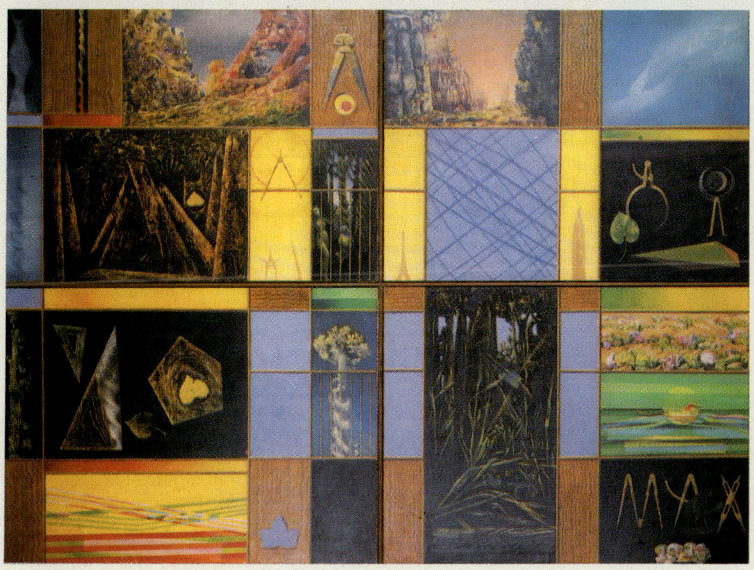

*RIGHT* Vox Angelica *(1943) is made up of four canvases each 76 x 101.5 cm (30 x 40 in). The work includes reference to all the techniques for which Ernst was known. Paris and New York are juxtaposed in the Empire State Building and the Eiffel Tower. Images such as the geometrical instruments and the drill recur in the painting. The image of the drill is paralleled in the images of the snakes entwined around trees; possibly references to the serpent in the Garden of Eden.*

# PIET MONDRIAN

*Composition with Red, Yellow, and Blue* (c. 1937-42)
Oil on canvas, 69cm × 72cm/27in × 28in

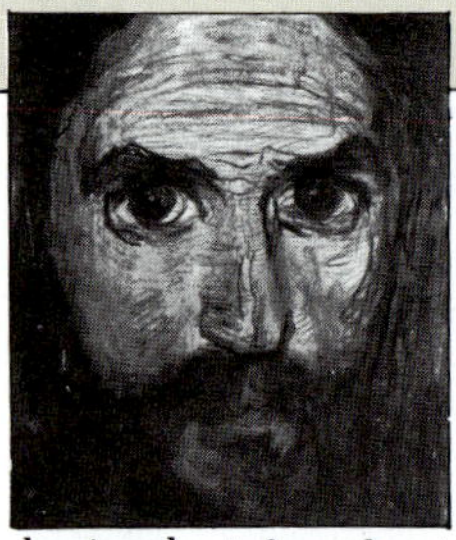

Piet Mondrian was born in Amersfort, near Amsterdam, Holland, in 1872 and subsequently worked in Holland, Paris and latterly New York where he died in 194 Mondrian was one of the greatest and certainly most single-minded exponents of abstract art. His rigorously abstract style looks extremely simple and an understanding of Mondrian's aesthetic views is important in order to grasp his technique and working methods. It is perhaps surprising that he began his career as a technically very proficient draughtsman and painter in the Dutch naturalistic tradition. However, between 1911 and 1919 Mondrian's art went through a lengthy process of reduction. He had come to equate naturalistic representation with subjectivity and he now wanted to achieve an objective vocabulary for art by abstracting colors and forms to the point where they became fundamental units in the construction of the painting. Colors became opaquely painted flat planes of primary color (red, blue and yellow) and non-color (white, black and gray), and forms were reduced to the straight line in what he termed 'its principal opposition', the right angle.

However, within these formal and aesthetic constraints, Mondrian's works remain highly personal. The subjective element asserts itself in the exact placing of the lines and blocks of color. In *Composition with Red, Yellow and Blue,* for example, adjustments can be seen around the four horizontal lines. These were made to ensure that the lines were in the right balance, in accordance with the artist's views on universal harmony. For implementing these metaphysical ideas, Mondrian used a grid system based on eight squares, like a chess-board.

While he worked in Paris his main tools for working out the painting were, according to his friend Michel Seuphor, a ruler and strips of transparent paper. However, when he went to New York, he began using other types of tape, both colored and adhesive, which he found extremely easy to move around when he was working on an upright canvas.

In addition to his artistic output, Mondrian is also remembered for founding the influential magazine *De Stijl* in 1917 with his fellow Dutch artist Theo van Doesburg. *De Stijl* provided a forum for Mondrian to develop his theories on abstract art.

**1.** Mondrian did not use a standard French format canvas. He favoured a vertical measurement which would divide into eight equal units of 9 cm (3·5 in).

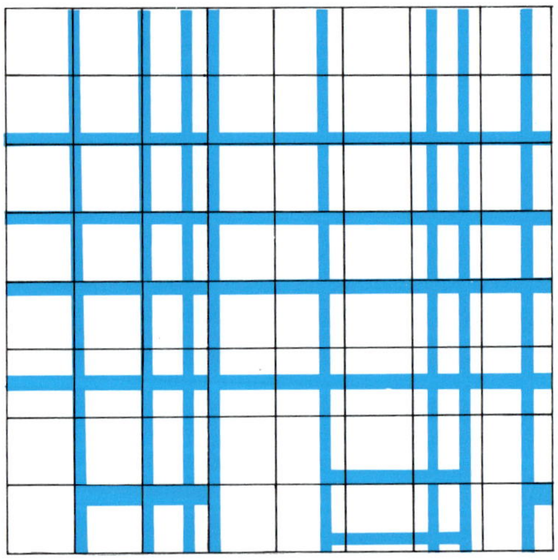

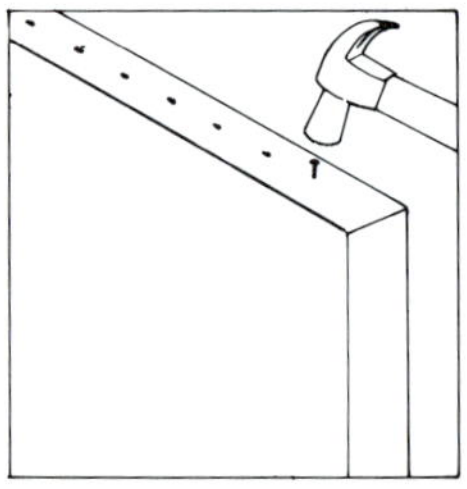

**2.** The finely woven linen canvas was attached to the stretcher by iron tacks and tape. A commercial ground of size and oil was then applied evenly over the whole canvas.

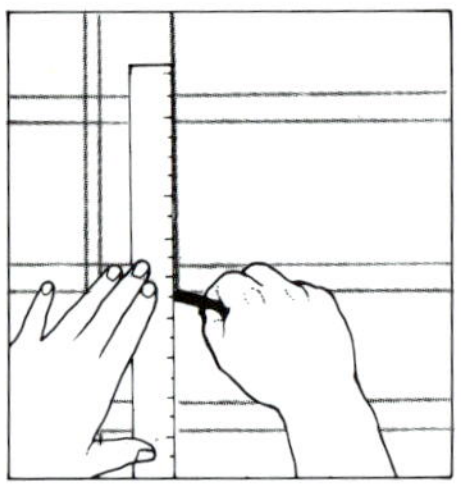

**3.** The projected grid structure, usually based on small sketches, was drawn on the canvas in charcoal.

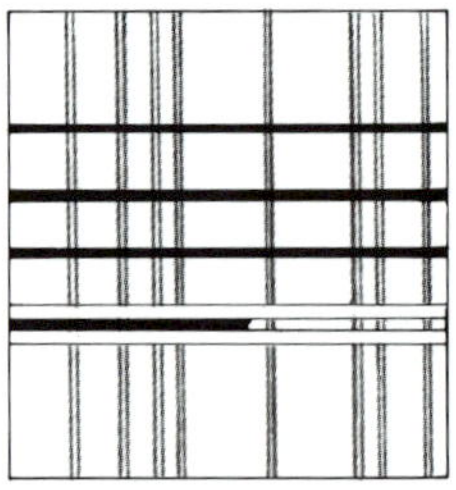

**4.** The 4 main horizontal lines, based on the division into 8 squares, were then painted in. Mondrian probably used strips of tape, possibly adhesive, to help him position the lines.

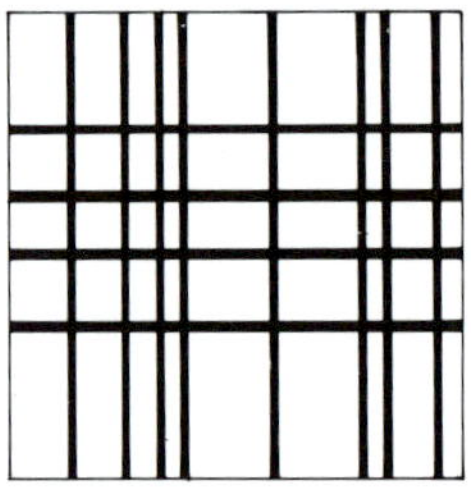

**5.** The 8 vertical lines were painted over the 4 horizontal lines and minute adjustments were made to ensure correct positioning.

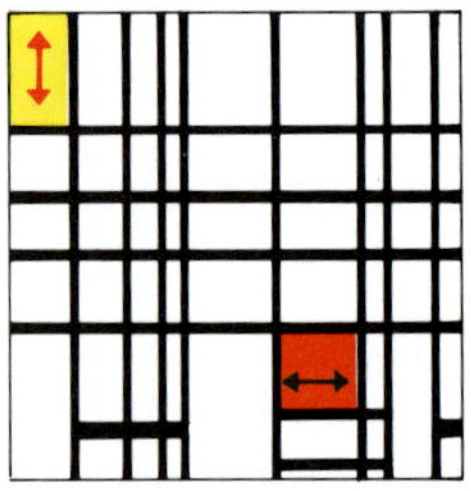

**6.** The cadmium yellow rectangle was brushed vertically and the main red square was brushed horizontally, as were the strips of cobalt blue and cadmium red, probably added later.

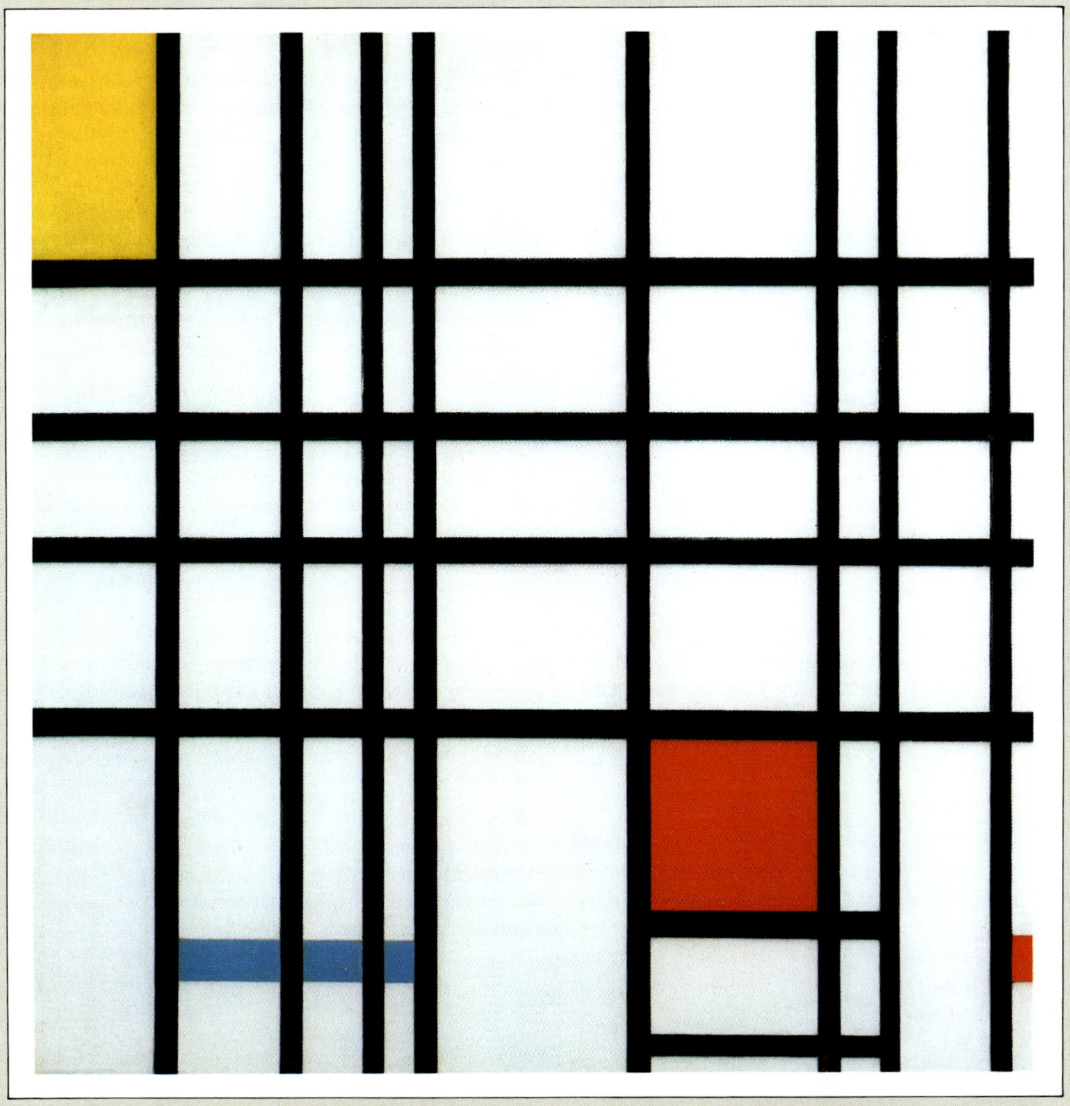

Composition with Red, Yellow and Blue *is an interesting example of Mondrian's constant modification and refinement of his technical means. The work was begun in Paris around 1937 and was completed in 1942, after Mondrian's move to New York. Mondrian's Paris studio was described by his friend Michel Seuphor, who thus gives an insight into the artist's working methods: 'The room was quite large, very bright, with a very high ceiling. . . . The actual work was done on the table. It stood in front of the large window facing the Rue du Départ, and was covered with a canvas waxed white and nailed to the underside of the boards. I often suprised Mondrian there, armed with a ruler and ribbons of transparent paper, which he used for measuring. I never saw him with any other working tool.' In New York, Mondrian began to use colored tapes which could be moved about the canvas easily while it was upright on an easel. His studio walls were covered with constantly changing rectangles of color to help give him inspiration.*

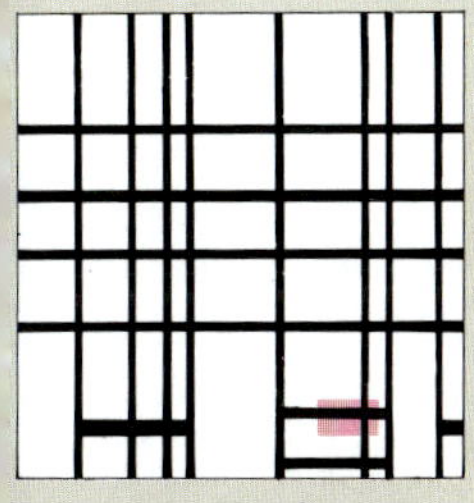

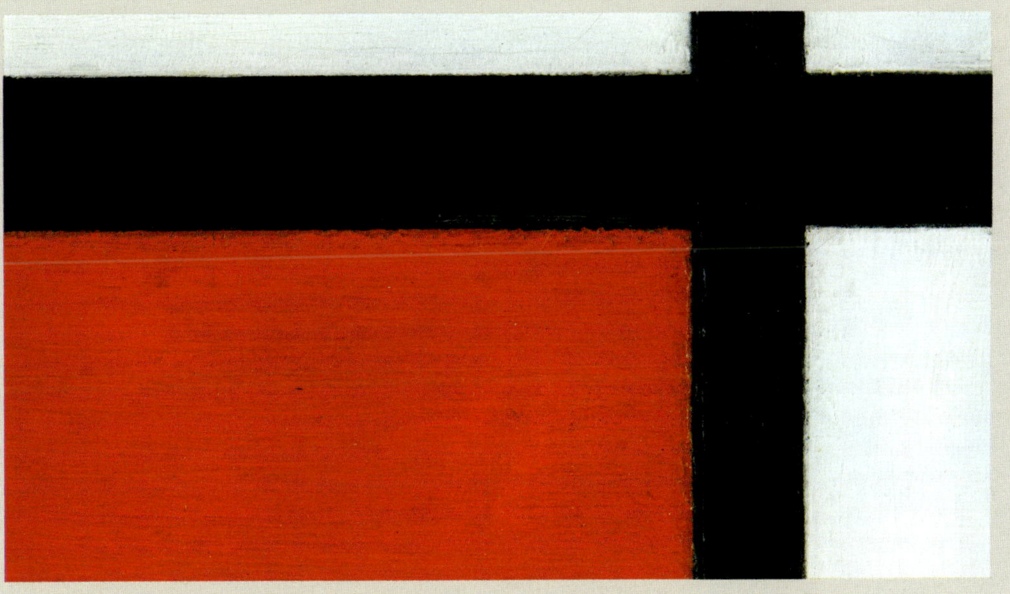

Actual size detail
*Mondrian so reduced his technical means that any changes in approach are extremely important. For example, there was an alteration to the bottom black line and the white overpainting can be clearly seen. The brushwork is horizontal in the red section and vertical in the narrower white oblong.*

# SALVADOR DALI

*Mountain Lake (1938)*
Oil on canvas
75cm × 92cm/28¾in × 36¼in

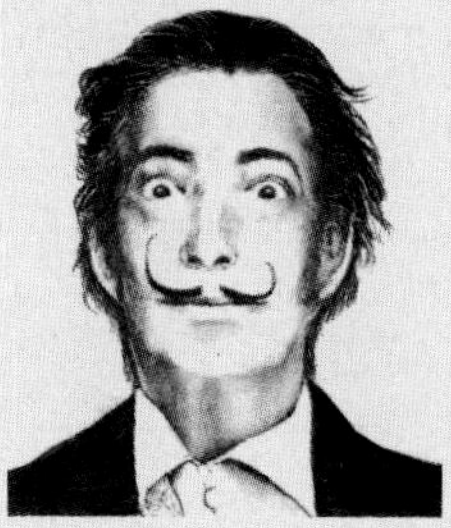

Dali's enormous appetite and talent for self-promotion and showmanship, his rhetorical and evasive writings,his gladiatorial capacity for debate and spectacle have so seduced the public imagination and the agencies of reproduction that he has some claim to being the most popular of twentieth-century painters. There has always been a wide gulf, however, between his popular and his art historical reputations. Far from allowing his work to stand as paradigms of the Surrealist spirit, critics have been quick to label him as a 'charlatan', as non-avant-garde in his rejection of modernist techniques and styles, and as a vulgar herald of 'the triumph of publicity over art'.

Salvador Dali was born in May 1904 in Figueras in north-eastern Spain. He retained vivid and powerful recollections of the local landscape. Dali's first instruction and interests were thoroughly academic and largely nineteenth century. In 1921 he entered the school of Fine Arts in Madrid, where he met the poet Frederico Garcí Lorca (1899-1936) and the future film maker Luis Buñuel (b 1900). During the late 1920s Dali became progressively enthralled by some of the ideas and experiments of Surrealism; but there is a sense in which he was never a real convert. His allegiance was eccentric, and his paintings, like the work of most of the 'visual' Surrealists, did not toe the line of André Breton's manifesto orthodoxy.

As an artist Dali has employed a bewildering range of media apart from the photographic or 'magic' realism for which he is so well known. His defence of the conceptual priority of ideas above the materials and techniques used to express them is an indication that he would accept no hierarchic order of importance for his various activities, and that he often considered words and sentences to be as effective carriers of information as, for example, oil painting. He worked in film, advertising, set and costume design for theater and ballet; he made jewelry, holographs, installations and a variety of Surrealist and other 'objects'. In more orthodox representational areas he used oil on board, panels, wood and canvas; mixed oil with collage and sand; drew on paper with ink, pencil and charcoal, and even put oil on embossed pewter. In 1958 he exhibited atomic 'anti-matter' paintings in New York. The list could go on.

Of all these techniques and styles, however, it was in oil on canvas and in the scrupulously detailed style of photographic realism which dominated his painting from about 1929 onwards that Dali found the suitable vehicle to express his alternative Surrealist theory of 'critical paranoia'. This self-induced state of delusion is evoked in a work such as *Mountain Lake* by the disparity of register between meticulous technical realism and the hallucinatory interruption of objects which subvert the normality of the 'scene'.

With typical erudition Dali wrote in *La Conquete de l'irrational (Conquest of the Irrational)* (1935) that: 'My whole ambition in the pictorial domain is to materialize the images of concrete irrationality with the most imperialist fury of precision in order that the world of imagination and concrete irrationality may be as objectively evident, of the same consistency, of the same durability, of the same persuasive, cognoscitive and communicable thickness as that of the exterior world of phenomenal reality.'

Dali thus took an anti-modernist position on the nature of his technique and materials. Rather than celebrating the canvas surface as the site of visual autonomy and indulging in the play of shape and color he communicated certain psychic effects as though his paint medium were transparent. It is, therefore, particularly difficult here to separate a technical analysis from other considerations.

The first impression of *Mountain Lake* is of the somber bluey, grey-green crepuscular atmosphere which saturates the picture, only to be enlivened by points and flashes of light and reflection. This tonal ubiquity is one of the several devices by which Dali attempts to persuade the view of the seamlessness of his paint application. The modulation of the vast area of darkening sky in opposition to the calculated specificity of the rocks and pebbles on the shore of the lake is another encouragement. A photograph of the work in raking light reveals minutely molded scumbling with careful tints of color, particularly in the cliff face to the left of center. All this technical virtuosity solicits an investment of belief in the image.

Practically, then, Dali did all he could to convince the viewer of the truth of the scene; a commercial white ground was applied to a standard-format closely woven canvas and then partially overlaid by a thin primary. The main contours were probably penciled onto the surface before color was applied with a variety of small sable brushes. In order to control the minutest of details Dali would rest his painting arm on a maulstick and scrutinize small areas with a jeweler's glass.

But these extravagant efforts at verisimilitude are merely the means for the communication of much broader ideas and paradoxes. In *Mountain Lake*, having registered the fairly blatant visual pun of the lake as a fish, one is left with the oblique and ironic allusion to the 1938 telephone conversations between Chamberlain and Hitler. The disconnected cable and the sedentary snails are eloquent testimonies to a series of non-sequiturs activated by the central opposition between dream and reality. This, in turn, is successful because of the technical seductiveness of the picture.

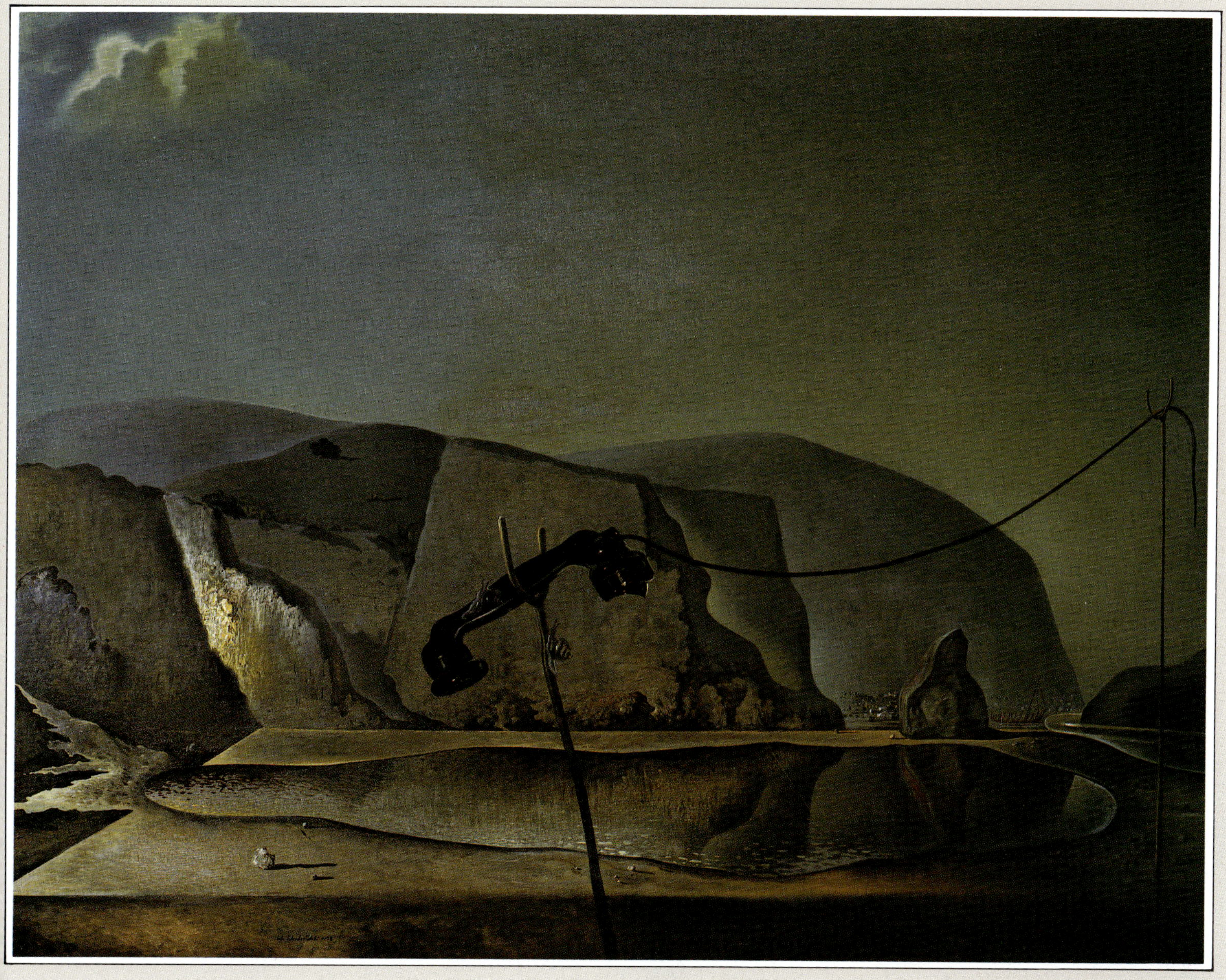

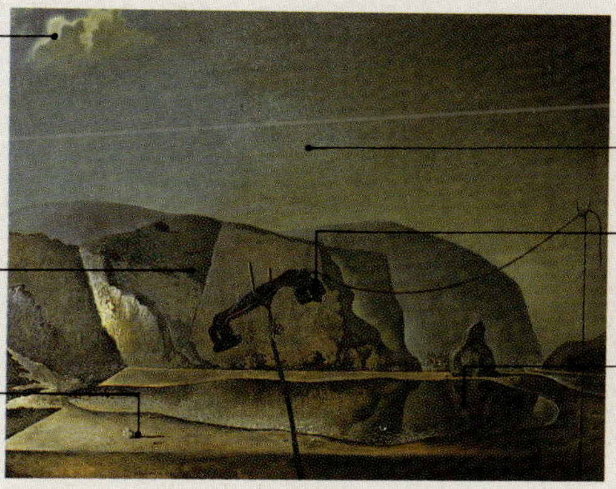


*Attention to the technical devices of Dali's* Mountain Lake *is apparently minimized by the scrupulously realistic execution; but expectations of 'reading through' the image are frustrated by formal as well as iconographic interruptions. The fish-shape of the lake, and the parallelogram which encloses it provide the best examples.*

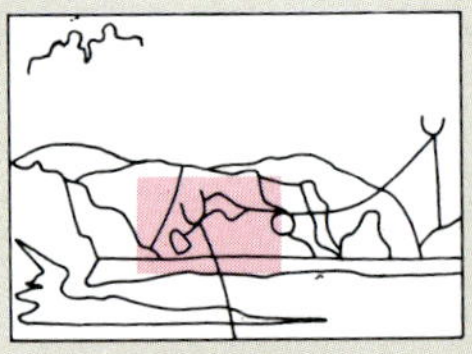

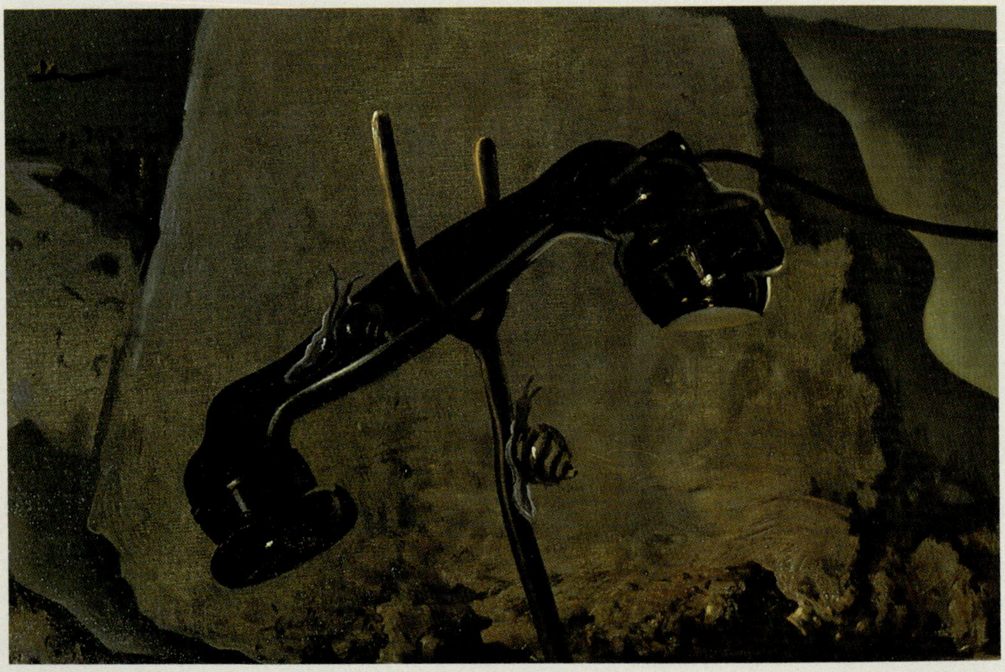

RIGHT The telephone and its impotent connecting lead are painted in an intensely reflective black, highlighted by flashes and ribbons of white. The incongruousness of the telephone is emphasized by the naturalistically executed snails. These are set-off by the lightly brushed rock-scape directly behind where the canvas weave is clearly visible. In contrast, the abstract quality of the sinuous curve to the left is accentuated by smudgy yellow shading.

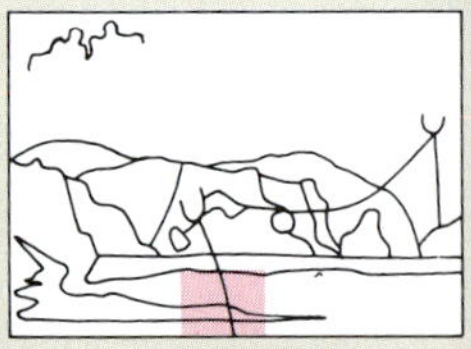

BELOW The black stem of the forked stick which supports the telephone cuts diagonally through five registers or layers. It has a skilfully managed transparency where the light hits the water and shore so that details behind the stick are glimpsed through it. Dali delights in effects of reflection. Water of mauve and light blue is merged into the creamy yellow-green shoreline. Multi-directioned flecks and dabs of paint are used to evoke the more fantastic rock forms of the lower mountains.

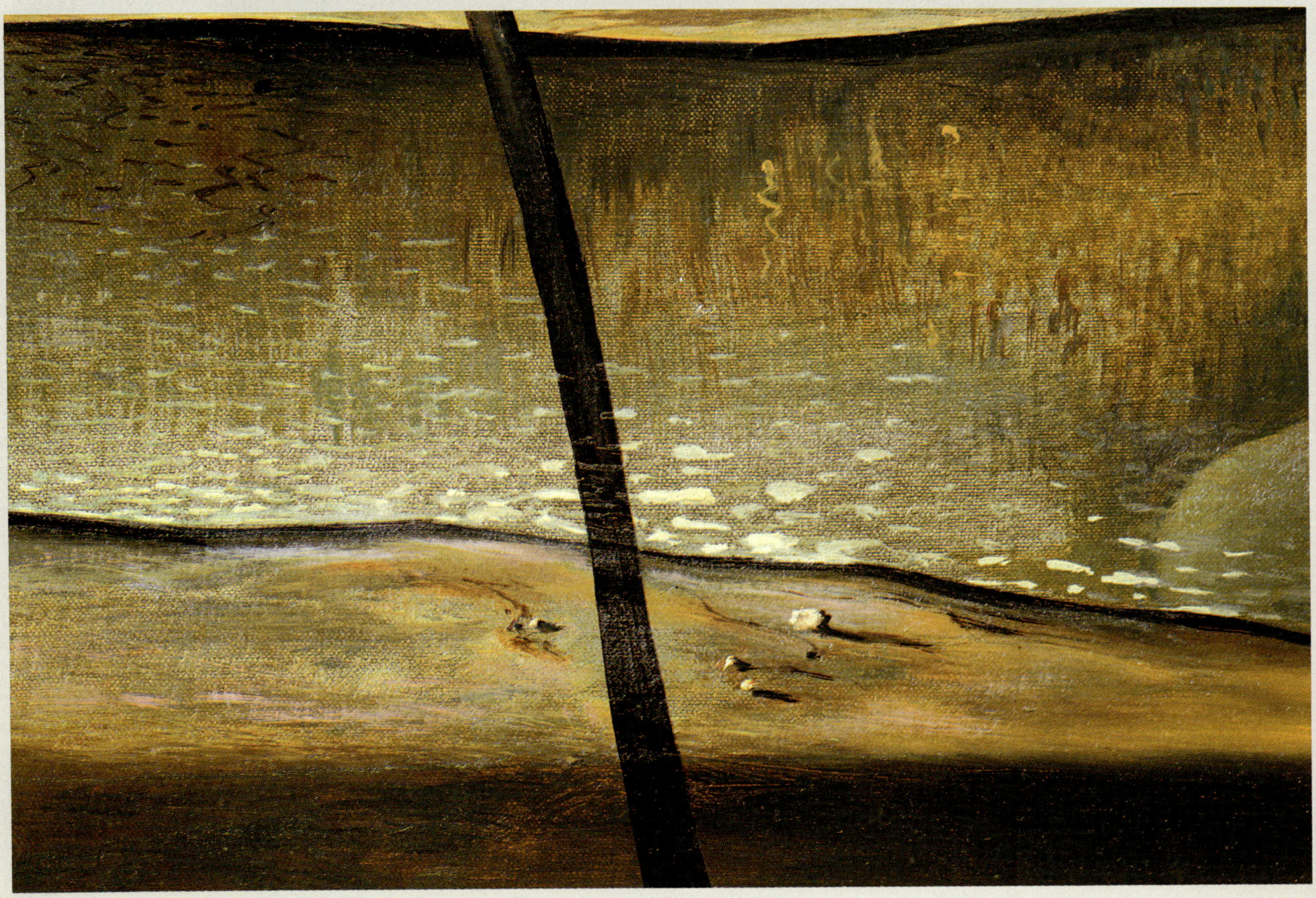

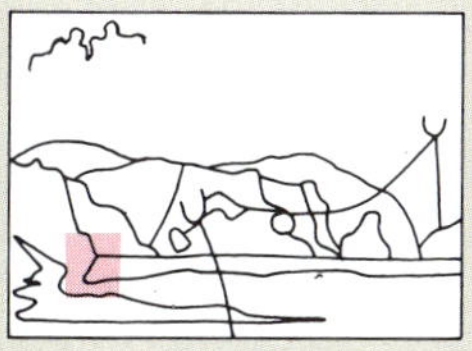

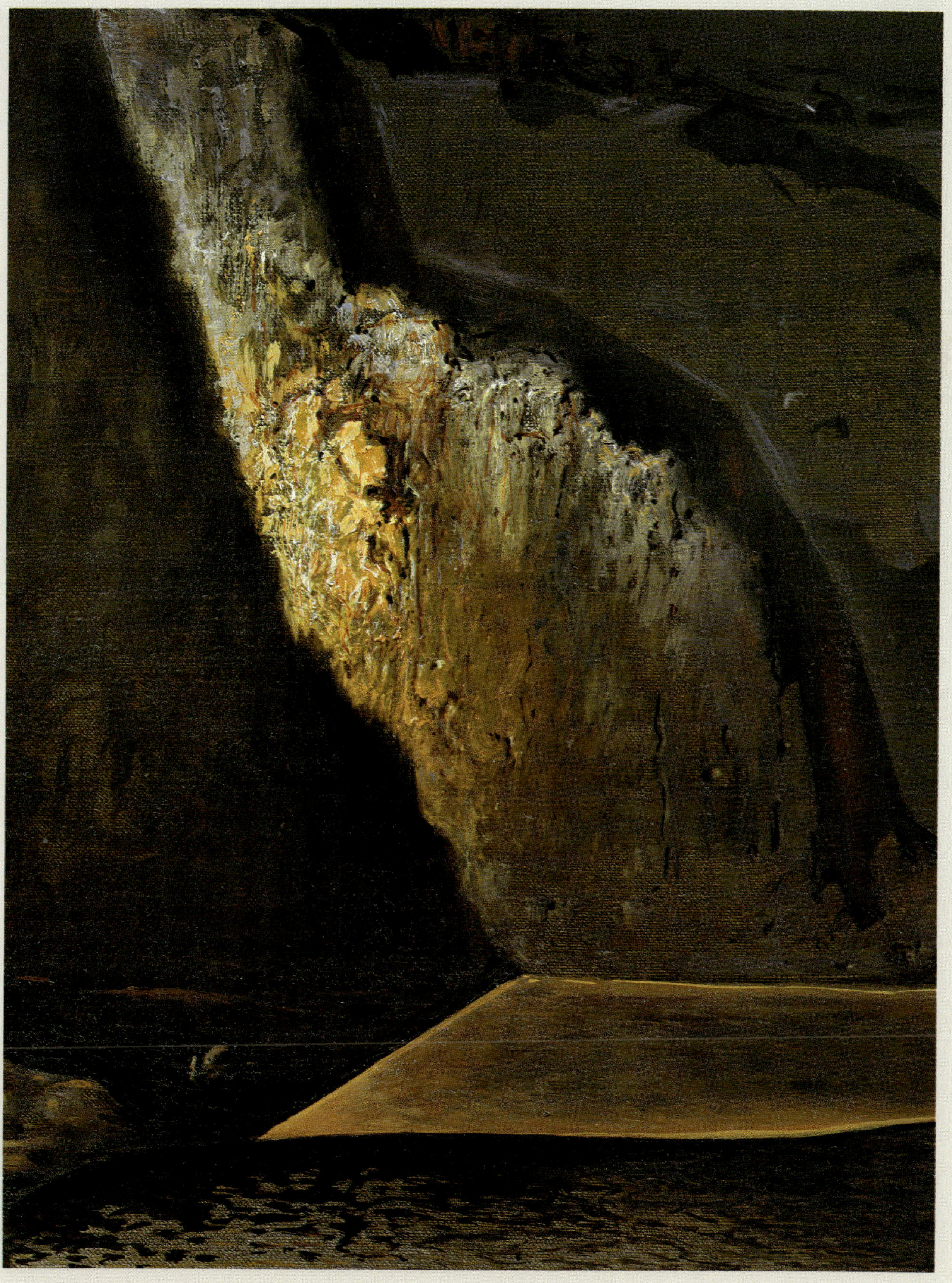

*ACTUAL SIZE DETAIL In the center of this detail Dali has almost 'sculpted a small field of impasto using both fine brushes and a blunt instrument (perhaps a palette knife or a fingernail). The layering of paint is graded out from a central focus of whites and creamy yellow, to the edges of the illuminated area where touches of greys and lavender diffuse the light intensity. The close-up reveals the artifice of Dali's 'naturalism', the lack of empirical logic which informs his choice of light-struck zones. It is not appropriate, then, for the straight line bounded area at the bottom right to be so entirely suffused with light while the dark rocks sloping up from right to left are uniformly unlit. Similarly, the mottling of the water at the bottom of the detail suggests that at this point it was more important to produce an impression of fish-scales than a convincing description of still water.*

# 1941 1960

## The New American painting

During the 1940s important new artistic movements began to develop in America, where until then painters had tended to follow European models or assume a provincial stance. The events which led to the Second World War indirectly contributed to this change, insofar as many European artists and intellectuals had been forced by the rise of Fascism to emigrate to the United States, and they soon proved to be a powerful source of inspiration for a younger generation. In New York this included young artists such as Jackson Pollock, Franz Kline (1910-1962), Willem de Kooning, Mark Rothko (1903-1970) and others; they evolved pictorial styles which drew upon earlier movements, particularly Cubism and Surrealism, but eventually went beyond these precedents in terms of original techniques and vision. The New American painting stressed the *manual* aspect of art, as well as the intense emotional response which it sought to provoke in the onlooker. One of its central aims was to combine a high degree of abstraction with expressive qualities: it is also therefore described as Abstract Expressionism.

Although individual Abstract Expressionists established entirely personal manners, they shared the desire to create images with an elemental impact that would challenge the uncertain climate of the wartime period. Initially, there was an interest in the tragic myths and art of primitive or ancient cultures because these were thought to contain a core of universal truth. It did not take long, however, for visual priorities to supersede literary references: instead, what came to the fore were dynamic methods of handling paint; the use of simplified forms, and canvases of enormous dimensions far exceeding those of the ordinary European easel picture. The big formats meant that the scale of the composition required novel attitudes to the application of pigment.

Jackson Pollock took the lead on that issue in 1947 when he extended the Surrealist technique of automatism to surprising limits, by laying his unstretched canvas support on the ground. He could then move rapidly around the picture from all sides and to assist his spontaneous approach he dispensed with brushes. Instead, Pollock poured and dribbled his highly diluted paint directly from the can, or used a stick to fling it on in whiplash strokes.

By such methods Pollock built up a dense web of lines suggesting a visual record of his turbulent, innermost feelings and also a reflection of the violent gestures which had brought the painting into existence. Yet a measure of intuitive control was present beneath this seeming chaos, as he remarked: 'When I am *in* my painting, I'm not aware of what I'm doing. It is only after a sort of "get acquainted" period that I see what I have been about. I have no fears about making changes, destroying

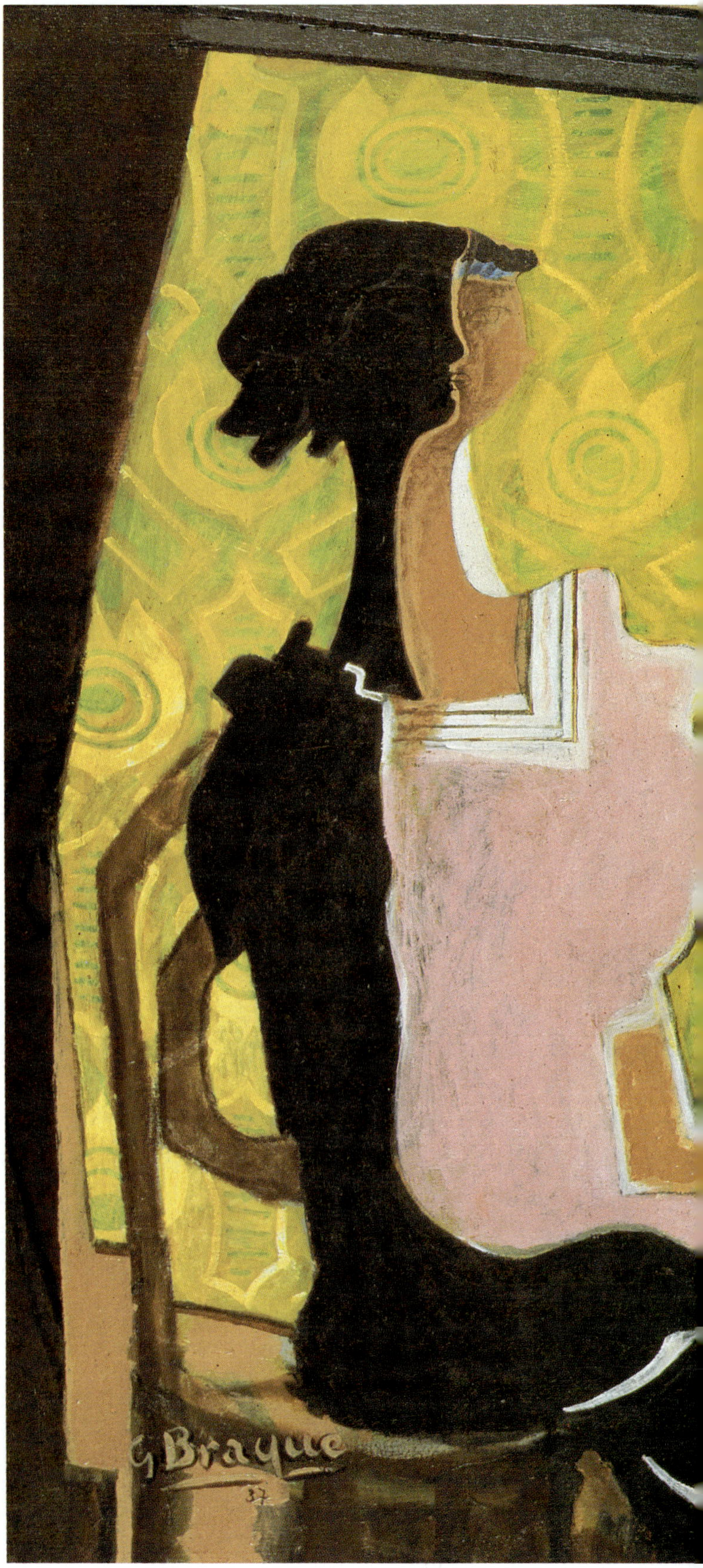

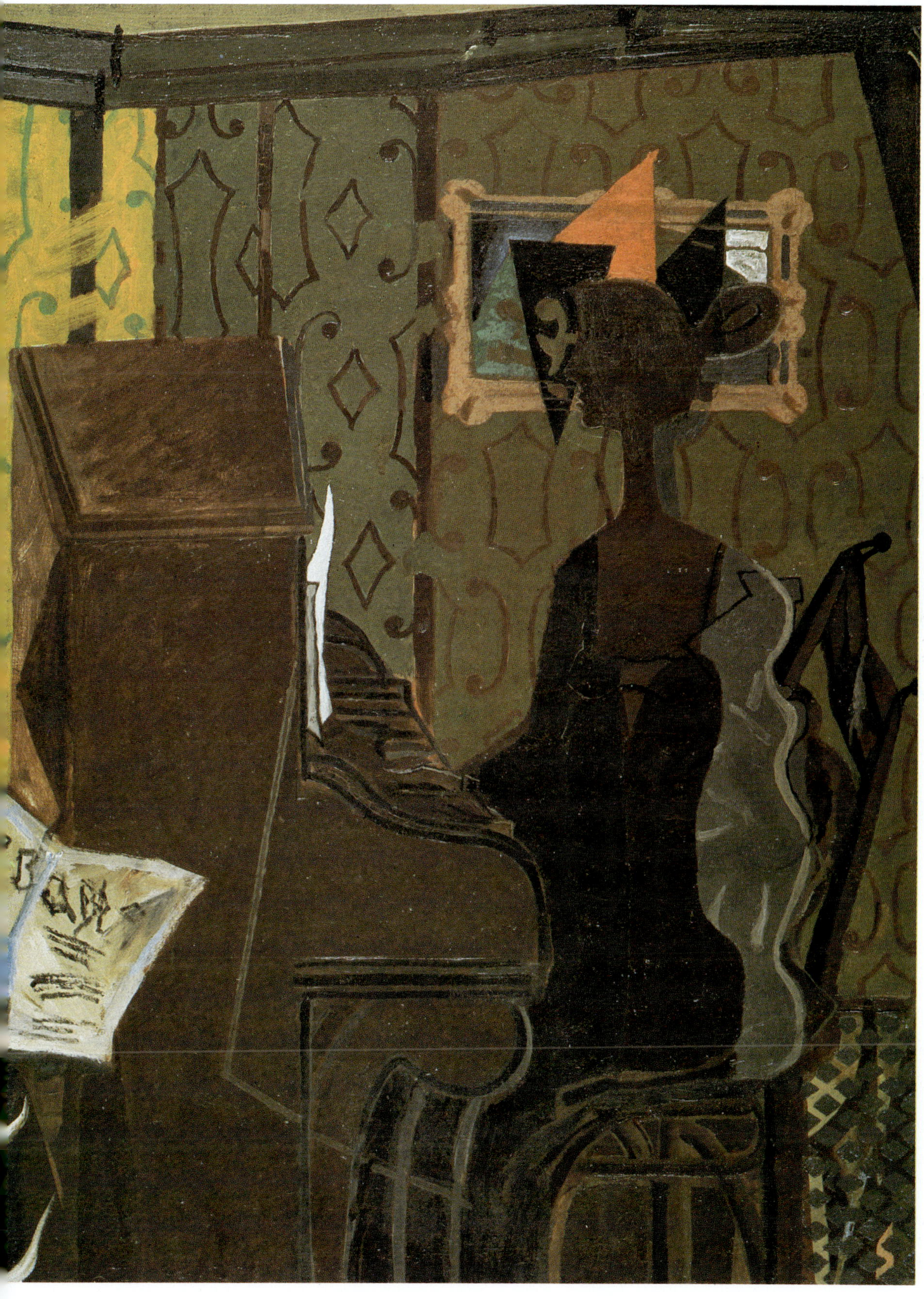

*LEFT* Duet *was painted in 1937, at a time when Braque was developing his combination of elegance and formal simplification that culminated in a series of* Oiseaux *done in the 1950s. Braque's mature work remains within the terms of Cubist easel painting. He made the structure of his vibrant surfaces more flexible and fuller, so that the subjects did not endanger the painting's constructive framework.*

the image, etc, because the painting has a life of its own. I try to let it come through. It is only when I lose contact with the painting that the result is a mess. Otherwise there is pure harmony, an easy give and take, and the painting comes out well.'

'I *am* nature', Pollock commented once,as if to say that his incorporation of physical movement into the act of painting signaled his own unity with the larger forces of the outside world. Indeed, he would occasionally introduce foreign elements – handprints, fragments of personal possessions and the like – into the surface of his compositions. These did not echo the role of the recognizable ingredients of Cubist collages, but were integrated with the pigment as reminders, perhaps, of the organic oneness Pollock felt between himself, nature and his creations.

Not every American affected by Surrealist automatism, particularly its fascination with chance and the unconscious, followed Pollock's unconventional extreme. Most did agree, however, that the manual factor about picture-making was of fundamental value, since it was the artist's gestures that were the crucial link between his or her inward experiences and how they were externalized on can-

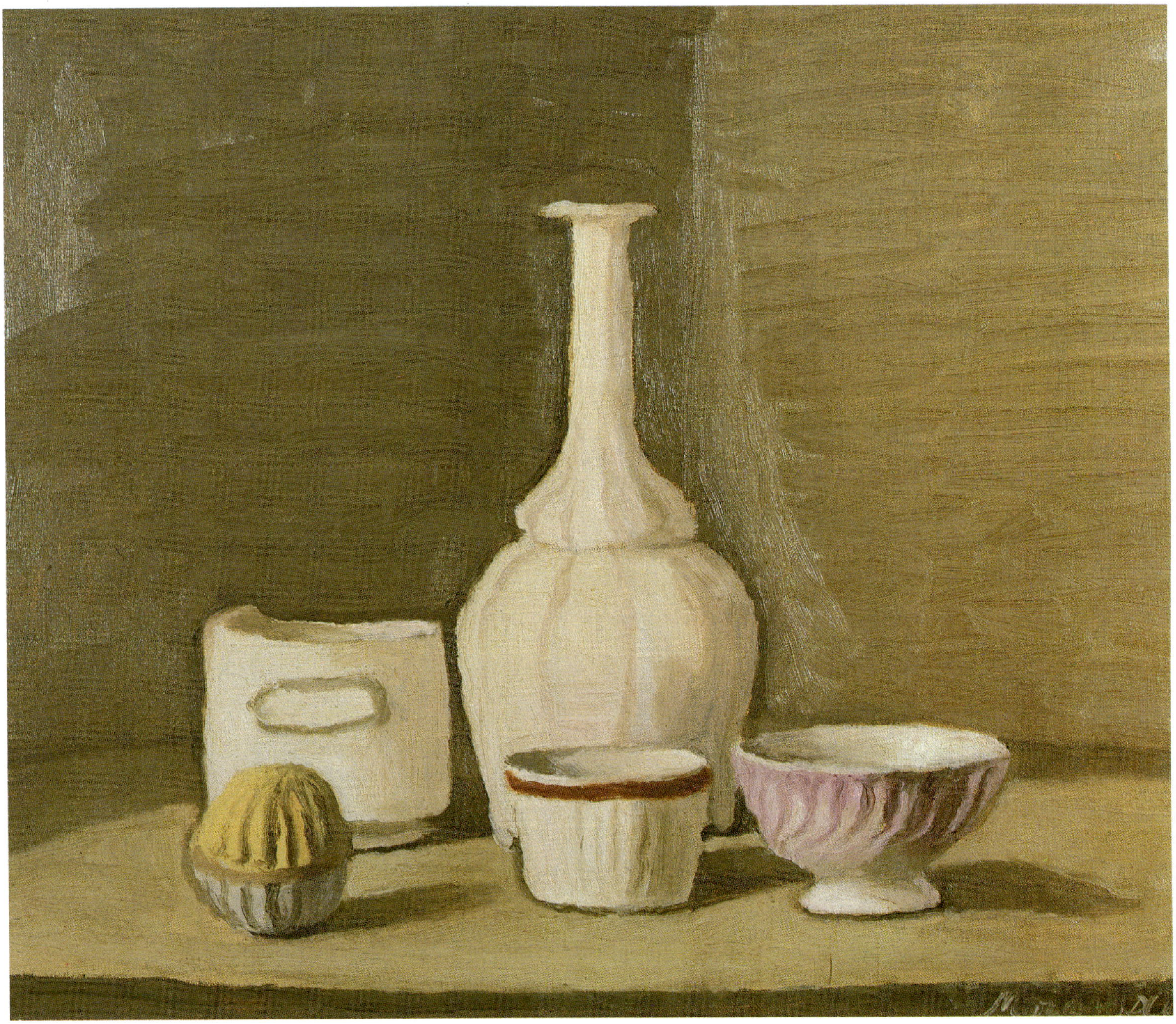

vas. On the West Coast, Mark Tobey (b 1890) produced networks of pale lines (often in the delicate tempera medium) on a smaller scale than Pollock's, yet they had a similar 'all-over' look: the entire work appeared to have been activated by the swift calligraphic touches of the brush. The results bear comparison with Pollock in their mysterious spatial aura too, because Tobey's Oriental mazes can be seen as both flat and infinitely deep. This impression was enhanced by Tobey's very soft colors, while Pollock sometimes chose the evanescence of silvery metallic paints.

The attitude underlying techniques such as those of Pollock and Tobey is usually termed 'gesturalism', denoting how the artist's dexterity, attack and physical movements in general contribute to the dynamism of his or her art. To New York painters, most notably de Kooning and Kline, gestural methods were ideal for expressing private tensions, the anxieties of modern urban life and the brutal immediacy of their materials. At moments their paintings appeared to have been left uncompleted, or else changes of mind and earlier stages were visible in the end product, which added to this unusually vigorous and aggressive feel.

In contrast to the ancient principle that artistic effort should be concealed, the gesturalists made it a tangible virtue. Hence their respect for *pentimenti* – the evidence that areas of a composition have been overpainted or reworked. During the early 1940s Pollock – who had yet to abandon brushes – deliberately

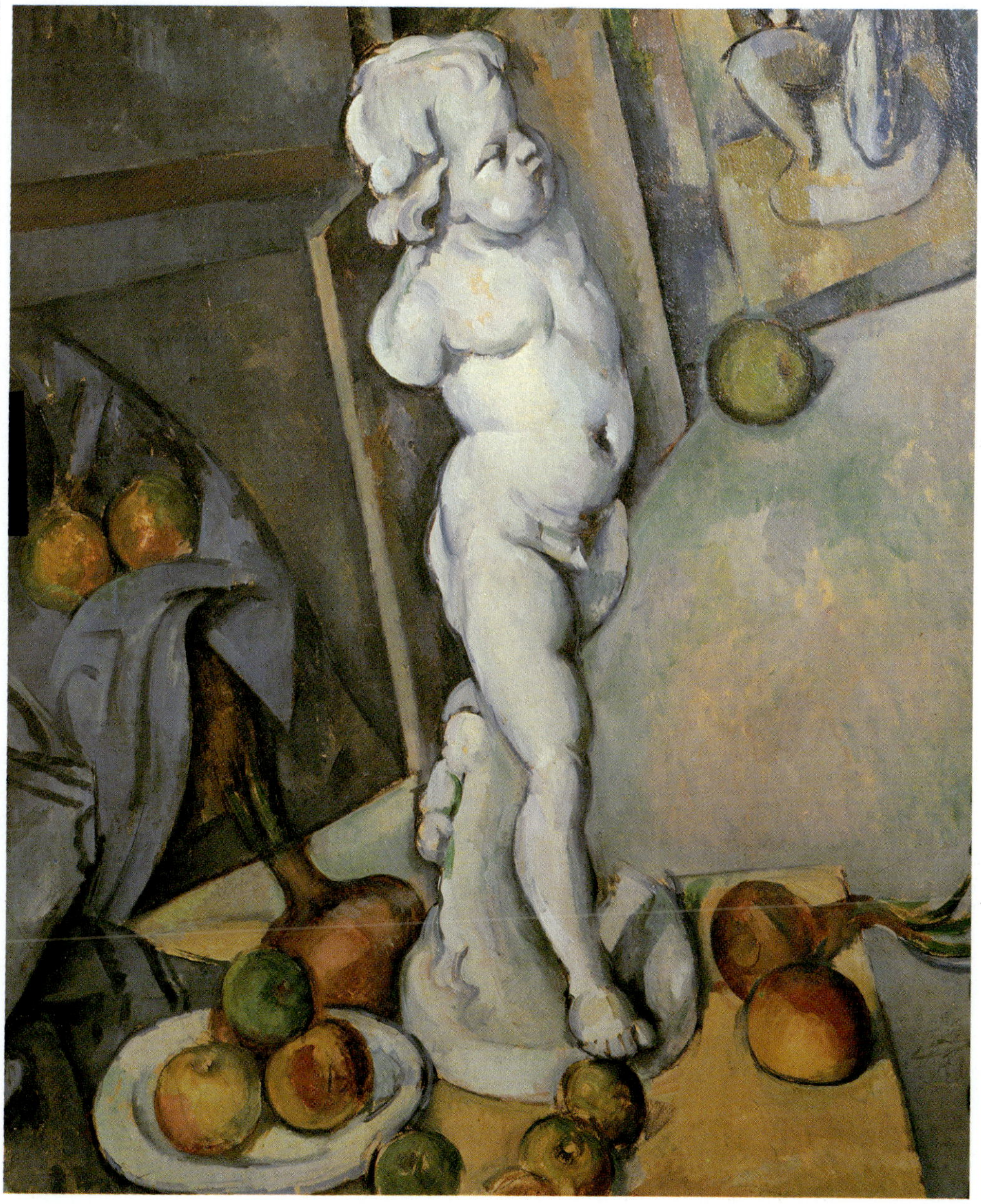

*By the time Giorgio Morandi painted his* Still Life *(LEFT) in 1946, he had perfected his contemplative style of depicting objects within a formal framework. He blurred the edges of the things in his paintings and their form is heavy and full of the essential value of the objects. Morandi's carefully observed everyday objects have a poetic impulse, but despite this lyricism there is an underlying pessimistic quality about his work. In contrast to Morandi's sparse formal arrangement Cézanne cluttered* Still Life with Plaster Cast *(1895) (RIGHT) with objects which have a slightly eclectic relationship with each other, and they are used in a complex spatial way. The apple Cézanne has placed in the background is the same size as those in the foreground, and has the effect of flattening the surface and halting the recession. While Morandi confined himself to a sober palette, Cezanne used subtly modulated contrasting colours which he applied in interlocking planes.*

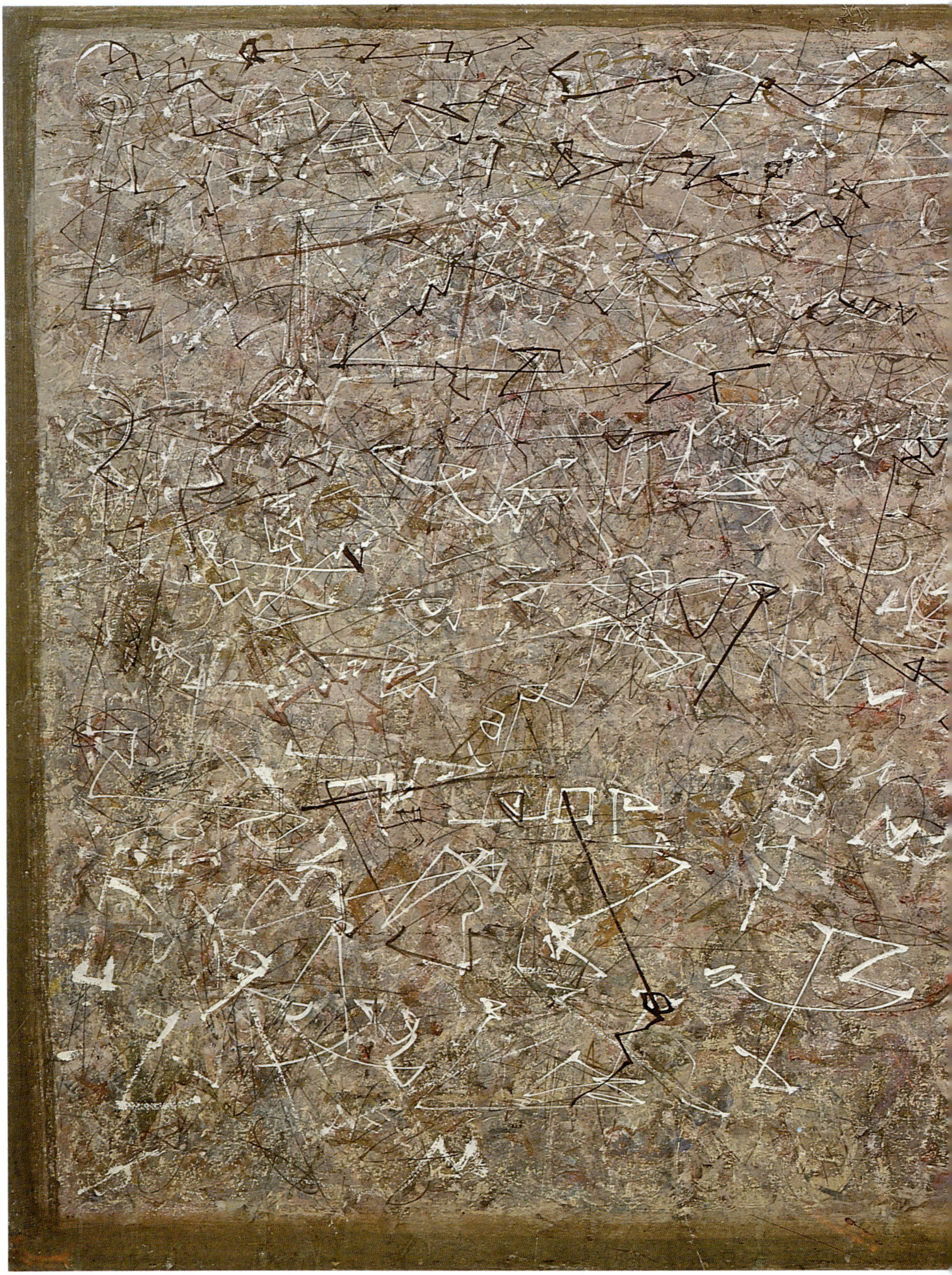

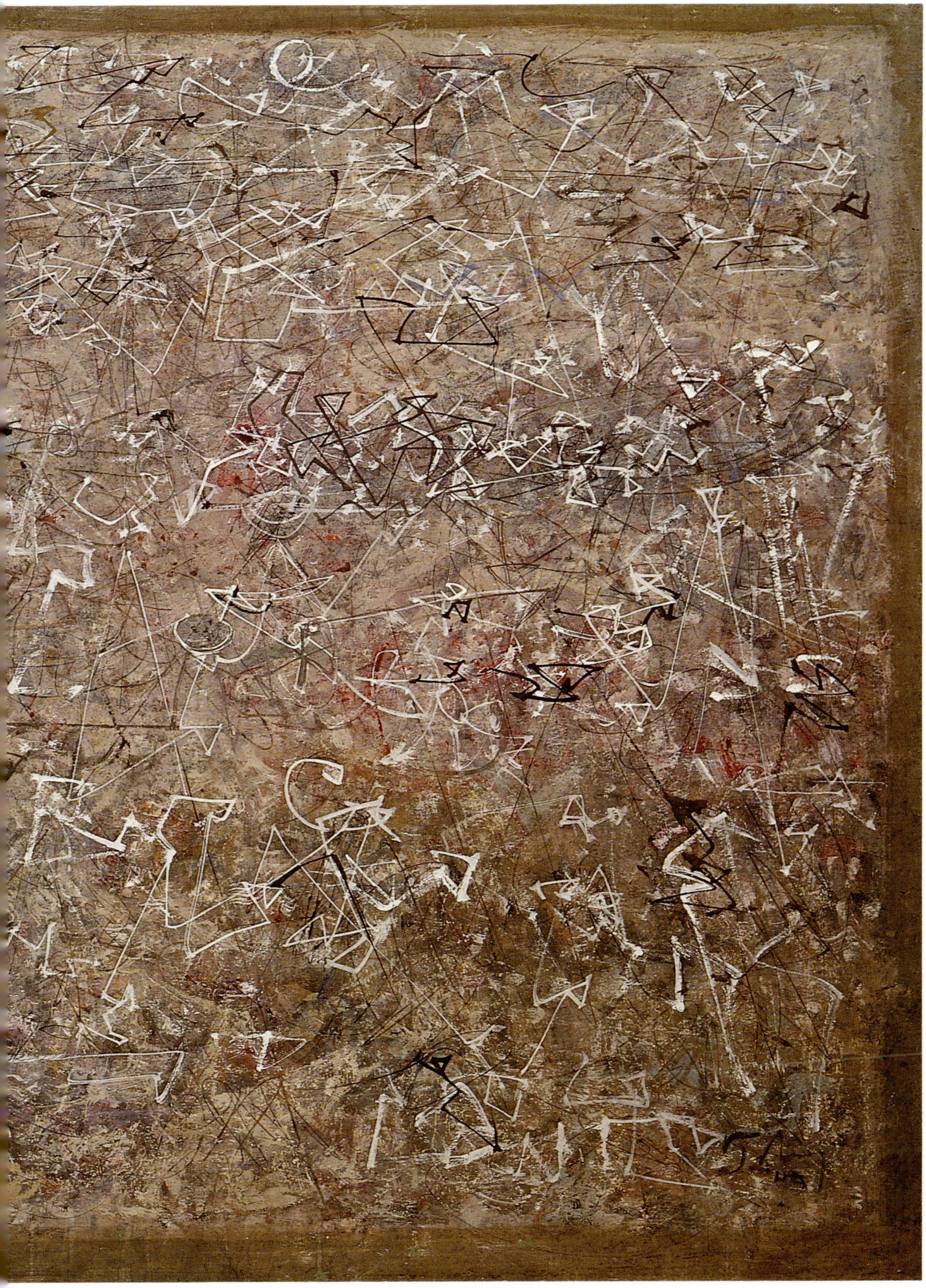

LEFT *Mark Tobey's* Universal Field *(1949) is an example of his remarkably powerful way of painting which concentrates on few expressional means. His style of 'gesturalism' evolved in complementary contrast to the emotive action paintings of Pollock and others. Tobey visited China and Japan in 1934 and studied Chinese calligraphy. By the next year he had developed his characteristic 'white writing' style. In Tobey's very individualistic kind of brush-writing — the calligraphic brush-stroke is considered to be a 'symbol of the spirit' by Zen philosophers — bewildering movements of white overlie dimly discerned suggestions of color beneath.*

overpainted the symbolic figures of works such as *Pasiphae* (1943) with successive layers of abstract markings. The resultant surface has a rich impasto permitting the viewer to discern Pollock, as it were, 'in action' as he progressed from figurative beginnings towards a near-abstract conclusion.

One influence on the rise of gesturalism, (or Action Painting, as it was called by the popular American critic Harold Rosenberg), was the art and teaching of the German-born emigré Hans Hofmann (1880-1966) who recommended fluent paint handling as an aid to spontaneity. Another starting point can be found in Arshile Gorky's later paintings where the colors are so thinned with medium that their almost liquid drips and washes form labyrinths associated with the mysterious depths of the artist's memory and unconscious. De Kooning and Kline, on the other hand, forged a more dramatic style that observers have linked to the violence and alienation of the contemporary American city.

In the 1940s both painters, like Pollock, dealt with the human figure and, through a study of Cubism, de Kooning fragmented it into planes and lines ranging over the entire composition. He simultaneously adopted enamel housepaints, mostly in black and white, because their easy flow enhanced rapid execution and added to the tough 'look' which he sought. These innovations in turn impressed Kline who in 1949 abstracted his figures into enormous strokes of black and white resembling magnified details from his previous imagery. Kline employed housepainter's brushes whose broad, flat edge produced marks which seemed to have been made with tremendous speed and forcefulness, particularly when some fail to stop within the edges of the composition and thus apparently hurtle beyond its boundaries altogether.

Despite the very different means of other Abstract Expressionists, such as Mark Rothko, Barnett Newman (1905-1970) and Clyfford Still (1904-1980), all of whom explored relatively static and sublime fields of color, it remained the gesturalist side of the movement that was most widely admired throughout the 1950s. Improvisatory working methods, loaded brushes, big formats and tactile surfaces came to represent the breakthrough of the New American Painting. Its impact caught the mood of the times and was soon felt outside America, although in lesser hands the techniques easily became confused with the end result. Following the example of Pollock and his colleagues, painters such as Georges Mathieu (b 1921) in France and the Dane Asger Jorn (1914-1973) brought a fierce intensity and heavy impasto to their work. By stressing the vitality of the manual act of painting, Abstract Expressionism also fostered new tendencies that would culminate in happenings and other unconventional approaches of more recent years, where physical performance is an essential and, perhaps, total part of the work of art.

**Figurative art in Europe**

The aftermath of the Second World War caused a resurgence of figurative art in Europe, just as the Great War had played a part in the rise of Expressionism. Anguish and doubt concerning human existence again moved many artists to project their unrest through new images of the human which were distorted or threatened by hostile forces. In certain instances, abstraction alone did manage to convey something of this outlook. The Spaniard Antonio Tapies (b 1923) and the Italian Alberto Burri (b 1915) respectively fashioned dark, rock-like reliefs and configurations of torn and burnt cloth that had a deeply pessimistic quality. On the other hand, the still lifes of Giorgio Morandi (1890-1964), despite their apparent calm, depict objects whose edges tremble slightly under a light of otherwise unnerving stillness. But the most extreme statements came from those who continued to see the figure as a focus of meaning. Existentialist thought justified this since it stressed a person's isolation and helpless vulnerability in an absurd universe.

Even those painters who had reached maturity long before the war exhibited a reawakened gravity of style during the mid-1940s. Pablo Picasso, for example, executed his large and unfinished *Charnel House* (1944-1945), based on photographs of concentration camp victims, in solemn shades of grey that hark back to the tones of *Guernica* (1937).

Less overtly horrific, but still fraught with tension were the paintings, mostly portraits, of the Franco-Swiss sculptor Alberto Giacometti (1901-1966). His colors were also limited, possibly reflecting a world devoid of human warmth. Moreover, Giacometti was obsessed by the conflict between a person and the space or void that surrounds him or her. In his sculpture Giacometti had implied this emptiness by reducing the figure to very slender proportions, as if it were eroded by its surroundings and he carried over this practice into oils and graphics after the war.

In England Francis Bacon (b 1909) offered an especially trenchant version of post-war malaise reinforced by a technique that many others have used, although Bacon maintained a pronounced originality. The people in Bacon's works are captured in extreme situations like cornered animals. This may partly explain the importance of photography to his procedures since the camera can record a moment of crisis so abrupt that it could otherwise escape notice. Bacon's major problem has therefore been to translate such perceptions into the substance of oil on canvas. His solu-

RIGHT *Although essentially a classical artist at a time of upheaval and change, Paul Delvaux painted works with an essential quality of modernity about them. This* Sleeping Venus *(1944) was one of several versions he painted, after becoming fascinated by two neighboring exhibits, a sleeping Venus and a skeleton, at the Musée Spitzner. This idea of the proximity of love and death recurred in many of his works.*

tion resembles that of the American gesturalists insofar as it involves quick brushwork and a grasp of how accidents may become positive features on account of their element of surprise. As Bacon noted in 1968: 'I think that you can make ... involuntary marks on the canvas which may suggest much deeper ways by which you can trap the facts you are obsessed by. If anything ever does work in my case it works from that moment when consciously I didn't know what I was doing.'

Bacon's imagery includes disturbing and unexpected juxtapositions, but it is the visual beauty that he brings to details such as a gaping wound or carcasses of meat behind a sitter that affords the greater shock. In this respect his style belongs to the tradition of 'painterly' artists – Velazquez, Rembrandt, Courbet – who have exploited juicy impasto and prominent brushwork. Yet if Bacon too celebrates the opulence of his materials,he is nonetheless a painter of this century because of the distinctly modern neuroses which the materials serve.

The idea that our place in the universe could no longer be taken for granted similarly

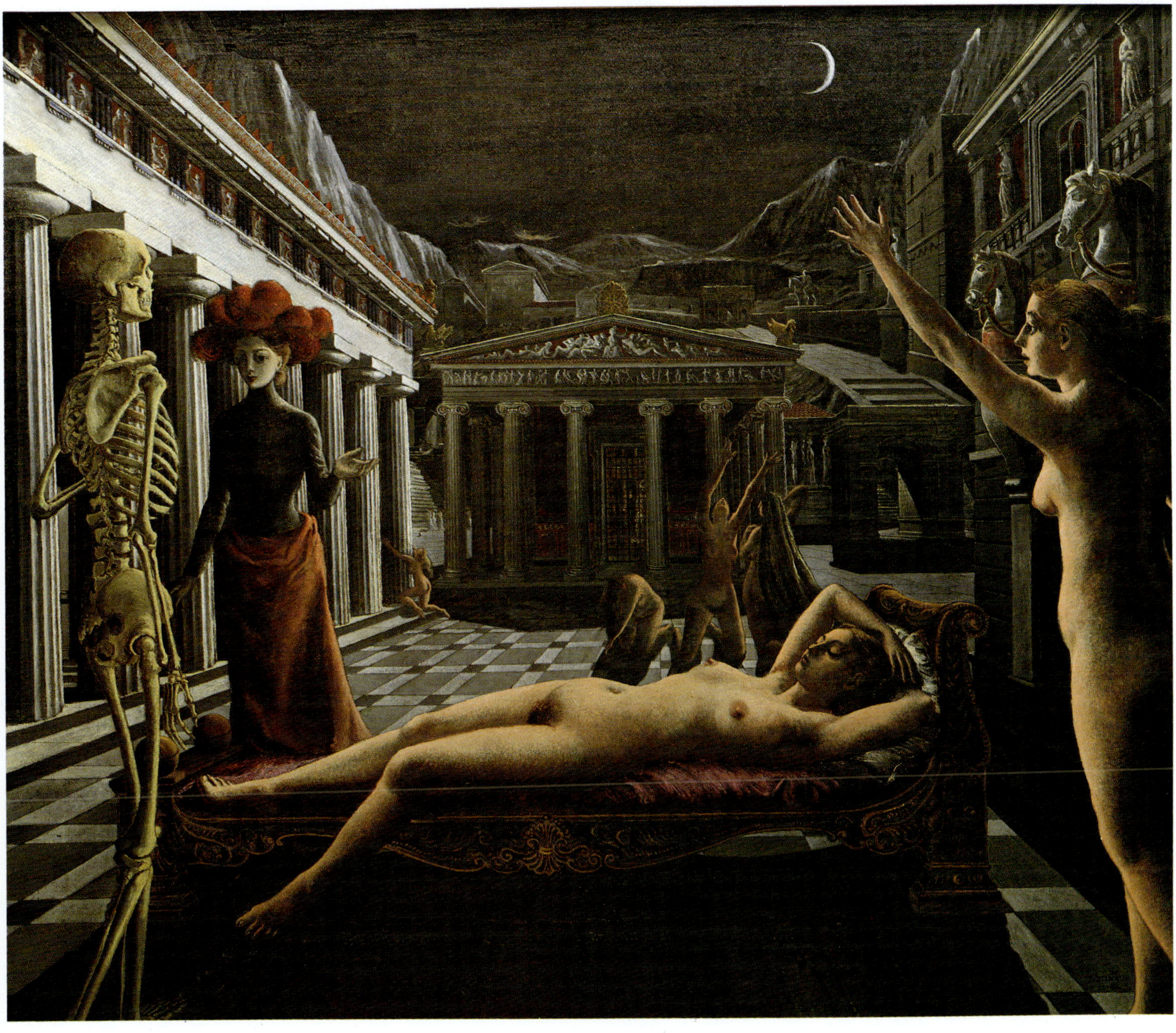

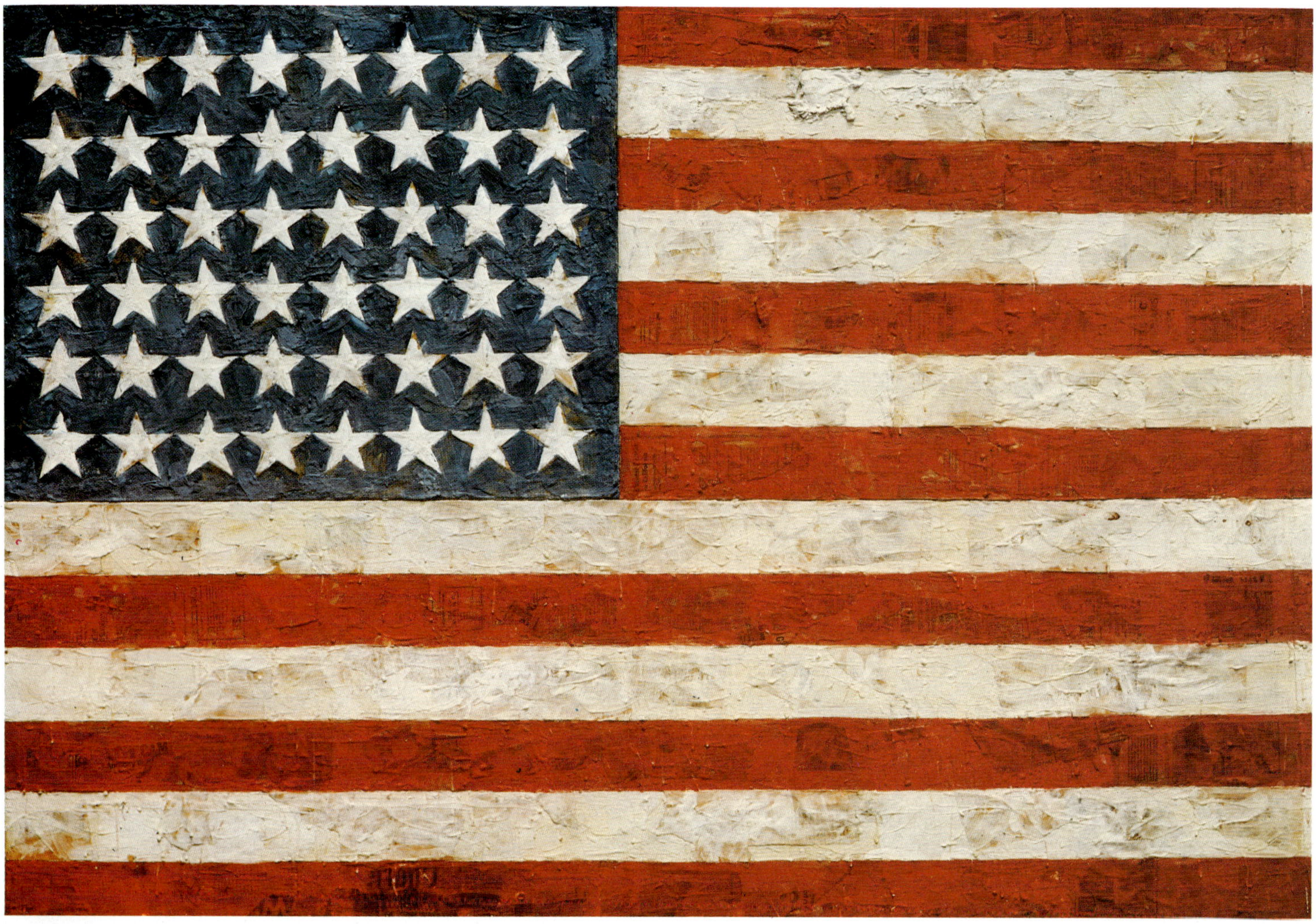

ABOVE *Jasper Johns began* Flag *(1955) in enamel or oil paint, then changed to using an encaustic technique. 'I wanted to show what had gone before in a picture, and what was done after. But if you put on a heavy brushstroke in paint and then add another stroke, the second stroke smears the first unless the paint is dry. And paint takes too long to dry ... someone suggested wax. It worked very well; as soon as the wax was cool I could put on another stroke and it would not alter the first.' Johns applied the paint with a brush or with material dipped into the hot medium.*

affected the Frenchman Jean Dubuffet (b 1901) and his development of what he called *art brut*, meaning rough or raw, as opposed to 'fine' art. The prototypes for *art brut* were found in the work of primitives, children and psychotics who all view reality in a different light to that of the supposedly civilized artist. Dubuffet – and to some extent his contemporaries such as Jean Fautrier (1898-1964) and Wols (1913-1951) – admired this lack of sophistication allied to a crude vigor. According to Dubuffet, no distinctions can be drawn between humanity and art and the matter of which they are both, in the last analysis, composed.

Dubuffet consequently chose banal subjects to avoid any pretensions to intellectual refinement, but his real discovery was to see paint as no longer *depicting* light, color or texture. Instead, its own material reality constituted the true purpose of the painting. To further this end Dubuffet added foreign substances, including leaves and earth, to his canvases and mixed the pigment with a filler such as plaster. The resultant surfaces are virtually low reliefs into which primitive outlines are scratched. Although *art brut* proved fairly short-lived, it counteracted the dry academic manner still popular as a legacy of Veristic Surrealism.

**Post-war developments in the use of color**

It is significant that those Europeans who continued to explore the resources of color were almost all from an earlier generation and so had either participated in Fauvism or were aware of its consequences. In France Raoul Dufy and Georges Rouault, for example, based their final works upon premises that had been current before the First World War. In Dufy's case this meant brilliant primaries and simplified design evolved from his Fauvist years, while Rouault maintained somber glowing shades set within encrusted paint surfaces.

Above all it was Henri Matisse who took the coloristic freedom, established early on by Fauvism, to its most radical conclusions in the last decade of his career. He had always recognized the inherent power of color to transcend its roots in nature. This partly explains the extraordinary liberties Matisse took with his palette from the turn of the century onwards, experimenting with extreme saturation, pure primary tones as well as the most subtle combinations. He seemed to be able to generate light rather than transpose it realistically into gradual changes from shade to tint. When Matisse reached his seventies, however, illness increasingly prevented his activities in the orthodox medium of oil on canvas. His solution was to use large sheets of paper that had already been colored to his own specifications. These were then cut as desired (hence the term *papier découpé*) and pasted on to a support. 'The cut-out paper allows me to draw in color. It is a simplification ... I am drawing directly in color; which will be the more measured as it will not be transposed. This simplification ensures an accuracy in the union of the two means.'

At face value *papier découpé* may resemble the Cubist collage technique but, in fact, the two have little in common. The Cubists were far less interested in color and reduction than Matisse was, and regarded *papier collé* as a means of constructing a complex interplay of meaning and spatial organization. On the contrary, Matisse could now limit every element of his design to its barest essentials. Color was the very substance of each shape. The breadth and directness of Matisse's methods contributed to the return of color as a primary factor in the art of the 1960s.

Yet perhaps an even more influential growth in the awareness of what color can achieve took place after the war in America. Gesturalism did not actually account for the whole of the New American painting, since three of its pioneers – Clyfford Still, Mark Rothko and Barnett Newman – had created large abstractions where brushstrokes tended to be less pronounced than the overall grandeur of the color fields. Still's technique was unique because he applied pigment with the palette knife in viscous layers, but Rothko and Newman kept their paint thin and fairly uniform so that texture did not interfere with the powerful hues. Newman, Still and Pollock in his later works also sometimes left parts of the canvas untouched to allow it to register as an individual color. Rather like Matisse, who had united drawing and color in his cut-outs, this approach permitted imagery to merge with the actual picture surface.

Such discoveries became especially relevant later when American artists reacted against what they considered the unnecessary sensationalism of action painting. They wanted to leave behind the loaded brush effects, turbulent composition and restricted palette. The formal beauty that abstract art can attain seemed a more urgent objective than any involvement with personal anguish or even the processes leading to the finished work.

BELOW *Norman Rockwell, probably the most widely known contemporary American artist in the 1950s, has never received critical acclaim to equal his popularity. His brand of Ruralism displayed in* The Country Agricultural Agent *(1948) was reproduced regularly on the cover of the high-circulation weekly magazine the* Saturday Evening Post.

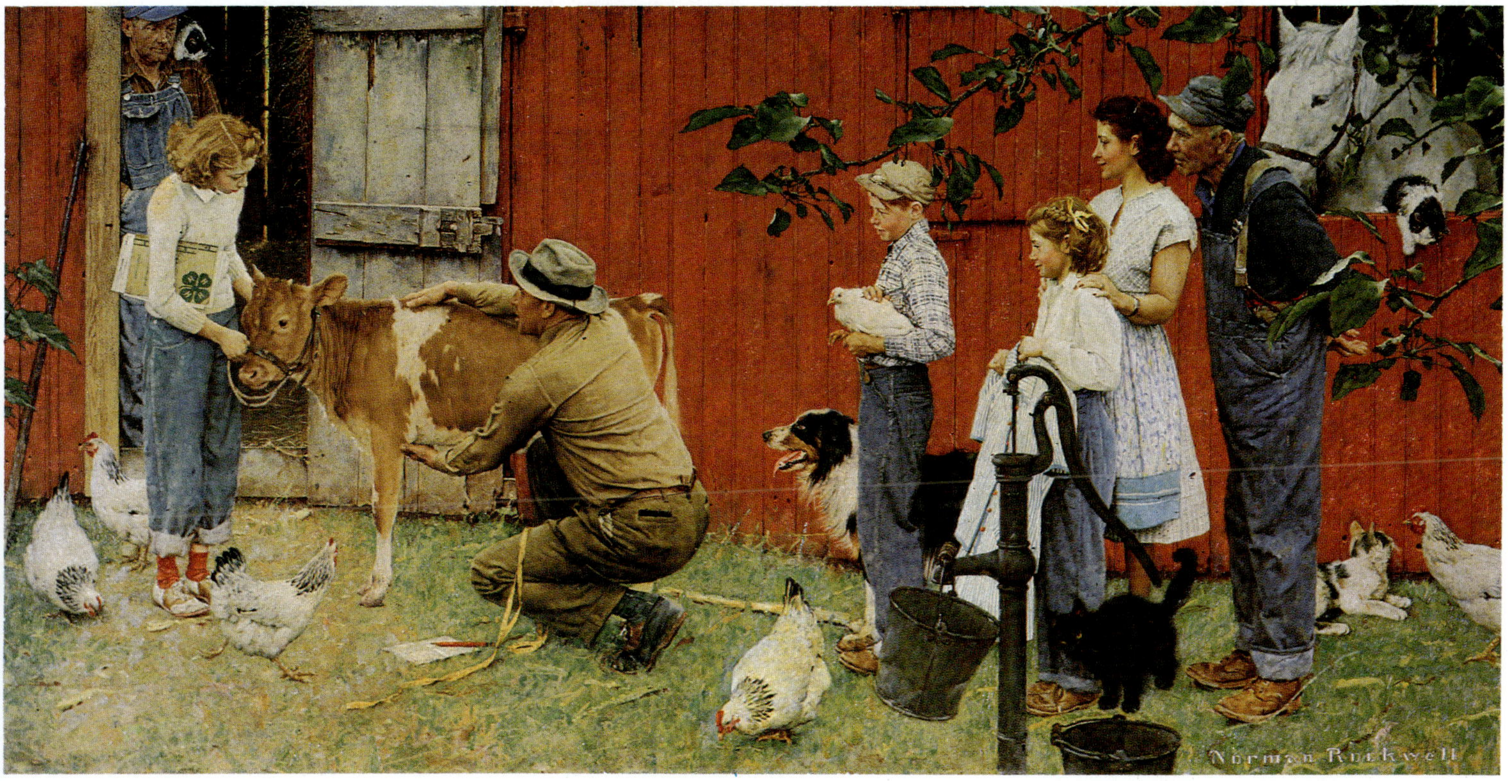

**Assemblage and mixed media approaches**
Perhaps the outstanding feature of the 1950s was the growth of the affluent society. Television, advertising and the media in general now reproduced images with a speed and insistence that brought visual information into the average person's routine as never before. Economic prosperity meant a surfeit of consumer goods and these helped to shape culture packed with an astonishing variety of products, both useful and disposable.

In this brash new climate, the high seriousness which motivated Abstract Expressionism looked increasingly out of place. Gesturalist art had been born of an era of social crisis and, although it was responsible for many technical innovations, it still upheld the basic assumption – largely unchanged since the Renaissance – that painting was a question of conveying emotion, illusion or ideas through marks on a flat surface. Yet one major alternative to this definition had arisen in the course of modern art. This was the Cubist notion that paper or other foreign materials could be used to *construct* rather than simply 'paint' a picture. From that realization grew not merely the three-dimensional Cubist construction but also the weird assemblages of found objects with which Dada and Surrealism blurred the boundaries of painting and sculpture. At a time when the British artist Peter Blake (b 1932) was introducing collage into his painting (which, however, was more akin to the Victorian scrapbook than to any Cubist work),the American Jasper Johns was revitalizing the notion of painting-sculpture, launching his ironic reply to the drama of action painting in the early 1950s.

Johns established his iconoclastic role on the New York art scene with pictures of deadpan motifs such as targets, numerals and flags. A possible key to these works is to interpret them as commentaries on the doctrine that paintings must have a meaning. By choosing signs that are always understood as part of a code – a target points to something, a number is only useful for what it measures – he deprived them of such meaning as the sole subject of a picture. Also, Johns depicted his designs with the agitated brushwork of a gesturalist, rather as if some monosyllable were repeated in a highly impassioned voice. To complete the contradictions he adopted the ancient technique of encaustic so that the normal flatness of a target, for instance, in fact become a low relief. Here was the start of an important modern tendency, continued by Larry Rivers (b 1923), Robert Rauschenberg (b 1925) and recent movements such as Conceptualism.

When Johns added plaster casts and similar artifacts to his compositions in the mid-1950s he anticipated a desire on the part of many artists to go beyond the conventions of the easel painting and its derivatives.

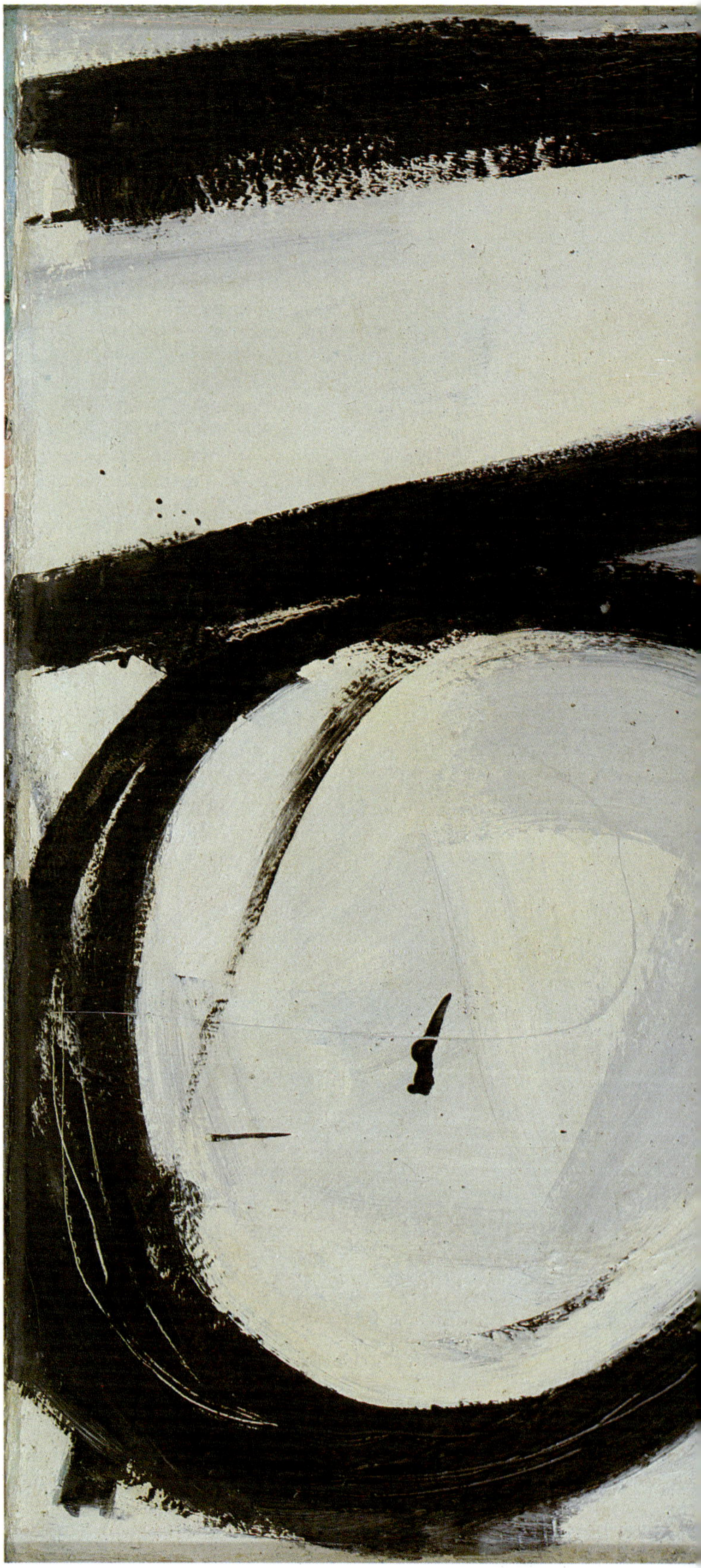

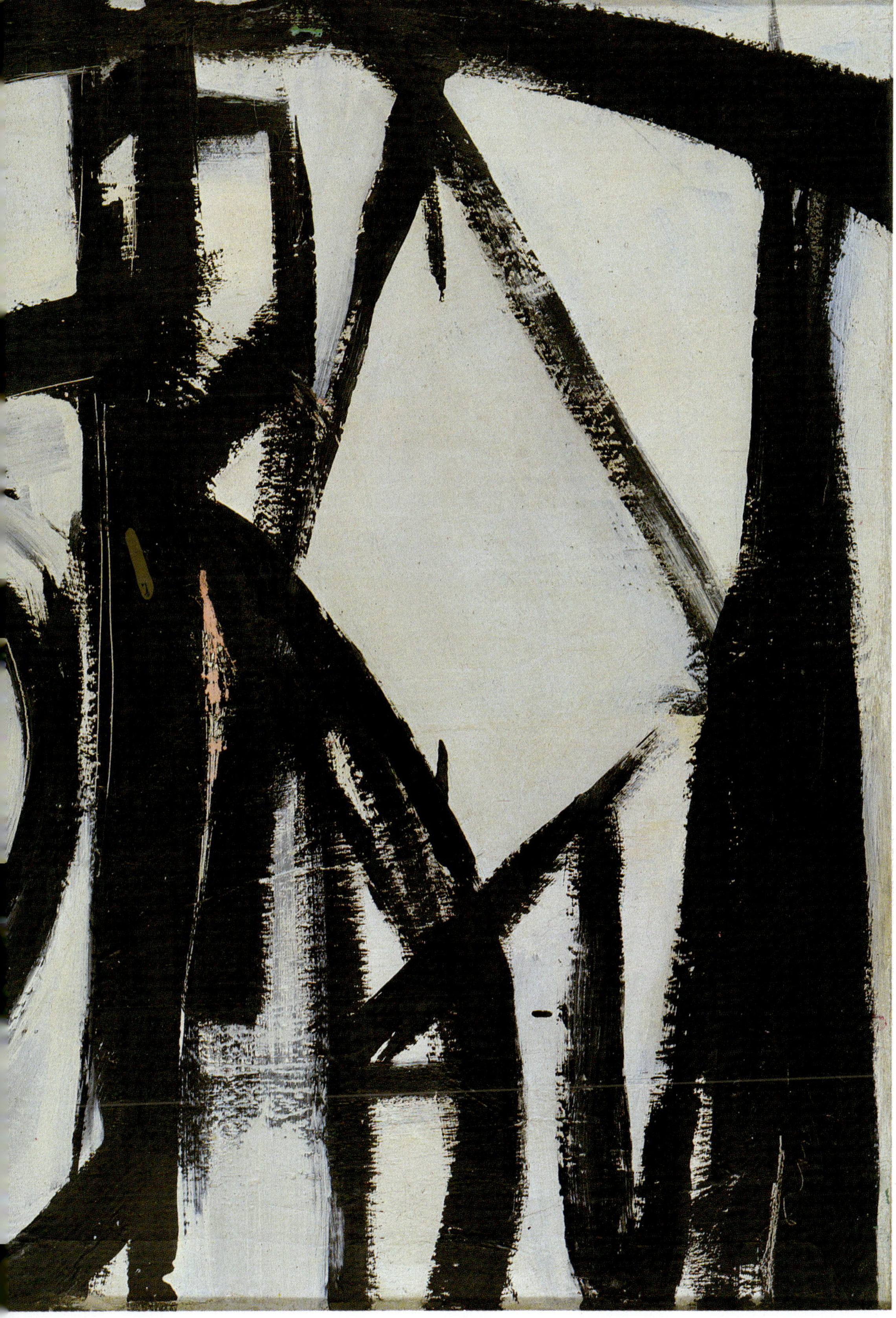

*LEFT In the 1940s Franz Kline was painting conservative canvases which developed into a bolder style based on traditional principles of abstract art. By the late 1940s and early 1950s, this abstraction evolved into a gesturalistic freedom of paint handling and brush-stroke, as well as a certain eastern quality of calligraphy.* Clock Face, *which he painted in 1950, is a canvas of tremendous boldness with its strong black strokes against a white background.* Kline *reduced his palette to black and white, and this, combined with his dramatic and enormous brushstrokes, conveyed a sense of the alienation and violence characteristic of the contemporary American city.*

# MAX ERNST

*Vox Angelica* (1943)
Oil on canvas, 152cm × 203cm/59in × 79in

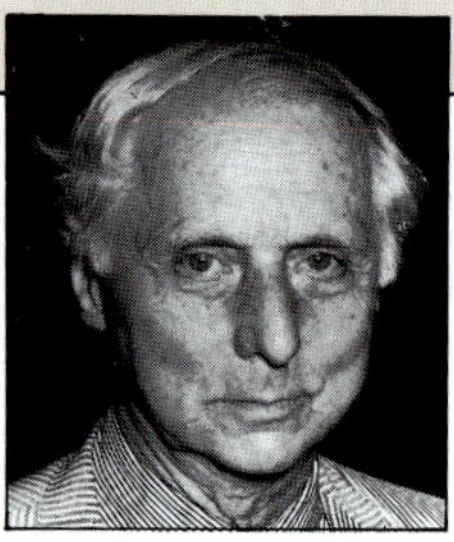

Max Ernst, one of the leading artists in both the Dada and Surrealist movements, can be regarded as perhaps the major technical innovator in twentieth century painting. He adapted and invented a whole variety of techniques. *Vox Angelica*, painted in Arizona in 1943 during his exile from Europe, summarizes his various, often picturesquely named, techniques – collage, illusionism, frottage, grattage, decalcomania and oscillation.

Ernst's first major technical contribution came in 1919 with his adaptation of collage to the transformation of commercial catalog sources. His first actual 'invention' was frottage, with which he experimented in Cologne in 1920 and 1921, and then developed in France in 1925 in response to the 1924 *First Surrealist Manifesto* by the poet André Breton. Ernst's description of frottage conveys something of the spirit which accompanied the invention. When sitting in a seaside inn, Ernst became 'obsessed' by the appearance of the well-scrubbed floorboards, so, in his words, 'to assist my contemplative and hallucinatory faculties, I took a series of drawings from the floorboards by covering them at random with sheets of paper which I rubbed with a soft pencil.' Frottage, which Ernst used extensively, is a drawing technique. In the winter of 1926 to 1927, Ernst adapted it to painting in a technique he called grattage, which involves scraping pigment over canvas placed on a heavily textured surface. The next significant automatic technique came a decade later with the invention of decalcomania by the Spanish Surrealist artist Oscar Dominguez. This technique involved painting gouache onto a piece of paper, covering it with another sheet and pressing it lightly with the hand. Next, the top sheet was peeled off slowly, like a transfer, and the process repeated until the color was almost dry. During 1939, Ernst experimented with a similar technique using oil paint and canvas. Ernst's last – and least successful – technical innovation was oscillation, in which a paint-filled tin can was suspended from a piece of thread or string and swung in varying directions over a flat piece of canvas. The Surrealist automatic techniques sought to eliminate the conscious element from the performance of the pen or brush as a way of stimulating or forcing the artist's inspiration.

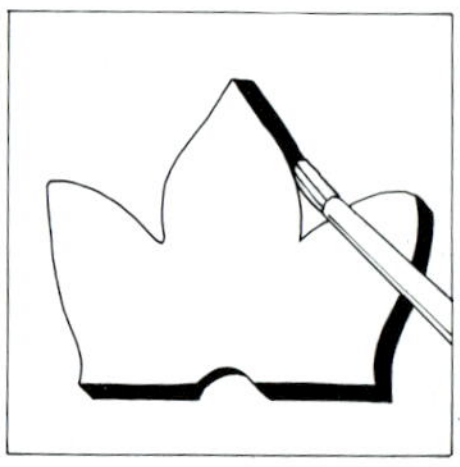

**1.** *Vox Angelica* sums up all the main techniques with which Ernst was associated. Collage is referred to parodistically in the illusionistic painting of the leaf, for example, which has been painted so that it appears to be stuck on.

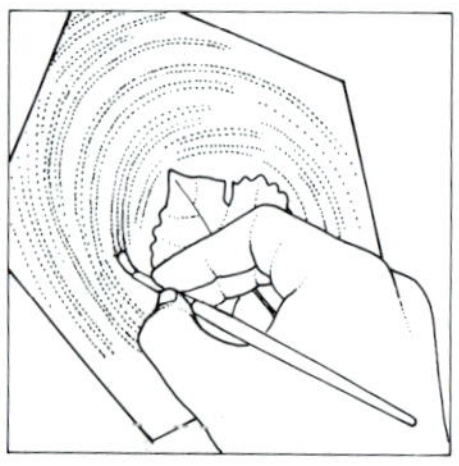

**2.** Frottage also features in a parodistic way. The appearance of floorboards was created by painting rather than by rubbing through paper with a soft pencil.

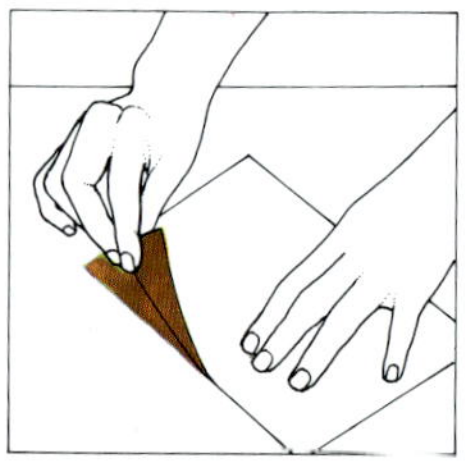

**3.** Ernst adapted the technique of decalcomania. The technique involves pressing a sheet of paper or similar material on to the paint-covered surface and peeling the sheet off again.

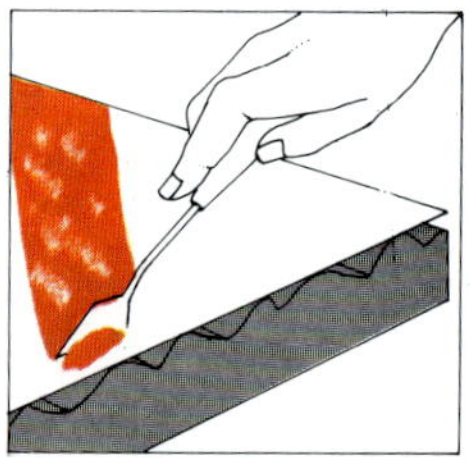

**4.** Grattage involves scraping pigment over canvas which has been placed on a heavily textured surface.

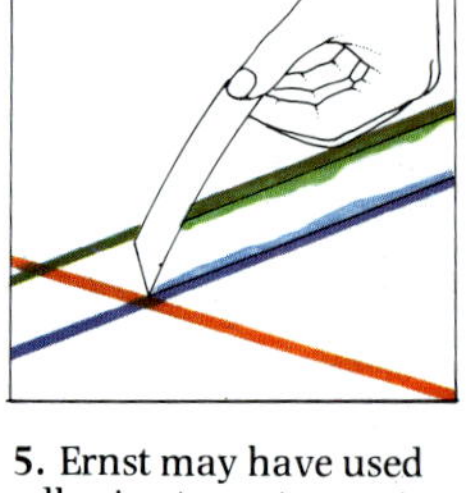

**5.** Ernst may have used adhesive tapes to create the straight, overlapping lines.

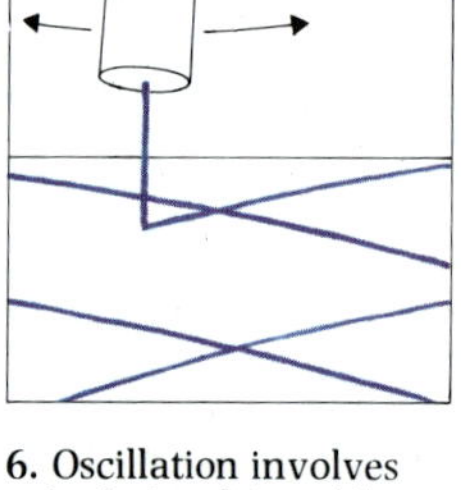

**6.** Oscillation involves paint being dripped frorr a can swung on the end of a piece of string.

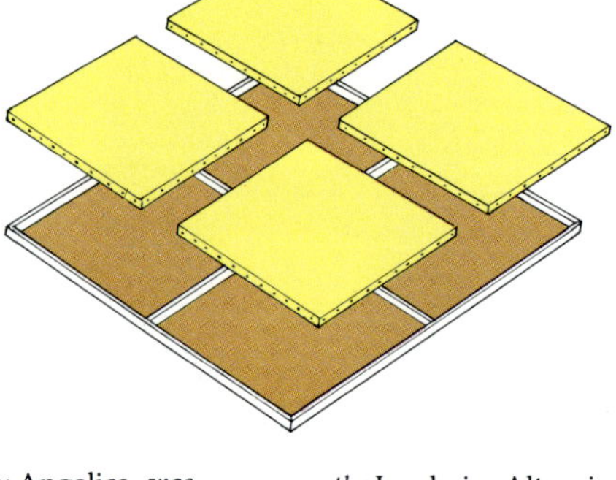

Vox Angelica *was painted on four canvases assembled in the same way as had been the parts of Grünewald's masterpiece, the* Isenheim Altarpiece *from a section of which Ernst's work took its name.*

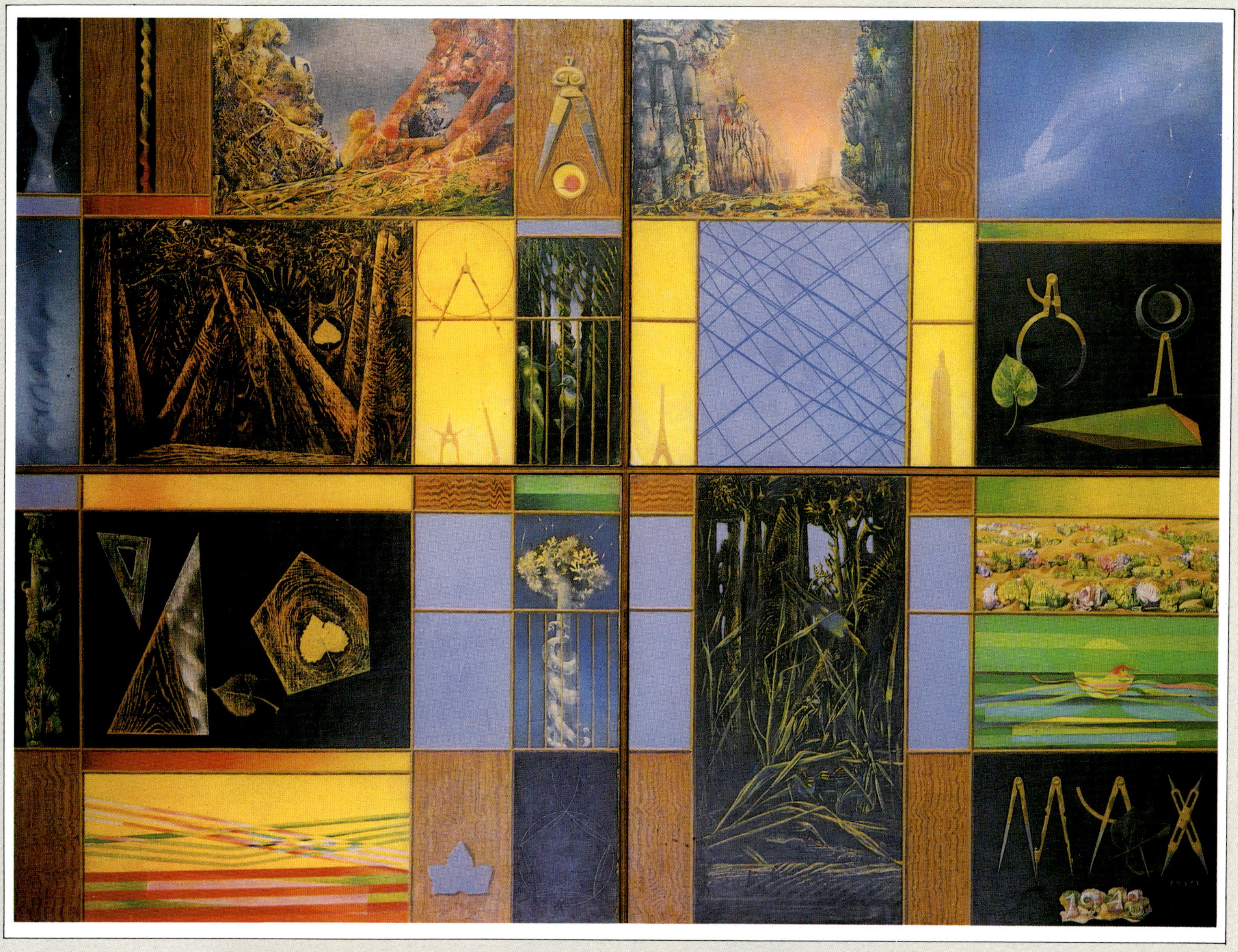

*Vox Angelica demonstrates all the techniques with which Max Ernst was associated* — collage, frottage, *decalcomania, illusionism,* grattage *and oscillation. However, the apparently collaged and frottaged elements were, in fact, painted in.*

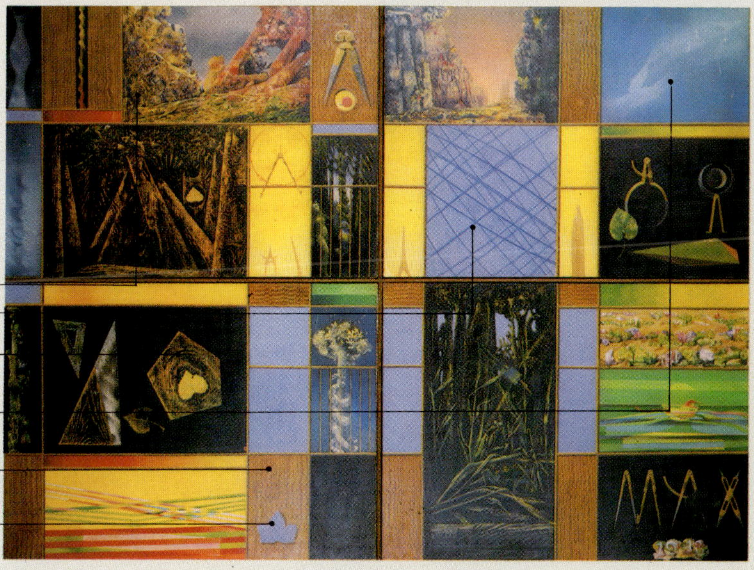


Vox Angelica *is made up of four canvases each measuring 30 × 40 in (76 × 101.5 cm). The canvases were assembled like the great* Isenheim Altarpiece *painted around 1515 by the sixteenth century German artist Mathias Grünewald. One part of the alterpiece is called* Concert of Angels, *and it was from this that* Vox Angelica *received its name. The work illustrates the vivid variety of effects which can be achieved through the conjunction of alien elements. The symmetrically structured painting is built up out of polarities of light and dark, and of ultramarine blue and yellow.* Vox Angelica *can even be seen as a parody on Ernst's previous achievements — it includes reference to all the techniques for which he was known. Paris and New York are juxtaposed in the Eiffel Tower and Empire State Building. Images recur in the painting, for example the geometrical instruments and the drill. The image of the drill is paralleled in the images of the snakes entwined around trees, which are perhaps references to the serpent in the Garden of Eden.*

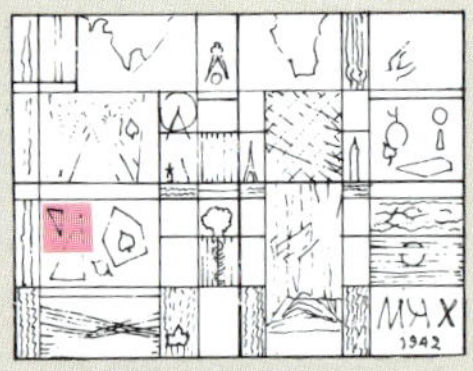

*This detail shows the fine brushwork with which the impression of* frottage *was evoked. It is possible that the texture of the spiral in the righthand set square was created using the* grattage *paint-scraping technique; but it is also possible that, like many of the other techniques in* Vox Angelica, *the effect of the actual procedure was mimicked rather than actually used.*

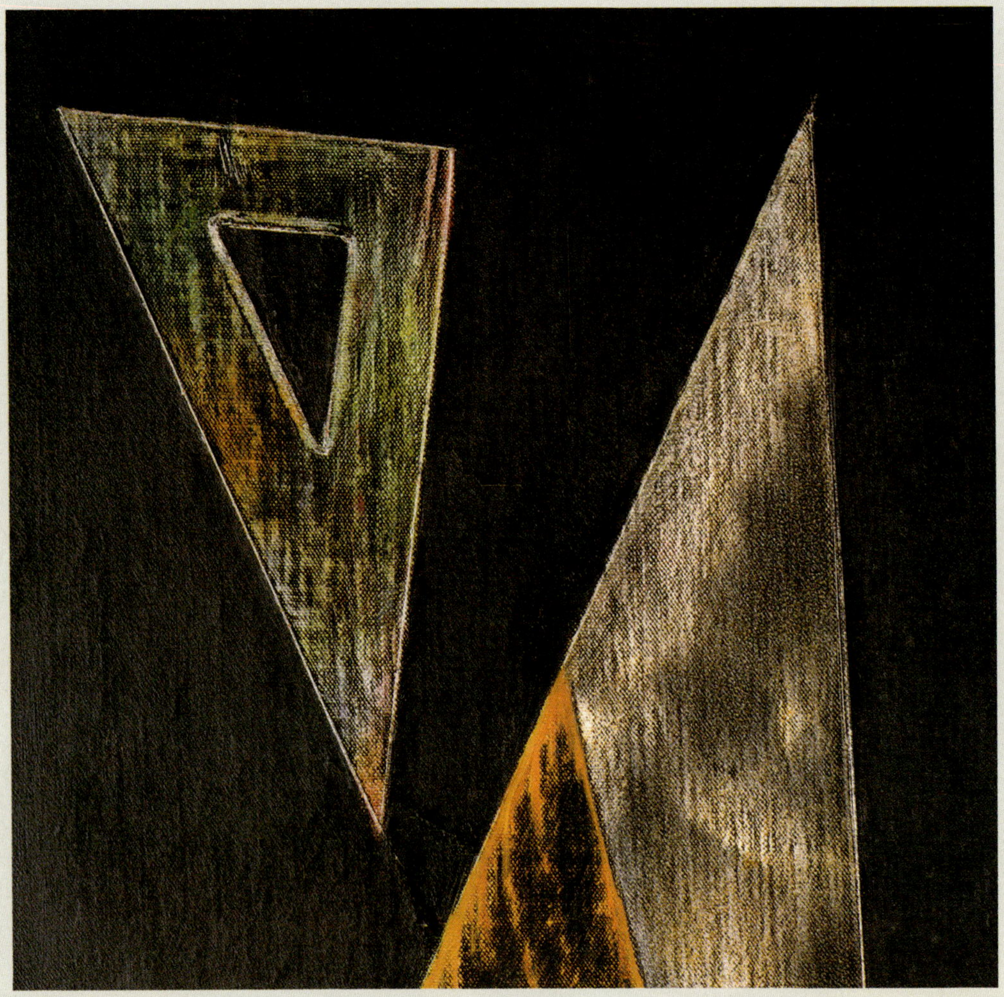

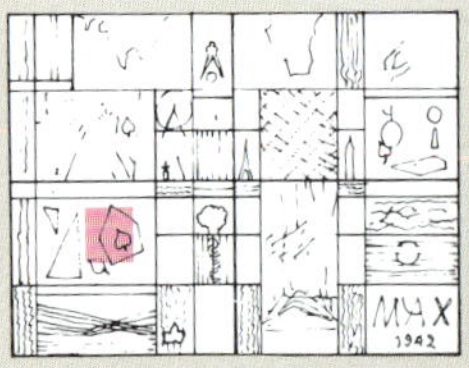

Actual size detail
*This detail shows the great precision of Ernst's technique. Here he has painted a leaf in an illusionistic way and placed it on top of a painting of a piece of wood. Although this image is painted, it is given the appearance of having been created using the technique of frottage, which involved making rubbings of floorboards for example. So, by painting a frottaged image, Ernst can be seen as parodying his previous achievements.*

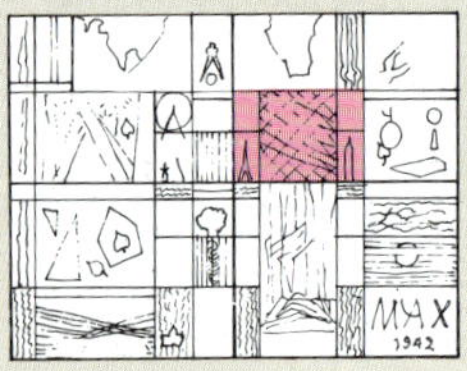

*This detail of* Vox Angelica *shows the overall yellow-blue contrast which characterizes the painting. The central section was painted using the oscillation technique, the pattern of lines being built up from paint dripped from a swinging can on the end of a piece of string. The juxtaposition of the Eiffel Tower and the Empire State Building symbolizes Ernst's own 'oscillation' between Paris and New York.*

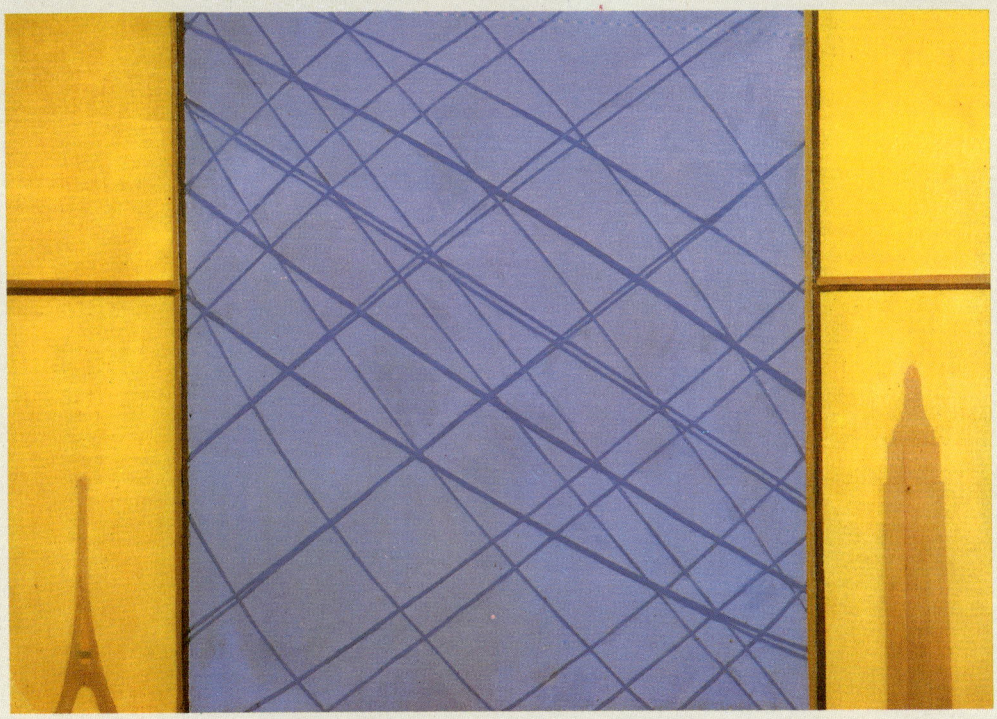

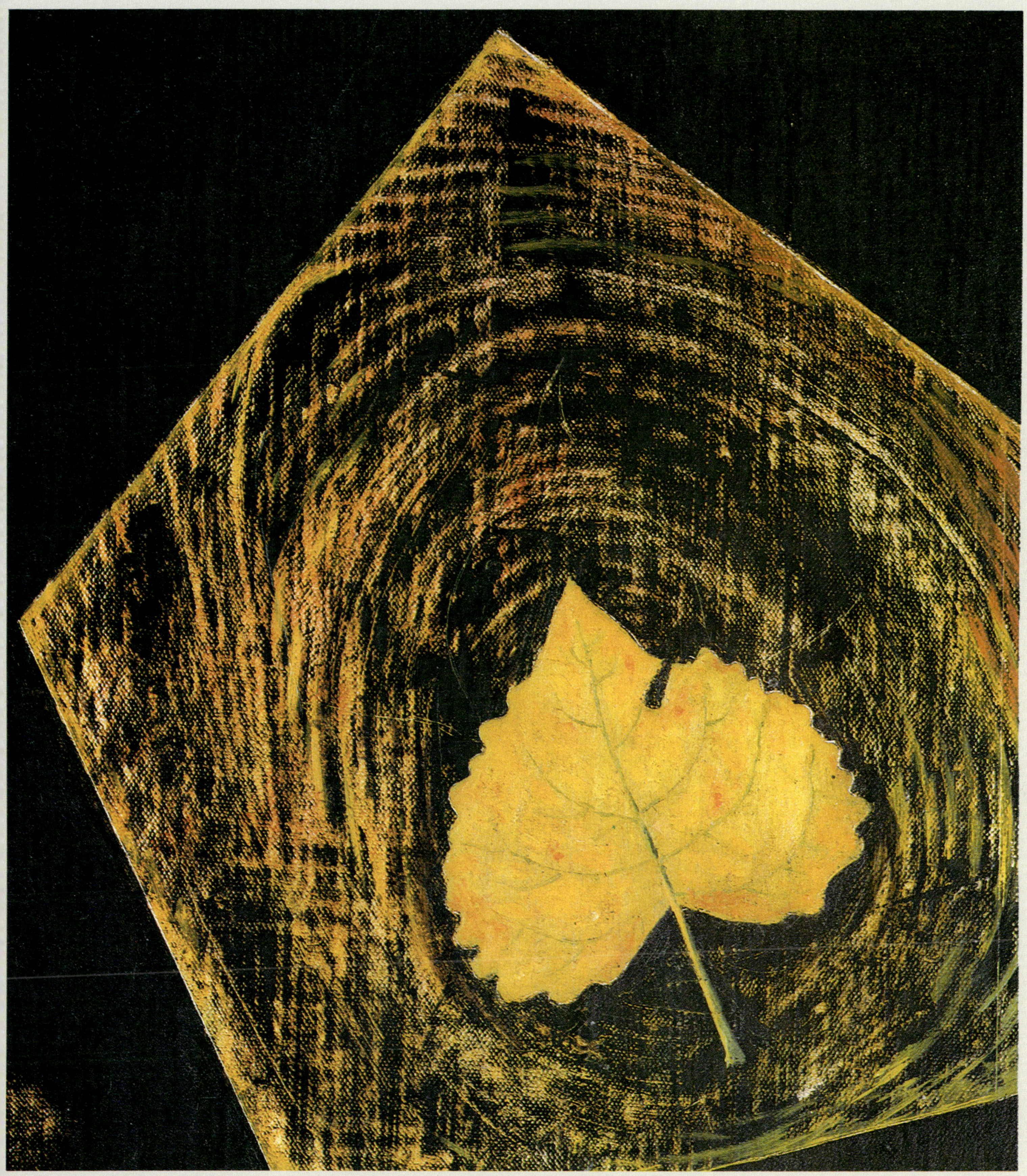

# FRANCIS BACON

*Figure in a Landscape (1945)*
Oil and pastel on canvas
144.7cm × 128.2cm/57in × 50½in

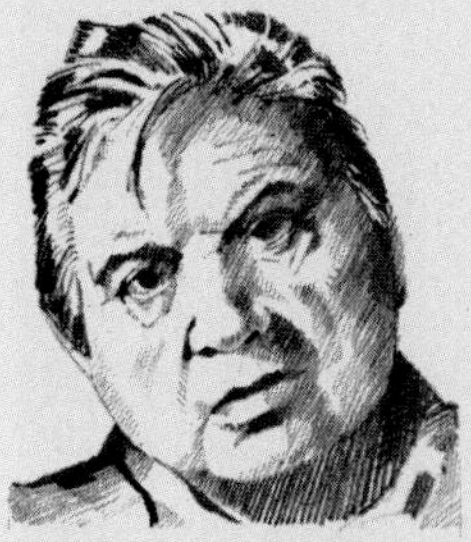

A peculiarly individual and isolated painter, Francis Bacon was born in Dublin in 1909. He moved with his parents to London when he was 16. He never received a formal art school training, but spent his twenties working as an interior designer making furniture and rugs. Throughout the 1930s he painted intermittently and in 1944 started to paint full-time.

A number of sources have recurred in his paintings. As prompts he employs X-ray photographs; Eadweard Muybridge's *The Human Figure in Motion* of 1887, showing the frozen movements of struggling or fighting pairs of men against a measured grid; film stills, as well as works by Rembrandt, Diego Velazquez (1590-1660) and Goya with particular reference to *chiaroscuro* areas of brilliant fluid brushwork emerging out of a dark field which provide drama and a sense of glimpsed movement.

*Figure in a Landscape* is an early example of Bacon's work, which had an enormous impact on post-war British painting. It is based on a photograph of his friend Eric Hall sitting astride a chair in Hyde Park, London.

Bacon frequently starts a painting with a controlled 'accident' of paint thrown at the canvas, which often evolves into a figure in violent movement in a disquieting domestic setting, or landscape. *Figure in a Landscape* was painted on a large white primed surface; probably some ivory black paint was 'accidently' splashed on the center of the canvas in the area now occupied by the figure. The next task was to create what Bacon refers to as an 'armature'. This is a two-dimensional framework upon which he almost literally 'hung' the paint. The link with the sculptor's wire armature is quite clear, but so is Bacon's experience of technical drawing and furniture design. These first lines can be traced raking horizontally across the center foreground in two parallel motions of thin black paint, also in an apparent railing curving in from the right, and later overpainted with two greens; and in the horizontal lines which slice across the center of the painting at the top of the chair back.

The central dark space was painted at an early stage, possibly echoing the shape created by the first controlled accident. Here Bacon used his knowledge of Matisse who had revealed that strong resonant blacks are possible only if laid directly on to the primed canvas. Any lighter paint underneath would have prevented its tendency to recede. He used broader brushes to put down the fields of buff-colored paint which dominate the entire upper half of the canvas but applied it more unevenly in the lower foreground where the primed canvas can be seen breaking through in many places.

The landscape behind the figure recalls a grid in movement, reminiscent of Eadweard Muybridge's experimental figure photographs. In the foreground it resembles a hot African grassland; Bacon has imaginatively transformed Hyde Park into a type of savannah. This is related to his interest in pictures of big game hunting, which have triggered off several other paintings.

Once this black/beige relationship had been laid down, the centers of focus could be established. The lapel, cuff and sleeve were put in as symbolic of a suit, Bacon's sense of commercial design enabling him to select the particular elements which would be universally recognizable. The wittiest piece of execution is at the lower knee where the cloying buff paint has been dragged over the now dry black underpaint so that the revealed canvas grain is 'read' as the assumed texture of the suit's cloth.

The area of greatest visual excitement occurs at the intersection of the four structures on the right, where Bacon creates a small explosion of scuffed paintwork using both his fingers and his brushes. This marks the introduction of alizarin crimson, which conveys a disturbing element of violence. Some of Bacon's most favored reference tools are medical manuals; from them he has developed the technique which gives this otherwise relaxed seated figure a new kind of violence and vulnerability. The seated figure is welded to the chair and pinned by the structures on the right, one like a machine gun. Again the technique is adapted to this purpose and some of the black paint has been aggressively scraped away revealing the canvas surface like a wound in the area inside the curving 'railing'.

Eric Hall's body is shown headless, a rare occurrence in Bacon's work, with a cavernous torso like a wheel arch painted in lamp, ivory and blue blacks. The body's presence in space is enforced by the broken patch of shadow behind the leg, put in with very thick impasto in two blacks and a deep ultramarine.

Bacon unified the painting in terms of color using alizarin crimson and cadmium red in a loose Divisionist speckling, in the red border at left and right of the figure and in the angled shadow at the lower right corner.

Cerulean blue was applied with a broad bristle brush in a broken strip across the top. This leads the eye to a flecked piece of raw sienna at top left. It functions as a color 'key', as it is the pure component of the dominant beige color of the landscape.

*Figure in a Landscape* is a brilliant example of the deliberate use of various methods and techniques, each shifting to accommodate Bacon's imaginative instincts in the different zones of the canvas. This activity entailed the visual destruction of a seated figure, yet was a highly organized disintegration which arose out of Bacon's stated 'desire for ordering and for returning fact on to the nervous system in a more violent way'.

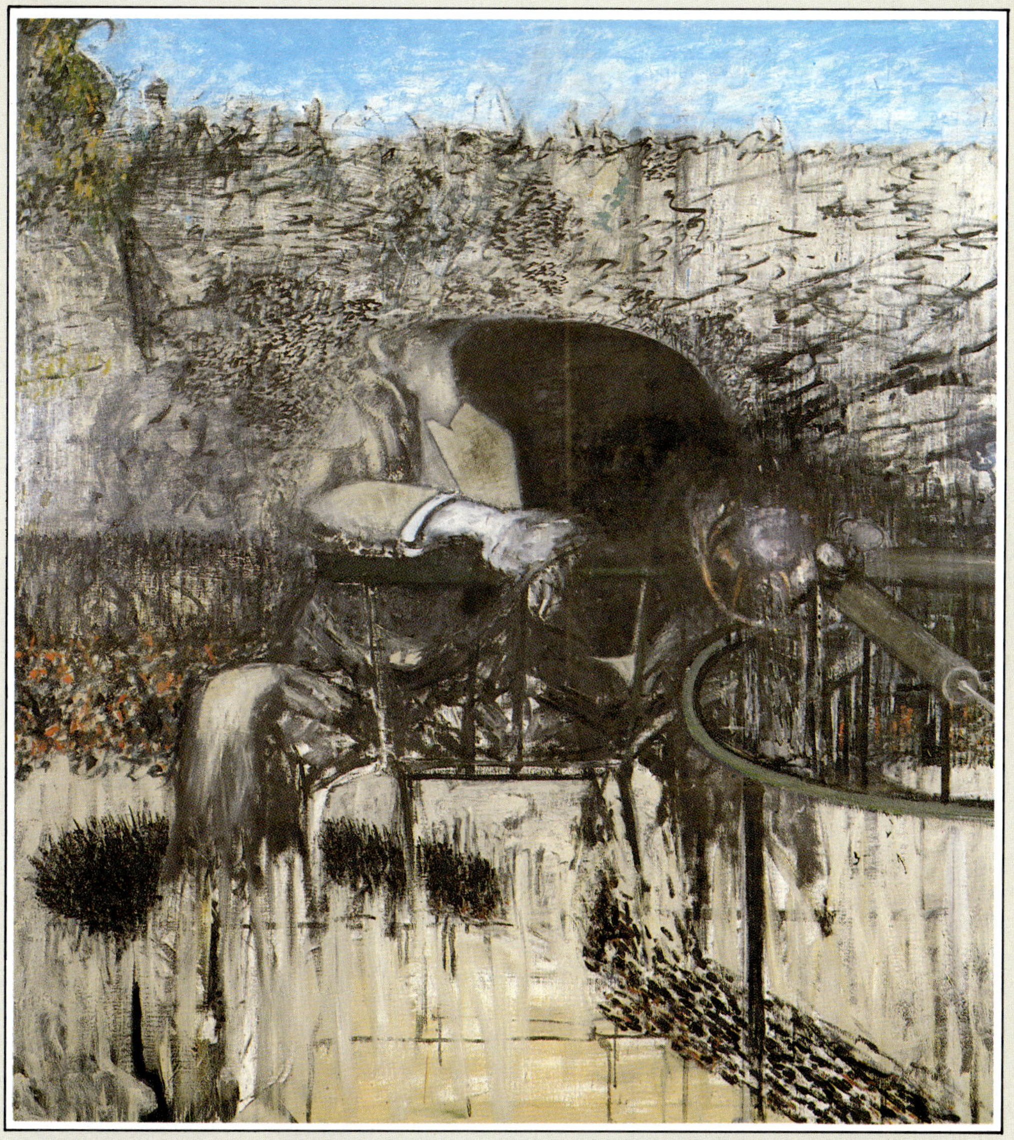

The Figure in a Landscape *is based on a snapshot of Eric Hall taken in Hyde Park. The photograph was used as a basis for a range of treatments of the surface of the canvas. Bacon aimed to give movement to the traditionally static seated figure, in order to make the picture act on 'the nervous system' with greater intensity. All technique was conspiring to create a cinematic view of the figure. The starting point for this work was probably a controlled accident (such as paint thrown at the canvas) — with most of Bacon's paintings. This is then brought under control by an extensive painted grid and successive glazes and overpainting.*

A Chinese brush was used to create a rapid calligraphic brushstroke with thinned black paint

A 'sgraffito' effect was achieved by a bunch of brush ends raking into wet paint, creating a ploughed effect

One of several areas of divisionist brushwork; a speckled broken area of color

White primed canvas breaks through in many areas of the painting to give air spaces to the composition

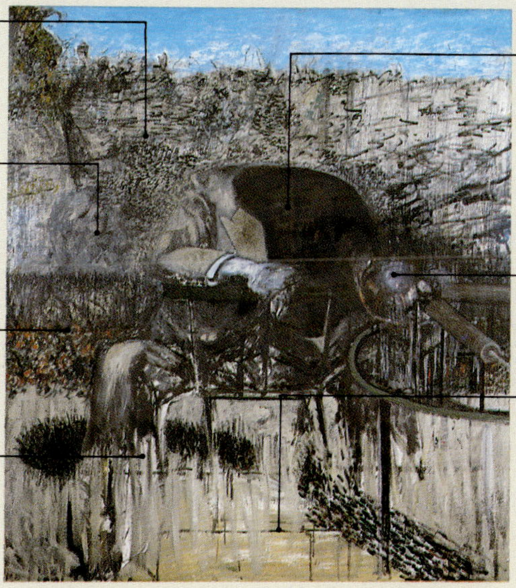

A lamp black, ivory black and pure ultramarine were used to give intensity to areas of deep shadow

Bacon used his fingers to blend the paint in several parts of the figure

Some traces of the initial black construction lines of the painting were left uncovered to give a sense of geometry controlling the composition

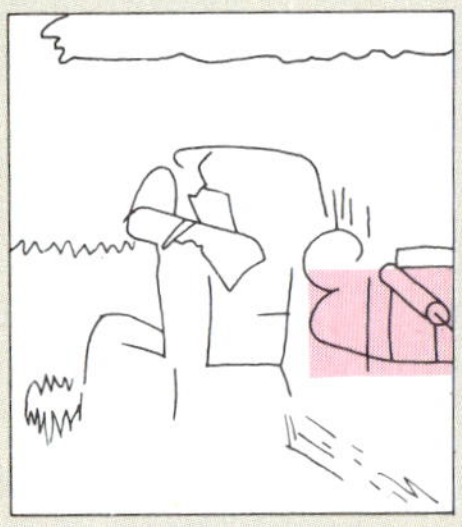

RIGHT *The paint was applied with some heavy impasto in the green 'railing' which was toned down from a shrill cadmium green to a cooler khaki tone which harmonizes with the hue of the tubular structure on the right. The area enclosed by this structure had some paint scraped away with a blunt knife in downwards motions, emphasized by a light strip thickly studded with ultramarine.*

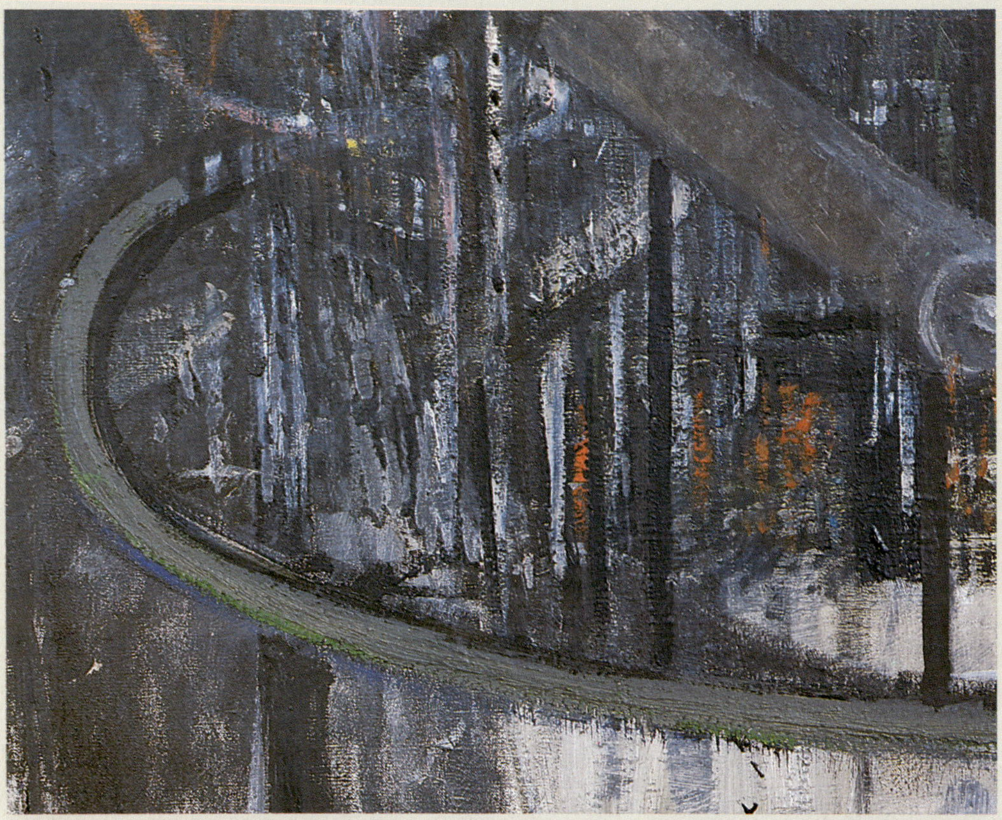

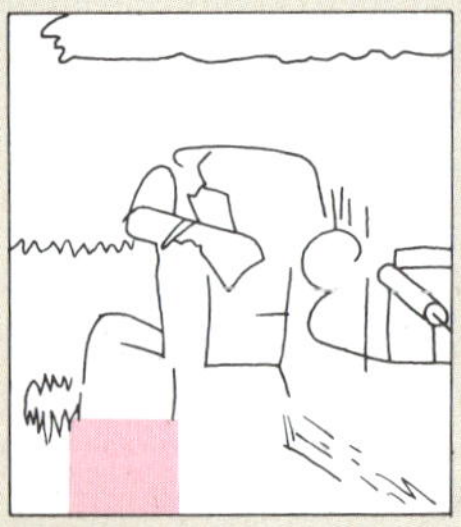

RIGHT *The figure's right leg is made to disintegrate into the foreground with a vertical smudging of beige paint over partly dry, black underpaint. Some of the initial understructure is allowed to break through the oil-thinned glaze of beige which is brushed in where a foot might appear. Some primed canvas appears in this area creating a sense of space and volume. A pool of shadow behind the leg was built up out of many small vertical brushstrokes in two blacks and ultramarine. This also conveys the texture of dry grass.*

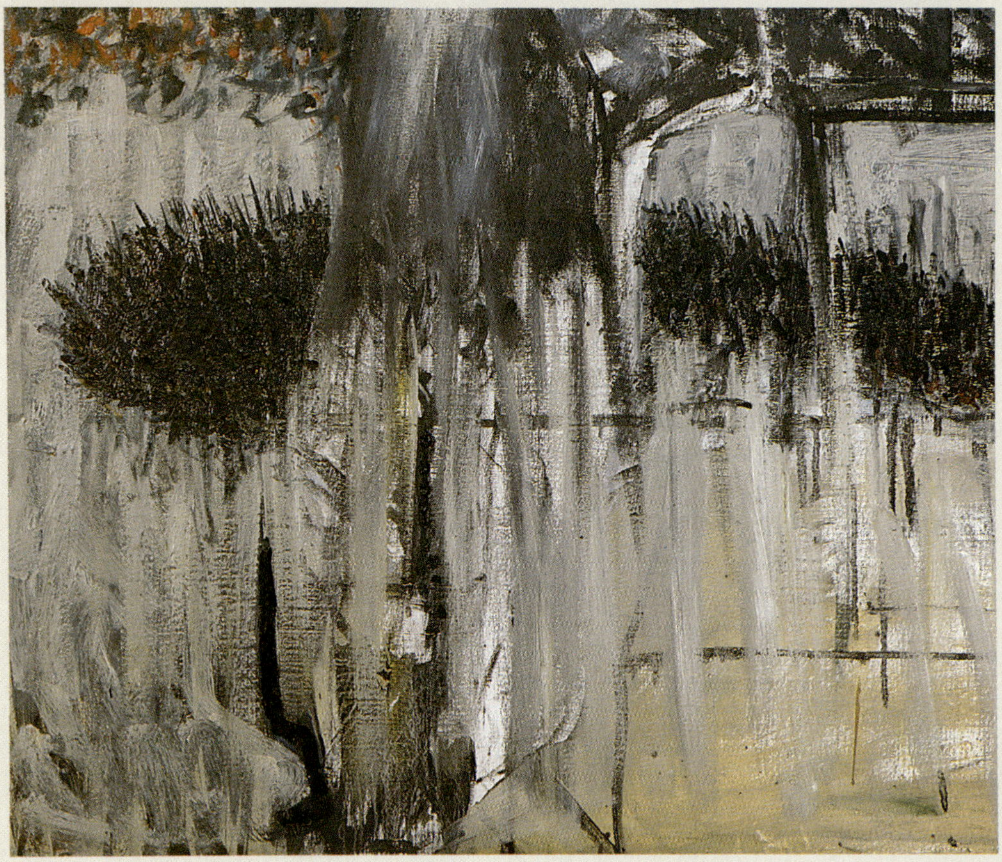

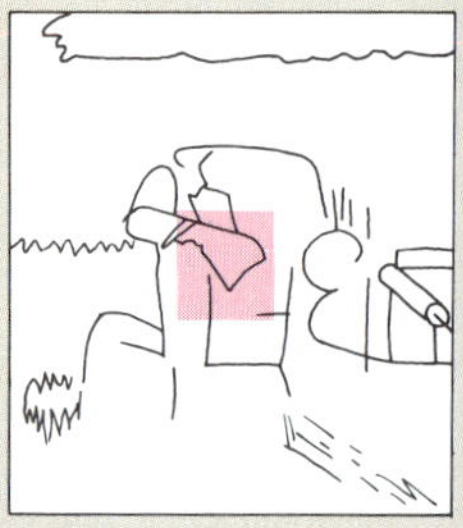

ACTUAL SIZE DETAIL *The hands of the figure resting on the back of the chair indicate the precise center point of the canvas. Bacon often uses a taut underlying geometry which is a result of his training as an interior designer. The upper hand has been painted and finger-smudged in a thinned flake white over raw sienna which had dried. The lower hand is merely drawn in with ivory black and is given some touches of thin white glazing on the knuckles to complement the light color of the primed canvas. The chair back has been brushed in as a horizontal line of pure viridian across the actual center line of the painting. The ivory and lamp blacks used in beneath this have been brushed in wet into wet. The flat side of the brush was dragged across the area depositing some random bristle prints to add movement and drama to the passage. Some unpainted canvas is also allowed to remain to give the impression of depth behind the chair struts.*

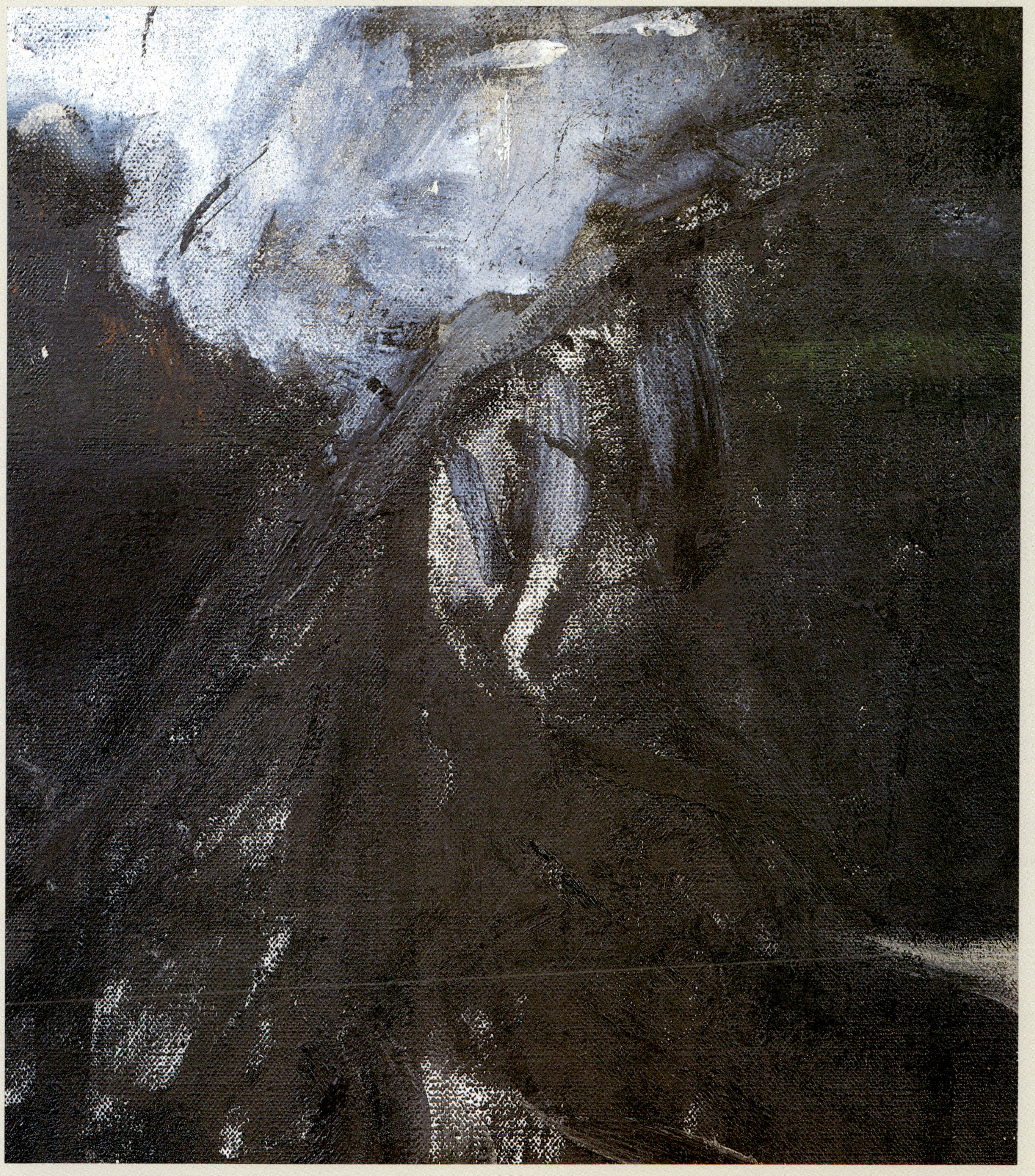

# JEAN DUBUFFET

*Dhotel nuancé d'abricot (1947)*
Oil on canvas
116cm × 89cm/45½in × 35in

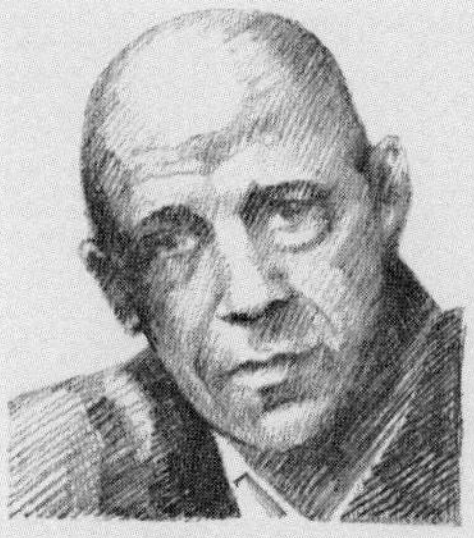

Dubuffet was born in 1901 in Le Havre. In 1918 he went to Paris where he gave up his course in painting at the Académie Julian after six months and started working on his own. He knew the painters Dufy and Léger and both had some influence on his otherwise 'self-taught' approach to art. By 1924 he had given up painting entirely and instead concentrated on running a wine business. In 1933 he started painting again, producing mainly puppets and masks, but in 1937 this creativity ended once again. It was only in 1942 that he finally devoted himself to painting and to the direction that he has continued since.

Dubuffet's return to painting was accompanied by a passion for primitive and naive art forms, as well as for paintings made by the psychologically disturbed. By 1945 he had started to collect so-called 'ugly art' or Art Brut, and in 1948 he founded a society to promote this type of work. He also wrote some important statements, criticizing the cultural aims of post-Renaissance Western art, in the place of which he advocated the more spontaneous, non-verbal, and spiritually potent qualities of primitive cultural expression. This resulted in a totemic approach to image-making which soon revealed itself in his first exhibition, where city life and images of men and women were presented with an aggressively simple and childish vigor. These paintings looked more like graffiti-covered walls or tribal emblems than conventional oil paint.

The driving force behind these early works was Dubuffet's entirely novel and extraordinary painting technique. He combined almost any element with the paint surface, including cement, tar, gravel, leaves, silver foil, dust and even butterfly wings. In defence of this technique he stated that 'art should be born from the materials and, spiritually, should borrow its language from it. Each material has its own language so there is no need to make it serve a language.' Such an approach has drawn him into the field of sculpture, using materials gathered at first from beside Parisian railway lines; by the 1970s he was creating enormous architectural environments in concrete.

In 1945 Dubuffet painted one of his first portraits, a drawing of Jean Paulhan, who later introduced the artist to the group of writers and intellectuals that frequently met at the house of Florence Gould. She persuaded him to make another portrait, of the writer Paul L'Eautaud. This developed into a series and eventually into the third of Dubuffet's major exhibitions entitled *Plus beaux qu'ils croient (portraits) (Better looking than they think). Dhotel nuancé d'abricot* was one of this group. André Dhotel is its subject.

The portraits are named after the sitters, whose most curious features have been deliberately emphasized by the artist. They combine caricature, imagery and some factual elements. Dubuffet explained that for a portrait to go well: 'it must be scarcely a portrait at all. It is then that it starts to function at full strength.'

Dubuffet's technique in *Dhotel nuancé d'abricot* can be reconstructed from a studio log book kept by him at the time. Laying the stretched canvas on the floor, he covered its entire surface with a thick, sticky *pâte* of light-colored oil paint applied with a spatula, like icing a cake. While it was still wet he took handfuls of ashes and sprinkled them over the whole area to darken the paint. Over this he dropped sand and then coal dust which would all, to a certain extent, sink into the surface. At this point some color was put on in the form of a thin 'apricot' mixture of yellow ochre, white and crimson brushed over the surface broadly. Some pure crimson was also put on, and is still visible through parts of the black crust.

The surface was now prepared to be totally covered with thick black paint troweled across with a palette knife, possibly with the addition of more ashes and dust. There was still no trace of the image at this stage – it would have looked instead like a plain smoke-blackened wall. With a broad spatula Dubuffet then carefully rubbed the materials into the surface and put the canvas on an easel to let any excess fall off.

It was only at this stage that the head was painted in with a cream white on a palette knife. Then, using a blunt point, he incised the contours of the head through this rich sandwich of paint and material, so that sometimes the canvas texture was revealed, as, for instance, on the side of the face to the left of the chin. The lines of the hair and the rest of the features were also drawn in with this instrument, sometimes lightly, as on the chin and spectacles, or deeply, as in the neck and shoulders, breaking through to the first thick impasto. A very thin mixture of 'apricot' paint and turpentine was then brushed over the face so that it ran into the gutters made by the ploughed lines, and stained the face with a warm glaze. Some of the original light paint of the face which was outside these boundaries was then blacked over. Finally, using a fine lettering brush the lines were enhanced with the addition of crimson, yellow ochre, black and white, in particular drawn into the trenches of the teeth, hair, nose and bow tie. These colors were used in a broader way in the earlier preparation of the surface, and thus the head and background appear unified visually.

The title of the work is, as usual with Dubuffet, an important final contribution. The result, in the case of *Dhotel nuancé d'abricot*, creates a humoros tension between what the viewer anticipated by the rather poetic description and what is actually confronted in the finished work with its primitive, earthy textures and skull-like gaze.

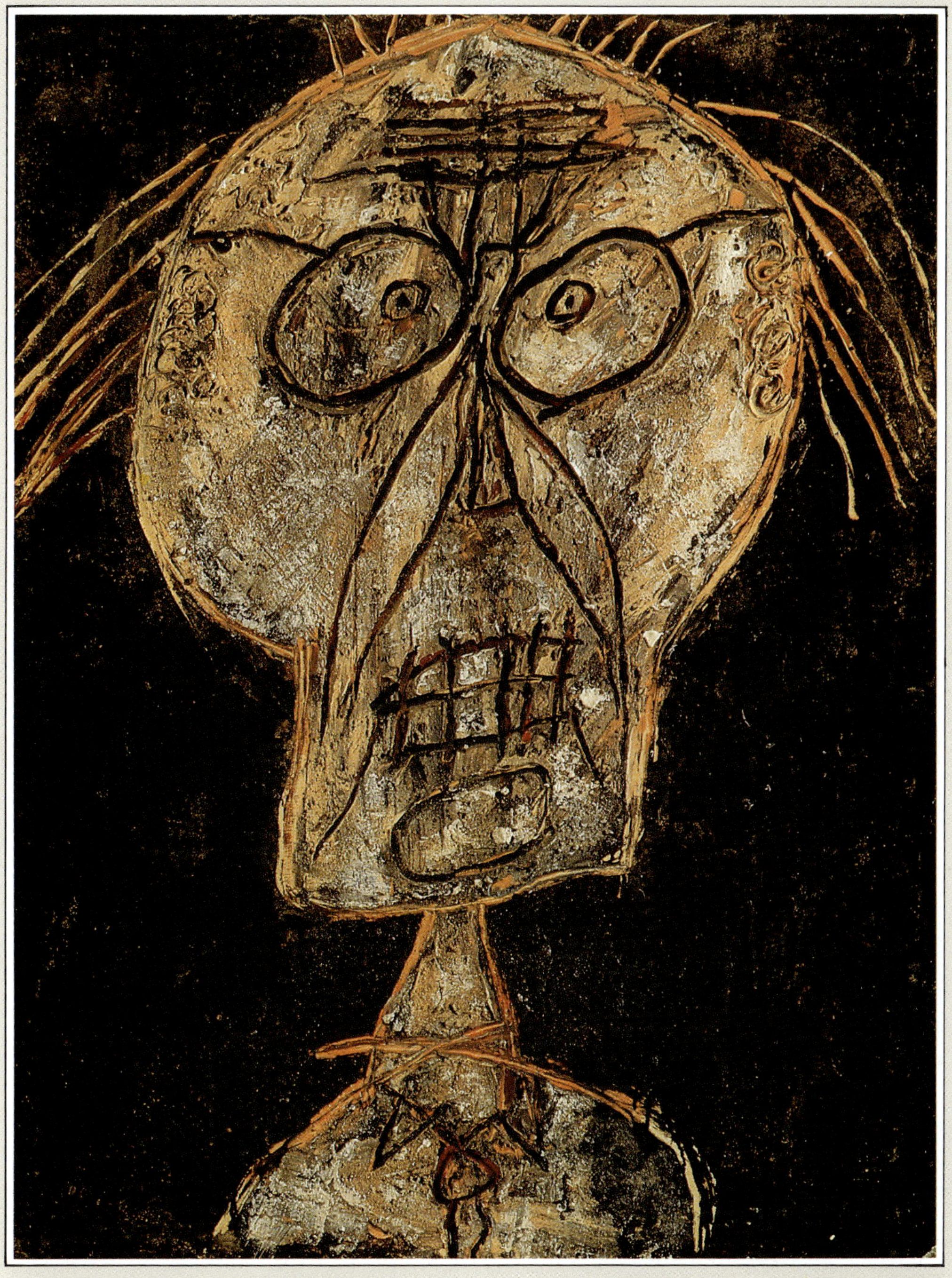

*Dubuffet gave this series of portraits the title 'Better looking than they think'. Despite the apparently childish graphic qualities of line, there was no intention to create a caricature, but rather to emphasize the features that the painter thought were worth remembering once in the studio. A sense of humor is also evident in the way the spectacle frames are echoed in the drawing of Dhotel's chin. Yet a slightly sinister skull-like quality is hinted at behind the frontal intensity of the gaze.*

Crimson underpainting of the background breaking through the final layer of black paint and material

Thick cream paint mixture dragged by a broad spatula over the crumbly surface of the paint and material

The dense black background is the result of an elaborate sandwich of oil paint, ashes, sand and coal-dust

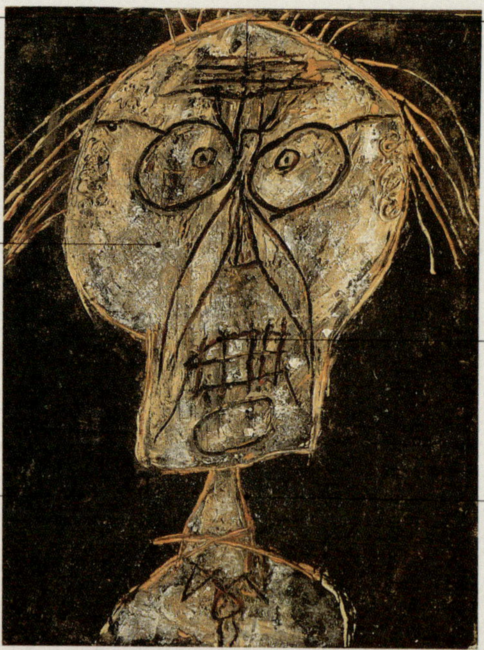

Thinned black paint and turpentine is painted with a fine lettering brush into the troughs made by a palette knife

Touches of pure crimson red added to the blackened lines

The palette knife produced all of the 'drawing' and, in places, has exposed the light color of the primed canvas

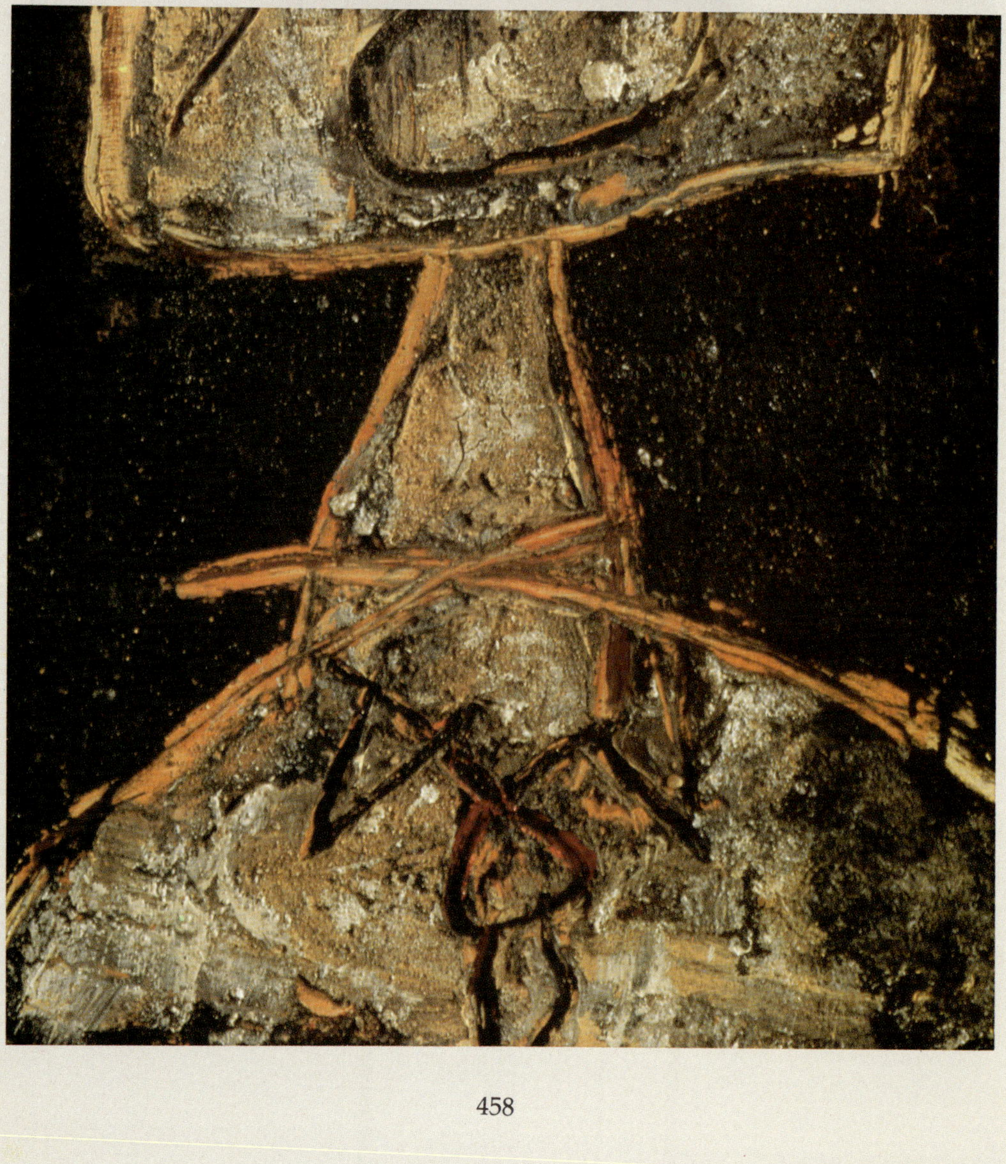

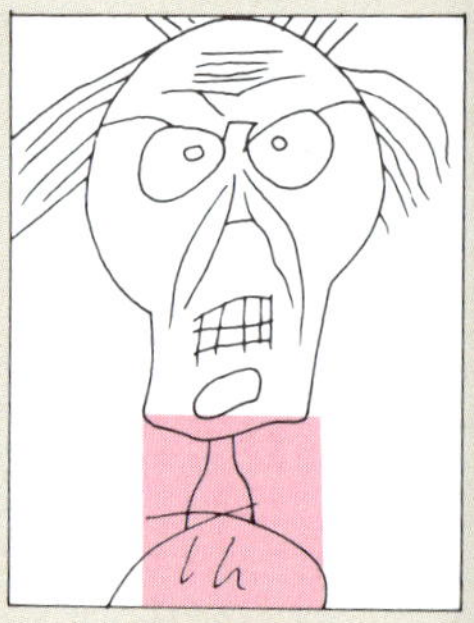

*LEFT Dubuffet's portrait of Dhotel is a good example of his use of* haute pâte *which required a thick mixture of oil paint, turpentine color washes and a limitless variety of granular raw material sprinkled over and mixed into the surface before any drawing was attempted. Here the head and shoulders required the final layer of cream color before the contours and features were drawn in with a palette knife.*

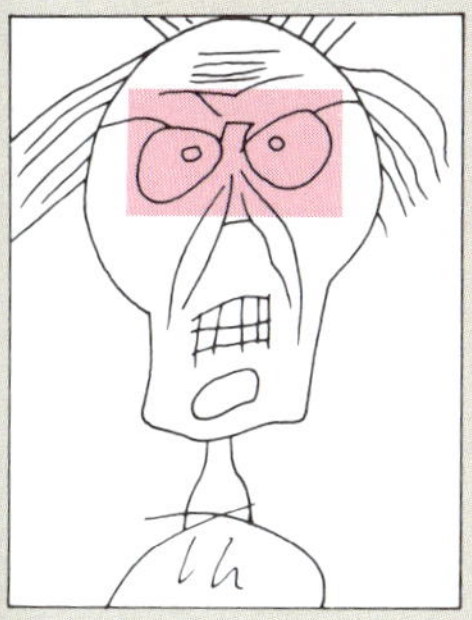

RIGHT Some of the successive processes in the assembly of haute pâte have been exposed by the furrows created by the palette knife. Here some of the texture of the primed canvas has been revealed. Dubuffet needed to paint this portrait with the canvas lying on the studio floor. When the portrait was put on the easel much excess material would fall off, then the main outlines and the finer brushwork could be added. Dubuffet was concerned to draw attention to the humblest raw materials and to give the commonplace elements of dust, ashes and sand a sense of value and beauty when employed in a painting. This aim is particularly successful in the combination of coal-dust and black paint in the background.

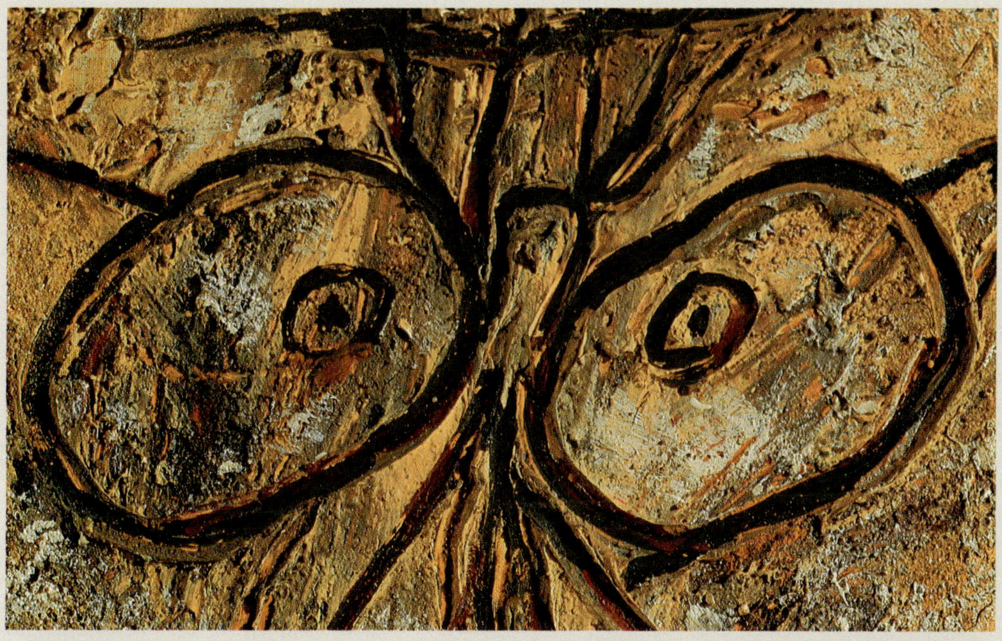

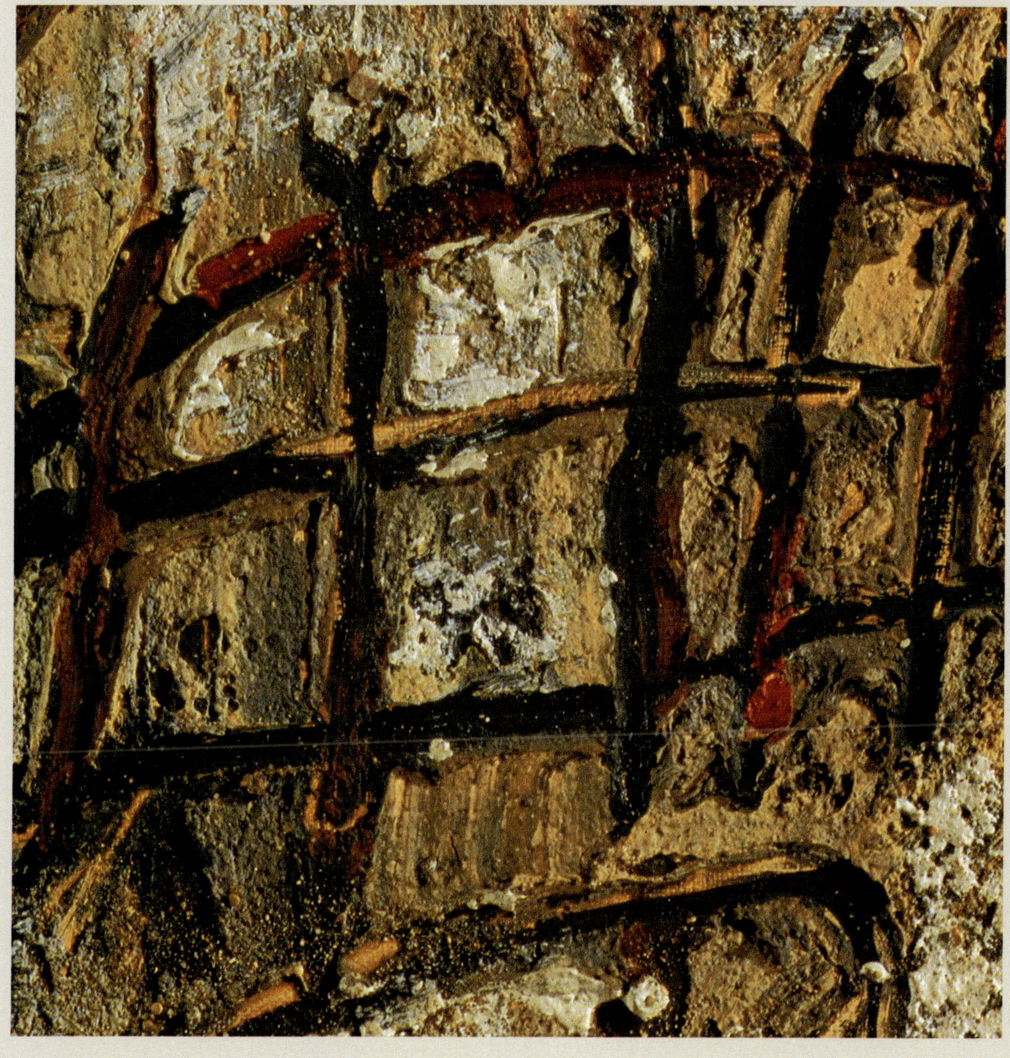

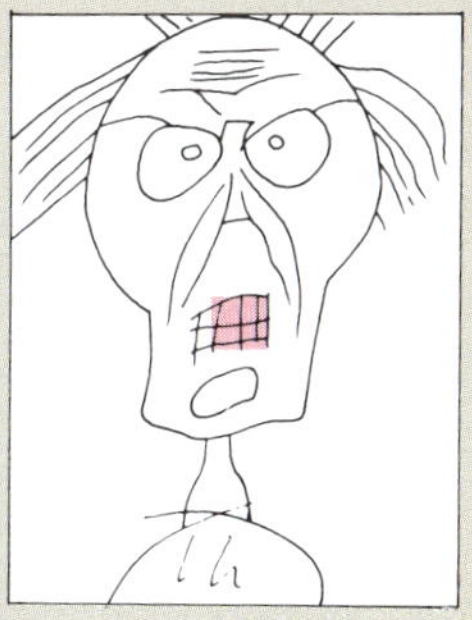

ACTUAL SIZE DETAIL The surface of the painting is approached like the form of map-making, a fact often declared by Dubuffet in the titles of some later paintings. A palette knife or blunt instrument was used to score into the thick paste which had been built up while the canvas lay on the studio floor. The apparent coarseness of the handling and the invitation to accident was then counteracted by the use of a fine lettering brush which was used, like a pen to reinforce the troughs in black and touches of crimson. The picture was probably completed within a day because the deep gouging was only possible while the pâte was still moist.

# JACKSON POLLOCK

*Full Fathom Five (1947)*
Oil on canvas with nails, tacks, buttons, coins, cigarettes etc
129cm × 76.5cm/50⅞in × 30⅛in

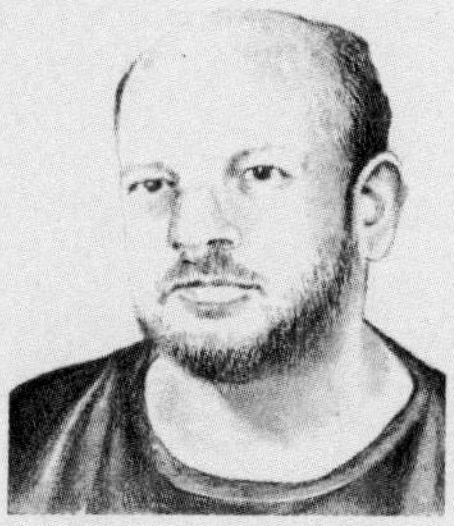

Jackson Pollock is held up as the tortured champion of American painting; the artist who, more certainly than any other, took the standard of the avant-garde from Paris to New York, a shift which is the most important single event in the history of post-war visual art. His technical and formal achievements, especially during the furiously innovative years 1947 to 1950, when he pioneered his famous drip technique, have been the most revolutionary since Cubism, and, some would claim, transcend even this. Most fertile of the Abstract Expressionists, Pollock took painting off the easel and finally cut the ties with imitation that are hidden in almost all modes of non-geometric abstraction prior to his.

He was born in January 1912 in Cody, Wyoming and spent his childhood largely in the west of the United States, in Arizona and California. He became interested in art through the influence of his eldest brother Charles, and he studied painting in Los Angeles at the same school as Philip Guston (b 1913), the future Abstract Impressionist.

The influences on Pollock's visual style and method have been the subject of much debate and controversy. Critic William Rubin presents the most extended and plausible argument, claiming that Pollock 'built simultaneously on such diverse and seemingly irreconcilable sources as Impressionism, Cubism and Surrealism', and arguing against the myth of instantaneousness started when critic Harold Rosenberg labeled Pollock's work as 'Action Painting'. Certainly, there is no doubt that Pollock was aware of the surface emphasis and scale of Monet, the stylistic and material experiments of Picasso and Braque, and the exploitation of 'automatic' procedures by Surrealist painters such as Joan Miró.

Possibly of relevance also, though notoriously difficult to detect precisely in the paintings themselves, is Pollock's known interests in mythology, religion and theosophy, and in particular the psychological writings of Carl Jung (1875-1961). From 1939 Pollock was in analysis and produced a variety of 'psychoanalytic drawings'. Ideas, then, of the untutored 'cowboy' from the West must be firmly resisted, as Pollock's attention to the art and writings of the past was extensive.

Such was the power and individuality of his achievement, however, that Pollock was more often reacted against than imitated in American and European art. Indeed he is difficult to imitate. Numerous attempts to fake his work appeared on the art market in the 1960s and they reveal the strength of the technical mastery Pollock developed over his own unique painting process. In fact the influence he did exert over subsequent generations was to provide artists with a final liberation from traditions of representation and from the controlled touch of the brush on canvas.

After a brief early flirtation with sculpture, Pollock became dedicated to painting, and his contribution technically was effected by experiment with the tools and means of application, mediating between the oil and canvas, or paper, rather than with the material constituents of these elements.

*Full Fathom Five* is one of the earliest masterpieces of Pollock's drip technique. The actual origins and initial development of this technique have never been fully explained, except by reading back from fuller photographic evidence produced about 1950, two or three years after this work was painted. Like other practical breakthroughs in twentieth-century painting, 'creative accident' seems likely to have played an important part, as Pollock probed and tested methods of paint application which promote the continuousness of line rather than the broken lines inevitable in the constant reloadings and readjustments of conventional brushwork. His solution was to pour from a can of domestic paint along a stick resting inside the container, so that a constant 'beam' of pigment came into contact with the canvas (which he left unstretched on the studio floor). The character of the line was determined by certain physical and material variables that could be combined in almost infinite permutations: the viscosity of the paint (controlled by thinning and dilution); the angle and hence speed of the pouring; and the dynamics of Pollock's bodily gestures, his sweep and rhythm, especially in the wrist, arm and shoulder. 'Like a seismograph', noted writer Werner Haftmann '[the painting] recorded the energies and states of the man who drew it.' In addition Pollock would flick, splatter and dab subsidiary colors on to the dominant linear configuration.

In *Full Fathom Five* the initial impression of a vibrant sea-green hue is relieved on inspection by the variety of shades and inflections which combine to produce an idea of water and of depth. A strenuous black calligraphy loops and curls round the volume of green; mottled and patchy areas of white interact with these, while the green is 'seasoned' with amounts of other colors.

Pollock has embedded nails, tacks, buttons, keys, coins, a torn cigarette, matches, and paint-tube tops into the surface – witnesses of the accidental nature of the 'painting' process and of the legitimacy of the trouser-pocket paraphernalia – as three-dimensional textural agents to amplify the signifying potential of the image. These alien materials, however, are subordinate to the overall design. They are, interestingly, almost invisible in normal reproductions of the painting; suffocated by the overwhelming presence of paint their function is analogous to the smears and touches of color, providing resistance and difference in the optical pattern.

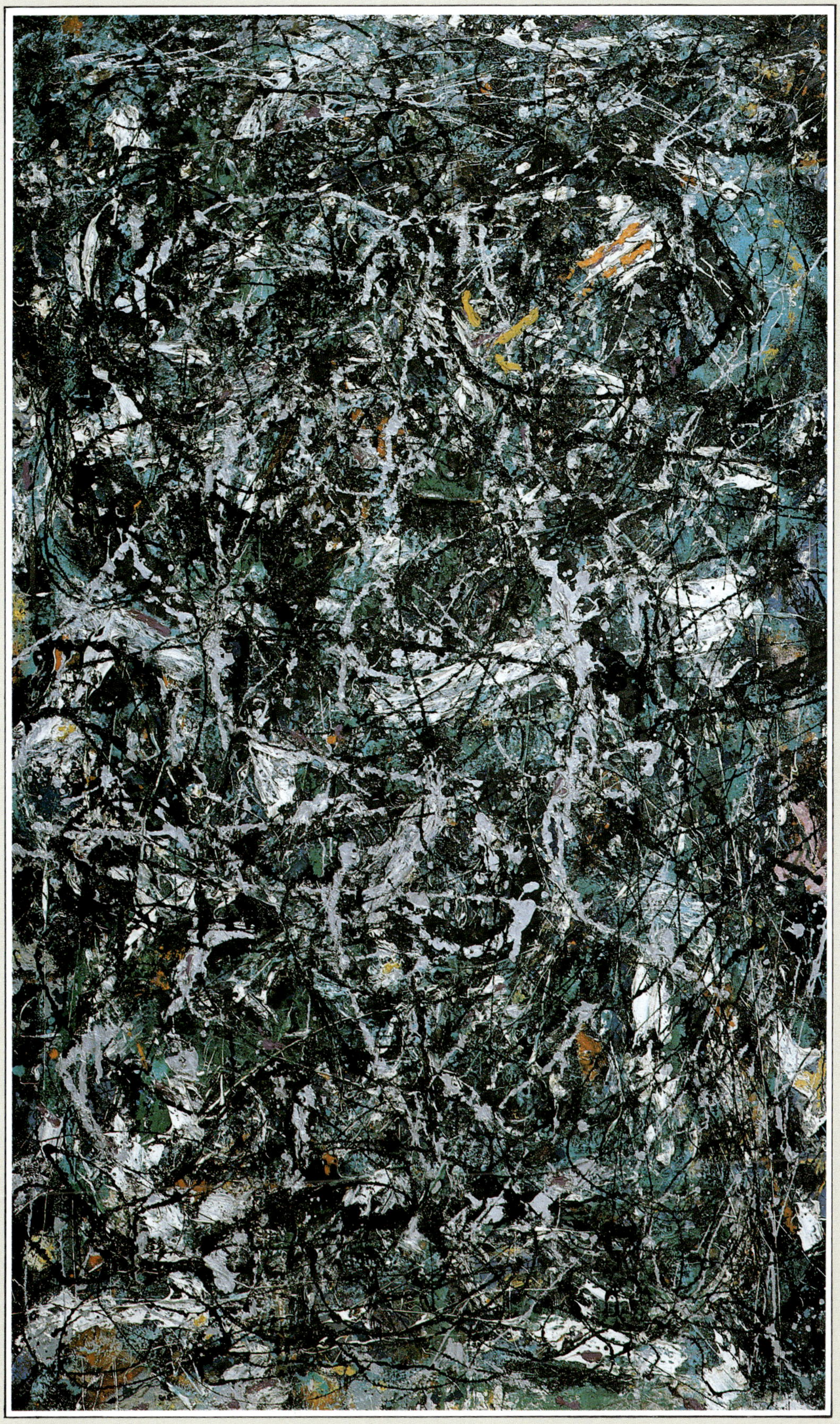

*Full Fathom Five is a boldly experimental early drip piece. The whole work however, has not been executed by pouring. There seem to be considerable areas, particularly in the various greens, that have been applied nearer to the surface. Liberal use has been made of aluminium paint whose sheen is skilfully exploited to contrast with the sharp white and more matt colors. Other colors are applied according to their hue and viscosity, as Pollock worked from all sides of his unstretched canvas, laid out on the studio floor. Unlike some later drip pieces such as* Autumn Rhythm *(1950),* Full-Fathom Five *is densely worked and multicolored and, even at the peripheries, often in Pollock the sites of slacker activity, there is scarcely a glimpse of the unprimed surface.*

Smears of yellow and orange, possibly the last and most deliberately applied pigments

Button embedded in the surface with paint

Thin, black tracery on a thick clot of white paint

Thick almost circular band of black, probably dripped and worked

Edge of composition with no linear drippings

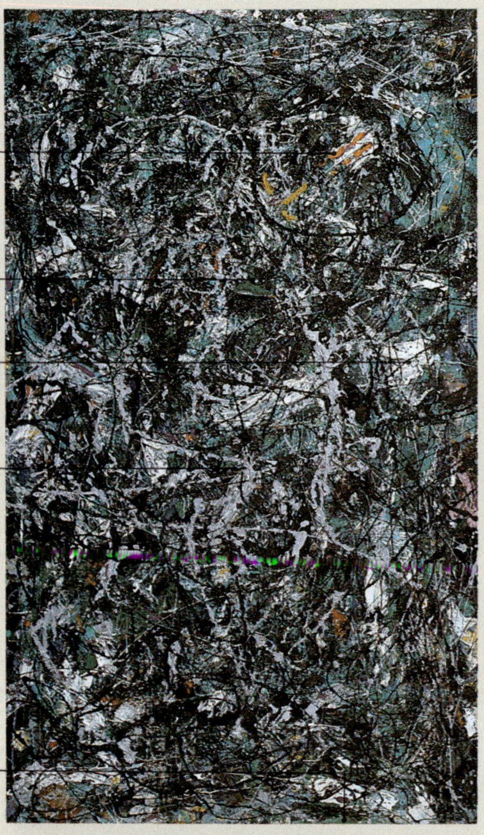

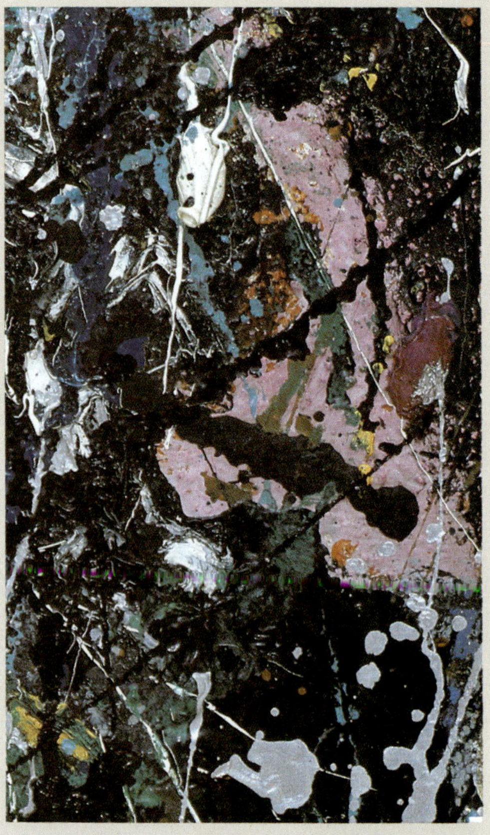

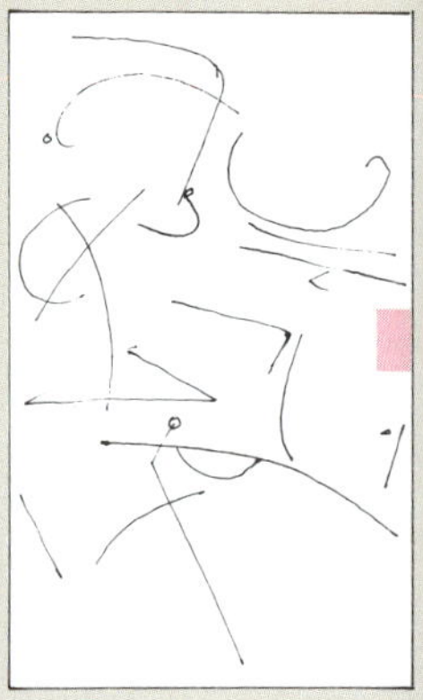

LEFT *The linear configuration in this detail is predominantly cursive and the color patches less discreet, invaded by other hues and effaced by later overpainting. The black calligraphy and metallic grey areas appear typically to have been added in the later stages of working. Small, but quite evenly rounded, paint flicks are visible over the whole surface.*

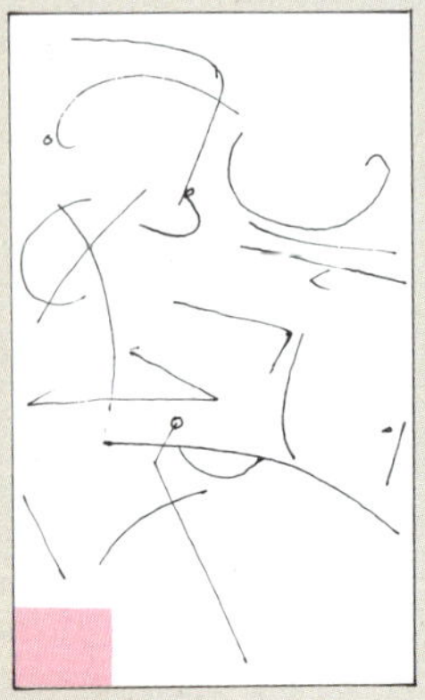

RIGHT *In a less heavily textured area such as this, the extreme delicacy of touch of Pollock's technique is clearly apparent. Minute spots and dabs of blue, yellow, orange and white inflect the mauve color patch, which is also traversed by all three of the main types of line used in the work, from the hair-thin sliver of white to the two thicker dribbled black lines.*

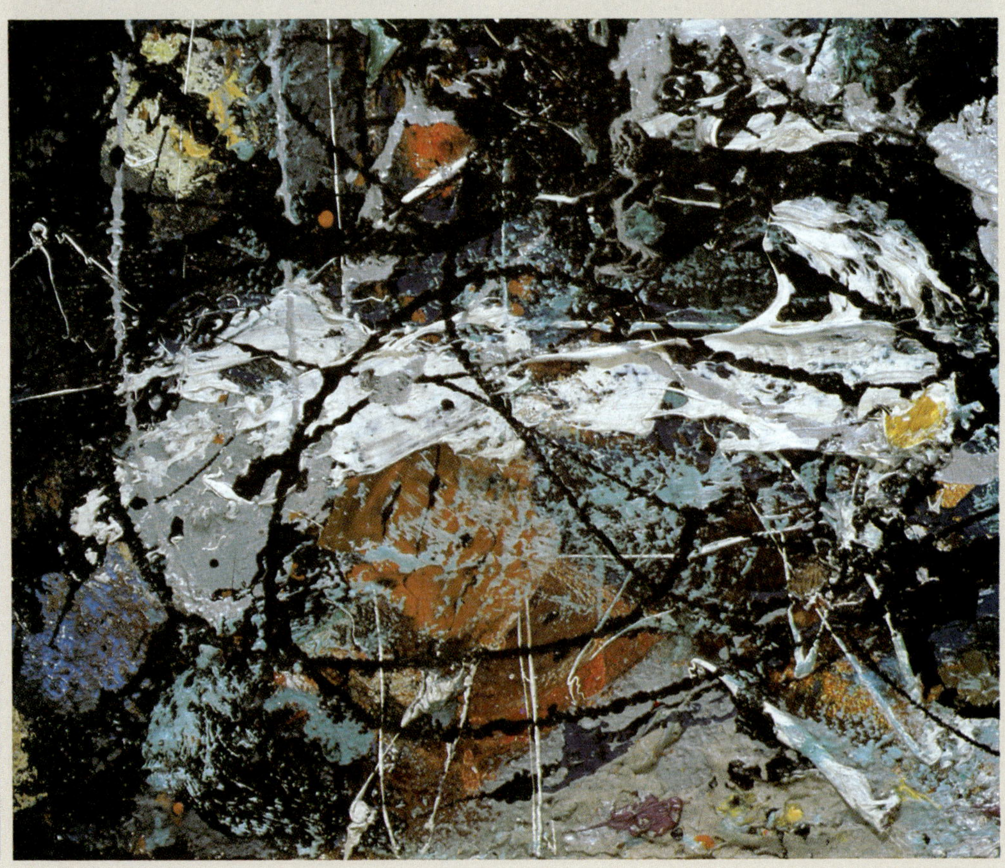

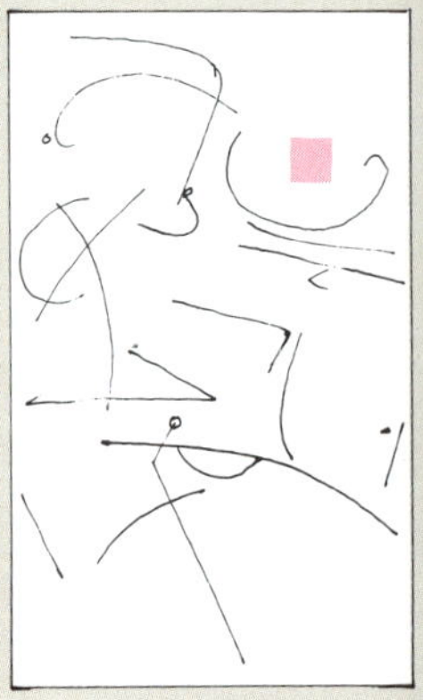

ACTUAL SIZE DETAIL *A number of marks, particularly the yellow and orange slabs with purple edging, appear to have been directly applied onto the surface, obscuring some of the black tracery. There is considerable variety of texture between the different modes of application; the thick smears of white, smaller touches, dots of paint flicked or applied from a distance, and continuously dripped lines.*

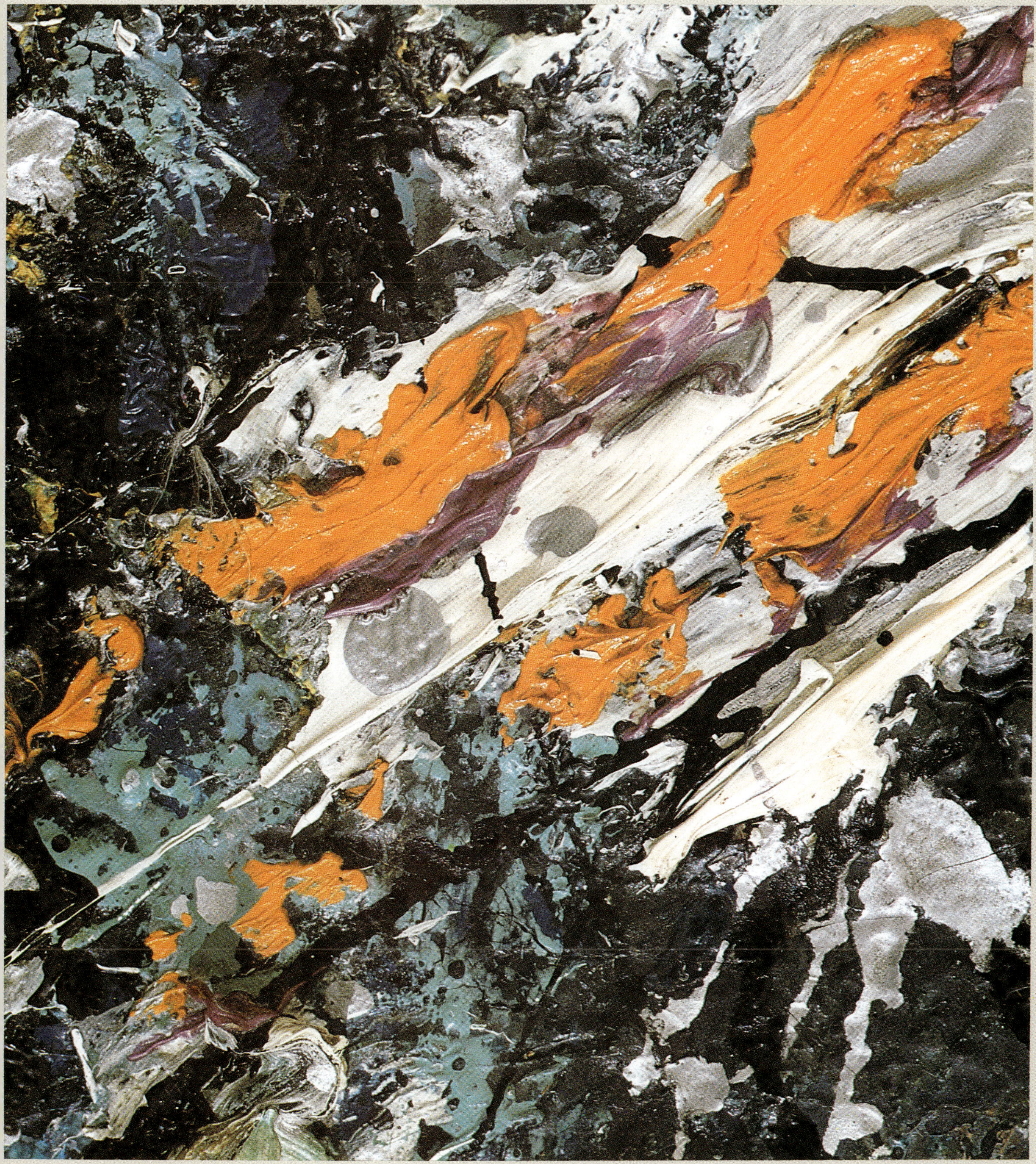

# JACKSON POLLOCK

*Autumn Rhythm* (1950)
Oil and enamel on canvas, 2m × 5m 38cm/8ft 10in × 17ft 8in

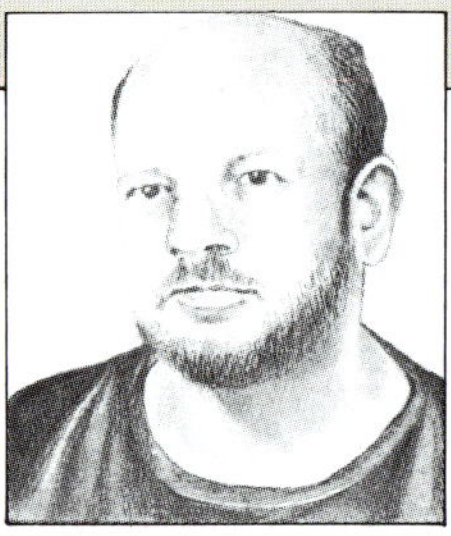

In 1947 Jackson Pollock began to create a series of paintings which filled the canvas with interlaced trickles, spatters, and puddles of paint which, as Willem de Kooning said, 'broke the ice' for what was to become Abstract Expressionism.

Prior to that time, Pollock's work had been figurative, symbolic and mythological. In 1946, after Pollock had finished with Jungian psychoanalysis, the mythological titles then gave way to titles referring to nature. It is apparent in these works that Pollock had begun to realize that the process of picture making could possibly take priority over the end results.

It was at this stage that Pollock felt the need to open up his paintings and, because he wanted to paint pictures beyond the range of outstretched arms, abandoned working from an easel. By placing his canvases on the floor or wall, adopting a drip technique and using dried out brushes, sticks and trowels as tools, Pollock was able to maintain an upright position and distance himself from the canvas. As he moved around the picture, working from all sides, the rhythm became expansive and involved long sweeping movements of the arm and hand to control the application of the paint. In 1951 Pollock said that 'My painting is direct . . . The method of painting is the natural growth out of a need . . . Technique is just a means of arriving at a statement. When I am painting I have a general notion as to what I am about. I can control the flow of paint: there is no accident just as there is no beginning and no end.' Technique was an inevitable solution to Pollock's search for self-expression and his methods and motives are best expressed in a statement made by him in 1948: 'My painting does not come from the easel. I hardly ever stretch my canvas before painting. I prefer to tack the unstretched canvas to the hard wall or floor, I need the resistance of a hard surface. On the floor I am more at ease. I feel nearer, more a part of the painting, since this way I can walk around it, work from the four sides and literally be *in* the painting . . . I continue to get further away from the usual painters' tools . . . I prefer sticks, trowels, knives and dripping fluid paint for a heavy impasto with sand, broken glass and other foreign matter added, . . . the painting has a life of its own. I try to let it come through.'

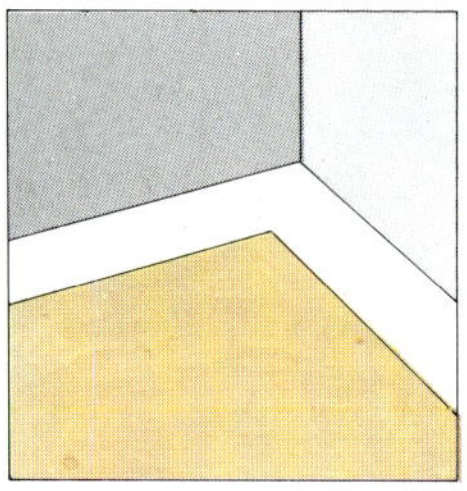

**1.** Unprimed canvas was either spread on the floor or tacked to a wall.

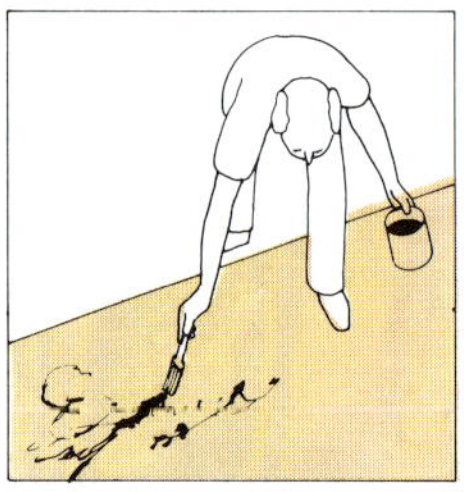

**2.** Pollock began painting in black enamel laying down the basic structure in a whirling net of splashes, splatters and dribbles.

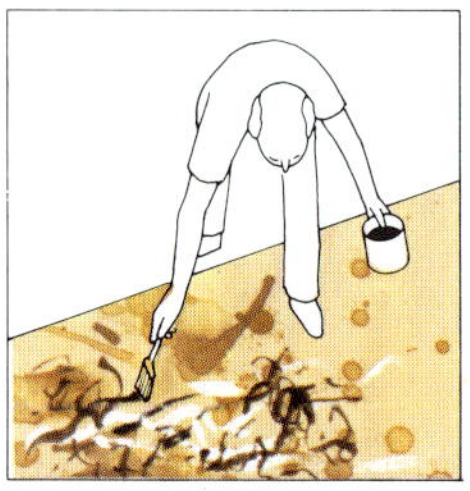

**3.** Light brown paint was used predominantly for splattering and staining the canvas; white paint was used similarly to black, and blue was used to make lines.

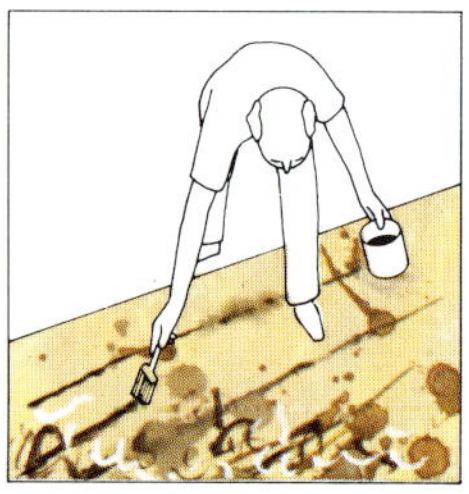

**4.** A thin line could be achieved by trailing the paint over a smooth dry area and thickened by allowing it to pass over and mix with still wet areas.

**5.** Large areas of bare canvas were used as a neutral color to stress the activity of the paint surface.

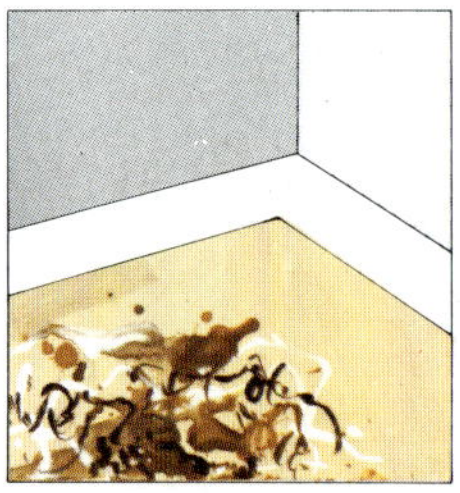

**6.** There is less paint around the edges with a noticeable easing of activity.

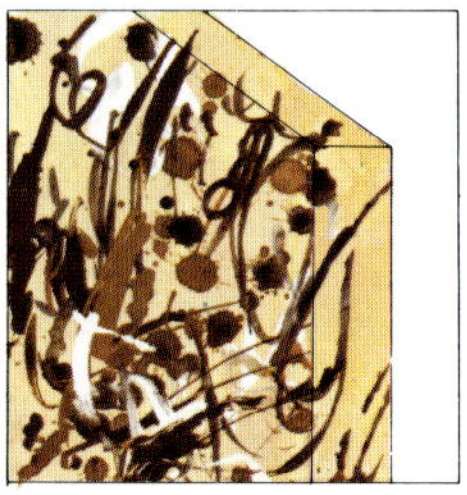

**7.** The dimensions of the painting were determined only on completion of the painting process. Finally Pollock stretched the canvas.

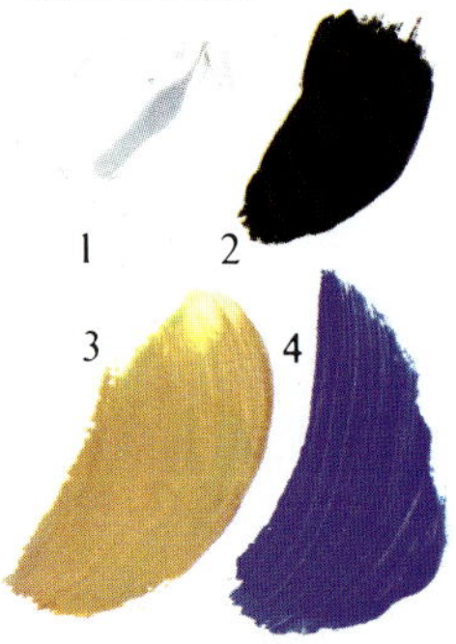


*In this work, Pollock used the following colors: white oil paint (1), black enamel (2), and light brown (3). Blue (4) was also used for lines.*

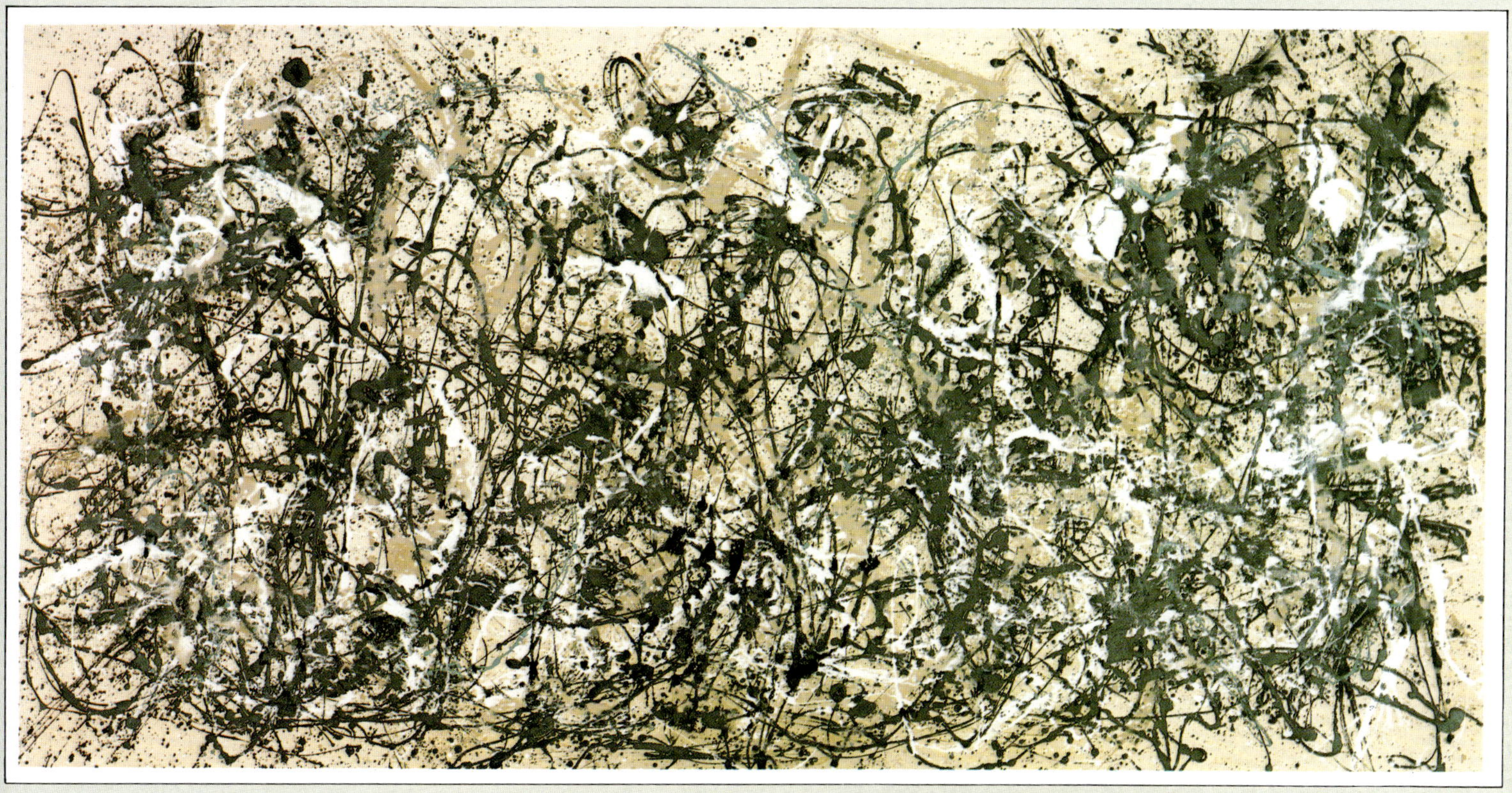

Autumn Rhythm *was executed in 1950 and shows Pollock's drip technique at its most elegant. Pollock worked from all sides of an unprimed canvas and emphasized each part of the painting equally but differently. Varying marks were made according to different methods of paint application. At what is now the top edge, the black and brown paint was thrown on to the canvas and splattered on impact, but the marks are also clearly directional. Along the lower edge the blacks and browns were allowed to run off a stick or brush and are more flowing, undulating and curvilinear. In some places, the paint was applied so thickly as to form pools which, in drying, formed skins in rippled surfaces. The skin which formed on the surface of open cans of paint was often either flung or carefully dropped on to the canvas.*

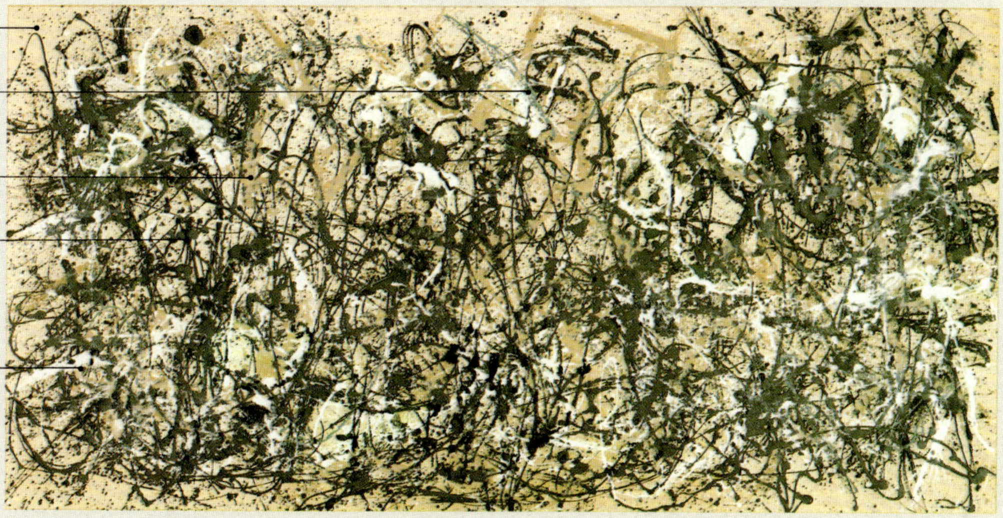

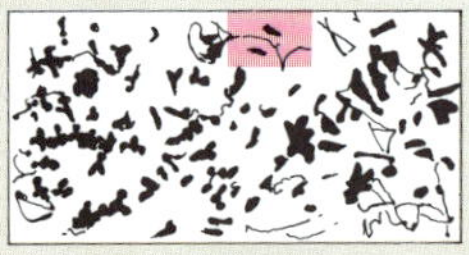

*As painting at an arm's length could not be sustained in Pollock's method of painting, he adapted his tools — dried brushes, sticks and trowels — to facilitate the painting process. Pollock would work his way around the canvas using his entire body to lay down the paint carefully but spontaneously. Gravity and the increased fluidity of the paint ensured that a picture made in this way would contain the kind of unexpected effects which Pollock desired. Concerning the prodigious control which Pollock exercised over his paintings, a friend stated that he had 'an amazing ability to quicken a line by thinning it, to slow it by flooding, to elaborate the simplest of elements — the line.'*

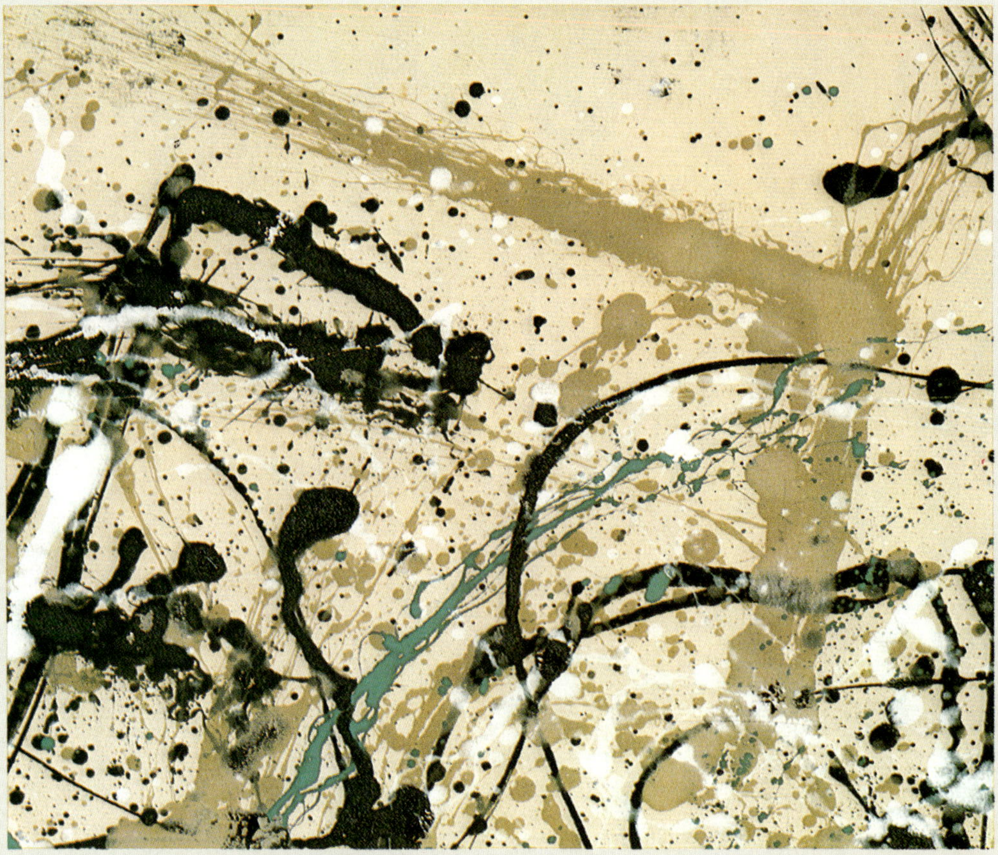

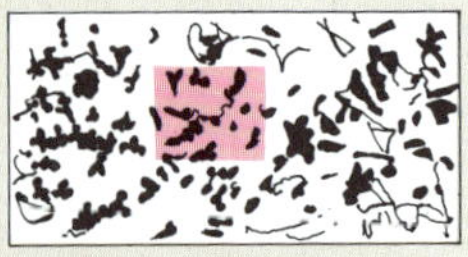

*Pollock used four colors to paint* Autumn Rhythm. *The viscosity of each of the paints determined to some extent the use which he made of it. Pollock started painting with black enamel, laying down a basic structure, a whirling interlaced net of splashes, splatters and dribbles which he then worked on in other colors.*

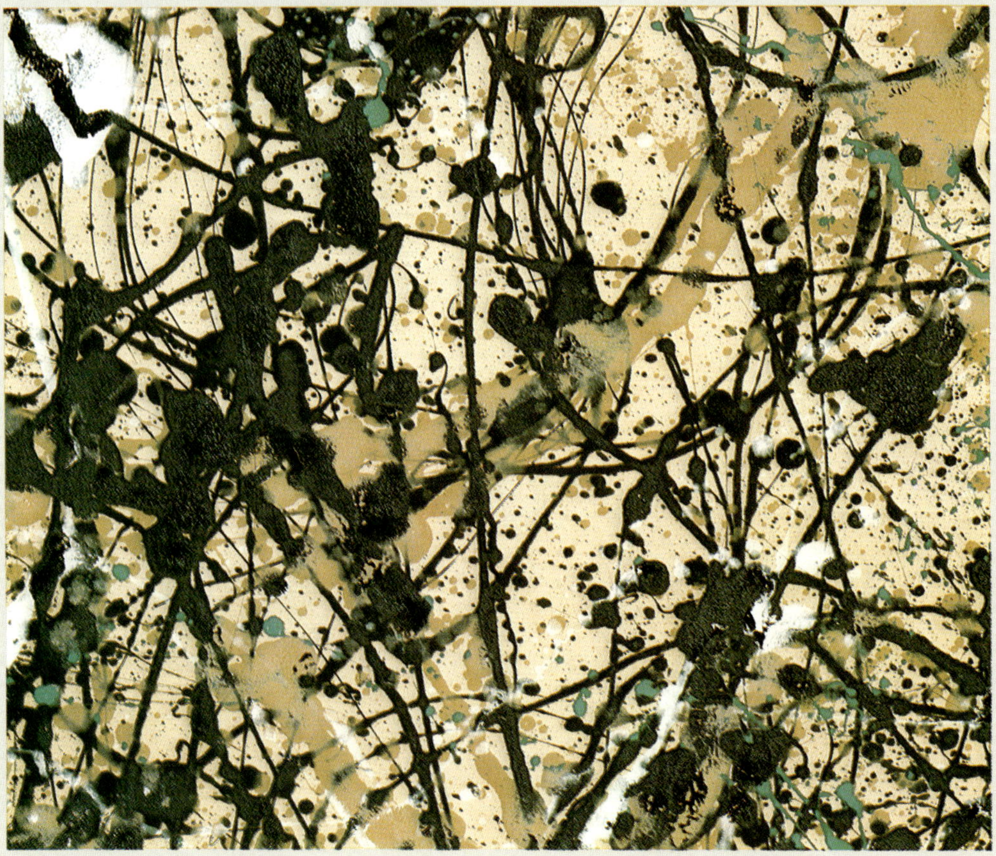

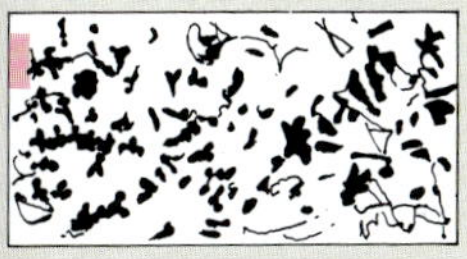

Actual size detail
*This detail of the top left edge of* Autumn Rhythm *clearly illustrates Pollock's innovative 'drip' technique. This method was used to achieve this spontaneous and flowing effect. The paint was thrown, splattered and dribbled on to the surface. However, while the paint was applied spontaneously and loosely, there is also a controlled and directive element. The black enamel has been used largely to create an active, flowing movement while the brown splatters create an effective background. The texture of the unprimed canvas provides the neutral surface for the paint which is the active element in the work. The painting was purposely stretched to continue around the sides to compensate for a lessening of paint activity at the outer edges of the canvas.*

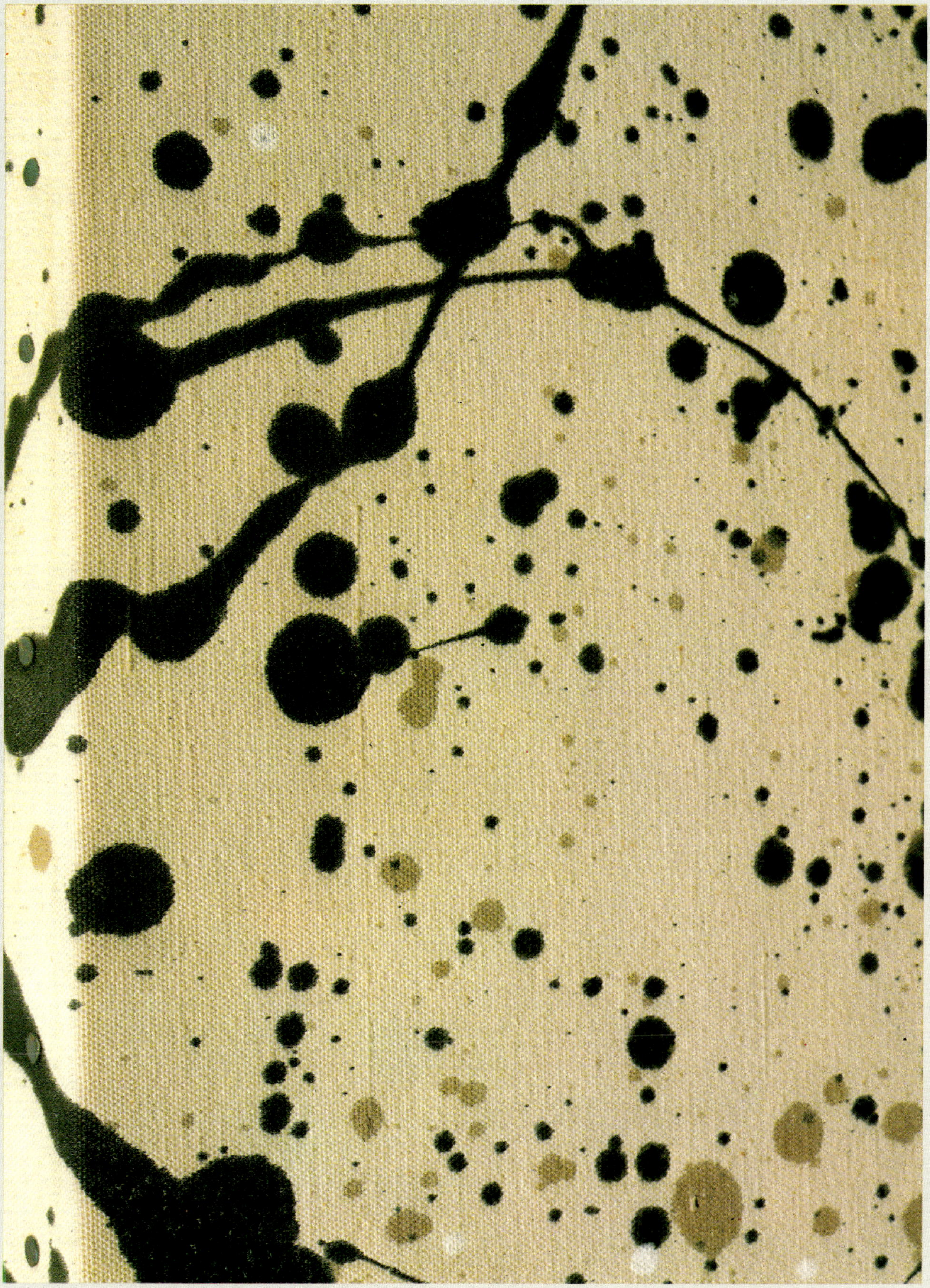

# HENRI MATISSE

*L'escargot (1953)*

Gouache on cut and pasted paper on heavy white cartridge paper
286.4cm × 287cm/112¾in × 113in

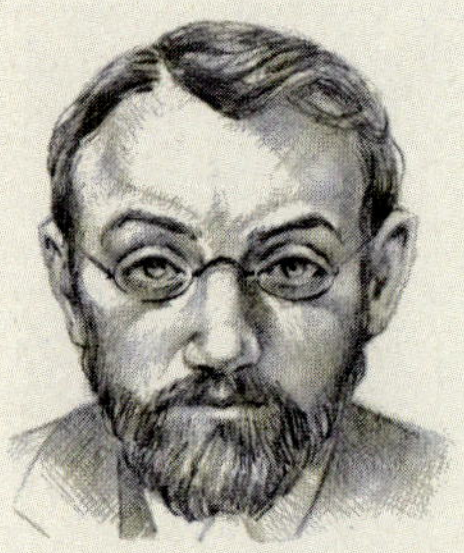

Born in 1869, Matisse did not become established as a painter until the first decade of this century, when, after a period of sustained study of still life and figure painting, including copying paintings in the Louvre, his works were exhibited with other Fauve painters in Paris. This group, including Derain, Vlaminck and Georges Rouault (1871-1958), adopted a very high-keyed approach to color which is evident in Matisse's early masterpiece, *Joie de Vivre* (1905-1906). This work features a group of strongly outlined nudes and a circle of dancers; motifs that were to concern him to the end of his life.

Matisse's studies of the nude led him to create, between 1904 and 1929, a series of four very large bronze sculptures *Backs* (of women) that became gradually more simplified and abstract. This process can also be traced in his studies for the Barnes Foundation murals of 1930-1932 where another group of gigantic nude dancers appear on an architecturally massive scale; he first used cut paper shapes in this project to help him plan out the mural. Matisse was given several other commissions in the decorative arts, such as tapestry, glass, interior decoration, a ballet set and the Chapelle du Rosaire at Vence. He also worked on a number of illustrated books; the most important is the 1947 *Jazz* which contains 20 brilliantly colored screenprints directly derived from some earlier small gouache and pasted paper cut-outs. This experience was to have great importance for the series of large cut gouaches of his last years. Matisse died in Nice in 1954, aged 84.

*L'escargot*, made the year before his death, was part of this series. It cannot be simply defined as either a conventional painting or a collage in the manner of the Cubists (who applied commercial or hand-prepared papers to their compositions and then added drawn or painted elements to unite the picture visually).

Matisse was here 'making' a painting in a process which he likened to sculpture, by cutting or tearing sheets of fine watercolor paper that had been prepared with opaque or semitransparent washes of high quality gouache, laid on with a broad brush in even strokes. He directed his assistants in the composition of these cut-out shapes which were pinned on to a temporary surface while he considered their arrangement. These pinholes are still visible in the corners of some pieces, as are several faint pencil lines and errant scissor cuts: all signs of the struggle of its making.

This technique had been used as early as 1930 in the Barnes murals where the cut-out dancers could be manoeuvred more effectively than unwanted charcoal drawing could be removed. However at that time, the paper was only a tool which was discarded once the desired outlines had been drawn in. It was only after the *Jazz* screenprints that Matisse developed this technique into a fully-fledged pictorial medium in its own right.

Two important processes had an influence on *L'escargot*. The first was printmaking, the second, architecture.

The cleanly cut edges of color, against a pure white background give *L'escargot* the appearance of some enormous screenprint. For *Jazz* Matisse had cut stencils for the color, thus blocking out areas of the white page which would have gleamed through as the whites do in this composition.

In 1947 Matisse was commissioned to do the entire decoration of a nuns' chapel, Chapelle du Rosaire, at Vence. He designed the building around stained glass windows which light the plain white-tiled interior. The subtle mathematical discipline of *L'escargot* derives from working with the proportions of the chapel space. In the painting a visual measurement is provided by the blue rectangle whose length equals the width of the large roll of paper that was being employed for the work. That same width is quietly apparent where the edges of the orange 'frame' meet on the left and right sides just above the center, and it can be traced in the proportions of several other shapes in the composition.

Other interesting structural elements in *L'escargot* are the two pieces of emerald which came from a single sheet, torn across, creating the only rough edges in the work; the rest of the pieces were cut with scissors or against a straight edge. In other large cut-outs in this series Matisse employed both the cut shape and its template as a piece of visual wit, creating echoes across the surface.

Matisse's palette was made up of nine colors which are held in position by a cadmium orange 'frame'. Gouache, a dense type of watercolor, can produce an infinite range of color, yet he chose simple primaries: a cobalt blue, a deep red and a warm cadmium yellow – and black and white – to which he linked five other complementary colors. Matisse controlled their strength with extraordinary precision. He said: 'simple colors can act upon the inner feelings with all the more force because they are simple. A blue, for instance, accompanied by the shimmer of its complementaries, acts upon the feelings like a gong.'

The musical simile is typical of Matisse. His reference to the function of blue is of special significance to *L'escargot* because it is the complementary color to the dominant orange. This is echoed by other contrasts: black against white; magenta against yellow, and even two greens against red. 'It's not enough to place colors, however beautiful, one beside the other; colors must also react on one another. Otherwise, you have cacophony,' noted Matisse. The result in *L'escargot* is a finely-tuned spiral of color that gives the 'snail's' shell a spiritual significance.

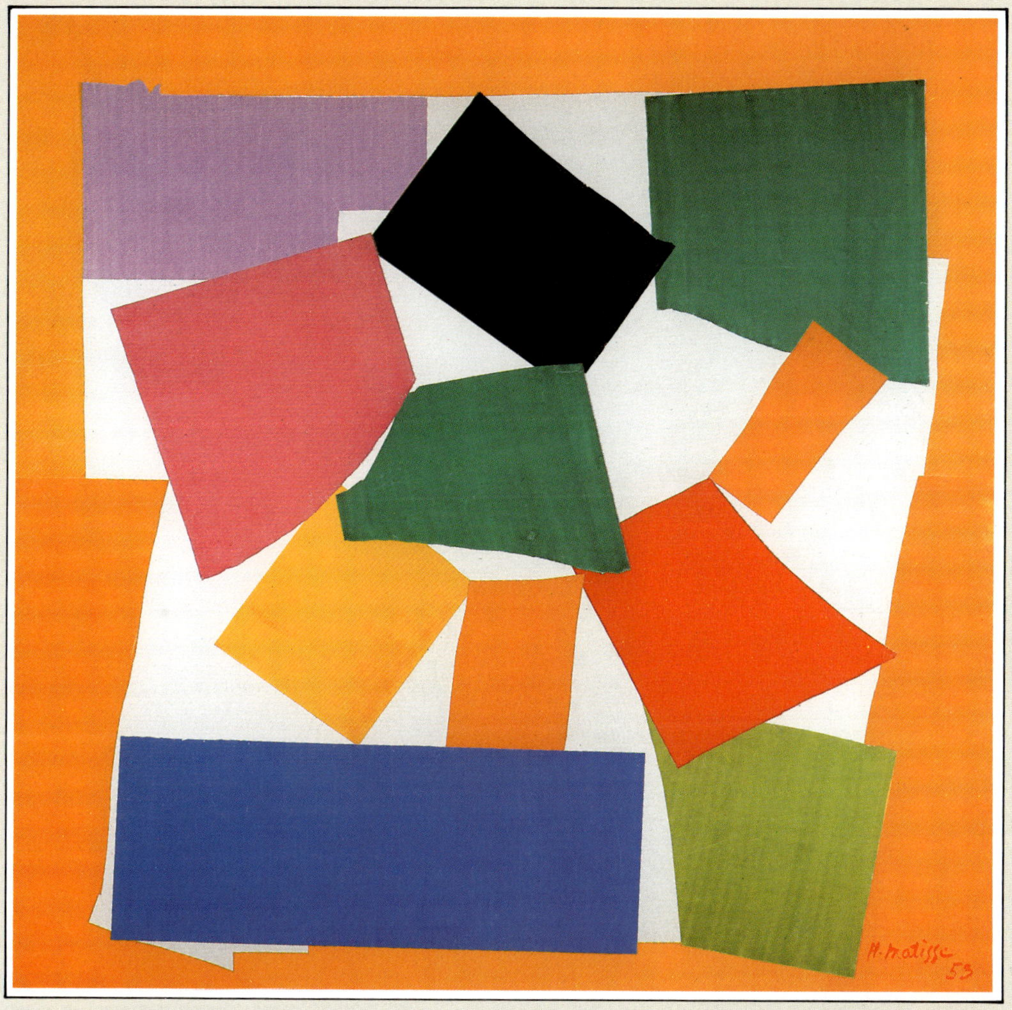

*L'escargot was one of a series of enormous papiers coupés that occupied Matisse at the end of his life. Their conception occurred during a series of earlier mural projects which involved the manipulation and changing of large dancing figures, made easier by cutting them out of paper and tracing round them. A series of screenprints called Jazz also formed the starting point of these gigantic works which look like very large prints. Matisse directed his helpers in the arrangement of the cut and painted papers which were temporarily pinned into position while the composition was considered. The color choice was governed by Matisse's realization that the feelings are affected by simple colors. Here they are arranged with an architectural subtlety and precision that has often eluded his imitators.*

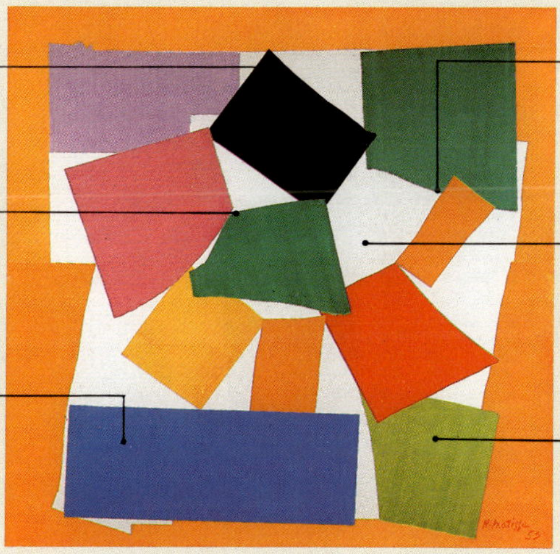

The black was painted on to appear very opaque, so that the white is totally covered

The meeting of the green and the crimson create a curving area which is completed at the left edge of the cobalt blue element

The width of the roll of watercolor paper is used like an architectural module in the length of the blue element

The torn edges of the two pieces of emerald painted paper show they were once unified

Plain, white, unpainted paper over 274cm (9ft) high makes a continuous surface for the painted papers

The brushmarks create a rhythm of their own in several pieces of paper

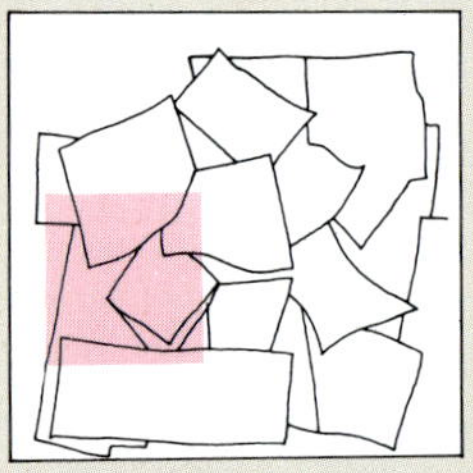

*RIGHT Matisse used scissors, knives, a straight-edge and random tears to provide a variety of profiles on each sheet. An error in the cutting of the cadmium orange border has been retained. The dimensions of the cadmium yellow sheet were sketched in pencil before it was cut.*

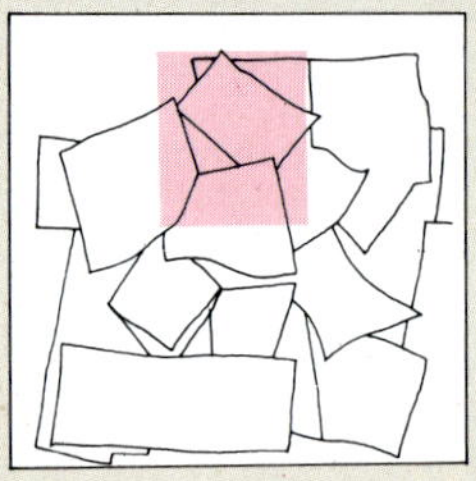

*BELOW The black gouache rectangle marks the summit of the 'snail's' back. It is always used as pure color in Matisse's palette. It is positioned to vibrate against the complementary white and orange and also creates two more echoing white triangles.*

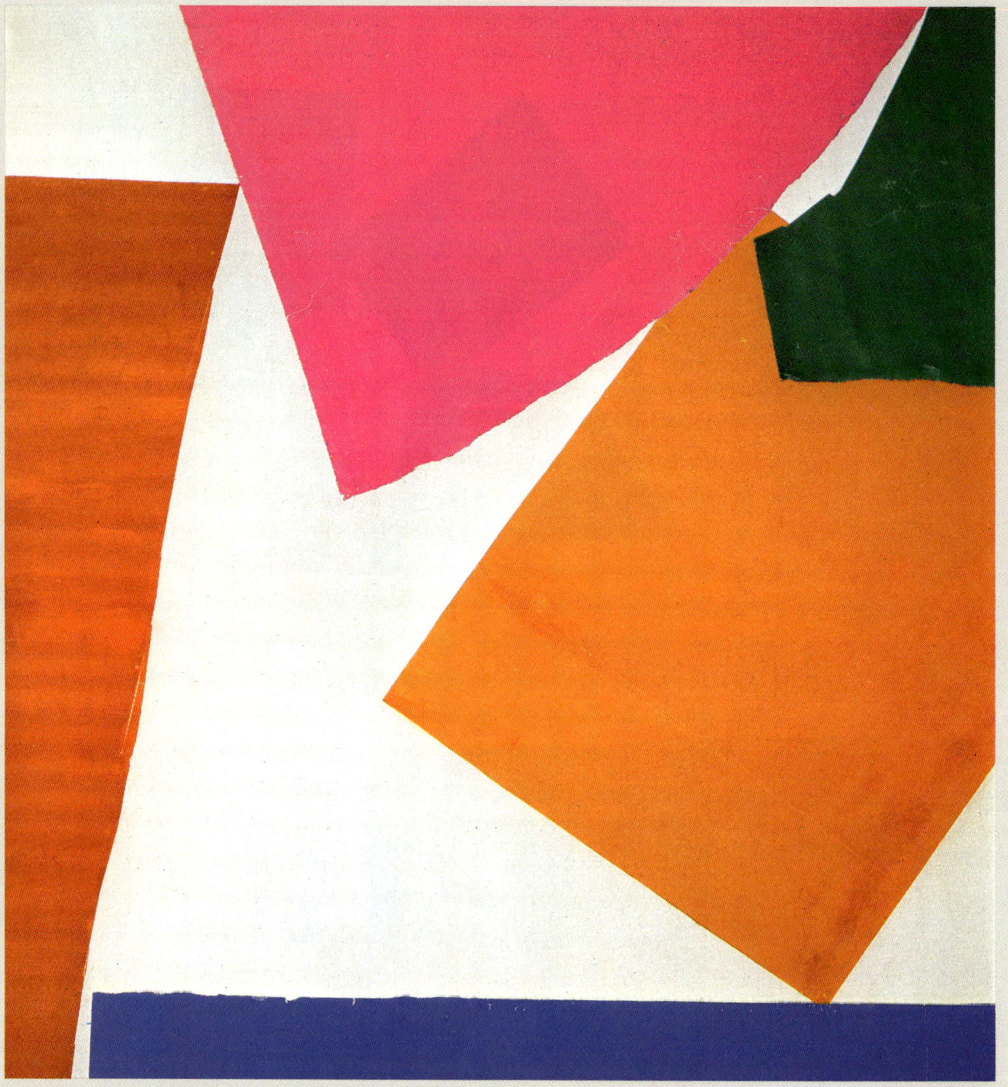

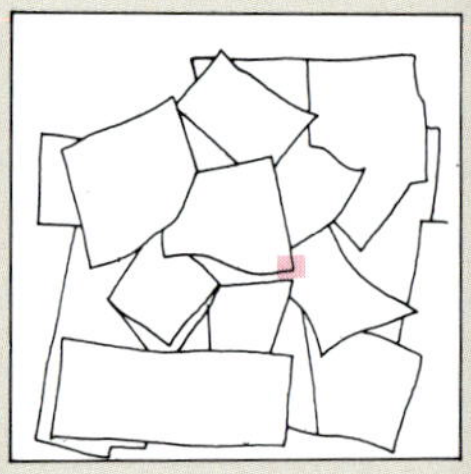

*ACTUAL SIZE DETAIL The struggle involved in the manipulation of the large sheets of paper has left its trace on L'escargot. Matisse's changes of mind are recorded in the large number of pin holes left in the torn corner of an emerald green sheet, as in the corresponding marks in the complementary crimson sheet which it overlaps. Other clues to its making can be found in pencil lines, folds and even thumbprints which were allowed to remain in the finished work.*

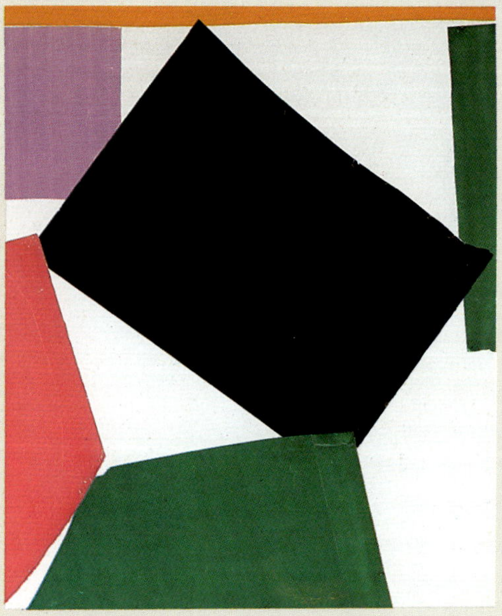

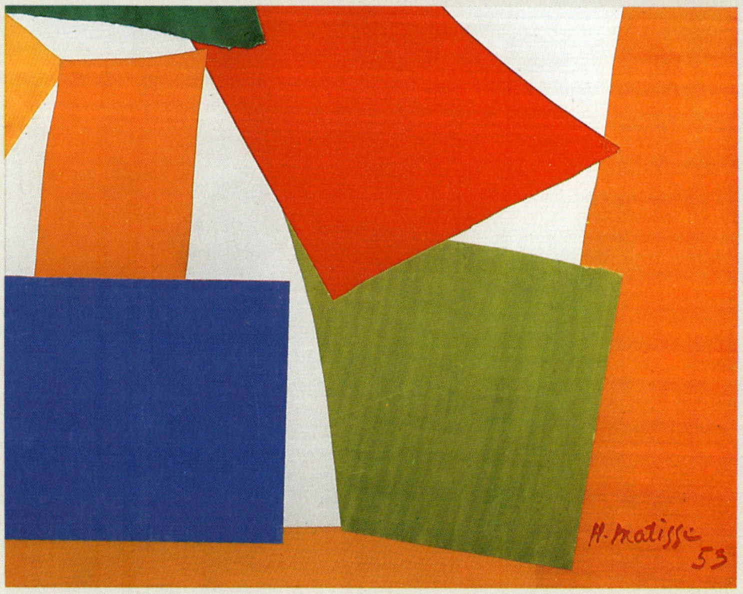


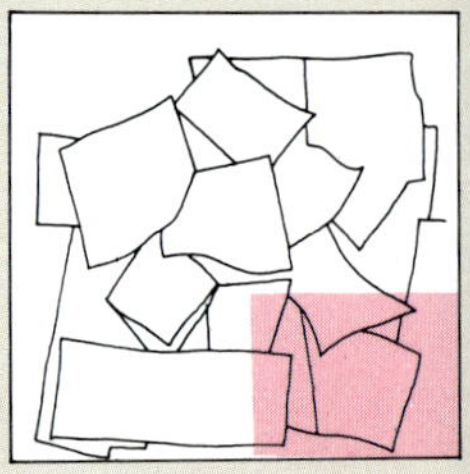

*LEFT At the age of 83 Matisse created this very large composition with extraordinary energy, using assistants to position the papers. His signature is always an important element in his paintings. It creates a quiet point of focus beside the architectural bulk of the complementary colors rotating beside it.*

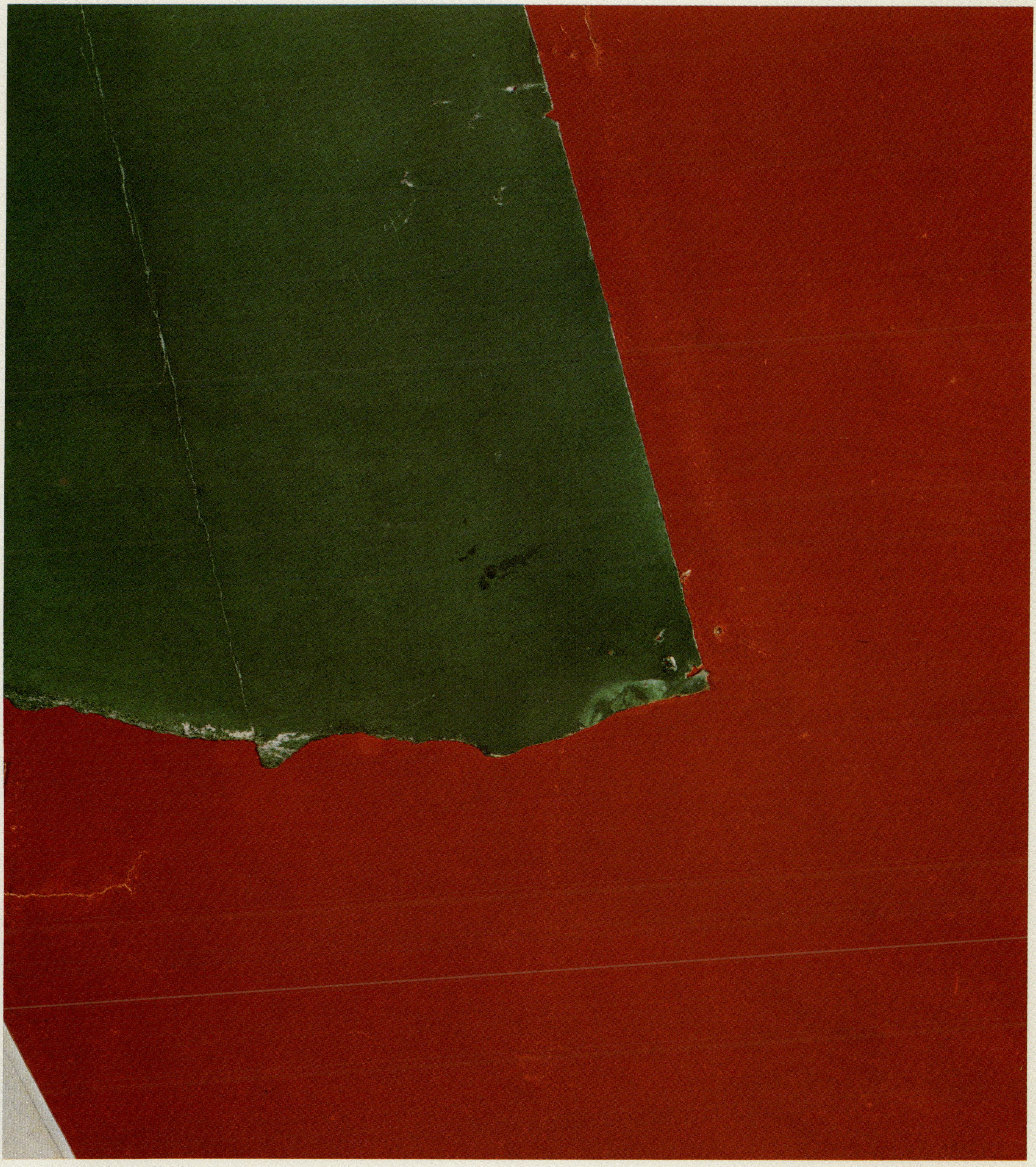

# ALBERTO GIACOMETTI

*Annette assise (1954)*
Oil on canvas
91.5cm × 64.1cm/36in × 25in

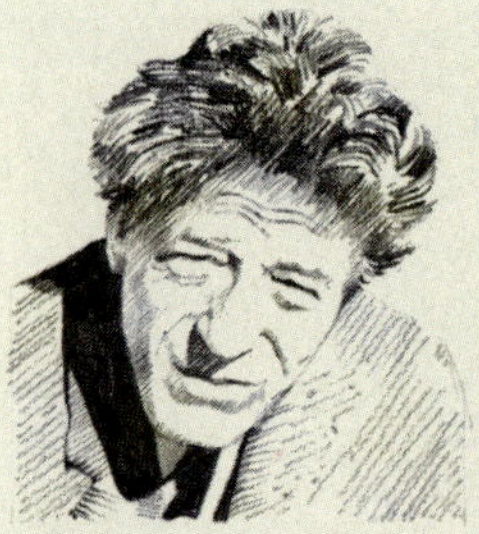

Alberto Giacometti was born in 1901 into an artistic family. His father Giovanni Giacometti was a well-known Swiss painter who worked in the Impressionist style. By the time he was a teenager, Alberto Giacometti was proficient in both painting and sculpture, and he briefly studied sculpture at the School of Arts and Crafts at Geneva. In 1922 he went to Paris, where he was to spend most of his working life, and again studied sculpture for three years, this time under Antoine Bourdelle (1861-1929).

Although he began his artistic career using models or working from the natural world, Giacometti found this approach burdensome, and for about 10 years from 1925, he worked from memory and imagination.

Sculpture was always Giacometti's primary activity, but from about 1946 until the end of his life in 1966, painting came to play a large role in his creative output. He seemed to turn to painting in order to approach the overwhelming problems he had in rendering reality from another angle: in his sculpture, he attempted to reproduce matter which then would act on and also be acted upon by its surrounding space; in his paintings, he had to create a pictorial space in order to find a way for the figure to come into existence.

The subject matter of Giacometti's paintings is nearly always the human figure. The figures either sit or stand, but always adopt a frontal pose, looking out and engaging the attention of the spectator, so that a relationship is formed between the two.

Giacometti's sculpture and paintings do not look like the work of any other artist: they are unique, and they reveal the path of artistic enquiry which he followed. He tried to convert precisely what he saw when he set up a figure in front of him; when a model was a certain distance away from him he attempted to render the model either in clay or in oil paint at the size that they actually appeared to be. Normally the mind involuntarily tells the eye that the figure one sees in the distance is life-size, like oneself, and thus conceptually alters its scale and dimensions. Giacometti tried to, and succeeded in, bypassing this mental trick, but then found that he had difficulties in determining the exact scale of his subject material when he tried to record it: '...the exact limits, the dimensions of this being become indefinable. An arm is as vast as the Milky Way, and this phrase has nothing mystical about it', he noted in despair, and '...the distance between one wing of the nose and the other is like the Sahara, without end, nothing to fix one's gaze upon, everything escapes.'

In his oil paintings, Giacometti eschewed bright hues, and kept to a range of greys and earth colors. This was because he felt that bright, primary colors would block his path, would create shapes and set up relationships outside of those he wished to entrap. He was aware that observers thought that his color range was limited, and that this limitation could be potentially harmful. His reply was that by choosing grey he was not limiting himself, but allowing himself an infinite richness: 'Already as a boy I got to know the colors on my father's palette and in his paintings; he really understood the primary colors. And when I was young I painted with those colors, too. Isn't grey a color, too? When I see everything in grey and in this grey all the colors I experience and thus want to reproduce, then why should I use any other color? I've tried it, because I never intended to paint only with grey and white or with any one single color at all. I have often put just as many colors on my palette as my colleagues when starting in to work; I've tried to paint like them. But as I was working I had to eliminate one color after another, no – one color after the other dropped out, and what remained? Grey! Grey! Grey!' For Giacometti the stuff of life and its representation in pigment was more than adequately served by this one color with all its variations. It would have been an artificial act for him to force himself deliberately to use blue and green, for example, and he set his aim upon truth.

In *Annette Assise* browns and greys are spread all over the canvas, and they seem to both cloud and create the image. A tension arises from the fact that Annette is seen far back in the picture space, set in a corner of the studio and pushed back in this imaginary space by illusory painted borders like overlapping mounts. Yet she emerges as a dense central core of matter, the most thickly painted part of the canvas, which thus projects forward from the picture surface into the real space of the observer. At a certain distance, the painted head takes on an almost tangible reality and the dark eyes have a gaze which is both robust and aloof. Yet a detail showing the head in close-up reveals that the eyes are not defined; the model's left eyebrow arch is marked by three parallel black strokes, and the forehead, nose, cheeks and chin stand out because of the white brushstrokes which traverse them. But the eyes and their sockets are rendered in the same way and in the same pigment as the shoulders and neck. Amazingly, their presence is marked by an actual absence of marks; they are formed by the treatment of the surrounding areas.

The very sketchy quality of the painting, the many attempts at an outline, the quickly brushed opaque background around the model, and the runnyness of the pigment in the border all testify to Giacometti's approach to oil painting. He did not use it for its sensual or decorative qualities: instead he saw it as a vehicle, with sculpture, in which to investigate and record spatial associations.

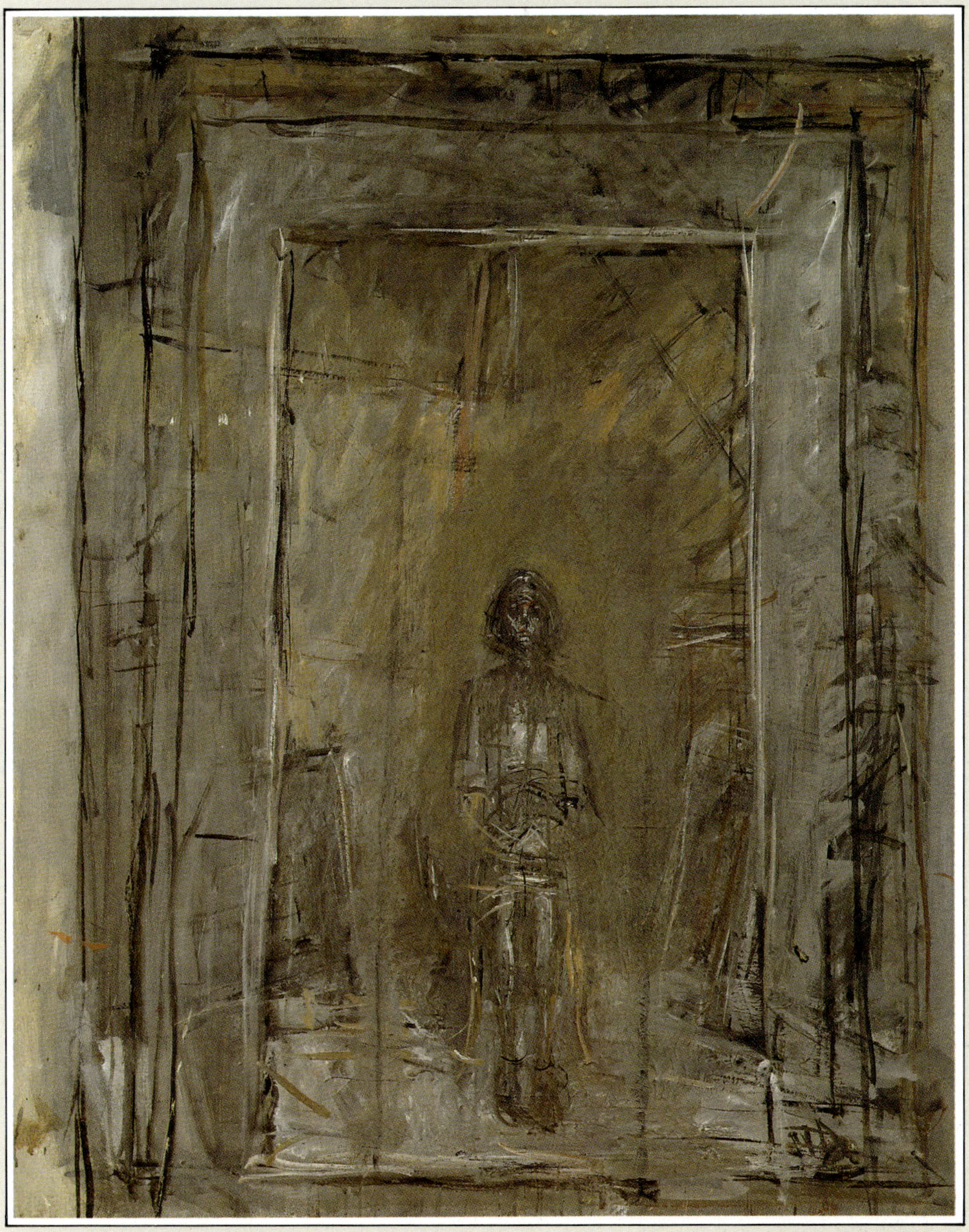

*The brushmarks, the physical evidence of the activity of Giacometti's hand and eye, are left very apparent in this painting. The palette chosen is a low-keyed range of earth colors, and the composition is deliberately kept simple, based on a vertical axis.*

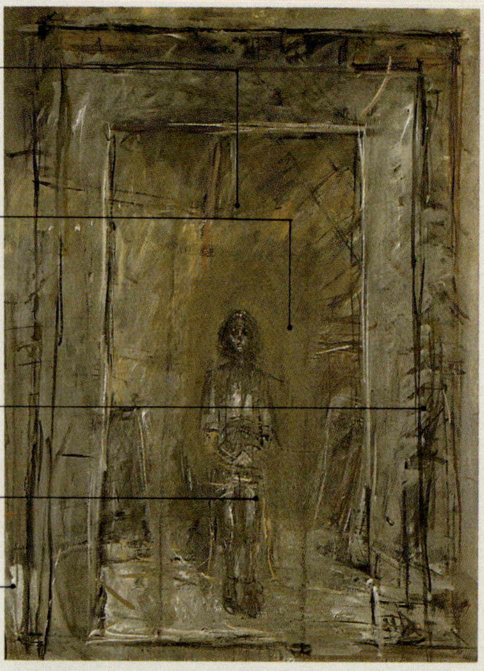


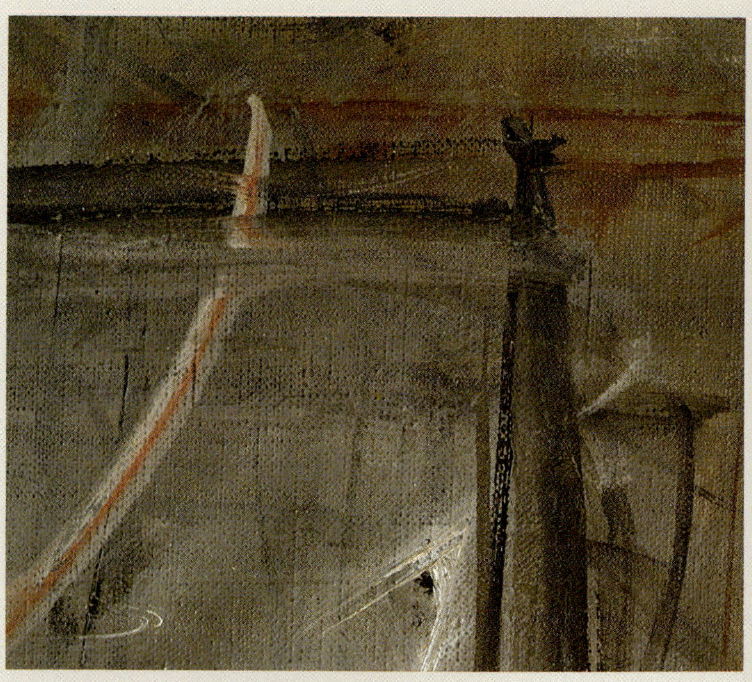

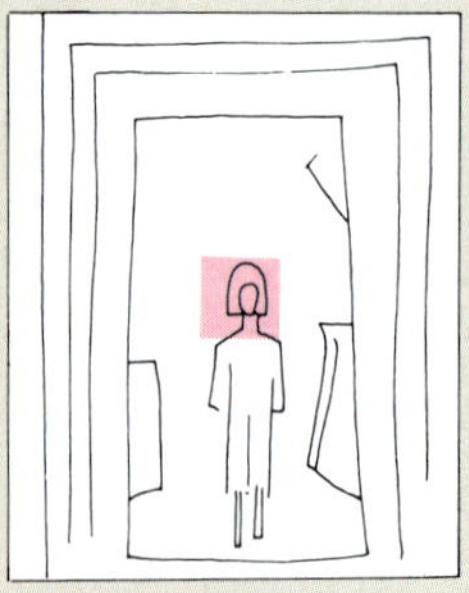

*RIGHT Giacometti found that if he tried to use any color other than grey he set up problems which he could not resolve. Bright colors seemed to stick to the surface of the canvas and prevent the creation of an image set in illusory space. Since he adds three touches of pure red, probably cadmium, which is not used anywhere else in the painting, he must have wished to emphasize the location of the brow and upper lip of the model.*

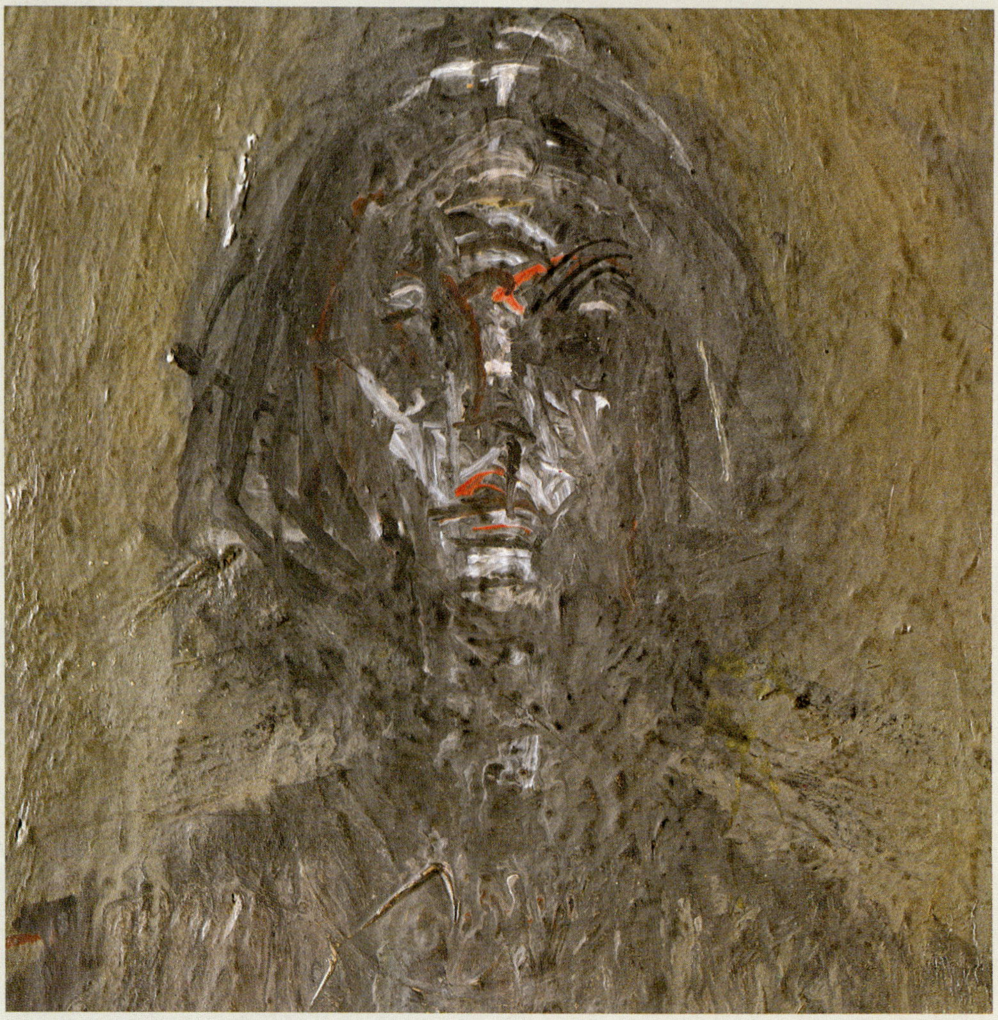

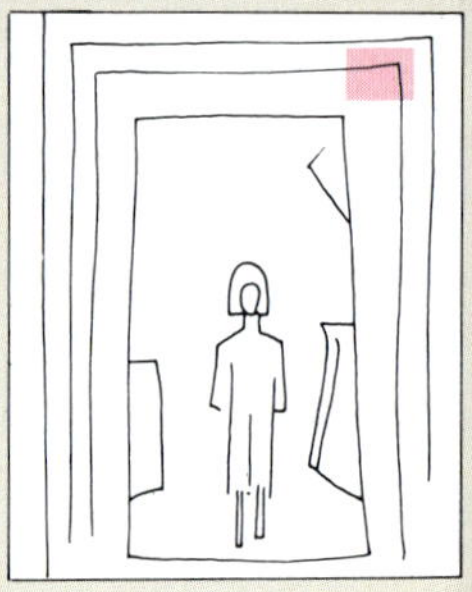

*ABOVE The several successive layers show because of the very diluted nature of the oil paint. Giacometti keeps close to his chosen all-purpose hue — grey — but horizontal lines of raw umber and an aggressive sweep of vermilion add their richness. The strong black right angle marks the corner of one of the three or four concentric borders.*

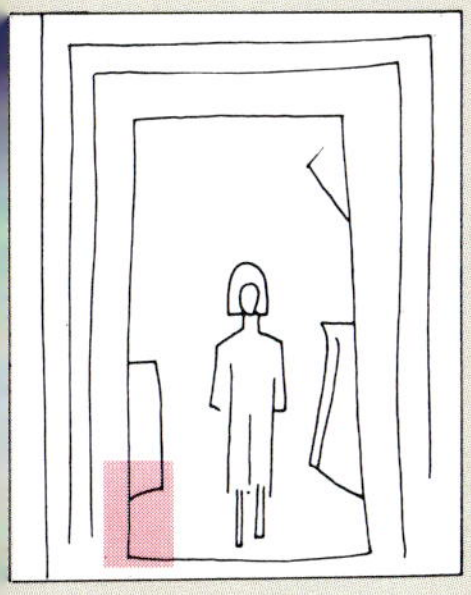

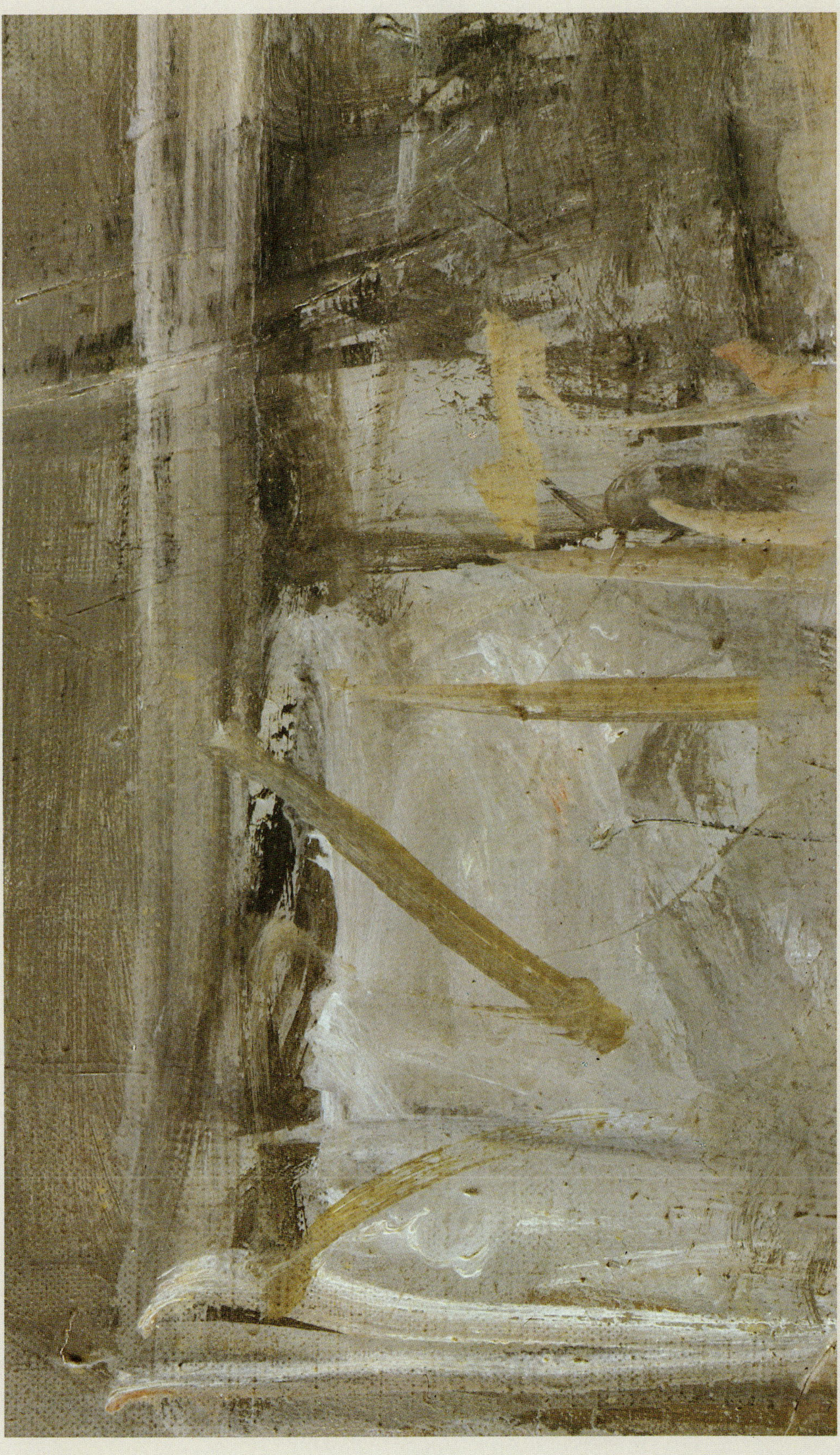

ACTUAL SIZE DETAIL
*This is not descriptive brushwork, and a great deal of it is loosely brushed, applied wet in wet. Some of the horizontal brushmarks carry more than one color, lifting the paint in that state straight from the palette. Giacometti kept his paintings loose since he liked to work over the complete canvas at one and the same time. For him, a final and finished painting was not necessary, what counted was the process of laying in marks and making them relate to the chosen motif. The short ochre dashes are part of the web of marks, which build up relationships throughout the canvas. Different size brushes have been used, the vertical strokes were painted with the widest one.*

# JASPER JOHNS

*Flag* (1955)
Encaustic, oil and collage on canvas, 106cm × 152cm/42¼in × 60⅝in

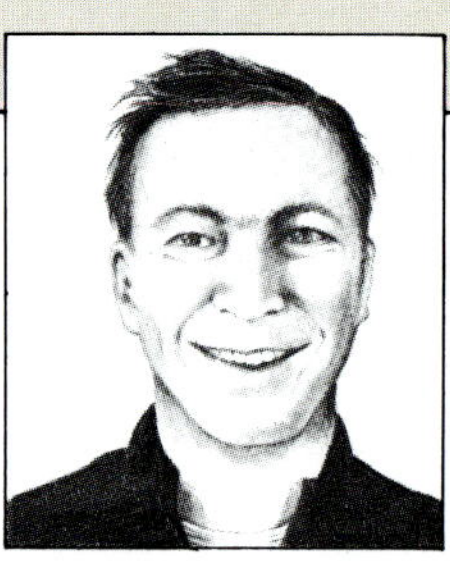

Jasper Johns began work on *Flag* at the end of 1954, but most of the picture was painted in 1955. *Flag* can be seen, in part at least, as Johns' reaction to the paralysis felt by many American artists during the Cold War. Johns started to work on the picture in a year of hysterical patriotism, and the picture can be interpreted either as a celebratory, chauvinistic gesture or an ironic comment. *Flag* is an extremely ambiguous and ambivalent work, as Johns himself asked, 'Is it a flag or a painting?' On the one hand, it has all the required elements of the national emblem of the United States of America – the red and white stripes which signify the 13 original colonies and the white stars on a blue background which denote the various states of the Union. On the other hand, *Flag* also has all the expected features of a work of art. Johns has maintained the flag was 'just a way of beginning, the painting was always about a flag, but it is no more about a flag than it is about a brushstroke, or about a color, or about the physicality of paint'. A third ambiguity – that of Johns' relationships with his contemporaries, the Abstract Expressionists – also remains unresolved.

The apparently simple, two-dimensional structure of *Flag* recalls the formalist approach of the American Abstract Expressionist painter Barnett Newman, and the gestural marks and drips seem to have been derived from the work of such Abstract Expressionists as the American Philip Guston and the Dutch-born American Willem de Kooning. However, Johns' relationship to Abstract Expressionism is still ambiguous. While *Flag* uses some of the approaches of this movement, it also questions the Abstract Expressionist conviction that painting must be either a representation of the artist's state of mind, anxieties and tensions or some kind of transcendental revelation expressed through brushwork and color. However, the most obvious reaction against the former generation was in the introduction of recognizable subject matter. Beginning with *Flag*, Johns started to develop a vocabulary of signs which eventually included not only American flags but targets, stencilled numbers and letters, words, the primary colors and their names, and objects from the home and studio. The art of the 1960s, particularly Pop Art, owes much to Johns.

**1.** The painting was begun in either enamel or oil paint on a bed sheet.

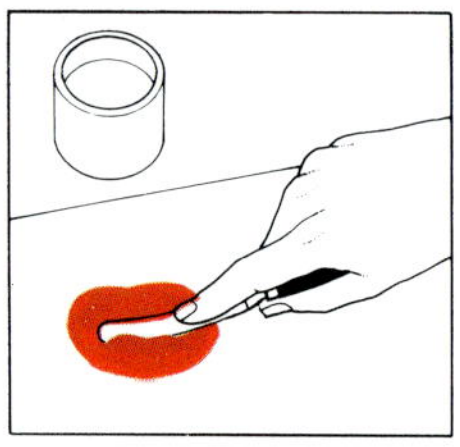

**2.** Johns was unsatisfied with this approach and changed to encaustic painting. The colors were made by mixing pigments with molten beeswax.

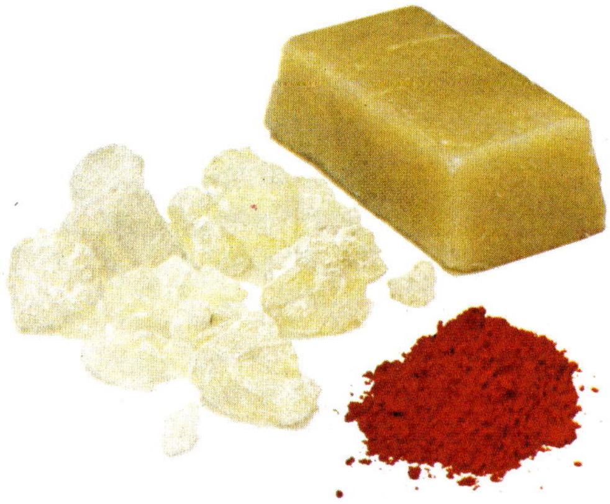

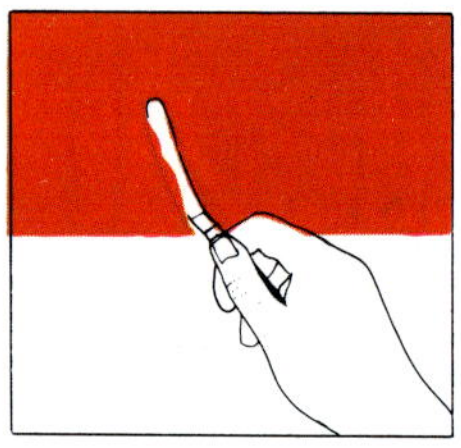

**3.** The colors were kept fluid and applied with either brushes or spatulate instruments.

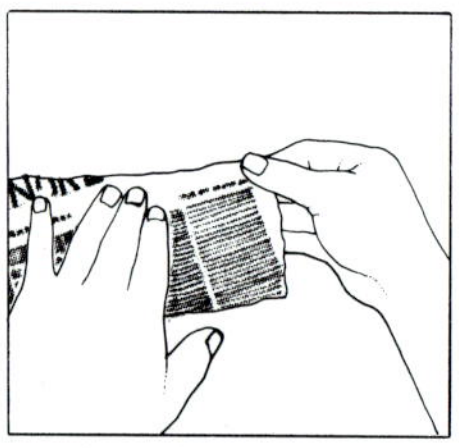

**4.** Johns also used collage, applying cut and torn pieces of newspaper with the hot wax. Paint was also applied using the collage material.

*Encaustic colors are made by mixing pigments with molten wax and, perhaps, a little resin. They are kept fluid and applied with either brushes or a palette knife. When all the colors have been applied, the panel or canvas is set face-up on a table and the colors are fused into an even film using a radiant heat source, such as an electric fire. As the paint cools, the resin helps to harden the paint film which can be given an extra gloss by polishing it with a soft cloth. Johns' technique, however, omits the thermal treatment. Johns chose to use this technique because of its speedy drying properties, so that he could superimpose brushstrokes quickly without those underneath being altered.*

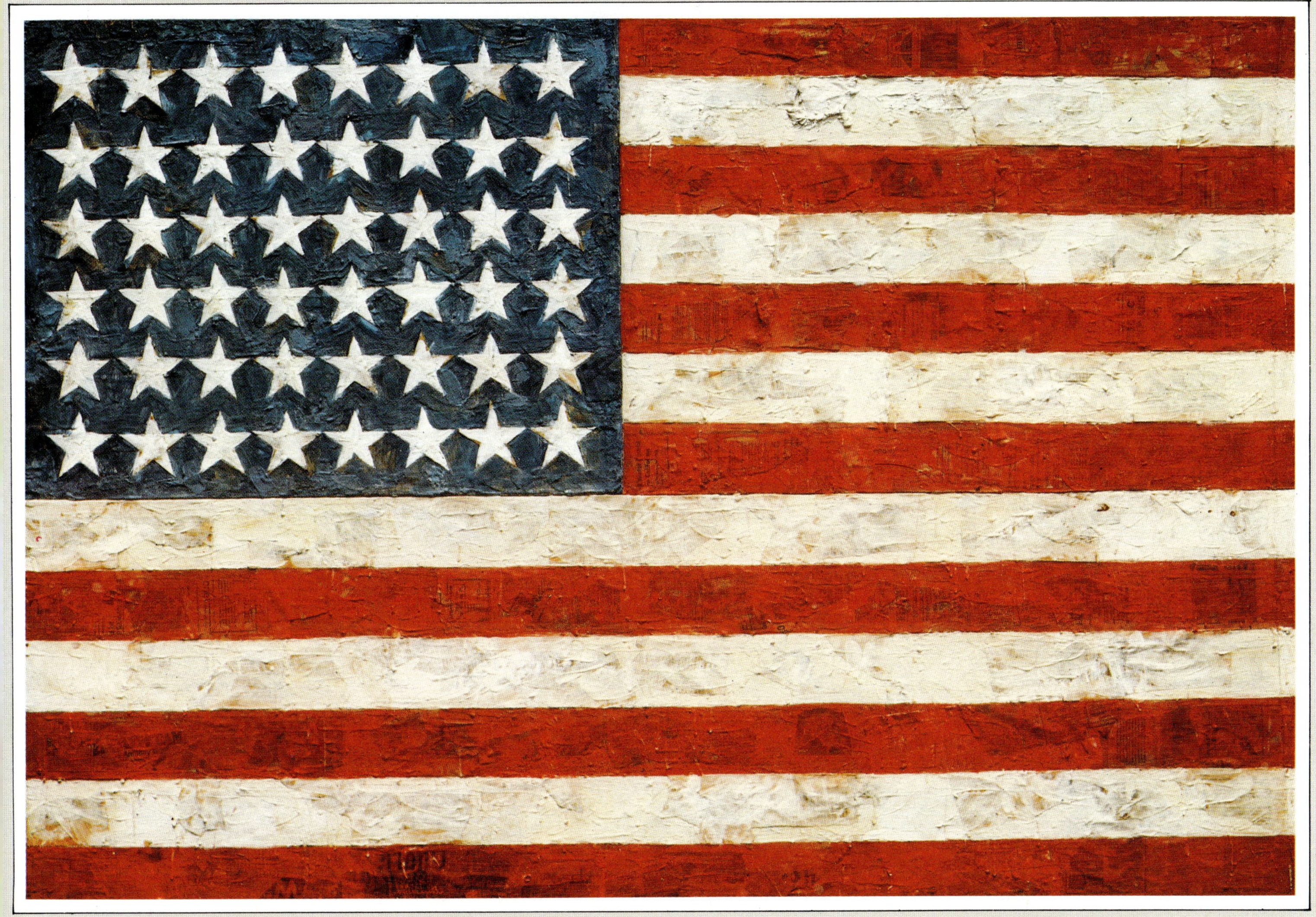

The complicated structure of *Flag* belies the apparent simplicity of the image.

Stars made as positive shapes set on top of blue or set into the blue field, as negative shape

Smaller pieces of collage laid on in different directions

Hem of the sheet

Large pieces of newsprint including a frame from a comic strip

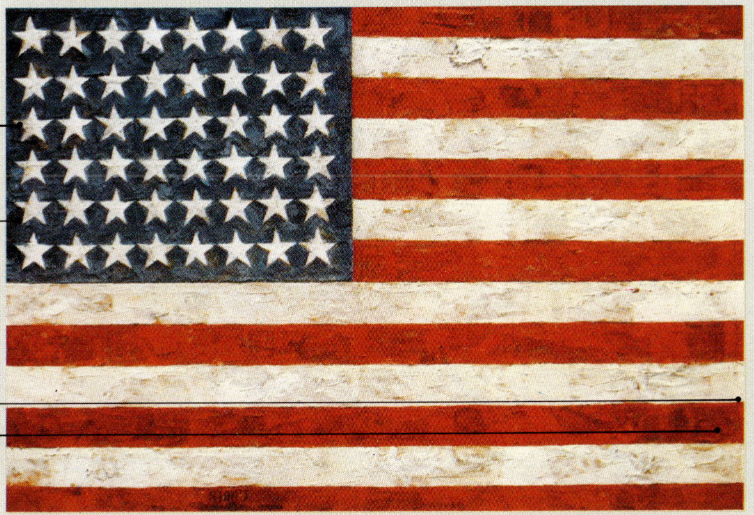

Having begun to paint *Flag* in enamel or oil paint, Johns changed to using an encaustic technique. He explained his reasons for this 'I wanted to show what had gone before in a picture, and what was done after. But if you put on a heavy brush-stroke in paint and then add another stroke, the second stroke smears the first unless the paint, is dry. And paint takes too long to dry. I didn't know what to do. Then someone suggested wax. It worked very well; as soon as the wax was cool I could put on another stroke and it would not alter the first.' Johns outlined the processes he used in painting *Flag*. These involved 'dipping pieces of paper and cloth into hot encaustic and fixing them to the surface before the encaustic solidified. In this way, some areas may or may not include the use of the brush. The two ways of applying paint – with a brush or with material dipped into the hot medium – have equal value and follow no particular sequence.'

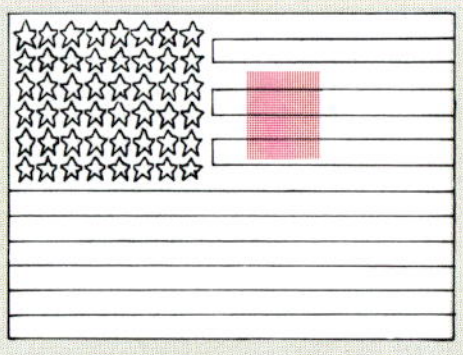

**Flag** *has been built up in a relatively uniform web of brushstrokes and encaustic, cut and torn collage elements which are laid over one another. In this way, Johns achieved an all-over textured surface. Drips and dribbles of encaustic run across edges of the stripes and link different parts of the design. The encaustic collage, which forms the red and white stripes, is less intricate than that used for the stars. The collage fragments are also longer, and set horizontally and vertically so that the lines of collaged text parallel and oppose the bands.*

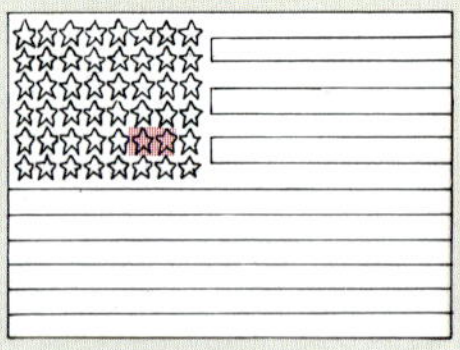

*Each star in* **Flag** *is unique. They are either cut out of a single piece of newsprint and brushed with white or they form negative shapes using the small pieces of newspaper which make up the blue field.*

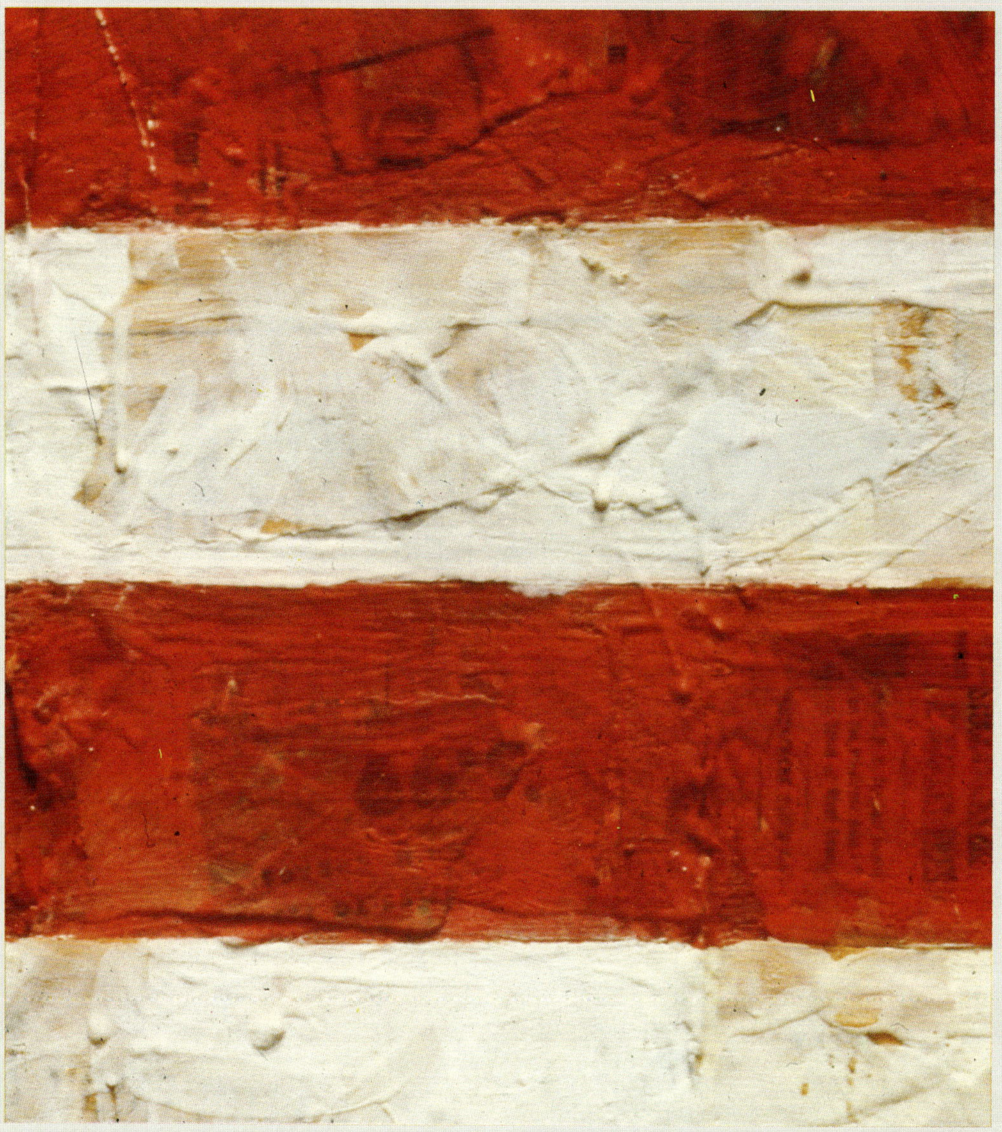

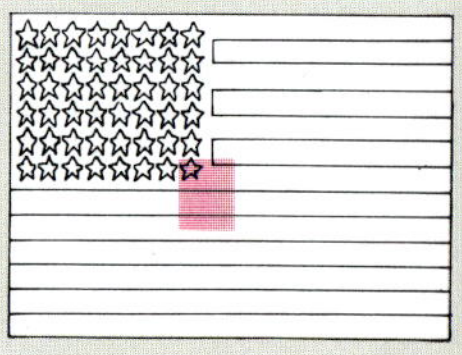

**Actual size detail**
**Flag** *is made of three separate canvases — one is used for the rectangle of stars, the second for the stripes immediately to the right of the stars and the third for the lower area of stripes. The transparency of the encaustic means that, in certain places, some of the collage material can be seen. One of the most obvious pieces of newsprint comes from a comic strip bearing the date February 15th 1956, which is at variance with the 1955 date Johns gave the painting. Evidently,* **Flag** *was damaged in Johns' studio in 1956 and was repaired by him with some contemporary pieces of newspaper.*

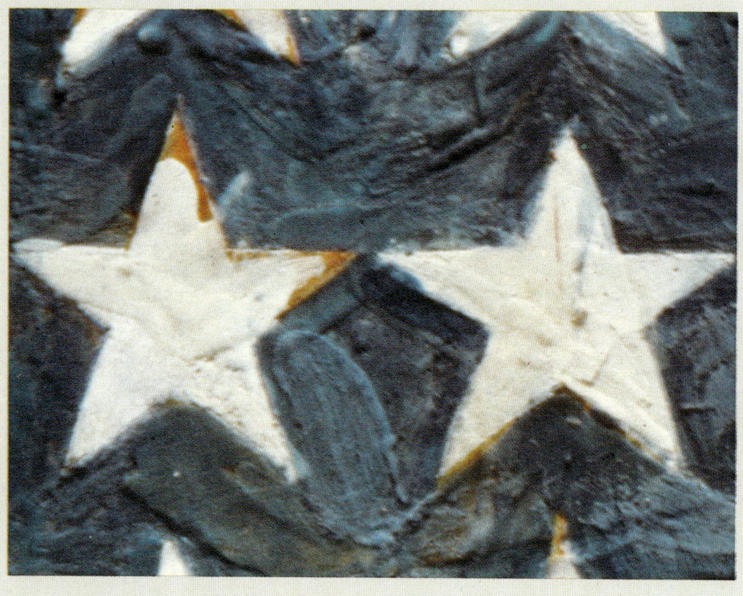

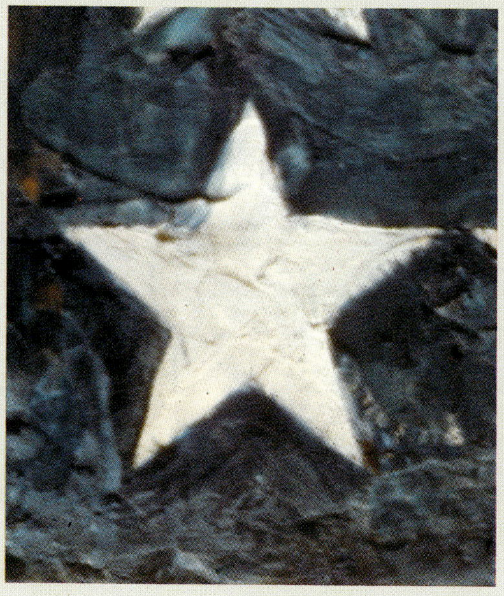

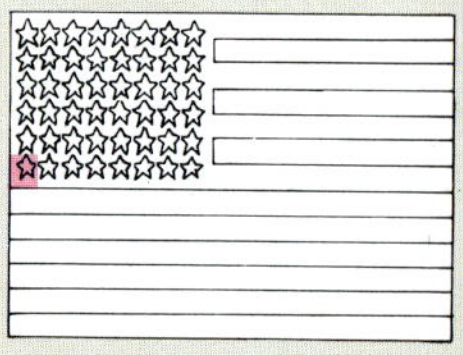

*These stars are made so that they are set into rather than on top of the blue field. The collage fragments are smaller and denser than those in the bands. They are also multi-directional and more varied in their coloration and tone.*

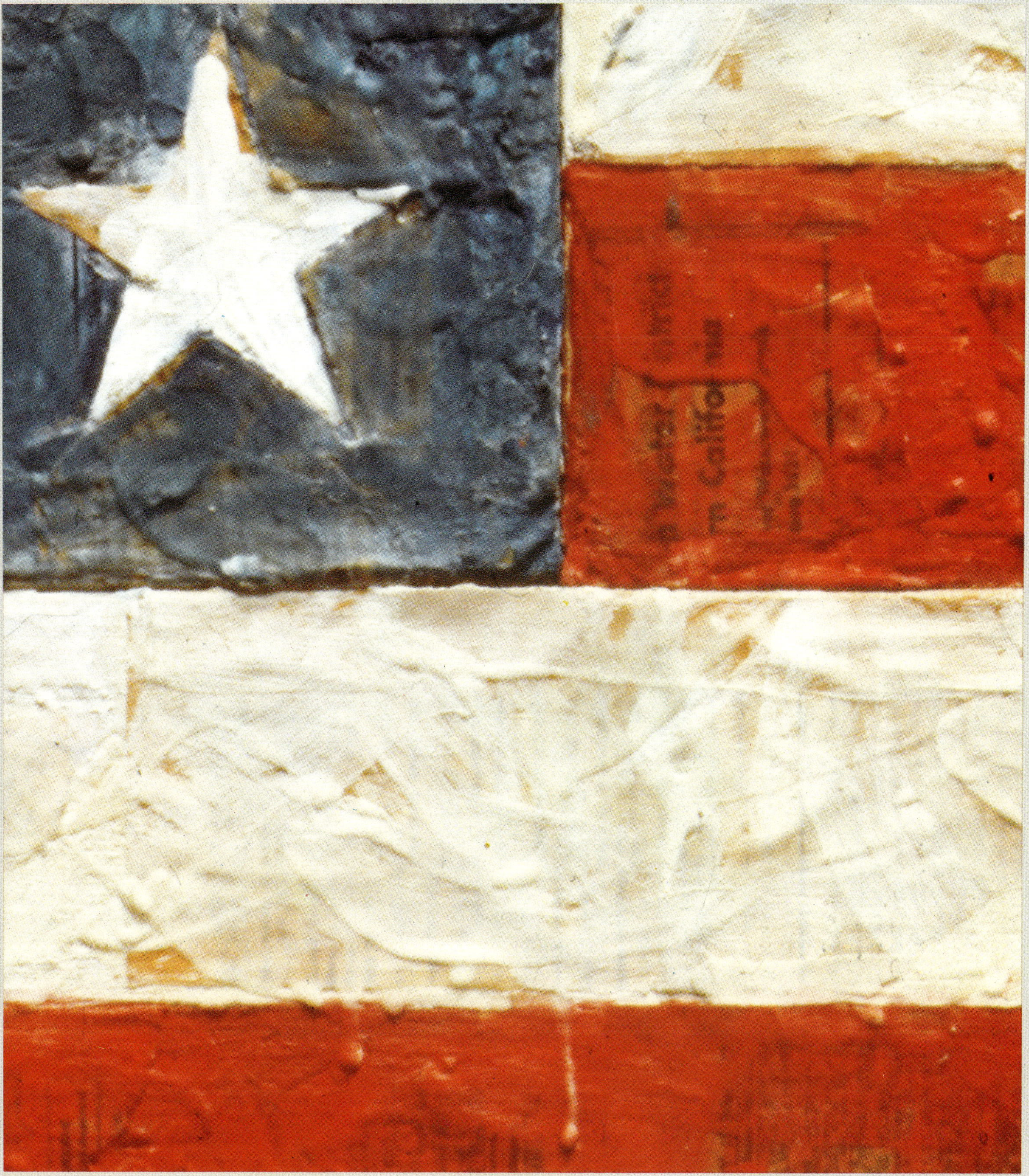

# JASPER JOHNS

*Target with Four Faces (1955)*
Encaustic and collage on canvas with plaster casts
75.5cm × 71cm × 9.7cm/29¾in × 26in × 3¾in

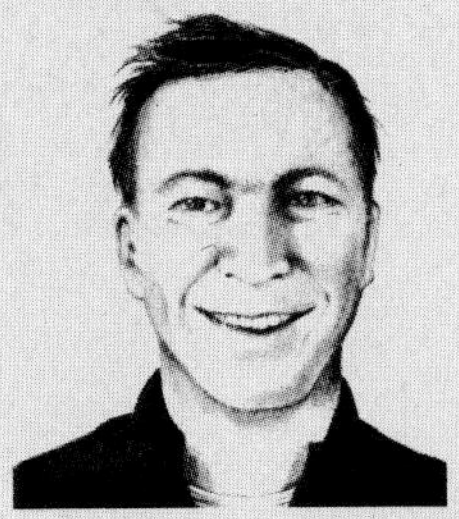

Jasper Johns's work, like that of Robert Rauschenberg (b 1925), played a crucial part in a watershed period of American painting, giving it a new, more objective approach than the then current Abstract Expressionist orthodoxy, which had reached its highpoint with Jackson Pollock's work.

Born on 15 May 1930, in Augusta, Georgia, Johns was brought up in Allendale, South Carolina, by a variety of relatives. His first limited training in art occurred while he was at the University of South Carolina. He settled in New York in 1952 when he began to paint seriously, and devoted himself full-time to art in 1958.

It was in New York that he formed life-long friendships that helped to foster both the appearance and the dominant concerns of his art. Chief among these was that with Robert Rauschenberg, through whom he met the composer John Cage and the dancer and choreographer Merce Cunningham. They introduced Johns to the idea of an opaque, impersonalized art, and, more particularly, through Rauschenberg's work, to a form of painting that used the bravura brushstrokes of the Abstract Expressionists, but drained them of dramatized self-exploration and emotional rhetoric. Rauschenberg was using common objects to enliven his work: 'junk art', was a technique that absorbed Johns increasingly.

Johns's work rapidly acquired its characteristic deadpan nature which overlaid a basic but sustaining creative tension between sardonic insolence and a more powerful seriousness. This arose from the issues suggested by his deceptively throwaway attitude: he was reported as suggesting that a painting of his should be accepted as an object, 'the same way you look at a radiator', leaving in the air both the distinction between a work of art and an everyday object, and the role of the observer in approaching a decision on the problem.

Johns began his career working in the encaustic medium but by 1959 was increasingly using oils, a step which corresponded to a more sustained use of pure color. Previously, his consistent interest (in a busy, well-worked surface texture) had been in paintings of predominantly pure tonality, and it is significant that *False Start* (1959), his first canvas in bright colors, was matched by the accompanying *Jubilee* (1959), virtually a *grisaille* commentary on the former. Apparently abandoning textural development, he turned to lithography in 1960; a rare, almost anachronistic medium at the time, but one that, in fact, maintained the concern for surfaces, that of the 'skin' of the lithographic stone. He also turned to sculpture: his first sculptures of 1958 were executed in sculp-metal, an easily modeled medium intended for the amateur, which he subsequently replaced with *pâpier-maché*.

Johns's primary importance has been in providing an alternative to the sterility of decaying Abstract Expressionism. Yet in many ways his work is too personal to supply a simple and sustained stylistic impetus to a new generation. However, his free use of materials and conventional consumer imagery, lettering and everyday objects, proved to be a significant ingredient in the iconography of Pop Art.

As Johns's career progressed, his additions to the flat picture plane became more complex. Objects and even furniture fragments were attached to the work and early letters and figures had become separate fixtures sometimes hinged on to the background setting. However, after an extended visit to Hawaii and Japan in 1964, Johns's work relaxed. He used many of his previous images, but in a much freer, more spontaneous way, and added more homely features, such as coffee cups and coat-hangers.

*Target with Four Faces* is from 1955, a highly productive year, and, as an earlier work, lacks the more sweeping brushwork and dramatically amplified addition of objects that Johns was to develop later. The subject of the target, an example of a favorite visual cliché, he has said, 'seemed to me to occupy a certain kind of relationship to seeing the way we see and to things in the world which we see... have clearly defined areas which could be measured and transferred to canvas.'

The use of encaustic here emphasizes the flatness and banality of the familiar subject while also, on closer examination, revealing (literally) hidden depths, visible layers which help to individualize this particular version. The encaustic technique involves mixing pigment with molten beeswax or resin; at which stage Johns added fragments of newspaper and fabric, applying the mixture and then drying it under a radiant heat, thus fusing the elements together. The immediate advantage was that of speed; the solution dried quickly and another layer could be added. There is, too, a degree of translucency which enables the viewer to see directly the various stages of work and the additional interest of collage elements embedded within the medium. As a glutinous medium encaustic is best applied with the palette knife and this gave Johns the opportunity to produce the heavy impastos which he so enjoys.

The use of plaster casts is an example of another favorite medium of the time: here they are taken from the same model, though carefully rearranged to avoid the impression of a sequence that had been inadvertently produced by the steady relaxation of the model's jaw throughout the casting, thus avoiding the impression of a mouth opening to speak. The wooden structure in which the casts are contained, despite its slightly sinister regimentation, provides another sort of the compartmentalization that Johns frequently employs.

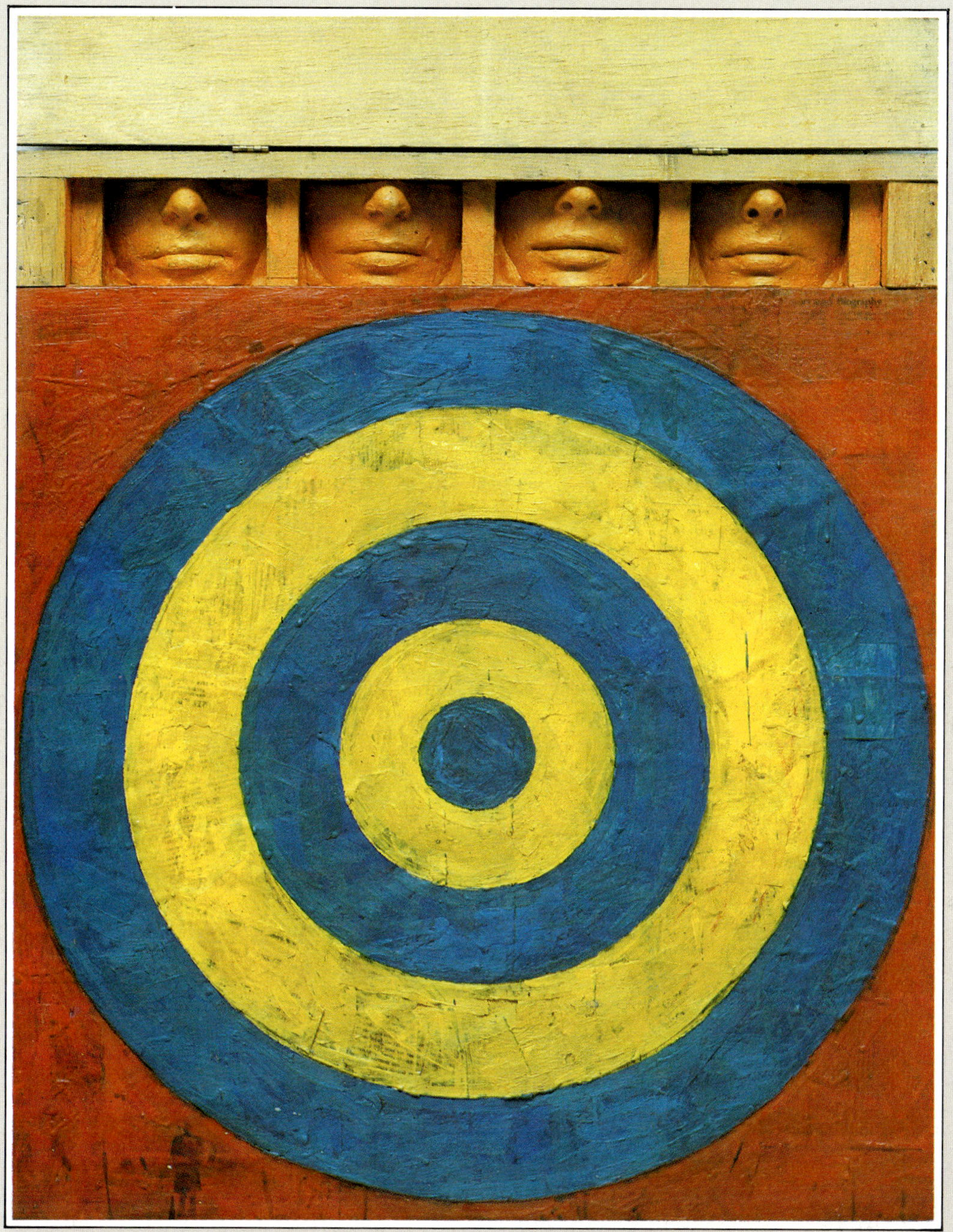

*While there are iconographic and formal precedents especially within early American modernism, for Johns's series of targets, first shown in 1958, the artist has denied any direct influence. This originality is seconded by the incorporation into the work here of colored plaster casts of faces, calculated material additions which dispel 'some of their identity as mere paintings'.* Target with Four Faces *(1955) was bought by A.H. Barr for the Museum of Modern Art in New York, a swift recognition of the reaction against Abstract Expressionism.*

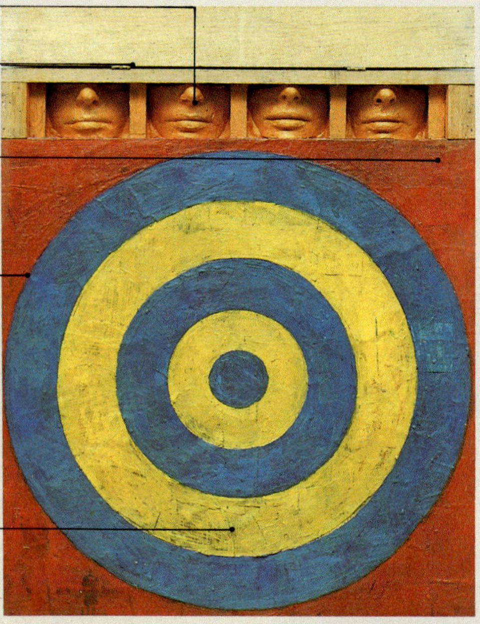


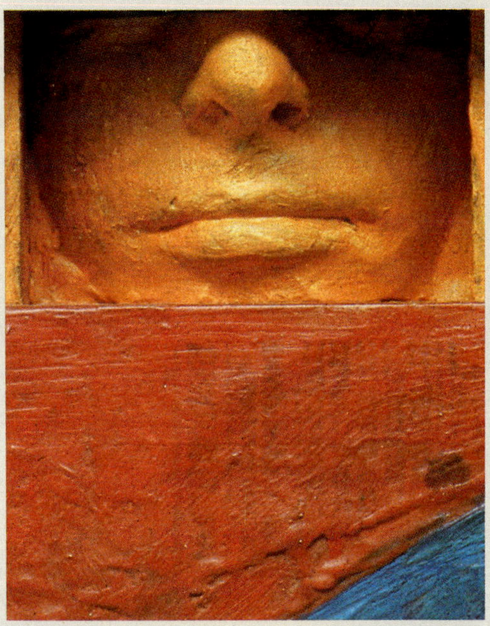

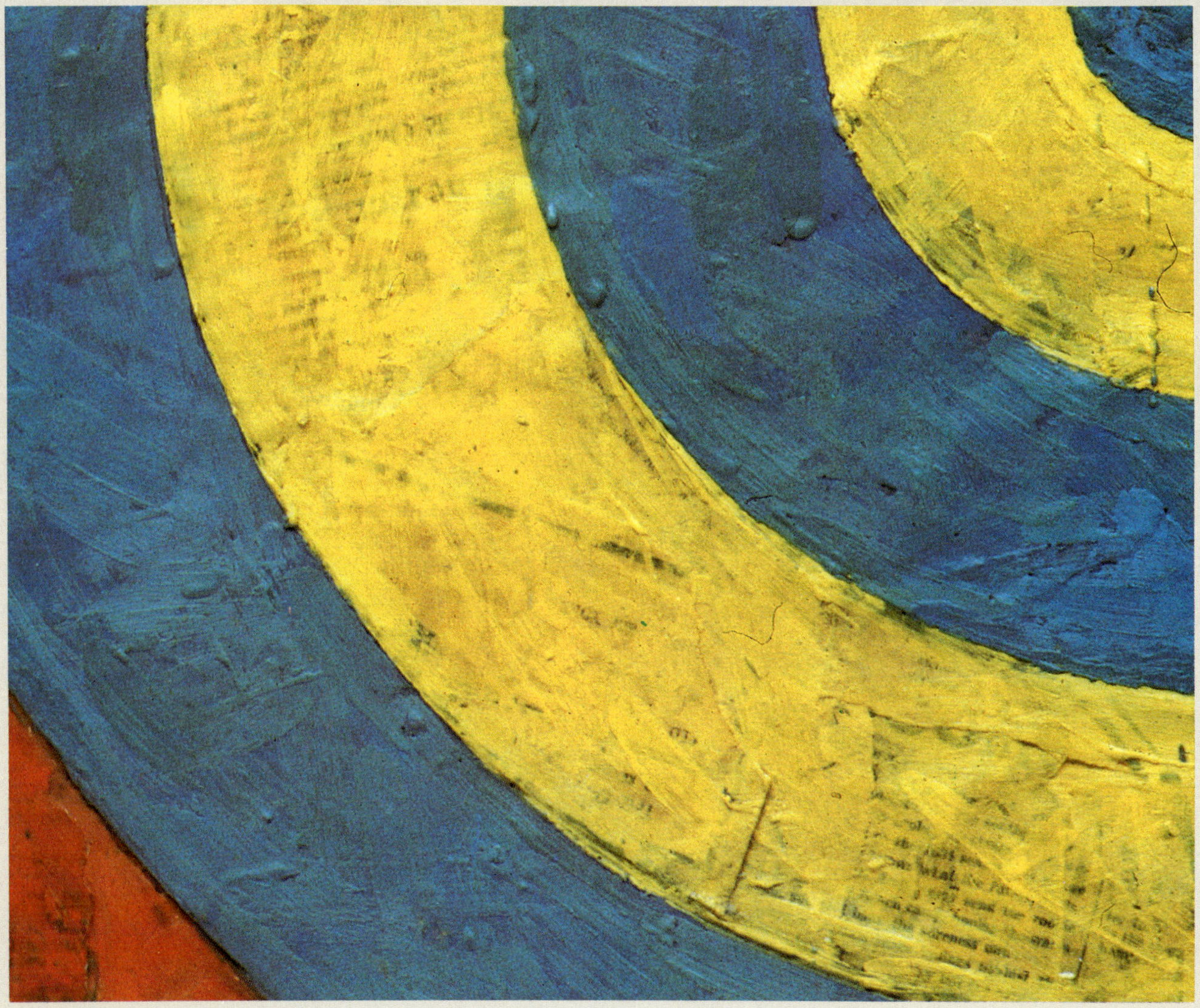

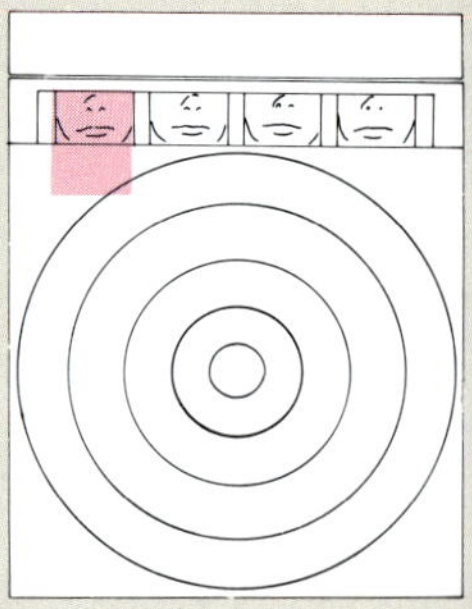

LEFT *The plaster casts have all been taken from the same model but slight physiognomic variations have been encouraged, both to prevent mechanical repetition and to add a typical hint of discontinuity and menace. This is augmented by the surreal appearance of the casts as if balanced on their flared nostrils. The texture of the casts is not unlike parts of the painted target, but contrasts sharply with the finished surface of the wooden compartment.*

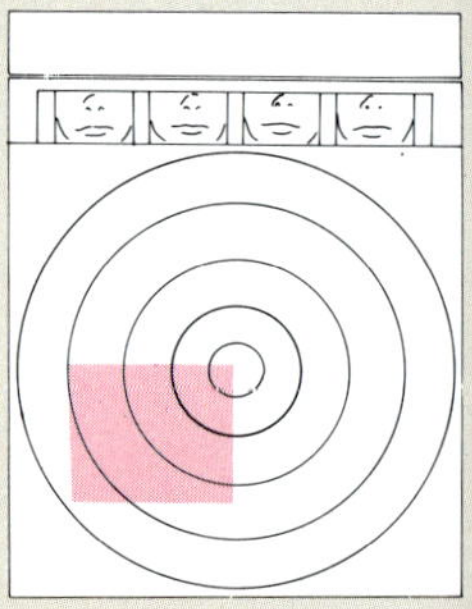

LEFT *The texture of* Target with Four Faces *is more densely worked than either* Target with Plaster Casts *or* Flag*, both of the same year. A further layer of collage and encaustic appears to have been added and worked in with a palette knife, producing scratches and inflections loosely aligned with the concentric circles of the target, but occasionally making straight lines. A patch of collaged material is clearly visible in the center of this excerpt, standing slightly proud of the surface.*

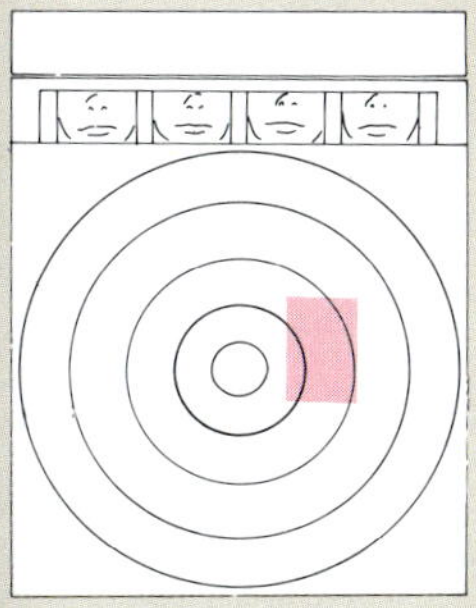

ACTUAL SIZE DETAIL
*Printed material is clearly visible through the transparent encaustic, but unlike similar additions in Cubist collage Johns has exposed the nature of his technique by providing a kind of 'horizon' by cross-section down into the upper layers of the surface. Paint is revealed as a skin over a more solid structure, and the whole surface is more like a miniature mountainscape than a flat canvas. Above the print is a crinkle or 'flaw' in the texture, probably the torn edge of a slightly corrugated collaged element.*

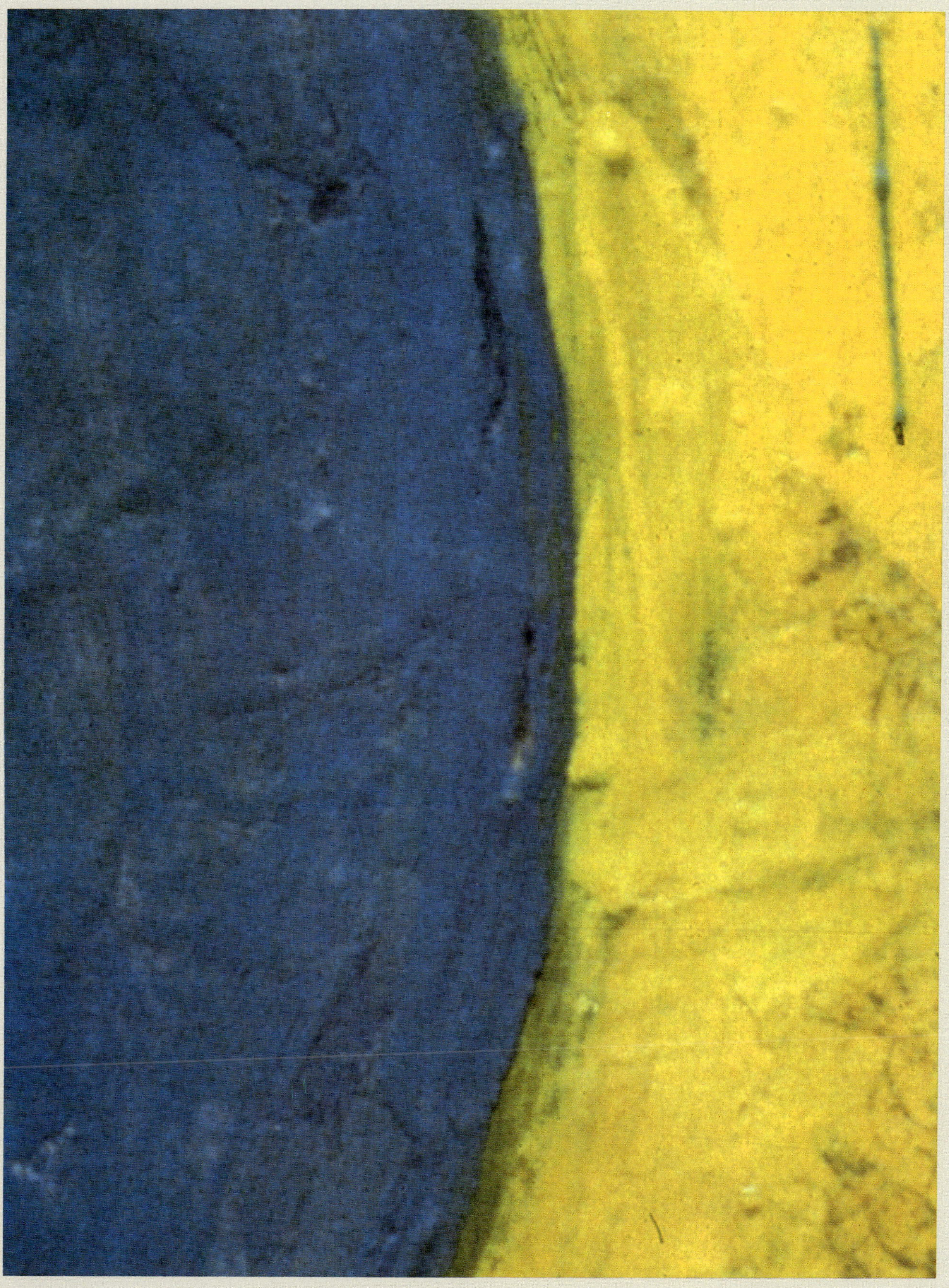

# PETER BLAKE

*On the Balcony (1955-1957)*
Oil on canvas
123cm × 90.8cm/47¾in × 35¾in

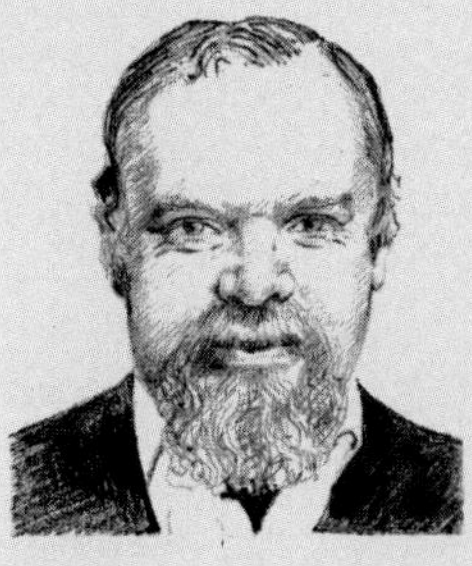

Although closely associated with Pop Art, Peter Blake is concerned with neither consumer goods nor technology. He sees the role of his art as not 'to make social comment in a critical way. It's purely to record.' Blake's art is rooted firmly in nostalgia: his subjects come from his own childhood and youth. But he is also conscious of both past and contemporary art and makes constant references to it.

With his discriminating sense of fantasy, Blake has annexed or incorporated the image of popular culture into the realms of modern British art. Bric-à-brac, Victoriana, photographs of film stars, plastic give-aways and children's comic strips – trivial in themselves – gain status and significance when gathered together by Blake. The identities of these objects and images are preserved but they are often modified by his way of painting which includes a formidable talent for sharp focus or *trompe l'oeil.*

Peter Blake was born in 1932 in Dartford, Kent. He studied graphic art, then fine arts at the Gravesend Technical and School of Art from 1945 to 1951, and attended the Royal College of Art in London from 1953 to 1956. As a painter, Blake could be classified as a pre-Cézannite, and as a practitioner of collage and assemblage, the heir, not of Cubist collage, but of the Victorian scrapbook. He has been influenced by the popular Victorian realists, including the Pre-Raphaelites, and by American Symbolic Realists, such as Ben Shahn (1898-1969) and Honoré Sharrer (b 1920). In fact Sharrer's painting *Workers and their Pictures,* in which contemporary workers hold famous paintings that they could never possess was the starting point for *On the Balcony.*

In Blake's painting there are no less than 27 different references to the balcony subject, which was set for the Royal College of Art's diploma in 1955, and many of these are references to art. The most obvious is the reproduction of Manet's *The Balcony* (1869) held by the figure on the left sitting on the park bench. The trio of paintings in the center bottom half of *On the Balcony* are Blake's idea of what three of his fellow students would have done with the same subject: behind the Royal Family is a 'Richard Smith', immediately below it is a small thin Robyn Denny, and at the bottom is a framed Leon Kossoff abstract.

At first glance parts of *On the Balcony* – the magazine covers and postcards, for example – appear to be collaged, a technique frequently employed by Blake. But every detail is painted: '. . . when I'm expected to paint it, I collage it, and when you might think I might collage it, I paint it – it's a kind of aesthetic game,' Blake commented. 'A picture like *On the Balcony* was purely a photo-realist, magic-realist picture where one was trying a *trompe l'oeil* technique – it wasn't about whether it should be collaged or not – it was just painting a picture and those questions came up afterwards.'

In the painting Blake is playing on the differences between reality and illusion. Side by side with his use of 'painted collage', items such as the cornflake packet and the two tables are painted in the traditional illusionistic way. This ambiguity is further underlined by the green background which could as easily be a noticeboard as a patch of lawn.

Interestingly, while he was working on *On the Balcony*, Blake was also studying West European folk art, and this could have been an important influence in the composition of the work and in his execution of the figures.

There are five figures in *On the Balcony*. One stands on the painter's table at the top left, and is cut off from the waist by the edge of the canvas. The four young figures sitting on the park bench wear the paraphernalia of the post-war, American-influenced youth – the 'I Love Elvis' and cinema club badges, fancy ties, sunglasses and jeans. The most interesting figure is that on the right, which looks like a self-portrait: the figure wears a portrait of John Minton, an artist who taught Blake at the Royal College and who committed suicide, and the painting he is holding is a work by Blake's brother.

A constant theme of Blake's work – which is evident in much of the British Pop Art – is his patriotism. Two of the figures on the bench are wearing Union Jacks and the Royal Family are represented no less than three times.

Blake paints slowly, gradually gathering images to incorporate into his work. He spent two years working on *On the Balcony*. Each of the objects he has included in it is in scale, but there are vast inconsistencies in the scale relationships to other objects in the work, rather like there would be in a magazine or book from which mechanically produced images might have been cut.

The canvas is attached to a pine stretcher with iron tacks, and it was prepared for Blake (not by him) with white oil ground through which the texture of the canvas is visible. Blake's medium is oil and gum and he has employed a variety of techniques to produce the mimetic effects of collage. The Leon Kossoff, for example, is painted in a 3-mm (⅛-in) thick impasto, while Manet's *Balcony* is executed in a lively Impressionistic manner, in contrast to the detailed photo-realistic *Life* covers.

The canvas has been left unvarnished and the artist has written in pencil on the reverse of the canvas's foldover edge: 'Blake RCA On the Balcony Unfinished'. It is common for Blake to regard a work as uncompleted. 'One of the reasons he may leave a picture unfinished or hesitate to complete it', noted art historian Michael Compton, 'is, simply, that he enjoys the visible brush strokes that will disappear or become almost completely integrated in the finished work.'

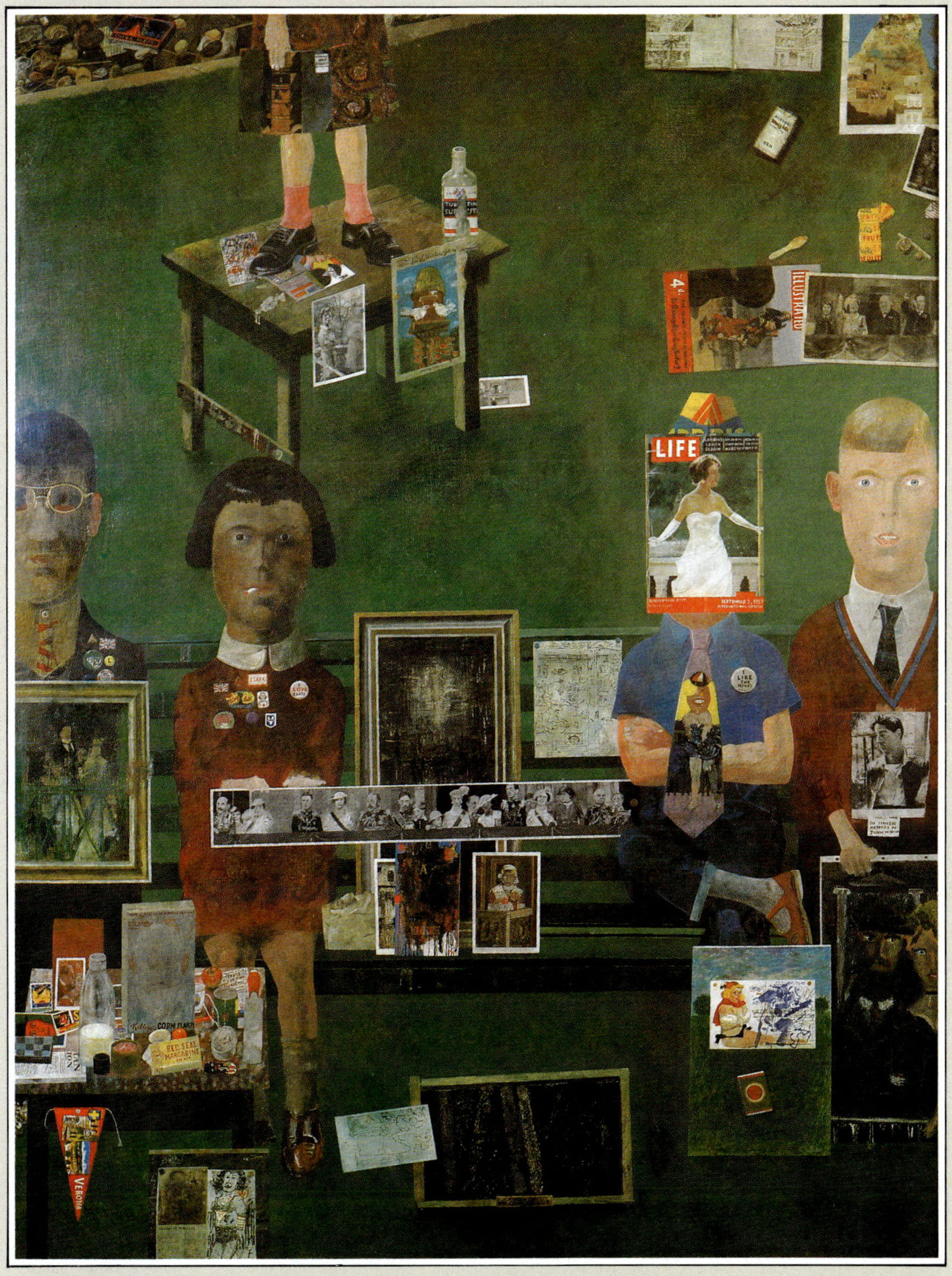


*On the Balcony is a tour de force of what might be called heterogeneous photographic realism. The technical representation of the wide variety of people, cloths, artworks and miscellaneous popular artefacts, is scrupulously attuned to the demands of each item so that the brush is motivated by a mass of particular contingencies, and imitates their own (supposed) modes of realism. The result is a remarkable interface between the visual art of the period and the habits, images and icons of its everyday life.*

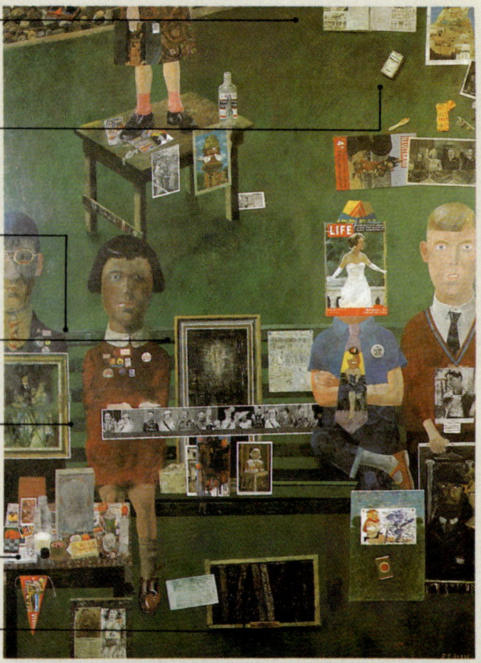


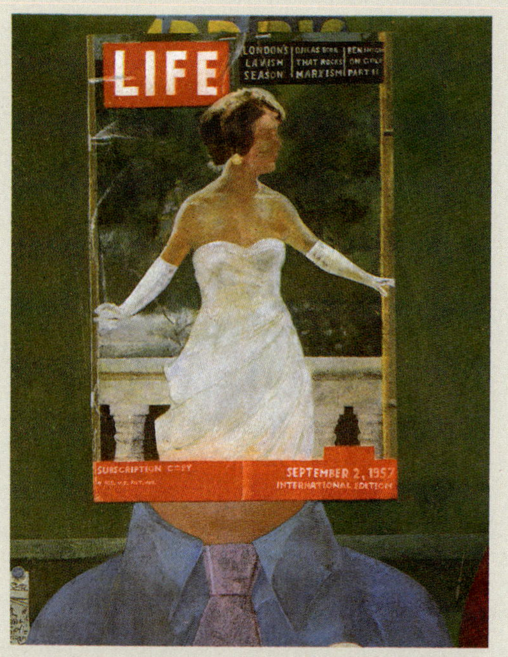


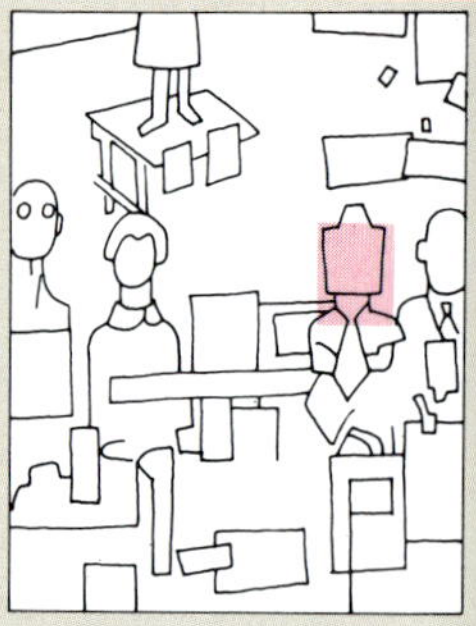

*LEFT The symbolic obliteration of the head of one of the four seated figures by the front cover of 'Life' magazine allows Blake scope for the most naturalist passage in the painting. Even the reflection creases are reproduced with sprays of the same white that builds up the princess's dress.*

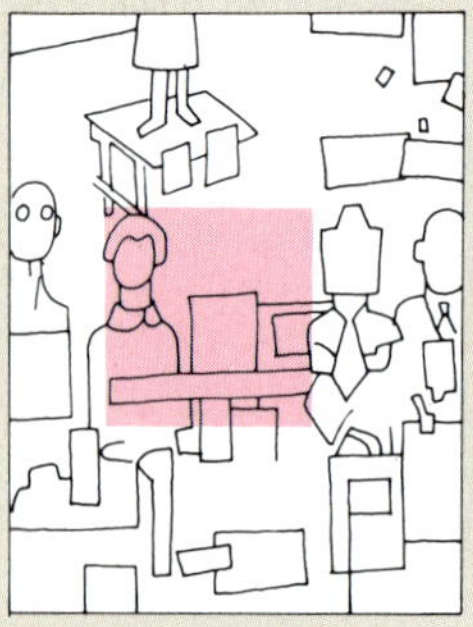

*RIGHT The full range of Blake's technical exuberance is revealed in this detail. While the dress of the seated woman is brushed loosely, her body stiff and disproportionate and the hands crudely reduced to pinkish smudges, the nine badges of diverse origin, which she wears, are rendered with the finest of touches. The images to the right of the woman are reproduced according to their own needs; the photograph of the royal family is worked up in black, white and grey, deviations from the 'real' photograph, being registered as caricatural effects. Below is a more coloristic modernist piece with stencilings, recalling the work of Jasper Johns.*

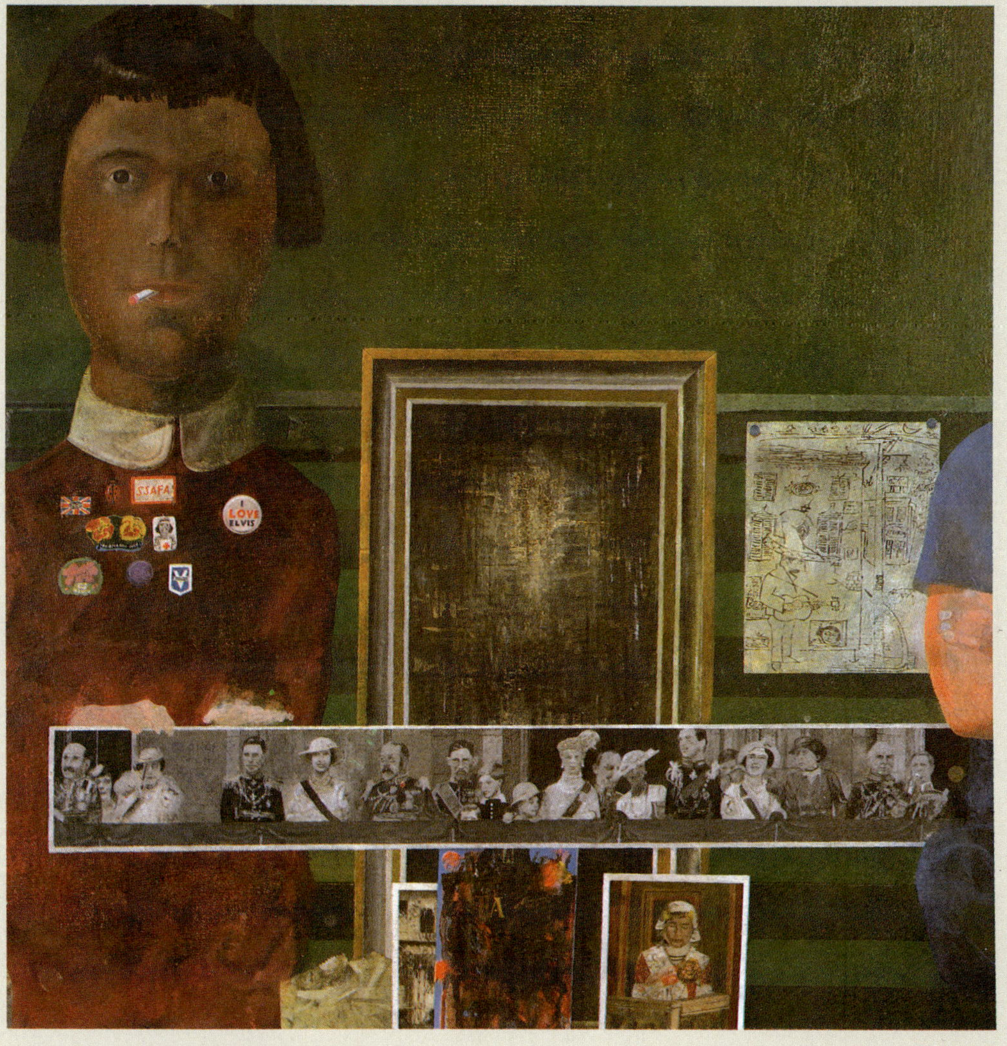

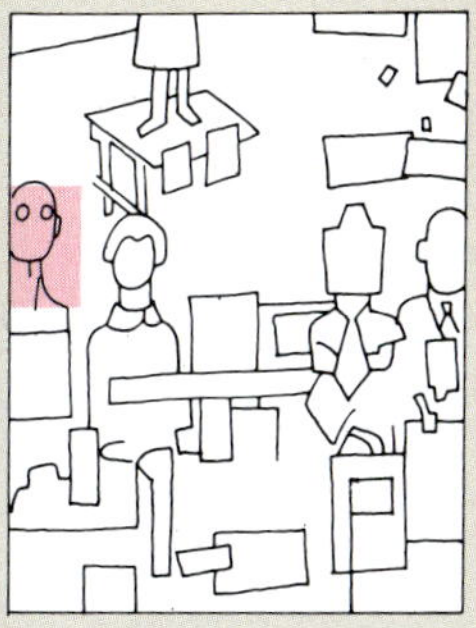

ACTUAL SIZE DETAIL *The head in the extreme left of the picture wears a familiar impassive expression which is, perhaps, analogous to Blake's painting technique itself. The differentiated thick-thin brush loads, and the different directions of stroke are apparent in the green background area. The hair is handled in a similar manner, but noticeable is a bold brush-swipe which produces furrows both to the right of the black hair and into the green painted zone adjacent. The original mark has been deftly overpainted to reassert the boundary, but, as often with Blake, this was done at a later stage and leaves the impasto ridges intact, but differently colored. A stereoscopic reflection of Blake at work is glimpsed in the mirror-lens sunglasses, apparently distorted by cross-reflections. The cheeks of the figure are pock-marked by the white pimples of canvas weave, as the face has been constantly rubbed and re-worked. His shoulders are appropriately decorated by the youthly insignia of a Y.H.A. badge and a Union Jack. The whole is a remarkable image of the obsessions and group identities of young people in the later 1950s, under the pressure of imported American popular culture, and through the technical mediation of an artist who was profoundly caught up in this moment; its manias, fantasies and illusions.*

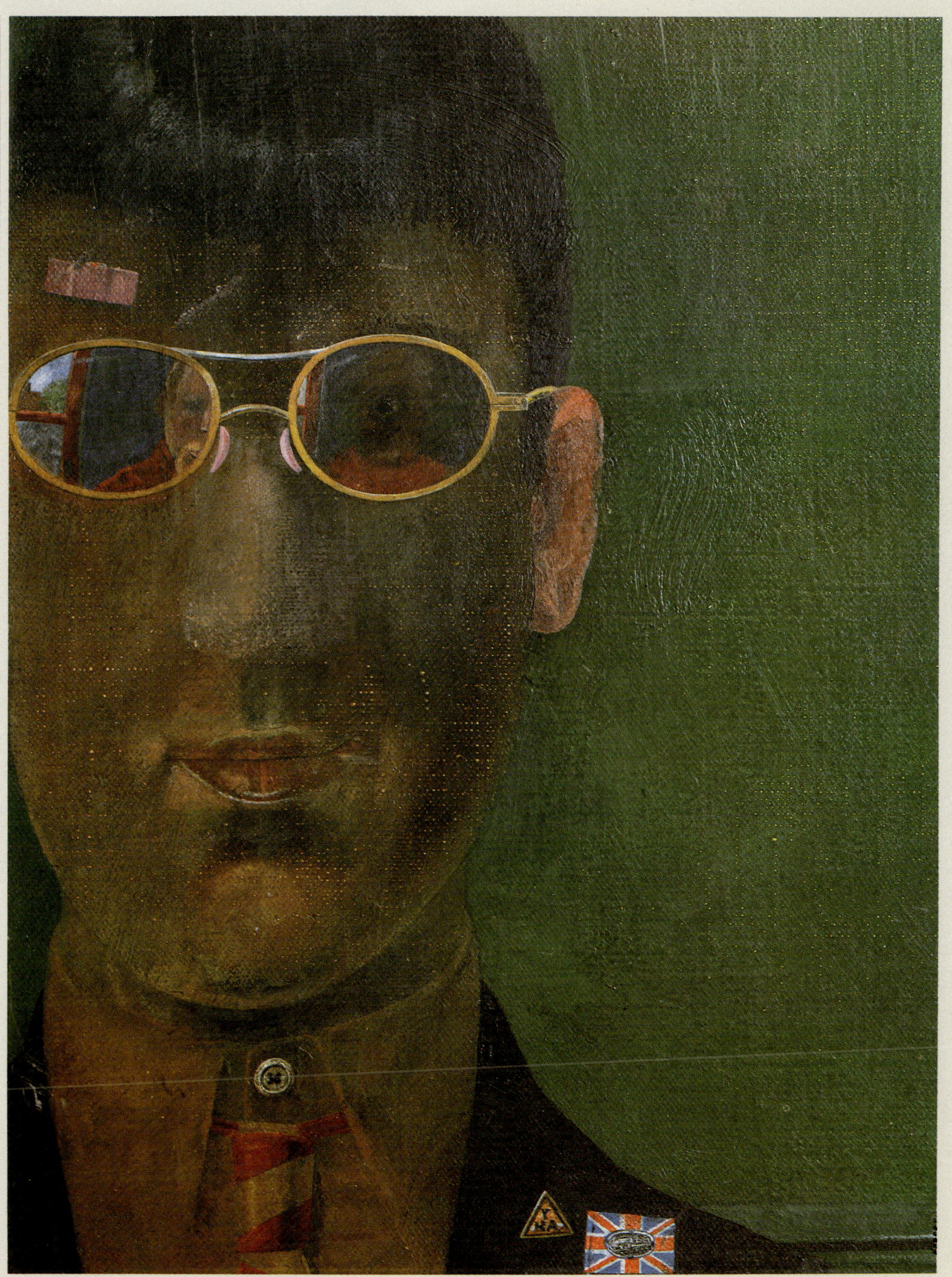

# FRANK STELLA

*Getty Tomb II* (1959)
Black enamel on canvas, 213cm × 243cm/84in × 96in

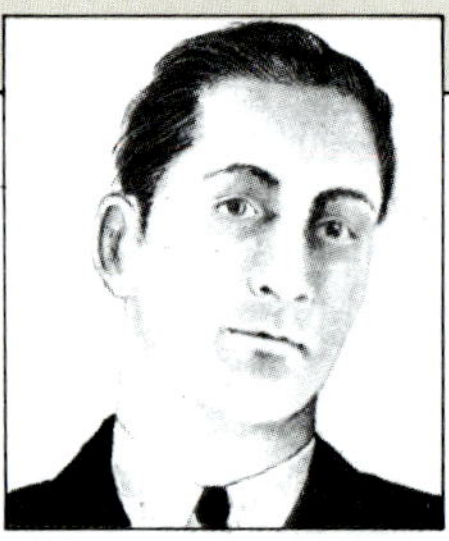

In 1958 Frank Stella began work on a series of pictures known as the *Black Paintings*. By 1960 he had completed 23 pictures, a body of work which proved to be the cornerstone of abstract art during the 1960s and 1970s. In 1958, Stella found the solution to certain problems in his painting practice in the paintings of the American artist Jasper Johns. He was impressed by the way in which, in his *Flag* painting, Johns 'stuck to the motif . . . the idea of stripes – the rhythm and interval – the idea of repetition.' The regulated symmetry Stella used in the *Black Paintings* kept the pictures flat and non-illusionistic. Stella's next problem was 'to find a method of paint application which followed and complemented the design solution.' This was achieved by the use of house painting techniques and tools.

Stella painted his pictures as he would a door or a wall, with a directness of approach – the paint was used straight from the can – and working from start to finish in one operation. Stella said of this technique: 'The painting must convince you at the level of the overall effect rather than by technical niceties, particularly the uniformity of the surface . . . If you look at my paintings, the technique was always at a fairly pedestrian level . . . They were never 'well painted' by any standards . . . but I do think that a good pictorial idea is worth more than a lot of manual dexterity.' Although Stella was convinced that virtuoso handling whether skillfuly spontaneous or skillfuly controlled, counted for nothing in the quality of his art, this did not mean that he was not concerned with the technical aspects of painting: 'I may have a flat-footed technique, or something like that, but still to me, the thrill, or the meat of the thing, is the actual painting. I don't get any thrill out of laying it out . . . I like the painting part, even when it's difficult.'

What type of object a painting was became a major issue among avant-garde artists of the 1950s and 1960s and Stella in particular was a subject of much controversy. Although Stella seemed to emphasize the status of his paintings as 'objects' by his use of color and common materials, the method by which he addressed his work as a 'thing' and his later use of unconventional, shaped canvases, he has always seen his work within the tradition of abstract painting.

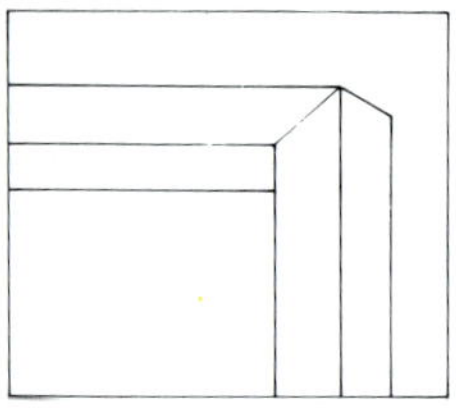

**1.** Stella used 3 in (7·5 cm) deep stretchers, which contributed to the picture's three-dimensionality.

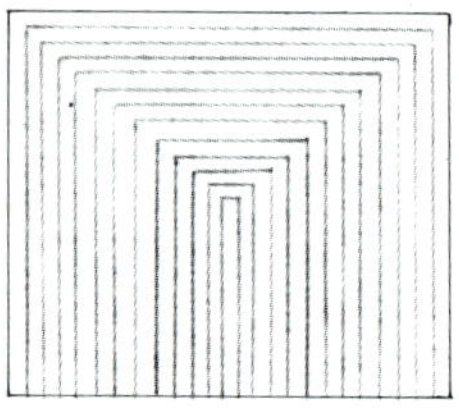

**2.** Earlier *Black Paintings* show no signs of underdrawing although later works initially had guidelines pencilled in.

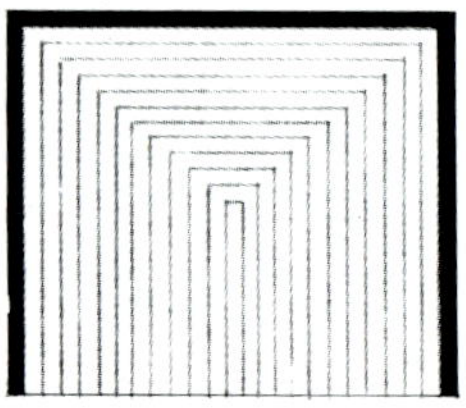

**3.** A commercial black enamel paint was applied to raw, unprimed canvas. The enamel was absorbed into the canvas and the gloss quality consequently diminished.

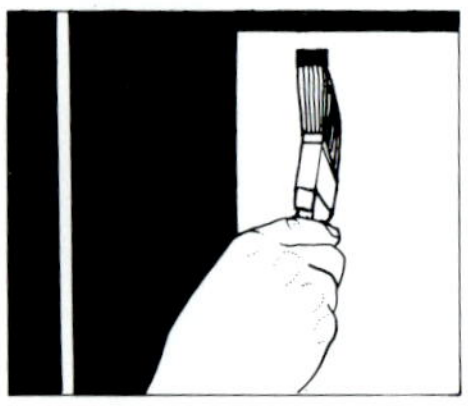

**4.** The paint was applied directly from the can using $2\frac{1}{2}$ in (6·25 cm) wide house-painter's brushes. Stella did not use masking tape to delineate the edges of the bands and no attempt was made to hide accidents or inconsistencies.

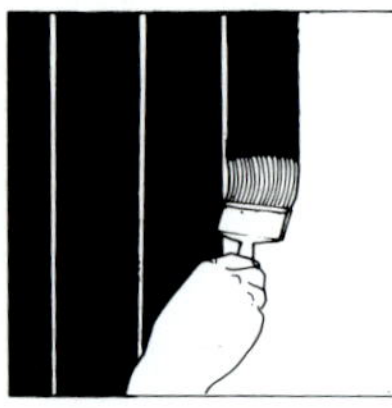

**5.** Stella worked from the outside edge of the painting inwards, painting each band individually.

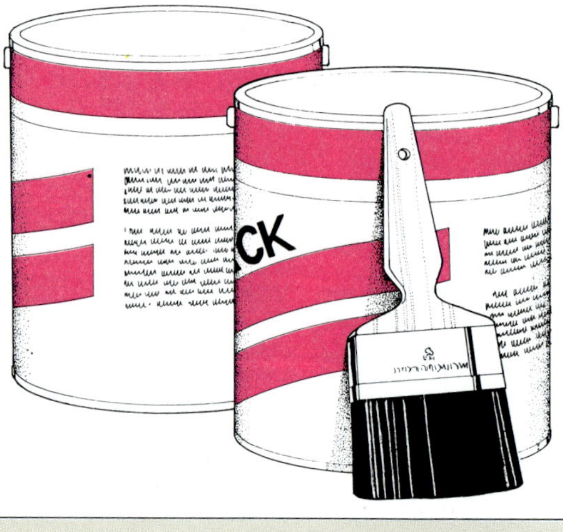


*Stella used commercial black enamel paint and applied it to the raw, unprinted canvas with a standard household paint brush. The enamel was absorbed by the cotton duck canvas and its gloss quality thus considerably reduced. The finish of* Getty Tomb II *varies according to how many layers of paint were applied. The degree of gloss increases if paint is applied on top of previous layers of paint, as opposed to directly onto the canvas.*

Getty Tomb II *was painted in two versions as Stella felt the first painting looked 'lopsided' and 'crooked'. The second version was 'blacker and straighter'.* Getty Tomb II *conveys a range of effects from matt to dull or low-gloss according to how many layers of paint were applied, the density of the paint in a particular area, and the effects of illumination. The paint has been applied directly with wide house painting brushes. In the earlier* Black Paintings *Stella worked directly on the canvas executing the bands from the outside edge to the center and rarely knew when he started a picture how many bands it would comprise.*
*Stella's movement towards three-dimensionality in his paintings was stressed by his preference for deep, wide stretchers which brought the painting into the realm of sculpture. Stella, however, always disagreed with this interpretation of his art: 'The deep stretchers lifted the pictures off the wall surface, so that they didn't fade into it as much. They created a bit of shadow and you knew that the painting was another surface. It seemed to me to actually accentuate the surface — to emphasize the two dimensionality of the painting's surface. Stella later added to this controversy by departing from the traditional canvas formats and stretching his canvas in unconventional shapes.*

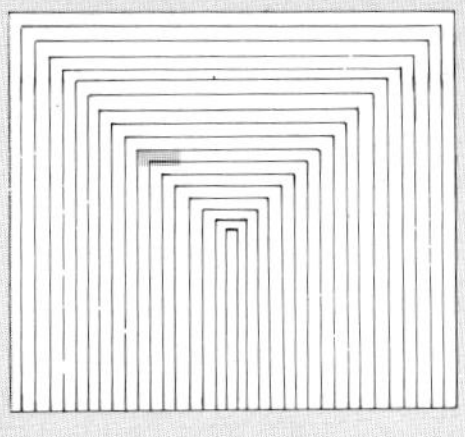

Actual size detail
*The contrast, shown in this detail, between the painted black bands and the unpainted interstices in Stella's paintings led some journalists to talk about the 'white pin stripes' or 'pin stripe painting'. Stella reacted against this interpretation in a letter written in 1961. Though humorous, the letter is not without its serious aspects and shows the importance which the artist attached to not using the brush to draw with : 'My own work . . . uses fairly broad stripes of black, and, more recently, aluminium or copper paint . . . I have never seen a 'white pin-stripe painting' . . . there is a distinction between what any artist DOES and does NOT do; and however it may lack journalistic appeal, this boundary is precisely the necessary limit without which no work of art can exist. With respect to my painting the case seems particularly simple; it is an observable fact that I have laid down paint in certain spaces, and have not done so in others.'*

# 1961 ONWARDS

Artists in these times have to face the weight and extension of art historical knowledge. To some this knowledge can be like the albatross was to the Ancient Mariner, while to others it is a stimulation and a challenge.

There was a period centered around 1970 when artists, feeling overwhelmed by information and images about earlier art, chose to reduce the amount, physical quality and content of their output. This phase has now been replaced by a kind of *horror vacui*: large canvases and complex painted sculptures appear – the canvases are filled to the point of saturation by pigment and heavyweight ideas, and the sculpture seems almost Baroque or Rococo in its largesse and decorative power. Today, mythological subject matter abounds – it is related to ancient mythology because both emerge from a concern with the basic human issues of love, death, power and sexuality – but it is too early to recognize the dominant themes; they remain too autobiographical and too expressive of the artists' particular stances.

We have experienced a full circle of development from 1950 to the present day. The Second World War was not a period conducive for work. Artists emerged from that time in a torpid state, their horizons diminished and their isolation increased. It was necessary to take stock – this resulted in an examination of art produced prior to the outbreak of war – and decisions had to be taken as to whether to continue as before or to start afresh.

The early 1950s found artists working in the Abstract Expressionist style; at the same time a new aesthetic was emerging, which played down personal expression and in its place proposed a dialog with the techniques and materials of mass media. Pop Art, as this new style became known, was clearly recognizable and capable of speedy assimilation. A total rejection of anything expressionistic was the extreme of this evolution, and the concept of minimal art was explored. Eventually the pendulum has swung right back towards a new expressionism, with a re-examination and assessment of the art of the past. Artists now feel able to plunder the art of the past and take what they personally feel was successful.

**Pop Art**

This movement developed simultaneously in England and America. Each country produced its own style, but to a great extent themes and materials were shared. The themes were those referring to mass or popular culture, hence the name of the movement. The name Pop Art was coined by the English critic Lawrence Alloway who identified the movement as originating among his friends: a group of artists, architects and designers who began to meet regularly for discussions at the Institute of Contemporary Arts (ICA), London, in the early 1950s. The group included Richard Hamilton (b 1922) and Eduardo Paolozzi (b 1924) and concentrated its attention upon commercial culture, finding in it a breadth and inventiveness which was in opposition to the élitist stance of the art world, which was promoting abstract, non-referential art.

Likewise in America, Pop Art arose partly as a reaction against the hermetic imagery and impassioned brushwork of Abstract Expressionism. Artists wanted to reintroduce figural imagery and to experiment with the new technical processes offered by commercial and industrial quarters.

A new alternative to oil paint began to be marketed in the 1950s. Originally developed for the household paint market, synthetically made acrylic paint emerged as a most useful medium for artists, just at the moment when they were looking for a way to produce colorful, hard-edged, somewhat impersonal works. Acrylic is soluble in water or a special thinner, and thus provides a great variety in the thickness of pigment available, as well as a finish which disguises the activity of the brush. It is quick drying and allows an artist to finish a work in a shorter time, since it is no longer necessary to wait while oil paint slowly dries.

As early as 1953, Morris Louis (1912-1962), a young painter from Baltimore, had begun using acrylics to explore a technique developed by Helen Frankenthaler (b 1928) of soaking washes of diluted paint into the canvas. Louis's first mature works consist of limpid color washes whose iridescence recalls not only Rothko but also the late *Waterlilies* of Monet. Where Louis differs from his predecessors is in the exceptionally transparent effects that his new materials made possible. His next series was the so-called *Unfurleds* (1961) where diagonal rivulets of intensely saturated color frame a central expanse of immaculate canvas which, by comparison, appears to radiate a pure white glow.

The hard-edged style which Louis pioneered in acrylics had a 'cool' rigor about it: the new synthetic pigment could be treated in a less sensual way than oil. There was a move towards objectivity and the more formal aspects of painting. The loose, painterly, often ugly brushwork of the Abstract Expressionists, with its concomitant ideas about truth and sincerity of personal feelings immediately and powerfully expressed (not always comprehended), gave way to a more impersonal approach to the handling of paint and a more anonymous subject matter.

Roy Lichtenstein (b 1923) and Andy Warhol (b 1930) were two of the artists who began to change the look of American painting by choosing a range of imagery from the most obvious visual aspects of American popular culture; imagery which did not belong to their private world but was already created by somebody else, for the public domain.

RIGHT *This extremely complex composition,* Calcium Light Night *is the result of a series of screenprints. Eduardo Paolozzi (b 1924) began with a matt black printing, over which he laid a translucent white, giving shape to the main abstract forms in a resulting grey. Slowly, detail and definition were added with subsequent layers of white, red, blue and white again, so building up a three-dimensional impression of organized unreality. The final opaque cream printing provided a vibrancy, while a varnish completed the picture.*

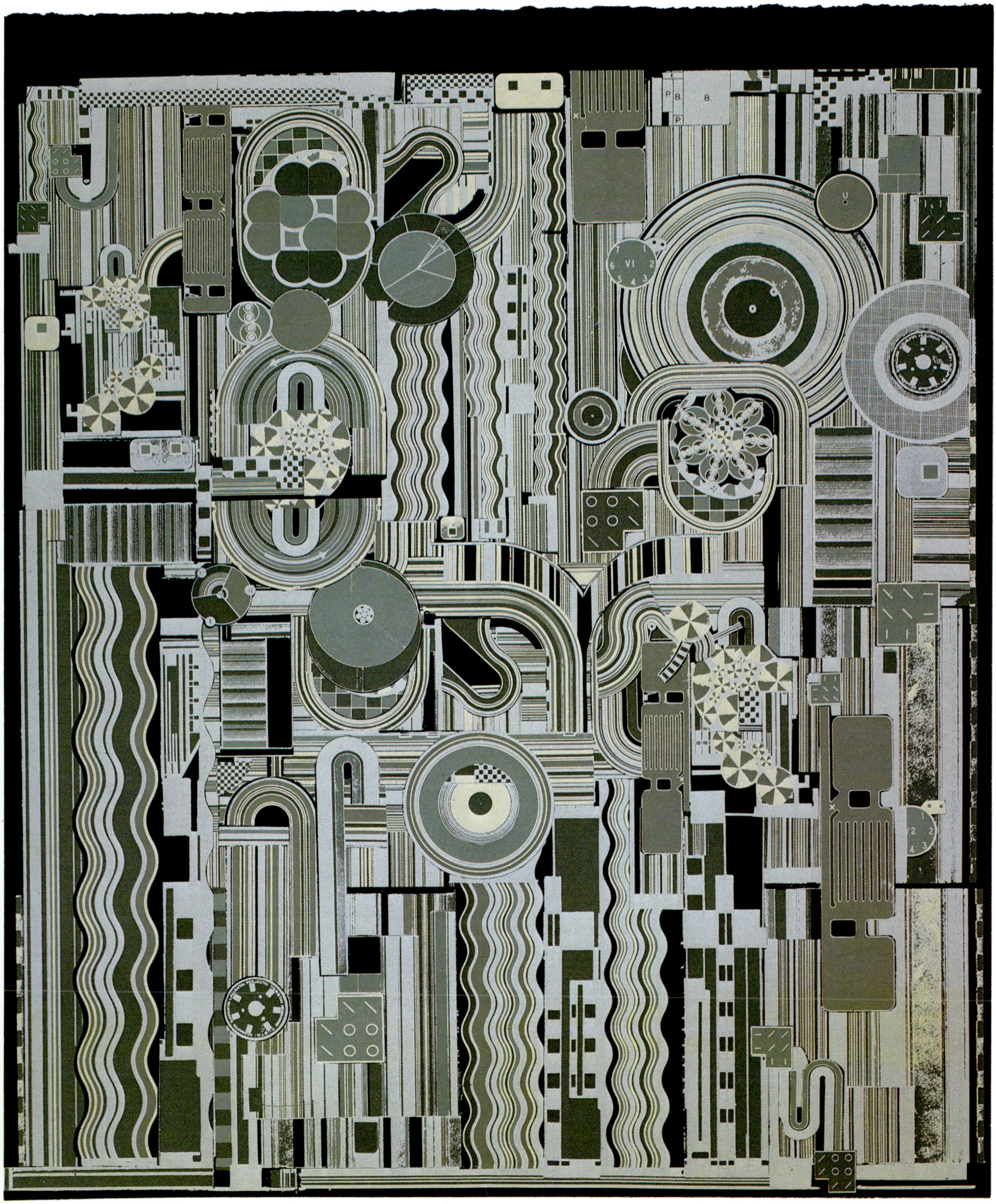

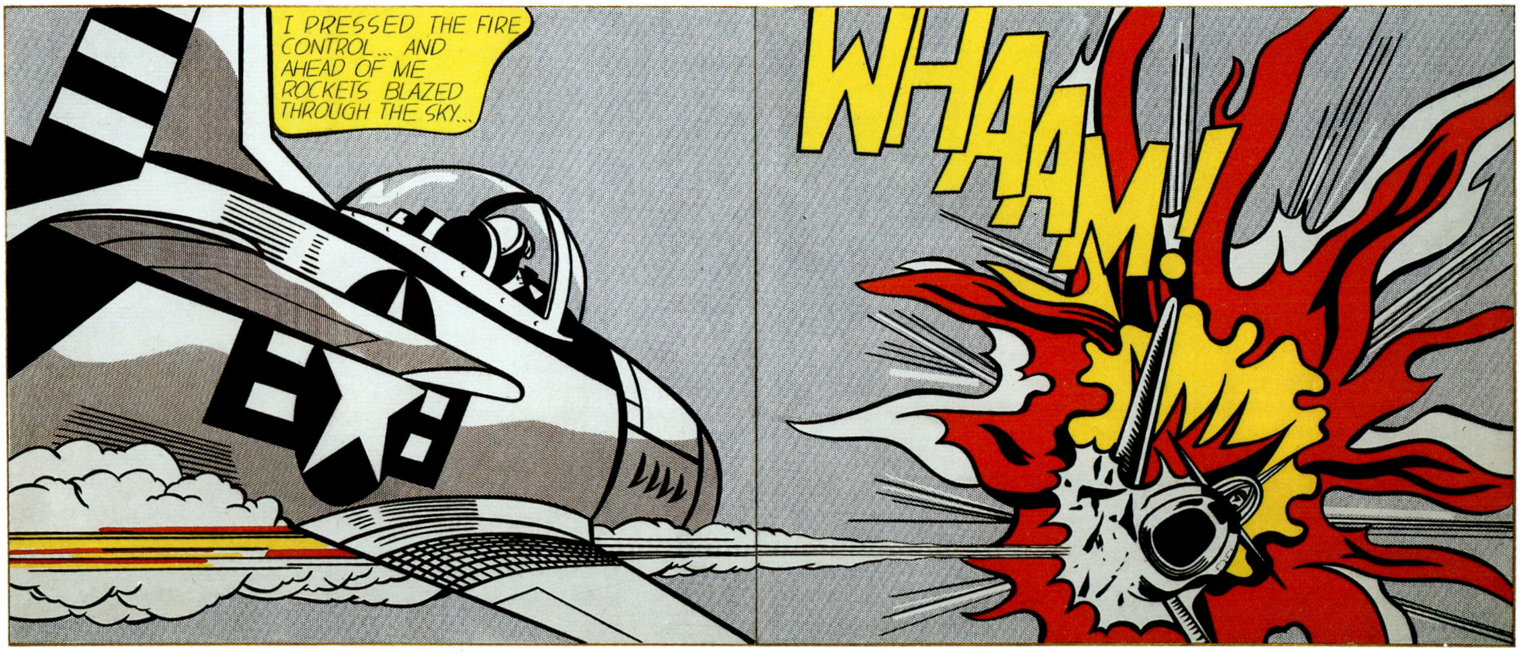


ABOVE Whaam! *(1963) by Roy Lichtenstein began as an idea for two separate paintings — one with a fighter plane attacking, and the other with a fighter plane being shot down. Then Lichtenstein decided that they would make more impact if he combined them. Thus the work is made up of two canvases identical in size, with the composition continuous across both. Lichtenstein began to use comic strip imagery in 1960, and the subject of* Whaam! *probably comes from a magazine he often used as source material — 'Armed Forces at War'. The strong, controversial subject-matter is in stark contrast to the dispassionate techniques used, yet both are derived from advertising and comic strips. Indeed the central divide between the two canvases can be read as a kind of echo of the divisions between pages. When the Tate Gallery acquired this work in 1966, the idea of paintings with bubbles full of words and large painted words of exclamation was still quite new.*

Lichtenstein purloined the work of major European artists, such as Monet, Picasso and Mondrian, and parodied their styles as though attempting to make their work as easily available as a bill-board advertisement. Lichtenstein and Warhol introduced an anti-Expressionist regime, subordinating the handling of paint.

Pop Art drew upon certain Dada precepts, and much that had been introduced by Marcel Duchamp. Distinctions between good and bad taste were avoided, and much that was tawdry, trivial or over-familiar in the late 1950s was converted into the material of art. Because art and life drew so close, objects from daily life found their way into art, either presented emblematically or standing as themselves (an appropriated piece of the real world).

Multi-media spectaculars began to enter the art world; artists themselves began to adopt a theatrical frame of reference, and perform their works as well as paint them. As Lawrence Alloway noted: 'The city with its inhabitants was not only the subject of much of this art, it was also literally, the *substance*, providing the texture and bulk of the material itself.' Thus objects from the real world, the debris and throw-away commonplaces of everyday life were used as artistic materials.

This is a link back to Dada, Cubism and Duchamp: Dada because the artists of that movement used provocative behavior as their mode of artistic creation; and Cubism and Duchamp because the Cubists introduced collage, and Duchamp was the inventor of the 'ready-mades' (objects selected at random from the oblivion of their existence in the everyday world, and accorded a new autonomy as artistic objects, yet which at the same time challenged the rules of art and proposed an anti-art value). Cubism, with its investigation of the use of *papier collé* and collage as artistic procedures, was an important ancestor. *Papier collé* and collage drew attention to the scraps of the real world which had been chosen to stand as artistic materials and were thus to be given a new scrutiny in terms of their technical properties.

Lichtenstein and Warhol produced works which lay an aggressive stress upon the picture surface, although neither chose to make much use of collage. One of Frank Stella's first works was a small collage entitled *The First Post-Cubist Collage* (1959). The arrogant title of this little work, which implied that there had been a fallow period in the use of collage since about 1914, shows that Stella was thinking deeply about the problems of space, flatness, color and texture.

Stella turned towards autonomous abstract art, a path critics of Cubism had always thought the movement would lead. He was working in America at the same time as Warhol, Lichtenstein, Jasper Johns (b 1930) and Robert Rauschenberg (b 1925), and contributed to the movement of anti-Expressionism, but he concentrated more on the interplay of geometry, structure and color to the exclusion of subject matter. He used commercial household paint to accentuate the flatness and surface tension of his canvases.

Thus Stella's aims were close to those of Warhol. But for Warhol subject matter was a better vehicle and he made much use of photographic images; by the early 1960s the camera and all its procedures emerged as a powerful artistic tool. Photographs have been used by artists as source material ever since photography was invented in the 1830s, but at first a photograph was used as a sketch, a way of noting reality and a jog for the memory. In the 1960s photographs began to be used as the basis of the image on the canvas: Warhol's *Marilyn Diptych* (1962) is made up from 50 silk-screened images printed from a publicity photograph, and Lichtenstein has recounted how he begins many paintings by projecting an image on to the canvas.

The British artists Richard Hamilton and David Hockney (b 1937) have enjoyed a fruitful involvement with photography. Hamilton plays upon the manipulative procedures involved in mass communication and advertising, and exaggerates many photographic techniques. His *Swinging London* series uses the same image which becomes modified with each new attempt, in much the same way that the images of Marilyn Monroe are in Warhol's *Marilyn Diptych*. Hamilton's small collage – *Just What Is It That Makes Today's Homes So Different, So Appealing?* (1956) – is a collection of images cut out from advertisements in magazines. In its subject matter and anti-traditional materials, it stands as a beacon to the British Pop Art movement.

Hamilton's move towards Pop Art actually predates anything produced across the Atlantic, but it was to America, and particularly American consumer goods and magazines, that British artists turned for their source material. Hockney turned to America for its glamorous subject matter, especially the hedonistic life of California, and then selected and painted things which interested him, just as Blake did. The paintings of Patrick Caulfield (b 1936), another British artist to whom the term Pop has been applied, shares more of the cool, impersonal American outlook. For a while like Hockney, Caulfield preferred to work in acrylic or commercial household paint. His work also has affinities with Lichtenstein, for Caulfield experiments with contrasting styles and methods of representation, and shows an interest in formalizing his composition into flat colors bounded by strong lines. He works from his own drawings done from real life and from photographs.

**Conceptual Art**

This blanket title has been used to cover art produced from the late 1960s until the late 1970s, which challenged the orthodoxy of the traditional media of painting and sculpture. Conceptual Art is not a totally satisfactory term, since it has to contain much that is contradictory, but its usefulness lies in the stress it places upon the *conceptual* rather than the practical, craftsmanship aspects of art practice.

In its breadth and voracity, the term has embraced other approaches such as idea art, process art, performance art, earth art, minimal art and Arte Povera. Conceptual Art has been seen as taking a reductive path: 'The world is full of objects, more or less interesting. I do not wish to add any more,' commented Conceptualist Douglas Huebler (b 1924) in 1968. Huebler's attitude, and the remark of Ad Reinhardt (b 1913) – 'sculpture is something you fall over when you step back to look at a painting' – contribute to the idea that art had reached a kind of impasse, because if the production of art objects were to continue unabated as it had done for previous centuries, the world would become clogged up with these precious commodities. Since Cubism and Dada, increasing importance has been attached to the choice of materials which are non-precious and ephemeral. Now the art object was thought of as dispensable too.

Returning to the ideas proposed by Marcel Duchamp as early as about 1913, Conceptual artists devoted their energies to creating an art of the mind. Art which could be conceived and appreciated in the mind did not necessarily need to be executed. But if it were to be executed then the materials used were to be commonplace and dispensable. Sometimes the work could only be satisfactorily comprehended in the mind, because the scale of the work prevented the viewer from ever experiencing it whole, at first hand.

Many works consisted of holes dug in the ground and then filled in again: Claes Oldenburg (b 1929), the American sculptor, had grave-diggers dig a hole and then fill it in again in Central Park, New York, as his contribution to a 1967 exhibition *Sculpture in Environment*. In 1969 Jachareff Christo (b 1935), the Bulgarian-born sculptor, wrapped part of the coastline near Sydney, Australia, with about 300,000 sq meters (1,000,000 sq ft) of industrial fabric and 500 km (36 miles) of rope; the previous year he had caused the Kunsthalle at Berne in Switzerland to be similarly packaged.

Minimal Art is one of the subdivisions of Conceptual Art. As the name implies, Minimalism means making do with less rather than more, usually in terms of the artist's intervention. The Americans Dan Flavin (b 1933), Don Judd (b 1928) and Carl André (b 1935) usually chose their material from industry–for example, Judd has used rolled steel, Flavin neon tubes, and Andre firebricks — and presented these materials organized into logical and systemized units. The materials are presented absolutely as themselves, leaving no room for misrepresentation, and no impression of any feeling or emotion of the artist. The subject matter of these Minimal works lies in awareness of the material. The essential properties of the chosen materials are permitted to speak more strongly in an art context than in their original, or unchosen, state. Also, the strength of the Minimal work often lies in its use of

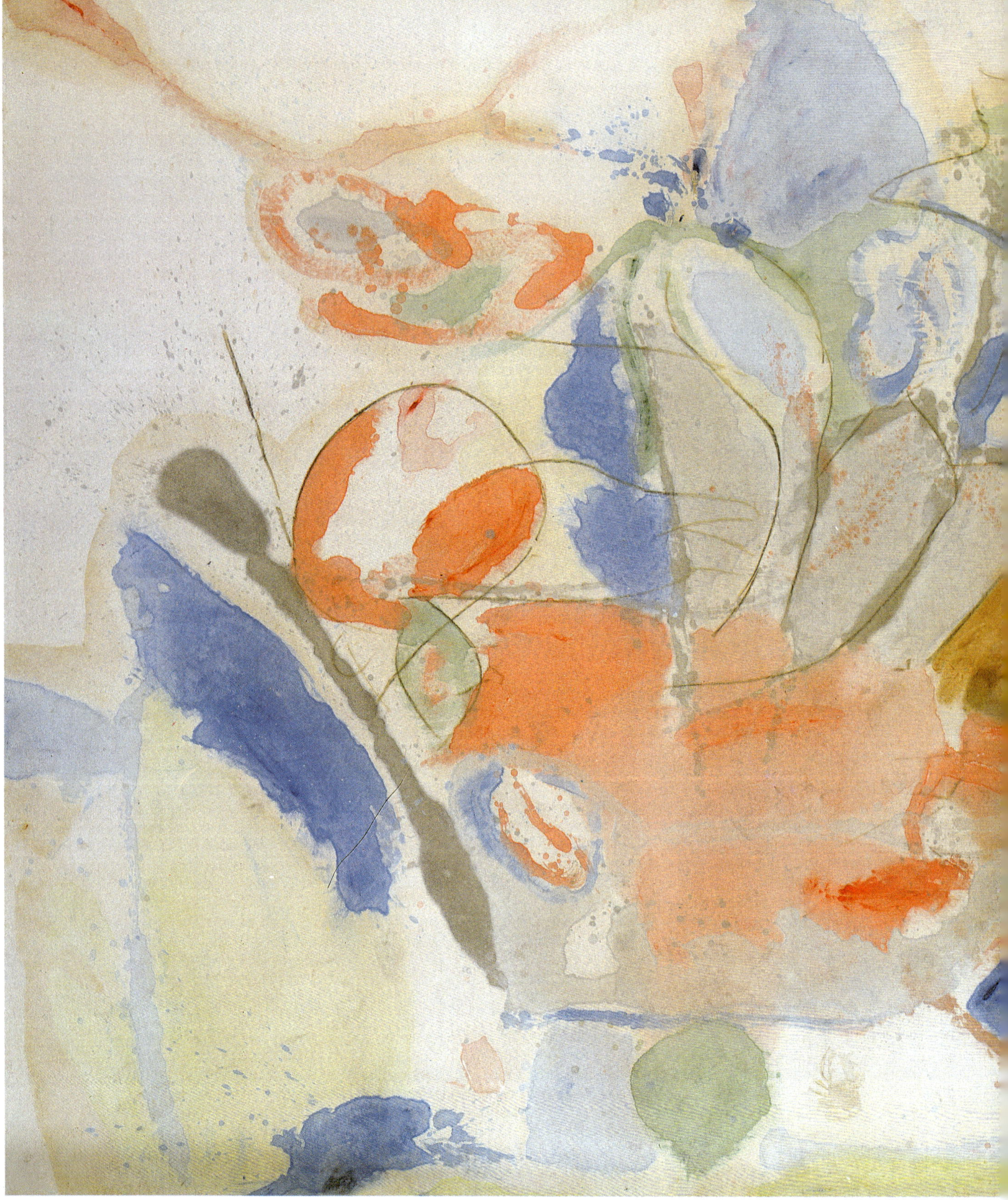

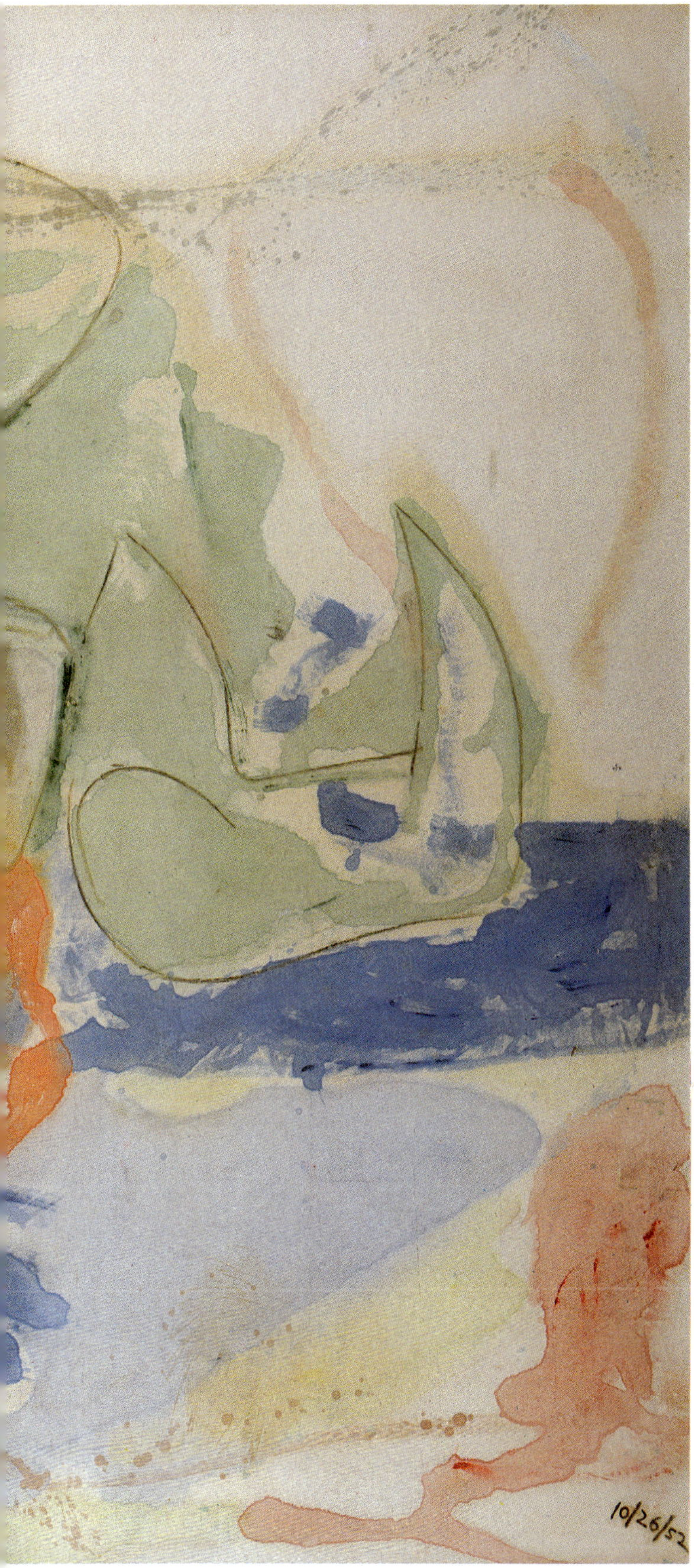

repetition of identical units.

One of the principles of Minimal Art was that the work need not be made by the artist: Don Judd's steel boxes were manufactured by others, and Sol LeWitt's serial wall drawings, which he initiated by producing one himself on the wall of the Paula Cooper Gallery, New York, in October 1968, are more usually drawn by draftsmen who work from a set of instructions provided by the artist.

In 1971, LeWitt provided 35 sentences on Conceptual Art as his contribution to the magazine *Flash Art*. Sentence eight reads: 'When words such as painting and sculpture are used, they connote a whole tradition and imply a consequent acceptance of this tradition, thus placing limitations on the artist who would be reluctant to make art that goes beyond the limitations.' These limitations were evidently overthrown in the late 1960s.

The main result was the physical disintegration of the art object. Often this involved inflicting violence upon the art object. Either deliberately mean materials were used – felt, twigs, mud – implying that the materials mattered less than the ideas (this manifestation was called Arte Povera), or else artists discharged their feelings by rupturing the standard processes. This could be done formally, for example Francis Bacon's distortions of subject matter, or materially. Lucio Fontana (1899-1968) slashed cuts into his canvases with a razor as early as 1957, in order to introduce a new concept of space: Gustav Metzger (b 1926) chose acid instead of paint, and nylon instead of canvas, so that when he created a painting by applying the acid to the nylon support, the acid caused the nylon to rot away, thus initiating the destruction of the piece.

Reduction, or destruction, of techniques and materials led to an enlargement of the role of the artist and his or her creative motivations and actions. Artists began nakedly to propose themselves, especially their bodies, as mat-

LEFT *Helen Frankenthaler (b 1928) is a member of the generation who followed after the pioneer work of the Abstract Expressionists, and thus a change of direction can be clearly seen. There is a calm and lyrical quality about* Mountains and Sea *(1952) also reflected in its title; works of this nature by Frankenthaler and her colleagues have been dubbed 'lyrical abstractions'. This is a large early canvas which shows the new techniques pioneered by her and taken up by other American artists in the 50s and 60s. She painted on raw unsized canvas, with the canvas laid on the floor rather than on an easel or wall. Since the canvas is unsized, the colors sink into and blend with the support.*

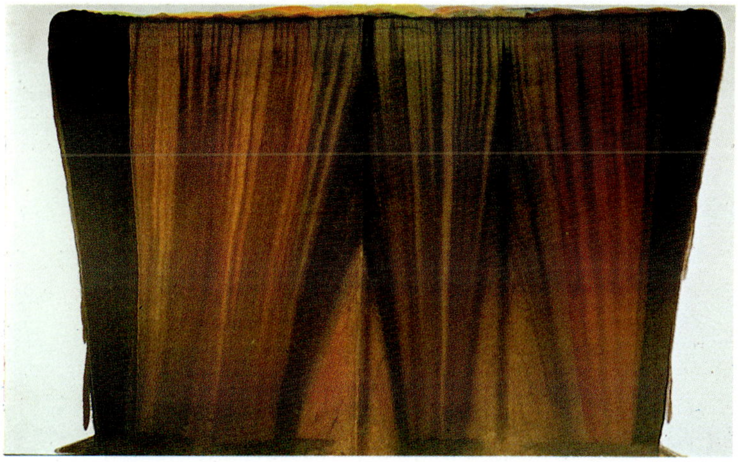

BELOW *Morris Louis was enabled to make such bold, color stained canvases — as here in* Golden Age *(1959) — by the dual influence of Frankenthaler's way of working and his own adoption of acrylic paint. Frankenthaler did not overlay her paints since oils would have caused opacity, but the water-soluble acrylic used by Louis allows veils of color to mingle within the fabric of the canvas, while still retaining their identities and without becoming muddied.*

*BELOW* Self-portrait with Badges *(1961) by Peter Blake has attracted the epithet 'pop' because it contains popular imagery, shown in the veritable plethora of metal badges. It is a strongly autobiographical work which provides much material about the artist in terms of emblems and symbols, and in this it recalls early English portraiture. Blakes likes to work his paintings up to a high state of finish, but not all areas need to be at the same time. The meticulous painting of the badges contrasts with the sketchy treatment of his left foot.*

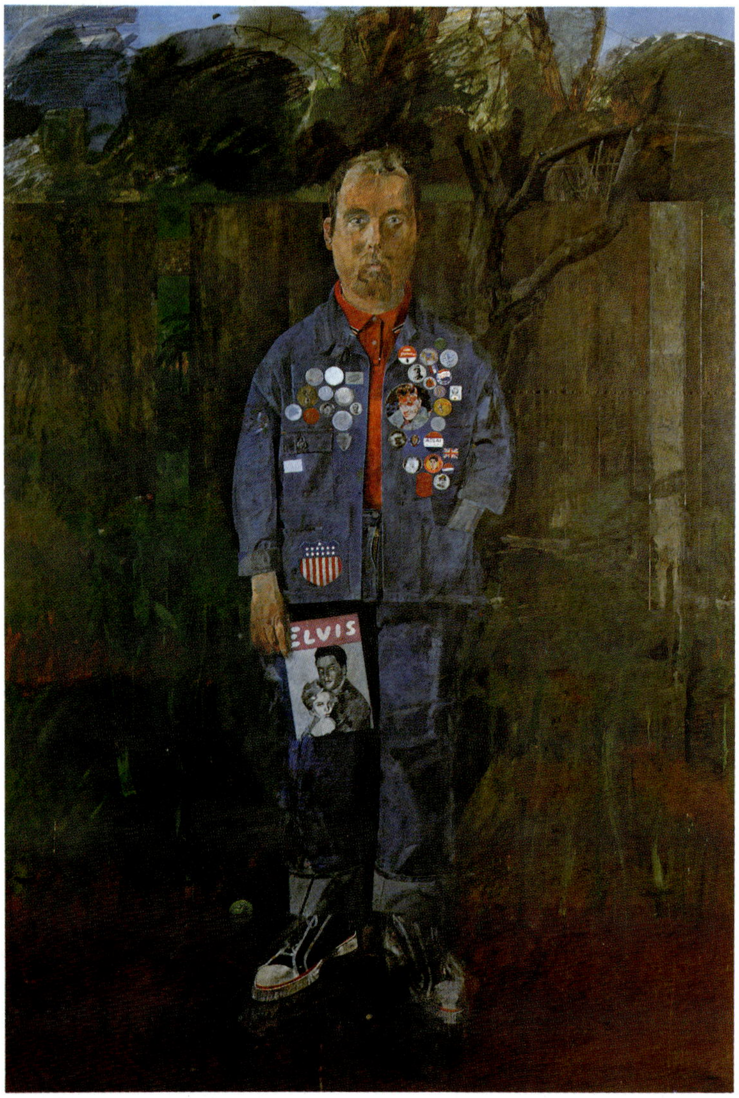


erial for artistic manipulation. This earned the term Performance Art. Artists such as Dennis Oppenheim (b 1938) and Vito Acconci (b 1940) subjected themselves to feats of endurance, strength, boredom and fear. Art and the life of the artist thus became indistinguishable.

Since many of the performance pieces were done privately, or involved an activity spread over a certain determined period – for example, Acconi's *Following Piece* which involved following people chosen at random on the New York streets for a one-month span – some kind of record or documentation was deemed necessary in order to prove the existence of the piece. Documentation was also necessary for Earth Art works. In 1970 Robert Smithson (1938-1973) designed a *Spiral Jetty* for Great Salt Lake, Utah, which was made out of earth by a construction team, and measured 450 meters (1,500 ft) long and 4.5 meters (15 ft) wide. The work would have remained quite private if Smithson had not exhibited his working drawings for it, and made a film revealing the context of the Jetty. Richard Long (b 1945) records his walks over unpopulated ground by providing the viewer with annotated maps, photographs and, more recently, a conjunction of place names and poetic incidents.

Joseph Beuys (b 1921) is an artist who believes in the value of teaching as an artistic commodity. Partly because of memories of experiences of the Russian front during the Second World War, he creates works which use animals; his performance work *How to Explain Pictures of a Dead Hare* (1965) consisted of Beuys cradling a dead hare in his arms, with his face covered by a layer of grease and gold-leaf. He wants such works to express metaphysical and social matters.

**New Expressionism**

During the mid-1970s it became apparent that there was a movement, or change of direction in art, which existed contemporaneously with Conceptual Art. This new approach contrasted strikingly with the methods, practices and techniques of the Conceptualists, because it represented a return to the traditional values of painting. Lucian Freud, who had been using oils exclusively for some time, was applying the paint with unconcealed brushstrokes, to sculptural effect. Several artists who had never subscribed to art as concept and who had continued to execute orthodox paintings, turned from using acrylic to oil paint, feeling that oils, with their classical central position in the history of painting, provided the painter with inbuilt, expressive, and even emotional qualities. If oils had served Rembrandt, Titian and van Gogh, then their value could only be enhanced by a conscious acknowledgement of this allegiance. Malcolm Morley (b 1931), a painter who had produced super-realist works from the mid-1960s, was one who changed from using acrylic paint with its precise, cool finish, to oils. One of the first canvases he painted using oil was *Piccadilly Circus* (1973), in which there is an obvious reference back to the work of the Abstract Expressionists: their loose, almost improvisatory painting style implied freedom of expression and, equally, placed great store upon the quality and quantity of the material used. Paint was applied thickly, quickly, with great texture and flourish. Often the subject was obscured or dominated by the pigment.

Nowadays, the younger artists of the 1980s take up much that was proposed by the Abstract Expressionists, but also look further back – to the German Expressionists, to van Gogh, Chaim Soutine (1893-1943) and even to the later style of de Chirico. Ernst Kirchner, cofounder of the German Expressionist Die Brücke group, wrote in 1906: 'We claim as our own everyone who reproduced directly and without falsification whatever it is that drives

*RIGHT* Mountain Indian *(1982) by Rainer Fetting is a large composition made up from two separately stretched pieces of canvas. Fetting chose to go to Berlin to pursue an artistic education, and in doing so he followed the path taken by the Dresden painters of Die Brücke, who moved to Berlin in 1911 in search of new creative experiences. The modern city, with its bars, shared flats, nightlife and aura of violence is usually the chosen subject matter, but in* Mountain Indian *a naked figure — Fetting himself? — stands before a lowering neo-romantic landscape. The overt subjective, emotional, autobiographical content of this painting, and indeed all of his work, looks back to the same choices made by the Die Brücke artists. They, and Fetting, record their activities in canvases with a range of color harmonies which is often lurid. The black, purple, green and yellow of* Mountain Indian *are just the choices that an artist like Kirchner would have made. Fetting has rejected both oil and acrylic paint as his medium, and works with powder paint — dry pigment which has to be mixed with a binder; traditionally this has been water, but a plastic medium is also possible. The rich purple and blue harmonies are reminiscent of those chosen by Symbolist painters, the young Picasso of the blue period included, and Fetting prefers works which are rich in psychological content. His paintings are not laboriously planned, but executed in a deft, hedonistic manner.*

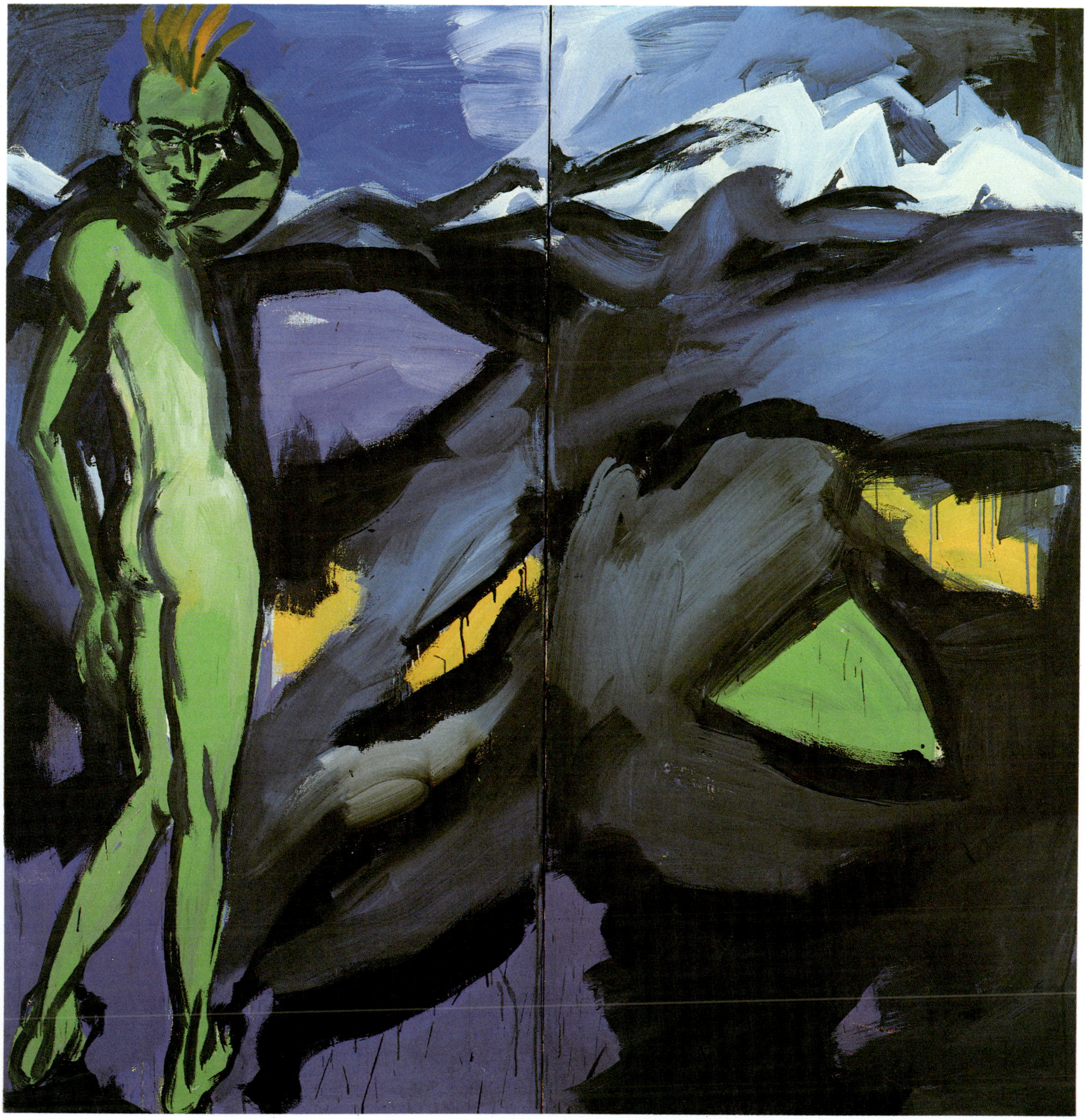

him to create.' The paintings of Karel Appel (b 1921), Asger Jorn (1914-1973), and the members of their Cobra group who worked towards the same aim from 1948 to 1951, also displayed spontaneity and emotion; they offered a more lyrical, witty kind of Expressionism which ran counter to the strength, violence and scale of the work of the American Abstract Expressionists.

Today, the international band of painters working in the New Expressionist idiom – they came from Germany, Italy, Britain and America – prefer the wild, violent approach. Canvases are large and their emotional content is high. Rainer Fetting (b 1949), for instance, has reworked the traditional theme of the crucifixion of Christ, and the choice of such subject matter is related to the sado-masochistic streak in his imagery. Identification with the suffering body is intensified by the way the paint is applied to the canvas and the image: maximum expressive *means* is wedded to maximum expressive *content*. Paintings can be triggered by an incident experienced or an image which fascinates; they express the claustrophobia and heady excitement of life in large cities, but they also give the idea of painter as observer, as anthropologist studying the wayward, sometimes incoherent activities of humans.

*RIGHT The title gives a clue to the form and content of* Entanglement Series: Perpetual Flux *(1981-1982) by Peter Phillips. He began making painted reliefs in 1963 and the entanglement can refer to the interpenetration of the three-dimensional elements which ride in front of a canvas-covered, painted backboard. The motifs are equally commixed: a fan, part of what looks like a cocktail dress, and the front half of subtly colored skis all take their palce. Phillips' mature style is one that revels in* trompe l'oeil *effects, and the mixing of 2-D and 3-D elements in this piece puzzle and delight.*

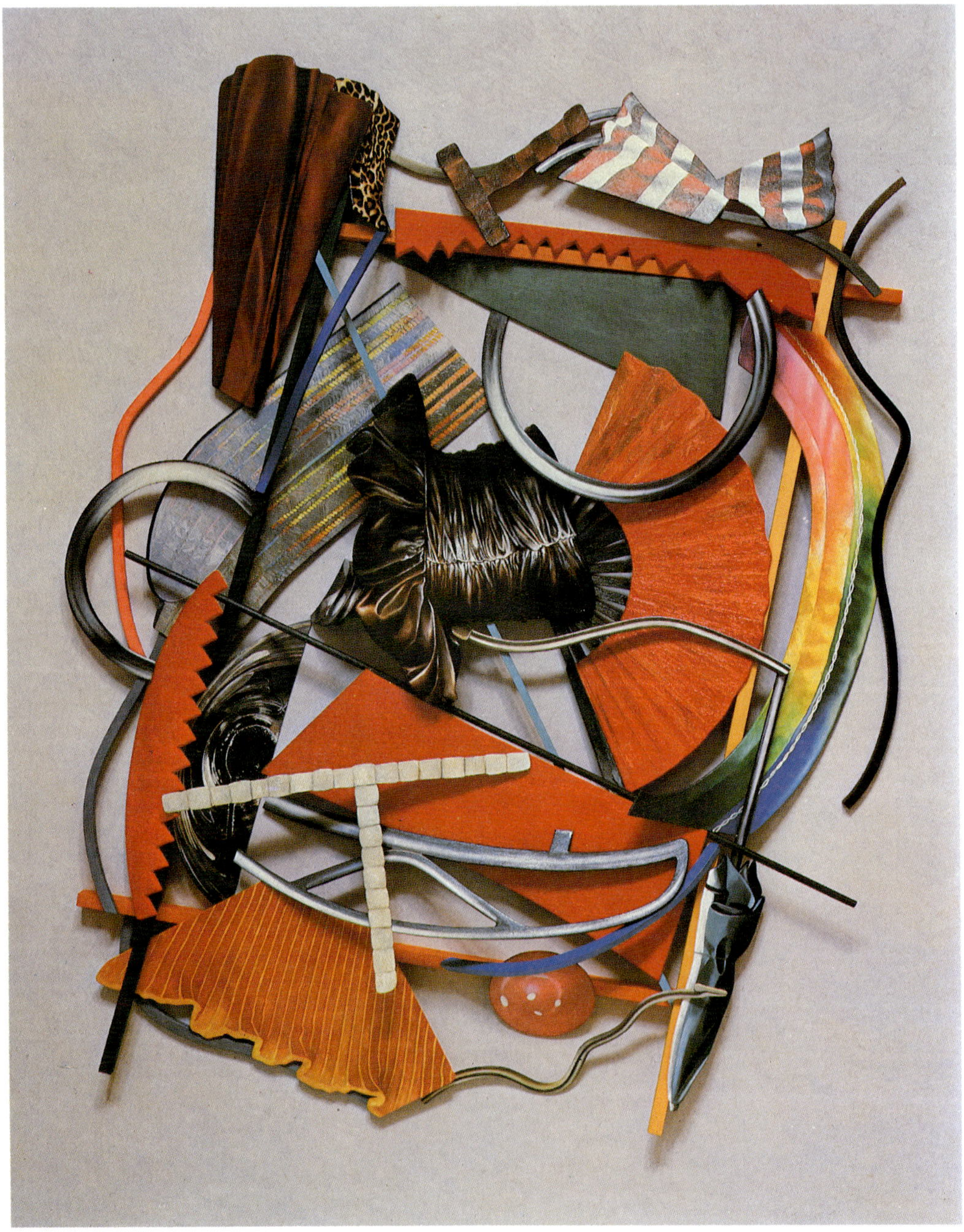

*RIGHT The subject of a dancer or dancers has long held a fascination for Allen Jones, as has the idea of a hermaphrodite image. In* Spanish Dancer *(1982) three figures are visible — two men, one in a dark grey and one in a red suit, and a dancer in a long blue dress. But the title of the piece is in the singular, implying that all the figures are fused into one. Following on from his early shaped canvases, and sections of relief in his panel paintings, Jones started to make free-standing painted sculpture in 1969. Then, as now, the strong, hard-edge of the contour of the plywood contrasts with the loose, expressionistic brushwork painted upon it.*

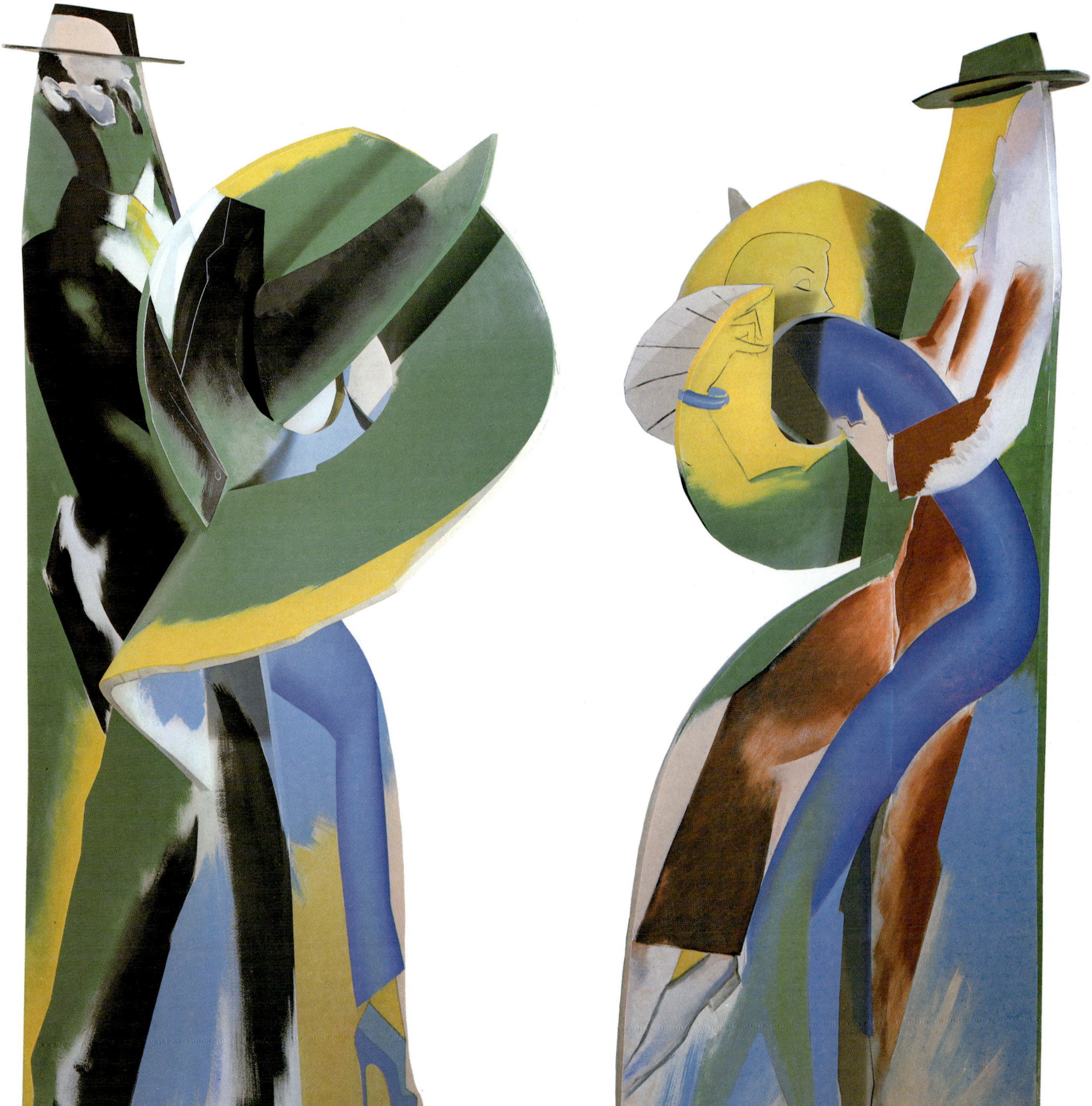

# MORRIS LOUIS

*Spawn (1959-1960)*
Acrylic on canvas
182.8cm × 243.8cm/72in × 96in

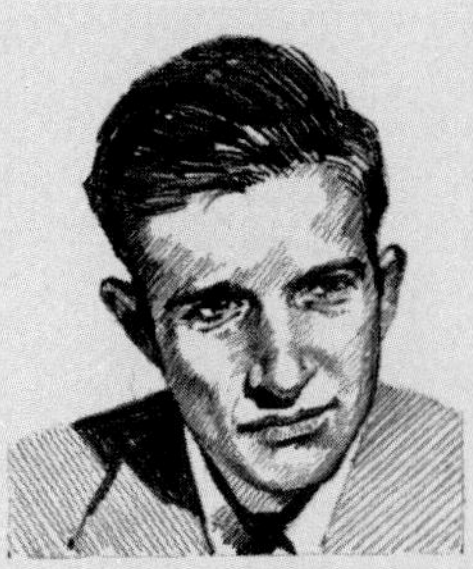

Morris Louis has been hailed as heir to Jackson Pollock's pictorial revolution, responsible for a real contribution to the liberating and abstracting tendencies of the art of the immediate post-war period, and as an artist who lived his life for painting with a dedication close at times to obsession. Under the championship of the critic Clement Greenberg, Louis took painting right into the fabric of the canvas and finally subverted decades of discussion about 'surface' and 'depth'. In the end he reacted against the 'gestural' practices of Action Painting and the seductive tactile qualities associated with it, in favor of the coolness, restraint and impersonality which became the mark of so much of the art of the 1960s.

Born in November 1912 in Baltimore, Maryland, Louis gained his knowledge of contemporary developments in painting, especially in the New York scene, mostly through a friendship with the artist Kenneth Noland, which began in the early 1950s. His style of painting up to about 1952 has been dismissed, perhaps over-hastily, as 'minor and provincial'. It reflects the influences of two close friends David Alfaro Siqueiros (1896-1974), the Mexican muralist, and of Arshile Gorky, the Abstract Surrealist, and finally of Pollock. But he was always experimenting during this 'preparatory' period with techniques such as Duco, and he first employed acrylic colors as early as 1948.

In 1953 Louis saw the *Mountains and Sea* (1952) of Helen Frankenthaler. This painting had been executed by pouring and staining, a color process developed by Frankenthaler after Pollock's dominantly black stainings which he produced from about 1951 to 1952 , and in combination with, his drip technique. Louis noted of Frankenthaler that 'she was the bridge between Pollock and what was possible'.

Frankenthaler's *Mountains and Sea* produced an almost visionary reaction in Louis and led him to annex and extend the technical possibilities of the staining method. By 1954 he had solved, to his own satisfaction, most of the practical problems of the technique.

The last eight years of his life were devoted to three general modes of staining canvas, differentiated both by the overall 'look' of the pictures and by definite shifts and nuances in the process of application. In 1954 and from 1958 to 1960 he painted *Veils* and *Florals*; in 1960 a concentrated series of *Unfurleds*, and from 1961 until his death from lung cancer in September 1962, a sequence called *Stripes*. These categories are not absolute and there are many 'marginal' works particularly from the years between 1955 to 1957 when Louis destroyed nearly all his work (because his methods allowed him to make no changes to the work).

Louis was a dedicated painter. Having used acrylic paint since the late 1940s, he was not really tempted by any other medium, except for a few collages (tissue paper and acrylic on upsom board) in 1953. There are several eloquent accounts of his mature technique but none from the artist himself.

The Magna paint which Louis used, distinguishes it from conventional oil paints and from the different acrylics used, for example, by David Hockney (b 1937). Magna is the trade name for an acrylic-based paint manufactured by Bocour Artist's Colors Inc., and contains a resin, a thinner, an emulsifying agent and pigment. Unlike oil, it is quick drying, non-acidic and can be thinned to flow and bind. Unlike the Liquitex water-based acrylic used by Hockney it is oil compatible and soluble in white spirit.

*Spawn* (part of the *Floral* series) was painted between 1959 and 1960, a crucial moment in the development of Louis' working procedure, as he became unhappy with a new formula Magna paint which was too viscous to flow and stain as he would have liked and the evidence from *Spawn* suggests a struggle with a somewhat recalcitrant medium.

The unprimed and probably unsized canvas which is not stained with color appears slightly scuffed and marked, possibly from the effort of manoeuver; the support would have had to have been tilted right round the compass angles – a movement greater and more complex than that necessitated by the *Veils* and *Stripes* with their dominant north-south or diagonal orientations.

The 'floral' effect of *Spawn* is achieved by the centrifugal movement of paint from a central depot (a stigma as it were), which is the point of focus for the composition. These colors were separated towards the peripheries where they were stopped and blunted or pointed, according to the volume and thickness of the acrylic (the 'petals'). A third, roughly concentric, band can be identified between the central nub and the one-color petals, where two or more hues merge and interact, producing a darker layered effect (the 'sepals').

The paint accumulated in the center of the work, an unusually dense area of impasto, has cracked on drying and stretching. To the left of center there are *frottage*-like tracks, created by the sweep of a swab or other implement across the surface as an aid to spreading. Slightly above the center there is a definite brushed radius, more consciously articulated. Elsewhere characteristic 'capillary scars' are visible round the boundaries of the color shapes, where the resin has become separated from the paint.

These various surface incidents, however, are only the technical constituents of a powerful coloristic sensibility, as significant in its own way as Robert Delaunay's early modern chromatic discs.

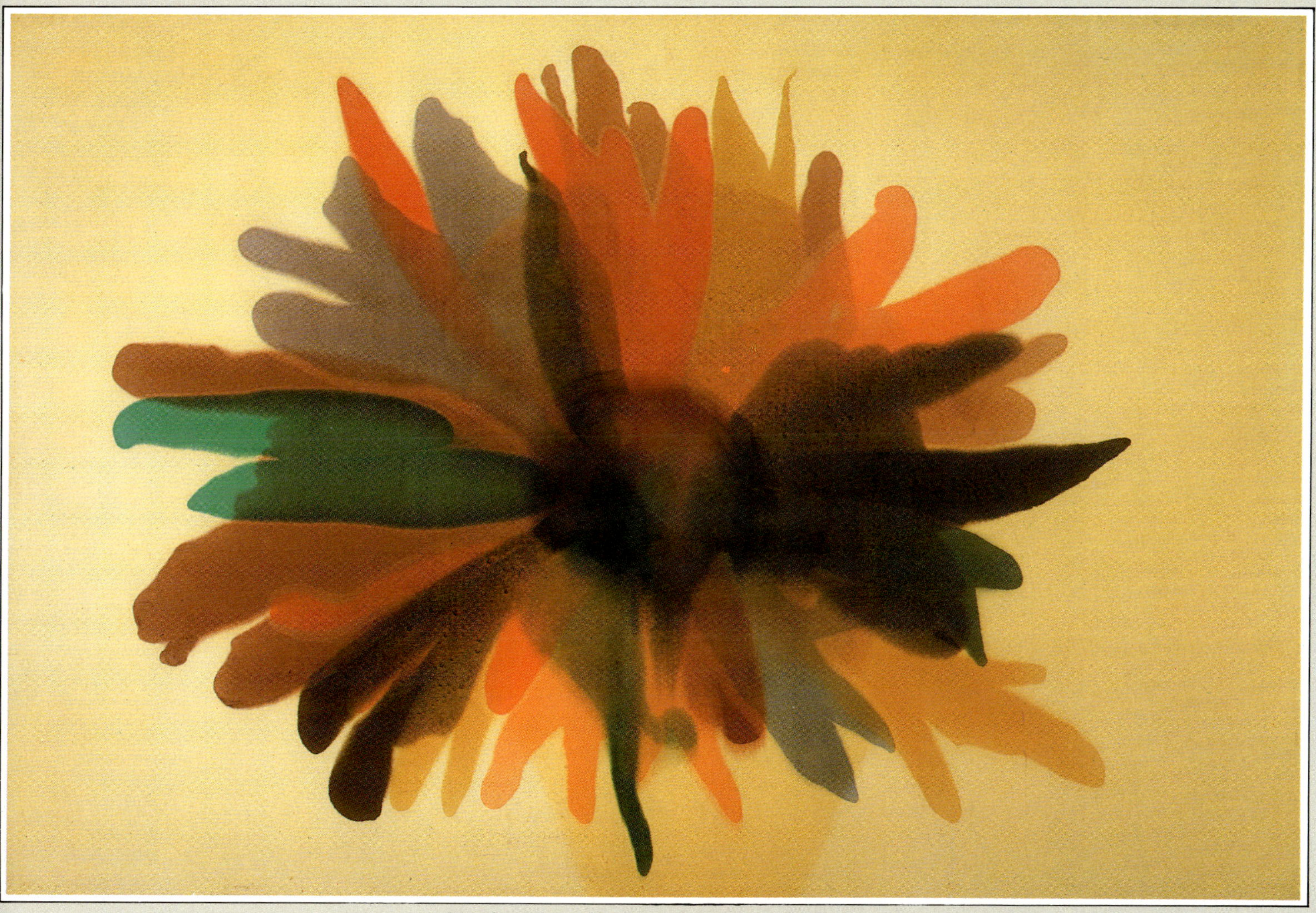

*The abstract but 'floral' appearance of* Spawn *belies a considerable number of technical incidents and decisions across the canvas surface. The work is not merely decorative, but is 'set-up' for the eye. It proposes not just the pleasurable experience of color combinations, but an experience which includes an apprehension of the very procedures which brought the painting into being.*

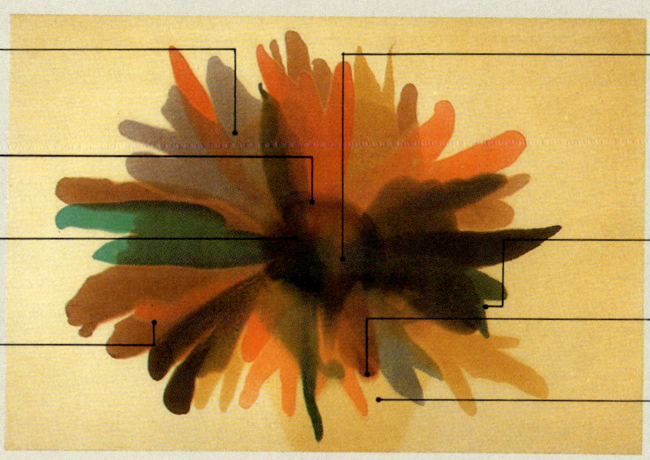

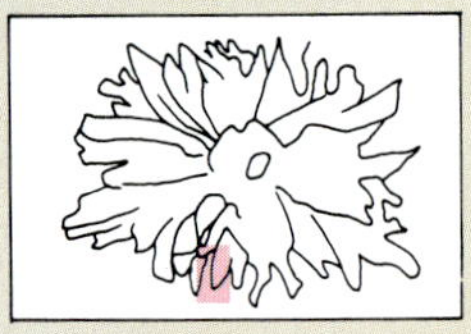

*ACTUAL SIZE DETAIL The relatively coarse weave is everywhere visible, with occasional tufts and irregularites in the fabric. There are no brushmarks, just boundaries and gradients between successive veils and pourings. The transition from the blunt finger of red-orange to the yellow paint in the bottom left corner of this detail shows how the eye reads the boundary as a continuous curve; in fact, close inspection reveals the zig-zag incursions that each color makes into the other's zone. Where color veils overlap there is a distinct tendency for individual knots of canvas to be colonized by a discrete hue, so that there is a kind of two-color Pointillist effect. This is particularly clear in the top right where the red-orange and darker green colors merge. The close-up masks, however, some of the tentacular extensions which stain downwards in vertical alignments. On the lefthand side there are two paint blisters clearly visible as dark circles enclosing lighter interiors.*

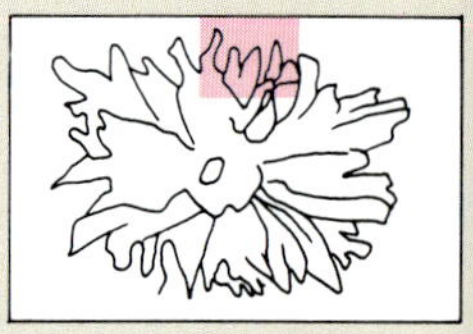

*RIGHT The 'top' section of* Spawn *has been stained carefully to produce a range of grouped pinnacles of paint. The poured prongs are more variously terminated than elsewhere in the work; the yellow finger to the left for example, is spectacularly attentuated in comparison to the normally blunted termini. On the left, a black stain ends with a strong dark zone the result of either the addition of a small dose of color, or the removal of paint by rubbing down from it. In the center, the 'pigeon-head' configuration of the brown stain was achieved by altering the angle of canvas tilt at the last moment. The capillary scars around the triple red prongs are particulary pronounced and evenly disposed.*

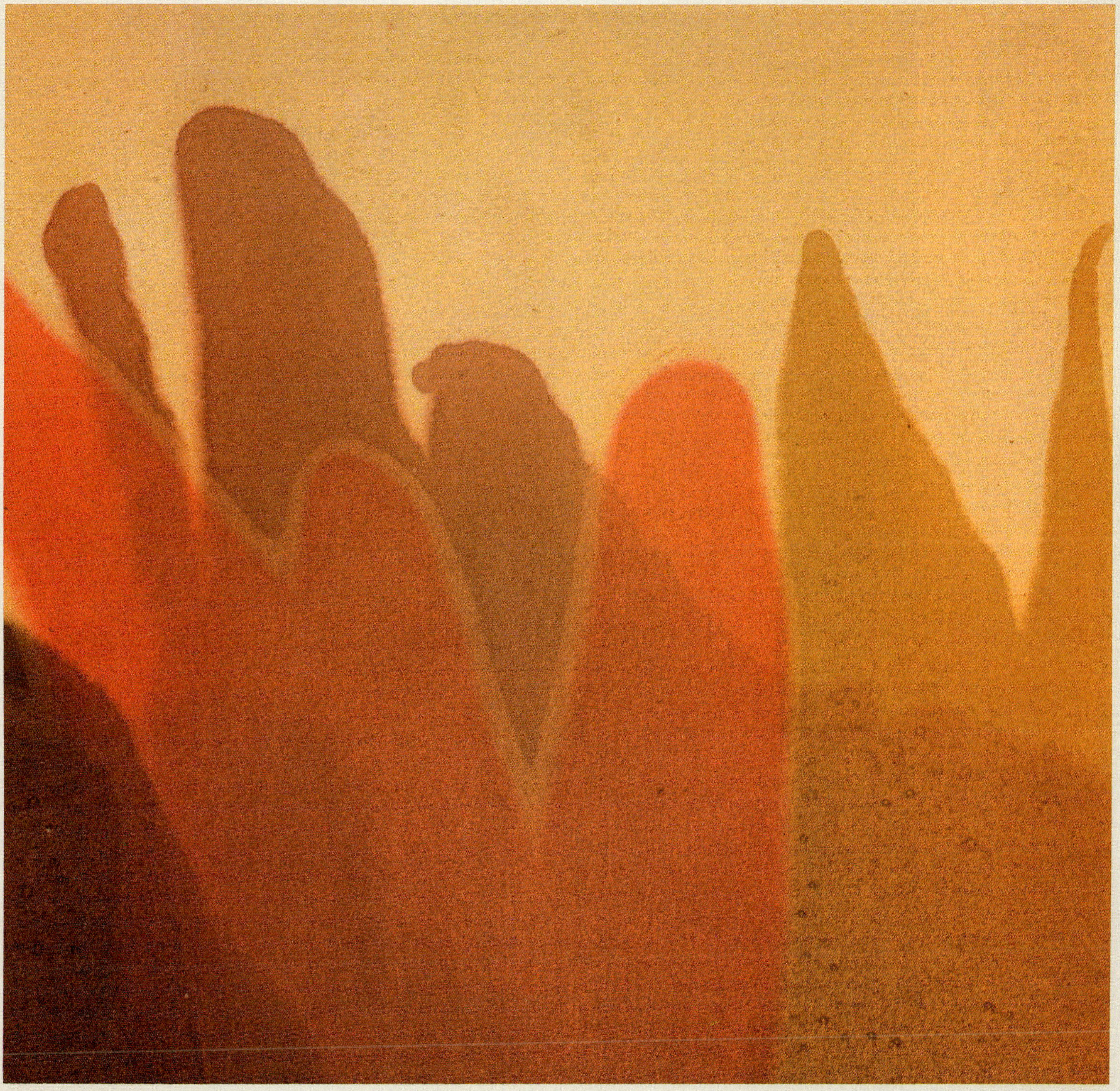

Metal spiral issuing from 'rupture' in fabric

Shreds of cloth 'dripping' into the brown zone

Electric light bulb with mains lead (switched on)

Cloth bag suspended from license plate

Automobile tyre pierced by wooden slat

Loose, thick white brushstrokes

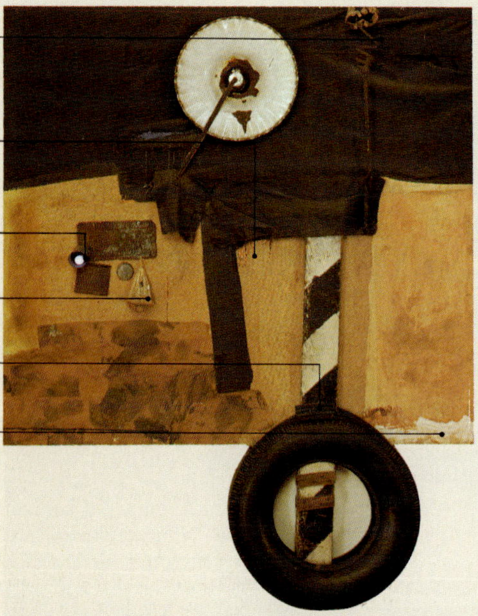

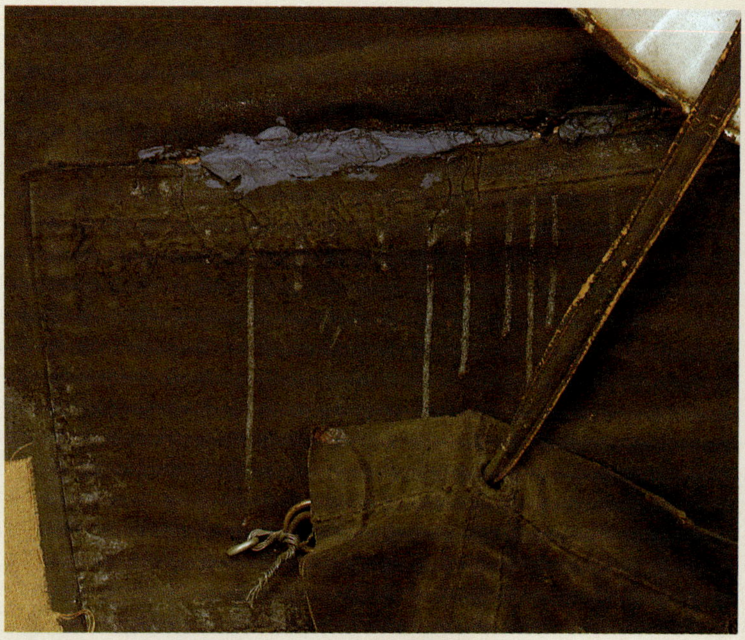

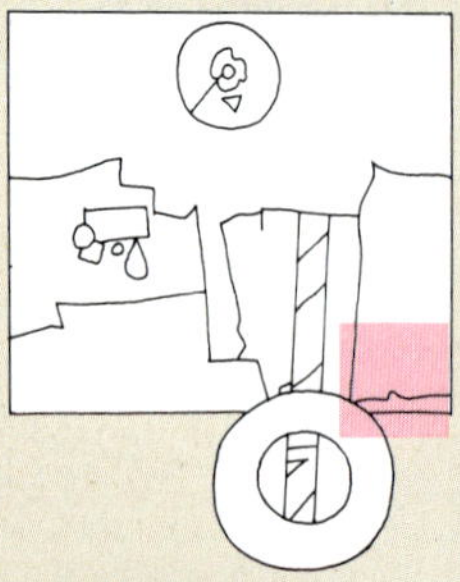

*RIGHT The commercial tyre projects inches from the composition board, while along the bottom to the right is the most richly painted section of the entire picture, a flourish of white and brown brushstrokes. Most of the detail, however, shows the disposition of lightly brushed marks creating an apparently random field, in which the play of activity somehow parallels the incorporation of more three-dimensional material elsewhere. But these highly non-referential painterly signs deliberately disavow the charged symbolic interpretations which have attended the similarly abstract-looking marks of the Abstract Expressionists; and also evade the structural suggestions which marks in this color elicited in Cubist compositions.*

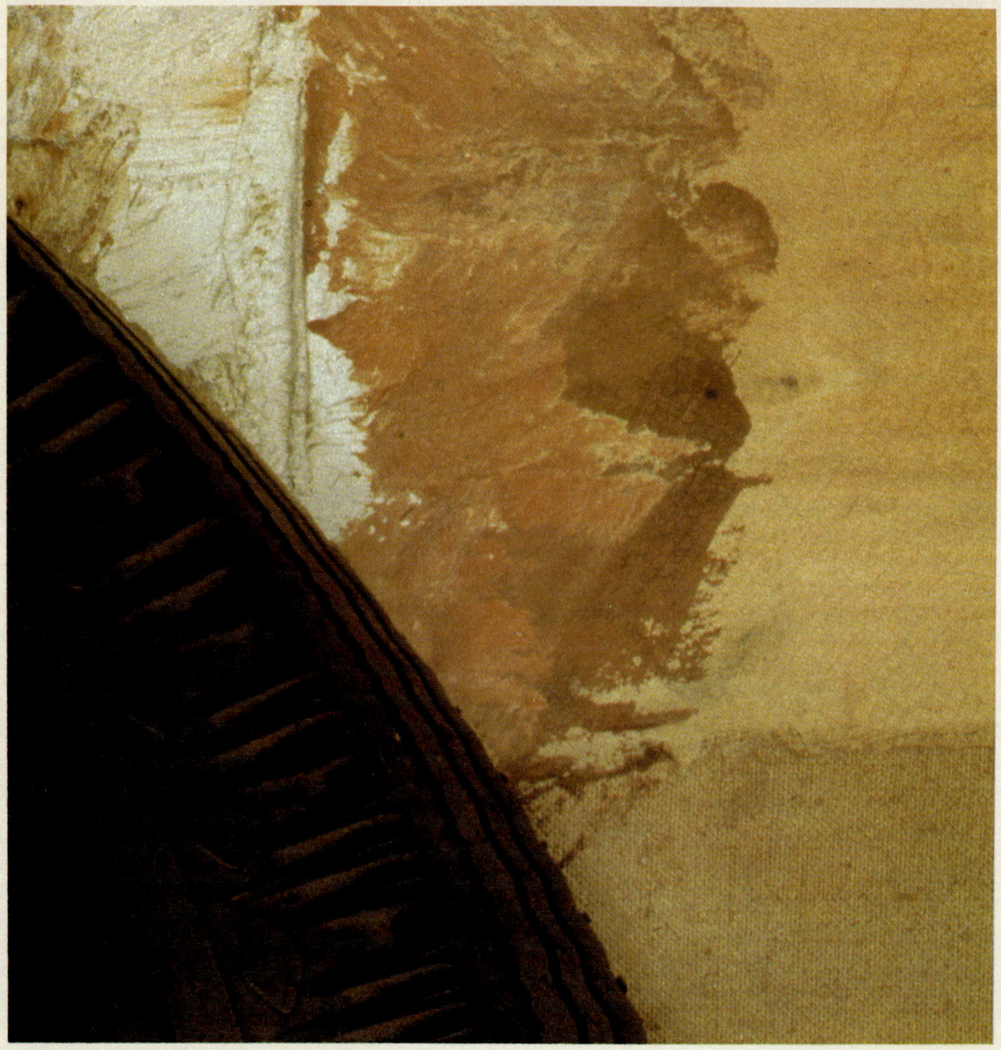

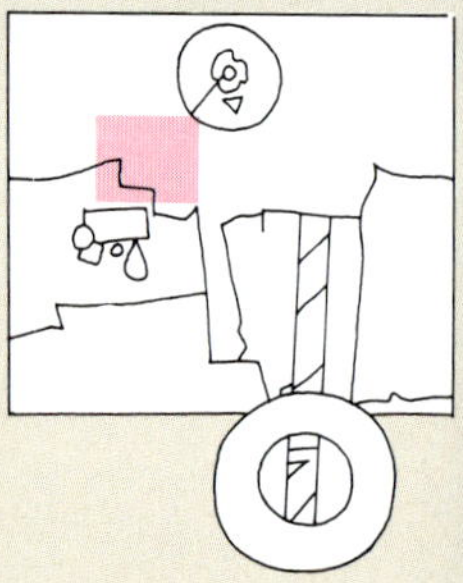

*ABOVE Rauschenberg used an extremely heterogeneous collection of materials: in this detail a reflector, a leather cable and a thick black cloth patch edged with a luminous stripe.*

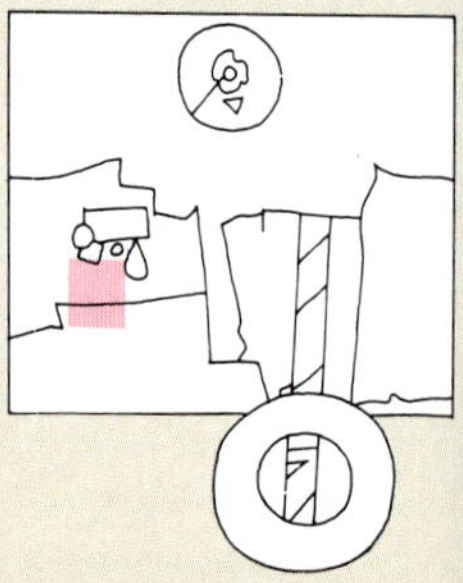

ACTUAL SIZE DETAIL
*Something of Rauschenberg's intricacy and anarchy is evident here. Folds, patches and creases of woven material are blended together and highlighted with dabs of white, black and red.*

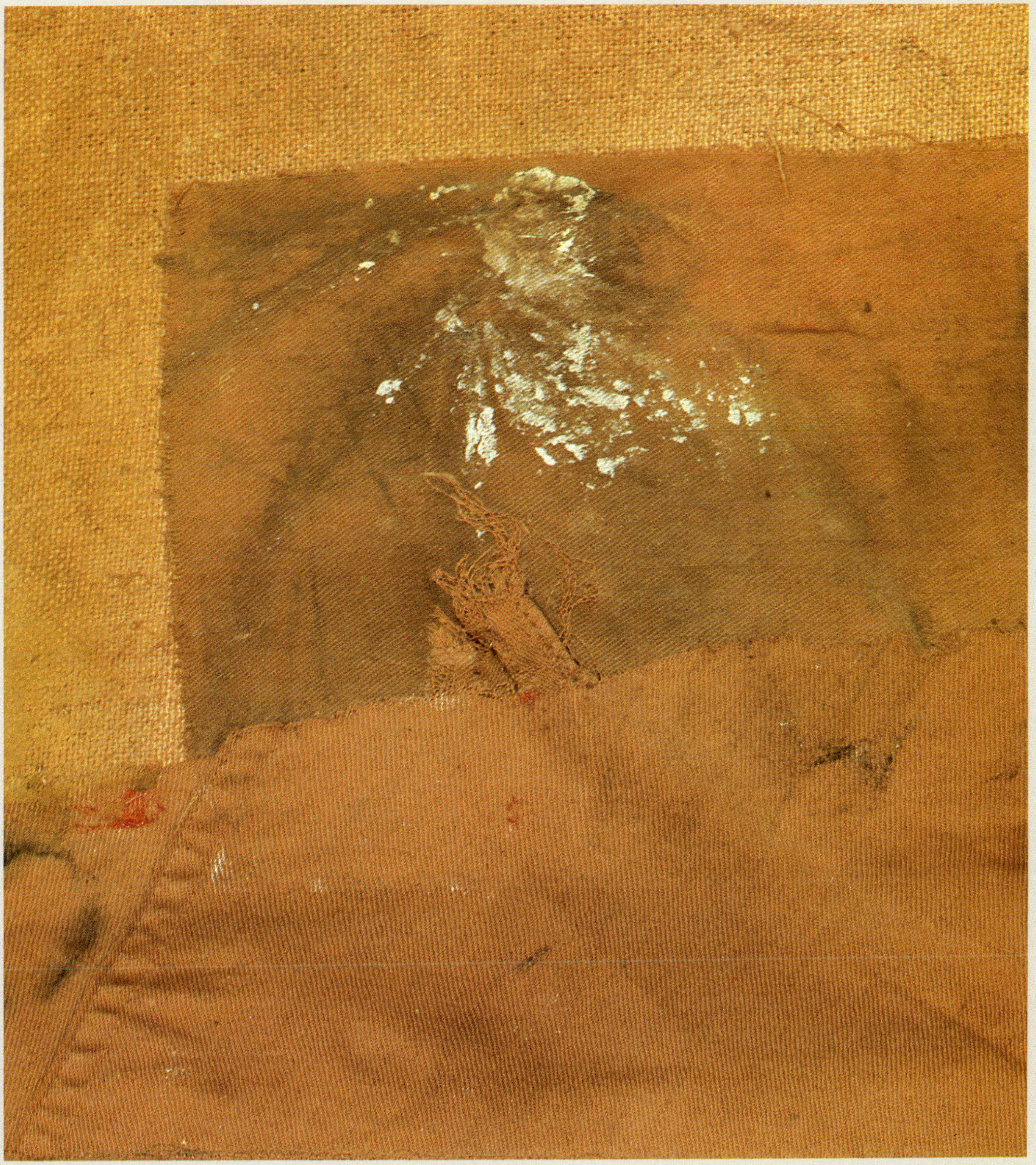

# RICHARD HAMILTON

*Towards a Definitive Statement . . .* (1962)
Mixed media, 61cm × 81.3cm/24in × 32in

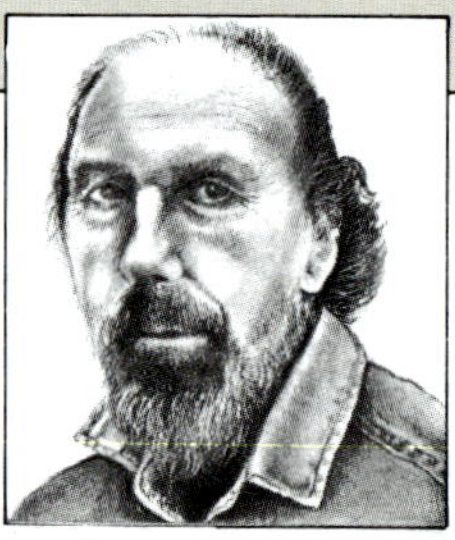

Richard Hamilton's art training began prior to World War II at the Royal Academy in London, and after the war, he continued his studies at the Academy and the Slade School of Art. However, it was not until the 1960s that he gained recognition through his association with the 'pop culture' of that period and as a founder of the Pop Art movement. Hamilton's return to more figurative work around 1951, as part of a search for contemporary relevance, was characterized by his use of visual sources such as photographs and graphics of commercial art. He commented that 'The return to nature came at second hand through the use of magazines rather than as a response to real landscape or still life objects or painting a person from life.'

He evolved an approach wherein elements were assembled from a plethora of daily visual material. This involved not only the juxtaposition of common images into new relationships, but also the mixing of visual conventions such as photography and technical drawing with more traditional styles and techniques of painting.

A consequence of using many elements composed of various materials is that their appearance alters to different degrees and in different ways over a period of time. For example, in *Towards a Definitive Statement . . .* which Hamilton painted in 1962, the color of the printed material taken from magazines and journals will fade with the exposure to light, and the white of the household undercoat paint which Hamilton used for this work will yellow more rapidly than will, for example, high-quality white artist's oil paint. This results in the uneven changing and alteration of relationships within the picture and the subsequent creation of new and unpredictable images. In this sense, the picture becomes a fluid and ever-changing vehicle. This demonstrates an attitude towards art which marks a radically different approach from the more traditional desire of the artist to retain the painting's original intentions and composition by the use of various solidifying agents such as varnish. Hamilton wanted the picture to remain an independent, constantly changing object and this element, combined with his use of non-traditional materials has marked him as an influential and innovative artist.

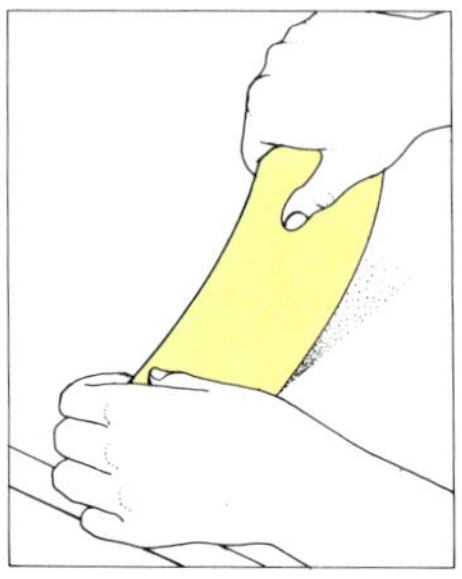

**1.** The hard-edged forms were taken from an optical diagram of a movie camera. First, pressure sensitive tape was applied to the unpainted ground.

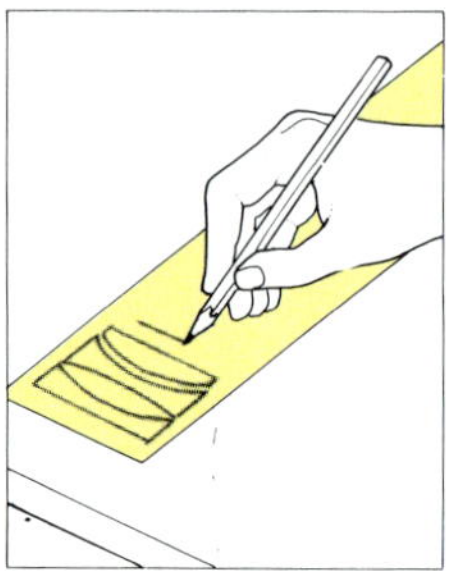

**2.** The design was drawn onto the tape.

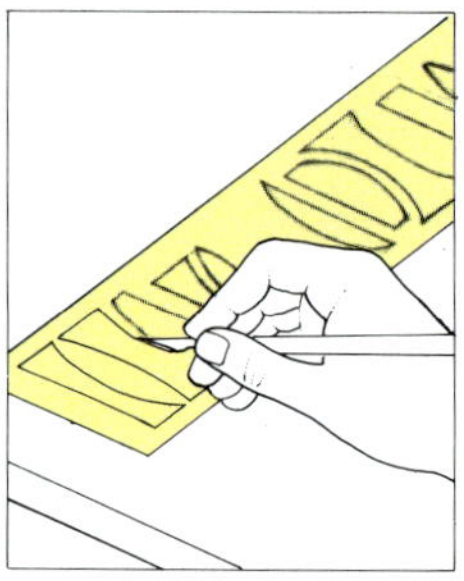

**3.** The drawn design was cut out with a scalpel.

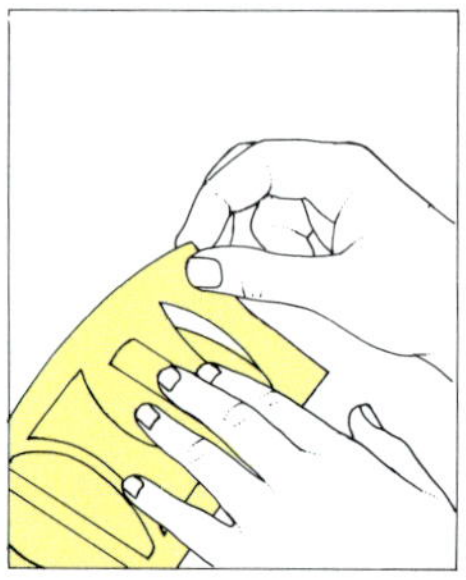

**4.** Excess tape was removed leaving the shape of the form.

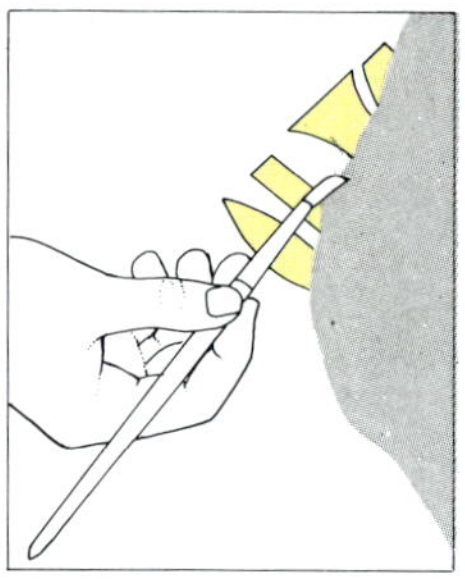

**5.** The area was painted over with silver paint.

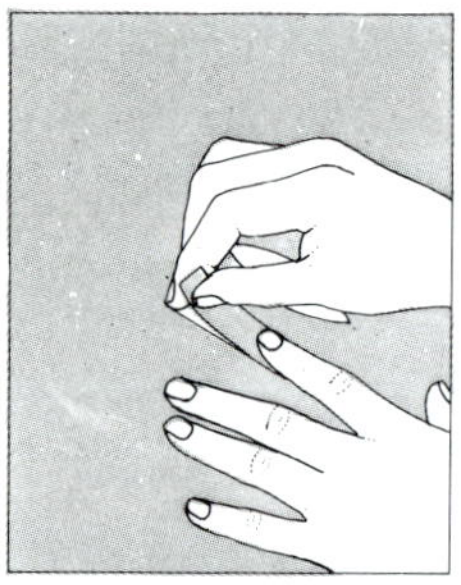

**6.** When the paint had dried, the tape was peeled away leaving the desired shape as unpainted ground.

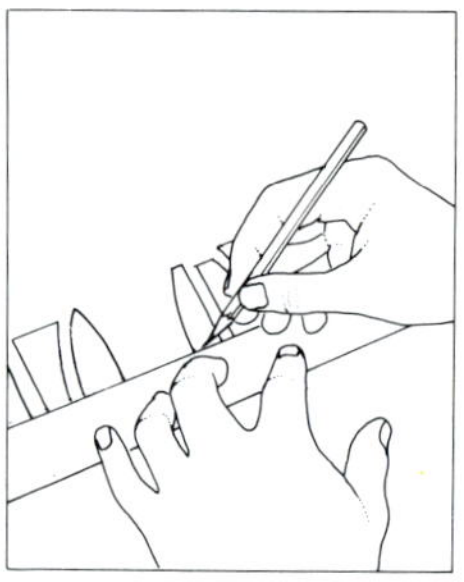

**7.** Linear elements were ruled in pencil and then white paint.

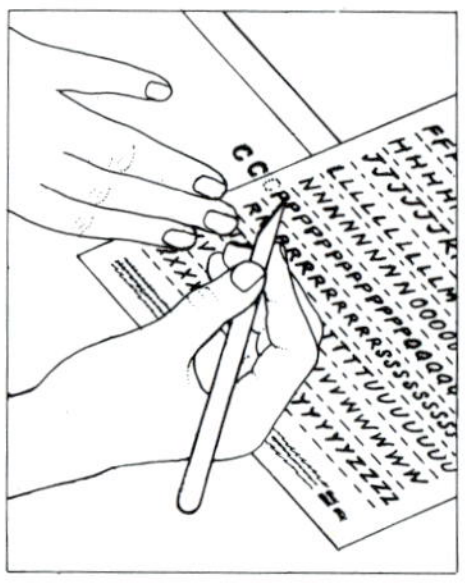

**8.** The letters 'CCCP' were applied by burnishing transfer lettering on to the painting.

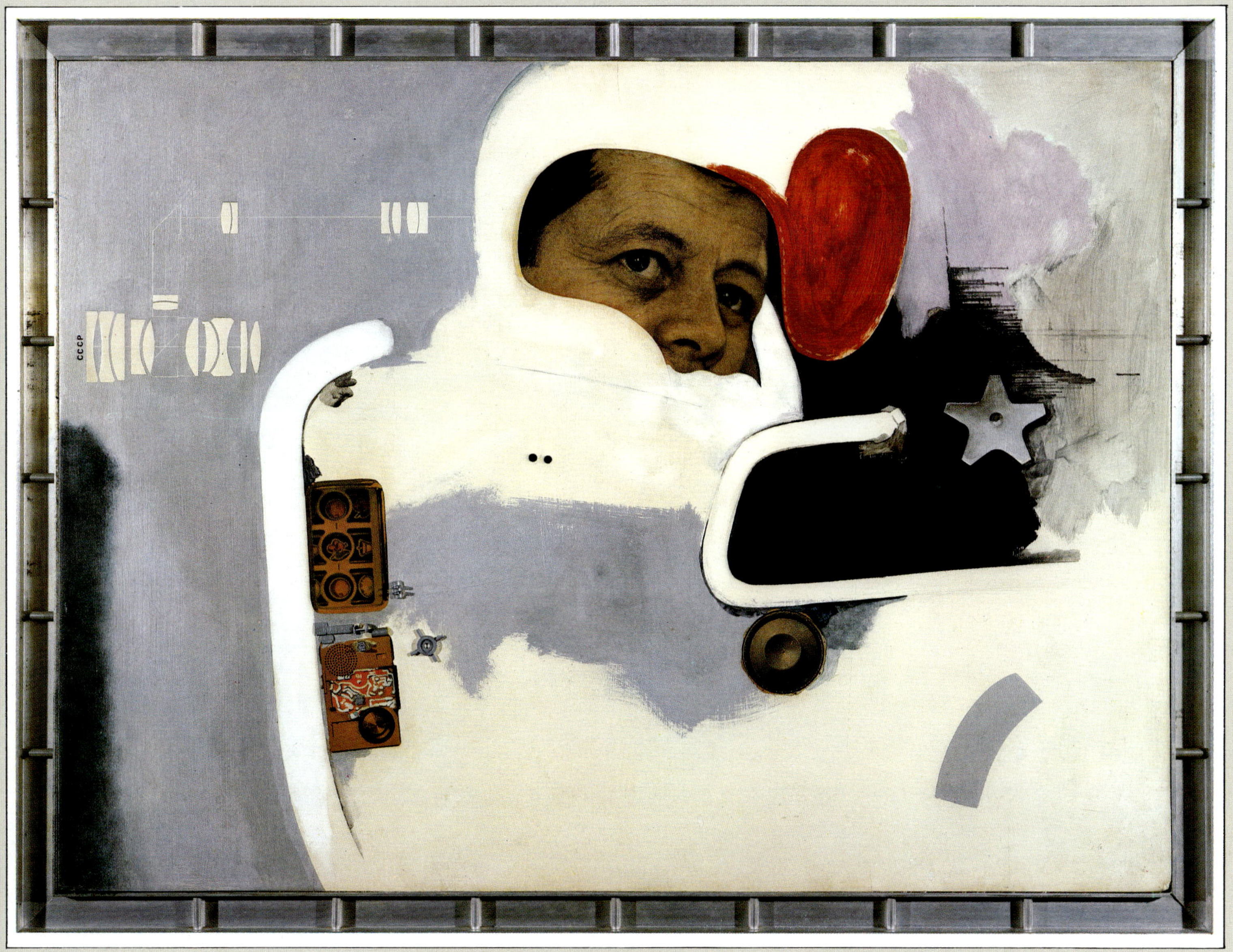

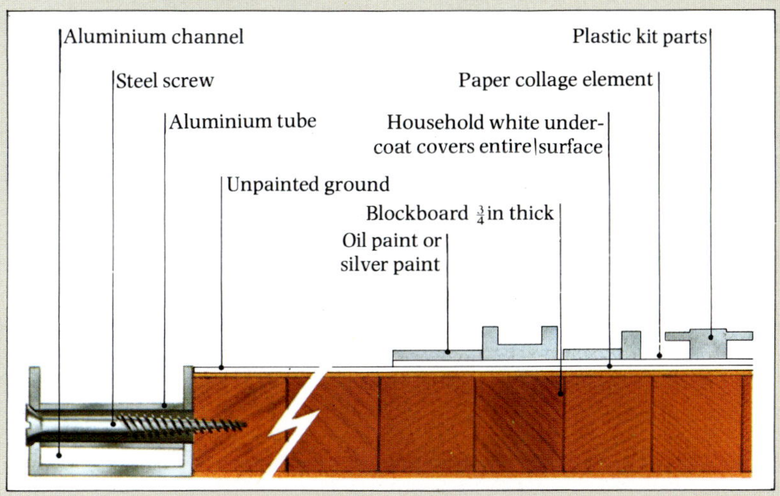


*The picture is on a support of wood blockboard prepared with an absorbent white undercoat. The ground has soft brushmarks and scratches and remains uncovered in many areas. The original design is in pencil. The photographic images are cut from color publications and stuck on to the board with paste and modified with overpainting. The painted areas are done in oil paint and 'silver' paint (probably an aluminum pigment in a synthetic resin medium). The application ranges from thick and opaque to thin glazed films. The hard-edged forms are achieved by stencilling. The metallic theme is carried in to the frame. 'The trick', said Hamilton, 'was to achieve a unity of disparate elements of similar size and shape.'*

*This sketch for the later work uses metal foil for the metallic effects. In the actual work, the softer, hazier effects are obtained from brushed silver paint. The reflections from this material are more in sympathy with the other surface qualities of the picture than the harsher silver foil.*

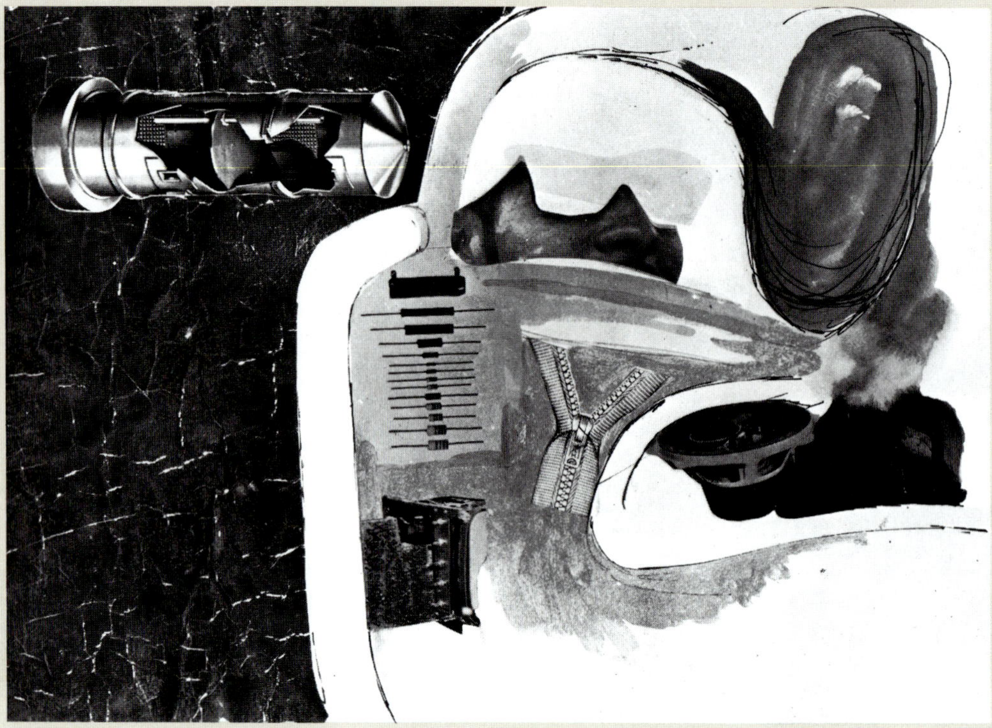

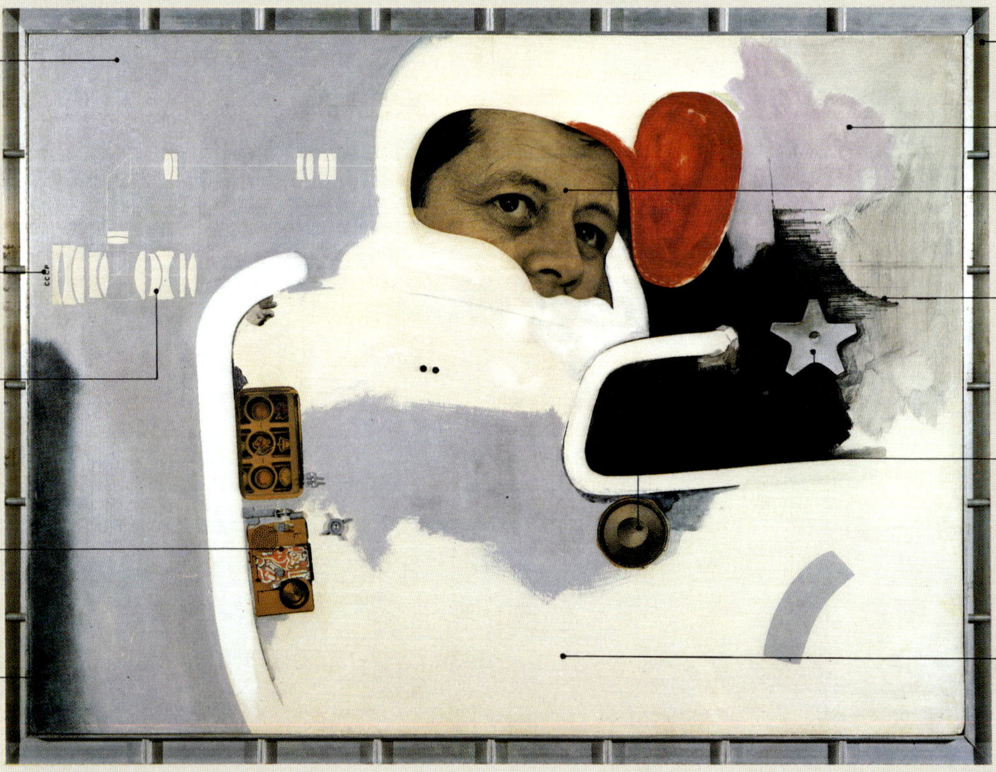

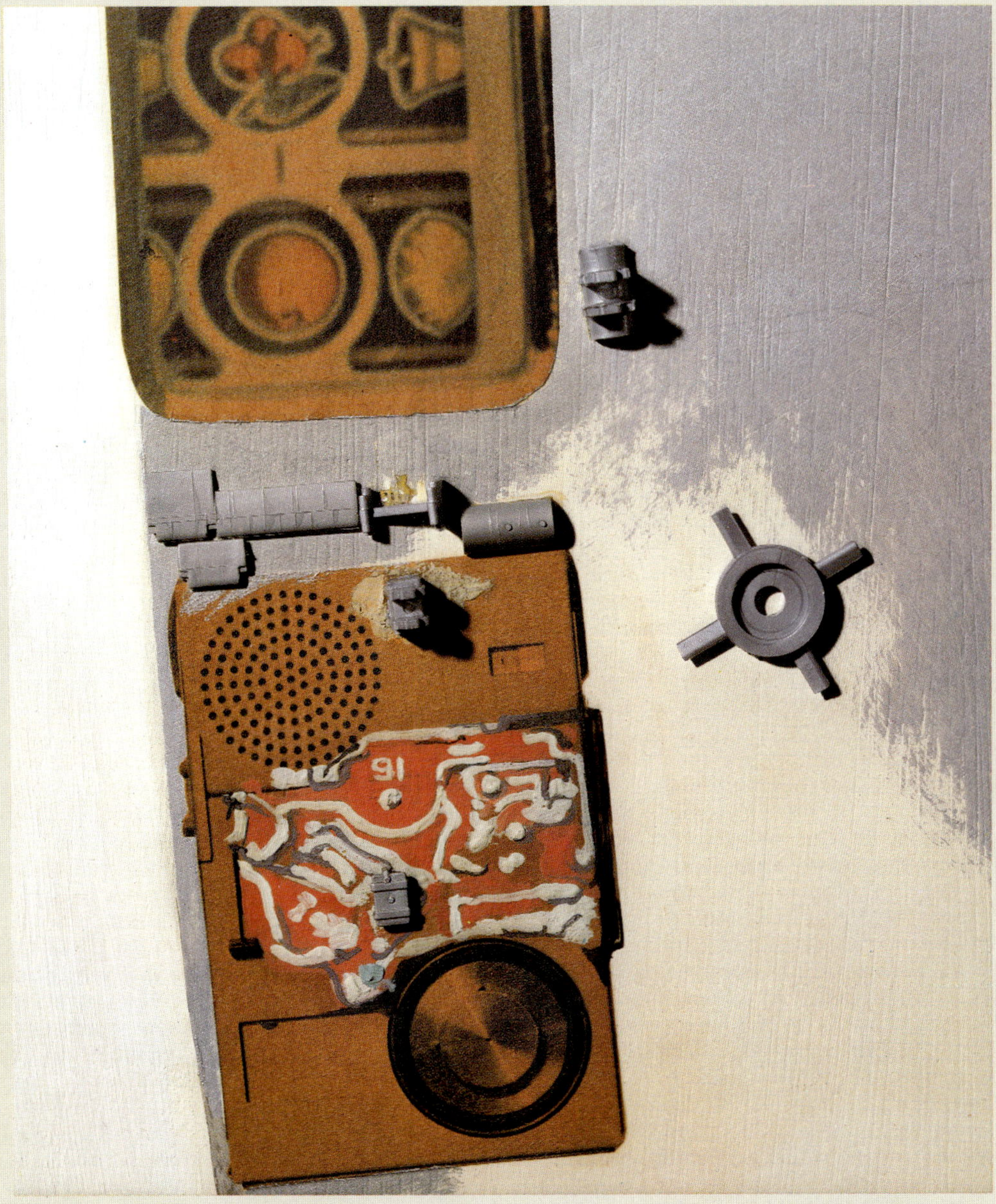

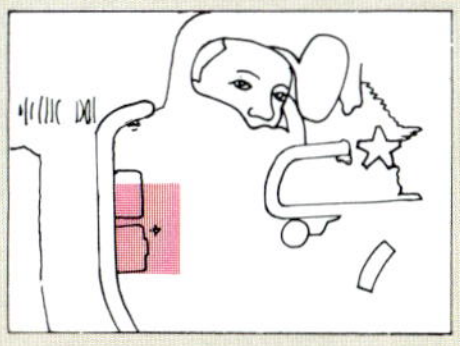

Actual size detail
*This detail is a good example of Hamilton's ability to mix and harmonize a variety of objects and techniques. He has incorporated a combination of graphic images, 'found' objects, and traditional paint media successfully to integrate and balance the picture plane. The uncovered ground which Hamilton used can be easily seen.*

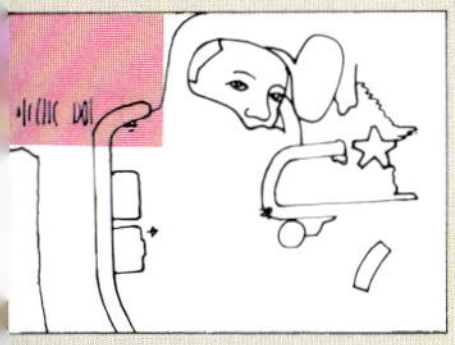

*This detail shows the vertical grain direction of the wood panel. The optical diagrams along the lower edge were created using a masking technique. The lettering is commercial dry transfer lettering. The hard-edged forms have been created by using a masking tape stencil and then overpainted to define the forms.*

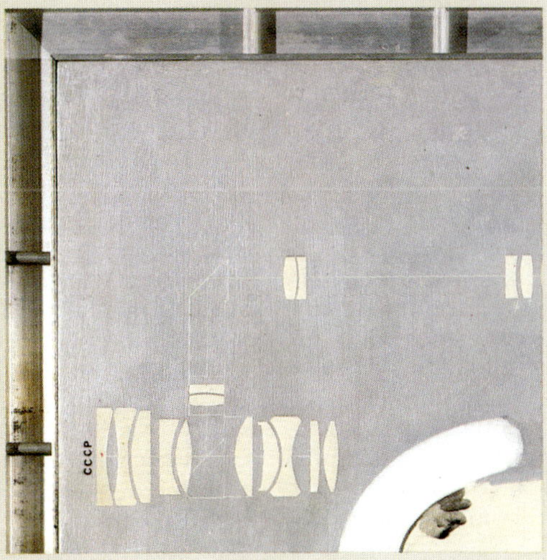

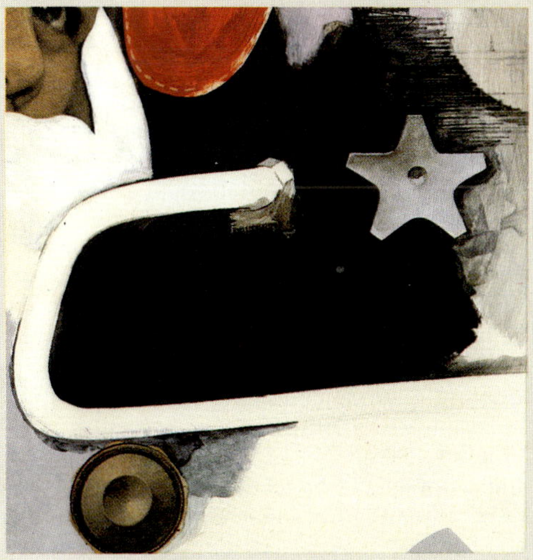

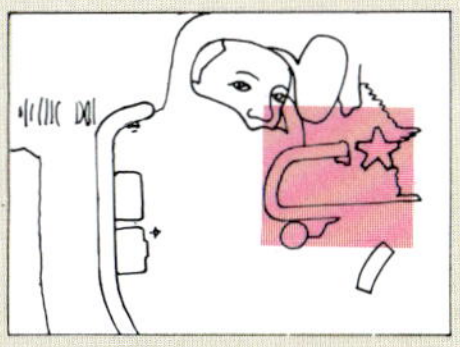

*In this section on the picture, the painted shape in the top righthand corner contrasts with the collaged element in the bottom lefthand corner. This juxtaposition of apparently disparate elements was one of the main techniques employed by Hamilton in this work.*

# ANDY WARHOL

*Marilyn Diptych (1962)*
Acrylic and silkscreen on canvas
208cm × 145cm/82in × 57in

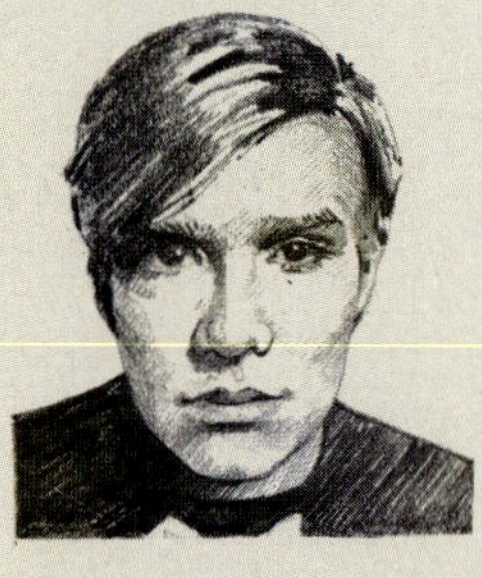

Andy Warhol was born in 1930 in Pittsburgh of immigrant Czech parents. He studied pictorial design at the Carnegie Institute of Technology, Pittsburgh, from 1945 to 1949, and then moved to New York, where he still lives and works. During his first 10 years in New York he worked as a commercial artist. 'The process of doing work in commercial art was machine-like, but the attitude had feeling to it.' Warhol found that, in working as a commercial artist, he had to be creative and original, and also had to satisfy those who were paying him.

Concurrently with his commercial work, Warhol held shows of his drawings in New York galleries and published six books of reproductions of thematic drawings. Although the books were printed in limited editions, the idea aped that of commercial art, and made his own art less exclusive, less unique and more accessible.

From 1960 to 1961 he took his subject matter from the category of mass communication – newspapers, comic strips and advertisements – and produced paintings which look bland and dispassionate. In his quest for an art that could be machine-like, that would look as though no human had produced it, he also wanted to encourage the idea that anybody and everybody could and should be able to produce art – 'I think everybody should be a machine.' In 1962 he executed some 'do-it-yourself' canvases; a seascape for example, in which the canvas is peppered with numbers placed in various areas, mimicking the popular pastime of painting-by-numbers.

In the same year he began using silkscreens to transfer readily available images on to his canvases. He spoke of this process with pleasure '... I'm using silkscreens now. I think somebody should be able to do all my painting for me . . . I think it would be so great if more people took up silkscreens so that no one would know whether my picture was mine or somebody else's.'

Warhol's image of Marilyn Monroe is taken from a publicity photograph by Gene Korman, used for the 1953 film *Niagara*. It was therefore a well-known public image and was already removed from her real life persona. By 1962 Marilyn Monroe was famous, not only through her films, but also through the manipulation and dissemination of printed images. These are the two approaches which Warhol has chosen as the basis for this work. Newspaper pictures are in black and white, and magazines in color; television sets and films also transmit images in both black and white and color. *Marilyn Diptych* could well be making a subtle comment about such differences. And for him more seems to be better than less; 50 images of Marilyn Monroe have a more powerful impact than two, because they emphasize Warhol's mechanical techniques.

Warhol probably worked on *Marilyn Diptych* on a horizontal surface and it would have been screenprinted and handpainted before being stretched. Whether or not the canvases were fixed to stretchers before or after the screenprinting process, Warhol has decided to give it an unplanned air by leaving the bottom few inches bare.

After the two canvases for *Marilyn Diptych* were prepared with a thin coat of off-white commercial paint, the multiple image of Marilyn was added by forcing paint through the prepared silkscreen. This is usually done with a squeegee, a fin of rubber rather like a windscreen wiper, which is pulled along the length of the screen. The trace it leaves depends on the amount of pigment which is squeezed on to the upper surface of the screen and on how the operator moves the squeegee. In the second vertical row of the righthand canvas, particularly the second image down, the silkscreen has been charged with far too much paint, and it has been forced through the mesh to finish up as a thick mess which almost blots out the image of Marilyn Monroe's face; it is also apparent that the edge of the squeegee was marred by something and thus prevented from making an even sweep. Where the screen has been overloaded with paint, the weave of the fabric is very apparent.

Both canvases of *Marilyn Diptych* would have had the same preliminary silkscreen printing. The righthand one was left at this stage, while further processes were applied to the lefthand canvas. Pencil lines drawn over the screenprint are visible on the righthand canvas, drawn as if to mark the limit of the dimensions of the screen. They serve little purpose on the righthand canvas, but it can be assumed that similar lines helped in guiding the application of color on the left and are now overpainted.

Six separate colors have been applied – pink for the face, yellow for the hair, turquoise for the eyeshadow and collar, red for the lips, white for the teeth, and orange for the background. The exact order of their application is difficult to determine since they do not overlay, but instead abut each other. In some images, however, the yellow overlaps the pink, and the orange overlaps the yellow. The application of each separate color must have been aided by some form of stencil which masked off the other areas. When all six colors had been painted on, again either by Warhol or assistants, a further layer of screenprinting was undertaken, since much of the detail and coherence of the image would have been lost under the color.

The cosmetic glamor of the lefthand painted canvas works as a necessary foil for the somber *grisaille* of the righthand one, which unrelieved might have been too raw a statement about a beautiful yet tragic victim.

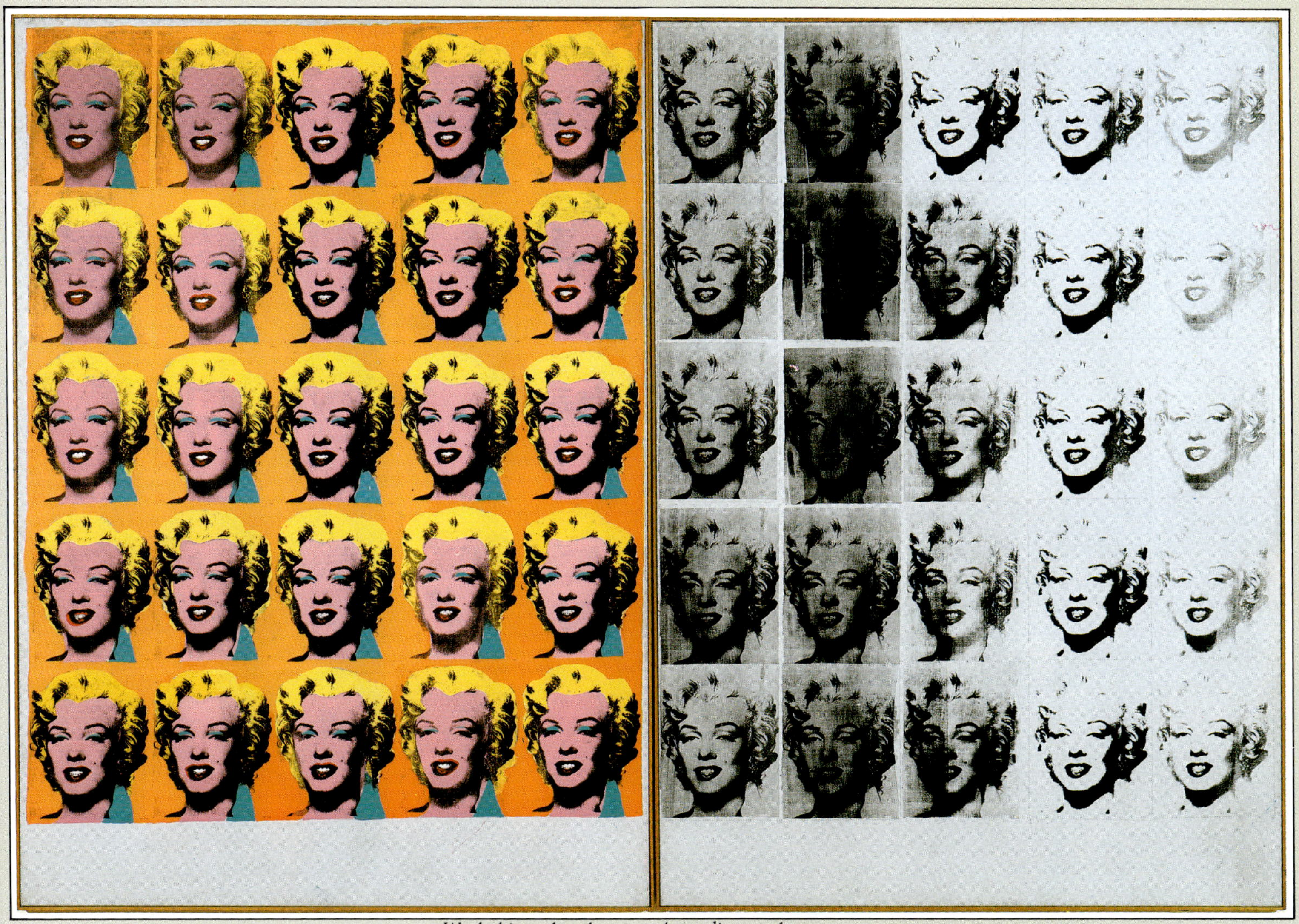

*Warhol introduced a new era of portraiture with this work. Not only did he successfully infuse a traditional genre, the portrait, with immediacy and power, he also brought to it new materials and techniques, acrylic paint and silkscreen printing.*

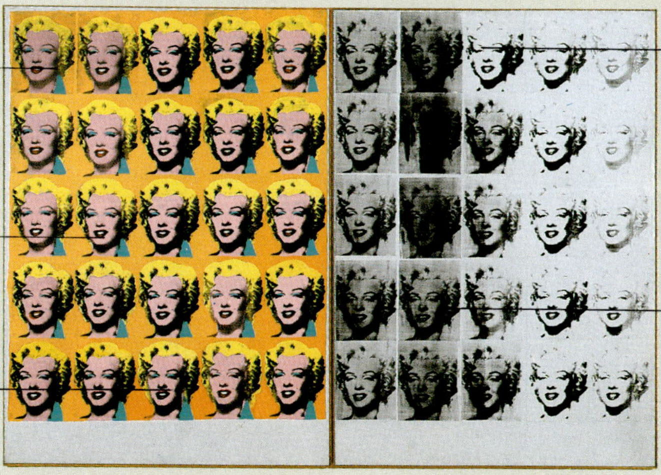

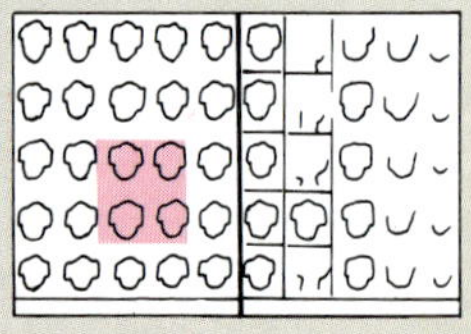

*RIGHT The differences caused by the application of acrylic paint by hand are noticeable here; the individual ways in which the yellow designates the hair, and the turquoise the stand-up collar, are the most obvious. The black pigment which was laid down by the silkscreen process shows no sign of manual application, but the strokes of a wide brush are visible in the yellow and orange.*

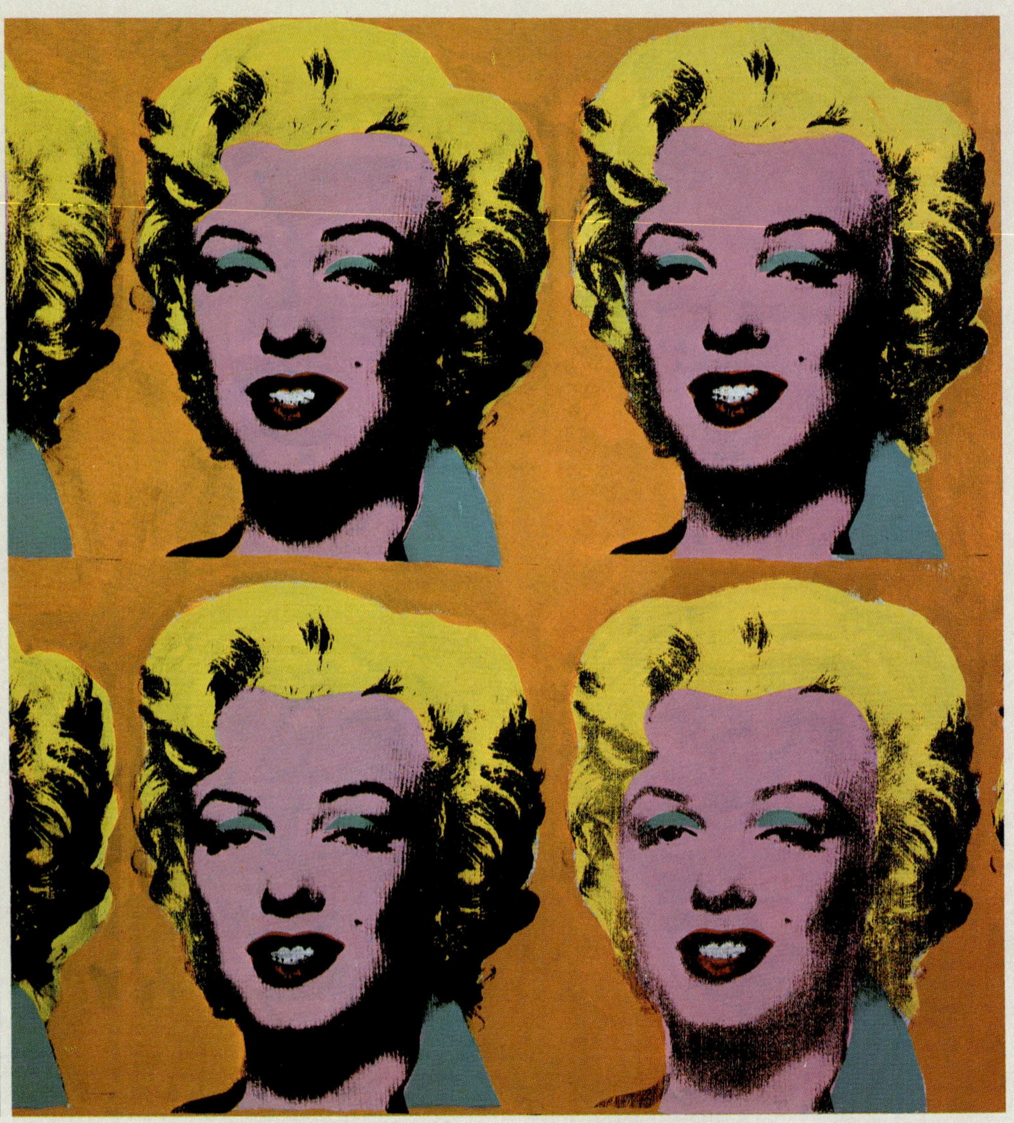

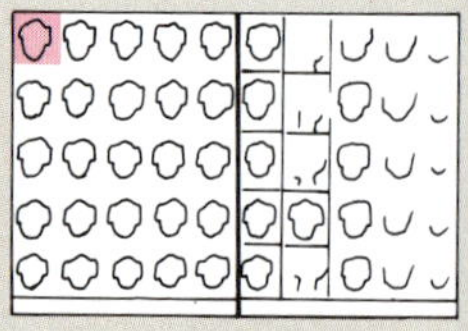

*ACTUAL SIZE DETAIL The six separate colors, pink, yellow, turquoise, red, white and orange, can be clearly seen. The colors are those of the advertising world, and do not conform to the standard range traditionally available to artists. The lefthand side of* Marilyn Diptych *was first printed with the silkscreen, painted with acrylic colors, and finally given a second layer of screenprint. The original silkscreen layer can be seen at the lefthand edge of the hair, where the overpainting with yellow and orange do not quite meet, revealing the earlier process. The order of laying on the paint can be gleaned by the way the yellow overlaps the pink at various points, and the orange the yellow.*

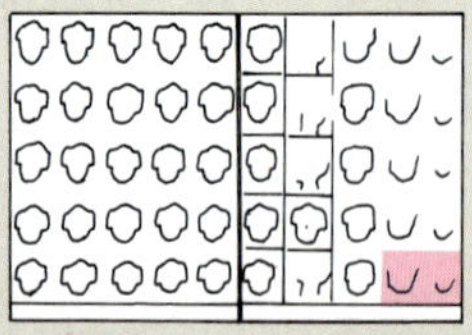

*BELOW These two images point up the different quantity of pigment with which the silkscreen was charged prior to printing. In the righthand image, the weave of the screen is apparent, and this is usually avoided in commercial printing.*

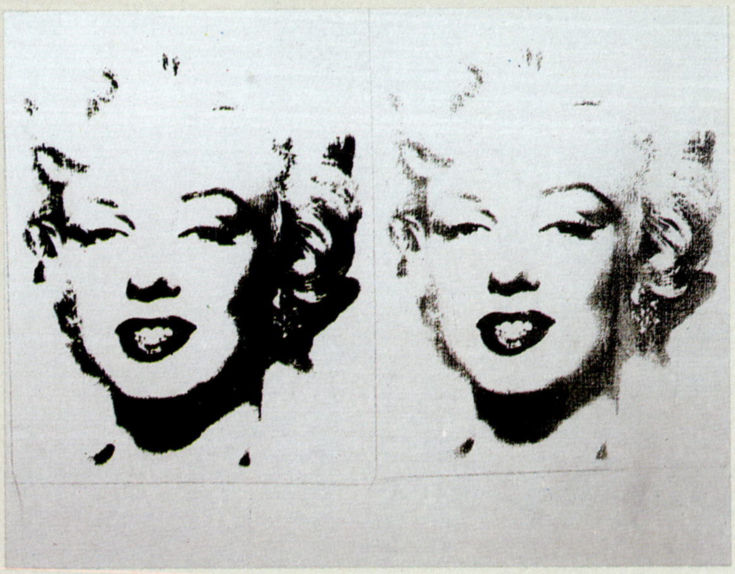

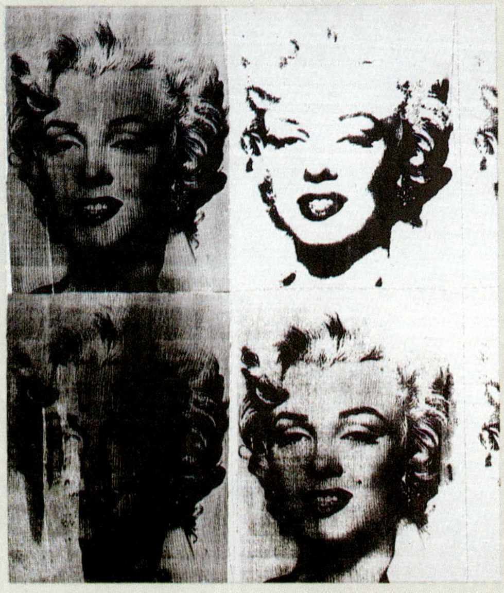

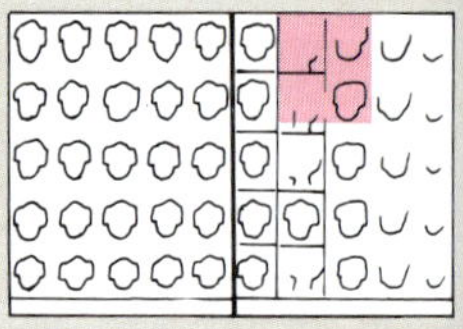

*LEFT The canvas, primed with a commercial off-white paint, shows through as a light ground between the dots of pigment laid down by the silkscreen. The result of adding far too much paint to the screen is seen in the bottom lefthand image, where it has forced its way through the mesh and almost obliterates the design.*

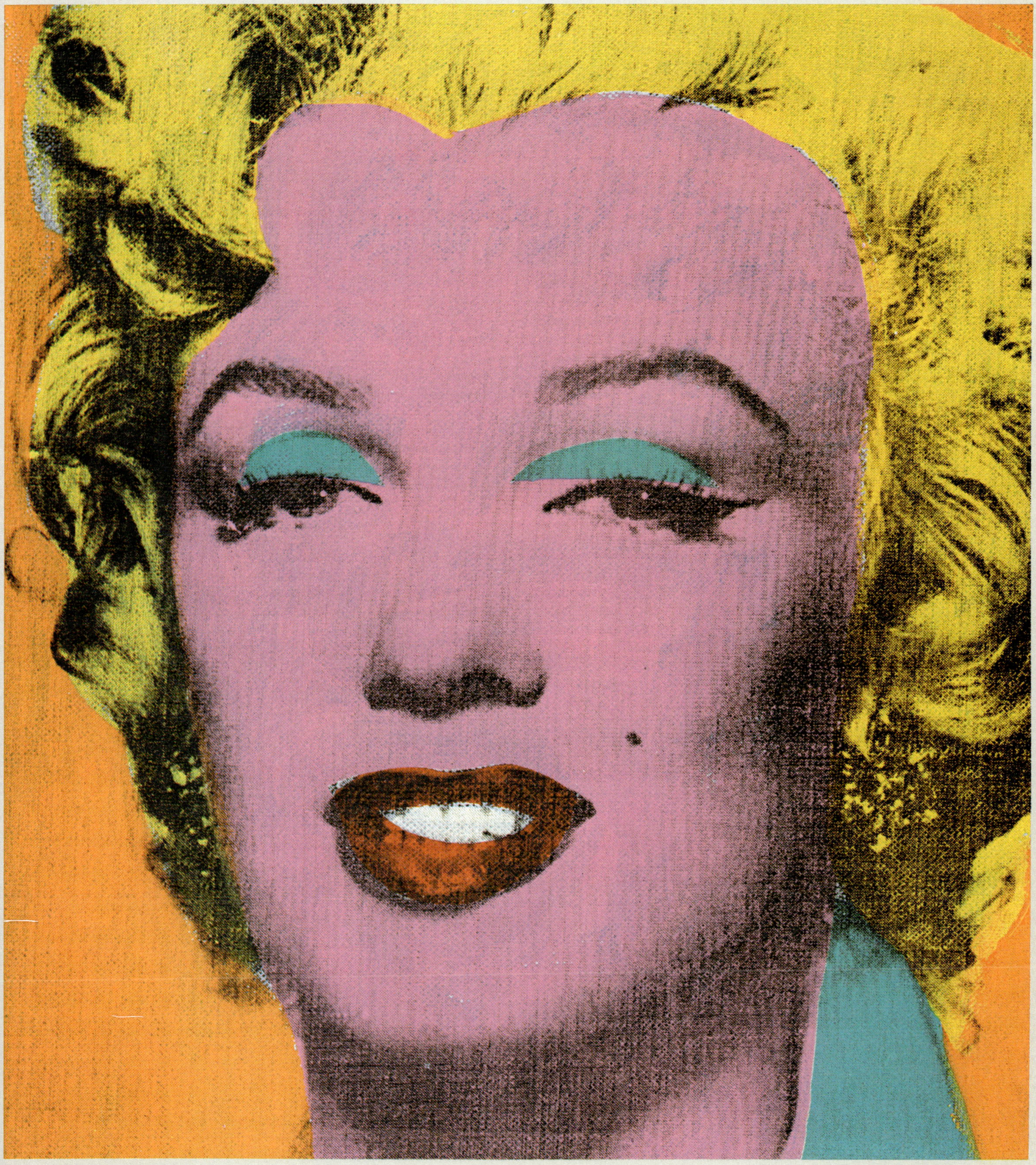

# FRANK STELLA

*Hyena Stomp (1962)*
Acrylic on canvas
195.6cm × 195.6cm/77in × 77in

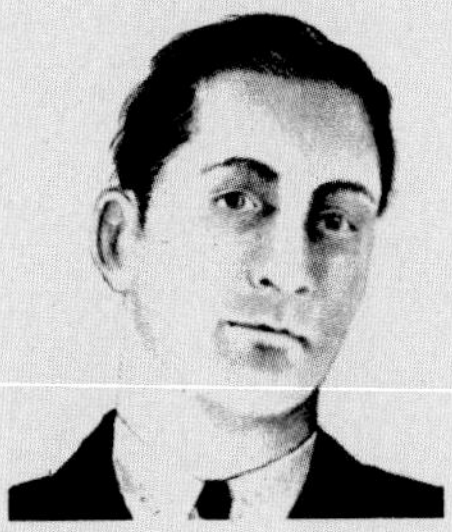

Born in 1936, Frank Stella grew up with a generation that witnessed the emergence of the New York 'school' of painting which drew world attention away from Paris, where most of the significant art revolutions had centered since the 1860s.

Stella was in close contact with the achievements of this group of American painters which included Pollock, Mark Rothko (1903-1970) and Louis; at art school in Princeton he became immersed in many of the technical and practical procedures that allowed this 'revolution' to take place, such as the use of acrylic and commercial paints which had, by 1960, eclipsed traditional oil painting in American art schools. While still a student Stella made some of his own paintings in the 'manner' of these recent masters; later he confessed that they 'tired' him both to make and to look at. His solution to this crisis was deceptively simple: to make the composition 'the same all over', like a type of enormous, yet simple, pattern. Stella's choice of materials for this was conditioned by his vacation jobs as a house painter; he used commercial brushes and equipment and enamel, motor vehicle paint and other industrial paints, as well as the usual acrylic and oil paints.

He first made his impact in 1959 when four of his plain black enamel striped paintings, some 3 meters (10 ft) high, were shown at the Museum of Modern Art, New York. These works contained variations on a repeating theme of brushed stripes within pencil-ruled margins, with a fine line of unprimed canvas between. In *Hyena Stomp*, painted in 1962, these bands are made crisp by the use of masking tape; in 1959 the edges were rough.

Stella needed to work through a series of at least 17 black paintings in order to explore all of the possible evolutions of his simple geometrical concept. *Hyena Stomp* forms part of a series painted between 1961 and 1964, for which Stella used the basis of a square, very often of 195.6cm (77 in) and it is a central work in this evolving series.

In an earlier square painting called *Sharpeville*, a decreasingly smaller set of striped squares shrinks towards a small central square; a rather predictable solution. Stella created a clockwise 'spiral' of stripes in *Hyena Stomp*. It enters from the top righthand corner in the form of the deep crimson stripe, taking the eye in decreasing lengths to a center that hooks up into itself, yet is made to look very complicated because it is cut into by the intersection of three diagonals, created and emphasized by the L-turns of the stripes.

Later paintings in this series were to play with only one diagonal or turn the stripes sideways to enter from the edge of the canvas in alternating colors. Another work, *Jasper's Dilemma* (1962 to 1963) repeats the structure and scale of *Hyena Stomp*, and then parodies it with a monochrome version which is painted directly to the left of it; the effect is like two large square eyes, one colorblind, the other garishly striped.

The structure of *Hyena Stomp* can be analyzed by visually isolating the triangle of stripes on the right, whose outer edge is composed of a deep crimson red, a pure lemon yellow and a cold mid-blue. This trio can be traced in ever-decreasing lengths spiraling in an anti-clockwise fashion into the center. Stella starts each new crimson stripe at the far right corner of the last blue stripe (facing towards the center).

There are eight more stripes, each of a different hue, before the red-yellow-blue combination occurs again, making a 'palette' of eleven shades in all. The more subtle tones of grey, orange-red, mid-red and the cadmium green could have been mixed from the stronger tones of blue, deep viridian, yellow and crimson in varying parts.

This structural analysis reveals that once Stella had decided upon the lefthand sequence of colors, for instance, the remaining three-quarters of the canvas was pre-determined with an almost automatic logic of its own. Once the paint had dried on one stripe the old masking tape could be pulled off and a new stripe masked off, leaving a constant gap between each.

The work was probably planned on graph paper, but the sheer scale of the canvas would have transformed its appearance. The impact can be contrasted with Matisse's *L'escargot* with its 'spiral' of saturated color, strangely both creating and destroying space.

Stella's paintings of the period of *Hyena Stomp* were exhibited with some Op art works in 1965, on the assumption that it attempted to dazzle with optical illusion. Certainly *Hyena Stomp* seems at one moment like a square tunnel, the next like an aerial view of an ancient Mesopotamian *ziggurat*, or stepped pyramid. But Stella's colors do not seem to have been selected simply because they occur in bands of vibrating complementaries, such as a blue against a yellow (its opposite), or a red against a green, but rather they also have a strange pre-selected appearance, comparable with a color manufacturer's chart and are not simply Op art shades. *Hyena Stomp* was painted in the same year as Andy Warhol's *Marilyn* and other works of Pop Art and Stella's colors recall those of a flag or a piece of commercial packaging. The title, which in every case was carefully chosen by the artist, reveals Stella's own attitude towards the work, and refers to his love of jazz. *Hyena Stomp*, as the name suggests, strikes the eye like an African-inspired jazz rhythm, attempting a fusion of two contradictory elements; rich, untamed color, caged in by a highly-disciplined and sophisticated structure.

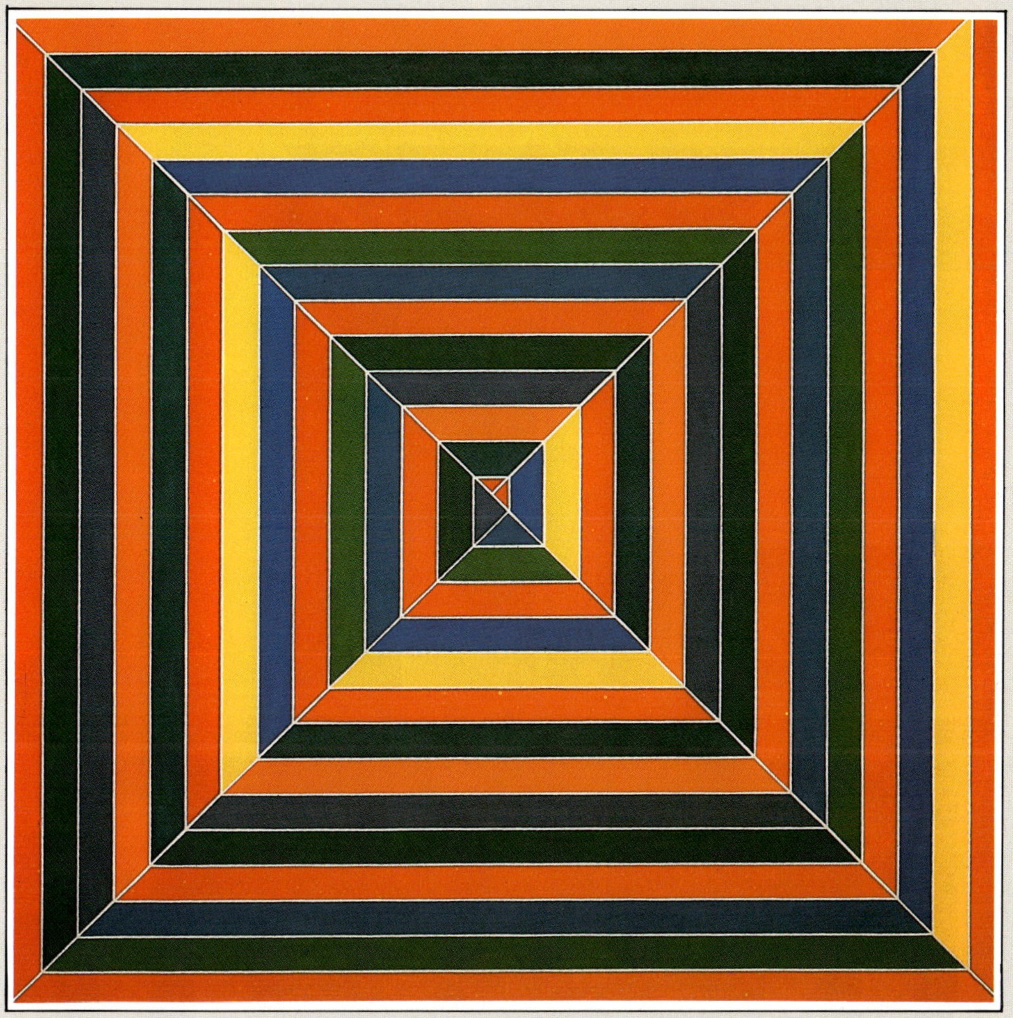

*A precise geometry is achieved by the use of measurement and masking tape combined with unvarying colored stripes which repeat themselves in sequences of groups of three.* Hyena Stomp *and similar works in the series have been likened to the appearance of a commercial color-maker's chart. Stella said that he tried to keep the paint 'as good as it was in the can'. Nevertheless, the diagonals seem to create an illusion of space which creates an illusionistic receding or emerging architecture, and denies any sense of flatness. The light-holding potential of the colors is also exploited to create a spiral towards the center which sets up another type of movement.*

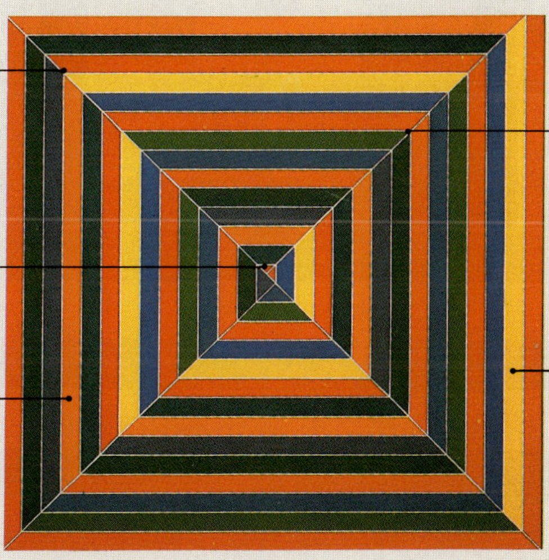

A constant gap of about 5mm (1/5in) of unprimed canvas is revealed between the lines

The spiral of stripes disrupts the placing of the third diagonal

The acrylic colors are mixed without white or black and brushed on without any modulation of tone within each stripe

A red-green complementary pair of stripes is arranged so they meet a similar pair of different hue and thus create a continuation rather than abrupt change

The cadmium yellow strip is the brightest color used and acts as a light source as it resonates against the red and blue primary colors next to it

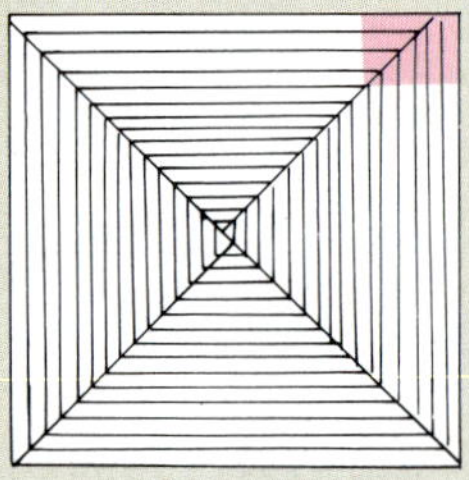

*RIGHT The upper right corner of the painting is unique as the deep red stripe is squared off by the frame, revealing the presence of a spiral and preventing the diagonal from meeting the corner. Stella uses a combination of primary colors on the right edge which reappear to the left and continue into the center. These groupings are often visually disrupted by their color affinities with neighboring stripes.*

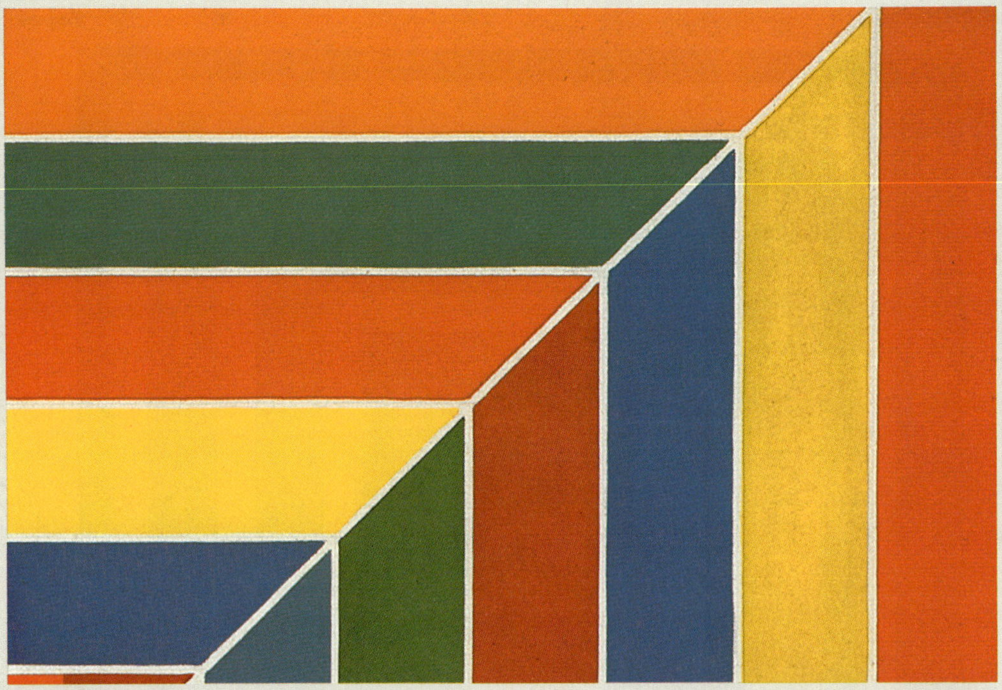

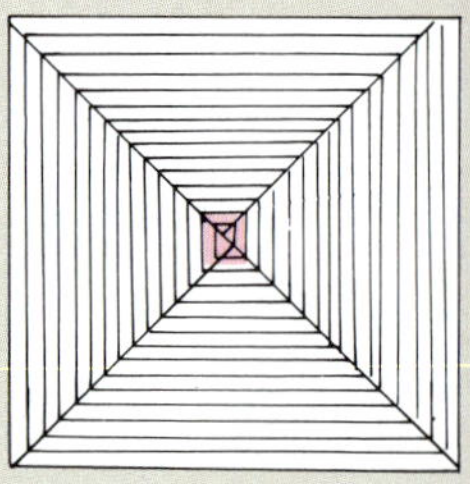

*ACTUAL SIZE DETAIL The intersection of the three diagonals at the center has created a set of four triangles which echo on a miniature scale the four large triangles of the composition of* Hyena Stomp. *The spiral system has been carefully calculated to preserve the widths of the line so that the center also appears to interlock into itself. The color combinations have been calculated so that a triangle of red appears to jump out of the very center. This is composed of two different hues of red, surrounded by a mesh of hues of blue, blue green, and shades of cadmium green. The acrylic color was brushed into areas that had been individually isolated with strips of masking tape which created the 'hard edge' style which was very popular in the painting of the 1960s.*

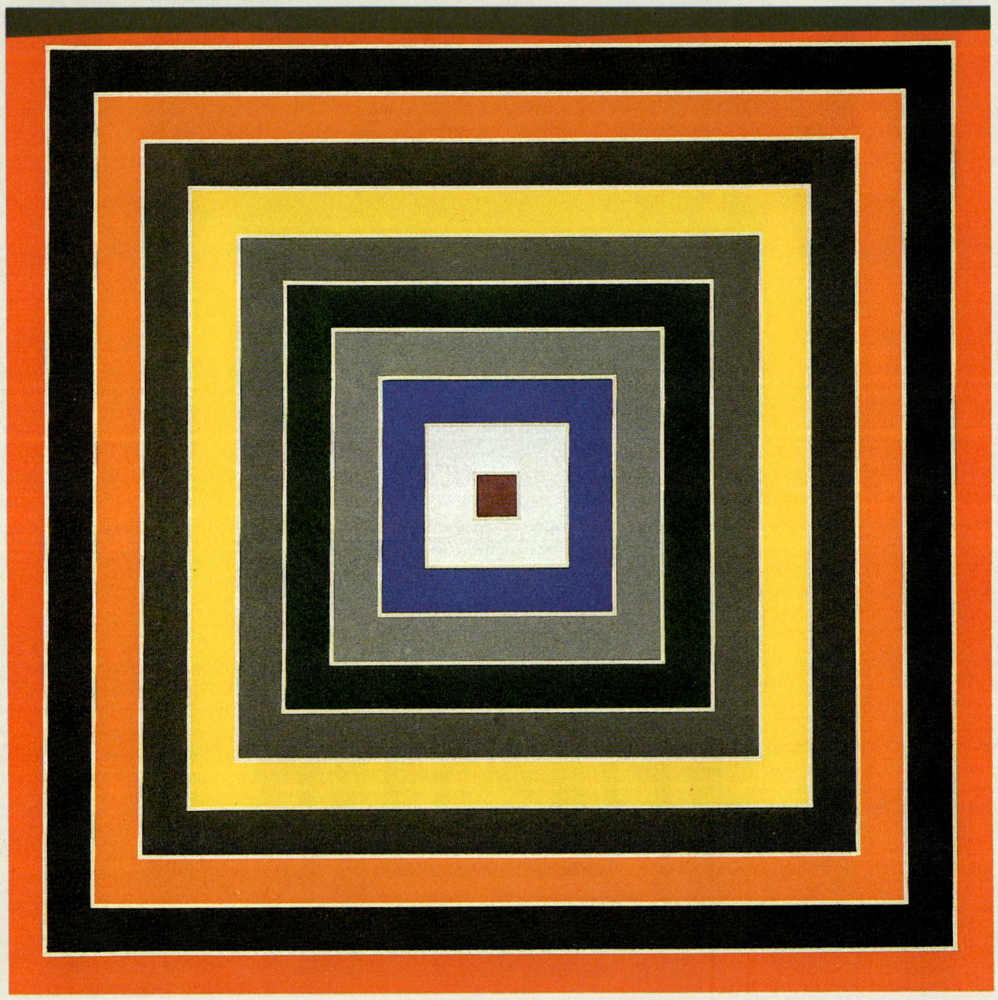

*RIGHT In 1959 Stella had produced a large rectangular painting of black enamel stripes called* Tomlinson Court Park *which anticipated the structure of this and* Hyena Stomp *by three years. This painting,* Untitled 1962, *like the larger* Sharpeville *(1962), broke away from the use of single color stripes in order to experiment with the optical force of stripes of different colors radiating from a central square, but here avoiding the use of diagonal lines. The result is both minimal and architectural and permits color to function as both light and space. It produced an image that has a neon quality suited to an urban setting and New York corporation architecture.*

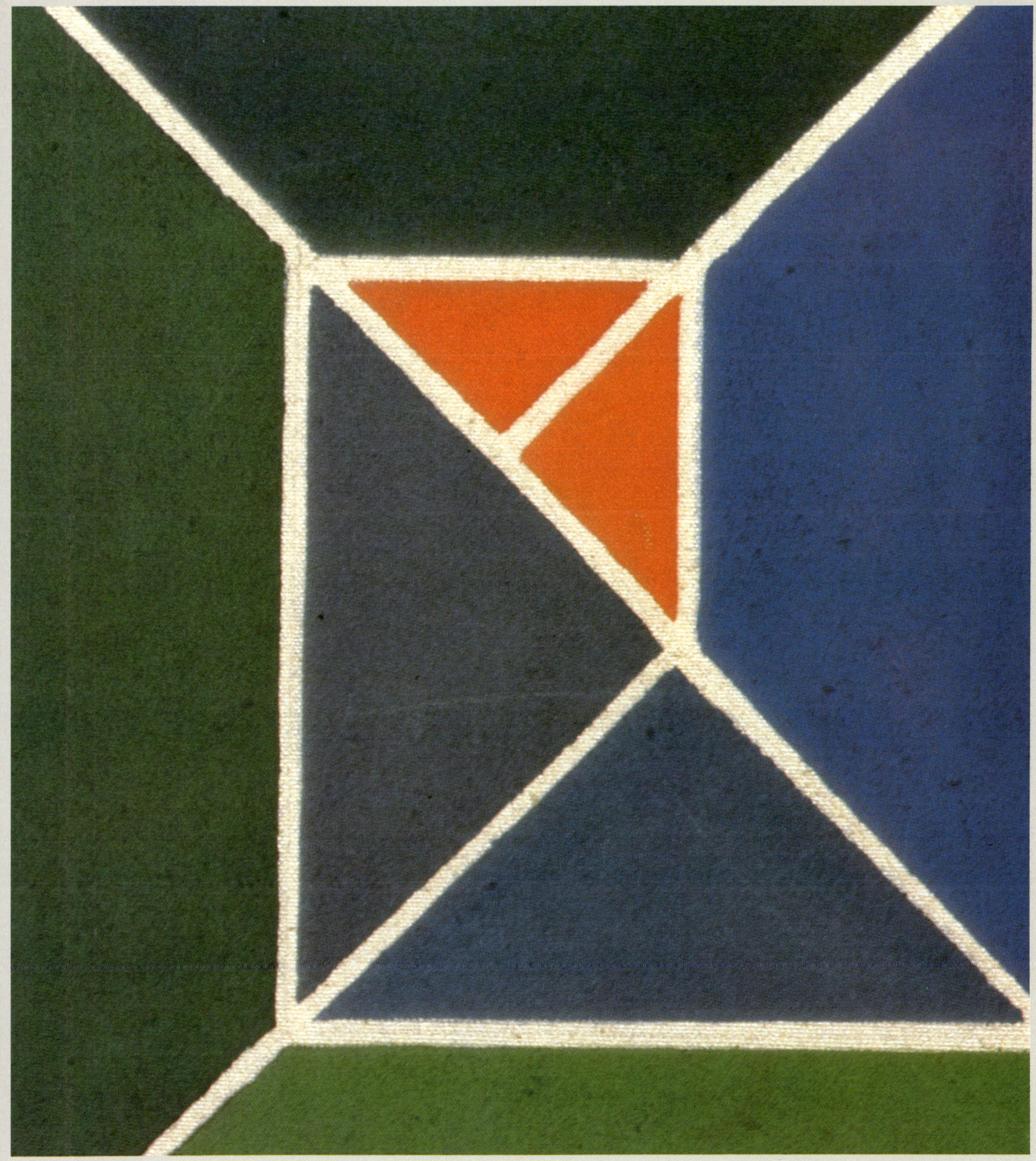

# Roy Lichtenstein

*Whaam!* (1963)

Magna on canvas (two canvases), 172cm × 269cm/68in × 106in

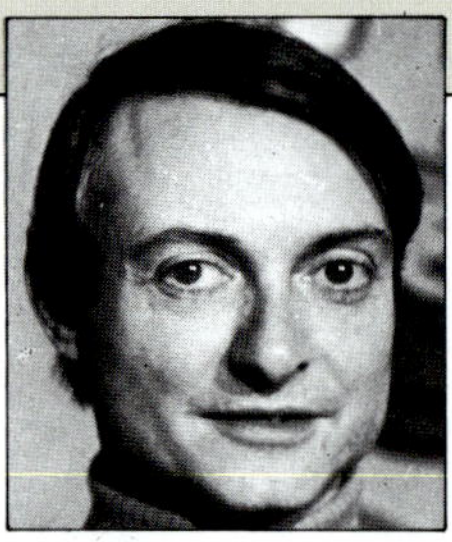

Roy Lichtenstein's work based on comic strips began in 1960 and marked a complete departure from his previous work which had been broadly in the Abstract Expressionist manner. By 1961 Lichtenstein's interest in cartoon elements, which had begun as a half-serious attempt to copy a cartoon without alteration, had come to dominate his work. In the period from 1961 to 1965, Lichtenstein made paintings derived from advertising imagery and common objects, of which the comic strip pictures are the most complex. They fall into three main groups – love and romance, science-fiction, and war and violence. The war paintings, of which *Whaam!* is one, are cinematographic close-up images of land warfare and aerial combat which emphasize explosions, the trajectories of bullets and the sounds of battle.

Lichtenstein does not simply magnify a frame from a comic strip. In some works he combined elements from several models, others, like *Whaam!*, were inventions. Lichtenstein uses the subject matter, stereotyped characters and situations of the comic strips. He also adapts certain linguistic conventions and mimics the mechanical printing process. However, Lichtenstein was not generally interested in using dialogue to tell a story; the words simply anchor the image. In *Whaam!*, the word on the right panel is not only the work's title but also expresses visually the sound of the explosion which is the subject of the picture.

*Whaam!*, like several of Lichtenstein's other war pictures, is made up of more than one canvas panel. It was painted in Magna, a type of acrylic. It is not difficult to tell a Lichtenstein from a comic strip, even if it is only reproduced in a book, while in an art gallery it is impossible to ignore the picture's size. Lichtenstein has not reproduced the mechanical dot shading and coloring technique used in comic-book production. In comics, the dots are of such a size and density that they are meant to be overlooked. In Lichtenstein's picture, the dots form clearly discernible abstract patterns on a two-dimensional surface. The two panels of *Whaam!* use images derived from war comics in a confident and technically very controlled way; they also have the humor, as Lichtenstein himself said, of 'one painting shooting another'.

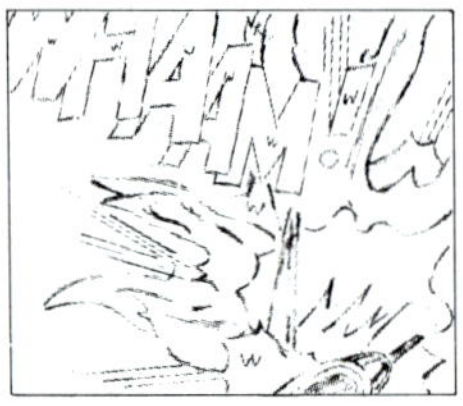

**1.** The artist first made a small pencil drawing which served as a guide for the major lines of the composition and coloring.

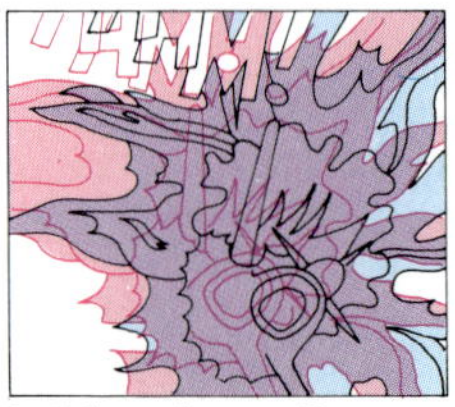

**2.** When the small drawing was transferred to the canvas, changes were made – two panels were used instead of one. The plane and burst of flames were greatly enlarged and the colors indicated on the drawing were altered.

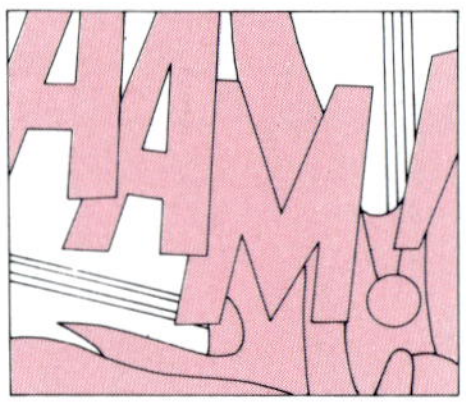

**3.** The dots were applied next. The areas which were not to receive the dot pattern were masked off.

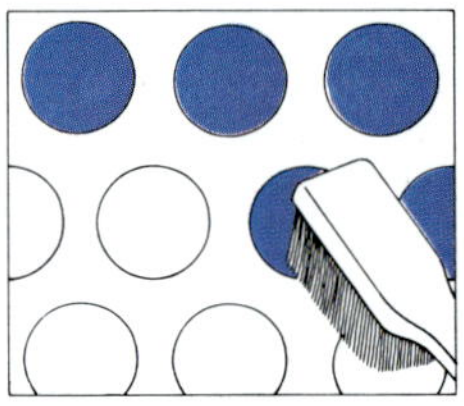

**4.** A perforated metal screen was placed on the canvas. The screen had regularly spaced holes through which the paint was brushed with a toothbrush.

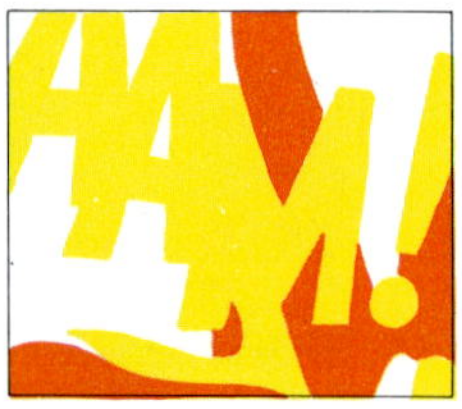

**5.** Lichtenstein then painted the areas of solid color, beginning with the lightest and working through to the darkest. For this, Lichtenstein used the primary colors associated with the comic strip.

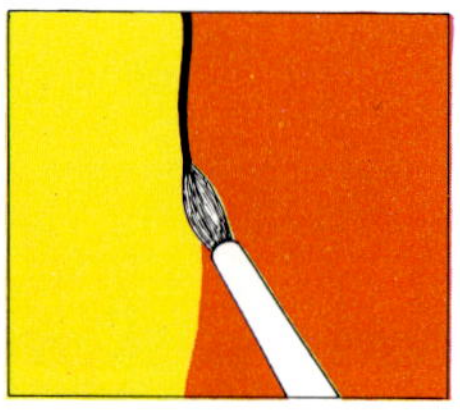

**6.** Finally, the black lines were painted over the primary colors and dots.

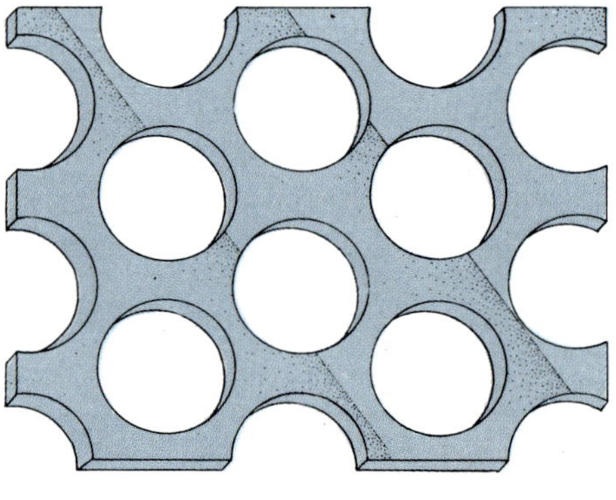

*Lichtenstein used a metal mesh screen to create the dot pattern in* Whaam!. *The screen was laid on the canvas and the paint brushed through the holes in it. When the screen was lifted off, the dot pattern was revealed.*

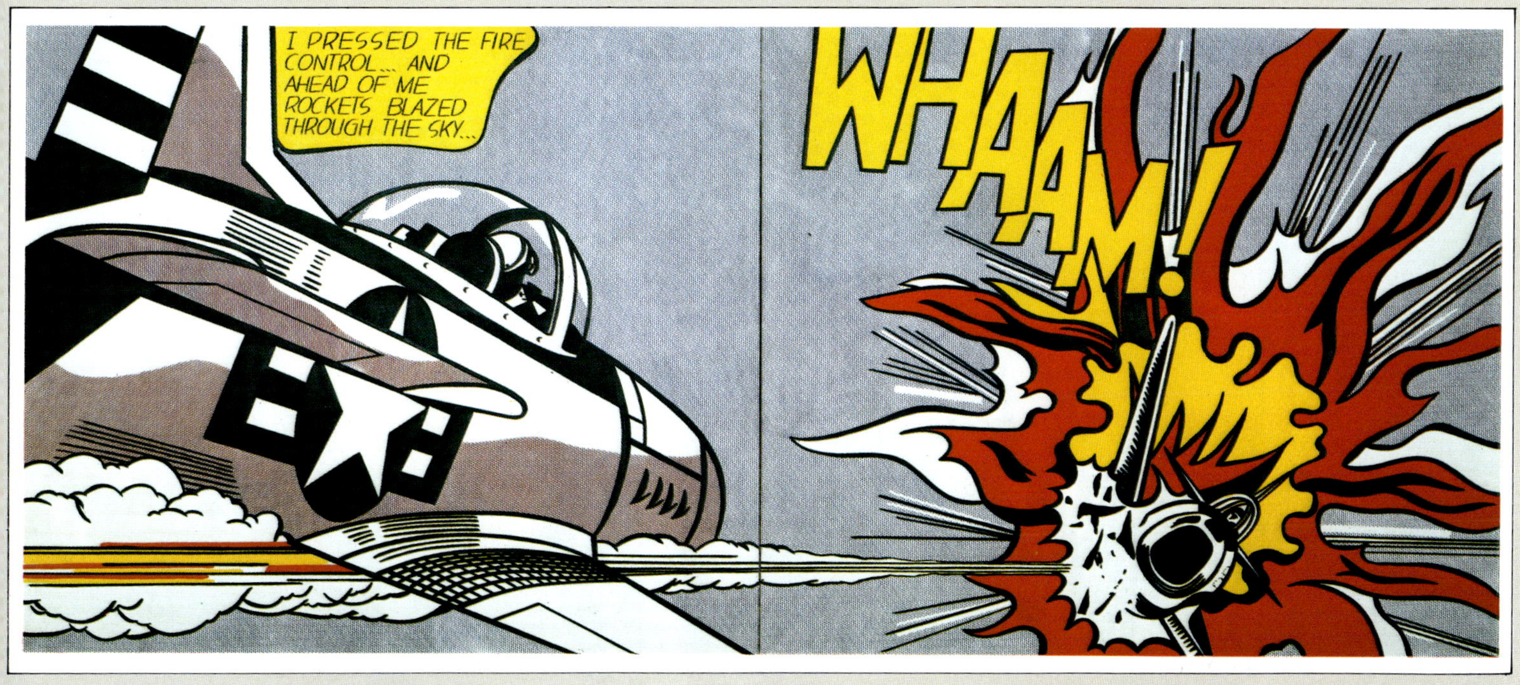


**Below** *This preparatory drawing for* Whaam! *shows that Lichtenstein did not adhere rigorously to his initial ideas. He had begun by thinking in terms of a single canvas; the two canvas format developed as the drawing was carried over onto a second piece of paper. Changes were also made as Lichtenstein transferred the drawing to the canvas. Both the plane and the burst of flames were enlarged so that they almost filled their respective canvases and so as to bring them closer together. The colors indicated on the drawing were also altered. 'Whaam!' on the sketch was noted as white, but was painted in yellow. The caption above the plane was also added.*

**Above** *Lichtenstein wanted his picture to look programed and, at first, his handling of paint might seem rigid and impersonal. However, this is not 'hard edge' painting; rather,* Whaam! *is freely drawn and painted. The black lines show the inflections of arm and wrist movements. The color areas often reveal the trackings of the brush, and pencil lines are rarely entirely concealed or eradicated. In some places the dots become paler and less clearly defined as the artist's stippling brush runs out of paint.*

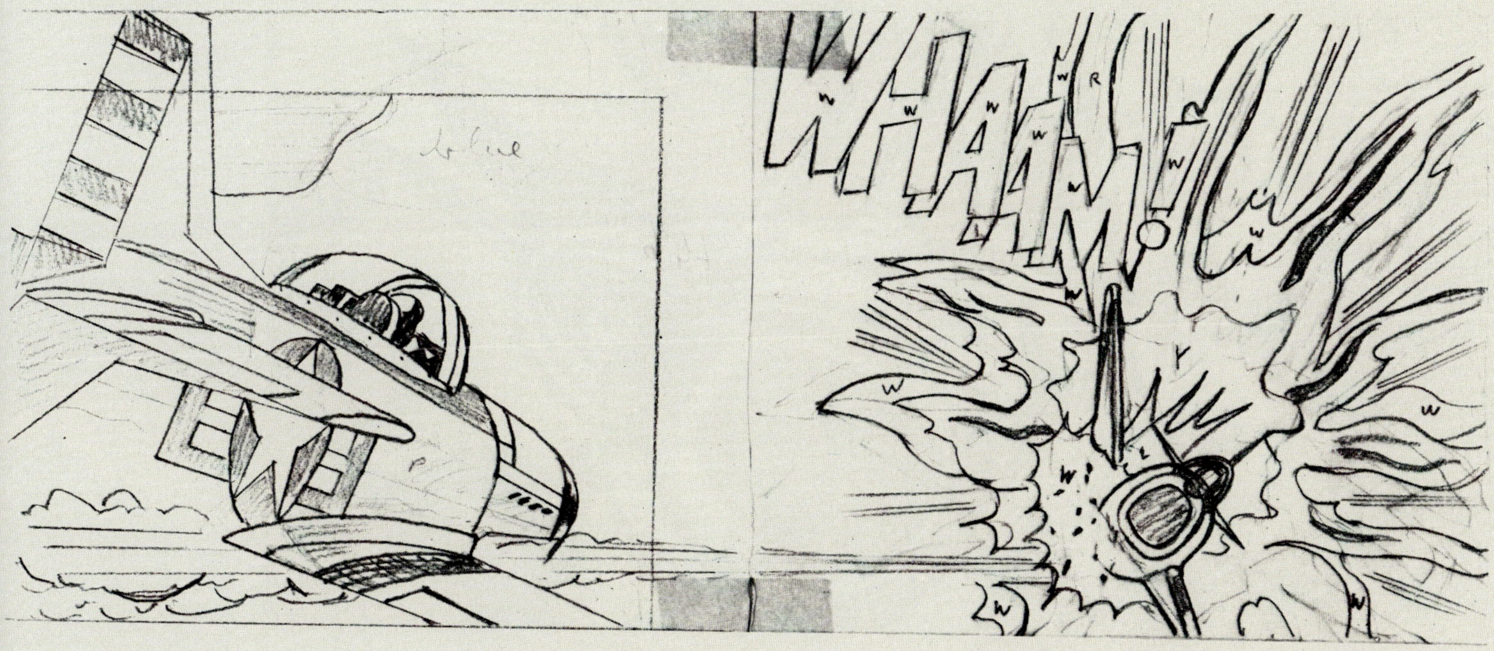

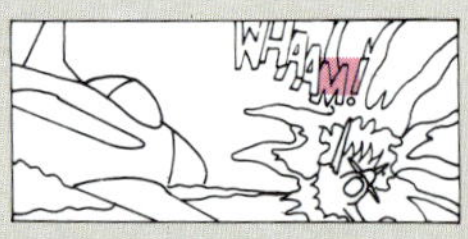

*This detail shows several of the elements in Lichtenstein's method of working. The white areas are created by masking them out with tape before the dots are applied through the screen. The blocks of solid color are applied next with a brush — the brushmarks can be seen in the yellow areas. The black lines are painted in last, and the relative freeness of the lines can be seen, as can rather smudged areas on some of the white. Lichtenstein used oil color and Magna acrylic on canvas. 'Magna' is the trade name for a brand of acrylic colors. Acrylic colors are made by dispersing pigments in an acrylic resin medium. Acrylics have gained quickly in popularity since they were first readily available commercially after the Second World War. These paints dry rapidly, do not yellow, and are easy to remove. The last quality enabled Lichtenstein to remove the paint if he wanted to make changes on the canvas, and to conceal any blemishes or stains by painting over in the same color as the canvas or the ground.*

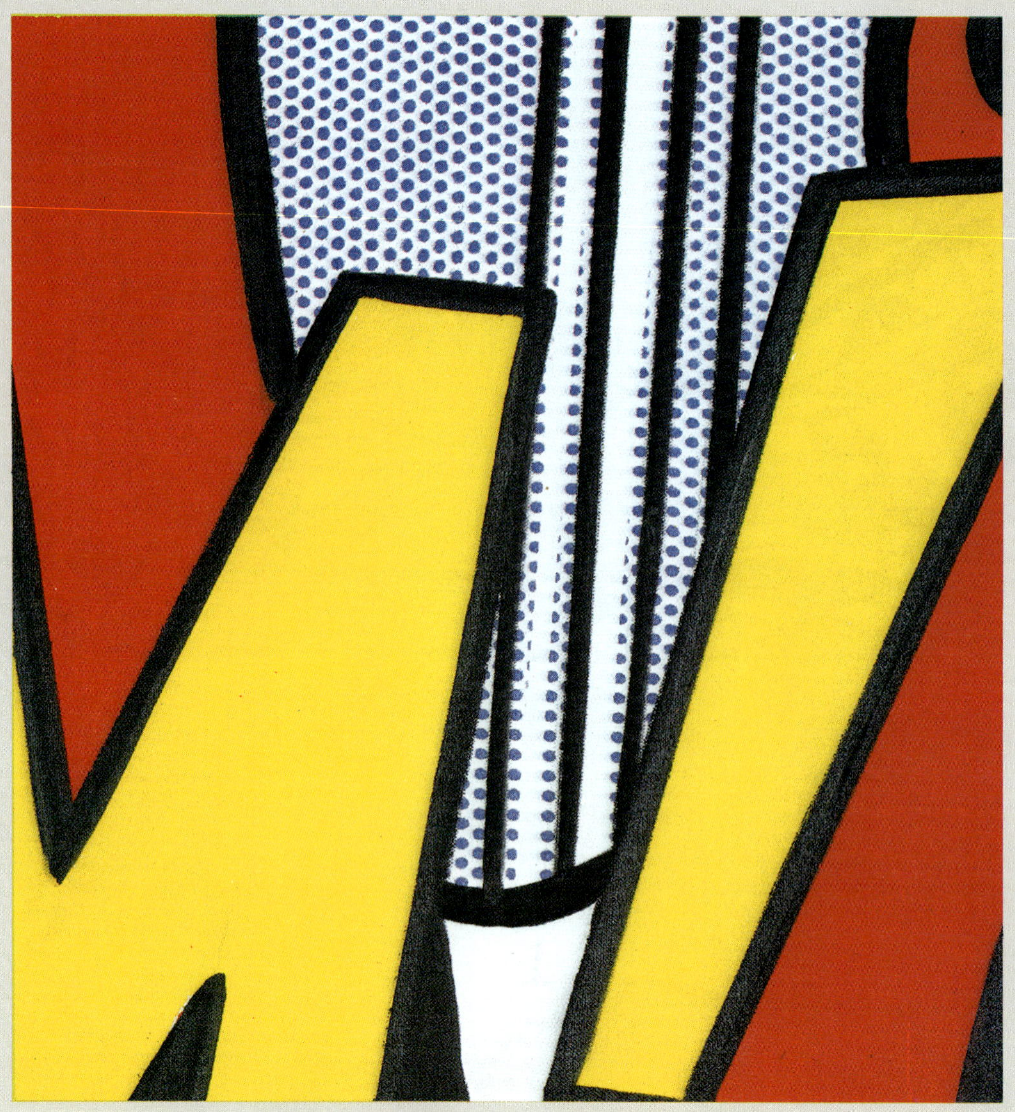

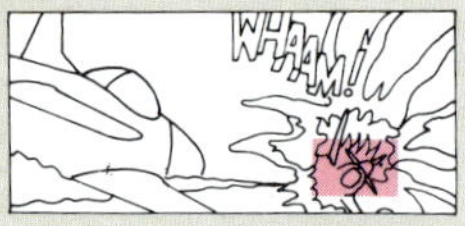

*Masking would probably have been used in this area. When Lichtenstein painted in the areas of solid color, he began with the lightest and worked through to the darkest. Explosions featured prominently in Lichtenstein's close-up comic strip images of warfare which were painted mainly between 1961 and 1965.*

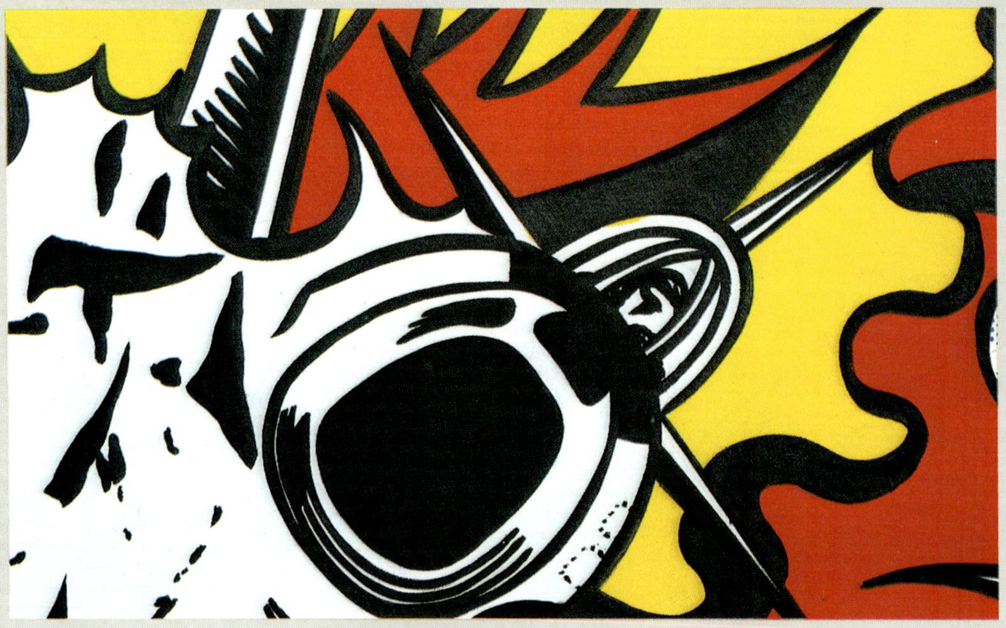

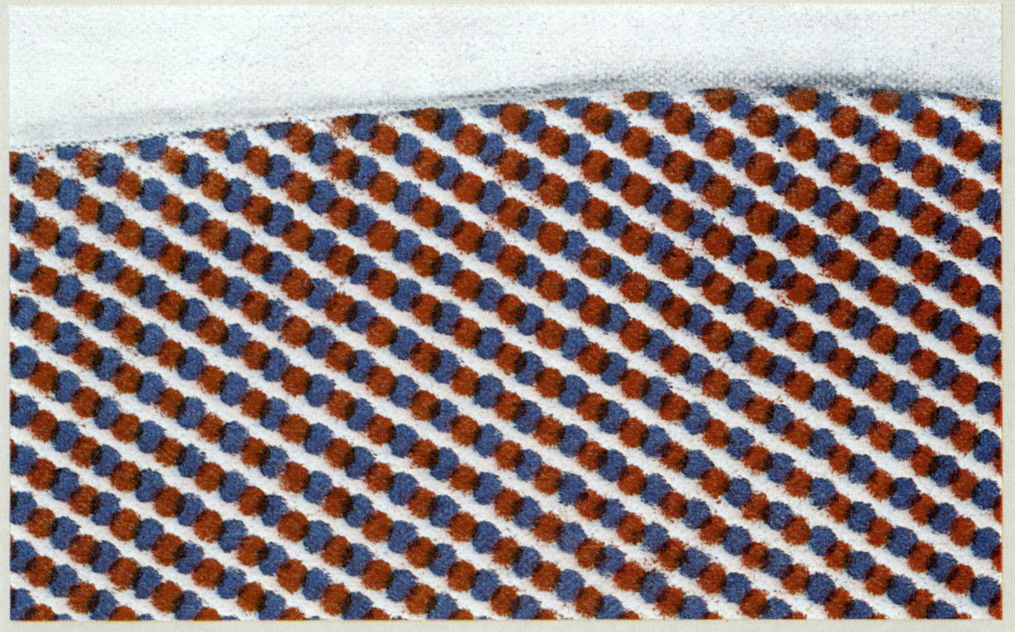

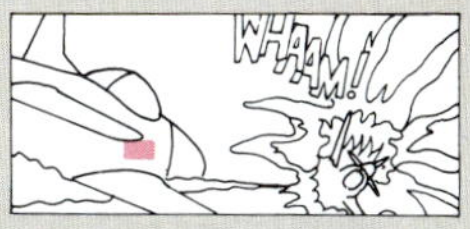

**Actual size detail**
*Lichtenstein does not reproduce the mechanical printing process in his work. In printing comics, the color is achieved using the Ben Day dot system in which dots, in a limited range oif colors — black, red, yellow and blue — are overlaid to produce different tones. Flesh color, for example, is either red dots on yellow or red on white. The dots are applied individually using a screen. When combined, these give the appearance of different tones. However, this actual size detail shows that Lichtenstein places the dots of solid color side by side. This detail also shows the underdrawing which still shows through on the finished painting.*

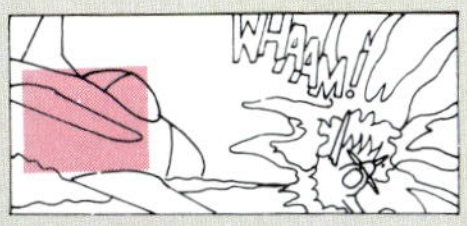

*The pattern of dots was created using a metal screen. The red and blue dots were laid side by side. Even when viewed from a slight distance, they begin to merge in the viewer's eye. The black lines were added last, after the solid blocks of color. Brushmarks and differences of pressure and line can be detected in them. The lines of the pencil underdrawing are rarely completely covered or eradicated.*

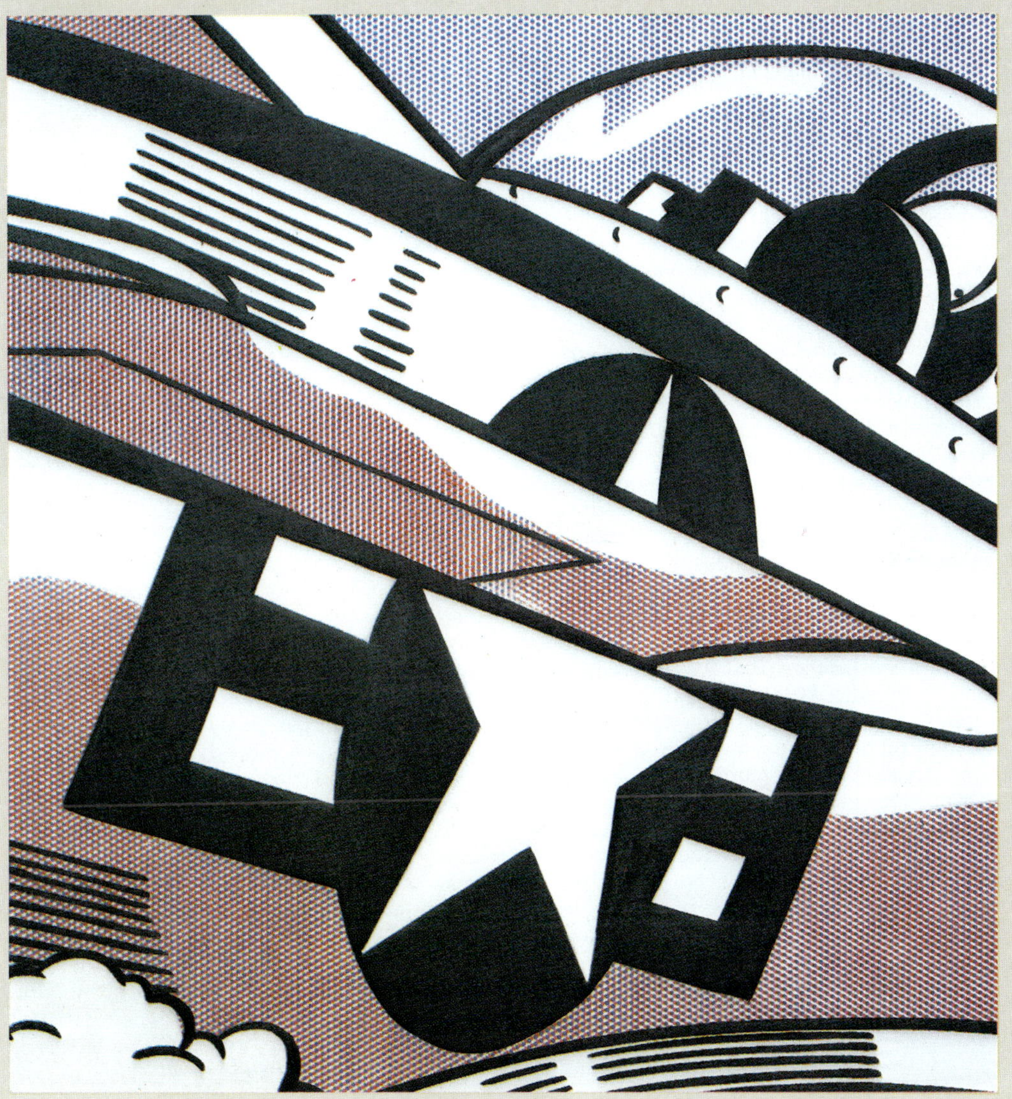

# ROY LICHTENSTEIN

*In the Car (1963)*
Magna on canvas
172cm × 203.5cm/67⅝in × 80⅛in

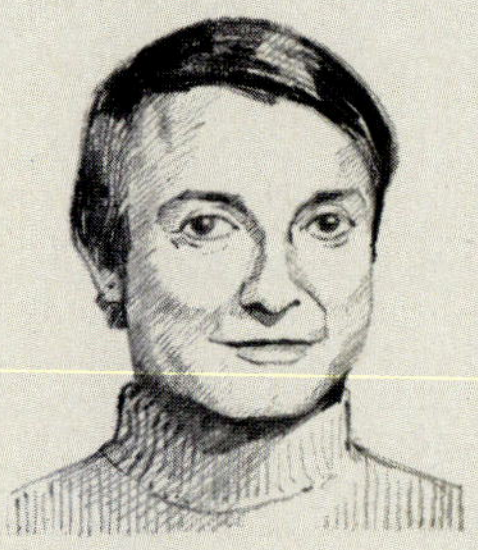

If Roy Lichtenstein's own definition of Pop Art is accepted – 'the use of commercial art as the subject matter in painting' – he must be counted, together with Andy Warhol, who was raiding graphic and mass-media sources at about the same time and more or less independently, as one of its leading protagonists. Lichtenstein is certainly the most technically consistent. Through this almost dispassionate consistency, his greatest achievement is to conjure the unexpected from a scrutiny of the commonplace; to 'make strange' the vulgar and the clichéd, to add uncertainty, paradox and elusiveness to our view of the world.

Born in New York City in 1923, Roy Lichtenstein first studied painting at the Art Students' League during his summer vacations. From 1940 he was enrolled in the School of Fine Arts, Ohio State University, where he came under the influence of H. L. Sherman's theories of the psychology of vision and illusionism. During the 1950s he worked as a commercial artist and freelance draftsman, while from 1957 to 1963 he taught, first at the New York State College of Education, Oswego, and then at Rutgers University, where he was a colleague of Allan Kaprow (b 1922), the creator of the environmental work *Happenings in 6 Parts* (1959). Lichtenstein resigned from Rutgers in 1964 to paint full-time. He soon became prominent in the New York Pop Art scene, loosely centered around the Leo Castelli Gallery.

Lichtenstein's early work was almost entirely in oil on canvas with occasional use of pastel. It betrayed a schooling in the vernacular of American Regionalism, unpretentious realists proud to celebrate aspects of American life. Gradually this early style gave way to a more expressive style and looser brushwork, which admitted influences from the Cubist and abstract idioms. In 1951 Lichtenstein exhibited a number of 'imagistic assemblages' at his first one-man show in New York. They were made up of a variety of materials, mainly discarded wood and metal objects clasped together. In the mid-1950s he experimented with painted wood constructions. His early comic-strip works were painted in oil on canvas without preliminary sketches. 1961 was the year when he first borrowed not merely the images of commercial art, but also the techniques of mechanical production, making use of Benday dots, lettering and balloons.

Since 1963 Lichtenstein's work has changed more in its subject matter and local style and scale, than in actual technique. The principal categories of his imagery derive from advertising, commonplace objects including foodstuffs, comic strip images, overt adaptions of works by other artists, classical ruins, land, sea, sky and moonscapes, paintings of brushstrokes and explosions. Lichtenstein has, however, produced a modest amount of glazed ceramic and other sculpture, and in 1977 exhibited a group of open-work silhouettes, cast in bronze and part painted.

By 1963, the year he painted *In the Car*, Lichtenstein had developed a sophisticated technique of projection which he has described to writer John Coplans: 'If I am working from a cartoon, photograph, or whatever, I draw a small picture – the size that will fit into my opaque projector – and project it on to the canvas. I don't draw a picture in order to reproduce it – I do it in order to recompose... I try to make the minimum amount of change... I project the drawing onto the canvas and pencil it in and then I play around with the drawing until it satisfies me. For technical reasons I stencil in the dots first... Then I start with the lightest colors and work my way down to the black line... I always end up erasing half the painting, redoing it and redotting it. I work in Magna color because it's soluble in turpentine... so that there is no record of the changes I have made. Then, using paint which is the same color as the canvas, I repaint areas to remove any stain marks from the erasures. I want my painting to look as if it had been programmed. I want to hide the record of my hand.'

*In the Car*, typically, is thinly painted with synthetic resin and oil so that the canvas pattern is strongly visible through a relatively rough surface. Dots were applied with a toothbrush through a perforated metal screen placed on the canvas, after areas which were not to receive them had been masked off. Areas of solid color were then blocked-in before the black bounding lines were added.

The work derives thematically from Lichtenstein's comic-strip paintings, and from his avowed interest in the representation of 'highly confectioned' women. But here the situation is untexted, and the viewer seems to be invited to write in a dialog from the disposition of the couple's eyes, their hair and the angle of their heads.

Lichtenstein's technique calls attention to the basic units of his design: blank areas, regularly dotted areas, blocked-in areas and lines. Particularizing details have been resisted, and each feature or configuration is registered by a simplified mode of working. Cutting into the composition, apparently both behind and in front of the couple, is the dynamic intrusion of speed-lines and reflection creases. The actual color areas set up a fugal relation between the three primaries, red, blue and yellow, and interact with the 'non-colors', black and white, in ways that are superficially reminiscent of Mondrian (whose work Lichtenstein 'subjected to his technique' a little later). Just as Lichtenstein separates out the elements of his own painting process, so the visibility of his surface, its magnification and its very friction on the viewer's eyes, records the disruptive and disquieting aims of his art.

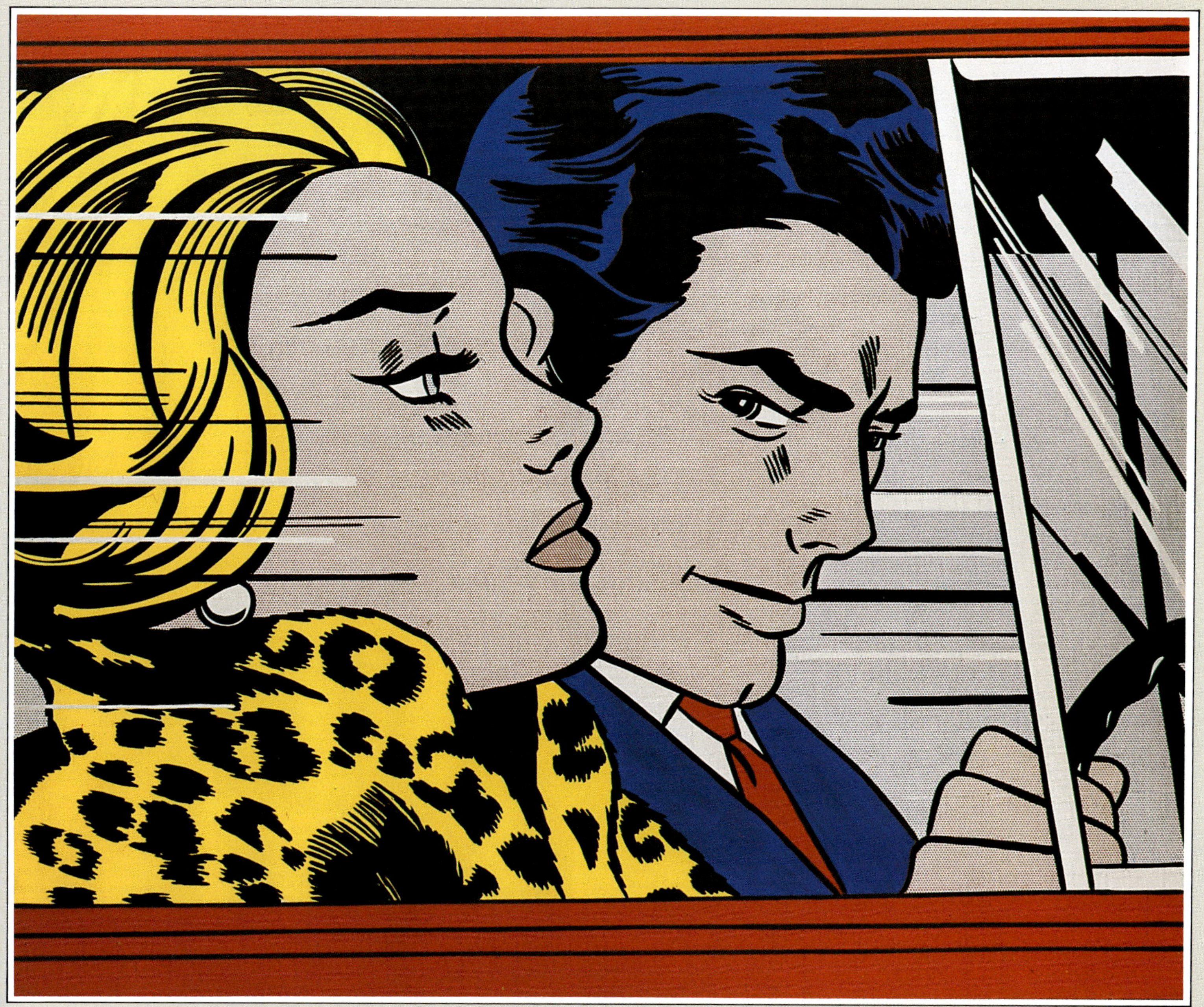

*Lichtenstein was constantly aware of the formal and structural significations of his work which accompany the manifest event or situation. For example, the color black functioning as infill, boundary pattern and shadow is counterpointed by the strong primary colors and by the 'negative' areas of white. Unlike a work such as* Whaam! *(1963) where their use is more diverse, dots are restricted here to three main areas — the flesh tints of the couple, the stronger red of the woman's lips, and the blue sky zone 'outside' the vehicle, which is echoed in her eye.*

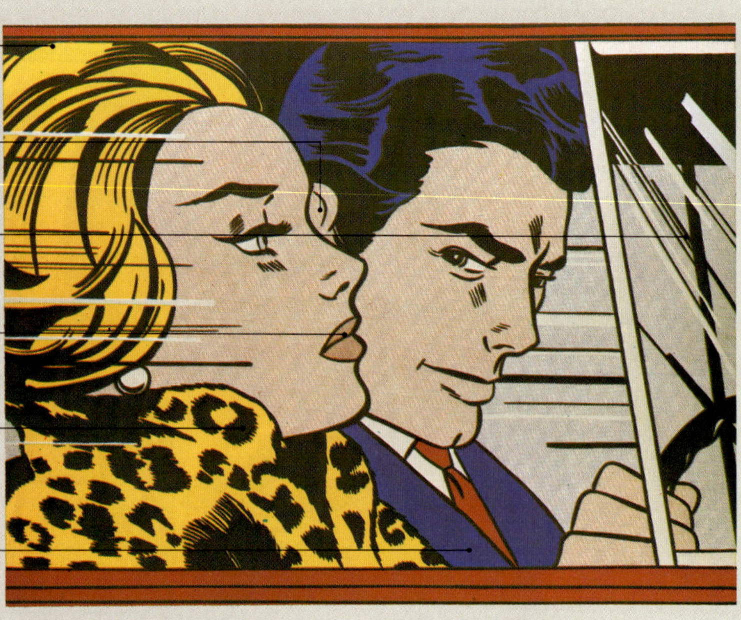

Slight gap between yellow of hair and black background shows ground

Man's ear 'behind' woman's face creates a zone of spatial ambiguity

Diagonal reflection lines evoke the change of angle from side window to windscreen

Dots of the same hue are bunched together to produce a stronger red effect

Irregular fringes of black suggest leopard spots, and echo the shadow marks on the faces of the couple

Slight diagonal brush sweeps visible

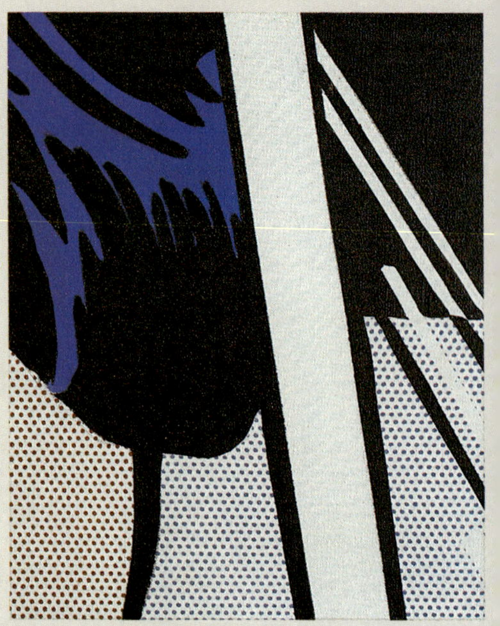

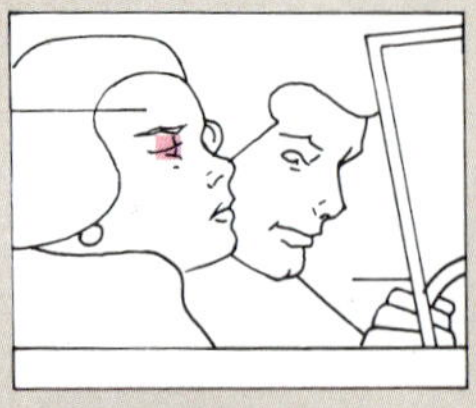

ACTUAL SIZE DETAIL *Quite loose pencil lines are visible as guiding marks throughout this extract, but the black paint does not completely infill them. The red and blue dots are evenly disposed in rows and diagonals, through the perforated metal screen, but are somewhat incomplete in places, particularly to the immediate right of the eye itself. This may have been the result of retouching after the removal of acrylic paint from the pupil or eyelash. Virtually all traces of the hand, magnified here, would be invisible at a normal viewing distance. The opacity of the black Magna paint, and the strong optical effect of the regular tessellation of dots are calculated technical strategies to promote this register of the gaze.*

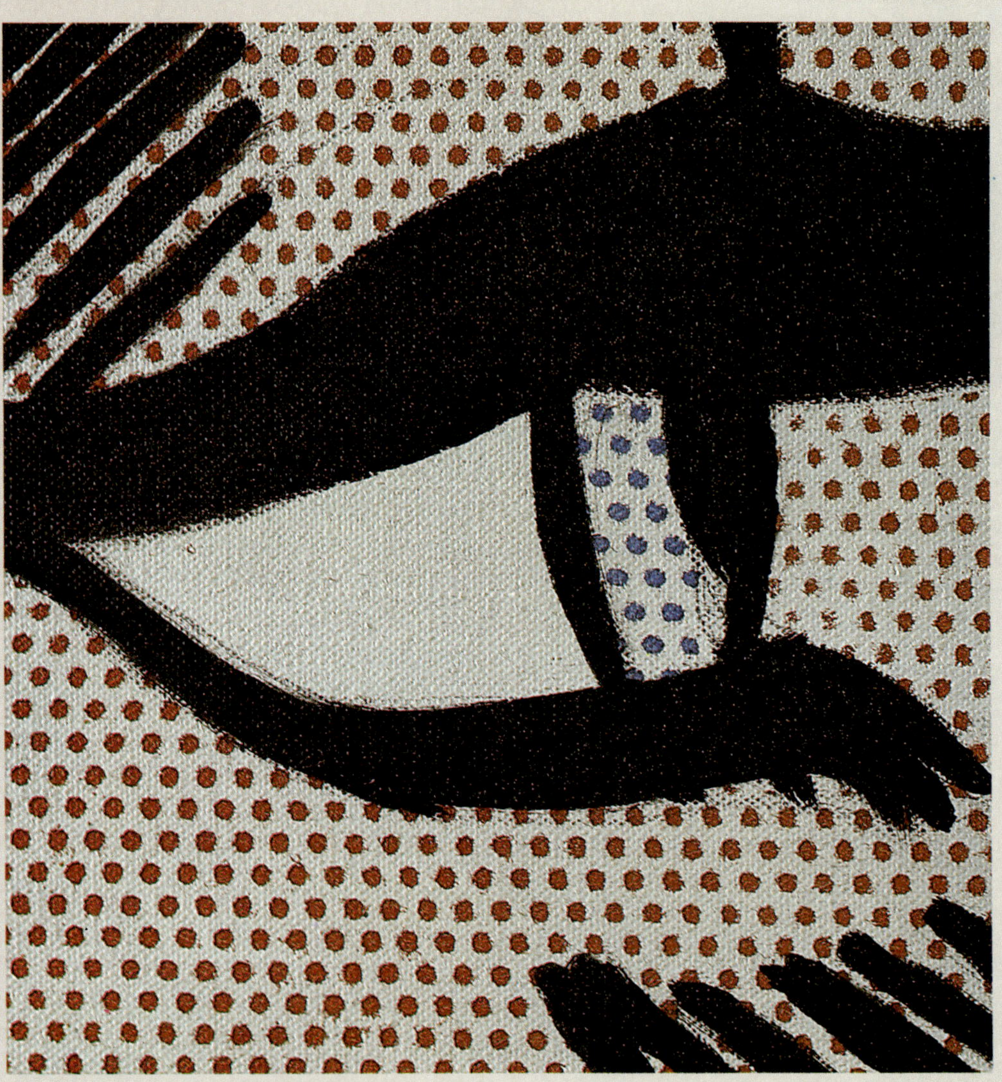

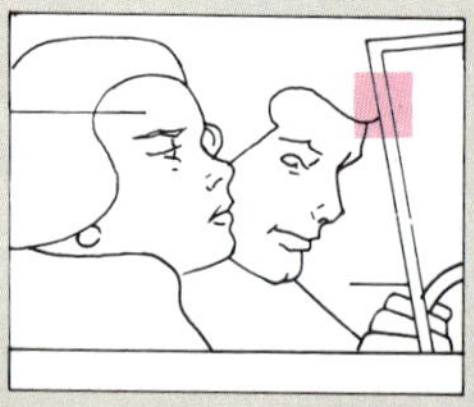

ABOVE *The strongly abstract nature of the element with which Lichtenstein worked is apparent here, as the signs for hair, eyebrow and reflections in eye glass are abbreviated and minimized. Traces of the original penciled design are visible along the fringes of the hair.*

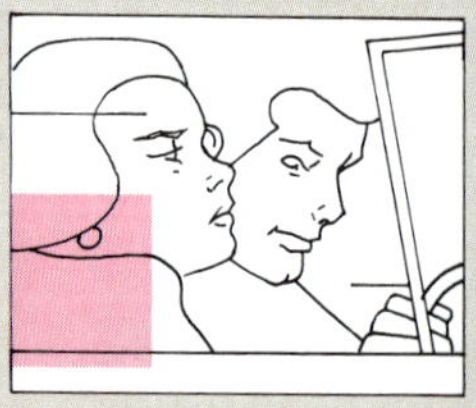

RIGHT *The black patches with ribboned edges which connote the texture of a leopard-skin coat are the most irregular paint marks in the picture. The blank space of the pearl and triangle of 'flesh' behind it echo and invert the form of the woman's eye.*

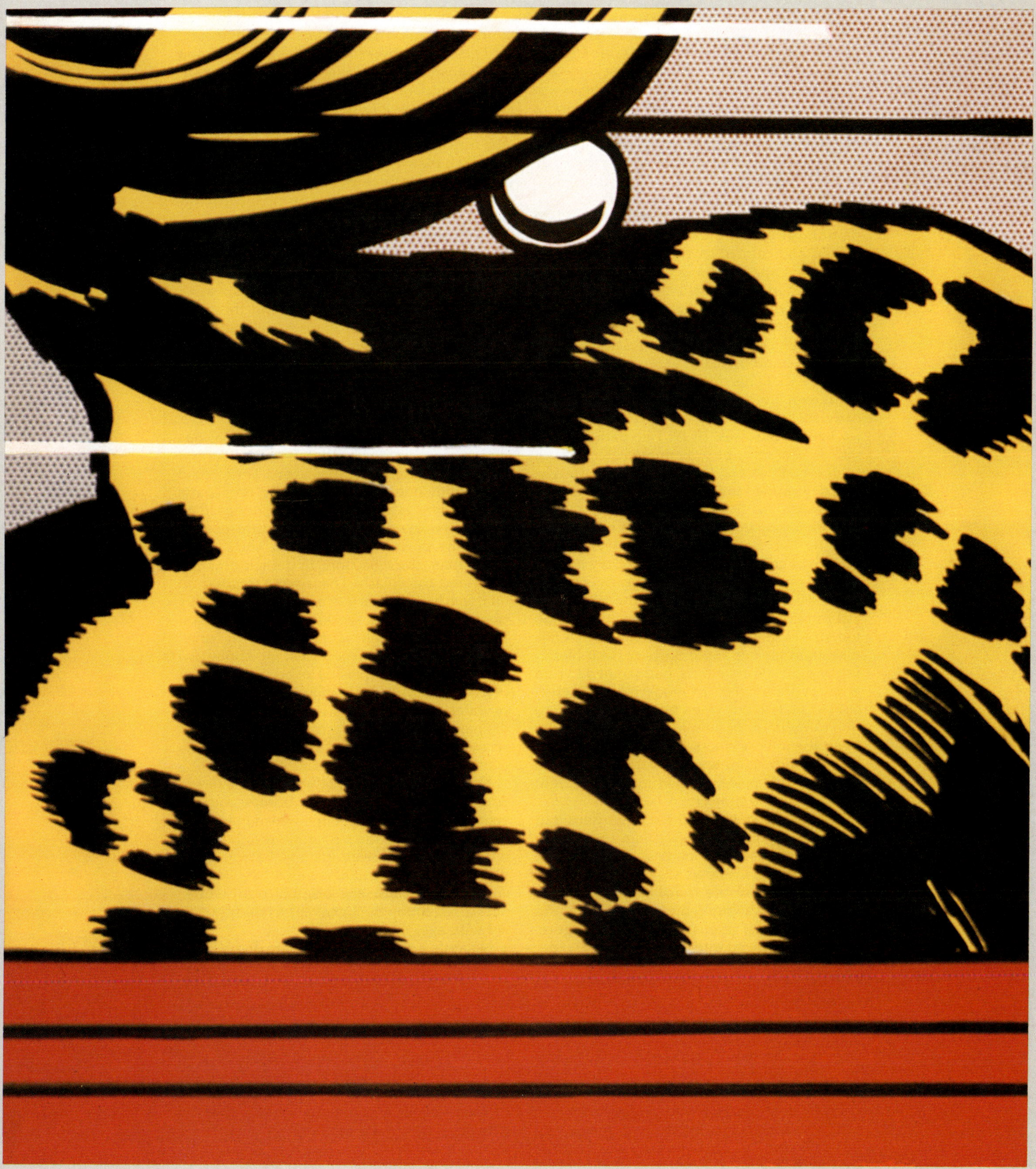

# DAVID HOCKNEY

*A Bigger Splash (1967)*
Acrylic on canvas
242.5cm × 243.9cm/95½in × 96in

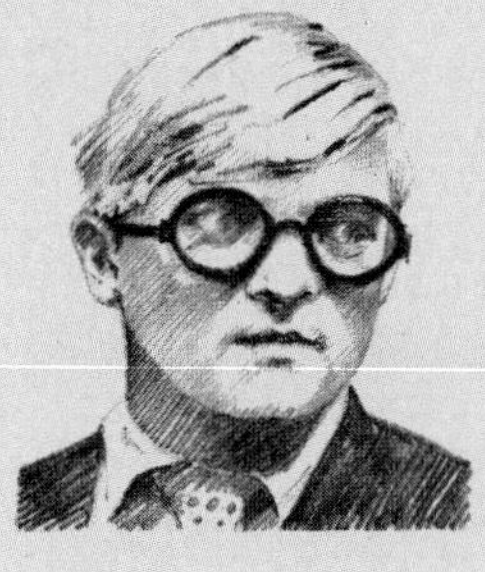

Since 1960 David Hockney has steadily emerged as one of the most popular and fêted painters in Europe. A review by critic Charles Harrison of a 1968 show by Hockney described a recent canvas, *Rocky Mountains and Tired Indians*, as 'unmistakably Hockney, a strange mixture of whimsy in its construction and disturbing reality in its effect.' Hockney's art, as Harrison noted, relies upon a marriage of wit, discipline, originality, invention, quirkiness and straightforward realism.

Born in Bradford in July 1937, he studied painting at Bradford College of Art from 1953 to 1957 and painted small oils, usually of portrait, landscape or urban subject matter. When he arrived in London in 1959, where he was a student at the Royal College of Art until 1962, he became under the powerful and then current influence of Abstract Expressionism. He tried his hand at painting in this style, but turned back to his original subject matter, that of his own life, its people and environment. As early as 1960 Hockney displayed a penchant for square canvases. In 1961 he paid his first visit to America; he was immediately struck by the freedom and originality of its lifestyle, and determined to return at regular intervals.

Hockney has visited California almost every year since 1963, first going there because he said he felt 'Somehow I instinctively knew that I was going to like it.' The literary quality of the London paintings of the early years of the 1960s disappeared with the arrival of Californian-based subject matter in 1964. So too, did Hockney's reliance on oil paint. Oils, with their greater possibilities of color blending and *chiaroscuro* effects, had seemed to him appropriate for the apt rendering of English subject matter, but when he turned his attention to California's swimming pools and palm trees, the intense colors of the American acrylic medium Liquitex, a water-based and water-soluble paint, seemed to him the right material for the subject.

*A Bigger Splash* was painted in California in the early summer of 1967. It is a record of a typical warm, sunny, cloudless day; from the position of the shadows cast by the eaves of the building and the chair, it appears to be midday when the sun is highest in the sky and the heat is most intense. The solitary figure, who has just dived into the pool, has been deliberately overwhelmed by the strength and composure of the rest of the composition. The hidden depths of this picture take longer to assimilate than its immediate joyful and decorative appeal.

*A Bigger Splash* is the third and last in a series of splash subjects which began with a small painting, *The Little Splash*, measuring 41×51 cm (16×20 in), in 1966, and progressed to *The Splash*, painted the same year, measuring 183×183 cm (72×72 in). Hockney was inspired to start this series by a photograph of a splash '...found in a book about how to build swimming pools... on a news stand in Hollywood.'

The only section to break the balanced and cool abstraction of the strong horizontals and verticals is the diagonally placed diving board and the splash. The spindly diagonal legs of the folding chair in the distance echo the thrust of the actual splash, while the point at which the swimmer entered the pool, creating the splash, is emphasized and delineated above by an odd thickening of the narrow white line along the roof.

Hockney recalls that he began the painting by drawing the basic lines of the composition; it is unclear whether he means that he actually drew by graphic means upon the canvas or that he mapped out the lines and the areas they enclose by using strips of self-adhesive masking tape. Certainly there is no evidence of a preliminary underdrawing. The painting is executed in Hockney's favorite Liquitex on white cotton duck canvas. Except for the splash, the paint surface is very flat.

Hockney applied the paint to the various geometric divisions with a paint roller, and gave each area two or three layers. The colored areas abut one another, and the only parts where there is overpainting, as opposed to successive layering of the same tint of pigment, are those of small details, such as the grass, trees, the reflections in the window, the chair and the splash. These were painted on afterwards with a variety of brushes. Hockney obviously enjoyed working on the splash, '...the splash itself is painted with small brushes and little lines; it took me about two weeks to paint the splash. I loved the idea, first of all, of painting like Leonardo, all his studies of water, swirling things. And I loved the idea of painting this thing that lasts for two seconds; it takes me two weeks to paint this event that lasts for two seconds.'

Not all of the canvas is painted, the areas uncovered being the wide border and the central narrow off-white line which marks the division between the pool edge and the pavement. The tonal relationships between the painted and unpainted sections have altered since 1967 because the original pure whiteness of the cotton duck canvas has slightly dulled with age.

Nevertheless, Hockney is aware of the value of technical craftsmanship, and of the importance of producing paintings which do not deteriorate rapidly. One of the reasons he turned to acrylic, besides that of its retention of color intensity, was because it is a stable and permanent medium – it has a good lasting quality and is less likely to crack or blister than oil paint. 'I didn't know anything about oil paint, I thought well, if people have paid £200 for paintings, then that's an awful lot of money. I should try to make sure that they don't fall to bits after six months.'

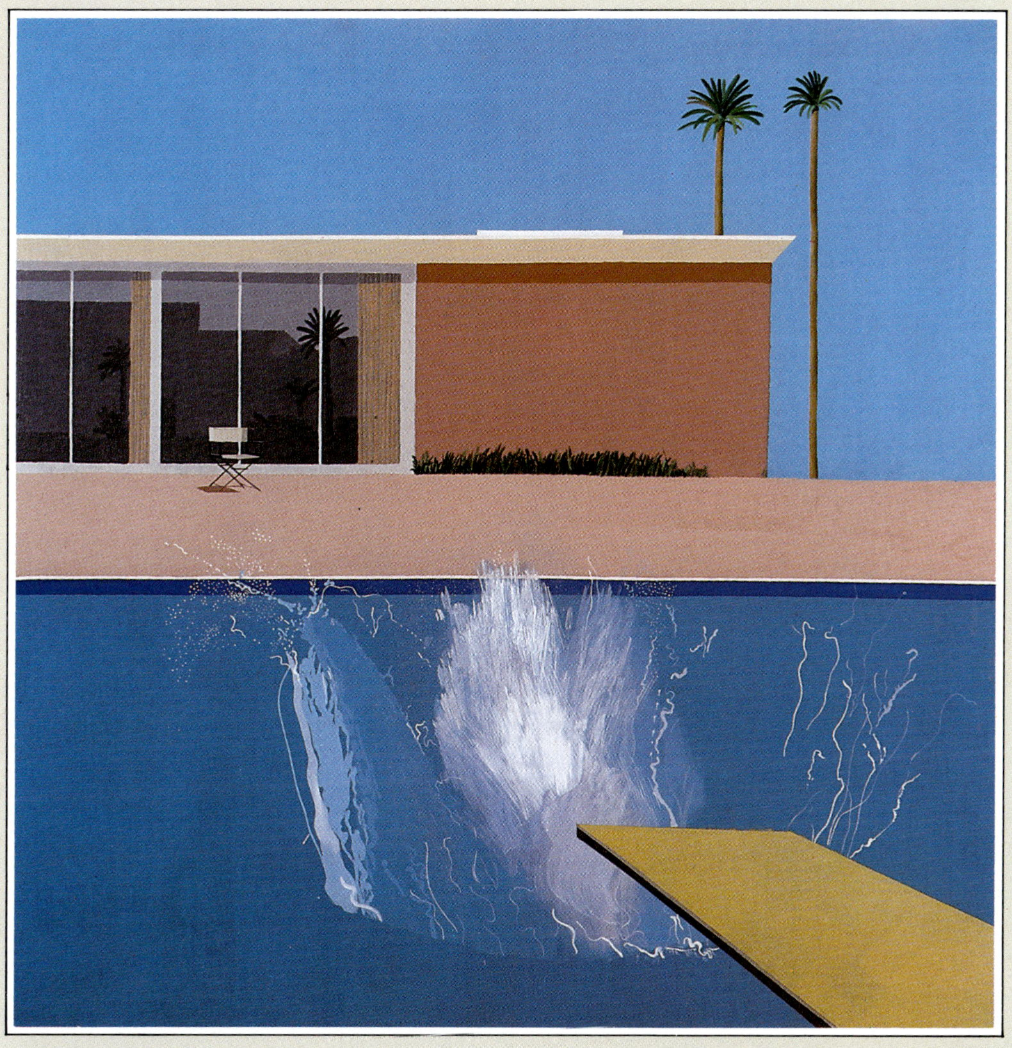

*The formal elegance of this painting is well matched by the hypnotic content. It is a highly organized composition, the design relying upon the taut oppositions of horizontal, vertical and diagonal elements. There is a tension too between the flatness of the smooth, broad-colored areas, and the illusory depth of the picture space. Hockney himself acknowledged this: '... if you take away the chair, for instance, and the reflection in the glass, it becomes much more abstract. You could even take away the glass, and then it becomes even more so...'*

Large, smooth areas of paint applied with a roller

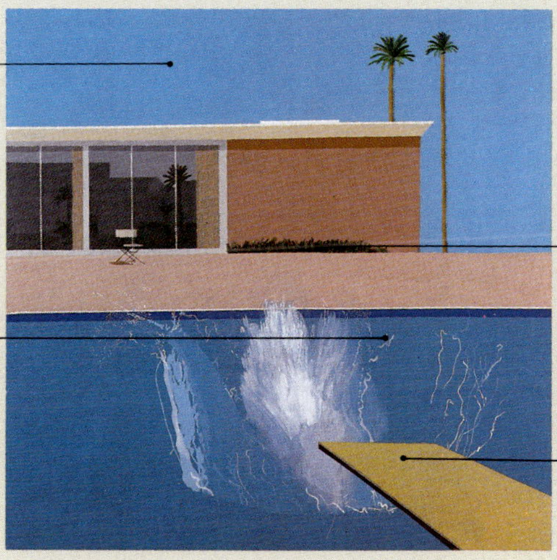

Foliage overpainted using green and raw umber

Lines and spots which make up the splash painted with small sable brushes

Colored areas mapped out with masking tape before paint application

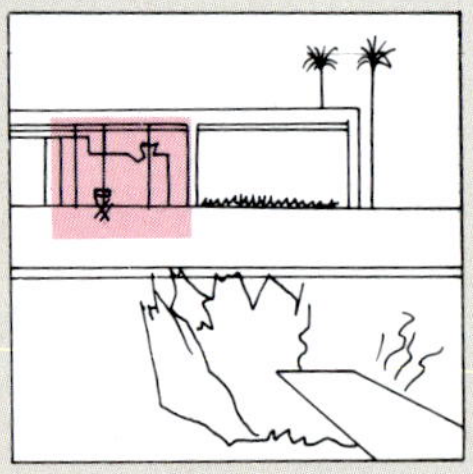

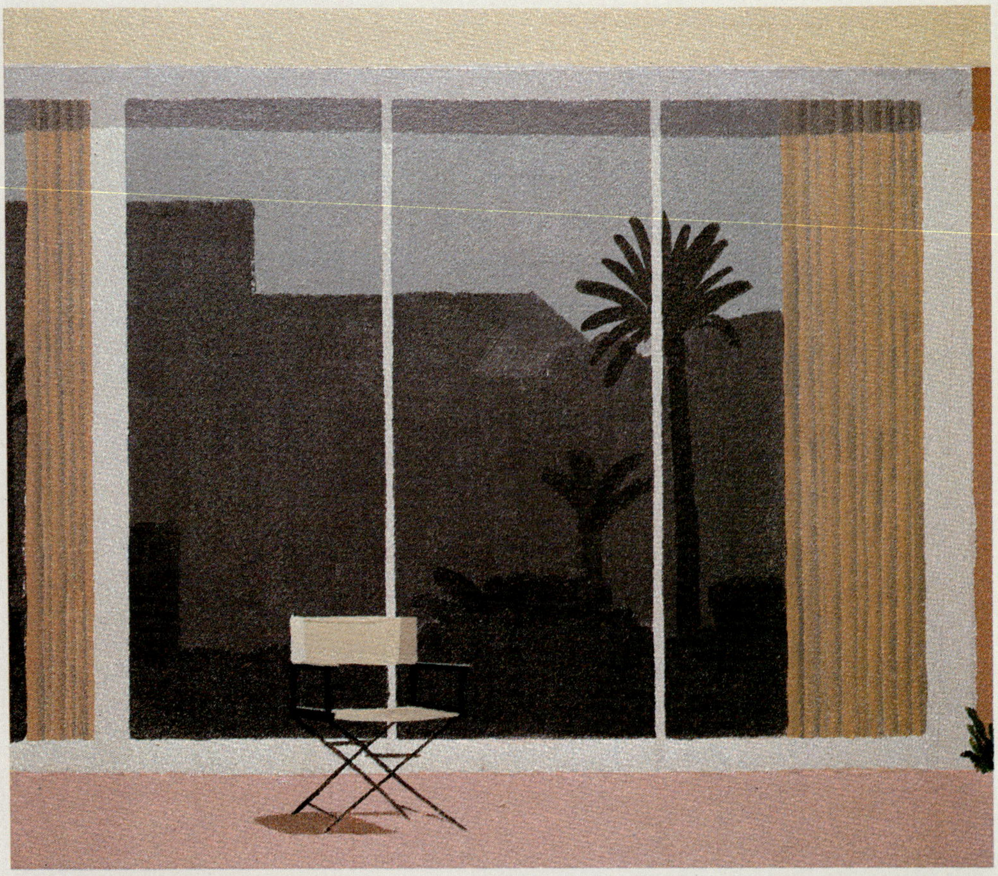

*RIGHT The burr caused by the paint piling up against the edge of the masking tape is visible along the top edge of the pink pavement. The masking tape technique allowed Hockney to paint colored areas edge to edge, but he chose to paint the small details, such as the chair, on top. The edges of the window jamb of the previous layer show through the chair back, and indicate that sequence. The paint which makes up the shadows on the glass is more diluted, and the light primed ground of the canvas shows through.*

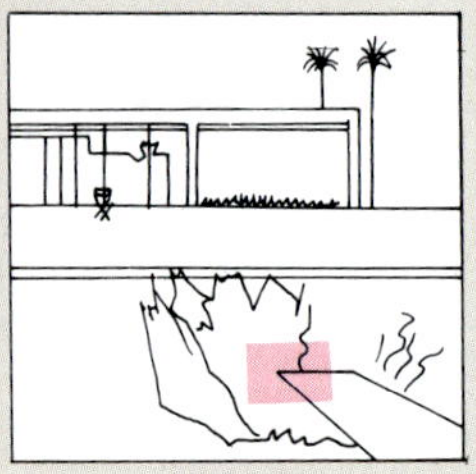

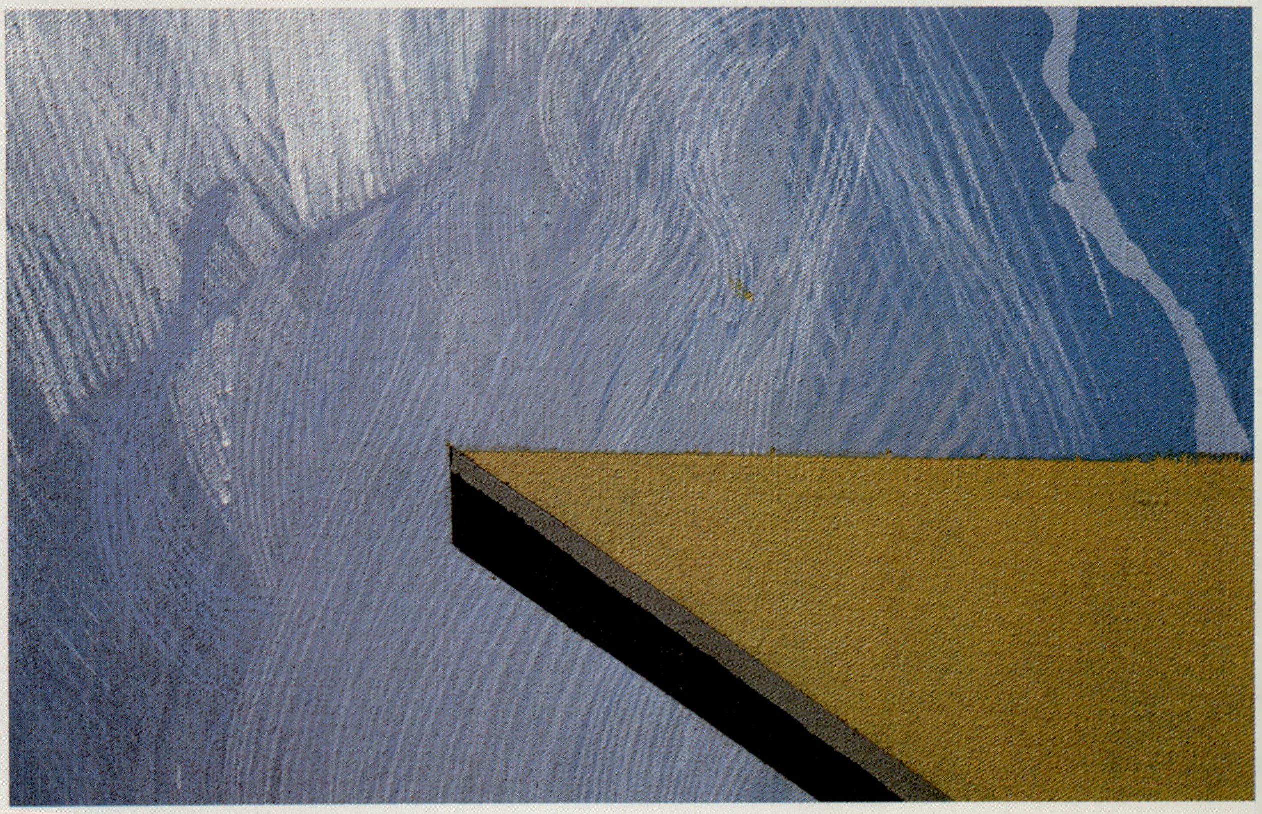

*RIGHT The Naples yellow paint used for the upper surface of the diving board was painted within an area masked off by self-adhesive masking tape. Because the tape was not pressed down so firmly along the top edge of the diving board, pigment seeped underneath and marred the otherwise crisp line. The most thickly painted area of the whole painting is that of the splash seen immediately behind the diving board, where at least four different colors have been used in succession.*

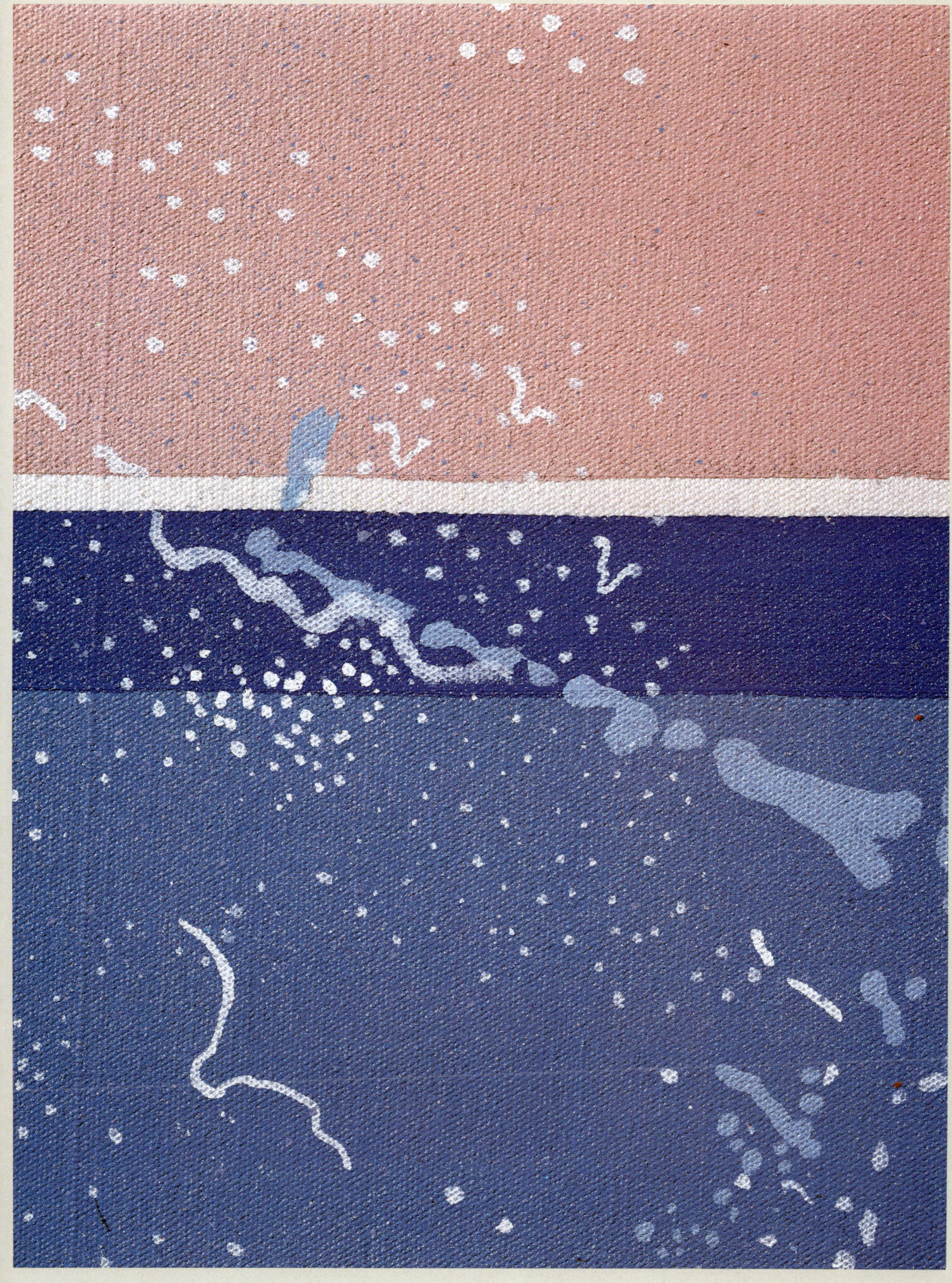

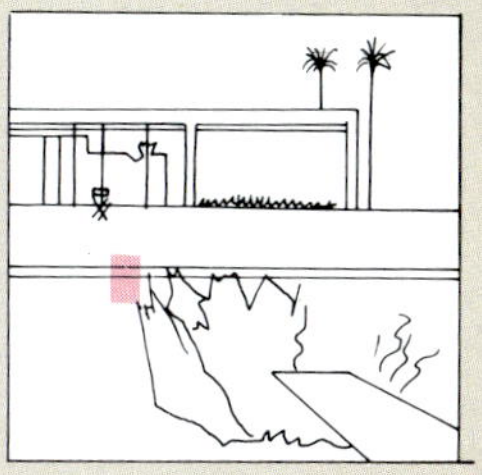

*ACTUAL SIZE DETAIL*
*Hockney recalls in his autobiography how the painting of the splash itself took him about two weeks; judging from the distribution of minute spots of different colored hues in this detail, the statement is eminently believable. This section of the canvas is divided into horizontal bands of pink, ultramarine and a cerulean-type blue all applied with a paint roller. The light tonal strip of the pool edge is actually the white primer layer left uncovered. The tiny spots of paint which go to make up the splash have a random air, almost as though this could be a detail of a drip painting by Jackson Pollock, but Hockney, with a photograph of a splash as a guide, will have planned their placemen. with care. The smallest of all spots in this detail, those in blue on top of the pink pavement, must have been executed with the point of a loaded brush.*

# DAVID HOCKNEY

*Mr and Mrs Clark and Percy* (1970)
Acrylic on canvas, 304cm × 213cm/120in × 84in

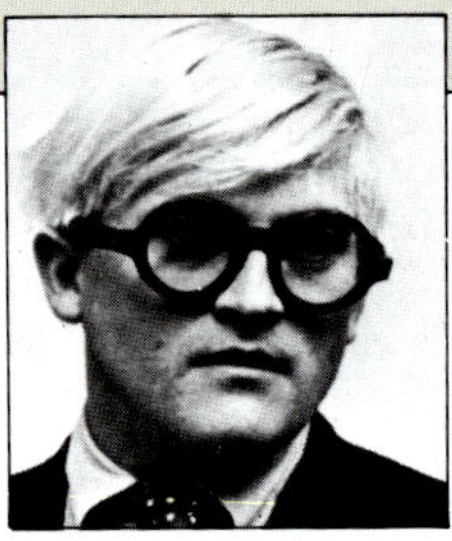

As a painter, draftsman, and illustrator, David Hockney has a popular reputation which extends worldwide. Throughout his painting career, Hockney has gathered subject matter from his own life, while his eclectic styles are largely borrowed from traditional art sources. In the early 1960s, Hockney's work, although largely figurative in content, made no attempt to provide a consistent illusion of reality. The expressionistic qualities of his painting are constantly brought to the viewer's attention through the way he used a wide variety of technical and stylistic devices.

In the middle 1960s, Hockney renewed his interest in literal representation and began to work increasingly from life. As well, he changed from oil paints to acrylics, which better suited the type of painting he wished to achieve.

During the 1960s and 1970s, portraiture began to occupy an increasingly important place in Hockney's work. None of these portraits were commissioned, but were generally of friends depicted in their normal, everyday environments which Hockney used to give hints to the sitter's character. These are not, however, 'snapshots' of life, but very carefully planned and organized pictures in which Hockney exploited his use of the acrylic medium to its limit. Hockney's portraits combine the concern for formality of his earlier works with an increasing interest in representational art and depicting natural space and color. They involved many preliminary drawings and paintings done both from photographs and real life. As many as a dozen studies of a particular part of the painting would be made before work on the final painting was begun.

Hockney paints on both primed and unprimed canvas and makes use of the different textural effects achieved by the two. He consistently uses successive applications of paint, each layer modifying rather than obscuring those beneath. Where extensive reworking has been done, the paint sometimes obliterates the texture of the canvas. To cope with the fast drying of the paint which hinders blending, Hockney devised the technique of spraying the surface with water to keep it wet. The painting, if executed on gessoed canvas, is usually covered with a generous film of acrylic medium, giving the painting a uniform glossiness and smoothness of finish.

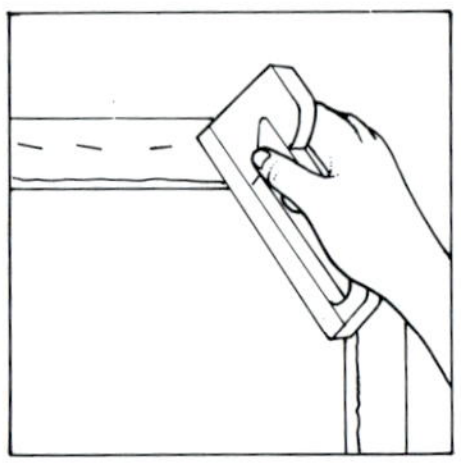

**1.** The painting was done on a plain weave cotton duck canvas, which was stretched over a pine stretcher and attached at the back with wire staples. It has been restretched, as Hockney used to unstretch and roll the canvas up in order to transport it.

**2.** The canvas was primed with thin white acrylic gesso, which was thin enough when applied to penetrate the back of the canvas in places. The priming reduces the effect of the canvas texture and provides a brilliant white reflective ground on which to paint.

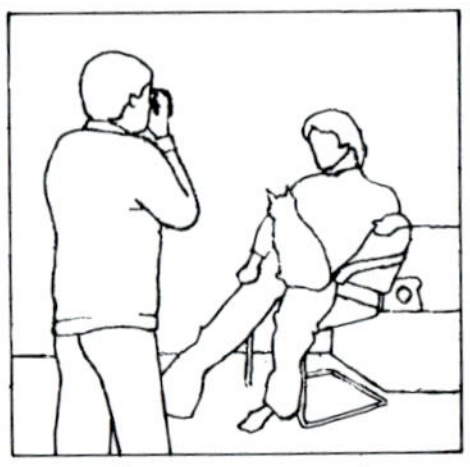

**3.** Preliminary work involved making small compositional drawings squared up to be transferred later to the canvas. Photographs were taken of the room and sitters so that preliminary drawings could be made.

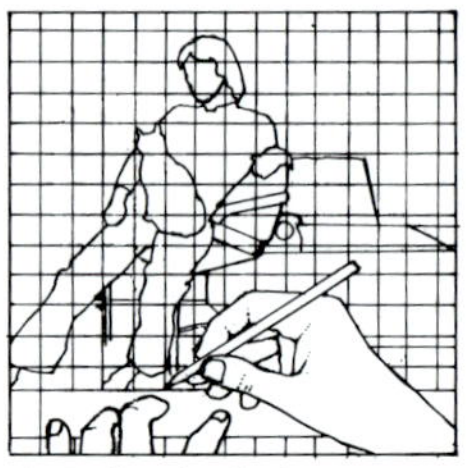

**4.** Individual objects, such as the vase of flowers, would be set up in the studio. Many portrait studies were done both from photographs and life.

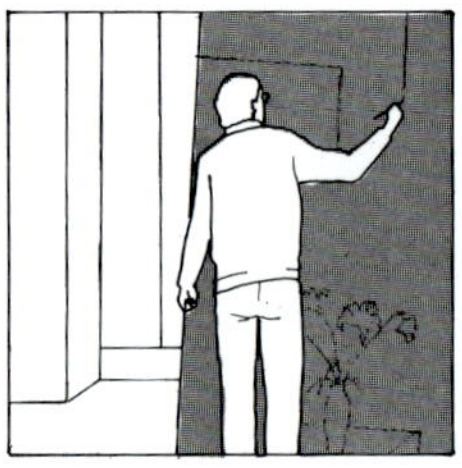

**5.** The compositional design was sketched on the canvas with the aid of preliminary studies.

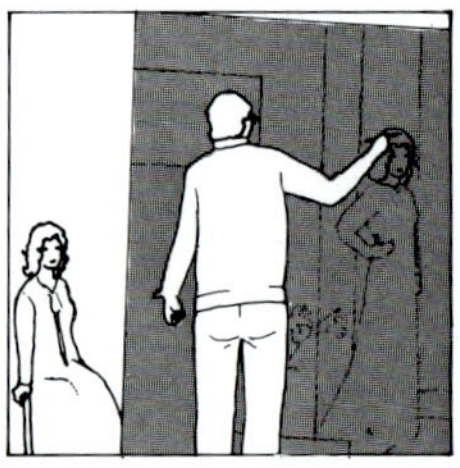

**6.** Hockney painted the sitter's heads from life.

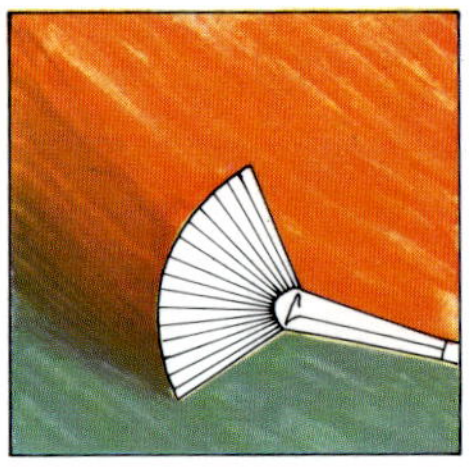

**7.** Soft edges were achieved by blending thin layers of acrylic with a fan brush.

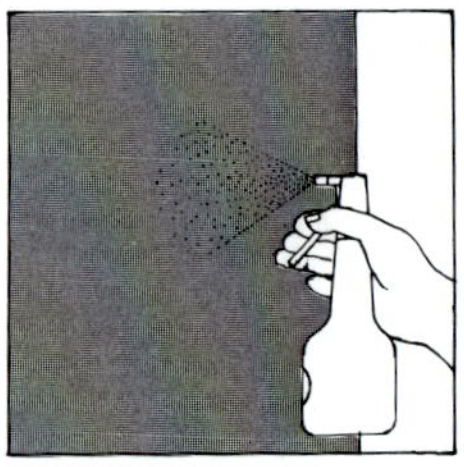

**8.** The final painting was sprayed with acrylic gloss medium or varnish. This saturated the colors and gives the surface a fairly uniform gloss.

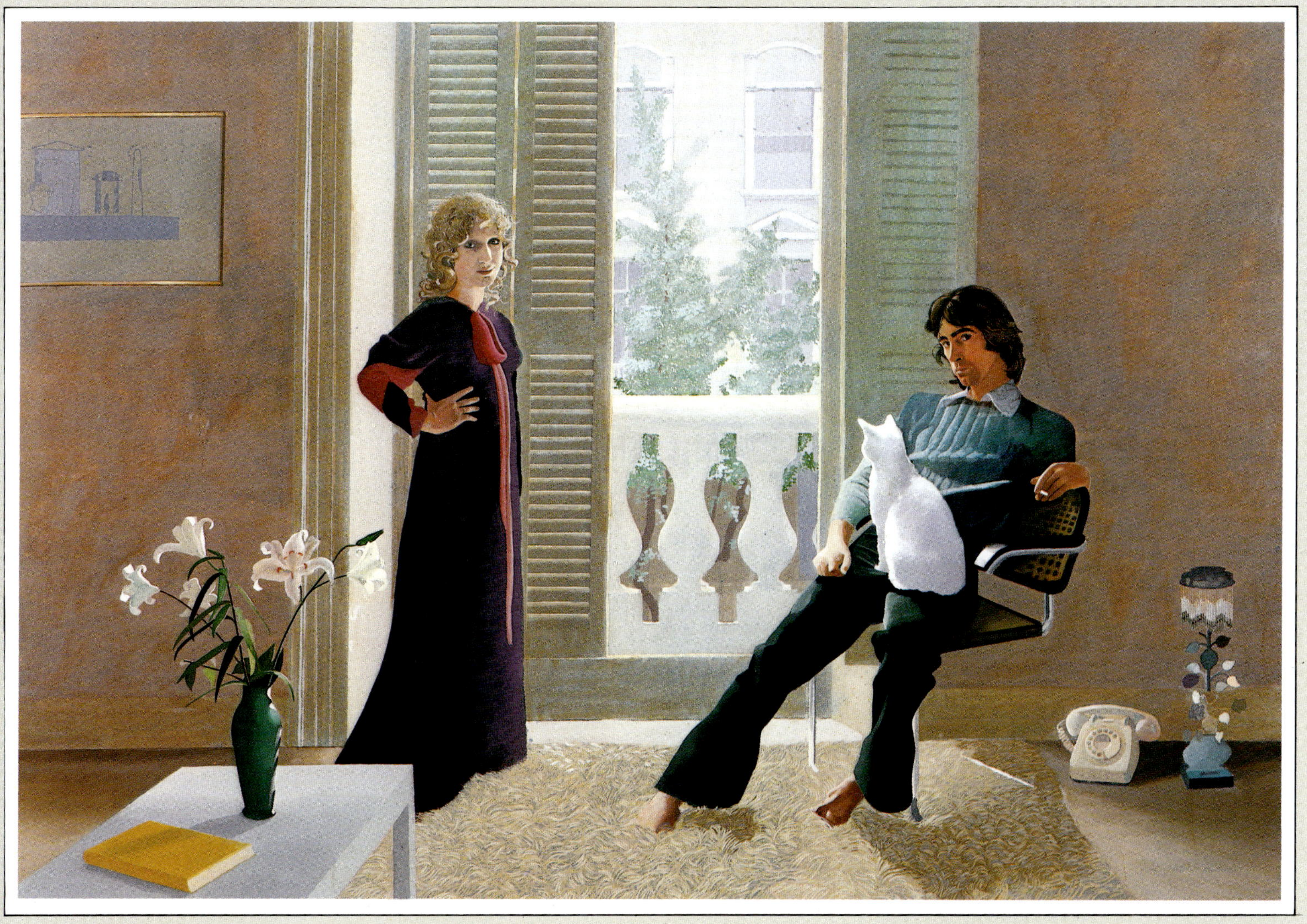

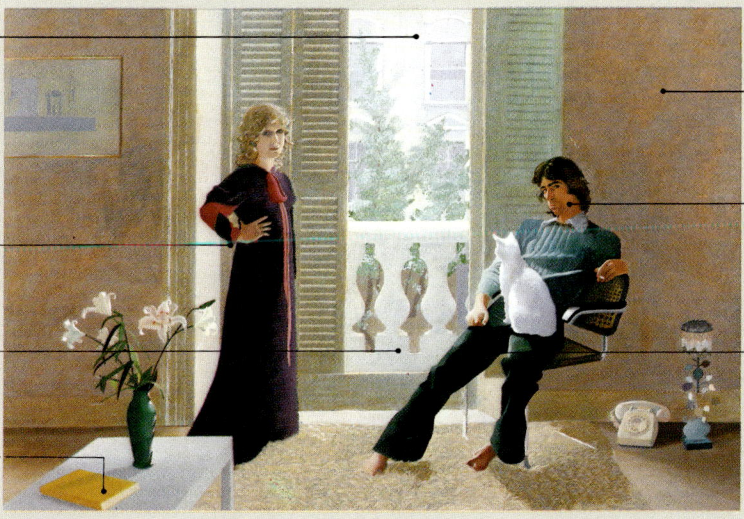

The exterior view is tonally lighter than the rest of the picture except for the highlights. It has a thin, white scumble over most of the surface.

Mrs Clark's dress is treated as a silhouette against the pale background.

The open section of the central window is the light source for the entire painting.

The few objects in the painting are greatly simplified in form.

Thin glazes and opaque layers are floated over one another to create a diffused light.

The eye level of the picture appears to be at the height of Mr Clark's head.

Mr Clark is orientated along the diagonal running from the centre of the bottom edge to the top right corner.

*Before starting this painting, Hockney worked extensively from photographs and life. The initial layout was done in pencil which remains visible in parts of the painting. Many thin glazes and opaque layers of paint were used to create the diffuse light of the background. The view through the window with its atmospheric unity was achieved by scumbling with a thin, white layer of paint. While the heads of the sitters have received more attention than the rest of the painting, freshness and translucency were retained by avoiding hard edges and the deft overlaying of thin layers of paint which Hockney blended quickly with a fan brush. The surface has been covered with a film of gloss medium which gives the painting a uniform glossiness.*

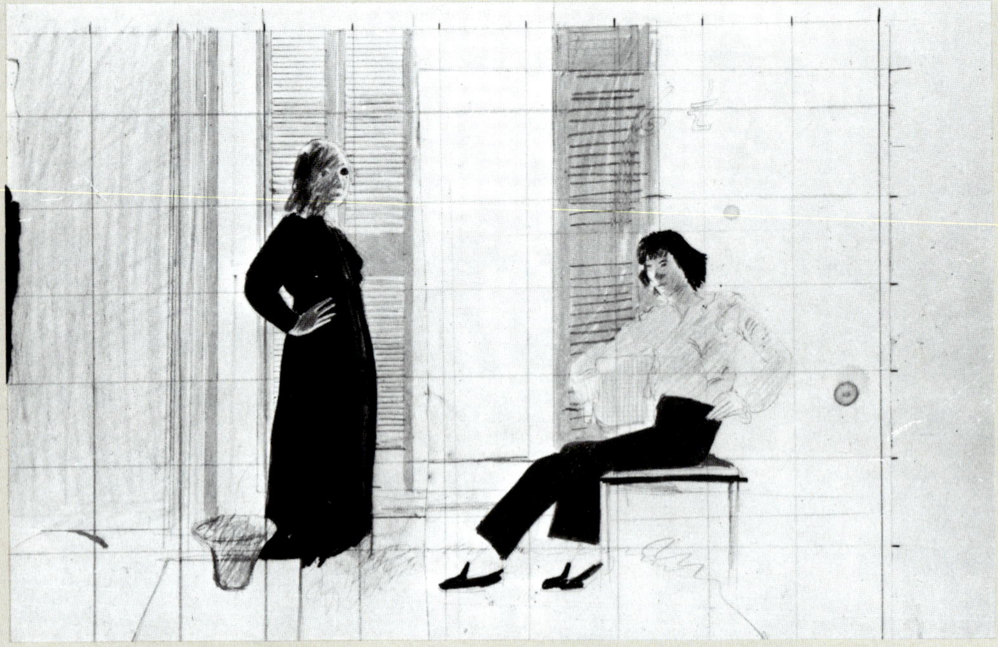

Hockney did many preparatory drawings for this painting which included sketches for the general composition showing the positions of the main figures (top). He also sketched the figure of Ossie Clark (middle right, center) as many as a dozen times. Hockney used photographs of the figures. Here he has drawn a grid on top of the photograph (middle right). This was to help transfer the image to the canvas.

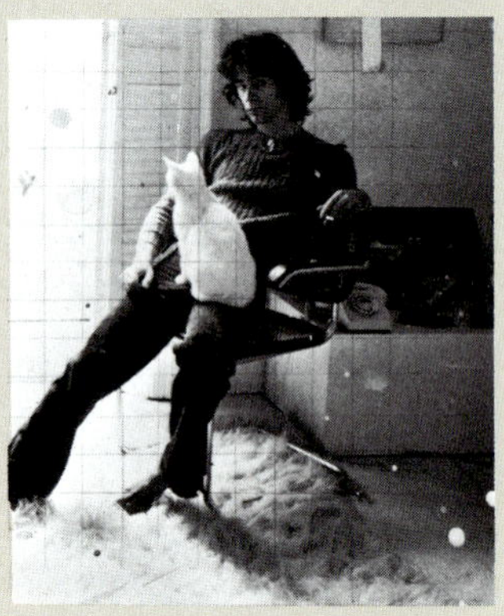

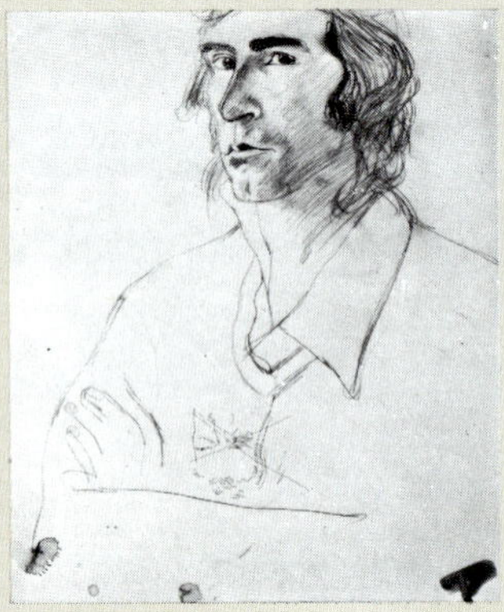

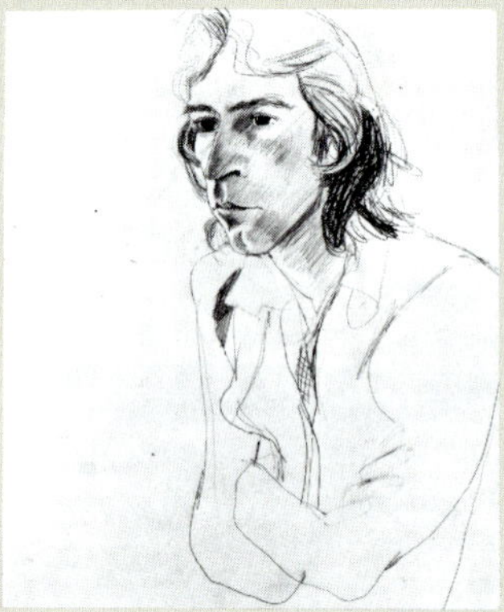

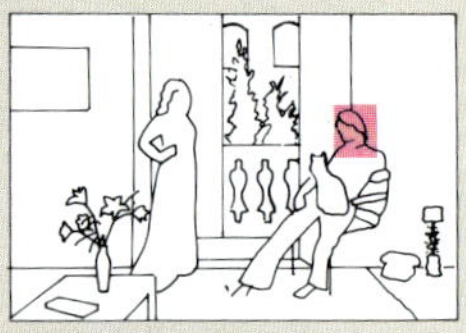

There is a very close resemblance between the head of Ossie Clark in the painting and the photograph. The portrait retains a freshness and translucency because the artist avoided painting hard edges by deftly overlaying thin applications of paint. While the uniformity and translucence of the painting allow the viewer to enter directly into the picture plane, he or she is brought abruptly back to its physical solidity by objects like Mr Clark's cigarette.

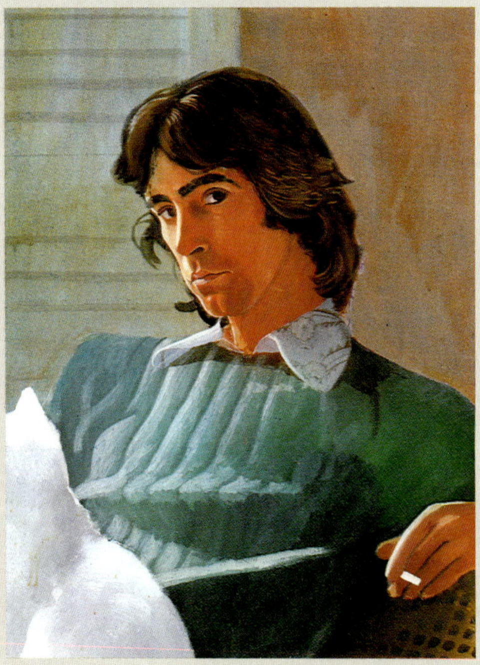

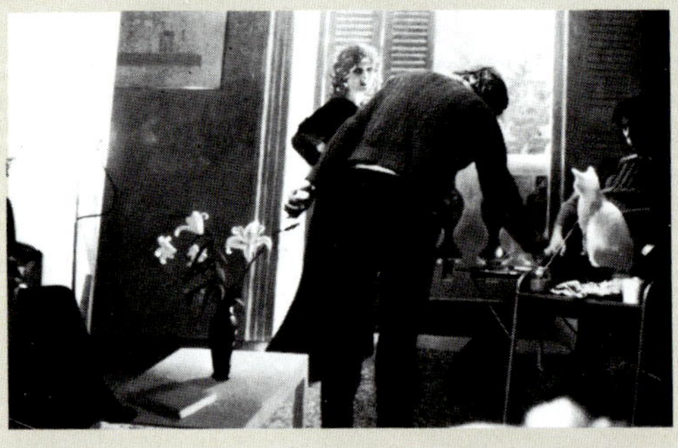

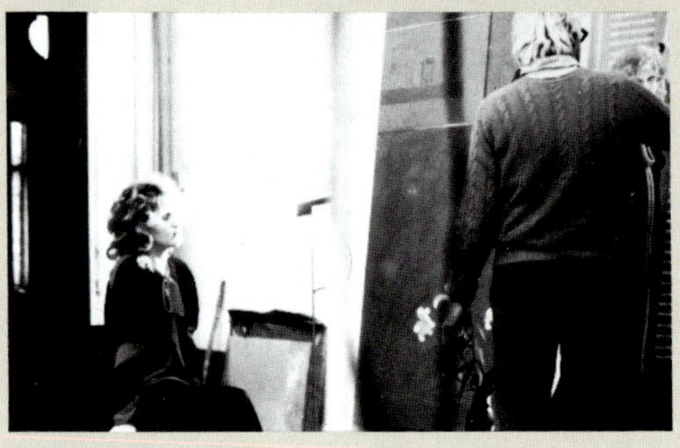

**Left** *These photographs show Hockney working on the picture. In the first (top), the table and vase of flowers create the illusion that Hockney is himself inside the picture. Hockney painted the vase of flowers from life in his studio, in which he also recreated the lighting conditions of the Clark's room. The second photograph (below) shows Celia Birtwell posing. Hockney recalls that both Celia and Ossie posed for a long time. The vase and flowers were painted in Hockney's studio. Care was taken to reproduce the light and atmosphere of the Clark's home even in the studio.*

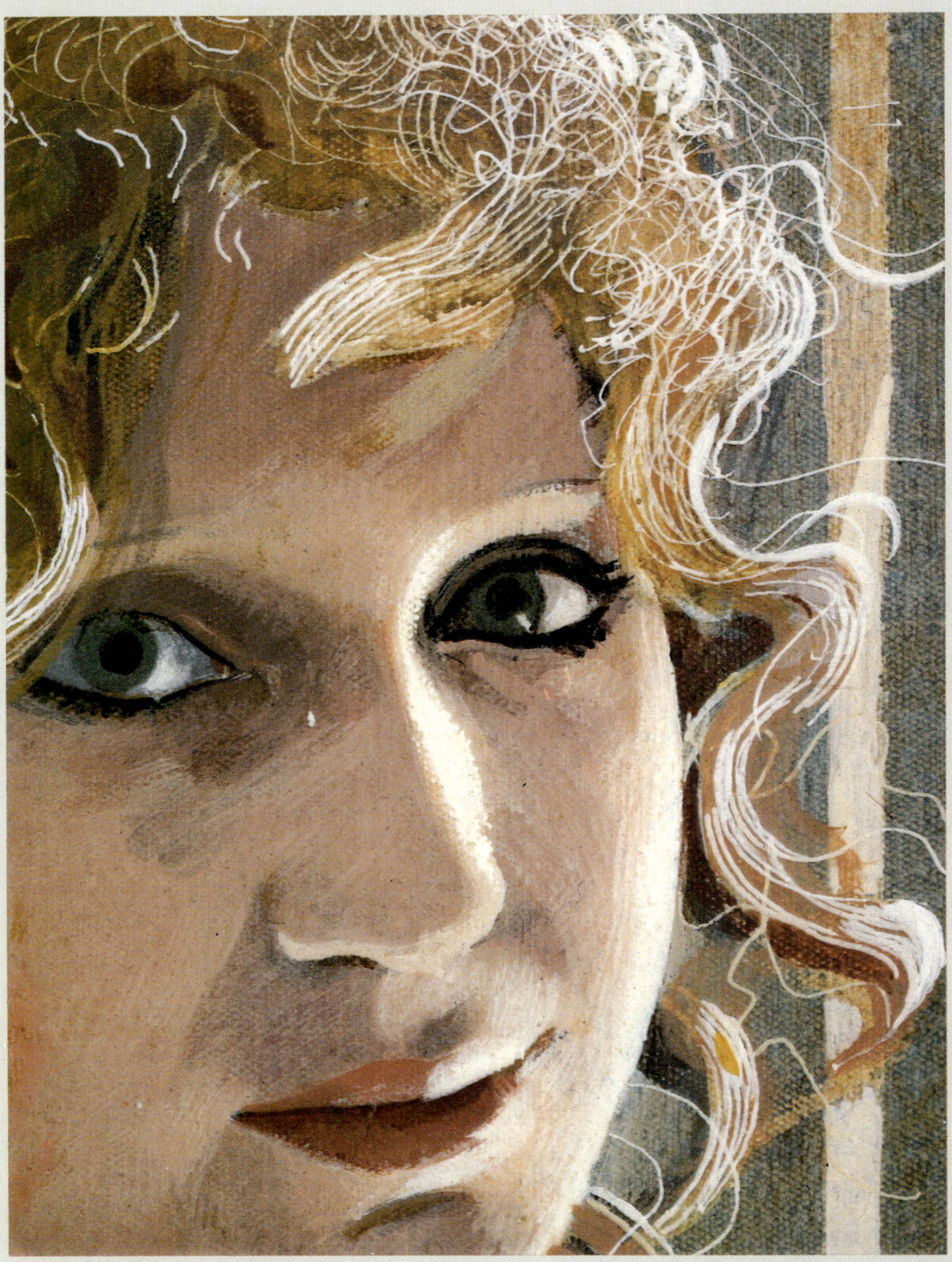

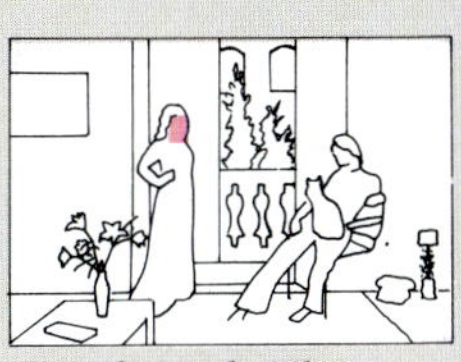

**Actual size detail** *The portrait heads of Mr and Mrs Clark have received more detailed work and reworking than other areas of the painting. The texture of Mrs Clark's hair was achieved by fine, linear arabesques applied in a light gold color over a darker underpainting. Other textural areas were also depicted by using a drawing brushstroke rather than a thick application of paint or glazes.*

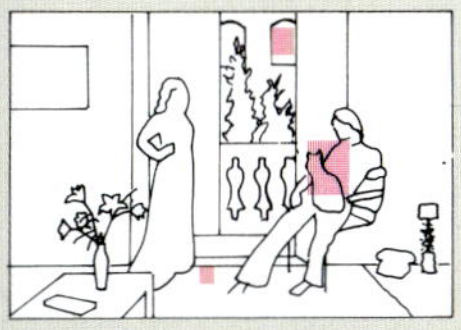

**Right** *The texture of the rug was created by laying down rhythmic curled strokes of cream over a dark gray. These give a sense of fullness and depth.*

**Middle** *The open section of the central window forms the light source for the scene. It is tonally lighter than most of the picture and has a white scumble worked over it.*

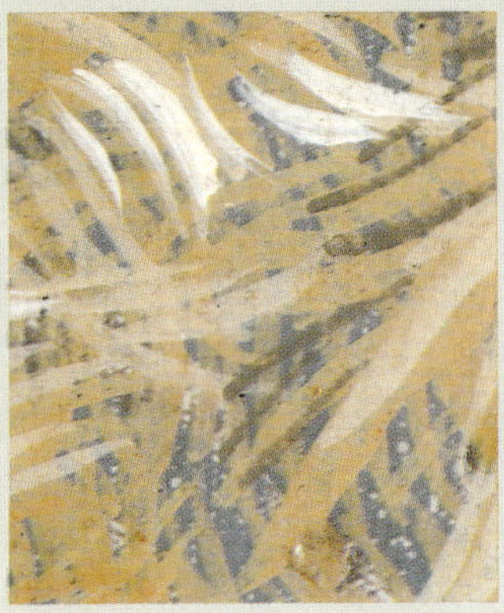

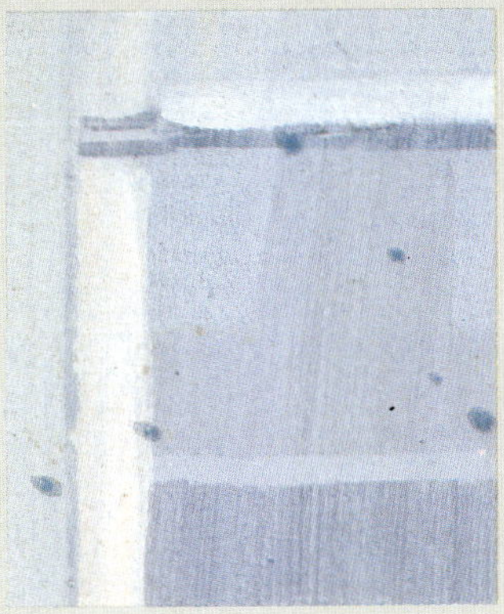

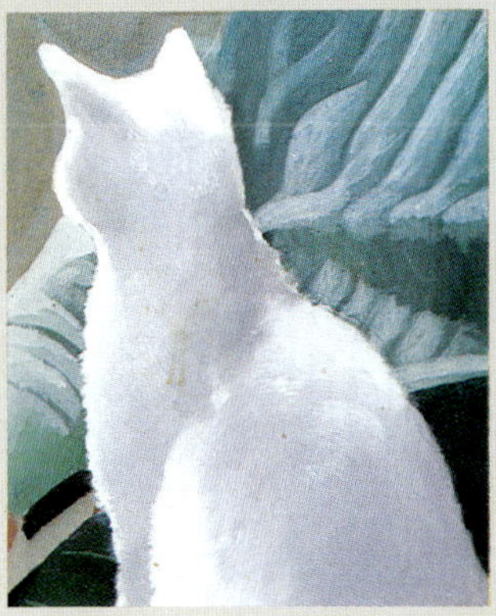

**Left** *In some parts of the painting, the gloss finish has been applied so liberally that it runs down the surface, as can be seen on the cat. A few areas of the painting have not been varnished at all and these are lighter and cooler in tone and have the eggshell finish characteristic of unvarnished acrylic.*

1961
ONWARDS

# SOL LEWITT

***Detail of: Fifteen Part Drawing using four colours and all variations (straight parallel lines, each colour in a different direction) (1970)***
**Graphite on wall surface**
**Dimensions variable**

Sol LeWitt is one of the foremost exponents of the Minimalist Art of the 1960s, which deliberately reduced expressiveness and illusion, as well as an extremely important precursor of Conceptualism, which relegates the material means of communication to promote content at the expense of form. LeWitt represents one of the few key figures who have bridged the avant-garde movements of the 1960s and 1970s successfully. Like many artists of his generation, LeWitt's work is accompanied by a formidable body of explanation, amplification and rhetoric, from critics, allies and himself.

LeWitt was born in 1928 in Hartford, Connecticut, and studied at Syracuse University, New York, from 1945 to 1949. By 1962 he had completely abandoned painting which had been more derivative than experimental. During the mid-1960s he worked in three dimensions, first making black and white reliefs and then various types of constructions. The best-known and most repeated of these forms is the serial variations on a cubic structure; open-frame, multicompartmental structures made of baked enamel on aluminium girders.

LeWitt had his first one-man show at the Daniels Gallery, New York, in 1965, wrote important texts on Conceptual Art, and taught at various institutions in New York. From 1968 he began an extended series of 'wall drawings', which included *Fifteen Part Drawing using four colors and all variations (straight parallel lines, each color in a different direction).*

LeWitt himself spoke of 'subconscious' reference material being his starting points; others have identified the forerunners of his 'grid' system in Cubism, in the work of Jackson Pollock and in that of the early Rationalist Agnes Martin (b 1912). The theory and practice of Constructivism and Jasper John's interrogation of Illusionism were also of some importance.

Such diverse influences and his friendship with contemporary sculptors Donald Judd (b 1928) and Robert Morris, who were engaged in exploring spatial and environmental relationships, gives LeWitt a pivotal position in recent art.

Sol LeWitt's first wall drawing was exhibited at the Paula Cooper Gallery, New York, in 1968. Some critics felt the long wall drawing series was as important for contemporary drawing as Jackson Pollock's use of the drip technique had been for painting in the 1950s.

LeWitt wrote that his overall motivating intention in the wall drawings was to be 'as two-dimensional as possible'. This demands a rejection of the conventional canvas and stretcher as unnecessary intermediaries between the viewer and the wall surface on which they are normally hung. Having, therefore, resolved to 'work directly on walls', LeWitt observes that 'the physical properties of the wall, height, length, color, material, architectural conditions and intrusions are a necessary part of the wall drawing', and that the differences and 'eccentricities' of various wall surfaces should not be reduced or equalized. The drawing is to be executed by one or more recognized draftsmen nominated by the owner of the 'certification' (a document providing diagram and instructions, written and signed by LeWitt, to be exhibited with the finished piece, although not an integral part of it).

LeWitt stipulates that 'the drawing is done rather lightly, using hard graphite so that the lines become, as much as possible, a part of the wall surface visually'. He allows that 'either the entire wall or a portion is used'. The actual kinds of line employed are straight and of four types; vertical, horizontal, 45 degrees diagonal left to right and 45 degrees diagonal right to left. The graphite colors used for colored drawings (restricted to what is commercially available) are yellow, red, blue and black (the colors used in printing); and 'a flat, white wall is preferable'.

*Fifteen Part Drawing* is number 52 in the chronological list of wall drawings; it was first executed at the Jewish Museum in May 1970 and exists in five other versions. Further, as one of the first wall drawings aimed at 'the entire wall from floor to ceiling' and one which makes calculated use of all the basic colors and their permutations, and all the four line directions, it has been considered by the artist himself as perhaps the most important wall drawing of its kind.

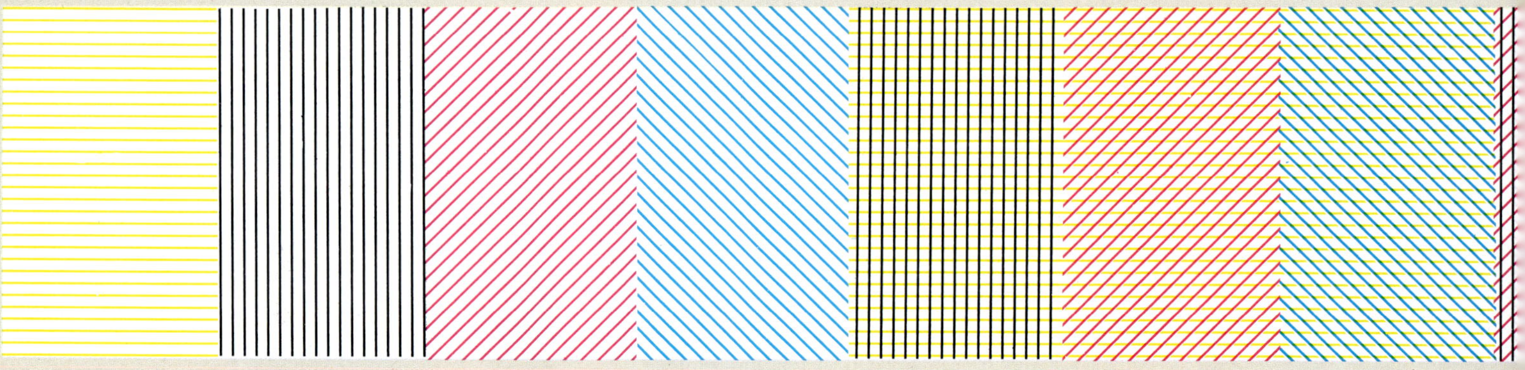

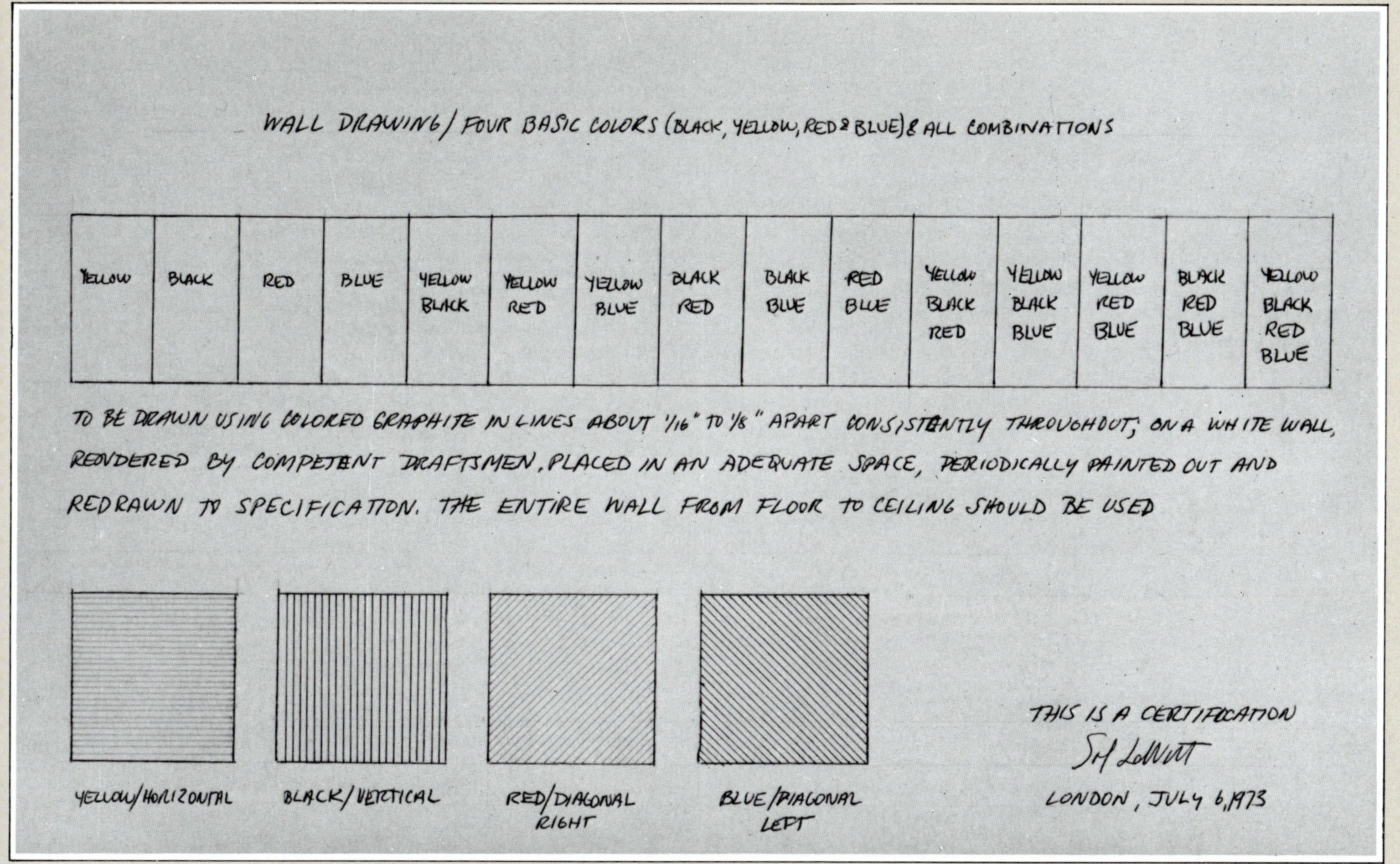

WALL DRAWING / FOUR BASIC COLORS (BLACK, YELLOW, RED & BLUE) & ALL COMBINATIONS

| | | | | | | | | | | | | | | |
|---|---|---|---|---|---|---|---|---|---|---|---|---|---|---|
| YELLOW | BLACK | RED | BLUE | YELLOW BLACK | YELLOW RED | YELLOW BLUE | BLACK RED | BLACK BLUE | RED BLUE | YELLOW BLACK RED | YELLOW BLACK BLUE | YELLOW RED BLUE | BLACK RED BLUE | YELLOW BLACK RED BLUE |

TO BE DRAWN USING COLORED GRAPHITE IN LINES ABOUT 1/16" TO 1/8" APART CONSISTENTLY THROUGHOUT; ON A WHITE WALL, RENDERED BY COMPETENT DRAFTSMEN, PLACED IN AN ADEQUATE SPACE, PERIODICALLY PAINTED OUT AND REDRAWN TO SPECIFICATION. THE ENTIRE WALL FROM FLOOR TO CEILING SHOULD BE USED

YELLOW/HORIZONTAL

BLACK/VERTICAL

RED/DIAGONAL RIGHT

BLUE/DIAGONAL LEFT

THIS IS A CERTIFICATION

Sol LeWitt

LONDON, JULY 6, 1973

*Any draftsman's true interpretation of Sol LeWitt's 'certification'* (ABOVE) *for* Fifteen Part Drawing *must necessarily be very precise; its success depends on fulfilling the artist's instructions. The composition graduates in complexity from left to right and is meant to fill the entire ceiling-to-floor wall space of a white-walled room.*

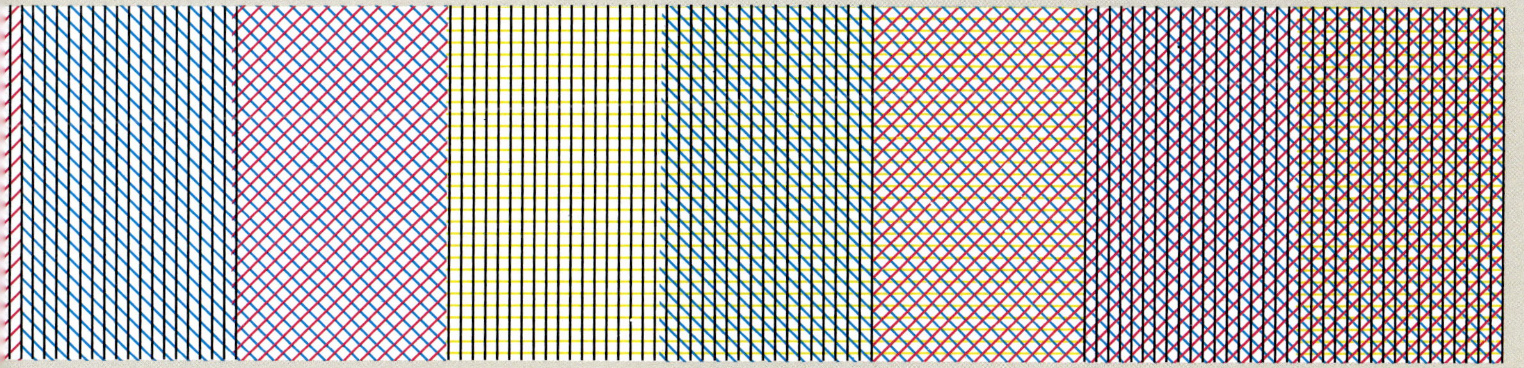

# LUCIAN FREUD

*Large Interior, W.9 (1973)*
Oil on canvas
91.5cm × 91.5cm/36in × 36in

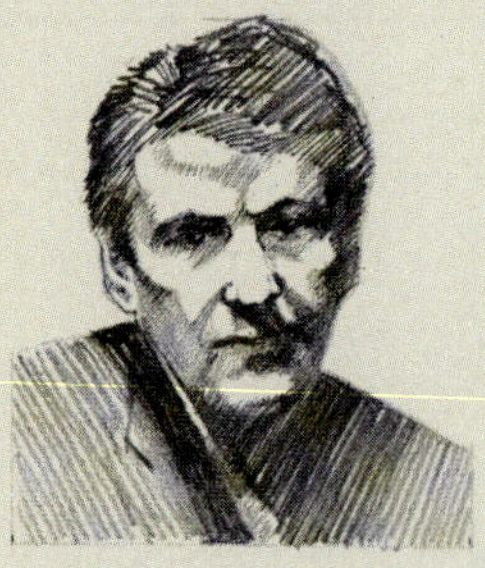

'The fascinated unblinking stare with which Lucian Freud fixed his subjects enabled him to represent them in a manner that makes it impossible for the spectator... ever to look at them casually: the eye is compelled to see them, down to the smallest detail, with something of the intensity with which he saw them himself,' art historian John Rothenstein commented. Much has been made of the fact that Lucian Freud is the grandson of Sigmund Freud, the inventor of psychoanalysis; and the grandson does seem to have inherited a passionate interest in the codification and seizure of states of mind from his grandfather.

Lucian Freud was born in Berlin in 1922 and was brought to England by his parents 10 years later. Lucian Freud drew and painted from an early age, and always wanted to become an artist. After a spell of making sculpture at school, he had a sporadic and varied period from 1939 to 1942 drawing and painting. By the middle of the 1940s his early style had been formed – it was at the same time sophisticated and naive, and reliant upon detailed draftsmanship.

A friendship with Francis Bacon and deep admiration for Bacon's work lead to Freud's discovery of how oil paint can be a magic equivalent for living flesh, and how the medium can actually mold and render its subject matter. He stopped drawing for a while in order to learn more about paint as a substance and as a vehicle. His style became broader in treatment and more concerned with volume and with flesh in its contrasts of lumpiness, density and pellucidity.

With the broadening of style came an equal change in the tools: 'I had stopped drawing and worked with bigger brushes, hog's hair instead of sable.' The bigger brushes, he discovered, enabled him to handle paint in a more generous manner, and the new power and strength of his brushes (hog's hair is much harder than sable) brought a different kind of technical virtuosity, allied to a more energetic vigilance in the depiction of his models.

Like so many of his canvases, *Large Interior, W.9* is square in its dimensions. Freud usually chooses canvases 60 or 90 cm (2 or 3 ft) square, but on occasion has also worked on a larger scale. It is painted in oil on canvas, oil being the *only* paint medium for Freud. He has not been tempted to try any of the newer synthetic media, but has in the past varied his supports – in the 1950s he painted in oil on both wood and copper bases. These hard, unyielding grounds were abandoned at about the time Freud's incisive, linear approach gave way to a broader, more painterly one.

'For him painting has to be, among other things, the collection of objects that he likes, the realizing of data that he values, an accumulation of what he enjoys or desires – it amounts to the same,' noted Lawrence Gowing, in *Lucian Freud* (1982), and went on to emphasize that the masterly technique and the content are inextricably allied. He has to have a relationship with the people he paints: 'If you don't know them it can only be like a travel book.' The seated figure is Lucie, Freud's mother, a status that puts her value beyond question. He first began to paint his mother in 1972, and this, one of 10 canvases of her, is the only one in which she does not appear alone. The half-naked model on the bed behind has also been painted several times by Freud. In this painting her admission into the mother-son intimacy subtly enriches the psychological situation, and at the same time enhances the formal values of the composition. The venue for their meeting, besides being the magic melding of oil paint upon canvas, is a corner of Freud's studio in Paddington, London.

Both figures would have been painted from life, both would have been required to pose for countless hours, but the fact that there is an odd relationship between the scale of the two figures (the head of the semi-naked model is as large as that of the mother and thus she does not take her place in the perspectival recession as she should) suggests that each model posed on their own.

From his earliest works, Freud has varied the scale of an object, usually a human figure, depending on how it works within the confines of the canvas and the setting, and within his sphere of interest.

The only other object in the corner of the studio, apart from the chair and bed which support the women, is a large pestle and mortar, containing a quantity of what seems to be freshly ground grey paint. Because Freud has held fast to the principle that'... the paint is the person. I want it to work for me just as flesh does', and because the mortar is positioned below his mother, with the grey paint being applied as the undercoat for her clothing, the pestle, mortar and paint could be read as a symbol for his mother. She is the paint and has endured what it has endured.

The clarity of Freud's perception, the 'realizing of data that he values', only works as well as it does because of his mastery of the technique of oil painting. In *Large Interior, W.9* different painterly approaches are used for different textures. The walls are thinly washed with color, allowing the light ground to shine through. With the wooden floor, the brushstrokes make and follow the grain, and with the figures thicker paint and larger brushstrokes model the forms.

'Freud has spoken about the images of the past', said Lawrence Gowing; 'which "are so powerful that one cannot imagine how anyone could have made them or how they could ever not have existed". That is how one feels about *Large Interior, W.9.*'

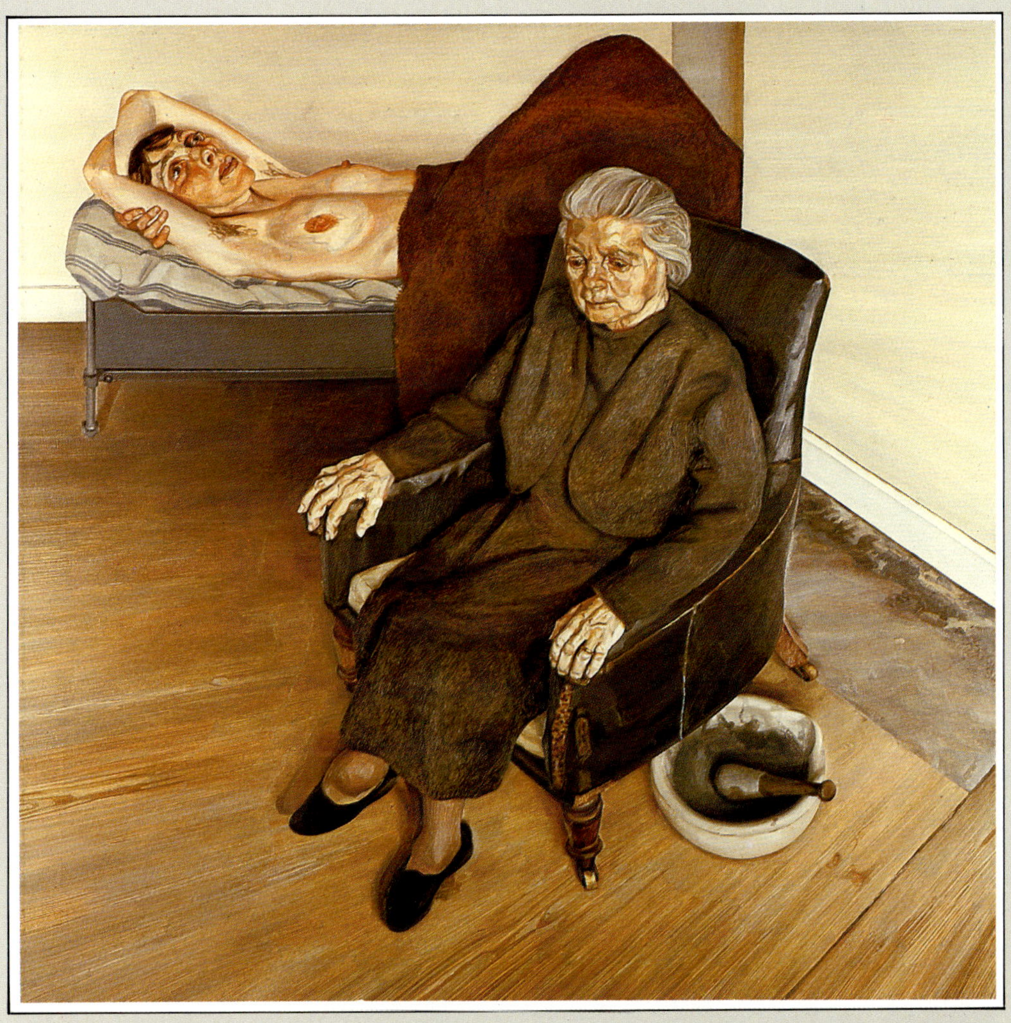

*Freud chooses to concentrate on the human figure as subject matter for his work. He brings such a close intensity and keenness to his work that even the spectator finds himself persuasively drawn into a relationship with the sitter.* Large interior, *W.9 is the culmination of a series of portraits by Freud of his mother, and is the only one to contain another figure. It is actually a juxtaposition of a younger and an older woman, both there to point up ideas about innocence, maturity and experience. The blanket thrown over the nude model acts as a shield and an extended wing of the chair to hide her from the mother, and as the shape of the blanket rises to an apex directly behind the mother's head it serves as a kind of halo or backcloth so that more attention is paid to the head.*

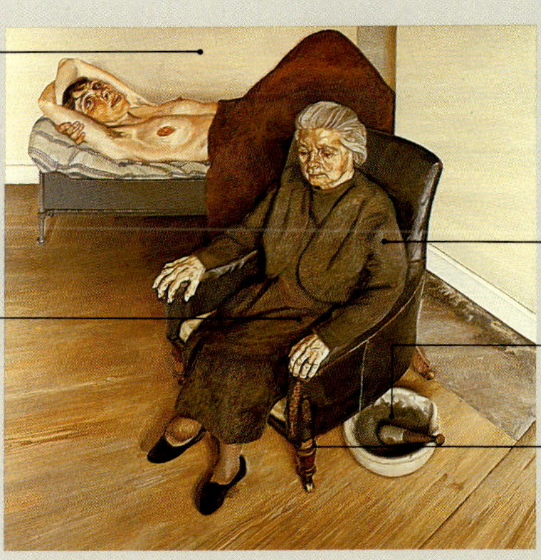

Large long straight brushstrokes of Naples yellow and white follow the direction of the walls

Color harmonies are built around the earth colors, siennas and umbers

Mid-grey is thinly painted over a burnt umber layer

The grey pigment in the pestle is used for the side of the bed

A concentrated dark-toned central area is offset by a paler surround

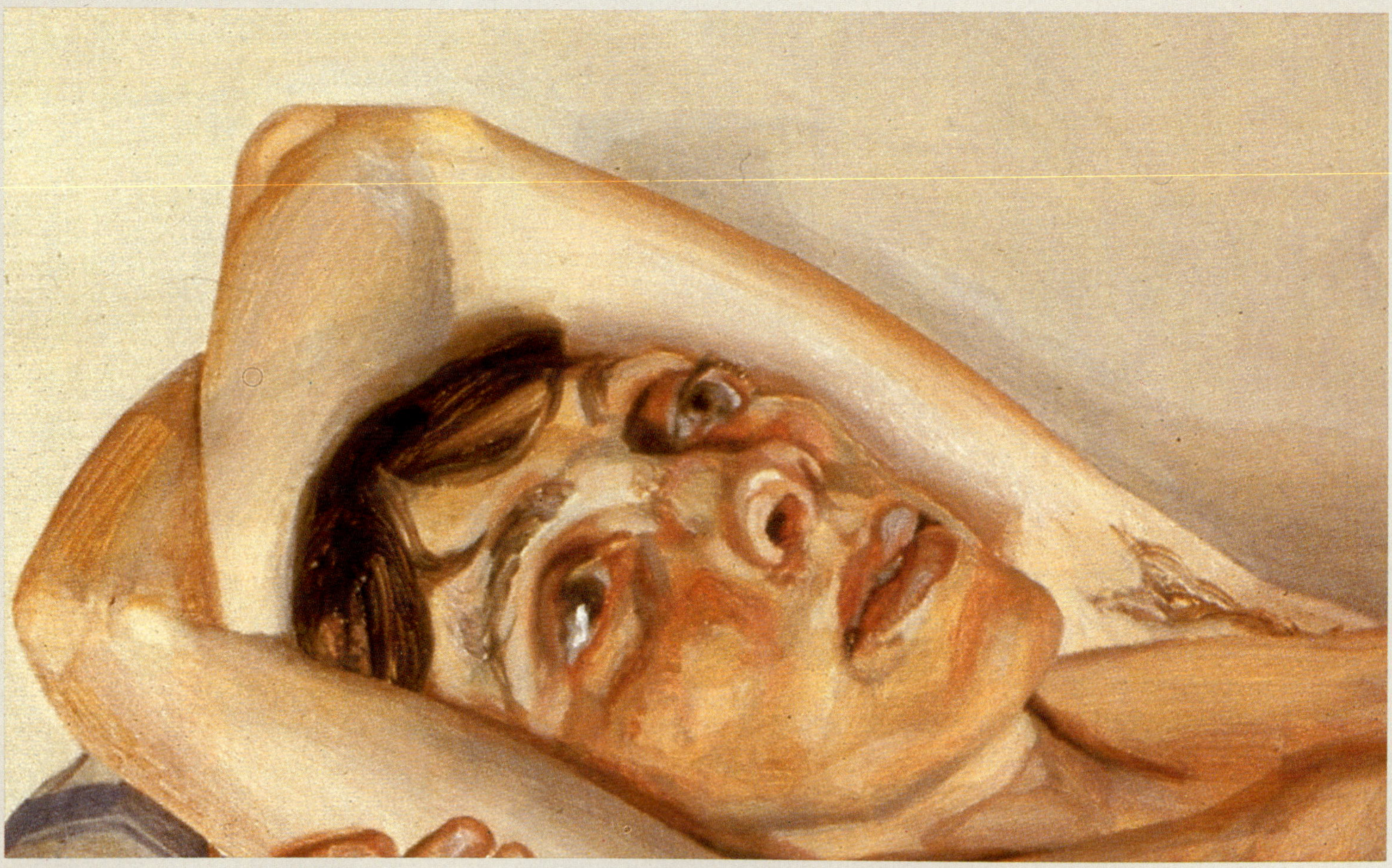

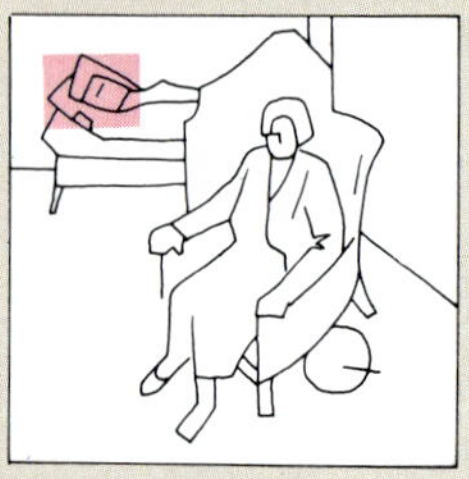

ACTUAL SIZE DETAIL
*Freud has painted this model before, and has also used this vulnerable pose which draws attention to the bare breasts. The blanket which covers the nude contains a high proportion of burnt sienna and the hot value of this color seems to be reflected throughout her flesh. The long streak of white in her eye is perhaps the reflection of a lit neon tube.*

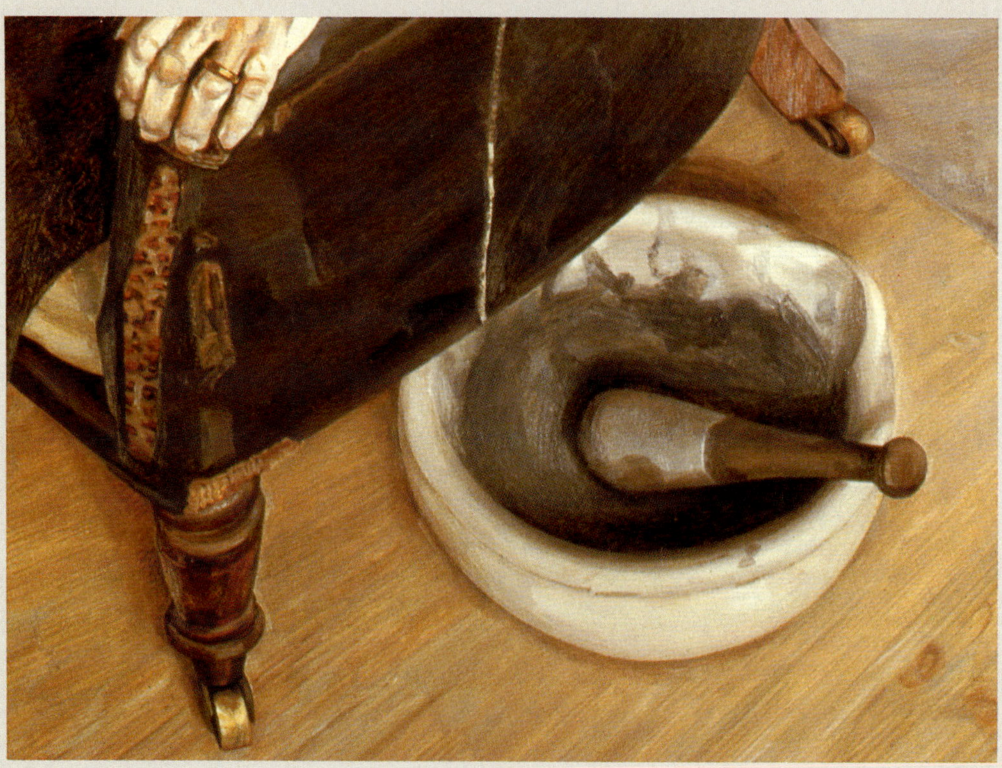

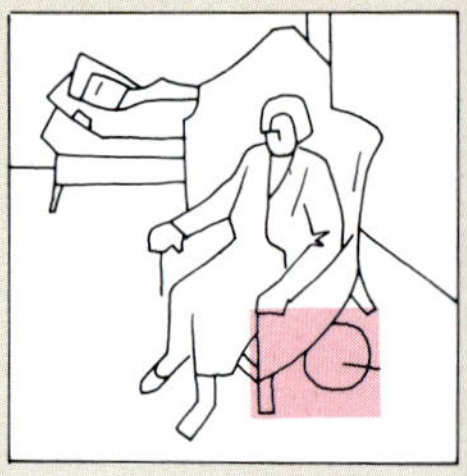

LEFT *This pestle and mortar must be one of Freud's possessions, kept in his studio. They stand as a reminder of one of the traditional tools of the artist's trade, a necessary piece of equipment when the artist had to grind his own pigment, in the days before it could be purchased ready prepared in tubes. The pigment it contains appears to have been mixed with a binder and is ready for use.*

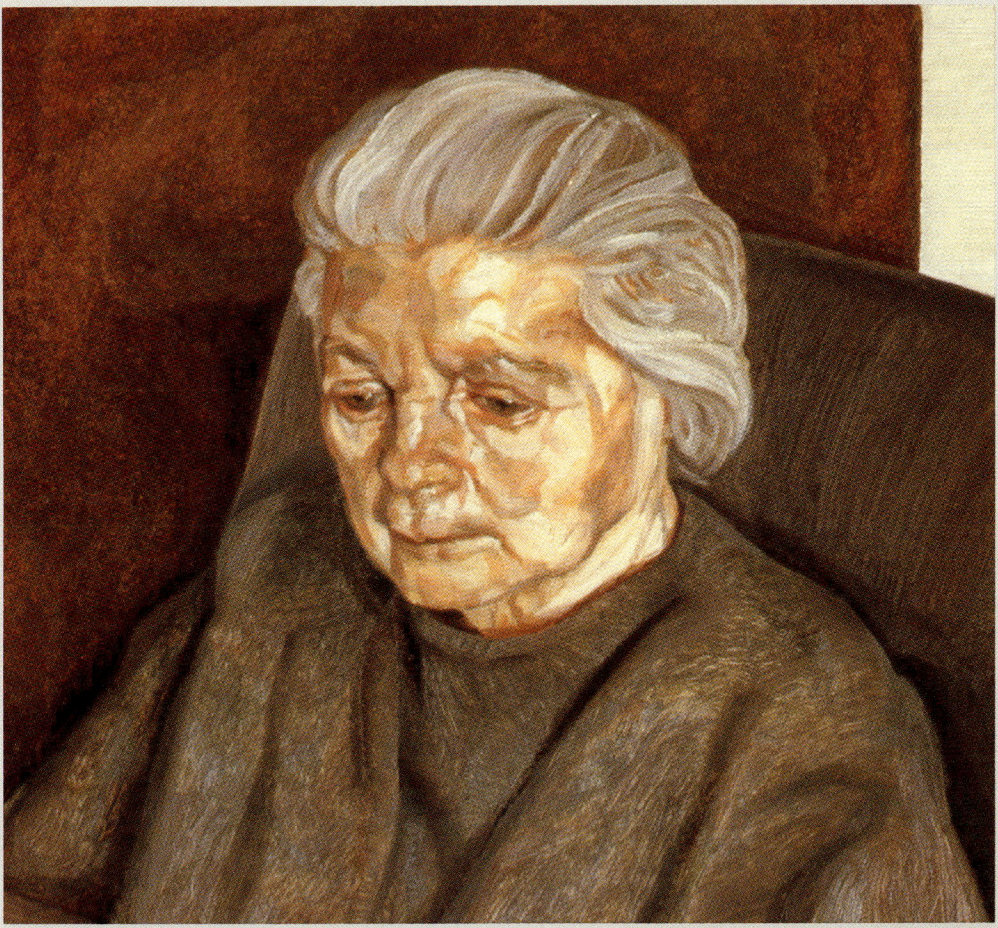

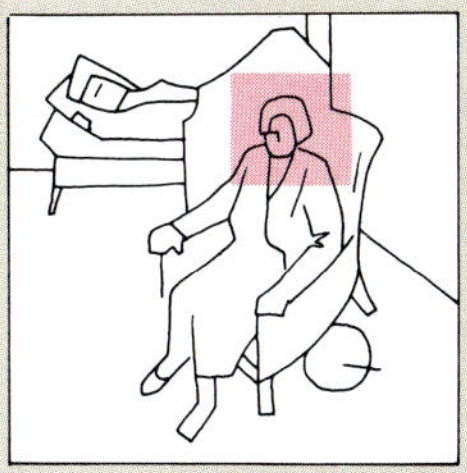

LEFT *Freud places his mother in one of this favorite studio props, a worn brown armchair with a hard reflective surface. As the model takes her color values from the blanket which clothes her, so Freud's mother wears a dress which shares the burnt umber hue used for the armchair. Possibly he asked her to sit to him wearing it so that this color relationship could be established, and it is echoed in hues chosen by Freud to capture the volumes of her face. The mother is lit from a strong light directly above; since he can work by both natural and electric light, and since the source of this light appears to be the ceiling, it is reasonable to assume that Freud painted this work under artificial lighting.*

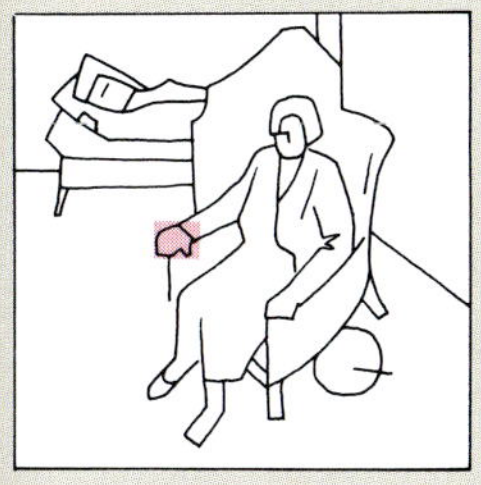

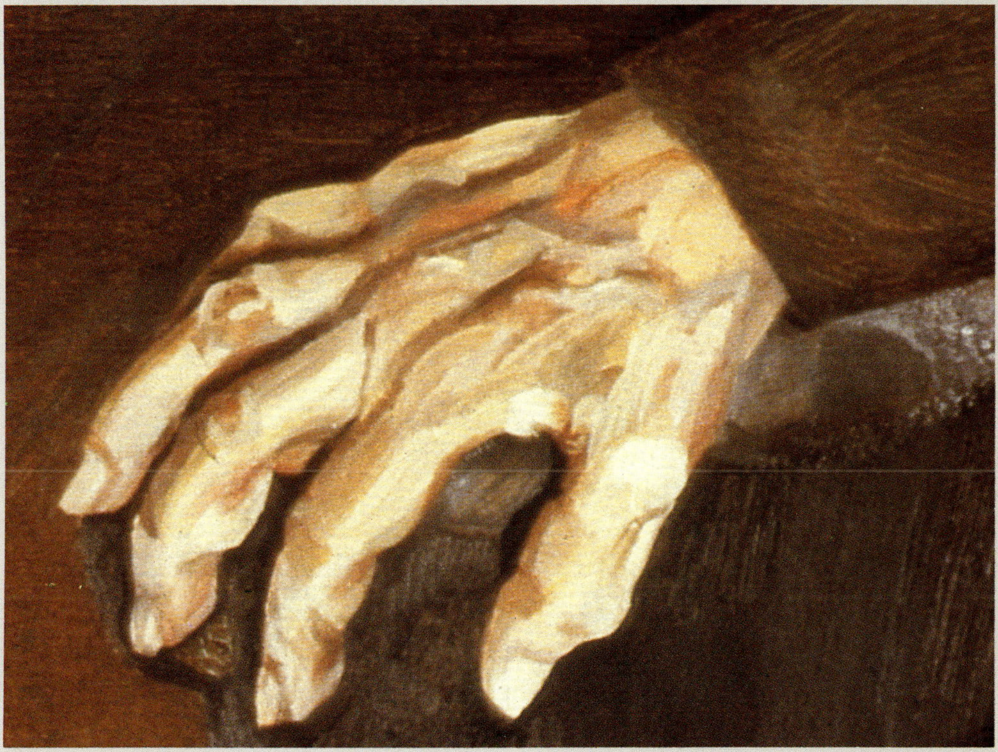

RIGHT *The mother's right hand with the fingers spread apart, constrasts with the left which is seen as a closed unit. The pose is strong and it is reinforced by deft, swift handling. Three long continuous brushstrokes in dark brown delineate the divisions of the back of the hand.*

# GLOSSARY

## A

**Abstract Art** A style of art that sees form and colour as holding the aesthetic values of art and not the naturalistic portrayal of subject matter. It is sometimes called *Concrete Art*.

**Abstract Expressionism** A form of *Abstract Art* and *Expressionism* which allows the subconscious to express itself. It is freed from the portrayal of everyday subject matter.

**Academic** This painting discipline was based on and conformed to the official standards set by the Academy. The Academy in France, first founded on Italian lines in the 1640s, was until 1863, in control of the Ecole des Beaux-Arts. This included jurisdiction over the Rome Prize and other awards and the official Salon exhibitions. The Academy was a conservative body, promoting a traditional, conservative style and method, based upon classical principles.

**Action Painting** (*Gesturalism*) A spontaneous action by the painter to express the subconscious in order to contribute to the personal dynamism of his or her work.

**Alizarin** A reddish purple *pigment* obtained from the root of the madder plant. Combined with salts of metals it creates the lake colors.

**Alla prima** *Alla prima* is an Italian phrase meaning painted solely wet in wet and usually, but not necessarily, at a single sitting. It is used most commonly with reference to oil painting.

**Ambient light** Broadly speaking, ambient light means the diffused and reflected light which fills the environment outdoors.

**Analytical Cubism** A phase of *Cubism* which sought to analyse nature by breaking down its subject matter, then reconstructing it again. It concentrated on the architecture of interlocking planes rather than on colour.

**Arriccio** A rough plaster surface consisting of lime and sand mixed in water. This is applied to a wall in the initial stages of *fresco* painting.

**Atelier** (studio) The *atelier* had two meanings in nineteenth century France. On the one hand, it meant the location where masters provided a setting and models for students who chose to study with them. This was a teaching studio. On the other hand, it simply meant the studio where individual artists executed their own work. Most nineteenth century studios were especially designed for the purpose, with the high ceilings and the high northern light which was preferred by most academic painters. Garrets were often used by poor painters for, although small, they had good light and were cheap.

**Automatism** A method of drawing where the pen is allowed to rove without any conscious planning.

**Azurite** A blue mineral derivative of copper often substituted for the very expensive *ultra-marine*.

## B

**Backlight** *see contrejour.*

**Baroque** A style of architecture, painting and sculpture which originated in Europe in the late sixteenth century and which lasted until the eighteenth. The movement succeeded *Mannerism* and turned away from the straight line and reason, in favor of curves, emotion and unidealized naturalism. Caravaggio, Rubens, Rembrandt and Velazquez represent different strains of Baroque art.

**Bauhaus** This was a German school of architecture, design and craftsmanship founded in 1919 and closed in 1933 by the Nazis. It was interested in fusing art with craft and the practicalities of daily life.

**Biomorphism** A form of *Abstract Art* which takes living organisms as its subject matter and not geometric shapes.

**Binder** *see medium.*

**Bitumen (asphaltum)** This transparent rich brown *pigment* never dries completely and causes deterioration and *craquelure* if used in *underpainting*. It was used, with frequently disastrous results, in the late eighteenth and nineteenth centuries. Rembrandt, amongst others, used it as a glaze, for which it is suitable.

**Bladders** Before the invention of metal tubes for artists' colors, leather bladders were used for storing paint. These were pricked by the artist when the paint was needed and then resealed to keep the paint fresh.

**Blanc, Charles** Charles Blanc was an influential nineteenth century art historian and theorist. In 1867, he published *Grammaire des arts du dessin* (*Grammar of the Art of Drawing*). An administrator in the Ecole des Beaux-Arts, Blanc was committed to the Renaissance tradition in art, yet his work was important for many young artists, including Seurat. Politically, Blanc was a utopian Socialist, which may have appealed to the radical Neo-impressionists.

**Blending** Blending is a term most commonly used with reference to academic painting practice to mean the blending together of separate touches of color for halftones, until the gradations of tone and the marks of the brush are imperceptible. The method most widely recommended was the deft slurring of each tone into the next by means of a touch of each of the tones on the brush. The blending brush was introduced in the nineteenth century especially to facilitate this process, but most authorities considered it a slick, softening and unsatisfactory alternative to the approved method. The soft fan-shaped blending brush was dragged dry across the wet paint of the halftones, blending them and obliterating the mark of the brush.

**Blocking-in** Blocking-in usually refers to the broad application of masses of light, shade, and color, in the early stages of a painting. It helped to obliterate rapidly the glaring brightness of the ground, permitting the artist to see the general effect in the painting more quickly. It is a term which normally has wider application than the very specific term *ébauche. See ébauche.*

**Blue rider (Der Blaue Reiter)** An influential group of German Expressionists formed in Munich in 1911 by Wassily Kandinsky, Paul Klee, August Macke and Franz Marc.

**Bouvier, P.L.** Bouvier was a painter of Swiss extraction who in 1827 published an influential volume called the *Manuel des jeunes artistes et amateurs en peinture* (*Handbook for Young Artists and Painting Amateurs*), which provides vital information on artistic practice and materials in early nineteenth century France.

**Broken color** A term covering a number of techniques in which several colors are used in their pure state rather than being blended or mixed. Usually the paint quality is stiff and thick and, when the paint is dragged across the surface, layers beneath show through. This term can also refer to the *Pointillist* technique.

**Die Brücke** An association of Expressionist-style artists established in Dresden in 1905. They were linked by their desire to discover new creative experiences.

## C

**Cadmiums** Brilliant permanent *pigments* which are suitable for most techniques. Cadmiums turn black when mixed with copper colors, such as *emerald green*, and brown when mixed with lime. The colors include cadmium yellow, green and red. The latter is considered the best substitute for *vermillion*.

**Camera obscura** A technical aid, widely used in the seventeenth and eighteenth centuries, which consisted of a darkened box or tent containing lenses and a mirror. The artist could project the image of an object or landscape onto the painting surface and then trace it out in charcoal or graphite.

**Casein** A strongly adhesive substance made from the curd of fresh milk.

**Casts** Casts are plaster copies taken from objects. Traditionally, art students have made drawing from casts. At the Ecole des Beaux-Arts, casts were usually made from suitable earlier sculpted masterpieces and antique sculpture. This was in order to educate the students' eyes in ideal beauty in the human form as well as to train them in drawing. Since plaster casts are more or less white, they simply present the student with a solid object devoid of color over which lights and darks play. Casts were thus used before the student graduated to work from the live model, to inculcate in them a knowledge of tone in drawing, which it was considered essential to learn before using color.

**Cennini, Cennino** A fifteenth century Florentine painter best known for his book *Libro dell'arte* (*The Craftsman's Handbook*). Written c. 1390, it contains valuable information on early *tempera* and *fresco* techniques.

**Chiaroscuro** The broad meaning of *chiaroscuro* in painting and drawing is the rendering of forms by a balanced contrast of light and shadow which serves to give relief to forms and an illusion of space and depth to the composition. It was a technique introduced in the Renaissance when it was perfected by

Leonardo da Vinci (145-1519). By the early nineteenth century, French academic painters were preoccupied with rendering the subtle gradations of tone which separated the highest lights and the deepest shadows. Ideally, the lights were opaque, and the shadows depicted with transparent paint. By this time, *chiaroscuro* was not simply a technical device, but also embodied a universal ideal of truth and beauty in art.

**Chroma** *see colour.*

**Chrome yellow** A brilliant colour, chrome yellow is made from lead chromate. It covers and dries well but tends to change tone with time.

**Chronophotography** The process of recording figures, animals and objects photographically in motion.

**Classicism** The term given to a style of art which is ultimately derived from the study of Greek and Roman artists. Classicism is often considered the antithesis of *Romanticism*.

**Collage** Derived from the French verb *coller* meaning 'to stick', collage is the technique of pasting cloth, paper or other materials onto a canvas or surface. It was first used by the Cubist artists.

**Color** (chroma) Color, chroma and hue are three terms used here synonymously to indicate the color of things as perceived by the eye — their appearance of redness or greenness for instance. Color is also used to refer to artists' colors, or paints ground with a binder for use in painting.

**Color grinding** In oil color grinding, dry pigment particles are ground with an oil medium or binder under friction, to achieve a thorough 'wetting' of each pigment particle, and a complete and even dispersal of all the particles in the binder.

**Color temperature** Color temperature refers to the identification of color by relative warmth or coolness. In broad terms, those colors on the blue half of the color circle are cool, while those on the red side are considered warm. Within this, a red, for example alizarin crimson, can be said to be cool relative to a hotter red like vermilion, because alizarin tends toward blue-violet in hue, while vermilion tends toward orange, another warm color.

**Complementary colors** Complementary colors are those found opposite each other on the color circle — red and green, yellow and violet, blue and orange. When these color pairs are placed side by side — especially when they are close in tonal value — they are mutually enhanced and appear to oscillate as the eye seeks to differentiate the two hues. Complementary or simultaneous contrast of tones takes place between blacks or grays, and whites. When juxtaposed these hues appear respectively darker or lighter where they join. The scientific basis for these phenomena, which had previously only been observed empirically, was laid by Eugène Chevreul in the 1830s in France.

**Composition** In painting the composition is the design or arrangement of, for example, lines, masses of light and shade, and colors, to form a coherent unity on the picture surface.

**Conceptual Art** A term for art in the late 1960s to late 1970s where the idea for a piece of work is more important than the execution and completion of the work.

**Concrete Art** see *Abstract Art.*

**Constructivism** A Russian movement developed from *Cubist collage* and founded by Vladimir Tatlin. It laid emphasis on the importance of movement in space rather than spatial volume. The movement died out in 1922.

**Contour** While the outline of a form is simply an invented line which follows the outer silhouette of the form, contour lines include lines inside the edges of the form, which suggest a three-dimensional quality.

**Contrejour** (back-light) *Contrejour* literally means 'against the daylight' and, as its name suggests, is a light source situated behind the artist's subject. It tends to throw the subject into silhouette, creating extremes of contrast between light and dark, usually with very limited halftones. This lighting was used to dramatic effect by Degas, for example in *Woman Against a Window* (c. 1872).

**Craquelure** This is the term used to designate the tiny cracks and fine lines covering the surface of most old paintings. They are caused by the shrinking and movement of the ground and the paint surface.

**Croquis** (thumbnail sketch) The small *croquis* is a free drawing often jotted down from the imagination in which the artist toys with ideas for poses for figures or groups of figures. These may be incorporated in the *esquisse. See esquisse.*

**Cross-hatching** A technique in which paint or another medium is laid down or drawn in a series of criss-crossing strokes to build up depth and tone.

**Cubism** An innovatory and influential abstract art movement begun in Paris around 1907 by Picasso and Braque. As a reaction against previous naturalistic painting traditions, the Cubists simultaneously depicted many different views of an object. They often represented forms as superimposed geometric planes with the intention of expressing the idea of an object rather than any particular aspect.

# D

**Dada** The French word for 'rocking horse'. A nihilistic movement which arose in 1915 in disillusionment at the First World War and lasted until 1922. It was anti-art and tended towards the absurd in its desire to shock and scandalize.

**Darks** The darks are those parts hidden from the fall of light in a painting. Traditionally, they were rendered thinly and with transparent earth colors. When treated with a loaded brush and opaque paint, transparent glazes of dark hues were added to give the darks depth and create an illusion of recession in painting. This is because it is hard to create an illusion of recession with opaque color, but dark transparent paint lends itself well to a sense of depth in a painting.

**De Piles, Roger** De Piles was an important seventeenth century art theorist. He published several volumes on art theory and practice, including *Les Premières élémens de la peinture pratique* (*First principles of Painting Techniques*) (Paris, 1684), which gives invaluable information on painting practice in France at that period.

**De Stijl** Originally a Dutch magazine (1917-1928) concerned with *Neo-Plasticism,* but also the name for the geometrical abstract ideas that the magazine advocated.

**Diluent** A diluent is the liquid used to dilute or thin a paint. For example, the diluent most commonly used with oil paints is turpentine, the diluent for watercolors is water.

**Distemper** An impermanent type of paint in which the pigments are mixed with *size.*

**Divisionism** A technique of applying small area of unmixed pigment onto the canvas, which optically combine for the spectator. It is also called *Pointillism.*

**Dragging** Dragging denotes the movement of a stiff bristle brush loaded with color, across a dry, rough surface. The roughness can come from the textured surface of a grainy primed canvas or irregularities resulting from previous applications of loaded paint which have dried. In dragging, the wet paints catches only on the raised parts of the dry surface texture, allowing the colors below to show through and create a vibrant, stippled effect of broken color.

**Drying oils** Drying oils are oils which have the property of forming a solid, elastic surface when exposed to air in thin layers. The drying oils most commonly used in oil painting were linseed oil, walnut oil and poppy oil. Examples of non-drying oils unsuitable for painting, are olive oil and almond oil.

# E

**Ebauche** (lay-in) The *ébauche* is the underpainting or thinly painted lay-in of the lines, broad masses of light and shade, and the halftones of the subject, which provided the base for the finished painting. The *ébauche* had to be completely dry, and then scraped down, before the final finishing or reworking of the painting began. The academic *ébauche* was normally executed in somber earth colors ranging in tone from deep browns to pale creams. The former were usually transparent, the latter always opaque. Progressive independent artists, like the Impressionists, avoided the dark *ébauche,* beginning their work in bright hues related to the local colors of their subject.

**Emerald green** This very poisonous color derived from copper arsenate will turn black if mixed with sulphur pigment. The Masters were aware of this danger and thus overpainted emerald green with varnish.

**Encaustic** A technique in which molten wax, mixed with pigments and sometimes resin, is applied to a surface. When dry, the colors have a glossy shine. This technique was most used in the first and third centuries, but has more recently been adapted by artists such as Jasper Johns.

**Esquisse** (sketch) This is the compositional drawing or painting which embodied the artist's first inspired idea or design for the final painting. Part of the academic painting procedure, the painted *esquisse* was normally preceded by drawn sketches and, if and when the final work was to be executed, the artist followed up the painted *esquisse* by carefully drawn and painted *études* or studies from life of individual elements in the composition. The compositional scheme was then transferred by drawing onto the final canvas, and the slow, meticulous process of executing the finished picture began. Careful finish was not expected for the *esquisse,* in which spontaneity and originality were the prime qualities sought. In 1816 a competition for the painted *esquisse* was introduced at the Ecole des Beaux-Arts as part of the Rome Prize system.

**Etude** (study) In academic figure painting the *esquisse* was the most freely and spontaneously executed stage, and the *études* were drawn or painted studies of individual compositional elements, relatively slowly and carefully worked under static studio lighting conditions. By contrast, in landscape painting, the *étude* formed the loosely worked stage, in which the artist's response to the natural effect was captured. The landscape *étude* was executed out of doors, and speed was essential to render the fast changing, ephemeral lighting effects which had to be translated into paint. In academic landscape painting, these small *études* from nature formed the raw material, the visual vocabulary, which aided the artist's memory when the final work was undertaken in the studio.

**Expressionism** A term applied to an art movement, founded in the twentieth century, which opposed the imitation of nature and *Impressionism.* Expressionists tend to stress emotion and feeling with strong color and line. Van Gogh is considered the great forerunner of Expressionism.

# F

**Fat** Fat oil color means paint which contains the maximum possible amount of oil, even in excess of that with which it was ground. The basic rule in oil painting is fat over lean. This means that paint with a high fat or oil content should only be applied late in the painting process. *See lean.*

**Fauve** A French word meaning 'wild beast'. The term 'fauves' referred to an association of painters formed between 1905 and 1908 with Matisse as one of its leading figures. Their main stylistic features were their excessive use of colour and frenzied brushstrokes as a means of expression.

**Fête galante** A term first used in the eighteenth century to describe a painting of a dream-like pastoral setting which shows people, often in extravagant costume, amusing themselves with dancing, music making and courtship. Watteau is referred to as a painter of 'fêtes galantes'.

**Figurative Art** The straightforward representation of life and individual objects as seen purely by the eye and with no artistic interpretation.

**Film color** Film color is a term used to indicate intangible color, like the atmospheric blue of the sky or the color reflected on the surface of water. Film color is thus distinct from surface color, which is the color visible on the surfaces of tangible objects. *See surface color.*

**Fixative** A thin varnish sprayed onto drawings and pastels to adhere the chalk to the surface and prevent rubbing and blurring.

**Florentine School** From the thirteenth century, the Florentines held a prominent position in the art world. They were particularly concerned with problems of design and their approach to art was scientific and intellectual. Giotto and Leonardo are among the many artists that Florence produced.

**Fresco** A method of wall-painting on a plaster *ground. Buon fresco,* or true fresco, was much used in Italy from the thirteenth to the sixteenth centuries. First, the *arriccio* is applied and upon this the design, or *sinopia,* is traced. An area small enough to be completed in one day — the *giornata* — is covered with a final layer of plaster, the *intonaco.* The design is then redrawn and painted with *pigments* mixed with water. *Fresco secco* is painted on dry plaster and suffers, like *distemper,* from impermanence.

**Frottage** A word taken from the French, *frotter,* meaning 'to rub'. It is the process of producing rubbings through paper from the surface of anything that has a textural pattern, such as wood.

**Fugitive color** A phrase used to describe a *pigment's* impermanence and tendency to fade or change color under the influence of natural effects such as sunlight.

**Full-face light** Full-face light falls directly onto the subject from behind the artist. Although some nineteenth century writers attributed the popularization of this type of lighting to the Impressionists, it was used by both Ingres and Manet before them. Full-face light, like *gris clair,* suppresses tonal contrasts outdoors, because shadows from objects are cast behind them, out of the artist's view. Full-face light is the most luminous and brilliant lighting effect, because maximum light is reflected off all available surfaces back into the viewer's eye. Because no shadows are visible under this type of light, it tends to flatten forms. This contrasts with side lighting which emphasizes the modeling of forms. *Contrejour* or backlighting is the opposite of full-face lighting. *See contrejour, side lighting.*

**Futurism** An explosive movement which started in 1909 as an attack on the stagnancy of Italian art. It praised speed, the machine and violence and scorned traditional values. A recurrent stylistic feature was the use of repetition of an image in a painting, in order to imply movement. The phase died out with the advent of the First World war.

# G

**Gamboge** A gum resin often used in watercolor. If applied in thick layers, it creates a gloss finish but it is not considered suitable for oil colors.

**Genre painting** A type of art which depicts scenes from everyday life. Two of the better known genre painters are the Dutch artist Vermeer and the Spaniard Velazquez.

**Gesso** A white, absorbent ground used in *tempera* and *oil painting.* In Italy during the early Renaissance, panels were first prepared with several coats of *gesso grosso* which is gesso mixed with *size.* On top of this coarse gesso was laid a coat of *gesso sottile.* This plaster and size mixture was brilliant white and gave a smooth surface.

**Gesturalism** see *Action Painting.*

**Glornata** A name given to an area in *fresco* painting which can be completed in one day.

**Glaze** A glaze is a thin, oil-rich application of transparent color in a liquid film over dry colors to adjust, enrich and unify them. In general, glazing was associated with academic practice, and was mainly avoided by the Impressionist painters. Glazing was normally the final stage in the painting procedure — as the glaze was rich in oil, no leaner paint could be added on top without risking the durability of the picture. This conforms to the oil painting rule — fat over lean. It is sometimes difficult to determine exactly the glazes used by the Old Masters because of previous restoration or cleaning, and also because of the similarity between the appearance of a glazed paint layer and varnish.

**Gold leaf** Gold which has been beaten into very thin sheets. This was often used to highlight and define forms in medieval manuscript illumination.

**Gouache** Gouache is opaque watercolor paint. It contains the same ingredients as watercolors, which are transparent, but with the addition of chalk. This makes the colors less saturated. As they are opaque, they reflect more light compared to the richer luminosity of watercolors used over white paper. The binder for watercolor is usually gum arabic in solution, while other ingredients may include sugar-water to aid flexibility, a wetting agent to give uniform flow of color on surfaces, and glycerin as a moistener, plus a preservative. In the late nineteenth century, honey was sometimes still in use as a moistener in watercolors and gouache colors.

**Grattage** A technique derived from *frottage,* where a painted canvas is pressed down onto an uneven surface, such as a grid, and then the paint is scraped away to reveal a negative image of the texture beneath.

**Green earths** These colors are similar to ochre and are among the oldest known painting colors. They were important in the Middle Ages and early Italian painting as middle and shadow tones in flesh.

**Grisaille** A *monochrome* painting executed in greyish colors.

**Gris clair** *Gris clair* is a French term used frequently in the nineteenth century to denote a particular quality of light. *Gris clair* meant the type of even, neutral light produced by a bright but overcast sky, where there is no direct sunlight and thus no shadows. Under this light, tones are close in value with extremes of light and shade suppressed, and local colors and their most pure and unmodified. This was one of the types of lighting preferred by the impressionists.

**Ground** (priming) These terms refer to the layer or layers with which the support is coated to prepare it to receive the paint. In oil painting on canvas, a glue size layer was usually followed by one, two or occasionally three layers of opaque oil-based paint. Absorbent grounds, made with chalk and glue, which had been popular in tempera painting, were revived in the early nineteenth century. In particular the Neo-Impressionists liked them. Most artists used commercially primed canvases in the nineteenth century. Priming refers both to the ground and to its application.

**Gum arabic** Gum obtained from the acacia plant. It is used as a binding agent in watercolors, gouache and pastels.

# H

**Halftones** Halftones refer to the gradations of tone in painting and drawing which separate the strongest lights from the deepest shadows. They are intended to soften the transition from lights to darks, creating an authentic illusion of relief on forms and suggesting solid objects in a 'real' space.

**Hatching** Hatching is a term normally used in drawing to indicate the use of parallel strokes or lines, generally placed close together to suggest halftones or shadow. The term is also occasionally used to refer to parallel, separate strokes of the brush in painting.

**Hessian** A type of canvas which generally has a coarse, thick weave.

**Highlights** *see lights.*

**Hue** *see color.*

# I

**Illusionism** A technique which deceives the eye into believing it is seeing a real object rather than its representation by the artist.

**Impasto** Paint applied in thick, raised daubs is called impasto. It can also refer to a generally loaded build-up of the paint layer, leaving brushmarks apparent, as distinct from a smooth, carefully blended, flat paint surface.

**Impressionism** A loose association of painters formed in Paris in 1874 for exhibiting purposes and as an alternative to the dry, academic Salon school. Monet, Renoir and Pissarro, amongst many others, depicted the natural, atmospheric effects of light in nature by painting out-of-doors in *broken colors.* They also painted shadows of objects in complementary colors. The Impressionist color theories have influenced all subsequent art movements.

**Independent** This fairly general term is now used to refer to artists, whether more or less innovatory in style and methods, who rejected academic standards or the academic teaching program which processed painters in the nineteenth century. Manet, for example, was an independent, but so was his non-academic teacher, Thomas Couture.

**Infra-red photography** A method of photography which can be used to examine thinly applied paint layers in a painting. The infra-red waves, which lie beneath the red end of the visible spectrum, penetrate the layers and can sometimes reveal the artist's original drawing.

**Intonaco** A smooth layer of fine plaster which is placed on top of the *arriccio* in *fresco.*

# L

**Lay-in** *see ébauche.*

**Lean** Lean oil color is paint in which the oil or fat content has been reduced, usually by indirect means such as diluting the paint with turpentine. In accordance with the oil painting rule fat over lean, the application of paint on the canvas should begin lean, and become progressively fatter or oilier with each successive layer. Artists like Degas and Toulouse-Lautrec made their oil color lean, quick drying and mat in finish by first placing the paint on blotting paper to soak out excess oil. This was then diluted with turpentine before being applied directly to the support in the form of a fluid colored wash. This was called *peinture à l'essence.* Other artists, including Monet and probably Pissarro, soaked oil out of their paint in the manner of Degas, but used it undiluted, in a stiffish paste to enhance chalky, dragged effects in their painting. *See fat.*

**Lights** (highlights) Lights are those parts directly illuminated by the fall of light depicted in a painting or drawing. They are normally depicted in painting by impasted opaque cream or off-white paint.

**Limning** An archaic term meaning to draw or paint, used particularly with reference to manuscript illumination and miniature painting.

**Lining** A conservation term for placing a new canvas on the back of a deteriorating original.

**Linseed oil** An oil, derived from the flax plant, which is mainly used as a painting medium and in tempera emulsions. Linseed oil gives a smooth effect to paint but it tends to yellow with age. As the Old Masters relied on a heavy layering of the paint surface, linseed oil was the best medium because of its fast drying time.

**Lithography** A method of printing from the surface of a slab of limestone called a lithographic stone. Greasy ink is applied to the stone and made permanent by the addition of chemicals. Water is applied, which is soaked up by the porous, non-greasy area of the limestone. This means that when the limestone is covered in greasy ink, only the drawn area is transferred in replica.

**Loaded** A picture is said to be loaded when it is painted thickly, often with a heavy impasto. A loaded brush is one charged to its full capacity with paint.

**Local color** Local color is the true color of an object when seen under neutral daylight. This is distinct from the apparent color of an object when modified by non-neutral light, for example reddish sunset lighting or colored light reflected from another object.

# M

**Madder lake** This purplish color is derived from the root of the madder plant and is impermanent. *Alizarin madder lake* is an artificial pigment and it is more permanent than natural madder lake.

**Mannerism** The artists of the Mannerist period (c 1520-1600) flouted the traditional 'rules' of classical and Renaissance art. The chief characteristics of the style are vivid and unnatural colours and elongated and exaggerated figures. Mannerism was supplanted by the *Baroque* period.

**Mastic resin** The best type comes from the pistachio tree. Mastic resin is used for making varnish and it prevents wrinkling, shrinkage and decay. It also gives depth and clarity to colors.

**Medium** (binder) The medium or binder is the substance which cements the pigment particles together in a form suitable for painting. Oil is the binder in oil painting, for example, and gum arabic that in watercolor and gouache. The binder also serves to make the paint adhere to the ground on drying. Painting medium can also refer to the substance or mixture of substances with which the artist alters the original consistency of the paint during the actual painting process. For example, Renoir used a mixture of linseed oil and turpentine as a painting medium. Medium has a third, more general usage, as the type of paint in which a picture is executed. Oil was the medium used by most Impressionists.

**Megilp** A drying oil which gives colors a buttery consistency.

**Merz** A variety of *Dada* invented by Schwitters in 1920. Like *collage,* it consisted of an arrangement of various materials merged into a work of art. Schwitters, however, used more diverse materials than those adopted in straightforward collage, and would take anything from iron bars to plastic, waste-disposal sacks.

**Metaphysical Painting** A movement that arose in Italy in 1915 with de Chirico. It was partly a reaction against the functionalist tendency of *Futurism.* The inner aspect of objects was sought by placing them in unusual and unexpected settings and creating a magical atmosphere of mystery and hallucination.

**Miniature painting** A small painting, usually a portrait, executed in gouache or a water-based medium. Miniatures were popular in the sixteenth and seventeenth centuries.

**Minimal Art** A style of art concerned with an awareness of the object itself as it is. It is an impersonal and neutral portrayal of an object.

**Modeling** In painting or drawing, modeling means the representation of three-dimensional form. The depiction of a fall of light and shade which 'models' the form is commonly used to achieve this effect. The Impressionists often used color contrasts or color temperature to suggest three-dimensional form, as opposed to the tonal contrasts of light and dark associated with academic modeling.

**Monochrome** A picture executed in just one color.

**Mordant** An adhesive used when pressing a material onto a surface, such as in the gold leafing of panels in medieval painting.

# N

**Naples yellow** A color which was popular with the Old Masters. Naples yellow is heavy and dense and so it has excellent covering properties. It is compatible with all other colors, unaffected by light and rarely cracks.

**Neo-Classicism** Neo-Classicism is the name given to an artistic movement which began in Rome in the mid eighteenth century and spread rapidly throughout Europe. It aimed to revive the art of antiquity. Unlike earlier revivals of classical art, actual examples of antique art were by then available as models for artists to emulate. This was because archeological work from the mid eighteenth century, for example at Pompeii and Herculaneum, had uncovered evidence of what antique art had really looked like. Antique sculpture and reliefs survived better than painting, and so Neo-Classical painting relied more heavily on examples of sculpture. Transferred into painting, this often resulted in a shallow pictorial space and a frieze-like distribution of figures across the picture surface. Figures and gestures often had a static, rather frozen quality, and flesh modeling was often reminiscent of carved stone. In Neo-Classical painting, color was restrained, and the composition usually balanced and symmetrical. Line and draftsmanship were important, and a high degree of finish with imperceptible brushwork was desired. The French artist Jacques-Louis David (1748-1825) is recognized as the purest exponent of the style.

**Neo-Impressionism** A late eighteenth-century style based on *Divisionism,* but concentrating on a more scientific and studied composition.

**Neo-Plasticism** A term coined by Mondrian in 1920 for his purely geometric style of art. He used only horizontal and vertical lines and the primary colors with black, white and grey. This was a movement closely connected with *De Stijl* magazine.

# O

**Oceanic Art** The art produced by the islands of the South Pacific.

**Ochres** Yellowish earth colors which tend to be impure. These pigments have a fairly good covering power and drying capacity, and they are very permanent when pure.

**Opaque** An opaque surface or color is one more or less impervious to rays of light, which are reflected back to the eye. Certain pigments are by nature opaque in an oil binder. These include some of the earth colors and lead white, which is acclaimed for its excellent hiding power. *See transparency.*

**Optical grays** Optical grays are achieved in oil painting by adding a thinly scumbled veil of opaque pale color over a darker, dry hue. The latter remains visible but is modified to a cool grayness by the pale veil of color on top. Warm effects can be created optically by laying a thin translucent veil of a darkish hue over a pale dry color below.

**Orphism** A style that arose from *Cubism* in 1913 and aimed to produce a more lyrical quality in its work than the severe intellectualism of Cubism.

**Orpiment yellow** A brilliant, poisonous yellow used by the Old Masters, *Cadmium yellow* has come to replace this *pigment.*

# P

**Paint layer** The paint layer is the actual layer or layers of color applied by the artist in the execution of the painting. However, this does not include the ground or preparation layer, or the final layer of varnish, if applied.

**Palette** Palette refers both to the flat surface on which an artist lays out and mixes colors, and to the particular range or selection of colors used by an artist for a particular painting. More generally, palette can be used to refer to a color range characteristic of an individual artist or school of artists. This would include, for example, the so called 'prismatic' palette associated with the Neo-Impressionists and the 'limited' palette referred to in discussions of Impressionist painting.

**Panel** A painting term for a rigid *support* such as wood. If wooden panels are used, they must first be *sized* to prevent the paint from being absorbed.

**Papier collé** A French term meaning 'stuck paper'. It is a type of *collage* which involves sticking layers of paper onto a support.

**Papier decoupé** A French term meaning 'cut paper', and used as a type of *collage.*

**Pastel** A pastel is a colored stick made of pigment mixed with just enough gum binder to hold the particles together. Pastels can vary in tint from the deepest pure pigment color, through a tonal range of increasing paleness achieved by adding more white chalk. Since they contain virtually no binder, pastels are very dusty and barely adhere to the support to which they are applied. Paper is the most popular support for pastel. As a result works executed in pastel are highly fragile, and need 'fixing' with a sprayed film of fixative. This can be made by dissolving a small amount of resin in a volatile solvent such as alcohol. Because pastels contain no binder, they are the most opaque and light-reflective of all colored media.

**Pentimento** Derived from the Italian meaning 'repentance', pentimenti are the changes in composition which a painter makes while producing a painting. These alterations are visible in *infra-red photographs* and are sometimes useful in determining forgeries.

**Performance Art** The art of the artist posing and proposing himself or herself for artistic manipulation.

**Photomontage** The technique of arranging and gluing photographic images onto a surface as a type of *collage.*

**Pictorial space** The pictorial space is the illusion of space created 'behind' the picture plane, to suggest 'real' space and depth. This may even include an illusionistic continuation of the real space of the spectator into the separate, constructed space of the painting.

**Picture plane** The picture plane is the plane occupied by the actual surface of the picture.

**Pigment** Pigment refers simply to the powder color from which paints are made. Pigments are insoluble in the liquid binder with which they are combined, and they give their colored effect by being spread over a surface. Dyes, or soluble colors, impart their coloring power by staining or being imbibed by the binder. Lake colors are pigments made by precipitating a dye on an inert, colorless base. The two chief categories of pigment are organic and inorganic. Organic pigments belong to the organic division of chemical compounds, such as those based on carbon, hydrogen, nitrogen or sulfur. Organic pigments derive mainly from vegetable sources, or may be made synthetically. They tend to be less stable and more fugitive than inorganic pigments. These derive from minerals and ores and are either found naturally or made synthetically.

**Pointillism** A painting technique developed by Georges Seurat out of the *Impressionist* theory of color. Dots or blobs of color were placed beside one another to create an 'optical mixture' in the viewer's eye. If a blue dot was placed beside a yellow one, it was said to create a more brilliant and intense green than if the two colors had been mixed on a *palette.*

**Polychromatic** A picture executed in many colors.

**Pop art** The dominant form of art in England and America in the late 1950s and early 1960s; the term is derived from the word 'popular'. Pop artists, such as Roy Lichtenstein, used material from comic-strips, advertising and films. The movement has been considered a direct challenge to *Abstract Expressionism* which preceded it.

**Post-Impressionism** A style that reacted against *Impressionism* and *Neo-Impressionism* and desired a return to the more Classical concepts of art and subject matter.

**Pre-Raphaelite Brotherhood** A group of nineteenth century English artists who sought to revive the ideals of fourteenth and fifteenth century Italian art. Their work generally involved the use of elaborate symbolism, bright colors and highly detailed painting.

**Priming** *see ground.*

**Prussian blue** A deep blue which has very strong coloring power and which is very permanent.

# Q

**Quattrocento** This term, the Italian word for 'four hundred', is used to denote the fifteenth century in Italy.

# R

**Rayonnism** A Russian style of art that believed in painting in a fourth dimension outside space and time. It used intersecting rays and lines of colour to achieve its ideal.

**Realism** Not to be confused with the naturalism of the landscape and rural painters. Realism was a nineteenth century movement in painting and literature which insisted that everyday life was a suitable subject for art. Courbet was the first major Realist painter.

**Red bole, Armenian** This natural clay was sometimes used as a ground in oil painting by artists such as Caravaggio. Since the Middle Ages, red bole has been used as a ground for gilding.

**Red Iron oxides** Artificial pigments made from iron ore or waste materials. They are closely related to the red earths and have similar properties such as good covering power and a quick drying time.

**Reflected light, reflected color** Reflected light is light which bounces off a surface and is therefore indirect. When that surface is colored, white light is tinted with that color, altering the color of any object on which the light then falls. Nineteenth century studio walls were often painted a muted hue to prevent reflected light disturbing the halftones and shadows across the model. Similarly, blue sky, green trees or red buildings, visible from the studio window, could tinge the light falling on the model. Academic artists in particular tried to avoid this type of reflected color, which fluctuated and altered the colors on the model. By contrast, complicated effects of reflected light and color were often actively sought out by Impressionist painters, as they were effects found naturally in outdoor conditions. Suppression of such effects in studio painting often resulted in an artificial, static or deadening effect in the work produced.

**Rubbing** *see scumbling*

**Rococo** Derived from the French word *rocaille* meaning 'shell-work'. Rococo is phase of decorative art which emerged in France during the reign of Louis XV. As a reaction against the Baroque style, Rococo artists, such as Watteau, emphasized pretty, ornamental curvilinear design.

**Romanticism** In art, a school of painting which was part of a far-reaching revolution which affected all artistic fields in the late eighteenth and early nineteenth centuries. Romantic paintings are often what their name implies, with their subject matter frequently derived from an extravagant, 'unreal' view of reality, particularly of the past. The French painter Delacroix was a major exponent of Romanticism.

# S

**Salon** This was the official art exhibition in Paris, established in 1667 by the Academy as the respectable venue where their work could be shown. It was named after the *Salon Carré* in the Louvre where exhibitions were originally held. From 1831 the Salon was usually held annually. The only year for which there was no jury regulating admission of work was 1848, the year of revolution. In 1863 a *Salon des Refusés*, an exhibition of work by those artists refused by the Salon jury, was held. This resulted in public and critical hostility and thus did not further the cause of the many independent artists like Manet who exhibited in it. The reactionary nature of the academic Salon finally prompted the emergence of alternative exhibitions, like those of the Impressionist group from 1874, and the *Salon des Artistes Indépendants* in 1884.

**Saturation** Saturation in color refers to its degree of intensity or vividness of hue. Full saturation suggests the absence of white or of neutralizing or dulling elements. In oil painting, full saturation is often taken to mean the richness of the color as it comes out of the tube. Unsaturated color tends toward a neutral pale grayness.

**Sauce** *Sauce* was a word commonly used in nineteenth century France to indicate fluid, dilute color applied usually in the *ébauche* stage of painting. *Sauce* was normally a dark, reddish-brown, transparent mixture to which turpentine and often also a boiled drying oil like linseed oil, which would dry relatively quickly, had been added. *Sauce* was often used derogatorily in the second half of the century to refer to paintings dominated by rich dark browns, which looked as if painted with 'gravy'. The dark *sauce* was often technically dangerous, as bitumen was frequently used in it, and it was avoided by independent painters who preferred pale, opaque paint layers.

**Scumbling** Scumbling is the rough application of thin opaque color over an earlier layer of paint or over the ground to modify the color below. Although the scumbled layer is opaque, it is applied so thinly that it is translucent, thus the color below can be seen as if through a veil. The scumbled layer is usually applied with a bristle brush and an irregular, coarse stroke so that the unevenness of color and the mark of the brush are left apparent. Rubbing is a comparable term used occasionally to describe the broad blocking-in of background color, especially during the *ébauche* stage of painting. *See glaze.*

**Sfumato** A subtle blending of colours in order to create a misty effect.

**Sgraffito** An Italian word meaning 'scratched'. It involves scratching away the top layer of plaster or paint to reveal a different colored layer below.

**Side lighting** This is light which falls from right to left or left to right across an object. It enhances the sense of form by giving balanced areas of light and shade with gradated halftones between. This type of lighting was preferred by academic painters because it stressed the modeling of forms.

**Sienna** A pigment named after the Italian city where it originated. Raw sienna is a yellowish brown ochre. Due to the amount of oil needed to create the paint, it may cause darkening. Burnt sienna is roasted to give a rich reddish brown color. It was often used with iron oxide by the Venetians to add warmth to flesh tones.

**Sinoper** This is a very light red ochre from Asia Minor. Used in ancient times and the Middle Ages, particularly in *fresco* painting, it is no longer available.

**Size** A mixture of powdered pigment and hot glue which is applied to the canvas to seal it against the corrosive action of subsequent layers of paint.

**Sketch** *see esquisse.*

**Smalt** A blue pigment made by powdering silica glass colored with cobalt oxide. As this color has poor covering power and tends to deteriorate, it is not generally used and cobalt blue is preferred.

**Socialist Realism** The official art of the Communist Party, which extolled the virtues of the party and work.

**Spatialism** A style that rejects traditional easel-painting for the development of color and form in space.

**Stand oil** Oil boiled with carbonic acid without the addition of a drying medium so that it dries more slowly than *linseed oil* but gives colors a high gloss. For painting, stand oil must be mixed with other mediums as it is very thick and fatty.

**Stretcher** The wooden frame on which a canvas is stretched. Stretched canvas is less prone to change with atmospheric variations and less susceptible to damage than unstretched canvas.

**Structure of a painting on canvas** The traditional structure of an oil painting is a series of layers. Working from the surface down these would usually consist of a varnish layer, colored glazes; a paint layer with pigment particles in an oil binder; the ground or preparation; a layer of glue size; and finally the canvas fabric. The different layers within the paint layer can usually be clearly differentiated because of the layered painting procedure. However, using wet-in-wet or *alla prima* techniques, the Impressionists often produced a much more unconventional paint layer, where separate coats of color are indistinguishable. They also preferred not to varnish their pictures. Monet, Cézanne, Renoir and Pissarro are the most noted for their anti-academic, unconventional methods of paint handling.

**Studio** *see atelier.*

**Study** *see étude.*

**Support** The support is the surface upon which the painting is executed. The most common supports for easel painting in nineteenth century France were canvas, wood panel, cardboard and paper. Canvas fabric — usually linen — was normally stretched onto wooden frames or 'stretchers', to make it sufficiently rigid to paint upon. Paper could be tacked to board or cardboard during painting and later glued or 'laid down' on canvas or panel to preserve it.

**Suprematism** A form of *Cubism* constructed from pure, geometric elements.

**Surface color** This is the color visible on the surfaces of objects, as opposed to film color. *See film color.*

**Surrealism** One of the most influential of twentieth century artistic movements, Surrealism set out to free the mind from all preconceived ideas by allowing the subconscious to assert itself. The Spanish Surrealist Salvador Dali is one of the major exponents.

**Symbolism** (*Syntheticism*) An artistic movement founded by a loose association of artists in the late nineteenth century. In a reaction which developed from *Impressionism* and *Realism*, Symbolists aimed to be both decorative and mystical. They tended to use bright, unnatural colors to express their ideas.

**Syntheticism** *see Symbolism.*

# T

**Tempera** This word actually describes a type of binder added to powdered pigment, but now refers to the egg tempera paints which were popular until the late fifteenth century. Being a quick-drying medium, tempera is difficult to work with but it dries to an almost impenetrable surface. The addition of oil to tempera emulsions brought about the eventual development of oil painting.

**Tenebrism** From the Italian *tenebroso* meaning 'murky'. Tenebrism is a style of painting which features an emphatic use of *chiaroscuro.* Spanish painters in the early seventeenth century who were influenced by the work of Caravaggio have been called Tenebrists, although they did not form a distinct group.

**Tesserae** The cubes used in creating mosaics.

**Thumbnail sketch** *see croquis.*

**Titanium white** Also known as titanium dioxide, this is a relatively new color with a good covering power. However, it does not dry well and it tends to yellow.

**Tone, tonal value** Tone or tonal value refers to the lightness or darkness of a color on a scale from white to black. The tonal value of a color is thus its position on a tonal scale gradated in steps from the lightest light through to the darkest dark. A color high in tonal value is thus very pale, high on the tonal scale meaning close to white. A pale tint means a color dominated by the presence of white. *See saturation, color.*

**Transparency** Transparency, as opposed to opacity, is the capacity of a color to transmit light. A transparent color is clear and unclouded like glass, water or stained glass. Such colors, like the red lakes, ultramarine or viridian green in an oil binder, can be used effectively for glazes. They produce an optical fusion of the color of the glazed layer with the color below. Transparent colors were rarely used by the Impressionists, who normally added white to them to render them opaque, light-reflective, and thus a good visual metaphor for effects of light in the atmosphere.

**Turpentine** This is the most common diluent in oil painting. It has no binding properties and, if too much is used, it tends to absorb colors creating a dull, dusty effect. Turpentine evaporates quickly and is used to accelerate drying. However, the paint surface will deteriorate if an excess is used.

# U

**Ultramarine** Made by powdering the semi-precious stone lapis lazuli, it has always been an expensive pigment which was only used sparingly.

**Underdrawing, underpainting** The preliminary technique of *blocking in* or laying in the drawing, composition, and often the tonal values of a painting. Occasionally color may be indicated in underpainting but it is generally used to lay down the basic structures of the picture before the more complex work begins.

# V

**Varnish** Varnish is a resin in solution in a volatile solvent, which, when applied in a thin coat on a surface, dries to a hard, glossy and normally transparent film. Varnish is usually the final coat added to protect an oil painting from dust and atmospheric pollution. During the 1880s in France, many artists preferred to frame their paintings under glass rather than varnish them. The glass protected the painting, while avoiding the immediate darkening and long-term yellowing which result from the addition of varnish to the paint surface. It also prevented the transformation of their intentionally mat paint layer into a glossy surface.

**Vellum** The skin of an animal, normally calf, which was often used in manuscript illumination in the Middle Ages and in *miniature painting* by artists such as Nicholas Hilliard.

**Venetian School** In the sixteenth century, artists such as Giorgione and Titian preferred a gentler, more sensuous approach to painting than had been adopted by the *Florentine School.* The Venetians used warm atmospheric tones.

**Veristic Surrealism** A tendency in *Surrealist* painting to depict the images of dreams.

**Vermilion** The favorite red of the Old Masters. When exposed to sunlight, vermilion tends to blacken so the Masters would often glaze *madder lake* over it to preserve and enhance its color.

**Vibert, Jéhan-Georges** Although undistinguished as a painter, Vibert undertook considerable research into artists' materials and methods, both historical and contemporary, which formed a series of talks given at the Ecole des Beaux-Arts probably in the late 1880s. In the early 1890s he published a volume on his research *La Science de la peinture* (*The Science of Painting*), which provides invaluable material on painting methods in the Impressionist period. Vibert produced some of his own materials, including a special ground based on chalk and cheese-glue for use under tempera painting on panel, which was marketed by the prominent French color merchants Lefranc et Cie.

**Vorticism** A type of *Cubism* where the diagonal was stressed like an imaginary vortex.

# W

**Wet-in-wet painting** Wet-in-wet painting means the application of one color over or into another before it is dry. Wet-in-wet painting, or the slurring of wet colors into each other leaving them partially mixed on the surface of the painting, is not necessarily synonymous with *alla prima* painting. Wet-in-wet handling can be used alongside wet-over-dry techniques in a painting which may be built up over an extended period.

**Wet-over-dry painting** Oil painting wet over dry indicates that color is applied over paint which has already been allowed to dry. Where these dry areas are executed in a vigorous or impasted technique, dragging often results when paint is added, especially if the paint is fairly stiff in consistency.

**White lead** A white pigment, also known as flake white, which is lead carbonate. The purity of the color is determined by the purity of the lead used. White lead has excellent covering, drying and mixing properties but it tends to yellow.

**Work from nature** Work from nature means work executed directly from the chosen subject, in front of any live or real subject in the real world. This is as opposed to subjects worked from the artist's imagination in the absence of a direct model, or work done from another art. With reference to the Impressionists, work from nature is often taken to mean work done out of doors or *en plein air* (in the open air), as opposed to landscapes painted in the studio.

# Z

**Zinc white** This was first introduced as an artist's color in 1840. It is economical, permanent and it does not yellow. Zinc white is an excellent pigment for tempera, watercolor and fresco painting.

# ACKNOWLEDGEMENTS

**Page 14** Portrait by Benedetto da Maiano, Duomo, Florence (Photo Scala, Florence); **15, 16, 17** Arena Chapel, Padua (Photo Scala); **19, 20, 21** National Gallery, London; **22** Self-portrait, National Gallery, London; **23, 24, 25** National Gallery, London; **27, 28, 29** National Gallery, London; **30** Self-portrait, Biblioteca Reale, Turin (Photo Scala); **31, 32, 33** National Gallery, London; **32**(*top*) Reproduced by gracious permission of Her Majesty Queen Elizabeth II (Windsor Castle, Royal Library); **34** Self-portrait, Codex de la Biblioteque d'Arras (Photo Giraudon, Paris); sketch, Berlin-Dahlem Kupferstickhkabinett, Inv. no. 550r (Photo Bildarchive Preussischer Kulturbesitz, Berlin); **34, 35, 36, 37** Museum voor Schone Kunsten, Ghent; **38** Self-portrait, Museo del Prado, Madrid (Photo M & W Fine Arts, Madrid); **39, 40, 41** National Gallery, London; **42** Self-portrait, and **43** Crown Copyright, Victoria and Albert Museum, London; **44** Portrait by Leoni, Biblioteca Marucelliana, Florence (Photo Scala); **45, 46, 47** National Gallery, London; **48** Self-portrait, Metropolitan Museum of Art, NY; **49, 50, 51** National Gallery, London; **52** Self-portrait, Uffizi, Florence (Photo Scala); **53, 54, 55** Wellington Museum, Apsley House, London; X-ray, National Gallery, London; **56** Self-portrait, Graphische Sammlung Arbetina, Vienna; **57, 58, 59** National Gallery, London; **60** Self-portrait, National Gallery, London; **61, 62, 63** National Gallery, London, **64** Self-portrait, and **65**(*bottom*), Kunsthistorisches Museum, Vienna; **65, 66, 67** The GLC as Trustees of the Iveagh Bequest, Kenwood, London; **68** Portrait by Boucher, Musée Condé, Chantilly (Photo Giraudon); **68, 69** National Gallery of Scotland, Edinburgh (Tom Scott Photography); **70** Self-portrait, Tate Gallery, London; **71, 72, 73** Tate Gallery, London; **74** Self-portrait, National Portrait Gallery, London; **75, 76, 77** Courtesy of the Trustees, Courtauld Institute Galleries, London; X-ray, Technical Department of the Courtauld Institute; **78** Portrait by J. Linnell, National Portrait Gallery, London; **79** Tate Gallery, London; **80** Portrait by D. Maclise, National Portrait Gallery; study, Crown Copyright, Victoria and Albert Museum, London; **81, 82, 83**, Tate Gallery, London; **84** Self-portrait, Uffizi, Florence (Photo Scala); **85** National Gallery, London; **86** Self-portrait, Uffizi, Florence (Photo Scala); **87**(*top*) Louvre, Paris; study, Cabinet des Dessins, Paris; **88** Self-portrait and paint box, Tate Gallery, London; **89, 90, 91** Tate Gallery, London; **93, 94, 95** Glasgow Art Gallery and Museums; **94**(*top*) Private Collection, Japan; **96** Portrait by W.B. Richmond, National Portrait Gallery, London; **97** Tate Gallery, London; **98** Self-portrait, Musée Petit Palais, Paris (Photo Cooper Bridgeman Library); **99, 100, 101** Musée Fabre, Montpellier (Photo Claude O'Sughrue; **104-105** Louvre, Paris (Photo Hubert Josse); **106** Dordrechts Museum, Dordrecht; **107** Museum of Fine Arts, Boston; **108, 109** A. Callen; **110, 111** Louvre, Paris (Photo Hubert Josse; **113** The Trustees, The Wallace Collection, London; **114, 115** Louvre, Paris (Photo Hubert Josse; **116** Collection Lefranc-Bourgeois, Le Mans; **117** The Phillipps Collection, Washington; **118, 119, 120** Courtauld Institute of Art, London; **121** Home House Society Trustees/Courtauld Institute Galleries, London; **122** Louvre, Paris (Photo Hubert Josse); **123** Victoria and Albert Museum/Crown Copyright reserved; **124, 125, 126** Musée du Jeu de Paume, Paris (Photo Hubert Josse; **127** Trustees of the British Museum, London; **128** Metropolitan Museum of Art, NY/Bequest of Mrs H.O. Havemeyer, 1929; **128**(*bottom*) Nationalmuseum, Stockholm; **129** Metropolitan Museum of Art, NY; **131, 132, 133** Finished work, Courtauld Institute Galleries; study, Louvre, Paris; **134** Southampton Art Gallery; **135, 136, 137** Louvre, Paris (Photo Hubert Josse); **139, 140, 141** Musée du Jeu de Paume Paris (Photo Hubert Josse); **143, 144, 145** National Gallery, London (Photo Mike Fear); **147, 148, 149** Wallraf-Richartz Museum, Cologne; **150** M. Marc Havel, Paris; **151, 152, 153** Musée du Jeu de Paume, Paris (Photo Hubert Josse); **155, 156, 157** National Gallery, London (Photo Mike Fear); **160, 161** National Gallery, London; **161**(*right*) M. Marc Havel, Paris; **162** National Gallery, London (Photo Mike Fear); **163** Home House Society Trustees, Courtauld Institute Galleries, London; **164**(*top*) Photo Ray Gardner; **164**(*bottom*) Metropolitan Museum of Art, NY/gift of Mr & Mrs Henry Ittleson, Jr., 1964; **165** Musée du Jeu de Paume, Paris (Photo Hubert Josse; **166** Fitzwilliam Museum, Cambridge; **167** Neue Pinakothek, Munich (Photo Bavaria Verlag); **169**(*top*), **170, 171** Metropolitan Museum of Art, Bequest of Lillian S Timken, 1959; **169**(*bottom*) Photo A. Callen; **172** Portrait by Renoir, Louvre (Photo Cooper Bridgeman Library); **173, 174, 175** Courtauld Institute Galleries, © SPADEM, Paris, 1980; **177, 178, 179** Musée de Jeu de Paume, Paris (Photo Hubert Josse); **181, 182, 183** National Museum of Wales, Cardiff (Photo Mike Fear); **184** Portrait, Snark International, Paris; **185, 186, 187** Courtauld Institute Galleries; **189, 190, 191** Home House Society Trustees/Courtauld

Institute Galleries, London; **193, 194, 195** Musée du Jeu de Paume, Paris (Photo Hubert Josse); **197, 198**(*top, bottom, left*), **199**(*top*) Ashmolean Museum, Oxford; **198**(*bottom right*) Home House Society Trustees/Courtauld Institute Galleries, London; **199**(*bottom*) Musée du Jeu de Paume, Paris (Photo Hubert Josse); **201, 202, 203** Chicago Art Institute; **205, 206, 207** Fitzwilliam Museum Cambridge/ Reproduced by kind permission of the Trustees of the Lord Butler of Saffron Walden, K.G., P.C., C.H. , F.R.S.L.; **209, 210**(*top*), **211** The Burrell Collection, Glasgow Museum and Art Galleries; **210**(*bottom*) Metropolitan Museum of Art, Rogers Fund, 1918; **212** National Gallery of Art, Washington; **213** The Burrell Collection, Glasgow Museum and Art Galleries; **214** Wadsworth Atheneum, Hartford, Connecticut; **215** Ohara Museum of Art, Kuranshiki, Japan; **216** Metropolitan Museum of Art/gift of Mrs Gardner Cassatt; **217**(*top*) Photo Ray Gardner; **217**(*bottom*) Minneapolis Institute of Arts/William H. Dunwoody Fund; **219**(*top*) Home House Society Trustees/ Courtauld Institute Galleries, London; **219**(*bottom*) Trustees of the British Museum (Photo Eileen Tweedy); **220** Tate Gallery, London (Photo Mike Fear); **221** Mary Evans Picture Library; **223, 224**(*top, left*), **225** National Museum of Wales, Cardiff (Photo Mike Fear); **224**(*right*) Courtauld Institute Galleries; **226** Portrait, Snark; **227, 228, 229** National Gallery, London, © SPADEM, Paris, 1980; **231, 232, 233** Museum of Fine Arts, Boston; **235, 236, 237** National Museum of Wales, Cardiff (Photo Mike Fear); **238, 239, 240, 241** Birmingham Museum and Art Gallery (Photo Mike Fear); **243, 244, 245** National Gallery, London (Photo Mike Fear); **251, 252, 253** Collection State Museum Kröller Müller, Otterlo, The Netherlands; **255, 256, 257** Museum of Fine Arts, Dallas; **259, 260, 261** Home House Society Trustees/ Courtauld Institute Galleries, London; **263, 264, 265** Tate Gallery, London; **267, 268, 269**(*bottom right*) Collection State Museum Kröller Müller, Otterlo, The Netherlands; **269**(*top, bottom left*) Yale University Art Gallery; **270** Tate Gallery, London (Photo Mike Fear); **271** National Museum Vincent van Gogh, Amsterdam; **272** National Gallery of Scotland, Edinburgh; **273**(*top*) Statens Museum for Kunst, Copenhagen (Photo Hans Peterson; **273**(*bottom*) Museum Folkwang, Essen; **274** Musée de Grenoble (Photo Ifot, Grenoble); **275** Private Collection, Switzerland; **156** Metropolitan Museum of Art, NY/ H.O. Havemeyer Collection; **277** National Gallery, London; **279, 280, 281** Home House Society Trustees/ Courtauld Institute Galleries, London; **282** Self-portrait, National Gallery, Oslo (Photo Cooper Bridgeman Library); **282, 283**, Rasmus Meyer Collection, Bergen; **284** Self-portrait, National Gallery, London; **284, 285, 286, 287** Courtauld Institute Galleries, London; **288** Self-portrait, Norton Simon Collection, Los Angeles (Photo Cooper Bridgeman Library); **289, 290, 291** Private Collection, Lausanne; **293, 294, 295, 297, 298, 299** Home House Society Trustees/Courtauld Institute Galleries, London; **301, 302, 303** National Gallery, London (Photo Mike Fear); **311** Tate Gallery, London (Photo Mike Fear); **312** Whitney Museum of Modern Art, NY; **313** Kunstsammlung Nordrhein-Westfalen, Dusseldorf; **314** Tate Gallery, London (Photo Mike Fear); **315** Private Collection (Photo Mike Fear), © ADAGP, Paris, 1983; **317** Tate Gallery, London (Photo Mike Fear); **318, 319** Kunstsammlung Nordrhein-Westfalen, Dusseldorf, © SPADEM, Paris, 1983; **321** Philadelphia Museum of Art, © ADAGP, Paris, 1983; **322** Anthony D'Offay Gallery, London; **323** Tate Gallery, London (Photo Mike Fear); **324** Musée National d'Art Moderne, Centre Georges Pompidou, Paris, © SPADEM, Paris, 1983; **325** Graves Art Gallery, Sheffield; **326** National Gallery, London; **327** Montpellier, Musée Fabre (Photo Claude O'Sughrue; **328** Museum of Fine Arts, Boston; **329** National Gallery, London (Photo Mike Fear); **330** Musée de Grenoble (Photo Ifot, Grenable), © SPADEM, Paris, 1983; **331** Bridgeman Art Library; **332** Yale University Art Gallery; **333** National Gallery, London; **334** British Library; **335**(*top*) Cinemathèque Français, Paris; **335**(*bottom*) Victoria and Albert Museum; **336** Stadtische Kunsthalle, Manheim, © ADAGP, Paris, 1983 (Photo © Cosmopress; **339, 340, 341** Courtauld Institute of Art, Home House Trustees; **343-349** Tate Gallery (Photo Mike Fear); **351, 352, 353** Tate Gallery, London (Photo Mike Fear), © ADAGP, Paris, 1983; **355, 356, 357** Museum of Modern Art, NY, gift of Nelson A. Rockefeller; **358** Self-portrait, The A.E. Galletin Collection, Philadelphia Museum of Art; **358, 359, 360, 361** Property of the French Nation, eventually to be housed in the Museum of Picasso, © SPADEM, Paris, 1980; **362** Portrait, Bettman Archive Inc, NY; **363** Museum of Modern Art, Paris, © ADAGP, Paris, 1980; **365, 366, 376** Tate Gallery, London (Photo Mike Fear), © ADAGP, Paris, 1983; **369, 370**(*bottom*), *371* Museum of Modern Art, NY, ©SPADEM, Paris, 1983; **370**(*right*) Philadelphia

Museum of Art © SPADEM, Paris, 1983; **373, 374**(*top*), 375 Guggenheim Museum, NY, © ADAGP, Paris, 1983; **374**(*bottom*) Arthothek/Baverlische Staatsgemaldesam-lungen, © ADAGP, Paris, 1983; **377, 378**(*top*), **379** Private Collection (Photo Mike Fear), © ADAGP, Paris, 1983; **378**(*bottom*) Museum of Modern Art, NY, © ADAGP, Paris, 1983; **381, 382, 383** Tate Gallery, London (Photo Mike Fear), © ADAGP, Paris, 1983; **384** Tate Gallery, London, © ADAGP, Paris, 1980; **389** Norton Simon Museum of Art at Pasadena; **390** Museum of Modern Art, NY, acquired through the Lillie Bliss Bequest; **392** Museum Ludwig, Koln; **393** Musée de Petit Palais, Paris (Photo Hubert Josse), © SPADEM, Paris, 1983; **394** Portrait, Musée National Fernand Léger, Biot; study, Private Collection, France; **395, 396, 397** Tate Gallery, © SPADEM, Paris, 1980; **398, 399**, Museum of Modern Art, NY; **401** *Museum of Modern Art, NY*, © ADAGP, Paris, 1983; **405, 406** Escher Foundation, Haags gemeentemuseum, The Hague, © SPADEM, Paris, 1983; **407** Tate Gallery, London; **409, 410**(*top*), **411** National Maritime Museum, London; **410** Graves Art Gallery, Sheffield; **413, 414, 415** Tate Gallery, London (Photo Mike Fear); **417** Norton Simon Museum of Art at Pasadena, © ADAGP, Paris, 1983; **419** Kunst-Museum, Bern, © ADAGP, Paris, 1983; **420, 421** Museum of Modern Art, NY, © ADAGP, Paris, 1980; **422** Self-portrait, Collection of Felix Klee, Bern; **423, 424, 425** Kunst-Museum, Bern (Photo Hinz), © Cosmopress, Geneve, and SPADEM, Paris, 1980; **427, 428, 429**(*top*) City of Manchester Art Gallery, © SPADEM, Paris, 1983; **429**(*bottom*) Acquarella Galleries, NY (Photo Otto Nelson, NY); **430** Self-portrait, Collection Haags Gemeentemuseum, The Hague; **431** Tate Gallery, © SPADEM, Paris, 1980; **433, 434, 435** Tate Gallery, London (Photo Mike Fear); **436, 437** Musée National d'Art Moderne, Centre Georges Pompidou, Paris; **438** Tate Gallery, London (Photo Mike Fear); **439** Courtauld Institute Art Galleries; **440, 441** Whitney Museum of American Art, NY, © ADAGP, Paris, 1983; **443** Tate Gallery, London (Photo Mike Fear), © SPADEM, Paris, 1983; **444** Museum of Modern Art, NY; **445** Collection University of Nebraska Art Galleries, gift of Nathan Gold; **446, 447** Private Collection; 448 Portrait, Popperfoto, London; **449, 450, 451** Acquarella Galleries, NY (Photo Otto Nelson, NY), © SPADEM, Paris, 1980; **453, 454, 455** Tate Gallery, London (Photo Mike Fear); **457, 458, 459** Musée National d'Art Moderne, Centre Georges Pompidou, Paris, © ADAGP, Paris, 1983; **461, 462, 463** Museum of Modern Art, NY; **465, 466, 467** Metropolitan Museum of Art, NY; **469, 470, 471** Tate Gallery, London (Photo Mike Fear), © SPADEM, Paris, 1983; **473, 474, 475** Lefevre Gallery, London, © ADAGP, Paris, 1983; **477, 478, 479** Museum of Modern Art, NY; **481, 482, 483** Museum of Modern Art, NY; **481, 482, 483** Tate Gallery, London (Photo Mike Fear) **489** Los Angeles County Museum of Art, purchased with Contemporary Art Council Funds; **491** Private Collection; **492** Tate Gallery, London; **494** Collection of the Artist (on loan to the National Gallery of Art, Washington DC; **496** Tate Gallery, London (Photo Mike Fear); **497** Anthony D'Offay Gallery, London; **498** Courtesy of the Artist; **499** Waddingtons/Courtesy of the Artist; **501, 502, 503** Private Collection, London; **505, 506, 507** Museum of Modern Art, NY, © SPADEM, Paris, 1983; **509, 510, 511** Tate Gallery, London; **510** Study, Private Collection; **517, 518**(*top*), **519** Tate Gallery, London (Photo Mike Fear); **518**(*bottom*) Photo courtesy Knoedler Gallery, London; **520** Portrait, Popperfoto, London; **521, 522, 523** Tate Gallery, London; **525, 526, 527** Scottish National Gallery of Modern Art, Edinburgh; **529, 530, 531** Tate Gallery, London (Photo Mike Fear); **532** Portrait, Popperfoto, London; **533, 534, 535** Tate Gallery, London, © The Artist; photographic study, Tate Gallery Archives, © The Artist; **537** Tate Gallery, London; **539** Courtesy of the Artist, reproduced by permisson of The Chatsworth Settlement Trustees.

# BIBLIOGRAPHY


**Arnason, H.H.** *History of Modern Art,* Thames & Hudson (1969)
**Arnheim, Rudolph** *Art and the Visual Perception,* University of California Press (1974)
**Bazin, Germain** *Corot,* Hachette (1973)
**Bradbury, Malcolm and McFarlane, James (eds)** *Modernism 1890-1930,* Penguin Books (1978)
**Boime, Albert** *The Academy and French Painting in the Nineteenth Century,* Phaidon (1973); *Thomas Couture and the Eclectic Vision,* Yale University Press (1980)
**Broude, Norma** *Seurat in Perspective,* Prentice-Hall (1978)
**Callen, Anthea** *Renoir,* Oresko Books (1978); *Courbet,* Jupiter Books (1980)
**Chipp, Herschel B. (ed)** *Theories of Modern Art,* University of California Press (1968)
**Doerner, Max** *The Materials of the Artist,* Hart-Davis, MacGibbon (1976)
**Dube, Wolf-Diter** *The Expressionists,* Thames & Hudson (1972)
**Duthuit, Georges** *The Fauvist Painters,* Wittenborn (1950)
**Elderfield, John** *Fauvism and its Affinities,* The Museum of Modern Art, NY (1976)
**Fermingier, André** *Pierre Bonnard* Thames & Hudson (1970)
**Gettens, R.J. and Stout, G.L.** *Painting Materials, A Short Encyclopedia,* Dover (1966)
**Gibson, James J.** *The Senses Considered as Perpetual Systems,* Allen & Unwin (1966)
**Golding, John** *Cubism: A History and an Analysis, 1907-14,* Faber (1959)
**Gombrich, Ernst** *Art and Illusion,* Phaidon (1962); *The Story of Art, Phaidon* (1950)
**Gowing, Lawrence** *Matisse,* Thames & Hudson (1979); *Lucien Freud,* Thames & Hudson (1982)
**Haffmann, Werner** *Painting in the Twentieth Century,* Lund Humphries (1961)
**Harrison, Charles** *David Hockney at Kasmin,* Studio International, vol 175, no 896 (Jan 1968)
**Havel, Marc** *La Technique du Tableau,* Dessin et Tolra (1974)
**Herbert, Robert** *Barbizon Revisited,* Museum of Fine Arts, Boston (1962)
**Hemmings, F.J.W.** *Culture and Society in France,* 1848-1898, Batsford 1971
**Homer, William I.** *Seurat and the Science of Painting,* The M.I.T. Press (1964)
**Hughes, Robert** *The Shock of the New,* British Broadcasting Corporation (1980)
**Isaacson, Joel** *Claude Monet, Observation and Reflection,* Phaidon (1978)
**Jean, Marcel and Meizei, Arpad** *History of Surrealist Painting,* Weidenfeld and Nicholson (1960)
**Kandinsky, Wassily and Marc, Franz (eds)** *The Blaue Reiter Almanac,* Thames & Hudson (1974)
**Lippard, Lucy R.** *Pop Art,* Praeger World Art Series (1966)
**Lloyd, Christopher** *Pissarro,* Skira, MacMillan (1981)
**Mayer, Ralph** *The Artist's Handbook,* Faber & Faber (1977)
**Minnaert, M.** *The Nature of Light and Color in the Open Air,* Dover (1954)
**Nadeau, Maurice** *The History of Surrealism,* Cape (1968)
**Nichlin, Linda** *Realism,* Penguin Books (1971); *Impressionism and Post-Impressionism,* Prentice-Hall (1966)
**Pollock, Griselda** *Mary Cassatt,* Jupiter Books (1980); *Millet* Oresko Books (1977); and **Orton, Fred** *Vincent van Gogh,* Phaidon (1978)
**Richter, Hans** *Dada: Art and Anti-Art,* Thames & Hudson (1968)
**Rothenstein, John** *Modern English Painters* — Vols II and III, MacDonald and Jane's
**Rubin, William (ed)** *Cézanne: The Late Years,* Thames & Hudson (1978)
**Rubin, William** *Frank Stella,* Museum of Modern Art, NY (1976)
**Shikes, R and Harper, P.** *Pissarro, His Life and Work,* Quartet (1980)
**Stangos, Nikos (ed)** *David Hockney,* Thames & Hudson (1976)
**Taylor, Joshua C.** *Futurism,* Museum of Modern Art, NY (1967)
**Waldman, Diane (intro)** *Roy Lichtenstein,* Thames & Hudson (1979)
**Wechsler, Judith** *Cézanne in Perspective,* Prentice-Hall (1975)
**Welsh-Ovcharov, Bogomila** *Van Gogh in Perspective,* Prentice-Hall (1974)
**Welsh, Robert** *Piet Mondrian* 1872-1944, Toronto: The Art Gallery (1966)
**Whiteley, Jon** *Ingres,* Oresko Books (1977)

**Museum Publications**
*Alfred Sisley,* Nottingham University Art Gallery (1971)
*Centenaire de l'Impressionnisme,* Editions des musées nâtionaux, Paris (1974)
*Jean-François Millet,* Hayward Gallery, London and Grand Palais, Paris (1975-76)
*Gustave Caillebotte: A Retrospective Exhibition,* Museum of Fine Arts, Houston and The Brooklyn Museum (1976-77)
*Post-Impressionism,* Weidenfeld and Nicolson and The Royal Academy of Arts, London (1979)
*Camille Pissarro,* Hayward Gallery, London and Museum of Fine Arts, Boston (1980-81)

# INDEX